The W~ Handbook

EDITOR
Barry Turner

M
MACMILLAN
REFERENCE
BOOKS

First published 1987 by
THE MACMILLAN PRESS LTD
London and Basingstoke

This edition published 1992

Associated companies in Auckland,
Delhi, Dublin, Gaborone, Hamburg,
Harare, Hong Kong, Johannesburg,
Kuala Lumpur, Lagos, Manzini,
Melbourne, Mexico City, Nairobi,
New York, Singapore, Tokyo

British Library Cataloguing in Publication
data is available for this book from the
British Library.

ISBN 0-333-57925-9

Typeset by Media Conversion Ltd, Ruislip
Printed by Richard Clay Ltd, Suffolk

Contents

Foreword   **vii**

Bringing the World to Book – Advice to the First Time Writer   **1**

First cards in a winning hand   **1**

  Markets   **1**

  Synopses   **2**

  Advances   **3**

Hold my hand   **3**

  Literary Agents   **3**

Friends at court   **5**

  Contracts and the Minimum Terms Agreement   **5**

  Royalties   **6**

UK Publishers   **9**

Publish and Be Ruined – The Law of Libel   **99**

Writing for Young People   **103**

Poetry   **109**

Formalism v The Rest   **109**

Publishers with poetry on their lists   **118**

Small/Poetry Presses   **119**

Little Magazines   **124**

Organisations of Interest to poets   **128**

Small Presses   **133**

UK Packagers   **148**

The Association of Authors' Agents – Code of Practice   **157**

UK Agents   **159**

What I Did in the Holidays – The Subtle Art of Travel Writing   **181**

National Newspapers   **187**

Regional Newspapers   **195**

Freelance Rates – Newspapers   **213**

Serial Killing   **215**

Magazines   **217**

Freelance Rates – Magazines   **302**

News Agencies   **304**

National and Regional Television 305
National Radio 315
Local Radio 319
Freelance Rates – Broadcasting 331
Look First, Read Later 334
Film, TV and Video Producers 337
Theatre Producers 377
Playwrights' Minimum Terms 401
Festivals 403
European Publishers 410
US Publishers 436
US Agents 455
US Press, Journals and Broadcasting 482
I Quote, You Plagiarise – The Law of Copyright 484
Professional Associations and Societies 489
Literary Societies 507
Arts Councils and Regional Arts Boards 513
The Postal Workshop 518
Independent Postal Workshops 520
Writers' Courses, Circles and Workshops 522
Editorial, Research and other Services 531
Press Cuttings Agencies 534
Bursaries, Fellowships and Grants 535
Prizes 542
Mellor, Can you Spare a Dime? – The Libraries and PLR 574
Library Services 577
Words with Pictures 595
Picture Libraries 598
Tax and the Writer 628
  Income Tax 628
  VAT 632
Index of Companies 637
Subject Index 669

Foreword

There seems to be nothing we can do to limit the size of *The Writer's Handbook*. In a year of deep recession throughout the media it was confidently predicted that the number of entries would fall sharply. But it hasn't happened that way. True, some publishers have gone down, many journals have closed and hardly a week has passed without a production company disappearing from the scene. In any other industry the news would be justifiably described as catastrophic. In the media, however, the positive more than cancels out the negative. For every company that slides into oblivion, a gaggle of newcomers begins the long climb up the slippery slope.

Hence, this year, as in every previous year of the Handbook's existence, we are justified in claiming more entries than ever before. Writers, actual or prospective, can take encouragement from the resilience of publishing in all its forms. But the multiplicity of companies — many with short track records — further complicates the business of finding the best market for a particular article, book or script. Guidelines on how to make a bid for fortune follow in the opening chapter but the ground rule is always to give close study to existing output. Editors are as one in complaining that too few of those who write in with ideas or submit manuscripts have actually thought very much about horses for courses.

My thanks and admiration go to Michèle Roche and Jill Fenner who have taken on the brunt of the research for the 1993 Handbook. In tackling an ever more complex task, they somehow manage to combine patience and understanding with a determination to get to the facts — an enviable quality. Grateful thanks to Penny Warren, our editor at Macmillan, who keeps us all in order and ties us down to an impossible schedule.

As ever, *The Writer's Handbook* has benefited greatly from the advice and support of Josephine Pullein-Thompson of **PEN**, Mark le Fanu of **The Society of Authors** and Walter Jeffrey of **The Writers' Guild**. Among the specialist contributors, particular thanks go to Peter Finch and A.P. Kernon for responding to the many demands we make on them.

For any errors or omissions, the Editor alone takes responsibility.

Barry Turner
September 1992

Bringing the World to Book

Advice for the First Time Writer

Publishers have been having a hard time of late. They are desperate to find authors who can break through the barrier of inertia that surrounds the book trade but they are more worried than ever about risking their money on unknowns.

Persuading a publisher that his fortune is bound up with yours can be a frustrating and tiring experience – rather like fighting a military campaign uphill. And as any old soldier will tell you, success in battle depends on planning, patience and perseverance. The would-be author needs great dollops of all three qualities.

We start with the idea. It is a grievous mistake to bash out eighty thousand words in the expectation that a publisher will be unable to resist such obvious dedication and effort. He will, only too easily – with a printed rejection slip which comes with a government health warning against self-induced depression and despair.

The fact is that too many weighty manuscripts are sent to publishers who have neither the time nor the optimism to wade through reams of what just might turn out to be the blockbuster of the century but more probably will not.

First cards in a winning hand

A synopsis and a sample chapter is all that are needed for a publisher to make a judgement. Preparation is critical. It is possible for a bad book to follow a good synopsis but it is rare for a good book to follow a poor synopsis. The publisher knows this better than anyone. So what is he looking for?

Begin with a few lines of justification. What is the book about? Why does it cry out to be written? Who are the likely purchasers?

It is not enough to claim that a book will appeal to the general reader. Every author likes to think that he is reaching out to the mass audience but in reality each book has a core appeal on which the sales potential will be judged.

Having identified the target readers, ask yourself if these people are really book buyers. There are strong specialist market sectors, ranging from cookery to steam railways, where a new book of any quality is almost certain to translate reader interest into counter sales. But other groups are not so quick to part with their money.

As for the author who sets out to scale the heights of the bestseller lists: even he must have in mind a clear image of the reader he seeks to attract. The task is not so horrendous as it sounds. To appreciate what makes a bestseller, just spend some time in the departure lounge of a large airport. This is where we find some of the busiest bookshops and the most eager buyers. One in every twenty books sold in Britain is sold at an airport. If the average citizen is the man on the Clapham omnibus, the typical book buyer is the passenger on the trans-Atlantic flight.

Having settled on a snappy justification, the synopsis can be used to describe the book in some detail. It is impossible to specify length – where a single page may suffice for a beginner's guide to beekeeping, a closely argued case for energy conservation might require several thousand words. What is essential is for the synopsis to be a clear and logical description of the book. It should end with a few pertinent details. What is the intended size of the book? This has an important bearing on production costs and thus on the sales forecast. The best estimate of size is the number of words, with the average book falling within the seventy to ninety thousand bracket.

Will there be illustrations? If so, what sort? Library pictures must be paid for, and can be very expensive. Commissioned drawings raise the question of the role and standing of the illustrator in the origination of the book.

What about an index? All too often a non-fiction writer who is new to the game will be so overwhelmed by the prospect of seeing his name in large type, that he will brush aside such petty-fogging questions. Any literate can throw together an index. Wrong. Indexing is a highly professional task and the quality of an index can make or break a reputation for creating what publishers are pleased to call 'user-friendly' books. If an indexer is to be engaged, his fee has to be built into the economics. Someone, author or publisher, needs to put cash in reserve.

And so to the most important question of all. When will the manuscript be delivered? Publishers are rightly suspicious of authors who think that it takes five years to create a saleable product. The trouble is that five years can so easily become seven years, which is to move out of range of any feasible sales forecast. What the publisher needs is a volume that he can put on to the market within two years at most. Allowing for the time it takes to print and promote a book (a minimum of six months), he is looking to an ideal delivery day of a year to eighteen months ahead.

Along with the synopsis should go a CV which points up writing experience and relevant specialist knowledge and, in the case of a first-time author, some sample material.

An insurance against prejudice, lazy reading or sheer incompetence ('Letter? What letter? It must have been lost in the post.'), it is as well to send the package to several publishers at the same time. If any one of them is at all interested, sooner or later (usually later) he will suggest a meeting. Don't be impatient. Writers are often sinned against but they can be unreasonable in their assumption of a quick decision on what, after all, is a risky investment.

If after three or four weeks, nothing is heard, a telephone call is justified. But a polite inquiry is more likely to get results than a demand to know 'what the hell is going on'. It helps to have sent material to a named editor. That way you avoid the risk of being sucked into the whirlpool of internal company communications.

If the outcome of the first meeting is encouraging, the next discussion should focus on the size of the advance. Any author who wants to make a living by writing must establish early on that his publisher is prepared to make a down payment on account of royalties. The bigger the advance the more likely the publisher will be to put his back into the marketing effort. Even if he winds up hating the book, he will want his money back.

Usually, an advance is split three ways, part on signature of contract, part on delivery of the script, and part on publication. Except in the case of a bestselling author, it is difficult to secure an advance much above the equivalent of 60% of the royalties likely to be payable on the first edition.

The advance may be on account of royalties on the publisher's own editions or on account of all income, including subsidiary rights. The former arrangement is preferable, but where the advance is substantial, it may be reasonable for the publisher to recoup his outlay from, say, the proceeds of a US or paperback deal. In either case the advance should be non-returnable except when the author fails to deliver a manuscript.

Contracts vary significantly from one company to another and, since they are all hideously complicated, the differences do not always show up to the unpractised eye. This is where an agent can be invaluable.

Hold my hand

The good agent understands the small print in a contract and, to greater advantage, spots the omissions such as the failure to allow for higher royalties beyond a certain minimum sale. The agented author has a say on book club deals, promotion budgets, cover design, the timing of publication, print number and on subsidiary rights – the latter capable of attracting earnings long after the book is out of print.The sheer range of potential subsidiary rights is mind-boggling – overseas publication (the publisher will try for world rights but when an agent is acting, US and translation rights are nearly always reserved to the ultimate benefit of the author), film and television adaptations, audio cassettes, video, information retrieval, to mention only the most obvious. Above all, the good agent keeps a watching brief long after the contract has been signed,

'One might expect, at a time of recession, that authors' problems would involve late payments, blundering dishonesty and general stinginess. These remain significant failings, but they lag well behind publishers' inability to communicate with their writers or adequately to market their books. Here, surely, is the ultimate proof of publishers' lunacy. The one area of their activities which costs nothing – simple, business-like civility towards authors – is the one which causes them most difficulty. The reason for this lack of manners is not hard to find. Over the past decade, the book business has become so fascinating with its takeovers, conglomerates and personality clashes, that the industry has become entirely inward-looking. Mesmerised by one another, publishers have forgotten that none of these excitements could take place without the efforts of writers.'
Terence Blacker
(*The Author*)

'There are just too many books about ex-college pals meeting up to be miserable; too many whimsies about Irish girls or summers in Tuscan villas; too much righteous indignation about South Africa . . .'
Roger Lewis
And too many books,
'. . . about bourgeois childhoods, divorce in NW3, about women in Conran dresses fretting over adultery, about – God Save Us All – literary London.'
D J Taylor (*A Vain Conceit*)

'Now that farmers are to be paid for *not* growing crops . . . might I suggest that this is a policy that the Arts Council Literature Committee could usefully adopt. Instead of subsidising authors to publish yet more unreadable tomes, they could pay writers not to produce books. This may seem a negative attitude but the only other alternative is to burn bad books – which would not be environmentally friendly . . . For Londoners it would be like living through an Arctic winter or a Kuwaiti summer.'
David M Bennie
(from a letter to *The Literary Review*)

always ready to challenge the publisher to do better on behalf of his author.

But where is the efficient and sympathetic agent to be found? There is no sure way of matching a writer and agent merely by glancing through the list of names and addresses. The famous names exercise the heaviest clout, of course, but the most powerful agencies are not necessarily suitable for a beginner who may feel the need for the close personal contact offered by a smaller agency. On the other hand, the smaller agency may already have taken on its full quota of newcomers. Those who are struggling for a toehold in publishing are by definition low earners who must, for a time, be subsidised by the more profitable sector of a client list. The agent who gets the balance wrong is heading for the bankruptcy court.

There are writers and publishers who swear by the **Association of Authors' Agents** (see page 489), members of which are designated in *The Writer's Handbook* list by an asterisk. To qualify, an agent must have been in business for three or more years and bring in average commissions totalling not less than £25,000 a year. The Association's code of practice rules that no member shall charge a reading fee and that all monies due to clients should be paid within 21 days of cheques being cleared.

Advice frequently given by the happily agented to the agentless is to seek out the opinion of authors who have been through the mill and to learn from their experiences. Writers' circles and seminars organised by the **Society of Authors** and the **Writers' Guild** are fruitful sources of gossip.

Having decided on a likely prospect, the best approach to an agent is to send an example of work in hand with a background letter and samples of published material. As with any business correspondence which calls for a personal response, it is bad practice to send out a duplicated letter to all and sundry. It is a strict rule of the agency business that round robins plummet straight into the waste bin.

When submitting a completed manuscript, state openly if any publishers have already turned it down. Most agents do not charge reading fees but a writer who sends a stamped addressed envelope with his material will be off to a good start. It has been argued, by writers as well as agents, that a reading fee is a guarantee of serious intent; that if an agent is paid to assess the value of a manuscript, he is bound to give it professional attention. Sadly, this is not necessarily the case. While there are respectable agents who deserve a reading fee, they are outnumbered by the charlatans who take the money and run.

Friends at court

The writer who handles his own affairs is not entirely alone. Having campaigned vigorously for ten years or more, the writers' unions have negotiated a Minimum Terms Agreement (MTA) with several leading publishers.

Contracts and the Minimum Terms Agreement. A copy of the MTA, which can be obtained from either the **Society of Authors** or the **Writers' Guild** (free of charge to members who send a stamped addressed envelope), is a useful standard against which to judge the virtue of a publisher's offer. When it comes to signing on the bottom line, you may feel you have had to give way on a few points, but if the general principles of the MTA are followed, the chances of securing a reasonable deal are much enhanced.

Probably the most important break from tradition contained in the MTA is the clause allowing for the length of licence granted by the author to the publisher to be negotiable. The custom is for the licence to run for the duration of copyright (i.e. the author's lifetime plus 50 years). The writers' unions have pressed for a 20-year licence and some publishers have agreed to this but an acceptable compromise is a review procedure which permits the contract to be revised every ten years. This gives the author the opportunity to claim, for example, improved royalties if the book has been a success.

Other basic principles covered by the MTA include:

- *Reversion of Rights.* As well as the author being able to recover rights after a book goes out of print (when fewer than 50 copies of the hardback or 150 copies of the paperback remain in stock), the author may also terminate the contract if sales fall below certain figures. This gives the author the opportunity to leave a publisher if a book is not being properly marketed.

- *Accounting.* The publishers must pay over to the author income from sub-licences straight away, once the advance has been earned.

- *Indexing.* The cost of indexing is shared equally with the publishers.

- *Free Copies.* The author receives twelve free copies of a hardback and twenty free copies of a paperback and is able to buy further copies at 50% discount.

- *Print-run.* The author is entitled to know the size of print-runs.

'An author is a brand name and you have to think of yourself as being Heinz or Sony or Audi. And if you are, whatever's got your logo on it has a market. Dick Francis could probably produce the bloodstock prices and it would sell.'
Celia Brayfield

'There are two sorts of writers. Those who write to make money and those who write because that is what they want to do. The second lot shouldn't complain about money.'
Anthony Cheetham

'Sit at a desk, pick up a pen, put the paper in front of you and start "Once upon a time..."'
Jeffrey Archer
(*on how to write a novel*)

The MTA offers some valuable guarantees on author involvement in the publication of their books. For example:

- There should be full discussion prior to signing the contract of illustrations, quotations, etc., the costs involved and who is to pay for them. Normally, the publishers will make a substantial contribution.
- There must be full consultation on all the illustrations, the jacket, blurb and publication date.
- The author must be consulted on publicity including the proposed distribution list for review copies and before any major sub-licences are granted by the publisher.

On the question of *royalties*:

- The basic hardback scale is 10% to 2,500 copies, $12^1/2$% on the next 2,500 copies and 15% thereafter – on the published price (home sales) or the publisher's receipts (exports). On certain small reprints the royalty may revert to 10%.
- On home (mass market) paperback sales the minimum royalty is $7^1/2$% of the published price, rising to 10% after 50,000 copies. On exports the minimum royalty is 6% of the published price. If paperback rights are sub-licenced, the author receives at least 60% of the income, rising to 70% at a point to be agreed.
- The author receives 85% of the income from the sale of American rights and 80% from translations.
- The author receives 90% from the first serial rights, TV and radio dramatisations, film and dramatic rights, etc. Other percentages to the author include: anthology and quotation rights, 60%; TV and radio readings, 75%; merchandising, 80%.

But bear in mind that the royalty percentages do not necessarily apply to all books. For example, heavily illustrated books are excluded and there are certain circumstances in which publishers may pay lower royalties (for example, long works of fiction published in short print-runs for libraries).

As a spot check on the acceptability of a contract, confirm four essential points before signature.

First, there should be an unconditional commitment to publish the book within a specified time, say, twelve months from delivery of the typescript or, if the typescript is already with the publisher, from signature of the agreement. It is also as well for the approximate published price to be specified.

The obligation to publish should not be subject to approval or acceptance of the manuscript. Otherwise what looks like a firm contract may be little more than an unenforceable declaration of intent to publish. It is equally important to watch that the words 'approval' or 'acceptance' do not appear in the clause relating to the advance payment. For example, if the advance, or part of it, is payable 'on delivery and approval' of the script, this might qualify the publisher's obligation to publish the work.

This point about the publisher's commitment to publishing a book is of vital importance, particularly since publishers' editors change jobs with increasing frequency. An author who has started a book with enthusiastic support from his editor may, when he delivers it, find he is in the hands of someone with quite different tastes and ideas. The publishers should satisfy themselves at the outset that the author is capable of writing the required book – if necessary by seeing and approving a full synopsis and sample chapter. Provided the book, when delivered, follows the length and outline agreed, the publishers should be under a contractual obligation to publish it, subject, possibly, to reasonable and specified changes to the typescript.

Secondly, there should be a proper termination clause. This should operate when the publishers fail to comply with any of the provisions of the contract or if, after all editions of the work are out of print or off the market, they have not, within six months of a written request, issued a new edition or impression of at least 1500 copies.

When, in any of these circumstances, rights revert to the author, this should be without prejudice to any claims for monies due. Occasionally, termination clauses state that if the publishers fail to reprint a new edition after due notice from the author, the rights shall terminate provided the author refunds any unearned balance of the advance and buys back blocks, stereoplates, etc., at a proportion of their original cost. Any such proviso should be deleted.

Thirdly, there should not be an option clause that imposes unreasonable restrictions on future work. The best advice is to strike out the option clause but if this proves impossible, an option should be limited to one book on terms to be mutually agreed (not 'on the same terms'). The publishers should be required to make a decision within, say, six weeks of delivery of the complete work in the case of fiction, or of submission of a synopsis and specimen chapter in the case of non-fiction.

It is as well to specify the type of work covered by the option, for example, fiction, non-fiction, or children's books, since you may want to publish different types of books with different publishers. Very occasionally, in the case of a new author, a publisher tries for a two-book option. In this case, if the publishers reject the first option book, they should automatically lose their option on the second.

Finally, the author should not be expected to contribute towards the cost of publication. Every writers' organisation warns against subsidised or vanity publishing. It is expensive (some vanity publishers charge up to £6000 for a modest print run), the quality of production is inferior to that offered by conventional publishers, and the promises of vigorous marketing and impressive sales are rarely borne out by experience.

So much for the practicalities. What is missing in all this is helpful advice on how to write. Sadly no one knows. Often the best authors are the worst teachers;they cannot explain their own supreme talents or pass on their trade secrets. The writing schools may claim otherwise but they have little to offer beyond a few basic rules and these can be got, easily enough, by referring back to the contribution from Frank Delaney to the late lamented *Punch*.

These are his ten best-kept secrets for author success:

1. Choose your setting carefully
2. Like your characters
3. It is 99% perspiration
4. Write from experience
5. Let your imagination go
6. Know your reader
7. It must also be entertaining
8. Study the classics
9. Know your limits
10. Make it new.

The rest is talent – and a load of luck.

UK Publishers

AA Publishing

The Automobile Association, Fanum House, Basingstoke, Hampshire RG21 2EA
☎0256 491574   Fax 0256 22575

Managing Director *John Howard*
Approx Annual Turnover £16 million

Publishes maps, atlases and guidebooks, motoring and leisure. About 100 titles a year.

Editorial Director *Michael Buttler* Unsolicited mss welcome.

Authors' Rating Benefiting from a clearly defined market, the AA has advanced strongly in the publication of maps and tour guides. Travel writers who really know their stuff are among the beneficiaries.

Abacus

See **Little, Brown & Co. (UK) Ltd**

ABC - All Books For Children

33 Museum Street, London WC1A 1LD
☎071–436 6300   Fax 071–240 6923

Managing Director *Sue Tarsky*

Created from the buyout of **Aurum Press**'s children's division. *Publishes* children's titles only; about 40 a year. TITLES include the successful *Angelina Ballerina* and *Sam's Worries*. *Specialises* in co-editions worldwide. Unsolicited material welcome; s.a.e. essential for reply.

IMPRINTS

SoftbABCks Paperback imprint launched 1991. *Royalties* paid twice yearly.

Aberdeen University Press

Farmers Hall, Aberdeen AB9 2XT
☎0224 641672/641663   Fax 0224 643286

Managing Director *Colin Kirkwood*

FOUNDED 1840, the company was restricted to printing until 1979. Now a member of Maxwell Macmillan Publishing. *Publishes* academic, with a particular interest in language, linguistics, history and literature, as well as books of Scottish cultural interest.

Editorial Head *Colin Kirkwood* TITLES *Concise Scots Dictionary; A Linguistic Atlas of Late Mediaeval English; The History of Scottish Literature; The Scots Thesaurus; The Scottish Dog.* Unsolicited mss will be considered if they fall within AUP's categories of interest. Synopses and ideas for books welcome.
Royalties paid annually.

Abington Publishing

See **Woodhead Publishing Ltd**

Absolute Press

14 Widcombe Crescent, Bath, Avon BA2 6AH
☎0225 316013   Fax 0225 445836

Managing Director *Jon Croft*

FOUNDED 1980. *Publishes* food and wine-related subjects. About 10 titles a year.

Editorial Director *Jon Croft*

IMPRINT

Absolute Classics Plays and theatre. Publishing neglected world masterpieces in English translation. About 10 titles a year. No unsolicited mss. Synopses and ideas for books welcome.
Royalties paid twice yearly.

Abson Books

Abson, Wick, Bristol, Avon BS15 5TT
☎0272 372446/0275 822446   Fax 0272 372446

Partners *A. Bickerton/P. McCormack*

FOUNDED 1970. *Publishes* original paperbacks: English language glossaries, literary puzzle books, West Country, general information. No fiction. About 5 titles a year.

Editorial Head *A. Bickerton* TITLES *American English; Rhyming Cockney Slang; Jane Austen Quiz and Puzzle Book; Into France with Ease; Job*

Hunters' Work Book. Unsolicited mss welcome but return postage essential.
Royalties either once or twice yearly. *Represented* in Europe.

Academic Press
See **Harcourt Brace Jovanovich Ltd**

Academy Books
35 Pretoria Avenue, London E17 7DR
☎081-521 7647   Fax 081-503 6655

Chairman/Managing Director *Tony Freeman*
Approx Annual Turnover £120,000

FOUNDED 1990 as a self-publishing venture for specialist transport titles. *Publishes* non-fiction, mostly historical and technological, with a strong bias towards transport and local history titles also. TITLES *Lost Voice of Queen Victoria; How To Trace the History of Your Car; Daimler: An Illustrated History; Lanchester Cars 1895–1956; Sir Joseph Bradney's History of Monmouthshire.* 13 titles in 1991. Unsolicited mss, synopses and ideas welcome. Synopses should be accompanied by sample chapter or example of previously published work. No fiction, arts or religion. Currently setting up a packaging division.
Royalties paid twice yearly.

Academy Editions
42 Leinster Gardens, London W2 3AN
☎071-402 2141   Fax 071-723 9540

Managing Director *Dr Andreas C. Papadakis*

FOUNDED 1967. Belongs to the Academy Group Ltd. *Publishes* books and magazines on art and architecture. Owns the London Art Bookshop in Holland Street, London W8.

Editorial Director *Dr Andreas C. Papadakis*
TITLES *Post-Modern Design* M. Collins; *The New Moderns* C. Jencks; *Richard Meier* K. Frampton, R. Meier & C. Jencks; *New Classicism Omnibus* A. Papadakis & H. Watson; *Architectural Design Magazine; Art & Design Magazine; The Journal of Philosophy and the Visual Arts; The UIA Journal.* No unsolicited mss but synopses and ideas welcome.
Royalties paid annually.

Acair Ltd
Unit 7, 7 James Street, Stornoway, Isle of Lewis, Scotland PA87 2QE
☎0851 3020   Fax 0851 3294

Manager/Editorial Director *Agnes Rennie*

Publishes Scottish culture, academic, biography and autobiography in Gaelic and English; children's Gaelic; plus educational and textbooks, history, music, poetry, reference and dictionaries, religious, sports and games. Unsolicited mss welcome.
Royalties paid twice yearly.

Accent Educational Publishers Ltd
17 Isbourne Way, Winchcombe, Gloucestershire GL54 5NS
☎0242 604466   Fax 0242 604480

Chairman *Duncan Prowse*
Managing Director *Richard Slessor*

FOUNDED 1990. *Publishes* educational books, especially language teaching materials for primary/secondary/tertiary education. Unsolicited mss, synopses and ideas welcome for language learning materials only.
Royalties paid annually.

Actinic Press
See **Cressrelles Publishing Co. Ltd**

Addison–Wesley Publishers Ltd
Finchampstead Road, Wokingham, Berkshire RG11 2NZ
☎0734 794000   Fax 0734 794035

Chairman *Don Hammonds*
Managing Director *Roderick Bristow*

A division of the Addison-Wesley European Publishing Group. Owned by Pearson since 1988, making it part of one of the biggest book publishers in the western world. *Publishes* scientific, technical, academic and senior school books, and is one of the leading computer science publishers. Several series covering computer science, microelectronics and international business, for the international market.

Head of Acquisitions *Andrew Ware* Unsolicited mss, synopses and ideas for books welcome.
Royalties paid twice yearly, in April and October.

Authors' Rating Addison-Wesley continues to buck the trend in educational publishing (a deal with **Economist Books** has pitched it into the MBA market). Benefits from a close knowledge of the education market on both sides of the Atlantic.

Adlard Coles Ltd
See **A & C Black (Publishers) Ltd**

Adlib Paperbacks
See **Scholastic Publications Ltd**

Agneau 2
See **Allardyce, Barnett, Publishers**

Airlife Publishing Ltd
101 Longden Road, Shrewsbury,
Shropshire SY3 9EB
☏ 0743 235651   Fax 0743 232944

Chairman/Managing Director *A. D. R. Simpson*
Approx Annual Turnover £2.5 million

Established to publish specialist aviation titles.
Publishes both technical and general titles for
pilots, historians and enthusiasts. About 30 titles a
year.

Editorial Head *John Beaton* TITLES *Fishing
Season; Robert Bateman: An Artist in Nature;
Flytier's Companion; Air Pilot's Manuals; Airforce:
The RAF in the '90s.*

IMPRINTS
Swan Hill Press *Specialises* in areas of country
sport, local interest, natural history, travel and
adventure. **Waterline Books** New imprint dedicated to nautical titles. **Chatsworth Library** Books
and stationery sourced from Chatsworth House
library. Unsolicited mss, synopses and ideas for
books welcome.
Royalties paid annually, twice yearly by arrangement.

The Alban Press
See **Curzon Press Ltd**

Ian Allan Ltd
Terminal House, Station Approach,
Shepperton TW17 8AS
☏ 0932 228950   Fax 0932 232366

Chairman *David Allan*
Chief Executive *Martin Kenny*
Publishing Director *S. Forty*

Publishes atlases and maps, aviation, biography
and autobiography, hobbies, guidebooks, defence
and militaria, nautical, reference and dictionaries,
transport, travel and topography. Unsolicited mss
considered. About 75 titles in 1992.

Allardyce, Barnett, Publishers
14 Mount Street, Lewes, East Sussex BN7 1HL
☏ 0273 479393

Publisher *Fiona Allardyce*
Managing Editor *Anthony Barnett*

FOUNDED 1981. *Publishes* art, literature and music,
previously with emphasis on substantial collections
by current English language poets. Recently
launched a new children's imprint called ABCD.
First title published 1992. 2 titles in 1991.

IMPRINTS
Agneau 2, ABCD. Unsolicited mss and synopses
discouraged.

J. A. Allen & Co. Ltd
1 Lower Grosvenor Place, Buckingham Palace
Road, London SW1W 0EL
☏ 071-834 0090   Fax 071-976 5836

Chairman/Managing Director *Joseph A. Allen*
Publishing Manager *Caroline Burt*
Approx Annual Turnover *c.* £600,000

Inaugurated in 1926 as part of J. A. Allen & Co.
(The Horseman's Bookshop) Ltd, and became a
separate independent company in 1960. *Publishes*
equine and equestrian non-fiction and fiction. 20
titles in 1991.

Editor *Jane Lake* Mostly commissioned titles, but
willing to consider unsolicited mss of technical/
instructional material related to all aspects of
horses and horsemanship. Also well-written equine
and equestrian fiction for age ranges 9–14 and teen
to adult.
Royalties paid twice yearly.

W. H. Allen & Co.
See **Virgin Publishing**

Allison & Busby
See **Virgin Publishing**

Alphabooks
See **A. & C. Black (Publishers) Ltd**

Amber Lane Press Ltd
Cheorl House, Church Street, Charlbury,
Oxon OX7 3PR
☏ 0608 810024   Fax 0608 810024

Chairman *Brian Clark*
Managing Director *Judith Scott*

FOUNDED 1979 *Publishes* plays and books on the
theatre. 4 titles in 1991.

Editorial Head *Judith Scott* TITLES *After Aida; The Best of Friends; The Dresser* (play texts); *Patterns of Postwar British Drama* Colin Chambers & Mike Prior; *The Sound of One Hand Clapping: A Guide to Writing for the Theatre* Sheila Yeger. No unsolicited mss. Synopses and ideas welcome.
Royalties paid twice yearly.

Amsco
See **Omnibus Press**

Anaya Publishers Ltd
3rd Floor, 44–50 Osnaburgh Street,
London NW1 3ND
☎071–383 2997   Fax 071–383 3076
Chairman *German Sanchez Ruiperez*
Managing Director *Colin Ancliffe*
Approx Annual Turnover £2 million

Part of Grupo Anaya, Spain. FOUNDED 1950. *Publishes* high-quality illustrated non-fiction. Currently expanding by about 20% each year. About 30 titles a year.

Editorial Head *Carey Smith* TITLES include *Victorian Needlepoint; Great Shots; Easy To Make: Pretty Things.* Unsolicited mss, synopses and ideas for books welcome.
Royalties paid twice yearly. *Overseas associates* in Spain, Italy, France and Mexico.

Andersen Press Ltd
20 Vauxhall Bridge Road, London SW1V 2SA
☎071–973 9720   Fax 071–233 6263
Managing Director/Publisher *Klaus Flugge*

FOUNDED 1976 by Klaus Flugge and named after Hans Christian Andersen. *Publishes* children's hardcover fiction. Seventy per cent of their books are sold as co-productions abroad.

Editorial Director *Denise Johnstone-Burt* **Fiction Editor** *Audrey Adams* TITLES Bestsellers include *Not Now Bernard* David McKee; *A Dark, Dark Tale* Ruth Brown; *I Want My Potty* Tony Ross; *Badger's Parting Gift* Susan Varley. Unsolicited mss are only welcome for picture books or young readers (up to age 12).
Royalties paid twice yearly.

Angus & Robertson (UK)
See **HarperCollins Publishers Ltd**

Antique Collectors' Club
5 Church Street, Woodbridge, Suffolk IP12 1DS
☎0394 385501   Fax 0394 384434
Managing Director *Diana Steel*

FOUNDED 1966. Has a five-figure membership spread throughout the world. It was in response to the demand for information on 'what to pay' that the price guide series was introduced in 1968 with the first edition of *The Price Guide to Antique Furniture.* Club membership costs about £17.50 per annum. Members buy the Club's publications at concessional rates. *Publishes* specialist books on antiques and collecting. Subject areas include furniture, silver/jewellery, metalwork, glass, textiles, art reference, ceramics, horology. Also books on architecture and gardening.

Editorial Adviser *John Steel* TITLES *Travels in China — A Plantsman's Paradise* Roy Lancaster; *Dictionary of British 20th Century Painters* Frances Spalding; *Jewellery 1789–1910* Shirley Bury. Unsolicited synopses and ideas for books welcome. No mss.
Royalties paid quarterly as a rule, but can vary.

Anvil Press Poetry Ltd
69 King George Street, London SE10 8PX
☎081–858 2946

FOUNDED 1968 to promote contemporary English and foreign poetry, both classic and contemporary, in translation. English list includes Peter Levi and Carol Ann Duffy. Anvil has now developed to the point at which most of its new titles are new volumes by their regulars. Preliminary enquiry required for translations. Unsolicited book-length collections of poems are welcome from writers whose work has appeared in poetry magazines.

Editorial Directors *Peter Jay/Julia Sterland*

Authors' Rating Distancing himself from the aggressive marketing tactics paraded by some other houses, Peter Jay is said to be the least likely of all publishers to sign a fashionable poet for merely commercial reasons but he has had great success with younger poets.

Apple
See **Quarto Publishing** under **UK Packagers**

Appletree Press Ltd
19–21 Alfred Street, Belfast, N. Ireland BT2 8DL
☎0232 243074   Fax 0232 246756
Managing Director *John Murphy*

FOUNDED 1974. Currently has about 150 books in print. *Publishes* cookery — the *Little Cookbook* series — and other small-format gift books, as well as general non-fiction of Irish interest.

Senior Editor *Douglas Marshall* **Cookery Editor** *Pat Scott* TITLES *Ireland: The Complete Guide; Northern Ireland: The Background to the Conflict; A Little French Cookbook; A Little English Cookbook* and about 30 other *Little Cookbook* titles. No unsolicited mss; send initial letter or synopsis.
Royalties paid twice yearly in the first year, annually thereafter.

Aquarian Press
See **HarperCollins Publishers Ltd**

Argus Books
Argus House, Boundary Way, Hemel Hempstead, Hertfordshire HP2 7ST
✆0442 66551　　　　　Fax 0442 66998

General Manager *Christine Basden*

The book publishing division of Argus Consumer Magazines. *Publishes* aviation, leisure and hobbies, modelling, electronics, health, wine and beer making, woodwork. Send synopses rather than completed mss.
Royalties paid twice yearly.

Aris & Phillips Ltd
Teddington House, Warminster, Wiltshire BA12 8PQ
✆0985 213409　　　　　Fax 0985 212910

Managing/Editorial Director *Adrian Phillips*

FOUNDED 1972 to publish books on Egyptology. A family firm which has remained independent. *Publishes* academic, classical, oriental and hispanic. About 20 titles a year.

Hispanic Classics Editor *Lucinda Phillips* With such a highly specialised list, unsolicited mss and synopses are not particularly welcome, but synopses will be considered.
Royalties paid twice yearly.

Ark
See **Routledge, Chapman & Hall Ltd**

Arkana
See **Penguin Books Ltd**

Armada
See **HarperCollins Publishers Ltd**

Arms & Armour Press
See **Cassell**

Edward Arnold
See **Hodder & Stoughton Ltd**

Arrow Books Ltd
See **Random House Publishing Group Ltd**

Artech House
6 Buckingham Gate, London SW1E 6JP
✆071-973 8077　　　　　Fax 071-630 0166

Managing Director (USA) *William M. Bazzy*

FOUNDED 1970. The European office of Artech House Inc., Boston. *Publishes* electronic engineering, especially telecommunications, optoelectronics and materials (books, software and videos). 48 titles in 1991.

Editorial Head *Dr Julie Lancashire* Unsolicited mss and synopses considered.
Royalties paid twice yearly.

Artemis Press
See **Vision Press Ltd**

Ashford, Buchan & Enright
31 Bridge Street, Leatherhead, Surrey KT22 8BN
✆0372 373355　　　　　Fax 0372 363550

Managing Director *John Mole*
Approx Annual Turnover £200,000

FOUNDED 1984. Taken over by Martins Printing Group in 1987 and became independent in January 1991. *Specialises* in countryside, field sports and nautical. TITLES include *Classic Game Shooting; Marine Electrics.* Unsolicited mss welcome if return postage included. Synopses and ideas for books considered. About 10 titles a year.
Royalties paid twice yearly.

Authors' Rating An exciting young company with a strong sense of marketing and promotion.

Ashgate Publishing Co. Ltd
Gower House, Croft Road, Aldershot, Hampshire GU11 3HR
✆0252 331551　　　　　Fax 0252 344405

Chairman/Managing Director *Nigel Farrow*

FOUNDED 1991. Owned by **Gower Publishing Group**. *Publishes* professional and academic books in social sciences, arts and humanities.

IMPRINTS
Avebury *Jo Gooderham* Research monographs on social sciences. **Ashgate** Professional monographs and reference publications on librarianship and information management *Sue McNaughton;* Social work and policy, transport and planning *Jo Gooderham;* Other technical subjects *John Hindley.* **Scolar Press** *Nigel Farrow* Academic and specialist books on fine art, music studies, books about books, bibliographies, etc. **Variorum** *John Smedley* Collected studies on history. Unsolicited mss welcome. Synopses and ideas for books considered.
Royalties paid as per contract.

Associated Publicity Holdings Ltd
Denmark House, Staples Corner, West Hendon, London NW9 7BW
☎081-202 2565   Fax 081-202 6736

Director of Publishing *Jonathan G. Harris*

FOUNDED 1988. Currently expanding. *Publishes* food, sport, directories and general non-fiction. Unsolicited mss, synopses and ideas for books, directories and one-off publications welcome.
Royalties paid twice yearly.

Associated University Presses (AUP)
See **Golden Cockerel Press Ltd**

Aston Publications
10 Claggy Road, Kimpton, Hertfordshire SG4 8QA
☎0438 832123   Fax 0438 833654

Publisher *Anthony Pritchard*

FOUNDED 1984. *Publishes* aviation, motoring, motorcycling, wildlife and travel. 19 titles in 1991.

Editorial Director *Keith Davey* TITLES include *Images of Wales* John R. Jones; *Italian Motorcycles* Mick Walker; *Aston Martin: The Post-War Competition Cars* Anthony Pritchard. Synopses and ideas within their subject areas considered.
Royalties paid twice yearly.

The Athlone Press
1 Park Drive, London NW11 7SG
☎081-458 0888

Managing Director *Brian Southam*

FOUNDED 1949 as the publishing house of the University of London. Now wholly independent, but preserves links with the University via an academic advisory board. *Publishes* archaeology, architecture, art, economics, history, medical, music, Japan, oriental, philosophy, politics, religion, science, sociology, zoology, women's/feminist issues. Anticipated developments in the near future: more emphasis on women's/ feminist studies and environmental/Green issues, including medicine. About 35 titles a year.

Editorial Head *Brian Southam* Unsolicited mss, synopses and ideas for academic books welcome. *Royalties* paid annually/twice yearly by arrangement. *Overseas associates* The Athlone Press, Atlantic Highlands, New Jersey, USA.

Atlantic Europe Publishing Co. Ltd
86 Peppard Road, Sonning Common, Reading, Berkshire RG4 9RP
☎0734 723751   Fax 0734 724488

Directors *Dr B. J. Knapp/D. L. R. McCrae*

Closely associated, since 1990, with Earthscape Editions packaging operation. *Publishes* full-colour, highly illustrated children's non-fiction for international co-edition markets only. Main focus is on national curriculum related titles, especially in the fields of mathematics, science, design and geography. 15 titles in 1991. Unsolicited synopses and ideas for books welcome but s.a.e. essential for return of submissions.
Royalties or fees paid depending on circumstance.

Atlantic Large Print
See **Chivers Press (Publishers)**

Attic Books
The Folly, Rhosgoch, Painscastle, Builth Wells, Powys LD2 3YJ
☎0497 851205

Managing Director *Jack Bowyer*

FOUNDED 1984 by its architect owners. *Publishes* books on building crafts, architecture and engineering. Mostly technical books for the industry, dealing mainly with restoration and conservation. 3 titles in 1992.

Editorial Head *Jack Bowyer*

IMPRINT
Orion Books TITLES *A History of Buildings* Jago V. Swillerton & Toomer. Unsolicited mss, synopses and ideas for books welcome.
Royalties paid annually.

Audio Books
See **Random House Publishing Group Ltd**

Aurum Press Ltd
10 Museum Street, London WC1A 1JS
☎ 071-379 1252   Fax 071-580 2469
Chairman *André Deutsch*
Managing Director *Bill McCreadie*

FOUNDED 1977. Formerly owned by Andrew Lloyd Webber's Really Useful Group, now owned jointly by Piers Burnett, Bill McCreadie and Sheila Murphy (Marketing & Rights Director), all of whom worked together in the 70s at **André Deutsch**. Committed to producing high-quality, illustrated and non-illustrated adult non-fiction books in the areas of biography and memoirs, visual arts, film, lifestyle and travel. About 40 titles a year.

Editorial Director *Piers Burnett*
Royalties paid twice yearly.

Austen Cornish
See **Mosby Year Book Europe Ltd**

Autolycus Press
See **Thames Publishing**

Avebury
See **Ashgate Publishing Co. Ltd**

Baillière Tindall
See **Harcourt Brace Jovanovich Ltd**

Bantam/Bantam Press
See **Transworld Publishers Ltd**

Arthur Barker Ltd
See **Orion Publishing Group**

Barny Books
The Cottage, Hough on the Hill, Near Grantham,
Lincolnshire NG32 2BB
☎ 040050 246

Managing Director *Molly Burkett*
Approx Annual Turnover £10,000

Founded with the aim of encouraging new writers and illustrators. *Publishes* children's books, and runs an advisory service to writers to encourage own publication (£10 fee to cover costs/postage).

Editorial Head *Molly Burkett* TITLES *The Welsh Witch* Molly Burkett; *Marie and the Octopus* Joy Mellins; *History of a Village School* Margaret Gregory. Too small a concern to have the staff/ resources to deal with unsolicited mss. Writers with strong ideas should approach Molly Burkett by letter in the first instance.
Royalties division of profits 50/50.

Authors' Rating The friendliest of small publishers, Barny Books is trying hard to remain a cottage industry but may soon be successful on a larger scale in spite of itself. Marketing and publicity are given a low priority on the principle that quality will always sell.

Baron Birch
See **Barracuda Books Ltd/Quotes Ltd**

Barracuda Books Ltd/Quotes Ltd
Meadows House, Well Street,
Buckingham MK18 1EW
☎ 0280 814441/2   Fax 0280 822986

Managing Directors *Clive Birch* (Barracuda)/
Carolyn Birch (Quotes)

Barracuda was formed in 1974, its sister company Quotes in 1985. The Sporting and Leisure Press imprint was launched in 1976, Saga in 1987 and Baron Birch in 1992. *Publishes* local and natural history, country and sporting life, military, transport, church, genealogical and institutional histories. About 30 titles a year.

DIVISIONS
Barracuda Books *Clive Birch* TITLES *The Book of Ely; The Nature of Warwickshire*. **Quotes Ltd** *Carolyn Birch* TITLES *Beside the Seaside: Lincolnshire in Camera; Cheltenham in Camera*. **Saga** Popular heritage TITLES *The Royal Veterinary College*. **Sporting & Leisure Press** *Crystal Palace FC: The Palace Centurions*. **Baron Birch** *Welcome Aboard: The Seamen's Hospital Society*. Synopses and ideas for books welcome.
Royalties paid annually.

Barrie & Jenkins Ltd
See **Random House Publishing Group Ltd**

Bartholomew
See **HarperCollins Publishers Ltd**

B. T. Batsford Ltd

4 Fitzhardinge Street, London W1H 0AH
☎ 071-486 8484   Fax 071-487 4296

Managing Director Peter Kemmis Betty
Editorial Director Timothy Auger
Approx Annual Turnover £5 million

FOUNDED 1843 as a bookseller, and began publishing in 1874. An independent company and world leader in books on chess, arts and craft. Publishes non-fiction: academic, archaeology, architecture, design and construction, cinema, crafts and hobbies, educational, equestrian, fashion and costume, graphic design, history and antiquarian, horticulture, botany and garden history, literary criticism and linguistics, local history, country sports and games, social work. Acquired **Christopher Helm**'s horticultural list from **A. & C. Black** at the beginning of the decade. About 150 titles a year, with a backlist of 1200.

DIVISIONS
Arts & Crafts TITLES Fabric Painting for Embroidery; Flowers for Weddings; The Complete Potter series; Needlepoint for the Home. **Archaeology & Ancient History** TITLES The English Heritage Book of Stonehenge (and others in the same series). **Chess** TITLES Batsford Chess Openings 2; How to Beat Your Computer. **Horticulture, Field Sports, Costume & Film** TITLES Alpines for the Open Garden; Fashions of a Decade (series); Quinlan's Illustrated Directory of Film Stars. **Architecture, Graphic Design, Cultural Studies** TITLES The Best in Office Interior Design, The Art and Architecture of Freemasonry. Unsolicited mss, synopses and ideas for books welcome.
Royalties paid twice in first year, annually thereafter.

Authors' Rating A traditional publisher and proud of it. Not a source of huge advances but plenty of strong sellers in the crafts and hobbies market.

Bay View Books Ltd

13A Bridgeland Street, Bideford,
Devon EX39 2QE
☎ 0237 479225/421285   Fax 0237 421286

Joint Managing Directors Charles Herridge/
Bridgid Herridge

FOUNDED 1986. Publishes transport books only, including series: all-colour classic car restoration guides; A-Zs of cars, motorcycles and racing cars. 7 titles in 1991.
Payment varies according to contract.

BBC Books

80 Wood Lane, London W12 0TT
☎ 081-576 2000   Fax 081-749 8766

Director of Books Christopher Weller
Joint Editorial Heads Sheila Ableman/Suzanne Webber
Approx Annual Turnover £15 million

BBC Books, a division of BBC Enterprises, has expanded its list to include books which, though linked with BBC television or radio, may not simply be the 'book of the series'. Books with no BBC link are of no interest.
TITLES Birth of Europe; Sea Trek; The Power and the Glory; The Victorian Flower Garden; Around the World in 80 Days — Michael Palin; Delia Smith's Christmas. Unsolicited mss (which come in at the rate of about 15 weekly) are rarely even read. If books are not commissioned, they are packaged and devised in consultation with known writers, or through known agents. Having said that, strong ideas well expressed will always be considered, and promising letters stand a chance of further scrutiny. About 150 titles a year.
Royalties paid twice yearly.

Authors' Rating With a near monopoly on such a fertile source of ideas, it is hardly likely that BBC Books has any need to go looking for produce. The best advice to authors is first to get your television series. Thereafter, one of the advantages of being published by the BBC is the prospect of fierce promotion to the watching millions and a short cut to the bestseller list. Sales of spoken word cassettes are up to £4.25 million and video sales to £23 million. This is where the growth is.

Bedford Square Press
See **NCVO Publications**

Belhaven Press
See **Pinter Publishers Ltd**

Belitha Press
See **UK Packagers**

Bellevue Books

Unit E4, Sunbury International Business Centre,
Brooklands Close, Sunbury on Thames,
Middlesex TW16 7DX
☎ 0932 765119   Fax 0932 765429

Chairman Howard Barkway
Approx Annual Turnover £20,000

FOUNDED 1991 to publish a book on the unsolved mystery of Rennes-le-Chateau. Now publishing unsolved natural and scientific mysteries, both ancient and modern. 1 title in 1991. Unsolicited mss, synopses and ideas welcome. Publishing output expanding; the company hopes to reach double figures by 1993.
Royalties paid quarterly.

Bellew Publishing Co. Ltd
Nightingale Centre, 8 Balham Hill,
London SW12 9EA
☎081-673 5611 Fax 081-675 3542

Chairman *Anthony Rainbird*
Managing Director *Ib Bellew*
Approx Annual Turnover £400,000

FOUNDED 1983. Publisher and packager. *Publishes* craft, art and design, fiction, illustrated non-fiction, general interest, religion and politics. Distributor and agent for Soho Press, New York, and distributor for Rex Collings Ltd. About 25 titles a year. No unsolicited mss. Synopses with specimen chapters welcome.
Royalties paid annually.

Bennett Books
See **Kingfisher Books**

Berg Publishers Ltd
150 Cowley Road, Oxford OX4 1JJ
☎0865 245104 Fax 0865 791165

Chairman/Managing Director *Marion Berghahn*
Approx Annual Turnover £600,000

Publishes scholarly books in the fields of history, economics, social sciences and humanities. About 70 titles a year.

Editorial Head *Marion Berghahn*

IMPRINTS
Oswald Wolff Books Scholary and general titles, including biography. TITLES *Leonard Bernstein* Gradenwitz; *Heinrich Böll* J. H. Reid. No unsolicited mss. Synopses and ideas for books welcome.
Royalties paid annually.

Berkswell Publishing Co. Ltd
PO Box 420, Warminster, Wiltshire BA12 9XB
☎0985 40189 Fax 0985 40189

Managing Director *John Stidolph*

FOUNDED 1974. Publisher and book packager. *Publishes* illustrated books, royalty, heritage, country sports, biographies and books with a flavour of

Wessex. No fiction. 4 titles in 1991. Unsolicited mss, synopses and ideas for books welcome.
Royalties paid according to contract.

Bestseller Publications
See **Studio Editions Ltd**

BFI Publishing
British Film Institute, 21 Stephen Street,
London W1P 1PL
☎071-255 1444 Fax 071-436 7950

Head of Trade Publishing *Edward Buscombe*
Approx Annual Turnover £250,000

FOUNDED 1982. Part of the **British Film Institute.** *Publishes* academic and general film/television-related books. About 20 titles a year.

Editorial Head *Edward Buscombe* TITLES *Sixties British Cinema* Robert Murphy; *Diary of a Young Soul Rebel* Colin MacCabe & Isaac Julien; *The Cinema of Jean Genet* Jane Giles; *Perspectives on Chinese Cinema* Chris Berry; *Popular Television in Britain* John Corner; *Queer Edward* Derek Jarman. Synopses and ideas preferred to complete mss.
Royalties paid annually.

Bible Society Publishing
Stonehill Green, Westlea, Swindon,
Wiltshire SN5 7DG
☎0793 513713 Fax 0793 512539

Executive Director *Neil Crosbie*
Approx Annual Turnover £6 million

The Bible Society was founded in 1804 to distribute scriptures worldwide. Granted a Royal Charter in 1948, it is now part of a worldwide fellowship of bible societies, working in over 180 countries. *Publishes* bibles, bible-related resources and group study materials. TITLES *The Good News Bible; The Bible in Stained Glass; Learn New Testament Greek.* 50 titles in 1991. Unsolicited synopses and ideas welcome. No Christian biography, fiction, poetry, general religious or bible commentaries.
Royalties paid twice yearly.

Clive Bingley Books
See **Library Association Publishing Ltd**

A. & C. Black (Publishers) Ltd
35 Bedford Row, London WC1R 4JH
☎071-242 0946 Fax 071-831 8478

Chairman *Charles Black*
Joint Managing Directors *Charles Black/David Gadsby*
Approx Annual Turnover £6.8 million

Acquisitions over the last few years have brought the Adlard Coles sailing list (ex-**Grafton/ HarperCollins**) and Christopher Helm books into A. & C. Black's stable. Christopher Helm set up his own imprint in 1986 following the takeover of Croom Helm by ABP academic publishers. His list, acquired by Black in 1990, has added specialist non-fiction titles (natural history and ornithology) to Black's core lists. *Publishes* children's and educational books, including music, for 3–15 years, arts and crafts, calligraphy, drama, fishing, ornithology, natural history, nautical, reference, sport, theatre and travel. About 160 titles a year.

IMPRINTS
Adlard Coles, Alphabooks, Christopher Helm, Nautical. TITLES *New Mermaid* drama series; *Who's Who; Writers' & Artists' Yearbook; Know the Game* sports series; *Blue Guides* travel series. Initial enquiry appreciated before submission of mss. *Royalties* payment varies according to contract.

Black Spring Press Ltd

63 Harlescott Road, Nunhead, London SE15 3DA
☎071-639 2492   Fax 071-639 2508

Managing Director *Simon Pettifar*

FOUNDED 1986. *Publishes* fiction, literary criticism, theatre and cinema studies, popular music. 5 titles in 1991.

Editor *Simon Pettifar* TITLES *And the Ass Saw the Angel* Nick Cave; *The Big Brass Ring* Orson Welles; *Beautiful Losers* Leonard Cohen; *Intimate Journals* Charles Baudelaire; *The Mortdecai Trilogy* Kyril Bonfiglioli. Send proposals rather than completed mss.
Royalties paid twice yearly.

Black Swan

See **Transworld Publishers Ltd**

Blackie & Son Ltd

No longer publishing. Blackie & Son Ltd disposed of its publishing interests in 1992. Blackie Children's Books was taken over by **Penguin**; Blackie Educational by **Thomas Nelson & Sons Ltd**.

Blackstaff Press Ltd

3 Galway Park, Dundonald, Belfast BT16 0AN
☎0232 487161   Fax 0232 489552

Directors *Michael Burns/Anne Tannahill*

FOUNDED 1971 by Jim and Diane Gracey and bought by Michael Burns in 1980. *Publishes* mainly, but not exclusively, Irish interest books, fiction, poetry, history, politics, illustrated and fine editions, natural history and folklore. About 25 titles a year.

Editorial Head *Anne Tannahill* Unsolicited mss, synopses and ideas welcome.
Royalties paid twice yearly.

Authors' Rating Winner of the *Sunday Times* Small Publisher of the Year Award for 1992, this Belfast publisher was praised for a superb backlist, the quality of new books and for its 'wonderfully well-presented catalogues and promotional material'.

Blackwell Publishers

108 Cowley Road, Oxford OX4 1JF
☎0865 791100   Fax 0865 791347

Chairman *Nigel Blackwell*
Managing Director *René Olivieri*
Approx Annual Turnover £2 million

Part of the Blackwell Group, Oxford. FOUNDED 1922 as an academic and educational publishing house; the early list included fiction, poetry and, perhaps curiously, Enid Blyton. Later expanded into journals and now publishes more than a hundred. Rapid growth followed in the 1970s and 1980s, including the establishment of a wholly-owned distribution company, the takeover of Martin Robertson and joint ventures with **Polity Press** and the National Computing Centre in Manchester. *Publishes* academic, economics, humanities, business and finance, professional and social sciences. About 300 titles a year.

DIVISIONS/IMPRINTS
Academic & General *Phillip Carpenter* **Journals** *Sue Corbett* **Shakespeare Head Press** *John Davey*. Unsolicited mss welcome; synopses with specimen chapter and table of contents preferred. *Royalties* paid annually. *Overseas associates* Basil Blackwell Inc., Cambridge, Massachusetts.

Authors' Rating Moving into the Nineties with a strong business and professional list aimed at the international market. Anyone who wants to write about MBA-related subjects would be well advised to think of Blackwell.

Blackwell Scientific Publications Ltd

Osney Mead, Oxford OX2 0EL
☎0865 240201   Fax 0865 721205

Chairman *Nigel Blackwell*
Managing Director *Robert Campbell*
Approx Annual Turnover (Group) £50 million

FOUNDED 1939. Part of the Blackwell Group which moved to Oxford in the 1960s, a period of growth and expansion for the group. The company then broadened its horizons further, in 1987, by buying **Collins**' professional list, and 1989 saw expansion into Europe with the acquisition of Medizinische Zeitschriften Verlagsgesellschaft (MZV), Vienna; Ueberreuter Wissenschaft Verlag (now Blackwell Wissenschafts-Verlag), Berlin; and Arnette, Paris. *Publishes* medical, professional and science. About 230 titles a year, plus 160 journals.

Editorial Director *Peter Saugman* TITLES *Diseases of the Liver and Biliary System* Sherlock & Dooley; *Essential Immunology* Hoffbrand. Unsolicited mss and synopses welcome.
Royalties paid annually. *Overseas associates* Blackwell Scientific Publications Inc., USA; Blackwell Scientific Publications Pty Ltd, Australia. *Subsidiaries* in Paris, Berlin and Vienna; editorial offices in London and Edinburgh.

Authors' Rating A tightly organised, highly competent publisher. Rewards may not be madly generous but they do pay on time.

Blake Publishing

158 Fulham Palace Road, London W6 9ER
☎081–748 7606   Fax 081–748 7613

Chairman *David Blake*
Managing Director *John Blake*
Approx Annual Turnover £1 million

FOUNDED January 1991. Rapidly expanding young company. *Publishes* fiction and mass market nonfiction. No cookery, children's, specialist or non-commercial. 4 titles in 1991. Unsolicited mss, synopses and ideas welcome.
Royalties paid twice yearly.

Blandford Publishing Ltd
See **Cassell**

Bloodaxe Books Ltd

PO Box 1SN, Newcastle upon Tyne NE99 1SN
☎091–232 5988   Fax 091–222 0020

Chairman *Simon Thirsk*
Managing Director *Neil Astley*

Publishes poetry, literature and criticism, theatre and drama, photography, politics, women's studies. Ninety per cent of their list is poetry. Recently launched a new series called *Bloodaxe Contemporary French Poets*. About 30 titles a year.

Editorial Director *Neil Astley* Unsolicited poetry mss welcome. Authors of other material should write first with details of their work.
Royalties paid annually.

Authors' Rating 'The liveliest and most innovative poetry house', according to the editor of *Poetry Review*. Strong on women's poetry and on translations.

Bloomsbury Books
See **Godfrey Cave Holdings Ltd**

Bloomsbury Publishing Ltd

2 Soho Square, London W1V 5DE
☎071–494 2111   Fax 071–434 0151

Chairman/Managing Director *Nigel Newton*

One of three major new imprints set up in 1986, Bloomsbury was founded by Nigel Newton, together with David Reynolds, Alan Wherry and Liz Calder. Less than three years after publication of its first titles, Bloomsbury had put 25 books on to *The Sunday Times* bestseller list, and its authors have been winning many of the most prestigious literary prizes. In 1991, Nadine Gordimer won the **Nobel Prize for Literature**.

Publishing Directors *David Reynolds/Liz Calder*
Editorial Director *Kathy Rooney* TITLES *Cat's Eye* Margaret Atwood; *And the Policeman Smiled* Barry Turner; *The Feathermen* Sir Ranulph Fiennes; *Ripley Under Water* Patricia Highsmith; *Leith's Cookery Bible*; *The English Patient* Michael Oondatje; *Going Back* Simon Weston; *Brightness Falls* Jay McInerney. Unsolicited mss and synopses welcome.
Royalties paid twice yearly (April/October).

Authors' Rating Coming up to its sixth birthday, Bloomsbury is celebrating a relatively painless emergence from recession with high-level investment in potential bestsellers. But there is a solid backlist and the reference division is proving its worth. Sadly, the original paperbacks, launched with a great fanfare two years ago, have not done well.

Blueprint Monographs
See **Fourth Estate Ltd**

Bobcat
See **Omnibus Press**

Bodley Head Childrens
See **Random House Publishing Group Ltd**

The Book Guild Ltd
Temple House, 25–26 High Street, Lewes, East
Sussex BN7 2LU
☎ 0273 472534   Fax 0273 476472

Chairman *Christine Lewis*
Managing Director *Carol Biss*

FOUNDED 1982. *Publishes* fiction, academic, general, juvenile, sport. Expanding paperback list. About
80 titles a year.

DIVISIONS/IMPRINTS
Fiction TITLES *Beethoven: The Crown of Martyrdom* Richard Newman; *Opfer* Claire Powell;
Pinstriped Predators Roger Kryss. **General** TITLES *I
Came Alone* Bertha Leverton & Schmuel
Lowensohn (winner of the **H. H. Wingate/
Jewish Quarterly Literary Prize);** *Columbus
and the Golden World of the Island Arawaks* D. J.
R. Walker; *The Real Joan of Arc* Nora Wooster.
Temple House Books TITLES *Mrs Murphy's Laws
of Gardening* Faith Hines & Gray Jolliffe; *More than
Winning* Alastair Aitken; *Our World in Transition*
Diarmuid O'Murchu. **Seagull Books** TITLES *Isamu
Noguchi: Aspects of a Sculptor's Practice* Tim
Threlfall. No unsolicited mss. Ideas and synopses
welcome.
Royalties paid twice yearly.

Authors' Rating Trawls for authors in the small
ads columns of the literary pages who may be
asked to contribute to the cost of publishing.

Bookmarks Publications
265 Seven Sisters Road, Finsbury Park,
London N4 2DE
☎ 081–802 6145

Managing Director *Duncan Blackie*
Approx Annual Turnover £75,000

FOUNDED 1979 to project the international socialist
movement. Has close links with the Socialist Workers Party and its internationally related organisations. *Publishes* politics, economics, labour history,
trade unionism, international affairs. About 5 titles
a year.

DIVISIONS
General Publishing *Duncan Blackie* TITLES *The
English People and the English Revolution* Brian
Manning; *Year One of the Russian Revolution*
Victor Serge; *Trotsky: Fighting the Rising Stalinist
Bureaucracy* Tony Cliff. Unsolicited synopses and
ideas welcome as long as they are compatible with
existing policy. No unsolicited mss.

Royalties paid annually. *Overseas associates* Chicago, USA; Melbourne, Australia.

Bounty Books
See **Reed International Books**

Bowker–Saur Ltd
60 Grosvenor Street, London W1X 9DA
☎ 071–493 5841   Fax 071–580 4089

Managing Director *Dr Shane O'Neill*

Part of Reed Reference Publishing, owned by US-based Reed International, Inc. *Publishes* library
reference, library science, bibliography, biography,
African studies, politics and world affairs.

Editorial Directors *Geraldine Turpie/Mark
Hudson* Unsolicited mss will not be read. Approach
with ideas only.
Royalties paid annually.

Boxtree
36 Tavistock Street, London WC2E 7PB
☎ 071–379 4666   Fax 071–836 6741

Chairman *Peter Roche*
Managing Director *Sarah Mahaffy*
Publishing Director *Adrian Sington*
Approx Annual Turnover £2.5 million

FOUNDED April 1987. Underwent a management
buy-out in 1990. *Specialises* in books linked to and
about television programmes. *Publishes* mass market paperbacks linked to film, TV, sports and rock
music events, plus children's. About 80 titles a year.
TITLES include *Dinosaur; The Angling Times
Library; The Making of London's Burning; The
Pirelli Album of Motor Racing Heroes; The
Simpsons; The Storyteller* Anthony Minghella, and
Walt Disney junior novels.
Royalties paid twice yearly.

Authors' Rating Having completed its management buy-out from **Reed**, Boxtree is expanding
output to 60 to 70 titles a year, most of them
television tie-ins. A recent deal links Boxtree originals to Disney film and video releases.

Marion Boyars Publishers Ltd
24 Lacy Road, London SW15 1NL
☎ 081–788 9522   Fax 081–789 8122

Managing Director *Marion Boyars*

FOUNDED 1975 as Calder and Boyars. *Publishes*
architecture and design, biography and autobiography, business and industry, economics, fiction, law,
literature and criticism, medical, music, philosophy,

poetry, politics and world affairs, psychology, religion and theology, sociology and anthropology, theatre and drama, film and cinema, travel, women's studies. About 30 titles a year.

Editorial Director *Marion Boyars* **Non-fiction Editor** *Ken Hollings* AUTHORS include Georges Bataille, Ingmar Bergman, Heinrich Böll, Jean Cocteau, Ken Kesey, Hubert Selby, Igor Stravinsky. Unsolicited mss not welcome for fiction; submissions from agents preferred. Unsolicited synopses and ideas welcome for non-fiction.
Royalties paid annually. *Overseas associates* Marion Boyars Publishers Inc., 237 East 39th Street, New York, NY 10016, USA.

Authors' Rating A publisher with an eye for originality. A refuge for talent which others have failed to appreciate but can be offhand with lesser mortals.

Boydell & Brewer Ltd
PO Box 9, Woodbridge, Suffolk IP12 3DF
☎0394 411320

Publishes non-fiction only. All books commissioned. No unsolicited material.

BPS Books
St Andrews House, 48 Princess Road East,
Leicester LE1 7DR
☎0533 549568   Fax 0533 470787

Publications Manager *Joyce Collins*

Book publishing division of **The British Psychological Society**. *Publishes* a wide range of academic and applied psychology, including specialist monographs, state-of-the-art reviews, textbooks for teachers, managers, doctors, nurses, lawyers, etc., and schools material; also general psychology. 10–15 titles a year.

Editor *Rochelle Serwator* **Assistant Editor** *Susan Pacitti* Proposals considered.

Bracken Books
See **Studio Editions Ltd**

Brampton Publications
See **S. B. Publications**

Nicholas Brealey Publishing Ltd
156 Cloudesley Road, London N1 0EA
☎071-713 7455   Fax 071-713 7455

Managing Director *Nicholas Brealey*

FOUNDED 1992. Independent non-fiction publisher focusing on high-profile practical books for business internationally. *Publishes* business and 'readable reference', including management, law, languages for business, training and human resources. The new company began life with a backlist of major titles from The Industrial Society's book publishing arm. TITLES *Mind Your Manners: Managing Culture Clash in the Single European Market; Brits at Work: The Inside Job on Management; Eurospeak: The Dictionary of the Single Market.* No fiction or leisure titles. No unsolicited mss; synopses and ideas welcome. *Royalties* paid twice yearly.

Martin Breese Publishing
164 Kensington Park Road, London W11 2ER
☎071-727 9426/9378   Fax 071-229 3395

Chairman/Managing Director *Martin Breese*
Editorial Director *Paul Houghton*

FOUNDED 1975 to produce specialist conjuring books and has since established a more general list, linking up with German, Italian, French and US publishers. *Publishes* fiction, crime, biography, self hypnosis, meditation, ESP and related fields, music and conjuring titles. 20 titles in 1992. No unsolicited mss; synopses and ideas welcome. If interested, mss will be read; if rejected and time allows, reasons will be given.

IMPRINTS
Breese Books TITLES *Even If They Fail* David Holbrook; *Rupert Brooke: The Splendour and The Pain* John Frayn Turner; *Exit Mr Punch* Russell Brennan. **Breese Books Paperbacks** TITLES *Self-hypnosis and other Mind Expanding Techniques* Charles Tebbetts; *Music Business Bastards* Russell Brennan.
Royalties paid twice yearly. *Represented* countrywide and distributed by Clipper Distribution.

Authors' Rating Quality publisher with a clear idea of what it wants to achieve. Among the latest titles is one submitted by a *Writer's Handbook* reader. We must be doing something right.

Martin Brian & O'Keeffe Ltd
78 Coleraine Road, London SE3 7PE
☎081-858 5164

Chairman *Timothy O'Keeffe*
Approx Annual Turnover £10,000

FOUNDED 1971. *Publishes* general non-fiction. No unsolicited mss, but synopses and ideas for books welcome. 1 title a year on average.

Editorial Head *Timothy O'Keeffe*
Royalties paid twice yearly.

Bridge Studios

Kirklands, The Old Vicarage, Scremerston, Berwick upon Tweed, Northumberland TD15 2RB
☎ 0289 302658/330274

Joint Managing Directors *Lynne Gray/Keith Allan*

FOUNDED 1987. Small general publisher interested mainly in local books and humour. No fiction or children's material. Also produces audio cassettes. About 5 titles a year. TITLES *Wild Oats & Wellingtons* Fordyce Maxwell; *Back to the Pulpit* Jack Richardson; *Dark Tales of Old Newcastle* Pamela Armstrong; *Newcastle Streets, Gateshead Perambulations* Desmond O'Donnell. Unsolicited mss welcome.
Royalties paid twice yearly.

Brimax Books

See **Reed International Books**

British Academic Press

See **I. B. Tauris & Co. Ltd**

The British Academy

20–21 Cornwall Terrace, London NW1 4QP
☎ 071-487 5966   Fax 071-224 3807

Publications Officer *J. M. H. Rivington*
Approx Annual Turnover £100,000

FOUNDED 1901. The primary body for promoting scholarship in the humanities, the Academy publishes 10–15 titles a year, mostly in series of source material stemming from its own longstanding research projects, or in series of lectures and conference proceedings. Main subjects include history, art and archaeology. SERIES *Auctores Britannici Medii Aevi; Early English Church Music; Fontes Historiae Africanae; Oriental and African Archives; Records of Social and Economic History.* Proposals for these series are welcome and are forwarded to the relevant project committees. 'The British Academy does not publish for profit; *royalties* are paid only when titles have covered their costs.'

British Association for Local History

See **Phillimore & Co. Ltd**

The British Library

Marketing & Publishing Office, 41 Russell Square, London WC1B 3DG
☎ 071-323 7732   Fax 071-323 7736

Managing Director *Jane Carr*
Publishing Manager *David Way*
Approx Annual Turnover £600,000

FOUNDED 1979 as the publishing arm of The British Library's London Collections to publish works based on the historic collections and related subjects. *Publishes* bibliographical reference, manuscript studies and book arts. TITLES *A History of Writing; Anglo-Saxon Manuscripts; The Doves Bindery.* 30 titles in 1991. Unsolicited mss, synopses and ideas welcome if related to the history of the book, book arts or bibliography. No fiction or general non-fiction.
Royalties paid annually.

British Museum Press

46 Bloomsbury Street, London WC1B 3QQ
☎ 071-323 1234   Fax 071-436 7315

Managing Director *Hugh Campbell*
Publishing Manager *Celia Clear*

The book publishing division of British Museum Publications Ltd. FOUNDED 1973; relaunched in 1991 as British Museum Press. *Publishes* history, archaeology, ethnography, art history, exhibition catalogues, and all official publications of the British Museum. 38 titles in 1991. TITLES *The British Museum Book of Ancient Egypt; Egypt: The Living Past; The Art of the Conservator; Medieval Craftsmen; Ancient Turkey: A Traveller's History; Interpreting the Past.* Synopses and ideas for books welcome. The Prometheus Award is presented annually for the best synopsis from new writers under 35; details from the marketing department on request.
Royalties paid twice yearly.

Brooks Books

23 Sylvan Avenue, Bitterne,
Southampton SO2 5JW
☎ 0703 434131   Fax 0703 434131

Chairman/Managing Director *Clive Brooks*

FOUNDED 1990. *Publishes* nautical, aviation and motoring. Subjects should have sound international appeal. Launching an educational list for the new National Curriculum and seeking teachers with good ideas. No unsolicited mss; synopses and ideas for books welcome if accompanied by s.a.e. or International Reply Coupons. Always interested in well thought out approaches accompanied by marketing and sales suggestions. Commissioned

works will have to be submitted both in hard copy print-out and on IBM-compatible 5¼" or 3½" computer disks, either in ASCII or Wordperfect 5 formats. Details for contributors provided at contract stage.
Royalties paid twice yearly.

Brown, Son & Ferguson, Ltd
4-10 Darnley Street, Glasgow G41 2SD
☏ 041-429 1234   Fax 041-420 1694

Chairman/Joint Managing Director *T. Nigel Brown*

FOUNDED 1850. *Specialises* in nautical textbooks, both technical and non-technical. Also Boy Scout/ Girl Guide books, and Scottish one-act/three-act plays. Unsolicited mss, synopses and ideas for books welcome.
Royalties paid annually.

Brown Watson Ltd
The Old Mill, 76 Fleckney Road, Kibworth Beauchamp, Leicestershire LE8 0HG
☏ 0533 796333   Fax 0533 796303

Managing Director *Michael B. McDonald*

FOUNDED 1980. A subsidiary of **Peter Haddock Ltd.** *Publishes* children's books only. 100 titles in 1992. Most books are commissioned and therefore unsolicited mss and synopses are not welcome.

Authors' Rating Children's books for the cheaper end of the market. Authors must work fast to make money.

Burns & Oates Ltd
See **Search Press Ltd**

Business Education Publishers Ltd
Leighton House, 10 Grange Crescent, Sunderland, Tyne & Wear SR2 7BN
☏ 091-567 4963   Fax 091-512 0145

Joint Managing Directors *P. M. Callaghan/ T. Harrison*
Approx Annual Turnover £300,000

FOUNDED 1981. *Publishes* business education, economics and law. Currently expanding into further and higher education, computing and books for the Health Service. TITLES *BTEC National Core Studies* Paul Callaghan, Tom Harrison & John Ellison; *Law for Housing Managers* Tom Harrison; *Computer Studies (for BTEC)* Knott, Waites, Callaghan & Ellison; *Transferable Personal Skills (for BTEC)* D. Hind; *Getting Started with Information Technology*

D. Eadson & K. Williams; *Employment Law* Tom Harrison. Unsolicited mss and synopses welcome.
Royalties paid annually.

Butterworth & Co. (Publishers) Ltd/ Butterworth Tax Publishers
See **Reed International Books**

Butterworth-Heinemann
See **Reed International Books**

Byway Books
Unit 3, Tweedbank Craft Centre, Haining Drive, Tweedbank, Selkirkshire TD1 3RU
☏ 0896 57869   Fax 0896 57869

Managing Director *W. F. Laughlan*

FOUNDED 1981. Small publishing house now concentrating on children's books. *Publishes* children's picture books in paperback series called *Byway Bairns.* TITLES *The Enchanted Boy* Mollie Hunter; *Nanny & Barnaby* series Mary Lightbody; *Nursery Rhyme People* George Gilfillan; *Sam Sees Edinburgh, Sam Sees a Steam Train* Ann Scott. All books are full-colour illustrated throughout. ILLUSTRATORS include Mahri Christopherson, Brigid Collins, Andrea Hellyar, Alison Johnston, Jennie McCall, Lesley McLaren, Ann Scott. No unsolicited mss; send synopses in the first instance.
Royalties paid twice yearly.

Cadogan Books Ltd
Mercury House, 195 Knightsbridge, London SW7 1RE
☏ 071-225 2050   Fax 071-225 3008

Chairman *Bill Colegrave*
Approx Annual Turnover £500,000

Publishes the *Cadogan Travel Guide* series. About 30 titles a year.

Editorial Director *Rachel Fielding* No unsolicited mss; send introductory letter with synopsis only. Synopses and ideas welcome.
Royalties paid twice yearly.

Calder Publications Ltd
9-15 Neal Street, London WC2H 9TU
☏ 071-497 1741

Chairman/Managing Director *John Calder*

A publishing company which has grown around the tastes and contacts of its proprietor/manager/ editorial director John Calder, the iconoclast of the literary establishment. The list has a reputation for controversial and opinion-forming publications; Samuel Beckett is perhaps the most prestigious name. Formerly John Calder (Publishers) Ltd but now trading as Calder Publications following voluntary liquidation and the transfer of assets to the Calder Education Trust in 1990/91. *Publishes* autobiography, biography, drama, literary fiction, literary criticism, music, opera, poetry, politics, sociology.

Editorial Head *John Calder* AUTHORS Marguerite Duras, P. J. Kavanagh, Robert Pinget, Alain Robbe-Grillet, Nathalie Sarraute, Julian Semyonov, Claude Simon, Howard Barker (plays), ENO opera guides. TITLES include all of Beckett's prose and poetry. No unsolicited material.
Royalties paid annually. *Overseas associates* Riverrun Press, New York. Distribution by Combined Book Services.

Authors' Rating In search of a more favourable intellectual climate, John Calder has moved to Paris but retains a London house.

California University Press
Avonlea, 10 Watlington Road, Cowley,
Oxford OX4 5NF
☎ 0865 748405 Fax 0865 748401

Director *James Clark* (USA)

Became part of The University Presses of Columbia & Princeton in 1987. *Publishes* academic, art, Asian studies, scholarly. About 200 titles a year. All editorial work is carried out in the USA.

Cambridge University Press
The Edinburgh Building, Shaftesbury Road,
Cambridge CB2 2RU
☎ 0223 312393 Fax 0223 315052

Chief Executive *A. K. Wilson*
Managing Director, Publishing *R. J. Mynott*

The oldest press in the world, and part of Cambridge University. Over the last few years CUP has been diversifying into reference and medical publishing and expanded its activities in Australia and the USA. *Publishes* academic/educational books for international English-language markets, at all levels from primary school to postgraduate. Also bibles and academic journals. 1566 titles in 1991.

DIVISIONS
Bibles *D. B. Forbes* **ELT** *C. J. F. Hayes* **Humanities** *A. M. C. Brown* **Social Sciences** *M. Y. Holdsworth* **Journals** *R. L. Ziemacki* **Reference** *A. du Plessis* **Education** *S. A. Seddon* **Sciences** *S. Mitton* **Eyre & Spottiswoode Publishers Ltd** Bibles, prayer books and religious

books. No unsolicited mss; synopses and ideas for books considered.
Royalties paid twice yearly.

Authors' Rating Smaller than its younger Oxford counterpart (no children's list, for example) but probably the best managed of all the academic presses.

David Campbell Publishers Ltd
79 Berwick Street, London W1V 3PF
☎ 071-287 0035 Fax 071-287 0038

Chairman *Alewyn Birch*
Managing Director *David Campbell*
Approx Annual Turnover £2.3 million

Independent publishing house FOUNDED 1990 with the acquisition of **Everyman's Library** (FOUNDED 1906) from **J. M. Dent**. *Publishes* literature classics. 47 titles in 1991. TITLES *Pride and Prejudice; 1984; Lolita; Red and Black; Anna Karenina*. No unsolicited mss; synopses/ideas welcome.
Royalties paid annually.

Authors' Rating Everyman Library was founded to produce cheap, pocket-size volumes of classic literature for 'every kind of reader', Everyman ended up on a backwater of **Weidenfeld** until, that is, David Campbell and Mark Bicknell raised £1 million to fund its acquisition and relaunch. The publishing brief obviously excludes new authors — unless they feel themselves to be associated with instant classical status. Marketing and promotions are handled by **Pimlico Books** (see **Random House**).

Canongate Press
14 Frederick Street, Edinburgh EH2 2HB
☎ 031-220 3800 Fax 031-220 3888

Managing Director *Stephanie Wolfe Murray*
Approx Annual Turnover £500,000

FOUNDED 1990 as Canongate Publishing. Maintains a healthy mix of newly published work and reprints, including poetry, both for its *Canongate Classics* series (adult paperbacks) and the *Kelpie* children's series, which includes *Kelpie Picture Books*, full-colour illustrated books for young children. About 50 titles a year. Synopses preferred to complete mss.
Royalties paid twice yearly.

Authors' Rating A buy-out from failed parent company Musterlin, Canongate has made an impressive new start in life with an interesting and varied list.

Jonathan Cape Ltd
See **Random House Publishing Group Ltd**

Carcanet Press Ltd
208 Corn Exchange Buildings,
Manchester M4 3BQ
☎061-834 8730   Fax 061-832 0084

Chairman *Kate Gavron*
Managing Director *Michael Schmidt*

Since 1969 Carcanet has grown from an undergraduate hobby into a substantial venture. Anglo-European in orientation, it is a Manchester-based operation. Robert Gavron bought the company in 1983. *Publishes* poetry, academic, literary biography, fiction, memoirs and translations. About 40 titles a year, plus the *P.N. Review* (six issues yearly).

Editorial Director *Michael Schmidt* AUTHORS John Ashbery, Edwin Morgan, Elizabeth Jennings, Iain Crichton Smith, Natalia Ginzburg, Stuart Hood, Leonardo Sciascia, Christine Brooke-Rose, Pier Paolo Pasolini, C. H Sisson, Donald Davie. *Royalties* paid annually.

Authors' Rating Carcanet is widely praised as a publisher which gives 'more attention to its books than to its balance sheet'. According to William Boyd: 'Carcanet is a vital and enlightened presence ... everything an independent publisher should be'.

Carlton Books Ltd
142 Wardour Street, London W1V 3AN
☎071-734 7338   Fax 071-434 1196

Managing Director *Jonathan Goodman*

FOUNDED 1992. Owned by Carlton Communications. *Publishes* illustrated leisure and entertainment. No unsolicited mss; synopses and ideas welcome. No fiction.
Royalties paid twice yearly.

Carnival
See **HarperCollins Publishers Ltd**

Frank Cass
Gainsborough House, 11 Gainsborough Road,
London E11 1RS
☎081-530 4226   Fax 081-530 7795

Managing Director *Frank Cass*

Publishes Africa, development, strategic and military studies, education, history, literature, Middle East, politics and world affairs.

Editorial Head *Norma Marson* TITLES *Churchill, the Great Game and Total War* David Jablonsky; *The Politics of Marginality* Tony Kushner & Kenneth Lunn; *Spy Fiction, Spy Films and Real Intelligence* Wesley K. Wark.

IMPRINTS
Woburn Press *Norma Marson* Educational. TITLES *History of Education* ed. Peter Gordon & Richard Szreter; *Dictionary of British Educationalists* ed. Richard Aldrich & Peter Gordon. **Vallentine, Mitchell** Jewish interest. TITLES *Second Exodus* Ze'ev Venia Hadari. Unsolicited mss considered but synopsis with covering letter preferred.
Royalties paid annually.

Cassell
Villiers House, 41–47 Strand, London WC2N 5JE
☎071-839 4900   Fax 071-839 1804

Chairman/Managing Director *Philip Sturrock*
Approx Annual Turnover £14.7 million

FOUNDED 1848 by John Cassell. Bought by Collier Macmillan in 1974, then by CBS Publishing Europe in 1982. Finally returned to independence in 1986 as Cassell plc and a string of acquisitions followed: Tycooly's book publishing division; Link House Books (now Blandford Publishing Ltd); Mansell; then Mowbray; and most recently Ward Lock, publisher of Mrs Beeton, which has been in print continuously since 1861 and for which the purchase price remained secret. *Publishes* business, education and academic, general non-fiction (a wide range across various imprints, see below), primary and secondary school books, poetry, religious. About 400 titles a year.

DIVISIONS

General Non-fiction *Clare Howell* IMPRINTS **Cassell** TITLES *The Golden Age of Travel; Victorian Interior Design; The Art of Balcony Gardening; The NeoClassical Source Book.* **Blandford Publishing** FOUNDED 1919, part of Cassell since 1987. Expansion of lists planned. *Publishes* animal care and breeding, acquaria, art and graphics, aviculture, crafts and hobbies, DIY, fishing, gardening, history, military, natural history, New Age, photography, popular music, popular science. About 50 titles a year. TITLES *Sketching with a Pencil* John Hamilton; *Parrots, Their Care and Breeding* Rosemary Low; *Encyclopaedia of Marine Animals* ed. Neville Coleman. **Ward Lock Ltd** FOUNDED 1854, acquired by Cassell in 1989. *Publishes* crafts, cookery, decorating and design, Mrs Beeton, walking, sports and gardening. About 100 titles a year. Also **Studio Vista** and **Wisley Handbooks**.

Educational, Religious & Reference *Stephen Butcher* IMPRINTS **Arms & Armour Press, Cassell,   Geoffrey   Chapman,   Mansell,**

Mowbray, New Orchard Editions. TITLES *Starting Design and Technology; Robert Runcie; The Cassell Directory of Publishing; Great Battles of the British Army* David Chandler; *Military Small Arms of the 20th Century.* **Arms & Armour Press** *Roderick Dymott* Aviation, military and war, nautical, politics and world affairs, transport. About 50 titles a year. **Mowbray** *Ruth McCurry* Theology, Christian paperbacks, handbooks for clergy and laity. FOUNDED 1858 and acquired by Cassell in 1988. About 30 titles a year.

Unsolicited mss and synopses welcome for most imprints but return postage should be included. Proposals with synopses preferred in most cases however. No fiction.

Royalties payment depends on sales potential and varies between imprints; generally twice yearly, but annually for Arms & Armour Press.

Authors' Rating Strong on academic and reference but the general books division has still to make its mark.

Kyle Cathie Ltd

3 Vincent Square, London SW1P 2LX
☎071-834 8027   Fax 071-821 9528

Managing Director *Kyle Cathie*

FOUNDED 1990 by three like-minded colleagues to publish and 'really promote books we have personal enthusiasm for'. *Publishes* mostly non-fiction: cookery, natural history, health, current affairs, philosophy and biography. 30 titles in 1992. No unsolicited mss. Synopses and ideas considered. *Royalties* paid twice yearly.

Authors' Rating A refugee from big-time publishing who has made good as a small independent producing books which really matter.

CBD Research Ltd

Chancery House, 15 Wickham Road, Beckenham, Kent BR3 2JS
☎081-650 7745   Fax 081-650 0768

Chairman *G. P. Henderson*
Managing Director *C. A. Henderson*
Approx Annual Turnover £250,000

FOUNDED 1961. *Publishes* directories and other reference/guides to sources of information. 2 titles in 1991 but looking to increase this to around 8 titles a year. No fiction. Unsolicited mss, synopses and ideas welcome.
Royalties paid quarterly.

Centaur Press Ltd

Fontwell, Arundel, West Sussex BN18 0TA
☎0243 543302

Managing Director *Jon Wynne-Tyson*

FOUNDED 1954. A one-man outfit publishing some 20 titles a year (literary, philosophical, classical, monographs) at its peak. Then became increasingly preoccupied with humane education and reduced its output to around 1–3 titles a year. After a semi-dormant decade — the Eighties — Centaur has just launched *The Kinship Library*, a series on the philosophy, politics and application of humane education, with special focus on the subject of animal rights and its relevance to the human condition. TITLES *The Universal Kinship; All Heaven in a Rage; The Life of Anna Kingsford; Seventy Years Among Savages; The Extended Circle; Food for A Future.* 6 titles in 1991.

IMPRINTS
Linden Press (no connection with **Simon & Schuster**'s later adoption). No unsolicited mss. New titles are commissioned.

Authors' Rating Given the limited range of its own output it may seem appropriate that Centaur offers a useful guide to Publishing Your Own Book (£3.50, revised edition).

Central Books Ltd

99 Wallis Road, London E9 5LN
☎081-986 4854   Fax 081-533 5821

Managing Director *William Norris*
Approx Annual Turnover £2 million

FOUNDED 1939, principally as book distributors. Now imports titles from Eastern Europe, the USA and West Germany, and distributes material from small presses. *Publishes* imported titles only (about 300 a year). No new material published. Distribution only.

Century Publishing

See **Random House Publishing Group Ltd**

Chadwyck-Healey Ltd

Cambridge Place, Cambridge CB2 1NR
☎0223 311479   Fax 0223 66440

Chairman *Sir Charles Chadwyck-Healey*

FOUNDED 1973. Established Chadwyck-Healey Inc., Washington DC, in 1974, Chadwyck-Healey France in 1985 and Chadwyck-Healey Espana in 1989. *Publishes* mainly on microform and CD-ROM, with a few reference works and guides for microform collections. Also publishes occasional monographs on fine art and architecture. About 50 titles a year.

Editorial Head *Alison Moss* TITLES *The English Satirical Print; Theatre in Focus; Index of Manuscripts in The British Library.* No unsolicited mss. Synopses and ideas for books welcome. *Royalties* paid annually.

W & R Chambers

43–45 Annandale Street, Edinburgh EH7 4AZ
☎031-557 4571
Fax 031-557 2936   Telex 727967

Chairman *John C. Clement*
Managing Director *T. Maurice Shepherd*
Approx Annual Turnover £2.5 million

FOUNDED in the early 1800s to publish self-education books, but soon diversified into dictionaries and other reference works. Having remained independent since 1832, Chambers was bought by Groupe de la Cité (publishers of the Larousse dictionaries in France) in 1989. Groupe de la Cité has expanded the company and widened its range of dictionaries and reference books. Acquisitions over the last two years have included **Richard Drew Publishing Ltd** of Glasgow and the **Harrap Publishing Group.** Chambers bought the copyrights and publishing licences of Harrap's core business: its bilingual dictionaries and language learning and reference publications for an undisclosed price in the spring of 1992. The acquisition strengthens its position in the dictionary market, adding bilingual titles covering almost all the major European languages, to its English language dictionaries. *Publishes* dictionaries, reference, school/college textbooks, Scottish non-fiction and self-help language guides. 50 titles in 1991. Send synopsis with accompanying letter rather than completed mss.
Royalties paid annually. *Overseas representation* by Chambers, Kingfisher and Graham, Inc. in North America, and various agents and publishers worldwide.

Authors' Rating After many quiet years, Chambers is expanding on three main fronts — reference, dictionaries and Scottish publishing.

Chapman

4 Broughton Place, Edinburgh EH1 3RX
☎031-557 2207

Managing Editor *Joy Hendry*

A new venture devoted to publishing books by young Scottish writers already known to readers of *Chapman* (see **Magazines**). The publishing side of the business grew organically out of the magazine and 'we intend to expand publishing activities considerably over the next two years'. *Publishes* poetry, short stories, books of contemporary importance in 20th-century Scotland. 4 titles in 1991. TITLES *Sting* George Gunn; *Singing Seals* Gordon Meade; *Conflict & Contexts* R. S. Silver. No unsolicited mss; synopses and ideas for books welcome. *Royalties* paid.

Geoffrey Chapman
See **Cassell**

Paul Chapman Publishing Ltd

144 Liverpool Road, London N1 1LA
☎071-609 5315   Fax 071-700 1057

Managing Director *Paul R. Chapman*
Editorial Director *Marianne Lagrange*

Publishes business, management, accountancy and finance, education, geography, planning and economics, for the academic and professional markets. A new list is being developed in human computer interaction. Books are marketed worldwide. Unsolicited mss and synopses welcome. *Royalties* paid twice yearly.

Chapman & Hall Ltd
See **Routledge, Chapman & Hall Ltd**

Chapmans Publishers

141–143 Drury Lane, London WC2B 5TB
☎071-379 9799   Fax 071-497 2728

Editor-in-Chief *Marjory Chapman*

FOUNDED 1989. *Publishes* fiction, biography, autobiography, travel, politics, current affairs, history, reference, some children's, crafts and cookery. No unsolicited mss.
Royalties paid twice yearly.

Authors' Rating Headed by Ian Chapman, former chairman of **Collins**, Chapmans aims for the mass market with such commercially illustrious names as Hammond Innes and Jack Higgins.

Chatsworth Library
See **Airlife Publishing Ltd**

Chatto & Windus Ltd
See **Random House Publishing Group Ltd**

Cherrytree Press Children's Books
See **Chivers Press (Publishers)**

Child's Play (International) Ltd
Ashworth Road, Bridgemead, Swindon,
Wiltshire SN5 7YD
☎0793 616286   Fax 0793 512795

Managing Director *Michael Twinn*

FOUNDED 1970. This Swindon-based publisher has pioneered learning-through-play since the early days of its inception. Recently signed a deal with like-minded Tamarind, founded by Verna Wilkins in 1989. Child's Play have taken over distribution of Tamarind titles. *Publishes* children's books — picture books, fiction, science, art, activity books and dictionaries. TITLES *Twins; How Small is an Ant?; Christmas Eve: The Prince and the Goosegirl; Animal Rights; Whizzers; Alf 'n' Bet.* Unsolicited mss welcome. S.a.e. essential for return/response. Expect to wait 1–2 months for a reply.
Royalties payment varies according to contract.

Chivers Press (Publishers)
Windsor Bridge Road, Bath, Avon BA2 3AX
☎0225 335336   Fax 0225 310771

Chairman *B. T. R. Scruby*
Managing Director *Roger H. Lewis*

Part of The Gieves Group. *Publishes* reprints for libraries mainly, including biography/auto-biography, children's, crime, fiction, large print editions, complete and unabridged, and spoken word cassettes. No unsolicited material. Reprints only for the time being.

IMPRINTS
Atlantic Large Print, Gunsmoke Westerns, Lythway Children's Large Print, Lythway Large Print, Paragon Softcover Large Print, New Portway Large Print, Swift Children's Books, Cherrytree Press Children's Books, Windsor Large Print, Black Dagger Crime; Scarlet Dagger Large Print. Cassette Imprints: **Chivers Audio Books, Chivers Children's Audio, Cavalcade Story Cassettes, Crimson Dagger Audio Books, Word-for-Word Audio Books, Sterling Audio Books.**
Royalties paid twice yearly.

Christian Focus Publications
Geanies House, Fearn, Tain, Ross-shire IV20 1TW
☎0862 87541   Fax 0862 87532

Chairman *R. W. M. Mackenzie*
Managing Director *William Mackenzie*
Editorial Head *Malcolm Maclean*

Approx Annual Turnover £300,000

FOUNDED 1979 to produce children's books for the co-edition market. Now a major producer of Christian books for the UK. *Publishes* Christianity, adult and children's, including some Christian fiction. 33 titles in 1991. Unsolicited mss, synopses and ideas welcome from Christian writers.
Royalties paid twice yearly.

Churchill Livingstone
Robert Stevenson House, 1–3 Baxter's Place, Leith Walk, Edinburgh EH1 3AF
☎031–556 2424   Fax 031–558 1278

Managing Director *Andrew Stevenson*
Publishing Director *Peter Richardson*
Journals Director *Sally Morris*

Formed from the amalgamation of E. & S. Livingstone and J. & A. Churchill in the early 1970s. Now part of the **Longman Group**. *Publishes* medical and nursing books, and medical journals. About 150 titles a year.

Publishing Managers *Timothy Horne/Mary Law.* No unsolicited mss. Synopses and ideas welcome. *Royalties* paid annually. *Overseas associates* Churchill Livingstone Inc., New York; Churchill Livingstone España, Madrid, Spain.

Authors' Rating Churchill Livingstone remains the leading medical publisher.

Cicerone Press
2 Police Square, Milnthorpe, Cumbria LA7 7PY
☎05395 62069   Fax 05395 63417

Managing Director *Dorothy Unsworth*

FOUNDED 1969. *Publishes* guidebooks and outdoor pursuit books only. About 30 titles a year. No fiction or poetry.

Editorial Director *Walt Unsworth* TITLES *The Cotswold Way; A Walker's Guide to the Lancaster Canal; Birdwatching in Mallorca; Modern Alpine Climbing; The Pyrenean Trail GR10; Lost Lancashire.* No unsolicited mss; synopses and ideas for books considered.
Royalties paid twice yearly.

John Clare Books
106 Cheyne Walk, London SW10 0DG
☎071–352 0636

Proprietor *M. Frost*

FOUNDED 1979. Parent company Interpress Features. Started with a wide general list and became increasingly specialised. *Publishes* non-fiction with an educational bias, and social education. TITLES *Mime over Matter* Pat Keysall; *Social Drama* Bert Amies. Synopses and ideas for books within their specialist field welcome. *Royalties* paid twice yearly.

Clarendon Press
See **Oxford University Press**

Claridge Press
27 Windridge Close, St Albans, Hertfordshire AL3 4JP
☎ 0727 869486

Chairman/Managing Director *Roger Scruton*
Managing Director *Andrea Downing*

FOUNDED 1987. Developed from the quarterly *Salisbury Review*. *Publishes* current affairs — political, philosophical and sociological — from a right-wing viewpoint.

Editorial Director *Roger Scruton* TITLES *Thinkers of our Time* and *Blasts* (both series); *Footsteps from the Finland Station; Collapse of Communism; Landscape Into Sound.* Unsolicited mss welcome within given subject areas.
Royalties according to contract.

Authors' Rating As the only house devoted to publishing the works of conservative thinkers, Claridge proclaims itself to be 'Britain's most backward-looking publisher'.

Robin Clark
See **Quartet Books**

T. & T. Clark
59 George Street, Edinburgh EH2 2LQ
☎ 031-225 4703   Fax 031-220 4260

Managing Director *Geoffrey Green*
Approx Annual Turnover £1 million

FOUNDED 1821. *Publishes* religion, theology, law and philosophy (academic only). About 35 titles a year, including journals.

Editorial Head *Geoffrey Green* TITLES *Church Dogmatics* Karl Barth; *A Textbook of Christian Ethics* ed. Robin Gill; *Scottish Law Directory; The Law of Arbitration in Scotland* R. L. C. Hunter. Unsolicited mss, synopses and ideas for books welcome.
Royalties paid annually.

Classic Words & Image
See **Elite Words & Image**

Clematis Press Ltd
18 Old Church Street, London SW3 5DQ
☎ 071-352 8755

Chairman/Managing Director *Clara Waters*

Distributors of imported books. No editorial facilities. No unsolicited mss.

Clio Press Ltd
55 St Thomas' Street, Oxford OX1 1JG
☎ 0865 250333   Fax 0865 790358

Chairman/Managing Director *John Durrant*
Approx Annual Turnover £2.5 million

Subsidiary of **ABC-Clio Inc.**, Denver, Colorado. FOUNDED 1971 in Oxford to publish academic reference works. *Publishes* social science and humanities; general fiction and non-fiction in large print; and unabridged talking books. About 220 titles in 1992.

DIVISIONS
Clio Press R. G. Neville TITLES *World Bibliographical Series; International Organisations Series; World Photographers Series; Clio Montessori Series.* **Art Bibliographies** J. Chibnall TITLES *Artbibliographies Modern* **Isis Large Print** V. Babington Smith **Isis Audio Books** V. Babington Smith.
Royalties paid twice yearly.

Frank Coleman Publishing
Maulden Road, Flitwick, Bedfordshire MK45 5BW
☎ 0525 712261   Fax 0525 718205

Managing Director *Neil Goldman*
Approx Annual Turnover under £100,000

Publishes children's books. Unsolicited mss welcome. Synopses and ideas for books considered.
Royalties paid annually.

Collins
See **HarperCollins Publishers Ltd**

Collins & Brown
Mercury House, 195 Knightsbridge, London SW7 1RE
☎ 071-584 2002   Fax 071-584 0138

Chairman *Cameron Brown*
Managing Director *Mark Collins*

Approx Annual Turnover £1 million

Independent publisher FOUNDED 1989. *Publishes* illustrated non-fiction: practical photography, crafts, gardening, illustrated letters and history. No fiction, children's, poetry or local interest. 50 titles in 1991.

DIVISIONS

Collins & Brown *Gabrielle Townsend* TITLES *Complete Guide to Video; Traditional Houses of Rural France; Complete Guide to Conservatory Plants*; **Juliet Gardiner Books** History, biography and literature titles *Juliet Gardiner* TITLES *Byron & Shelley*; **History Today Books** *Juliet Gardiner* TITLES *Age of Chivalry; Russia and Europe*. No unsolicited mss; send outlines with s.a.e. *Royalties* paid twice yearly.

Columbia University Press

Avonlea, 10 Watlington Road, Cowley, Oxford OX4 5NF
☎0865 748405   Fax 0865 748401

Director *John Moore* (USA)

Publishes academic books, especially social sciences, Asian studies and reference. 200 titles a year. Editorial department in the US. Represents American University in Cairo Press and East European Monographs.

Commonword Ltd

Cheetwood House, 21 Newton Street, Manchester M1 1FZ
☎061–236 2773

Chairman *Christina Hill*
Approx Annual Turnover £9000

Manchester-based publishing and writing project established in 1977. Develops, supports and publishes new writing in the North-west. Books are sold and distributed nationally under the Crocus imprint launched in 1988. 3 titles in 1991. Unsolicited mss welcome from writers in the North-west for poetry, short stories, novels and autobiography. Synopses preferred for novels.

IMPRINTS

Crocus *Cathy Bolton/Helen Windrath* Poetry, short stories and fiction.
Royalties not paid.

Condé Nast Books

See **Random House Publishing Group Ltd**

Condor

See **Souvenir Press Ltd**

Conran Octopus

See **Reed International Books**

Constable & Co. Ltd

3 The Lanchesters, 162 Fulham Palace Road, London W6 9ER
☎081–741 3663   Fax 081–748 7562

Chairman/Join Managing Director *Benjamin Glazebrook*
Publishing Director/Joint Managing Director *Robin Baird-Smith*
Approx Annual Turnover £2.34 million

FOUNDED in 1890 by Archibald Constable, a grandson of Walter Scott's publisher. Controlling interest was bought by Benjamin Glazebrook in 1967 and Random Century (now **Random House**) bought the remaining 48% in 1989. Small but select publisher whose list includes Muriel Spark and John Julius Norwich. *Publishes* archaeology, architecture and design, biography and autobiography, cookery, fiction, guidebooks, history and antiquarian, natural history, psychology, sociology and anthropology, travel and topography, wines and spirits. About 75 titles a year. TITLES *Symposium* Muriel Spark; *Howling at the Moon* Paul Sayer; *The Ant Colony* Francis King. Unsolicited mss, synopses and ideas for books welcome.
Royalties paid twice yearly.

Authors' Rating Exercising a strong appeal to authors who enjoy a personal style of management. Distinguished by paying authors at least two thirds of income from the sale of paperback rights. Contrary to the impression given in the last edition of *Writer's Handbook*, Constable is not limiting itself to agented projects. To quote Robin Baird-Smith, 'as a middle-sized resolutely independent publishing house, we put great store on publishing first novels and fresh, original non-fiction books.'

Consumers' Association

2 Marylebone Road, London NW1 4DF
☎071–486 5544   Fax 071–383 7044/935 1606

Director *Dr John Beishon*

FOUNDED 1957 as a consumer research organisation, funded by subscription sales of *Which?* and other publications. Now a registered charity. *Publishes* non-fiction: information, reference, how-to, including travel, gardening, health, personal finance, consumer law, food, education, crafts, DIY. Titles must offer direct value or utility to the UK consumer. 26 titles in 1991.

DIVISIONS

Which? Books *Gill Rowley* TITLES *Good Food Guide; Good Skiing Guide; Good Walks Guide; Which? Travel Guides; Which? Consumer Guides.* No unsolicited mss; send synopses and ideas only. *Royalties* paid twice yearly; but owing to in-house editorial development of many titles, royalties are not always applicable.

Leo Cooper

See **Pen & Sword Books Ltd**

Corgi

See **Transworld Publishers Ltd**

Cornerhouse Publications

70 Oxford Street, Manchester M1 5NH
☎061-228 7621   Fax 061-236 7323

Managing Director *Dewi Lewis*
Approx Annual Turnover £120,000

Part of Manchester's film and visual arts centre, Cornerhouse. Publishing activities began in 1987 and in 1990 Cornerhouse was winner of the *Sunday Times* Small Publisher of the Year Award. *Publishes* illustrated books and critical texts on the visual arts, photography, design and media. 12 titles in 1991. Unsolicited material welcome though 'we rarely commission work'. Not interested in anything outside its subject areas.
Royalties paid annually.

Cornwall Books

See **Golden Cockerel Press Ltd**

Coronet Books

See **Hodder & Stoughton Ltd**

Council for British Archaeology

112 Kennington Road, London SE11 6RE
☎071-582 0494   Fax 071-587 5152

President *Dr P. V. Addyman*
Director *Richard Morris*
Approx Annual Turnover £25,000

FOUNDED in 1944 to represent and promote archaeology at all levels. Its aims are to improve the public's awareness in and understanding of Britain's past; to carry out research; to survey, guide and promote the teaching of archaeology at all levels of education; to publish a wide range of academic, educational, general and bibliographical books. *Publishes* academic archaeology reports and monographs; archaeology and education. No unsolicited mss; synopses and ideas for books welcome.

Editorial Head *Christine Pietrowski* Located at CBA Northern Office, The King's Manor, York YO1 2EP. Tel: 0904 433925. TITLES *Welsh Industrial Heritage; The Archaeology Resource Book; An Anglo-Saxon Watermill at Tamworth.*

IMPRINTS
The Archaeology of York TITLES *The Coppergate Helmet; Non-ferrous Metalworking from Coppergate.* **The Archaeology of Lincoln** TITLES *St Mary's, Guildhall.*
Royalties not paid.

Countryside Books

6 Pound Street, Newbury, Berkshire RG14 6AB
☎0635 43816

Publisher *Nicholas Battle*

FOUNDED 1976. *Publishes* mainly paperbacks on regional subjects, generally by county. Local history, genealogy, walking and photographic, some transport. 44 titles in 1991. Unsolicited mss and synopses welcome.
Royalties paid twice yearly.

Crabtree Publishing

73 Lime Walk, Headington, Oxford OX3 7AD
☎0865 67575   Fax 0865 742024

President *Peter Crabtree*

FOUNDED 1980. *Publishes* ecological and educational books in series. 12 titles in 1992.

Editorial Director *Bobbie Kalman* SERIES include *Animals and Their Ecosystems; Lands, Peoples and Culture; The Arctic World; Endangered Animals; Historic Communities; Crabtree Environment; Primary Ecology.* Synopses and ideas for books welcome.
Royalties paid twice yearly.

Cressrelles Publishing Co. Ltd

311 Worcester Road, Malvern,
Worcestershire WR14 1AN
☎0684 565045

Managing Director *Leslie Smith*

Publishes general and children's books.

DIVISIONS/IMPRINTS
Actinic Press Specialises in books on chiropody; **Kenyon-Deane; J. Garnett Miller Ltd** (see entry).

Crime Club
See **HarperCollins Publishers Ltd**

Crocus
See **Commonword Ltd**

The Crowood Press Ltd
The Stable Block, Crowood Lane, Ramsbury,
Marlborough, Wiltshire SN8 2HR
☏ 0672 20320   Fax 0672 20280

Chairman/Publisher *John Dennis*
Publishing Director *Ken Hathaway*

FOUNDED 1982 by John Dennis as a one-man concern. *Publishes* sport and leisure including animal and land husbandry, climbing and mountaineering, country sports, equestrian, fishing and shooting. Also chess and bridge, crafts, dogs, gardening, health and social issues, military, motor and travel. 70 titles in 1992. Preliminary letter preferred in all cases. Synopses and ideas for books welcome.
Royalties paid annually.

Crucible
See **HarperCollins Publishers Ltd**

James Currey Publishers
54B Thornhill Square, London N1 1BE
☏ 071-609 9026   Fax 071-609 9605

Chairman/Managing Director *James Currey*

FOUNDED 1985. A small specialist publisher. *Publishes* academic books on Africa, the Caribbean and Third World: history, anthropology, economics, sociology, politics and literary criticism. Approach in writing with synopsis if material is 'relevant to our needs'.
Royalties paid annually.

Curzon Press Ltd
264 Pentonville Road, London N1 9JY
☏ 071-837 8027

Managing Director *Malcolm G. Campbell*

Scholarly and specialised publishing house with imprints on Asian and African studies. *Publishes* academic and scholarly, history and archaeology, languages and linguistics, Oriental and African studies, philosophy, religion and theology, sociology and anthropology. Unsolicited mss considered.

IMPRINTS
The Alban Press.
Royalties according to contract.

Dalesman Publishing Co. Ltd
Clapham, Lancaster LA2 8EB
☏ 05242 51225   Fax 05242 51708

Editorial Manager *David Joy*

Publishers of the well-established county magazine of the same name, and also *Cumbria* magazine. *Publishes* crafts and hobbies, geography and geology, guidebooks, history and antiquarian, humour, transport, travel and topography. Unsolicited mss considered on all subjects. About 25 titles a year.
Royalties paid twice yearly.

Terence Dalton Ltd
Water Street, Lavenham, Sudbury,
Suffolk CO10 9RN
☏ 0787 247572   Fax 0787 248247

Chairman *Terence R. Dalton*
Director *Elisabeth Whitehair*

FOUNDED 1967. Part of Lavenham Holdings plc. A family company. *Publishes* non-fiction: aviation and maritime history, river series and East Anglian interest. 7 titles in 1991.

Editorial Head *Elisabeth Whitehair* TITLES *Smacks and Bawleys* John Leather; *Two Horse Power* John Hewitt; *The River Tees* Bob Woodhead; *Pathfinder Bennett, Airman Extraordinary* Capt. A. S. Jackson; *The Suffolk Coast* Russell Edwards; *Thames Cavalcade* L. M. Bates; *The Beloved Coast* R. A. Whitehead. No unsolicited mss; send synopsis with two or three sample chapters. Unsolicited ideas for books welcome.
Royalties paid annually.

The C. W. Daniel Co. Ltd
1 Church Path, Saffron Walden, Essex CB10 1JP
☏ 0799 521909   Fax 0799 513462

Managing Director *Ian Miller*
Approx Annual Turnover £750,000

FOUNDED in 1902 by a man who apparently knew and was an admirer of Tolstoy. The company was taken over by its present directors in 1973 and has since acquired the Health Science Press imprint (1980), health and healing titles, and Neville Spearman Publishers (1985) who specialised in metaphysical titles. *Publishes* New Age: alternative healing and metaphysical. 13 titles in 1991. No fiction, books on diet or cookery. Unsolicited

synopses and ideas welcome; no mss. Expansion planned.
Royalties paid twice yearly.

IMPRINT
Daybreak *Morag Reeve.*
Royalties paid twice yearly.

Darf Publishers Ltd

13 Prince of Wales Terrace, London W8 5PG
☎071-937 1974 Fax 071-937 2580
Chairman/Managing Director *M. B. Fergiani* ·
Approx Annual Turnover £500,000

FOUNDED 1982 to publish books and reprints on the Middle East, history, theology and travel. Now *publishing* geography, history, language, literature, oriental, politics, theology, travel and sport. About 50 titles a year.

Editorial Head *A. Bentaleb* TITLES *Moslems in Spain; Travels of Ibn Battuta; Sudan, Death of a Dream; The Barbary Corsairs; First Footsteps in East Africa; A Pilgrimage to Nejd; Teaching of the Qur'an; Elementary Arabic; They All Played at Lords.* Unsolicited mss, synopses and ideas for books welcome.
Royalties paid twice yearly. *Overseas associates* Dar Al-Fergiani, Cairo and Tripoli.

Dartmouth Publishing Co. Ltd

Gower House, Croft Road, Aldershot, Hampshire GU11 3HR
☎0252 331551 Fax 0252 344405
Managing Director *John Irwin*

FOUNDED 1989. Part of the **Gower Publishing Group**. *Publishes* books and reference works on international law and international relations, politics and management. Unsolicited mss, synopses and ideas welcome.
Royalties paid according to contract.

Darton, Longman & Todd Ltd

89 Lillie Road, London SW6 1UD
☎071-385 2341 Fax 071-381 4556
Managing Director *Christopher Ward*
Approx Annual Turnover £1 million

FOUNDED by Michael Longman who broke away from Longman Green in 1959 when they decided to cut their religious list. Became a common ownership business in July 1990. *Publishes* Christian books of all types. About 50 titles a year.

Editorial Director *Mary Jean Pritchard* TITLES *Jerusalem Bible; New Jerusalem Bible; God of Surprises; The God Who Speaks* Ian Petit. Unsolicited mss, synopses and ideas for books welcome.

David & Charles Publishers

Brunel House, Forde Road, Newton Abbot, Devon TQ12 4PU
☎0626 61121 Fax 0626 64463
Managing Director *Terry Stubbs*

FOUNDED 1960 as a specialist company. Family controlled until 1990 when it was acquired by the **Reader's Digest Association Ltd**. *Publishes* practical crafts, gardening, hobbies, popular art and natural history. No fiction, poetry, memoirs or children's. About 60 titles a year.

Editorial Director *Piers Spence* TITLES *Picture it in Cross Stitch; Painting Detail in Watercolour; Tales of the Old Gamekeepers; The Hillier Manual of Trees and Shrubs; Making Dolls' Houses; Understanding Britain's Wildlife.* Unsolicited mss, synopses and ideas welcome. *Author's Guide* available on receipt of a first class stamp.
Royalties paid annually; twice yearly in first two years on request.

Authors' Rating Relaunched as a front rank publisher of illustrated non-fiction titles, David & Charles plans to bring out around 60 titles a year, an 80 per cent cutback on the previous output. To compensate, it is said that sales per title have doubled.

Christopher Davies Publishers Ltd

PO Box 403, Sketty, Swansea, West Glamorgan SA2 9BE
☎0792 648825

Managing Director *Christopher T. Davies*
Approx Annual Turnover *c.*£100,000

FOUNDED 1949 to increase the output of Welsh language publications. By the 1970s this had reached the level of over 50 titles a year. The drop in Welsh sales in that decade led to the establishment of a small English list, which has continued. *Publishes* biography, cookery, history and literature of Welsh interest. About 6 titles a year.

Editorial Head *Christopher Davies* TITLES *English/Welsh Dictionaries; Abbeys and Priories of Wales; Historic West Wales.* No unsolicited mss. Synopses and ideas for books welcome.
Royalties paid twice yearly.

Authors' Rating A favourite for Celtic readers and writers.

Daybreak
See **Darton, Longman & Todd Ltd**

Debrett's Peerage Ltd
73–77 Britannia Road, PO Box 357,
London SW6 2JY
☎ 071-736 6524   Fax 071-731 7768

Chairman *Ian McCorquodale*
Managing Director *R. M. Summers*
General Manager *Patricia Ellis*

FOUNDED 1769. The company's main publications
(in conjunction with **Macmillan**) are the quin-
quennial *Debrett's Peerage and Baronetage* (next
publication 1995), and *Debrett's People of Today*
(annual). Debrett's general books are published
under licence through **Headline Book
Publishing**.
Royalties paid twice yearly.

Dedalus Ltd
Langford Lodge, St Judith's Lane, Sawtry,
Cambridgeshire PE17 5XE
☎ 0487 832382   Fax 0487 832382

Chairman *Juri Gabriel*
Managing Director *George Barrington*
Approx Annual Turnover £125,000

FOUNDED 1983. First titles included *The Arabian
Nightmare*. Nearly all their titles are what they
describe as literary fantasy. Most successful titles
tend to be 'outré, fantastic or decadent works'.
Publishes contemporary European fiction and classics, literary fantasy anthologies and original literary fantasy. Interested in translators' suggestions
for European fiction; synopses and ideas for books
welcome in the field of literary fantasy only. 20
titles in 1991.

DIVISIONS/IMPRINTS
Literary Fantasy *Robert Irwin/Brian Stableford*
TITLES *Dedalus Book of British Fantasy/French
Fantasy/German Fantasy, etc.* **Dedalus European
Classics** TITLES *Devil in Love* Cazotte; *The Angel
of the West Window* Meyrink. **Decadence from
Dedalus** TITLES *Senso* Camillo Boito; *Angels of
Perversity* Remy de Gourmont; *The Dedalus Book
of Russian Decadence* ed. Natalia Rubenstein. **A
Dedalus Nobel Prize Winner** TITLES *One, No-
body and One Hundred Thousand* Pirandello.
Europe 1992 TITLES *The Black Cauldron*
Heinesen; *History of a Vendetta* Yorgi
Yatromanolakis; *The Architect of Ruins* Herbert
Rosendorfer.
Royalties paid annually. *Overseas associates*
Hippocrene Books, New York.

Authors' Rating One-time writer, Eric Lane, became so frustrated at the difficulty he and other
aspiring authors had in getting into print, he set up
his own publishing house. Against the odds
(Dedalus was originally known by the trade as
Dead Loss), he succeeded in launching several first
novelists and in making a living.

Delacorte Press
See **Transworld Publishers Ltd**

J. M. Dent
See **Orion Publishing Group**

André Deutsch Ltd
105–106 Great Russell Street, London WC1B 3LJ
☎ 071-580 2746   Fax 071-631 3253

Chairman/Managing Director *T. G. Rosenthal*
Submissions *Esther Whitby*
Approx Annual Turnover £2.5 million

FOUNDED in 1950 by André Deutsch, the original
list included *Books are Essential, To Live in Man-
kind* and *Jewish Cookery*. A major fiction list
followed, with writers like V. S. Naipaul, Philip Roth
and Norman Mailer. André Deutsch sold the company in 1990 and finally severed his association
with it in September 1991. *Publishes* art illustrated,
fiction and non-fiction, poetry and general, particularly biography, current affairs, history, politics and
photographic. About 130 titles a year. Sold its
highly regarded children's list to **Scholastic Publications Ltd** in 1991.

DIVISIONS
Adult books *Esther Whitby* AUTHORS John
Updike, Paul Erdman, Penelope Lively, Carlos
Fuentes, William Gaddis, Gore Vidal, Dan
Jacobson, Gerald Priestland, Malcolm Bradbury,
Dale Spender, Gail Godwin, Bohumil Hrabal,
George V. Higgins, Clive Sinclair, Molly Keane.
Unsolicited mss, synopses and ideas for books
welcome.
Royalties paid twice yearly.

André Deutsch Children's Books
See **Scholastic Publications Ltd**

Diadem
See **Hodder & Stoughton Ltd**

Dinosaur
See **HarperCollins Publishers Ltd**

Dolphin Book Co. Ltd
Tredwr, Llangrannog, Llandysul, Dyfed SA44 6BA
☎0239 654404

Managing Director *Martin L. Gili*
Approx Annual Turnover £5000

FOUNDED 1957. A small publishing house specialising in Spanish and South American academic books. TITLES *The Late Poetry of Pablo Neruda* Christopher Perriam; *Galdós' House of Fiction* (papers given at the Birmingham Galdós Colloquium). 1 title in 1991; 2 planned for 1992. Unsolicited mss not welcome. Approach by letter. *Royalties* paid annually.

John Donald Publishers Ltd
138 St Stephen Street, Edinburgh EH3 5AA
☎031-225 1146　　　　Fax 031-220 0567

Managing Director *Donald Morrison*
Publisher *Gilly Basan*

Publishes academic and scholarly, agriculture, archaeology, architecture and design, business and industry, economics, educational and textbooks, guidebooks, history and antiquarian, languages and linguistics, military, music, religious, sociology and anthropology, sports and games, transport. About 40 titles a year. Unsolicited mss considered. *Royalties* paid annually.

Dorling Kindersley Ltd
9 Henrietta Street, London WC2E 8PS
☎071-836 5411　　　　Fax 071-836 7570

Chairman *Peter Kindersley*
Deputy Chairman *Christopher Davis*

FOUNDED 1974. Packager for the international market, and publisher of illustrated non-fiction on subjects such as cookery, crafts, gardening, health, natural history and children's information books. Launched a new US imprint in autumn 1991. About 175-200 titles a year.

DIVISIONS

Adult; Children's; Direct; Vision (video); **Education; Multimedia.** TITLES *Eyewitness Guides; BMA Complete Family Health Encyclopedia; RHS Gardener's Encyclopedia of Plants & Flowers; Reader's Digest Complete Guide to Cookery.* Unsolicited synopses/ideas for books welcome.

Authors' Rating Lavish, high-quality books which sell massively on the international market. To date, Dorling Kindersley has published 300 books which have sold 75 million copies, or 250,000 per book. Bucking the trend, Dorling Kindersley announced its conversion to the Net Book Agreement with vociferous opposition to Dillons' 'tawdry' price cuttings. At the time of going to press, there were plans for a stock market flotation to raise up to £30 million for further development, particularly of interactive CDs.

Doubleday
See **Transworld Publishers Ltd**

D. P. Publications Ltd
Aldine Place, 142-144 Uxbridge Road,
London W12 8AW
☎081-746 0044　　　　Fax 081-743 8692

Managing Director *R. J. Chapman*

FOUNDED 1972. Part of BPP Holdings plc. *Publishes* accounting, business, computing and mathematics textbooks for higher and further education.

Editorial Director *Catherine Tilley* Unsolicited synopses and ideas for books welcome. Authors sought for active learning material in business, accounting and computing in further and higher education.
Royalties paid twice yearly.

Dragon's World
26 Warwick Way, London SW1V 1RX
☎071-976 5477　　　　Fax 071-976 5429

Managing Director *Hubert Schaafsma*

FOUNDED 1975. *Publishes* fantasy art, natural history, children's non fiction (ages 7-11), contemporary album cover art, fine art, design, craft, photography, DIY, folklore, illustrated children's classics and fables. 25 titles in 1991.

IMPRINTS

Dragon's World General illustrated non-fiction, notably natural history, with a major pocket guide series. **Paper Tiger Books** Fantasy art. Unsolicited mss, synopses and ideas for books welcome.

Drake Educational Associates
89 St Fagans Road, Fairwater, Cardiff CF5 3AE
☎0222 560333　　　　Fax 0222 554909

Contact *R. G. Drake*

Educational publishers. A member of the Drake Group of Companies.

Richard Drew Publishing Ltd
See **W & R Chambers**

Gerald Duckworth & Co. Ltd

The Old Piano Factory, 48 Hoxton Square,
London N1 6PB
☎071-729 5986   Fax 071-729 0015

Managing Director *Colin Haycraft*

FOUNDED 1898. Owned jointly by the Rowntree
Trust, Duckworth author Michael Estorick and a
private investor. Authors on their early list included
Hilaire Belloc, August Strindberg, Henry James and
John Galsworthy. *Publishes* mainly academic, with
some fiction. About 60 titles a year.

IMPRINT
Paperduck Paperback imprint. Unsolicited synopses and ideas for books welcome. Enclose s.a.e. or
return postage for response/return.
Royalties paid twice yearly at first, annually thereafter.

Authors' Rating With rumours of the impending
departure of the idiosyncratic Colin Haycraft, there
is some confusion as to the policy of this small
general publisher.

Martin Dunitz Ltd

The Livery House, 7–9 Pratt Street,
London NW1 0AE
☎071-482 2202   Fax 071-267 0159

Chairman/Managing Director *Martin Dunitz*
Publisher *Stuart McRobbie*

FOUNDED 1978 publishing popular health, flying
and sailing books. Moved into medical publishing
in the early 1980s and sold its *Positive Health
Guides* to **Macdonald/Optima**, following the success of the series. Now concentrating solely on
specialist medical books aimed at an international
market, with co-editions for the USA and Europe.
Recently won the Queen's Award for Export
Achievement (1991). *Publishes* medical and dental
titles only. 15 titles in 1991. Unsolicited synopses
and ideas welcome but no mss.
Royalties paid twice yearly.

Dunrod Press

8 Brown's Road, Newtownabbey, Co.
Antrim BT36 8RN
☎0232 832362   Fax 0232 848780

Managing Director *Ken Lindsay*

FOUNDED 1979. *Publishes* politics and world affairs.
About 3 titles a year.

Editorial Head *Ken Lindsay* Preliminary letter
essential. Synopses and ideas for books welcome.
Royalties paid annually. *Overseas associates*
Dunrod Press, Republic of Ireland.

Eagle

See **Inter Publishing Ltd**

Earthscan Publications Ltd

See **Kogan Page Ltd**

East-West Publications

8 Caledonia Street, London N1 9DZ
☎071-837 5061   Fax 071-278 4429

Chairman *L. W. Carp*
Managing Director *B. G. Thompson*
Approx Annual Turnover £250,000

FOUNDED in the early Seventies. *Publishes* Eastern
religions and philosophy, children's books and
stationery. 6 titles in 1991. No 'romance, pot-
boilers, mindless leftish political tracts, books on
chiropody, farm management, differential calculi,
etc.' Unsolicited mss, synopses and ideas discouraged.

DIVISIONS

East-West Publications *L. W. Carp* TITLES *The
Sacked Mountain; Nirvana Tao; Nada Brahma;*
Gallery Children's Books *B. G. Thompson*
TITLES *A Child's Garden of Verses; Our Old Nursery
Rhymes.*
Royalties paid twice yearly.

Ebury Press

See **Random House Publishing Group Ltd**

Economist Books

Axe & Bottle Court, 70 Newcomen Street,
London SE1 1YT
☎071-403 9328   Fax 071-403 9485

Publishing Director *Sarah Child*
Approx Annual Turnover £1.5 million

Owned by *The Economist. Publishes* business and
finance, management studies, economics, guidebooks, politics and world affairs, reference books.
About 12 titles a year.

Editorial Director *Stephen Brough* Unsolicited
mss considered.
Royalties paid twice yearly.

Authors' Rating Powerful marketing via *The
Economist* distribution network. Strong on direct
sales.

Edinburgh University Press

22 George Square, Edinburgh EH8 9LF
☎031-650 4218/Polygon: 650 4689
Fax 031-662 0053
Chief Editor *Vivien Bone*

Publishes academic and scholarly books: anthropology, archaeology, biology and zoology, computer science, history, Islamic studies, law, linguistics, literary criticism, philosophy, physics, social sciences. 95 titles in 1992.

IMPRINTS
Polygon A creative writing and Scottish studies imprint. *Publishes* international fiction and poetry. SERIES include *Sigma* (aphorisms, anarchisms and surreal); *Determinations* (Scottish cultural polemics); *Living Memory* (oral history). No unsolicited mss for EUP titles; mss welcome for Polygon but must be accompanied by s.a.e. for reply/return; letter/synopsis preferred in the first instance, particularly for EUP.
Royalties paid annually.

Edward Elgar Publishing Ltd

Suite 2, Fairview Court, Fairview Road,
Cheltenham, Gloucestershire GL52 2EX
☎0242 226934   Fax 0242 262111
Managing Director *Edward Elgar*

FOUNDED 1986. Part of the **Gower Publishing Group**. *Publishes* books and reference publications on economics and other social sciences. Unsolicited mss, synopses and ideas welcome.
Royalties paid according to contract.

Elite Words & Image

PO Box 24, Sherborne, Dorset DT9 3SN
☎0935 816410   Fax 0935 816409
Publisher *Ali Burns-Hill*

FOUNDED 1990. *Publishes* childcare and parenting, health, women's interests, some illustrated humour and artistic literature. No general fiction. Unsolicited mss, synopses and ideas welcome with s.a.e. 1 title in 1991; 5 planned for 1993.

IMPRINTS
Classic Words & Image TITLES *The Rime of the Ancient Mariner*.
Royalties paid twice yearly.

Elliot Right Way Books

Kingswood Buildings, Lower Kingswood,
Tadworth, Surrey KT20 6TD
☎0737 832202   Fax 0737 830311

Joint Managing Directors *Clive Elliot/Malcolm G. Elliot*

FOUNDED 1946 by Andrew G. Elliot. All the early books were entitled *The Right Way to . . .*, but this format became too restrictive. However, most books are still *How to* titles, instruction books illustrated with line drawings, published in Paperfronts. *Publishes* how-to books on car repairs, cooking, DIY, family financial and legal matters, family health and fitness, fishing, looking after pets and horses, motoring, popular education, puzzles, jokes and quizzes.

IMPRINTS
Paperfronts Unsolicited non-fiction mss, synopses and ideas for books welcome.
Royalties paid annually.

Aidan Ellis Publishing

Cobb House, Nuffield, Henley-on-Thames,
Oxon RG9 5RT
☎0491 641496   Fax 0491 641678
Partners/Editorial Heads *Aidan Ellis/Lucinda Ellis*
Approx Annual Turnover £350,000

FOUNDED in 1971 by Aidan Ellis. *Publishes* fiction and general trade books. 22 titles in 1992.

DIVISIONS
Fiction Current authors include Dana Fuller Ross, Vivian Stuart, Jose Roig, Neil Church and Philip Sayetta Jacobs. **Non-Fiction** TITLES *Foreign Policy Standpoints* Mauno Koivisto, President of Finland; *Dear Departed* Marguerite Yourcenar (part 1 of a three-part autobiography); *The Saving of Kenwood and the Northern Heights* John Carswell; *Peter Lanyon* Andrew Causey. Unsolicited mss, synopses and ideas for books welcome.
Royalties paid twice yearly. *Overseas associates* in Australia and New Zealand, Europe, Far East, Africa, South America and South Africa.

Elm Publications

Seaton House, Kings Ripton, Huntingdon,
Cambridgeshire PE17 2NJ
☎04873 254/238   Fax 04873 359
Managing Director *Sheila Ritchie*

FOUNDED 1977. *Publishes* textbooks, namely business management, teaching aids, educational resources (especially history), educational software and languages for adult learners and business. First approach in writing with outline/ideas for books. 'We usually commission books and teaching/ training resources to meet business, management and other syllabi.' About 30 titles a year. Ideas always welcome for new textbooks. *Royalties* paid annually.

Elsevier Science Publishers Ltd

Crown House, Linton Road, Barking,
Essex IG11 8JU
📞 081-594 7272   Fax 081-594 5942

Managing Director *Brian D. Scanlan*

Parent company Elsevier Science Publishers, Amsterdam. *Publishes* scientific and technical books, journals and magazines. There was considerable expansion into the scientific journals market at the turn of the decade with the acquisition of over 400 titles from **Pergamon**. About 170 titles a year, plus journals.

DIVISIONS
Applied Science *Dr Robert Lomax* **Advanced Technology** *Chris Lloyd* **Elsevier Trends Journals** *David Bousfield*. Unsolicited mss, synopses and ideas for books welcome.
Royalties paid annually.

Authors' Rating An offshoot of the largest Dutch publisher. Refreshingly open with authors in the tradition of northern European publishers — early news on print-runs and royalties paid promptly.

Elvendon Press

The Old Surgery, High Street, Goring on Thames,
Reading RG8 9AW
📞 0491 873003   Fax 0491 874233

FOUNDED 1978. *Specialises* in producing publications (books, magazines and booklets) for government departments, national organisations, media & PR agencies, and blue-chip companies. Database facility welcomes publication of directories, yearbooks & exhibition programmes. All general subjects considered except fiction. Keen to branch out into other areas. Synopses and ideas for books welcome.

Editorial Head *Ray Hurst* No unsolicited mss. Preliminary letter essential.

Emap Business Publishing Ltd

Meed House, 21 John Street, London WC1N 2BP
📞 071-404 5513   Fax 071-831 3540

Chairman *Colin Morrison*

Leading UK publisher of professional and business magazines, with over 65 titles and directories on its list, including market leaders such as *PC User; Architects' Journal; Designers' Journal; Media*

Week; Television Week; Money Week; What Personal Computer. Operating subsidiaries: Emap Architectural Press; Emap Computing; Emap Business Information; Emap Heighway; Emap Media; Emap Maclaren; Emap Response.

Enitharmon Press

36 St George's Avenue, London N7 0HD
📞 071-607 7194   Fax 071-607 8694

Director *Stephen Stuart-Smith*

FOUNDED 1969 by Alan Clodd and soon established itself as one of Britain's most enterprising poetry presses. One of the leaders in its field. Publication of Beckett, Lorca and Borges gave Enitharmon an international reputation but it has also fostered new talent in this country. *Publishes* poetry, literary criticism, art and photography. 30 titles in 1992–93. TITLES include new poetry collections by Duncan Forbes and Martyn Crucefix; *A Sprinkle of Nutmeg* (letters to Christopher Fry); Catherine Reilly's anthology of Victorian women poets; David Gascoyne's *Selected Verse Translations*; Jeremy Reed's *Pop Stars* (with photos by Mick Rock); and collaborations involving the poets Neil Curry and Paul Durcan with the artists Jim Dine and Patrick Caulfield. No unsolicited mss.
Royalties paid according to contract. *Distribution* in the UK and Ireland by Password (Books) Ltd, Manchester; in the USA by Dufour Editions Inc., Chester Springs, PA 19425.

Ensign Publications

2 Redcar Street, Southampton SO1 5LL
📞 0703 702639   Fax 0703 785251

Managing Director *David Graves*
Approx Annual Turnover £500,000

FOUNDED 1988 to publish local history and regional books based on Central Southern England (i.e. Hampshire and the Isle of Wight, Dorset, Sussex, Wiltshire). *Publishes* local history, topography, shipping, transport, naval, business, countryside, true crime, customs and folklore. TITLES *One Hundred Years of Roads and Rails Around the Solent; Fast Boats and Flying Boats: A Biography of Hubert Scott-Paine; Pub Walks in the New Forest.* No unsolicited mss; send synopses in the first instance. No fiction. 11 titles in 1991.
Royalties paid annually.

Epworth Press

Hartley Victoria College, Luther King House,
Brighton Grove, Manchester M14 5JP
📞 061-224 2215   Fax 061-248 9201

Chairman *Graham Slater*
Editor *Rev. Dr C. S. Rodd*

Formerly based in Cambridge, Epworth has only recently relocated its operation to Manchester. *Publishes* Christian books only: philosophy, theology, bibles, pastoralia and social concern. No fiction, poetry or children's. Epworth's new series of Commentaries on Bible is now well launched. About 10 titles a year. TITLES *An Easier Yoke? A Perspective on Christian Ministry* Trevor Rowe; *The Truth in Tradition: A Free Church Symposium* Keith Clements, Rupert E. Davies & David Thompson; *Looking on Glass: Thoughts for Every Day* Nancy Blamires; *Free to Dance with the Lord of the Dance* Mary Austin; commentaries on *The Johannine Epistles* William Loader; *I Corinthians* Nigel Watson. Unsolicited mss considered; please write to enquire first. Authors wishing to have their mss returned should send sufficient postage. *Royalties* paid annually.

Erskine Press/Bluntisham Books

PO Box 3, Harleston, Norfolk IP20 0BH
☎ 0986 86359   Fax 0986 868181

Chief Executive *Stephen Easton*

Publishes Antarctic exploration titles. No unsolicited mss or synopses, but ideas always welcome on Antarctic-related titles. About 2–3 titles a year. *Royalties* paid twice yearly.

estamp

204 St Albans Avenue, London W4 5JU
☎ 081-994 2379   Fax 081-995 9131

Contact *Silvie Turner*

Independent publishing company set up specifically to publish books about the fine art of printmaking, papermaking and bookmaking. Books are designed and written for people with special or professional interest in the inter-related crafts of papermaking, artists' books and original prints. TITLES *A Printmaker's Handbook; Which Paper?; Printsafe; Directory of Printmaking Workshops.* Approach in writing in first instance.

Euromonitor

87–88 Turnmill Street, London EC1M 5QY
☎ 071-251 8024   Fax 071-608 3149

Chairman *R. N. Senior*
Managing Director *T. J. Fenwick*
Approx Annual Turnover £3 million

FOUNDED 1972 as an international business information publisher specialising in library and professional reference books. Now also handling market reports, electronic databases and journals. *Publishes* business reference, market analysis and information directories only. 77 titles in 1991.

DIVISIONS

Market Direction *S. Holmes* TITLES *Credit & Charge Cards: The International Market;* **Reference Books & Reports** *S. Leckey* TITLES *Europe in the Year 2000; European Marketing Handbook;* **Directories** *M. McGrath* TITLES *European Directory of Trade and Business Associations; World Retail Directory and Sourcebook.*
Royalties payment is generally by flat fee.

Europa Publications Ltd

18 Bedford Square, London WC1B 3JN
☎ 071-580 8236   Fax 071-636 1664

Chairman *C. H. Martin*
Managing Director *P. A. McGinley*
Approx Annual Turnover £4 million

Owned by Staples Printers Ltd. FOUNDED 1926 with the publication of the first edition of *The Europa Year Book.* *Publishes* annual reference books on political, economic and commercial matters. No fiction, biography or poetry. No unsolicited mss; synopses and ideas welcome. 2 titles in 1991. *Royalties* paid annually.

Europe 1992

See **Dedalus Ltd**

Evans Brothers Ltd

2A Portman Mansions, Chiltern Street, London W1M 1LE
☎ 071-935 7160   Fax 071-487 5034

Managing Director *Stephen Pawley*
Approx Annual Turnover £2 million

FOUNDED 1908 by Robert and Edward Evans. Originally published educational journals, books for primary schools and teacher education. After rapid expansion into popular fiction and drama, both lists were sacrificed to a major programme of educational books for schools in East and West Africa. A new UK programme was launched in 1986 and **Hamish Hamilton**'s children's non-fiction list was acquired in 1990. *Publishes* UK children's and educational books, adult travel, educational books for Africa, Caribbean and Far East. 35 titles in 1991.

International Publishing Director *Brian Jones*
Primary Commissioning Editor
Jean Coppendale

DIVISIONS
Overseas TITLES *Agriculture for Senior Secondary Schools; Modern History of Nigeria.* **UK Publishing** TITLES *Repairing the Damage: Earthquakes, Hurricanes & Storms; Take Ten Years 1980s; Holy Cities: Rome/Jerusalem/...* Unsolicited mss, synopses and ideas for books welcome.
Royalties paid annually. *Overseas associates* Kenya, Cameroon, Sierra Leone, Evans Bros (Nigeria Publishers) Ltd.

Everyman
See **Orion Publishing Group**

Everyman's Library
See **David Campbell Publishers Ltd**

University of Exeter Press
Reed Hall, Streatham Drive, Exeter EX4 4QR
☎ 0392 263066　　　　　　Fax 0392 264420
Contact *The Secretary*

FOUNDED 1956. *Publishes* academic books: archaeology, classical studies, mining, history, maritime studies, English literature (especially medieval), linguistics, modern languages and literature, American and Commonwealth arts, and books on Exeter and the South West. 21 titles in 1991. Publishing proposals from within and outside Exeter University welcome.
Royalties not paid.

Exley Publications Ltd
16 Chalk Hill, Watford, Hertfordshire WD1 4BN
☎ 0923 248328　　　　　　Fax 0923 818733
Managing Director *Helen Exley*

FOUNDED 1976. An independent family company. *Publishes* gift books and humour in series. No individual titles. Has a very substantial children's non-fiction list. About 40 titles a year.

Editorial Director *Helen Exley* TITLES *The World's Greatest Composers; People Who Have Helped the World; Organisations That Help the World.* No unsolicited mss but synopses (accompanied by s.a.e.) considered.

Eyre & Spottiswoode Publishers Ltd
See **Cambridge University Press**

Faber & Faber Ltd
3 Queen Square, London ˙WC1N 3AU
☎ 071-465 0045　　　　　　Fax 071-465 0034

Chairman/Managing Director *Matthew Evans*
Approx Annual Turnover £8.8 million

Geoffrey Faber and Richard de la Mare founded the company in the 1920s, with T.S. Eliot as an early recruit to the board. The original list was based on contemporary poetry and plays (the distinguished backlist includes Eliot, Auden and MacNeice). *Publishes* poetry and drama, art, children's, fiction, nursing and medical, music, specialist cookery, and a growing number of miscellaneous one-offs. The new blood of recent years has led to Faber looking to new areas, such as film/ screenplays. Unsolicited mss will be considered; synopses and ideas for books welcome.

DIVISIONS
Art *Giles de la Mare* **Children's** *Janice Thomson* AUTHORS Gene Kemp, Helen Cresswell. **Cookery** *Tracey Scoffield* TITLES *Simple French Cuisine; Pastability.* **Fiction** *Robert McCrum* AUTHORS P.D. James, Peter Carey, William Golding, Milan Kundera, Mario Vargas Llosa, Garrison Keillor, Paul Auster. **Music** *Andrew Clements/Tracey Scoffield* **Nursing & Medical** *Roger Osborne* Specialist titles and popular books. **Plays & Filmscripts** AUTHORS Samuel Beckett, David Hare, Tom Stoppard, John Boorman, Woody Allen, Martin Scorsese. **Poetry** *Christopher Reid* AUTHORS Seamus Heaney, Ted Hughes, Douglas Dunn, Tom Paulin. **Non-fiction** *Susanne McDadd* TITLES *Live From Number 10; Good & Faithful Servant; Saddams's War.*
Royalties paid twice yearly. *Overseas office* Boston.

Authors' Rating The quaint traditional image of Faber as a literary establishment publisher has long since given way to sharp commercialism. Some may regret the change but there is little doubt that authors and readers have benefited. Faber paperbacks with their distinctive jackets now account for 60% of turnover, yet it is not so long ago that the very idea of venturing beyond hardback was regarded as heresy. A third of the company is owned by a trust representing staff, one of a number of safeguards to protect Faber against predators.

Facts On File
Collins Street, Oxford OX4 1XJ
☎ 0865 728399　　　　　　Fax 0865 244839
Contact *Alan Goodworth*

Subsidiary of **Facts On File Inc.**, New York. *Specialises* in information and reference books, including series, on virtually any subject from antiques to zoology for age range 8 plus. Claims to be 'in an excellent position to adopt world English language rights in titles for simultaneous publication worldwide'. Publishes up to 125 books a year, with a growing backlist (currently 700 titles).

DIVISIONS
Trade/Reference/Academic/Professional/ Educational TITLES *Cultural Atlas* (series); *The Elements* (series); *Wetlands; Madagascar: A Natural History; The Visual Dictionary; Encyclopedia of Shakespeare; World Political Almanac.* Approach with ideas.
Royalties paid twice yearly. *Represented* in the UK by **Roundhouse Publishing**, Oxford.

Falmer Press
Rankine Road, Basingstoke, Hampshire RG24 0PR
☎0256 840366/071–405 2237 Fax 0256 479438

Managing Director *Malcolm Clarkson*

Publishes educational books/materials for all levels. Largely commissioned.

Editorial Director *Malcolm Clarkson* Unsolicited mss considered.
Royalties paid annually.

Farming Press Books
Wharfedale Road, Ipswich, Suffolk IP1 4LG
☎0473 241122   Fax 0473 240501

Chairman *Derek Barton*
Manager *Roger Smith*

Owned by United Newspapers plc, publishers of the *Daily Express, Sunday Express* and *Daily Star. Publishes* specialist books on farming, plus a range of humorous and countryside books. No unsolicited mss; synopses and ideas for books welcome provided material is within their specific field. 10 titles in 1991.
Royalties paid twice yearly.

Fernhurst Books
33 Grand Parade, Brighton, East Sussex BN2 2QA
☎0273 623174   Fax 0273 623175

Chairman/Managing Director *Tim Davison*

FOUNDED 1979. For people who love boats mainly. *Publishes* practical, highly illustrated handbooks on sailing, watersports, skiing and motoring. 14 titles in 1991. TITLES *Sailing: A Beginner's Manual* John Driscoll; *The Prudential Book of Sailing: A Guide for the under-16s* Gary & Steve Kibble; *The Catamaran Book* Brian Phipps; *Motorcycling: A Beginner's Manual* Jerry Matthews. No unsolicited mss; synopses and ideas welcome.
Royalties paid twice yearly. *Distributed* by **Reed**

International, one of the world's largest publishing groups.

Flamingo
See **HarperCollins Publishers Ltd**

Floris Books
15 Harrison Gardens, Edinburgh EH11 1SH
☎031–337 2372   Fax 031–346 7516

Managing Director *Christian Maclean*
Editor *Christopher Moore*
Approx Annual Turnover £250,000

Trading since 1977. *Publishes* books related to the Steiner movement, including arts & crafts, children's, the Christian Community, history, religious, science, social questions.

IMPRINTS
Floris Classics *Christopher Moore* No unsolicited mss. Synopses and ideas for books welcome.
Royalties paid annually.

Fodor
See **Random House Publishing Group Ltd**

Fontana
See **HarperCollins Publishers Ltd**

Forest Books
20 Forest View, Chingford, London E4 7AY
☎081–529 8470   Fax 081–524 7890

Managing Director *Brenda Walker*
Approx Annual Turnover £70,000

FOUNDED 1984 to promote international cultural links through publishing. *Publishes* literary translations, poetry, anthologies, fiction and plays. Particularly keen to publish works from minority languages and ethnic groups whose literatures are not widely spread. A number of books are published in collaboration with UNESCO. *Specialises* in books from Eastern Europe. TITLES *Call Yourself Alive?* Nina Cassian; *Modern French Poetry* ed. Martin Sorrell; *Vlad, Dracula, the Impaler* Marin Sorescu. Unsolicited mss discouraged unless they fall firmly within subject interests; synopses and ideas welcome subject to the same criteria. No non-fiction of any kind or writing from Britain. International works only.
Royalties paid twice yearly.

G. T. Foulis & Co Ltd
See **Haynes Publishing Group**

W. Foulsham & Co.
Yeovil Road, Slough, Berkshire SL1 4JH
☎0753 526769   Fax 0753 858699

Chairman *R. S. Belasco*
Managing Director *B. A. R. Belasco*
Approx Annual Turnover £1.7 million

FOUNDED 1816 and now one of the few remaining
independent family companies to survive takeover.
Publishes non-fiction on most subjects including
astrology, gardening, cookery, DIY, business, hobbies, sport, health and New Age. No fiction.
Unsolicited mss, synopses and ideas welcome. 60
titles in 1991.
Royalties paid twice yearly.

Fount
See **HarperCollins Publishers Ltd**

Fountain Press Ltd
Queensborough House, 2 Claremont Road,
Surbiton, Surrey KT6 4QU
☎081-390 7768   Fax 081-390 8062

Managing Director *Mr H. M. Ricketts*
Approx Annual Turnover £600,000

FOUNDED 1923 when it was part of the Rowntree
Trust Group. Owned by the British Electric Traction
Group until 1982 when it was bought out by the
present managing director. *Publishes* mainly
photography; also crafts and hobbies, DIY, military
and aviation, graphics and design. TITLES
*Photography Yearbook; Camera Manuals Series;
On the Spot Guides.* Unsolicited mss and synopses
are welcome. About 25 titles a year.
Royalties paid twice yearly.

Fourth Estate Ltd
289 Westbourne Grove, London W11 2QA
☎071-727 8993   Fax 071-792 3176

Chairman/Managing Director *Victoria Barnsley*
Approx Annual Turnover £1.5 million

FOUNDED 1984. Independent publishers, with the
emphasis on literary fiction and well-designed
upmarket non-fiction. Strong on high media profile
books and design. *Publishes* current affairs, design,
fiction, humanities, humour, popular culture, reference (hardback and trade paperback). About 50
titles a year.

DIVISIONS/IMPRINTS
Fiction/Non-fiction   *Giles O'Bryen/Christopher
Potter* TITLES *Fables of the Irish Intelligentsia* Nina
Fitzpatrick; *Shoot the Women First* Eileen
MacDonald; *Republic of Love* Carol Shields; *Judy
Garland* David Shipman. **Non-Fiction** *Victoria
Barnsley* TITLES *John Major* Bruce Anderson.
Guardian Books Joint imprint with *The Guardian*
newspaper. Entirely non-fiction: reference, current
affairs, humour, the arts and travel guides. TITLES
Notes & Queries, The Election: A Voter's Guide.
Blueprint Monographs ed. *Deyan Sudjic* Joint
imprint with *Blueprint* magazine: a series of mono-
graphs on leading international designers and
architects. TITLES *Javier Mariscal: Designing the
New Spain* Emma Dent Coad. Unsolicited mss,
synopses and ideas for books welcome.
Royalties paid twice yearly.

Authors' Rating Now approaching its tenth birthday, Fourth Estate has become the model for small
publishing ventures.

Foxbury Press
See **St Paul's Bibliographies**

Franklin Watts
See **The Watts Group**

Free Association Books
26 Freegrove Road, London N7 9RQ
☎071-609 5646   Fax 071-700 0330

Managing Director *Robert M. Young*

Publishes psychoanalysis and psychotherapy; critical books on the social implications of science and
technology, and cultural studies; biography, autobiography and memoirs. Very selective. Write a letter
in the first instance; unsolicited mss not accepted.

Editorial Head *Robert M. Young* TITLES
Psychoanalytic Politics; Black Athena.
Royalties paid twice yearly. *Overseas associates*
Columbia University Press, USA; Astam, Australia.

W. H. Freeman & Co. Ltd
20 Beaumont Street, Oxford OX1 2NQ
☎0865 726975   Fax 0865 790391

President *Linda Chaput* (New York)

Part of W. H. Freeman & Co., USA. *Publishes*
academic, agriculture, animal care and breeding,
archaeology, artificial intelligence, biochemistry,
biology and zoology, chemistry, computer science,
economics, educational and textbooks, engineering, geography and geology, mathematics and

statistics, medical, natural history, neuroscience, paleontology, physics, politics and world affairs, psychology, sociology and anthropology, and veterinary. Freeman's editorial office is in New York (Oxford is a sales and marketing office only) but unsolicited mss can go through Oxford. Those which are obviously unsuitable will be sifted out; the rest will be forwarded to New York.
Royalties paid annually.

Samuel French Ltd

52 Fitzroy Street, London W1P 6JR
☎ 071-387 9373   Fax 071-387 2161

Chairman *M. A. Van Nostrand*
Managing Director *John Bedding*

FOUNDED 1830 with the object of acquiring acting rights, and publishing plays. Part of **Samuel French Inc.**, New York. *Publishes* plays only; about 50 titles a year. Unsolicited mss considered only after initial submission of synopsis and specimen scene. Such material should be addressed to the Performing Rights Department.
Royalties paid twice yearly.

Authors' Rating Unlike some drama publishers who limit themselves to critically approved plays, Samuel French takes a more liberal view of what makes a publishable text. A boon to playwrights and amateur dramatic societies alike.

David Fulton (Publishers) Ltd

2 Barbon Close, Great Ormond Street,
London WC1N 3JX
☎ 071-405 5606   Fax 071-831 4840

Chairman/Managing Director *David Fulton*
Approx Annual Turnover £350,000

FOUNDED 1987. *Publishes* non-fiction: teacher training at B.Ed and PGCE levels for primary; geography for postgraduate and professional; plus computer skill training manuals. No unsolicited mss; synopses and ideas for books welcome. 34 titles in 1991.
Royalties paid twice yearly.

Funfax/Junior Funfax

See **Henderson Publishing Ltd**

Gaia Books Ltd

66 Charlotte Street, London W1P 1LR
☎ 071-323 4010   Fax 071-323 0435

Managing Director *Joss Pearson*

FOUNDED 1983. *Publishes* ecology, health, natural living and the mind, mainly in illustrated reference form. About 10 titles a year. TITLES *Book of Massage; The Gaia Atlas of Planet Management.* No unsolicited mss; outlines accepted. Most projects conceived in-house.
Royalties paid.

Gairm Publications

29 Waterloo Street, Glasgow G2 6BZ
☎ 041-221 1971

Chairman *Prof. Derick S. Thomson*

FOUNDED 1952 to publish the quarterly Gaelic periodical *Gairm* and soon moved into publishing other Gaelic material. Acquired an old Glasgow Gaelic publishing firm, Alexander MacLaren & Son, in 1970. Now publishing a wide range of Gaelic and Gaelic-related books: dictionaries, grammar, handbooks, children's, fiction, poetry, music and song.

Gallery Children's Books

See **East-West Publications (UK) Ltd**

Juliet Gardiner Books

See **Collins & Brown**

J. Garnet Miller Ltd

311 Worcester Road, Malvern WR14 1AN
☎ 0684 565045

Managing Director *Leslie Smith*

FOUNDED 1951 from the drama section of Frederick Muller Ltd and later expanded with the acquisition of Steele's Play Bureau and Pinker & Sons Ltd. Now owned by **Cresrelles Publishing**. *Specialises* in plays and theatre textbooks. Unsolicited mss, synopses and ideas welcome.

DIVISIONS
Plays (Children and Adult) *Simon Smith* TITLES *Italian Straw Hat; Pride and Prejudice; Alice in Wonderland.* **Theatre** TITLES *Stage Management and Theatrecraft; Choreographing the Stage Musical; Adaptable Stage Costume.*
Royalties paid twice yearly.

Gateway Books

The Hollies, Wellow, Bath, Avon BA2 8QJ
☎ 0225 835127   Fax 0225 840012

Publisher *Alick Bartholomew*

FOUNDED 1982. Formerly Turnstone Press. *Publishes* popular psychology, spirituality, holistic health, self-help, ecology, crop circles and earth energies, metaphysics and New Age titles. Unsolicited mss, synopses and ideas for books welcome. About 12 titles a year.
Royalties paid annually or twice yearly.

The Gay Men's Press (GMP Publishers Ltd)

PO Box 247, London N17 9QR
☎ 081-365 1545   Fax 081-365 1252
Managing Director *David Fernbach*

Publishes primarily books by gay authors about gay-related issues: art, photography, biography and autobiography, literary fiction and popular (historical romance to crime and science fiction), poetry, health and leisure. Works should generally be submitted by the author on disk.

DIVISIONS
Art & Photography *Aubrey Walter*. All other enquiries to *David Fernbach*. TITLES *Mother Clap's Molly House* Rictor Norton; *Halfway Home* Paul Monette; *Gaveston* Chris Hunt; *Trouble with the Law?* Caroline Gooding; *Rodeo Pantheon* Delmas Hale; *Younger Days* Ian David Baker. Send synopses with sample chapters rather than complete mss. *Royalties* One-off payments rather than royalties. Terms open to negotiation.

Geographia
See **HarperCollins Publishers Ltd**

Robert Gibson & Sons
17 Fitzroy Place, Glasgow G3 7SF
☎ 041-248 5674   Fax 041-221 8219
Chairman/Managing Director *R. D. C. Gibson*

Began life in 1850; went public in 1886. *Publishes* educational books only, and has been agent for the Scottish Certificate of Education Examination Board since 1902. Unsolicited mss preferred to synopses/ ideas. About 40 titles a year.
Royalties paid annually.

Ginn
See **Reed International Books**

Mary Glasgow Publications Ltd
Avenue House, 131-133 Holland Park Avenue, London W11 4UT
☎ 071-603 4688   Fax 071-602 5197

Managing Director *Chris Blake*

Now part of the Wolters Kluwer Group, Mary Glasgow Publications was founded in 1956. Apart from a regular output of foreign language magazines in French, Spanish and German and for EFL studies, there is an established and continually expanding list of secondary school main course, text and teacher-support materials in foreign languages, geography, music, media studies, design and technology.

DIVISIONS
Books *Geneviève Talon* **Magazines** *Sally Gray* No unsolicited mss. Synopses and ideas for books considered.

Authors' Rating At the time of going to press, there were talks of a merger with **Stanley Thornes (Publishers) Ltd**.

Godfrey Cave Holdings Ltd
42 Bloomsbury Street, London WC1B 3QJ
☎ 071-636 9177   Fax 071-636 9091
Managing Director *John Maxwell*

Subsidiary companies: Godfrey Cave Associates Ltd; Godfrey Book Sales; Omega Books Ltd; Benson Books Ltd. The list consists entirely of remainders and reprints of black and white reference and illustrated books. No new books are undertaken but up to 100 out of print titles are reissued per year. In addition to reprinting works from publishers, as a wholly-owned subsidiary of **Penguin Books Ltd**, the company also reprints out of print Penguin titles in hardcover.

IMPRINTS
Bloomsbury Books (no connection with **Bloomsbury Publishing**), **Omega Books**.

Golden Cockerel Press Ltd
25 Sicilian Avenue, London WC1A 2QH
☎ 071-405 7979   Fax 071-405 7979
Chairman/Managing Director *Thomas Yoseloff* (USA)

Originally set up in London in 1980 to distribute books published by its overseas associate company, Associated University Presses Inc., New Jersey. Now acts as a full academic publishing house, with its own editorial function. *Publishes* art, collecting, film, history, Judaica, literary criticism, music, philosophy, sociology, special interest. About 80 titles a year.

Editorial Head *Tamar Yoseloff*

IMPRINTS
AUP US member presses publishing scholarly and

academic: Bucknell, Delaware, Fairleigh Dickinson, Folger Shakespeare Library. **Cornwall Books** Trade hardbacks. **Balch Institute Press, Lehigh University Press, Susquehanna University Press**. Unsolicited mss, synopses and ideas for academic books welcome.
Royalties paid annually.

Victor Gollancz Ltd
14 Henrietta Street, London WC2E 8QJ
☎071-836 2006   Fax 071-379 0934
Chairman/Managing Director *Stephen Bray*
Publisher *Liz Knights*
Approx Annual Turnover £6.53 million

FOUNDED 1928 by Victor Gollancz as a general publishing company. Became famous for its political books during the 1930s and 1940s (*Left Book Club*). After 60 years of independence, Gollancz was bought in 1989 by **Houghton Mifflin Co.**, of Boston. It was their intention to 'fully retain the firm's literary traditions and standing'. *Publishes* biography and memoirs, bridge, children's, current affairs, detective stories and thrillers, general fiction, history, music, science fiction, fantasy and horror, travel and vernacular architecture. **H. F. & G. Witherby Ltd** is a wholly-owned subsidiary which publishes angling, natural history, ornithology, travel, wine and sport.

DIVISIONS

Children's *Chris Kloet;* **Science Fiction** *Richard Evans;* **Thrillers** *Julia Wisdom;* **Vernacular Architecture & Bridge** *Peter Crawley;* **Music & Sport** *Richard Wigmore.* Send typescripts preceded by descriptive letter. Unsolicited synopses and ideas for books also welcome.
Royalties paid twice yearly.

Authors' Rating With big brother **Houghton Mifflin** watching progress, Gollancz has been struggling to re-establish its reputation as a leading general publisher. A thorough shakeup of its list has opened the way to a broader range of titles.

Gomer Press
Wind Street, Llandysul, Dyfed SA44 4BQ
☎0559 362371   Fax 0559 363758
Chairman *J. Huw Lewis*
Managing Director *J. Huw Lewis*

FOUNDED 1892. *Publishes* adult fiction and non-fiction in English and Welsh, plus children's fiction and educational material in Welsh. About 100 titles a year (80 Welsh; 20 English).

DIVISIONS/IMPRINTS
Gomer Press *Dr Elis-Gruffydd* **Pont Books** *John Spink.* No unsolicited mss, synopses or ideas.
Royalties paid twice yearly.

Gordon & Breach Science Publishers
PO Box 197, London WC2E 9PX
☎071-836 5125   Fax 071-379 0800
Chairman *Martin Gordon*
Manager (UK) *Roger Greene*
Editor-in-Chief *John Gillman*

FOUNDED 1961. *Publishes* books and journals across a wide range of disciplines, including engineering and technology, mathematics and computer science, physics, chemistry, biomedicine, psychology, social science, economics, music, visual arts and dance. Over 200 titles a year. Unsolicited mss and synopses welcome.
Royalties paid annually. *Overseas office* Gordon & Breach Publishers Inc., New York.

Gower Publishing Ltd
Gower House, Croft Road, Aldershot, Hampshire GU11 3HR
☎0252 331551   Fax 0252 344405
Chairman *Nigel Farrow*
Managing Director *Christopher Simpson*

FOUNDED 1967. *Publishes* books, manuals, films and other training resources on business, management and human resource development. Unsolicited mss, synopses and ideas welcome.
Royalties paid according to contract. *Overseas associates* in the US, Australia, Hong Kong and Singapore.

GPC Books
See **University of Wales Press**

Grafton Books Ltd
See **HarperCollins Publishers Ltd**

Graham & Trotman Ltd
Sterling House, 66 Wilton Road, London SW1V 1DE
☎071-821 1123   Fax 071-630 5229
Managing Director *Alastair M. W. Graham*

FOUNDED 1974. Owned by the Wolters Kluwer Group since 1986. *Publishes* books, directories, journals and looseleaf in the fields of international business and law. About 60 titles a year, with plans to increase output.

DIVISIONS
Business *Alastair Graham* **Law** *Fergal Martin.* Unsolicited mss, synopses and ideas for books welcome.
Royalties paid twice yearly. *Overseas sister company* Kluwer Inc., Boston, USA; Wolters Kluwer Academic Publishers, The Netherlands.

Graham-Cameron Publishing
10 Church Street, Willingham,
Cambridge CB4 5HT
☏0954 60444   Fax 0954 61453

Editorial Director *Mike Graham-Cameron*
Art Director *Helen Graham-Cameron*

FOUNDED 1984, originally as a packaging operation. *Publishes* illustrated books: for children, institutions and business; also biography, education and social history. TITLES *Up From the Country; In All Directions; The Holywell Story.* No unsolicited mss. *Royalties* paid annually. *Subsidiary company*: Graham-Cameron Illustration.

Granta Publications
2–3 Hanover Yard, Noel Road, London N1 8BE
☏071-704 9776   Fax 071-704 0474

Managing Director *Derek Johns*
Editor *Bill Buford*

FOUNDED 1989. *Publishes* literary magazines and literary fiction, reportage and travel.

Granville Publishing
102 Islington High Street, London N1 8EG
☏071-226 2904

Managing Director *John Murray-Browne*
Approx Annual Turnover 'very small'

FOUNDED 1983. Part of a bookshop. *Publishes* literature reprints only. No unsolicited mss.

Green Books
Ford House, Hartland, Bideford, Devon EX39 6EE
☏0237 441621   Fax 0237 441203

Chairman *Satish Kumar*
Approx Annual Turnover £70,000

FOUNDED in 1987, with the support of a number of Green organisations. Closely associated with *Resurgence* magazine. *Publishes* high-quality books (on recycled paper wherever possible), on a wide range of Green issues, particularly those concerned with ideas, philosophy and the practical application of Green values.

Managing Editor *John Elford* TITLES *Forest Gardening* Robert A. de J. Hart; *The Ultimate Heresy* John Seymour; *Fighting Like the Flowers* Lawrence D. Hills; *The Living Tree* John Lane; *Tongues in Trees* Kim Taplin. No unsolicited mss. Synopses and ideas for books welcome.
Royalties paid twice yearly.

Green Print
See **Merlin Press Ltd**

Greenhill Books/Lionel Leventhal Ltd
Park House, 1 Russell Gardens,
London NW11 9NN
☏081-458 6314   Fax 081-905 5245

Managing Director *Lionel Leventhal*

FOUNDED 1987 by Lionel Leventhal (ex-**Arms & Armour Press**). *Publishes* aviation, military and naval, and a Napoleonic Library series. Synopses and ideas for books welcome. No mss.
Royalties paid twice yearly.

Greenpeace Books Ltd
See **UK Packagers**

Gresham Books
PO Box 61, Henley-on-Thames, Oxon RG9 3LQ
☏0734 403789   Fax 0734 403789

Managing Director *Mary V. Green*
Approx Annual Turnover £100,000

Bought by Mary Green from Martins Publishing Group in 1980. A small specialist one-woman publishing house. *Publishes* hymn and service books for schools, also craftbound orchestral, choir and Record of Achievement folders. TITLES include *The Headmasters' Conference Hymnbook.* No unsolicited material or ideas. Deals with schools and music publishers only.

Grevatt & Grevatt
9 Rectory Drive, Newcastle upon Tyne NE3 1XT

Chairman/Editorial Head *Dr S. Y. Killingley*

Part-time business established in 1981 as an alternative publisher of works not normally commercially viable. Authors waive royalties on the first 500 copies; and three books have appeared with financial backing from professional bodies. *Publishes* academic books, especially on language, linguistics and religious studies, plus some poetry. In 1988 a new series of rewritten conference proceedings at the University of Newcastle was launched, entitled

The Sanskrit Tradition in the Modern World (STIMW) Papers. The first volume of the series was *Aurobindo and Zaehner on the Bhagavad-Gītā* by Yvonne Williams & Michael McElvaney. Subsequent titles include: *Rammohun Roy in Hindu and Christian Tradition* (the 1990 Teape lectures) by Dermot Killingley; *Ritual and Society* by Shirley Firth and others. Publications are reviewed in many prestigious international journals, including *Language, Lingua; Bulletin de la Société de Linguistique de Paris; Leuvense Bijdragen; Journal of Child Language; World Literature Today; Journal of the Royal Asiatic Society; Revue Biblique; The Times Educational Supplement*. In 1991, Dr Killingley was elected editor of the *British Linguistic Newsletter* by the Linguistics Association of Great Britain (initially for three years). No unsolicited mss. Synopses and ideas should be accompanied by s.a.e.
Royalties paid annually (after the first 500 copies).

Grey Seal Books

28 Burgoyne Road, London N4 1AD
☎ 081-340 6061

Chairman *John E. Duncan*

Began publishing in December 1991. *Publishes* religion, Islam, history and politics. No unsolicited mss; synopses and ideas welcome. 7 titles in 1991. *Royalties* paid annually.

Grisewood & Dempsey

See **Kingfisher Books**

Grosvenor Books

54 Lyford Road, Wandsworth, London SW18 3JJ
☎ 081-870 2124   Fax 081-871 9239

Managing Director *David W. Locke*

FOUNDED 1964. Owned by Grosvenor Productions Ltd. Publishers for Moral Rearmament. *Publishes* biography, children's, contemporary issues, educational and religious. 3 titles in 1991. TITLES *The Muslim Mind* Dr Charis Waddy; *Cast Out Your Nets* Garth Lean; *Boy on a Bus* W. Cameron-Johnson. No unsolicited mss; synopses considered. *Royalties* paid yearly. *Overseas associates* in Australia, New Zealand, USA, Canada.

Grotius Publications

PO Box 115, Cambridge CB3 9BP
☎ 0223 323410   Fax 0223 311032

Managing Director *C. J. Daly*

FOUNDED 1979 for the publication of the *International Law Reports* and other related titles in the international law sphere.

Editorial Director *S. R. Pirrie* TITLES *Terrorism & Hostages in International Law* J. Lambert; *The Kuwait Crisis, Basic Documents* E. Lauterpacht, C. J. Greenwood, M. Weller & D. Bethlehem. Unsolicited mss, synopses, and ideas for books welcome if within specialist framework.
Royalties paid annually.

Grub Street

The Basement, 10 Chivalry Road,
London SW11 1HT
☎ 071-924 3966   Fax 071-738 1009

Joint Managing Directors *John Davies/Anne Dolamore*

FOUNDED 1982. Publishers and packagers of cookery, humour, gift and aviation history books. 12 titles in 1992. TITLES *The Low-Risk Cancer Cookbook; Torpedo Leader; 99 Donts*. Unsolicited mss and synopses welcome.
Royalties paid twice yearly.

Grune & Stratton

See **Harcourt Brace Jovanovich Ltd**

Guardian Books

See **Fourth Estate Ltd**

Guinness Publishing Ltd

33 London Road, Enfield, Middlesex EN2 6DJ
☎ 081-367 4567   Fax 081-367 5912

Chairman *Ian Chapman CBE*
Managing Director *Mark J. Cohen*

FOUNDED 1954 to publish *The Guinness Book of Records*, now the highest-selling copyright book in the world, published in 35 languages. In the late 1960s the company set about expanding its list with a wider range of titles, and now publishes about 50 titles a year.

Editor *Peter Matthews* Ideas and synopses for books welcome if they come within their fields of sport, human achievement (with the emphasis on facts and feats) and family reference.

Authors' Rating Any idea must seem inferior to the first book — in itself a record breaker. However the company is broadening its base and has the resources to back ambitious ideas.

Gunsmoke Westerns
See **Chivers Press (Publishers)**

Peter Haddock Ltd
Pinfold Lane Industrial Estate, Bridlington,
E. Yorks YO16 5BT
☎ 0262 678121   Fax 0262 400043

Managing Director *Peter Haddock*
Contact *Pat Hornby*

FOUNDED 1952. *Publishes* children's picture stories
and activity books. About 200 series a year. Ideas
for picture books welcome.
Royalties payments vary according to each contract.

Authors' Rating Cheap end of the market. Writers need to work fast to make a living.

Peter Halban Publishers
42 South Molton Street, London W1Y 1HB
☎ 071-491 1582   Fax 071-629 5381

Directors *Peter Halban/Martine Halban*

Independent publisher. FOUNDED 1986 by Peter
and Martine Halban. *Publishes* literary fiction, biography, autobiography and memoirs, history, philosophy, theology, religion, politics, literature and
criticism, world affairs. Unsolicited material welcome provided it is accompanied by return postage. 5 titles in 1991.
Royalties paid twice yearly for first two years,
thereafter annually in December.

Robert Hale Ltd
Clerkenwell House, 45–47 Clerkenwell Green,
London EC1R 0HT
☎ 071-251 2661   Fax 071-490 4958

Chairman/Managing Director *John Hale*

Family-owned company FOUNDED 1936. *Publishes*
adult fiction (most types) and non-fiction, plus
some poetry. No specialist material (education,
law, medical or scientific). Over 300 titles a year.
TITLES *The Pleasures of Love* Jean Plaidy; *Late
Harvest* Pamela Street; *The Gardener's Quotation
Book* Jennifer Taylor. Unsolicited mss, synopses
and ideas for book welcome.
Royalties paid twice yearly.

Authors' Rating Takes good care of authors but
can be tough on advances. Favours the popular
end of the fiction market.

The Hambledon Press
102 Gloucester Avenue, London NW1 8HX
☎ 071-586 0817   Fax 071-483 4541

Chairman/Managing Director *Martin Sheppard*

FOUNDED 1980. *Publishes* English and European
history, from post-classical to modern. Currently
expanding its list to include history titles with a
wider appeal. 25–30 titles a year.

Editorial Head *Martin Sheppard* TITLES *Studies in
Medieval Thought from Abelard to Wyclif* Beryl
Smalley; *Godly People: Essays on English Protes-
tantism and Puritanism* Patrick Collinson. No unso-
licited mss; send preliminary letter. Synopses and
ideas for books welcome.
Royalties paid annually. *Overseas associates* The
Hambledon Press (USA), Ohio.

Hamish Hamilton Ltd
See **Penguin Books Ltd**

Hamlyn/Hamlyn Children's Books
See **Reed International Books**

Harcourt Brace Jovanovich Ltd
24–28 Oval Road, London NW1 7DX
☎ 071-267 4466   Fax 071-482 2293/485 4752

Managing Director *Joan Fujimoto*

Parent company **Harcourt Brace Jovanovich
Inc.**, New York. *Publishes* academic, accountancy
and taxation, archaeology, biology and zoology,
business and industry, chemistry, computer science, economics, educational and textbooks, EFL,
geography and geology, languages and linguistics,
mathematics and statistics, medical, physics, psychology, religious, sociology and anthropology,
veterinary and health science. No unsolicited mss.

IMPRINTS
**Academic Press, Baillière Tindall, Grune &
Stratton, Holt Rinehart and Winston, W. B.
Saunders, Saunders Scientific Publications,
Surrey University Press** (acquired 1992 from
Blackie & Son Ltd following Blackie's disposal of its
publishing interests).
Royalties paid twice yearly.

Harley Books
Martins, Great Horkesley, Colchester,
Essex CO6 4AH
☎ 0206 271216   Fax 0206 271182

Managing Director *Basil Harley*

FOUNDED 1983. Natural history publishers specialising in entomological books. Definitive, high-quality illustrated reference works. TITLES *The Moths and Butterflies of Great Britain and Ireland; Spiders of Great Britain and Ireland; Dragonflies of Europe.* Royalties paid twice yearly in the first year, annually thereafter.

HarperCollins Publishers Ltd

77–85 Fulham Palace Road, London W6 8JB
☎081–741 7070   Fax 081–307 4440
Freepost PO Box, Glasgow G4 0NB
☎041–772 3200   Fax 041–306 3119

Executive Chairman *Terry Kitson*
Chief Executive/Publisher *Eddie Bell*
Approx Annual Turnover £188 million

Settling down after restructure following the acquisition in 1990 of Thorsons Publishing Group and Unwin Hyman Ltd (including all of Tolkein's works) and subsequent trimming down of its book divisions, with the sale of its academic and ELT titles in 1991. (Academic lists have been sold to **Routledge, Chapman & Hall Ltd**; ELT has gone to **Thomas Nelson & Sons Ltd**). Initially tied in with Grafton Books, Thorsons has now become a stand-alone division within the Group and Unwin Hyman titles are being phased out, along with Angus & Robertson (an earlier purchase), with titles being incorporated into relevant imprints across other divisions: Unwin Hyman trade titles into Grafton or Thorsons; Unwin Hyman educational into Collins. Grafton Hardbacks, a trade imprint, is also being phased out in favour of the HarperCollins imprint. A proposed Pandora management buy-out collapsed after five months of negotiation and the imprint has now transferred back to Thorsons.

DIVISIONS

Trade Division *Jonathan Lloyd* Hardbacks and paperbacks. IMPRINTS **Crime Club, Flamingo, Fontana, Fontana Press, Grafton Hardbacks, Grafton Paperbacks, HarperCollins, Harvill, Mariners' Library, Paladin Books, Tolkein.** Hardbacks are published mostly under HarperCollins Publishers; paperbacks under either Grafton (fiction, non-fiction and poetry) or Fontana. **Deputy Publisher** *John Boothe;* **Publishing Director, Fiction** *Malcolm Edwards;* **Publishing Directors, Non-fiction** *Michael Fishwick/Stuart Proffitt;* **Harvill** *Christopher MacLehose;* **Crime Club** *Elizabeth Walter.* Over 400 titles a year.

Thorsons *Eileen Campbell* IMPRINTS **Aquarian Press, Crucible, Mandala, Pandora Press, Thorsons, Unwin Hyman**. Astrology, divination, esoteric teachings, healing, mythology, occultism and the paranormal, tarot, self-development (Aquarian Press); philosophy and new science, psychology and psychotherapy, religion and spirituality, women's spirituality and men's consciousness (Mandala); fiction and non-fiction by and for women (Pandora); complementary medical, health, vegetarian cookery and special diets, positive thinking, parenting, organic gardening and conservation, pets and animal rights (Thorson's); health, childcare, yoga, parenting (Unwin Hyman, but being transferred now to Thorsons).

Children's Division *Roy Davey* IMPRINTS **Armada, Carnival, Dinosaur, HarperCollins, HarperCollins Audio, Jets, Lions, Picture Lions, Tracks, Young Lions**. About 385 titles a year.

Reference Division *Robin Wood* IMPRINTS **Collins, Collins Cobuild, Collins English Dictionaries, Collins English Library, Collins Gift Classics, Collins New Naturalist, CollinsGems, CollinsWillow**. Includes the major range of English/bilingual dictionaries, with every combination of English, French, German, Italian and Spanish; plus a new range of paperback subject dictionaries (mathematics, economics, biology, artificial intelligence, philosophy, etc); quotation dictionaries, phrase books and holiday guides; natural history pocket and field guides; and a wide range of special interest publications.

Collins Educational *Roy Davey* IMPRINTS **Collins Educational, Holmes McDougall**. Textbook publishing for schools (5–18 year-olds); all subjects for primary, with main strengths in secondary being English, history, geography, science and technology. Holmes McDougall is being phased out: no new titles; reprints are being incorporated under Collins Educational.

Religious Division *Ron Chopping* A broad-based and committed religious publisher of bibles and liturgical books. IMPRINTS **HarperCollins Religious, Collins Liturgical Books, Collins Bibles, Fount, Marshall Pickering**. Extensive list covering both popular and academic spirituality, Christian fiction, poetry, music and reference (Marshall Pickering); missals, prayer books, etc (Collins Liturgical Books).

Bartholomew/Times *Barry Winkleman* The newly-formed cartographic division, with Bartholomew and Times Books now joined as one division, but operating from two addresses: Bartholomew from Edinburgh (12 Duncan Street, Edinburgh EH9 1TA. Tel: 031-667 9341. Fax: 031-662 4282); Times Books from Fulham Palace Road (as above). IMPRINTS **Bartholomew, Bartholomew Clyde, Bartholomew Holiday Maps, Collins, Collins Longman, Geographia, Nicholson (Robert) Publications Ltd,**

Nicholson/Ordnance Survey, Times Bartholomew Guides, Times Atlases, Times Books, Invincible Press, HarperCollins Audiobooks. Maps, atlases and guides (Bartholomew; Collins; Collins Longman; Geographia; Times Bartholomew Guides; Times Atlases); Leisure maps (Bartholomew Clyde, but soon to be incorporated into the new Bartholomew Holiday Maps imprint); Educational titles (Collins Longman); London titles (Nicholson (Robert) Publications Ltd); Waterway guides (Nicholson/Ordnance Survey); Sports titles for *The Sun* and *News of the World* (Invincible Press); Some reference and non-fiction (Times Books). The Geographia imprint, which includes large-scale maps, is also being phased out, in favour of Bartholomew or Nicholson. About 55 titles a year.

Authors' Rating Dedicated to rough-house skills of best selling, HarperCollins has confounded the pundits, who thought the days of giant advances had passed, by signing up Barbara Taylor Bradford on a £17 million three-book deal. Confidence seems justified by sales figures which buck the recessionary slide. In Britain, Harper Paperbacks has advanced ahead of target but academic publishing (Unwin Hyman) has been trimmed. Paladin and Flamingo are to merge. The strongest areas are children's books, reference and religious publishing.

Harrap Publishing Group Ltd
See **W & R Chambers**

Harvard University Press
14 Bloomsbury Square, London WC1A 2LP
☎ 071-404 0712   Fax 071-404 0601

Director *William Sisler*
General Manager *Ann Sexsmith*

Part of **Harvard University Press**, USA. *Publishes* academic and scholarly works in history, politics, philosophy, economics, literary criticism, psychology, sociology, anthropology, women's studies, biological sciences, astronomy, history of science, art, music, film, reference. All mss go to the American office: 79 Garden Street, Cambridge, MA 02138.

Harvill
See **HarperCollins Publishers Ltd**

Haynes Publishing Group
Sparkford, near Yeovil, Somerset BA22 7JJ
☎ 0963 40635   Fax 0963 40825

Chairman *John H. Haynes*
Approx Annual Turnover £12 million

FOUNDED in 1960 by John H. Haynes. A family-run business which does its own typesetting and printing on the premises. The mainstay of its programme has been the *Owners' Workshop Manual*, first published in the mid 1960s and still running off the presses today. Keeping a strong bias towards motoring and transport titles, Haynes have expanded their lists, incorporating more general titles into its fold. *Publishes* DIY workshop manuals for cars and motorbikes, railway, aviation, military, maritime, model making, and general leisure under the Oxford Illustrated Press imprint.

IMPRINTS
G. T. Foulis & Co. Cars and motoring-related books; **J. H. Haynes & Co. Ltd** *P. Ward* Workshop manuals; **Oxford Illustrated Press** Photography, sports and games, gardening, travel and guidebooks; **Oxford Publishing Co.** Railway titles; **Patrick Stephens Ltd** *Darryl Reach* Motoring, rail, aviation, military, maritime, model making. Unsolicited mss welcome if they come within the subject areas covered.
Royalties paid annually. *Overseas associates* Haynes Publications Inc., California, USA.

Authors' Rating When car sales plummeted, so did Haynes. The knock-on was inevitable though John Haynes is honest enough to admit his company was 'slow to respond to the intensity and speed of the UK recession'. Now, after a cutback in the publishing programme and other economies, a return to healthy business is confidently predicted.

Hazleton Publishing
3 Richmond Hill, Richmond, Surrey TW10 6RE
☎ 081-948 5151   Fax 081-948 4111

Chairman/Managing Director *R. F. Poulter*

Publishers of *Autocourse*, the world's leading Grand Prix annual, now in its 42nd edition. *Publishes* high-quality motor sport titles including annuals. No unsolicited mss; synopses and ideas welcome. Not interested in technical or personality motor sport titles. 8 titles in 1991.
Royalties payment varies.

Headline Book Publishing
Headline House, 79 Great Titchfield Street, London W1P 7FN
☎ 071-631 1687   Fax 071-631 1958

Managing Director *Tim Hely Hutchinson*
Approx Annual Turnover £11.5 million

FOUNDED 1986 with substantial City funding. Major expansion followed with the appointment of Alan

Brooke as director of non-fiction, setting up a new non-fiction division, and in 1990 the company acquired the main backlist paperback and fiction copyrights from **W. H. Allen**. 1992 saw the acquisition of certain sports and yearbook titles from Macdonald as that company reverted into **Little, Brown & Co.** in the spring. The titles, 34 in total, mostly yearbooks, including market leaders such as *Rothman's Football Yearbook* and *Playfair Cricket Annual*, were published under the **Queen Anne Press** imprint and will now be incorporated under Headline's own imprint. (The remaining Queen Anne Press titles were sold to **Lennard Publishing**). Headline has also just taken over the Debrett's series from **Webb & Bower**. *Publishes* commercial fiction, hardback and paperback, and non-fiction, particularly biography, cinema, design and film, food and wine, countryside and TV tie-ins, and sports yearbooks. 400 titles in 1992.

Publishing Director, Non-fiction *Alan Brooke*
Editorial Director, Fiction *Jane Mayeth* TITLES *The Summer of the Danes* Ellis Peters; *Hideaway* Dean R. Koontz; *The Girl from Cotton Lane* Harry Bowling; *The Palace Affair* Una-Mary Parker; *The Covenant of the Flame* David Morrell; *Heartbeat* Nicholas Rea; *Ginger! My Story* Ginger Rogers; *English Villages* John Timpson; *Debrett's Etiquette and Modern Manners; Debrett's Correct Form.* Unsolicited mss and synopses welcome. *Royalties* paid twice yearly.

Authors' Rating One of the rare companies to fit the bankers' category of the 'cash rich'. With money raised by a highly successful flotation, Headline is pumping up its output to 400 titles a year, quite an achievement for a company still three years short of its tenth birthday. Open to ideas for formula fiction and popular non-fiction. Came out third in a recent **Society of Authors** and **Writers' Guild** survey of authors' relationships with their publishers.

Headway
See **Hodder & Stoughton Ltd**

William Heinemann/Heinemann Educational/Heinemann International/ Heinemann Young Books
See **Reed International Books**

Helicon Publishing
42 Hythe Bridge Street, Oxford OX1 2EP
☎0865 204204   Fax 0865 204205

Managing Director *David Attwooll*
Editorial Director *Michael Upshall*

FOUNDED 1992 from the management buy-out of Random Century's (now **Random House**) reference division. Led by David Attwooll, the buy-out (for an undisclosed sum) includes the Hutchinson Encyclopedia titles and databases, along with other reference titles. Helicon management and staff will hold the largest share, with backing from ex-Harrap owner Nicholas Berry, Tim Waterstone and Klett-Cotta of Stuttgart. Random will maintain a close relationship, however, representing Helicon to the trade. Mr Attwooll plans to increase the range of titles and further promote the Hutchinson lead in electronic publishing.

Christopher Helm Publishers Ltd
See **A. & C. Black (Publishers) Ltd**

Henderson Publishing Ltd
Tide Mill Way, Woodbridge, Suffolk IP12 1BY
☎0394 380622   Fax 0394 380618

Managing Director *Barrie Henderson*
Commissioning Editor *Hazel Jones*

FOUNDED January 1990. *Publishes* children's books. Unsolicited mss, synopses and ideas for books welcome.
IMPRINTS
Funfax, Junior Funfax, Panda Books, Loony Balloonies.
Royalties paid twice yearly.

Ian Henry Publications Ltd
20 Park Drive, Romford, Essex RM1 4LH
☎0708 749119

Managing Director *Ian Wilkes*

FOUNDED 1976. *Publishes* local history, transport history and Sherlockian pastiches. No unsolicited mss; synopses and ideas for books welcome. TITLES include *An Ilford Boyhood; Doctor Watson and the Invisible Man; The Casebook of Sherlock Doyle.* 10 titles in 1991.
Royalties paid twice yearly.

The Herbert Press Ltd
46 Northchurch Road, London N1 4EJ
☎071-254 4379   Fax 071-254 4332

Managing Director *David Herbert*

Publishes archaeology, architecture and design, biography, crafts and hobbies, fashion and costume, fine art and art history, natural history, photography, travel and topography. 9 titles in 1991.

Editorial Director *David Herbert* Unsolicited mss welcome.
Royalties paid twice yearly.

Nick Hern Books
See **Random House Publishing Group Ltd**

Highland Books
See **Inter Publishing Ltd**

Hippo Books
See **Scholastic Publications Ltd**

Hippopotamus Press
See **Poetry, Small Presses**

HMSO Books
St Crispins, Duke Street, Norwich,
Norfolk NR3 1PD
☎ 0603 622211   Fax 0603 695582
Controller *Dr Paul Freeman*

FOUNDED 1786. Government publisher of material sponsored by Parliament, government departments and other official bodies. No unsolicited material. The Controller is responsible for the administration of Crown and parliamentary copyright. The contact point for any copyright queries is 0603 695506.

Hobsons Publishing
Bateman Street, Cambridge CB2 1LZ
☎ 0223 354551   Fax 0223 323154
Executive Chairman *Adrian Bridgewater*
Chief Executive *Martin Morgan*
Approx Annual Turnover £11 million

FOUNDED 1973 by Adrian Bridgewater. Now wholly owned by Daily Mail and General Trust, who bought all shares in the company in 1990. *Publishes* textbooks, course and career guides, computer software, directories and specialist publishing work for employers and government departments. TITLES include *Recommended Hotels in UK* (ex-Johansen Publications which was bought by Hobsons in 1987); *Graphics Catalogue; Freelance Directory; Bloodstock Sales Review.* About 360 titles a year.

Authors' Rating Formula publishing based on a close and shrewd analysis of the education and business markets.

Hodder & Stoughton Ltd
47 Bedford Square, London WC1B 3DP
☎ 071-636 9851   Fax 071-631 5248
Academic (Edward Arnold): Mill Road, Dunton Green, Sevenoaks, Kent TN13 2YA. Tel 0732 450111. Fax 0732 460134 (Edward Arnold 0732 461321)

Chairman *Philip Attenborough*
Chief Executive *Patrick Wright*
Approx Annual Turnover £60 million

FOUNDED 1868. An independent company engaged in a diverse range of publishing, but best known, perhaps, as a successful publisher of fiction and non-fiction (particularly personal adventure and explorations). Most of its leading authors are published first in hardcover and then in one of Hodder's three paperback imprints (Coronet, New English Library, Sceptre). *Publishes* academic, educational, children's, fiction, non-fiction, medical, religious, mountaineering. About 750 titles a year.

Publisher *Michael Attenborough*
Deputy Publisher *Eric Major*

DIVISIONS/IMPRINTS
Non-fiction *Ion Trewin* IMPRINTS **Sceptre Paperbacks. Fiction** *Clare Bristow* IMPRINTS **Coronet, New English Library** Paperback imprints. AUTHORS John le Carré, Jeffrey Archer, Jean M. Auel, Melvyn Bragg, James Clavell, Thomas Keneally, Stephen King, James Herbert, Gavin Lyall, Mary Stewart. **Children's** *David Grant* IMPRINTS **Knight Books** Paperbacks AUTHORS R. Goscinny/A. Uderzo (*Asterix*), Mick Inksen. **Educational** *Brian Steven* IMPRINTS **Teach Yourself Series, Headway. Academic (Edward Arnold)** *Richard Stileman* Academic, humanities, scientific and technical, medical. **Religious** *Eric Major* TITLES include the *NIV Bible.* **Diadem** Specialist mountaineering/exploration list. Hodder & Stoughton actively discourages the submission of unsolicited mss, though 'the company is very willing to assess synopses and sample chapters.'
Royalties paid twice yearly. *Overseas associates* Australia, New Zealand and a widespread network of overseas agencies.

Authors' Rating After two miserable years when Hodder took the brunt of the recession — and was honest enough to confess its troubles — there are signs of recovery with fiction and paperback publishing leading the way. The organisation has been streamlined and investment has held up, notably in education. Authors speak fondly of happy editorial relationships and open dealing. The balance sheet is said to look healthier after the sale of *Lancet* to **Elsevier.**

The Hogarth Press Ltd
See **Random House Publishing Group Ltd**

Holmes McDougall
See **HarperCollins Publishers Ltd**

Holt Rinehart & Winston
See **Harcourt Brace Jovanovich Ltd**

Horizon Books
See **Northcote House Publishers**

How To Books Ltd
Plymbridge House, Estover Road, Plymouth,
Devon PL6 7PZ
☎0752 735251/695745   Fax 0752 695699

Publisher/Managing Director Roger
Ferneyhough

The first How To books were published in 1986 by
Northcote House Publishers. By 1991 the list
had grown so much and was expanding at such a
rate that Roger Ferneyhough set up a separate
company, with 25 titles in print and a programme
of some 20 new titles a year. TITLES take the form
of 'how to achieve a specific goal or benefit' in the
areas of employment, business, education and self-
development: How to Buy & Run a Shop; How to
Get a Job Abroad; How to Live & Work in Spain;
How to Make it in Films & TV. Well structured
proposals from qualified and experienced professionals welcome.
Royalties paid annually.

Hulton Educational
See **Stanley Thornes (Publishers) Ltd**

Human Horizons
See **Souvenir Press Ltd**

Hunt & Thorpe
66 High Street, Alton, Hampshire GU34 1ET
☎0426 83301   Fax 0426 83432
Approx Annual Turnover £1 million

Publishes children's and religious titles only. Unsolicited material welcome. 15 titles in 1991.

C. Hurst & Co.
38 King Street, London WC2E 8JT
☎071-240 2666   Fax 071-240 2667

Chairman/Managing Director Christopher Hurst

FOUNDED 1967. An independent company, active
in trade affairs. Aims to cultivate a small publisher's
concern for literacy, detail and the visual aspects of
the product. Publishes contemporary history, politics and social science, with an emphasis on the
developing world. About 18 titles a year.

Editorial Heads Christopher Hurst/Michael
Dwyer TITLES A History of Modern Algeria; The
Discourse of Race in Modern China; Governing
from the Centre (Dutch Politics); Parties and Voters
in France; The Economy of United Germany. No
unsolicited mss. Synopses and ideas for books
welcome.
Royalties paid twice yearly in first year, annually
thereafter.

Hutchinson Books
See **Random House Publishing Group Ltd**

Hutchinson Reference
See **Helicon Publishing**

IBC Publishing
57–61 Mortimer Street, London W1N 7TD
☎071-637 4383   Fax 071-580 2975

Chairman Jonathan Bloch

Owned by International Business Communications
(Holdings) plc. Publishes Banking Technology
magazine and a range of business to business
books, newsletters and directories, aimed at senior
management. Unsolicited synopses and ideas welcome, but initial approach in writing preferred.
About 5 titles a year, plus monthly newsletters.
Royalties paid twice yearly.

Inter Publishing Ltd
Williams Building, Woodbridge Meadows,
Guildford, Surrey GU1 1BH
☎0483 306309   Fax 0483 33880

Chairman Peter Davies
Managing Director David Wavre
Approx Annual Turnover £300,000

FOUNDED 1990. The first titles appeared in March
1991 and output has been considerable since, with
30 titles a year now planned. Publishes religious
books only. Unsolicited mss, synopses and ideas
for books welcome.

IMPRINTS
Eagle, Highland Books.
Royalties paid quarterly.

Invincible Press
See **HarperCollins Publishers Ltd**

Isis Large Print/Isis Audio Books
See **Clio Press Ltd**

Jai Press Ltd
118 Pentonville Road, London N1 9JN
☎071-833 1778   Fax 071-837 2917

Chairman *Herbert M. Johnson*
Managing Director *Piers R. Allen*

Owned by Jai Press, Inc., USA. FOUNDED 1976.
Publishes high-quality scholarly publications in
business, economics, social sciences, computer
sciences, chemistry and life sciences. Aims to span
the complete range of social and economic sciences, natural, pure and applied physical sciences.
Specialises in the publication of research serials
and monograph series, as well as journals. TITLES
*Advances in Biosensors; Research in Organization-
al Behavior; Research in Third World Accounting;
Advances in Solid-State Chemistry*. No undergraduate texts. Unsolicited synopses discouraged. Synopses and ideas welcome. 140 titles a year.
Royalties paid annually. *Overseas associates* Jai
Press, Inc., Greenwich, Connecticut, USA.

Arthur James Ltd
1 Cranbourne Road, London N10 2BT
☎081-883 1831/2201; 0386 446566
Fax 081-883 8307/0386 446566

Managing Director *Denis Duncan*
Approx Annual Turnover £100,000

FOUNDED 1944 by a Fleet Street journalist, A. J.
Russell. *Publishes* day books, devotional classics,
psychological, religious, social work and *New
Testament* translations.

Editorial Head *Denis Duncan* AUTHORS include
William Barclay, Leslie Weatherhead, J. B. Phillips,
Denis Duncan, Betty Brooke, George Bennett,
Howard Booth, Stanley Booth-Clibborn. No
unsolicited mss.
Royalties paid annually. *Overseas associates*
Buchanan, Australia; Omega, New Zealand.

Jane's Information Group
163 Brighton Road, Coulsdon, Surrey CR5 2NH
☎081-763 1030   Fax 081-763 1005

Managing Director *Michael Goldsmith*
Approx Annual Turnover £25 million

FOUNDED 1898 by Fred T. Jane with publication of
All The World's Fighting Ships. Now part of the
Thomson Corporation. For the last few years
management has been focusing on growth opportunities in its core business and in enhancing the
performance of initiatives like Jane's yearbooks on
CD-ROM. *Publishes* reviews and yearbooks on
defence, aerospace and transport topics, with
details of equipment and systems; plus directories
and strategic studies. TITLES include the leading
international defence magazine, *Jane's Defence
Weekly.*

DIVISIONS
Defence Magazines *Simon Kay* TITLES *Jane's
Defence Weekly; International Defence Review;
Jane's Intelligence Review.* **Aerospace Maga-
zines** *Rob Ropelewski* TITLES *Interavia Aerospace
Review; Jane's Airport Review; Air Letter; Aviation
Ground Equipment Market.* **Data Division** *Bob
Hutchinson* TITLES *Defence Aerospace Yearbooks*
(hard copy and CD-ROM); *Defence Aerospace
Directories/ Binders.* Unsolicited mss, synopses
and ideas for books welcome.
Royalties paid twice yearly. *Overseas associates*
Jane's Information Group Inc., USA; Interavia Pub-
lishing Group SA, Switzerland.

Jarrold Publishing
Whitefriars, Norwich, Norfolk NR3 1TR
☎0603 763300   Fax 0603 662748

Chairman *Peter Jarrold*
Managing Director *Antony Jarrold*
Approx Annual Turnover £4 million

Part of Jarrold & Sons Ltd, long-established
printing/publishing company. *Publishes* travel, leisure and light poetry, and is a major publisher of
calendars also. Material tends to be of a high
pictorial content. No novels, or biography unless it
has specific local interest. About 30 titles a year.

Editorial Head *Julie Beesley* Unsolicited mss,
synopses and ideas welcome.
Royalties paid twice yearly.

Jets
See **HarperCollins Publishers Ltd**

Michael Joseph Ltd
See **Penguin Books Ltd**

Kahn & Averill
9 Harrington Road, London SW7 3ES
☎081-743 3278

Managing Director M. Kahn

FOUNDED 1967. Originally published juvenile titles but gradually began to specialise in music titles. A small independent publishing house. *Publishes* music and some general non-fiction. No unsolicited mss; synopses and ideas for books considered. *Royalties* paid twice yearly.

Karnak House

300 Westbourne Park Road, London W11 1EH
☎071-221 6490   Fax 071-221 6490
Chairman *Dada Imarogbe*
Managing Director *Amon Saba Saakana*
Approx Annual Turnover £75,000

FOUNDED 1979. *Publishes* anthropology, education, Egyptology, history, language and linguistics, literary criticism, music, parapsychology, prehistory, poetry, fiction and children's stories. No poetry at present. No humour or sport. No unsolicited mss; send introduction or synopsis with one sample chapter. Synopses and ideas welcome. 12 titles in 1991.
Royalties paid twice yearly. *Overseas subsidiaries* Karnak House, Illinois, USA.

Kenilworth Press Ltd

Addington, Buckingham MK18 2JR
☎0296 715101   Fax 0296 715148
Chairman/Managing Director *David Blunt*
Approx Annual Turnover £500,000

FOUNDED 1989 with the acquisition of Threshhold Books. Developed a specialisation in equestrian publishing and is now the UK's principal instructional equestrian publisher, producing the official books of the British Horse Society and the Pony Club. Recently moved offices from London to premises adjacent to the International Dressage and Training Centre at Addington Manor. Unsolicited mss, synopses and ideas welcome. Not interested in anything not concerned with the care or riding of horses or ponies. 10 titles in 1991.

IMPRINTS
Kenilworth Books TITLES *Mark Todd's Cross-Country Handbook; The International Warmblood Horse; Course Design & Construction for Horse Trials.* **Threshold Books** TITLES *Threshold Picture Guides 1-22.*
Royalties paid twice yearly.

The Kensal Press

Riverview, Headington Hill, Oxford OX3 0BT
☎0865 750302   Fax 0865 62922

Managing Director *Mrs Betty Millan*
General Manager *Miss Georgina Shomroni*

FOUNDED 1982. *Publishes* mainly historical biographies. TITLES *Richard of England* D. M. Kleyn; *No Peace Without Spain* J. A. C. Hugill; *Where Have You Been All Your Life?* Dr Anne Gray. 2 titles in 1991. Send synopses rather than completed mss. Full in-house editorial services.
Royalties paid twice yearly for the first year, annually thereafter.

Kenyon-Deane

See **Cressrelles Publishing Co. Ltd**

Kime Publishing

PO Box 1, Hunstanton, Norfolk PE36 5JY
☎048525 347

Owner *Dr Clive Layton*

FOUNDED 1988. *Publishes* martial arts and sports psychology. Unsolicited mss, synopses and ideas for books welcome.

Laurence King

71 Great Russell Street, London WC1B 3BN
☎071-831 6351   Fax 071-831 8356
Chairman *Robin Hyman*
Managing Director *Laurence King*

Publishing imprint of **Calmann & King Ltd** (see **UK Packagers**). LAUNCHED 1991 to publish art books. *Publishes* full-colour illustrated books on art history, the decorative arts, photography and design. Unsolicited material welcome.
Royalties paid twice yearly.

Kingfisher Books

Elsley House, 24-30 Great Titchfield Street, London W1P 7AD
☎071-631 0878   Fax 071-323 4694
Chairman *Daniel Grisewood*
Managing Director *Duncan Baird*

Publishing imprint of **Grisewood & Dempsey Ltd** (see **UK Packagers**). *Publishes* children's books: stories, rhymes and picture books, fiction and poetry anthologies, young non-fiction, activity books, general series, reference and natural history. 169 titles in 1991.

IMPRINTS
Bennett Books Fiction and non-fiction.
Kingfisher Books.
Royalties paid twice yearly.

Authors' Rating One of the star turns in children's non fiction where, following the packaging principles of its parent company, the emphasis is on mass sale co-editions. Its *Children's Encyclopedia* is the big success but there is strong investment in other reference titles.

Jessica Kingsley Publishers Ltd

118 Pentonville Road, London N1 9JN
☎071-833 2307   Fax 071-837 2917

Managing Director *Jessica Kingsley*
Approx Annual Turnover £400,000

FOUNDED 1987. Independent publisher of social and behavioural sciences, including arts therapies, psychotherapy and higher education policy. TITLES include the *Journal of Access Studies.*

Kingsway Publications

Lottbridge Drove, Eastbourne, East Sussex BN23 6NT
☎0323 410930   Fax 0323 411970

Chairman *Peter Fenwick*
Executive Director *John Paculabo*
Approx Annual Turnover £1.3 million

Part of Kingsway Trust Group Ltd, owned by a charitable trust with Christian objectives. *Publishes* Christian literature including fiction, children's, bibles, drama, songbooks, missions, church growth, devotional, biography, biblical reference tools, management. 55 titles in 1992.

IMPRINTS
Kingsway, Minstrel, Phoenix. TITLES include *The Life Application Bible; The Father Heart of God* Floyd McClung; *Rolling in the Aisles* Murray Watts; *Hagbane's Doom* John Houghton. Unsolicited mss welcome, but partial submissions/synopses preferred. All submissions should be addressed to the Editorial Department.
Royalties paid annually.

Kingswood Press

See **Reed International Books**

Kluwer Academic Publishers

PO Box 55, Lancaster LA1 1PE
☎0524 34996   Fax 0524 32144

Managing Director *Mr A. Visser*
Publishing Director *Dr Peter Clarke*
Approx Annual Turnover £1.5 million

A member of Wolters Kluwer Academic Publishers, publisher of approximately 200 scholarly journals and 500 titles a year, in an extensive range of scientific disciplines. Kluwer Academic (UK) specialises in medical, scientific and technical publishing at the postgraduate level. *Publishes* research monographs, postgraduate textbooks, colour atlases and texts for family physicians. Particular areas of medical specialisation include cardiology, nephrology, radiology, oncology, pathology, neurosciences and immunology.

Knight Books

See **Hodder & Stoughton Ltd**

Charles Knight Publishing

See **Tolley Publishing Co. Ltd**

Kogan Page Ltd

120 Pentonville Road, London N1 9JN
☎071-278 0433   Fax 071-837 3768/6348

Managing Director *Philip Kogan*
Managing Director, Earthscan *Kate Griffin*
Approx Annual Turnover £5.2 million

FOUNDED 1967 by Philip Kogan, publishing *The Industrial Training Yearbook.* A member of the Euro Business Publishing Network. Recently launched a series of business audio tapes and acquired controlling interest in Earthscan Publications which has now joined Kogan Page at its Pentonville Road site. Earthscan will remain editorially independent of its parent and will continue to concentrate on its specialised list (see below). *Publishes* business and management, education and careers, marketing, personal finance, personnel, small business, training and industrial relations, transport, plus journals. Continuing to expand, particularly in the professional and human resource areas, yearbooks and directories.

DIVISIONS
Kogan Page *Pauline Goodwin/June Lines/Peter Chadwick/Dolores Black.* TITLES *Working for Yourself* series; *BIM* books; *Professional* paperbacks; *Careers* series; *Stoy Hayward Business Tax Guide; European Business* titles; *Better Management Skills* series; *Training Directory.*
Earthscan Publications *Kate Griffin* Close associations with the International Institute for Environment and Development and with the Worldwide Fund for Nature. *Publishes* Third World issues and their global implications, taking the inescapable link between poverty and environmental degradation as a starting point, and general environmental titles, both popular and academic. 30 titles in 1991. Unsolicited mss, synopses and ideas for books welcome.
Royalties paid twice yearly.

Authors' Rating Now the largest independent business publisher, Kogan Page is expanding into environmental issues. The purchase of Earthscan Publications with its 80 Green titles includes the bestselling *Blueprint for a Green Economy*. Phil Kogan says that he is in bullish mood.

Ladybird Books Ltd

Beeches Road, Loughborough,
Leicestershire LE11 2NQ
☎0509 268021
Fax 0509 234672   Telex 341347

Chair *Paula Kahn*
Managing Director *A. D. Forbes Watson*
Approx Annual Turnover £17 million

FOUNDED in the 1860s. Part of the **Longman Group**. The Ladybird name and format was established as a result of the development of a children's list during the First World War. In the early 1960s the commercial print side of the operation was abandoned in favour of publishing Ladybird titles only and in 1971 the company was bought by the Pearson Longman Group. *Publishes* children's trade books and some school titles. 110 titles in 1991.

Publishing Director *M. H. Gabb* IMPRINTS **Ladybird, Disney, Sunbird, Balloon Books**. TITLES *Well Loved Tales; Ladybird Dictionary; Read with Me Series; Activity Books; Learning to Read; Read it Yourself; Rupert; Disney; Beatrix Potter; Ladybird Tell-a-Tale* cassette/book series. Although most material is generally commissioned once publication programme has been determined, unsolicited mss relating to published areas are welcome. *Overseas associates* Ladybird Books, Auburn, Maine, USA.

Authors' Rating Ladybird is dumping its old-fashioned image with a commitment to broaden its product range.

Allen Lane The Penguin Press

See **Viking**

Lawrence & Wishart Ltd

144A Old South Lambeth Road, London SW8 1XX
☎071-820 9281   Fax 071-587 0469

Managing Director *Sally Davison*

FOUNDED 1936. An independent publisher with a substantial backlist. *Publishes* current affairs, cultural politics, economics, history, politics and education. 15–20 titles a year.

Editors *Matt Seaton/Sally Davison/Vicky Grut* TITLES *New Times: The Changing Face of Politics in*

the 1990s; The Big Market: The Future of the European Community; What Future for Education? Synopses preferred to complete mss. Ideas welcome.
Royalties paid annually, unless by arrangement.

Authors' Rating One of the few genuine left-wing publishers. Authors should expect to surrender profit to principles.

Leading Edge Press & Publishing Ltd

See **UK Packagers**

Leicester University Press

Fielding Johnson Building, University of Leicester,
University Road, Leicester LE1 7RH
☎0533 523333   Fax 0533 522200

Publisher *Alec McAulay*

Part of **Pinter Publishers Ltd** but still a university press. *Publishes* academic books in archaeology, defence studies, history, law, museum studies, literature, politics and international relations. 35 titles in 1991. Unsolicited mss considered if on appropriate subjects. Synopses and ideas for books welcome.
Royalties paid annually.

Authors' Rating Strong but small academic list which was under threat until Pinter Publishers injected some urgently needed funds.

Lennard Publishing

Windmill Cottage, Mackerye End, Harpenden,
Hertfordshire AL5 5DR
☎0582 715866   Fax 0582 715121

Chairman/Managing Director *Adrian Stephenson*
Approx Annual Turnover £100,000

FOUNDED 1986 by Adrian Stephenson. The book publishing division of Lennard Associates Ltd which also owns **Lennard Books** (see **UK Packagers**). About 5 titles a year.

Editorial Head *Adrian Stephenson* TITLES *Cricketers' Who's Who* ed. Iain Sproat; *Rosa Tidy's Pasta Book* Rosa Tidy; *London Villages* Paul Barkshire. Limited publishing programme envisaged for the next two years. No unsolicited mss.

IMPRINTS
Queen Anne Press Bought from Macdonald in mid 1992, following Macdonald's absorption into **Little, Brown & Co.** The list consists of about 80 sporting titles (34 were previously bought by

Headline Publishing prior to Lennard's acquisition). Some titles will be sold off, and there are plans to develop the yearbook titles in particular. *Royalties* paid twice yearly.

Charles Letts & Co. Ltd

Publishing Division, Letts of London House, Parkgate Road, London SW11 4NQ
☎071-407 8891   Fax 071-403 6729

Managing Director *Carole Saunders*
Editorial Head *Cortina Butler*
Approx Annual Turnover *c.* £5 million

A subsidiary of Charles Letts (Holdings) Ltd. The Publishing Division was formed in January 1990. Charles Letts was founded in 1796 as a diary publisher. In 1979 the company moved into educational publishing and sold its educational list twelve years later to BPP. Publishing activities are now concentrated on general leisure and home interest titles. *Publishes* gardening, self-help, natural history, travel, leisure, cookery, crafts and hobbies, cake decorating, gifts. No children's, fiction, biography, technical or educational. No unsolicited mss; synopses and ideas welcome. 50 titles in 1991. *Royalties* paid twice yearly.

Lionel Leventhal Ltd

See **Greenhill Books/Lionel Leventhal Ltd**

John Libbey & Co. Ltd

13 Smiths Yard, Summerley Street, London SW18 4HR
☎081-947 2777   Fax 081-947 2664

Chairman/Managing Director *John Libbey*

FOUNDED 1979. *Publishes* media and medical books only. TITLES *Progress in Obesity Research 1990; Television and the Gulf War.* Unsolicited mss normally welcome for media titles. Synopses and ideas welcome for both specialist areas. 50 titles in 1991.
Overseas subsidiaries John Libbey Eurotext Ltd, France; John Libbey-Cic, Italy.

Liber Press

Cuttlebrook House, Charlton Village, Wantage, Oxford OX12 7HE
☎02357 68798   Fax 02357 60603

Chairman/Managing Director *John Skinner*
Approx Annual Turnover £250,000

Independent publishing company established 1971 by John and Judith Skinner. *Publishes* children's fiction and non-fiction, with a bias towards picture books for the very young. Not interested in anything which would not sell to either children or their parents. TITLES *Exploring the World; Bear Books; Liber Readers* (broad range of storytelling for 7-9-year-olds); *Age Range Series.* Unsolicited mss, synopses and ideas welcome. 20 titles in 1992; 30 titles planned for 1993. *Royalties* paid twice yearly.

Library Association Publishing

7 Ridgmount Street, London WC1E 7AE
☎071-636 7543   Fax 071-636 3627

Chairman *E. M. Broome OBE*

Publishing arm of **The Library Association**. *Publishes* library and information science, monographs, reference, textbooks and bibliography. 35 titles in 1991.

DIVISIONS
Library Association Publishing *Barbara Jover* TITLES *Walford's Guide to Reference Material* **Clive Bingley Books** *Barbara Jover* TITLES *Basics of Librarianship.* Unsolicited mss, synopses and ideas welcome provided material falls firmly within the company's specialist subject areas. *Royalties* paid annually.

Lime Tree

See **Reed International Books**

Frances Lincoln Ltd

Apollo Works, 5 Charlton Kings Road, London NW5 2SB
☎071-482 3302   Fax 071-485 0490

Managing Director *Frances Lincoln*
Editorial Directors *Erica Hunningher* (Adult non-fiction)/*Janetta Otter Barry* (Children's)

FOUNDED 1977. *Publishes* highly illustrated non-fiction: gardening, interiors, health and crafts; plus children's books. About 35 titles a year. TITLES *Child Development* Richard Lansdown & Marjorie Walker; *Mozart* Catherine Brighton; *What Colour?* Anthea Sieveking. Synopses and ideas for books considered.
Royalties paid twice yearly.

Linden Press

See **Centaur Press Ltd**

Lion Publishing

Peter's Way, Sandy Lane West, Oxford OX4 5HG
☎0865 747550   Fax 0865 747568

Approx Annual Turnover £6.5 million

FOUNDED 1971. Went public in 1975. A Christian book publisher, strong on illustrated books for a popular international readership, with rights sold in 74 languages worldwide. *Publishes* a diverse list with Christian viewpoint the common denominator. All ages, from board books for children to multi-contributor adult reference, children's fiction and non-fiction, educational, paperbacks and colour co-editions. 70 titles in 1991. Unsolicited mss welcome provided they have a positive Christian viewpoint intended for a wide general and international readership. Synopses and ideas for books also welcome. Adult material should be addressed to the *Editorial Department*; children's material to *Ms Su Box*.
Royalties paid twice yearly. *Overseas associates* Lion Publishing, USA.

Authors' Rating Came out ahead in a 1988 **Society of Authors** survey of author/ publisher relationships. Much praised for straight dealing and for taking care of authors.

Lions/Picture Lions/Young Lions
See **HarperCollins Publishers Ltd**

Little, Brown & Co. (UK) Ltd
165 Great Dover Street, London SE1 4AA
☎071-334 4800   Fax 071-334 4905

Managing Director *Philippa Harrison*
Approx Annual Turnover £18 million

FOUNDED 1988 as a wholly owned subsidiary of Little, Brown (USA), selling imported titles from the US, and launched its own illustrated non-fiction list in 1990. Part of Time-Warner Inc., Little Brown took over Macdonald & Co. in mid 1992 and has transferred its operation to 'he former Macdonald offices while looking for new premises for the new structure. *Publishes* hardback and paperback fiction, literary fiction, crime, science fiction and fantasy; and general non-fiction, including illustrated: architecture and design, fine art, photography, biography and autobiography, cinema, gardening, history, humour, travel, crafts and hobbies, reference, cookery, wines and spirits, DIY, guidebooks, natural history, nautical, alternative health, ecology and popular psychology.

Publishing Director *Barbara Boote*

DIVISIONS/IMPRINTS
Abacus *Richard Beswick* Literary fiction and non-fiction paperbacks; **Optima** *Hilary Foakes* Alternative health, women's and popular psychology, mostly in B-format paperbacks; **Orbit** *Colin Murray* Science fiction and fantasy; **Little Brown** and **Warner** *Alan Samson/Barbara Boote/Hilary*

Hale Mass market fiction and non-fiction; **Warner-Futura** *Hilary Hale/Barbara Boote* Crime paperbacks; **Illustrated** *Vivien Bowler* Hardbacks. Unsolicited synopses and ideas for books welcome.
Royalties paid twice yearly.

Authors' Rating Originally sold only titles imported from the US but launched its own illustrated non-fiction list in 1990, scoring a hit with *HRH The Prince of Wales Watercolours*. Now entering its third phase with the purchase of Macdonald from the deflated Maxwell empire. Cries of anguish from Macdonald authors excluded from the deal who must now join the sad ranks of Maxwell creditors.

Liverpool University Press
Senate House, Abercromby Square, PO Box 147, Liverpool L69 3BX
☎051-794 2232/37   Fax 051-708 6502

Managing Director *Robin Bloxsidge*

The principal activity of LUP, since its foundation in 1899, has been in the humanities and social sciences. *Publishes* academic and scholarly hardback and paperback books in the fields of archaeology, education, geography, ancient and modern history, English literature, Hispanic languages and literature, town planning and veterinary medicine. 13 titles in 1991.

Editorial Head *Robin Bloxsidge* TITLES *The Eighteenth Century in Spain; Ideological Hesitancy in Spain 1700-1750; The Crimean Doctors: A History of the British Medical Services in the Crimean War; Brass Plate and Brazen Impudence: Dental Practice in the Provinces 1755-1855; Conquerors and Chroniclers of Early Medieval Spain; The Goths in the Fourth Century; Services for Shelter; A Mastitis Handbook for the Dairy Practitioner.* Unsolicited mss, synopses and ideas for books welcome.
Royalties paid annually.

Livewire Books for Teenagers
See **The Women's Press**

Lochar Publishing Ltd
The High Street, Moffat, Dumfriesshire DG10 9ED
☎0683 20916   Fax 0683 21183

Chairman *Gordon Campbell*
Managing Directors *Michael De Luca/Neil Wilson*

FOUNDED 1985. *Publishes* adult non-fiction: leisure, biography, outdoor pursuits, food and drink, Scottish interest, sport and pocket books. No unsolicited mss; send initial letter with synopsis/ideas in the first instance. TITLES include *Malt Whisky Almanac; Encyclopaedia of World Rugby; Real Ale Drinker's Almanac.* 40 titles in 1991. *Royalties* paid annually.

Authors' Rating Set up by Neil Wilson and Mike de Luca in 1985 as a distinctly Scottish imprint, Lochar is trying hard to extend its appeal south of the border by moving on to titles of national interest.

Longman Group Ltd

Longman House, Burnt Mill, Harlow, Essex CM20 2JE
☎ 0279 426721   Fax 0279 431059

Chair/Chief Executive *Paula Kahn*

FOUNDED 1724 by Thomas Longman. Now the biggest educational publishing house in the English-speaking world (outside the United States). Longman Group (UK) is the largest of the 31 subsidiaries within the Longman Group, itself a wholly owned subsidiary of Pearson plc. It is an international company, exporting over half its sales to subsidiaries, partners and booksellers worldwide. *Publishes* English language teaching, medical, business and professional (including law, tax, finance, industry, training), dictionaries and educational.

DIVISIONS
ELT *Tim Hunt* **Business & Professional** *Peter Warwick* **Medical** *Robert Duncan* **Education** *Peter Warwick*.

IMPRINTS
Churchill Livingstone (based in Edinburgh, see entry), **Ladybird Books Ltd** (based in Leicestershire, see entry), **Longman ELT, Longman Law, Tax & Finance, Longman Industry & Public Service Management, Longman Training, Longman Higher Education, Longman Education, Longman Logotron, Oliver & Boyd, Pitman** (based in London, see entry).
All unsolicited mss should be addressed to the Contracts & Copyright Manager *David Lea*.
Royalties paid annually. *Overseas associates* worldwide.

Authors' Rating Longman is now out of trade publishing (including the Chronicle partnership) and is concentrating on educational, medical, professional and ELT books. Dominates over large sectors of the education market. Strong on sales overseas.

Loony Balloonies

See **Henderson Publishing Ltd**

Lund Humphries Publishers Ltd

Park House, 1 Russell Gardens,
London NW11 9NN
☎ 081–458 6314   Fax 081–905 5245

Chairman *Lionel Leventhal*

Publisher of fine art books; first titles appeared in 1895. *Publishes* art, architecture, design, graphics and language guides. 16 titles in 1991. There are plans to expand the graphic arts and design list in the years to come. Unsolicited mss welcome but initial introductory letter preferred. Synopses and ideas for books considered.
Royalties paid twice yearly.

The Lutterworth Press

PO Box 60, Cambridge CB1 2NT
☎ 0223 350865   Fax 0223 66951

Managing Director *Adrian Brink*

The Lutterworth Press dates back to the 18th century when it was founded by the Religious Tract Society. In the 19th century it was best known for its children's books, both religious and secular, including *The Boys' Own Paper*. In 1984 it was bought by James Clarke & Co. Ltd of Cambridge. *Publishes* general non-fiction: antiques and collecting, architecture and design, children's books, educational and textbooks, fine art and art history, gardening, environmental, natural history, religion and theology. 19 titles in 1991. TITLES *Camping with the Prince; Other tales of Science in Africa* Thomas A. Bass; *Hogarth: Volumes I/II* Ronald Paulson; *British Sport: A Social History* Dennis Brailsford; *The World of Dinosaurs: Animals and Landscapes to Make Yourself* Bernd Burkart; *The Miracles of Jesus; The Parables of Jesus* Tomie dePaola. Initial letter with s.a.e. advised before submitting mss.
Royalties paid annually.

Authors' Rating The list is expanding but it still has its anchor in evangelical publishing. Imaginative children's list.

Lythway Large/Children's Large Print

See **Chivers Press (Publishers)**

Macdonald & Co. Ltd

See **Little, Brown & Co. (UK) Ltd**

McGraw-Hill Book Co. Europe

McGraw-Hill House, Shoppenhangers Road,
Maidenhead, Berkshire SL6 2QL
☎ 0628 23432   Fax 0628 770224

Managing Director *Stephen White .*

FOUNDED 1899 in London and moved to Maidenhead in 1963. Parent company **McGraw-Hill Inc.**, New York. The British publishing programme started in 1965. *Publishes* business and economics, engineering, computer science, business computing and secretarial studies for the academic, student and professional markets. 103 titles in 1991. Unsolicited mss, synopses and ideas welcome. All submissions should be addressed to *Roger Horton* (Editorial Director).
Royalties paid twice yearly.

MCM Publishing

60 Oakwood Avenue, Southgate,
London N14 6QL

Publisher *Mary Martinez*
Editorial Head *Francoise Budd*

Owned by the **M. C. Martinez Literary Agency.**
Publishes adult and children's fiction.

Macmillan Publishers Ltd

4 Little Essex Street, London WC2R 3LF
☏071-836 6633   Fax 071-370 4204

Chairman *Nicholas Byam Shaw*
Approx Annual Turnover £190 million

Holding company of the recently restructured Macmillan UK publishing operation which is divided into three main divisions: Macmillan Press Ltd; Pan Macmillan Ltd; Macmillan Magazines Ltd.

DIVISIONS

Macmillan Press Ltd *Adrian Soar* Houndmills, Basingstoke, Hampshire RG21 2XS. Tel: 0256 29242. Fax 0256 479476. Textbooks, monographs and works of reference in academic, professional and vocational subjects; medical and scientific journals, directories, ELT, education. About 800 titles a year.
DIVISIONS
Medical & Scientific Journals *H. Holt;* **Postgraduate & Scholarly** *T. M. Farmiloe;* **Reference & Financial** *J. F. K. Ashby;* **Directories** *D. Robertson;* **Scientific Reference** *R. Foster;* **Social Sciences Texts** *S. Kennedy;* **Further Education** *J. Winkler;* **Overseas Education** *A. Brown;* **ELT** *S. Holden.* Unsolicited mss welcome.

Pan Macmillan Ltd *Alan Gordon Walker* 18-21 Cavaye Place, London SW10 9PG. Tel: 071-373 6070. Fax: 071-370 0746. Represents the adult and children's trade publishing divisions.
DIVISIONS
Pan Books Ltd *Ian S. Chapman* Mass market

paperback house. FOUNDED 1944. IMPRINTS **Pan** Fiction *Susanne Baboneau* Non-fiction *Catherine Hurley;* **Picador** *Peter Strauss.* Published its first list in 1947 and in 1961 had its first million-selling title with *The Dam Busters.* The first Pan bookshop opened in the Fulham Road in 1975. Macmillan took over warehousing and distribution in 1981 and bought all shares in the company in 1987. *Publishes* adult fiction and non-fiction across a comprehensive range: archaeology, architecture, design, atlases and maps, biography and autobiography, business and industry, cinema and video, cookery, crafts, hobbies, economics, gardening, guidebooks, history and antiquarian, humour, languages and linguistics, literature and criticism, medical, military and war, natural history, philosophy, photography, politics and world affairs, psychology, reference and dictionaries, sports and games, theatre and drama, travel and topography, wines and spirits. About 300 titles a year. Mss, synopses and ideas welcome.
Pan Macmillan Children's Books *Mary Tapissier* Picture books and fiction. IMPRINTS **Piccolo** Nonfiction; **Piper** Fiction. Having sold off its children's education and reference list to **Heineman Educational**, Macmillan merged its own trade list with that of Pan's children's operation. About 100 titles a year. Mss and ideas welcome.
Macmillan London Ltd *Felicity Rubinstein* Fiction and general non-fiction. **Publishing Director** *Roland Philipps.* Biography and autobiography, fiction, cookery, crime (*Maria Rejt*), gardening, guidebooks, health and beauty, history and antiquarian, humour, literature and criticism, music, natural history, politics and world affairs, psychology, sports and games, theatre and drama, wines and spirits. Unsolicited mss and synopses welcome.
Sidgwick & Jackson Ltd *William Armstrong* FOUNDED 1906 and bought by Macmillan, from Lord Forte, in 1986. *Publishes* astronomy, autobiography, cinema and theatre, cookery, crafts, current affairs, humour, illustrated classics and gift books, business and management, military history, pop and rock, sport, and some fiction. About 30 titles a year. TITLES include *Superwoman* Shirley Conran; *Is That It?* Bob Geldof; *Our Story* Reg & Ron Kray. Unsolicited mss are always welcome but rarely published; send synopsis with sample chapter. Titles tend to be commissioned, submissions via agents or from staff contacts.

Macmillan Magazines Ltd *Raymond Barker* Magazine publishing division. TITLES include *Nursing Times* and *Nature.*

Royalties paid annually or twice yearly depending on contract. *Overseas associates* worldwide.

Authors' Rating Having completed its merger with Pan, Britains's largest privately owned publishing company has shifted away from UK education (the source of its strength for many generations) towards general publishing. But future prosperity is tied to the 'multi-million' investment in reference works and in particular, the long-awaited art encyclopedia.

Julia MacRae Books
See **Random House Publishing Group Ltd**

Magi Publications
112 Whitfield Street, London W1P 5RU
☎ 071-387 0610   Fax 071-383 5003
Correspondence to: 55 Crowland Avenue, Hayes, Middlesex UB3 4JP

Publisher *Monty Bhatia*
Editor *Linda Jennings*
Approx Annual Turnover £500,000

FOUNDED 1987. *Publishes* children's picture books only. Unsolicited mss, synopses and ideas welcome. 12 titles in 1991; 20–24 planned for 1993. *Royalties* paid annually.

Mainstream Publishing Co. (Edinburgh) Ltd
7 Albany Street, Edinburgh EH1 3UG
☎ 031-557 2959   Fax 031-556 8720

Directors *Bill Campbell/Peter MacKenzie*
Approx Annual Turnover £1.5 million

Publishes autobiography, biography, current affairs, fiction, health, history, illustrated and fine editions, literature and criticism, military and war, photography and sport, politics and world affairs, popular paperbacks. Over 60 titles a year. Ideas for books considered, but they should be preceded by a letter, synopsis and s.a.e. or return postage. *Royalties* paid twice yearly.

Authors' Rating A Scottish company aiming for a British profile. Keen on finding authors who 'can develop with us'.

Mammoth
See **Reed International Books**

Manchester University Press
Oxford Road, Manchester M13 9PL
☎ 061-273 5539   Fax 061-274 3346

Publisher/Chief Executive *Francis Brooke*
Approx Annual Turnover £1.4 million

FOUNDED at the turn of the century and now Britain's third largest university press, with a list marketed and sold internationally. Originally based on history, MUP's list has expanded to cover the humanities, social sciences and academic books from A-level texts to research monographs. *Publishes* academic and educational books in literature, cultural and media studies, history, art and architecture, politics, international law, economics, modern languages, anthropology and special education. Also more general books, notably on genealogy, history and the North-west of England. About 100 titles a year, plus journals.

DIVISIONS
Humanities *Anita Roy* **History** *Jane Carpenter* **Politics** *Richard Purslow* **Economics** *Francis Brooke* **Arts** *Katharine Reeve*. Unsolicited mss welcome.
Royalties paid annually.

Mandala
See **HarperCollins Publishers Ltd**

Mandarin
See **Reed International Books**

George Mann Books
PO Box 22, Maidstone, Kent ME14 1AH
☎ 0622 759591

Chairman *George Mann*
Managing Director *John Arne*

FOUNDED 1972, originally as library reprint publishers, but has moved on to other things with the collapse of the library market. *Publishes* selected reprints and some original non-fiction. No new fiction. No unsolicited mss; send preliminary letter with synopsis, enclosing by-return postage/ s.a.e. if by-return response is wanted. Material which is not accompanied by return postage is neither read nor returned.

IMPRINTS
George Mann, Arnefold, Recollections New imprint for subsidised, non-commercial, prestigious publications of short-run, strictly limited editions of true books of adventure and experience of a biographical/autobiographical nature. Unlimited editorial advice and assistance provided for this. Send preliminary letter enclosing large s.a.e. Outside of envelope should be marked 'Recollections'. *Royalties* paid twice yearly.

Mansell
See **Cassell**

Marc
See **Monarch Publications**

Mariners' Library
See **HarperCollins Publishers Ltd**

Marshall Pickering
See **HarperCollins Publishers Ltd**

Masks/Masks Noir
See **Serpent's Tail**

Kenneth Mason Publications Ltd
12 North Street, Emsworth, Hampshire PO10 8DQ
☎0243 377977/8   Fax 0243 379136

Chairman *Kenneth Mason*
Managing Director *Piers Mason*
Approx Annual Turnover £500,000

FOUNDED 1958; its first title, *What's Where in London*, by D. Parsons, sold 100,000 copies. *Publishes* nautical books and general non-fiction, namely diet, health and fitness. No poetry. Initial approach by letter with synopsis preferred. TITLES include *Count Your Calories; Low Fat Meals; Hip and Thigh Exercises*. 12 titles in 1991. *Royalties* paid twice yearly (Jun/Dec) in first year, annually (Dec) thereafter.

Meadow Books
22 Church Meadow, Milton under Wychwood, Oxford OX7 6JG
☎0993 831338

Managing Director *C. O'Neill*

FOUNDED 1990. *Publishes* social history of hospitals, etc. TITLES *A Picture of Health; More Pictures of Health* Cynthia O'Neill. Unsolicited mss welcome if accompanied by return postage in full. *Royalties* by arrangement.

The Medici Society Ltd
34–44 Pentonville Road, London N1 9HG
☎071-837 7099   Fax 071-837 9152

Managing Director *John Gurney*

FOUNDED 1908. *Publishes* children's fiction, art and nature. No unsolicited mss; send synopses with specimen illustrations only. 7 titles in 1991. *Royalties* paid annually.

Melrose Press Ltd
3 Regal Lane, Soham,
Ely Cambridgeshire CB7 5BA
☎0353 721091   Fax 0353 721839

Chairmen *Dr Ernest Kay/Richard A. Kay*
Managing Director *Nicholas S. Law*
Approx Annual Turnover £1.5 million

Publisher of *Who's Who*. FOUNDED in London in 1960. Took on its present name in 1969 and moved to Cambridge in 1972. *Publishes* biographical Who's Who reference only. 7 new editions in 1991.

DIVISIONS
International Biographical Centre *Jocelyn Timothy* TITLES *International Authors and Writers Who's Who; International Who's Who in Music; Who's Who in Australasia & the Far East; World Who's Who of Women; Dictionary of International Biography*. Plus 17 other Who's Who titles. Ideas welcome.

Mercat Press
c/o James Thin Booksellers, 53 South Bridge,
Edinburgh EH1 1YS
☎031-556 6743   Fax 031-557 8149

Chairman/Managing Director *D. Ainslie Thin*

FOUNDED 1971 as an adjunct to the large Scottish bookselling chain of James Thin. Began by publishing reprints of classic Scottish literature but has since broadened to include new books of general and academic interest. *Publishes* Scottish classics reprints and non-fiction of Scottish interest, mainly historical and literary. An injection of new titles is planned over the next couple of years.

Editorial Heads *Tom Johnstone/Seán Costello* TITLES *The Campaigns of Montrose* Stuart Reid; *The New Makars* ed. Tom Hubbard; *History of the Highland Clearances* A. MacKenzie. Unsolicited synopses and ideas for books, preferably with sample chapters, are welcome. No complete mss. *Royalties* paid annually.

Mercury Business Books
Gold Arrow Publications Ltd, 862 Garratt Lane,
London SW17 0NB
☎081-682 3858   Fax 081-682 3859

Managing Director *Nicholas Dale-Harris*
Approx Annual Turnover £1 million

FOUNDED 1987 to develop a range of books for executives and managers working in the modern world of business, supplemented with information through other media like seminars, audio and video. *Publishes* business and management, company histories and sponsored titles. 40 titles in 1991.

Editorial Head *Robert Postema* Unsolicited mss, synopses and ideas for books welcome.
Royalties paid twice yearly.

Authors' Rating A recent entry to the growing business books market, Mercury is expanding with the help of a £250,000 loan under the Business Expansion Scheme.

Merehurst Ltd
Ferry House, 51–57 Lacy Road,
London SW15 1PR
☎ 081-780 1177   Fax 081-780 1714

Group Managing Director *Nicolas Wright*
Group Editorial Director *Shirley Patton*
Approx Annual Turnover £3 million

Owned by Australian media group J. B. Fairfax International Ltd. *Publishes* books for the creative, leisure and home reference markets, namely crafts (needlecraft and hard crafts), cake decorating and cookery. About 30 titles a year. Synopses and ideas for books welcome; no unsolicited mss.
Royalties paid twice yearly.

Merlin Press Ltd
10 Malden Road, London NW5 3HR
☎ 071-267 3399   Fax 071-284 3092

Directors *Martin Eve/Jon Carpenter*
Approx Annual Turnover £280,000

FOUNDED 1956 by Martin Eve. *Publishes* ecology, economics, history, philosophy, left wing politics. AUTHORS Georg Lukacs, Ernest Mandel, Istvan Meszaros, Ralph Miliband, E. P. Thompson. About 20 titles a year. No unsolicited mss; preliminary letter essential before making any type of submission. No fiction.
IMPRINTS
Green Print *Jon Carpenter,* **Seafarer.**
Royalties paid twice yearly.

Mermaid Books
See **Penguin Books Ltd**

Methuen/Methuen Children's Books
See **Reed International Books**

Midland Publishing Ltd
24 The Hollow, Earl Shilton, Leicester LE9 7NA
☎ 0455 847256   Fax 0455 841805

Director *N. P. Lewis*

Publishes aviation, military and railways. No unsolicited mss; synopses and ideas welcome. No wartime memoirs.
Royalties paid quarterly.

Milestone Publications
62 Murray Road, Horndean, Waterlooville,
Hampshire PO8 9JL
☎ 0705 592255   Fax 0705 591975

Managing/Editorial Director *Nicholas J. Pine*

Sister company of **Scope International Ltd.** *Publishes* antiques and collecting, business, economics, military, war and reference. No unsolicited mss. Approach in writing in first instance.
Royalties paid twice yearly.

Millenium
See **Orion Publishing Group**

Miller's Publications
See **Reed International Books**

Mills & Boon Ltd
Eton House, 18–24 Paradise Road, Richmond,
Surrey TW9 1SR
☎ 081-948 0444   Fax 081-940 5899

Chairman *John T. Boon*
Managing Director *R. J. Williams*

FOUNDED 1908. Owned by the Canadian-based Torstar Group. *Publishes* romantic fiction and historical romance. Over 600 titles in 1991.

Editorial Director *Frances Whitehead*

IMPRINTS
Mills & Boon Romances Traditional love stories, with happy endings assured. **Mills & Boon Temptation** *Linda Fildew* Modern, sensual storylines; temptation and choices with satisfying resolutions. **Medical Romances & Masquerade** *Elizabeth Johnson* Established in the 1950s, and still very popular. Love stories set in a realistic medical world (Medical Romances); Historical romances, slightly longer than usual (Masquerade). **Worldwide** *Linda Fildew* Individual women's fiction (minimum 100,000 words). **Silhouette Desire, Special Edition, Sensation** imprints are handled by Silhouette Books, 300 E. 42nd St, 6th Floor, New York, NY 10017, USA. (No unsolicited

mss; query letter in first instance. Tip sheets available from this address.) Unsolicited mss welcome for other imprints listed above. A guide to writing romantic novels is available from Mills & Boon (*Behind the Hearts and Flowers*, £7.50 incl. VAT, p&p) containing practical advice on preparing a manuscript, plus an audio tape *And Then He Kissed Her*. *Royalties* paid twice yearly.

Authors' Rating A success story which runs and runs, Mills & Boon is preparing to launch a series of made-for-television romantic blockbusters, a romantic music collection and glossy magazine. If by some terrible mischance all this goes wrong, the company can always fall back on its loyal book readership of four million who buy something like 15 million copies of Mills & Boon titles. Mills & Boon editors 'are genuinely interested in new writers', particularly those who acknowledge that 'there is more to writing a romantic novel than creating a heroine, a hero and incorporating a couple of quarrels with a happy ending'.

Minerva
See **Reed International Books**

Minstrel
See **Kingsway Publications**

The MIT Press Ltd
14 Bloomsbury Square, London WC1A 2LP
☎ 071-404 0712   Fax 071-404 0601

Director *F. Urbanowski*
General Manager *A. Sexsmith*

Part of **MIT Press**, USA. *Publishes* academic, architecture and design, bibliography, biography and autobiography, biology and zoology, business and industry, chemistry, cinema and video, computer science, economics, educational and textbooks, engineering, fine art and art history, geography and geology, history and antiquarian, languages and linguistics, law, mathematics and statistics, medical, music, natural history, philosophy, photography, physics, politics and world affairs, psychology, reference, scientific and technical, sociology and anthropology, neurobiology and neuroscience, and topography. All mss go to the American office: 55 Hayward Street, Cambridge, Mass. 02142.

Mitchell Beazley
See **Reed International Books**

Mitre
See **Monarch Publications**

Monarch Publications
Owl Lodge, Langton Road, Speldhurst,
Kent TN3 0NP
☎ 0892 863129   Fax 0892 863129

Directors *Tony & Jane Collins*

Formerly part of **Kingsway Publications** but broke away from that company in 1992 to publish an independent list of Christian books across a wide range of concerns. About 30 titles a year.

IMPRINTS
Monarch Upmarket social concern issues list covering a wide range of areas from gay rights to future studies, politics, etc., all with a strong Christian dimension. **Marc** Leadership, mission and church growth titles. **Mitre** Creative writing imprint: fiction, humour and drama with a Christian dimension. Unsolicited mss, synopses and ideas welcome.

Mondo
See **Titan Books**

Moorland Publishing Co. Ltd
Moorfarm Road, Airfield Estate, Ashbourne,
Derbyshire DE6 1HD
☎ 0335 44486   Fax 0335 46397

Managing Director *Mr C. L. M. Porter*
Approx Annual Turnover £1 million

FOUNDED 1971. *Publishes* travel and countryside guides. Expanding list, with the main thrust still being the production of travel guides. SERIES *Visitor's Guide; Off The Beaten Track*.

Editorial Head *Dr J. Robey* Unsolicited mss will be considered, but synopses accompanied by letters of introduction preferred. *Royalties* paid annually.

Mosby Year Book Europe Ltd
Brook House, 2–16 Torrington Place,
London WC1E 7LT
☎ 071-636 4622   Fax 071-637 3021

Chairman *Timothy Hailstone*
Managing Director, Publishing *Elizabeth Horne*
Publishing Director *Dr Geoffrey Greenwood*
Approx Annual Turnover £11 million

Part of Times Mirror Corporation, USA. Embraces Wolfe Publishing, now an imprint for international colour atlases, and texts in medicine, dentistry and veterinary science. Also publishes books, journals and day studies for nurses. About 40 titles a year. TITLES *A Colour Atlas of the Brain & Spinal Cord* M. England; *A Colour Atlas of Allergy* W. F. Jackson & R. Cerio; *The Ward Sister's Survival Guide* ed. E. M. Horne; JOURNALS *Professional Nurse; Journal of the British Contact Lens Association; Care of the Critically Ill.*

IMPRINTS
Wolfe Publishing, Austen Cornish Nursing titles. Synopses and ideas for books and journal articles welcome.
Royalties paid twice yearly.

Motor Racing Publications
Unit 6, The Pilton Estate, 46 Pitlake, Croydon, Surrey CRO 3RY
☎ 081-681 3363   Fax 081-760 5117
Chairman *John Blunsden*
Approx Annual Turnover £500,000

FORMED soon after the end of World War II to concentrate on motor racing titles. Fairly dormant in the mid 1960s but was re-activated in 1968 by a new shareholding structure. John Blunsden later acquired a majority share and major expansion followed in the 1970s. About 12 titles a year. *Publishes* motor sporting history, classic car collection and restoration, road transport, motorcycles, off-road driving and related subjects.

Editorial Head *J. B. Blunsden*

IMPRINTS
Fitzjames Press, Motor Racing Publications TITLES *The Supertrucks of Scammell; Classic Hauliers; Grand Prix People* Gerald Donaldson; *Stage by Stage: Rallying with Russell Brookes; VW Power and Style* Ian Kuah. Unsolicited mss, synopses and ideas in specified subject areas welcome.
Royalties paid twice yearly.

Mowbray
See **Cassell**

Muller
See **Random House Publishing Group Ltd**

John Murray (Publishers) Ltd
50 Albemarle Street, London W1X 4BD
☎ 071-493 4361   Fax 071-499 1792
Chairman *John R. Murray*
Managing Director *Nicholas Perren*

FOUNDED 1768 and has remained independent ever since. *Publishes* general trade books, educational (secondary school and college textbooks) and success studybooks.

DIVISIONS
General Books *Grant McIntyre* **Educational Books** *Nicholas Perren.* Unsolicited material discouraged.
Royalties paid annually.

Authors' Rating One of the few remaining independent publishers of any size, this 'most dynastic of houses' is led by Jack Murray (now into his eighth decade) who quotes with approval a correspondent who described him as the 'only publisher in whose company a failed author could sit with ease'.

Nautical
See **A. & C. Black (Publishers) Ltd**

NCVO Publications
8 Regents Wharf, All Saints Street, London N1 9RL
☎ 071-636 4066   Fax 071-436 3188
Approx Annual Turnover £100,000

NCVO Publications, set up in 1992, is the new publishing imprint of the National Council for Voluntary Organisations. It combines the former Bedford Square Press list with NCVO's many other publications. The list reflects NCVO's role as the representative body for the voluntary sector. *Publishes* directories, management, legal, fundraising and employment titles of primary interest to the voluntary sector. Representation by Troika.
TITLES *The Voluntary Agencies Directory; Grants from Europe; Volunteering and Society: Principles and Practice.* Unsolicited mss, synopses and ideas for books welcome.
Royalties paid twice yearly.

Thomas Nelson & Sons Ltd
Nelson House, Mayfield Road, Walton-on-Thames, Surrey KT12 5PL
☎ 0932 246133   Fax 0932 246109
Managing Director *Michael Thompson*
Approx Annual Turnover £30 million

FOUNDED 1798. Part of the Thomson Corporation. *Publishes* educational (infant, primary, secondary), school atlases and dictionaries, English language teaching and educational books for the Caribbean market. Having acquired **Edward Arnold**'s ELT list in 1990, Thomas Nelson went on to buy the Collins ELT imprint from **HarperCollins** in 1991 along with **Macmillan**'s children's education list (school books) and **Blackie**'s educational list (Blackie's disposed of its publishing interests altogether last year). Nelson's position in the education and ELT markets has thus been strengthened considerably over the last two years.

Development Director *Pamela Hutchinson* TITLES *GAIA: Geography, An Integrated Approach; Synthesis; Story Chest; Maths Chest; Tricolore; Zickzack; Deutsch Heute; Breakaway; Vaya!* Unsolicited mss and synopses welcome. *Royalties* paid twice yearly.

Authors' Rating Having tightened its hold on the ELT market with the purchase of HarperCollins' list, Thomas Nelson is exceptional among publishers in showing confidence in the future of educational publishing. In a recent **Society of Authors** and **Writers' Guild** survey, Thomas Nelson was rated poorly for author-publisher relationships.

New English Library
See **Hodder & Stoughton Ltd**

New Holland (Publishers) Ltd
37 Connaught Street, London W2 2AZ
☎071–258 0204   Fax 071–262 6184

Chairman *John Grant*
Managing Director *John Beaufoy*
Approx Annual Turnover £1.3 million

FOUNDED as The Holland Press in 1956 and underwent a change of name and editorial identity in 1987. New directions and rapid expansion followed, transforming the small specialist imprint into a publisher of high-quality illustrated books for the international market. *Publishes* illustrated non-fiction, specialising in natural history, travel, cookery, cake decorating, crafts and gardening.

Editorial Head *Charlotte Parry-Crooke* TITLES *Field Guide to the Birds of Britain and Europe; Wild Malaysia.* No unsolicited mss; synopses and ideas welcome.
Royalties paid twice yearly.

New Orchard Editions
See **Cassell**

New Portway Large Print
See **Chivers Press (Publishers)**

Nexus
See **Virgin Publishing**

NFER-NELSON Publishing Co. Ltd
Darville House, 2 Oxford Road East, Windsor, Berkshire SL4 1DF
☎0753 858961   Fax 0753 856830
Managing Director *Michael Jackson*

FOUNDED 1981. Jointly owned by the Thomson Corporation and the National Foundation for Educational Research. *Publishes* educational and psychological tests and training materials.

Editorial Head *Keith Nettle* Main interest is in educational, clinical and occupational assessment and training material. Unsolicited material welcome.
Royalties vary according to each contract.

Nicholson
See **HarperCollins Publishers Ltd**

90s
See **Serpent's Tail**

Nonesuch Press
See **Reinhardt Books Ltd**

Northcote House Publishers Ltd
Plymbridge House, Estover Road, Plymouth, Devon PL6 7PZ
☎0752 705251   Fax 0752 695699
Managing Director *Brian Hulme*

FOUNDED 1985, following the purchase of 100 titles from **Longman** and **Mitchell Beazley**, to develop titles for business education and training for schools and further education. *Publishes* careers and education management, business, critical studies in literature, dance, drama and travel titles. 15 titles in 1992. 'Well thought out proposals with marketing arguments welcome.'

IMPRINTS
Horizon Books Travel and leisure imprint established 1986. Titles must be information based rather than pictorial or narrative. **Northcote House.** Unsolicited mss welcome; outlines preferred. Ideas welcome too.
Royalties paid annually.

Oak
See **Omnibus Press**

Oberon Books

521 Caledonian Road, London N7 1RH
☎071-607 3637

Publishing Director *James Hogan*
Managing Director *Charles D. Glanville*

Publishes play texts (highly original material and specialist theatre books). *Specialises* in contemporary plays and translations of European classics. AUTHORS/TRANSLATORS include Marguerite Duras, Giles Havergal, Graham Greene, Roland Rees, Dick Edwards, Colin Winslow.

Octagon Press Ltd

PO Box 227, London N6 4EW
☎081-348 9392   Fax 081-341 5971

Managing Director *George R. Schrager*
Approx Annual Turnover £100,000

FOUNDED 1972. *Publishes* philosophy, psychology, travel, Eastern religion, translations of Eastern classics and research monographs in series. Unsolicited material not welcome. 5 titles in 1991, with a backlist of around 140.
Royalties paid annually.

Octopus Publishing

See **Reed International Books**

Oliver & Boyd

See **Longman Group Ltd**

Michael O'Mara Books Ltd

9 Lion Yard, Tremadoc Road, London SW4 7NQ
☎071-720 8643   Fax 071-627 8953

Chairman *Michael O'Mara*
Managing Director *Lesley O'Mara*
Editorial Director *David Roberts*
Approx Annual Turnover £2 million

FOUNDED 1985 by Michael and Lesley O'Mara. Independent trade publisher whose first two titles were bestsellers: *The ITN Book of the Queen Mother; In Person, The Prince and Princess of Wales* by Alastair Burnet. *Publishes* general trade fiction and non-fiction, royalty, murder and mystery, illustrated classics, children's, anthologies and reference (including the *ITN Factbook*). Unsolicited mss, synopses and ideas for books welcome.
Royalties paid twice yearly.

Omega Books

See **Godfrey Cave Holdings Ltd**

Omnibus Press

Book Sales/Music Sales Ltd, 8–9 Frith Street, London W1V 5TZ
☎071-434 0066   Fax 071-439 2848

FOUNDED 1971 by Robert Wise. Independent publisher of music books, rock and pop biographies. Also produces song sheets/books, educational tutors, cassettes, videos and software.

Editorial Head *Chris Charlesworth*

IMPRINTS
Amsco, Bobcat, Oak, Omnibus, Proteus, Wise, Zomba. Unsolicited mss, synopses and ideas for books welcome.
Royalties paid twice yearly. *Overseas associates* Music Sales Corporation, New York; Music Sales Pty, Sydney.

Open Books Publishing Ltd

Beaumont House, Wells, Somerset BA5 2LD
☎0749 677276   Fax 0749 670760

Managing Director *Patrick Taylor*

FOUNDED 1974. *Publishes* academic and general. No unsolicited material; all books are commissioned.
Royalties paid twice yearly.

Open Gate Press

51 Achilles Road, London NW6 1DZ
☎071-431 4391   Fax 071-431 5088

Managing Directors *Jeannie Cohen/Elisabeth Petersdorff/Morris Kahn*

FOUNDED 1989 by a group of psychoanalysts, social psychiatrists and artists to provide a forum for psychoanalytic, social and cultural studies. *Publishes* psychology, philosophy, social sciences, politics. 3 titles in 1991. TITLES *Psychoanalysis and Society*. Unsolicited mss, synopses and ideas for books welcome.
Royalties paid twice yearly.

Open Letters

147 Northchurch Road, London N1 3NT
☎071-359 4078   Fax 071-359 4078

Chairman *Gillian Hanscombe*
Managing Director *Ros de Lanerolle*

FOUNDED by a group of women, most of whom were previously from **The Women's Press**' and left in 1991. *Publishes* mainly non-fiction, dealing with women's studies and issues of gender in relation to cultural studies, literature, history, development studies and politics. First title published

1992. Unsolicited mss discouraged; preliminary letter with outline preferred in the first instance. Interested only in books suitable for simultaneous publication into an academic and trade market. No fiction as yet unless of a specialist nature with a potential market in lesbian or development studies. 10 titles in the first year; about 20 planned for 1993. *Royalties* paid twice yearly (March/September).

Open University Press
22 Ballmoor, Buckingham MK18 1XW
☏ 0280 823388   Fax 0280 823233

Managing Director *John Skelton*
Approx Annual Turnover £2 million

FOUNDED 1977 as an independent imprint of the Open University's course materials. *Publishes* academic and professional books in the fields of education, health studies, politics, psychology, women's studies. Not interested in anything outside the social sciences, and no economics or anthropology. No unsolicited mss; enquiries/proposals only. 105 titles in 1992.
Royalties paid annually.

Optima
See **Little, Brown & Co. (UK) Ltd**

Orbit
See **Little, Brown & Co. (UK) Ltd**

Orchard Books
See **The Watts Group**

Orion Books
See **Attic Books**

Orion Publishing Group
Orion House, 5 Upper St Martin's Lane,
London WC2H 9EA
☏ 071-240 3444   Fax 071-240 4822

Managing Director *Peter Roche*

FOUNDED 1992 by Anthony and Rosemary Cheetham, ex-Random Century (now **Random House**). Incorporates Weidenfeld & Nicolson Ltd, J. M. Dent and Arthur Barker Ltd.

DIVISIONS/IMPRINTS
Orion *Rosemary Cheetham* Hardcover and mass market fiction. IMPRINTS **Orion** *Rosemary*

Cheetham; **Millenium** *Deborah Beale* Science fiction and fantasy; **Phoenix** *Maggie McKernan* Literary fiction. Unsolicited mss welcome.
Weidenfeld & Nicolson General and illustrated non-fiction. **Illustrated Books** *Michael Dover* IMPRINTS **Weidenfeld & Nicolson, Weidenfeld Paperbacks**. Subjects include biography, autobiography, history and travel. Illustrated books, with a strong emphasis on the visual and upmarket design, include cookery, wine, gardening, art and architecture, natural history and personality-based books. No unsolicited mss; approach in writing in the first instance.
J. M. Dent *William Mitchell* Adult non-fiction and children's (fiction and non-fiction). IMPRINTS **J. M. Dent, Everyman, Paperbacks** *Hilary Lawrie;* **Reference** *David Swarbick/Anna Hodson;* **Academic** *Ben Buchan;* **Music** *Julia Kellerman;* **Children's** *Fiona Kennedy.*

Authors' Rating Following his unceremonious departure from Random Century, the supremely entrepreneurial Anthony Cheetham set up his own company and thus proceeded to surprise everyone with a buy-out of Weidenfeld & Nicolson. The result is a major new publisher spreading across mass market fiction, science fiction, literary fiction and non-fiction. 300 books are forecast for the first year's programme. Paperback first novels are promised at competitive prices.

Osprey
See **Reed International Books**

Peter Owen Ltd
73 Kenway Road, London SW5 0RE
☏ 071-373 5628/370 6093   Fax 081-373 6760

Chairman *Peter Owen*
Senior Editor *Michael Levien*

FOUNDED 1951. Known for its literary fiction, English and translated. *Publishes* biography, general books, literary fiction, sociology. No middlebrow romance, thrillers or children's. AUTHORS include Fiona Pitt-Kethley, Jeremy Reed, Shusaku Endo, Paul Bowles, Anais Nin, Jane Bowles, Anna Kavan, Peter Vansittart. 40 titles in 1991. Unsolicited synopses welcome; mss should be preceded by a descriptive letter or synopsis with s.a.e.
Royalties paid annually. *Overseas associates* worldwide.

Authors' Rating A true internationalist, Peter Owen has a great knack of spotting world-class literature — to the extent of having seven **Nobel Prize** winners on his list. But this does not bring huge profits, or in some years, any profit at all. Of the 80 or so books on Peter Owen's current fiction list, 50 are translations. No other publisher would take the risk. No wonder Francis King proclaims him a cause for rejoicing.

Owl Press

PO Box 315, Downton, Salisbury,
Wiltshire SP5 3YE
☎ 0725 22553

Managing Editors *Annie Musgrove/Catherine Jones*

FOUNDED 1990. *Publishes* books of military interest, either historical or humorous, and general titles written by authors with strong military connections. TITLES *Gumboots and Pearls; The Backstabber's Guide; Bullets and Bandsmen.* Unsolicited mss welcome. No poetry.
Royalties paid.

Oxford Illustrated Press/Oxford Publishing Co.
See **Haynes Publishing Group**

Oxford University Press

Walton Street, Oxford OX2 6DP
☎ 0865 56767   Fax 0865 56646

Chief Executive *Professor Sir Roger Elliott*
Approx Annual Turnover £150 million

A department of the university for several hundred years, the Press grew from the university's printing works and developed into a major publishing business in the 19th century. *Publishes* academic books in all categories: student texts, scholarly journals, schoolbooks, ELT material, dictionaries, reference, music, bibles, imported titles from the USA and beyond, as well as paperbacks, poetry, general non-fiction and children's books. 2900 titles in 1991, with a backlist of about 20,000.

DIVISIONS
Arts and Reference *I. S. Asquith* TITLES include the *Concise Oxford Dictionary*. **Educational** *F. E. Clarke* Courses for the National Curriculum. **ELT** *P. R. Mothersole* ELT courses and dictionaries. **Science, Medical & Journals** *J. R. Manger* TITLES include the *Birds of the Western Paleartic*.

IMPRINTS
Clarendon Press Monographs in humanities, science and social science. **Oxford Paperbacks** The trade paperback list. **Oxford Science Publications, Oxford Medical Publications, Oxford Electronic Publications.**

OUP welcomes first-class academic material in the form of proposals or accepted theses.

Royalties paid once/twice yearly. *Overseas subsidiaries* Sister company in USA; also branches in Australia, Canada, East Africa, Hong Kong, India, Japan, New Zealand, Pakistan, Singapore, South Africa. Offices in Argentina, Brazil, France, Germany, Greece, Italy, Mexico, Spain, Taiwan, Thailand, Turkey, Uruguay. Joint companies in Malaysia, Nigeria and Germany.

Authors' Rating Winner of the Queen's Award for Export Achievement, OUP sells over half its output overseas. One of the finest academic lists in the world headed by the *Oxford English Dictionary*, a 20-volume heavyweight which, despite selling 10,000 sets, turns in a substantial loss. No matter, the prestige of the *OED* is worth millions.

Paladin
See **HarperCollins Publishers Ltd**

Pan Books Ltd
See **Macmillan Publishers Ltd**

Panda Books
See **Henderson Publishing Ltd**

Pandora Press
See **HarperCollins Publishers Ltd**

Paper Tiger Books
See **Dragon's World**

Paperduck
See **Gerald Duckworth & Co Ltd**

Paperfronts
See **Elliot Right Way Books**

Paragon Softcover Large Print
See **Chivers Press (Publishers)**

Partridge Press
See **Transworld Publishers Ltd**

Paternoster Press Ltd

3 Mount Radford Crescent, Exeter,
Devon EX2 4JW
☎ 0392 50631   Fax 0392 413317

Chairman/Managing Director *Jeremy H. L. Mudditt*
Approx Annual Turnover £400,000

FOUNDED 1935 by the present chairman's father. *Publishes* religion, including learned and church/life-related journals. About 10 titles a year.

Editorial Head *Jeremy Mudditt* TITLES *The New International Dictionary of New Testament Theology* (4 vols) ed. Colin Brown; *Commentary on the Greek Text of Luke* Howard Marshall; *Paul — Apostle of the Free Spirit* F. F. Bruce; *Matthew: Evangelist & Teacher; New Testament Interpretation.* Unsolicited mss, synopses and ideas for books welcome.
Royalties paid annually.

Pavilion Books Ltd
196 Shaftesbury Avenue, London WC2H 8HL
☎ 071-836 1306   Fax 071-240 7684

Joint Chairmen *Tim Rice/Michael Parkinson*
Managing Director *Colin Webb*

Publishes biography, children's, cookery, gardening, art, sport and travel. About 50 titles a year. Unsolicited mss not welcome. Non-fiction synopses and ideas considered in all above areas except children's.
Royalties paid twice yearly.

PBI Publications
Britannica House, High Street, Waltham Cross, Hertfordshire EN8 7DY
☎ 0992 23691
Fax 0992 641225   Telex 23957

Chairman/Managing Director *Dr D. G. Hessayon*

Paperback publisher of gardening and agricultural books by Dr D. G. Hessayon. TITLES *The Bedding Plant Expert; Be Your Own Greenhouse Expert; The Armchair Book of the Garden; The Home Expert; The Indoor Plant Spotter; The Garden DIY Expert*, etc. No unsolicited material.

Pelham Books
See **Penguin Books Ltd**

Pen & Sword Books Ltd
190 Shaftesbury Avenue, London WC2H 8JL
☎ 071-836 3141   Fax 071-240 9247

Chairman *Sir Nicholas Hewitt*
Managing Director *Leo Cooper*

FOUNDED 1990 following the acquisition by parent company Barnsley Chronicle Holdings of the Leo Cooper imprint from **Octopus**. *Publishes* military history, autobiography and biography. About 35 titles a year. Unsolicited mss, synopses and ideas welcome but return postage must be included with all submissions.

IMPRINTS
Leo Cooper.
Royalties paid twice yearly. *Associated company* **Wharncliffe Publishing Ltd**.

Penguin Books Ltd
27 Wrights Lane, London W8 5TZ
☎ 071-416 3000/3100
Fax 071-416 3099/3293/3295

Chief Executive *Peter Mayer*
Managing Director *Trevor Glover*
Approx Annual Turnover (Group worldwide) £300 million

Owned by Pearson. *Publishes* general and academic books of all kinds: biography, autobiography and memoirs, business, children's, fiction, classics, crime, thrillers, crafts, DIY, guidebooks and handbooks, health, history, ELT, literature and criticism, theatre, reference and dictionaries, science, mathematics, sports, travel, women's studies, science fiction and fantasy, astrology, environment, New Age, mysticism and spirituality, current affairs and politics. Penguin recently (1992) acquired the whole of the share capital of **Ventura Publishing** for an undisclosed sum. Ventura is best known for *Spot*, the international bestselling children's character created by Eric Hill and published by Puffin since 1983. The Pelican imprint and Peregrine have been phased out over the last few years, with Pelican titles going over to Penguin's non-fiction list.

Editor-in-Chief, Adult Publishing *Peter Carson*
Publishing Director, Children's *Elizabeth Attenborough*
Publishing Director, Penguin *Tony Lacey*

DIVISIONS/IMPRINTS

Penguin Fiction and non-fiction. **Puffin** Leading UK children's paperback list, publishing in virtually all general fields: fiction, non-fiction (limited), picture books, poetry. Over 1700 titles in print. **ROC** Science fiction and fantasy imprint launched 1991. **Signet** Mass market paperback fiction and non-fiction.

Arkana *Robin Waterfield/Janice Brent/Caroline Muir* (astrology) Eastern and Western mysticism, spirituality and religious tradition, complementary medicine, astrology, new science, environmentalism, women's spirituality, transpersonal psychology and speculative philosophy. 16 titles in 1991.

Blackie Children's Books *Martin West* General fiction, from pre-school upwards, hardback and paperback, including the *Topsy & Tim* series.

Hamish Hamilton *Andrew Franklin* IMPRINTS **Hamish Hamilton** *Alexandra Pringle;* **Hamish Hamilton Children's** *Jane Nissen.* FOUNDED 1931. Bought by Penguin in 1985. *Publishes* biography, children's, current affairs, fiction, history, literature, politics, theatre and travel. AUTHORS Peter Ackroyd, Isabel Allende, Bill Bryson, Germaine Greer, Paul Theroux, Barry Unsworth, Peter Mayle, Sarah Paretsky; CHILDREN'S Raymond Briggs, Eric Carle, Anne Fine, Susan Hill. Unsolicited mss, synopses and ideas welcome.

Authors' Rating With Peter Mayle, how can you go wrong? Easy enough to say now but three years ago Hamish Hamilton was close to extinction. Many of its best authors had left with Christopher Sinclair-Stevenson and sweeping editorial changes upset those who remained. It was a long haul for Andrew Franklin who took command, cutting back on output and dropping the paperback list. But confidence has been restored and imaginative publishing is back in fashion.

Michael Joseph Ltd *Susan Watt* IMPRINTS **Mermaid Books, Pelham Books.** FOUNDED 1936. *Publishes* biography and memoirs, belles-lettres, current affairs, fiction, history, humour, travel, crafts, DIY, sports and sports biographies, handbooks and general leisure. About 150 titles a year. The **Pelham Books** imprint, established 1961 to publish *Pears Cyclopaedia* when the rights were bought from Lever Bros., is Penguin's primary vehicle for sport and leisure titles. **Mermaid Books** is a paperback imprint publishing illustrated non-fiction titles. AUTHORS include Dick Francis, Denis Healey, A. Wainwright. Unsolicited mss discouraged; synopses/ideas welcome.

Ventura *Robin Ellis* Producers and packagers of children's novelty books, *Spot* titles being the mainstay of its programme. Under new owner, Penguin, the title is likely to benefit from the Group's larger international profile in children's books and merchandising, both in print and non-print products. Already, since its first publication in 1980, it has been sold in over 100 countries, in 62 languages, including minority ones, and in Braille and sign language editions.

Viking *Clare Alexander/Elizabeth Attenborough* IMPRINTS **Allen Lane The Penguin Press, Viking, Viking Children's Books.** FOUNDED 1983 as the hardback imprint of Penguin, Viking has developed a distinct identity over the last decade. *Publishes* biography, autobiography, history, travel,

popular science, literary and commercial fiction (including thrillers), general non-fiction and children's. The relatively new **Allen Lane** imprint, in fact a revival of an old imprint, was launched in 1988 to publish a small range of significant academic books. Recent titles include *The Complete Essays of Montaigne* trans. M. A. Screech; *The Penguin Book of Renaissance Verse; Selected Letters of Bertrand Russell; The Tyranny of History* W. J. F. Jenner; *Consciousness Explained* Daniel Dennett. **Viking** Adult and children's fiction and non-fiction. The children's hardcover imprint mirrors much of Penguin's Puffin range, with a particular emphasis on quality fiction. AUTHORS include John Mortimer, Dirk Bogarde, Ruth Rendell, William Trevor, Margaret Drabble, Edna O'Brien, Howard Jacobson, Michael Frayn, Claire Tomalin, Christopher Hibbert.

Frederick Warne *Sally Floyer Publishes* classic children's books, Beatrix Potter, adult non-fiction, and the *Observer Series* (transport, hobbies, natural history, pets). TITLES *Orlando The Marmalade Cat; Huxley Pig; Flower Fairies; Beatrix Potter.* No unsolicited mss; send letter in the first instance. Most books are by commission.
Royalties paid twice yearly. *Overseas associates* in Australia, Canada, India, New Zealand and USA. Associate companies throughout the world including New American Library, Dutton and Dial.

Authors' Rating Having tightened up on its publishing programme and cut back on output, Penguin is launching its comeback with the **Signet** mass market imprint, responsible for up to 30 titles a year. A sign of the times is contained within the latest Pearson results which show that 55 per cent of the Group's turnover comes from Penguin USA, making it the fourth largest American trade publisher. Puffin continues a successful formula with a magnificent backlist of children's book. Accounting for half the total of Penguin sales, Puffin sells 12 million books annually, of which two million are accounted for by 19 Roald Dahl titles.

Penny Press
176 Greendale Road, Coventry CV5 8AY
☎0203 542277

Publisher *Philip J. Brown*

FOUNDED 1988. *Publishes* science and technology, computer user manuals, and integrated science against a background of the history of the universe. No unsolicited mss; synopses and ideas welcome especially for science and technology subjects. Currently developing titles for its *History of Natural Creation* series. TITLES *Global Vision: A History of the Universe; Introduction to Basic Science; Review*

of Current World Problems; Thoughts about the Future.
Royalties paid twice yearly.

Pergamon Press

Headington Hill Hall, Oxford OX3 0BW
☎0865 794141   Fax 0865 60285
Managing Director *M. Boswood*

FOUNDED 1948. *Publishes* academic and professional text and reference books and journals in agriculture, bibliography and library service, biology and zoology, business and industry, chemistry, computer science, economics, education, engineering, geography and geology, languages and linguistics, mathematics and statistics, medical, open learning, philosophy, physics, politics and world affairs, psychology, sociology and anthropology, vocational training and careers. 200 titles a year.

DIVISIONS
Social Sciences & Humanities *Barbara Barrett*
Life Sciences & Medicine *Norman Paskin*
Physical Sciences & Engineering *Peter Shepherd.* Unsolicited mss welcome if within specialist range.
Royalties paid annually. *Overseas associates* in USA, Korea, Japan.

Phaidon Press Ltd

140 Kensington Church Street, London W8 4BN
☎071-221 5656   Fax 071-221 8474
Chairman *Richard Schlagman*
Approx Annual Turnover £5 million

Owned by Mark Futter and Richard Schlagman. *Publishes* quality books on the visual arts, including fine art, art history, architecture, design, practical art, lifestyle and photography. 60 titles in 1992.

Editorial Heads *J. Skipworth/M. Jordan/D. Jenkins/P. Iley/R. Sears* Unsolicited mss welcome but 'only a small amount of unsolicited material gets published'.
Royalties paid twice yearly.

Authors' Rating Settling in under new ownership, Phaidon has celebrated its move to London with a smart new look to its books. The list is as before — upmarket art — but there are reports of ambitious plans for expansion.

George Philip

See **Reed International Books**

Phillimore & Co. Ltd

Shopwyke Hall, Chichester, West
Sussex PO20 6BQ
☎0243 787636   Fax 0243 787639

Chairman/Managing Director *Philip Harris*
Approx Annual Turnover £1 million

FOUNDED 1870 by W. P. W. Phillimore, Victorian campaigner for local archive conservation in Chancery Lane, London. Soon became the country's leading publisher of historical source material and local histories, and became a limited company in 1897. Somewhat run down by the 1960s, it was revived by Philip Harris who moved the company to Chichester in 1968. *Publishes* British local and family history, including histories of institutions, buildings, villages, towns and counties, plus guides to research and writing in these fields. No unsolicited mss; synopses/ideas welcome for local or family histories. 40 titles in 1991.

DIVISIONS/IMPRINTS
Phillimore *Noel Osborne* TITLES *Domesday Book; A History of Essex/Carlisle; The Royal Hampshire Hospital; Channel Island Churches.* **British Association for Local History** *Noel Osborne* TITLES *Running a Local History Society; Writing Local History.*
Royalties paid annually.

Phoenix

See **Orion Publishing Group**

Phoenix (Kingsway)

See **Kingsway Publications**

Piatkus Books

5 Windmill Street, London W1P 1HF
☎071-631 0710   Fax 071-436 7137
Managing Director *Judy Piatkus*
Approx Annual Turnover £2.75 million

FOUNDED 1979. *Publishes* business, childcare and parenting, cookery, fiction, health, mind, body and spirit, popular psychology, practical, women's interests. 110 titles in 1991 (60 of which were fiction). TITLES *The Complete Style Guide from the Colour Me Beautiful Organisation; The Curry Club* (cookbook range); *The Complete Time Management System.*

DIVISIONS
Fiction *Judy Piatkus* TITLES *A Woman Possessed* Malcolm Ross; *The Immaculate* Mark Morris. **Non-fiction** *Gill Cormode* TITLES *Perfectly Legal Tax Loopholes* Stephen Courtney; *Dare to Connect*

Susan Jeffers. Unsolicited mss, synopses and ideas for books welcome.
Royalties paid twice yearly.

Authors' Rating Piatkus Books has grown from a one-room band to a thriving independent list. The company claims to give commitment to each book they take on and to treat every non-fiction title as a lead. Authors are cheered by fast decision-making and by the policy of frequent small reprints which keeps titles in print for much longer than average.

Picador
See **Pan Books Ltd**

Piccadilly Press
5 Castle Road, London NW1 8PR
☎071-267 4492   Fax 071-267 4493

Managing Director *Brenda Gardner*
Approx Annual Turnover £500,000

FOUNDED 1983 by Brenda Gardner. Small independent publisher who plans to stay small, publishing about 25-30 titles a year, with a total staff of three. *Publishes* children's hardbacks, picture and story books, teenage non-fiction and humour for age range 9-90! Unsolicited synopses and ideas for books (with s.a.e.) welcome.
Royalties paid twice yearly.

Piccolo
See **Pan Books Ltd**

Pictorial
See **Souvenir Press Ltd**

Picture Publishing Co. Ltd
108 Clarendon Road, London W11 2HR
☎071-727 4388   Fax 071-727 3918

Managing Director *Jeremy Hamp*

FOUNDED 1989. *Publishes* video/book packages in a variety of fields. No unsolicited mss; send synopses and ideas for books in first instance.

Pimlico
See **Random House Publishing Group Ltd**

Pinter Publishers Ltd
25 Floral Street, London WC2E 9DS
☎071-240 9233   Fax 071-379 5553

Managing Director *Frances Pinter*

Publishes academic social sciences, physical sciences and environmental policy. About 130 titles a year.

Editorial Director *Iain Stevenson*

IMPRINTS
Belhaven Press Environmental science. **Leicester University Press** (see entry).
Royalties paid annually.

Authors' Rating With Belhaven as the only scholarly imprint devoted to environmental issues, Pinter Publishers are attracting authors and titles more usually associated with bigger companies.

Piper
See **Pan Books Ltd**

Pitkin Pictorials
See **Reed International Books**

Pitman Publishing
128 Long Acre, London WC2E 9AN
☎071-379 7383   Fax 071-240 5771

Managing Director *Henry Reece*

Part of the **Longman Group**. FOUNDED 1837 as the publisher of the Pitman Shorthand System. Pitman has now joined **Longman** as its specialist Business Education and Information Technology and Management Skills publishing house. *Publishes* textbooks, reference and dictionaries in business education: secretarial, business studies, management and professional studies; also books for business professionals. 147 titles in 1991.

DIVISIONS
Educational *Simon Lake* **Professional** *Helen Pilgrim*

IMPRINTS
Pitman, M & E, Financial Times, NatWest Business Handbooks, BIM Guides. Unsolicited mss, synopses and ideas for books welcome.
Royalties paid annually.

Authors' Rating Formerly a medical publisher of note, some authors were unhappy when they were hived off to other parts of the Longman empire. But Pitman are reasserting themselves with a growing reputation for good quality business books.

Plenum Publishing Ltd
88-90 Middlesex Street, London E1 7EZ
☎071-377 0686   Fax 071-247 0555

Chairman *Martin E. Tash* (USA)
Managing Director *Dr Ken Derham*

FOUNDED 1966. A division of **Plenum Publishing**, New York; the London office is the editorial and marketing base for the UK and Europe. *Publishes* postgraduate, professional and research level scientific, technical and medical monographs, conference proceedings and reference books. About 325 titles (worldwide) a year.

Editorial Head *Dr Ken Derham* (UK and Europe)

IMPRINTS
Consultants Bureau, IFI Plenum Data Company, Plenum Medical Company, Plenum Press, Human Sciences Press. Synopses preferred to finished mss.
Royalties paid annually.

Plexus Publishing Ltd
26 Dafforne Road, London SW17 8TZ
☎081-672 6067   Fax 081-672 1631

Chairman *T. C. Porter*
Managing Director *S. M. Wake*

FOUNDED 1973. *Publishes* high-quality illustrated books, specialising in international co-editions with an emphasis on art and cinema, biography, popular culture and popular music. Unsolicited mss, synopses and ideas welcome.
Royalties paid twice yearly.

Pluto Press Ltd
345 Archway Road, London N6 5AA
☎081-348 2724   Fax 081-348 9133

Managing Director *Roger Van Zwanenberg*

FOUNDED 1970. Developed a reputation for innovatory publishing in the field of non-fiction. Acquired the Journeyman Press when Journeyman ceased trading at the end of 1989. *Publishes* academic and scholarly books across a range of subjects including cultural studies, politics and world affairs, social sciences and socialist, feminist and Marxist books. About 50–60 titles a year.

Editorial Director *Anne Beech* Synopses and ideas welcome.

Authors' Rating Zwan takeover led to a radical editorial rethink. Now less cultural (no more theatre, cinema, literary criticism), much more political.

Polity Press
65 Bridge Street, Cambridge CB2 1UR
☎0223 324315   Fax 0223 461385

FOUNDED 1984. All books are published in association with **Blackwell Publishers**. *Publishes* archaeology and anthropology, criminology, economics, feminism, general interest, history, human geography, literature, media and cultural studies, medicine and society, philosophy, politics, psychology, religion and theology, social and political theory, sociology. Unsolicited mss, synopses and ideas for books welcome.
Royalties paid annually.

Polygon
See **Edinburgh University Press**

Pop Universal
See **Souvenir Press Ltd**

Popular Dogs
See **Random House Publishing Group Ltd**

Presentations
See **Souvenir Press Ltd**

Princess House
See **Studio Editions Ltd**

Princeton University Press
Avonlea, 10 Watlington Road, Cowley,
Oxford OX4 5NF
☎0865 748405   Fax 0865 748401

Director *Walter Lippincott* (USA)

Wide range of academic books, especially biology, history and literature. Over 200 titles a year. Editorial department based in the US (see entry **US Publishers**).

Prism Press Book Publishers Ltd
2 South Street, Bridport, Dorset DT6 3NQ
☎0308 27022   Fax 0308 421015

Managing Director *Julian King*

FOUNDED 1974 by Julian King and Colin Spooner. *Publishes* alternative medicine, architecture, building, conservation, environment, farming, feminism, health, law, mysticism, occult, philosophy, politics and wholefood cookery. 15 titles in 1991.
TITLES *Solar Architecture in Europe EEC; Your Health Our World* Diane Wiesner; *Dictionary of Mysticism* Nevill Drury. Unsolicited mss, synopses and ideas welcome.

Royalties paid twice yearly. *Overseas associates* Prism Press, USA.

Proteus
See **Omnibus Press**

Puffin
See **Penguin Books Ltd**

Quartet Books
27–29 Goodge Street, London W1P 1FD
☏ 071-636 3992   Fax 071-637 1866

Chairman *Naim Attallah*
Approx Annual Turnover £1.4 million

FOUNDED 1972 by four ex-Granada employees and bought by Naim Attallah in 1976. Part of the Namara Group, which also includes the **Women's Press**. *Publishes* classical music books, fiction, jazz, literary biography, literature in translation (most European languages including East European), photography and popular non-fiction. About 80 titles a year.

Editorial Director *Stephen Pickles*

IMPRINTS
Robin Clark, Quartet Encounters (series of European literature, prose only, in translation.) TITLES *Memoirs* Leni Riefenstahl; *Maria Callas* Jürgen Kesting; *Letters 1940–54, Vol 1* Pier Paolo Pasolini; *The Honour of the Tribe* Rachid Mimouni; *Anathemas & Admirations* E. M. Cioran; *Captain Nemo's Library* Per Olor Enquist; *A Time To Kill* Ennio Flaiano; *Farewells & A Grave with No Name* Juan Carlos Onetti. Unsolicited mss, synopses and ideas for books welcome. No crime fiction.
Royalties paid twice yearly.

Authors' Rating A high-profile company riding on the flamboyant reputation of its owner, Naim Attallah, whose publishing interests include the best of the book journals, *The Literary Review*. Writers are encouraged to think big but payments can be erratic.

Queen Anne Press
See **Lennard Publishing**

Quiller Press
46 Lillie Road, London SW6 1TN
☏ 071-499 6529
Fax 071-381 8941   Telex 21120

Managing Director *Jeremy Greenwood*

Specialises in sponsored books and publications sold through non-book trade channels or bookshops, but not vanity publishing. *Publishes* architecture, biography, business and industry, children's, cookery, crafts and hobbies, DIY, gardening, guidebooks, humour, reference, sports, travel, wine and spirits. 15 titles in 1991.

Editorial Director *Jeremy Greenwood* TITLES *Memorable Dinners* Derek Nimmo; *They Will Always Meet At Eleven* Jim Meads; *Entrée Guides* Patricia Finn; *Superscrooge* Malcolm Stacey. Unsolicited mss not welcome; ideas nearly always originated in-house. Distributed by ABS.
Royalties paid twice yearly.

Quotes Ltd
See **Barracuda Books Ltd**

RAC Publishing
RAC House, Bartlett Street, South Croydon, Surrey CR2 6XW
☏ 081-686 0088   Fax 081-688 2882

Publisher *C. Milsome*

Publishes maps, atlases and travel guides. Synopses and ideas for books considered.

Radius
See **Random House Publishing Group Ltd**

The Ramsay Head Press
15 Gloucester Place, Edinburgh EH3 6EE
☏ 031-225 5646

Joint Managing Directors *Conrad Wilson/Mrs Christine Wilson*

A small independent family publisher. FOUNDED 1968 by Norman Wilson OBE. *Publishes* biography, cookery, Scottish fiction and non-fiction. About 3–4 titles a year. TITLES *The Happy Land* Howard Denton & Jim C. Wilson; *Seven Valleys* Tessa Ransford. Synopses and ideas for books welcome if they come within their range (Scottish).
Royalties paid twice yearly.

Random House Publishing Group Ltd
Random House, 20 Vauxhall Bridge Road, London SW1V 2SA
☏ 071-973 9000   Fax 071-233 6058

Chief Executive *Gail Rebuck*
Managing Director *Brian Robertson*

The Random House Publishing Group Ltd is the new name for the trading company of Random House UK Ltd; the former Century element has now been dropped. There has been further restructuring within the Group and perhaps the most significant change that has occurred is the management buy-out of the Group's reference division. All titles including the Hutchinson Encyclopedia range will now be published under a new company and imprint, **Helicon Publishing**, led by David Attwooll and based in Oxford (see entry). The buy-out is in line with Random's increasing focus on its trade publishing, both here and in the US. Trade publishing now consists of eight sub-divisions as outlined below.

DIVISIONS/IMPRINTS

Arrow Books Ltd *Simon Master* Tel: 071-973 9700. Fax: 071-233 6127. IMPRINTS **Arrow, Century, Vintage** (upmarket fiction and non-fiction aimed at the 20-40 age group). Arrow incorporates the old Century fiction titles and is phasing out the Rowan and Legend imprints. *Publishes* fiction, non-fiction, children's, reference, science fiction and fantasy, crime and detective fiction. No unsolicited mss; submissions should be made via agents.

Jonathan Cape Ltd *David Godwin* Tel: 071-973 9730. Fax: 071-233 6117. IMPRINTS **Jonathan Cape, Shanbhala**. *Publishes* archaeology, biography and memoirs, current affairs, drama, economics, fiction, history, philosophy, poetry, sociology and travel.

Century Business *Kate Parkin* Tel: 071-973 9670. Fax: 071-233 6125. *Publishes* business management, advertising, communication, marketing, selling, investment and financial titles.

Chatto & Windus Ltd *Carmen Callil* Tel: 071-973 9740. Fax: 071-233 6123. IMPRINTS **Chatto & Windus, The Hogarth Press**. *Publishes* archaeology, art, belles-lettres, biography and memoirs, cookery, crime, current affairs, drama, essays, fiction, history, illustrated and fine editions, poetry, politics, psychoanalysis, translations and travel. Hardback and paperbacks. No unsolicited mss.

Authors' Rating Keeping one step ahead with its new list of paperback originals, Chatto editors have an eye for offbeat titles, fiction and non-fiction.

Random House Children's Books *Piet Snyman* Tel: 071-973 9750. Fax: 071-233 6058. All of the Group's children's imprints have been operating under a single division since 1991. IMPRINTS **Bodley Head Children's, Hutchinson Children's, Random House, Jonathan Cape Children's, Tell-a-Story, Julia MacRae Books, Red Fox. Publishing Directors** *Clare Conville/ Caroline Roberts/ Alison Berry/Julia MacRae/Tom Maschler*. *Publishes* picture books, fiction, non-

fiction and books on audio cassette. Red Fox is the division's paperback imprint.

Ebury Press *Amelia Thorpe/Fiona McIntyre* Tel: 071-973 9690. Fax: 071-233 6057. IMPRINTS **Ebury Press Stationery** (ex-Century Benham) *Romie Sinfield*, **Barrie & Jenkins Ltd** (art, architecture, photography, antiques and collecting) *Julian Shuckburgh*, **Rider** *Tessa Strickland*, **Vermilion** *Rowena Webb*, and **Condé Nast Books**. *Publishes* cookery, health and beauty, photography, travel, transport, humour, crafts, antiques, hobbies, gardening, natural history, DIY, diaries, gift stationery and Condé Nast titles. Ebury is also the publishing vehicle for National Magazine Co. book tie-ins. About 150 titles a year. Unsolicited mss, synopses and ideas for books welcome.

Hutchinson Books Ltd *Simon King* Tel: 071-973 9680. Fax: 071-233 6129. IMPRINTS **Hutchinson, Radius, Stanley Paul, Popular Dogs, Nick Hern Books, Pimlico, Muller**. *Publishes* belles-lettres, biography, memoirs, thrillers, crime, current affairs, essays, general fiction, history, illustrated books, poetry, politics, translations and travel. Hardback and paperback. **Stanley Paul, Popular Dogs** *Roddy Bloomfield Publishes* sports, games, hobbies, sporting biographies, animals, practical books on breeding, care, training and general management of dogs. **Nick Hern Books** *Nick Hern* Tel: 071-973 9670. Fax: 071-223 6125. *Publishes* Playtexts, theatre and the performing arts. Unsolicited mss, synopses and ideas in the realm of the performing arts welcome. Not interested in unperformed plays.

Random House Enterprises IMPRINTS **Fodor's, Audio Books, TSR** (audio books also).

Royalties paid twice yearly for the most part but may vary from within the Group from one division/ imprint to another.

Authors' Rating By far the largest general trade publisher, Random House has undertaken a massive reorganisation which encompasses a new non-fiction trade paperback imprint (Pimlico) which is expected to be 'one of the most successful publishing enterprises in London'. Barrie & Jenkins has dropped its general list to concentrate on antiques and Nick Hern is being allowed to do what he does best — books on the theatre. Century Business is bravely going where few other publishers dare to go — into audio, video and CDs. Hutchinson is a rarity in that *Writer's Handbook* readers have made a point of complimenting the high standards of editorship.

R & B Publishing

PO Box 200, Harrogate, North Yorkshire HG2 9RB
☎ 0423 507545   Fax 0423 507545

Chairman/Managing Director *C. Brown*

FOUNDED 1990. Independent publisher of humour and recreation titles. TITLES *The Hangover Handbook; The Ancient Art of Farting.* 6 titles in 1991. Unsolicited mss, synopses and ideas for books welcome. Full editorial and production services to authors (hard copy or disk). *Royalties* paid twice yearly.

Reader's Digest Association Ltd

Berkeley Square House, Berkeley Square, London W1X 6AB
☎071-629 8144   Fax 071-236 5956

Managing Director *Neil McRae*
Approx Annual Turnover £119 million

Publishes gardening, natural history, cookery, DIY, travel and word books. About 10 titles a year.

DIVISIONS
Reader's Digest General Books *Robin Hosie*
TITLES *Family Medical Adviser; The Gardening Year; Nature Lover's Library; New DIY Manual; The Repair Manual.* Unsolicited mss, synopses and ideas for books welcome.
Royalties paid according to contract.

Red Fox

See **Random House Publishing Group Ltd**

Reed International Books

Michelin House, 81 Fulham Road, London SW3 6RB
☎071-581 9393   Fax 071-589 8419

Chairman *Paul Hamlyn*
Chief Executive *Ian Irvine*
Approx Annual Turnover £333.6 million

Owned by Reed International, Inc., whose book publishing operation is divided into two parts: Reed International Books and Reed Reference Publishing. Reed International Books is the consumer, professional and educational arm of Reed's book publishing business. (Reed Reference Publishing incorporates the UK-based **Bowker-Saur Ltd**).

DIVISIONS

Reed Consumer Books Ltd *Richard Charkin* Comprises all the consumer publishing imprints acquired by Reed since 1987 (including **Octopus** trade, children's and illustrated titles) and the new Mandarin and Minerva paperback imprints launched in 1989.
IMPRINTS/DIVISIONS
Bounty Books *Sally-ann Platts* (Michelin House) Tel: 071-581 9393. Fax: 071-225 0873. Now mass market and hardback adult and children's fiction and non-fiction.
Brimax Books *Patricia Gillette* Units 4/5, Studland Park Industrial Estate, Exning Road, Newmarket, Suffolk CB8 7AU. Tel: 0638 664611. Fax: 0638 665220. Mass market picture books for children. TITLES *The Children's Book of Verse; Teddy Bear's Counting Book; Teddy Bears Tell the Time.* Unsolicited mss considered; synopses preferred.
Conran Octopus *Alison Cathie* 37 Shelton Street, London WC2H 9HN. Tel: 071-240 6961. Fax: 071-836 9951. **Editorial Director** *Anne Furniss* Quality illustrated books, particularly lifestyle, cookery, gardening. TITLES *Terence Conran's New House Book; The Complete Mothercare Manual; Creating Small Gardens; 10 Minute Cuisine.* Synopses/ideas welcome.
Hamlyn *Emma Blackley* (Michelin House) Tel: 071-581 9393. Fax: 071-581 9553. Popular illustrated non-fiction, particularly cookery, gardening, craft, sport, film tie-ins, rock'n'roll, road atlases. TITLES *Larousse Gastronomique; Variety Movie Guide; Sunday Times Chronicle of Sport; Jean Moss Designer Knits Collection.* Synopses/ideas welcome; no mss.
Hamlyn Children's Books *John Moulder* 38 Hans Crescent, London SW1X 0LZ. Tel: 071-581 9393. Fax: 071-581 9553. Illustrated non-fiction and reference books for children. TITLES *Children's All Colour Bible; The Animal Encyclopedia; The See Through History* series; *The Giant Board Book* series. Synopses/ideas welcome.
William Heinemann *Helen Fraser* (Michelin House) Tel: 071-581 9393. Fax: 071-589 8437. **Editorial Directors** *Tom Weldon* (Non-fiction); *Max Eilenberg* (Fiction) TITLES *The Liar* Stephen Fry; *Orwell* Michael Shelden; *Requiem* Clare Francis; *Turning Back the Sun* Colin Thubron. Synopses/ideas welcome.
Heinemann Young Books *Ingrid Selberg* 38 Hans Crescent, London SW1X 0LZ. Tel: 071-581 9393. Fax: 071-584 2022. Books for children, including quality picture books, novels, anthologies and TV tie-ins. TITLES *Thomas The Tank Engine; Where's Spot; The Jolly Postman.* Synopses/ideas welcome; no mss.

Authors' Rating Economies of scale are sought by the organisational changes which bring Heinemann and its paperback imprint, Mandarin, under the same management. A tighter structure should benefit authors.

Kingswood Press *Neil Tunnicliffe* (Michelin House) Tel: 071-581 9393. Fax: 071-589 8450. Sport: cricket, fishing, etc. TITLES *The Official Rules of Sports and Games; The Board of Coal Rugby League Yearbook; Match of My Life.* Synopses/ideas welcome.
Lime Tree *Elsbeth Lindner* (Michelin House) Tel:

071-581 9393. Fax: 071-589 8450. Music, women's titles, fiction and general non-fiction. TITLES *By Heart, The Autobiography of Elizabeth Smart* Rosemary Sullivan; *Listening to Music* Jonathan Kramer; *B Monkey* Andrew Davies; *Live, In the Flesh* Katie Campbell. Synopses/ideas welcome.

Mammoth *Ingrid Selberg* 38 Hans Crescent, London SW1X 0LZ. Tel: 071-581 9393. Fax: 071-584 2022. **Editorial Director** *Gill Evans* Children's paperbacks. TITLES *Winnie the Pooh; The Little House in the Big Woods; Frog and Toad.* No unsolicited mss; ideas in writing welcome.

Mandarin *Helen Fraser* (Michelin House) Tel: 071-581 9393. Fax: 071-589 8437. **Editorial Directors** *Tom Weldon* (Non-fiction); *Max Eilenberg* (Fiction) Paperback fiction and general non-fiction. TITLES *The Silence of the Lambs* Thomas Harris; *You'll Never Eat Lunch in This Town Again* Julia Phillips; *Churchill* Martin Gilbert; *Revolving Jones* Leslie Thomas. No unsolicited mss; ideas/synopses welcome.

Methuen *Geoffrey Strachan* 7 Kendrick Mews, London SW7 3HG. Tel: 071-581 9393. Fax: 071-225 0933. **Editorial Directors** *Ann Mansbridge/Pamela Edwardes* Drama, humour and general non-fiction. TITLES *Families and How to Survive Them* Robin Skynner & John Cleese; *Monty Python's Big Red Book; The Secret Diary of Adrian Mole Aged 13 3/4* Sue Townsend; *From Zia with Love* Wole Soyinka; plays by Bertholt Brecht, Edward Bond, Caryl Churchill, Joe Orton. Synopses welcome; no mss.

Methuen Children's Books *Ingrid Selberg* 38 Hans Crescent, London SW1X 0LZ. Tel: 071-581 9393. Fax: 071-823 9406. Books for children, including quality picture books and fiction for babies to early teens. TITLES *Winnie The Pooh; Babar; Tintin; The Wind in the Willows.* Ideas welcome.

Minerva *Helen Fraser* (Michelin House) Tel: 071-581 9393. Fax: 071-589 8437. **Editorial Director** *Geoff Mulligan* Paperback literary fiction and non-fiction. TITLES *Vineland* Thomas Pynchon; *The Book of Evidence* John Banville; *A Dance to the Music of Time* Anthony Powell; *India* V. S. Naipaul. Mss, synopses and ideas welcome.

Mitchell Beazley *Simon McMurtrie* (including **Miller's Publications**) (Michelin House) Tel: 071-581 9393. Fax: 071-584 8268. Illustrated encyclopedias and quality illustrated books, including wine. TITLES *Hugh Johnson's Pocket Wine Book; The World Atlas of Wine; The New Joy of Sex; Miller's Antiques Price Guide.* Mss, synopses and ideas welcome.

Osprey *Nick Collins* (Michelin House) Tel: 071-581 9393. Fax: 071-589 8419. Militaria, aviation, automotive, natural history. TITLES *MG; Racing the Silver Arrows; F14 Tom Cats Forever; Waterloo, The 100 Days.* Mss, synopses/ideas welcome.

George Philip *John Gaisford* (Michelin House) Tel: 071-581 9393. Fax: 071-589 8419. Atlases, maps, travel guides, astronomy. TITLES *Philips' Atlas of the World; Philips' Road Atlas of Britain; Philips' Guide to the Night Sky; Philips' London.* Mss, synopses/ ideas welcome.

Pitkin Pictorials *Ian Corsie* Healey House, Dene Road, Andover, Hants SP10 2AA. Tel: 0264 334303. Fax: 0264 334110. Illustrated souvenir guides. TITLES *Britain's Kings and Queens; The Queen and Her Family; Cathedral Guides; City Guides.* Ideas welcome.

Secker & Warburg *Dan Franklin* (Michelin House) Tel: 071-581 9393. Fax: 071-589 8421. Literary fiction and general non-fiction. TITLES *The Van* Roddy Doyle; *Paradise News* David Lodge; *An Act of Terror* Andre Brink; *Neither Here Nor There* Bill Bryson. Mss and synopses welcome.

Authors' Rating Making great play of publishing paperback originals. Quality fiction supported by a formidable backlist.

Sinclair-Stevenson *Christopher Sinclair-Stevenson* 7 Kendrick Mews, London SW7 3HG. Tel: 071-581 1645. Fax: 071-225 1699. Fiction and general non-fiction. TITLES *Jesus* A. N. Wilson; *Bertrand Russell* Caroline Moorhead; *Sacred Country* Rose Tremain; *The Mist in the Mirror* Susan Hill. Mss and synopses welcome.

Authors' Rating Originally trumpeted as a classy independent, Christopher Sinclair-Stevenson has responded to economic pressures with a sell-out to Reed. However, the independence is said to be preserved and judging by the author list, enduring classiness cannot be denied. Came out first in a recent **Society of Authors** and **Writers' Guild** survey on author-publisher relationships.

Professional Division: Butterworth & Co. (Publishers) Ltd *Neville Cusworth* Borough Green, Sevenoaks, Kent TN15 8PH. Tel: 0732 884567. Fax: 0732 884079.
IMPRINTS/DIVISIONS

Butterworth Law Publishers *David Summers* 88 Kingsway, London WC2B 6AB. Tel: 071-405 6900. Fax: 071-405 1332. **Publishing Directors** *Jane Allen/Paul Brown/David Millet* Legal books, journals and loose-leaf services. TITLES *Halsbury's Laws of England; All England Law Reports; Stone's Justices Manual; The Discipline of Law* Lord Denning. Synopses/ideas welcome.

Butterworth Tax Publishers *Peter Robinson* (Kingsway: address, telephone and fax as above). **Publishing Director** *Christine Durman.* Tax and accountancy books, journals and loose-leaf services. TITLES *Simon's Taxes; Butterworth's Business Tax Service; Butterworth's Personal Tax Service; Butterworth's Yellow/ Orange Handbooks.* Synopses/ideas welcome.

Butterworth-Heinemann *Doug Fox* Linacre House, Jordan Hill, Oxford OX2 8DP. Tel: 0865

310366. Fax: 0865 310898. **Publishing Directors** *Peter Dixon* (Technical); *Charles Fry* (Medical); *Kathryn Grant* (Business). Scientific, technical, medical and business books and journals. TITLES *Human Cross-Sectional Anatomy* Harold Ellis, Bari Logan & Adrian Dixon; *Plant Engineering Reference Book; Managing Data Protection; Quality Management Handbook* Max Hand & Brian Ploughman. Synopses/ideas welcome.

Reed Educational Division *Stephen Warshaw* Halley Court, Jordan Hill, Oxford OX2 8EJ. Tel: 0865 311366. Fax: 0865 310043.
DIVISIONS/IMPRINTS
Heinemann Educational *Bob Osborne* (Halley Court: address, telephone and fax as above). **Publishing Directors** *Stephen Ashton* (Primary); *Kay Symons* (Secondary). Textbooks, literature and other educational resources for primary and secondary schools and further education. Mss, synopses and ideas welcome.
Ginn *William Shepherd* Prebendal House, Parson's Fee, Aylesbury, Bucks HP20 2QZ. Tel: 0296 88411. Fax: 0296 25487. **Editorial Director** *Ann Foster* Textbooks and educational resources for primary schools. Titles tend to be commissioned; no mss. Ideas welcome.
Heinemann International *Mike Esplen* (Halley Court). **Publishing Director** *Yvonne de Henseler* English language teaching books and materials. Mss, synopses and ideas welcome.
Heinemann International Literature & Textbooks *Vicky Unwin* (Halley Court) Textbooks and literature for schools in Africa and the Caribbean. Mss, synopses and ideas welcome.
Royalties paid twice yearly/annually, according to contract.

Authors' Rating We must get used to these new corporate titles. But just because Reed Consumer Publishing encompasses names like Heinemann and Secker & Warburg, do not assume that it is simply an amalgam of chips off the old block. Under Richard Charkin's leadership, Reed is now one of the sharpest acts in the business. The somewhat impersonal, no-nonsense approach does not suit all authors but no one has been heard to complain about increased royalty cheques — the result of tougher and more imaginative marketing. Reed was first in line to support Terry Maher and the Pentos Group in their fight against the Net Book Agreement. It has been quieter on that front of late but the marketing push that led to the Reed break with the NBA is now showing up in the establishment of a telephone sales unit, to service any business interested in selling books, and a direct sales operation. Richard Charkin has even thought of exploring the backlist to revive former strong sellers under a new format — obvious enough to most authors but an idea of startling originality to most publishers. Tighter management has brought

its own rewards with a strong advance against the recessionary trend. An indication of change is the advance of Bounty Books, formerly a reprint specialist, now a mass-market publisher.

Reinhardt Books Ltd
27 Wrights Lane, London W8 5TZ
☎ 071-938 1253/416 3000 ext. 2474
Fax 071-416 3293

Chairman/Managing Director *Max Reinhardt*
Directors *Joan Reinhardt/John Hews*

FOUNDED 1887 as H. F. L. (Publishers). Acquired its present identity in 1987 under Max Reinhardt, ex-**Chatto, Bodley Head, Cape**. Established by 'a team of friends and colleagues publishing for pleasure'. First publication was in September 1988 with Graham Greene's *The Captain and the Enemy*. *Publishes* biography, children's books and fiction. AUTHORS include Maurice Sendak, Alistair Cooke and Mitsumasa Anno.

Assistant Publisher *Amanda Hargreaves*
Editorial Consultant *Judy Taylor*

IMPRINTS
Nonesuch Press After a period of dormancy began republishing in 1989 with limited editions of Graham Greene's *Why The Epigraph?* and the definitive edition of Robert Louis Stevenson's *The Wrong Box*.
Royalties paid according to contract.

Rider
See **Random House Publishing Group Ltd**

Robinson Publishing
11 Shepherd House, Shepherd Street,
London W1Y 7LD
☎ 071-493 1064   Fax 071-409 7226

Managing Director *Nick Robinson*

FOUNDED 1983. *Publishes* general fiction and non-fiction trade paperbacks, and some hardbacks. Specialist areas include true crime, fantasy, health, film, general and science fiction. SERIES include *Mammoth Books, Dark Fantasy, Writer's Workshop, Best New* and *Classic Authors*. About 20 titles a year.

Editorial Head *Nick Robinson* No unsolicited mss.
Royalties paid twice yearly.

Robson Books Ltd

Bolsover House, 5-6 Clipstone Street,
London W1P 7EB
☏ 071-323 1223

Managing Director *Jeremy Robson*

FOUNDED 1973 by Jeremy Robson. *Publishes* mainly general non-fiction, including biography, cinema, cookery, gardening, guidebooks, health and beauty, humour, sports and games, theatre and drama, travel and topography. About 60 titles a year.

Editorial Head *Louise Dixon* Unsolicited mss, synopses and ideas for books welcome (s.a.e. essential).
Royalties paid twice yearly.

Authors' Rating The hard-pressed gift buyers' favourite publisher. A Robson book is always good for a laugh.

Rosendale Press Ltd

Suite 320, Premier House, 10 Greycoat Place,
London SW1P 1SB
☏ 071-222 8866 Fax 071-799 1416

Chairman *Timothy S. Green*

FOUNDED 1985. Independent publisher of non-fiction and illustrated books, namely food and drink, travel, business, and family health. 9 titles in 1991.

Editorial Director *Maureen P. Green* TITLES *The Top 100 Pasta Sauces; Favourite Indian Food; The Prospect for Gold; The Gold Companion; Understanding Your Baby.* Synopses and ideas for books considered within their specialist fields only.
Payment varies according to contract.

Roundhouse Publishing Ltd

PO Box 140, Oxford OX2 7SF
☏ 0865 59594 Fax 0865 59594

Publisher *Alan T. Goodworth*
Managing Director *William R. Gills*

Publisher of cinema, theatre and other media-interested titles; biography and autobiography; photography and general interest non-fiction. Fiction interests include English translations of the Modern Greek Writers Series. TITLES *Loser Take All: The Comic Art of Woody Allen; Italian Cinema: From Neo-realism to the Present; The Cinema of Stanley Kubrick.* Also sales and distribution agents for a range of publishers in the UK and US.
Royalties paid twice yearly.

Routledge, Chapman & Hall Ltd

11 New Fetter Lane, London EC4P 4EE
☏ 071-583 9855 Fax 071-583 0701

Managing Director *Robert Kiernan*
Approx Annual Turnover (Group worldwide) £15 million

Owned by International Thomson since 1987. Routledge is composed of Croom Helm, Methuen Academic, Routledge & Kegan Paul and Tavistock Publications; Chapman & Hall embraces the old ABP (Associated Book Publishers were the previous owner): E&FN Spon, Van Nostrand Reinhold (New York), Blueprint, HK Lewis Medical, and BMMR. In 1991, **HarperCollins** sold its academic list to Routledge, Chapman & Hall. This incorporates former Unwin Hyman and Harper & Row nursing titles and consists of textbooks and monographs in a variety of subjects, namely sociology, politics, history, geography, life sciences, earth sciences, cultural and media studies, economics and business. All in all a substantial list to add to its stable.

DIVISIONS
Routledge (New Fetter Lane) **Managing Director** *David Croom* George Routledge set up business as a bookseller in 1836 and began publishing the same year. Acquired Kegan Paul, Trench, Trübner, a soundly-based academic list in 1911 and gradually increased its academic list. Became Routledge & Kegan Paul in 1977 and was bought by ABP in 1985. *Publishes* access, addiction, anthropology, archaeology, art, Asian studies, busines and management, classical heritage and studies, counselling, criminology, development and environment, dictionaries, economics, education, geography, health, history, Japanese studies, library science, linguistics, literary criticism, media and culture, Middle East, philosophy and religion, politics, political economy, psychiatry, psychology, reference, social administration, social studies and sociology, women's studies and journals. No poetry, fiction, travel or astrology. 638 titles in 1991. DIVISIONS/IMPRINTS **Economics, Education, Politics, Geography, Middle East, Soviet, Critical Assessments** *Peter Sowden;* **Social and Behavioural Studies** *David Stonestreet;* **Humanities** *Janice Price;* **Reference** *Wendy Morris;* **Ark** *Elizabeth White.* Send synopses with sample chapter and c.v. rather than complete mss.
Chapman & Hall Ltd 2-6 Boundary Row, London SE1 8HN. Tel: 071-865 0066. Fax: 071-522 9623. **Managing Director** *David Inglis Publishes* science, technology, medicine and professional reference, and journals. About 300 titles a year. DIVISIONS **Science, Technology & Medicine** *Anthony Watkinson* **E&FN Spon** *Phillip Read* **University & Professional** *Dominic Recaldin.* Unsolicited mss and synopses welcome in above specialist fields only.

Royalties paid annually for Routledge titles; twice yearly for Chapman & Hall.

Saga
See **Barracuda Books Ltd/Quotes Ltd**

Sage Publications Ltd
6 Bonhill Street, London EC2A 4PU
☎ 071-374 0645   Fax 071-374 8741

Managing Director *David Hill*

FOUNDED 1971. *Publishes* academic, scholarly and professional.

Editorial Director *Stephen Barr* TITLES *Robert Colquhoun* Raymond Aron. Unsolicited mss and synopses welcome.
Royalties paid twice yearly.

David St John Thomas Publisher
PO Box 4, Nairn, Scotland IV12 4HU
☎ 0667 54441   Fax 0667 54401

Chairman *David St John Thomas*
Approx Annual Turnover £70,000

FOUNDED 1982 by the founder and chairman of **David & Charles Publishers** to provide an outlet for special interest publications. *Publishes* railway, Scottish interest, and instructional writing books in conjunction with *Writers News* magazine. 5 titles in 1991. Unsolicited mss, synopses and ideas for books welcome.
Royalties paid annually.

St Paul Publications
St Paul's House, Middlegreen, Slough, Buckinghamshire SL3 6BT
☎ 0753 520621   Fax 0753 574240

Managing Director *Karamvelil Sebastian*
Approx Annual Turnover £500,000

Publishing division of the Society of St Paul. Began publishing in 1914 but activities were fairly limited until around 1948. *Publishes* religious material only: theology, scripture, catechetics, prayer books, children's material and biography. Unsolicited mss, synopses and ideas welcome. 52 titles in 1991.
Royalties paid annually. *Overseas subsidiary* St Pauls, Maynooth, Republic of Ireland.

St Paul's Bibliographies
1 Step Terrace, Winchester, Hampshire SO22 5BW
☎ 0962 860524   Fax 0962 842409

Chairman/Managing Director *Robert Cross*
Approx Annual Turnover £70,000

FOUNDED 1982. *Publishes* bibliographical reference books only. 3 titles in 1991.

IMPRINTS
St Paul's TITLES *Eric Gill: A Bibliography*.
Foxbury Press TITLES *British Library History: Bibliography 1985–89*. Unsolicited mss, synopses and ideas welcome.
Royalties paid twice yearly.

Salamander Books Ltd
129–137 York Way, London N7 9LG
☎ 071-267 4447   Fax 071-267 5112

Managing Director *Ray Bonds*
Editor-in-Chief *Graham Smith*

FOUNDED 1973. Independent publishing house. *Publishes* collecting, cookery and wine, crafts, military and aviation, pet care, sport, transport, technical and children's non-fiction. About 55 titles a year. Unsolicited synopses and ideas for books welcome.
Royalties outright fee paid instead of royalties.

Sangam Books Ltd
57 London Fruit Exchange, Brushfield Street, London E1 6EP
☎ 071-377 6399   Fax 071-247 1817

Executive-In-Charge *Anthony de Souza*

Traditionally educational publishers, at school and college levels, but also publishes books on art, India, medicine, science, technology and social sciences. Some fiction in paperback list.

W. B. Saunders/Saunders Scientific Publications
See **Harcourt Brace Jovanovich Ltd**

S. B. Publications
Unit 2, The Old Station Yard, Pipe Gate, Market Drayton, Shropshire TF9 4HY
☎ 0630 647200

Managing Director *Steve Benz*
Approx Annual Turnover £200,000

FOUNDED 1987, initially on a part-time basis. Rapid expansion led to full-time publishing in January 1990. *Specialises* in local history, including themes illustrated by old picture postcards and photographs; also travel, maritime history and railways. 40 titles in 1991.

IMPRINTS
Brampton Publications *Steve Benz* TITLES
Potteries Picture Postcards. **Ship Pictorial Publications** *A. S. Mallett* TITLES *The Cunard Line*.
Unsolicited mss, synopses and ideas for books
welcome.
Royalties paid annually.

Scarlett Press

5 Montague Road, London E8 2HN
☎071-241 3702 Fax 071-729 3591

Directors *Belinda Budge/Christine Considine/Avis
Lewallen/Ann Treneman/ Victoria Wilson*

FOUNDED 1989. Independent publishing house supported by **Pluto Press**. *Publishes* feminist non-fiction covering politics, autobiography, social policy, arts, leisure, history, lesbian and gay studies.
Unsolicited mss, synopses and ideas welcome. No
fiction or any 'non-woman' centred material. TITLES
The European Women's Almanac Paula Snyder;
Superwomen and the Double Burden ed. Chris
Corrin; *Women and Bisexuality* Sue George. 8 titles
in 1992.
Royalties paid annually.

Sceptre Paperbacks
See **Hodder & Stoughton Ltd**

Scholastic Publications Ltd

Villiers House, Clarendon Avenue, Leamington
Spa, Warwickshire CV32 5PR
☎0926 887799 Fax 0926 883331

Chairman *M. R. Robinson*
Managing Director *David Kewley*
Approx Annual Turnover £16.5 million

FOUNDED 1964. One of four international subsidiaries of **Scholastic Inc**. The company has three
main divisions: Educational Publishing; Children's
Trade Publishing; Direct Marketing to Schools.
Publishes education for primary school teachers,
children's fiction and non-fiction.

DIVISIONS/IMPRINTS
Educational Publishing (Villiers House) *Annie
Turrell/ Regina Nuttall* Professional books and
classroom materials for primary teachers, plus
magazines such as *Child Education, Junior Education, Art & Craft, Junior Projects, Infant Projects*
and *Perspective*.
Direct Marketing to Schools The largest school-based book club operator in the UK, selling to
children via their schools through four book clubs:
See-Saw, Lucky, Chip and *Scene*, covering ages
5–13, and to teachers through *Criterion*. Also
operates *Scholastic Book Fairs*, a complementary

school marketing operation which sells books to
children in schools.
Children's Trade Publishing 7–9 Pratt Street,
London NW1 0AE Tel: 071-284 4474. Fax:
071-284 4234. *David Fickling* Acquired **André
Deutsch's** children's list in 1991. IMPRINTS
Scholastic Hardcover, Adlib Paperbacks (12+
fiction), **Hippo Books** (paperbacks), **André
Deutsch Children's Books**. TITLES *Postman Pat;
Rosie & Jim; Foxwood Tales; Point Horror*.
Royalties paid twice yearly.

Authors' Rating Strong on direct sales (Scholastic has four book clubs), the children's list has
expanded with the acquisition of André Deutsch's
children's books. Restructuring of editorial and
management teams suggests further expansion
within a year or so.

SCM Press Ltd

26–30 Tottenham Road, London N1 4BZ
☎071-249 7262/5 Fax 071-249 3776

Managing Director *Rev. Dr John Bowden*
Approx Annual Turnover £1 million

Publishes mainly religion and theology with some
ethics and philosophy. About 40 titles a year.
Unsolicited mss and synopses considered if sent
with s.a.e.
Royalties paid annually.

Authors' Rating Leading publisher of religious
ideas with well-deserved reputation for fresh thinking. At SCM, 'questioning theology is the norm'.
The recent deal with Trinity Press of New York,
requiring both to work as a single organisation,
publishing under both imprints means that SCM
authors can now be published worldwide.

Scolar Press
See **Ashgate Publishing Co. Ltd**

Scope International Ltd

62 Murray Road, Horndean, Waterlooville,
Hampshire PO8 9JL
☎0705 592255 Fax 0705 591975

Managing/Editorial Director *Nicholas J. Pine*

Sister company of **Milestone Publications**.
Publishes business, finance, specialist and exclusive personal management. Unsolicited mss not
welcome. Approach in writing essential in first
instance.
Royalties paid twice yearly.

Scorpion Publishing Ltd

Victoria House, Victoria Road, Buckhurst Hill,
Essex IG9 5ES
☎081-506 0606   Fax 081-506 0553

Managing Director *Leonard Harrow*

FOUNDED 1976. *Publishes* books on the Middle East
and Orient: architecture, politics, history, culture
and travel.

Editorial Director *Leonard Harrow* Unsolicited
mss and synopses welcome if they come within
their specialist subject areas.
Royalties vary according to contract.

Scottish Academic Press

56 Hanover Street, Edinburgh EH2 2DX
☎031-225 7483   Fax 031-225 7662

Managing Editor *Dr Douglas Grant*

FOUNDED 1969. *Publishes* academic: architecture,
education, geology, history, journals, literature,
poetry, social sciences, theology. Works in conjunction with Handsel Press and distributes titles
for **Sussex University Press**. Most books are
commissioned but unsolicited mss and synopses
will be considered.
Royalties paid annually.

B. A. Seaby Ltd

7 Davies Street, London W1Y 1LL
☎071-495 2590   Fax 071-491 1595

Chairman *Dr Jerome M. Eisenberg*
Managing Director *Bobby Cox*
Approx Annual Turnover £750,000

FOUNDED 1926. Began life as a coin dealer and has
now moved into antiquities and publishing.
Publishes numismatics, archaeology and history.
No unsolicited mss; synopses and ideas welcome.
12 titles in 1991.
Royalties paid annually.

Seafarer

See **Merlin Press Ltd**

Seagull Books

See **The Book Guild Ltd**

Search Press Ltd/Burns & Oates Ltd

Wellwood, North Farm Road, Tunbridge Wells,
Kent TN2 3DR
☎0892 510850   Fax 0892 515903

Managing Director *Countess de la Bédoyère*

FOUNDED 1847. Publishers to the Holy See.
Publishes (Search Press) full-colour art, craft, cookery, needlecrafts and organic gardening; (Burns &
Oates) philosophy, theology, history, spirituality,
educational, reference.

DIVISIONS
Academic *Paul Burns* TITLES include the
Liberation & Theology series, currently ten volumes. **Craft** *Julia Rowlands* Books on papermaking
and papercrafts, painting flowers on silk, calligraphy and embroidery, and the *Organic Handbooks*
series. Unsolicited mss, synopses and ideas for
books welcome.
Royalties paid annually.

Secker & Warburg

See **Reed International Books**

Serpent's Tail

4 Blackstock Mews, London N4 2BT
☎071-354 1949   Fax 071-704 6467

Contact *Pete Ayrton*
Approx Annual Turnover £350,000

FOUNDED 1986. Winner of the *Sunday Times* Small
Publisher of the Year Award for 1989 and the Ralph
Lewis Award for New Fiction in 1992. Serpent's
Tail has introduced to British audiences a number
of major internationally-known writers who had
been neglected by UK publishers. A strong emphasis on design — including flaps on paperback
covers in the continental style — and an eye for
the unusual. *Publishes* contemporary fiction, including works in translation, crime, popular culture
and biography. No poetry, science fiction or fantasy. 40 titles in 1992.

IMPRINTS
Masks TITLES *Motion Sickness* Lynne Tillman;
Appearances Gianni Celati. **Serpent's Tail** TITLES
They Still Shoot Models My Age Susan Moncur; *The
Best of Cosmopolitan* ed. Kate Figes. **90s** New
writing series launched 1990. TITLES *Nudists May
Be Encountered* Mary Scott; *Transmission* Atima
Srivastava. **Masks Noir** TITLES *Devil in a Blue Dress*
Walter Mosley. Unsolicited ideas for books wel-
come. Send synopsis and 50 pp text, along with
s.a.e. Prospective authors who are not familiar with
Serpent's Tail should try to find out something
about the list before submitting proposals. Cata-
logue available.
Royalties normally paid yearly.

Authors' Rating Praised for 'daring', sophisticated and good-looking books. Publishes in
paperback only.

Settle Press
10 Boyne Terrace Mews, London W11 3LR
☎071-243 0695

Chairman/Managing Director D. Settle

FOUNDED 1981. *Publishes* travel, guidebooks, general non-fiction and fiction. About 16 titles a year. Unsolicited synopses and ideas for books welcome. No mss.

DIVISIONS
Travel/Tourist Guides/General D. Settle TITLES *City Break Series* (Paris, Moscow, Leningrad, etc.); *Where to Go Series* (Romania, Turkey, America, etc.). **Fiction** M. Carter TITLES *Trewenno; The Falklands Factor.*
Royalties paid by arrangement.

Severn House Publishers
35 Manor Road, Wallington, Surrey SM6 0BW
☎081-773 4161   Fax 081-773 4143

Chairman Edwin Buckhalter

FOUNDED 1974, a leader in library fiction publishing. Several bestsellers both in the UK and overseas. *Publishes* hardcover fiction: romance, science fiction, horror, fantasy, crime. About 140 titles a year. No unsolicited material. Synopses/proposals through bona fide literary agents only.
Royalties paid twice yearly. *Overseas associates* Severn House Publishers Inc., New York.

Shakespeare Head Press
See **Blackwell Publishers**

Shanbhala
See **Random House Publishing Group Ltd**

Sheba Feminist Press
10A Bradbury Street, London N16 8JN
☎071-254 1590   Fax 071-249 5351

Editor & Rights Michelle McKenzie

FOUNDED 1980. Collectively-run publishing house – one of Britain's few remaining independent feminist publishers. 'We have built our reputation around a passionate commitment to feminism, to open and critical debate, to a recognition of the differences between women, and to change now and in the future. ' Sheba, now twelve years old, is run by a racially mixed group of women who have put behind them a strong backlist including Audre Lorde's *Zami* and *Serious Pleasure*, the first collection of lesbian erotica published in the country. *Publishes* anti-sexist/anti-racist children's books,

adult fiction and theoretical works by black women, working class women, new writers and lesbians. TITLES *Talking Back: Thinking Feminist/ Thinking Black* Bell Hooks; *Playbook for Kids about Sex*; *More Serious Pleasure: Lesbian Erotic Stories and Poetry* ed. Sheba; *People in Trouble* Sarah Schulman; *Positively Women* ed. Gilchrist, O'Sullivan & Thomson; *Wild Hearts: Contemporary Lesbian Melodrama*. Unsolicited mss, synopses and ideas for books welcome.
Royalties paid annually.

Sheldon Press
See **Society for Promoting Christian Knowledge**

Shepheard-Walwyn (Publishers) Ltd
Suite 34, 26 Charing Cross Road, London WC2H 0DH
☎071-240 5992   Fax 071-379 5770

Managing Director Anthony Werner
Approx Annual Turnover £140,000

FOUNDED 1972. 'We regard books as food for the mind and want to offer a wholesome diet of original ideas and fresh approaches to old subjects.' *Publishes* general non-fiction in three main areas: Scottish interest; gift books in calligraphy and/or illustrated; history, political economy, philosophy and religion. 4 titles in 1991. Synopses and ideas for books welcome.
Royalties paid twice yearly.

Ship Pictorial Publications
See **S. B. Publications**

Shire Publications Ltd
Cromwell House, Church Street, Princes Risborough, Aylesbury, Buckinghamshire HP17 9AJ
☎08444 4301   Fax 08444 7080

Commissioning Editor Jackie Fearn

FOUNDED 1967. *Publishes* original non-fiction paperbacks. 31 titles in 1991. No unsolicited material; send introductory letter with detailed outline of idea.
Royalties paid annually.

Sidgwick & Jackson Ltd
See **Macmillan Publishers Ltd**

Signet
See **Penguin Books Ltd**

Silent Books
Boxworth End, Swavesey, Cambridge CB4 5RA
☎ 0954 31000/32199   Fax 0954 32199

Managing Director Carole A. Green

FOUNDED 1985 by Carole and Geoff Green. *Publishes* general art titles, gardening and community care. Unsolicited mss, synopses and ideas welcome. No fiction. 6 titles in 1991. *Specialises* in realistically priced, high-quality books. Winners of various awards.

Simon & Schuster Ltd
West Garden Place, Kendal Street,
London W2 2AQ
☎ 071-724 7577   Fax 071-402 0639

Managing Director Nick Webb

FOUNDED 1986. Offshoot of the leading American publisher, **Simon & Schuster,** New York. *Publishes* general hardbacks and trade/mass market paperbacks. Fiction, non-fiction, children's and school publishing, the latter a more recent departure following the acquisition of educational and ELT lists from **Blackwell** and **Cassell** respectively. No pure academic or technical.

Editorial Directors Maureen Waller/Carol O'Brien
Royalties paid twice yearly.

Authors' Rating Best known in the States for its technology list, Simon & Schuster has made its British reputation with new fiction and children's books. Expansion into school publishing which started with the purchase of Blackwell's education list has continued with the takeover of Cassell's ELT list.

Sinclair-Stevenson
See **Reed International Books**

Skoob Books Publishing Ltd
11A-15 Sicilian Avenue, Southampton Row,
London WC1A 2QH
☎ 071-404 3063   Fax 071-404 4398
Editorial office: 43 Old Bethnal Green Road, London E2 6PR
☎ 071-729 7564   Fax 071-404 4398

Publishes literature, poetry in translation, lost classics of English poetry, autobiography of poets, gothic fiction from the 1790s, esoteric, and some

picture books. Approach by letter in the first instance.

DIVISIONS
Literary Lucien Jenkins **Esoteric** Christopher Johnson TITLES George Eliot, Collected Poems; Rainer Maria Rilke: The Sonnets to Orpheus; The Truth About the Tarot Gerald Suster. 22 titles in print.

Smith Gryphon Ltd
Swallow House, 11-21 Northdown Street,
London N1 9BN
☎ 071-278 2444   Fax 071-278 1677

Chairman/Managing Director Robert Smith

Family-owned company. FOUNDED 1990 by Robert Smith, ex-**Sidgwick & Jackson** and **Ebury Press**. *Publishes* biography, autobiography, music (mostly rock), cinema, true crime, topical issues, finance and business, personality-led fiction, wine, food and cookery, and illustrated. 10 titles in its first year; 20-25 in 1992. No unsolicited mss; ideas and synopses welcome.
Royalties paid twice yearly. *Represented* by **Sinclair-Stevenson**.

Colin Smythe Ltd
PO Box 6, Gerrards Cross,
Buckinghamshire SL9 8XA
☎ 0753 886000   Fax 0753 886469

Managing Director Colin Smythe
Approx Annual Turnover £650,000

FOUNDED 1966. *Publishes* Anglo-Irish literature, poetry and criticism, history. No unsolicited mss; send synopses and ideas for books in first instance. 15 titles in 1991.
Royalties paid annually/twice yearly.

Society for Promoting Christian Knowledge (SPCK)
Holy Trinity Church, Marylebone Road,
London NW1 4DU
☎ 071-387 5282   Fax 071-388 2352

Approx Annual Turnover £1.5 million

FOUNDED 1698, SPCK is the oldest religious publisher in England. *Publishes* academic theology, general religious titles and pastoral books, including popular self-help. About 80 titles a year.

Editorial Director Judith Longman

IMPRINTS
SPCK Philip Law TITLES The Study of Spirituality; Science and Creation; Dictionary of Pastoral Care;

Approaches to Prayer. **Triangle** *Rachel Boulding* TITLES *Prayers for Everyone; Living With Anger.* **Sheldon Press** *Joanna Moriarty* TITLES *Helping Children Cope with Grief; Curing Arthritis — The Drug-Free Way.* No unsolicited material. Enquiries only.
Royalties paid annually.

Authors' Rating Religion with a strong social edge.

Solo Books Ltd

49–53 Kensington High Street, London W8 5ED
☏ 071–376 2166   Fax 071–938 3165

Chairman/Managing Director *Don Short*
Senior Editor *Don Coolican*
Approx Annual Turnover (Group) £1.3 million

Solo Books is the publishing arm of parent company, **Solo Syndication**, literary agents. First registered in 1981, it has only recently become active in publishing. *Specialises* in biography/autobiography and celebrity books as well as other non-fiction works. Also expanding into corporate works, with a projected output across the two areas of 15 titles in 1993. No fiction. Unsolicited mss not welcome; approach in writing with synopses/ideas. 1 title in 1991.
Royalties paid quarterly.

Souvenir Press Ltd

43 Great Russell Street, London WC1B 3PA
☏ 071–580 9307/8 & 637 5711/2/3
Fax 071–580 5064

Chairman/Managing Director *Ernest Hecht*

Independent publishing house. FOUNDED 1952. *Publishes* academic and scholarly, animal care and breeding, antiques and collecting, archaeology, autobiography and biography, business and industry, children's, cookery, crafts and hobbies, crime, educational, fiction, gardening, health and beauty, history and antiquarian, humour, illustrated and fine editions, magic and the occult, medical, military, music, natural history, philosophy, poetry, psychology, religious, sociology, sports, theatre and women's studies. About 60 titles a year. Souvenir's *Human Horizons* series for the disabled and their carers is one of the most pre-eminent in its field and recently celebrated fifteen years of publishing for the disabled.

Senior Editor *Tessa Harrow* TITLES *The Goddess of the Stones: The Language of the Megaliths* Dr George Terence Meaden; *Unfit for Human Consumption* Professor Richard Lacey; *Singing From the Soul* José Carreras; *Closer to the Light: Learning from Children's Near Death Experiences* Dr Melvyn

Morse; *Know Yourself Through Your Cat* Vivienne Angus.

IMPRINTS
Condor, Pictorial, Presentations, Pop Universal, Human Horizons. Unsolicited mss welcome; initial letter of enquiry preferred though.
Royalties paid twice yearly.

Authors' Rating One of the best independent publishers in London. Since there are now so few independents left, this may not seem much of a compliment. But Ernest Hecht does manage to combine sensitivity towards authors with commercial acumen — a rare combination.

SPCK

See **Society for Promoting Christian Knowledge**

Spellmount Ltd

12 Dene Way, Speldhurst, Near Tunbridge Wells, Kent TN3 0NX
☏ 0892 862860   Fax 0892 863861

Managing Director *Ian Morley-Clarke*
Approx Annual Turnover £300,000

FOUNDED 1983. Jointly owned by Ian and Kathleen Morley-Clarke and Vale Packaging Ltd of Tonbridge. *Publishes* non-fiction hardback titles; biographies (composers, cricketers); militaria (*Military Machine* series); companion guides to music and the arts including the *London Library Guide* series. About 18 titles a year.

DIVISIONS
Composers' Biographies & Militaria *Kathleen Morley-Clarke/ Robert Hardcastle* **Cricket Biographies** *Ian Morley-Clarke* **London Guides** *Edwin Webb*. No unsolicited mss. Synopses/ideas for books welcome in above specialist fields only.
Royalties paid annually.

Spindlewood

70 Lynhurst Avenue, Barnstaple, Devon EX31 2HY
☏ 0271 71612

Managing Director *Michael Holloway*

FOUNDED 1980. *Publishes* children's books. No unsolicited mss; send synopsis with sample chapter or two. 4 titles in 1991.
Royalties paid according to contract.

E&FN Spon

See **Routledge, Chapman & Hall Ltd**

Sporting & Leisure Press
See **Barracuda Books Ltd/Quotes Ltd**

Springfield Books Ltd
Norman Road, Denby Dale, Huddersfield, West Yorkshire HD8 0LS
☏ 0484 864955   Fax 0484 865443

Chairman/Managing Director *Brian Lewis*
Editorial Head *Paula Yates*
Approx Annual Turnover £1.2 million

FOUNDED 1984. *Publishes* sport and leisure titles only. TITLES *Progressive Weight Training for Women; Mountain Bike Racing; Mountain Bike Maintenance and Repair; Cycle Racing.* Unsolicited mss, synopses and ideas welcome if they fall within range of subject areas above. 8 titles in 1991. *Royalties* paid twice yearly.

Stainer & Bell Ltd
PO Box 110, 23 Gruneisen Road, London N3 1DZ
☏ 081-343 3303   Fax 081-343 7351

Chairman *Bernard A. Braley*
Managing Directors *Carol Y. Wakefield/Keith M. Wakefield*
Publishing Manager *Nicholas Williams*
Approx Annual Turnover £605,000

FOUNDED 1907 to publish sheet music. Now *publishes* music and religious subjects, mainly related to hymnody. Mss welcome only if preceded by letter enclosing brief précis. Unsolicited synopses/ideas for books welcome. *Royalties* paid annually.

Stam Press
See **Stanley Thornes (Publishers) Ltd**

Stanley Paul
See **Random House Publishing Group Ltd**

Harold Starke Publishers Ltd
Pixey Green, Stradbroke, Near Eye, Suffolk IP21 5NG
☏ 0379 388334   Fax 0379 388335
203 Bunyan Court, Barbican, London EC2Y 8DH
☏ 071-588 5195

Directors *Harold K. Starke/Naomi Galinski*

Publishes adult non-fiction, medical and reference. No unsolicited mss. *Royalties* paid annually.

Patrick Stephens Ltd
See **Haynes Publishing Group**

Stone Flower Ltd
2 Horder Road, London SW6 5EE
☏ 071-736 0477

Chairman *J. Norman*
Managing Director *L. G. Norman*

Set up by Lee Norman 'to commission and publish books that he wanted to read but which had not been written'. First publication 1992. *Publishes* biography, fiction, humour and legal. 'No anthropomorphism. No hype.' Unsolicited synopses and ideas welcome. No mss. *Royalties* paid twice yearly.

Stride
See **Small Presses**

Studio Editions Ltd
Princess House, 50 Eastcastle Street, London W1N 7AP
☏ 071-636 5070   Fax 071-580 3001

Managing Directors *Kenneth Webb/Roderick Webb*
Approx Annual Turnover £8 million

FOUNDED 1982 as Bestseller Publications; changed its name in 1992. *Publishes* illustrated non-fiction: fine and decorative art, military history, natural history and the plant world, travel and topography, children's books, social stationery. Unsolicited mss, synopses and ideas for books welcome. Over 85 titles a year.

IMPRINTS
Studio Editions Trade publishing, **Bracken Books** Promotional reprints, **Princess House** *Jackie Fortey* Children's, **Studio Designs** Social stationery. TITLES *Moule's Illustrated County Maps of Old England; Impressionism: The Painters and the Paintings; Oliver Goldsmith's History of the Natural World; The Wallchart of World History.* *Royalties* paid according to contract.

Studio Vista
See **Cassell**

The Sumach Press
29 Mount Pleasant, St Albans, Hertfordshire AL3 4QY
☏ 0727 47032   Fax 0727 50479

Chairman *David Godwin*
Managing Director *Heather Godwin*
Approx Annual Turnover £80,000

FOUNDED 1990. A small imprint set up in partnership with Random Century (now **Random House**), to publish a maximum of 10 titles a year. *Publishes* non-fiction: country matters, county histories, countryside and landscape, and some fiction. No complete mss; send sample chapters only. Synopses and ideas for books welcome. *Royalties* paid twice yearly.

Summersdale Publishers

PO Box 49, Chichester, West Sussex PO19 4LF
☎0243 779327   Fax 0243 782033

Manager *Alastair Williams*
Editor *Stewart Ferris*

FOUNDED 1990. *Publishes* non-fiction, especially travel, cookery, humour, arts/ entertainment, and student-related topics. TITLES *Don't Lean Out of the Window!* (Surviving Europe on a Train); *The Student Grub Guide; The Busker's Guide to Europe; From Horizontal to Vertical* (Working with the Paralysed in Bangladesh); *Watch My Back.* 7 titles in 1992. Unsolicited mss welcome if preceded by letter.
Royalties paid.

Sunflower Books

12 Kendrick Mews, London SW7 3HG
☎071-589 1862   Fax 071-225 1033

Joint Managing Directors *Pat Underwood/John Seccombe*

FOUNDED 1981. *Publishes* countryside guides for walkers and motorists covering popular European holiday destinations. No unsolicited mss; prepared to look at synopses and ideas, but 'our main efforts are directed towards extending our existing *Landscapes* series'. 5 titles in 1992.
Royalties paid annually.

Surrey University Press

See **Harcourt Brace Jovanovich Ltd**

Sussex University Press

See **Scottish Academic Press**

Alan Sutton Publishing Ltd

Phoenix Mill, Far Thrupp, Stroud,
Gloucestershire GL5 2BU
☎0453 731114   Fax 0453 731117

Managing Director *Alan Sutton*
Approx Annual Turnover £3 million

FOUNDED 1978. Owned by Guernsey Press. *Publishes* academic, archaeology, biography, countryside, history, regional interest, local history, pocket classics (lesser known novels by classic authors), topography, transport, travel. 190 titles in 1991.

Publishing Director *Peter Clifford* Send synopses rather than complete mss.
Royalties paid twice yearly.

Authors' Rating Unusually for a small publisher, Alan Sutton handles his own sales and distribution and even typesetting and production. Strong on history with illustrated books leading the expansion programme.

Swan Hill Press

See **Airlife Publishing Ltd**

Sweet & Maxwell Ltd

South Quay Plaza, 183 Marsh Wall,
London E14 9FT
☎071-538 8686   Fax 071-538 8625

Managing Director *David Evans*

Part of International Thomson Professional Information Ltd. *Publishes* legal and professional books, loose-leaf works, journals and law reports. About 130 titles a year, with live backlist of over 400 titles.

Publishing Director *Carol Tullo* Writers with legal/professional projects in mind are advised to contact the company at the earliest possible stage in order to lay the groundwork for best design, production and marketing of a project. Catalogues available on application. List, though basically legal and professional, is extremely varied and contains many academic titles as well as treatises and reference works in the legal and professional fields. *Royalties* vary according to contract.

Swift Children's Books

See **Chivers Press (Publishers)**

Tabb House

7 Church Street, Padstow, Cornwall PL28 8BG
☎0841 532316 (no calls between 1.00–3.00 pm)
Fax 0841 532316

Director *Caroline White*

FOUNDED 1980, publishing hardback and paperback titles to promote the literary and cultural ideas and values of the country in particular. *Publishes* fiction, memoirs, children's poetry, country, literature and local history. No commerce, occult, science fiction, technical or academic. Unsolicited mss discouraged but tolerated. Ideas and synopses preferred in the first instance. 4 titles in 1991. *Royalties* paid twice yearly.

Tarragon Press

Moss Park, Ravenstone, Whithorn, Scotland DG8 8DR
☎ 098 885 368

Director/Editorial Head *David Sumner*

FOUNDED 1987. *Publishes* medical and scientific for the layperson. About 3 titles a year. Unsolicited mss, synopses and ideas for books welcome. *Royalties* paid annually.

I. B. Tauris & Co. Ltd

45 Bloomsbury Square, London WC1A 2HY
☎ 071-916 1069   Fax 071-916 1068

Chairman/Publisher *Iradj Bagherzade*

Independent publisher FOUNDED 1984. Once tipped by *The Observer* 'to be the Publisher of the Nineties'. *Publishes* general non-fiction and academic in the fields of international relations, current affairs, history, Middle East, East-West relations and Soviet studies. TITLES *The Third Revolution: Environment, Population and a Sustainable World* Paul Harrison; *Palestine Reborn* Walid Khalidi (intro. Albert Hourani); *The Intelligence Game* James Rusbridger; *Offshore, Britain and the European Idea* Giles Radice; *Dictionary of Third World Terms* Kofi Buenor Hadjor.

IMPRINTS
Tauris Parke Books Elegant illustrated books on architecture, travel, design and culture. **British Academic Press** High-level academic monographs. Unsolicited mss, synopses and ideas for books welcome.
Royalties paid twice yearly.

Teach Yourself Books

See **Hodder & Stoughton Ltd**

Temple House Books

See **The Book Guild Ltd**

Thames and Hudson Ltd

30–34 Bloomsbury Street, London WC1B 3QP
☎ 071-636 5488   Fax 071-636 4799

Managing Director *Thomas Neurath*

Publishes art, archaeology, architecture and design, biography, crafts, fashion, history and antiquarian, illustrated and fine editions, mythology, music, photography, popular culture, travel and topography. Over 150 titles a year.

Editorial Head *Jamie Camplin* TITLES *World of Art, New Horizons* and *Photofile* series; *The Shock of the New; The Complete Tutankhamun; Mozart: The Golden Years; The Chronicle of Western Costume; Design After Dark*. Send preliminary letter and outline before mss.
Royalties paid twice yearly.

Authors' Rating One of the few publishers to realise the true potential of new technology — albeit with a French initiative to spur them on. New Horizons, a series with an eclectic choice of subjects from Beethoven to dinosaurs, enhances reader appeal with superb in-depth illustrations.

Thames Publishing/Autolycus Press

14 Barlby Road, London W10 6AR
☎ 081-969 3579

Managing Director *John Bishop*

FOUNDED 1970. Thames *publishes* music (serious) and books about English music; Autolycus *publishes* autobiography, biography, poetry and humour. No unsolicited mss; send synopses and ideas in first instance. 4 titles in 1991.

Stanley Thornes (Publishers) Ltd

Old Station Drive, Leckhampton, Cheltenham, Gloucestershire GL53 0DN
☎ 0242 228888   Fax 0242 221914

Managing Director *David Smith*
Approx Annual Turnover £10 million

FOUNDED 1972 by Stanley Thornes. Merged with Kluwer NV of the Netherlands in 1976. Now part of the Wolters-Kluwer Group. *Publishes* across the whole secondary and college curriculum and covers complete school range from age five upwards. About 200 titles a year. Unsolicited mss, synopses and ideas for books welcome if appropriate to specialised list.

IMPRINTS
Hulton Educational EFL list. **Stam Press** Technical books.
Royalties paid annually.

Authors' Rating At the time of going to press, there were talks of a merger with **Mary Glasgow Publications**.

Thornhill Press

24 Moorend Road, Cheltenham,
Gloucestershire GL53 0EU
☎0242 519137   Fax 0594 564984

Directors *Desmond Badham-Thornhill/M. F. Badham-Thornhill/John Pemberthy/Bryan Robinson*
Approx Annual Turnover £50,000

FOUNDED 1972. *Publishes* mainly walking and touring guides, English heritage, sport, and some general titles. No fiction or poetry. About 6 titles a year.

Editorial Head *Desmond Badham-Thornhill* TITLES *The Old Straight Tracks of Wessex* Paul Devereux & Laurence Main; *Discovering Ancient Dean & The Wye Valley* Brian Walters; *In and Out of the Forest* Winifred Foley. Unsolicited mss, synopses and ideas for books welcome.
Royalties paid twice yearly. *Sales & Distribution Office*: Unit 3, Fountain Way, Parkend, Near Lydney, Glos GL15 4HH. Tel: 0594 564984.

Thorsons

See **HarperCollins Publishers Ltd**

Three Hills Books

Unit 3, Tweedbank Craft Centre, Haining Drive, Tweedbank, Galashiels, Selkirkshire TD1 3RU
☎0896 57869   Fax 0896 57869

Partners *Ann Laughlan/Bruce Harrison*

FOUNDED 1988. Small publishing house specialising in children's picture books. Publishers of the popular *Maisie* series about a kilted kitten and her adventures. Also distributor for **Byway Books**. No unsolicited mss.

Threshold Books

See **Kenilworth Press Ltd**

Times Books

See **HarperCollins Publishers Ltd**

Titan Books

19 Valentine Place, London SE1 8QH
☎071-620 0200   Fax 071-620 0032

Managing Director *Nick Landau*

FOUNDED 1981 by Nick Landau and has grown considerably over the last decade to become the largest publisher of graphic novels and graphic albums in the UK. *Publishes* comic books and graphic novels, cartoon strips, film and television titles, science fiction and fantasy, and true crime under its newly launched Mondo imprint. About 70–80 titles a year.

Managing Editor *Katy Wild*

IMPRINTS
Titan Books, Mondo New imprint specialising in true crime and the bizarre extremes of human behaviour. TITLES *Clive Barker's Nightbreed Chronicles; The Hellraiser Chronicles; Golden Age of Children's Television; Batman; Judge Dredd; Best of 2000 AD; Star Trek; Star Trek: The Next Generation; Doctor Who; Gerry Anderson* range. Although little new material handled, unsolicited ideas will be considered. Send synopsis/outline with sample chapter.
Royalties paid twice yearly.

Tolkein

See **HarperCollins Publishers Ltd**

Tolley Publishing Co. Ltd

Tolley House, 2 Addiscombe Road, Croydon, Surrey CR9 5AF
☎081-686 9141   Fax 081-686 3155

Chairman *G. J. S. Wilson*
Managing Director *Harry L. King*

Part of United Newspapers plc, publishers of the *Daily Express, Sunday Express* and *Daily Star. Publishes* taxation, accounting, legal, business, technical and professional books. Unsolicited mss, synopses and ideas welcome.

DIVISIONS
Tolley Publishing, Charles Knight Publishing, Benn Technical Books, Taxation Publishing.

Tracks

See **HarperCollins Publishers Ltd**

Transworld Publishers Ltd

61–63 Uxbridge Road, London W5 5SA
☎081-579 2652
Fax 081-579 5479   Telex 267974

Managing Director *Paul Scherer*
Deputy Managing Director (Publishing) *Mark Barty-King*

FOUNDED 1950. A subsidiary of **Bantam, Doubleday, Dell Publishing Group**., New York, which is a wholly owned subsidiary of Bertelsmann in Germany. *Publishes* general fiction and non-fiction, children's books, sports and leisure.

Bantam *Anthony Mott* **Bantam Press** *Ursula Mackenzie* **Black Swan** *Patrick Janson-Smith* **Corgi** *Patrick Janson-Smith* **Doubleday** *Marianne Velmans* **Partridge Press** *Debbie Beckerman* AUTHORS include Isaac Asimov, Sally Beauman, Martin Bell, Charlotte Bingham, Emma Blair, Geoffrey Boycott, Michael & Marilyn Clayton, Pat Conroy, Catherine Cookson, Jilly Cooper, Bill Cosby, Frederick Forsyth, Robert Goddard, Joseph Heller, John Irving, Ludovic Kennedy, Judith Krantz, Rosalind Laker, Terry McMillan, Naguib Mahfouz, Armistead Maupin, Anne McCaffrey, Shirley Maclaine, Tim Sebastian, Danielle Steel, Joanna Trollope, Joseph Wambaugh, Mary Wesley.

Children's & Young Adults Books *Philippa Dickinson* TITLES Young Adult series: *Saddle Club; Sweet Dreams; Sweet Valley High.* Children's series: *Choose Your Own Adventure; Sweet Valley Kids.* Hardcover imprints: *Doubleday, Delacorte Press.* Paperbacks: **Picture Corgi, Yearling, Young Corgi, Corgi, Corgi Freeway** AUTHORS/ ARTISTS include Frank Asch, Emilie Boon, John Cunliffe, Terrance Dicks, Diane Duane, Dick King-Smith, Frank Muir, Robert Swindells, Jean Ure. Unsolicited mss welcome only if preceded by preliminary letter.
Royalties paid twice yearly. *Overseas associates* Transworld Australia/ New Zealand, Trans-South Africa Book Distributors.

Authors' Rating Still riding high on *A Brief History of Time* (older readers will remember when it was not in the bestseller lists), Transworld continues to invest heavily in big-name authors like Frederick Forsyth who has been paid a 'big, very big' advance for his next two novels.

Trentham Books Ltd
Westview House, 734 London Road, Stoke on Trent, Staffordshire ST4 5NP
☎0782 745567   Fax 0782 745553
Chairman/Managing Director *Dr John Eggleston*
Editorial Head *Gillian Klein*
Approx Annual Turnover £250,000

Publishes education (nursery, school and higher), social sciences, intercultural studies, design and technology education. Unsolicited mss, synopses and ideas welcome if relevant to their interests. About 20 titles a year.
Royalties paid annually.

Triangle
See **Society for Promoting Christian Knowledge**

Trotman & Co. Ltd
12 Hill Rise, Richmond, Surrey TW10 6UA
☎081-940 5668   Fax 081-948 9267
Managing Director *Andrew Fiennes Trotman*
Approx Annual Turnover £2.5 million

Particularly active in the educational resources market, producing recruitment (brochures and organising careers fairs. *Publishes* general careers books, higher education guides, teaching support material, education. Unsolicited material welcome. About 10 titles a year. TITLES *Getting into University; Getting into Polytechnic; How to Complete Your UCCA/ PCAS Form; Survey of HND Courses; Survey of Polytechnics; Your GCSE Decisions.*
Royalties paid twice yearly.

Two-Can Publishing Ltd
346 Old Street, London EC1V 9NQ
☎071-613 3376   Fax 071-613 3371
Chairman *Andrew Jarvis*
Managing Director *Ian Grant*
Approx Annual Turnover £3 million

FOUNDED 1987 to publish innovative, high-quality material for children. *Publishes* non-fiction, *Playdays* (weekly infants' magazine) and *Young Telegraph* (weekend supplement for 9–12-year-olds).

DIVISIONS
Books *Ian Grant* **Magazines** *Andrew Jarvis.* No unsolicited mss; send synopses and ideas in the first instance.
Royalties paid twice yearly.

Unicorn Books
16 Laxton Gardens, Paddock Wood, Kent TN12 6BB
☎0892 833648   Fax 0892 833577
Managing Director *Raymond Green*
Approx Annual Turnover £100,000

Part of Factwell Ltd. FOUNDED 1985 to publish railway and transport history titles, and photographic essays relating to lines, counties and company histories. Unsolicited synopses and ideas for books welcome. About 3 titles a year.
Royalties paid twice yearly.

Unwin Hyman
See **HarperCollins Publishers Ltd**

Usborne Publishing Ltd

83–85 Saffron Hill, London EC1N 8RT
☎071-430 2800   Fax 071-430 1562

Managing Director *T. Peter Usborne*
Approx Annual Turnover £14 million

FOUNDED 1975. *Publishes* primarily non-fiction books for children, young adults and parents. Up to 100 titles a year.

Editorial Director *Jenny Tyler* Books are written in-house to a specific format and therefore unsolicited mss are not welcome. Ideas which may be developed in-house are considered. Keen to hear from new illustrators and designers.

DIVISIONS
Usborne Books at Home Oasis Park, Eynsham, Oxford OX8 1TP.
Royalties paid twice yearly.

Authors' Rating One of the best publishers of information books for children. Potential authors must believe that knowledge can be fun.

Vallentine, Mitchell

See **Frank Cass**

Variorum

See **Ashgate Publishing Co. Ltd**

Ventura Publishing Ltd

See **Penguin Books Ltd**

Vermilion

See **Random House Publishing Group Ltd**

Verso Ltd

6 Meard Street, London W1V 3HR
☎071-434 1704/437 3546   Fax 071-734 0059

Chairman *Robin Blackburn*
Managing Director *Colin Robinson*
Directors *Robin Blackburn/Colin Robinson/Ellen Wood*

Formerly New Left Books which grew out of the *New Left Review. Publishes* politics, history, sociology, economics, philosophy, cultural studies, feminism. TITLES *Ideology* Terry Eagleton; *Deterring Democracy* Noam Chomsky; *City of Quartz* Mike Davis; *Postmodernism, or, the Cultural Logic of Late Capitalism* Fredric Jameson. Unsolicited synopses and ideas for books welcome. No memoirs. No unsolicited mss.
Royalties paid annually.

Overseas office in New York.

Authors' Rating As a radical book publisher, Verso won the 1991 *Sunday Times* Small Publisher of the Year Award.

Viking

See **Penguin Books Ltd**

Vintage

See **Random House Publishing Group Ltd**

Virago Press Ltd

Centro House, 20–23 Mandela Street,
London NW1 0HQ
☎071-383 5150   Fax 071-383 4892

Chairman *Carmen Callil*
Managing Director *Harriet Spicer*
Approx Annual Turnover £2.75 million

Escaped from the Cape, Virago, Bodley Head and Chatto group just before the latter was taken over by **Random House**. FOUNDED 1973 by Carmen Callil, with the aim of publishing a wide range of books which illuminate and celebrate all aspects of women's lives. Most titles are published in paperback; a distinguished reprint list makes up one third of these, with two thirds original titles commissioned across a wide range of interest: autobiography, biography, crime, fiction, history, non-fiction, philosophy, poetry, politics, psychology, reference, women's studies, young adult (non-fiction). About 100 titles a year.

Editorial Director *Lenore Goodings* TITLES *On the Golden Porch* Tatyana Tolstaya; *Let it Be Told: Essays by Black Women Writers in Britain* ed. Lauretta Ngcobo; *The Drama of Being a Child* Alice Miller; *All My Days* Kathleen Dayus. Unsolicited mss welcome but synopsis and a few sample chapters preferred in the first instance.
Royalties paid twice yearly.

Authors' Rating The leading feminist publisher, eager to find new women writers with something to say.

Virgin Publishing

338 Ladbroke Grove, London W10 5AH
☎081-968 7554   Fax 081-968 0929

Chairman *Robert Devereux*
Managing Director *Robert Shreeve*
Approx Annual Turnover £5 million

Formerly W. H. Allen & Co., established in the early 1800s. The W. H. Allen imprint has now been dropped and general publishing takes place under the company's own imprint, Virgin. *Publishes* popular culture generally, particularly film, TV, showbiz, music, biography, autobiography, popular reference and humour.

IMPRINTS
Virgin *Sally Holloway* **Allison & Busby** *Peter Day* Literary fiction, poetry and non-fiction. **Nexus** *Peter Darvill-Evans* Erotic fiction. **True Crime** New mass market imprint launched 1992. **Dr Who** *Peter Darvill-Evans*. Unsolicited mss, synopses and ideas for books welcome.
Royalties paid twice yearly.

Authors' Rating In a recent **Society of Authors** and **Writers' Guild** survey, Virgin scored poorly for author-publisher relationships.

Vision Press Ltd
28 Phillimore Walk, London W8 7SA
☎071-938 2929   Fax 071-938 2929 (eves)

Managing Director *Alan Moore*

FOUNDED 1947. *Publishes* academic and educational. 5 titles in 1991.

IMPRINTS
Artemis Press TITLES *GCSE Guidance & Answers* series. No unsolicited mss but synopses and ideas for books welcome.
Royalties paid annually.

Volcano Press
PO Box 139, Leicester LE2 2YH
☎0533 706714   Fax 0533 706714

Chairman *A. Hussain*
Managing Director *F. Hussain*

FOUNDED 1992. *Publishes* academic non-fiction in the following areas: Islam, women's studies, human rights, Middle East, strategic studies and socio-political works. TITLES *Islam in Britain; Sociology of Islam; Twentieth Century Islamic Thinkers; Muslim Resource Book of the United Kingdom*. No unsolicited mss; synopses and ideas welcome. No fiction, poetry or plays. 1 title in 1991; 10 planned for 1993.
Royalties paid twice yearly.

University of Wales Press
6 Gwennyth Street, Cathays, Cardiff CF2 4YD
☎0222 231919   Fax 0222 230908

Director *E. M. Thomas*
Approx Annual Turnover £300,000

Set up as an extension of the university in 1922. *Publishes* academic and scholarly books, in English and Welsh, mainly within the humanities, modern languages and social sciences. Also works of Celtic scholarship. Co-publishes with North American presses and on behalf of learned bodies. 50 titles in 1991.

IMPRINTS
GPC Books, Gwasg Prifysgol Cymru, University of Wales Press. TITLES *Japanese Manufacturing Investment in Wales* Max Munday; *Newspaper French* Adrian C. Ritchie; *A Pocket Guide to the History of Wales* J. Graham Jones. Unsolicited mss considered.
Royalties paid annually; more frequently by negotiation.

Walker Books Ltd
87 Vauxhall Walk, London SE11 5HJ
☎071-793 0909   Fax 071-587 1123

Approx Annual Turnover £23 million

FOUNDED 1979. *Publishes* illustrated children's books and fiction. About 300 titles a year.

Editors *Wendy Boase/David Lloyd/Caroline Royds/Sally Christie/Amanda McCardie/Lucy Ingrams/Sally Foord-Kelcey* TITLES *Where's Wally?* Martin Handford; *Five Minutes' Peace* Jill Murphy; *Can't You Sleep, Little Bear?* Martin Waddell & Barbara Firth; *We're Going on a Bear Hunt* Michael Rosen & Helen Oxenbury; *Why Weeps the Brogan?* Hugh Scott. Unsolicited mss welcome.
Royalties paid twice yearly.

Authors' Rating Walker, the publisher that 'knows how to talk to children', continues to thrive with sales increases well ahead of its main competitors. The deal with Sainsbury's supermarkets accounts for ten per cent of turnover and income from America is now ahead of the UK figure. Known as Candlewick Press, the US offshoot will launch its own list in early 1993. Authors, illustrators and staff benefit from a trust which owns half the company and last year paid out £1000 per member. Came out second in a recent **Society of Authors** and **Writers' Guild** survey on author-publisher relationships.

Ward Lock Ltd
See **Cassell**

Ward Lock Educational
1 Christopher Road, East Grinstead, West Sussex RH19 3BT
☎0342 318980   Fax 0342 410980

Owner *Ling Kee*
Director *Vincent Winter*

FOUNDED 1952. *Publishes* educational books (primary, middle, secondary, teaching manuals) for all subjects, specialising in maths, science, geography and English.
Royalties paid annually.

Frederick Warne
See **Penguin Books Ltd**

Warner Chappell Plays Ltd
129 Park Street, London W1Y 3FA
☏071-629 7600   Fax 071-499 9718

General Manager *Michael Callahan*

Publishes theatre scripts in paperback. Preliminary letter essential. Also agents (see **UK Agents**).
Royalties paid twice yearly.

Warner/Warner-Futura
See **Little, Brown & Co. (UK) Ltd**

Waterline Books
See **Airlife Publishing Ltd**

The Watts Group
96 Leonard Street, London EC2A 4RH
☏071-739 2929   Fax 071-739 2318

Managing Director *Marlene Johnson*

A division of Grolier Ltd, owned by Grolier, Inc., Connecticut. *Publishes* general non-fiction, reference, information and children's (fiction, picture and novelty). 300 titles in 1992.

IMPRINTS
Franklin Watts Non-fiction and information *Chester Fisher.* **Orchard Books** Children's fiction — picture and novelty *Judith Elliott.* Unsolicited mss, synopses and ideas for books welcome.
Royalties paid twice yearly. *Overseas representation* in the Caribbean, Scandinavia, Germany, France, Japan, South Korea, N. Ireland, Eire, S. Africa. *Overseas associates* in Australia and New Zealand, US and Canada.

Wayland (Publishers) Ltd
61 Western Road, Hove, East Sussex BN3 1JD
☏0273 722561   Fax 0273 29314

Managing Director *John Lewis*
Approx Annual Turnover £6 million

Part of the Wolters Kluwer Group, Zwolle. FOUNDED 1969. *Publishes* a broad range of subjects including colour illustrated non-fiction for children of 5 years and upwards. About 300 titles a year.

Editorial Director *Stephen White-Thomson* No unsolicited mss or synopses as all books are commissioned.
Royalties paid annually. *Overseas associates* Bookright Press Inc., USA.

Weavers Press Publishing
Tregeraint House, Zennor, St Ives,
Cornwall TR26 3DB
☏0736 797061   Fax 0736 797061

Managing Director *John T. Wilson*

Publishes business, educational, careers, hobbies, directories and guidebooks. Production service available to self-publishers. A member of the **Independent Publishers Guild**.

Webb & Bower (Publishers) Ltd
5 Cathedral Close, Exeter, Devon EX1 1EZ
☏0392 435362   Fax 0392 211652

Managing Director *Richard Webb*

Webb & Bower has reverted to its original role of licensing books to other publishers. It has ceased publishing under its own imprint and its distribution agreement with **Penguin Books Ltd** ended in March 1992. Eight new projects in 1992.

Weidenfeld & Nicolson Ltd
See **Orion Publishing Group**

Wharncliffe Publishing Ltd
47 Church Street, Barnsley, South
Yorkshire S70 2AS
☏0226 734222   Fax 0226 734444

Chairman *Sir Nicholas Hewitt*
Managing Director *T. G. Hewitt*
Approx Annual Turnover £62,000

Part of Barnsley Chronicle Holdings Ltd. Wharncliffe is the book and newspaper publishing arm of an old-established, independently owned newspaper publishing and printing house. *Publishes* local and regional interest and activities, field sports and related material.

Editorial Head *J. B. Bayne* Unsolicited mss, synopses and ideas welcome but return postage must be included with all submissions.
Royalties paid twice yearly. *Associated company* **Pen & Sword Books Ltd**.

Which? Books
See **Consumers' Association**

Whittet Books Ltd
18 Anley Road, London W14 0BY
☎ 071-603 1139   Fax 081-994 1533

Managing Director *Annabel Whittet*

Publishes natural history, rural interest and transport. Unsolicited mss, synopses and ideas for books welcome.
Royalties paid twice yearly.

John Wiley & Sons Ltd
Baffins Lane, Chichester, West Sussex PO19 1UD
☎ 0243 779777   Fax 0243 775878

Chairman *W. Bradford Wiley* (USA)
Managing Director *Michael Foyle*
Publishing Director *Dr John Jarvis*
Approx Annual Turnover £24 million

Part of John Wiley & Sons, New York. FOUNDED 1807, with the London office opening in 1960. *Publishes* professional, reference and textbooks, scientific, technical and biomedical. Currently making a move into general publishing with titles lifted from its US parent company catalogue. 180 titles in 1991, plus 100 periodicals.

DIVISIONS
Behavioural & Professional Sciences *Michael Coombs* **Physical Sciences** *Dr Ernest Kirkwood* **Biomedical & Natural Sciences** *Dr Michael Dixon* **Technology** *Ian McIntosh*. Unsolicited mss welcome, as are synopses and ideas for books. *Royalties* paid annually.

The Windrush Press
Windrush House, 12 Main Street, Adlestrop, Moreton-in-Marsh, Gloucestershire GL56 0YN
☎ 0608 658075/658018   Fax 0608 658860

Managing Director *Geoffrey Smith*

Independent company set up in 1987. *Publishes* travel, biography, memoirs, history, general, local history. About 10 titles a year.

Editorial Head *Victoria Huxley* TITLES *Learning Not to Be First: A Life of Christina Rossetti; Sardinia; A Windrush Island Guide; A Traveller's History of England*. Send synopsis and letter in first instance.
Royalties paid twice yearly.

Windsor Large Print
See **Chivers Press (Publishers)**

Wise
See **Omnibus Press**

Wisley Handbooks
See **Cassell**

H. F. & G. Witherby Ltd
See **Victor Gollancz Ltd**

Woburn Press
See **Frank Cass**

Wolfe Publishing
See **Mosby Year Book Europe Ltd**

Oswald Wolff Books
See **Berg Publishers Ltd**

The Women's Press
34 Great Sutton Street, London EC1V 0DX
☎ 071-251 3007   Fax 071-608 1938

Publishing Director *Kathy Gale*
Approx Annual Turnover £1 million

Part of the Namara Group. First titles appeared in 1978. *Publishes* women only: quality fiction and non-fiction. Fiction usually has a female protagonist and a woman-centred theme. International writers and subject matter encouraged; some novels appear in translation. Non-fiction: general subjects of interest to feminists, both practical and theoretical, and to women generally; art books, feminist theory, health and psychology, literary criticism. About 40 titles a year. Also publishes the *Women Artists' Diary*.

DIVISIONS
Women's Press Crime, Women's Press Science Fiction, Handbooks.

IMPRINTS
Livewire Books for Teenagers *Carole Spedding* Fiction and non-fiction series for the teenage market. Synopses and ideas for books welcome. 'No mss without previous letter, synopsis and sample material please.'
Royalties paid twice yearly, in September and March.

Authors' Rating Upheaval last year in the wake of serious losses brought staff changes and tighter budgeting. Authors must be devoted to the feminist cause. In a recent **Society of Authors** and

Writers' Guild survey, came out poorly for author-publisher relationships.

Woodhead Publishing Ltd

Abington Hall, Abington, Cambridge CB1 6AH
☎ 0223 891358   Fax 0223 893694

Chairman *Alan Jessup*
Managing Director *Martin Woodhead*
Approx Annual Turnover £750,000

FOUNDED 1989. *Publishes* engineering, electronics, finance and investment. TITLES *The TWI Journal* (welding research); *Advanced Composites Letters; The International Grain/Nickel/Zinc/Tin/Silver Trade* series; *Electrical Interference Technology; RFI/EMI Shielding Materials.* Unsolicited material welcome. 20 titles in 1991.

DIVISIONS
Woodhead Publishing *Martin Woodhead*
Abington Publishing *Amanda Thomas.*
Royalties paid annually.

Wordwright Books

See **UK Packagers**

World International Publishing Ltd

Egmont House, PO Box 111, 61 Great Ducie Street, Manchester M60 3BL
☎ 061-834 3110   Fax 061-834 0059

Chairman/Managing Director *Tony Palmer*

Part of the Egmont Group, Denmark. *Specialises* in children's books for home and international markets. Owned by the Egmont H. Petersen Foundation, a Danish charity organisation which has over 90 companies in Europe and the US. Over 300 titles a year.

Managing Editor *Nina Filipek*

DIVISIONS
Activity Books TITLES *Cub Scout Puzzle Book; Flags Sticker Atlas.* **Humour Books** TITLES *1000 Stoopid Jokes.* **Licensed Character Books** TITLES Roger Hargreaves' *Mr Men* and *Little Miss* series; *Enid Blyton Library.* **Little Owl Series** TITLES *Easy Learners; Ready for Reading; Bible Stories.* **Classic Library** TITLES *Black Beauty; Treasure Island; Hard Times.* **Information Books** TITLES *Working with Animals; Children's Concise Encyclopedia of Science.* **Religious** TITLES *Children's Illustrated Bible; The Christmas Story.* **Annuals** TITLES *Football Association; Count Duckula.* Unsolicited material rarely used. Titles tend to be commissioned once programme has been finalised.

Yale University Press (London)

23 Pond Street, London NW3 2PN
☎ 071-431 4422   Fax 071-431 3755

Managing Director *John Nicoll*

UK operation of **Yale University Press**, USA. FOUNDED 1961. *Publishes* academic and humanities. About 160 titles (worldwide) a year.

Editorial Director *John Nicoll* Unsolicited mss and synopses welcome if within specialised subject areas.
Royalties paid annually.

Roy Yates Books

40 Woodfield Road, Rudgwick, Horsham, West Sussex RH12 3EP
☎ 0403 822299   Fax 0403 823012

Chairman/Managing Director *Roy Yates*
Approx Annual Turnover £80,000

FOUNDED 1990. Incorporates Baker Books (est. 1982) and Ingham Yates (est. 1986). *Publishes* children's books only, and is involved in wholesale and retailing of children's books in foreign and dual language editions. No unsolicited material as books are adaptations of existing popular classics suitable for translation into dual language format. *Royalties* paid quarterly.

Yearling

See **Transworld Publishers Ltd**

Yorkshire Arts Circus Ltd

School Lane, Glass Houghton, Castleford, West Yorkshire WF10 4QH
☎ 0977 550401

Approx Annual Turnover £180,000

Became a limited company in 1987 and a registered charity in 1992. Small publishing operation which specialises in publishing new writing by first-time authors. *Publishes* autobiography, community books, fiction, short stories and books with local (Yorkshire/ Humberside) connection. No children's stories, reference, local history or nostalgia. TITLES *No Option but to Fight* Maggi Chapman; *Barbed Lines* ed. Debjani Chatterjee & Rashida Islam. Unsolicited mss discouraged; authors should send for fact sheet in the first instance. 6 titles in 1991. There are plans to introduce a new fiction imprint in 1993.

Young Library Ltd

3 The Old Brushworks, 56 Pickwick Road,
Corsham, Wiltshire SN13 9BX
☎ 0249 712025   Fax 0249 715558

Managing Director *Roger Cleeve*

FOUNDED 1982. *Publishes* children's information
books. No unsolicited mss; send synopsis/ideas in
the first instance. 12–20 titles a year.
Royalties paid annually.

Zed Books Ltd

57 Caledonian Road, London N1 9BU
☎ 071-837 4014   Fax 071-833 3960

Approx Annual Turnover £750,000

FOUNDED 1976. *Publishes* international and Third
World affairs, development studies, women's studies and specific area studies, namely the Middle
East, Africa, Asia, Latin America and the Caribbean. No fiction or children's. 43 titles in 1991.

DIVISIONS
Development & Environment *Robert Molteno*
TITLES *The Development Dictionary* ed. Wolfgang
Sachs. **Women's Studies** *Anna Gourlay* TITLES
Staying Alive Vandana Shiva. **Middle East Studies**
Michael Pallis TITLES *An A–Z of the Middle East.* No
unsolicited mss; synopses and ideas welcome
though.
Royalties paid annually.

Zomba

See **Omnibus Press**

Publish and be Ruined

The Law of Libel

Robert Maxwell should be an example to us all. During his long and inglorious career he employed an army of lawyers to protect him from what he was inclined to call 'grievous libels' and everybody else described as the unvarnished truth. That he is now revealed as a crooked manipulator of the first order is an unchallengeable indictment against our libel laws. By putting the burden of proof on journalists and authors, and imposing draconian penalties on those who venture too far into murky waters, the law does a great disservice to democracy. And seems to do it, moreover, with its eyes wide open.

In one of Maxwell's legal battles with *Private Eye*, he was awarded £5000 compensatory damages and a further £50,000 in exemplary or punitive damages. This was to punish the magazine for not having accepted the convention of silence. It had continued to write about Maxwell while the case was pending.

As Auberon Waugh reminds us:

> 'This "gagging" writ is a well-known device used by crooks to prevent any newspaper or magazine from exposing their nefarious activities. Maxwell had 60 such writs out at the time of his death. The reason that *Private Eye* was the only one taken to court was that it was the only defendant which dared defy the crook, who went on swindling and lying and stealing to his heart's content, backed up to the hilt by our legal system.
>
> 'Hundreds of people must have known exactly what he was doing. None dared say a word. One wonders how many Robert Maxwells there are now enjoying the same protection.'

Reformers are clear as what needs to be done. Following the wisdom of Sir Neville Faulks, whose recommendations were published all of fifteen years ago, the court should have discretion to decide whether a trial should be with or without a jury. In the event of a jury trial, the responsibility of the jury should be limited to indicating whether damages should be substantial, moderate, nominal or contemptuous. The judge would then decide on the appropriate figure.

But the Lord Chancellor, Lord Mackay, is not ready for this. In a recent meeting with an authors' delegation, he discounted the prospect of a new Defamation Bill while offering amendments to the existing law.

The most important change is in the role of the Court of Appeal. It will now be able to substitute its own finding when it disagrees with a jury's estimate of damages. At present, all the Court of Appeal can do is to set aside an award, leaving the plantiff to start all over again – assuming he has the stomach and the purse for a re-run.

Lord Mackay also promises that the Court of Appeal will clarify considerations to be taken into account by juries when deciding damages. This holds open the possibility of extending the rule currently applicable in Scotland, that the plaintiff has to prove a damaged reputation. Current English practice is far harsher in that once the words are shown to be libellous, hefty damages can be obtained even if no real harm has resulted.

Any degree of liberalisation is to be welcomed but it is disturbing that even with the more active involvement of the Court of Appeal we are still a long way from the open society of democratic ideals.

In America, where the spirit of inquiry is less inhibited, any public figure who sues is liable to be reminded of the adage about avoiding the heat of the kitchen. For damages to be awarded in an American court, someone must publish untruths knowing them to be untrue. In Britain, a statement which is genuinely believed to be true and indeed is true at base in part may still be libellous. Hence the whacking sums that are handed down to compensate for damage to reputations that were hardly snowy pure before they were libelled.

Journalists never like to find themselves in court but they at least have the comfort of knowing that they are covered by their employers, who generally take on the whole cost of a libel action. Authors, on the other hand, are more exposed to the rigours of legal censorship. A typical publishing contract includes a warranty clause which entitles the publisher to be indemnified by the author against damages and costs if any part of the work turns out to be libellous.

Publishers excuse their weakness of backbone by arguing that only the author is in a position to know whether or not a work is libellous and that the onus should be on the author to check facts before they are published. But why, asks Mark Le Fanu of the **Society of Authors**, should the risk be borne by the author alone when a publisher deliberately gambles on making money out of a book?

> 'While it is true that a writer of fiction is much more likely than the publisher to know whether or not a person has been defamed (whether intentionally or unintentionally), the issue is much less clear-cut with non-fiction. Authors are not experts in the arcane mysteries of the 'fair comment' defence to a libel claim. Publishers are well aware that certain sorts of books (e.g. biographies of the living, business exposés, etc.) inevitably carry a libel risk.'

In fairness, it must be said that the indemnity is rarely invoked against an author unless the publisher feels he has been deceived or misled. The wise and economical course is to check out the hazards before a manuscript goes to print.The litmus test for libel is to ask, 'Would the words complained of tend to lower the plaintiff in the estimation of right-thinking members of society?' Or, more simply, 'Would you like it said about you?' If a novel features a corrupt member of parliament, a financier who fiddles his tax or a vicar with an obsessive interest in choirboys, it is as well to check in the directories that the names given to these characters do not correspond to flesh and blood people. Since one cannot libel the dead, a valuable and safe source of names is *Who Was Who*?

If this is thought to be over-cautious, listen to the wise words of the columnist known as The Weasel who writes in *The Independent Magazine*:

'A case brought by one Artemus Jones against the *Sunday Chronicle* in 1908 established that "a writer may be guilty of libel without knowing the existence of the person he has libelled". The Defamation Act of 1952 was meant to put an end to such nonsense by decreeing that anyone who had "innocently" libelled an unknown person could avoid liability by publishing an apology. However, the definition of "innocence" was so strict that the Act proved all but useless. In 1956 an actress, June Sylvaine, sued the publishers of Antonia White's novel *The Sugar House* because it included a character called June Sylvaine, who was described as "fat". Both sides agreed that the coincidence of names was accidental, and the real Sylvaine admitted that it had done her no discernible harm. Nevertheless, she was awarded damages.'

In book publishing it is the biographers of contemporary or near-contemporary figures who tread the narrowest line. To state a known fact about an individual, that he behaved deviously or dishonestly for example, may raise questions about his friends, associates or family which they feel bound to contest. In such cases the best hope for the writer is the plaintiff's awareness that publicity generated by his action will cause him yet more pain. As Dr Johnson reminds us, 'Few attacks either of ridicule or invective make much noise but with the help of those they provoke.'

Where a libel has been committed unintentionally or 'innocently', it is possible to alleviate the consequences by an 'offer to make amends'. This usually involves a published apology and a settlement of costs. Otherwise, unless it can be established that a statement, however defamatory, is true in substance and fact (a difficult trick to pull off), the defence against libel will probably turn on the assertion that the words complained of are fair comment on a matter of public interest. This is where the wheel turns full circle because writers, who are themselves inclined to rush to law when they feel aggrieved, often hear the 'fair comment' defence from reviewers who have savaged their work. The perimeters of 'fair comment' are supposed to protect the principles of free speech, so that, according to precedent, 'However wrong the opinion expressed may be in point of truth, or however prejudiced the writer, it may still be within the prescribed limit'. In other words, it is one thing to argue that a person's *views* are lunatic but quite another to assert that *he* is a lunatic.

At the very least, the author of a controversial work should insist that his publisher has the manuscript read for libel and he should make sure his contract does not allow for unlimited liability.

In one important respect, authors and publishers suffer more than anyone from the application of the libel laws. At the root of the problem is the ease with which determined plaintiffs can get a book withdrawn from circulation. David Hooper, author of the entertainingly instructive *Public Scandal, Odium and Contempt* (**Coronet**) points out that the position of distributors in such situations is extremely perilous.

'They have no means of knowing whether the book is in fact libellous. All they know is that any profit they might have made – and more – will find its way smartly into the hands of their lawyers.'

The remedy, says David Hooper, is for anyone seeking to get a book withdrawn to be required to undertake to pay damages if their claims turn out to be without substance.

Is there anything to be said for those who bring libel actions? It is hard to disagree with Bernard Levin who asserts 'If I were libelled (I have frequently been) and were given the choice of suing or having all my toenails pulled out with red-hot pincers while listening to *Pelléas et Mélisande*, I think it would be a close run thing.'

Writing for Young People

As a writer for seven-to-seventeen-year-olds, I'm well used to being treated as an object of curiosity, amusement and even pity. Yet after nearly thirty years, I am still occasionally dumbfounded by the tactlessness of people, rarely writers themselves, who take it for granted that I've failed in my chosen field and have bravely settled for second best.

I first came across this attitude while in hospital waiting for the results of tests and X-rays. A friendly young doctor seemed intrigued to find me propped up by my pillows, frantically scribbling the deadlined final episode of a magazine serial for eleven-year-olds. Several weeks and two major, but miraculously successful, brain operations later, he appeared at my bedside again. 'Now you'll be able to write for grown-ups,' he said cheerfully. Of course he was joking, at least I hope he was, but the gist of his remark has been echoed countless times since then by cynics of a far more irritating kind. I cope more or less by clinging on to my sense of humour, in and out of working hours, but if my tormentors persist in refusing to believe that any right-minded person would actually choose to write for kids, let alone enjoy trying to make a living out of it – as I most certainly do – it sometimes helps to remind them, and myself, of such masters as Oscar Wilde, C. S. Lewis and Roald Dahl, whose stories for young readers, along with their less fanciful works for adults, will be valued and talked about for generations to come. Who would dare suggest that these gems of imagination were not written partly, if not wholly, for the sheer pleasure of writing them?

I am by no means alone in thinking that anyone starting on their first book for teenagers or younger children should be warned that job satisfaction is not so much a fringe benefit but more a basic necessity. Victoria Eldon, senior commissioning editor for **Pan Books**, told me that her more successful authors of 'young' novels often showed give-away signs of putting enjoyment before money.

When asked for tips for new writers, she said, 'Don't be put off by rejections, recessions or anything else. If something is good, it will eventually come through. Try other publishers and, while waiting for their verdicts, read a lot and write a lot, because nearly everyone improves with practice.' Among Victoria's pet hates are writers who take an issue and try to write a story round it. 'It's far better to have the same issue coming out of what is first and foremost a good story in its own right.' After mentioning how children resented being talked down to, she added, 'I don't like books with overly dogmatic or preachy, two-dimensional characters.

'Make sure the work's easy on the eye', she advised, emphasising the folly of poor presentation. 'Avoid worn-out typewriter ribbons, use double spacing always and keep scribbled-in alterations to a minimum. It's a sensible plan to start by submitting two chapters and a careful outline of the plot to your chosen publisher who, if interested, may have suggestions to make about the way you continue the story.'

The choosing of a publisher deserves both time and care and it is wise to start researching almost as soon as the seeds of a book idea have germinated in your head. A hunt through the children's section of a public library or bookshop will reveal the names and addresses of publishers whose titles cover subjects compatible with yours for the age group you have in mind. When picking off-peak times for my own research, I've found the assistants happy to guide me to the right shelves, pointing out books which might be of interest and telling me of young readers' current likes and dislikes.

Once you've made your first choice, be sure you have a copy of your own in case of loss before sending off your manuscript to the Children's Editorial Department, enclosing a stamped addressed envelope of adequate size for its return and a brief covering letter. Normally, you will receive a printed acknowledgement of receipt fairly soon, but if you've heard nothing after a couple of weeks, a quick phone call to the publisher's office is permissible, just to make sure your work is in the right hands. After that, be prepared for a wait of up to six months and resist the temptation to ring or write on any pretext, during that time. It's a sad fact that few things irritate a busy editor more than anxious pleas about a manuscript he or she has not yet had time to consider properly.

Of course, an agent will cut out much of the bother and heartache of selecting a publisher, seeking other possible buyers for rejected work and negotiating a fair deal. The well-known problem for new writers is finding someone willing to take them on. Says literary agent Maggie Noach:

'I am here first and foremost to sell saleable material, thinking not so much of the children who will eventually read it, but of the parents, teachers and other adults – usually with pre-conceived ideas of their own – who choose and buy the books for them.'

'There's a big difference between writing to sell and writing for kids you know well,' she continued, mentioning that, in common with other reputable agents, she was at present finding herself forced to turn down over 90 per cent of applications from would-be clients. With children's writers, this was sometimes because they simply hadn't made any preliminary study of the market for themselves, and even seemed unsure of the age group they were aiming at. 'These days young people are more age-conscious than ever before, and a book which pleases an eight-year-old is likely to be of little or no interest to readers approaching their teens. It is simply not good enough for an author to say vaguely that his or her work will suit children of all ages,' she insisted.

This last remark reminded me of the time I was busily tackling my first novel: one of a series for twelve-to-thirteen-year olds. I'd just about reached the halfway stage when I received an anxious call from the publisher telling me to go easy on the romance scenes, as research had shown that the series was being read by girls as young as ten. That caused no hassle, because I hadn't really been thinking in terms of red-hot passion, but before I started my second novel, I phoned to ask if the rule still applied. The answer came loud and clear: 'Oh yes please. We've just heard that the readers now include *eight*-year olds . . .'

Diane Elliot, junior librarian in one of the bigger London libraries, passed on some useful information about the types of book young readers preferred at different ages, pointing out that it was impossible to be precise because no two children were alike in taste and maturity. (Rather like adults, I thought.) On the whole, she said, up to the ages of seven or eight, girls and boys seemed to read the same authors, and enjoyed puzzle and activity books as well as fiction. From eight or nine, girls often turned their attention to pony and school stories – the *Chalet School* books were still popular – while boys chose adventure, science fiction and more sophisticated activity books such as the **Puffin** *Fighting Fantasy* series. Soon, the girls were demanding teenage romances, devouring them avidly until ready for adult novels. 'I've even caught boys dipping into the romances,' said Diane, 'though high adventure stays top favourite with most of them.' (If you're thinking gloomily that all this borrowing from libraries won't help to sell your books, don't forget the Public Lending Right scheme; last February, when I was beginning to accept that royalties from my novels had dried up, I received over £200 in PLR money, which came in highly useful at a very bleak time.)

Because there was so much talk about the popularity of activity books, I decided to find out more from Patrick Burston, who writes the **Walker Books** *Which Way?* series for young children. 'Kids want to be involved,' he said. 'I know I did – as far back as I remember – and I still do.' It was through his enduring love of projects and involvement that he hit on the idea of encouraging his readers to take an active part in his stories, giving them puzzles to solve, a choice of pages to turn to, and the feeling of having a say of their own in the dénouement. Patrick didn't believe people had to be parents or teachers to become successful writers for children. 'My big advantage', he explained, 'is that I still seem to think and feel as a child, myself.'

'It's exactly the same with me,' admitted Mary Hooper, lecturer at evening classes on the subject of Writing to Sell. Author of many books for teenage and younger readers, she works part-time assisting the editor of a teens-and-twenties magazine. 'I'm quite frivolous – convinced I'm immature – and feel certain this has helped me more than anything else when writing for kids.' After explaining how part of her job was to help wade through piles of unsolicited manuscripts, she said, 'Amusing stories are in great demand, but nothing's worse than false humour. I'm all for a bit of anarchy, here and there, but I don't like goody-goodies and nor do our readers.'

If your aim is to write non-fiction for young people, many rules are the same as those for fiction, but it is essential to know your subject backwards – especially if you've no formal qualifications – and to practise the art of writing in simple words without a hint of bossiness. By all means add a sprinkling of humour, but beware of sounding like a pompous schoolteacher generously allowing your pupils a short break for laughter. I'll always be grateful for the advice given me by my one-time journalist boss when I was a very junior publicity writer: 'Whatever your subject, show a real interest in it, temporarily at any rate. The more excited and absorbed you become yourself, the better chance you stand of injecting your readers with enthusiasm, too.' And that, I now realise, is one of the secrets of success in creative writing of any kind.

New writers, dubious about their readiness to attempt a full-length book, may find it less daunting to start off by writing short stories or articles. I'll now try to illustrate why it's a big mistake to feel there's anything second-rate or unprofessional about writing fact or fiction for the cheaper magazines and comics . . .

It was because I'd written countless stories and an apparently never-ending serial for a teenage magazine, that I was commissioned to write my first teenage novel, on the strength of two chapters and a synopsis. Largely thanks to all the picture stories I'd written when my daughters were small, I was given the opportunity to write one of a series of half-hour TV plays for older schoolchildren. By showing evidence of my experience as cookery columnist (unpaid) on a local charity newspaper, I've sold several recipe features to national magazines. The moral here is that it can be a great advantage to have a clip or two of previously published work to send to prospective editors and publishers along with the story or feature idea you hope they'll accept. For this reason it may be unwise, at first at any rate, to argue too hotly about matters of fees and copyright.

The simplest way to begin is by scouring the bookstalls for a publication you feel you might be able to write for, and then looking it up in the magazine section of this book to discover what you can about the editor's requirements: type and length of stories, for example. Next, buy or borrow a recent copy and read it carefully, noting the subject matter, format and style (such as whether single or double quotation marks are used) before thinking up a theme or plot of your own. Now get busy typing, bearing in mind that features editors usually prefer to be sent a brief outline of your idea, before giving the go-ahead for the article itself. Fiction editors understandably expect short stories to be submitted in full.

Writing for picture and photostory papers can be enormous fun, but a dedicated old Scots editor once told me that his more prized scriptwriters were born with a kind of visual ability which could rarely be taught. Contributors are sometimes needed for the flimsy but colourful comics aimed at schoolchildren (with titles such as *Mandy* or *Roy of the Rovers*). It is essential to have an ear for the spoken word and current junior jargon because, rather like a play, the story is told by way of dialogue. An occasional one-line caption moves things along and the writer is expected to begin each frame with a brief but carefully thought-out description of the picture required from the artist or photographer. If all this seems highly confusing, it may be worth writing to the editor of your chosen publication asking about the availability of a scriptwriting guidelines sheet. The staff at D. C. Thomson (Albert Square, Dundee, DD1 9QJ) are usually very helpful over this kind of request.

In my search for more advice, I spoke to the editors of two very different magazines for older teenagers. After stressing that clear, clean copy was more important than ever now they were computerised, Lorna Read of *Loving Monthly* said,

'We use more fiction than features and, as the name suggests, love is the main ingredient. School stories are never considered and heroines are always over sixteen, although some of the readers may be younger. Because I've a very small staff, please submit only one manuscript at a time and even if my reply includes a few tips and comments, don't send a rewrite unless I've asked for one. I'm usually on the lookout for 1000-word sting-in-tail stories, but be warned that these are notoriously tricky to write.'

Lorna added that two of her *bêtes noires* were faulty grammar and stories written from an animal's viewpoint.

More! is a fortnightly magazine, mostly devoted to features about relationships, sex, careers and such practicalities as finding a first flat. There is also a page for male writers entitled 'Always by Men'. Editor Fiona Gibson told me that the vast majority of unsolicited manuscripts were turned down because of unsuitable material.

'It is essential to study the mag, because most of the articles are written to fit into ready-established slots. The style should be fast but straightforward – cheeky, yes, but tongue-in-cheek, never. Always submit an idea first, because the subject may have already been covered in a recent issue. Lots of people don't realise that we work just a month ahead,' she went on, 'so I rarely go wild over the likes of Valentine's Day notions received in June.'

Almost all of us like having writer friends to talk things over with, and some (but not all) beginners find encouragement from writers' circles (see **Writers' Courses, Circles and Workshops**) and evening classes. (Find out more from your local paper and library notice-board.) Books can be helpful, too, especially some of the ones written by successful authors. Dianne Doubtfire's books are widely praised, but be wary of sermonising offerings by little known writers, who seem to think that talent can be taught by way of strings of tedious but, in many people's view, time-wasting exercises.

Several of my friends have derived great benefit from residential courses, finding that the students often include experienced authors as well as learner-writers. I had a particularly interesting talk with Sally Worboyes, founder-director of the **Fen Farm** five-day writing courses held in the wilds of Suffolk, who said

'We meet lots of children's writers here, and at one TV and radio drama course, two of our students were tackling plays for young people. A talented girl brought the first pages of her book for adults to a recent novel-writing course tutored by Stan Barstow, but went home even more enthusiastic about the promising start she'd made while here, on a rollicking teenage romance.'

(For more details see **Writers' Courses, Circles and Workshops** Section and study writers' magazines and national papers for news of other courses.)

You may have heard some of Sally's own plays on Radio 4, but she has written drama for children, too, and was Residential Writer for the Norfolk Young People's Theatre. She said there were at present more openings in radio than in TV for plays for young listeners, but that the going was tough and new writers would have to be prepared to 'write, write and rewrite' on their road to recognition. She advised them to glue their ears to Radio 5 and to spend as much time as possible in the company of kids of the right age – by offering help at a local youth organisation or school, perhaps – soaking up the 'in' expressions, interests and crazes. (Rosemary Horstmann's paperback, *Writing for Radio*, **A & C Black**, gives useful addresses and know-how information.)

Our talk reminded me, for some reason, of another comment I frequently receive from curious friends: 'You must love children an awful lot . . .' The truth is that I like *some* children immensely, but find a few of them unlovable in almost every way. This is no problem, because my plots would be pathetically lukewarm if there were no baddies to stir up trouble for my never entirely saintly goodies. The need, I think, is not so much for fondness, but empathy.

Ann de Gale

Formalism vs the Rest

Peter Finch

In what state do we find poetry in this last decade of the twentieth century? As flush with innovation and excitement as it was in its first? Hardly. In America the battle between the proponents of free verse and the new formalists rages. Over here our long love of conventional metrication once again rises to the top. 'Formalism is great and a reality,' says Simon Armitage. 'A continuation of original streams,' affirms Mike Horovitz. In school we are taught to create now, not just to dissect, so it's all OK. Modernism for many may have come and gone but watch out. Not every new voice wants to sound like Hardy. John Ashbery and his followers are staking their territory. Poetry will continue to be full of sparks.

As many as 12% of the UK population now claims to read verse and of these two-thirds are female. No one is sure how many write – too many, according to most editors. Positive discrimination towards women in competitions, anthologies and events can make it a disadvantage to be anything but. If in doubt drop your first name and stick to initials.

A straw poll among organisers and practitioners tells us that despite continued high sales of works like Philip Larkin's *Collected Poems* (more than 40,000 copies now) and with Wendy Cope's *Serious Concerns* riding at the top of the paperback bestsellers list, interest in poetry is actually flattening. There have been a couple of successful large-scale poetry readings at festivals and at the National Theatre, but far less mid-range activity, no emerging new little mags of significance and, despite new technology, a steadying of small press output. 'Historically speaking, the ratio of poetry's audience to the rest of society is not in the former's favour,' said Joseph Brodsky in his Poet Laureate of the USA acceptance speech. Thus it has always been.

Yet, at core, activity is as real as ever. **Chadwyck-Healey**'s recent CD–ROM publication *The English Poetry Full-Text Database*, which reprints some 4500 volumes onto four disks, might make the rest of the business look a little superfluous, but it does cost £22,000 a copy. The majority of contemporary poetry is eminently affordable. So it should be. The Arts Minister recently claimed that as much as £1.5 million was spent supporting it. What we need now are more readers. If you produce poetry you should make it your business to be a consumer too. Buy books, attend events, subscribe to magazines. The very real fear felt by some new poets that they might contaminate their ideas by reading those of others should be overcome immediately. The poetry business is not a melting pot where everything turns a uniform grey, but a salad bowl where the 'tossed and marinated ingredients subtly lend each other taste and flavour'. Slice your tomato, start now.

Commercial Publishers

Down in the market place the recession appears to have made little difference to poetry's meagre flow. Since sales are minute anyway, any reduction is difficult to measure. Those who try, continue, and although there may be quite a number of trade publishers with poetry of sorts in their catalogues, those with an active interest remain at five – still producing too many titles, argue the critics – but for the poets, never enough. **Faber & Faber**, since T. S. Eliot's days as editor, has the most enviable list anywhere. It must be so. They say it themselves. 'The great tradition continues', runs their promotional material. Heaney, Hughes, Dunn, Motion, Larkin – British poetry's world-beating face. New editor Christopher Reid, a post-modern generation poet like his predecessor Craig Raine, promises a run of new names: Simon Armitage, Susan Wicks, Martin Turner, but it's hardly a flood. **Chatto** was revived by Andrew Motion and is now in the hands of former *Poetry Review* editor Mick Imlah. Anthologies such as their *The Chatto Book Of Love Poems* have a high profile. Poets Alan Jenkins, Carol Rumens, Norman McCaig, John Fuller are staples. New books include Mark Ford, Robert Crawford and the inimitable Peter Reading. **Hutchinson** do better out of their 'inspirational' versifiers Patience Strong and Helen Steiner Rice than they do out of their 'real' poets. Dannie Abse and Gavin Ewart remain in there, although all of interest to appear recently has been Hutchinson's annual anthology for the **Poetry Book Society**. **Oxford University Press** represent the traditional centre of English verse but surprising to some have a fair roster of contemporary names – Porter, Stevenson, Enright, Scupham, Shuttle – together with new voices such as Jamie McKendrick, Sean O'Brien and Jo Shapcott. Under editor Jaqueline Simms they put out at least a dozen titles a year. **Secker & Warburg** has had a long-held interest in modern poetry. Under editor Robin Robertson its list is rich in contemporary names with a commendable lack of attendant anthologies. Centrepieces are Michael Longley and Peter Redgrove with cracking back-up from Sharon Olds, John Burnside, Matthew Sweeney, David Hartnett and others. But even Seckers is now less eager than in the past to consider new poets.

Other Chances?

Elsewhere there is little. **Jonathan Cape**, whose reputation used to be strong has reduced its names to Roger McGough, Derek Walcott and the increasingly popular Heathcote Williams. **Collins-Harvill** do Michael Hulse. **Methuen** has Michèle Roberts and Katie Campbell. **Robson Books** makes money out of broadcaster Nigel Forde and adds culture with ex-boxer Vernon Scannell. Dabblers all. Only in **Sinclair-Stevenson**, a new commercial company, are there glimmerings – C. Day Lewis, Fiona Pitt-Kethley and Jon Silkin.

The Paperbackers

By definition paperback houses produce cheap softback editions of hardbacks previously marketed by others and with the exception of one company have traditionally never been a great outlet for new work, although recent years have seen that rule bend a little. **Penguin**, who probably sell more poetry in this country than anyone else, might initially appear to present a flourishing market for potential contributors. The list is thick with thematic, national and historic anthologies, translations, classic authors, splendid compilations of contemporary practice and an enviable range of books by present-day poets such as Peter Redgrove, U. A. Fanthorpe and Roger McGough. How many speculative submissions they receive I have no idea, but the evidence is that they publish none. Like the good mass market house it is, Penguin sticks with track records. Tony Harrison, James Fenton, Geoffrey Hill, Andrew Motion *et al* have all made their reputations elsewhere. **Paladin**, on the other hand, takes greater risks. Its controversial anthology *The New British Poetry* was a ground-breaking original. In addition to mainstream post-modernists Paz, Ashbery, Middleton and Ensenberger, the imprint's slowly building list now includes stalwarts of the official opposition: Iain Sinclair, Douglas Oliver, Lee Harwood, Tom Raworth, Barry Macsweeney, Chris Torrance and Bill Griffiths – inhabitors of the fringes all. How long this will continue now that the imprint has been merged with **HarperCollins**'s Flamingo list is anybody's guess. Elsewhere there isn't much. Both **Picador** and **Abacus** have produced the occasional title. Feminist presses such as **Virago** and **The Women's Press** publish a small amount as part of an overall strategy: Gillian Allnutt, Grace Nichols, Maya Angelou. Not a lot. Beginners beware.

The Specialists

The great gap in the poetry business has been vigorously filled by a group of seven semi-commercial independents known generically as the Specialists. They all began life as classic small presses, in the late Seventies and early Eighties, but soon outgrew the restraints of back-bedroom offices and under-the-stairs warehousing. All now have national representation of some sort; a number use *Password* (23 New Mount Street, Manchester M4 4DE), who issue a very useful catalogue. Most (but not all) receive substantial grant aid, without which their publishing programmes would be sunk. They are models of what poetry publishing should be – active, alert and exciting. The problem is that they are too few. Leader of the pack **Carcanet** is by now almost indistinguishable from its trade competitiors. It has over 500 titles in print and 'reps' in 42 countries. Run by Michael Schmidt, the press has its own magazine, *PN Review*, and concentrates on producing substantial editions, making a poet's whole oeuvre available alongside cheap selected poems and new titles from both the untried and the famous. Typical of its list are John Ash, Edwin Morgan, Gillian Clarke, and bestseller Elizabeth Jennings, whose *Selected Poems* has now sold in excess of 10,000 copies. Carcanet has an air of studied seriousness about it, and in a frivolous world that can be no bad thing.

    Littlewood Arc is a much smaller operation resulting from the merger of two independents: Tony Ward's avant garde Arc and John Killick's more mainstream Littlewood Press. The upshot is a sturdy imprint keen on new voices and the work of minorities, and full of northern grit. Ivor Cutler, Michael Hulse and Myra Schneider do best here, with Cutler's sales outstripping those of many a commercial house's best.

    Enitharmon Press represents quality. Its books are produced to the highest of standards and it has little interest in fashion, preferring 'poetry of the human spirit' which exhibits 'moral imagination'. Owner Stephen Stuart-Smith successfully continues founder Alan Clodd's policy of promoting new writers and reviving the reputations of the neglected. Typical poets include David Gascoyne, Frances Bellerby, Paul Duncan and Jenny Joseph.

    Harry Chamber's **Peterloo Poets** proves that the alternative to mainstream need not be avantgarde. Concentrating on new writers, many late starters, whose work is 'accessible to all who can read and have feelings', Chambers has pulled a whole series of poetry bestsellers out of the non-metropolitan hat. The press produces six new titles a year along with a house journal called *Poetry Matters*, and every other year publishes the *Peterloo Preview*, which acts as an introduction to the work of newcomers. Peterloo bestsellers include Dana Gioia, Michael Laskey and John Mole.

Peter Jay's **Anvil Press** was for years a classic, alternative publisher set up almost in formal opposition to the Fabers and OUPs of the world. His interest in writers like Harry Guest, Peter Levi, Anthony Howell and Heather Buck continues, although the focus has now clearly shifted to work in translation, much of it European. Anvil brings out around nine titles a year, is open to the work of the unknown and 'does its best according to eclectic lights'. This means on the one hand taking the market by storm, with translations of Verlaine and Baudelaire, on the other running to three print-runs of Carol Ann Duffy.

Seren Books (Poetry Wales Press until 1988 when founder Cary Archard decided that poetry alone would never keep them afloat) remains committed to new verse, concentrating on material originating in its native Wales. Leslie Norris, John Tripp, Tony Curtis, Robert Minhinnick, Sheenagh Pugh and Jean Earle are among bestsellers.

Bloodaxe Books, run from Newcastle upon Tyne, likes to think of itself as revolutionary. Begun a little over a decade ago with a pamphlet by Ken Smith, the press now reckons to sell more poetry than anyone except OUP, Penguin and Faber. Like many small publishers, owner Neil Astley became disillusioned with a scene, as he saw it, run by academics, full of dust and boredom. He wanted to read poetry which was so startling that it would lift the hairs on the back of his neck. Bloodaxe, with the air of new writers, innovative marketing and a deal of panache, set out to find it. A decade later the evidence is that they succeeded. Winner of the 1990 *Sunday Times Small Publisher of the Year Award*, they have a 'ferocious reputation'. Perhaps the most open of the independents, Bloodaxe is not afraid to mix world figures with upstart newcomers. It approaches poetry broadside, takes risks, produces a high number of first volumes (many from the North) and is a force to be reckoned with. Its sampler anthology, *Poetry With An Edge*, takes some beating.

The Traditional Outlets

There exists a small, traditional market for new poetry – *The Times Literary Supplement, Encounter*, now and again the quality Sunday papers, *London Magazine, The Spectator, The London Review of Books, The Literary Review, New Statesman and Society*, the occasional spot in magazines like *The Lady* and *The Countryman* – all paying outlets which sounds quite reassuring. But the truth is that were poetry to vanish overnight, these publications would continue to flourish without a flicker. Who, other than the poets, would notice?

The Small Press and the Little Magazine

Amateur publishing ventures have been around for quite a long time. Virginia Woolf began **The Hogarth Press** this way – literally on the kitchen table. But it was not until well after the Second World War and the rise of what the

Americans called the mimeo revolution, that poetry magazine and pamphlet publishing really took off. Recent advances in technology have seen the revolution move on considerably. Computer-literate poets are everywhere. Publishing has been stripped of its mystery. Access to photocopiers, laser printers and desktop publishing packages are commonplace. Disposable income has increased. More and more poets are able and willing to set up competent one-person publishing operations and turn out neat professional-looking titles on a considerable scale.

These are the small presses and the little magazines. They sell to new and often non-traditional markets and rarely find space on bookshop shelves where they are regarded as unshiftable nuisances. Instead they sell hand to hand at poetry readings, creative writing classes and literary functions, or via subscription, and are liberally exchanged among all concerned. The question remains: is there anyone out there, not directly concerned with poetry, who is actually reading it? But that is another story.

Numerically the small presses and the little magazines are the largest publishers of new poetry, both in terms of their range of titles and total sales. They operate in a variety of shapes and sizes, everywhere from Cardiff to Caithness and Lewes to Llandudno. The present wave of enthusiasm has thrown up a variety of support organisations to which new poets can direct initial enquiries. Both the **Association of Little Presses** and the **Small Press Group** (see entries **Professional Associations**) produce catalogues, as well as running bookfairs and events around the country.

The country's best known poetry magazines all began as classic titles. Between them *PN Review, Ambit, Agenda, Outposts, Orbis, Poetry Review, Rialto* and *Stand* do not come up to over half the circulation of journals like *Shooting Times* and *Yachting World* – which says a lot about the way we value our poetry. Nonetheless they manage to get to almost everyone who matters. In the second division (in terms of sales) lie the regional or genre specialists such as *Poetry Wales, Lines Review, Salmon, Oxford Poetry, Poetry Ireland, New Welsh Review, Poetry Nottingham, Talus, Gairfish* and *Borderlines*. All are well-produced, often with the help of grants, and all are representative of a specific point of view. In Wales there is *Barddas* for poets using the strict meters and in Scotland *Lallans* for poets writing in Lowland Scots. The vast majority of small mags, however, owe no allegiance and range from fat irregulars like *Joe Soap's Canoe* or *Slow Dancer* to fleeting pamphlets like *Rhinoceros, Bare Wires* 'for the non-professional serious writer', *Understanding* and *Scratch*. Some, such as the experimentally-orientated *Tak Tak Tak*, puts out accompanying cassettes of performance work; others like the irreverent *Agog* provide a computer disk supplement (usable only if you own an Applemac).

Among pressses and small publishers there is a similar range of variety. **Allardyce, Barnett** represent the innovative writers included in the anthology, *A Various Art* (Paladin), publishing fine, hefty editions of J. H. Prynne, Andrew Crozier and Douglas Oliver; Bob Cobbing's **Writers Forum** sticks to mainstream experimental; **Forest Books**, run with panache by Brenda Walker and bringing out just as many new titles as the specialists, concentrates on English translations of foreign, often East-European texts; **Dangaroo**, Bogle L'Ouverture, **Peepal Tree Press** and **Katabasis** have Third World and ethnic concerns; **Smith/Doorstop** captures the Northern voice in its series of double-header pamphlets; **Honno** supports Welsh women; Woodfield Publishing Services has Tamar Segal, 'the new Patience Strong'; **Jane Publishing** is into performance work; Equinox Press has a strong interest in haiku; **Y Lolfa** publishes unofficial bards; **Envoi** brings out the accessible; and Hunter House only publishes Janet Rutherford's poetry. For the new writer these are the places to try first. Indeed, many have. Who published T. S. Eliot's first? A small publisher. Likewise Dannie Abse, Peter Redgrove, James Fenton and Dylan Thomas. R. S. Thomas, Ezra Pound and Edgar Allen Poe didn't even go that far. They published themselves.

Cash

A lot of writers new to the business are surprised to learn that their poetry will not make them much money. Being a poet is not much of an occupation. You get better wages delivering papers. There will be the odd pound from the better-heeled magazine, perhaps even as much as £40 from periodicals lucky enough to be in receipt of a grant, but generally it amounts to no more than free copies of the issues concerned and thank you letters. Those with collections published by a subsidised, specialist publisher can expect a couple of hundred pounds as an advance on royalties; those using the small presses can look forward to a few dozen complimentary copies. The truth is that poetry itself is undervalued. You can earn money writing about it, reviewing it, lecturing on it or giving public recitations. In fact most things in the poetry business will earn better money than the verse itself. Expect to spend a lot on stamps and a fair bit on sample copies. Most of the time all you get in return is used envelopes.

Readings

Since the great beat-generation Albert Hall reading of 1964, an ever-expanding phenomenon, poets on platforms are reading or reciting their stuff to an audience that can be anywhere between raptly attentive and asleep. There is a magic in the spoken poem. The music lives, the images echo. But for some writers the reading has devolved so far as to become a branch of the entertainment industry; yet for others it is an essential aspect of what they do. Whichever way you view it it is certainly an integral part of the business and one which the beginner is going to need to engage in sooner or later. Begin by attending, see how others manage. Watch out for local events advertised at your library or ring your local arts board (see **Arts Councils and Regional Arts Boards**). Poets with heavy reputations can often turn out to be lousy performers while many an amateur can really shake it down. Don't expect to catch every image as you listen. Readings do not go in for total comprehension but more for glancing blows. Treat it as fun and it will be. If you are trying things yourself for the first time make sure you've brought your books along to sell, stand upright, drop the shoulders, gaze at a spot at the back of the hall and blow.

Competitions

Poetry competitions have been the vogue for more than a decade now, with the most unlikely organisations sponsoring them. The notion here is that anonymity ensures fairness. Entries are made under pseudonyms so that if your name happens to be Miroslav Holub, it won't help you very much. Results seem to bear this out. The big competitions such as the one run biennally by the **Arvon Foundation** (with the help of *The Observer* and Duncan Lawrie Ltd), or the **Poetry Society**'s National attract an enormous number of entries and usually throw up quite a number of unknowns among the winners. And why do people bother? Cash prizes can be large – thousands of pounds – but it costs at least a pound a poem to enter. But if it is cash you want, then horses are a better bet. And there has been a recent trend for winners to come from places like Cape Girardeau, Missouri and Tibooburra, Australia. The odds are getting longer. Who won the 1986 Arvon? I don't remember. But if you do fancy a try, it's a fairly innocent activity. You tie up a poem for a few months and spend a couple of pounds in doing so. Watch the small mags for details, write to your local arts board, check out **Quartos** (see entry **Magazines** section), look on the notice board at your local library, or write for a list to the **Poetry Library** in London (see entry **Library Services**). The really keen will have a copy of the **Book Trust**'s *Guide to Literary Prizes, Grants and Awards in Britain and Ireland* which lists all the major events.

Where to start

Probably the best place will be locally. Find out through the library or regional arts board which writers' groups meet in your area. There you will run into others of a like mind, encounter whatever locally produced magazines there might be, and get a little direct feedback on your work. 'How am I doing?' is a big question for the emerging poet and although criticism is not all that hard to come by, do not expect it from all sources. Magazine editors, for example, will rarely have the time to offer advice. Be wary of that offered by friends and relations – they will no doubt be only trying to please. Writers' groups present the best chance for honest mutual criticism but if you want a more detailed, written analysis of your efforts and are willing to pay a small sum for it, you should apply to the service operated nationally by the **Poetry Society** (22 Betterton Street, London WC2), in Wales by the Welsh Arts Council via Oriel (The Friary, Cardiff), or to one run on an area basis by your local arts association or board. There are also a number of non-subsidised critical services, which are advertised in writers' magazines.

If you have decided to publish your work, the first thing to do is a little market research. Although the business is overstocked with periodicals and publications, you will not find many of these in your local W.H. Smith. Most poetry reaches its public via the specialist. Begin by reading a few newly published mainstream books and ask your bookseller for recommendations. Enquire at the library; try selecting a recent anthology of *contemporary* verse. To get a broad view of what's going on, not only should you read Blake Morrison and Andrew Motion's *Penguin Book of Contemporary British Poetry*, Edward Lucie-Smith's *British Poetry since 1945*, and perhaps Seamus Heaney and Ted Hughes's *The Rattle Bag* (Faber), but also Andrew Crozier and Tim Longville's *A Various Art* (Paladin), *The New British Poetry* (Paladin), Jeni Couzyn's *The Bloodaxe Book of Contemporary Women Poets*, James Berry's *News for Babylon*, Donald Allen and George F. Butterick's *The Postmoderns; The New American Poetry Revised* (Grove) and *In The American*

Tree, a language poetry anthology edited by Ron Silliman (NPF). The last two might be hard to find but are well worth the effort. Move on then to the literary magazine. Write off to a number of the magazine addresses which follow this article and ask the price of sample copies. Enquire about subscriptions; expect to pay a little but not a lot. It is important that poets read not only to familiarise themselves with what is currently fashionable and to increase their own facility for self-criticism, but also to help support the activity in which they wish to participate. Buy, read, and if it's all still a mystery to you try Tony Curtis's *How to Study Modern Poetry* (Macmillan) or my own *How to Publish Your Poetry* (**Allison & Busby**), and only then, if appropriate, think about sending something in.

How To Do It

Increase your chances of acceptance by following this simple, standard procedure:

- Type, single side of the paper, A4-size, single-spacing, with double between stanzas, *exactly* as you'd wish your poem to appear when printed.
- Give the poem a title, clip multi-page works together, include your name and address at the foot of the final sheet.
- Keep a copy, make a record of what you send where and when, and leave a space to note reaction.
- Send in small batches: six is a good number, and include a brief covering letter saying who you are. Leave justification, apology and explanation for the writers' circle.
- Include a self addressed, stamped envelope of sufficient size for reply and/or return of your work.
- Be prepared to wait weeks for a response. Don't pester. Be patient. Most magazines will reply in the end.
- Never send the same poem to two places at the same time.
- Send your best. Work which fails to fully satisfy even the author is unlikely to impress anyone else.

Where?

Try the list which follows. The total market is vast – 200 or so addresses here – over a thousand in *Small Presses and Little Magazines of the UK and Ireland* (Oriel, The Friary, Cardiff, £5.50 including postage), literally thousands and thousands worldwide in Judson Jerome's *Poet's Market* (Writer's Digest Books) and Len Fulton's *Directory of Poetry Publishers* (Dustbooks) – the two main American directories. The British Council has also published *British Literary Periodicals – A Selected Bibliography* which covers some titles along with scholarly journals.

The Next Step

Once you have placed a few poems you may like to consider publishing a booklet. There are as many small presses around as there are magazines. Start with the upmarket professionals by all means – **Secker & Warburg, Oxford**

University Press, Chatto & Windus, Hutchinson, Faber & Faber, Virago – but be prepared to compromise. The specialists and the small presses are swifter and more open to new work.

If all else fails you can do it yourself. Blake did, so did Walt Whitman. Modern technology puts the process within the reach of us all; if you can put up a shelf, there's a fair chance that you'll be able to produce a book to put on it. Read my *How To Publish Yourself* (Allison & Busby) and *Into Print*, the BBC book from its TV series on desktop publishing. For more detailed information and case studies, have a look at Audrey & Philip Ward's *The Small Publisher* (Oleander Press).

What to Avoid – The Vanity Presses

Requests which should make you suspicious: *Poems wanted for new anthology; Publisher seeks new authors and poets for well established list; Authors wanted; Publisher seeks new material. Special interest in autobiography, war memoirs and poetry.* Small ads like these are scattered through the classifieds of Sunday papers and in the Personal sections of large circulation magazines. You can tell that something is wrong by the fact that they are there at all. No reputable publisher needs to advertise for poetry. The natural state of affairs is that there is always too much.

Vanity presses are shady businesses run by sharks interested in fleecing the unsuspecting. There are no considerations of literary worth here. The system works by making the amateur writer feel significant. You send in your work and receive a glowing response by return. 'The editor has read your poems with interest and is pleased to report that they show considerable talent. We would like to include them in our forthcoming anthology *Pageant of the British Muse*. This important anthology of new verse will be circulated among the editors of national newspapers such as the *Daily Mirror*, the *Daily Express* and the *Daily Mail* as well as being put on the shelves of the libraries of Oxford University, Cambridge University, Trinity College Dublin, The National Library of Wales at Aberystwyth and the British Library in London. Leading critics use our anthologies as touchstones. Inclusion is a considerable achievement.' It sounds terrific. You are dancing round the room. There follows a lot of hoo-hah about copyright, assignment of author's rights, royalties, etc., all bound up in the form of a legal-sounding document with words like 'upon this day . . . the . . . of . . . witnessed the undersigned . . .', and so forth. The importance of the deal is made abundantly clear. The sting is in the small print at the bottom. 'In order to help defray publisher's overheads in this period of increasing printing costs we are asking you for a small contribution of £40 per poem printed . . .' And by the time you get to this you are so enraptured with the success of your obvious talent that you pay up without a murmur.

It is a deception, of course. Hundreds of others have received the same letter. The anthology will be badly set, poems crammed in like sardines, and it will not be sold in bookshops (no shop owners will stock it), not bought by libraries (those mentioned are copyright libraries and by law need to receive a copy of everything printed), ignored by newspapers (those listed never review poetry anyway), in fact bought and read by no one bar the contributors themselves.

Criticise the presses for this piece of bamboozlery and they will tell you that they are doing no more than providing a service. People want their names in print and are willing to pay to see that happen. The establishment of vanity presses is the inevitable consequence. The immorality is that those who participate are always the inexperienced – often the young and the very old – generally those least able to pay. The vanity presses provide no value judgement on work submitted. There is no discrimination – they print everything they receive. As a test one press was sent a poem by Gerard Manley Hopkins, a cut-up from the *Daily Star*, jottings by a 7-year-old, and a piece assembled from overheard conversations in a launderette. The whole lot was accepted.

Variations and embellishments on the vanity press theme include offers to put your poetry to music, setting you off on the road to stardom, or readings of your verse by actors with deep voices to help you break into the local radio market (there isn't one), and further requests for cash to help pay for your collection in book form, usually bound in expensive leather with your name gold-blocked on the front. Don't pay a single penny. If a publisher asks you for money, forget it. This is not the way things should be done.

Subsidy Publishing

This is the half-legitimate brother of the vanity press. Here authors of completed books (often poets), help out the publisher by providing some (or all) of the initiation costs with the idea that they will subsequently share any profits. The system has a long history. Dickens did it, as did Jane Austen, and so too T. S. Eliot and R. S. Thomas. In the world of small presses it is common practice but potential participants should take care. Genuine self-publishing is almost always a cheaper alternative.

If you are approached for money in this context it is imperative that you check the publisher's credentials carefully. Look at their list and get in touch with one or more of their authors. Find out how the deal worked for them. Ask about reputations at your local library and bookshop. The kind of money involved can run into thousands.

The Listings

None of the lists of addresses which follow are exhaustive. Publishers come and go with amazing frequency. There will always be the brand new press on the lookout for talent and projected magazine desperate for contributions. For up-to-the-minute information check **Organisations of Interest To Poets** in the lists which follow. Poetry has a huge market. It pays to keep your ear to the ground.

Commercial Publishers with poetry on their lists

(For addresses, see **UK Publishers**.)
  Allardyce, Barnett, Publishers
  Blackstaff Press Ltd
  Marion Boyars Publishers Ltd
  Calder (Publications) Ltd

Canongate Publishing Ltd
Cassell
Chapman
André Deutsch Ltd
Edinburgh University Press
Faber & Faber Ltd
The Gay Men's Press (GMP) Publishers Ltd
Robert Hale Ltd
HarperCollins Publishers Ltd
Oxford University Press
Penguin Books Ltd
Random House Publishing Group Ltd
Chatto & Windus Ltd
Hutchinson Books
Reed International Books
Secker & Warburg
Scottish Academic Press
Skoob Books Publishing Ltd
Souvenir Press Ltd
Virago Press Ltd
Virgin Publishing
George Weidenfeld & Nicholson Ltd

The Specialists

Anvil Press Poetry Ltd *Peter Jay*, see **UK Publishers**

Bloodaxe Books Ltd *Neil Astley*, see **UK Publishers**

Carcenet Press *Michael Schmidt*, see **UK Pub;ishers**

Enitharmon Press *Stephen Stuart-Smith*, see **UK Publishers**

Littlewood Arc *John Killick*, see **Small Presses** (page 141)

Peterloo Poets *Harry Chambers*, 2 Kelly Gardens, Calstock, Cornwall PH8 9SA

Seren Books (formerly Poetry Wales Press) *Mick Felton*, Andmor House, Trewsfield Industrial Estate, Tondu Road, Bridgend CF3 4LJ

Small Poetry Presses

Aard Press see **Small Presses** (page 133)

The Ada Press *Andrew Hale*, 31 Ada Road, Canterbury, Kent CT1 3TS

Adelphi Press 4–6 Effie Road, London SW6 1TD

Agenda Editions *William Cookson/Peter Dale*, 5 Cranbourne Court, Albert Bridge Road, London SW11 4PE

AK Press see **Small Presses** (page 133)

Alembic Press see **Small Presses** (page 133)

Aloes *Jim Pennington*,69 Lancaster Rd, London N4 4PL

Alun Books *Sally Jones*, 3 Crown Street, Port Talbot, West Glamorgan

Amra Imprint see **Small Presses** (page 133)

BB Books see **Small Presses** (page 134)

Bedlam Press *David Moody*, Church Green House, Old Church Lane, Pateley Bridge, Harrogate HG3 5LZ

Big Little Poem Books *Robert Richardson*, 42 Peaksfield Avenue, Grimsby, South Humberside DN32 9QF

Blue Bridge Press *David Tipton*, 24 Aireville Road, Frizinhall, Bradford BD9 4HH

Bradgate Press 15 Court Farm Road, Warlingham, Surrey CR6 9BL

Brainwave Communications Hindburn House, Main Street, Wray, Lancs LA2 8QB

Brentham Press see **Small Presses** (page 135)

Businesslike Publishing see **Small Presses** (page 135)

Chrysalis Books *John Howard*, 12 Priory Road, Bruton, Somerset BA10 0DZ

CNP Publications see **Small Presses** (page 136)

Crescent Moon Publishing see **Small Presses** (page 136)

Curlew Press Hare Cottage, Kettlesing, Harrogate HG3 2LB

Dangaroo Books PO Box 186, Coventry CV4 7HG

Dark Diamond Publications see **Small Presses** (page 136)

Dedalus Poetry Press *John F. Deane*, 24 The Heath, Cypress Downs, Dublin 6

Diamond Press see **Small Presses** (page 136)

Dollar of Soul/Chicken Sigh Press *Owen Davis*, 15 Argyle Road, Swanage, Dorset BH19 1HZ

Dog and Bone Publishers 175 Queen Victoria Drive, Scotstown, Glasgow G12 9BP

Downlander Publishing *Derek Bourne-Jones*, 88 Oxenden Gardens, Lower Willingdon, Eastbourne, East Sussex BN22 0RS

Dragonfly Press see **Small Presses** (page 136)

Echo Room Press *Brendan Cleary*, 45 Bewick Court, Princess Street, Newcastle upon Tyne NE1 8EG

Eden Centre Books 38 Lee Rd, Lynton, Devon EX35 6BS

Ember Press *Patricia Oxley*, 6 The Mount, Furzeham, Brixham, Devon

Envoi Poets *Anne Lewis Smith*, 2 Penfordd, Newport, Dyfed SA42 0QT

Equofinality 147 Selly Oak Road, Bournville, Birmingham B30 1HN

Feather Books see **Small Presses** (page 137)

Ferry Press Bridges Farmhouse, Laughton, Lewes, East Sussex

Flambard Press 4 Mitchell Ave, Jesmond, Newcastle-upon-Tyne, NE2 3LA

Forest Books *Brenda Walker*, 20 Forest View, Chingford, London E4 7AY

Fox Press see **Small Presses** (page 138)

Galdragon Press 136 Byres Road, Glasgow G12 8TD

Gallery Press *Peter Fallon*, 19 Oakdown Road, Dublin 14

Gavarnie Publications *Val Fethney*, 41 Legion Way, East Wittering, Chichester, West Sussex PO20 8PP

Genera Editions *Colin Simms*, Temperance Farm, Halton Lea Gate, Carlisle, Cumbria CA6 7LB

Gild of St George 17 Hadassah Grove, Liverpool L17 8XH

Gomer Press *John Lewis*, Llandysul, Dyfed SA44 4BQ

Greville Press Emscote Lawn, Astborn, Warwick CV34 5QD

Greylag Press *Jim Vollmar*, 20 Grove Street, Higham Ferrars, Northants NN9 8HX

Gryphon Press 38 Prince Edward Rd, Lewes, Sussex BN7 1BE

Hangman Books *Billy Childish*, 32 May Road, Rochester, Kent ME1 2HY

Hard Pressed Poetry *Billy Mills*, 1st Floor, 80 Ashford Rd, Eastbourne BN21 3TE

Hastings Arts Pocket Press *Margaret E. Rose*, 25 St Mary's Terrace, Hastings, East Sussex TN34 3LS

Headland Publications 38 York Avenue, West Kirby, Wirral, Merseyside

Hearing Eye *John Rety*, Box 1, 99 Torriano Avenue, London NW5

Hippopotamus Press *Roland John*, 22 Whitewell Rd, Frome, Somerset BA11 4EZ

Hilltop Press see **Small Presses** (page 139)

Honno Ailsa Craig, Heol y Cawl, Dinas Powys, South Glamorgan

Hub Editions *Colin Blondell*, 9 The Ridgeway, Flitwick, Bedfordshire MK45 1DH

Indelible Inc see **Small Presses** (page 140)

Interim Press *Peter Dent*, 3 Thornton Close, Budleigh Salterton, Devon EX9 6PJ

International Concrete Poetry Archive *Paula Claire*, 11 Dale Close, Thames Street, Oxford OX1 1TU

Iron Press *Peter Mortimer*, 5 Marden Terrace, Cullercoats, North Shields, Tyne and Wear NE30 4PD

Jackson's Arm Press *Michael Blackburn*, PO Box 74, Lincoln LN1 1QC

Jane Publishing 23 Bright Street, York YO2 4XS

Katabasis *Dinah Livingstone*, 10 St Martin's Close, London NW1 0HR

KQBX *James Sale*, 30 Fitzroy Avenue, Luton LU3 1RS

KRAX 63 Dixon Lane, Wortley, Leeds LS12 4RR

K.T. Publications 16 Fane Close, Stamford, Lincolnshire PE9 1HG

Kwemarabak Publications 77 Mary Datchelor Close, Camberwell, London SE5 7DY

Larklane Poetry Books 80 Lark Lane, Liverpool L17 BU4

Leaves/Scales PO Box 664, London E5 0JW

Lobby Press *Richard Tabor*, 1 Dairy Cottages, Compton Road, Yeovil, Somerset BA22 7EZ

Lomond Press *R. L. Cook*, 4 Whitecraigs, Kinneswood, Kinross, Scotland KY13 7JN

Lymes Press Greenfields, Agger Hill, Finrey Green, Newcastle, Staffordshire ST5 6AA

Magenta Press *Maggie O'Sullivan*, Middle Fold Farm, Colden, Heptonstall, West Yorkshire HX7 7PG

Mammon Press *Fred Beake*, 12 Dartmouth Avenue, Bath, Avon BA2 1AT

Manchester Poets *Dave Tarrant*, 122 Petersburg Road, Edgeley Park, Stockport, Cheshire SK3 9RB

Manderville Press *Peter Scupham/John Mole*, 2 Taylor's Hill, Hitchin, Hertfordshire

Mannamead Press *Geoff Holland*, 77A Mannamead Road, Mannamead, Plymouth PL3 4SX

The Many Press *John Welch*, 15 Northcott Road, London N16 7BJ

Mariscat Press *Hamish Whyte*, 3 Mariscat Road, Glasgow G41 4ND

Menard Press *Anthony Rudolf*, 8 The Oaks, Woodside Avenue, London N12 8AR

Merseyside Poetry Circuit *Dave Calder*, 38 Canning Street, Liverpool L8 7NP

Microbridgade *Ulli Freer*, 74 Lodge Lane, Finchley Park, London N12 8JJ

Midnag Publications Northumberland Technical College, College Road, Ashington, Northumberland NE63 9RG

Morning Star Publications *Alec Finlay*, 14 Clerk Street, Edinburgh EH8 9MX

Mother Tongue Publishing Co-op Carlton-Bolling College, Undercliffe Lane, Bradford BD3 0DJ

New Beacon Books 76 Stroud Green Road, London N7 5EN

New Broom Private Press *Toni Savage*, 78 Cambridge Street, Leicester LE3 0JP

New River Project Unit P8, Metropolitan College of Craftsmen, Enfield Road, London N1 5AZ

North and South *Peterjon Skelt*, 23 Egerton Road, Twickenham, Middlesex TW2 7SL

Northern House 19 Haldane Terrace, Newcastle upon Tyne NE2 3AN

Oasis Books *Ian Robinson*, 12 Stevenage Road, London SW6 6ES

Oscars Press *Peter Daniels*, BM Oscars, London WC1N 3XX

Overdue Books *Jan Maloney*, 37 Melbourne Street, Hebden Bridge, West Yorkshire HX7 6AS

Overdrawn Books 63 Gordon Road, Enfield, Middlesex EN2 0PZ

P.B.B. *Paul Beasley*, 57 Effingham Road, London SE12 8NJ

Paranoia Press see **Small Presses** (page 142)

Peepal Tree Books see **Small Presses** (page 143)

Permanent Press *Rbt Vas Dias*, 108 Hemingford Road, London N1 1DE

Phoenix Press *Bruce Barnes*, 19a Marriott Road, London N4 3QN

Pig Press *Ric Caddel*, 7 Cross View Terrace, Neville's Cross, Durham DH1 4JY

Poetical Histories 27 Sturton Street, Cambridge CB1 2QC

Poetry Business see **Small Presses** (page 143)

Poetry Now 2–3 Wilfric Square, North Bretton, Peterborough PE3 8RF

Portlight Press 53 Knutsford Drive, Belfast BT14

Prebendal Press PO Box 30, Thame, Oxon OX9 3AD

Prest Roots Press *P.E. Larkin*, 34 Alpine Court, Kenilworth CV8 2GP

Previous Parrot Press See **Small Presses** (page 143)

Primitive Poetry Press *Ruskin Watts*, The Cottage, Longnor, Near Buxton SK17 0LA

Purple Heather Publications *Richard Mason*, 16 Rokeby Gardens, Headingley, Leeds LS6 3JS

Queen-Spark Books see **Small Presses** (page 144)

Raven Arts *Dermot Bolger*, PO Box 1430, Finglas, Dublin 11

Reality Studios 4 Howard Court, Peckham Rye, London SE15 3PH

Red Candle Press 9 Milner Road, Wisbech PE13 2LR

Red Sharks Press *Christopher Mills*, 122 Clive Street, Grangetown, Cardiff CF1 7JE

Redbeck Press *David Tipton*, 24 Aireville Road, Frizinghall, Bradford BD9 4HH

Re-Verb *Paul A Green*, 5 Sycamore Grove, New Maldon, Surrey, KT3 3DN

Rivelin Grapheme Press *Snowdon Barnett*, The Annex, Kennet House, 19 High Street, Hungerford, Berkshire RG17 0NL

Rockingham Press 11 Musley Lane, Ware, Hertfordshire SG12 7EN

Satis *Malcolm Rutherford*, 14 Greenhill Place, Edinburgh EH10 4BR

Satori Books 27 Court Leet, Brinley Woods, Coventry

Satori Press 149 Bower St, Bedford MA40 3RA

Ship of Fools *Robert Sheppard*, 239 Lessingham Avenue, London SW17 8NQ

Slow Dancer Press *John Harvey*, 58 Rutland Rd, Bridgford, Nottingham NG2 5DG

Smith/Doorstop see **Small Presses** (page 145)

Solaris 23 Egerton Rd, Twickenham, Middlesex TW2 7SL

Spanner *Allen Fisher*, 14 Hopton Road, Hereford HR1 1BE

Spectacular Diseases *Paul Green*, 83B London Road, Peterborough PE2 9BS

Stingy Artist/Last Straw Press 8 Chelmsford Street, Weymouth, Dorset DT4 7HR

Street Editions *Wendy Mulford*, 31 Panton Street, Cambridge CB2 1HL

Stride see **Small Presses** (page 146)

Swansea Poetry Workshop 124 Overland Road, Mumbles, Swansea SA3 4EU

Sycamore Press *John Fuller*, 4 Benson Place, Oxford OX2 6QM

Taurus Press of Willow Dene *Paul Peter Piech*, 11 Limetree Way, Danygraig, Porthcawl, Mid Glamorgan CF36 5AU

Taxus Press see **Stride, Small Presses** (page 146)

Torque Press *Peter Middleton*, 43 Kirigston Street, Cambridge CB1 2NU

Tuba Press *Peter Ellison*, Tunley Cottage, Tunley, Near Cirencester, Gloucestershire GL7 6LW

Turret Books *Bernard Stone*, 42 Lamb's Conduit Street, London WC1N 3LJ

Underground Press 9 Lanelay Tce, Maesycoed, Pontypridd

Vigil Publications *John Howard*, 12 Priory Road, Bruton, Somerset BA10 0DZ

Wellsweep Press *John Cayley*, 719 Fulham Road, London SW6 5UL

The Wide Skirt Press *Geoff Hattersley*, 28 St Helen's Street, Elsecar, Barnsley, S. Yorks S74 8BH

Word and Action (Dorset) Ltd 43 Avenue Road, Wimborne, Dorset BH21 1BS

Writers Forum *Bob Cobbing*, 89A Petherton Road, London N5 2QT

Zena Publications Croesor, Gwynedd LL48 6SR

Zora Press PO Box 33, Kingsland High Street, London E8 2NF

Little Magazines

Acumen see **Magazines**

Agenda *William Cookson*, 5 Cranbourne Court, Albert Bridge Road, London SW11 4PE

Agog *Ed Jewasinski*, 116 Eswyn Road, Tooting, London SW17 8JN

Aireings 24 Brudenell Road, Leeds LS6 1BD

Ambit see **Magazines**

Aquarius *Eddie S. Linden*, Flat 10, 116 Sutherland Avenue, London W9

Bare Wires The Basement, Station Road, Bolton-on-Dearne, Rotherham S63 8JB

Bête Noire *John Osborne*, Dept of American Studies, The University of Hull, Cottingham Road, Hull HU6 7RX

Bogg *George Cairncross*, 31 Belle Vue Street, Filey, Yorkshire YO14 9HU

Borderlines *Dave Bingham*, 20 Hodgebower, Ironbridge TF8 7QG

The Bound Spiral Open Poetry Conventicle, 72 First Avenue, Bush Hill Park, Enfield EN1 1BW

Bradford Poetry Quarterly *Clare Chapman*, 9 Woodvale Road, Bradford BD7 2SJ

The Bridge 112 Rutland Street, Grimsby, South Humberside DN32 7NF

Briggistane *Shetland Arts Trust*, 22–24 North Road, Lerwick, Shetland

Calliope Women's Writing 53 Wyndham Road, Canton, Cardiff

Cencrastus 34 Queen Street, Edinburgh EH2 1JX

Chapman *Joy M. Hendry*, see **Magazines**

Chester Poets *Dr P. Higson*, 1 Westlands Avenue, Newcastle, Staffordshire

Clanjam Frie *Giles Sutherland*, Blairlogie Cottage, Blairlogie, Stirling FK9 5PX

Cobweb *Peter Kenny*, 7 Isis Court, Grove Park Road, London W4 3SA

Cyphers *Pearse Hutchinson*, 3 Selskar Tee, Ranelagh, Dublin 6

Distaff *Jennifer Brice*, c/o London Women's Centre, Wesley House, 4 Wild Court, Kingsway, London WC2

A Doctor's Dilemma *Peter Godfrey*, Flat 3, 32 Brunswick Terrace, Hove, East Sussex BN3 1JH

The Echo Room *Brendan Cleary*, 45 Bewick Court, Princess Street, Newcastle upon Tyne NE1 8EG

Ecuatorial *Will Rowe*, Dept of Spanish, Kings College, Strand, London WC2 2LS

Envoi *Roger Elkin*, 44 Rudyard Road, Biddulph Moor, Stoke-on-Trent ST8 7JN

Exile *Herbert Marr*, 38 Emerald Street, Saltburn-by-the-Sea, Cleveland TS12 1ED

Figs *Tony Baker*, 1 The Flats, East Bank, Winster, Derbyshire

First Offense *Tim Fletcher*, Syringa, The Street, Stodmarsh, Canterbury, Kent CT3 4BA

First Time *Josephine Austin*, 4 Burdett Place, George Street, Hastings TN34 3ED

Five Leaves Left 16 Rokeby Gardens, Headingley, Leeds LS6 3JS

Folded Sheets 14 Foster Clough, Heights Road, Hebden Bridge, West Yorkshire HX7 5QZ

Foolscap *Judi Benson*, 78 Friars Road, East Ham, London E6 1LL

Fragmente *Andrew Lawson/Anthony Mellors*, 9 Hertford Street, Oxford OX4 3AJ

The Frogmore Papers *Jeremy Page*, 42 Morehall Avenue, Folkestone, Kent CT19 4EF

Gairfish *W.N.Herbert*, 45 Hazelwood Road, Bridge-of-Weir, Strathclyde PA11 3DX

Gallery *Valerie Sinason*, 3 Honeybourne Road, London NW6 1HH

Global Tapestry Journal *Dave Cunliffe*, 1 Springbank, Longsight Road, Salebury, Blackburn, Lancashire BB1 9EU

The Green Book 49 Park Street, Bristol BS1 5NT

Haiku Quarterly *Kevin Bailey*, 39 Exmouth St, Swindon SN1 3PU

Hat *Ian Hogg*, 1A Church Lane, Croft, Near Skegness, Lincolnshire

The Honest Ulsterman 159 Lower Braniel Road, Belfast BT5 1NN

Illuminations *Simon Lewis*, Ryde School, Queens Road, Ryde, Isle of Wight

Impressions 84 Colwyn Road, Northampton NN1 3PX

Inkshed *Anthony Smith*, Flat 4, 387 Beverly Road, Hull HU5 1LF

Inverse *George Wickes*, 41 Finborough Road, Stowmarket, Suffolk IP14 1PS

Iota *David Holliday*, 67 Hady Crescent, Chesterfield, Derbyshire SH1 0EB

Irish Review *Kevin Barry*, Cork University Press, University College, Cork, Eire

Iron *Peter Mortimer*, 5 Marden Terrace, Cullercoats, North Shields, Tyne and Wear NE30 4PD

Issue One *Ian Brocklebank*, 2 Tewkesbury Drive, Grimsby, South Humberside DN34 4TL

Joe Soap's Canoe *Martin Stannard*, 30 Quiller Road, Felixstowe, Suffolk IP11 7JJ

Krax *Andy Robson*, 63 Dixon Lane, Leeds LS12 4RR

Krino The Paddocks, Glenrevagh, Corrandulla, Co. Galway, Eire

Kunapipi PO Box 186, Coventry CV4 7HG

Label *Paul Beasley*, 57 Effingham Road, Lee Green, London SE12 8NT

Lines Review Macdonald Publishing, Edgefield Road, Loanhead, Midlothian EH20 9SY

London Magazine see **Magazines**

Mar Flat 1, 81 Back Road East, St Ives, Cornwall

Memes *Norman Jope*, 38 Molesworth Road, Plympton, Plymouth, Devon PL7 4NT

Momentum *Jeff Bell*, Glan Lynn, Glyn Ceiriog, Llangollen, Clwyd LL20 7AB

Moonstone *Talitha Clare*, BM Moonstone, London WC1N 3XX

Naked City *Dee Rimband*, 27 Castle Street, Edinburgh EH2 3DN

New Departures *Mike Horovitz*, Piedmont, Bisley, Stroud, Gloucestershire GL6 7BU

New Hope International *Gerald England*, 20 Werneth Avenue, Gee Cross, Hyde, Cheshire SK14 5NL

New Welsh Review *Robin Reeves*, Room 1-8, 49 Park Place, Cardiff

The North see **Magazines**

North Magazine *John Hughes*, 10 Stranmillis Park, Belfast BT9 5AY

Northlight 136 Byres Road, Glasgow G12 8TD

Nutshell *Tom Roberts*, 12 Canal Buildings, Leicester Row, Coventry CV1 2LH

Oasis *Alan Robinson*, 12 Stevenage Road, London SW6 6ES

Odyssey Coleridge Cottage, Nether Stowey, Somerset

Orbis see **Magazines**

Ore *Eric Ratcliffe*, 7 The Towers, Stevenage, Hertfordshire SG1 1HE

Ostinato PO Box 522, London N8 7SZ

Otter Parford Cottage, Chegford, Newton Abbot, Devon

Outposts *Roland John*, 22 Whitewell Road, Frome, Somerset BA11 4EL

Oxford Poetry Magdalen College, Oxford OX1 4AU

Paraphernalia *Harvey Doctors*, 41 Maynard Road, Walthamstow, London E17 9JE

Pen: umbra *David Rushmer*, 1 Beeches Close, Saffron Walden, Essex CB11 4BU

Pennine Ink *J. McEvoy*, c/o MPAA, The Gallery Downstairs, Yorke Street, Burnley, Lancashire

Pennine Platform *Brian Merrikin Hill*, Ingmanthorpe Hall Farm Cottage, Wetherby, West Yorkshire LS22 5EQ

The People's Poetry *P.G.P. Thompson*, 71 Harrow Crescent, Romford, Essex RM3 7BJ

People to People West Midlands Arts, 82 Granville Street, Birmingham B1 2LH

Planet *John Barnie*, PO Box 44, Aberystwyth, Dyfed

PN Review *Michael Schmidt*, 208–212 Corn Exchange Buildings, Manchester M4 3BQ

Poetica *Anthony Barnett*, 14 Mount Street, Lewes, East Sussex BN7 1HL

Poetry and Audience *Jonathan Ward*, School of English, University of Leeds, Leeds LS2 9JT

Poetry Durham *Michael O'Neill*, Dept of English, University of Durham, Elvet Riverside, New Elvet, Durham DH1 3JT

Poetry Ireland Review *John Ennis*, 44 Upper Mount Street, Dublin 2

Poetry Nottingham Summer Cottage, West Street, Shelford, Notts NG12 1EJ

Poetry Review see **Magazines**

Poetry World 69 King George Street, London SE10 8PX

Poets Voice *Fred Beake*, 12 Dartmouth Avenue, Bath, Avon BA2 1AT

Printer's Devil S.E. Arts, 10 Mount Ephraim, Tunbridge Wells, Kent TN4 8AS

Psychopoetica *Geoff Lowe*, Dept of Psychology, University of Hull, Hull HU6 7RX

Quartos Magazine see **Magazines**

Quest 69 Thackarey Road, Bradford, W. Yorks BD10 0JR

Renaissance 10 Argyle Gardens, Upminster, Essex

Rhinoceros Flat 3, 90 University St, Belfast

The Rialto *John Wakeman*, 32 Grosvenor Road, Norwich NR2 2PZ

Roads 49 Meynell Heights, Leeds LS11 9PY

Salmon Literary Magazine Auburn House, Upper Fairhill, Galway, Eire

Salopoet 6 Avondale, Lawly Bank, Telford, Shropshire TF4 2LW

Scratch *Mark Robinson*, 24 Nelson Street, The Groves, York YO3 7NJ

Shearsman *Tony Frazer*, 47 Dayton Close, Plymouth PL6 5DX

Slow Dancer *John Harvey*, 58 Rutland Road, Bridgford, Nottingham NG2 5DG

Smiths Knoll *Roy Blackman* and *Michael Laskey*, 46 Glebe Way, Burnham-on-Crouch, Essex CM0 8QJ

Smoke *Dave Ward*, 40 Canning Street, Liverpool L8 7NP

Sol 44 Station Road, Rayleigh, Essex SS6 7HL

South 43 Avenue Road, Wimborne, Dorset BH21 1BS

Spectacular Diseases *Paul Green*, 83B London Road, Peterborough, Cambridge PE2 9BS

Spokes *Donald Atkinson*, The Orchard House, 45 Clophill Road, Upper Gravenhurst, Bedford MK45 4JH

Stand Magazine see **Magazines**

Staple Magazine *Bob Windsor*, Gilderoy East, Upper Wood Road, Matlock Bath, Derbys DE4 3PD

Sunk Island Review see **Magazines**

Swansea Review University College Swansea, Singleton Park, Swansea SA2 8PP

Tak Tak Tak PO Box 7, Bulwell, Nottingham NG6 0HW

Tears in the Fence *David Caddy*, 38 Hod View, Stourpaine, Near Blandford Forum, Dorset DT11 8TN

Tees Valley Writer see **Magazines**

Tenth Decade 12 Stevenage Road, London SW6

10th Muse 33 Hartington Road, Southampton, Hants SO2 0EW

The Third Half *Kevin Troop*, 16 Fane Close, Stamford, Lincolnshire PE9 1HG

Understanding 20A Montgomery Street, Edinburgh EH7 5JS

Verse *Robert Crawford*, Dept of English, The University, St Andrews, Fife KY16 9AL

Verse, (Glasgow) Dept of English Literature, University of Glasgow G12 8QQ

Vision *Louis Foley*, 32 Gilchrist Avenue, Corby, Northamptonshire NN17 1BA

West Coast Magazine *Kenny Mackenzie*, Dolphin Arts Centre, 7 James Street, Bridgeton, Glasgow G40 1BZ

Westwords *Dave Woolley*, 15 Trelawney Road, Peverell, Plymouth, Devon PL3 4JS

Weyfarers *Margaret Pain*, Hilltop Cottage, 9 Whiterose Lane, Woking, Surrey GU22 7JA

The White Rose Literary Magazine *Nancy Whybrow*, 14 Browning Road, Temple Hill, Dartford, Kent DA1 5ET

The Wide Skirt *Geoff Hattersley*, 28 St Helen's St, Elsacar, Barnsley, S. Yorks S74 8BH

Working Titles see **Magazines**

Writer's Rostrum see **Magazines**

Writers' Own Magazine *Eileen M. Pickering*, 121 Highbury Grove, Clapham, Bedford MK41 6DU

Writing Women 10 Mistletoe Road, Newcastle upon Tyne NE2 2DX

Organisations of Interest to Poets 1993

A survey of some of the societies, groups and other bodies in the UK which may be of interest to practising poets. Organisations not listed should send details of themselves to the editor to facilitate inclusion in future editions.

Apples & Snakes Unit A11, Hatcham Mews Business Centre, Hatcham Mews Park, London SE14 5QA (Tel 081–639 9656). A unique, independent promotional organisation for poetry and poets – promoting poetry as an innovative and popular medium and as a vital community and cross-cultural activity. A&S organises an annual programme of over 150 events including tours, residencies and festivals and operates a Poets in Education Scheme and a non-profit booking agency for poets. Contacts are *Paul Beasley & Ruth Harrison*.

The Association of Little Presses See **Professional Associations**.

The Arvon Foundation See **Professional Associations**.

The British Haiku Society formed in 1990 promotes the appreciation and writing within the British Isles of haiku, senyru, tanka and renga, by way of tutorials, workshops, exchange of poems, critical comment and information. It publishes a quarterly journal, *Blithe Spirit*, and administers the annual James W. Hackett Award for haiku. Secretary is *David Cobb*, Sinodun, Shalford, Braintree, Essex CM7 5HN (Tel 0371 851097).

European Association for the Promotion of Poetry is situated at European Poetry House 'The Seven Sleepers', Coutereelstraat 76, B–3000 Leuven, Belgium and is the home of the European Poetry Library and Centre for Research, Translation and Documentation, obviously the place for us all now we are fully fledged Europeans. The Association works in at least four European languages, runs the annual European Poetry Festival at Leuven, administers the **European Prize for the Translation of Poetry** as well as publishing bi-lingual volumes of European poets and a poetry magazine *Pi*. Membership costs 1000 BF.

Federation of Worker Writers and Community Publishers See **Professional Associations**.

The Little Magazine Collection and Poetry Store housed at University College London Library, are the fruits of Geoffrey Soar and David Miller's interest in UK alternative publishing with a strong emphasis on poetry. The Little Mags Collection runs to over 3000 titles mainly in the more experimental and avant-garde areas. The Poetry Store consists of over 6000 small press items, mainly from the sixties onwards, again with some stress on experimental work. In addition there are reprints of classic earlier little magazines, from *Symbolism* through to the present. Anyone who is interested can consult the collections, and it helps if you have some idea of what you want to see. Bring evidence of identity for a smooth ride. The collections can be accessed by visiting the Manuscripts and Rare Books Room at University College in Gower Street, London WC1E 6BT between 10.00 am and 5.00 pm on weekdays (Tel 071–380 7796). Most items are available on inter-library loans.

The National Convention of Poets and Small Presses An accessible, some might say disorganised, weekend jamboree of writers and poetry publishers held at a different venue each year. The amateur status of the event is undisputed but it can be good fun for those with enough stamina to last out the marathon readings. There is no central organising committee – bids to host future conventions being made in person at the event itself. So far it has visited Liverpool, Hastings, Corby, Dartford, Stamford, Norwich and North Shields. For information on the next Convention contact *Derrick Woolf*, Odyssey Magazine, Coleridge Cottage, Nether Stowey, Somerset TA5 1NQ.

Northern Arts Poetry Library Free membership open to residents of Northumberland, Durham, Tyne and Wear, Cleveland and Cumbria. Associate membership is available to residents of Scotland. Housed at the County Central Library, The Willows, Morpeth, Northumberland NE61 1TA, the collection has over 12,000 volumes including virtually all poetry published in the UK since 1968. Loans may be made by post.

National Poetry Foundation is the rather grand sounding title for the poetry organisation run by *Jonathon Clifford* from 27 Mill Road, Fareham, Hants PO16 0TH (Tel 0329 822218). With the financial assistance of Rosemary Arthur who has so far put £20,000 into the kitty, the NPF attempts to encourage new writers through a criticism scheme and a series of rather well produced poetry books. Membership costs £16 which in addition gives subscribers access to *Pause*, the organisation's internal magazine. The NPF has a strong interest in the professional poetry recital as a fund raising device for the furtherance of its work. Eight small mags and a number of individual poets have to date benefited from NPF financial aid. Grants are small, unrenewable and directed at that sector of the poetry community traditionally ignored by other bodies.

Oriel Bookshop The Friary, Cardiff. Owned and run by the **Welsh Arts Council**. Publishes at regular intervals *Small Presses and Little Magazines of the UK and Ireland – An Address List*, specialises in twentieth century poetry, operates a mail order service, runs a critical service for writers, hosts poetry readings and provides information on local competitions, workshops, groups and literary activities.

The Poetry Association of Scotland Formerly the Scottish Association for the Speaking of Verse, founded in 1924 by John Masefield. Current President: *Norman MacCaig*, Secretary: *Robin Bell*. Promotes poetry through readings and related activities from its headquarters at 38 Dovecot Road, Edinburgh EH12 7LE.

The Poetry Bookshop run by *Allen Halsey* from 22 Broad Street, Hay-on-Wye HR3 5DB (Tel 0497 820305). Holds a large stock of modern and contemporary poetry – British, Irish, American, translations, concrete, etc, – mostly second-hand but including some new small press material and poetry magazines. Deals extensively by post and produces a regular catalogue.

The Poetry Book Society Can't choose? This is one way to increase your reading of mainstream poetry. For an annual fee of £24 members receive a quarterly new volume of verse, selected by experts, an annual anthology and a quarterly bulletin. Members are also able to buy from a vast selection of PBS Recommendations, all at reduced prices. If that's not enough membership 'B' costing £105, will bring you 21 new books annually. Write to PBS manager, *Martha Smart*, at 10 Barley Mow Passage, London W4 4PH.

The Poetry Business is a resource centre run by *Peter Sansom* and *Janet Fisher* from 51 Byram Arcade, Westgate, Huddersfield HD1 1ND (Tel 0484 434840). The Business operates a small bookshop, a critical reading service, runs competitions (see **Poetry Business Competition** under **Prizes**) and organises monthly writing Saturdays. Publishes *The North* magazine and books, pamphlets and cassettes under the Smith/Doorstop imprint. Send for their catalogues.

Poetry Ireland 44 Upper Mount Street, Dublin 2 (Tel 01 610320). The national Irish poetry organisation, supported by both Arts Councils in Ireland. It publishes a quarterly magazine, *Poetry Ireland Review*, offers poetry books at reduced prices to members, produces a bi-monthly newsletter of upcoming events and competitions, as well as organising tours and readings by Irish and foreign poets. Administers the Austin Clark Library, a collecton of over 6000 volumes. Director is *Theo Dorgan*; Administrator is *Niamh Morris*.

The Poetry Library see **Library Services**

Poetry Listing compiled by *David Hart*. An annual publication which attempts with admirable success to list and comment on the whole panoply of available, contemporary English language poetry worldwide. The survey is total, not limiting itself to the recently published. The result is doubly useful. Issues 1–4 so far still available. Copies cost £2.90 from Wood Wind Publications, 42 All Saints Road, Kings Heath, Birmingham B14 7LL.

Poetry London Newsletter A publication for and about poetry activity in the capital. Quarterly it surveys all current poetry groups, listing specialisms; runs articles on funding, how to start your own group, how to put on a reading etc, as well as features on major poets, examples of work and reviews of little and mainstream poetry presses. Invaluable at £10 for four issues. Write to *Leon Cych* at 26 Clacton Road, London E17 8AR.

The Poetry Society, at 22 Betterton Street, London WC2H 9BU (Tel 071–240 4810). Founded in 1909 which ought to make it venerable. Centre of the poetry universe for some, a total anathema for others. The PoSoc is the poetry world's answer to the Royal National Theatre. In the UK we value our verse far less than our orchestras – the Society has to scrape its way by. It does sterling work nonetheless. Current activities include:

- A national events programme incorporating tours, one-off events and co-operation with Britain's many literature festivals.

- A quarterly magazine of new verse, views and criticism, *Poetry Review*, edited by Peter Forbes.

- An advice and information service offering a wide range of help to both the public and those working with poetry. Also produces the Poetry Society Newsletter.

- The Poetry Society Education Department, now run in conjunction with the Schools' Poetry Association, offering a termly journal, *School's Poetry Review*, newsletters, an information and support service, regular competitions, courses for teachers and discounts on the Society INSET scheme. In addition the Society offers a Poets in Schools Scheme, sponsored by W.H.Smith, designed to encourage young people to write and enjoy poetry.

- A critical service which provides detailed reports on submitted work. Current charges are £25 per 200 lines (cheaper for members).

- Spoken poetry and prose examinations taken by 1000s of young people annually.

- Competitions and awards including the annual **National Poetry Competition** with a first prize of £1000.

Society Chairman: *Sebastian Barker*. Director and General Secretary: *Chris Green*. Membership costs £22 (London) or £18 (elsewhere).

Quartos Magazine (see **Magazines**) – 'bi-monthly magazine for creative writers'. Subscription £12 from BCM-Writer, 27 Old Gloucester Street, London WC1N 3XX. A reliable source of information on poetry competitions.

Regional Arts Boards For full list of addresses see page 513. Most are of invaluable interest to poets as a source of information on local activities, poetry groups, competitions, publications, readings and creative writing weekends.

Many publish a magazine of their own, a number run critical services for writers. Some provide fellowships for poets, paying for school visits or for poet's workshops to be established. Service varies from region to region depending on demand and the influence and interest of the local literature officer.

Schools' Poetry Association see **Poetry Society** above.

Scottish Poetry Library see **Library Services**.

Small Press Group of Britain see **Professional Associations**.

Ty Newydd run by the Taliesin Trust, an independent, Arvon-style residential writing centre at Llanystumdwy, Criccieth, Gwynedd LL52 0LW in North Wales. Courses have a strong poetry content. Fees start at £96 for weekends and £196 for week courses. Tutors to date have included Tony Curtis, Gillian Clarke, Fleur Adcock, Wendy Cope, Robert Minhinnick, Carol Ann Duffy and Anne Stevenson. (Also see **Writers Courses, Circles & Workshops**.)

Small Presses

'As a direct result of being listed in your Handbook last year we have been offered several very interesting manuscripts and hope to publish these in the coming year.'

Colin Stanley, Paupers' Press

Aard Press

c/o Aardverx, 31 Mountearl Gardens,
London SW16 2NL

Managing Editor *D. Jarvis*

FOUNDED 1971. *Publishes* experimental or visual poetry, artists' bookworks, comix, thrillers, 'zines', ephemera and documents mail-art projects. TITLES *I, Jade Green; Jade's Ladies; Jade AntiJade* (thrillers); *Phoedra Kelly; Dawn Redwood; Petal Jeffrey* (collected poems); *PunKomik* (mail-art); *Eos.* No unsolicited material or proposals. *Royalties* not paid.

AK Press/AKA Books

3 Balmoral Place, Stirling FK8 2RD

Managing Editor *Ramsey Kanaan*

AK Press grew out of the activities of AK Distribution which distributes a wide range of radical (anarchist, feminist, etc.) literature (books, pamphlets, periodicals, magazines), both fiction and non-fiction. Long-term goal is to have some sort of high-street retail outlet for radical material. *Publishes* politics, history, situationist, fiction and poetry in both book and pamphlet form. TITLES *Terrorising the Neighbourhood* Noam Chomsky; *Poll Tax Rebellion* Danny Burns; *Leonard's Shorter Catechism* Tom Leonard; *The Bigger Tory Vote: The Covert Sequestration of the Bigotry Vote* Nick Toczek. 12 titles in 1992/3. Unsolicited mss, proposals and synopses welcome provided they fall specifically within the above areas of interest. *Royalties* paid.

Richard Alan Publications

118 Watling Street, Grendon, Atherstone,
Warwickshire CV9 2PE
℡ 0827 713360

Managing Editor *Dr Alan Barnes*

FOUNDED 1990. *Publishes* books about historic musical instruments mainly, particularly church organs, chamber organs in stately homes, etc. TITLES *The 18th Century Chamber Organ in Kedleston Hall, Derbyshire; The 1777 Chamber*

Organ by John Snetzler in Merevale Church. 2 titles in 1991. No unsolicited mss; synopses and ideas for books welcome. *Payment* flat fee.

The Alembic Press

139 Upper Road, Oxford OX1 5LR
℡ 0865 730381   Fax 0865 327368

Owner *Claire Bolton*

FOUNDED 1976. Self-publisher of hand-produced books by traditional letterpress methods. Short print runs. *Publishes* bibliography, book arts and printing, miniatures and occasional poetry. TITLES *Maziarczyk Paste Papers; A Winchester Bookshop & Bindery; The Alembic Press Guide; Some Cats Help!; Awa Gami.* No unsolicited mss, ideas or proposals. 5 titles in 1991.

Amra Imprint

21 Alfred Street, Seaham, Co. Durham SR7 7LH
℡ 091-581 6738

Managing Editor *Bill Griffiths*

FOUNDED 1990 to continue an earlier series issued in the early 1970s called Pirate Press. *Publishes* modern poetry, Anglo-Saxon studies and local history. TITLES *A User-Friendly Dictionary of Old English* ed. Bill Griffiths; *Metrical Cookery* Bill Griffiths; *Anglo-Saxon Times; The Patrick Poems* Ian Davidson. 6 titles in 1991. No unsolicited mss, synopses or ideas. *Royalties* not paid.

Apparition Press

See **Stride**

Atlas Press

BCM Atlas Press, London WC1N 3XX

Managing Editor *Alastair Brotchie*

FOUNDED 1983. *Publishes* prose translations from French and German. TITLES include *Selected Works of Raymond Roussel* and *Aurora* Michel Leiris. 12

titles in 1991. Interested in translations of 19th and 20th century writers only. Do not send unsolicited mss; write first.
Royalties paid.

Aussteiger Publications
8 Back Skipton Road, Barnoldswick, Lancashire BB8 5NE
℡ 0282 812741

Managing Editor *John Leonard Dixon*

FOUNDED 1990. *Publishes* historical and archaeological walking guides and historical town/area guides. Through the medium of walking, Aussteiger aims to bring the neglected economic and social history of the North of England to the fore in its 'journeys of exploration'. TITLES *Historic Walks Around the Pendle Way; The Forest of Bowland; Journeys Through Brigantia, Vols 1-7.* 1 title in 1991. All work is commissioned. Synopses and ideas welcome.
Royalties not paid (10% of trade price).

M. & M. Baldwin
24 High Street, Cleobury Mortimer, Near Kidderminster, Worcestershire DY14 8BY
℡ 0299 270110

Managing Editor *Dr Mark Baldwin*

FOUNDED 1978. *Publishes* local interest and history, and inland waterways books. TITLES *Idle Women; Tom Rolt & The Cressy Years; Voyage in a Bowler Hat; Cleobury Mortimer: The Past in Pictures.* 1 title in 1991. Unsolicited mss, synopses and ideas for books welcome.
Royalties paid.

Barton House Publishing
9 Barton Orchard, Bradford on Avon, Wiltshire BA15 1LU
℡ 02216 7705   Fax 02216 7763

Managing Editor *Jane Chrzanowska*

FOUNDED 1990. *Publishes* New Age titles, holistic health, metaphysics, and mind, body and spirit. TITLES *The Wind of Change; The Cosmic Dance* Julie Soskin. 3 titles in 1991. Unsolicited mss welcome. Not interested in synopses or ideas which have not yet been developed.
Royalties paid.

BB Books
Spring Bank, Longsight Road, Copster Green, Blackburn, Lancashire BB1 9EU
℡ 0254 249128

Managing Editor *Dave Cunliffe*

FOUNDED 1962 as Screeches Publications, a platform for 'an emergent literary counter-culture and a voice for the Sixties British poetry renaissance'. Published *The New British Poetry* in 1965. *Poetmeat* magazine and collections of UK, European and North American poetry were what established the press in the mid 1960s. Today it is funded from a variety of sources on which it depends to effect its publishing programme. A non-commercial literary press publishing mainly post-Beat-orientated writing, plus a small number of poetry pamphlets a year, and *Global Tapestry* magazine. TITLES *Love Juice* (transformations from Ikkyu's Chinese poetry, with calligraphy and paintings); *Here We Go* (poetry celebration of soccer); *Garden World* (folio of prints by the celebrated anarchist painter Arthur Moyse). Unsolicited mss, synopses and ideas for books welcome.
Royalties not paid (authors get 10% of print-run).

The Book Castle
12 Church Street, Dunstable, Bedfordshire LU5 4RU
℡ 0582 605670   Fax 0582 662431

Managing Editor *Paul Bowes*

FOUNDED 1986. Principally a retail bookseller but proprietor's previous experience in publishing led to the formation of a small press in 1985. *Publishes* non-fiction, mostly of local interest (Bedfordshire, Hertfordshire, Buckinghamshire, Northamptonshire, the Chilterns). TITLES *North Chilterns Camera; Whipsnade — My Africa; Journeys into Bedfordshire; John Bunyan.* Unsolicited mss, synopses and ideas for books welcome. 6 titles in 1991.
Royalties paid.

Bozo
BM Bozo, London WC1N 3XX
℡ 0234 211606

Managing Editor *John Nicholson*

FOUNDED 1981. Began by producing tiny pamphlets (*Patriotic English Tracts*) and gained its reputation as England's foremost pamphleteer. Has earned much praise, too, in the US, for its magazine titles (*The Fanatic; Heretic Visions; Small Companion*). Particular areas of interest: historical analyses, apocalyptic rants, wry/savage humour, and political 'filth'. Currently embarking on considerable expansion of titles due to John Nicholson's departure from his post as chairman of the **Small Press Group**. No unsolicited mss, synopses or ideas.
Royalties not paid.

Bracken Press

2 Roscoe Street, Scarborough, North
Yorkshire YO12 7BX
☎ 0723 371708   Fax 0723 371708

Managing Editor *Michael Atkin*

FOUNDED 1974. *Publishes* limited edition, artist-originated fine art books printed on handmade paper: etchings, lithographs, silkscreen and wood engravings. TITLES *Beggar's Bridge; Blue*. No unsolicited mss but interested in proposals and ideas for books (finances permitting).
Royalties not paid.

Brentham Press

40 Oswald Road, St Albans,
Hertfordshire AL1 3AQ
☎ 0727 835731

Managing Editor *Margaret Tims*

FOUNDED 1974 with the object of publishing items of literary, artistic and social value outside the mass commercial market. *Publishes* mainly poetry and some criticism. No fiction. TITLES *Poet's England* (regional verse series); *Ruskin and Siena* Anthony Harris (Ruskin Lectures series); *Strawberries in the Salad* May Ivimy (verse). No unsolicited mss; preliminary letter essential. Synopses and ideas considered but must be accompanied by return postage. 4 titles in 1992.
Royalties by arrangement.

Broadside

68 Limes Road, Tettenhall,
Wolverhampton WV6 8RB
☎ 0902 753047

Managing Editor *Jon Raven*

Published its first book in 1963 and has been actively publishing regional material ever since. *Publishes* Black Country/Birmingham/West Midlands folklore, folk song and history; and general ethnic English folklore and songs. Produces a catalogue of West Midland and Folk Songs of England recordings. TITLES *The Book of the Black Country; Victoria's Inferno* (industrial songs); *Black Country Towns and Villages* (an A-Z). 3 titles in 1991. No unsolicited mss; synopses and ideas welcome.
Royalties paid.

Businesslike Publishing

Burnside, Station Road, Beauly, Inverness-shire IV4 7EQ
☎ 0463 782258

Managing Editor *Iain R. McIntyre*

FOUNDED 1989 in London with the aim of printing a bi-monthly magazine, *The Civil Service Author*. Went on to provide a printing and publishing service for members of the **Society of Civil Service Authors**. *Publishes* poetry, short stories, art, cartoons, plays and magazines. Currently producing the *Focus* series, poetry anthologies for the poetry workshop of the Society of Civil Service Authors which since its inception extended its membership to poets and short story writers. TITLES *Shelf Life; A Favour, Lord?; Some Aspects of Far Eastern Painting; Rags of Time*. 4 titles in 1991. Unsolicited mss welcome. Not interested in ideas/synopses.
Royalties not paid.

Castleden Publications

11 Castlegate, Pickering, North
Yorkshire YO18 7AX
☎ 0751 76227

FOUNDED 1986 as a private press for publication of own work. *Publishes* local history and guidebooks. TITLES *Pickering Through the Ages; Thornton Dale Throught the Ages; Pike's Visitor's Guide to Pickering*. 1 new title in 1992. No unsolicited material, synopses or ideas.
Royalties not paid.

Chapter Two

13 Plum Lane, Plumstead Common,
London SE18 3AF
☎ 081-316 5389

Managing Editor *E. N. Cross*

FOUNDED 1976 as a book agent but went on to become bookseller/dealer and publisher. Chapter Two's chief activity is the propagation of the Christian faith through the printed page. *Publishes* exclusively on Plymouth Brethren. TITLES *Those Who Love God; Jacob's Last Words; The Church Infiltrated*. 5 titles in 1991. No unsolicited mss, synopses or ideas. Enquiries only.
Royalties not paid.

The Cheverell Press

Manor Studios, Manningford Abbots, Pewsey,
Wiltshire SN9 6HS
☎ 0672 63163   Fax 0672 64301

Managing Editor *Sarah de Larrinaga*

Started life as a self-publisher. Now publishing other authors. *Publishes* careers, particularly with regard to drama and related areas, and how-to books. No fiction. No unsolicited mss; brief synopses only. TITLES *How to Become a Working Actor; The Guide to Drama Training in the UK*. Currently undergoing slow and steady expansion and moving into areas other than drama. 6 titles planned for 1992 in Cheverell's *Pocket Guidebook* series (about 20–30,000 words, heavily factual, not anecdotal). Ideas welcome. Happy to advise on self-publishing, but write rather than phone. *Royalties* paid.

CNP Publications/Lyfrow Trelyspen

Roseland, Gorran, St Austell, Cornwall
☎ 0726 843501   Fax 0726 843501

Managing Editor *Dr James Whetter*

CNP: FOUNDED 1975. *Publishes* poetry, political essays, local Cornish interest and Celtic design. Its main publication, *An Baner Kirnwick (The Cornish Banner)*, is a quarterly magazine of local interest. **Lyfrow Trelyspen**: FOUNDED 1989. *Publishes* Cornish local history and biography only. TITLES *Cornish Weather and Cornish People in the 17th Century; Thomas Holloway: Victorian Philanthropist*. 2 titles in 1991. Unsolicited mss, synopses and ideas welcome for both imprints. *Royalties* not paid.

Crescent Moon Publishing

18 Chaddesley Road, Kidderminster,
Worcestershire DY10 3AD

Managing Editor *Jeremy Robinson*

FOUNDED 1988, concentrating mainly on critical studies of literary figures such as D. H. Lawrence, Thomas Hardy, André Gide and Robert Graves. A small press publishing literature, criticism, art, painting, poetry, travel, guidebooks, cinema and some fiction. Expansion into fiction planned over the next couple of years. TITLES *Glorification: Religious Abstraction in Renaissance and 20th Century Painting; Love and Tragedy: A Study of Thomas Hardy; The Passion of DH Lawrence; Gide: Fiction and Fervour; The Passion of Colours: Travels in Mediterranean Lands*. 4 titles in 1991. Unsolicited mss, synopses and ideas welcome. *Royalties* negotiable.

Daniels Publishing

38 Cambridge Place, Cambridge CB2 1NS
☎ 0223 467144   Fax 0223 467145

Managing Editor *Lisa MacGregor*

Educational press specialising in photocopy master A4-packs on health, social education and medicine for schools, health authorities and colleges. Also training materials for the pharmaceutical industry. Unsolicited mss, synopses and ideas welcome.

Dark Diamonds Publications

1 St John's View, Boston Spa, Wetherby, West Yorkshire LS23 6NQ

Managing Editor *Andrew Cocker*

FOUNDED 1987. Its first publication, *Dark Diamonds Magazine*, now has a readership across 15 countries. *Publishes* social, political, ecological concerns, plus poetry and art anthologies. All publications have small print-runs of between 500–1000. TITLES *Dark Diamonds 3/4* (a collection of essays on contemporary Third World issues); *A Riot of Emotions 2* (poetry/art anthology). 1 title in 1991. Unsolicited poetry and short story mss welcome (2000 words max). Synopses and ideas also welcome. *Royalties* not paid.

Diamond Press

5 Berners Mansions, 34–36 Berners Street, London W1P 3DA
☎ 071-580 0767

Managing Editors *Geoffrey Godbert/Jay Ramsay*

An author-publisher cooperative. FOUNDED 1985 'to put back the heart, spirit and soul into published poetry'. *Publishes* poetry and poetry-related material, including a poetry pamphlet series currently being developed. TITLES include *First Things* Lizzie Spring; *Interpreting The Tree* Carolyn Askar; *Sea of Glass* Diana Durham; *For Now* Geoffrey Godbert & Jay Ramsay; *The Burning Word* Jehanne Mehta. About 2–3 titles a year. Unsolicited mss welcome. *Royalties* not paid.

The Dragonby Press

15 High Street, Dragonby, Scunthorpe DN15 0BE
☎ 0724 840645

Managing Editor *Richard Williams*

FOUNDED 1987 to publish affordable bibliography for reader, collector and dealer. *Publishes* bibliographical works only. TITLES *Collins Crime Club: A Checklist*. 3 titles in 1991. Unsolicited mss, synopses and ideas welcome on bibliographical projects only. *Royalties* paid.

Dragonfly Press

2 Charlton Cottages, Barden Road, Speldhurst, Tunbridge Wells, Kent TN3 0LH
☎ 0892 862395

Managing Editor *C. Bell*

FOUNDED 1989. A division of publishing service company Words & Images. *Publishes* local history, literary fiction, poetry and how-to titles. TITLES *The Writer's Guide to Self-Publishing; Ask a Silly Question About Your IBM Computer; A History of Knockholt in the County of Kent; Fe-Fi-Fo-Fum* (poems with an animal conservation theme). No unsolicited material. Commissions only. 3 titles in 1991.
Royalties paid where applicable.

Education Now Publishing Cooperative Ltd

113 Arundel Drive, Bramcote Hills,
Nottingham NG9 3FQ
☎0602 257261

Managing Editors *Dr Roland Meighan/Philip Toogood*

A non-profit making venture set up in reaction to 'the totalitarian tendencies of the 1988 Education Act'. It sets out to report positive initiatives in education, providing a platform for fresh and lively ideas. Its aim is to widen the terms of the debate about education. Its point of reference extends overseas as well as in the UK and so far it has reported on initiatives such as flexi-schooling, home-based education and democratic schooling. *Publishes* books on education only. TITLES include *Small Schools* ed. Philip Toogood; *Learning All the Time* John Holt; *Anatomy of Choice in Education* Roland Meighan & Philip Toogood. 3 titles in 1991. Not interested in unsolicited material or ideas. Enquiries only.
Royalties generally not paid but on occasion.

Egotist Press

BM Egotist, London WC1N 3XX
☎0734 420668

Managing Editor *John Mackay*

FOUNDED 1989 to publish intellectual theory, literature and propaganda, modernist or not. Essentially intellectual titles rather than academic ones. TITLES *Sade; Brute; Skin; Mad; Aryan* Jonathan Bowden. 2 titles in 1991. Unsolicited mss, synopses and ideas welcome. The company hopes to expand considerably over the next 12 months.

Ellenbank Press

The Lathes, Selby Terrace, Maryport,
Cumbria CA15 6LX
☎0900 817773   Fax 0900 817546

Contact *Dr Ian Francis/Kelly Davis*

FOUNDED 1991. One of its first titles that year, *Coleridge Walks The Fells* by Alan Hankinson, won the **Portico Prize** for best book set in North-west England. *Publishes* travel, history and natural history of local interest: Lake District/North of England. 3 titles in 1992. Unsolicited mss, synopses and ideas on appropriate subjects of interest are welcome.
Royalties paid twice yearly.

Feather Books

Fair View, Old Coppice, Lyth Bank, Shrewsbury,
Shropshire SY3 0BW
☎074372 2177

Managing Editor *Rev. John Waddington-Feather*

FOUNDED 1980 to publish the poetry and biography of a particular writers' group, Feather has since expanded into children's fiction. *Publishes* children's environmental fiction, good poetry (mainly, but not exclusively, religious), biography, local history and short stories. Material has a Christian content. TITLES *The Harry Hedgehog Series; Leeds: The Heart of Yorkshire; Dreams and Nightmares.* No unsolicited mss, synopses or ideas. *Overseas associates* (children's fiction) John Muir Publications, Santa Fe, New Mexico, USA. 2 titles in 1992.
Royalties paid.

Ferry Publications

12 Millfields Close, Pentlepoir, Kilgetty, Pentlepoir,
Pembrokeshire SA68 0SA
☎0834 813991   Fax 0834 813991

Managing Editor *Miles Cowsill*

FOUNDED 1987 to publish ferry and shipping books. TITLES *The Townsend Thoresen Years; The Hoverspeed Story; Folkestone-Boulogne.* 5 titles in 1991. Unsolicited mss, synopses and ideas welcome.
Royalties paid.

Fitzgerald Publishing

PO Box 804, London SE13 5JJ
☎081-690 0597

Managing Editor *Tim Fitzgerald*

FOUNDED 1974. *Publishes* entomological and arachnological scientific books only. TITLES *Baboon Spiders: Tarantulas of Africa; Stick Insects of Europe & The Mediterranean; How To Keep Tarantulas; How To Keep Scorpions.* 2 titles in 1991. Unsolicited mss, synopses and ideas for books welcome.
Royalties paid.

Footmark Publications
12 The Bourne, Fleet, Hampshire GU13 9TL
☎0252 621431

Managing Editor *R. Rose*

FOUNDED 1990 to publish its *Family Walks* series.
TITLES *Family Walks Around Hook and Hartley
Wintney*. 1 title a year. No unsolicited material.
Royalties not paid.

Forth Naturalist & Historian
University of Stirling, Stirling FK9 4LA
☎0259 215091
30 Dunmar Drive, Alloa, Clackmannan-
shire FK10 2EH

Honorary Editor *Lindsay Corbett*

FOUNDED by the collaboration of members of
Stirling University and the Central Regional Council
in 1975 to promote interests and publications on
central Scotland. *Publishes* naturalist, historical and
environmental studies and maps. TITLES *Alloa in
Days of Prosperity; The Lure of Loch Lomond; The
Ochil Hills; Mines and Minerals of the Ochils.*
Unsolicited mss, synopses and ideas welcome.
Royalties not paid.

Fortress Books
PO Box 141, London E2 0RL
☎081-985 7394

Managing Editor *T. Andrews*

FOUNDED 1987 with the purpose of publishing
material related to Liverpool and its struggles and
has gone from strength to strength. *Publishes*
politics, political and social history. TITLES include
*Liverpool: A City That Dared to Fight; Out of the
Night; Month of Revolution: France 1968; Towards
A New Revolution — Workers of the Soviet Union
Speak; Whose Choice — Working Class Women
and the Control of Fertility.* No unsolicited mss,
synopses or ideas.
Royalties paid.

Fox Press
Oak Tree, Main Road, Colden Common, Near
Winchester, Hampshire SO21 1TL
☎0703 692309

Managing Editor *Beryl Bron*

FOUNDED 1986. *Publishes* poetry, local interest and
animal welfare. No fiction. TITLES *As the Months
Go By* Donald Christie; *No Bitter Springs* Jeanette
Arnold; *Fettered Kingdoms* John Bryant; *Poetry My*

Pleasure (anthology). No unsolicited material.
About 2 titles a year.
Royalties paid.

Frontier Publishing
Windetts, Kirstead, Norfolk NR15 1BR
☎0508 58174

Managing Editor *John Black*

FOUNDED 1983. *Publishes* travel, photography and
literature. TITLES *Calling From Kashgar: A Journey
Through Tibet; Francis' Wife; Travellers on a Trade
Wind.* No unsolicited mss; synopses and ideas
welcome. About 2–3 titles a year.
Royalties paid.

Galactic Central Publications
Imladris, 25A Copgrove Road, Leeds, West
Yorkshire LS8 2SP

Managing Editor *Phil Stephensen-Payne*

FOUNDED 1982 in the US and became a joint UK/US
company five years ago. *Publishes* science fiction
bibliographies. TITLES *Gene Wolfe: Urth-Man
Extraordinary; Andre Norton: Grand Master of
Witch World.* 4 titles a year. All new publications
originate in the UK. Unsolicited mss, synopses and
ideas welcome.
Royalties paid.

Geological Society Publishing House
Unit 7, Brassmill Enterprise Centre, Brassmill Lane,
Bath BA1 3JN
☎0225 445046   Fax 0225 442836

Managing Editor *Mike Collins*

Publishing arm of the Geological Society which was
founded in 1807. *Publishes* undergraduate and
postgraduate texts in the earth sciences. 10 titles a
year. Unsolicited mss, synopses and ideas welcome.
Royalties not paid.

Glosa
PO Box 18, Richmond, Surrey TW9 2AU
☎081-948 8683

Managing Editors *Wendy Ashby/Ronald Clark*

FOUNDED 1981. *Publishes* textbooks and dictionaries for the teaching and speaking of Glosa (an
international auxiliary language); also a newsletter
and journal. TITLES *Glosa 6000 Dictionary; Introducing Euro-Glosa; Eduka-Glosa.* Unsolicited mss
and ideas for books welcome. Currently expanding

into translations and more dictionaries. 2 titles in 1992.

Gothic Press

PO Box 542, Highgate, London N6 6BG

Managing Editor *Robin Crisp*

Formed as a small specialist publisher for largely, but not exclusively, gothic titles and productions in high-quality case editions. Its list features non-fiction only at the moment but fiction may come on board in the not too distant future. *Publishes* occult, religious, biography, history, supernatural. TITLES *The Highgate Vampire; Mad, Bad and Dangerous to Know.* No unsolicited mss; synopses and ideas may be welcome. *Royalties* not paid.

Grant Books

Victoria Square, Droitwich,
Worcestershire WR9 8DF
☎0905 778155   Fax 0905 794507

Managing Editor *H. R. J. Grant*

Began publishing in 1978. *Publishes* golf-related titles only: golf architecture, history, biographies, etc, but no instructional material. New titles and old, and limited edition publications. TITLES *The Parks of Musselburgh; The Murdoch Golf Library; The History of Olton Golf Club.* 4 titles in 1991. Unsolicited mss, synopses and ideas welcome. *Royalties* paid.

Haunted Library

Flat 1, 36 Hamilton Street, Hoole,
Chester CH2 3JQ
☎0244 313685

Managing Editor *Rosemary Pardoe*

FOUNDED 1979. *Publishes* an annual ghost story magazine and booklets. Mostly in the antiquarian tradition of M. R. James. The magazine publishes stories and articles; booklets tend to be single-author collections. TITLES *Ghosts & Scholars* (the magazine); *The James Gang; The Reluctant Ghost-Hunter; Spirits of Another Sort. Ghosts & Scholars,* 14 issues to date, will be published twice yearly from 1993. 4 titles in 1991. Unsolicited mss welcome; synopses and ideas for non-fiction welcome also. *Royalties* not paid.

Heart of Albion Press

2 Cross Hill Close, Wymeswold,
Loughborough LE12 6UJ
☎0509 880725

Managing Editor *R. N. Trubshaw*

FOUNDED 1990 to publish and distribute books and booklets on the East Midlands area. *Publishes* local history and earth mysteries. TITLES *Drayton Manor & Village: Home of the Peels; Around Foxton: Memories of an Edwardian Childhood; Good Gargoyle Guide.* 10 titles in 1991. No unsolicited mss but synopses and ideas welcome. *Royalties* not usually paid.

Hermitage Publishing

PO Box 1383, London N14 6LF
☎081-886 1414

Managing Editor *C. Street*

FOUNDED 1990 as a self-publishing venture to publish *Earthstars.* 1 title to date. Not interested in publishing other people's work at present. No mss, synopses or ideas.

Hilltop Press

4 Nowell Place, Almondbury, Huddersfield, West Yorkshire HD5 8PB

Managing Editor *Steve Sneyd*

FOUNDED 1966 to publish *Riding West* magazine. Following its demise in 1969, began publishing individual poetry booklets, anthologies and some prose but since 1988 has been specialising in science fiction poetry and related reference material. TITLES *Icons of Starchasm; War of the Words; The Cambodunum Chapbook Companion.* 3 titles in 1991. No unsolicited mss. Limited resources make prospects of acceptance relatively low, but synopses and ideas relevant to SF poetry are welcome. *Royalties* not paid.

Hisarlik Press

4 Catisfield Road, Enfield Lock,
Middlesex EN3 6BD
☎0992 700898   Fax 0902 700898

Managing Editors *Dr Jeffrey Mazo/Georgina Clark-Mazo*

FOUNDED 1991. *Publishes* academic books and journals: folklore, local history and medieval Scandinavia. TITLES *With Disastrous Consequences: London Disasters 1830–1917; The Maiden Who Rose From The Sea and Other Finnish Folktales;*

Contemporary Legend (journal). 1 title in 1991. No unsolicited mss; synopses and ideas welcome. *Royalties* paid.

Indelible Inc
BCM 1698, London WC1N 3XX
☎0924 892661

Managing Editor *Roberta McKeown*

FOUNDED 1988, from the Enterprise Allowance Scheme, to publish children's books. First titles were limited editions, followed by the *The Black & White & Read All Over* series. Now expanding into more academic and neglected areas including Renaissance poetry and literary pamphlets. TITLES include *The Overthrow of the Gout* (a 16th-century scientific poem) and *Monstrous Births* (an illustrated introduction to early English teratology). Also publishes *Massacre* magazine (new fiction and literary criticism strictly related to anti-naturalism, for example, Dada and surrealism), published annually. Suitable submissions welcome. Unsolicited material, synopses and ideas welcome in subject areas which have previously been neglected, e.g. criticism of avantgarde literature.
Royalties paid, though since print runs are so small, this does not amount to much.

Institute For Social Inventions
20 Heber Road, London NW2 6AA
☎081-208 2853   Fax 081-452 6434

Managing Editor *Nicholas Albery*

FOUNDED 1985. *Publishes* a quarterly social inventions journal; also books and booklets dealing with new and imaginative non-technological ideas and projects for improving the quality of life, tackling social problems, or bringing about a more human scale to society. TITLES *The Forest Garden; Can Civil Wars Be Avoided? Learning Computer Programming in 1 Day; Alternative Moscow.* No unsolicited mss. Synopses and ideas welcome but not returned: all ideas are automatically entered in the Institute's annual Social Inventions Competition in June (prize £1000), and some are featured in the Institute's journal or annual *Book of Visions*. The Institute also runs a self-publishing service.
Royalties 10% of any surplus once printing, posting and advertising costs are paid.

Intellect Books
108–110 London Road, Headington,
Oxford OX3 9AW
☎0235 528726   Fax 0235 528726

Managing Editor *Masoud Yazdani*

FOUNDED 1984. *Publishes* books and journals in advanced technologies such as artificial intelligence, hypertext, multimedia, computers related to writing and language disciplines. Currently trying to build up two themes/series: *The Art and Science of ... and Computers and ....* TITLES *The Art and Science of Computer Animation; Hypertext: State of the Art; Computers & Writing.* 12 titles in 1991. Unsolicited mss, synopses and ideas welcome. *Royalties* paid.

Iolo
38 Chaucer Road, Bedford MK40 2AJ
☎0234 270175   Fax 0234 270175

Managing Director *Dedwydd Jones*

Campaigns for a Welsh National Theatre. Produces a series of *Black Books on the Welsh Theatre*, with number 5 in the series published in March 1992. Correspondence on Welsh themes encouraged.

Kittiwake Press
Tŷ Capel, Darowen, Machynlleth,
Montgomeryshire SY20 8NS
☎0650 511314   Fax 0650 511602

Managing Editor *David Perrott*

FOUNDED 1986. Part of Perrott Cartographics. *Publishes* guidebooks only, with emphasis on good design and production. TITLES *Guide to the Western Islands of Scotland; Outer Hebrides Handbook; Dyfi Valley Way; Oxfordshire Trek.* Unsolicited mss, synopses and ideas welcome. *Royalties* paid.

Korvet Publishing and Distribution
GPO Box 115, Priory Terrace, Leamington Spa,
Warwickshire CV31 1AA
☎0926 315262
Fax 0926 450973 attn Sarah Garrett

Joint Managing Editors *Sarah Garrett/John Briton*

FOUNDED 1991 with the publication of *Marks of Courage*, a major historical reference work on the Korean War (1950–53). Two more Korean War titles followed, along with *One Man's Look at Arthritis*, spearhead of the company's 1992 programme. *Publishes* mainly historical and autobiographical works, specialising in Korean War titles. No unsolicited mss; synopses and ideas welcome. *Royalties* not paid.

Littlewood Arc

The Nanholme Centre, Shaw Wood Road,
Todmorden, Lancashire OL14 6DA
☎0706 818419   Fax 0706 818948
Editor *John Killick*

Arc Publications was founded by Tony Ward in
1969; Littlewood by John Killick in 1982 as a
poetry pamphlet publisher. The two joined forces
in April 1990. *Publishes* perfect-bound collections,
new poetry mainly, plus some fiction and anthologies. TITLES *The Dream of Intelligence* Sebastian
Barker; *The Fire in the Tree* Donald Atkinson;
Northern Stories Three ed. Berlie Doherty & Stanley
Middleton. Unsolicited mss, synopses and ideas
welcome. 12 titles in 1992. Represented by Password.
Royalties paid twice yearly.

Logaston Press

Logaston, Woonton, Almeley,
Herefordshire HR3 6QH
☎05446 344

Managing Editor *Andy Johnson*

FOUNDED 1985. *Publishes* walking guides, natural
history, social history, local history, regional cookery. TITLES *Is It Still Raining in Aberfan? A Pit and
its People; The Humble-Bee: Its Life History and
How to Domesticate It; Alfred Watkins, A Herefordshire Man; Walks in Southern Powys & The
Borders.* 3 titles in 1991. Unsolicited mss, synopses
and ideas welcome.
Royalties paid.

Luath Press Ltd

Barr, Ayrshire KA26 9TN
☎046 586 636

Managing Editor *T. W. Atkinson*

FOUNDED 1980 to publish books on Scotland.
Publishes guidebooks and general books with a
Scottish connection. TITLES include *Seven Steps in
the Dark* (autobiography of a Scottish miner);
Mountain Days and Bothy Nights. 6 titles in 1991.
Unsolicited mss, synopses and ideas welcome.
Royalties paid.

Lyfrow Trelyspen

See **CNP Publications**

Mandrake

PO Box 250, Oxford OX1 1AP
☎0865 243671

Managing Editor *Chris Morgan*

Publishes occult, surreal, magical art, sexology,
heretical and radically new ideas. TITLES *Surrealism
and the Occult* Nadia Choucha; *Visual Magick* Jan
Fries; *The Books of Beast* Tim D'Arch-Smith. 5 titles
in 1991. No mss; send synopsis first with return
postage. There are plans to expand the list into
specialist fiction and new science.
Royalties paid.

Marine Day Publishers

64 Cotterill Road, Surbiton, Surrey KT6 7UN
☎081-399 7625   Fax 081-399 1592

Managing Editor *Stephen H. Day*

FOUNDED 1990 as part of The Marine Press Ltd.
Publishes local history only. TITLES *Malden, Old
and New; Malden, Old and New Revisited; King-
ston and Surbiton, Old and New.* 1 title in 1991.
Unsolicited synopses and ideas welcome; no mss.
Royalties not paid.

Maypole Editions

57 Cowley Road, Ilford, Essex
☎081-554 7258

Owner *Barry Taylor*

Self-publisher of fiction and poetry in the main.
Unsolicited mss welcome provided return postage
is included. 3 titles a year. TITLES *Memento Mori,
Cock Robin; Metallum Damnantorum and Other
Poems; X and the Glawkoid Party; Love Sonnets.*
Catalogue available.

Meridian Books

40 Hadzdr Road, Oldbury, Warley, West
Midlands B68 9LA
☎021-429 4397

Managing Editor *Peter Groves*

FOUNDED 1985 as a small home-based enterprise
following the acquisition of titles from Tetradon
Publications Ltd. *Publishes* local history, walking
and regional guides. TITLES *Waterside Walks in the
Midlands* ed. Peter Groves; *Beyond the Bars: Ten
Walks from York City Walls* Ivan E. Broadhead;
*Streetwise: Street Names in and around Birming-
ham* Vivian Bird. 4 titles in 1991. Unsolicited mss,
synopses and ideas welcome if relevant. Send s.a.e.
if ms is to be returned.
Royalties paid.

Minority Rights Group

379 Brixton Road, London SW9 7DE
℡ 071-978 9498   Fax 071-738 6265

Managing Editor *Kaye Stearman*

FOUNDED in the late 1960s, MRG has offices in many other countries and through its publications and the United Nations, works to raise awareness of minority issues worldwide. *Publishes* books, reports and educational material on minority rights. TITLES *The Kurds: A Nation Denied; Somalia: A Nation in Turmoil*. 9 titles in 1991. No unsolicited mss; synopses/ideas welcome.
Royalties not paid.

National Poetry Foundation

(Registered Charity No: 283032)
See **Poetry**

New Arcadian Press

13 Graham Grove, Burley, Leeds, West Yorkshire LS4 2NF
℡ 0532 304608

Managing Editor *Patrick Eyres*

FOUNDED 1981 to publish artist-writer collaborations in journal form on landscape and garden themes (each being limited edition collector's items). TITLES *The New Arcadian Journal; Castle Howard; The Wentworths; A Cajun Chapbook*. No unsolicited mss, synopses or ideas.
Royalties not paid.

Norvik Press Ltd

School of Modern Languages & European History, University of East Anglia, Norwich NR4 7TJ
℡ 0603 56161 ext. 2142   Fax 0603 58553

Managing Editors *James McFarlane/Janet Garton*

Small academic press. *Publishes* the journal *Scandinavica* and books related to Scandinavian literature. TITLES *Literary History and Criticism* (series); *English Translations of Works of Scandinavian Literature* (series); *Ibsen and Meaning* James McFarlane; *An Aquarium of Women* Bjorg Vik; *Strindberg and Autobiography* Michael Robinson. Interested in synopses and ideas for books within the *Literary History and Criticism* series. No unsolicited mss. 4 titles a year.
Royalties paid.

NRB Publications

91 Hawksley Avenue, Chesterfield, Derbyshire S40 4TJ

Managing Editor *N. R. Bradley*

FOUNDED 1987 to promote the dissemination of information on graphology and other methods of understanding personality, particularly by research. *Publishes* books on handwriting, graphology and the psychology of handwriting. TITLES *What Your Handwriting Shows* Saudek; *100 Studies in Handwriting & Related Topics* Bradley; *Papers of the First British Symposium on Graphological Research*. 1 title in 1991. No unsolicited mss; synopses/ideas welcome, 'particularly works which fit into the format of treating a subject in short one-page summaries, e.g. 99 tips on any topic'. There are plans to expand the range of titles over the next couple of years.
Royalties paid.

Oriflamme Publishing

125 Station Road, Mickleover, Derby DE3 5FN
℡ 0332 510230/071-263 2195

Managing Editor *Edward Marsh*

FOUNDED 1982 to publish science fiction and fantasy but now concentrating on a few successful ranges of educational textbooks, mainly English and mathematics. Some fiction and special interest also. TITLES *The Rules of Maths; Help Yourself to English*, both series. 6 titles in 1991. No unsolicited mss; synopsis/ideas welcome but must be brief and preferably of educational/textbook nature. There were plans to set up an imprint (Days Eye) in mid 1992 to offer 'genuine' shared-cost publishing to authors whose material is outside the mainstream and whose work could not otherwise be handled.
Royalties paid.

Paranoia Press (Teesside)

35 Percy Street, Middlesbrough, Cleveland TS1 4DD
℡ 0642 224617   Fax 0642 251495

Contact *Editorial Manager*

Emerged as the book imprint of *Mind's i* magazine and subsequently survived the magazine's demise, establishing itself as a viable separate entity. Moved up to Teesside in the late 1980s to become the region's main quality press. Strong local roots, but very much open to material from other parts of the country, Ireland or the US. *Publishes* poetry mainly, prose and drama, political and literary criticism. Books tend to be perfect-bound but larger, flat-spined collections of both poetry and prose are planned. Good new writing encouraged: 'Editors are given a brief to be alive to exciting new writers'. Unsolicited material welcome if accompanied by return postage/ s.a.e. No unsolicited proposals or synopses. TITLES *Flowers of Morning* Sheila

Holligon; *Fear of Language* Brian Burr; *The Teesside Beowulf* M. F. Rutter. 4 titles in 1992. *Royalties* paid.

Partizan Press

26 Cliffsea Grove, Leigh on Sea, Essex SS9 1NQ
☎ 0702 73986

Managing Editor *David Ryan*

Established to cater for the growing re-enactment and wargaming market. *Publishes* military, history and local history, with particular regard to the 17th and 18th Centuries, or earlier. TITLES *Officers and Regiments of the Royalist Army; Scots Armies of the Seventeenth Century; Discovery of Witchcraft.* Unsolicited mss welcome. 20 titles in 1991. *Royalties* paid.

Paupers' Press

27 Melbourne Road, West Bridgford, Nottingham NG2 5DJ
☎ 0602 815063

Managing Editor *Colin Stanley*

FOUNDED 1983. *Publishes* extended essays (about 15,000 words) in literary criticism in booklet form, and philosophy. Also acts as distributor for selected titles from small US publishers and recently began publishing limited hardback editions of their bestselling titles (2 planned for 1992). TITLES *David Lindsay's Vision* David Power; *Human Nature Stained: Colin Wilson and the Existential Study of Modern Murder* Jeffrey Salmon; *Marriage and London* Colin Wilson; *Sex, America and Other Insights* Colin Wilson. No unsolicited mss but synopses and ideas for books welcome. 6 titles in 1991. *Royalties* paid.

Peepal Tree Books

17 King's Avenue, Leeds, West Yorkshire LS6 1QS
☎ 0532 451703   Fax 0532 300345

Managing Editor *Jeremy Poynting*

FOUNDED 1985. Run as a one-person operation producing 22 titles until 1991 when **Arts Council** funding provided development opportunities. *Specialises* in Caribbean, Black British, African and South Asian writing. *Publishes* fiction, poetry, drama and academic studies. TITLES *You Alone Are Dancing* Brenda Flanagan; *Essays on Indentured Indians in Natal* ed. S. Bhana; *Watercourse* Anthony Kellman; *Janjhat* Rooplall Monar. 15–18 titles a year planned, along with expansion into a broader range of Black/Third World fiction; about to launch a series of literary critical titles in this area. Approach by letter with synopsis and sample

chapters in the first instance. Synopses and ideas for books welcome. *Royalties* paid.

Peterloo Poets

See **Poetry, The Specialists**

The Poetry Business

51 Byram Arcade, Westgate, Huddersfield, West Yorkshire HD1 1ND
☎ 0484 434840   Fax 0484 426566

Managing Editors *Peter Sansom/Janet Fisher*

FOUNDED 1986. *Publishes* poetry only, under the **Smith/Doorstop** imprint, and *The North* magazine. Also runs a resource centre, reading service, etc. (For more details on this, see **Organisations of Interest to Poets**). Unsolicited mss and ideas welcome. *Royalties* not paid.

Power Publications

1 Clayford Avenue, Ferndown, Dorset
☎ 0202 875223

Contact *Mike Power*

FOUNDED 1989. *Publishes* local interest and pub walk guides. TITLES *Pub Walks in Dorset/West Sussex; Ferndown: A Look Back; Dorset Coast Path.* 2 titles in 1991. Unsolicited mss, synopses and ideas welcome. *Royalties* paid.

Previous Parrot Press

The Foundry, Church Hanborough, Oxford OX7 2AB
☎ 0993 881260

Managing Editor *Dennis Hall*

Publishes illustrated editions of poetry and prose, and books about book illustration. TITLES *Clay Cuts* Jack Clemo; *Haslewood Books* Peter Tucker (on the books produced by Frederick Etchells and Hugh Macdonald 1921–30). 3 titles in 1991. Unsolicited mss, synopses and ideas welcome if relevant.
Royalties paid where appropriate.

Pythia Press

7 Silver Street, Glastonbury, Somerset BA6 8BS
☎ 0234 211606

Owner *Cecilia Boggis*

Reprints of rare writing by remarkable women. Correspondence welcome. No submissions or mss. *Royalties* not paid.

QED Books

1 Straylands Grove, York YO3 0EB
☏ 0904 424381

Managing Editor *John Bibby*

Publishes maths, education and travel, plus learning aids. TITLES include *The Mathematics Calendar; The Great Barrier Reef; Joy of Maths.* Synopses (3pp) and ideas for books welcome. QED arranges publicity for other small presses and has many contacts overseas.
Royalties 20% after breakeven point.

Quay Books Exeter

Tuck Mill Cottage, Payhembury, Near Honiton, Devon EX14 0HF
☏ 0404 84388

Managing Editor *Chris Smith*

FOUNDED 1990 to publish **BBC Radio Devon**'s *Village Profiles,* based on a Down Your Way type series broadcast on the station. *Publishes* local history and general fiction by Devon authors. 1 title in 1991. There are plans to expand the list. No unsolicited mss; synopses and ideas welcome but opportunities are limited at present. S.a.e. essential with submissions.
Royalties paid.

QueenSpark Books

Lewis Cohen Urban Studies Centre, 68 Grand Parade, Brighton, East Sussex BN2 2JY
☏ 0273 571916

A community writing and publishing group run mainly by volunteers who work together to write and produce books. Since the early 1970s they have published 26 titles, mainly local autobiographies but also humour, poetry, history and politics. Free workshops held on a regular basis and new members welcome.

Quilliam Press Ltd

80 Lamble Street, London NW5 4AB
☏ 071–267 7567   Fax 071–284 0860

Managing Editor *Tim Winter*

FOUNDED 1989 to commemorate the centennial of the establishment of the first British Muslim community, created by Abdallah Quilliam, a Liverpool solicitor. Its objective is to provide a new generation of UK Muslims, both Asian and converts, with access to traditional wisdom. Vigorously opposed to fundamentalism, and any other modern deviation. *Publishes* religion, with some emphasis on British writers who have converted to Islam; also spirituality and mysticism in a series called *Classics of Muslim Spirituality* which includes translations of some of the best known Islamic devotional and mystical works. TITLES *Islam: Religion of Life* Abdul Wadod Shalabi (a brief introduction to Islam for Westerners by leading Egyptian religious figure); *The Book of Assistance* Abdallah al-Haddad (on mysticism). Unsolicited mss, synopses and ideas welcome on Islam and the Muslim world.
Royalties paid occasionally depending on project.

Reaper Books

11 Brockley Acres, Eastcombe, Stroud, Gloucestershire GL6 7DU
☏ 0452 770440

Reaper Books is the self-publishing imprint of writer/artist Leo Baxendale. No unsolicited mss, synopses or ideas.

Red Earth Publications

7 Silver Street, Marton, Ulverston, Cumbria LA12 0NQ
☏ 0229 64172

Managing Editor *Anne McFadzean*

FOUNDED 1987 as a self-publishing venture and extended its list to include other work in 1990. *Publishes* local history, geology, industrial archaeology and Lakeland interest. TITLES *Lead Miners of Helvellyn; The Iron Moor; Force Crag; Beneath the Lakeland Fells.* There are plans to broaden the scope to include fiction, poetry and other subjects over the next few years. Unsolicited mss, synopses and ideas welcome.
Royalties paid.

The Redlake Press

Brook House, Clun, Shropshire SY7 8LY
☏ 0588 640524

Managing Editor *Ursula Freeman*

FOUNDED 1974. Produces limited, hand printed edition poetry books. TITLES *Calendar* Simon Rae; *The Secret Garden* (anthology, Brotherhood of Ruralists); *Pavement Poems* for St Martin in the Fields. 1 title in 1991. Unsolicited mss welcome but must be very good.
Royalties depending on contract.

Redstone Press

7A St Lawrence Terrace, London W10 5SU

☎071-221 5219   Fax 071-243 1455

Managing Editor *Julian Rothenstein*

FOUNDED 1987. *Publishes* art and literature. No unsolicited mss; synopses and ideas welcome but familiarity with Redstone's list advised in the first instance. About 5 titles a year.
Royalties paid.

The Robinswood Press

30 South Avenue, Stourbridge, West Midlands DY8 3XY

☎0384 397475   Fax 0384 440443

Managing Editor *Christopher J. Marshall*

FOUNDED 1985. *Publishes* educational, particularly remedial and Steiner education. TITLES *Waldorf Education, An Introduction; Take Time* (exercises for children with learning difficulties). 5 titles in 1991. Unsolicited mss, synopses and ideas welcome.
Royalties paid.

Romer Publications

170 Brick Lane, London E1 6RU

☎071-247 3581   Fax 071-247 3581

Managing Editor *Hubert de Brouwer*

FOUNDED 1986. *Publishes* academic and educational, specialising in scholarly studies about 'the myth of superdominant ideologies of Western culture'. Particularly interested in material which undermines the religious doctrines of established institutions. TITLES *In the Footsteps of St Paul to Lydney; Fascism Down the Ages: From Caesar to Hitler; The Decline of the House of Herod; Matter and Gravitational Waves.* 2 titles in 1991. Unsolicited mss, synopses and ideas relevant to Romer's particular areas of interest only are welcome.
Royalties paid.

Seren Books

See **Poetry, The Specialists**

Sherlock Publications

6 Bramham Moor, Hill Head, Fareham, Hampshire PO14 3RU

☎0329 667325

Managing Editor *Philip Weller*

FOUNDED to supply publishing support to various Sherlock Holmes societies. *Publishes* Sherlock Holmes publications only. TITLES *The Dartmoor of The Hound of The Baskervilles; Sherlock Holmes and Scotland Yard; The Baker Street Pillar Box.* 8 titles in 1991. No unsolicited mss; synopses and ideas welcome.
Royalties not paid.

Smith/Doorstop

See **The Poetry Business**

Southover Press

2 Cockshut Road, Southover, Lewes, East Sussex BN7 1JH

☎0273 473038

Managing Editor *Ann Haly*

Caters for those interested in the history of food and recipes, etc. *Publishes* biographies of great cooks, collections/reprints of historic recipes/cookery books with scholarly introductions. Also historic housekeeping books and related subjects. TITLES *Alexis Soyer: Cook Extraordinary* Elizabeth Ray; *The London Art of Cookery* John Farley; *Dr William Kitchiner: Regency Eccentric* Tom Bridge & Colin Cooper English; *The Culinary Campaign* Alexis Soyer. Interested in old cookbooks for reprint. Synopses and ideas welcome (include s.a.e. for return). No mss.
Royalties paid as appropriate.

Spacelink Books

115 Hollybush Lane, Hampton, Middlesex TW12 2QY

☎081-979 3148

Managing Director *Lionel Beer*

FOUNDED 1986. Named after a UFO magazine published in the 1960/70s. *Publishes* titles connected with UFOs, Fortean phenomena and paranormal events. TITLES *The Moving Statue of Ballinspittle and Related Phenomena.* No unsolicited mss; send synopses and ideas. Distributors also.
Royalties and fees paid according to contract.

Stepney Books Publications

19 Tomlins Grove, Bow, London E3 4NX

Contact *Jenny Smith*

FOUNDED 1976. A community publishing project run on a part-time basis. Heavily reliant on fundraising and grants for each new publication of which there is one about every 18 months. *Publishes* history and autobiography of Tower Hamlets in London. TITLES *Memories of Old Poplar; Children of the Green.* Unsolicited material considered but 'any publication we undertake to do can take years to get to press whilst we raise the money to fund it'. 1 title in 1991.

Stride

37 Portland Street, Newtown, Exeter EX1 2EG
☎ 0392 435087

Chairman/Managing Director *Rupert Loydell*

FOUNDED 1979 to publish *Stride Magazine*. Committed to innovative poetry and fiction. Since the mid 1980s Stride has published over a hundred books of imaginative new writing. *Publishes* fiction, poetry, prose-poetry, theology, art criticism, music criticism, thematic anthologies and books for children. TITLES *The Slack-Jawed Camel* John Coldwell; *Alive & Kicking* (featuring the work of young Devon writers); *Etchings* John Kavanagh; *Snowfruit* Mary Maher. Took over the Taxus Press imprint in the late 1980s, maintaining its focus upon the landscape, a sense of place, and the spiritual. 18 titles in 1991. Unsolicited mss, synopses and ideas welcome. S.a.e essential for reply/return. No memoirs, war, romantic or historical fiction, biography or autobiography. Regularly funded by **South West Arts**, and has received a publicity grant from the **Arts Council**.

IMPRINTS
Taxus Press, Trombone Press, Apparition Press, Stride.
Royalties paid annually.

Tamarind Ltd

PO Box 296, Camberley, Surrey GU15 1QW
☎ 0276 683979   Fax 0276 685365

Managing Editor *Verna Wilkins*

FOUNDED 1987 to publish material in which black children are given an unselfconscious, positive profile. *Publishes* books and other educational material (puzzles, sequencing, recipes, maps) which removes the division between schoolbook and homebook, by producing a good read which is educational and fun in both environments. TITLES *Abena and the Rock* (Ghanaian story); *Just A Pile of Rice* (Chinese story); *The Snowball Rent* (Scottish story); *Five Things to Find* (Tunisian story) — four tradition stories which give a global perspective to National Curriculum primary science. Published from BBC Schools programmes. No unsolicited mss.

Taxus Press
See **Stride**

Temple Press Ltd

PO Box 227, Brighton, East Sussex BN2 3GL
☎ 0273 679129   Fax 0273 621284

FOUNDED 1988 to establish a sub-cultural forum for occultural synthesis. Projects include magazine publishing and distribution. *Publishes* occult literature, poetry and radical. TITLES *The Correct Sadist* Terence Sellers; *The Stratagem and other stories* Aleister Crowley; *Ratio:3, Vol 1, Media Shamans; Ratio:3, Vol 2, Transmediators-Z'Ev*. 3 titles in 1991. Unsolicited material welcome with return postage.
Royalties paid.

Terminus Publications

592A Chatsworth Road, Chesterfield,
Derbyshire S40 3JX
☎ 0246 566406

Managing Editor *A. R. Kaye*

FOUNDED 1981. Formerly known as Lowlander Publications. *Publishes* general transport titles and 'then & now' type illustrated books. TITLES *Great Central Railway North of Nottingham; Cromford & High Peak Railway, Final Years; Chesterfield Through the Years; Riding with Hulleys of Baslow*. 4 titles in 1991. Unsolicited mss, synopses and ideas can't always be considered, but are sometimes welcome.
Royalties paid.

Third House (Publishers)

69 Regent Street, Exeter, Devon EX2 9EG
☎ 0392 432479

Managing Editors *David Rees/Peter Robins/Dave Royle*

FOUNDED 1986. *Publishes* gay fiction. First publication was the highly acclaimed *Oranges and Lemons* anthology. TITLES *The Freezer Counter; The Colour of His Hair; Letters to Dorothy; Flux*. No unsolicited material. 3 titles in 1992.
Royalties paid.

Trombone Press
See **Stride**

The Tufnell Press

47 Dalmeny Road, London N7 0DY
☎ 071-272 4861

Managing Editor *Robert Digby*

Publishes pamphlets and books in education, sociology, health education, HIV/AIDS, gender studies and politics. TITLES *Sex, Risk and Danger; Equal Opportunities in the New Era.* 10 titles in 1991. Unsolicited mss, synopses and ideas welcome. *Royalties* paid.

Tyrannosaurus Rex Press
BM Box 1129, London WC1N 3XX
☏ 0923 229784

Managing Editor *Dr Keith Seddon*

The people running TRP are already published authors with big commercial publishers. TRP was established to create a forum for their own and others' 'uncommercial' work — the type that would not interest 'the big boys'. Most titles published 'will reflect our deep dissatisfaction with modern society, some of it hopefully promoting new and better ways of seeing and living'. *Publishes* literary fiction mostly and non-fiction (philosophy and religion). Unsolicited mss welcome. Send hard copy in the first instance but any book accepted for publication will have to be supplied later on disk. Unsolicited ideas and synopses are welcome. Authors should send an intelligent explanatory letter with c.v. Return postage essential
Royalties paid.

Wakefield Historical Publications
19 Pinder's Grove, Wakefield, West Yorkshire WF1 4AH
☏ 0924 372748

Managing Editor *Kate Taylor*

FOUNDED 1977 by the Wakefield Historical Society to publish well-researched, scholarly works of regional (namely West Riding) historical significance. TITLES *Aspects of Medieval Wakefield; Landscape Gardens in West Yorkshire 1680–1880; Coal Kings of Yorkshire; The Aire and Calder Navigation.* 2 titles in 1991. Unsolicited mss, synopses and ideas for books welcome. *Royalties* not paid.

Whyld Publishing Co-op
Moorland House, Kelsey Road, Caistor, Lincolnshire LN7 6SF
☏ 0472 851374   Fax 0472 851374

Managing Editor *Janie Whyld*

Having taken over former ILEA titles which would otherwise have vanished, Janie Whyld has gone on to publish a specialist list of educational materials, with an emphasis on equal opportunities, anti-sexist titles, counselling and assertiveness. TITLES *Using Counselling Skills to Help People Learn; Anti-Sexist Work with Boys and Young Men.* 1 title in 1991. Short runs only, with a progressive approach to

education. Mss, synopses/ideas which meet these requirements welcome. *Royalties* nominal.

Works Publishing
12 Blakestones Road, Slaithwaite, Huddersfield, West Yorkshire HD7 5UQ

Managing Editor *Dave W. Hughes*

One-man operation publishing two magazines: *Works* (science fiction) and *The Modern Dance* (music review). Unsolicited mss (with s.a.e) welcome; no synopses/ideas. *Royalties* not paid.

Yoffroy Publications
7 Upper Dumpton Park Road, Ramsgate, Kent CT11 7PE
☏ 0843 851419

Managing Editor *Frank Foy*

FOUNDED 1988. *Publishes* non-fiction and educational, plus information packs in various subject areas, including music and games. TITLES *Employment in Europe, A Guide; Music Network Guide* (to the music industry); *Play It Now!* (electric guitar tutor manual). 2 titles in 1991. Unsolicited mss, synopses and ideas welcome. Educational game material of interest.
Royalties paid depending on contract.

Zzero Books
BCM ZZero, London WC1N 3XX

Managing Editor *Steven Holmes*

FOUNDED 1990 to publish new types of critical material that might otherwise not find a voice: 'not cultist, political, mystical, science fiction, feminist, not anarchist or silly, but *sincere*'. *Publishes* philosophical, critical (new ideas and social theories), pychological (not self-improvement). TITLES *Triumph (States of Mind)* John Flash; *The Evolution of Decency* John Flash; *Matter of Life and Death* Joe Bidder. Send brief letter in the first instance. Definitely not interested in anyone who is not 'genuinely revolutionary and concerned with ideas'. Send £1.25 in stamps for 64-page sampler of published books.
Two new guides to Self-Publishing have appeared: *The Writer's Guide to Self-Publishing* by Charlie Bell, 24pp, £2.25 (incl p&p) available from **Dragonfly Press** (see entry) and the *Brief Guide to Self-Publishing* by Ann Kritzinger, 16pp, £2.50 (incl p&p) from 20 Shepherds Hill, London N6 5HA.

UK Packagers

The Albion Press Ltd

PO Box 52, Princes Risborough, Aylesbury,
Buckinghamshire HP17 9PR
☎ 08444 4018   Fax 08444 3358

Chairman/Managing Director *Emma Bradford*

FOUNDED 1984 to produce high-quality illustrated
titles. CLIENTS include **Collins**, **Blackie**,
Chapmans, **Cassell**, **Heinemann** and **Michael
Joseph**. *Commissions* illustrated trade titles, par-
ticularly English literature, social history, art, chil-
dren's. 14 titles in 1992.
TITLES *The Darling Buds of May Book of the
Seasons* H. E. Bates; *A Child's Book of Prayers*
Linda Yeatman; *A New Treasury of Poetry* Neil
Philip. Unsolicited synopses and ideas for books
not generally welcome.
Royalties paid; fees paid for introductions and
partial contributions.

Alphabet & Image Ltd

Alpha House, South Street, Sherborne,
Dorset DT9 3LU
☎ 0935 814944   Fax 0935 816717

Chairman/Managing Director *Anthony Birks-
Hay*
Approx Annual Turnover £200,000

FOUNDED 1968. Established the Alphabooks imprint which was subsequently sold to **A. & C.
Black** in 1987 and resumed its book packaging
activities in 1989. *Commissions* horticulture, history, architecture, ceramics. 5 titles in 1991.

Editorial Head *Leslie Birks-Hay* Unsolicited
synopses and ideas for books welcome.
Royalties paid twice yearly, or flat fee in lieu of
royalties.

Andromeda Oxford Ltd

11–15 The Vineyard, Abingdon, Oxon OX14 3PX
☎ 0235 550296   Fax 0235 550330

Managing Director *Mark Ritchie*
Group Publishing Director *Michael Desebrock*
Approx Annual Turnover £7 million

FOUNDED 1986. *Commissions* adult and junior
international illustrated reference, both single volume and series. About 20 titles a year.

DIVISIONS
Future Programme *Lawrence Clarke* (Publishing
Director); **Nature & Geography** *Graham
Bateman* (Editorial Director); **Medicine & Psy-
chology** *Stuart McCready* (Editorial Director);
History *Peter Furtado* (Senior Editor). TITLES
*Encyclopedia of Personal Relationships; World of
Science; Encyclopedia of World Geography; Cultur-
al Atlases; Junior Science Encyclopedia; Encyclo-
pedia of World History*. Approach by letter in the
first instance.

Archival Facsimiles Ltd

PO Box 3, Harleston, Norfolk IP20 0BH
☎ 098686 359   Fax 098686 8181

Contact *Stephen Easton/Cris de Boos*

FOUNDED 1986. Produces reprints of scholarly
works for the British Library among others, plus
high-quality limited edition publications for prestigious academic/business organisations from Europe
and America, ranging from leather-bound folios of
coloured reproductions of period prints to small
illustrated booklets. Also publishes under the
Erskine Press imprint (see **UK Publishers**). No
unsolicited mss.
Payment usually fees.

AS Publishing

73 Montpelier Rise, London NW11 9DU
☎ 081–458 3552   Fax 081–458 0618

Managing Director *Angela Sheehan*

FOUNDED 1987. *Commissions* children's illustrated
non-fiction. No unsolicited synopses or ideas for
books, but approaches welcome from experienced
authors, editors and illustrators in this field.
Fees paid.

Aspect

33A High Street, Thatcham, Newbury,
Berkshire RG13 4JG
☎0635 71802   Fax 0635 71803

Managing Director *Graham Jones*

FOUNDED 1984. *Commissions* books on health and
medicine. Recently developed in to packaging due
to demand.
Payment royalties/fees.

Autumn Publishing Ltd

Studio 2/3, Appledram Barns, Birdham Road,
Appledram, Near Chichester, West
Sussex PO20 7EQ
☎0243 531660   Fax 0243 774433

Managing Director *Campbell Goldsmid*

FOUNDED 1976. Highly illustrated non-fiction: mainly children's, including activity books, and books
with a sporting slant. About 10 titles a year.

Editorial Director *Ingrid Goldsmid* Unsolicited
synopses and ideas for books welcome if they
come within relevant subject areas.
Payment varies according to contract; generally a
flat fee.

Beanstalk Books Ltd

The Gardens House, Hever Castle Gardens,
Threshersfield, Chiddingstone, Kent TN8 7NE
☎0892 870912   Fax 0435 872850

Directors *Shona McKellar/Penny Kitchenham*

FOUNDED 1983. Works in three main areas: for
publishers, own-brand retailers, and commercial
firms who want a book created to their own
requirements. *Commissions* children's illustrated
fiction and non-fiction, plus highly illustrated adult
non-fiction. Unsolicited synopses and ideas for
books welcome, particularly children's novelty,
poetry and activity titles with overseas co-edition
potential. Interested in writers and artists from
ethnic minorities and Third World countries.
Royalties paid twice yearly and/or fees.

Belitha Press Ltd

31 Newington Green, London N16 9PU
☎071-241 5566   Fax 071-254 5325

Managing Director *Martin Pick*

FOUNDED 1980. Packages books for **Barrie &
Jenkins, André Deutsch, Hamish Hamilton,
HarperCollins, Little, Brown & Co., Methuen,**
and **Franklin Watts**. Belitha also now publishes
books independently, with its own educational

selling operation in the UK, as part of an international co-edition packaging business. All titles are
expected to sell in at least four co-editions.
Commissions children's non-fiction and occasional
general titles, with strong interest in natural history
and environmental issues. About 20 titles a year.

Editorial Director *Neil Champion* TITLES Belitha
Information Library: *Flying Start Science; Science
Discoveries; Michelangelo & The Creation of the
Sistine Chapel; Introducing Michelangelo.* No unso-
licited mss. Synopses and ideas for books welcome
from experienced children's writers.

IMPRINTS
1993 Series: *The Silk and Spice Routes* (4 titles;
co-production with Unesco); *Environmental Atlases: Animals and Places; Introducing Picasso;
What is a Bird?*.

David Bennett Books Ltd

94 Victoria Street, St Albans,
Hertfordshire AL1 3TG
☎0727 55878   Fax 0727 864085

Managing Director *David Bennett*

FOUNDED 1989. Children's books — picture books,
non-fiction and education. Synopses and ideas for
books welcome.
Payment both fees and royalties.

Berkswell Publishing Co. Ltd

PO Box 420, Warminster, Wiltshire BA12 9XB
☎0985 40189   Fax 0985 40189

Managing Director *John Stidolph*
Approx Annual Turnover £250,000

FOUNDED 1974. *Commissions* biographies of country people and books about Wessex; illustrated
books on the royal family, country sports, British
heritage, martial arts, English artists, wines and
spirits, and photography. 4 titles in 1991. Unsolicited synopses and ideas for books welcome. No
fiction.
Royalties or fees paid according to terms of
contract.

Bison Books Ltd

Kimbolton House, 117A Fulham Road,
London SW3 6RL
☎071-823 9222   Fax 071-823 8863

Chairman *Sydney L. Mayer*

Part of the Bison Group, one of the world's largest
book packagers. *Commissions* large format illustrated books on art, history, militaria, transport,
travel, entertainment, sport, wildlife and cookery.

About 100 new titles and 200 reprint and foreign editions a year.

Editorial Head *Jane Alexander* TITLES *Ukiyo-e; Art Deco in Europe; Harley Davidson; History of the World.* Unsolicited mss not welcome. The vast majority of titles originate by commission but synopses/ideas are considered. *Royalties* by arrangement.

BLA Publishing Ltd
1 Christopher Road, East Grinstead, West Sussex RH19 3BT
☎ 0342 318980   Fax 0342 410980

Owner *Ling Kee*
Director *Vincent Winter*

Packagers of multi-volume encyclopedias for younger readers and information book series on various topics.

DIVISION
Thames Head Illustrated general non-fiction.
Payment varies according to contract (reference books tend to be flat fees; royalties for single author or illustrator).

Book Packaging and Marketing
3 Murswell Lane, Silverstone, Towcester, Northamptonshire NN12 8UT
☎ 0327 858380   Fax 0327 858380

Contact *Martin F. Marix Evans*

FOUNDED 1989. Essentially a project management service, handling books demanding close designer/editor teamwork of complicated multi-contributor administration, putting books together for publishers, business 'or anyone who needs one'. Clients pay contributors direct and get world rights. Mainly illustrated adult non-fiction including travel, historical, home reference, coffee table books. No fiction or poetry. 2 titles in 1991. Proposals always considered; and writers are often required for projects in development. TITLES *A Lady's Commonplace Book* (for **Letts**; a sort of decorated notebook); *Paris* (guidebooks for **Pitkin Pictorials**); *Royal College of Nursing Manual of Family Health; The Golfers Diary 1993.*
Payment Authors contract direct with client publishers; fees paid on first print usually and royalties on reprint but this depends on publisher.

Breslich & Foss
Golden House, 28–31 Great Pulteney Street, London W1R 3DD
☎ 071–734 0706   Fax 071–494 0854

Director *Paula Breslich*
Approx Annual Turnover £1 million

Packagers of a wide variety of non-fiction subjects including art, children's, crafts, gardening, sport and health. Unsolicited mss welcome but synopses preferred. Always include s.a.e. with submissions. *Royalties* paid twice yearly.

Brooke Associates (Manchester) Ltd
21 Barnfield, Urmston, Manchester M31 1EW
☎ 061–746 8140   Fax 061–746 8132

Chairman *W. R. Mills*
Director *Dr M. Z. Brooke*
Approx Annual Turnover £200,000

Part of Orbis Publishing Ltd. Began life as a research and writing agency and developed into packaging and publishing by client demand. Unsolicited synopses and ideas for books not welcome at present.
Payment generally by author's fee.

Brown Wells and Jacobs Ltd
2 Vermont Road, London SE19 3SR
☎ 081–653 7670   Fax 081–771 1765

Managing Director *Graham Brown*

FOUNDED 1979. *Commissions* non-fiction, novelty, pre-school and first readers, natural history and science. 56 titles in 1991. Unsolicited synopses and ideas for books welcome.
Fees paid.

Calmann & King Ltd
71 Great Russell Street, London WC1B 3BN
☎ 071–831 6351   Fax 071–831 8356

Chairman *Robin Hyman*
Managing Director *Laurence King*
Approx Annual Turnover £2.5 million

FOUNDED 1976. *Commissions* books on art, design and nature. About 20 titles a year. Unsolicited synopses and ideas for books welcome.
Royalties paid twice yearly.

Cameron Books (Production) Ltd
PO Box 1, Moffat, Dumfriesshire DG10 9SU
☎ 0683 20808   Fax 0683 20012

Directors *Ian A. Cameron/Jill Hollis*
Approx Annual Turnover £350,000

Commissions natural history, social history, decorative arts, fine arts, collectors' reference, educational reference, gardening, cookery, conservation,

countryside, film, design. About 6 titles a year. Unsolicited synopses and ideas for books welcome.
Payment varies with each contract.

Chancerel Publishers Ltd

40 Tavistock Street, London WC2E 7PB
☎071-240 2811   Fax 071-836 4186

Managing Director *W. D. B. Prowse*

FOUNDED 1976. *Commissions* educational books and publishes language teaching materials in most languages. Language teachers/writers often required as authors/consultants, especially native speakers other than English.
Payment generally by flat fee but royalties sometimes.

Philip Clark Ltd

53 Calton Avenue, Dulwich, London SE21 7DF
☎081-693 5605   Fax 081-299 4647

Managing Director *Philip Clark*

A founder member of the **Book Packagers Association**, Philip Clark's first title, *The Industrial Heritage of Britain*, was published by **Ebury Press** in 1982. Since then the company has produced heavily illustrated books on a variety of subjects for some thirty publishers in the UK and overseas. TITLES include *The Complete Guide to Windsurfing*, which sold over 100,000 copies worldwide; and the *Travellers' Wine Guides*, which have already appeared in Danish, German, Swedish, UK and US editions. Unsolicited synopses and ideas for books, particularly on international subjects, welcome.
Fees paid.

Creative Comics

80 Silverdale, Sydenham, London SE26 4SJ
☎081-699 7725

Proprietor *Denis Gifford*

Specialises in children's comic strips, producing custom-made single strips or complete comics, cartoon booklets, paperbacks, etc., especially promotional and giveaway comics. Past projects include a weekly comic supplement in *Reveille* and a full-colour comic for National Savings. No unsolicited material. Has 100 freelance cartoonists on its books.

Curtis Garratt Ltd

The Old Vicarage, Horton cum Studley,
Oxon OX9 1BT
☎086735 536   Fax 086735 8844

Directors *Neil Curtis* (Editorial)/*Richard Garratt* (Design)

FOUNDED 1983. General illustrated non-fiction trade books, with full DTP service available. 28 titles in 1991. TITLES *Chronicle of the First World War, Volume 2 (1917–1918); Madagascar: A Natural History; I-Spy Series; Consumer's Guide to Over-the-Counter Medicines*. Synopses and ideas for books considered, but most work stems from own ideas or from publishers.
Payments both royalties and fees.

Diagram Visual Information Ltd

195 Kentish Town Road, London NW5 8SY
☎071-482 3633   Fax 071-482 4932

Managing Director *Bruce Robertson*

FOUNDED 1967. Library, school, academic and trade reference books. About 10 titles a year. Unsolicited synopses and ideas for books welcome without obligation to pay for sample material.
Fees paid.

Eddison Sadd Editions

St Chad's Court, 146B King's Cross Road,
London WC1X 9DH
☎071-837 1968   Fax 071-837 2025

Managing Director *Nick Eddison*
Editorial Director *Ian Jackson*
Approx Annual Turnover £2.5 million

FOUNDED 1982. Produces a wide range of popular illustrated non-fiction titles for an ever-increasing range of publishers around the world, with books published in 25 countries. Ideas and synopses are welcomed but must have international appeal. Catalogue available on request.
Royalties paid twice yearly; flat fees paid when appropriate.

Gardenhouse Editions Ltd

15 Grafton Square, London SW4 0DQ
☎071-622 1720   Fax 071-720 9114

Managing Director *Lorraine Johnson*
Approx Annual Turnover £350,000

Commissions practical and art-related books on fashion, gardening, interior design, architecture, cookery. About 6 titles a year.

DIVISIONS
Knitwear & Gardening *Louisa McDonnell*
Architecture *Elisabeth Haldane/Bridget Harney*
TITLES *The Garden Wall; A Table in Tuscany/Provence; Architectural Guides For Travellers.* Unsolicited synopses and ideas for books welcome.

Royalties paid as agreed; fees paid in addition to or instead of royalties.

Greenpeace Books

5 Baker's Row, London EC1R 3DB
☎ 071-833 0600   Fax 071-837 6606
Publishing Manager *Peter Wright*

FOUNDED 1987. Produces books across the entire area of environmental concerns and publishes books for Greenpeace.

Editorial Director *John May* TITLES *The Greenpeace Book of Antarctica; The Greenpeace Book of the North Sea; The Greenpeace Global Warming Report.* No unsolicited mss; synopses and ideas for books considered.
Fees paid.

Grisewood & Dempsey Ltd

Elsley House, 24–30 Great Titchfield Street, London W1P 7AD
☎ 071-631 0878   Fax 071-323 4694

Chairman *Daniel Grisewood*
Managing Director *Duncan Baird*

FOUNDED 1973. Packagers and publishers of general children's fiction and non-fiction in hardcover and paperback. 60 titles in 1991.

IMPRINTS
Kingfisher Books (see entry **UK Publishers**); **Rainbow Books** *Henryk Wesolowski* (Managing Director)/*Jim Miles* (Publishing Director). Mass-market trade list, launched 1990.

Grub Street

See **UK Publishers**

Hamilton House Mailings Ltd

17 Staveley Way, Brixworth Industrial Estate, Northampton NN6 9EL
☎ 0604 881889   Fax 0604 880735

Managing Director *Tony Attwood*
Approx Annual Turnover £1 million

FOUNDED 1979. Often works in collaboration with inexperienced authors, repackaging material, clearing copyright, etc., before selling the infant product on. Distributors for other publishers and book packagers for educational (secondary school), TV and radio tie-ins, directory and diary titles. *Commissions* business, employment, careers. About 10 titles a year. Approach by letter in first instance. Less involved at present with the packaging side of its operation but synopses and ideas for

books are considered if accompanied by s.a.e. No unsolicited mss. Happy to advise.
Royalties paid annually.

Holtkamp and Whitlam Ltd

40 Tavistock Street, London WC2E 7PB
☎ 071-240 8500   Fax 071-836 4186

Managing Director *John Whitlam*
Approx Annual Turnover £70,000

FOUNDED in 1988 to provide packaging services specifically in the field of bilingual reference. Works for some of Europe's major dictionary publishers and employs freelance editors with experience of lexicography and/or translation. Knowledge of foreign languages, including native speaker knowledge is essential. Increasingly involved with database and Wordstar formats and therefore favours editors with computing knowledge and facilities. *Commissions* bilingual dictionaries and related works, such as phrase books, etc.
Fees paid.

Ilex Publishers Ltd

29–31 George Street, Oxford OX1 2AY
☎ 0865 723148   Fax 0865 791267

Managing Director *Chris Aworth*

FOUNDED 1986. Highly-illustrated colour information books for children and adults covering the whole information spectrum. About 25 titles a year.

Publisher *Peter Sackett* TITLES *Children's World Atlas* Series; *20th Century Atlas of the World; Issues Atlas Series: World/Social/Environment/Economic; How? Why? What? Where? Series; How It Works Series; Pictorial Atlas Series.* No unsolicited material. All ideas are generated in-house.
Payment outright fee.

Ink Inc. Ltd

1 Anglesea Road, Kingston on Thames, Surrey KT1 2EW
☎ 081-549 3174   Fax 081-546 2415

Managing Director *Richard Parkes*
Editorial Head *Barbara Leedham*
Approx Annual Turnover £600,000

Undertakes virtually any type of publishing assignment: research, writing, design and packaging. Packaging activities include a considerable number of general interest illustrated titles, plus yearbooks and directories. Also consultancy work and the supply of colour repro and print from the UK, Hong

Kong, Portugal and Eastern Europe. Unsolicited submissions not welcome. *Fees* paid.

Leading Edge Press & Publishing Ltd

Old Chapel, Burtersett, Hawes, North Yorkshire DL8 3PB
☎ 0969 667566   Fax 0969 667788

Chairman/Managing Director *Stan Abbott*
Approx Annual Turnover £300,000

Primarily a commercial magazine/brochure/ newsletter design and production house but, since its formation in 1984, has steadily increased its turnover in book publishing to dovetail with its core activity. Book publishing now accounts for about a quarter of the company's activities. Synopses and ideas for books welcome subject to prior contact by phone. *Commissions* transport and outdoor leisure, including walking. 10 titles in 1992. *Royalties* paid thrice yearly and/or fees.

Lennard Books

Windmill Cottage, Mackerye End, Harpenden, Hertfordshire AL5 5DR
☎ 0582 715866   Fax 0582 715121

Chairman/Managing Director *Adrian Stephenson*

FOUNDED 1979 by Adrian Stephenson. The book packaging division of Lennard Associates Ltd which also owns **Lennard Publishing**. *Specialises* in sport, humour and personality books, plus a number of television associated titles. TITLES include *The Whitbread Rugby World* and *The Official TCCB Cricket Statistics* for **Queen Anne Press**, now owned by Lennard Associates who bought the Press and all its assets (with the exception of 34 titles which had already been sold to **Headline Publishing**), following Macdonald's takeover by **Little, Brown & Co.** in 1992.
Payment both fees and royalties by arrangement.

Lexus Ltd

205 Bath Street, Glasgow G2 4HZ
☎ 041-221 5266   Fax 041-226 3139

Managing Director *P. M. Terrell*

FOUNDED 1980. *Commissions* bilingual reference, language and phrase books. About 20 titles a year.

Editorial Director *P. M. Terrell* TITLES *Chambers Travelmate Series; Collins Italian Concise Dictionary; Harrap Study Aids; Hugo's Phrase Books; Hamlyn Phrase Books; Harrap Shorter French Dictionary* (revised). No unsolicited material. Books are mostly commissioned. Freelance contributors employed for a wide range of languages.
Payment generally flat fee.

Lionheart Books

10 Chelmsford Square, London NW10 3AR
☎ 081-459 0453   Fax 081-451 3681

Senior Partner *Lionel Bender*
Approx Annual Turnover £250,000

A design/editorial packaging team. CLIENTS include most of the major children's book publishers. Titles are either conceived by the partnership or commissioned from publishers. Highly illustrated non-fiction for children aged 8-14, mostly natural history, history and general science. 30 titles in 1990. Lionel Bender is himself a writer of children's science books, with over 30 titles to date.
Payment generally flat fee.

Market House Books Ltd

2 Market House, Market Square, Aylesbury, Buckinghamshire HP20 1TN
☎ 0296 84911   Fax 0296 437073

Directors *Dr Alan Isaacs/Dr John Daintith*

FOUNDED (as Laurence Urdang Associates) in 1970. Dictionaries, encyclopedias and reference. 15 titles in 1991. TITLES *Concise Macmillan Encyclopedia; Brewer's 20th Century Phrase and Fable; Oxford Dictionary for Science Writers and Editors; Concise Dictionary of Business; The Collins English Dictionary; The Macmillan Encyclopedia.* Unsolicited material not welcome as most books are compiled in-house.
Fees paid.

Marshall Cavendish Books Ltd

119 Wardour Street, London W1V 3TD
☎ 071-734 6710   Fax 071-734 6221

Director *Hooi Kwee Sum*
Approx Annual Turnover £10 million

Part of the Marshall Cavendish Group of companies founded in 1968, primarily to exploit partwork material in book form; now, however, said to originate about 60% of its material. *Commissions* illustrated non-fiction. About 100 titles a year. Unsolicited synopses and ideas for books welcome.
Fees paid, not royalties.

Marshall Editions Ltd

170 Piccadilly, London W1V 9DD
☎ 071-629 0079   Fax 071-834 0785

Managing Director *Bruce Marshall*

FOUNDED 1977. *Commissions* non-fiction, including thematic atlases, leisure and self improvement.

Managing Editor *Ruth Binney* TITLES *The Atlas of Mysterious Places; The 35mm Photographer's Handbook; The Natural History of the Universe.*

MM Productions Ltd

8B East Street, Ware, Hertfordshire SG12 9HJ
☎ 0920 466003   Fax 0920 462267

Chairman/Managing Director *Mike Moran*
Approx Annual Turnover £1 million

Started as a packager for publishers; now also involved in mainstream (electronic) publishing. *Commissions* fiction, technical and scientific, medical, naval & military, sport, games and pastimes, travel and adventure, directories. Publishers of MM Publisher Database and MM Printer Database, available in UK, European and international editions. 7 titles in 1991. Unsolicited synopses and ideas for books welcome.
Fees paid to authors in addition to royalties which are paid twice yearly.

Morgan Samuel Editions

11 Uxbridge Street, London W8 7TQ
☎ 071-229 9339   Fax 071-243 2886

Proprietor/Editorial Director *Nigel Perryman*

FOUNDED 1987. Packagers of illustrated non-fiction titles in all subject areas. TITLES *A History of Medicine; A History of Forensic Science; The Amateur Astronomer's Pathfinder; The Amateur Fossil Hunter's Pathfinder; Cossack; Samurai; Zulu; Finger Food; An Encyclopedia of the 60s; The World of Model Railways; Behind the Scenes in Motor Racing; Behind the Scenes in Horse Racing.* 12 titles in 1992. No unsolicited mss.
Payment both fees and royalties.

Neil & Ting Morris

27 Riverview Grove, London W4 3QL
☎ 081-994 1874

Partners *Neil Morris/Ting Morris*

FOUNDED 1979. Mainly children's fiction and non-fiction. 20 titles in 1991. No unsolicited mss but interested in seeing examples of illustrators' work.
Royalties usually paid.

New England Editions Ltd

2-6 Ellington Place, Ellington Road,
London N10 3DG
☎ 081-444 0505   Fax 081-444 0695

Contact *Charles Perkins*

Former imprint of **Wordwright Books**, now independent but still associated. *Commissions* natural history, environmental, science, art, younger readers, and general books.

Oyster Books Ltd

Sparrow Hill Way, Weare, Near Axbridge,
Somerset BS26 2LA
☎ 0934 732251   Fax 0934 732514

Managing Director *Jenny Wood*

FOUNDED 1985. Packagers of activity and information books for children of pre-school age to ten years old. No fiction. 20 titles in 1991. Synopses and ideas for books welcome.
Payment usually fees.

Parke Sutton Publishing Ltd

Hi-Tech House, 10 Blackfriars Street,
Norwich NR3 1SF
☎ 0603 667021   Fax 0603 760284

Managing Director *Ian S. McIntyre*

FOUNDED 1982. Produces newspapers, magazines and reference books for organisations and training offices; and packages books for publishers, including **David & Charles**, **Simon & Schuster**, **AA Publishing**, **BBC Books**, **Hutchinson Books**. *Commissions* non-fiction books in the leisure field in its broadest sense, with particular interest in titles requiring strong design emphasis. Design and production departments utilise the latest in Applemac technology. Unsolicited synopses and ideas for books welcome strictly within their field and if accompanied by s.a.e. 12 titles in 1991.
Royalties paid twice yearly; fees sometimes paid rather than royalties.

Playne Books

New Inn Lane, Avening, Tetbury,
Gloucestershire GL8 8NB
☎ 0453 835 155   Fax 0453 835 590

Director *David Playne*
Editor *Gill Davies*

FOUNDED 1987 as a sister company to Playne Design and Playne Photographic to look after the book packaging and commercial book side of the

business. *Commissions* highly illustrated and practical books on any subject. Unsolicited synopses and ideas for books welcome.
Royalties paid 'on payment from publishers'. Fees sometimes paid instead of royalties.

Mathew Price Ltd

Old Rectory House, Marston Magna, Yeovil, Somerset BA22 8DT
☏0935 851158   Fax 0935 851285

Chairman/Managing Director *Mathew Price*
Approx Annual Turnover £1 million

Commissions high-quality, full-colour picture books and fiction for young children; also novelty and non-fiction. Unsolicited synopses and ideas for books welcome.
Fees sometimes paid instead of royalties.

Quarto Publishing

The Old Brewery, 6 Blundell Street, London N7 9BH
☏071-700 6700/333 0000
Fax 071-700 4191/700 0077

Chairman *Laurence Orbach*
Approx Annual Turnover £14 million

FOUNDED 1976. Went public in 1986 and has shown phenomenal growth since. Now Britain's largest book packaging company, and since 1986 the company has been publishing under the **Apple** imprint. *Commissions* illustrated non-fiction, including painting, graphic design, visual arts, history, cookery, gardening, crafts. Unsolicited synopses/ideas for books welcome.
Payment flat fees paid.

Roxby Press Ltd

Aura House, 53 Oldridge Road, London SW12 8PP
☏081-675 3336   Fax 081-673 9494

Chairman/Managing Director *Hugh Elwes*
Approx Annual Turnover £1.6 million

FOUNDED 1974. Part of Roxby & Lindsey Holdings Ltd. *Commissions* illustrated non-fiction titles for international co-edition market. About 6 titles a year. Unsolicited synopses and ideas for books welcome 'provided the author is prepared to work with the editors to prepare any material submitted for the international markets'.
Royalties paid annually. Fees paid only for books with many different contributors.

Sadie Fields Productions Ltd

3D West Point, 36–37 Warple Way, London W3 0QR
☏081-746 1171   Fax 081-746 1170

Directors *David Fielder/Sheri Safran*

FOUNDED 1981. Quality children's books. Conceives, designs and produces pop-ups, three-dimensional, novelty, picture and board books. Several books have won awards in the UK and USA. Concentrates on books with international co-edition potential. About 20 titles a year. Approach with preliminary letter and sample material in the first instance.
Royalties based on a per copy sold rate and paid in stages.

Salariya Book Company Ltd

25 Stanford Road, Brighton, East Sussex BN1 5DH
☏0273 551122   Fax 0273 541527

Managing Director *David Salariya*

FOUNDED 1989. Children's information books — fiction, history, art, music, science, architecture, education and picture books. No unsolicited material.
Payment by arrangement.

Savitri Books Ltd

115J Cleveland Street, London W1P 5PN
☏071-436 9932   Fax 071-580 6330

Managing Director *Mrinalini S. Srivastava*
Approx Annual Turnover £200,000

FOUNDED 1983. Keen to work 'very closely with authors/illustrators and try to establish long-term relationships with them, doing more books with the same team of people'. *Commissions* high-quality, illustrated non-fiction, mainly nature, natural history and craft. About 4 titles a year. Unsolicited synopses and ideas for books 'very welcome'.
Royalties between 10–15% of the total price paid by the publisher. 'Rarely work on a flat fee basis except in the case of some books for which the text would be compiled in-house and an illustrator commissioned to do a series of pictures. In such a case, and should the illustrator's contribution to the book have been of great importance, a small royalty may be paid on subsequent editions.'

Sheldrake Press Ltd

188 Cavendish Road, London SW12 0DA
☏081-675 1767   Fax 081-675 7736

Managing Director *Simon Rigge*
Approx Annual Turnover £1 million

Subsidiary of Sheldrake Publishing. *Commissions* illustrated non-fiction: cookery, travel, style, history of technology and stationery. TITLES *Victorian House Book; The Shorter Mrs Beeton; The Power of Steam; The Railway Heritage of Britain; Wild France; The Kate Greenaway Baby Book.* Synopses and ideas for books welcome.
Fees paid.

Templar Company

Pippbrook Mill, London Road, Dorking,
Surrey RH4 1JE
☎0306 876361   Fax 0306 889097

Chairman/Managing Director *Richard Carlisle*
Approx Annual Turnover £3 million

FOUNDED 1981. Produces children's illustrated non-fiction, educational and story books. Synopses and ideas for books welcome. 40 titles in 1992.

Editorial Head *Amanda Wood*
Royalties by arrangement.

Thames Head

See **BLA Publishing Ltd**

Toucan Books Ltd

Albion Courtyard, Greenhills Rents,
London EC1M 6BN
☎071-251 3921   Fax 071-251 1692

Managing Director *Robert Sackville-West*
Approx Annual Turnover £400,000

FOUNDED 1985. Originally specialised in international co-editions, now focusing on fee-based editorial, design and production services to film. *Commissions* illustrated non-fiction only. 15 titles in 1991. TITLES *Leith's Cookery Bible; Henry VIII; Wetlands; Collins' Racegoers' Encyclopedia; People and Places.* Unsolicited synopses and ideas for books welcome. No fiction or non-illustrated titles. *Royalties* twice yearly; fees paid in addition to or instead of royalties.

Twin Books UK Ltd

Kimbolton House, 117A Fulham Road,
London SW3 6RL
☎071-823 9222   Fax 071-244 7139

Chairman *Sydney L. Mayer*

FOUNDED 1986. *Specialises* in children's books: picture books, leisure and fiction. TITLES include

Disney The Little Mermaid; Beauty and the Beast; Babar (TV series); *Babar and His Friends.* No unsolicited material.
Payment both fees and royalties.

Victoria House Publishing Ltd

4 North Parade, Bath BA1 1LF
☎0225 463401   Fax 0225 460942

Managing Director *Derek Hall*
Approx Annual Turnover £5 million

Part of the Reader's Digest Group. *Commissions* children's novelty, pop-up, jigsaw books and plastic bath books. About 200 titles a year.
Royalties or flat fee according to contract.

Wordwright Books

2-6 Ellington Place, Ellington Road,
London N10 3DG
☎081-444 0505   Fax 081-444 0695

Contact *Charles Perkins*

FOUNDED by ex-editorial people; hence words tend to be more important here than elsewhere. *Commissions* illustrated non-fiction: social history and comment, military history, women's issues, sport. About 10-12 titles a year. Unsolicited synopses/ideas (a paragraph or so) welcome for illustrated non-fiction. *Payment* usually fees but royalties (twice-yearly) paid over a certain agreed number of copies.

Zoe Books Ltd

15 Worthy Lane, Winchester,
Hampshire SO23 7AB
☎0962 851318   Fax 0962 843015

Managing Director *Imogen Dawson*

FOUNDED 1990. Packaging company established by former **Macmillan** employees. *Specialises* in full-colour information and reference books for children, the family and schools. Also publishing consultants for UK trade and educational markets, and providers of production/editorial services to UK and US publishers. About 40 titles a year. Tends to generate own ideas but happy to hear from freelance writers and editors.
Fees paid.

The Association of Authors' Agents

Code of Practice

The code runs as follows:

(a) No member shall knowingly represent an author who is the client of another agency, without the agreement of such agency, whether or not that agency is a member of the Association. Failure to enquire as to an author's agency relationship shall be considered negligence and a violation of this rule.

(b) No member of the Association shall charge a reading fee on his/her own behalf to an author except in circumstances approved by a majority of the Committee.

(c) All members shall account faithfully to their authors, paying within not more than 21 days of the money being cleared in the member's bank account, for all sums due to their authors unless instructed otherwise by their authors or unless such sums total less than £25.

(d) Members shall furnish promptly to their authors any information and material which the author may reasonably request in connection with his/her business.

(e) No member shall act for an author after his/her authority to do so, whether oral or written, has terminated, except that

   (i) the member shall not be debarred from continuing to act if so instructed in writing by the author and

   (ii) the member shall continue to take commission in respect of agreements entered into previously with third parties by the member on the author's behalf and appropriate commission in respect of negotiations carried out on the author's behalf which are subsequently concluded by the author or a new agent.

(f) No member shall charge a fee to an author beyond his/her regular commission as notified to the Association without the author's prior consent in writing.

A member may not, without informing his/her author in writing in advance, represent in any transaction both his/her author as vendor of services or copyright material and any other interest as purchaser of such material and must declare to the author in writing any proprietary or profitable interest in any contract apart from that of normal agency commission.

A member may in exceptional circumstances make special commission arrangements with an author provided that he/she obtains the author's prior consent in writing. Members are strongly advised to consult the Committee if they are in any doubt whatsoever as to the propriety of such special arrangement. The Committee shall have power to decide on the acceptability to the Association of any such special arrangement which comes to its notice and to require the member in question to amend to its satisfaction any such arrangements which in its unanimous view it deems unacceptable.

Applicants must furnish the Association with a statement of their commission rates and, if elected, notify the Association of any changes in them, which shall be recorded by the Committee.

(g) A member shall not use or communicate to others information relating to an author's affairs confidentially given to him/her except as required by law.

(h) A member shall allow his/her authors at all reasonable times the right to verify and authenticate any statement of account concerning that author and shall submit promptly and regularly to the author full details of any transaction handled by the member.

(i) All members shall establish a bank account for their client's monies separately from the member's general business and personal accounts except in circumstances notified to and approved by a majority of the Committee.

All complaints made against members for alleged violation of any provision of the code of practice shall be considered by the full Committee of the Association who shall have the right to expel any member against whom a significant and material breach of the code of practice is upheld. Such a decision shall be taken unanimously by the full Committee. Any member against whom a complaint has been lodged shall have the right to appear in person before the Committee to hear and answer such complaint. In the event of a dispute between member agencies over a matter of professional practice, other than an alleged violation of any provisions of the code of practice, the Committee may, if requested by the parties, act as arbitrators.

UK Agents

Members of the **Association of Author's Agents** (see entry **Professional Associations and Societies**) are marked with an asterisk.

Abacus Literary Agency

298 Manchester Road, West Timperley, Altrincham, Cheshire WA14 5NB
☎061-962 9749

Contact *Cliff South*

FOUNDED 1989; active since 1991. *Handles* fiction, non-fiction and scripts. Particularly interested in books with a strong moral Christian theme, especially early readers. *Specialises* in psychology, theology, topography, natural history, westerns and romantic fiction. No sex or violence for its own sake: 'If Mrs Whitehouse wouldn't approve, neither would we'. Unsolicited mss welcome but initial approach by letter, accompanied by sample chapters, preferred in the first instance. ASCII disks by arrangement. No reading fee. *Commission* Home 10%; USA 20%; Translation by arrangement.

Aitken & Stone Ltd*

29 Fernshaw Road, London SW10 0TG
☎071-351 7561   Fax 071-376 3594

Contact *Gillon Aitken/Brian Stone*

FOUNDED 1984 from the amalgamation of Gillon Aitken Ltd and Hughes Massie Ltd. *Handles* fiction and non-fiction. No plays or scripts unless by existing clients. Send preliminary letter, with synopsis and return postage, in the first instance. No reading fee. CLIENTS include Agatha Christie, Germaine Greer, Susan Howatch, V. S. Naipaul, Piers Paul Read, Salman Rushdie, Paul Theroux. *Commission* Home 10%; US 15%; Translation 20%. *Overseas office* Wylie, Aitken & Stone Inc., 250 West 57th Street, New York, NY 10107, USA.

Jacintha Alexander Associates*

47 Emperor's Gate, London SW7 4HJ
☎071-373 9258   Fax 071-373 4374

Contact *Jacintha Alexander/Julian Alexander*

FOUNDED 1981. *Handles* full-length general and literary fiction and non-fiction of all kinds. No plays, poetry, textbooks or science fiction. Film and TV scripts handled for established clients only. Preliminary letter with s.a.e. essential. *Commission* Home 15%; US 20%; Translation 20%. *Overseas associates* in New York, Los Angeles, Japan, and throughout Europe.

Darley Anderson Books

Estelle House, 11 Eustace Road, London SW6 1JB
☎071-385 6652   Fax 071-386 5571

Contact *Darley Anderson/Louise Schweitzer* (short stories/journalism)

Run by an ex-publisher who is an experienced and highly professional negotiator with a sympathetic touch and a knack for encouraging talent. He recently negotiated a £150,000 UK advance for a first-time novelist. *Handles* commercial fiction & non-fiction; also scripts for TV, radio and theatre. No academic books. *Special interests* Fiction: all types of women's fiction including glitzy, family sagas, thrillers and horror, crime, fantasy and comedy; non-fiction: celebrity autobiographies, biographies, popular psychology, health, beauty and fashion, gardening, cookery and religious. Send letter and outline with 1–3 chapters, plus return postage. Brief synopsis and first chapter giving a strong flavour of the book preferred. CLIENTS Beryl Kingston, Barbara Cartland, Tessa Barclay, Martina Cole, Joseph Corvo, Janet Filderman, Adrian Plass, Fred Secombe, Christine Thomas. *Commission* Home 15%; US 20%; Translation 20%; Radio/TV/ Film 15%; Journalism/ Short stories 25%. *Overseas associates* 'too numerous' to list. Works with major foreign agents worldwide.

Aquarius Literary Agency & Picture Library

PO Box 5, Hastings, East Sussex TN34 1HR
☎0424 721196   Fax 0424 717704

Contact *Gilbert Gibson*

FOUNDED 1955. *Handles* non-fiction only, with an emphasis on the entertainment world and its history: autobiography, biography, memoirs, pictorial collections from the world of show business (cinema, stage and TV), pop music, motion pictures, the cinema. No scripts except 'in very specific and specialised cases'. No unsolicited mss;

introductory letter with synopsis and opening chapters (three) preferred. No reading fee. Picture library also. *Commission* Home 10%; USA 20%; Translation 20%. *Overseas associates* Cosmos, Tokyo; Aquarius, Beverly Hills.

Aspect

33A High Street, Thatcham, Newbury, Berkshire RG13 4JG
☎ 0635 71802   Fax 0635 71803

Contact *Graham Jones*

FOUNDED 1984. *Handles* health and medicine only, dealing with articles, booklets and books. Syndicates articles worldwide. No reading fee. *Commission* Home 15%; Syndication 50%.

Yvonne Baker Associates

8 Temple Fortune Lane, London NW11 7UD
☎ 081–455 8687   Fax 081–458 3143

Contact *Yvonne Baker*

FOUNDED 1987. *Handles* scripts for TV, theatre, film and radio. Books extremely rarely. No poetry. Approach by letter giving as much detail as possible, including s.a.e. No reading fee. *Commission* Home 10%; US 20%; Translation 20%.

Blake Friedmann Literary Agency Ltd*

37–41 Gower Street, London WC1E 6HH
☎ 071–631 4331   Fax 071–323 1274

Contact *Carole Blake* (books)/*Julian Friedmann* (film/TV)/*Conrad Williams* (original scripts/radio)

FOUNDED 1977. *Handles* all kinds of fiction from genre to literary; a varied range of specialised and general non-fiction; some juvenile titles; plus scripts for TV, radio and film. No poetry. *Special interests* thrillers and commercial women's fiction. Unsolicited mss welcome but initial letter with synopsis and first two chapters preferred. Letters should contain as much information as possible on previous writing experience, aims for the future, etc. No reading fee. CLIENTS include Gilbert Adair, Ted Allbeury, John Gordon Davis, Barbara Erskine, Maeve Haran, John Trenhaile, Pamela Vandyke Price. *Commission* Books: Home 15%; US 20%; Translation 20%; Radio/TV/film: 15%; Journalism/ short stories: 25%. *Overseas associates* throughout Europe, Asia and USA.

David Bolt Associates

12 Heath Drive, Send, Surrey GU23 7EP
☎ 0483 721118   Fax 0483 222878

Contact *David Bolt*

FOUNDED 1983. Ex-**David Higham**. *Handles* fiction and general non-fiction. No books for small children or verse (except in special circumstances). No scripts. *Special interests* fiction, African writers, biography, history, military, theology. Preliminary letter with s.a.e. essential. Reading fee for unpublished writers. Terms on application. CLIENTS include Chinua Achebe, Carol-Ann Courtney, Eilis Dillon, Frank Graves, Arthur Jacobs, James Purdy, Joseph Rhymer, Colin Wilson. *Commission* Home 10%; US 19%; Translation 19%.

Bookworms Literary Agency

London House, Llanddewi Brefi, Tregaron, Dyfed SY25 6RL
☎ 0974 298719   Fax 0974 298719

Contact *Hilary Harvey*

FOUNDED 1990. *Handles* fiction and non-fiction including travel, biography, investigative and women's books, plus children's. No scripts. No specialist or technical. Approach by letter in first instance. Mss should be accompanied by return postage and s.a.e. for response. No reading fee. *Commission* Home 10%; US 15%.

Rosemary Bromley Literary Agency

Avington, Near Winchester, Hampshire SO21 1DB
☎ 0962 78656   Fax 0962 864649

Contact *Rosemary Bromley*

FOUNDED 1981. *Handles* fiction and non-fiction. Also scripts for TV and radio. No poetry or short stories. *Special interests* natural history, leisure, biography and cookery. No unsolicited mss. Send preliminary letter with full details. Enquiries unaccompanied by return postage will not be answered. CLIENTS include Elisabeth Beresford, Jean Buchanan, Gwen Chewell, Teresa Collard, Fanny Cradock, Cécile Curtis, Christine Franklin, Jacynth Hope-Simpson, Keith West, Ron Wilson. *Commission* Home 10%; US 15%; Translation 20%.

Felicity Bryan*

2A North Parade, Banbury Road, Oxford OX2 6PE
☎ 0865 513816   Fax 0865 310055

Contact *Felicity Bryan*

FOUNDED 1988. *Handles* fiction of various types and non-fiction with emphasis on history, biography, science and current affairs. No scripts for TV, radio or theatre. No crafts, how-to, science fiction or light romance. No unsolicited mss. Best approach by letter. No reading fee. CLIENTS include John Julius Norwich, Roy Strong, Miriam Stoppard,

Rosamunde Pilcher, Anthony Hyde, Barbara Trapido, Liza Cody. *Commission* Home 10%; US 20%; Translation 20%. *Overseas associates* Lennart Sane (Scandinavia); Andrew Nurnberg (Europe); **Curtis Brown** (USA).

Peter Bryant (Writers)

3 Kidderpore Gardens, London NW3 7SS
☎071-794 1019

Contact *Peter Bryant*

FOUNDED 1980. *Special interests* TV, film, theatre and radio scripts. Also children's fiction. No reading fee for these categories but s.a.e. essential for all submissions. CLIENTS include Roy Apps, Ruth Silvestre, Owen Holder, George Tarry. *Commission* Home 10%; US 10%. *Overseas associates* Hartmann & Stauffacher, Germany.

Diane Burston Literary Agency

46 Cromwell Avenue, Highgate, London N6 5HL
☎081-340 6130

FOUNDED 1984. *Handles* general non-fiction and fiction, namely women's, crime, historical and westerns. No scripts. No poetry, children's, thrillers or spy fiction. No unsolicited mss. Telephone or write in the first instance. Reading fee for complete mss; none for synopses with sample chapters. CLIENTS include Margaret James, L. D. Tetland, Geoff Viney. *Commission* Home 10%; US 15%; Elsewhere 20%.

Bycornute Books

76A Ashford Road, Eastbourne, East Sussex BN21 3TE
☎0323 26819   Fax 0323 649053

Contact *Ayeshah Haleem*

FOUNDED 1987. *Handles* illustrated books on art, archaeology, cosmology, symbolism and metaphysics, both ancient and modern. No scripts. No unsolicited mss. Send introductory letter outlining proposal. No reading fee. *Commission* Home 10%; USA 10%.

Campbell Thomson & McLaughlin Ltd*

31 Newington Green, London N16 9PU
☎071-249 2971   Fax 071-923 1375

Contact *John McLaughlin/Charlotte Bruton*

FOUNDED 1931. *Handles* book-length mss (excluding children's, science fiction and fantasy). No plays, film scripts, articles or poetry. Short stories

from existing clients only. No reading fee. No unsolicited mss. Send preliminary letter with s.a.e. in the first instance. *Overseas associates* Fox Chase Agency, Philadelphia and **Raines & Raines**, New York.

Carnell Literary Agency*

Danescroft, Goose Lane, Little Hallingbury, Hertfordshire CM22 7RG
☎0279 723626

Contact *Pamela Buckmaster*

FOUNDED 1951. *Handles* fiction and general non-fiction, specialising in science fiction and fantasy. No poetry. No scripts except from published authors. No unsolicited mss. Send preliminary letter with brief synopsis and first two chapters (include s.a.e. for acknowledgement). No reading fee. *Commission* Home 10%; US and Translation 19%. Works in conjunction with agencies worldwide.

Casarotto Ramsay Ltd

National House, 60–66 Wardour Street, London W1V 3HP
☎071-287 4450   Fax 071-287 9128

Contact *Jenne Casarotto* (Film and television)/ *Tom Erhardt* (Stage)/ *Greg Hunt/Henrietta Lees & Margaret Hanbury* (books)

Took over the agency responsibilities of Margaret Ramsay Ltd in 1992, incorporating a strong client list, with names like Alan Ayckbourn, Caryl Churchill, Willy Russell and Muriel Spark. *Handles* scripts for TV, theatre, film and radio, plus general fiction and non-fiction. No poetry or books for children. No unsolicited material without preliminary letter. CLIENTS include J. G. Ballard, Robert Bolt, Edward Bond, Donald Clarke, David Hare, Judith Lennox, Prof. Paul Preston, Julian Rathbone, David Yallop. *Commission* Home 10%; US and Translation 20%. *Overseas associates* worldwide.

Judith Chilcote Agency

8 Wentworth Mansions, Keats Grove, London NW3 2RL
☎071-794 3717   Fax 071-794 7431

Contact *Judith Chilcote*

FOUNDED 1990. *Handles* commercial fiction, non-fiction, celebrity books, TV tie-ins, illustrated cookery and health. No scripts. No academic, science fiction, children's or poetry. No unsolicited mss. Send letter with c.v., synopsis, three chapters and s.a.e. for return. No reading fee. CLIENTS Ann Chubb, Robert Farago, Unity Hall, Mavis Klein, Douglas Thompson. *Commission* Home 15%; US

20%; Translation 25%. *Overseas associate* in the US, plus overseas agents.

Teresa Chris Literary Agency

16 Castellain Mansions, Castellain Road,
London W9 1HA
☎071-289 0653

Contact *Teresa Chris*

FOUNDED 1989. *Handles* general and literary fiction, and non-fiction: crime, health, business, travel, cookery, sport and fitness. *Specialises* in crime. No scripts. Film and TV rights handled by co-agent. No poetry, short stories, fantasy, science fiction or horror. Unsolicited mss welcome. Send query letter with sample material, including s.a.e., in first instance. No reading fee. CLIENTS include Tania Alexander, Marlena Spieler, Deborah Valentine. *Commission* Home 10%; US 15%; Translation 20%. *Overseas associates* Thompson & Chris Literary Agency, California; representatives in most other countries.

Serafina Clarke*

98 Tunis Road, London W12 7EY
☎081-749 6979   Fax 081-740 6862

Contact *Serafina Clarke/Jan Ward*

FOUNDED 1980. *Handles* fiction: romance, horror, thrillers, literary; and non-fiction: travel, cookery, gardening and biography. Only deals in scripts by authors already on its books. *Special interests* gardening, history, country pursuits. No unsolicited mss. Introductory letter with synopsis (and return postage) essential. No reading fee. *Commission* Home 10%; US 20%; Translation 20%. *Represents* Permanent Press, USA; Second Chance Press, USA.

Robert Clarson-Leach

29 Ravensbourne Park Crescent, London SE6 4YJ
☎081-690 4616   Fax 081-690 4616

Contact *Robert CLarson-Leach/Daphne Adams*

FOUNDED 1985. *Handles* biography, education, finance, humour, plus other non-fiction; also some full-length fiction, but rarely. Film/TV rights negotiated. Revision of texts suggested where appropriate. No unsolicited mss. Send preliminary letter with s.a.e. first. No reading fee. CLIENTS Bernard Cashman, Mick Gilbert, Susan Hastings, Elizabeth James, Stephen Jenkins, Donald Laming, Robert Leach, Christine Turner. *Commission* Home 10%; US 20%; Translation by arrangement. *Overseas associates* Almar Press, New York.

Jonathan Clowes Ltd*

10 Iron Bridge House, Bridge Approach,
London NW1 8BD
☎071-722 7674   Fax 071-722 7677

Contact *Brie Burkeman*

FOUNDED 1960. Pronounced 'clewes'. Now one of the biggest fish in the pond, and not really for the untried unless they are true high-flyers. Fiction and non-fiction, plus scripts. No textbooks or children's. *Special interests* situation comedy, film and television rights. No unsolicited mss; authors come by recommendation or by successful follow-ups to preliminary letters. CLIENTS include Kingsley Amis, David Bellamy, Len Deighton, Carla Lane, Doris Lessing, David Nobbs. *Commission* Home 10%; US 15%; Translation 19%. *Overseas associates* Andrew Nurnberg Associates; Lennart Sane Agency; Tuttle Mori Agency and Japan Uni, Japan.

Elspeth Cochrane Agency

11–13 Orlando Road, London SW4 0LE
☎071-622 0314   Fax 071-622 0314

Contact *Elspeth Cochrane/Donald Baker*

FOUNDED 1960. *Handles* fiction, biography and autobiography. Subjects include Lord Olivier, Leonard Rossiter, Sir Ralph Richardson, Shakespeare, Sir John Gielgud, Dame Peggy Ashcroft, Dirk Bogarde. Also handles scripts for all media. *Special interest* drama. No unsolicited mss. Preliminary letter with a description of the work, a brief outline, and s.a.e., is essential in the first instance. No reading fee. CLIENTS include John Charters, David Pinner, Royce Ryton, Robert Tanitch. *Commission* Home 12½%; US 12½%; Translation 12½% ('but this can change – the % is negotiable, as is the sum paid to the writer').

Dianne Coles Agency

The Old Forge House, Sulgrave, Banbury,
Oxon OX17 2RP
☎0295 760692   Fax 0295 760692

Contact *Dianne Coles/Philip Gosling*

FOUNDED 1980. *Handles* non-fiction, including investigative journalism, craft and leisure, biography, travel and human interest. Preliminary letter and return postage essential. *Commission* Home 15%; Radio/TV/Film 15%; Journalism/Short stories 25%; Translation 20%; Overseas 20%. *Overseas office* in the US.

Rosica Colin Ltd

1 Clareville Grove Mews, London SW7 5AH
☎071-370 1080   Fax 071-244 6441

Contact *Joanna Marston*

FOUNDED 1949. *Handles* all full-length mss, plus theatre, film, television and sound broadcasting. Preliminary letter with return postage essential; writers should outline their writing credits and whether their mss have previously been submitted elsewhere. Takes 3–4 months to consider full mss; synopsis preferred in the first instance. No reading fee. *Commission* Home 10%; US 15%; Translation 20%.

Comstock-Smith Literary Agency

141 Wilberforce Road, London N4 2SX
☏071-354 0615   Fax 071-226 9828

Contact *Elizabeth Comstock-Smith*

FOUNDED 1992. In association with **Cecily Ware Literary Agents**. *Handles* children's books and theatre scripts mainly; plus some radio and a little television. No non-fiction or poetry. *Specialises* in Irish theatre. No unsolicited scripts; first approach in writing. No reading fee. *Commission* Home 10%; US 15%. *Overseas associates* **Susan Schulman Agency**, New York.

Vernon Conway Ltd

5 Spring Street, London W2 3RA
☏071-262 5506/7

Contact *Vernon Conway*

FOUNDED 1977. *Special interests* novels, biographies, plays. No textbooks or academic. Send introductory letter with return postage in the first instance. No reading fee. CLIENTS include Anne Born, Ian Grimble, David Halliwell, Monty Haltrecht, Thomas Marty, Angela Meyer, Elizabeth Morgan, Aled Vaughan. *Commission* 10% on all sales.

Jane Conway-Gordon*

1 Old Compton Street, London W1V 5PH
☏071-494 0148   Fax 071-287 9264

Contact *Jane Conway-Gordon*

FOUNDED 1982. In association with **Andrew Mann Ltd**. *Handles* fiction and general non-fiction, plus occasional scripts for TV/radio/theatre. No poetry or science fiction. Unsolicited mss welcome; preliminary letter and return postage preferred though. No reading fee. *Commission* Home 10%; US 20%; Translation 20%. *Overseas associates* **McIntosh & Otis Inc.**, New York; plus agencies throughout Europe and Japan.

Creative Tone Ltd

2nd Floor, 1–2 Great Chapel Street,
London W1V 3AG
☏071-287 2448   Fax 071-287 2449

Contact *John Rowe* (Manager)

Agents and managers for writers of TV drama, documentaries and drama features. 'We are particularly interested in new works and first-time writers, and use our wide range of contacts in television and film to promote them as extensively as possible.' Unsolicited material welcome.

Rupert Crew Ltd*

1A King's Mews, London WC1N 2JA
☏071-242 8586   Fax 071-831 7914

Contact *Doreen Montgomery/Shirley Russell*

FOUNDED 1927 by F. Rupert Crew. International representation, handling fiction and non-fiction for volume publication. Limited interest in major newspaper or magazine features/series and short fiction. No plays or poetry. No unsolicited mss. Preliminary letter essential. No reading fee. *Commission* Home (books) 10–15%; Overseas 20%.

Cruickshank Cazenove Ltd

97 Old South Lambeth Road, London SW8 1XU
☏071-735 2933   Fax 071-820 1081

Contact *Harriet Cruickshank*

FOUNDED 1983. *Handles* fiction, general non-fiction and scripts for TV/radio/ film. No unsolicited mss. Preliminary letter with synopsis and s.a.e. essential. *Commission* Home 10%; US and Translation varies according to contract. *Overseas associates* Works with various foreign agents abroad.

Curtis Brown Group Ltd

162–168 Regent Street, London W1R 5TB
☏071-872 0331   Fax 071-872 0332

Contact *Material should be addressed to the Company.*

Long-established literary agency, whose first sales were made in 1899. Merged with **John Farquharson**, forming the Curtis Brown Group Ltd in January 1989. *Handles* a wide range of subjects including fiction, general non-fiction, children's and specialist, scripts for film, TV, theatre and radio. Send synopsis with covering letter and c.v. rather than complete mss. No reading fee. *Commission* Home 10%; US 15%; Translation 20%. *Overseas offices* Curtis Brown (Australia) Pty Ltd; **Curtis Brown Ltd**, New York/Los Angeles; Curtis

Brown, Toronto; **John Farquharson Ltd**, New York.

Judy Daish Associates Ltd

83 Eastbourne Mews, London W2 6LQ
☏ 071-262 1101   Fax 071-706 1027

Contact *Judy Daish/Louise Cooper/Sara Stroud/ Debora Harwood*

FOUNDED 1978. Theatrical literary agent only. Scripts for film/TV/ theatre/radio. No books. Preliminary letter essential. No unsolicited mss.

Caroline Davidson and Robert Ducas Literary Agency

5 Queen Anne's Gardens, London W4 1TU
☏ 081-995 5768   Fax 081-994 2770

Contact *Caroline Davidson/Robert Ducas*

FOUNDED 1988. Caroline Davidson works in London; Robert Ducas works in New York. *Handles* art, architecture, biography, cookery, design, fiction, gardening, travel, history, investigative journalism, natural history, photography, reference, science. Many highly illustrated books. No science fiction, occult, plays or poetry. Writers should telephone or send an initial letter giving details of the project together with c.v. and s.a.e. CLIENTS Philip Beresford, Robert Baldock, Hazel Evans, Paul Hillyard, Mary Hollingsworth, Tom Jaine, Huon Mallalieu, Brigid Murray, Gemma Nesbitt, Sri Owen, Jehanne Wake. *Commission* Home/ Commonwealth/US 12½%; occasionally more (20% if sub-agents have to be used).

Merric Davidson Literary Agency

Oakwood, Ashley Park, Tunbridge Wells, Kent TN4 8UA
☏ 0892 514282   Fax 0892 514282

Contact *Merric Davidson*

FOUNDED 1990. *Handles* fiction and general non-fiction. No scripts. No children's, academic, short stories or articles. Particularly keen on contemporary fiction, thrillers and popular music titles. No unsolicited mss. Send preliminary letter with synopsis and biographical details. S.a.e. essential for response. No reading fee. CLIENTS include Faith Addis, Elizabeth Harris, Valerie Singleton. *Commission* Home 10%; US 15%; Translation 20%.

Reg Davis-Poynter

118 St Pancras, Chichester, West Sussex PO19 4LH
☏ 0243 779047

Contact *R. G. Davis-Poynter/Anne Payne*

Handles books only. *Special interests* autobiography, biography, history, politics, sociology, theatre. No children's or religious. No unsolicited mss. Writers should approach with preliminary letter, sample chapter and synopsis (including return postage) in the first instance. No reading fee. *Commission* Home 15%, US 20%; Translation 15%; Theatre/Film/Television/Radio 15%. *Overseas associates* in Germany, Scandinavia, Japan, Italy, France and USA.

Felix de Wolfe

Manfield House, 376-378 The Strand, London WC2R 0LR
☏ 071-379 5767   Fax 071-836 0337

Contact *Felix de Wolfe*

FOUNDED 1938. *Handles* quality fiction only, and scripts. No non-fiction or children's. No unsolicited mss. No reading fee. CLIENTS include S. Campbell-Jones, Robert Cogo-Fawcett, Brian Glover, Derek Haddinott, Jennifer Johnston, John Kershaw, Bill MacIlwraith, Angus Mackay, Gerard McLarnon, Braham Murray, Charles Savage, Alan Sievewright, Julian Slade, David Thompson, Dolores Walshe. *Commission* Home 12½%; US 20%.

Denniston & Lownie

16A Inverleith Row, Edinburgh EH3 5LS
☏ 031-556 8949   Fax 031-558 3853

Contact *Robin Denniston*

FOUNDED 1991. *Handles* non-fiction, mainly biography, history and philosophy. No fiction, scripts, poetry or children's. *Specialises* in Scottish writers of serious non-fiction. Particularly interested in secret intelligence and spies. Approach by letter with synopsis, sample chapters and return postage. No reading fee. CLIENTS include Bishop T. Huddleston, Rebecca Ridgway. *Commission* Home 10%; US 25%; Translation (including sub-agent's commission) 35%.

Dorian Literary Agency

Upper Thornehill, 27 Church Street, St Marychurch, Torquay, Devon

Contact *Dorothy Lumley*

FOUNDED 1986. *Handles* both mainstream and commercial full-length adult fiction, especially science fiction, fantasy and horror, women's (including sagas), crime and thrillers. Also limited non-fiction: primarily environmental issues and media-related subjects; plus scripts for TV and radio. No poetry, children's, theatrical scripts, short stories, academic or technical. Introductory letter with synopsis/ outline essential. No reading fee. CLIENTS include Harriet Hudson, Brian Lumley, Amy Myers. *Commission* Home 10%; US 15%; Translation 20-25%. Works with agents in most countries for translation; submit direct to the States.

Colleen Doyle

9 The Ridings, Epsom, Surrey KT18 5JQ
☎0372 722367   Fax 0372 722367
Contact *Colleen Doyle*

FOUNDED 1989. *Handles* commercial fiction and non-fiction. *Special interests* women's fiction, thrillers, crime, science fiction and fantasy, humorous fiction, celebrity autobiography, biography, lifestyle and relationships, film and television. No short stories, poetry, plays or academic work. No unsolicited mss; send introductory letter with synopsis, first three chapters and return postage. *Commission* Home 10%; US & Translation 20%.

Anne Drexl

8 Roland Gardens, London SW7 3PH
☎071-244 9645

Contact *Anne Drexl*

FOUNDED 1988.*Handles* commercially orientated full-length mss for romantic fiction, general, family sagas and crime. Ideas welcome for business related books, how-to, DIY, hobbies and collecting. Strong interest too in juvenile fiction, including children's games, puzzles and activity books. Writers should approach with preliminary letter and synopsis (including s.a.e.). No reading fee. *Commission* Home 12½%; US and Translation 20% (but varies depending on agent used).

Toby Eady Associates Ltd

18 Park Walk, London SW10 0AQ
☎071-352 4450   Fax 071-352 3627
Contact *Toby Eady/Grace Cheetham/Xandra Hardie*

In association with **Xandra Hardie**. *Handles* books on Africa, the Middle East, India, China, fishing, fiction, non-fiction and poetry. No scripts. No unsolicited mss. Approach by letter first. No reading fee. CLIENTS include Julia Blackburn, John Carey, Jung Chang, Bernard Cornwell, Mark Daniel, Angela Fisher & Carol Beckwith, Esther Freud, Kuki Gallmann, Alasdair Gray, Sean Hardie, Michael Hofmann, Tim Jeal, Rana Kabbani, Mary Keen, Lee Langley, Russell Lucas, Patrick Marnham, Matthew Parris, Shona Ramaya. *Commission* Home 10%; US 20%; Translation 20%. *Overseas associates* La

Nouvelle Agence; Mohr Books; The English Agency, Tokyo; Jan Michael and Rosemarie Buckman.

Faith Evans Associates*

5 Dryden Street, London WC2E 9NW
☎071-829 8425/8409   Fax 071-240 5600
Contact *Faith Evans/Rosie Gilbey*

FOUNDED 1987. Small selective agency specialising in editorial support as well as representation. *Handles* fiction and non-fiction. No scripts or unsolicited mss; preliminary letter essential. CLIENTS include Eleanor Bron, Helena Kennedy, Roger Mugford, Sheila Rowbotham. *Commission* varies according to degree of editorial involvement required.

John Farquharson*

See **Curtis Brown Group Ltd**

Film Link Literary Agency

31 Oakdene Drive, Tolworth, Surrey KT5 9NH
☎081-330 3182

Contact *Yvonne Heather*

FOUNDED 1979. *Handles* fiction, general non-fiction, children's fiction and scripts for TV/radio. *Special interest* women's fiction. No film, poetry or short stories. Send synopsis and sample pages, accompanied by s.a.e. No reading fee. CLIENTS include Tommy Boyd, Michael Elder, Ann McManus, Margaret Sunley. *Commission* Home 10%; Overseas 15-20%.

Laurence Fitch Ltd

483 Southbank House, Black Prince Road, Albert Enbankment, London SE1 7ST
☎071-735 8171

Contact *Laurence Fitch/Brendan Davis*

FOUNDED 1954. *Handles* scripts for theatre, film, TV and radio only. No fiction; dramatists only. Unsolicited mss welcome. No reading fee. CLIENTS include Indy Allen, John Chapman, John Graham, and the Dodie Smith estate. *Commission* Home 10%; US 15% (maximum); Translation 20%. *Overseas associates* worldwide.

Jill Foster Ltd

3 Lonsdale Road, London SW13 9ED
☎081-741 9410   Fax 081-741 2916

Contact *Jill Foster/Alison Finch/Ann Foster*

FOUNDED 1976. *Handles* scripts only, mainly TV, drama and comedy. No fiction, short stories or poetry. No unsolicited mss; approach by letter in the first instance. No reading fee. CLIENTS include James Hendrie, Paul Hines, Julia Jones, Chris Ralling, Colin Bostock-Smith, Susan Wilkins. *Commission* Home 12½%; US 15%; Translation 15%.

Fox & Howard Literary Agency
4 Bramerton Street, London SW3 5JX
☎071-352 0561   Fax 071-352 8691
Contact *Chelsey Fox/Charlotte Howard*

FOUNDED 1992. *Handles* fiction: women's, literary and thrillers; general non-fiction: biography, health, sport, naval and military history, business, humour, self-help, true crime and travel; educational and reference: GCSE and A-level texts. No scripts. No poetry, plays, short stories, children's, science fiction, fantasy and horror. Particulary keen on educational and reference material. No unsolicited mss; send letter, synopsis and sample chapter with s.a.e. for response. No reading fee. CLIENTS Sir Rhodes Boyson, Claire Gillman, Dr Graham Handley, John Winton. *Commission* Home 10%; US 20%; Translation 20%.

French's
24 St Anselm's Place, London W1 1FG
☎071-495 1598
Contact *John French*

FOUNDED 1973. *Handles* novels and factual material; and scripts for all media. No religious or medical books. No unsolicited mss. 'For unpublished authors we offer a reading service at £35 per mss, exclusive of VAT and postage.' Interested authors should write a letter in the first instance. CLIENTS include James Duke, Gillian Hanna, Barry Heath, Susanna Hughes, Mal Middleton, Shaun Prendergast. *Commission* Home 10%.

Vernon Futerman Associates
Garden Flat A, 159 Goldhurst Terrace,
London NW6 3EU
☎071-625 9601   Fax 071-372 1282
Contact *Vernon Futerman* (academic/politics/ current affairs/show business)/ *Wendy Futerman* (educational/history)/*Jenny Goodstone* (fiction/ art)

FOUNDED 1984. *Handles* fiction and non-fiction, including academic, art, educational, politics, history, current affairs, show business, travel, business and medicine. Also scripts for film, TV, theatre and radio. No short stories, science fiction, crafts, hobbies or gardening. No unsolicited mss; send preliminary letter with detailed synopsis and s.a.e. No reading fee. CLIENTS Nora Beloff, Dr Juliet Barker, Dr Michael Ward, Ernie Wise. *Commission* Home 12½–17½%; USA 17½–22½%; Translation 17½–25%. *Overseas associates* Brigitte Axster, Germany & Scandinavia; Sabine Balland, France.

Jüri Gabriel
35 Camberwell Grove, London SE5 8JA
☎071-703 6186
Contact *Jüri Gabriel*

Handles fiction and non-fiction; also, more recently, scripts for TV/ radio. No short stories generally, unless in exceptional circumstances or a collection, and no articles, verse or books for children. Unsolicited mss welcome if accompanied by return postage and letter giving sufficient information about author's writing experience, aims, etc. CLIENTS Robin Adshead, Mark Brown, Nigel Cawthorne, Col. John Cross, Alfred Draper, Robert Irwin, Leslie McDonnell, John Outram, Philip Roberts, Major Ewen Southby-Tailyour, Adisakdi Tantimedh, Dr Terence White, Herbert Williams, John Wyatt, Dr Robert Youngson. *Commission* Home 10%; US 20%; Translation 20%.

Kerry Gardner Management
15 Kensington High Street, London W8 5NP
☎071-937 4478/3142   Fax 071-376 2587
Contact *Nicola McArdle*

FOUNDED 1975. *Handles* scripts for theatre, film, radio and television. No fiction. Unsolicited mss welcome but written approach preferred in the first instance. CLIENTS Michael Axinn, Michael Black, Vince Foxall, David Punford. *Commission* Home 10%. *Overseas associates* Susan Smith & Associates, Beverly Hills; Artists and Writers, Beverly Hills.

Pamela Gillis Management
46 Sheldon Avenue, London N6 4JR
☎081-340 7868
Contact *Pamela Gillis*

FOUNDED 1975. TV scripts and radio material. No books. No unsolicited mss. *Commission* Home and Abroad 10%.

Eric Glass Ltd
28 Berkeley Square, London W1X 6HD
☎071-629 7162   Fax 071-499 6780

Contact *Eric Glass/Janet Crowley*

FOUNDED 1934. *Handles* fiction, non-fiction and scripts for publication or production in all media. No poetry. No unsolicited mss. No reading fee. CLIENTS include Philip King, Wolf Mankowitz and the estates of Jean Cocteau, Jean-Paul Sartre, Robin Maugham and Warwick Deeping. *Commission* Home 10%; US 15%; Translation 20% (to include sub-agent's fee). *Overseas associates* in USA, Germany, Scandinavia, France, Italy, Spain, Czechoslovakia, Holland, Greece, Poland, Australia, South Africa, Japan.

Christine Green (Authors' Agent) Ltd*
2 Barbon Close, London WC1N 3JX
☎071-831 4956   Fax 071-831 4840
Contact *Christine Green*

FOUNDED 1984. *Handles* fiction (general and literary) and general non-fiction. No scripts, poetry or children's. No unsolicited mss; initial letter and synopsis preferred. No reading fee but return postage essential. *Commission* Home 10%; US 15%; Translation 20%.

Elaine Greene Ltd*
37 Goldhawk Road, London W12 8QQ
☎081-749 0315   Fax 081-749 0318
Contact *Elaine Greene/Carol Heaton*

A small agency that likes to involve itself with its authors. *Handles* fiction, general non-fiction and children's books. No original scripts for theatre, film or TV. *Special interest* crime writing. No unsolicited mss without preliminary letter. CLIENTS include Sybille Bedford, Kate Charles, Jan Dalley, Colin Forbes, P. D. James, Mary Morrissy, Conor Cruise O'Brien, William Shawcross. *Commission* Home 10%; US 20%; Translation 20%.

Gregory & Radice Authors' Agents*
Riverside Studios, Crisp Road, London W6 9RL
☎081-741 3646   Fax 081-846 9039
Contact *Jane Gregory/Dr Lisanne Radice/Reva Harini*

FORMED 1986, incorporating the former Jane Gregory Agency. *Handles* fiction and non-fiction. *Specialises* in crime, thrillers and politics. No plays, film scripts, science fiction, poetry, academic or children's. No unsolicited mss. Preliminary letter with synopsis and a couple of sample chapters (plus return postage) essential. No reading fee. *Commission* Home 15%; Newspapers 20%; US & Translation 20%. *Represents* three American companies, and is itself represented in most countries.

David Grossman Literary Agency Ltd
110–114 Clerkenwell Road, London EC1M 5SA
☎071-251 5046   Fax 071-490 2702
Contact *Material should be addressed to the Company.*

FOUNDED 1976. *Handles* full-length fiction and general non-fiction — good writing of all kinds and anything controversial. No verse or technical books for students. No original screenplays or teleplays (only sold for performance rights works existing in volume form). Generally works with published writers of fiction only but always pleased to consider 'truly original, well-written novels from beginners'. Best approach by preliminary letter giving full description of the work. No unsolicited mss. No reading fee. *Commission* rates vary for different markets. *Overseas associates* throughout Europe, Japan, Brazil and USA.

June Hall Literary Agency Ltd
See **The Peters Fraser & Dunlop Group Ltd**

Maggie Hanbury*
See **Casarotto Ramsay Ltd**

Roger Hancock Ltd
Greener House, 66–68 Haymarket,
London SW1Y 4AW
☎071-839 6753   Fax 071-930 8458
Contact *Material should be addressed to the Company.*

FOUNDED 1961. *Special interests* drama and light entertainment. Scripts only. No books. Unsolicited mss not welcome. Initial phone call required. No reading fee. *Commission* 10% throughout.

Xandra Hardie Literary Agency
See **Toby Eady Associates Ltd**

A. M. Heath & Co. Ltd*
79 St Martin's Lane, London WC2N 4AA
☎071-836 4271   Fax 071-497 2561
Contact *Mark Hamilton/Michael Thomas/Bill Hamilton/Sara Fisher*

FOUNDED 1919. *Handles* fiction and general non-fiction. No scripts or poetry. Preliminary letter and synopsis essential. No reading fee. CLIENTS include Saul Bellow, Anita Brookner and Jean Plaidy. *Commission* Home 10%; US 20%; Translation 20%; Film & TV 15%. *Overseas associates* in USA, Europe, South America, Japan.

David Higham Associates Ltd*

5-8 Lower John Street, Golden Square,
London W1R 4HA
☏ 071-437 7888   Fax 071-437 1072

Contact *Anthony Goff/John Rush* (Scripts)/
Elizabeth Cree

FOUNDED 1935. *Handles* fiction and general non-fiction: biography, history, current affairs, art, music, etc. Also scripts. Preliminary letter with synopsis essential in first instance. No reading fee. CLIENTS include John le Carré, Stephen Fry, James Herbert, Alice Walker. *Commission* Home 10%; US 15%; Translation 19%.

Pamela Hodgson Writers' Agency*

38 Westminster Palace Gardens, Artillery Row,
London SW1P 1RR
☏ 071-222 4468   Fax 071-222 4468

Contact *Pamela Hodgson*

FOUNDED 1991. *Handles* children's books only. No scripts. No unsolicited mss. Phone first or send preliminary letter with s.a.e. for return. No reading fee. *Commission* Home 15%; US 15%.

Vanessa Holt Associates Ltd

59 Crescent Road, Leigh-on-Sea, Essex SS9 2PF
☏ 0702 73787/714698   Fax 0702 471890

Contact *Vanessa Holt*

FOUNDED 1989. Ex-**John Farquharson/Curtis Brown**. *Handles* general adult fiction and non-fiction. No scripts, poetry, academic or technical. *Specialises* in commercial and crime fiction; social issues in non-fiction. No unsolicited mss. Approach by letter in first instance. No reading fee. *Commission* Home 10%; US 20%; Translation 20%. *Overseas associates* in USA, Europe, South America and Japan.

Valerie Hoskins

The Noel Gay Organisation, 19 Denmark Street,
London WC2H 8NA
☏ 071-836 3941   Fax 071-379 7027

Contact *Valerie Hoskins*

FOUNDED 1983. *Handles* scripts for film, theatre, television and radio. *Special interests* feature films. No unsolicited scripts; preliminary letter of introduction essential. No reading fee. CLIENTS include Daniel Boyle, Kit Hesketh-Harvey, Robin Miller, Jeff Povey, Gillian Richmond, Stephen Wyatt. *Commission* Home 15%; US 20% (maximum).

Howard Seddon Associates

BM Box 1129, London WC1N 3XX
☏ 0923 229784

Contact *Dr Keith Seddon*

FOUNDED 1988. *Handles* full-length general and literary fiction, general non-fiction and academic. No scripts. No poetry, crime, glitzy women's, short stories, gardening, cooking or children's. *Specialises* in fantasy, gothic, horror and literary fiction; folklore, New Age, occult, philosophy, religion, social issues. Unsolicited mss welcome. Return postage essential. Preferred approach is by letter including sample pages of mss together with c.v. £25 reading fee charged to unpublished authors. CLIENTS Jocelyn Almond, Ravan Christchild, Sheila Holligon, Gabriel Vane. *Commission* Home 15%; US 20%; Translation 20%.

Tanja Howarth*

19 New Row, London WC2N 4LA
☏ 071-240 5553/836 4142   Fax 071-379 0969

Contact *Tanja Howarth/Charlotte Oldfield*

FOUNDED 1970. Interested in taking on both fiction and non-fiction from British writers. No children's books, plays or poetry, but all other subjects considered providing the treatment is intelligent. No unsolicited mss. Preliminary letter preferred. No reading fee. Also an established agent for foreign literature, particularly from the German language. *Commission* Home 10%; Translation 15%.

ICM

Oxford House, 76 Oxford Street,
London W1R 1RB
☏ 071-636 6565   Fax 071-323 0101

Contact *Ian Amos/Amanda David*

FOUNDED 1973. *Handles* film/TV/theatre scripts. No books. No unsolicited mss. Preliminary letter essential. No reading fee. *Commission* 10% throughout. *Overseas associates* ICM New York and Los Angeles.

Michael Imison Playwrights Ltd

28 Almeida Street, Islington, London N1 1TD
☏ 071-354 3174   Fax 071-359 6273

Contact *Michael Imison/Sarah McNair*

FOUNDED 1944. Michael Imison is an ex-TV director and script editor for the BBC. *Handles* plays and books based on scripts, e.g. *Yes Minister;* also film, TV, radio and theatre. No fiction or general books. *Special interest* in writers motivated primarily by writing for the theatre, and translations, particularly from Russian and Italian. Unsolicited mss not welcome. Initial letter (plus s.a.e.) with recommendation from a known theatre professional essential. No reading fee. CLIENTS David Edgar, Dario Fo, Timberlake Wertenbaker, the Nöel Coward estate. *Commission* Home 10%; US and Translation 15%.

International Copyright Bureau Ltd
22A Aubrey House, Maida Avenue,
London W2 1TQ
☎071-724 8034   Fax 071-724 7662

Contact *Joy Westendarp*

FOUNDED 1905. *Handles* scripts for TV/theatre/film/radio exclusively. No books. Preliminary letter for unsolicited material essential. *Commission* Home 10%; US 19%; Translation 19%. *Overseas agents* in New York and most foreign countries.

International Scripts
1 Norland Square, Holland Park,
London W11 4PX
☎071-229 0736   Fax 071-792 3287

Contact *Bob Tanner/Yvonne Weaver/Jill Lawson*

FOUNDED 1979 by Bob Tanner. *Handles* all types of books and scripts for all media. No poetry. Complete mss preferred. CLIENTS include Masquerade (USA), Barrons (USA), Peter Haining, Robert A. Heinlein, Dean R. Koontz, Richard Laymon, Jean Moss, John Spencer. *Commission* Home 10–15%; US 20%; Translation 20%. *Overseas associates* include Ralph Vicinanza, Spectrum, USA; Thomas Schluck, Germany; Irina Reylander, Italy; Eliane Benisti, France; Ulla Lohren, Scandinavia; Gerd Plessl, Eastern Europe; Artisjus, Hungary.

Gordon Jarvie, Literary Agent
81 Comiston Drive, Edinburgh EH10 5QT
☎031-447 3417

Contact *Gordon Jarvie/Frances Jarvie*

FOUNDED 1990. *Handles* fiction: children's and adult; educational and ELT; and non-fiction: biography, history, current affairs. Also theatre scripts. No radio, film or TV scripts; no science fiction, technical books or journalism. Particularly interested in Irish and Scottish material, both fiction and non-fiction; and in children's books. Unsolicited mss welcome but initial approach by letter preferred, including synopsis of idea/text and s.a.e. for return. No reading fee. CLIENTS Myrtle Simpson, Fred Urquhart, and the George Friel estate. *Commission* Home 15%; US 15%; Translation 20%.

Jane Judd Literary Agency*
18 Belitha Villas, London N1 1PD
☎071-607 0273   Fax 071-607 0623

Contact *Jane Judd*

FOUNDED 1986. *Handles* general fiction and non-fiction: historical sagas, crime, fantasy, thrillers, literary fiction, cookery, humour, pop/rock, biography/autobiography, investigative journalism, health, women's interests and travel. 'Looking for good sagas/women's read but not Mills & Boon-type'. No scripts, academic, gardening or DIY. Approach with letter, including synopsis, sample chapter and return postage in first instance. Initial telephone call helpful in the case of non-fiction. CLIENTS Patrick Anthony, John Brunner, Jillie Collings, John Grant, Heather Hay, Jill Mansell, Jeremy Pascall, John Pidgeon, Elliot Philipp, Jonathon Porritt. *Commission* Home 10%; US 20%; Translation 20%.

Juvenilia
Avington, Near Winchester, Hampshire SO21 1DB
☎0962 78656   Fax 0962 864649

Contact *Rosemary Bromley*

FOUNDED 1973. *Handles* young/teen fiction, picture books, and non-fiction. Also scripts for TV and radio. No poetry or short stories unless part of a collection or picture book material. No unsolicited mss. Send preliminary letter with full details of work and biographical outline in first instance. Preliminary letters unaccompanied by return postage will not be answered. Phone calls not advised. CLIENTS include Stephanie Baudet, Elisabeth Beresford, Denis Bond, Terry Deary, Linda Dearsley, Elizabeth Edmonson, Cecilia Fitzsimons, Gaye Hicyilmaz, Chris Masters, Marc Meltonville, Helen Morgan, Marjorie Newman, Kelvin Reynolds, Enid Richemont, Peter Riley, Malcolm Rose, Maureen Spurgeon, Cathy Simpson, Keith West, Jennifer Zabel. *Commission* Home 10%; US 15%; Translation 20%.

Frances Kelly*
111 Clifton Road, Kingston upon Thames,
Surrey KT2 6PL
☎081-549 7830   Fax 081-547 0051

Contact *Frances Kelly*

FOUNDED 1978. *Handles* non-fiction, including illustrated: biography, history, art, self-help, food & wine, complementary medicine and therapies, New Age; and academic non-fiction in all disciplines. No scripts except for existing clients. No unsolicited mss. Approach by letter with brief description of work or synopsis, together with c.v. and return postage. *Commission* Home 10%; US 20%; Translation 20%.

Knight Features
20 Crescent Grove, London SW4 7AH
☏071-622 1467   Fax 071-622 1522
Contact *Peter Knight/Robin Mackay Miller/Ann King-Hall*

FOUNDED 1985. *Handles* motor sports, cartoon books for both adults and children, puzzles, factual and biographical material, and scripts (on a very selective basis) occasionally. No poetry, science fiction or cookery. No unsolicited mss. Send letter accompanied by c.v. and s.a.e. with synopsis of proposed work. Reading fee charged. CLIENTS Christopher Hilton, Frank Dickens, Michael Crozier, Frederic Mullally. *Commission* dependent upon authors and territories. *Overseas associates* United Media (USA); Auspac Media (Australia).

Lemon, Unna and Durbridge Ltd
24–32 Pottery Lane, London W11 4LZ
☏071-727 1346   Fax 071-727 9037
Directors *Sheila Lemon/Stephen Durbridge/ Wendy Gresser/Girsha Reid/Nigel Britten/Bethan Evans*
Contact *Nigel Britten/Bethan Evans*

Writers' agency which was formed from the merger in 1989 of Lemon & Durbridge Ltd with Harvey Unna & Stephen Durbridge Ltd. *Handles* theatre, TV, film and radio scripts. No unsolicited mss; preliminary letter and outline essential. No reading fee. *Commission* Home 10%; US and Translation varies. *Overseas associates* worldwide.

L'Epine Smith & Carney Associates
10 Wyndham Place, London W1H 1AS
☏071-724 0739   Fax 071-724 3725
Contact *Terry Carney*

FOUNDED 1957. Only interested in plays and TV scripts. Send synopsis in the first instance. *Commission* Terms on application.

Barbara Levy Literary Agency*
21 Kelly Street, London NW1 8PG
☏071-485 6037   Fax 071-284 0292
Contact *Barbara Levy/John Selby*

FOUNDED 1986. *Handles* general fiction, non-fiction and scripts for TV and radio. No unsolicited mss. Send detailed preliminary letter in the first instance. No reading fee. *Commission* Home 10%; US 20%;

Translation by arrangement, in conjunction with **Marsh & Sheil Ltd**. *US associates* Arcadia Ltd, New York.

Christopher Little
49 Queen Victoria Street, London EC4N 4SA
☏071-236 5881   Fax 071-236 7625
Contact *C. J. Little/B. Godfrey/J. Hytner*

FOUNDED 1979. *Handles* full-length fiction, non-fiction, and film/TV scripts. *Special interests* crime, thrillers, historical fiction. Reading fee of £40.25 (incl. VAT), plus postage. CLIENTS include Erin Pizzey, A. J. Quinnell, Carolyn Terry, W. Wright (alias David Graham), Peter Holt, Alastair MacNeill, Simon Gandolfi. *Commission* Home 20%; US 20%; Translation 20%.

London Independent Books Ltd
1A Montagu Mews North, London W1H 1AJ
☏071-706 0486   Fax 071-486 3470
Contact *Mrs C. Whitaker*

FOUNDED 1971. A self-styled 'small and idiosyncratic' agency. *Handles* fiction and non-fiction reflecting the tastes of the proprietors. All subjects considered (except computer books), providing the treatment is strong and saleable. Scripts handled only if by existing clients. *Special interests* boats, travel, travelogues, commercial fiction. No unsolicited mss; letter, synopsis and first two chapters with return postage the best approach. No reading fee. CLIENTS 'none are household names, yet!' *Commission* Home 15%; US 20%; Translation 20%.

Bill McLean Personal Management
23B Deodar Road, Putney, London SW15 2NP
☏081-789 8191
Contact *Bill McLean*

FOUNDED 1972. *Handles* scripts only, for all media. No books. No unsolicited mss. Phone call or introductory letter essential. No reading fee. CLIENTS Dwynwen Berry, Jane Galletly, Tony Jordan, David Lane, Bill Lyons, John Maynard, Glen McCoy, Michael McStay, Les Miller, Jeffrey Segal, Frank Vickery, Mark Wheatley. *Commission* Home 10%.

Eunice McMullen Children's Literary Agent Ltd
38 Clewer Hill Road, Windsor, Berkshire SL4 4BW
☏0753 830348   Fax 0753 833459

Contact *Eunice McMullen*

FOUNDED 1992. *Handles* all types of children's material from picture books to teenage fiction, plus some non-fiction. Some scripts (provided they are for children). Particularly interested in children's fiction and illustrated texts. Send preliminary letter with s.a.e., outline and biographical details in the first instance. No unsolicited scripts; sample chapters only initially. No reading fee. CLIENTS Mark Foreman, Simon James, Sue Porter, James Riordan, David Wood. *Commission* Home 10%; US 15%; Translation 20%.

Andrew Mann Ltd*

1 Old Compton Street, London W1V 5PH
☎071-734 4751   Fax 071-287 9264

Contact *Anne Dewe/Tina Betts*

In association with **Jane Conway-Gordon**. FOUNDED 1975. *Handles* fiction, general non-fiction, and film/TV/theatre/radio scripts. No unsolicited mss. Preliminary letter, synopsis and s.a.e. essential. No reading fee. *Commission* Home 10%; US 19%; Translation 19%. *Overseas associates* various.

Manuscript ReSearch

PO Box 33, Bicester, Oxon OX6 8BU
☎0869 252992

Contact *Graham Jenkins/V. Miller*

FOUNDED 1988. *Handles* fiction: thrillers, historical novels, crime and general; biographies, children's and scripts for TV/radio. No technical, religious, science fiction, poetry or short stories unless from established clients. *Special interests* revision/rewriting scripts for selected clients. Optional criticism service available, including professional line-by-line editing and laser printing. Approach by letter with s.a.e. in first instance. No reading fee. CLIENTS include Tom Barrat, Richard Butler, Nicholai Kollantoy, Val Manning, Peter Pook. *Commission* Home 10%; US 20%.

Marjacq Scripts Ltd

32 Cumberland Mansions, Nutford Place,
London W1H 5ZB
☎071-724 0565   Fax 071-723 3405

Contact *Jacqui Lyons*

FOUNDED 1974. Fiction and non-fiction, plus radio and TV scripts. No children's or religious. Unsolicited mss welcome with s.a.e. but phone call in the first instance preferred. No reading fee. *Commission* Home 10%; US 10%; Translation 20%.

Marsh & Sheil Ltd

19 John Street, London WC1N 2DL
☎071-405 7473   Fax 071-405 5239

Contact *Paul Marsh/Susanna Nicklin*

FOUNDED 1985. Marsh & Sheil deals in translation rights only, on behalf of selected British and American agents. No unsolicited mss, ideas or synopses. CLIENTS include **Anthony Sheil Associates**, F. Joseph Spieler, Don Congdon Associates, Watkins Loomis and Harriet Wasserman. *Commission* Translation 10%.

Judy Martin

20 Powis Mews, London W11 1JN
☎071-229 8764   Fax 071-792 3635

Contact *Judy Martin*

FOUNDED 1990. *Handles* fiction, including science fiction; non-fiction: travel, history, humour; children's books; journalism; and scripts for radio, film and television. No theatre, poetry or photography. Unsolicited mss welcome. Include letter giving past publishing history and details of rejections, together with s.a.e. for reply or return of mss. No reading fee. *Commission* Home 10%; US 20%; Translation 20%. *Foreign rights* **Marsh & Sheil Ltd**.

M. C. Martinez Literary Agency

60 Oakwood Avenue, Southgate,
London N14 6QL
☎081-886 5829

Contact *Mary Caroline Martinez/Francoise Budd*

FOUNDED 1988. *Handles* high-quality fiction, children's books, arts and crafts, interior design, DIY, cookery, travel and business. Also scripts for TV, radio and theatre. *Specialises* in fiction, children's and travel. No unsolicited mss. Preliminary letter with synopsis and s.a.e. is advised. No reading fee. DTP service also available. *Commission* Home 15%; US 20%; Translation 20%. Works in conjunction with several foreign agencies.

Blanche Marvin

21A St John's Wood High Street,
London NW8 7NG
☎071-722 2313   Fax 071-722 2313

Contact *Blanche Marvin*

FOUNDED 1968. *Handles* general non-fiction and scripts for film/radio/TV/ theatre. No poetry. Send c.v. and outline of the work in the first instance. No reading fee. *Commission* 12½% throughout.

MBA Literary Agents Ltd*

45 Fitzroy Street, London W1P 5HR
☏ 071-387 2076/4785   Fax 071-387 2042

Contact *Diana Tyler/John Richard Parker/Meg Davis/Ruth Needham*

FOUNDED 1971. *Handles* fiction and non-fiction. No poetry or children's fiction. Also scripts for film, television, radio and theatre. CLIENTS include Jeffrey Caine, Glenn Chandler, Neil Clarke, Valerie Georgeson, Andrew Hodges, BS Johnson (estate), Roy Lancaster, Paul J. McAuley, Anne McCaffrey, Anne Perry, Iain Sinclair, Tom Vernon, Douglas Watkinson, Freda Warrington, Patrick Wright, Valerie Windsor. No unsolicited mss. No reading fee. Preliminary letter with outline and s.a.e. essential. *Commission* Home 10%; US 20%; Translation 20%; Theatre/TV/ Radio 10%; Film 10-15%. *Overseas associates* in USA, Japan, and throughout Europe. Also rights representative in the UK for the Donald Maass Agency and **Ethan Ellenberg Agency**, New York.

Millstone Lit

17 Broombank, Birkby Park, Huddersfield, West Yorkshire HD2 2DJ
☏ 0484 512817

Contact *Reggie Byram*

FOUNDED 1991. *Handles* adult fiction and non-fiction only. No children's. No unsolicited mss. Approach by letter or phone; synopses (with s.a.e.) considered. No reading fee. CLIENTS include Hope Dubé and James Lansbury. *Commission* Home 10%; US 15%.

Richard Milne Ltd

28 Makepeace Avenue, London N6 6EJ
☏ 081-340 7007

Contact *R. M. Sharples/K. N. Sharples*

FOUNDED 1956. *Specialises* in drama and comedy scripts for radio, film and television but not presently in the market for new clients as 'fully committed in handling work by authors we already represent'. No unsolicited mss. *Commission* Home 10%; US 15%; Translation 25%.

William Morris Agency UK Ltd*

31-32 Soho Square, London W1V 5DG
☏ 071-434 2191   Fax 071-437 0238

Contact *Stephen M. Kenis* (films)/*Jane Annakin* (television/theatre)/ *Lavinia Trevor* (books)

FOUNDED 1965. Worldwide theatrical and literary agency with offices in New York, Beverly Hills and Nashville; associates in Rome, Munich and Sydney. *Handles* theatre, television, film and radio scripts; fiction and general non-fiction. Writers should approach by letter with synopsis/ sample chapters and s.a.e. No unsolicited material. No reading fee. *Commission* Film/TV/Theatre/UK Books 10%; US 20%; Translation 20%.

Michael Motley Ltd*

42 Craven Hill Gardens, London W2 3EA
☏ 071-723 2973   Fax 071-262 4566

Contact *Michael Motley*

FOUNDED 1973. *Handles* all subjects except short mss (e.g. freelance journalism), some poetry, and original dramatic material. No scripts. *Special interest* crime novels. Mss will be considered but must be preceded by a preliminary letter with s.a.e. No reading fee. CLIENTS include Simon Brett, Doug Nye, K. M. Peyton, Barry Turner. *Commission* Home 10%; US 15%; Translation 20%. *Overseas associates* in all publishing centres.

The Maggie Noach Literary Agency*

21 Redan Street, London W14 0AB
☏ 071-602 2451   Fax 071-603 4712

Contact *Maggie Noach*

FOUNDED 1982. Ex-**A. P. Watt** and pronounced 'no-ack'. *Handles* a wide range of books including literary fiction, general non-fiction and some children's. Also film/TV rights in association with **Seifert Dench Associates**. No scientific, academic or specialist non-fiction. No romantic fiction, poetry, plays or books for the very young. Recommended for promising young writers but few new clients taken on as it is considered vital to give individual attention to each author's work. Unsolicited mss not welcome. Approach by letter giving a brief description of the book and enclosing a few sample pages. Return postage essential. No reading fee. *Commission* Home 10%; US 20%; Translation 20%.

Andrew Nurnberg Associates Ltd*

Clerkenwell House, 45-47 Clerkenwell Green, London EC1R 0HT
☏ 071-251 0321   Fax 071-251 0584

Directors *Andrew Nurnberg/Klaasje Mul/Sarah Nundy*

FOUNDED in the mid-1970s. *Specialises* in foreign rights, representing leading authors and agents.

Alexandra Nye

45 Blackheath Road, Greenwich,
London SE10 8PE
☏ 081-691 9532

Contact *Alexandra Nye*

FOUNDED 1991 by Alexandra Nye, former director of Maclean Dubois. 'New agency with a real interest in taking on first-time novelists.' *Handles* fiction and topical non-fiction. *Special interests* literary fiction, biography, thrillers. No children's, horror or crime. No scripts, poetry or plays. Unsolicited mss welcome (s.a.e. essential for return). Preliminary approach by letter, with synopsis, preferred. Reading fee for supply of detailed report on mss. CLIENTS include Robin Jenkins, Dr Tom Gallagher. *Commission* Home 10%; US 20%; Translation 15%.

David O'Leary Literary Agents

10 Lansdowne Court, Lansdowne Rise,
London W11 2NR
☏ 071-229 1623   Fax 071-221 7185

Contact *David O'Leary*

FOUNDED 1988. *Handles* fiction, both popular and literary, and non-fiction. Areas of interest include ecology, history, popular science, Russia and Ireland (history and fiction). No scripts, poetry or children's. No unsolicited mss but happy to discuss a proposal. Ring or write in the first instance. No reading fee. CLIENTS include James Barwick, Roy MacGregor-Hastie, Don Robins, Douglas Sutherland. *Commission* Home 10%; US 10%. *Overseas associates* Lennart Sane, Scandinavia, Spain and South America; Tuttle Mori, Japan.

Deborah Owen Ltd*

78 Narrow Street, Limehouse, London E14 8BP
☏ 071-987 5119/5441   Fax 071-538 4004

Contact *Deborah Owen/Rosemary Scoular*

FOUNDED 1971. Small agency specialising in representing authors direct around the world. *Handles* international fiction and non-fiction (books which can be translated into a number of languages). No scripts, poetry, science fiction, children's or short stories. No unsolicited mss. No new authors at present. CLIENTS include Amos Oz, Ellis Peters, Delia Smith, Murray Smith. *Commission* Home 10%; US 15%; Translation 15%.

Mark Paterson & Associates*

10 Brook Street, Wivenhoe, Colchester,
Essex CO7 9DS
☏ 0206 825433   Fax 0206 822990

Contact *Mark Paterson/Mary Swinney*

FOUNDED 1961. *Specialises* in psychoanalysis and psychotherapy. No song or play scripts. No articles. No unsolicited mss; preliminary letter preferred. May charge reading fee. CLIENTS include Hugh Brogan, Vivian Cook, Sir Arthur Evans, Peter Moss, Dorothy Richardson, Hugh Schonfield, D. W. Winnicott, and the estate of Sigmund Freud. *Commission* 20% throughout (including sub-agent's commission).

John Pawsey

60 High Street, Tarring, Worthing, West
Sussex BN14 7NR
☏ 0903 205167   Fax 0903 205167

Contact *John Pawsey*

FOUNDED 1981. Experience in the publishing business has helped to attract some top names here, and develop new talent too. *Handles* non-fiction: biography, politics, current affairs, show business, gardening, travel, sport, business and music; and fiction: thrillers, crime, women's and contemporary. *Special interests* sport, politics, current affairs and popular fiction. No scripts, poetry, short stories, journalism or academic. Preliminary letter with s.a.e. essential. No reading fee. CLIENTS include Trevor McDonald, Simon Barnes, David Lewis, David Rayvern Allen, Caroline Fabre, Ben Bova, Orson Scott Card. *Commission* Home 10–15%; US 19%; Translation 19%. *Overseas associates* in USA, Japan and throughout Europe.

Maggie Pearlstine

31 Ashley Gardens, Ambrosden Avenue,
London SW1P 1QE
☏ 071-828 4212   Fax 071-834 5546

Contact *Maggie Pearlstine*

FOUNDED 1989. *Handles* full-length fiction: thrillers, crime, horror, sagas, contemporary, women's; and general non-fiction: home and leisure, cookery, gardening, craft, health, biography, history, current affairs, business. *Specialises* in commercial fiction and illustrated lifestyle. No children's or poetry. Send preliminary letter with synopsis and s.a.e. in the first instance. No reading fee. CLIENTS Roy Hattersley, Glorafilia (Carole Lazarus & Jennifer Berman), Catherine Neal, Prof. Robert Winston. *Commission* Home 12½% (fiction), 10% (non-fiction); US 20%; Translation 20%.

Penman Literary Agency

175 Pall Mall, Leigh-on-Sea, Essex SS9 1RE
☏ 0702 74438

Contact *Leonard G. Stubbs*

FOUNDED 1950. *Handles* fiction mainly, plus a small amount of non-fiction (biography and autobiography). No unsolicited mss. Send preliminary letter with synopsis. No reading fee. *Commission* Home 10%; Overseas 15%.

Peters Fraser & Dunlop Group Ltd*

503–504 The Chambers, Chelsea Harbour, Lots Road, London SW10 0XF
☎071–376 7676   Fax 071–352 7356/351 1756

Contact *Michael Sissons* (books)/*Anthony Jones* (film/TV)/*Pat Kavanagh* (books and serial)/*Norman North* (TV drama/fiction)/ *Caroline Dawnay* (books)/*Charles Walker* (TV documentary/ books)/ *Araminta Whitley* (books)/*Kenneth Ewing & Gordon Dickerson* (theatre)/*Tim Corrie* (film/TV)/ *Richard Wakeley* (film/TV)/*Mark Lucas* (books)/ *Maureen Vincent & Ginette Chalmers* (artists)/ *Lucinda Culpin/Rosemary Canter/Laura Fleminger* (books/June Hall Agency)/*Rosemary Canter* (children's/June Hall Agency)

Contact *June Hall* ☎ 071–352 4233

FOUNDED April 1988 as a result of the merger of A. D. Peters & Co. Ltd and Fraser & Dunlop, and was later joined by the June Hall Literary Agency. Michael Sissons (married to Julian Barnes) and Anthony Jones are one of the most high-powered teams in London. With Fraser & Dunlop bringing their experience as a show business agency to the group, this is a truly comprehensive source of contact with all branches of the media. *Handles* all sorts of books including fiction and children's, plus scripts for film, theatre, radio and TV material. *Special interests* 'Building careers for writers of talent.' No third-rate DIY. No unsolicited mss. Prospective clients should write 'a full and honest letter, with a clear account of what he/she has done and wants to do.' No reading fee. CLIENTS include Sally Beauman, Margaret Drabble, Clive James, Robert McCrum, John Mortimer, Douglas Reeman, Ruth Rendell, Anthony Sampson, Gerald Seymour, Tom Stoppard, and the Evelyn Waugh estate. *Commission* Home 10%; US 20%; Translation 20%.

Laurence Pollinger Ltd

18 Maddox Street, London W1R 0EU
☎071–629 9761   Fax 071–629 9765

Contact *Gerald J. Pollinger/Margaret Pepper/ Romany van Bosch/Juliet Burton* (negotiating editor)/*Lesley Hadcroft* (children's books)

FOUNDED 1958. A successor of Pearn, Pollinger & Higham. *Handles* all types of books including

children's, but no pure science, academic or technological. Good for crime and romantic fiction. No plays. ACCOUNTS include the estates of H. E. Bates, Scott Fitzgerald, Graham Greene, D. H. Lawrence and other notables. Unsolicited mss welcome if preceded by letter. No phone calls. A contribution of £10 is requested towards editorial costs. *Commission* Home 15%; US 15%; Translation 20%.

Murray Pollinger*

222 Old Brompton Road, London SW5 0BZ
☎071–373 4711   Fax 071–373 3775

Contact *Murray Pollinger/Gina Pollinger/Sara Menguc*

FOUNDED 1969. Part of the Pollinger dynasty (Murray is the youngest son of Laurence), with a particularly strong name for new writers. Securely based on Roald Dahl and one or two big-selling literary novelists. *Handles* all types of general fiction and non-fiction. No poetry, plays or travel, and no scripts of any kind. No unsolicited mss; writers should send a letter with synopsis and names of other agents and publishers previously approached. CLIENTS include Charlotte Bingham, J. M. Coetzee, John Gribbin, Molly Keane, Penelope Lively, Lyall Watson, and the estate of Roald Dahl. *Commission* Home 10%; Foreign 20%. *Overseas associates* in all major cultural centres.

Shelley Power Literary Agency Ltd

PO Box 149A, Surbiton, Surrey KT6 5JH
48 Kings Road, Long Ditton, Surrey KT6 5JF
☎081–398 7723   Fax 081–398 8723

Contact *Shelley Power*

FOUNDED 1976. *Handles* general commercial fiction, quality fiction, business books, self-help, true crime, investigative exposés, film and entertainment. No scripts, short stories, children's or poetry. Preliminary letter with brief outline of project (plus s.a.e.) essential. Send to PO Box, not Kings Road address. No reading fee. CLIENTS include Michael Beer, Steven Corbin, Stephen Gray, Sutherland Lyall, Donald McRae, Neville Sherriff, Gina Stewart, Madge Swindells, Roger Wilkes. *Commission* Home 10%; US/Translation 19%.

PVA Management Ltd

Hallow Park, Hallow, Worcester WR2 6PG
☎0905 640663   Fax 0905 640663

Contact *Laraine King*

FOUNDED 1978. *Handles* mainly non-fiction, plus some fiction and scripts. Send preliminary letter with synopsis and return postage. *Commission* Home and Abroad 15%.

Radala & Associates

17 Avenue Mansions, Finchley Road,
London NW3 7AX
☎071-794 4495   Fax 081-209 1231
Contact *Richard Gollner/Neil Hornick/Anna Swan*

FOUNDED 1970. *Handles* quality fiction, non-fiction, drama, performing and popular arts, psychotherapy, writing from Eastern Europe. Also provides editorial service, initiates in-house projects and can recommend independent professional readers if unable to read or comment on submissions. Does *not* handle 'poetry, screenplays, epic sword 'n' sorcery fantasies, Mills 'n' Boonish romance, Raymond Chandler and John Le Carré pastiches, or any pre-Yeltsin Cold War thrillers, semi-autobiographical tales of youthful angst in suburbia or anything beginning with the hero waking up with a terrible hangover; no sub-literate novels by advertising executives featuring lusty execs bedding dolly birds between drinking bouts; no rollicking reminiscences of lower-deck life in the 1950's Merchant Navy; no novels or sitcoms featuring characters with names like Kevin Crapper and Butch Beerbelly; no esoteric studies written for a target readership of three fellow enthusiasts in Surrey.' Prospective clients should send a shortish letter plus synopsis (maximum 2 pages), first two chapters (double-spaced, numbered pages) and s.a.e. for return. *Commission* Home 10%; US 15-20%; Translation 20%. *Overseas associates* **Writers House Inc.** (Al Zuckermann), New York, plus agents throughout Europe.

Margaret Ramsay Ltd

See **Casarotto Ramsay Ltd**

Jim Reynolds Associates

Westbury Mill, Westbury, Near Brackley,
Northamptonshire NN13 5JS
☎0280 701582   Fax 0280 703706
Contact *Ann Reynolds*

FOUNDED 1988. *Handles* military history, biography, Middle East, cricket, crime, current affairs, social and political studies, and investigative journalism. No scripts. No fiction, instructional, technical, scientific and business, DIY, children's or poetry. No unsolicited mss; send preliminary letter describing proposed mss or project, together with note on author's relevant qualifications. S.a.e. essential. No reading fee. CLIENTS Michael Adeney, Paul Beg, John Bulloch, Gavin Hewitt, Harvey

Morris, Keith Skinner, Brian Wilkins. *Commission* Home 10%; US 19%; Translation 19%. *Overseas associates* **Robert Ducas**, USA; Peter Fritz, Germany; Mary Kling, France; Menno Kohn, Holland.

Patricia Robertson

Flat 1, 87 Caledonian Road, London N1 9BT
☎071-278 9982   Fax 071-837 3486
Contact *Patricia Robertson*

FOUNDED 1985. *Handles* fiction: general, crime, historical, fantasy; and non-fiction: craft, biography and memoirs, history and social history. Some collaboration on scripts with Mike Sharland of the **Sharland Organisation**. No poetry, short stories or specialist technical books. Unsolicited mss welcome but preliminary letter enclosing s.a.e. much preferred. No reading fee. CLIENTS include Phil Drabble, B. M. Gill. *Commission* Home 10%; US 15%; Translation 20%. *Overseas associates* Harold Ober Associates Inc. (USA); Liepman AG; Robert Fouques du Parc; Rosemarie Buchman; Tuttle Mori.

Rogers, Coleridge & White Ltd*

20 Powis Mews, London W11 1JN
☎071-229 3717   Fax 071-229 9084
Contact *Deborah Rogers/Gill Coleridge/Patricia White/Ann Warnford Davis* (foreign rights)

FOUNDED 1967. *Handles* fiction, non-fiction and children's books. No poetry, plays or technical books. Rights representative in UK for several New York agents. *Commission* Home 10%; US 15%. *Overseas associates* ICM, New York.

Herta Ryder

c/o Toby Eady Associates, 18 Park Walk,
London SW10 0AQ
☎081-948 1010
Contact *Herta Ryder*

FOUNDED 1984. *Handles* fiction and non-fiction, including children's (particularly older children's), music (lives rather than specialist), military history and German books of quality (Herta Ryder is London representative for Liepman AG, Zurich). No scripts, poetry, individual short stories, technical, textbooks or articles. Unsolicited mss considered but explanatory letter preferred in the first instance. CLIENTS include Judy Blume, Gwyneth Jones (Ann Halam), Adrienne Kennaway, Jean Morris, Farley Mowat, David Henry Wilson. *Commission* Home 10%; US 15%; Translation 20%. *Overseas associates* Harold Ober Associates, New York, plus associates in most other countries.

Ian Sales Associates

5 Spains Hall Place, Woodlands, Basildon,
Essex SS16 5UR
☎0268 531353   Fax 0268 524605

Contact *Ian Sales/Ken Ford/Richard Langham*

FOUNDED 1990. *Handles* scripts for TV (including documentary), film and theatre. No radio. No books. Particularly interested in TV comedy. Mss welcome. Send letter with synopsis (and s.a.e.) in the first instance. No reading fee. CLIENTS Neil Antony, Simon Basham, Debbie Sayer. *Commission* ·Home 10%; US 10%.

Tessa Sayle Agency*

11 Jubilee Place, London SW3 3TE
☎071-823 3883   Fax 071-823 3363

Contact *Tessa Sayle/Rachel Calder* (books)/*Penny Tackaberry* (drama)

FOUNDED 1976 under present ownership. *Handles* fiction: literary novels rather than category fiction; non-fiction: current affairs, social issues, biographies, historical; and drama (TV, film and theatre): contemporary social issues or drama with comedy, rather than broad comedy. No poetry, children's, textbooks, science fiction, fantasy, horror or musicals. No unsolicited mss. Preliminary letter essential, including a brief biographical note and a synopsis. No reading fee. CLIENTS include (books) Stephen Amidon, Ronan Bennett, Peter Benson, Rose Boyt, Pete Davies, Margaret Forster, Georgina Hammick, Paul Hogarth, Mark Illis, Thomas Keneally, Andy Kershaw, Phillip Knightley, Rory MacLean, Ann Oakley, Kate Pullinger, Ronald Searle, Alan Sillitoe, William Styron, Mary Wesley; (drama) Janet Barron, Ann Marie Di Mambro, Sarah Dunant, Stuart Hepburn, Robert David McDonald, Geoff McQueen, Nigel Moffatt, Ayshe Raif, Trix Worrell. *Commission* Home 10%; US 20%; Translation 20%. *Overseas associates* in USA, Japan and throughout Europe.

Seifert Dench Associates

24 D'Arblay Street, London W1V 3FH
☎071-437 4551   Fax 071-439 1355

Contact *Linda Seifert/Elizabeth Dench*

FOUNDED 1972. *Handles* scripts for television and film only. Unsolicited mss will be read, but a letter with sample of work and c.v. (plus s.a.e.) is preferred. CLIENTS include Peter Chelsom, Tony Grisoni, Michael Radford, Stephen Volk. *Commission* Home 15%. *Overseas associates* William Morris, Sanford Skoura & Gross (Los Angeles).

James Sharkey Associates Ltd

3rd Floor, 15 Golden Square, London W1R 3AG
☎071-434 3801   Fax 071-494 1547

Contact *Cat Ledger*

FOUNDED 1983. Actors' and literary agency. *Handles* adult fiction and non-fiction. No scripts. Preliminary letter and synopsis with s.a.e. essential in the first instance. No reading fee. *Commission* 10%.

The Sharland Organisation Ltd

9 Marlborough Crescent, Bedford Park,
London W4 1HE
☎081-742 1919   Fax 081-995 7688

Contact *Mike Sharland/Alice Sharland*

FOUNDED 1988. *Handles* fiction, non-fiction and scripts for TV, radio and theatre. Also markets books for film and handles stage, radio, film and television rights for authors. No scientific or technical books. *Specialises* in national and international film and TV negotiations. No unsolicited mss. Preliminary enquiry by letter or phone essential in the first instance. *Commission* Home 15%; US 20%; Translation 20%. *Overseas associates* various.

Vincent Shaw Associates

20 Jay Mews, Kensington Gore, London SW7 2EP
☎071-581 8215   Fax 071-225 1079

Contact *Vincent Shaw/Lester McGrath*

FOUNDED 1954. *Handles* TV, radio, film and theatre scripts only. Unsolicited mss welcome. Approach in writing enclosing s.a.e. No phone calls. *Commission* Home 10%; US and Translation by negotiation. *Overseas associates* Herman Chessid, New York.

Sheil Land Associates Ltd*

43 Doughty Street, London WC1N 2LF
☎071-405 9351   Fax 071-831 2127

Contact *Anthony Sheil/Sonia Land/Giles Gordon/ Mic Cheetham/Vivien Green/Jane Villiers* (film/ drama/TV); *Paul Marsh/Susie Nicklin* (Marsh & Sheil/foreign).

FOUNDED 1962. Formerly traded under the name of Anthony Sheil Associates. Incorporated the Richard Scott Simon Agency in 1989. *Handles* full-length general and literary fiction, biography, travel, cookery and humour. Also theatre, film, radio and TV scripts. One of the UK's most dynamic agencies, Sheil Land represents over 270 established clients and welcomes approaches from new clients looking either to start or to develop their careers to the top with a highly professional, innovative and caring agency. Known to negotiate sophisticated contracts with publishers. Preliminary letter with s.a.e. appreciated. No reading fee CLIENTS include Peter Ackroyd, Melvyn Bragg, Catherine Cookson, **Field Day Theatre Company**, John Fowles, Susan Hill, HRH The Prince of Wales, Michael Ignatieff, John Keegan, Richard Mabey, Michael Moorcock, Tom Sharpe, Anthony Sher, Rick Smolan, Sue Townsend, Rose Tremain. *Commission* Home 10%; US 20%; Translation 20%. *Overseas associates* **Georges Borchardt Inc.** (Richard Scott Simon); **Sanford J.Greenburger Associates** (Sheil Land Associates). UK representatives for **Farrar, Straus & Giroux Inc.** *Consultant* Film/Drama/TV *Lynda Myles.*

Caroline Sheldon Literary Agency*

71 Hillgate Place, London W8 7SS
☎071-727 9102

Contact *Caroline Sheldon*

FOUNDED 1985. *Handles* adult fiction, in particular women's, both commercial sagas and literary novels. Also full-length children's fiction. No TV/ film scripts unless by clients who also write books. Send letter with all relevant details of ambitions and four chapters of proposed book (enclose large s.a.e.). No reading fee. *Commission* Home 10%; US 20%; Translation 20% (handled by Jennifer Luithlen, The Rowans, 88 Holmfield Road, Leicester).

Jeffrey Simmons

10 Lowndes Square, London SW1X 9HA
☎071-235 8852   Fax 071-235 9733

Contact *Jeffrey Simmons*

FOUNDED 1978. *Handles* biography and autobiography, cinema and theatre, fiction (both quality and commercial), history, law and crime, politics and world affairs, parapsychology, sport and travel (but not exclusively). No children's books, cookery, crafts, hobbies or gardening. Film scripts handled only if by book-writing clients. *Special interests* personality books of all sorts and fiction from young writers (i.e. under 40) with a future. Writers become clients by personal introduction or by letter, enclosing a synopsis if possible, a brief biography, a note of any previously published books, plus a list of any publishers and agents who have already seen the mss. CLIENTS include Michael Bentine, Billy Boy, Clive Collins, Doris Collins, Adrienne Corri, Daniel Easterman, John Feltwell, Philippe Frossard, Fred Lawrence Guiles, Jim Haskins, Keith W. Wright. *Commission* Home 10-15%; US 15-20%; Translation 20%.

Richard Scott Simon Agency

See **Sheil Land Associates Ltd**

Carol Smith Literary Agency

25 Hornton Court, Kensington High Street, London W8 7RT
☎071-937 4874   Fax 071-938 5323

Contact *Carol Smith*

FOUNDED 1976. Ex-**A. P. Watt.** *Handles* general fiction of all sorts and general non-fiction. Scripts for TV/film only rarely. No technical material of any kind. Reputed to be good on encouraging talented young novelists. Unsolicited mss welcome with return postage. Introductory letter preferred. No reading fee. CLIENTS include John Cornwell, Alexander Frater, Sarah Harrison, Denise Robertson, Katie Stewart, Mike Wilks. *Commission* Home 10%; US 20%; Translation 20%.

Solo Syndication & Literary Agency Ltd

49-53 Kensington High Street, London W8 5ED
☎071-376 2166   Fax 071-938 3165

Contact *Don Short* (Chairman)/*John Appleton* (Senior Executive & Accounts)/*Trevor York* (Syndication Manager)/*Don Coolican* (Senior Editor)

FOUNDED 1978. *Handles* non-fiction. *Special interests* celebrity autobiographies, unauthorised biographies, sports and adventure stories, wildlife, nature & ecology, crime, fashion, beauty & health. Also some fiction but only from established authors. No unsolicited mss. Preliminary letter essential. CLIENTS include Britt Ekland, Michael Gatting, James Oram, Fred Perry. *Commission* Home 15%; US 20%; Translation 20-30%.

Specialises also in worldwide newspaper syndication of photographs, features and cartoons. Professional contributors only. CLIENTS in this field include the *Daily Mail, Mail on Sunday, YOU Magazine, Evening Standard, Guinness Book of Records, Woman's Own, Woman, Woman's Realm, Woman's Weekly,* plus News Limited of Australia and many others including fifty Fleet Street and international freelance journalists. *Commission* 50%.

Elaine Steel

110 Gloucester Avenue, London NW1 8JA
☎071-483 2681   Fax 071-483 4541

Contact *Elaine Steel*

FOUNDED 1986. Scripts and screenplays only. No technical or academic. Initial phone call preferred. CLIENTS include Les Blair, Michael Eaton, Troy Kennedy Martin, G. F. Newman, Rob Ritchie. *Commission* Home 10%; US 20%; Translation 20%.

Abner Stein*

10 Roland Gardens, London SW7 3PH
☎ 071-373 0456/370 7859   Fax 071-370 6316

Contact *Abner Stein*

FOUNDED 1971. *Handles* full-length fiction and general non-fiction. No scientific, technical, etc. No scripts. Send letter and outline in the first instance rather than unsolicited mss. *Commission* Home 10%; US 20%; Translation 20%.

Micheline Steinberg Playwrights' Agent

110 Frognal, London NW3 6XU
☎ 071-433 3980   Fax 071-794 8355

Contact *Micheline Steinberg*

FOUNDED 1988. *Specialises* in plays for stage, TV, radio and film. Best approach by preliminary letter (with s.a.e.) in the first instance. Dramatic associate for **Laurence Pollinger Ltd**. *Commission* Home 10%; Abroad 15%.

Belinda Sugg Literary Agency

Other End Cottage, Upper Moor, Wyre Piddle, Pershore, Worcestershire WR10 2JR
☎ 0386 860892   Fax 0386 556218

Contact *Belinda Sugg/Steven Sheppard/Mary Wills*

FOUNDED February 1989. *Handles* full-length fiction and non-fiction. Will consider most subjects at their discretion. No scripts, poetry, technical, religious or short stories. Claims to have adopted a more human approach with clients, giving individual help and encouragement to new writers by written assessment, and personal attention for all clients on their lists. First approach by letter or phone call. Assessment fee £147.00. CLIENTS include Ginny Graham, Paul Doherty, Terry Piper. *Commission* Home 15%; US 15%.

Peter Tauber Press Agency

94 East End Road, London N3 2SX
☎ 081-346 4165

Directors *Peter Tauber/Robert Tauber*

FOUNDED 1950. *Handles* women's fiction, especially family sagas and glitz; well-researched thrillers aimed at the international market; ingenious whodunnits and original fantasy; literature by Oxbridge or similar graduates; auto/biographies of the famous. No poetry, short stories, plays, children or foreign books. Preliminary letter with synopsis, author's c.v., copies of all previous rejections and s.a.e. essential. Only interested in British or Commonwealth authors under fifty; forty for literary fiction. *Commission* 20% worldwide.

J. M. Thurley

213 Linen Hall, 162–168 Regent Street, London W1R 5TA
☎ 071-437 9545/6   Fax 071-287 9208

Contact *Jon Thurley/Patricia Preece*

FOUNDED 1976. *Handles* all types of fiction, non-fiction, coffee-table books, etc. Also scripts for TV/film/radio/theatre. No short stories or children's illustrated books. No unsolicited mss; approach by letter in the first instance. No reading fee. *Commission* Home 10%; US 15%; Translation 15%.

Vardey & Brunton Associates*

Studio 8, 125 Moore Park Road, London SW6 4PS
☎ 071-384 1248   Fax 071-384 1246

Contact *Carolyn Brunton/Lucinda Vardey*

FOUNDED 1985. Now specialising in representation for US & Canadian publishers and agents including **Addison-Wesley**, Knox Burger Associates, Grove Weidenfeld, Penguin Canada, Madison Press, **Sagalyn Agency**, Lucinda Vardey Agency. No unsolicited mss.

Ed Victor Ltd*

162 Wardour Street, London W1V 3AT
☎ 071-734 4795   Fax 071-494 3400

Contact *Ed Victor/Graham Greene/Maggie Phillips/Sophie Hicks*

FOUNDED 1977. *Handles* a broad range of material from Iris Murdoch to Jack Higgins, Erich Segal to Stephen Spender. Leans towards the more commercial ends of the fiction and non-fiction spectrums. No scripts, no academic. Takes on very few new writers. After trying his hand at book publishing and literary magazines, Ed Victor, an ebullient American, found his true vocation. Strong opinions, very pushy and works hard for those whose intelligence he respects. Loves nothing more than a good title auction. Preliminary letter essential, setting out very concisely and clearly what the book aims to do. No unsolicited mss. CLIENTS include Douglas Adams, Jack Higgins, Erica Jong, Iris Murdoch, Erich Segal, Stephen Spender, and the estates of Raymond Chandler and Irving

Wallace. *Commission* Home 15%; US 15%; Translation 20%.

S. Walker Literary Agency
96 Church Lane, Goldington, Bedford MK41 0AS
☎0234 216229

Contact *Cora-Louise Oldfield*

FOUNDED 1939. *Handles* full-length fiction and some non-fiction. No poetry, short stories or short topical articles. No unsolicited mss. Preliminary letter enclosing synopsis and return postage essential. *Commission* Home 10%; US 20%; Translation 20%. *Overseas associates* Works in conjunction with agencies in most European countries and also negotiates directly with foreign publishers. *Consultant* E. K. Walker.

Cecily Ware Literary Agents
19C John Spencer Square, Canonbury,
London N1 2LZ
☎071-359 3787   Fax 071-226 9828

Contact *Cecily Ware/Gilly Schuster*

In association with **Comstock-Smith Literary Agency**. FOUNDED 1972. Primarily a film and television script agency representing work in all areas: drama, children's, series/serials, adaptations, comedies, etc. Also radio. Very few new clients being taken on. No unsolicited mss or phone calls. Approach in writing only. No reading fee. *Commission* Home 10%; US 10–20% by arrangement.

Warner Chappell Plays Ltd
129 Park Street, London W1Y 3FA
☎071-629 7600   Fax 071-499 9718

Contact *Michael Callahan*

Formerly the English Theatre Guild, Warner Chappell are now both agents and publishers of scripts for the theatre. No unsolicited mss; introductory letter essential. No reading fee. CLIENTS include Ray Cooney, Arthur Miller, John Steinbeck. *Commission* Home 10%; US 20%. *Overseas representatives* in USA, Canada, Australia, New Zealand, India, South Africa and Zimbabwe.

Watson, Little Ltd*
12 Egbert Street, London NW1 8LJ
☎071-722 9514   Fax 071-586 7649

Contact *Sheila Watson/Mandy Little*

Handles fiction and non-fiction. *Special interests* popular science, psychology, self-help, military history and business books. No scripts. Not interested in authors who wish to be purely academic writers. Send preliminary ('intelligent') letter rather than unsolicited synopsis. £10 administrative fee for unpublished authors. *Commission* Home 10%; US 19%; Translation 19%. *Overseas associates* **McIntosh & Otis**, New York; Mohrbooks, Zurich; La Nouvelle Agence, Paris; Agenzia Letteraria Internazionale, Milan; T & L Literary Agents, Amsterdam; Suzanne Palme, Scandinavia; Carmen Balcells, Barcelona & Rio de Janeiro; Tuttle-Mori, Tokyo. *Dramatic associate* **The Sharland Organisation**, London.

A. P. Watt Ltd
20 John Street, London WC1N 2DR
☎071-405 6774   Fax 071-831 2154

Contact *Hilary Rubinstein/Caradoc King/Rod Hall* (drama and media)/ *Imogen Parker/Lisa Eveleigh*

FOUNDED 1875. The oldest established literary agency in the world. *Handles* full-length typescripts, including children's books, screenplays for film and TV, and plays. No poetry, academic or specialist works. Unsolicited mss and outlines welcome but must be preceded by introductory letter, plus return postage. No reading fee. CLIENTS include Evelyn Anthony, Martin Gilbert, Nadine Gordimer, Michael Holroyd, Garrison Keillor, Alison Lurie, Timothy Mo, Jan Morris, Frank Muir, Ben Okri, Graham Swift. Also, the estates of Wodehouse, Graves and Maugham. *Commission* Home 10%; US 20%; Translation 20%. *Overseas associates* **Ellen Levine Inc.(USA)**.

Dinah Wiener Ltd*
27 Arlington Road, London NW1 7ER
☎071-388 2577   Fax 071-388 7559

Contact *Dinah Wiener*

FOUNDED 1985. *Handles* fiction and general non-fiction: auto/biography, popular science, cookery. No scripts, children's or poetry. Approach with preliminary letter in first instance, giving full but brief c.v. of past work and future plans. Mss submitted must include s.a.e. and be typed in double-spacing. CLIENTS include David Deutsch, Tania Kindersley, Dalene Matthee, Daniel Snowman, Michael Thornton. *Commission* Home 15%; US 20%; Translation 20%.

Michael Woodward Creations Ltd
Parlington Hall, Aberford, West
Yorkshire LS25 3EG
☎0532 813913   Fax 0532 813911

Contact *Michael Woodward*

FOUNDED 1990 to develop and handle characters and concepts for licensing with in-house studio facilities. New artists should forward samples, character profiles and concept synopses.

The Write Stuff

19 Cheval Place, London SW7 1EW

☎ 0222 465689   Fax 0222 465648

Contact *Richard Rees*

FOUNDED 1990. Celebrity press agency representing freelance journalists in the UK and US. No books or scripts. Approach in writing or by fax. No unsolicited material. CLIENTS *Empire, Hello!, Daily Express, Daily Mail,* Rusconi Editore, ACP. *Commission* Home 20%; US 50%. *Overseas associates* The Write Stuff, Los Angeles/Hollywood.

What I Did in the Holidays

The Subtle Art of Travel Writing

When I was twenty and a student I went to Turkey for the summer, teaching English in a little language school on the shores of the Black Sea. It was the height of the Cold War and a time when 'brain-washing' was much discussed. This fearsome technique, as you may remember, had supposedly been required to persuade US pilots captured in Korea to convert to communism; and William Sargent had written a memorable book on just this subject. It was called *Battle for the Mind* and my Turkish employer, seeing me reading it, begged to keep it when I left. 'It will help me so much to control the teachers and the classes.'

This was one insight. I felt I had gained others when I was involved in a car crash in the Taurus Mountains; when I was entertained in Konya, home of the whirling dervishes, by a manufacturer of torch batteries; and when I swam in the hot springs of Pammukale among the tombs of long-departed Romans. Except for my employer and an unfortunate encounter with a Turkish army officer, scary in memory even after thirty years, almost all the people whom I met had been friendly and fascinating, positively Homeric in their hospitality. In short, I felt I had really been travelling, had had some exceptional adventures and, since I was especially sensitive and had ambitions to be a writer, it was pretty obvious my first book – the first, that is, in a series of Dickensian proportions – would be my impressions of that summer in Turkey.

I must have been twenty-two and no longer a student when I threw away the manuscript containing my first efforts. Every sentence I had tried to write had plunged me deeper and deeper into an abyss of uncertainty and aridity, into a perfect confidence I had nothing whatever to say on this or any subject. As for sensitivity, others might have it, not I. And Dickens – forget him. Even the humblest of travel writers were so far over the horizon I was unfit to read them.

Looking back now I see it was appropriate to have some modesty about my own ability. But I also see a host of things I did not do which would have made my undertaking realistic, if not easy.

I had kept no systematic notes or journal. I had read little on Turkey, thinking the play of place and character would be enough. Rather than researching in a positive spirit, I had accepted my experiences passively, believing that the writer's 'reality' was what came at him in the ordinary course of events.

Put most simply, I had relied on genius, not work. Deciding only after the event to write about the summer, I had failed entirely to treat it, during the time that I was travelling, as a job, a project to be studied and accomplished, not perfectly, but so far as I was able. To have done so would have given shape and focus to whatever sensitivity I had.

I know now that you cannot even start to be a travel writer until you see it as a task, relating to the world out there, requiring all your intelligence, the hard sweat of research in libraries and on the ground, the discipline of note-taking and the greater discipline of writing, then rewriting patiently, until you have got as far as you can in rendering down your subject matter in the form that suits it – or suits your market.

That once realised, there opens up a type of work which is not well rewarded financially but is – if you care for travel, place and people – utterly and endlessly fascinating. Travel writers may grot and grind for a living and complain about it in an unseemly manner, given how privileged an existence it appears from the outside, but they do it because they love it, a cliché and a truth.

As for myself, my first travel book was written only when I had passed the age of thirty, requiring in the event five years and an infinity of notebooks. For the past six years I have earned my living as a full-time travel writer, dallying over other full-length books and churning out articles and guidebooks as quickly as I can, consistent, I hope with professionalism. This is the basic condition of the journalist. All three functions of the travel writer – books, articles and guidebooks – have rather different ground rules and it is worth looking at each separately.

Travel Articles for Newspapers and Magazines

The first question people always ask is 'How do I get my work published?' – to which there is no easy answer, though I will attempt an answer of sorts in just a moment. A much better opening question is 'What shall I write and how do I go about it?'

First, I think, you decide what places and what aspects of travel interest you and what kind of style you would like to write in – which may be anything from the moderately elevated, as in papers like *The Observer*, to the popular, as in magazines like *Bella*. This gives you a target, and if you are short of ideas plenty of publications are listed in this handbook.

Look quite closely at your target publications and ask yourself whether they stand in need of the ideas you are thinking of. Do they specialise in beach reports or lingering evocations of the monsoon? Are the articles literary or consumer-oriented or a mixture of both approaches? (The latter is often the case, with each article divided into a longer 'good read' section and a supplementary 'side-bar' or 'fact box' with all the necessary back-up information.) Now, in the light of a growing knowledge of the market, you try to marry your own interests and preferences to the gaps and opportunities you see. The object is to write freshly, but not naïvely. 'It's not where you've been, but how you've been there,' says Shona Crawford Poole, Travel Editor of *The Times*.

My own recommendation is that you should start by writing one foreign piece and one piece based in Britain. The foreign one will show that you can actually get yourself abroad and get your pen around something 'other', far from yourself. Conversely, the advantage of writing about travel and holidays in Britain is that many journalists turn up their noses at it and editors are often short of copy in this important department of travel-writing.

Unless you are rich, you will certainly have to work up the foreign piece while notionally on holiday. But you will have to remember that *you yourself are not on holiday*. You are there to collect material and think it through, not to enjoy yourself except as a by-product and not to entertain your spouse, your lover or five children. There are certainly good travel stories which feature husbands, wives and children, but you will only be able to write these on the basis of, ideally, sharp and, possibly, humorous observation of your partner or your children. The condition of the travel writer is one of perpetual observation, whether at home or abroad. You should also realise that the travel writer is set apart from his subject-matter by the fact that he or very often she is rushing madly from place to place trying to fit as much as possible into every expensive day abroad. There is remarkably little lolling about involved, and often, even in a hot country where every fibre longs for it, no time even for a swim.

Travel stories set in the UK follow all the same rules as foreign ones but are made rather harder by the need to create the kind of atmosphere which comes so much more easily when you are writing of foreign places.

For both kinds of article, you need to use guidebooks and any material published by tourist offices, if only to understand the basic background and to make sure you are not missing anything important. If there are general books on the area, it is useful to have read them in advance – but only in the broad sense of culture and awareness. Journalism goes so quickly that you won't have a chance to do a great deal of new reading; and if you do, there is always the possibility you will bog your writing down with unassimilated material. (Almost all travel editors will tell you that the greatest and most persistent fault of the unpractised writer is trying to put too much into a single article.)

Now, it is perfectly possible that when you survey the market you will decide that they have more than enough of what you want to offer. You will probably be quite right, since travel writing is, alas, a buyers' market and editors have drawers full of usable articles quite often queueing for anything up to a year for inclusion in the paper. So then you will want to look around for something a little different – which may be, unromantically, in the field of service journalism. There are respected travel writers who not only write about places – known as 'destinations' in the travel trade – but who have carved out a speciality for themselves in a practical area such as travel insurance, caravanning, ferries or even ideas for weekends. Then there are activity holidays. Think of it: walking, sailing, riding, just anything at all to do with horses, fishing, photography classes, bell-ringing or flower arrangement in funny places. The range is huge. Skiing is another subject on which many thousands of articles are published each year.

By the time you have thought about all this and written an article or two to your own satisfaction, you will be starting to professionalise yourself in what is often more a craft than an art. You will also have material ready to offer outside the home and possibly some photographs – but only if photography is a special interest. (If it isn't, you will take unusable pictures and distract yourself fatally from your writing. If you *are* a photographer, you should know that papers increasingly and magazines most certainly will want colour slides rather than black and white or colour prints. All must be briefly captioned.)

It is now, with articles in hand, that the hard part begins. Unless you know somebody who knows somebody – which remains, unfortunately, the easiest way to get a start – you will simply have to send your work off to the travel editor of your choice and await judgement. Travel editors receive huge quantities of unsolicited 'spec' pieces but most are hard-working folk who do eventually write back. Don't telephone – everybody in newspapers is always in a panic. Don't send the articles to two papers at once – an easy way to embarrass yourself if both accept you – and do be resilient enough to accept rejection and send them on to another paper immediately, amended if necessary in the light of any comments. And while you are waiting, write two more so as to send a second round to the recipient of your first efforts. This is much more likely to convince them you are serious than a single mail-shot out of the blue.

But it is, I'm afraid, incredibly difficult to get in. What actually happens is that travel editors are busy making patterns. This month they may be looking for material on America for a four-page binge on US family holidays and they will not give a second thought to your efforts on birdwatching in Iceland. Next month it may be all the other way around. The trouble is, you never know, nor, even if you get to know them well, do the editors ever get round to telling you. Even as a regular freelance, you are almost always in the position of having to suggest ideas against a wall of ignorance about what is really wanted.

Apart from seeing your work in print and getting paid for it, the great importance of getting published is that you may in due course reach a position where the newspaper itself sends you, or accepts an offered travel trade freebie on your behalf (which you should accept but treat like a free book offered for review. Some journalists still see a freebie as a chance to swill away, then write an article of grovel rather than evaluation. But that, I'm glad to say, is increasingly the exception.)

The fact, though, is that unless you become established, the systematic writing of travel articles is impossible because of the ruinous expense of gathering material. This means, for better or for worse, that would-be entrants sink or swim quite quickly. On the other hand, there is nothing that pleases an editor so much as unexpected material coming from a new source and requiring minimal editing. That in the end is the big ground for hope.

Writing Guidebooks

A quick trip to the bookshop will tell you, if you didn't know already, that the flood tide of travel guides has not yet ebbed, incredibly enough in view of the recession that began in 1989/90 and a market that looks to the unprofessional eye as if it must be totally saturated. But there it is – the publishers publish the guides and the public still seems to buy them, in all their gaudy colours and often crude attempts to catch the eye. It can't last much longer, but while it does, this is a lively option for the travel writer.

The best way in is via writing articles. Then you may be offered work by a publisher who has noticed you, or at least, if you approach a publisher yourself, you have some status. You should keep an ear to the ground so that you hear of new series, new formats, and know which companies need writing done. Even if you are still unpublished, another possibility is to put yourself forward directly to a likely publisher – but only if you happen to know a particular country or city extremely well. In this case you will certainly be asked to write a sample chunk or chapter.

I've logged up several guidebooks now, both short and long, and it is clear that writing them is a mixed pleasure. You get a fixed sum of money, which is a plus, given the uncertainty of writing articles. But on the other hand guidebooks are hideously difficult to write well. Articles rely on selectivity; guidebooks depend on knowing it all. The need for inclusiveness pushes up the blood-pressure as you try to get round every castle and museum, every bar and boutique and every hotel with its beastly phone number and fax, and all before the money runs out and the project becomes a loser. The writing is often unsatisfying because it has to be in short 'takes' rather than a grand continuum. Yet on the other hand you do feel by the end that you have really got to know a good deal more about a place than you ever imagined that you would. And you begin to appreciate the layers of accumulated understanding that lie behind the better guides.

If most travel writers are driven by curiosity, then curiosity is richly rewarded by guidebook writing, despite the *angst* and bouts of boredom. But there is no glamour in it and little prestige and it is a mug's game if you do it for a company which does not take the genre seriously.

Writing Travel Books

Every cobbler to his last; for me, travel books are the whole *raison d'être* and all the rest is a means to this one end, a support to the learning process and a kind of underlay to the different ways of thinking that you need for the longer run. In fact, it could well be argued that you would do best to keep completely clear of newspaper travel and specially of such hackwork as guidebooks if you want to write a travel book that sings in the reader's mind and memory.

Travel books, of course, come in all shapes and forms. Many are about adventures, the crazier the better, cycling in the Andes or power-boating down quite ridiculously ferocious gorges. These call for a lively sense of narrative, and often a trace of self-mockery. They are in my view a distinctly minor genre. Then there are quests, quests for a lost tribe or even, quite directly, for the writer's soul and self. These may be tremendous, searing works of literature. There are family stories, stories of childhood, stories of youth in faraway places; there are deep studies of civilisations, evocations of art, analyses of social change, and, above all, portrayals of people. More perhaps than in any other national school, British writers have made travel a major branch of literature and to this there apply all the same rules as to any other kind of book writing. You do it at your peril. Disappointment and financial difficulty are constant attendants. But you do it if it is in you and if you have regrets you hide them. This is the real McCoy – and long live travel writing.

Adam Hopkins

Adam Hopkins is a travel writer for national newspapers and magazines. His most recent book, Spanish Journeys: a portrait of Spain *is published by Viking at £16.99. It will appear as a Penguin paperback in spring 1993.*

National Newspapers

Daily Express

Ludgate House, 245 Blackfriars Road,
London SE1 9UX
☎071-928 8000   Fax 071-620 1654

Owner *United Newspapers*
Editor *Sir Nicholas Lloyd*
Circulation 1.54 million

The general rule of thumb is to approach in writing with an idea; all departments are prepared to look at mss without commitment. Unsolicited mss welcome but already receives many which are 'too numerous to count'.

News Editor *Michael Parry*
Diary Editor *Ross Benson*
Features Editor *Heather McGlone*
Literary Editor *Peter Grosvenor*
Sports Editor *David Emery*
Women's Page *Janet Menzies*

Forty Eight Hours: Saturday supplement.
Features Editor *Heather McGlone*

Planning Editor (News Desk) should be circulated with copies of official reports, press releases, etc., to ensure news desk cover at all times.
Payment depends on the nature of the article accepted.

Daily Mail

Northcliffe House, 2 Derry Street, Kensington,
London W8 5TT
☎071-938 6000   Fax 071-937 4463

Owner *Lord Rothermere*
Editor *Paul Dacre*
Circulation 1.69 million

In-house feature writers and regular columnists provide much of the material. Photostories and crusading features often appear; it's essential to hit the right note to be a successful *Mail* writer. Close scrutiny of the paper is strongly advised. Not a good bet for the unseasoned.

News Editor *Ian Monk*
Diary Editor *Nigel Dempster*
Features Editor *Peter Wright*
Sports Editor *Vic Robbie*
Women's Page *Tessa Hilton*

Accepts news on savings, building societies, insurance, unit trusts, legal rights, tax and small businesses.

Daily Mirror

Holborn Circus, London EC1P 1DQ
☎071-353 0246   Fax 071-822 3405

Owner *Mirror Group Newspapers*
Editor *Richard Stott*
Circulation 2.89 million

No freelance opportunities for the inexperienced but strong writers who understand what the tabloid market demands are always needed.

News Editor *Stephen Lynas*
Diary Editor *Garth Gibbs*
Features Editor *Roger Collier*
Literary Editor *George Thaw*
Political Editor *Alastair Campbell*
Sports Editor *Keith Fisher*
Women's Page *Mary Riddell*

Daily Record

Anderston Quay, Glasgow G3 8DA
☎041-248 7000   Fax 041-242 3145/6

Owner *Mirror Group Newspapers*
Editor *Endell J. Laird*
Circulation 780,000

Mass-market Scottish tabloid.

News Editor *M. B. Speed*
Features Editor *R. Steel*
Education *Mike Ritchie*
Political Editor *David King*
Women's Page *Elsa McAlonan*

Daily Sport

19 Great Ancoats Street, Manchester M60 4BT
☎061-236 4466   Fax 061-236 4535

Owner *Sport Newspapers Ltd*
Editor *Peter Grimsditch*
Circulation 300,000

Features Editor *John Stead*
Sports Editor *Steve Millar*

Daily Star
Ludgate House, 245 Blackfriars Road,
London SE1 9UX
☎071–928 8000   Fax 071–922 7960

Owner *United Newspapers*
Editor *Brian Hitchen*
Circulation 849,814

At one time in competition with *The Sun* for most
flesh and least hard news, but returned to more
family fare in its attempt to halt a slide in circulation figures. Freelance opportunities almost non-
existent. Most material is written in-house or by
regular outsiders.

News Editor *Graham Jones*
Entertainments *Pat Codd*
Features Editor *Mike Parker*
Sports Editor *Phil Rostron*
Women's Page *Carole Malone*

The Daily Telegraph
1 Canada Square, Canary Wharf, London E14 5DT
☎071–538 5000   Fax 071–538 6242

Owner *Conrad Black*
Editor *Max Hastings*
Circulation 1.06 million

Unsolicited mss not generally welcome — 'all are
carefully read and considered, but only about one
in a thousand is accepted for publication'. As they
receive about 20 weekly, this means about one a
year. Contenders should approach the paper in
writing making clear their authority for writing on
that subject. No fiction.

News Editor *Tom Pride* Tip-offs or news reports
from *bona fide* journalists. Must phone the news
desk in first instance. Maximum 200 words.
Payment minimum £10 (tip).
Arts Editor *Nigel Reynolds*
Business Editor *Roland Gribben*
Diary Editor *Quentin Letts* Always interested in
diary pieces; contact *Peterborough* (Diary column).
Education *John Clare*
Environment *Charles Clover*
Features Editor *Veronica Wadley* Most material
supplied by commission from established contribu-
tors. New writers are tried out by arrangement with
the features editor. Approach in writing. Maximum
1500 words.
Literary Editor *John Coldstream*
Political Editor *George Jones*
Sports Editor *David Welch* Occasional opportu-
nities for specialised items.
Women's Page *Veronica Wadley*
Payment by arrangement.

Telegraph Magazine: Saturday colour supplement.

Editor *Nigel Horne*
Payment About £300-500 per 1000 words.

The European
1st Floor, Orbit House, 5 New Fetter Lane,
London EC4A 1AP
☎071–822 2002   Fax 071–377 4773

Owner *The Barclay Brothers*
Editor *Charles Garside*
Circulation 167,146 (excl. US sales)

LAUNCHED May 1990 as a colour weekly aimed at a
European weekend market. News and current
affairs, business, sport, European affairs, society
and politics, plus european arts and lifestyle section, *eLAN*. Returned to a three-section format in
May 1992 after a period of readjustment following
new ownership. Freelance contributions will be
considered. First approach in writing.

News *Simon de Bruxelles*
Features *Mike Maclay*
Business *John Phelps*
eLAN *Sebastian O'Kelly*
Payment by arrangement.

Financial Times
1 Southwark Bridge, London SE1 9HL
☎071–873 3000   Fax 071–873 3076

Owner *Pearson*
Editor *Richard Lambert*
Circulation 287,423

FOUNDED 1888. Business and finance-orientated
certainly, but by no means as featureless as some
suppose. All feature ideas must be discussed with
the department's editor in advance. Not snowed
under with unsolicited contributions — they get
less than any other national newspaper. Approach
in writing with ideas in the first instance.

News Editor *Alain Cass*
Arts Editor *J.D.F. Jones*
Business Editor *Peter Martin*
City/Financial Editor *Rod Oram*
Diary Editor *Christine Burton*
Education *Andrew Adonis*
Environment *John Hunt*
Features Editor *Andrew Gowers*
Literary Editor *Anthony Curtis*
Political Editor *Philip Stephens*
Small Businesses *Charles Batchelor*
Sports Editor *Michael Thompson-Noel*
Women's Page *Lucia van der Post*
Payment About £180 per 1000 words.

The Guardian

119 Farringdon Road, London EC1R 3ER
☏ 071-278 2332   Fax 071-837 2114/833 8342

Owner *The Scott Trust*
Editor *Peter Preston*
Circulation 411,324

Of all the nationals *The Guardian* probably offers the greatest opportunities for freelance writers, if only because it has the greatest number of specialised pages which use freelance work. But mss must be directed at a specific slot.

News Editor *Paul Johnson* No opportunities except in those regions where there is presently no local contact for news stories.

Arts Editor *Helen Oldfield*
City/Financial Editor *Alex Brummer*
Computer Guardian *Jack Schofield* A major part of Thursday's paper, almost all written by freelancers. Expertise essential — but not a trade page; written for 'the interested man in the street' and from the user's point of view. Mss on disk or by electronic mail appreciated.

Diary Editor *Andrew Moncur*

Education Editor *Stephen Bates* Expert pieces on modern education welcome.

Environment *John Vidal*

Features Editor *Alan Rusbridger* Receives up to 30 unsolicited mss a day; these are passed on to relevant page editors.

Grassroots *John Course* Manchester-based forum page dealing with a wide variety of subjects: 'the only rule of thumb is: nothing to do with London', and ordinarily not by London writers. However, the page is heavily oversubscribed; probably only 1% of contributions are successful.

Guardian Society *David McKie* Social welfare, psychology and theology, both academic and popular. Experts who write well, rather than journalists. Forward-looking, off-beat. Maximum of 12 pieces weekly.

Literary Editor *Richard Gott*

Media *Georgina Henry* Approximately four pieces a week, plus diary. Outside contributions are considered. All aspects of modern media, advertising, PR, consumer trends in arts/entertainments. Background insight important. Best approach with a note, followed by phone call.

Political Editor *Ian Aitken*

Sports Editor *Mike Averis*

Women's Page *Louise Chunn* Daily since the revamp. Unsolicited mss used if they show an appreciation of the page in question.

Saturday: *Guardian Weekend* is now accompanied by a substantial new section, *Outlook*.
Payment about £200 per 1000 words.

The Herald (Glasgow)

195 Albion Street, Glasgow G1 1QP
☏ 041-552 6255   Fax 041-552 2288

Owner *Caledonian Newspaper Publishing*
Editor *Arnold Kemp*
Circulation 127,636

The oldest national newspaper in the English-speaking world, The Herald, which dropped its 'Glasgow' prefix in February 1992, returned to Scottish hands in mid-1992 following a management buy-out and the establishment of the newly created company, Caledonian Newspaper Publishing. Lively, quality Scottish daily described by Arnold Kemp as a 'pluralist' paper. Keen to expand the paper into a truly national Scottish broadsheet.

News Editor *Robert Sutter*
Arts Editor *John Fowler*
Business Editor *R. E. Dundas*
Diary *T. Shields*
Education *Barclay McBain*
Environment *Liz Buie*
Sports Editor *E. Rodger*
Women's Page *Anne Simpson*

The Independent

40 City Road, London EC1Y 2DB
☏ 071-253 1222   Fax 071-956 1435

Owner *Newspaper Publishing*
Editor *Andreas Whittam Smith*
Circulation 375,110

FOUNDED October 1986. The first new quality national in over 130 years and the first newspaper to be so precisely targeted and researched before its launch. Aimed at a professional/office-working readership, better educated and more affluent than their parents. Content is geared towards those who only have time to dip into a paper at odd times during the day. Particularly strong on its arts/media coverage, with a high proportion of feature material. Theoretically, opportunities for freelancers are good. However, unsolicited mss are not welcome; most pieces originate in-house or from known and trusted outsiders. Ideas should be submitted in writing.

News Editor *John Price*
Arts Editor *Thomas Sutcliffe*
Business Editor *Christopher Huhne*
City/Financial Editor *Clare Dobie*
Education *Colin Hughes*
Environment *Nicholas Schoon*

Features Editor *David Robson*
Literary Editor *Robert Winder*
Political Editor *Anthony Bevins*
Sports Editor *Paul Newman*

The Independent Magazine: Saturday colour supplement.
Editor *Alexander Chancellor*
Payment About £175 per 1000 words.

The newspaper also runs annual travel writing awards. Details, which vary from year to year, are advertised in the paper.

The Independent on Sunday

40 City Road, London EC1Y 2DB
☎071-253 1222   Fax 071-415 1333

Owner *Newspaper Publishing*
Editor *Ian Jack*
Circulation 375,716

FOUNDED 1986. Freelance contributions welcome in all areas.

News Editor *David Felton*
Arts Editor *Tim De Lisle*
Commissioning Editor, Features *Sue Matthias*
City/Financial Editor *Jeremy Warmer*
Environment *David Nicholson-Lord*
Political Editor *Don MacIntyre*
Sports Editor *Simon O'Hagan*
Payment About £200 per 1000 words.

International Herald Tribune

181 avenue Charles de Gaulle, 92200 Neuilly-sur-Seine, France
☎01033-1 4637 9300   Fax 01033-1 4637 9338

Editor *John Vinocur*
Circulation 174,200

Published in France, Monday to Saturday, and circulated in Europe, the Middle East, North Africa, the Far East and the USA. General news, business and financial, arts and leisure.

News Editor *Walter Wells*

The Mail on Sunday

Northcliffe House, 2 Derry Street, Kensington, London W8 5TS
☎071-938 6000   Fax 071-937 3829

Owner *Lord Rothermere*
Editor *Jonathan Holborrow*
Circulation 1.94 million

Sunday paper with a high proportion of newsy features and articles. Experience and judgement required to break into its band of regular feature writers.

News Editor *Jon Ryan*
City/Financial Editor *Clive Wolman*
Diary Editor *Nigel Dempster*
Features Editor *Graeme Gourlay*
Literary Editor *Paula Johnson*
Political Editor *Peter Dobbie*
Sports Editor *Roger Kelly*

You - The Mail on Sunday Magazine: colour supplement. Many feature articles, supplied entirely by freelance writers.

Editor *Dee Nolan*
Commissioning Editors *Peter Watson/Vicci Bentley/John Chenery*
Payment About £450 per 1000 words.

Morning Star

1-3 Ardleigh Road, London N1 4HS
☎071-254 0033   Fax 071-254 5950

Owner *Peoples Press Printing Society*
Editor *Dr Tony Chater*
Circulation 25,000

Not to be confused with the *Daily Star*, the *Morning Star* is the farthest left national daily. Those with a penchant for a Marxist reading of events and ideas can try their luck, though feature space is as competitive here as in the other nationals.

News Editor *Roger Bagley*
Arts/Features Editor *Paul Corry*
Political Editor *Mike Ambrose*
Sports Editor *Tony Braisby*
Women's Page *Billie Bex*

The News of the World

1 Virginia Street, London E1 9XR
☎071-782 4000   Fax 071-583 9504

Owner *Rupert Murdoch*
Editor *Patsy Chapman*
Circulation 4.84 million

Highest circulation Sunday paper.

News Editor/City & Financial/Diary *Robert Warren*
Features Editor *Tony Harris*
Literary Editor *Roy Stockdill*
Sports Editor *Bill Bateson*
Women's Page *Unity Hall*

Sunday Magazine: colour supplement. Showbiz interviews and strong human-interest features make up most of the content, but there are no strict rules

about what is 'interesting'. Unsolicited mss and ideas welcome.
Editor *Sue Carroll*

The Observer

Chelsea Bridge House, Queenstown Road, London SW8 4NN
☏071-627 0700   Fax 071-627 5570

Owner *Lonrho*
Editor *Donald Trelford*
Circulation 556,505

FOUNDED 1791. Occupies the middle ground of Sunday newspaper politics. Unsolicited mss are not generally welcome, 'except from distinguished, established writers'. Receives far too many unsolicited offerings already. No news, fiction or special page opportunities. Occasional feature opportunities.

News Editor *Paul Routledge*
Arts Editor *Gillian Widdicombe*
City/Financial/Business Editor *Melvyn Marckus*
Diary Editor *Richard Brooks*
Education *Barry Hugill*
Features Editor *Bob Low*
Literary Editor *Michael Ratcliffe*
Political *Nicholas Wapshott*
Women's Page *Yvonne Roberts*
Observer Magazine: Freelance writers are used extensively, but they tend to come from an experienced and comprehensive pool of writers. Only very strong ideas and demonstrable talent are likely to succeed here.
Editor *Simon Kelner*
Commissioning Editors *Madeline Lim/Sheila McNamara/Richard Askwith*
Payment Living Section: about £250 per 1000 words.

The newspaper runs annual competitions which change from year to year. Previously this has been a travel writing competition. Details are advertised in the paper.

The People

Holborn Circus, London EC1P 1DQ
☏071-353 0246   Fax 071-822 3864

Owner *Mirror Group Newspapers*
Editor *William Hagerty*
Circulation 2.24 million

Slightly up-market version of *The News of the World*. Keen on exposés and big-name gossip.

News Editor *Phil Hall*
City/Financial Editor *Peter Prendergast*
Arts Editor *Maurice Krais*
Features Editor *Geri Hosier*

Political Editor *Nigel Nelson*
Sports Editor *Bill Bradshaw*
Women's Page *Cathy Galvin*

People Magazine: colour supplement.
Editor *Kathy Galvin*
Senior Commissioning Editors *Heidi Kingstone/Victor Oliver*

Scotland on Sunday

20 North Bridge, Edinburgh EH1 1YT
☏031-225 2468   Fax 031-220 2443

Owner *Thomson Regional Newspapers Ltd*
Editor *Andrew Jaspan*

Launched late 1988.

News Editor *William Peakin*
Features Editor *Nigel Billen*
Education *Steve Briggs*
Political *John Forsyth*

Scotland on Sunday Magazine: colour supplement launched April 1989. Features on personalities, etc.

The Scotsman

20 North Bridge, Edinburgh EH1 1YT
☏031-225 2468   Fax 031-226 7420

Owner *The Scotsman Publications Ltd*
Editor *Magnus Linklater*
Circulation 90,000

Scotland's national newspaper. Many unsolicited mss come in, and stand a good chance of being read, although a small army of regulars supply much of the feature material not written in-house.

News Editor *Mark Douglas-Home*
City/Financial Editor *Clifford German*
Education *Douglas Fraser*
Environment *Auslan Cramb*
Features Editor *Robert Campbell* The features page carries a great variety of articles. The tabloid *Weekend* and *Listings* section ditto, including book reviews and travel articles.
Literary Editory *Catherine Lockerbie*
Women's Page *Gillian Glover*

The Sun

1 Virginia Street, London E1 9XP
☏071-782 4000   Fax 071-488 3253

Owner *Rupert Murdoch*
Editor *Kelvin Mackenzie*
Circulation 3.69 million

Highest circulation daily. Right-wing, populist outlook; very keen on gossip, pop stars, TV soap, scandals and exposés of all kinds. Not much room for feature writers; 'investigative journalism' of a certain hue is always in demand, however.

News Editor *Tom Petrie*
Features Editor *Neil Wallace*
Sports Editor *David Balmforth*
Women's Page *Caroline Graham*

Sunday Express
Ludgate House, 245 Blackfriars Road, London SE1 9UX
☎ 071-928 8000   Fax 071-620 1656

Owner *United Newspapers*
Editor *Eve Pollard*
Circulation 1.65 million

FOUNDED 1918. Unsolicited mss are generally welcome. Approach in writing with ideas.

News Editor *Rowena Webster* Occasional news features by experienced journalists only. All submissions must be preceded by ideas. 750 words.

Features Editor *Charles Golding* General features (1000 words); profiles of personalities (900 words); showbiz features (1000-1500 words).

Literary Editor *Graham Lord*
Sports Editor *Peter Watson*
Women's Page *Daphne Broadhead*

Sunday Express Magazine: colour supplement. No unsolicited mss. All contributions are commissioned. Ideas in writing only.

Editor *Jean Carr*
'Style' Editor *Vinny Lee*
Payment negotiable.

Sunday Mail
Anderston Quay, Glasgow G3 8DA
☎ 041-248 7000   Fax 041-242 3145/6

Owner *Mirror Group Newspapers*
Editor *James Cassidy*
Circulation 880,958

Popular Scottish Sunday paper.

News Editor *Brian Steel*
Environment *A. MacKay*
Features Editor *Ken Laird*
Political *Chris Mullinger*
Women's Page *Melanie Reid*

Sunday Mail Magazine: monthly colour supplement.
Editor *James Cassidy*

Sunday Mirror
Holborn Circus, London EC1P 1DQ
☎ 071-353 0246   Fax 071-822 2160/3405/3864

Owner *Mirror Group Newspapers*
Editor *Bridget Rowe*
Circulation 2.81 million

Receives anything up to 100 unsolicited mss weekly. In general terms, these are welcome, though the paper patiently points out it has more time for contributors who have taken the trouble to study the market. Initial contact in writing preferred, except for live news situations. No fiction.

News Editor *John McShane* The news desk is very much in the market for tip-offs and inside information. Contributors would be expected to work with staff writers on news stories.
City/Financial Editor *John Husband*
Features Editor *Sally Morris* 'Anyone who has obviously studied the market will be dealt with constructively and courteously.' Cherishes its record as a breeding ground for new talent.
Literary Editor *Keith Richmond*
Sports Editor *Bob Harris*
Women's Page *Gill Martin*

Sunday Mirror Magazine: colour supplement.
Editor *Bridget Rowe*

Sunday Post
144 Port Dundas Road, Glasgow G4 0HZ
☎ 041-332 9933   Fax 041-331 1595

Owner *D. C. Thomson & Co. Ltd*
Editor *Russell Reid*
Circulation 1.48 million

The highest circulation Scottish Sunday paper. Contributions should be addressed to the editor.

News Editor *Iain MacKinnon*

Sunday Post Magazine: monthly colour supplement.
Editor *Maggie Dun*

Sunday Sport
3rd Floor, Marten House, 39-47 East Road, London N1 6AH
☎ 071-251 2544   Fax 071-608 1979

Owner *David Sullivan*
Editor *Ian Pollock*
Circulation 368,091

FOUNDED 1986. Sunday tabloid catering for a particular sector of the male 18-35 readership. As concerned with 'glamour' (for which, read: 'page 3') as with human interest, news, features and sport. Unsolicited mss are welcome; receives about

90 a week. Approach should be made by phone in the case of news and sports items, by letter for features. No fiction. All material should be addressed to the news editor.

News Editor *Gary Thompson* Off-beat news, human interest, preferably with photographs.

Features Regular items: glamour, showbiz and television, as well as general interest.

Sports Hard-hitting sports stories on major soccer clubs and their personalities, plus leading clubs/ people in other sports. Strong quotations to back up the news angle essential.
Payment negotiable and on publication.

Sunday Telegraph
1 Canada Square, Canary Wharf, London E14 5DT
☎071-538 5000 Fax 071-538 1330

Owner *Conrad Black*
Editor *Trevor Grove*
Circulation 567,672

Right-of-centre quality Sunday paper (meaning it has the least tendency to bend its ear to the scandals of the hour). Traditionally starchy and correct, it has been trying to pep up its image to attract a younger readership. Editorial resources of *The Daily Telegraph* and *Sunday Telegraph* have been pooled to create a seven-day news-gathering operation. The move aims to inject more of *The Daily Telegraph's* editorial punch behind the *Sunday Telegraph.*

News Editor *Kim Fletcher*
City/Financial Editor *John Jay*
Features Editor *Jon Connell*
Arts Editor *John Preston*
Literary Editor *Miriam Gross*
Diary Editor *Kenneth Rose*
Sports Editor *David Grice*

The Sunday Times
1 Pennington Street, London E1 9XW
☎071-782 5000 Fax 071-782 5658

Owner *Rupert Murdoch*
Editor *Andrew Neil*
Circulation 1.15 million

FOUNDED 1820. Generally right-of-centre, with a strong crusading investigative tradition. Unsolicited mss are always welcome, especially on the features pages. Approach the relevant editor with an idea in writing. Close scrutiny of the style of each section of the paper is strongly advised before sending mss. No fiction. All fees by negotiation.

News Editor *Rosemary Collins* Opportunities are very rare.

Payment About £180 per 1000 words.

City/Financial Editor *Jeff Randall*
Features Editor *Robert Tyrer* Submissions are always welcome, but the paper commissions its own, uses staff writers or works with literary agents, by and large. The features sections where most opportunities exist are Screen, Look, Leisure and Spectrum.
Payment About £250-300 per 1000 words.

Arts Editor *David Mills*
Business Editor *John Cassidy*
Education *Charles Hyman*
Environment *Sean Ryan*
Literary Editor *John Walsh*
Political (Atticus) *Michael Jones*
Sports Editor *Chris Nawrat*
Women's Page *Kate Carr*

Sunday Times Magazine: colour supplement. No unsolicited material. Write with ideas in first instance.
Editor *Philip Clarke*

The Times
1 Pennington Street, London E1 9XN
☎071-782 5000 Fax 071-488 3242

Owner *Rupert Murdoch*
Editor *Peter Stothard*
Circulation 388,819

Generally right (though columns/features can range in tone from diehard to libertarian). *The Times* receives a great many unsolicited offerings. Writers with feature ideas should approach by letter in the first instance. No fiction.

News Editor *Alan Copps*
Arts Editor *Richard Morrison*
Business Editor *John Bell*
City/Financial Editor *Michael Tate*
Diary Editor *Nigel Williamson*
Education *Greg Hadfield*
Environment *Michael McCarthy*
Executive Features Editor *Brian MacArthur*
Literary Editor *Daniel Johnson*
Political Editor *Robin Oakley*
Sports Editor *Tom Clarke*
Women's Page *Brigid Callaghan*

Supplements include *Life & Times*, a new daily arts and features supplement, plus the *Saturday Review* and *Weekend Times* sections.
Features Editor, Life & Times *Brigid Callaghan*
Payment About £190 per 1000 words.

Today
1 Virginia Street, Wapping, London E1 9BS
☎071-782 4600 Fax 071-782 4822

Owner *Rupert Murdoch*
Editor *Martin Dunn*
Circulation 467,407

The first of the new technology papers. Originally middle-of-the-road but has turned sharply to the right under Rupert Murdoch. Feature opportunities look to be declining fast.

News Editor *Fiona Wyton*
Business/City/Financial Editor *George Campbell*
Education *Alison Brace*
Features Editor *Juliet Ashworth*
Political *Paul Wilenius*
Sports Editor *Mike Crouch*

Accepts news on tax, insurance, unit trusts, building societies, small businesses, legal rights and investments.

Wales on Sunday

Thomson House, Havelock Street,
Cardiff CF1 1WR
☎0222 223333   Fax 0222 342462

Owner *Thomson Regional Newspapers Ltd*
Editor *Peter Hollinson*

Launched March 1989. 24-page sports tabloid, 40-page broadsheet newspaper and colour supplement magazine.

News/Features Editor *Denis Gane*
Sports Editor *Chris Baldock*
Women's Page *Mike Smith*

Regional Newspapers

Regional newspapers are listed in alphabetical order under town. Thus the *Evening Standard* appears under 'L' for London; the *Lancashire Evening Post* under 'P' for Preston.

Northcliffe Newspapers Group Ltd
31-32 John Street, London WC1N 2QB
☎071-242 7070

Central office of the regional papers belonging to the group: *The Citizen* (Gloucester); *Hull Daily Mail; Derby Evening Telegraph; Evening Sentinel* (Stoke); *Gloucestershire Echo* (Cheltenham); *Grimsby Evening Telegraph; Herald Express* (Torquay); *Leicester Mercury; Lincolnshire Echo; Scunthorpe Evening Telegraph; South Wales Evening Post*. See separate listings for details.

Thomson Regional Newspapers Ltd
Hannay House, 39 Clarendon Road, Watford, Hertfordshire WD1 1JA
☎0923 255588   Fax 0923 817020

Central office of the group which owns the following regional daily papers: *Belfast Telegraph; Evening News* (Edinburgh); *Evening Chronicle* (Newcastle); *Evening Express* (Aberdeen); *Evening Gazette* (Middlesbrough); *Evening Post* (Reading); *The Journal* (Newcastle); *Chester Chronicle; The Press & Journal* (Aberdeen); *South Wales Echo* (Cardiff); *Sunday Life* (Belfast); *Sunday Sun* (Newcastle); *Western Mail* (Cardiff). Also the following national Sunday papers: *Scotland on Sunday* and *Wales on Sunday*. See separate listings for details. City editors of *The Press & Journal* (Aberdeen); The Journal (Newcastle) and the *Western Mail* (Cardiff) are based at 52 St John Street, Smithfield, London EC1 (Tel: 071-490 5581).

Aberdeen

Evening Express (Aberdeen)
PO Box 43, Lang Stracht, Mastrick,
Aberdeen AB9 8AF
☎0224 690222   Fax 0224 699575

Owner *Thomson Regional Newspapers Ltd*
Editor *Richard J. Williamson*
Circulation 80,764

Circulates in Aberdeen and the Grampian region. Local, national and international news and pictures, family finance and property news. Unsolicited mss welcome 'if on a controlled basis'.

News Editor *David Smith* Freelance news contributors welcome.
Features Editor *Raymond Anderson* Women, fashion, showbiz, health, hobbies, property — anything will be considered on its merits.
Sports Editor *Jim Strachan*
Women's Page *J. Mackie*
Payment £30-40.

The Press & Journal
PO Box 43, Lang Stracht, Mastrick,
Aberdeen AB9 8AF
☎0224 690222   Fax 0224 699575

Owner *Thomson Regional Newspapers Ltd*
Editor *Harry Roulston*
Circulation 112,862

Circulates in Aberdeen, Grampians, Highlands, Tayside, Orkney, Shetland and the Western Isles. A well-established regional daily which is said to receive more unsolicited mss a week than the *Sunday Mirror*. Unsolicited mss are nevertheless welcome; approach in writing with ideas. No fiction.

News Editor *Dan Hewitt* Wide variety of hard or off-beat news items, relating to the northern half of Scotland. 500 words.
Features Editor *Norman Harper* Tightly-written topical pieces, preferably with a Scottish flavour. 1000 words.
Sports Editor *Colin Farquharson*
Women's Page *Stephanie Smith*
Payment by arrangement.

Barrow in Furness

North West Evening Mail
Abbey Road, Barrow in Furness,
Cumbria LA14 5QS
☎0229 821835   Fax 0229 832141

Owner *Cumbrian Newspapers Ltd*
Editor *Keith Sutton*
Circulation 23,157

All editorial material should be addressed to the editor.

News Editor *Mike Rushton*

Basildon

Evening Echo
Newspaper House, Chester Hall Lane, Basildon, Essex SS14 3BL
☎0268 522792   Fax 0268 532060

Owner *Westminster Press*
Editor *Jim Worsdale*
Circulation 62,363

Relies almost entirely on staff and regular outside contributors, but will consider material sent on spec. Approach the editor in writing with ideas.

Bath

Evening Chronicle (Bath)
33 Westgate Street, Bath, Avon BA1 1EW
☎0225 444044   Fax 0225 445969

Owner *Wessex Newspapers*
Editor *Paul Deal*
Circulation 26,172

News Editor *John McCready*
Features Editor *Pamela Kelt*

Belfast

Belfast Telegraph
Royal Avenue, Belfast BT1 1EB
☎0232 321242   Fax 0232 242287

Owner *Thomson Regional Newspapers Ltd*
Editor *Roy Lilley*
Circulation 140,000

Weekly business supplement.

News Editor *Norman Jenkinson*
Features Editor *Janet Devlin*
Sports Editor *Sammy Hamill*
Women's Page *Jane Bell*

The Irish News
Donegall Street, Belfast BT1 2GE
☎0232 242614   Fax 0232 231282

Owner *Irish News Ltd*
Editor *Nick Garbutt*
Circulation 43,609

All material to appropriate editor (phone to check), or to the news desk.

News Editor *Pauline Reynolds*
Features Editor/Women's Page *Nick Garbutt*
Sports Editor *P. J. McKeefry*

Sunday Life (Belfast)
124–144 Royal Avenue, Belfast BT1 1EB
☎0232 331133   Fax 0232 248968

Owner *Thomson Regional Newspapers Ltd*
Editor *Edmund Curran*
Circulation 60,500

News Editor *Jim Flanagan*
Sports Editor *Lindsay Kilpatrick*

Sunday News (Belfast)
51–67 Donegall Street, Belfast BT1 2GB
☎0232 244441   Fax 0232 230715

Owner *Century Newspapers Ltd*
Editor *Chris Harbinson*
Circulation 60,157

Bi-monthly supplement: *Accent.*

News Editor/Features *Paul Connolly*
Sports Editor *Nigel Ballantine*
Women's Page *Una Brankin*

Ulster News Letter
Donegall Street, Belfast BT1 2GB
☎0232 244441   Fax 0232 230715

Owner *Century Newspapers Ltd*
Editor *Geoff Martin*
Circulation 105,000

Supplements: *Farming Life* (weekly); *Shopping News; Belfast Newsletter.*

Acting Editor *Dan Kinney*
News/Features Editor *Harry Robinson*
Sports Editor *Brian Millar*
Women's Page *Niki Hill*

Birmingham

Birmingham Evening Mail
28 Colmore Circus, Queensway,
Birmingham B4 6AX
☎021-236 3366   Fax 021-233 0271

Owner *Birmingham Post & Mail Ltd*
Editor *Ian Dowell*
Circulation 235,852

News Editor *Tony Dickens*
Features Editor *Paul Cole*
Women's Page *Fiona Murray*

Freelance contributions are welcome, particularly
topics of interest to the West Midlands and Wom-
en's Page pieces offering original and lively comment.

Birmingham Post
28 Colmore Circus, Queensway,
Birmingham B4 6AX
☎021-236 3366   Fax 021-233 0271

Owner *The Birmingham Post & Mail Ltd*
Editor *Terry Page*
Circulation 28,500

One of the country's leading regional newspapers.
Freelance contributions are welcome. Topics of
interest to the West Midlands and pieces offering
lively, original comment are particularly welcome.

News Editor *David Jester*
Features Editor *Danny Barton*
Women's Page *Jo Ind*

Metro News
78-79 Francis Road, Edgbaston,
Birmingham B16 8SP
☎021-454 8800   Fax 021-455 9458

Owner *Reed Midland Newspapers*
Editor *Mark Higgitt*
Circulation 276,486

FOUNDED 1984. Britain's first free daily newspaper.
Unsolicited mss generally welcome. Approach the
editor in writing in the first instance.

~~**News Editor** *Linda Green*~~

Sunday Mercury (Birmingham)
28 Colmore Circus, Birmingham B4 6AZ
☎021-236 3366   Fax 021-233 0271

Owner *Birmingham Post & Mail Ltd*
Editor *Peter Whitehouse*

Circulation 168,024

News Editor *Bob Haywood*
Features Editor *Keith Kendrick*
Sports Editor *Roger Skidmore*
Women's Page *Pam Thompson*

Blackburn

Lancashire Evening Telegraph
Telegraph House, High Street, Blackburn,
Lancashire BB1 1HT
☎0254 678678   Fax 0254 680429

Editor *Peter Butterfield*
Circulation 57,627

News stories and feature material with an East
Lancashire flavour welcome. Approach· in writing
with an idea in the first instance. No fiction.

News Editor *Nick Nunn*
Features Editor *Nick Nunn* Either a local angle,
or material written by local people.
Women's Page *Nick Nunn*

Blackpool

Evening Gazette (Blackpool)
PO Box 20, Preston New Road, Blackpool,
Lancashire FY4 4AU
☎0253 839999   Fax 0253 66799

Owner *United Newspapers*
Editor *Peter Charlton*
Circulation 52,000

In theory unsolicited mss are welcome. Approach
in writing with an idea. Publishes a motoring
supplement called *Wheels.* Other weekly supplements: *Financial & Business* (Tuesday); *Women*
(Monday); *Property* (Thursday); *Weekend* (leisure
and entertainment, Saturday).

News Editor *Charles Stewart*
Sports Editor *Tony Durkin*
Women's Page *Jackie Heap*

Bolton

Bolton Evening News
Newspaper House, Churchgate, Bolton,
Lancashire BL3 4SQ
☎0204 22345   Fax 0204 365068

Owner *Northern Counties Newspapers*
Editor *Chris Walder*
Circulation 90,655

Business, children's page, travel, local services, motoring, fashion and cookery.

News Editor *Melvyn Horrocks*
Features Editor *Derrick Grocock*
Women's Page *Angela Kelly*

Bournemouth

Evening Echo
Richmond Hill, Bournemouth BH2 6HH
☎ 0202 554601   Fax 0202 292115

Owner *Southern Newspapers Ltd*
Editor *Gareth Weekes*
Circulation 57,076

FOUNDED 1900. Has a very strong features content and invites specialist articles, particularly on unusual and contemporary subjects. Payment on publication. Supplement: *Prime Time.* Business diary, gardening, motoring, weddings, property, women, books, finance. All editorial material should be addressed to the news editor.

News Editor *Andy Bissell*

Bradford

Telegraph & Argus (Bradford)
Hall Ings, Bradford BD1 1JR
☎ 0274 729511   Fax 0274 723634

Owner *Bradford & District Newspapers*
Editor *Mike Glover*
Circulation 79,596

Unsolicited mss not welcome. Approach in writing with samples of work. No fiction.

News Editor *John Meehan*
Features Editor *Peter Anderson* Local features and general interest. Showbiz pieces. 600–1000 words (maximum 1500).
Sports Editor *Alan Birkinshaw*
Women's Page *Peter Anderson*
Payment NUJ rates for members; negotiable for others.

Brighton

Evening Argus
89 North Road, Brighton, East Sussex BN1 4AU
☎ 0273 606799   Fax 0273 607215

Owner *Southern Publishing (Westminster Press) Ltd*
Editor *Chris Fowler*
Circulation 85,602

News Editor *Andrew Drinkwater*
Features Editor *Mike Bacon*
Sports Editor *John Freemantle*
Women's Page *Winifred Blackmore*

Bristol

Evening Post
Temple Way, Bristol BS99 7HD
☎ 0272 260080   Fax 0272 279568

Owner *Bristol United Press Ltd*
Editor *Adrian Faber*
Circulation 109,790

Unsolicited mss welcome; receives about a dozen a week. Approach in writing with ideas. Monthly supplement: *Home & Garden.*

News Editor *Rob Stokes*
Features Editor *Brian Feeney*
Sports Editor *Peter Godsiff*
Women's Page *Julia Foot*

Western Daily Press
Temple Way, Bristol BS99 7HD
☎ 0272 260080   Fax 0272 279568

Owner *Bristol United Press Ltd*
Editor *Ian Beales*
Circulation 76,964

News Editor *Steve Hughes*
Features Editor *David Webb*
Sports Editor *Bill Beckett*
Women's Page *Lynda Cleasby*

Burton upon Trent

Burton Mail
65–68 High Street, Burton upon Trent, Staffordshire DE14 1LE
☎ 0283 512345   Fax 0283 510075/550482

Owner *Burton Daily Mail Ltd*
Editor *Brian Vertigen*
Circulation 22,478

Motoring (Tuesday & Friday); property (Thursday); what's on (Friday & Saturday); women's world (Wednesday); leisure (Saturday); farming (Friday); rock (Wednesday); financial/money page (Monday); fashion (Monday); health (Monday); consumer (Tuesday); wildlife (Monday); environment (Monday); shopping (Wednesday); nostalgia (Monday).

News/Features Editor *Andrew Parker*
Sports Editor *Rex Page*
Women's Page *Corry Adger*

Cambridge

Cambridge Evening News
51 Newmarket Road, Cambridge CB5 8EJ
☎ 0223 358877   Fax 0223 460846

Owner *Cambridge Newspapers Ltd*
Editor *Robert Satchwell*
Circulation 46,056

News Editor *Chris Elliott*
Sports Editor *Mike Finnis*
Women's Page *Pauline Hunt*

Cardiff

South Wales Echo
Thomson House, Cardiff CF1 1WR
☎ 0222 223333   Fax 0222 383886

Owner *Thomson Regional Newspapers Ltd*
Editor *Patrick Pilton*
Circulation 100,704

Circulates in South and mid Glamorgan.

News Editor *Stuart Minton*
Features Editor *John Scantlebury*
Sports Editor *Richard Williams*

Western Mail
Thomson House, Cardiff CF1 1WR
☎ 0222 223333   Fax 0222 220238

Owner *Thomson Regional Newspapers Ltd*
Editor *John Humphries*
Circulation 78,140

Circulates in Cardiff, Merthyr Tydfil, Newport, Swansea and towns and villages throughout Wales. Mss welcome if of a topical nature, and preferably of Welsh interest. No short stories or travel. Approach in writing to the editor. 'Usual subjects already well covered, e.g. motoring, travel, books, gardening. We look for the unusual.' Maximum 1000 words. Opportunities also on women's page. Supplement: *TV Wales.*

News/Features Editor *Roger Dobson*
Sports Editor *John Kennedy*
Women's Page *Julie Coulson*

Carlisle

Evening News & Star
Newspaper House, Dalston Road,
Carlisle CA2 5UA
☎ 0228 23488   Fax 0228 512828

Owner *Cumbrian Newspaper Group Ltd*
Editor *R. W. J. Harris*

News Editor *Steve Johnston*
Features Editor *J. Reynolds*
Sports Editor *Chris Brader*
Women's Page *Jane Loughran*

Chatham

Kent Evening Post
395 High Street, Chatham, Kent ME4 4PG
☎ 0634 830600   Fax 0634 829479

Owner *Kent Messenger Group*
Editor *Graham Cole*
Circulation 29,500

News Editor *Mrs Lee Wells*
Sports Editor *Neil Webber*
Women's Page *Liz Dickens*

Cheltenham

Gloucestershire Echo
1 Clarence Parade, Cheltenham,
Gloucestershire GL50 3NZ
☎ 0242 526261   Fax 0242 578395

Owner *Northcliffe Newspapers Group Ltd*
Editor *Anita Syvret*
Circulation 29,512

News Editor *John Flint*

All material, other than news, should be addressed to the editor.

Chester

Chester Chronicle
Chronicle House, Commonhall Street,
Chester CH1 2BJ
☎ 0244 340151   Fax 0244 340165

Owner *Thomson Regional Newspapers Ltd*
Editor-in-Chief *Bob Adams*
Editor *David Parry-Jones*

All unsolicited feature material will be considered.

Colchester

Evening Gazette (Colchester)
Oriel House, 43–44 North Hill, Colchester,
Essex CO1 1TZ
☎ 0206 761212   Fax 0206 769523

Owner *Essex County Newspapers*
Editor *Martin McNeill*
Circulation 31,913

Unsolicited mss not generally used. Relies heavily
on regular contributors.

News Editor *Irene Kettle*
Features Editor *Iris Clapp*

Coventry

Coventry Evening Telegraph
Corporation Street, Coventry CV1 1FP
☎ 0203 633633   Fax 0203 550869

Owner *Coventry Newspapers Ltd*
Editor *Neil Benson*
Circulation 86,585

Owned by American press baron, Ralph Ingersoll.
Unsolicited mss are read, but few are published.
Approach in writing with an idea. No fiction.

Features Maximum 600 words. All unsolicited
material should be addressed to the editor.

News Editor *Peter Mitchell*
Features Editor *Diane Chalmers*
Sports Editor *Roger Draper*
Women's Page *Barbara Argument*
Payment negotiable.

Darlington

The Northern Echo
Priestgate, Darlington, Co. Durham DL1 1NF
☎ 0325 381313   Fax 0325 380539

Owner *North of England Newspapers*
Editor *Peter Sands*
Circulation 88,372

FOUNDED 1870. DAILY. Freelance pieces welcome
but telephone first to discuss submission.

News Editor *Peter Barron* Interested in reports
involving the North-east or North Yorkshire.
Preferably phoned in.
Features Editor *Jenny Needham* Background
pieces to topical news stories relevant to the area.
Must be arranged with the features editor before
submission of any material.
Local industrial reports *Ian Green*
Sports Editor *Nick Helliwell*
Women's Page *Sharon Griffiths*
Payment and length by arrangement.

Derby

Derby Evening Telegraph
Northcliffe House, Meadow Road,
Derby DE1 2DW
☎ 0332 291111   Fax 0332 290280

Owner *Northcliffe Newspapers Group Ltd*
Editor *Mike Lowe*
Circulation 81,804

Weekly business supplement.

News Editor *Steve Hall*
Features Editor *Martin Wells*
Sports Editor *Steve Nicholson*
Women's Page *Lucy Orgill*

Devon

Herald Express
See **under** *Torquay*

Doncaster

The Doncaster Star
40 Duke Street, Doncaster DN1 3EA
☎ 0302 344001   Fax 0302 329072

Owner *Sheffield Newspapers Ltd*
Editor *Iain Lovell*

Sports Editor *Steve Hossack*
Women's Page *J. Makinson*

All other editorial material to be addressed to the editor.

Dundee

The Courier and Advertiser

80 Kingsway East, Dundee DD4 8SL
☎0382 23131   Fax 0382 27159

Owner *D. C. Thomson & Co. Ltd*
Editor *Iain Stewart*
Circulation 129,605

Circulates in Dundee, Tayside and Fife. Features welcome on a wide variety of subjects, not solely of local/Scottish interest. Two pages devoted to features each weekend, supplied by freelancers and in-house. Finance, insurance, agriculture, EEC topics, motoring, women, modern homes. Only rule of thumb is to keep it short. Maximum 500 words.

News Editor *Steve Bargeton*
Features Editor *Shona Lorimer*
Sports Editor *Ian Wheeler*
Women's Page *Sandra Scott*

Evening Telegraph & Post

80 Kingsway East, Dundee DD4 8SL
☎0382 23131   Fax 0382 454590

Owner *D. C. Thomson & Co. Ltd*

Editor *Harold Pirie*
Circulation 48,395

Circulates in Tayside, Dundee and Fife. All material should be addressed to the editor.

East Anglia

East Anglian Daily Times

See **under** *Ipswich*

Eastern Daily Press

See **under** *Norwich*

Edinburgh

Evening News

20 North Bridge, Edinburgh EH1 1YT
☎031-225 2468   Fax 031-225 7302

Owner *Thomson Regional Newspapers Ltd*
Editor *Terry Quinn*
Circulation 123,356

FOUNDED 1873. Circulates in Edinburgh, Fife, Central and Lothian. Coverage includes: lifestyle (Monday–Saturday); motoring column (Tuesday); entertainments (daily); gardening, computers, book reviews, DIY, historical memories, shopping, fashion, nature, show business, and *The Doctor* (health). Unsolicited feature material welcome. Approach the appropriate editor by telephone.

News Editor *Murray Morse*
Features Editor/Women's Page *Helen Martin* Weekender magazine supplement of broad general/historical interest. Occasional Platform pieces (i.e. sounding off, topical or opinion pieces). Maximum 1000 words.
Sports Editor *Paul New*
Payment NUJ/house rates.

Exeter

Express & Echo

160 Sidwell Street, Exeter, Devon EX4 6RS
☎0392 73051   Fax 0392 221566

Owner *Express & Echo Publications Ltd*
Editor *Rachael Campey*
Circulation 36,210

Weekly supplements: *Devon Business News; Property Scene; Wheels.*

News Editor *Sue Kemp*
Features Editor *Dave Murdock*
Sports Editor *Tim Dixon*
Women's Page *Susannah Cooper*

Glasgow

Evening Times

195 Albion Street, Glasgow G1 1QP
☎041-552 6255   Fax 041-553 1355

Owner *Lonrho*
Editor *George McKechnie*
Circulation 187,091

Circulates in the Strathclyde region. Supplement: *Evening Times Sport.*

News Editor *Robbie Wallace*
Features Editor *Russell Kyle*
Sports Editor *Alistair Nicol*
Women's Page *Marian Pallister*

The Herald (Glasgow)
See **National Newspapers**

Gloucester

The Citizen
St John's Lane, Gloucester GL1 2AY
☎ 0452 424442   Fax 0452 307238

Owner *Northcliffe Newspapers Group Ltd*
Editor *Hugh Berlyn*
Circulation 38,800

All editorial material to be addressed to the news editor.

News Editor *Michael Gubbins*

Gloucestershire Echo
See **under** *Cheltenham*

Greenock

Greenock Telegraph
2 Crawfurd Street, Greenock PA15 1LH
☎ 0475 26511   Fax 0475 83734

Owner *Dunfermline Press*
Editor *Kenneth Thomson*
Circulation 21,799

Circulates in Greenock, Port Glasgow, Gourock, Kilmacolm, Langbank, Bridge of Weir, Inverkip, Wemyss Bay, Skelmorlie, Largs. Unsolicited mss considered 'if they relate to the newspaper's general interests'. No fiction. All material to be addressed to the editor or the news editor.

News Editor *David Carnduff*

Grimsby

Grimsby Evening Telegraph
80 Cleethorpe Road, Grimsby, South Humberside DN31 3EH
☎ 0472 359232   Fax 0472 358859

Owner *Northcliffe Newspapers Group Ltd*
Editor *Peter Moore*
Circulation 74,000

Sister paper of the *Scunthorpe Evening Telegraph.* Unsolicited mss generally welcome. Approach in writing. No fiction. Monthly supplement: *Businsess Telegraph.* All material to be addressed to the news editor.

News Editor *S. P. Richards* Hard news stories welcome. Approach in haste by telephone.

Guernsey

Guernsey Evening Press & Star
Braye Road, Vale, Guernsey, Channel Islands
☎ 0481 45866   Fax 0481 48972

Owner *Guernsey Press Co. Ltd*
Editor *Dave Prigent*
Circulation 16,883

Special pages include children's and women's interest, gardening, and fashion.

News Editor *Richard Diggard*
Features Editor *Nick Le Messurier*
Sports Editor *John Le Poidevin*
Women's Page *Julie Mosley*

Halifax

Evening Courier
PO Box 19, Halifax, West Yorkshire HX1 2SF
☎ 0422 365711   Fax 0422 330021

Owner *Halifax Courier Ltd*
Editor *Edward Riley*
Circulation 37,873

News Editor *John Kenealy*
Features Editor *William Marshall*
Sports Editor *Ian Rushworth*
Women's Page *Diane Crabtree*

Hartlepool

Mail (Hartlepool)

Clarence Road, Hartlepool, Cleveland TS24 8BU
☎ 0429 274441   Fax 0429 869024

Owner *Northeast Press Ltd*
Editor *Andrew C. Smith*
Circulation 29,153

News Editor *Steve Hartley*
Features Editor *Bernice Saltzer*
Sports Editor *Neil Watson*
Women's Page *Margaret O'Rourke*

Huddersfield

Huddersfield Daily Examiner

Queen Street South, Huddersfield, West
Yorkshire HD1 2TD
☎ 0484 430000   Fax 0484 423722

Editor *Ivan M. Lee*
Circulation 41,914

Home improvement, home heating, weddings, dining out, motoring, fashion, services to trade and industry.

News Editor *P. D. Hinchcliffe*
Features Editor *Malcolm Cruise*
Sports Editor *John Gledhill*
Women's Page *Hilarie Stelfox*

Hull

Hull Daily Mail

Blundell's Corner, Beverley Road, Hull HU3 1XS
☎ 0482 27111   Fax 0482 584353

Owner *Northcliffe Newspapers Group Ltd*
Editor *Michael Wood*
Circulation 108,022

News/Features Editor *Mike Gilson*
Sports Editor *Chris Buckley*
Women's Page *Jo Davison*

Ipswich

East Anglian Daily Times

30 Lower Brook Street, Ipswich, Suffolk IP4 1AN
☎ 0473 230023   Fax 0473 225296

Owner *East Anglian Daily Times Co. Ltd*
Editor *Ken Rice*
Circulation 51,354

FOUNDED 1874. Unsolicited mss generally not welcome; three or four received a week and almost none are used. Approach in writing in the first instance. No fiction. Supplement: *Anglia Business Scene*; plus specials: Property and industry in East Anglia; and Look at the Land.
News Editor *Steve Russell* Hard news stories involving East Anglia (Suffolk, Essex particularly) or individuals resident in the area are always of interest.
Features Editor *Richard Brown* Mostly in-house, but will occasionally buy in when the subject is of strong Suffolk/East Anglian interest. Photo features preferred (extra payment). Special advertisement features are regularly run. Some opportunities here. Maximum 1000 words.
Sports Editor *Tony Garnett*
Women's Page *Pat Small*

Evening Star

30 Lower Brook Street, Ipswich, Suffolk IP4 1AN
☎ 0473 230023   Fax 0473 225296

Owner *East Anglian Daily Times Co. Ltd*
Acting Editor *David Henshall*
Circulation 36,664

News Editor *Terry Hunt*
Sports Editor *Mike Horne*

Jersey

Jersey Evening Post

PO Box 582, Five Oaks, St Saviour, Jersey, Channel
Islands JE4 8QX
☎ 0534 73333   Fax 0534 79681

Owner *Jersey Evening Post Ltd*
Editor *Mike Bisson*
Circulation 25,174

Special pages: *Mainly Feminine; On the House;* also off-licence, gardening, motoring, farmers and growers, property, boating, computer and office, video, young person's (16–25); plus weekend supplement.

News Editor *Philip Jeune*
Features Editor/Women's Page *Pauline Faiers*
Sports Editor *Alan Carter*

Kent

Kent Evening Post
See **under** *Chatham*

Kent Messenger
See **under** *Maidstone*

Kent & Sussex Courier
See **under** *Tunbridge Wells*

Kettering

Evening Telegraph
Northfield Avenue, Kettering,
Northamptonshire NN16 9JN
☎ 0536 81111   Fax 0536 85983

Owner *EMAP*
Editor *Colin Grant*
Circulation 42,804

Business Telegraph (daily); *Weekender* supplement (Saturday), featuring travel, TV, gardening, pop music, reviews, books and arts; two monthly supplements: *Gardening & Home*, and *New Cars*.

News/Features Editor *Jackie May*
Sports Editor *Ian Davidson*
Women's Page *Kate Roddis*

Lancashire

Lancashire Evening Post
See **under** *Preston*

Lancashire Evening Telegraph
See **under** *Blackburn*

Leamington Spa

Leamington Courier
32 Hamilton Terrace, Leamington Spa CB32 4LY
☎ 0926 888222   Fax 0926 451690

Owner *Courier Publishing*
Editor *Martin Lawson*
Circulation 19,232

News Editor *John Wilson*

Unsolicited feature articles considered, particularly on court and legal matters with local angle. Telephone with idea first.

Leeds

Yorkshire Evening Post
Wellington Street, Leeds, West Yorkshire LS1 1RF
☎ 0532 432701   Fax 0532 443430

Owner *Yorkshire Post Newspapers Ltd*
Editor *Christopher Bye*
Circulation 149,405

News Editor *Ian Hamilton*
Features Editor *Anne Pickles*
Sports Editor *Melvyn Jones*
Women's Page *Anne Patch*

Evening sister of the *Yorkshire Post.*

Yorkshire Post
Wellington Street, Leeds, West Yorkshire LS1 1RF
☎ 0532 432701   Fax 0532 443430

Owner *Yorkshire Post Newspapers Ltd*
Editor *Tony Watson*
Circulation 93,418

A serious-minded, quality regional daily with a generally conservative outlook. three or four unsolicited mss arrive each day; all will be considered but initial approach in writing preferred. All submissions should be addressed to the editor. No fiction. Quarterly supplement: *Preview.*

News Editor *Richard Clark*
Features *Robert Cockroft* Open to suggestions in all fields (though ordinarily commissioned from specialist writers).
Sports Editor *Bill Bridge*
Women's Page *Jill Armstrong*

Leicester

Leicester Mercury
St George Street, Leicester LE1 9FQ
☎ 0533 512512   Fax 0533 530645

Owner *Northcliffe Newspapers Group Ltd*
Editor *Alex Leys*
Circulation 134,328

Monthly supplement: *The Merc.*

News Editor *Jon Myles*
Features Editor *Joan Stephens*

Lincoln

London

Lincolnshire Echo

Brayford Wharf East, Lincoln LN5 7AT
☎0522 525252   Fax 0522 545759

Owner *Northcliffe Newspapers Group Ltd*
Editor *Cliff Smith*
Circulation 32,528

Best buys, holidays, motoring, dial-a-service, restaurants, sport, leisure, home improvement, women's page, record review, gardening corner, stars. All editorial material to be addressed to the news editor.

News Editor *Nick Oldham*

Liverpool

Daily Post

PO Box 48, Old Hall Street, Liverpool L69 3EB
☎051-227 2000   Fax 051-236 4682

Owner *Liverpool Daily Post & Echo Ltd*
Editor *Keith Ely*
Circulation 78,000

Unsolicited mss welcome. Receives about six a day. Approach in writing with an idea. No fiction. Local, national/international news, current affairs, profiles – with pictures. Maximum 800-1000 words.

News Editor *Alistair Coull*
Features Editor *Trevor Willis*
Sports Editor *Len Capeling*
Women's Page *Margaret Kitchen*

Liverpool Echo

PO Box 48, Old Hall Street, Liverpool L69 3EB
☎051-227 2000   Fax 051-236 4682

Owner *Liverpool Daily Post & Echo Ltd*
Editor *John Griffith*
Circulation 204,202

One of the country's major regional dailies. Unsolicited mss welcome; initial approach with ideas in writing preferred.

News Editor *Alf Green*
Assistant Editor (Features) *Eric Stokes* Maximum 1000 words.
Sports Editor *David Jones*
Women's Page *Maria McGeoghan*

Evening Standard

Northcliffe House, 2 Derry Street, Kensington, London W8 5EE
☎071-938 6000   Fax 071-937 3193

Owner *Lord Rothermere*
Editor *Stewart Steven*
Circulation 483,626

Long-established and staunchly conservative evening paper, serving Londoners with both news and feature material. Genuine opportunities for London-based features.

News Editor *Stephen Clackson*
Features Editor *Sarah Sands*
Sports Editor *Michael Herd*

ES - The Evening Standard Magazine: monthly colour supplement.
Editor *Michael Watts*

Maidstone

Kent Messenger

6 & 7 Middle Row, Maidstone, Kent ME14 1TG
☎0622 695666   Fax 0622 757227

Owner *Kent Messenger Group*
Editor *John Evans*
Circulation 47,000

For economic reasons, very little freelance work is being commissioned.

Manchester

Manchester Evening News

164 Deansgate, Manchester M60 2RD
☎061-832 7200   Fax 061-832 5351

Owner *Manchester Evening News Ltd*
Editor *Michael Unger*
Circulation 289,528

One of the country's major regional dailies. Initial approach in writing preferred. No fiction opportunities. *Property World* (second and fourth Tuesday each month); holiday feature (Tuesday); *Lifestyle* (Saturday).

News Editor *Paul Horrocks*
Features Editor *Ken Wood* Regional news features, personality pieces and showbiz profiles considered. Maximum 1000 words.

Sports Editor *Neville Bolton*
Women's Page *Dianne Robinson*
Payment based on house agreement rates.

Middlesbrough

Evening Gazette
Borough Road, Middlesbrough,
Cleveland TS1 3AZ
☎ 0642 245401   Fax 0642 232014

Owner *Thomson Regional Newspapers Ltd*
Editor *Ranald Allan*
Circulation 77,000

Special pages: business, motoring, home, computing.

News Editor *David Lorimer*
Features Editor *Alan Sims*
Sports Editor *Alan Boughey*
Women's Page *Liz Coggins*

Mold

Evening Leader
Mold Business Park, Wrexham Road, Mold,
Clwyd CH7 1XY
☎ 0352 700022   Fax 0352 700048

Owner *North Wales Newspapers*
Editor *Reg Herbert*
Circulation 34,000

Circulates in Clwyd, Deeside and Chester. Special pages/features: motoring, travel, arts, women's, children's, photography, local housing, information and news for the disabled, music and entertainment.

News Editor *Steven Rogers*
Features Editor *Jeremy Smith*
Sports Editor *Doug Mortimer*
Women's Page *Gail Cooper*

Newcastle upon Tyne

Evening Chronicle
Thomson House, Groat Market, Newcastle upon Tyne NE1 1ED
☎ 091-232 7500   Fax 091-232 2256

Owner *Thomson Regional Newspapers Ltd*
Editor *Graeme Stanton*
Circulation 147,691

Receives a lot of unsolicited material, much of which is not used. 'Motors Mart', 'Print Out' (computers), women's page, amateur photography, gardening, pop, fashion, cooking, consumer, films and entertainment guide, home improvements, motoring, property, angling, sport and holidays. Approach in writing with ideas.

News Editor *Tim Pedley*
Features Editor *Ian Wilson* Limited opportunities due to full-time feature staff. Maximum 1000 words.
Sports Editor *John Gibson*
Women's Page *Alison Blair*

The Journal
Thomson House, Groat Market, Newcastle upon Tyne NE1 1ED
☎ 091-232 7500   Fax 091-232 2256

Owner *Thomson Regional Newspapers Ltd*
Editor *Neil Fowler*
Circulation 59,000

Daily platforms include farming and business. Monthly full-colour business supplement: *The Journal Northern Business Magazine*.

News/Features Editor *Tom Patterson*
Sports Editor *Paul Nunn*
Women's Page *Jennifer Wilson*

Sunday Sun
Thomson House, Groat Market, Newcastle upon Tyne NE1 1ED
☎ 091-232 7500   Fax 091-230 0238

Owner *Thomson Regional Newspapers Ltd*
Editor *Chris Rushton*
Circulation 125,058

All material should be addressed to the appropriate editor (phone to check), or to the editor.

News Editor *Mike McGiffen*
Features Editor *Keith Dufton*
Sports Editor *Mark Dawson*
Women's Page *Yvonne Ridley*

Newport

South Wales Argus
Cardiff Road, Maesglas, Newport,
Gwent NP9 1QW
☎ 0633 810000   Fax 0633 810100

Owner *South Wales Argus Ltd*
Editor *Steve Hoselitz*
Circulation 40,000

Circulates in Newport, Gwent and surrounding areas.

News Editor *Peter John*
Features Editor/Women's Page *Lesley Williams*
Sports Editor *Robin Davey*

North of England

The Northern Echo

See **under** *Darlington*

Northampton

Chronicle and Echo

Upper Mounts, Northampton NN1 3HR
☎ 0604 231122   Fax 0604 233000

Owner *Northampton Mercury Co. Ltd*
Editor *Clive Hutchby*
Circulation 35,000

Unsolicited mss are 'not necessarily unwelcome but opportunities to use them are rare'. Some 3 or 4 arrive weekly. Approach in writing with an idea. No fiction. Supplement: *Property Chronicle* (Wednesday); property, pop page (Thursday); holidays, environment page (Tuesday); business and commerce (Friday); plus motoring.

News Editor *Jennie Oldfield*
Features Editor/Women's Page *Alison Bott*
Sports Editor *David Jones*

Northamptonshire Evening Telegraph

See **under** *Kettering*

Norwich

Eastern Daily Press

Prospect House, Rouen Road, Norwich,
Norfolk NR1 1RE
☎ 0603 628311   Fax 0603 612930

Owner *Eastern Counties Newspapers*
Editor *Lawrence Sear*
Circulation 85,508

Unsolicited mss welcome. Approach in writing with ideas. News (if relevant to Norfolk), and features up to 900 words. Other pieces by commission only. Supplements: *Eastern Daily Press Business & Personal Finance* (daily); what's on (daily); employment (weekly); motoring (weekly); business

(weekly); property pages, industrial property (monthly); plus motoring, agriculture, and arts focus.

News Editor *Paul Durrant*
Features Editor *Peter Hannam*
Sports Editor *Keith Peel*
Women's Page *Lyndsey Hewison*

Evening News

Prospect House, Rouen Road, Norwich,
Norfolk NR1 1RE
☎ 0603 628311   Fax 0603 612930

Owner *Eastern Counties Newspapers*
Editor *Tim Bishop*
Circulation 49,789

Previously listed as *Eastern Evening News*. Includes special pages on local property, motoring, children's page, pop, fashion, arts, heavy entertainments and TV, gardening, local music scene, home and family.

News Editor *Tom Bodden*
Features Editor *Roy Strowger*
Sports Editor *Steve Snelling*

Nottingham

Evening Post Nottingham

Forman Street, Nottingham NG1 4AB
☎ 0602 482000   Fax 0602 484116

Owner *T. Bailey Forman Ltd*
Editor *Barrie Williams*
Circulation 133,161

Unsolicited mss welcome. Send ideas in writing. Supplements: *Car Buyer* (thirteen issues a year); *Citizens Guide* (annual); *Homemaker* (thirteen issues a year); *Post Extra* (weekly); monthly colour supplement; business, holidays and travel supplement; money matters and food page.

News Editor *Gordon Boreland*
Features Editor *Jerry Lewis* Good local interest only. Maximum 800 words. No fiction.
Sports Editor *Trevor Frecknall*
Women's Page *Lynne Dixon*

Oldham

Evening Chronicle

PO Box 47, Union Street, Oldham,
Lancashire OL1 1EQ
☎ 061-633 2121   Fax 061-627 0905

Owner *Hirst Kidd & Rennie Ltd*
Editor *Philip Hirst*
Circulation 42,274

'We welcome the good but not the bad.' Motoring, food and wine, women's page, business page.

News Editor *Mike Attenborough*
Women's Page *Ron Fletcher*

Oxford

Oxford Mail
Osney Mead, Oxford OX2 0EJ
☎ 0865 244988   Fax 0865 243382

Owner *Oxford & County Newspapers*
Editor *Eddie Duller*
Circulation 38,023

Unsolicited mss are considered but a great many unsuitable offerings are received. Approach in writing with an idea, rather than by phone. No fiction. All fees negotiable.

News Editor *John Chipperfield* Telephone first.
Features Editor *Tom Strathdee* Any features of topical or historical significance. Maximum 800 words.
Sports Editor *Stuart Earp*
Women's Page *Fiona Tarrant*

Paisley

Paisley Daily Express
14 New Street, Paisley, Scotland PA1 1XY
☎ 041-887 7911   Fax 041-887 6254

Owner *Scottish & Universal Newspapers Ltd*
Editor *Murray Stevenson*
Circulation 13,010

Circulates in Paisley, Linwood, Renfrew, Johnstone, Elderslie, Raiston and Barrhead. Unsolicited mss welcome only if of genuine local (Paisley) interest. The paper does not commission work, and will consider submitted material. Maximum 1000–1500 words. All submissions to the editor.

Peterborough

Evening Telegraph
Telegraph House, 57 Priestgate,
Peterborough PE1 1JW
☎ 0733 555111   Fax 0733 555188

Owner *EMAP*
Editor *Kie Miskelly*
Circulation 35,000

Unsolicited mss not welcome. Approach in writing with ideas. Special pages include fashion, farming, motoring, property, women, gardening, pop, travel, television, books and film. Plus weekly lifestyle supplement.

Features Editor *Mike Colton*
Sports Editor *Bob French*
Women's Page *Rosie Sandall*

Plymouth

Evening Herald
Leicester Harmsworth House, 65 New George Street, Plymouth, Devon PL1 1RE
☎ 0752 266626   Fax 0752 267580

Owner *Western Morning News Co. Ltd*
Editor *Alan Cooper*
Circulation 60,608

News Editor *Mike Bramhall*

All editorial material to be addressed to the news editor or the editor.

Sunday Independent
Burrington Way, Plymouth, Devon PL5 3LN
☎ 0752 777151   Fax 0752 780680

Owner *West of England Newspapers Ltd*
Editor *John Noble*
Circulation 50,198

Fashion, what's on, gardening, computers, DIY, business, home improvements, motoring, furniture, food and wine, out and about, property, photography, hobbies, insulation, health and beauty, kitchens, motor cycles. All editorial material should be addressed to the editor.

Western Morning News
Leicester Harmsworth House, 65 New George Street, Plymouth, Devon PL1 1RE
☎ 0752 266626   Fax 0752 267580

Owner *Western Morning News Co. Ltd*
Editor *Colin Davison*
Circulation 58,000

Unsolicited mss welcome, but best to telephone features editor first. Special pages include West country matters, books, antiques, lifestyle and arts.

News Editor *Philip Bowern*
Features Editor *Janet Wooster* Mostly local interest, 600–1000 words. Must be topical.
Sports Editor *Ross Taylor*
All other editorial material to be addressed to the editor.

Portsmouth

The News
The News Centre, Hilsea, Portsmouth PO2 9SX
☎0705 664488   Fax 0705 673363

Owner *Portsmouth Printing & Publishing Ltd*
Editor *Geoffrey Elliott*
Circulation 94,043

Unsolicited mss not generally welcome. Approach by letter.

News Editor *Mark Acheson*
Features Editor *Paul Bithell* General subjects of SE Hants interest. Maximum 600 words. No fiction.
Sports Editor *Colin Channon* Sports background features. Maximum 600 words.
Women's Page *Bryony Jones*

Preston

Lancashire Evening Post
Olivers Place, Eastway, Fulwood, Preston, Lancashire PR2 4ZA
☎0772 54841   Fax 0772 563288

Owner *United Newspapers Publications Ltd*
Acting Editor *Philip Welsh*
Circulation 71,364

Unsolicited mss are not generally welcome; many are received and not used. All ideas in writing to the editor.

Reading

Evening Post
PO Box 22, Tessa Road, Reading, Berkshire RG1 8NS
☎0734 575833   Fax 0734 599363

Owner *Thomson Regional Newspapers Ltd*
Editor *David Murray*
Circulation 30,272

Unsolicited mss welcome; one or two received every day. Interested in finished copy only — no phone calls or written ideas. Fiction very rarely used. Special pages include travel (Saturday); motoring and motorcycling (Tuesday); gardening, rock (Saturday); women (Monday/ Thursday); junior readers and theatre (Saturday); business (Wednesday); citizens' guide (periodically).

News Editor *Tony Johnston*
Features Editor *Brian Sansome* Topical subjects, particularly of Thames Valley interest. Maximum 800–1000 words.
Women's Page *Rosalind Renshaw*

Scarborough

Scarborough Evening News
17–23 Aberdeen Walk, Scarborough, North Yorkshire YO11 1BB
☎0723 363636   Fax 0723 354092

Owner *Yorkshire Regional Newspapers Ltd*
Editor *Neil Speight*
Circulation 18,785

Special pages include property (Monday); women (Tuesday); motoring (Tuesday/Friday); pop (Thursday).

News Editor/Women's Page *Elizabeth Johnson*
Arts Editor/Music *Gillian Enlund*
Motoring *G. F. Exley*
Sports *Charles Place*
All other material should be addressed to the editor.

Scotland

Daily Record (Glasgow)
See **National Newspapers**

Scotland on Sunday
See **National Newspapers**

The Scotsman
See **National Newspapers**

Sunday Mail (Glasgow)
See **National Newspapers**

Sunday Post (Glasgow)
See **National Newspapers**

Scunthorpe

Scunthorpe Evening Telegraph
Doncaster Road, Scunthorpe DN15 7RE
☎ 0724 843421 Fax 0724 853495

Owner *Northcliffe Newspapers Group Ltd*
Editor *P. L. Moore*
Circulation 74,000

News Editor *Russell Ward*

All correspondence should go to the news editor.

Sheffield

Star
York Street, Sheffield S1 1PU
☎ 0742 767676 Fax 0742 725978

Owner *United Newspapers*
Editor *Michael Corner*
Circulation 140,683

Unsolicited mss not welcome, unless topical and local.

News Editor *Paul License* Contributions only accepted from freelance news reporters if they relate to the area.
Features Editor *Philip Andrews* Very rarely require outside features, unless on specialised subject.
Sports Editor *Derek Fish*
Women's Page *Alison Hurndall*
Payment negotiable.

Shropshire

Shropshire Star
See **under** *Telford*

South Shields

Gazette
Chapter Row, South Shields, Tyne & Wear NE33 1BL
☎ 091-455 4661 Fax 091-456 8270

Owner *Northeast Press Ltd*
Editor *Ian Holland*
Circulation 28,091

News Editor *Neil McKay*
Sports Editor *John Cornforth*
Women's Page *Joy Yates*

Southampton

The Echo
45 Above Bar, Southampton SO9 7BA
☎ 0703 634134 Fax 0703 630289

Owner *Southern Newspapers Ltd*
Editor *Patrick Fleming*
Circulation 75,500

Unsolicited mss 'tolerated'. Approach in writing with strong ideas; staff supply almost all the material. All correspondence should be addressed to the editor.

Stoke on Trent

Evening Sentinel
Sentinel House, Etruria, Stoke on Trent, Staffordshire ST1 5SS
☎ 0782 289800 Fax 0782 280781

Owner *Northcliffe Newspapers Group Ltd*
Editor *Sean Dooley*
Circulation 102,191

Weekly sports final supplement.

News Editor *Michael Wood*

All material should be sent to the news editor.

Sunderland

Sunderland Echo
Pennywell Industrial Estate, Pennywell, Sunderland, Tyne & Wear SR4 9ER
☎ 091-534 3011 Fax 091-534 5975

Owner *Sunderland & Hartlepool Publishing Ltd*
Editor *Andrew Hughes*
Circulation 67,347

All editorial material to be addressed to the news editor.

Swansea

South Wales Evening Post
Adelaide Street, Swansea, Glamorgan SA1 1QT
☎0792 650841   Fax 0792 655386

Owner *Northcliffe Newspapers Group Ltd*
Editor *Nick Carter*
Circulation 71,155

Circulates throughout South West Wales.

News Editor *Simon Orrell*
Sports Editor *David Evans*
Women's Page *Betty Hughes*

Swindon

Evening Advertiser
100 Victoria Road, Swindon, Wiltshire SN1 3BE
☎0793 528144   Fax 0793 542434

Owner *Wiltshire Newspapers*
Editor *John Mayhew*
Circulation 34,839

Finished copy much preferred to ideas. 'All material must be strongly related or relevant to the town of Swindon, borough of Thamesdown or the county of Wiltshire.' Little scope for freelance work. Fees vary depending on material.

News Editor *David Gledhill*
Features Editor *Pauline Leighton*
Sports Editor *Alan Johnson*
Women's Page *Shirley Mathias*

Telford

Shropshire Star
Ketley, Telford, Shropshire TF1 4HU
☎0952 242424   Fax 0952 254605

Owner *Shropshire Newspapers Ltd*
Editor *Warren Wilson*
Circulation 98,161

Unsolicited mss not welcome. Approach the editor with ideas in writing in the first instance. No news or fiction. Monthly supplement: *Star Magazine*.

News Editor *Andy Wright*
Features Editor *Dai Lewis* Limited opportunities here; uses mostly in-house or syndicated material. Maximum 1200 words.
Sports Editor *P. Byram*
Women's Page *Shirley Tart*

Torquay

Herald Express
Harmsworth House, Barton Hill Road,
Torquay TQ2 8JN
☎0803 213213   Fax 0803 313093

Owner *Northcliffe Newspapers Group Ltd*
Editor *J. C. Mitchell*
Circulation 31,000

Drive scene, property guide, Monday sports, special pages, rail trail, Saturday surgery, nature and conservation column, Saturday children's page. Supplements: *Curriculum* (quarterly); *Lifestyle* (weekly); *Gardening* (quarterly); *Visitor's Guide* (monthly); *Antiques & Collectables* (monthly); *Healthcare News* (quarterly). Unsolicited mss generally not welcome. Receives about 2 dozen a year. All editorial material should be addressed to the editor in writing.

Tunbridge Wells

Kent & Sussex Courier
Longfield Road, Tunbridge Wells, Kent TN2 3HL
☎0892 526262   Fax 0892 543181

Owner *Courier Printing & Publishing Co. Ltd*
Editor *Martin Oxley*

Very little freelance work commissioned at present.

Wales

South Wales Argus
See **under** *Newport*

South Wales Echo
See **under** *Cardiff*

South Wales Evening Post
See **under** *Swansea*

Wales on Sunday
See **National Newspapers**

Western Mail
See **under** *Cardiff*

West of England

Express & Echo
See **under** *Exeter*

Western Daily Press
See **under** *Bristol*

Western Morning News
See **under** *Plymouth*

Weymouth

Dorset Evening Echo
57 St Thomas Street, Weymouth, Dorset DT4 8EU
☎0305 784804   Fax 0305 782593

Owner *Southern Newspapers*
Editor *Michael Woods*
Circulation 24,000

Farming, by-gone days, films, arts, showbiz, brides, teens page, children's page, and video.

News Editor *Paul Thomas*
Sports Editor *Jack Wyllie*

Wolverhampton

Express & Star
Queen Street, Wolverhampton, West
Midlands WV1 3BU
☎0902 313131   Fax 0902 21467

Owner *Midlands News Association*
Editor *Keith Parker*
Circulation 235,633

News Editor *Derek Tucker*
Features Editor *Garry Copeland*
Sports Editor *Brian Clifford*
Women's Page *Marion Brennan*

Worcester

Evening News
Berrow's House, Hylton Road,
Worcester WR2 5JX
☎0905 748200   Fax 0905 429605

Owner *Reed Midland Newspapers Ltd*
Editor *Malcolm Ward*
Circulation 29,256

Pulse pop page (Tuesday); leisure (Wednesday); property (Thursday); weekend news (Saturday). Supplements: *Midweek News* (weekly); *Motoring News* (weekly); *Weekend News and Entertainment* (weekly).

News Editor *John Murphy*
Features Editor/Women's Page *Chris Lloyd*
Sports Editor *Paul Ricketts*

Yorkshire

Yorkshire Evening Post
See **under** *Leeds*

Yorkshire Post
See **under** *Leeds*

Freelance Rates – Newspapers

Freelance rates vary enormously. The following should be treated as guidelines. Minimum rates recommended by the **National Union of Journalists** represent an overall increase of 5% on last year's rates. Most work can command higher fees from employers whether or not they have NUJ agreements. It is up to free-lancers to negotiate the best deal they can.

National Newspapers and News Agencies

Words

(A premium of 50 per cent should be added to all the rates listed below for exclusive coverage.)

Home news: £21 per 200 words or part thereof
Foreign news: £21 per 100 words
City and business news: £21 per 100 words
Sports match reports: Minimum payment for match reports: £63

National Daily Papers:
Features: £210 per 1000 words
Reviews: £163 per 1000 words
Listings: £131 per 1000 words
Gazette: £200 per 1000 words

Sunday Papers:
Features: £247 per 1000 words
Reviews: £184 per 1000 words

Diary paragraphs: Gossip column items, art reviews and notices: these attract a higher fee than the minimum per word since they are of restricted length. Lead items – about £100, others £44.

Photographic Fees

National papers: day rate £126, half-day £73.50 (some papers may work on an assignment rate rather than half-day rates).

Studio or location work or commissions requiring special equipment/techniques (e.g. aerial): £550 per day.

Black and White reproduction fees for one British use only in a national paper:

Up to (sq in):	20	20-30	30-50	50-80	Over 80
Minimum	£63	£73.50	£84	£94.50	by negotiation

Colour reproduction fees: by negotiation.
Cover and front page: 50 per cent extra.
Photographs ordered and accepted but not used: at least £63.
Print fee: at least £4 delivery charges.

Cartoons and Illustrations

Cartoon size: 1 column £87, thereafter subject to individual negotiation.

Colour: Double the above rate.
(All rates quoted are for one British use.)

Colour Supplements

Words
A fee should not be less than £236 for up to1000 words.

Photographic Fees
Commissioned work should be in the region of £262 a day plus expenses; £147 per half day.
Studio work: £605.
Colour reproduction fees:

Up to:	¹/₄ page	¹/₂ page	³/₄ page	full page
Minimum	£157.50	£220	£262	£315

Cartoons, Illustrations, Crosswords
Should be at least double the national newspaper rate.

Provincial Newspapers

Words
Minimum News Lineage Rate Weekly newspapers: £1.38 for up to and including 10 lines; 13.8p per line thereafter. Daily, Evening & Sunday newspapers; £2.40 for up to and including 10 lines; 20.2p per line thereafter.
Minimum Feature Rate (for features submitted on spec.) Weekly newspapers: £1.51 for up to and including 10 lines; 18.9p per line thereafter. Daily, Evening & Sunday newspapers: £2.66 for up to and including 10 lines; 21p per line thereafter.
Commissioned features Weekly newspapers: £126; Daily & Sunday newspapers: £177; Regional and Evening newspapers: £145.

Photographic Fees
Commissions Provincial evening newspapers: £44 for up to 4 hours; £74.55 for up to 8 hours. Weekly, Regional, Daily and Sunday newspapers: £50 for up to 4 hours; £99.75 for up to 8 hours.

Black and White	Daily/Evening/Sunday	Freesheet/Weekly
Up to 10 sq in	£16.40	£10.00
Over 10 and up to 50 sq in	£21.50	£12.60
Over 50 and up to 80 sq in	£33.20	£20.20
Over 80 and up to 150 sq in	£40.40	£26.80

Colour Daily newspapers: minimum rate of £22 for colour pictures of less than 8 sq in which do not exceed single column width. For other colour pictures, minimum fees will be as for black and white above, plus 25% subject to a minimum rate of £27 for daily and Sunday papers, £15.75 for weeklies.

Cartoons
Single Frame: at least £44.
Feature Strip (up to 4 frames): £81.

Serial Killing

A recent trade promotion for Peter Mayle's *A Year in Provence* reveals the publisher in self-congratulatory mood.

'*A Year in Provence* was first published in hardback by Hamish Hamilton in 1989. It was quietly received and sold 3500 copies.'
  'It was published in paperback by Pan in 1990 and has now sold 750,000 copies.'

We get the message. All praise to the sharp-eyed marketing people at Pan for detecting the hidden potential in Mr Mayle's excursion into Gallic whimsy. But the copywriter omits a significant detail. In the period between the respectful reviews and Peter Mayle's canonisation as travel writer of the year, *A Year in Provence* was serialised in *The Sunday Times Magazine*, one chapter a month for twelve months on the run. With such exposure – the equivalent say of a million-pound-plus advertising campaign – Mayle's future was assured. If anyone deserves credit for turning Provence into a literary wonderland, it is Brian MacArthur, then executive editor of *The Sunday Times*, who was first in line to buy serialisation rights.

Pan's reluctance to share the glory is understandable. There are not nowadays so many success stories in publishing that they can afford to be generous. But another, more subtle factor, may be at work. Publishers have never quite come to terms with the press. They put a high value on publicity but dread the journalists' power to make or break reputations. The ambivalence shows up most obviously in the uneasy relationship between publishers and critics. If criticism is part of literature (an argument strengthened by the fact that many critics are themselves authors) then, say the publishers, it is the solemn duty of critics to write nice things about the books they review so that lots of people will rush out to buy. The tougher-minded critics will have none of this. As they see it, they have a twin responsibility to give their version of the truth (it was Bernard Shaw who said that a criticism written without personal feeling is worthless) within the compass of a good read. Which is why a critic's byline is invariably printed in bolder type than either the title of the book or the name of the author he is reviewing.

As a generator of suspicion and misunderstanding, serialisation runs a close second to criticism. On the face of it, serialisation in a large circulation newspaper brings benefits all round. Author and publisher share a sizeable cheque (in the not so far off days of media boom payments of £100,000 plus were not exceptional), the book is fanfared throughout the land, readers are attracted to the newspaper, book buyers place their orders. At best, it is a highly profitable formula. But it doesn't always work like that.

Newspaper extracts are not of themselves a guarantee of shop sales. Readers may feel that, after wading through a few thousand words over Sunday breakfast, they can very easily do without the full unexpurgated version of the book.

The chances of this happening have been greatly increased of late by the editorial policy of gutting books for serialisation. In the old days, a newspaper would do the decent thing by running a chapter or two as appetisers, leaving the reader with the vague feeling that if he didn't buy the book he could be missing out on the best part of the story.

It is a measure of just how long it takes publishers to catch up with events, that some of them fondly imagine that this is still the recognised procedure. Not so. When a newspaper bids for serialisation it is on the clear understanding that the manuscript can be pulled apart, sliced up and reassembled, even to some extent rewritten, to make a running story of two or three parts. This means reducing, say, an eighty-thousand-word tome to, at most, twelve thousands words – a pruning exercise which calls for an energetic wielding of the editorial hatchet.

There are publishers, not to mention authors, who balk at such wanton vandalism though, reminded of the bird in the hand, their complaints usually stop short of returning the cheque. If then the book goes on to make the bestseller list, resentment disappears. If the book dives towards the remainder merchants, guess who is held to blame?

On the experience of having two of my own books serialised, one in *The Mail*, the other in *The Sunday Times* and of serialising the work of other writers to the tune of some thirty books, I can sympathise with any author who feels artistically abused by the system but only to the extent of pointing out that, as with literary criticism, it is an illusion to believe that the press is there to serve the interests of publishing. Its own readers come first.

There is a follow-up argument. If serialisation proves anything it is that most books are far too long and that many are not best organised to attract reader interest. As every young journalist learns, the first rule of his trade is to grab attention with the first paragraph, the first line, even the first word. The cherry goes on the top, as Lord Beaverbrook used to say. Fiction writers acquire this knack – the successful ones, anyway. But over wide areas of non-fiction where serialisation is most in prospect, the tendency to waffle is endemic. Political memoirs are a case in point. The former cabinet minister who goes into print is a one-product salesman. His book will be judged on the strength of what he has to say about his hour upon the stage – not, most emphatically not, on reprints of committee minutes or languid accounts of manoeuvring in the West Wittering Conservative Association. By cutting such guff the serialiser does great service to the discerning book buyer who naturally refuses to part with ready cash for what he knows to be mere padding.

Which brings us back to *A Year in Provence*. Not that Peter Mayle is guilty of overwriting. His style is spare and deceptively simple – proof, no doubt, that his early life as an advertising copywriter was not in vain. Moreover, he knows how to beguile the reader who, having begun, feels compelled to finish the chapter, if not the entire book. As everybody now agrees, *A Year in Provence* opens irresistibly.

'The year started with lunch.'

You just have to know more. Brian MacArthur saw this, which is why the book went into a mammoth *Sunday Times* serialisation. But why did it take so long for the publishers to catch up? Could it be that they need to shake up their ideas on what makes a good read?

Magazines

Accountancy

40 Bernard Street, London WC1N 1LD
☎071-833 3291   Fax 071-833 2085

Owner *Institute of Chartered Accountants in England and Wales*
Editor *Brian Singleton-Green*
Circulation 74,654

FOUNDED 1889. MONTHLY. Written ideas welcome.

Features *Peter Carty* Accounting/tax/business-related articles of high technical content aimed at professional/managerial readers. Maximum 2000 words.
Payment by arrangement.

News *Julia Irvine* Approach by phone with news items.

Accountancy Age

32-34 Broadwick Street, London W1A 2HG
☎071-439 4242   Fax 071-437 7001

Owner *VNU Publications*
Editor *Peter Williams*
Circulation 77,000

FOUNDED 1969. WEEKLY. Unsolicited mss welcome. Ideas may be suggested in writing provided they are clearly thought out.

Features Topics right across the accountancy/business/financial world. Maximum 1800 words.
Payment NUJ rates.

Active Life

Aspen Specialist Media, Christ Church, Cosway Street, London NW1 5NJ
☎071-262 2622 ext. 265   Fax 071-706 4811

Owner *Aspen Specialist Media*
Editor *Helene Hodge*

FOUNDED 1990. QUARTERLY magazine aimed for readership aged 55 and over. General consumer interests including travel and leisure. Opportunities for freelancers in all departments, including fiction. Approach in writing with synopsis of ideas. Authors' notes available.

Acumen

6 The Mount, Higher Furzeham, Brixham, South Devon TQ5 8QY
☎0803 851098

Owner *Acumen Publications*
Editor *Patricia Oxley*
Circulation 800

FOUNDED 1985. TWICE-YEARLY literary magazine with a bias towards poetry; but also including extensive review section, short stories, literary articles and graphics. Unsolicited mss welcome. Approach with ideas in writing. Particularly interested in poetry, short stories. literary and biographical pieces, or the occasional academical article on poetry or specific writers. Most of the magazine's interviews (one per issue) are devoted to 'poets on poetry', and are generally commissioned. No overtly political or religious material; no heavy academic copy, or anything sectarian.

Features *William Oxley/Patricia Oxley*
Fiction *Patricia Oxley* Short stories welcome.
Other/Special Pages *Glyn Pursglove/Patricia Oxley*
Payment Cash payments are exceptional; as a rule payment is in the form of complimentary copies.

ADviser

Hamilton Press Ltd, Quayside House, Pedders Way, Ashton, Preston, Lancashire PR2 0XS
☎0772 733333   Fax 0772 721044

Owner *British Dietetic Association*
Editor *Neil Donnelly*
Circulation *c. 3500*

FOUNDED 1981. QUARTERLY. Unsolicited mss welcome from dietitians and nutritionists. Make initial approach in writing. All pieces should be appropriate to dietitians. Maximum 1200 words.
Payment £40-50.

African Affairs

Dept of Politics, University of Reading, White Knights, PO Box 218, Reading RG6 2AA
☎0734 875123   Fax 0734 314404

Owner *Royal African Society*
Editors *David Killingray/Peter Woodward*
Circulation 2250

FOUNDED 1901. QUARTERLY learned journal publishing articles on contemporary developments on the African continent. Unsolicited mss welcome.

Features Should be well researched and written in a style that is immediately accessible to the intelligent lay reader. Maximum 8000 words.
Payment for non-academics may be up to £40 per 1000 words. No payment for academics.

Air International

PO Box 100, Stamford, Lincolnshire PE9 1XQ
☎0780 55131   Fax 0780 57261

Owner *Key Publishing Ltd*
Editor *Barry Wheeler*

FOUNDED 1971. MONTHLY. Civil and military aircraft magazine. Unsolicited mss welcome but initial approach by phone or in writing preferred.

Airforces Monthly

PO Box 100, Stamford, Lincolnshire PE9 1XQ
☎0780 55131   Fax 0780 57261

Owner *Key Publishing Ltd*
Editor *David Oliver*
Circulation 33,000

FOUNDED 1988. MONTHLY. Modern military aircraft magazine. Unsolicited mss welcome but initial approach by phone or in writing preferred.

Amateur Film and Video Maker

33 Gassiot Way, Sutton, Surrey SM1 3AZ
☎081-644 0839   Fax 081-644 0839

Owner *Film Maker Publications*
Editor *Tony Pattison*
Circulation 3000

FOUNDED 1930. BI-MONTHLY of the Institute of Amateur Cinematographers. Reports news and views of the Institute. Unsolicited mss welcome but all contributions are unpaid.

Amateur Gardening

Westover House, West Quay Road, Poole,
Dorset BH15 1JG
☎0202 680586   Fax 0202 674335

Owner *IPC Magazines Ltd*
Editor *Graham Clarke*
Circulation 103,850

FOUNDED 1884. WEEKLY. New contributions are welcome provided that they have a professional approach. Of the twenty unsolicited mss received each week, ninety per cent are returned as unsuitable. All articles/news items are supported by colour pictures (which may or may not be supplied by the author).

Features Topical and practical gardening articles. Maximum 800 words.

News Compiled and edited in-house generally.
Payment negotiable.

Amateur Golf

PO Box 12, Wetherby, West Yorkshire LS22 4SR
☎0937 583181   Fax 0937 583181

Owner *Park View Publications Ltd*
Editor *John Lelean*
Circulation 12,000

MONTHLY journal of the English Golf Union. UK coverage of amateur golf interests, club events and international matches, plus European golf from June 1992. Unsolicited mss considered. Approach with ideas in writing or by phone.

Features Golf course management and equipment, golf holidays, profiles and general amateur golf concerns. Maximum 2000 words.

Other Always interested in golf cartoons.
Payment negotiable in all cases.

Amateur Photographer

King's Reach Tower, Stamford Street,
London SE1 9LS
☎071-261 5000   Fax 071-261 5404

Owner *IPC Magazines Ltd*
Editor *Keith Wilson*
Circulation 62,219

For the competent amateur with a technical interest. Freelancers are used but writers should be aware that there is ordinarily no use for words without pictures.

Amateur Stage

83 George Street, London W1H 5PL
☎071-486 1732   Fax 071-224 2215

Owner *Platform Publications Ltd*
Editor *Charles Vance*

Some opportunity here for outside contributions (in writing only). Topics of interest include amateur premières, technical developments within the amateur forum and items relating to landmarks/ anniversaries in the history of amateur societies. *No payment.*

Ambit

17 Priory Gardens, Highgate, London N6 5QY
☏ 081-340 3566

Owner *Martin Bax*
Editor *Martin Bax*
Circulation 2000

FOUNDED 1959. QUARTERLY literary magazine. *Publishes* short stories, experimental fiction, poetry and original drawings. No features, conventional short stories, or traditional poems. 'An idiosyncratic magazine with its own taste and flavour... We like to publish material by some well-established writers alongside work by new writers in each number and much of the material is illustrated by artists who regularly work for Ambit. Authors wishing to submit are strongly advised to have a look at the magazine before doing so because much totally unsuitable material is received.' Approach in writing, not by phone.

Editors Prose *J. G. Ballard;* Poetry *Edwin Brock/ Carol Ann Duffy/Henry Graham*

The American

114-115 West Street, Farnham, Surrey GU9 7HL
☏ 0252 713366   Fax 0252 716792

Owner *British American Newspapers Ltd*
Editor *Robert Pickens*
Circulation 15,000

FOUNDED 1976. FORTNIGHTLY community newspaper for US citizens resident in the UK and as such requires a strong American angle in every story. 'We are on the look-out for items on business and commerce, diplomacy and international relations, defence and 'people' stories.' Maximum length '5 minutes read'. First approach in writing with samples of previous work.
Payment 'modest but negotiable'.

Angling Times

Bretton Court, Bretton, Peterborough,
Cambridgeshire PE3 8DZ
☏ 0733 266222   Fax 0733 265515

Owner *EMAP Pursuit Publications*
Editor *Keith Higginbottom*
Circulation 126,155

Do not send your fishing stories here: this weekly is more concerned with angling news than feature material, most of which is provided by their large staff. Occasional features from outsiders.
Payment varies.

Animal World

Causeway, Horsham, West Sussex RH12 1HG
☏ 0403 64181   Fax 0403 41048

Owner *RSPCA*
Editor *Michaela Miller*
Circulation 70,000

BI-MONTHLY RSPCA Junior membership magazine. Articles (pet care, etc.) are written in-house. Good-quality animal photographs welcome.

Annabel

80 Kingsway East, Dundee DD4 8SL
☏ 0382 462276   Fax 0382 452491

Owner *D. C. Thomson & Co. Ltd*
Editor *Emil Pacholek*
Circulation 162,185

A good bet for freelancers. Apart from the domestic content of the magazine, material is supplied mainly by freelance writers which is typical of a D. C. Thomson publication. Although 'the slush pile' does not generally yield much in the way of ready-made features, it can provide openings for new writers. Currently aiming at women aged 35 and over.

Features Editor *Karen Donnelly* General women's interest features, interviews and topical articles. Plus fiction — which doesn't have to be about marriage — 'we've also published Fay Weldon'. Maximum 3000 words.
Payment negotiable.

Antique and New Art

10-11 Lower John Street, London W1R 3PE
☏ 071-434 9180   Fax 071-287 5488

Owner *Antique Publications*
Editor *Alistair Hicks*
Circulation 22,000

FOUNDED 1986. QUARTERLY. Amusing coverage of antiques and art. Unsolicited mss not welcome. Approach by phone or in writing in the first instance. Interested in freelance contributions on international art news items.

The Antique Collector

Eagle House, 50 Marshall Street,
London W1V 1LR
☏ 071-439 5000   Fax 071-439 5177

Owner *National Magazine Co. Ltd*
Editor *David Coombs*
Circulation 14,500

FOUNDED 1930. MONTHLY. Opportunities for free-lance features. Submit ideas in writing. Feature articles have a set format: maximum 2000 words with eight illustrations in colour and/or black and white. Acceptance depends primarily on how authoritative and informative they are. Topical and controversial material is always welcome. *Payment* negotiable.

The Antique Dealer and Collectors' Guide

PO Box 805, Greenwich, London SE10 8TD
☎081-318 5868

Owner *Statuscourt Ltd*

Publisher *Philip Bartlam*
Circulation 13,900

FOUNDED 1946. MONTHLY covering all aspects of the antiques and fine art world. Unsolicited mss welcome.

Features Practical but readable articles on the history, design, authenticity, restoration and market aspects of antiques and fine art. Maximum 2000 words.

News *Philip Bartlam* Items on events, sales, museums, exhibitions, antique fairs and markets. Maximum 150 words.
Payment £76 per 1000 words.

Aquarist & Pondkeeper

9 Tufton Street, Ashford, Kent TN23 1QN
☎0233 621877   Fax 0233 645669

Owner *Dog World Ltd*
Editor *John Dawes*
Circulation *c.* 25,000

FOUNDED 1924. MONTHLY. Covers all aspects of aquarium and pondkeeping: conservation, herpetology (study of reptiles and amphibians), news, reviews and aquatic plant culture. Unsolicited mss welcome. Ideas should be submitted in writing first.

Features *John Dawes* Good opportunities for writers on any of the above topics or related areas. 1500 words (maximum 2500), plus illustrations. 'We have stocks in hand for up to two years, but new material and commissioned features will be published as and when relevant (average lead-in 4–6 months).'

News *John Dawes* Very few opportunities.

Architects' Journal/The Architectural Review

33–39 Bowling Green Lane, London EC1R 0DA
☎071-837 1212   Fax 071-278 4003

Owner *EMAP Architectural Press*

WEEKLY (Architects' Journal) and MONTHLY (The Architectural Review) trade magazines dealing with all aspects of the industry. No unsolicited mss. Approach in writing with ideas. The Architectural Review was previously published by MBC Architectural Press and was acquired by EMAP Business Publishing in 1992.

Architectural Design

42 Leinster Gardens, London W2 3AN
☎071-402 2141   Fax 071-723 9540
Editor *Dr Andreas Papadakis*
Circulation 12,000

FOUNDED 1930. BI-MONTHLY. Theoretical architectural magazine. Unsolicited mss not generally welcome. Copy tends to come from experts in the field only.

The Architectural Review
See **Architects' Journal/The Architectural Review**

Arena

3rd Floor, Block A, Exmouth House, Pine Street, London EC1R 0JL
☎071-837 7270   Fax 071-837 3906

Owner *Wagadon Ltd/Condé Nast Publications*
Editor *Dylan Jones*

Style and general interest magazine for the trendy man about town — male fashion and intelligent feature articles.

Features Editor *Dylan Jones* Wide range of subject matter: film, television, politics, business, music, media, design, art, architecture and theatre. Both profiles and articles. Fiction occasionally. *Payment* £150 per 1000 words.

Art & Craft

Scholastic Publications Ltd, Villiers House, Clarendon Avenue, Leamington Spa, Warwickshire CV32 5PR
☎0926 887799   Fax 0926 883331

Owner *Scholastic Publications Ltd*
Editor *Eileen Lowcock*
Circulation 23,000

FOUNDED 1936. MONTHLY aimed at a specialist market — the needs of primary school teachers and pupils. Ideas and synopses considered for commission.

Features *Eileen Lowcock* Most of our contributors are primary school teachers or art and craft specialists familiar with the needs of our specialised market. Insufficient research from outside contributions is often a problem.

News Handled by in-house staff. No opportunities.

Art & Design
42 Leinster Gardens, London W2 3AN
☎071-402 2141   Fax 071-723 9540
Editor *Dr Andreas Papadakis*
Circulation 12,000

FOUNDED 1985. BI-MONTHLY. Theoretical art magazine. Unsolicited mss not generally welcome. Copy tends to come from experts in the field.

Art Monthly
Suite 17, 26 Charing Cross Road,
London WC2H 0DG
☎071-240 0389

Owner *Britannia Art Publications*

Editor *Peter Townsend*
Circulation 4000

FOUNDED 1976. TEN ISSUES YEARLY. News and features of relevance to those interested in modern art. Unsolicited mss welcome. Contributions should be addressed to the editors.

Features Alongside exhibition reviews: usually 600–1000 words and almost invariably commissioned. Articles of up to 3000 words on art theory (e.g. modernism, post-modernism), individual artists, modern art history and issues affecting the arts (e.g. funding and arts education). Book reviews of 600–1000 words, occasionally more (up to 3000). *Payment* in all cases negotiable.

News Brief reports (250–300 words) on conferences, public art, etc.

The Art Newspaper
Mitre House, 44-46 Fleet Street,
London EC4Y 1BN
☎071-936 2886   Fax 071-583 6897

Owner *Umberto Allemandi & Co. Publishing*
Editor *Anna Somers Cocks*
Circulation 15,000

FOUNDED 1990. MONTHLY. Broadsheet format with up-to-date information on the international art market, news, museums, exhibitions and current debate topics. No unsolicited mss. Approach with ideas in writing. Commissions only.

Features *Anna Somers Cocks* Opportunities for experienced journalists with knowledge of the art world and art market.
Payment £120 per 1000 words.

News *Anna Somers Cocks* Maximum 400 words.

The Artist
Caxton House, 63–65 High Street, Tenterden,
Kent TN30 6BD
☎05806 3673   Fax 05806 5411

Owner *Irene Briers*
Editor *Sally Bulgin*
Circulation 17,000

FOUNDED 1931. MONTHLY.

Features *Sally Bulgin* Art journalists, artists, art tutors and writers with a good knowledge of art materials are invited to write to the editor with ideas for practical and informative features about art, materials, techniques and artists.

Athletics Weekly
Bretton Court, Bretton, Peterborough PE3 8DZ
☎0733 261144   Fax 0733 265515

Owner *EMAP Pursuit Publications*
Editor-in-Chief *Paul Richardson*
Circulation 17,000

FOUNDED 1945. WEEKLY. Features news and articles on track and field athletics, road running and cross-country. Includes interviews, profiles, historical articles and exclusive news.
Payment by arrangement.

The Author
84 Drayton Gardens, London SW10 9SB
☎071-373 6642

Owner *The Society of Authors*
Editor *Derek Parker*
Manager *Kate Pool*
Circulation 6000

FOUNDED 1890. QUARTERLY journal of **The Society of Authors**. Unsolicited mss not welcome.

Autocar & Motor
38-42 Hampton Road, Teddington,
Middlesex TW11 0JE
☎081-943 5013   Fax 081-943 5653

Owner *Haymarket Magazines Ltd*
Editor *Shaun Campbell*
Circulation 96,500

FOUNDED 1895. WEEKLY. All news stories, features, interviews, scoops, ideas, tip-offs and photographs welcome.

Features *Mark Harrop*

News *Michael Harvey*
Payment from £150 per 1000 words/negotiable.

Baby Magazine

The Publishing House, Highbury Station Road, London N1 1SE
☎ 071-226 2222   Fax 071-226 1255

Owner *Harrington Kilbride*
Editor *Jane Harrington*

QUARTERLY for mothers with children up to school age (0-5 years). Always interested in new writers. Contact *Alice Westgate* with any ideas. No unsolicited mss. Telephone or send synopsis of feature with covering letter in the first instance. Unsolicited material is not returned.

Back Brain Recluse (BBR)

PO Box 625, Sheffield S1 3GY

Owner *Chris Reed*
Editor *Chris Reed*
Circulation 3000 + (worldwide)

International QUARTERLY speculative fiction magazine providing opportunity for new writers. 'We strongly recommend familiarity with our guidelines for contributors, and with recent issues of *BBR*, before any material is submitted. All correspondence must be accompanied by s.a.e. or international reply coupons.'
£5 per 1000 words.

Balance

British Diabetic Association, 10 Queen Anne Street, London W1M 0BD
☎ 071-323 1531   Fax 071-637 3644

Owner *British Diabetic Association*
Editor *Lesley Hallett*
Circulation 150,000

FOUNDED 1935. BI-MONTHLY. Unsolicited mss welcome if relevant to diabetes. Initial approach in writing preferred.

Features *Lesley Hallett* Medical and lifestyle features written by people with diabetes or an interest and expert knowledge in the field. General features

are mostly based on experience or personal observation. Maximum 2000 words.
Payment £75 per 1000 words.

News *Lesley Hallett* Short pieces about activities relating to diabetes and the lifestyle of diabetics. Maximum 150 words.
Payment £75 per 1000 words.

Young Balance *Ed Barrett* Any kind of article written by those under 18 and with personal experience of diabetes. Also book, film, drama, music, etc. reviews. Maximum 1500 words.
Payment varies.

The Banker

102-108 Clerkenwell Road, London EC1M 5SA
☎ 071-251 9321   Fax 071-251 4686

Owner *Financial Times Business Information*
Editor *Gavin Shreeve*
Circulation 13,847

FOUNDED 1926. MONTHLY. News and features on banking, finance and capital markets worldwide.

Barclaycard Magazine

Direct Marketing, Barclaycard, Northampton NN1 1SG
☎ 0604 252296   Fax 0604 253389

Owner *Barclaycard*
Editor *Marian Reidy*
Circulation c. 4 million

FOUNDED 1988. THRICE-YEARLY publication. Practical product-orientated features, e.g. fashion, holidays, food and drink, theme parks, etc. No unsolicited mss. Approach in writing with ideas.

BBC Gardeners' World Magazine

101 Bayham Street, London NW1 0AG
☎ 071-331 8000   Fax 071-331 8030

Owner *Redwood Publishing*
Editor *Adam Pasco*
Circulation 318,000

FOUNDED 1991. MONTHLY. Gardening advice, ideas and inspiration. No unsolicited mss. Approach by phone or in writing with ideas.

BBC Good Food

101 Bayham Street, London NW1 0AG
☎ 071-331 8000   Fax 071-331 8001

Owner *Redwood Publishing*
Editor *Mitzie Wilson*
Circulation 491,178

FOUNDED 1989. MONTHLY food magazine with television and radio links. No unsolicited mss.

BBC WILDLIFE Magazine
Broadcasting House, Whiteladies Road, Bristol BS8 2LR
☎ 0272 732211   Fax 0272 467075

Owner *BBC Enterprises Ltd*
Editor *Rosamund Kidman Cox*

FOUNDED 1963 (formerly *Wildlife*, née *Animals*). MONTHLY. Unsolicited mss not welcome.

Competition The magazine runs an annual competition for professional and amateur writers with a first prize of £1000 (see entry under **Prizes**).

Features Most features commissioned from writers with expert knowledge of wildlife or conservation subjects. Unsolicited mss are usually rejected. Maximum 3500 words. *Payment* £120–350.

News Most news stories commissioned from known freelancers. Maximum 800 words. *Payment* £40–100.

Bedfordshire Magazine
50 Shefford Road, Meppershall, Bedfordshire SG17 5LL
☎ 0462 813363

Owner *White Crescent Press*
Editor *Betty Chambers*
Circulation 2400

FOUNDED 1947. QUARTERLY. Unsolicited material welcome on Bedfordshire — history, biography, natural history and arts. No general interest articles. Approach by phone or in writing in the first instance.

Features Nothing in the way of consumer features.

News Very little.

Fiction Occasional poems of county interest only.

Special Pages Primarily historical material on Bedfordshire. Optimum 1500–2000 words. *Payment* nominal.

Bee World
18 North Road, Cardiff CF1 3DY
☎ 0222 372409   Fax 0222 665522

Owner *International Bee Research Association*
Editor *Dr P. A. Munn*
Circulation 1700

FOUNDED 1919. QUARTERLY. High-quality factual journal with international readership. Features apicultural science and technology. Unsolicited mss welcome.

Bella
H. Bauer Publishing, Shirley House, 25–27 Camden Road, London NW1 9LL
☎ 071–284 0909   Fax 071–485 3774

Owner *H. Bauer Publishing*
Editor *Sharon Brown*
Circulation 1.3 million

FOUNDED 1987. German launch into the women's weekly magazine market. Contributions welcome.

Features *Sue Reid* Maximum 1200–1300 words.

Fiction *Linda O'Byrne* Maximum 1200–4000 words. Send s.a.e. for guidelines. *Payment* varies, about £300 per 1000 words.

Best
10th Floor, Portland House, Stag Place, London SW1E 5AU
☎ 071–245 8700   Fax 071–245 8825

Owner *G & J (UK)*
Editor *Caroline Richards*
Circulation 660,000

FOUNDED 1987. WEEKLY women's magazine and stablemate of the magazine *Prima*. Multiple features, news, short stories on all topics of interest to women. Important for would-be contributors to study the magazine's style which differs from most women's weeklies. Approach in writing with s.a.e.

Features Maximum 1500 words. No unsolicited mss.

Fiction 'Five-Minute Story' and 'Romantic Fiction' slots: maximum 1500 words. Mss accepted in April and October only. *Payment* £100.

Bicycle
Northern & Shell Building, PO Box 381, Millharbour, London E14 9TW
☎ 071–987 5090   Fax 071–987 2160

Owner *Northern & Shell*
Editor *Ben Orme*
Circulation 17,000

FOUNDED 1981. MONTHLY for cyclists and cycling enthusiasts. Unsolicited mss, outlines and ideas welcome.

Features Interested in tours at home and abroad, local events, bike tests, health, fitness and training articles, and various cycling issues. Maximum 3000 words. Send covering letter with every submission. Make sure each page of mss is identifiable and indicate for how long article may be held. Colour transparencies preferred.
Payment £85 per 1000 words.

The Big Paper
The Design Council, 28 Haymarket,
London SW1Y 4SU
☎071–839 8000   Fax 071–925 2130

Owner *The Design Council*
Editor *Laurie Johnston*
Circulation 11,000

FOUNDED 1987. Published THRICE YEARLY (for each school term). Features design-related topics of interest and use to primary schools and teachers. Gets its name from its centre pages, which unfold from A3 to A2 to A1, to create a large worksheet-cum-poster. Ideas welcome from writers with an interest in primary education and design technology. Approach in writing in first instance, with outline of idea and supporting artwork.

Features *Laurie Johnston* Mostly commissioned or written in-house but unsolicited mss are welcome from writers with genuine interest in primary education and design technology.

News *Laurie Johnston* Maximum 100 words.
Payment £120 per 1000 words.

Birds
The Lodge, Sandy, Bedfordshire SG19 2DL
☎0767 680551   Fax 0767 692365

Owner *Royal Society for the Protection of Birds*
Editor *R. A. Hume*
Circulation 510,000

QUARTERLY magazine which covers not only wild birds but also wildlife and related conservation topics. No interest in features on pet birds. Mss or ideas welcome. On the look-out for photofeatures (colour transparencies) from photographers. Especially interested in unusual bird behaviour. 'No captive birds, please.'

Black Beauty & Hair
Hawker Consumer Publications Ltd, 13 Park House, 140 Battersea Park Road,
London SW11 4NB
☎071–720 2108   Fax 071–498 3023

Owner *Hawker Consumer Publications Ltd*
Editor *Irene Shelley*

Circulation 21,006

QUARTERLY beauty and fashion magazine. Unsolicited contributions welcome.

Features Beauty and fashion from writers with a knowledge of the Afro-Caribbean beauty scene. Emphasis on humorous but authoritative articles that relate to clothes, hair, lifestyle, sexual politics, women's interests. Minimum 1500 words.
Payment £85 per 1000 words.

Blueprint
26 Cramer Street, London W1M 3HE
☎071–486 7419   Fax 071–486 1451

Owner *Wordsearch Ltd*
Editor *Deyan Sudjic*
Circulation 10,000

FOUNDED 1983. TEN ISSUES YEARLY. Features on design and architecture. Maximum 1500 words. Unsolicited mss not welcome as 'the odds are against people getting the tone right without talking to us first'. Approach by phone in the first instance.
Payment negotiable.

Boat International
5–7 Kingston Hill, Kingston upon Thames,
Surrey KT2 7PW
☎081–547 2662   Fax 081–547 1201

Owner *Edisea Ltd*
Editor *Jason Holtom*
Circulation 24,000

FOUNDED 1983. MONTHLY. Unsolicited mss welcome. Approach with ideas in writing.

Features Maximum 2500 words.
Payment £100 per 1000 words.

News Maximum 300 words.
Payment £100 per 1000 words.

Book and Magazine Collector
43–45 St Mary's Road, Ealing, London W5 5RQ
☎081–579 1082   Fax 081–566 2024

Owner *Diamond Publishing Group Ltd*
Editor *John Dean*
Circulation 11,900

FOUNDED 1984. MONTHLY. Unsolicited feature items welcome. Approach in writing with ideas. Maximum 3000 words.
Payment £35 per 1000 words.

Bookdealer

Suite 34, 26 Charing Cross Road,
London WC2H 0DH
☎071-240 5890   Fax 071-379 5770
Editor *Barry Shaw*

WEEKLY trade paper which acts almost exclusively
as a platform for people wishing to buy or sell rare/
out-of-print books. Six-page editorial only; occasional articles and book reviews by regular freelance writers.

Books

43 Museum Street, London WC1A 1LY
☎071-404 0304   Fax 071-242 0762
Editor *Rodney Burbeck*
Circulation *c.* 200,000

Formerly *Books and Bookmen*. A consumer
magazine, dealing chiefly with features on authors
and reviews of books.
Payment negotiable.

The Bookseller

12 Dyott Street, London WC1A 1DF
☎071-836 8911   Fax 071-836 6381

Owner *J. Whitaker & Sons Ltd*
Editor *Louis Baum*

Trade journal of the publishing and book trade.
Essential guide to what is being done to whom.
Trade news and features, including special features, company news, publishing trends, etc. Unsolicited mss rarely used as most writing is either
done in-house or commissioned from experts within the trade. Approach in writing first.

Features *Penny Mountain/Helen Paddock*

News *Penny Mountain*

Brides and Setting Up Home

Vogue House, Hanover Square, London W1R 0AD
☎071-499 9080   Fax 071-493 1345

Owner *Condé Nast Publications Ltd*
Editor *Sandra Boler*
Circulation 72,700

BI-MONTHLY. Freelance contributions considered if
relevant. Much of the magazine is produced in-
house but a good feature (maximum 1000 words)
on cakes, jewellery, music, flowers, etc. is always
welcome. Prospective contributors should telephone with idea in the first instance.
Payment £120.

Bridge Magazine

London Road, Wheatley, Oxon OX9 1YR
☎08677 4111   Fax 08677 5383

Owner *Chess & Bridge Ltd*
Editor *Glyn Liggins*
Circulation 10,000

Formerly Pergamon Bridge. Recently relaunched in
a bright new illustrated format, and includes articles on bidding and play. A blend of instruction,
competitions, tournament reports and humour.
Coverage of world events welcome from qualified
journalists.

The British Bandsman

The Old House, 64 London End, Beaconsfield,
Buckinghamshire HP9 2JD
☎0494 674411   Fax 0494 670932

Owner *Austin Catelinet*
Editor *Peter Wilson*

FOUNDED 1887. WEEKLY. News on brass bands.
Features on brass instruments and music. Contributions welcome, but no payment.

British Birds

Fountains, Park Lane, Blunham,
Bedford MK44 3NJ
☎0767 40025   Fax 0767 40025

Owner *British Birds Ltd*
Editor *Dr J. T. R. Sharrock*
Circulation 11,000

FOUNDED 1907. MONTHLY ornithological magazine
published by non-profit-making company. Features
annual *Report on Rare Birds in Great Britain* and
sponsored competitions for Bird Photograph of the
Year and Bird Illustrator of the Year. Unsolicited
mss welcome from ornithologists only.

Features Well-researched, original material relating to Western Palearctic birds welcome. Maximum
6000 words.

News *Mike Everett/Robin Prytherch* Items ranging
from conservation to humour. Maximum 200
words.
No payment.

British Book News

10 Spring Gardens, London SW1A 2BN
☎071-930 8466   Fax 071-839 6347

Owner *The British Council*
Editor *Jennifer Creswick*
Circulation 7000

FOUNDED 1940. MONTHLY survey for librarians, booksellers and bookbuyers worldwide, including review articles, features and news of professional interest to book professionals, plus annotated listings of around 1000 new titles monthly. No unsolicited mss. Approach with ideas by phone or in writing.

Features *Jennifer Creswick* Interested in topics of interest to the professional book trade and library community, e.g. production matters, conservation, book export, developments in book-related technologies, publishing trends in Britain, and related topics. Maximum 2500 words. *Payment* negotiable.

News No real opportunities. News is gathered by the editor and a regular team of freelancers.

Special Pages *Jennifer Creswick* **Book Surveys**: regular series of two per month, with about 50 titles 'surveyed'. Authors should have special expertise in chosen field for review. About 2000 words, plus related bibliography. *Payment* negotiable.

British Chess Magazine
9 Market Street, St Leonards-on-Sea, East Sussex TN38 0DQ
☎ 0424 424009   Fax 0424 435439

Owner *British Chess Federation/M. Chandler*
Editor *Bernard Cafferty*

FOUNDED 1880. MONTHLY. Particularly interested in tournaments, the history of chess, and chess-related literature. Unsolicited mss not welcome unless from qualified chess experts and players. Ideas welcome. Approach in writing.

British Journalism Review
Cassel, Villiers House, 41–47 Strand, London WC2N 5JE
☎ 071-839 4900

Owner *British Journalism Review Ltd*

Editors *Geoffrey Goodman/Hugo Young/Philip Whitehead/Robin Lustig*
Circulation 2000+

FOUNDED 1989. QUARTERLY. Aims to create a vehicle for academic consideration of British journalism, establishing a critical forum for media matters. Best approach by writing. Unsolicited material welcome.

News/Features Contact **Publisher** *Colin Simpson* Will consider any article about journalism, journalists or broadcasting. Specific areas of interest include ethics, censorship and training. *Payment* £100 or by negotiation.

Book Reviews *Mark Hollingsworth* On issues specified above and usually by commission only. *Payment* £50/negotiable.

British Medical Journal
BMA House, Tavistock Square, London WC1H 9JR
☎ 071-387 4499   Fax 071-383 6418

Owner *British Medical Association*
Editor *Dr Richard Smith*

No market for freelance writers.

Broadcast
7 Swallow Place, London W1R 7AA
☎ 071-491 9484   Fax 071-355 3177

Owner *International Thomson*
Editor *Marta Wohrle*
Circulation 10,200

FOUNDED 1960. WEEKLY. Opportunities for freelance contributions. Write to the relevant editor in the first instance.

Features Any broadcasting issue. Maximum 1500 words.
Payment £130 per 1000 words.

News *Quentin Smith* Broadcasting news. Maximum 400 words.
Payment £130 per 1000 words.

Brokers' Monthly & Insurance Adviser
7 Stourbridge Road, Stourbridge, West Midlands DY9 7DG
☎ 0384 895228   Fax 0384 893666

Owner *John C. N. Sadler*
Editor *Brian Susman*
Circulation 8000

FOUNDED 1950. MONTHLY. No unsolicited material. Approach by phone in first instance.

Features Very few but willing to consider contact from specialist insurance writers. Maximum 2000 words.

The Brownie
17–19 Buckingham Palace Road, London SW1W 0PT
☎ 071-834 6242   Fax 071-828 8317

Owner *Guides Association*
Editor *Marion Thompson*
Circulation 28,000

FOUNDED 1962. MONTHLY. Aimed at brownies aged 7-10.

Articles Crafts and simple make-it-yourself items using inexpensive or scrap materials.

Features Of general interest (500-600 words). *Payment* £40 per 1000 words pro rata.

Fiction Brownie content an advantage. No adventures involving unaccompanied children in dangerous situations — day or night. Maximum 1000 words. *Payment* £40 per 1000 words pro rata.

Budgerigar World

County Press Buildings, Bala, Gwynedd LL23 7PG
☎0678 520262   Fax 0678 521262

Owner *Budgerigar World Ltd*
Editorial Director *G. H. Evans*

FOUNDED 1982. MONTHLY magazine for those breeding and exhibiting budgerigars. Unsolicited mss welcome.

Features *Terry A. Tuxford* Areas of interest include bird health, aviaries and individual budgerigars.

Building

Builder House, 1 Millharbour, London E14 9RA
☎071-537 2222   Fax 071-537 2007

Owner *The Builder Group*
Editor *Peter Bill*
Circulation 21,500

FOUNDED 1842. WEEKLY. Features articles on aspects of the modern building industry. Unsolicited mss not welcome but freelancers with specialist knowledge of the industry often used.

Features Focus on the modern industry. No building history required. Maximum 1500 words. *Payment* by arrangement.

News Maximum 500 words. *Payment* by arrangement.

The Burlington Magazine

6 Bloomsbury Square, London WC1A 2LP
☎071-430 0481   Fax 071-242 1205

Owner *The Burlington Magazine Publications Ltd*
Editor *Caroline Elam*

FOUNDED 1903. MONTHLY. Unsolicited contributions welcome on the subject of art history provided they are previously unpublished. All preliminary approaches should be made in writing.

Exhibition Reviews Usually commissioned, but occasionally unsolicited reviews are published if appropriate. Maximum 1000 words. *Payment* £100 (maximum).

Main Articles Maximum 4500 words. *Payment* £100 (maximum).

Shorter Notices Maximum 2000 words. *Payment* £50 (maximum).

Business Life

Greater London House, Hampstead Road, London NW1 7QQ
☎071-377 4633   Fax 071-383 7570

Owner *HHL Publishing*
Editor *David Taylor*
Circulation 110,000

MONTHLY. Glossy business magazine with few opportunities for freelancers. Unsolicited mss not welcome. Approach with ideas in writing only.

Business Traveller

388-396 Oxford Street, London W1N 9HE
☎071-629 4688   Fax 071-629 6572

Owner *Perry Publications*
Editor *Gillian Upton*
Circulation 39,161

MONTHLY. Opportunities for freelance writers but unsolicited contributions tend too often to be 'irrelevant to our market'. Would-be contributors are advised to study the magazine first. Approach in writing with ideas. *Payment* varies.

Cambridgeshire Life

County Life Ltd, PO Box 81, Lincoln LN5 7DY
☎0522 77567   Fax 0522 77463

Owner *A. L. Robinson*
Editor *Hilary Hammond*
Circulation 2500

FOUNDED 1965. MONTHLY county magazine featuring geographically relevant articles. Maximum 1000-1500 words. Contributions welcome and should be supported by three or four good-quality photographs. Approach in writing. *Payment* varies.

Camcorder User

57-59 Rochester Place, London NW1 9JU
☎071-485 0011   Fax 071-482 6269

Owner *W. V. Publications*
Editor *Ian Campbell*
Circulation 35,061

FOUNDED 1988. MONTHLY. Covers the expanding interest in camcorders with features on creative technique, shooting advice, new equipment, accessory round-ups and interesting applications on location. Unsolicited mss welcome.
Payment £80 plus illustrations.

Campaign

22 Lancaster Gate, London W2 3LY
☎071-413 4036   Fax 071-413 4507

Owner *Haymarket Publishing*
Editor *Dominic Mills*
Circulation 23,008

FOUNDED 1968. WEEKLY. Lively magazine serving the advertising and related industries. Freelance contributors are best advised to write in the first instance.

Features Articles of up to 1500-2000 words.
Payment negotiable.

News Relevant news stories of up to 300 words. Material should be addressed to the news desk.
Payment £35-£50.

Camping and Caravanning

Greenfields House, Westwood Way,
Coventry CV4 8JH
☎0203 694995   Fax 0203 694886

Owner *Camping and Caravanning Club*
Editor *Peter Frost*
Circulation 96,528

FOUNDED 1901. MONTHLY. Interested in journalists with camping and caravanning knowledge. Write with ideas for features in the first instance.

Features Outdoor pieces in general and items on specific regions of Britain. Maximum 1200 words. Illustrations to support text essential.

Camping Magazine

Link House, Dingwall Avenue, Croydon CR9 2TA
☎081-686 2599   Fax 081-760 0973

Owner *Link House Magazines Ltd*
Editor *David Roberts*

FOUNDED 1961. MONTHLY magazine with features on walking and camping. Aims to reflect this enjoyment by encouraging readers to appreciate the outdoors and to pursue an active camping holiday whether as a family in frame tent or as a lightweight backpacker. Articles that have the flavour of the camping lifestyle without being necessarily expeditionary or arduous are always welcome. Study of the magazine is advised in the first instance. Ideas welcome.

Canal and Riverboat

Stanley House, 9 West Street, Epsom,
Surrey KT18 7RL
☎0372 741411   Fax 0372 744493

Owner *A. E. Morgan Publications Ltd*
Editor *Norman Alborough*
Circulation 26,000

All aspects of waterways, narrow boats and cruisers. Contributions welcome. Make initial approach in writing.

Features *Norman Alborough* Aspects of waterways, narrow boats and motor cruisers, including cruising reports, practical advice, etc. Unusual ideas and personal comments are particularly welcome. Maximum 2000 words.
Payment around £50.

Fiction Considered only if subject matter is relevant. Maximum 1500 words.
Payment around £35.

News *Norman Alborough* Items of up to 300 words on the Inland Waterways System, plus photographs if possible.
Payment £10.

Capital Gay

38 Mount Pleasant, London WC1X 0AP
☎071-278 3764   Fax 071-278 3250

Owner *Stonewall Press Ltd*
Editor *Michael Mason*
Circulation 17,756

FOUNDED 1981. WEEKLY newspaper with social and political news and features for London's gay community. Some opportunities for freelance work. Approach in writing first.

Arts & Entertainments *Pas Paschali* Maximum 250 words.

Features *Michael Mason* Maximum 1800 words.

News *Andrew Saxton* Maximum 400 words.
Payment £70 per 1000 words.

Car

FF Publishing, 97 Earls Court Road,
London W8 6QH
☎071-370 0333   Fax 071-244 8692

Owner *FF Publishing Ltd*
Editor *Gavin Green*
Circulation 132,000

FOUNDED 1962. MONTHLY. Unsolicited mss of at least 1000 words welcome.

Features Usually commissioned from staff and known writers but outside material on new and old cars, special events and travel experiences considered. Maximum 3000 words.

Soapbox Special column for readers' stories on any matter concerning motoring, be it an experience or opinion. Maximum 1000 words.
Payment £200.

News Items (up to 250 words) with photographs always welcome, especially on new car models.
Payment £200 per 1000 words/negotiable.

Car Mechanics

PO Box 213, Crawley, West Sussex RH10 4YL
☎0342 715802   Fax 0342 715802

Owner *EMAP National Publications Ltd*
Editor *Grahame Steed*
Circulation 55,051

MONTHLY. Practical guide to performance tuning. Unsolicited mss welcome 'at sender's risk'. Ideas preferred. Approach by phone. Interested in anything related to performance tuning.

Features Good, technical, entertaining and well-researched features. Awareness of the tuning and bodystyling market is essential. Maximum 2500 words.
Payment by arrangement.

Caravan Magazine

Link House, Dingwall Avenue, Croydon CR9 2TA
☎081-686 2599   Fax 081-760 0973/781 6044

Owner *Link House Magazines Ltd*
Editor *Barry Williams*
Circulation 29,017

FOUNDED 1933. MONTHLY. Unsolicited mss welcome. Approach in writing with ideas. All correspondence should go direct to the editor.

Features Touring features with strong caravan bias and technical/DIY features. Maximum 1500 words.
Payment by arrangement.

Cars and Car Conversions Magazine

Link House, Dingwall Avenue, Croydon,
Surrey CR9 2TA
☎081-686 2599   Fax 081-760 0973

Owner *Link House Magazines Ltd*
Editor *Nigel Fryatt*
Circulation 70,000

FOUNDED 1965. MONTHLY. Unsolicited mss welcome but prospective contributors are advised to make initial contact by telephone.

Features *Nigel Fryatt* Technical articles on current motorsport and unusual sport-orientated roadcars. Length by arrangement.
Payment negotiable.

Cat World

10 Western Road, Shoreham-by-Sea, West Sussex BN43 5WD
☎0273 462000   Fax 0273 455994

Owner *D. M. & J. H. Colchester*
Editor *Joan Moore*
Circulation 19,000

FOUNDED 1981. MONTHLY. Unsolicited mss welcome but initial approach in writing preferred.

Features Lively first-hand experience features on every aspect of the cat. Breeding features and veterinary articles by acknowledged experts only. Maximum 1000 words.
Payment £25 per 1000 words.

News Short, concise, factual or humorous items, concerning cats. Maximum 100 words.
Payment £5.

Poems Maximum 50 words.
Payment £6.

Catch

D. C. Thomson & Co. Ltd, Albert Square, Dundee DD1 9QJ
☎0382 23131   Fax 0382 22214

Owner *D. C. Thomson & Co. Ltd*
Editor *Lesley Fenwick*

FOUNDED 1990. MONTHLY magazine for girls aged 17–21: typical reader viewed as 17 and single. Aims to have a much broader editorial base than *Looks*, going beyond the beauty and personality profile pages, and hopes to bridge the gap between magazines like *Just Seventeen* and titles for the older woman.

Catholic Herald

Lamb's Passage, Bunhill Row, London EC1Y 8TQ
☎071-588 3101   Fax 071-256 9728

Editor *Peter Stanford*
Circulation 30,000

Interested not only in straight Catholic issues but also in general humanitarian matters, social policies, the Third World, the arts, and books.
Payment by arrangement.

Caves & Caving

342 The Green, Eccleston, Chorley,
Lancashire PR7 5TP
☏ 0257 452763   Fax 0772 884687

Owner *British Cave Research Association*
Editor *Andy Hall*
Circulation 3000

FOUNDED 1970. QUARTERLY. Covers news on British and foreign caving activities, equipment reports, reviews, letters, expeditions, etc.

Features Expedition reports, new exploration in the UK, history of exploration articles. Maximum 1500–2000 words.

News Regional items from all over the UK. Maximum 1000 words. Unsolicited material welcome.

Certified Accountant

Granary House, Rutland Street, Cork, Republic of Ireland
☏ 010 353 21313 855   Fax 010 353 21313 496

Editor *Brian O'Kane*
Circulation 40,000

MONTHLY. Specialist, professional readership; unsolicited mss not welcome. Make initial contact in writing. Most features tend to be commissioned. No fiction.

Features Maximum 3000 words.
Payment £150.

Chacom

9–10 Eastway Business Village, Fulwood, Preston, Lancashire PR2 4WT
☏ 0772 653000   Fax 0772 655544

Owner *Central & West Lancashire Chamber of Commerce & Industry*
Editor *Babs Murphy*
Circulation 3000

FOUNDED 1984. MONTHLY for commerce and industry. Unsolicited mss welcome.

Features Various topical areas of business, exports, Chamber of Commerce business, etc.

News Items on commerce and industry. Maximum 1500 words.
Payment nominal.

Challenge

Revenue Buildings, Chapel Road, Worthing, West Sussex BN11 1BQ
☏ 0903 214198   Fax 0903 217663

Owner *Challenge Literature Fellowship*
Editor *Donald Banks*
Circulation 70,000

FOUNDED 1958. MONTHLY Christian newspaper which welcomes contributions. Send for sample copy of writers' guidelines in the first instance.

Fiction Short children's stories. Maximum 600 words.

News Items of up to 500 words (preferably with pictures) 'showing God at work', and human interest photostories. 'Churchy' items not wanted.
Payment negotiable.

Chapman

4 Broughton Place, Edinburgh EH1 3RX
☏ 031-557 2207

Owner *Joy M. Hendry*
Editor *Joy M. Hendry*
Circulation 2000

FOUNDED 1970. QUARTERLY. Scotland's quality literary magazine. Features poetry, short works of fiction, criticism, reviews, and articles on theatre, politics, language and the arts. Unsolicited material welcome if accompanied by s.a.e. Approach in writing unless discussion is needed.

Features *Joy Hendry* Topics of literary interest, especially Scottish literature, theatre, culture or politics. Maximum 5000 words.
Payment £16 per 1000 words.

Fiction *Joy Hendry* Short stories, occasionally novel extracts if self-contained. Maximum 6000 words.
Payment £16 per 1000 words.

Special Pages *Joy Hendry* Poetry, both UK and non-UK in translation (mainly, but not necessarily, European).
Payment £9 per published page.

Chat

King's Reach Tower, Stamford Street,
London SE1 9LS
☏ 071-261 6565   Fax 071-261 6534

Owner *IPC Magazines Ltd*
Editor *Terry Tavner*

FOUNDED 1985. WEEKLY general interest women's magazine. Unsolicited mss considered (about 100 received each week). Approach in writing with ideas.

Features *Karen Swayne* Human interest, humour. Not interested in contributors 'who have never bothered to read *Chat* and don't therefore know what type of magazine it is'. Maximum 1000 words. *Payment* up to £250 maximum.

Fiction *Johnathan Courtenay* Maximum 900 words.

Cheshire Life

The Old Custom House, 70 Watergate Street, Chester CH1 2LA
☎ 0244 345226   Fax 0244 348430

Owner *Oyston Publications*
Editor *Patrick O'Neill*
Circulation 10,000

FOUNDED 1934. MONTHLY. Features articles on homes, gardens, personalities, business, farming, conservation, heritage, books, fashion, arts, science — anything which has a Cheshire connection somewhere. Unsolicited mss welcome. Maximum 500–1500 words.

News 'Not a lot — small diary items only.' First approach in writing. Maximum 150 words.
Payment £15–20.

Chess

London Road, Wheatley, Oxon OX9 1YR
☎ 08677 4111   Fax 08677 5383

Owner *Chess & Bridge Ltd*
Editor *Jimmy Adams*
Circulation 12,000

FOUNDED 1935. MONTHLY magazine which reviews the international chess scene in an entertaining and light-hearted style. Coverage of world events welcome from qualified journalists.

Child Education

Scholastic Publications, Villiers House, Clarendon Avenue, Leamington Spa, Warwickshire CV32 5PR
☎ 0926 887799   Fax 0926 883331

Owner *Scholastic Publications*
Editor *Gill Moore*
Circulation 68,000

FOUNDED 1923. MONTHLY magazine aimed at nursery, pre-school playgroup, infant and first teachers. Articles relating to education for 4–7-year age group, written by teachers, are welcome.

Maximum 1700 words. First approach in writing with synopsis. No unsolicited mss.

Choice

3rd Floor, 2 St Johns Place, St Johns Square, London EC1M 4DE
☎ 071–490 7070   Fax 071–253 0393

Owner *EMAP/Bayard Presse*
Editor *Wendy James*
Circulation 130,000

MONTHLY full-colour magazine for people aged 50–69. Puts forward a positive approach to third age. Unsolicited mss are not welcome; approach in writing only.

Deputy Editor *June Weatherall*

Features *Janet Horwood* People and places of interest to active men and women who seek to widen their horizons in retirement through learning, activities, travel, etc. No travel articles commissioned.

Rights/News All items affecting the magazine's readership are written by experts: pensions, state benefits, health, money, property, legal, and caring for elderly relatives.
Payment by arrangement.

Christian Herald

Herald House, 96 Dominion Road, Worthing, West Sussex BN14 8JP
☎ 0903 821082   Fax 0903 821081

Owner *Herald House Ltd*
Editor *Colin Reeves*
Circulation 23,000

FOUNDED 1866. WEEKLY. Conservative evangelical Christian magazine aimed at adults with families. Theological and spiritual articles which tend to be commissioned.
Payment Herald House rates.

Church of England Newspaper

12–13 Clerkenwell Green, London EC1R 0DP
☎ 071–490 0898   Fax 071–490 0861

Owner *Parliamentary Communications Ltd*
Editor *John K. Martin*
Circulation 10,500

FOUNDED 1828. WEEKLY. Almost all material is commissioned but unsolicited mss are considered. Some fiction and poetry but rarely.

Features *James Tweed* Preliminary enquiry essential. Maximum 1200 words.

News *Colin Blakely* Items must be sent promptly and should have a church/Christian relevance. Maximum 200–400 words.
Payment NUJ/IOJ rates.

Church Music Quarterly
151 Mount View Road, London N4 4JT
☎ 081-341 6408   Fax 081-340 0021

Owner *Royal School of Church Music*
Editor *Trevor Ford*
Circulation 15,000

QUARTERLY. Contributions welcome. Telephone in the first instance.

Assistant Editor *Marianne Barton*

Features *Trevor Ford* Articles on Church music or related subjects considered. Maximum 2000 words.
Payment £60 per page.

Church Times
33 Upper Street, London N1 6PN
☎ 071-359 4570   Fax 071-226 3073

Owner *Hymns Ancient & Modern*
Editor *John Whale*
Circulation 42,158

FOUNDED 1863. WEEKLY. Unsolicited mss considered.

Features *John Whale* Articles (700–1200 words) on religious topics.
Payment £80 per 1000 words.

News *John Whale* Occasional reports (commissions only) on out-of-London events.
Payment by arrangement.

City Limits
66-67 Wells Street, London W1P 3RB
☎ 071-636 4444   Fax 071-637 2471

Owner *City Limits (London) Ltd*
Editor *Sam Taylor*
Circulation 20,000

FOUNDED 1981. WEEKLY independent London publication with news, reviews and features. Recommend first approach by telephone. 'We have a lead period of six weeks so we advise would-be contributors to contact us well in advance.'

Features Maximum 1500–2000 words.
Payment from £85 per 1000 words.

Reviews Maximum 150 words.
Payment £20 per review.

Classical Guitar
Olsover House, 43 Sackville Road, Newcastle upon Tyne NE6 5TA
☎ 091-276 0448   Fax 091-276 1623

Owner *Ashley Mark Publishing Co.*
Editor *Colin Cooper*

FOUNDED 1982. MONTHLY.

Features *Colin Cooper* Usually written by staff writers. Maximum 1500 words.
Payment by arrangement.

News *Thérèse Wassily Saba* Small paragraphs and festival concert reports welcome.
No payment.

Reviews *Chris Kilvington* Concert reviews of up to 250 words. Approach in writing.

Classical Music
241 Shaftesbury Avenue, London WC2H 8EH
☎ 071-836 2383   Fax 071-528 7991

Owner *Rhinegold Publishing Ltd*
Editor *Keith Clarke*

FOUNDED 1976. FORTNIGHTLY. A specialist magazine using precisely targeted news and feature articles. Unsolicited mss are not welcome. Freelance contributors may approach in writing with an idea but should familiarise themselves beforehand with the style and market of the magazine.
Payment negotiable.

Climber and Hill Walker
The Plaza Tower, East Kilbride, Glasgow G74 1LW
☎ 03552 46444   Fax 03552 63013

Owner *George Outram & Co. Ltd*
Editor *Cameron McNeish*
Circulation 15,000

FOUNDED 1962. MONTHLY. Unsolicited mss welcome (they receive about ten a day). Ideas welcome.

Features Freelance features (maximum 2000 words) are accepted on climbing, mountaineering and hillwalking in UK and abroad. The standard of writing must be extremely high.
Payment negotiable.

News No freelance opportunities as all items are handled in-house.

Club International
2 Archer Street, London W1V 7HE
☎ 071-734 9191
Fax 071-734 0614   Telex 22638

Owner *Paul Raymond*
Editor *Stephen Bleach*
Circulation 180,000

FOUNDED 1972. MONTHLY. Features and short humorous items in the style of *Viz, Private Eye, Punch,* etc.

Features Maximum 2500 words.
Payment negotiable.

Shorts 200–750 words.
Payment negotiable.

Coin Monthly
See **Coin News**

Coin News
Token Publishing Ltd, 84 High Street, Honiton, Devon EX14 8JW
☎ 0404 45414   Fax 0404 45313

Owner *J. W. Mussell*
Editor *J. W. Mussell*
Circulation 10,000

FOUNDED 1964. MONTHLY. Incorporating *Coin News* and *Banknote News.* Contributions welcome. Approach by phone in the first instance.

Features Articles welcome only from well-informed authors 'who know the subject and do their homework'. Maximum 2500 words.
Payment £20 per 1000 words.

Commerce Magazine
Station House, Station Road, Newport Pagnell, Milton Keynes MK16 0AG
☎ 0908 614477   Fax 0908 616441

Owner *Holcot Press Group*
Group Editor *Bryan Jones*
Circulation 30,000

MONTHLY. Ideas welcome. Approach by phone or in writing first.

Features *Simon Redley/Nick Edwards* By-lined articles frequently used. Generally 750–800 words with photos.

News Handled in-house.

Special Pages Throughout the year — media and marketing; building and construction; finance and professional; office update. 750–800 words with photos.
No payment.

Company
National Magazine House, 72 Broadwick Street, London W1V 2BP
☎ 071-439 5000   Fax 071-439 5117

Owner *National Magazine Co. Ltd*
Editor *Mandi Norwood*
Circulation 220,972

Glossy women's MONTHLY. Appealing to the independent and intelligent young woman. A good market for freelancers: 'we've got more space for them, as we have fewer staff feature writers'. 1500–2000 words. Keen to encourage bright new young talent, but uncommissioned material rarely accepted. Feature outlines are really the only sensible approach in the first instance.
Payment £150 per 1000 words.

Computer Weekly
Quadrant House, The Quadrant, Sutton, Surrey SM2 5AS
☎ 081-652 3122   Fax 081-652 8979

Owner *Reed Business Publishing*
Editor *John Lamb*
Circulation 112,000

FOUNDED 1966. Freelance contributions welcome. No fiction.

Features *Lindsay Nicolle* Always looking for good new writers with specialised industry knowledge. Special show features for industry events (e.g. previews) welcome. Maximum 1200 words.

News *David Bicknell* Some openings for regional or foreign news items. Maximum 300 words.
Payment £150 per 1000 words.

Computing
32–34 Broadwick Street, London W1A 2HG
☎ 071-439 4242   Fax 071-437 3516

Owner *VNU Publications*
Editor *Sarah Underwood*
Circulation 116,000

WEEKLY. More of a newspaper than a magazine. New contributors welcome. Approach in writing with ideas in the first instance.

Contemporary Review
61 Carey Street, London WC2A 2JG
☎ 071-831 7791

Owner *Contemporary Review Co. Ltd*
Editor *Dr Richard Mullen*

FOUNDED 1866. MONTHLY. One of the first periodicals to devote considerable space to the arts.

Liberal without any specific political affiliations. Covers a wide spectrum of interests including home affairs and politics, literature and the arts, history, travel and religion.

Literary Editor *Betty Abel* Monthly book section with reviews which are generally commissioned. Unsolicited material welcome. Maximum 3000 words. No fiction.

Cornish Life

45 Queen's Street, Exeter EX4 3SR
℡ 0392 216766   Fax 0392 71050

Owner *Today Publications*
Editor *Neville Hutchinson*
Circulation 4500

FOUNDED 1972. MONTHLY. Features articles on any aspect of life in Cornwall. Unsolicited mss welcome. Maximum 2000–2500 words. Initial approach in writing preferred.
Payment about £35.

Corporate Clothing & Textile Care

578 Kingston Road, Raynes Park,
London SW20 8DR
℡ 081-540 8381   Fax 081-540 8388

Owner *Nesthill Printers Ltd*
Editor *Lorna O'Driscoll*

Only magazine in the UK dedicated to the corporate clothing industry. Unsolicited mss welcome on any aspect of business uniforms and corporate clothing.

Cosmopolitan

National Magazine House, 72 Broadwick Street,
London W1V 2BP
℡ 071-439 5000   Fax 071-439 5016

Owner *National Magazine Co. Ltd*
Editor *Marcelle D'Argy Smith*
Circulation 472,480

Popular mix of articles on relationships and careers, and strong fiction designed to appeal to the mid-twenties, modern-minded female. Known to have a policy of not considering unsolicited mss but do look sometimes at those received as always on the look-out for 'new writers with original and relevant ideas and a strong voice. Send short synopsis of idea. All would-be writers should be familiar with the magazine.'
Payment About £200 per 1000 words.

Cotswold Life

West One House, 23 St George's Road,
Cheltenham, Gloucestershire GL50 3DT
℡ 0242 226367/226373

Owner *Beshara Press*
Editor *John Drinkwater*
Circulation *c.* 10,000

FOUNDED 1968. MONTHLY. News and features on life in the Cotswolds. Most news written in-house but contributions welcome for features.

Features Interesting places and people, reminiscences of Cotswold life in years gone by, and historical features on any aspect of Cotswold life. Approach in writing in the first instance. Maximum 1500–2000 words.
Payment by negotiation after publication.

Country Homes and Interiors

King's Reach Tower, Stamford Street,
London SE1 9LS
℡ 071-261 6433   Fax 071-261 6895

Owner *SouthBank Publishing Ltd/IPC Magazines Ltd*
Editor *Julia Watson*
Circulation 90,000

FOUNDED 1986. MONTHLY. The best approach for prospective contributors is with an idea in writing as unsolicited mss are not welcome.

Features *Victoria Hinton* Monthly personality interview of interest to an intelligent, affluent readership (both women and men), aged 25–44. Maximum 1200 words.
Payment negotiable.

Travel *Caroline Suter/Victoria Hinton* Articles 1200 words. Also hotel reviews, leisure pursuits, week-ending pieces in England and abroad. Length 750 words.
Payment negotiable.

Country Life

King's Reach Tower, Stamford Street,
London SE1 9LS
℡ 071-261 7058   Fax 071-261 5139

Owner *IPC Magazines Ltd*
Editor *Jenny Greene*
Circulation 46,200

Features which relate to the countryside, wildlife, rural events, sports and pursuits, and are of interest to well-heeled country dwellers, are welcome. Strong informed material rather than amateur enthusiasm.
Payment from £120 per 1000 words.

Country Living

National Magazine House, 72 Broadwick Street,
London W1V 2BP
☎071-439 5000   Fax 071-439 5093

Owner *National Magazine Co. Ltd*
Editor *Francine Lawrence*
Circulation 175,000

Upmarket, people-orientated magazine which takes living in the country seriously. Covers people, conservation, wildlife, houses, gardens, animals, country businesses, etc. Often uses 'named writers'.
Payment negotiable, but usually upwards of £200 per 1000 words.

Country Quest

North Wales Newspapers, Business Park, Mold,
Clwyd CH7 1X4
☎0352 700022   Fax 0248 354793

Owner *North Wales Newspapers*
Editor *Ray Bower*

FOUNDED 1960. MONTHLY. Unsolicited material and approaches in writing welcome. Maximum 750–1000 words with photos and illustrations dealing with the Welsh countryside, nature and the environment (in Wales), Welsh history and personalities. Welsh border country included.
Payment negotiable.

Country Sports

59 Kennington Road, London SE1 7PZ
☎071-928 4742   Fax 071-620 1401

Owner *British Field Sports Society*
Editor *Peter Atkinson*
Circulation 84,000

FOUNDED 1983. THRICE-YEARLY magazine on matters relating to field sports. No unsolicited mss.

The Countryman

Sheep Street, Burford, Oxon OX18 4LH
☎0993 822258   Fax 0993 822703

Owner *United Consumer Magazines*
Editor *Christopher Hall*
Circulation 68,000

FOUNDED 1927. SIX ISSUES YEARLY. Unsolicited mss with s.a.e. welcome; about 120 received each week. Prospective contributors are advised to make initial approach in writing, having first read a few issues of the magazine to understand its character.

Country-Side

48 Russell Way, Higham Ferrers,
Northamptonshire NN9 8EJ
☎0933 314672   Fax 0933 314672

Owner *British Naturalists' Association*
Editor *Dr D. Applin*
Circulation *c.* 15,000

FOUNDED 1905. QUARTERLY. Conservation and natural history magazine. Unsolicited mss and ideas for features welcome on conservation, environmental and natural history topics only. Approach in writing with ideas. Maximum 1400 words.
Payment £40 (with pictures).

Creative Camera

Battersea Arts Centre, Old Town Hall, Lavender
Hill, London SW11 5TF
☎071-924 3017   Fax 071-978 5207

Owner *Registered Charity*
Editor *David Brittain*
Circulation *c.* 6000

FOUNDED 1968. BI-MONTHLY. Most of the magazine's content is commissioned but new contributors are welcome, and are best advised to approach in writing.

Features Reviews of photographic books and exhibitions. Maximum 750 words.
Payment by arrangement.

Creative Review

50 Poland Street, London W1V 4AX
☎071-439 4222   Fax 071-734 6748

Editor *Lewis Blackwell*

The trade magazine of advertising and related industries, including film, design and illustration. Expert contributors only. Send in samples of work, whether published or not. Feature needs are organised on a commission basis and writers of talent may be taken up.

Crescendo & Jazz Music

Broadway Chambers, 1 Cranbrook Road, Ilford,
Essex IG1 4EA
☎081-553 0860   Fax 081-553 0827

Owner *Limelight Publishing Group*
Editor *Dennis H. Matthews*
Circulation 15,000 (readership)

FOUNDED 1962. SEVEN ISSUES YEARLY. Big band and jazz music coverage, plus technical articles for musicians. Unsolicited mss welcome. Approach in writing or by phone with ideas. No pop.

Features Top names in the big band and jazz worlds. Writers should have informed knowledge of music.
Payment by arrangement, but limited resources available.

The Cricketer International

Third Street, Langton Green, Tunbridge Wells, Kent TN3 0EN
☎0892 862551   Fax 0892 863755

Owner *Ben G. Brocklehurst*
Editor *Peter Perchard*
Circulation 40,000

FOUNDED 1921. MONTHLY. Unsolicited mss considered. Ideas in writing only. No initial discussions by phone. All correspondence should be addressed to the editor.

Cumbria

Dalesman Publishing, Clapham, Lancaster LA2 8EB
☎05242 51225   Fax 05242 51708

Owner *Dalesman Publishing Co. Ltd*
Editor *Hilary Gray*
Circulation 15,600

FOUNDED 1951. MONTHLY. County magazine of strong, regional and countryside interest only. Unsolicited mss welcome. Maximum 1000 words. Approach in writing or by phone with feature ideas.

Cycling Weekly

King's Reach Tower, Stamford Street, London SE1 9LS
☎071-261 5588   Fax 071-261 5758

Owner *IPC Magazines Ltd*
Editor *Andrew Sutcliffe*
Circulation 39,243

FOUNDED 1891. WEEKLY. All aspects of cycle sport covered. Unsolicited mss and ideas for features welcome. Approach in writing with ideas. Fiction rarely used.

Features Cycle racing and related areas. Maximum 2000 words. Most work commissioned but interested in seeing new work.
Payment £55-75 per 1000 words (quality permitting).

News Short news pieces, local news, etc. Maximum 300 words.
Payment £12 per story.

The Dalesman

Dalesman Publishing, Clapham, Lancaster LA2 8EB
☎05242 51225   Fax 05242 51708

Owner *Dalesman Publishing Co. Ltd*
Editor *David Joy*
Circulation 56,000

FOUNDED 1939. Now the biggest-selling regional publication of its kind in the country. MONTHLY magazine with articles of specific Yorkshire interest. Unsolicited mss welcome; receive approximately ten per day. Initial approach in writing preferred. Maximum 2000 words.
Payment negotiable.

Dance & Dancers

214 Panther House, 38 Mount Pleasant, London WC1X 0AP
☎071-837 2711   Fax 071-837 2711

Owner *Dance & Dancers Ltd*
Editor *John Percival*
Deputy Editor *Nadine Meisner*

FOUNDED 1950. MONTHLY magazine covering ballet and modern dance throughout the world.

'There is opportunity for good writers with good knowledge of dance', but preliminary discussion is always advisable.
Payment 'low'.

Dance Theatre Journal

Laban Centre for Movement Dance, Laurie Grove, London SE14 6NH
☎081-694 9620   Fax 081-694 8749

Owner *Laban Centre for Movement & Dance*
Co-Editors *Chris de Marigny/Deirdre McMahon*

FOUNDED 1983. QUARTERLY. Interested in features on every aspect of the contemporary dance scene. Unsolicited mss welcome. Especially interested in articles concerning issues such as the funding policy for dance, as well as critical assessments of choreographers' work and the latest developments in the various schools of contemporary dance. 1000-3000 words.
Payment varies 'according to age and experience'.

The Dancing Times

Clerkenwell House, 45-47 Clerkenwell Green, London EC1R 0BE
☎071-250 3006   Fax 071-253 6679

Owner *The Dancing Times Ltd*
Editor *Mary Clarke*

FOUNDED 1910. MONTHLY. Freelance suggestions welcome from specialist dance writers and photographers only. Approach in writing.

Darts World

241 High Street, Beckenham, Kent BR3 1BN
☎081-650 6580   Fax 081-650 2534

Owner *World Magazines Ltd*
Editor *A. J. Wood*
Circulation 24,500

Features Single articles or series on technique and instruction. Maximum 1200 words.

Fiction Short stories with darts theme of no more than 1000 words.

News Tournament reports and general or personality news required. Maximum 800 words.
Payment negotiable.

Dateline Magazine

23 Abingdon Road, London W8 6AL
☎071-938 1011   Fax 071-937 3146

Owner *John Patterson*
Editor *Lorraine Furneaux*
Circulation 23,000

FOUNDED 1976. MONTHLY magazine for single people. Unsolicited mss welcome; ideas in writing only.

Features Anything of interest to, or directly concerning, single people. Maximum 2500 words.
Payment from £40-45 per 1000 words.

News Items required at least six weeks ahead. Maximum 2500 words.
Payment from £40-45 per 1000 words.

David Hall's Coarse Fishing Magazine

60 Hillmorton Road, Rugby,
Warwickshire CV22 5AF
☎0788 535218   Fax 0788 541845

Owner *Chrisreel Ltd*
Editor *David Hall*
Deputy Editor *Roger Mortimer*
Circulation 21,000

FOUNDED 1985. MONTHLY. Unsolicited mss welcome but initial approach by phone or in writing preferred.

Features Any general angling interest accepted. Maximum 1000-2000 words.

Other Product reviews always welcome.
Payment £50.

David Hall's Match Fishing Magazine

60 Hillmorton Road, Rugby,
Warwickshire CV22 5AF
☎0788 535218   Fax 0788 541845

Owner *Chrisreel Ltd*
Publisher *David Hall*
Editor *Roger Mortimer*
Circulation 22,000

FOUNDED 1987. MONTHLY. Dealing with all aspects of match fishing. News and features on pollution, fishing matches, events and general fishing topics. Unsolicited mss welcome. Maximum 2000 words.
Payment £50.

Day by Day

Woolacombe House, 141 Woolacombe Road,
Blackheath, London SE3 8QP
☎081-856 6249

Owner *Loverseed Press*
Editor *Patrick Richards*
Circulation 24,000

FOUNDED 1963. MONTHLY. News commentary and digest of national and international affairs, and review of the arts. Unsolicited mss welcome (s.a.e. essential). Approach in writing with ideas. Contributors are advised to study the magazine in the first instance.

News *Ronald Mallone* Themes connected with non-violence and social justice only. Maximum 600 words.
Payment negotiable.

Features No scope for freelance contributions here.

Fiction *Michael Gibson* Very rarely published.

Poems *Michael Gibson* Short poems in line with editorial principles considered. Maximum 20 lines.
Payment negotiable.

Decanter

Priory House, 8 Battersea Park Road,
London SW8 4BG
☎071-627 8181   Fax 071-738 8688

Editor *David Rowe*
Circulation 32,000

FOUNDED 1975. Glossy wines and spirits magazine. Unsolicited material welcome but an advance telephone call is appreciated. No fiction.

News/Features All items and articles should concern wines, spirits or food and related subjects.

Derbyshire Life and Countryside

Lodge Lane, Derby DE1 3HE
☎ 0332 47087   Fax 0332 290688
Owner *B. C. Wood*
Editor *Vivienne Irish*
Circulation 12,098

FOUNDED 1931. MONTHLY county magazine for Derbyshire. Unsolicited mss and photos on and of Derbyshire welcome, but written approach with ideas preferred.

Descent

51 Timbers Square, Roath, Cardiff, South Glamorgan CF2 3SH
☎ 0222 486557   Fax 0222 486557
Owner *Ambit Publications*
Editor *Chris Howes*
Assistant Editor *Judith Calford*

FOUNDED 1969. BI-MONTHLY magazine for cavers. Submissions welcome from freelance contributors who can write accurately and knowledgeably on any aspect of caves, mines or underground structures.

Features Maximum 2500 words. General interest articles of under 1000 words also welcome, especially if supported by photographs/illustrations.
Payment on publication according to page area filled.

Design

The Design Council, 28 Haymarket,
London SW1Y 4SU
☎ 071–839 8000   Fax 071–925 2130
Owner *The Design Council*
Editor *Marion Hancock*
Circulation 13,000

FOUNDED 1949. MONTHLY magazine of larger-than-A4 format. Unsolicited mss not welcome; approach by phone or in writing.

Book Reviews Various lengths.
Payment approximately £150 per 1000 words.

Features Most design-related areas, including product and consumer goods design, graphics and packaging, furniture and lighting. Also interviews with designers, managers and consultancies. Maximum 1500 words.
Payment £150 per 1000 words.

Designers' Journal

33–39 Bowling Green Lane, London EC1R 0DA
☎ 071–837 1212   Fax 071–278 4003

Owner *EMAP Architectural Press*

MONTHLY trade magazine dealing with all aspects of the industry. No unsolicited mss. Approach in writing with ideas.

DESIGNING

The Design Council, 28 Haymarket,
London SW1Y 4SU
☎ 071–839 8000   Fax 071–925 2130
Owner *The Design Council*
Editor *Debra Staplehurst*
Circulation 7000

Published THRICE YEARLY (for each school term). A 32-page A3 colour magazine for secondary school teachers and students, with news, features, book reviews and special supplements on a wide range of design-related topics and design work in schools. Contributions welcome from writers with an interest in education and design. Approach in writing with ideas of subjects covered.

Book Reviews *Debra Staplehurst*
Payment £25 per review.

Features *Debra Staplehurst* All design-related topics and design work in secondary schools. Length 800–1200 words.
Payment £120 per 1000 words.

News *Debra Staplehurst* Short paragraphs on relevant events. Length 100–300 words.
Payment £120 per 1000 words.

Devon Life

45 Queen's Street, Exeter, Devon EX4 3SR
☎ 0392 216766   Fax 0392 7105
Owner *Today Publications*
Editor *Neville Hutchinson*
Circulation 5500

FOUNDED 1965. MONTHLY. Features articles on an aspect of life in Devon. Unsolicited mss welcome. Approach in writing with ideas. Maximum 2000–2500 words. Four sister magazines each for different county: *Cornish Life; Somerset & Avon Life; Exeter Life; Wiltshire Life.*
Payment about £35.

Dimensions

Greater London House, Hampstead Road,
London NW1 7QQ
☎ 071–377 4633   Fax 071–383 7486/757
Owner *MICP*
Editor *Michael Imeson*
Circulation 400,000

FOUNDED 1989. QUARTERLY National Westminster Bank magazine on money matters and lifestyle. Most articles are commissioned. Unsolicited mss are rarely used.

Special Pages Possible openings for cartoonists here.
Payment by arrangement.

Director

Mountbarrow House, Elizabeth Street, London SW1W 9RB
☏071-730 6060   Fax 071-235 5627

Editor *Stuart Rock*
Circulation 40,000

1991 Business Magazine of the Year. Published by the Institute of Directors for its members. Wide range of features, from political and business profiles and management thinking to employment and financial issues. Also book reviews. Regular contributors used. Letter with synopsis/published samples preferred to unsolicited mss. Strictly no 'lifestyle' writing.
Payment negotiable.

Dirt Bike Rider (DBR)

PO Box 100, Stamford, Lincolnshire PE9 1XQ
☏0780 55131   Fax 0780 57261

Owner *Key Publishing Ltd*
Editor *Mike Greenough*
Circulation 21,000

FOUNDED 1981. MONTHLY. Off-road dirt bikes (motorcross, enduro, trial and trail). Unsolicited mss and ideas in writing welcome. Particularly interested in personality features.

Disability Now

12 Park Crescent, London W1N 4EQ
☏071-636 5020   Fax 071-436 2601

Publisher *The Spastics Society*
Editor *Mary Wilkinson*
Circulation 28,000

FOUNDED 1984. MONTHLY. Leading publication for disabled people in the UK, reaching people with a wide range of physical disabilities, their families and carers, and relevant professionals. No unsolicited material but freelance contributions welcome. Approach in writing.

Features Covering new initiatives and services, achievements and general issues of interest to a wide national readership. Maximum 1200 words. Disabled contributors welcomed.

News Maximum 500 words.

Disabled Driver

DDMC, Cottingham Way, Thrapston, Northamptonshire NN14 4TN
☏08012 4724   Fax 08012 3816

Owner *Disabled Drivers' Motor Club*
Contact *Mrs J. E. Jones*
Circulation 14,500

BI-MONTHLY publication of the Disabled Drivers' Motor Club. Includes information for members, members' letters. Approach in writing with ideas. Unsolicited mss welcome.

Dog World

9 Tufton Street, Ashford, Kent TN23 1QN
☏0233 621877   Fax 0233 645669

Owner *Dog World Ltd*
Editor *Simon Parsons*
Circulation 32,740

FOUNDED 1908. WEEKLY newspaper for people 'seriously interested in pedigree dogs'. Unsolicited mss considered but initial approach in writing preferred.

Features Well-researched historical items or items of unusual interest concerning dogs. Maximum 1000 words. Photographs of unusual 'doggy' situations often of interest.
Payment up to £40.

News Freelance reports welcome on court cases, local government issues, etc., involving dogs.

Fiction Very occasionally.

Dorset Life

23 Market Street, Crewkerne, Somerset TA18 7JU
☏0460 78000/0458 250827   Fax 0460 76718

Owner *Smart Print Publications Ltd*
Managing Editor *Jack Rayfield*
Circulation 6500

FOUNDED 1977. MONTHLY magazine with features on any subject of interest (historical, geographical, arts, crafts) to people living in Dorset. Length 1000-1500 words. Unsolicited mss welcome but initial approach in writing preferred.
Payment negotiable.

Duty Free Magazine

Sea Containers House, 20 Upper Ground,
London SE1 9PF
☎ 071-928 2111   Fax 071-620 1594

Editor *Alison Booth*
Circulation 2 million +

TWICE-YEARLY magazine of Sealink Ferries, distributed to those travelling with the company. Formerly *Connections*, but changed its name in 1991 to *Duty Free Magazine*. Carries around three articles per issue, mostly connected with places en route. Unsolicited material and ideas not generally welcome; happy with current contributors and commission when necessary.

Early Music

c/o Oxford University Press, 7-8 Hatherley Street,
London SW1P 2QT
☎ 071-233 5466   Fax 071-233 6638

Owner *Oxford University Press*
Editor *Dr Tess Knighton*

FOUNDED 1973. QUARTERLY. Scholarly articles on medieval, renaissance and baroque music, especially performance practice. Record, book and music reviews, salesroom reports, etc. Unsolicited mss welcome. Approach in writing with ideas. Not interested in concert reviews, forthcoming concert news, or very topical items (being a quarterly).

Early Times

London & North Surrey Newspapers, 12 Skerne Road, Kingston upon Thames, Surrey KT2 5AF
☎ 081-546 2261   Fax 081-541 3743

Owner *Argus Newspapers*
Editor *Alison Haymonds*
Circulation 27,000

WEEKLY quality newspaper aimed at bright enquiring children. First issue in January 1988 sold out on the day of issue. Originally conceived for the 8-14 age group but now attracting a wider age range. News and features on national and international issues.
Payment £100 per 1000 words.

The Ecologist

Agriculture House, Bath Road, Sturminster Newton,
Dorset DT10 1DU
☎ 0258 73476   Fax 0258 73748

Owner *Ecosystems Ltd*
Editors *Edward Goldsmith/Nicholas Hildyard*
Circulation 8000

FOUNDED 1970. BI-MONTHLY. Unsolicited mss welcome but initial approach in writing preferred.

Features *Nicholas Hildyard* Content tends to be of an academic nature for the most part. Subjects have included the military and the environment; green consumerism; ecofeminism; women's blood: development and taboo. Writers are advised to study the magazine for style. Maximum 5000 words.
Payment £20 per 1000 words.

The Economist

25 St James's Street, London SW1A 1HG
☎ 071-839 7000   Fax 071-839 2968

Owner *Financial Times/individual shareholders*
Editor *Rupert Pennant-Rea*
Circulation 480,000 (worldwide)

FOUNDED 1843. WEEKLY. Unsolicited contributions not welcome. Approaches should be made in writing to the editor.

Edinburgh Review

22 George Square, Edinburgh EH8 9LF
☎ 031-650 4215   Fax 031-662 0053

Owner *Polygon Books*
Editor *Murdo Macdonald*
Circulation 1500

FOUNDED 1969. TWICE YEARLY. Articles and fiction on Scottish and international literary, cultural and philosophical themes. Unsolicited contributions are welcome (1600 are received each year), but prospective contributors are strongly advised to study the magazine first. Return of material is not guaranteed.

Features Articles do not have to be tied in to a recent anniversary; interest will be shown in accessible articles on philosophy and its relationship to literature.

Fiction Maximum 6000 words. Particularly interested in translations from little-known world writers.

Encyclopedia Supplement Approximately twenty pages of short items on matters of cultural and political importance which aim to show knowledge and ideas to be 'the collective property of humankind'. Entries vary in length from just a few words to a maximum of 1000.

Education

21-27 Lamb's Conduit Street, London WC1N 3NJ
☎ 071-242 2548   Fax 071-831 2855

Owner *Longman Group*
Editor *George Low*
Circulation 33,000

WEEKLY journal read by educational administrators and professionals. Only interested in articles which appeal to these groups. Areas of interest include practical administration and how schools are run, plus comment on the state of administration at the present time. Freelancers used but tend to be regulars.
Payment NUJ rates.

Education & Training

62 Toller Lane, Bradford, West Yorkshire BD8 9BY
☎ 0274 499821   Fax 0274 547143

Owner *MCB University Press Ltd*
Editor *Dr Richard Holden*
Circulation 1500

FOUNDED 1959. SEVEN ISSUES YEARLY. Journal focusing on the vital and rapidly changing interface between education and training, relating in particular to the 16–18 age group. Unsolicited mss welcome provided they are practically orientated, not academic.
No payment.

Electrical Times

Quadrant House, The Quadrant, Sutton, Surrey SM2 5AS
☎ 081-652 3115   Fax 081-652 8972

Owner *Reed Business Publishing Group*
Editor *Bill Evett*
Circulation 18,000

FOUNDED 1891. MONTHLY. Aimed at electrical contractors, power generators and distributors, and the industry in general. Unsolicited mss welcome but initial approach by phone preferred.

Elle

Rex House, 4–12 Lower Regent Street, London SW1Y 4PE
☎ 071-930 9050   Fax 071-839 2762

Owner *Hachette*
Editor *Angela Palmer*
Circulation 250,000

FOUNDED 1985. MONTHLY glossy. Prospective contributors should approach the relevant editor in writing in first instance, including cuttings.

Features *Miranda Carter* Maximum 2000 words.

News *Susie Forbes* **Insight**: short articles on current/ cultural events with emphasis on national and not just London-based readership. Maximum 500 words.
Payment £150 per 1000 words.

Embroidery

PO Box 42B, East Molesley, Surrey KT8 9BB
☎ 081-943 1229   Fax 081-977 9882

Owner *Embroiderers' Guild*
Editor *Valerie Campbell-Harding*
Circulation 14,500

FOUNDED 1933. QUARTERLY. Features articles on embroidery techniques, historical and foreign embroidery, and specific artists' work with illustrations. Also reviews. Unsolicited mss welcome. Maximum 1000 words.
Payment negotiable.

Empire

42 Great Portland Street, London W1N 5AH
☎ 071-436 5430   Fax 071-637 7031

Owner *EMAP Metro*
Editor *Barry McIlheney*

LAUNCHED 1989 at the Cannes Film Festival. MONTHLY guide to the movies which aims to 'cover the world of films in a comprehensive, adult, intelligent and witty package'. Although the majority of *Empire* is devoted to films and the people behind them, it also looks at the developments and technology behind television and video. Wide selection of in-depth features and stories on all the main releases of the month, and reviews of over 200 films and videos. Contributions welcome but must approach in writing first.

Features *Philip Thomas* Short features on behind the scenes in films.
Payment £125 per 1000 words.

The Engineer

30 Calderwood Street, London SE18 6QH
☎ 081-855 7777   Fax 081-316 3040

Owner *Morgan Grampian Ltd*
Editor *Chris Barrie*
Circulation 40,000

FOUNDED 1856. WEEKLY news magazine for engineers and managers.

Features *Colin Macilwain* Most outside contributions are commissioned but good ideas are always welcome. Maximum 2000 words.
Payment by arrangement.

News *Chris Barrie* Some scope for specialist regional freelancers, and for tip-offs. Maximum 500 words.
Payment by arrangement.

Techscan *Kam Patel* Technology news. Freelance opportunities available as for news. Maximum 500 words.
Payment by arrangement.

Engineering
The Design Council, 28 Haymarket, London SW1Y 4SU
☎071-839 8000   Fax 071-925 2130

Owner *The Design Council*
Editor *Andy Pye*
Circulation 22,000

FOUNDED 1866. MONTHLY. Unsolicited mss not welcome. Prospective contributors may approach by telephone with an idea and should be prepared to follow up afterwards with a written synopsis.

Features *Andrew Beevers* Developments in technology, product design, marketing and trade. Maximum 1800 words.
Payment £200.

News *Andrew Beevers* Little opportunity for freelancers here but 'outstanding new developments in technology' always considered. Maximum 350 words.
Payment £40.

Specials Applications of advanced plastic composite materials are of great interest — good stories in this area always required. Maximum 1800 words.
Payment £200.

English Heritage Magazine
Paragon Communications Ltd, Film House, 142 Wardour Street, London W1V 3AU
☎071-734 6030   Fax 071-437 6085

Managing Editor *Nick Weiss*

FOUNDED 1984. QUARTERLY for members of the English Heritage Organisation, responsible for the conservation and preservation of historic buildings. Interested in outside contributions; send synopsis of proposal in first instance.

ES (Evening Standard magazine)
See **Regional Newspapers**

Escape: The Career Change Magazine
Tregeraint House, Zennor, St Ives, Cornwall TR26 3DB
☎0736 797061   Fax 0736 797061

Owner *Weavers Press Publishing*
Editor *John T. Wilson*
Circulation 3500

SIX ISSUES YEARLY. Articles, news, features, reviews, personal experience and information for teachers, nurses and other public servants who wish to get out of public service into a new career or self-employment. Length 500-1200 words. No work considered unless accompanied by s.a.e.
Payment £20 per 1000 words.

Esquire
National Magazine Co. Ltd, 72 Broadwick Street, London W1V 2BP
☎071-439 5000   Fax 071-439 5067

Owner *National Magazine Co. Ltd*
Editor *Rosie Boycott*
Circulation (target) 70,000

MONTHLY launched March 1991. Aimed at men aged 25-44. Synopses for features welcome provided they are in keeping with the magazine's style.

Essentials
Elme House, 133 Long Acre, London WC2E 9AD
☎071-836 0519   Fax 071-836 3644

Owner *G E Publishing*
Editor *Gilly Cubitt*
Circulation 519,000

FOUNDED 1988. MONTHLY. Unsolicited mss (not originals) welcome if accompanied by s.a.e. Initial approach in writing preferred.

Features *Clare Weatherall* Prospective contributors should study the magazine thoroughly before submitting anything. Maximum 2000 words double-spaced on A4.

Fiction *Valery McConnell* 'We are looking for something outside the mainstream of romantic fiction, which reflects life in the 90s for busy women in their 20s and 30s. The subject matter should preferably reflect the features in the rest of the magazine, which could be about credit card debts, the ozone layer, or how to tell if your wardrobe is out of date!'. Length: 1800-2500 words, double-spaced on A4.
Payment negotiable, but minimum £100 per 1000 words.

Essex Countryside
Wenden Court, Wendens Ambo, Saffron Walden,
Essex CB11 4LB
☎0799 41675　　　　　　Fax 0799 41682

Owner *Market Link Publishing Ltd*
Editor *Meg Davis-Berry*
Circulation 15,000

FOUNDED 1952. MONTHLY. Unsolicited material of
Essex interest welcome. No general interest material.

Features Countryside, culture and crafts in Essex.
Maximum 1500 words.
Payment £40.

Essex Life
See **Suffolk Life**

Euromoney
Nestor House, Playhouse Yard, London EC4V 5EX
☎071-779 8888

Owner *Euromoney Publications*
Editor *Garry Evans*

FOUNDED 1969. MONTHLY. World finance and economics. Unsolicited mss welcome. Ideas should be
submitted in writing.

European Medical Journal
Lynmouth, Devon EX35 6EE
☎027188 2235　　　　　Fax 027188 2235

Owner *Dr Vernon Coleman*
Editor *Dr Vernon Coleman*
Circulation 1100

FOUNDED 1991. QUARTERLY. Critical medical review
published in English, French, Italian and German
simultaneously. Approach in writing after careful
study of journal. No unsolicited mss. Send s.a.e. for
reply.

Evergreen
PO Box 52, Cheltenham,
Gloucestershire GL50 1YQ
☎0242 577775　　　　　Fax 0242 222034

Editor *R. Faiers*
Circulation 66,000

FOUNDED 1985. QUARTERLY magazine featuring
articles and poems about Britain. Unsolicited contributions welcome.

Features Britain's natural beauty, towns and villages, nostalgia, wildlife, traditions, odd customs,

legends, folklore, crafts, etc. Length: 250-2000
words.
Payment £15 per 1000 words; poems £4.

Everywoman
34 Islington Green, London N1 8DU
☎071-359 5496

Editor *Barbara Rogers*
Circulation 15,000

Feminist magazine which provides general news
and features geared towards women's interests in
current affairs and practical concerns such as
health, employment, money and relationships, rather than traditional consumer lifestyle pursuits.
Contributors must study the magazine, show an
understanding of its point of view, and indicate
which section submissions are intended for. Approach in writing, not by phone.

Executive Strategy
29 Tivoli Road, Brighton, East Sussex BN1 5BG
☎0273 565505　　　　　Fax 0273 550072

Owner *Policy Publications Ltd*
Editor *Peter Bartram*
Circulation 4116

Business and management magazine. Unsolicited
mss welcome. Approach in writing with ideas.

Executive Travel
Francis House, 11 Francis Street,
London SW1P 1BZ
☎071-828 8989　　　　　Fax 071-798 9710

Editor *Mike Toynbee*
Circulation 40,000

FOUNDED 1979. MONTHLY. Aimed specifically at
business travellers. Unsolicited mss welcome.

Exeter Life
See **Devon Life**

The Expatriate
56A Rochester Row, London SW1P 1JU
☎071-834 9192　　　　　Fax 071-630 0194

Owner *FMI Publishers*
Editor *Philip Coles*
Circulation *c.* 500

FOUNDED 1977. MONTHLY serving the British expatriate community. Wholly owned by Colin McAskill

(First Market Intelligence Ltd). Unsolicited mss welcome.

Features Special features on working in particular countries, and international travel. Psychological problems for spouses, education difficulties, pensions, investment and taxation features, health matters. Maximum 2000 words.

News Information on special facilities for expatriates, e.g. mail-order presents, financial services, relocation agents, etc. Maximum 1000 words.

Export Sales and Marketing

Nat West House, 31 Upper George Street, Luton, Bedfordshire LU1 2RD
☏0582 456767 Fax 0582 453640

Owner *ISE Publications Ltd*
Editor *Jane Parker*
Circulation 13,000

MONTHLY. Aimed at the export sector of sales and marketing with the single European market in mind. Unsolicited mss welcome, provided they are relevant, and typed in double-line spacing. Initial approach in writing preferred.

Features Export sales techniques, training, technology and modern management practices.
Payment negotiable.

Expression

20–26 Brunswick Place, London N1 6DJ
☏071-490 1444 Fax 071-490 0494

Editor *Sue Thomas*
Circulation 600,000

Upmarket glossy mailed to American Express card members. Ideas for features welcome. Material produced both in-house and by regular freelancers. Unsolicited articles rarely used.

Features Travel, food, wine and general consumer matters — anything of genuine interest to the discerning with a disposable income.
Payment about £250 per 1000 words.

The Face

3rd Floor, Block A, Exmouth House, Pine Street, London EC1R 0JL
☏071-837 7270 Fax 071-837 3906

Owner *Wagadon Ltd*
Editor *Sheryl Garratt*
Circulation 73,202

FOUNDED 1980. Perhaps the ultimate magazine of the style generation, concerned with who's what and what's cool. Profiles, interviews and stories. No

fiction. Acquaintance with the 'voice' of *The Face* is essential before sending mss on spec.

Features New contributors should write to the editor with their ideas. Maximum 3000 words.
Payment £110 per 1000 words.

Diary No news stories.

Family Circle

King's Reach Tower, Stamford Street, London SE1 9LS
☏071-261 5000 Fax 071-261 5929

Owner *IPC Magazines Ltd*
Editor *Gilly Batterbee*
Circulation 406,190

FOUNDED 1964. 13 ISSUES PER YEAR. Little scope for freelancers: most of the magazine's material is produced in-house. Unsolicited material is rarely used, but it is considered. Prospective contributors are best advised to send written ideas to the relevant editor.

Beauty *Janine Steggles*

Cookery *Petra Jackson*

Fashion *Janine Steggles*

Features *Deborah Murdoch* Very little outside work commissioned. Maximum 2500–3000 words.

Fiction *Dee Remmington* Short stories: 1000–3000 words.

Home *Caroline Rodriguez*

News (Full Circle) *Caroline Rodriguez*
Payment for all contributions not less than £100 per 1000 words.

Family Tree Magazine

15–16 Highlode, Ramsey, Huntingdon, Cambridgeshire PE17 1RB
☏0487 814050

Owner *J.M. & M. Armstrong*
Editor *Avril Cross*
Circulation 24,500

FOUNDED 1984. MONTHLY. News and features on matters of genealogy. Unsolicited mss considered but not interested in any more material on 'own family' histories. Keen to receive articles on unusual sources of genealogical research. Approach in writing with ideas. All material should be addressed to *Michael Armstrong*.

Features Maximum 3000 words on genealogically related subjects only.

Special Pages Subject-related crossword puzzles or similar.
Payment £18 per 1000 words (news and features); negotiable (crossword pages).

Farmers Weekly

13th Floor, Quadrant House, Sutton,
Surrey SM2 5AS
☎081-652 4911   Fax 081-652 8901

Owner *Reed Business Publishing Group*
Editor *Stephen Howe*
Circulation 265,000

WEEKLY. For practising farmers. Unsolicited mss considered.

Features A wide range of material relating to farmers' problems and interests: specific sections on arable and/or livestock farming, farm life, practical and general interest.

News General interest farming news.
Payment negotiable.

Farming News

Morgan Grampian House, 30 Calderwood Street,
London SE18 6QH
☎081-855 7777   Fax 081-854 6795

Owner *Morgan Grampian Farming Press Ltd*
Editor *Donald Taylor*
Circulation 102,000

Freelance writers used occasionally.

FarmWatch

20 Lavant Street, Petersfield,
Hampshire GU32 3EW
☎0730 264208   Fax 0730 260791

Owner *Compassion in World Farming*
Editor *Anne Wignall*
Circulation 4000

FOUNDED 1991. THRICE YEARLY. Covers all major animal welfare/ rights issues, environmental and vegetarian concerns. Aimed at the 10–18 age group and published to coincide with school terms. News, articles and short stories welcome. Maximum 1000 words. Also interested in good quality photographs. Unsolicited mss welcome. Approach in writing with ideas.
Payment nominal, but negotiable.

Fast Car

Argosy House, High Street, Orpington,
Kent BR6 0LW
☎0689 874025/870541

Fax 0689 876438/896847

Owner *Security Publications*
Editor *Danny Morris*
Circulation 60,000

FOUNDED 1987. MONTHLY. Concerned with the modification of road and race vehicles, with technical data and testing results. Unsolicited mss welcome. Approach in writing with ideas. No kit-car features, race reports or road test reports of standard cars.

Features *Jim Blackstock* Innovative feature ideas in line with the magazine's title. Generally about five pages in length.

News Any item in line with magazine's title. Copy should be as concise as possible.
Payment negotiable.

Fast Lane

Perry Motor Press, 388–396 Oxford Street,
London W1N 9HE
☎071-629 4688   Fax 071-629 6572

Owner *Perry Motor Press*
Editor *Andrew English*
Circulation 55,000

FOUNDED 1984. MONTHLY car magazine. Many unsolicited mss are received but few are ever used. Prospective contributors are advised to make initial approach in writing.

The Field

10 Sheet Street, Windsor, Berkshire SL4 1BG
☎0753 856061   Fax 0753 831086

Owner *Daily Mail/General Trust*
Editor *J. Young*

FOUNDED 1853. MONTHLY magazine for those who are serious about the British countryside and its pleasures. Unsolicited mss and transparencies welcome but preliminary approach should first be made in writing.

Features Exceptional work on any subject concerning the countryside. Most work tends to be commissioned.
Payment varies according to material.

Fifty Plus

Millbank Publications, 25 Catherine Street,
London WC2B 5JW
☎071-379 3036   Fax 071-240 6840/836 1900

Owner *Millbank Publications*
Editor *Paul Newbon*
Circulation 20,000

FOUNDED 1982. QUARTERLY. Opportunities in news and features only. Approach in writing with s.a.e.

Features Well-illustrated (good-quality colour/b&w transparencies) items on travel, finance, leisure pursuits, personalities, second careers, crafts and hobbies. Maximum 1500 words. *Payment* negotiable.

News Maximum 1500 words. *Payment* negotiable.

Film Monthly

Argus House, Boundary Way, Hemel Hempstead, Hertfordshire HP2 7ST
☏0442 66551   Fax 0442 66998

Owner *Argus Specialist Publications*
Editor *Dave Reader*
Circulation 14,523

MONTHLY. Covering the film, video and television scenes. Unsolicited material welcome. S.a.e. essential for return of material. *Payment* by arrangement.

Film Review

Orpheus Publications, 4th Floor, Centro House, Mandela Street, London NW1 0DU
☏071-387 3848   Fax 071-388 8532

Owner *Orpheus Publications*
Editor *David Aldridge*
Circulation 37,000

MONTHLY. Profiles, interviews and special reports on films. Unsolicited material considered.

First Choice

Greater London House, Hampstead Road, London NW1 7QQ
☏071-388 3171   Fax 071-387 9518

Owner *Headway Home & Law Publishing Group Ltd*
Editor *Debbi Scholes*
Circulation 3.5 million

TWICE YEARLY. Items of women's/family interest, including humorous. Also recipes, etc. Unsolicited mss considered provided they tie in with planned editorial. Initial approach by phone preferred.

First Down

The Spendlove Centre, Enstone Road, Charlbury, Chipping Norton, Oxon OX7 3PQ
☏0608 811266   Fax 0608 811380

Owner *Mediawatch Ltd*
Editor *Stephen Anglesey*
Circulation 21,188

FOUNDED 1986. WEEKLY American football magazine. Unsolicited mss welcome.

Features *Stephen Anglesey* Ideas for commission are welcome.

News *Neil Rowlands* Tip-offs and news items relating to American football in the UK. Maximum 300 words. *Payment* negotiable.

Flight International

Quadrant House, The Quadrant, Sutton, Surrey SM2 5AS
☏081-652 3882   Fax 081-652 3840

Owner *Reed Business Publishing Group*
Editor *Allan Winn*
Circulation 60,000

FOUNDED 1909. WEEKLY. International trade magazine of the aerospace industry, including civil, military and space. Unsolicited mss welcome. Phone with ideas, and follow up with letter.

Features *David Learmount* Technically informed articles and pieces on specific geographical areas with international appeal. Analytical, in-depth coverage required, preferably supported by interviews. Maximum 1800 words.

News *Andrew Chuter* Opportunities exist for news pieces from particular geographical areas on specific technical developments. Maximum 350 words. *Payment* NUJ rates.

Flora

46 Merlin Grove, Eden Park, Beckenham, Kent BR3 3HU
☏081-658 1080

Owner *Maureen Foster*
Editor *Russell Bennett*
Circulation 15,000

FOUNDED 1974. BI-MONTHLY magazine for flower arrangers and florists. Unsolicited mss welcome. Approach in writing with ideas. Not interested in general gardening articles. Fully illustrated features, preferably with b&w photos, or illustrations/colour transparencies, welcome. Personality profiles, news, relevant book reviews and features.

Features Floristry items written with practical knowledge and well illustrated are particularly welcome. Maximum 2000 words. Also features on flower arranging, flower gardens and flowers. *Payment* £30 per 1000 words.

FlyPast

PO Box 100, Stamford, Lincolnshire PE9 1XQ
☎0780 55131   Fax 0780 57261

Owner *Key Publishing Ltd*
Editor *Ken Ellis*
Circulation 41,144

FOUNDED 1981. MONTHLY. Historic aviation, mainly military and Second World War. Unsolicited mss welcome but initial approach by phone or in writing preferred.

Folk Roots

PO Box 337, London N4 1TW
☎081-340 9651   Fax 081-348 5626

Owner *Southern Rag Ltd*
Editor *Ian A. Anderson*
Circulation 13,000

FOUNDED 1979. MONTHLY. Unsolicited mss welcome but a large number are received and not used. Initial phone call is preferred.

Features Folk and roots music, and musicians. Maximum 3000 words.
Payment c. £40 per 1000 words.

Football Monthly

28 Croydon Road, Reigate, Surrey RH2 0PG
☎0737 221158   Fax 0737 223047

Owner *Proud Print Ltd*
Editor *Tony Pullein*
Circulation 35,000

FOUNDED 1951. MONTHLY.

Features 'All contributions are considered. Prefer interviews with current players/managers.' Maximum 1600 words. Historical items compiled by team of regular contributors.
Payment from £30 depending upon topicality, etc.

Fortean Times: The Journal of Strange Phenomena

PO Box 2409, London NW5 4NP
☎071-485 5002   Fax 071-485 5002

Owner *Bob Rickard/Paul Sieveking*
Editors *Bob Rickard/Paul Sieveking*
Circulation 15,000

FOUNDED 1973. BI-MONTHLY. Accounts of strange phenomena and experiences, curiosities, mysteries, prodigies and portents. Unsolicited mss welcome. Approach in writing with ideas. No fiction, poetry, rehashes or politics.

Features Well researched and referenced material on current or historical mysteries, or first-hand accounts of oddities. Maximum 3000 words. Preferably with good illustrations. Always interested in good relevant photos.

News Concise copy with full source references essential.
Payment negotiable.

Foundation: The Review of Science Fiction

SF Foundation, Polytechnic of East London, Longbridge Road, Dagenham, Essex RM8 2AS
☎081-590 7722   Fax 081-590 7799

Owner *Science Fiction Foundation*
Editor *Edward James*

TRIENNIAL publication devoted to the critical study of science fiction. Available by subscription.
Payment rates available on request.

The Freelance

NUJ, Acorn House, 314 Gray's Inn Road, London WC1X 8DP
☎071-278 7916   Fax 071-837 8143

BI-MONTHLY published by the **National Union of Journalists**. Contributions welcome.

Freelance Market News

Cumberland House, Lissadell Street, Salford, Manchester M5 6GG
☎061-745 8850   Fax 061-745 8827

Owner *Arthur Waite*
Editor *Saundrea Williams*
Circulation 2200

MONTHLY. News and information on the freelance writers' market, both inland and overseas. Includes market information on competitions, seminars, courses, overseas openings, etc. Unsolicited contributions welcome.

Freelance Writing & Photography

Tregeraint House, Zennor, St Ives, Cornwall TR26 3DB
☎0736 797061   Fax 0736 797061

Owner *Weavers Press Publishing*
Editor *John T. Wilson*

Articles, features, reviews, interviews, competitions, tips, hints, market news for the freelance writer and photographer. 250–1000 words. No

work considered unless accompanied by s.a.e.
Ideas in writing preferred in first instance.
Payment £20 per 1000 words.

Garden Answers

Apex House, Oundle Road,
Peterborough PE2 9NP
☏ 0733 898100   Fax 0733 898433

Owner *EMAP National Publications Ltd*
Editor *Lynne Barber*
Circulation 98,130

FOUNDED 1982. MONTHLY. 'It is unlikely that unsolicited manuscripts will be used, as writers rarely consider the style and format of the magazine before writing.' Prospective contributors should approach the editor in writing. Always interested in hearing from gardening writers on any subject, whether flowers, fruit, vegetables, houseplants or greenhouse gardening.

Garden News

Apex House, Oundle Road,
Peterborough PE2 9NP
☏ 0733 898100   Fax 0733 898433

Owner *EMAP Apex Publications Ltd*
Editor *Alan Durose*
Circulation 114,564

FOUNDED 1958. Britain's biggest-selling gardening WEEKLY. News and advice on growing flowers, fruit and vegetables, plus colourful features on all aspects of gardening for the committed gardener. News and features welcome, especially if accompanied by photos or illustrations. Contact the editor before submitting any material.

Gay Times

Ground Floor, Worldwide House, 116–134 Bayham Street, London NW1 0BA
☏ 071–482 2576   Fax 071–284 0329

Owner *Millivres Ltd*
Editor *John Marshall*

Covers all aspects of gay life, and general interest likely to appeal to the gay community, with art reviews and news section. Regular freelance writers used. Unsolicited contributions welcome. Some fiction.

Features *Peter Burton*

News *David Smith*
Payment negotiable.

Gibbons Stamp Monthly

Stanley Gibbons, 5 Parkside, Ringwood,
Hampshire BH24 3SH
☏ 0425 472363   Fax 0425 470247

Owner *Stanley Gibbons Magazines Ltd*
Editor *Hugh Jefferies*
Circulation 22,000

FOUNDED 1890. MONTHLY. News and features. Unsolicited mss welcome. Approach first in writing or by phone to avoid disappointment.

Features *Hugh Jefferies* Unsolicited material of specialised nature or general stamp features welcome. Maximum 3000 words but longer pieces could be serialised.
Payment £17–35 per 1000 words.

News *Michael Briggs* Any philatelic news item. Maximum 500 words.
No payment.

Girl About Town

175–179 St John's Street, London EC1V 4RP
☏ 071–490 1166   Fax 071–490 2518

Owner *Girl About Town Magazine Ltd*
Editor *Claire Gillman*
Circulation 125,000

FOUNDED 1972. WEEKLY free distribution magazine for women. Unsolicited mss 'useful'. No fiction.

Features Standards are 'exacting'. Commissions only. Very little chance, if any, of unknown writers being commissioned but unsolicited material is considered. Maximum 1600 words.
Payment approx. £100 per 1000 words.

News Some, including film, music, fashion and beauty. Maximum 200 words.

Giroscope

Downside House, Shepton Mallet,
Somerset BA4 4JL
☏ 0749 342516   Fax 0749 344956

Owner *IPS Ltd*
Editor *Ned Halley*
Circulation 1.3 million

BI-MONTHLY. Girobank's magazine for customers. Girobank financial information and general interest features. Contributions welcome on consumer-interest topics: housing, personal finance, holidays and leisure.
Payment negotiable.

Golf Monthly

King's Reach Tower, Stamford Street,
London SE1 9LS
☎071-261 7237   Fax 071-261 7240

Owner *IPC Magazines Ltd*
Editor *Colin Callander*
Circulation 94,809

FOUNDED 1911. MONTHLY. Player profiles, golf instruction, general golf features and columns. Not interested in instruction material from outside contributors. Unsolicited mss welcome. Approach in writing with ideas.

Features Maximum 1500-2000 words.
Payment by arrangement.

Golf Weekly

Advance House, 37 Millharbour, London E14 9TX
☎071-538 1031   Fax 071-537 2053

Owner *Golf World Ltd*
Editor *Neil F. C. Elsey*
Circulation 20,000

FOUNDED 1890. WEEKLY. Unsolicited material welcome from full-time journalists only. For features, approach in writing in first instance; for news, fax or phone.

Features Maximum 1500 words.

News Maximum 300 words.
Payment negotiable.

Golf World

Advance House, 37 Millharbour, London E14 9TX
☎071-538 1031   Fax 071-538 4106

Owner *New York Times*
Editor *Robert Green*
Circulation 108,075

FOUNDED 1962. MONTHLY. Unsolicited mss not welcome. Approach in writing with ideas.

Good Food Retailing

5 Mulgrave Chambers, 26-28 Mulgrave Road,
Sutton, Surrey SM2 6LE
☎081-770 7337   Fax 081-770 7283

Owner *Robert Farrand*
Editor *Jennifer Muir*
Circulation 8500

FOUNDED 1980. MONTHLY. Serves the food retailing industry. Unsolicited mss welcome.

Good Holiday Magazine

1-2 Dawes Court, 93 High Street, Esher,
Surrey KT10 9QD
☎0372 469799   Fax 0372 466365

Managing Editor *John Hill*
Editor *Mary Burrell*
Circulation 100,000

FOUNDED 1986. QUARTERLY. Synopses/articles welcome but mss are generally found to be unsuitable. 'We cannot promise to publish them.' Articles should be biased towards holiday-makers rather than travellers as this is a holiday magazine and in all cases the price of everything from teas and coffees to major purchases should be included along with the relevant rates of exchange. All articles should be illustrated by either high-quality slides or well-printed colour prints. 'Do not send originals as we cannot guarantee immediate return.' Worldwide destinations, including Europe and domestic. Any queries regarding work/ commissioning must be in writing.
Payment negotiable.

Good Housekeeping

National Magazine House, 72 Broadwick Street,
London W1V 2BP
☎071-439 5000   Fax 071-439 5591

Owner *National Magazine Co. Ltd*
Editor-in-Chief *Sally O'Sullivan*
Circulation 391,449

FOUNDED 1922. MONTHLY glossy. Unsolicited mss read but not encouraged. Write with ideas in the first instance to the appropriate editor.

Features *Hilary Robinson* Most work is commissioned but original ideas are always welcome. Send short synopsis, plus relevant cuttings, showing previous examples of work published.

Fiction *Hilary Robinson* Tends to come via agents or publishers but unsolicited mss will be read.

Newslines *Alison Pylkkanen* Four pages of short news stories on subjects ranging from food and travel to film stars and money. Maximum 350 words.

Good Ski Guide

1-2 Dawes Court, 93 High Street, Esher,
Surrey KT10 9QD
☎0372 469799   Fax 0372 466365

Publisher *John Hill*
Editor *John Hill*
Circulation 350,000

FOUNDED 1976. QUARTERLY. Unsolicited mss welcome from writers with a knowledge of skiing and

ski resorts. Prospective contributors are best advised to make initial contact in writing as ideas and work need to be seen before any discussion can take place.
Payment negotiable.

ASSOCIATED TITLES *A-Z Resorts Guide* and *A-Z Fashion and Equipment Guide.*

Good Stories

23 Mill Crescent, Kingsbury,
Warwickshire B78 2LX
☏ 0827 873435

Owner *Oakwood Publications*
Editor *Andrew Jenns*
Circulation 5000

FOUNDED 1990. QUARTERLY of A5 format featuring approximately fifteen short stories in each issue, plus crossword, letters and various filler columns. Unsolicited mss welcome but contributors are strongly advised to study the magazine's style in the first instance.

Fiction Short stories of any kind. Maximum 2500 words but shorter (1000 words or less) always needed.
Payment about £20 per 1000 words.

News Brief paragraphs of interest to readership and readers of short fiction in general.

Special Pages Readers' Letters: preferably humorous. Maximum 100 words. Crosswords: not too complex, and suitable for use as Prize Crosswords for readers; also other word puzzle games from time to time. Fillers: Short and humorous, based on true-life incidents (maximum 100 words); plus cartoons.
Payment Readers' letters: up to £5; Crosswords: £5-10 depending on complexity; Fillers: up to £10.

GQ

Vogue House, Hanover Square, London W1R 0AD
☏ 071-499 9080   Fax 071-495 1679

Owner *Condé Nast Publications Ltd*
Editor *Michael VerMeulen*

FOUNDED 1988. MONTHLY. No unsolicited material. Phone with an idea in first instance.

Features *Angus Mackinnon/Philip Watson*

Special Pages *John Morgan* Small news, grooming and style items.

Gramophone

177-179 Kenton Road, Harrow HA3 0HA
☏ 081-907 4476   Fax 081-907 0073

Editor *James Jolly*
Circulation 72,488

Classical music magazine, of which ninety-five per cent is reviews. At any time they are using around 50 regular freelance writers, who provide classical music reviews, and on occasion, features or interviews. Reviewing is the starting place on the magazine, however. Submit samples of work, whether published or not, to the editor.

Granta

2-3 Hanover Yard, Noel Road, London N1 8BE
☏ 071-704 9776   Fax 071-704 0474

Managing Director *Derek Johns*
Editor *Bill Buford*

FOUR ISSUES YEARLY. Literature and politics magazine published in book form in association with **Penguin**. Highbrow, diverse and contemporary, with a thematic approach. Unsolicited mss (including fiction) considered. A lot of material is commissioned. Important to read the magazine first to appreciate its very particular fusion of cultural and political interests. No reviews.
Payment depends on length, but not less than £150 per 1000 words.

The Great Outdoors

The Plaza Tower, East Kilbride, Glasgow G74 1LW
☏ 03552 46444   Fax 03552 63013

Owner *George Outram & Co. Ltd*
Editor *Cameron McNeish*
Circulation 26,000

FOUNDED 1978. MONTHLY. Deals with walking, backpacking and countryside topics. Unsolicited mss are welcome.

Features Well-written and illustrated items on relevant topics. Maximum 2000 words.
Payment about £80-120.

News Short topical items (or photographs). Maximum 300 words.
Payment £10-20.

Green Magazine

Northern & Shell Building, PO Box 381,
Millharbour, London E14 9TW
☏ 071-987 5090   Fax 071-538 3690

Owner *Northern & Shell*
Editor *Alistair Townley*
Circulation 55,000

FOUNDED 1989. MONTHLY. Environmental issues on an international scale. Unsolicited mss considered.

Interested in topical, national, international and exclusive material. Approach with ideas in writing.

Features *Rufus Bellamy* Write in the first instance with synopsis. Maximum 2500 words.
Payment £120 per 1000 words.

Greenscene
Parkdale, Dunham Road, Altrincham,
Cheshire WA14 4QG
☎061-928 0793   Fax 061-926 9182

Owner *Vegetarian Society UK Ltd*
Editor *Juliet Gellatley*
Circulation 9000

FOUNDED 1988. Aimed at 10–18 age group. Unsolicited contributions welcome, particularly non-fiction stories with animal welfare, environmental or vegetarian angle, and animal rights issues. Also short stories.
Payment nominal but negotiable.

Gridiron
The Spendlove Centre, Enstone Road, Charlbury,
Chipping Norton, Oxon OX7 3PQ
☎0608 811266   Fax 0608 811380

Owner *Mediawatch Ltd*
Editor *David Smith*
Circulation 10,794

MONTHLY. Unsolicited mss welcome.

Features *David Smith* Ideas for commission welcome.

News *Neil Rowlands* Tip-offs and news items relating to American football in the UK welcome. Maximum 300 words.
Payment negotiable.

Guide Patrol
17–19 Buckingham Palace Road,
London SW1W 0PT
☎071-834 6242   Fax 071-828 8317

Owner *Guides Association*
Editor *Deborah Fulham*
Circulation 20,000

FOUNDED 1992. MONTHLY aimed at Guides aged 10–14 years. Unsolicited mss welcome.

Features/Fiction General interest with a guiding background. Maximum 1000 words.
Payment £40 per 1000 words.

Guiding
17–19 Buckingham Palace Road,
London SW1W 0PT
☎071-834 6242   Fax 071-828 8317

Owner *Guides Association*
Editor *Nora Warner*
Circulation 33,000

FOUNDED 1914. MONTHLY. Unsolicited mss welcome provided topics relate to the movement, and/or women's role in society. Ideas in writing appreciated in first instance.

Features Topics that can be useful in the Guide programme, or special interest features with Guide link. Maximum 1300 words.
Payment £50–70 per 1000 words.

News Guide activities. Maximum 100–150 words.
Payment £50 per 1000 words.

Special Pages Outdoor activity, information pieces, Green issues. Maximum 1400 words.
Payment £50–70 per 1000 words.

Hair
Room 1414, King's Reach Tower, Stamford Street,
London SE1 9LY
☎071-261 6975   Fax 071-261 6697

Owner *IPC Magazines Ltd*
Editor *Annette Dennis*
Circulation 168,000

FOUNDED 1980. BI-MONTHLY hair and beauty magazine. No unsolicited mss, but always interested in good photographs. Approach with ideas in writing.

Features *Jacki Wadesa* Fashion pieces on hair trends. Maximum 1000 words.
Payment £150.

Hairflair
178–184 Pentonville Road, London N1 9LB
☎071-278 4393   Fax 071-837 8219

Owner *Shaw Publications*
Editor *Sue Rouse*
Circulation 45,000

FOUNDED 1982. MONTHLY Original and interesting hair-related features written in a young, lively style to appeal to a readership aged 16–35 years. Unsolicited mss not welcome. Write with ideas.

Features Maximum 1000 words.
Payment £100 per 1000 words.

Halifax Building Society Magazine
Greater London House, Hampstead Road,
London NW1 7QQ
☎071-377 4633   Fax 071-383 7570

Owner *HHL Publishing*
Editor *Steven Day*
Circulation 500,000

FOUNDED 1983. QUARTERLY. Customer magazine for the Halifax Building Society, biased towards home and general interest topics. Most articles are commissioned. Unsolicited mss rarely used.

Hampshire, The County Magazine
74 Bedford Place, Southampton, SO1 2DF
☎0703 333457/223591   Fax 0703 227190

Owner *Paul Cave Publications Ltd*
Editor *Dennis Stevens*
Circulation 9350

FOUNDED 1960. MONTHLY. Of regional interest only. Unsolicited mss welcome. Approach with ideas in writing.

Features Hampshire life, people, history and activities. 500-2000 words, preferably illustrated.

Handgunner
Seychelles House, Brightlingsea, Essex CO7 0NN
☎0206 305204

Owner *J. A. Stevenson*
Editor *J. A. Stevenson*
Assistant Editor *Richard A.I. Munday*
Circulation 25,000

FOUNDED 1980. BI-MONTHLY. Unsolicited mss are welcome but material should be incisive and in-depth. Make initial contact by telephone.

Features Firearms in economic, political, industrial, police, military and technical fields. Top-quality material only. Length is dictated by subject matter.
Payment about £20 per page.

Harpers & Queen
National Magazine House, 72 Broadwick Street,
London W1V 2BP
☎071-439 5000   Fax 071-439 5506

Owner *National Magazine Co. Ltd*
Editor *Vicki Woods*
Circulation 82,767

MONTHLY. Up-market glossy combining the Sloaney and the streetwise. Approach in writing (not phone) with ideas.

Features *Lucinda Bredin* Ideas only in the first instance.

Fiction *Selina Hastings* Fiction welcome. Maximum 6000 words.

News Snippets welcome if very original.
Payment negotiable.

Health and Efficiency
28 Charles Square, Pitfield Street, London N1 6HP
☎071-253 4037   Fax 071-253 0539

Owner *Peenhill Publishers Ltd*
Editor *Jane Hendy-Smith*
Circulation 120,000

FOUNDED 1900. MONTHLY, QUARTERLY and BI-ANNUAL editions in three languages. Preliminary letter advised for prospective contributors.

Features Naturist travel, especially if accompanied by photos; human and sexual relationships; personal experiences of nudity, naturism or relationship problems; plus occasional health and fitness, and food. Maximum 2000 words (1000 preferred).
Payment £40 per 1000 words.

Health & Fitness
Finsbury Business Centre, 40 Bowling Green Lane,
London EC1R 0NE
☎071-278 0333   Fax 071-837 7612

Owner *Hudson Brothers Publishers Ltd*
Editor *Sharon Walker*
Circulation 35,000

FOUNDED 1983. MONTHLY. Freelance contributions welcome. Ideas in writing preferred.

Health Now
Seymour House, South Street, Godalming,
Surrey GU7 1BZ
☎0483 426064
Fax 0483 426005   Telex 859511

Editor *Alice Peet*
Circulation 350,000

FOUNDED 1977. BI-MONTHLY. Unsolicited mss welcome only if related to the specialised interests of the magazine. Prospective contributors are advised to make their first approach in writing.

Hello!
Wellington House, 69-71 Upper Ground,
London SE1 9PQ
☎071-334 7404   Fax 071-334 7411

Owner *Hola!* (Spain)
Editor *Maggie Goodman*
Circulation 444,257

LAUNCHED 1988. WEEKLY. Sister magazine to its Spanish counterpart *Hola!*. Showbusiness, celebrity and royalty features and gossip. No unsolicited material. Approach with an idea in first instance.

Features *Melanie Hart* Particularly interested in personality-based features and exclusive interviews from generally unapproachable personalities.

Here's Health

Victory House, 14 Leicester Place,
London WC2H 7BP
☎071-437 9011   Fax 071-436 1515

Owner *EMAP Consumer Magazines Ltd*
Editor *Mandy Francis*
Circulation 28,753

FOUNDED 1956. Full-colour MONTHLY dealing with alternative medicine, nutrition, natural health, wholefoods, supplements, organics and the environment. Prospective contributors should bear in mind that this is a specialist magazine with a pronounced bias towards alternative/ complementary medicine, using expert contributors.

Features Length varies.
Payment negotiable.

Hertfordshire Countryside

4 Mill Bridge, Hertford SG14 1PY
☎0992 553571   Fax 0992 587713

Owner *Martin Small*
Editor *Ken Washbrook*
Circulation 14,000

FOUNDED 1946. MONTHLY. Emphasis on county affairs but also regular features on finance, antiques, the arts, fashion, motoring, gardening, property, home interests and dining out. A strong Green presence also, with features on conservation, wildlife and environmental issues. Unsolicited mss welcome but initial approach with ideas in writing preferred. Contributions from freelance writers particularly welcome for articles with an historic background about local towns, villages and surrounding countryside.

Features Maximum 1000 words.
Payment £25.

News Maximum 1000 words.
Payment £25.

Hi-Fi News & Record Review

Link House, Dingwall Avenue, Croydon,
Surrey CR9 2TA
☎081-686 2599   Fax 081-781 6046

Owner *Link House Magazines Ltd*
Editor *Steve Harris*
Circulation 39,000

FOUNDED 1956. MONTHLY. Write in the first instance with suggestions based on knowledge of the magazine's style and subject. All articles must be written from an informed technical or enthusiast viewpoint.

Music *Christopher Breunig*

News *Trevor Butler*

Payment negotiable, according to technical content.

High Life

Greater London House, Hampstead Road,
London NW1 7QQ
☎071-377 4633   Fax 071-383 7570

Owner *HHL Publishing*
Editor *William Davis*
Circulation *c.* 275,000

MONTHLY glossy. British Airways in-flight magazine. Almost all the content is commissioned. No unsolicited mss. Few opportunities for freelancers but ideas in writing always considered.

HIM

Worldwide House, 116-134 Bayham House,
London NW1 0BA
☎071-482 2576   Fax 071-284 0329

Owner *Millivres Ltd*
Editor *Pas Paschali*

MONTHLY gay magazine. Pin-ups, features, fiction, news, reviews, ads, etc. Approach by phone in first instance.

Features *Pas Paschali*

News *David Smith*
Payment negotiable.

History Today

83-84 Berwick Street, London W1V 3PJ
☎071-439 8315

Owner *History Today Ltd*
Editor *Gordon Marsden*
Circulation 30,086

FOUNDED 1951. MONTHLY. Approach in writing only, with synopsis or outline of proposal. Definitely no unsolicited mss.

Features Cross-current pieces linking current events, affairs and issues with their historical contexts. Maximum 1400–1800 words. Mainline articles on all aspects of history with a scholarly bias and emphasis on reinterpretation. Maximum 3000–3500 words.
Payment by negotiation.

News News-orientated pieces about excavations, forthcoming heritage activities and discoveries or reassessments in the historical and archaeological fields. Maximum 600–750 words.

Holiday Which?
2 Marylebone Road, London NW1 4DF
☏ 071-486 5544   Fax 071-935 1606

Owner *Consumers' Association*
Editor *Patricia Yates*
Circulation 170,000

QUARTERLY. All research and writing is done by permanent staff, with occasional outside commissions in special circumstances. No real opportunities for freelancers. Unsolicited mss not considered. Also publishers of travel guidebooks, however, for which material is sometimes commissioned.

Home and Country
104 New Kings Road, London SW6 4LY
☏ 071-731 5777   Fax 071-736 4061

Owner *National Federation of Women's Institutes*
Editor *Penny Kitchen*
Circulation 95,000

FOUNDED 1919. Official MONTHLY journal of the Federation of Women's Institutes, containing articles on a wide range of subjects of interest to women. Strong environmental country slant. Unsolicited mss, photos and illustrations welcome.
Payment by arrangement.

Home & Family
The Mothers' Union, Mary Sumner House, 24 Tufton Street, London SW1P 3RB
☏ 071-222 5533
Fax 071-222 5533 ext. 200 (day);
  071-222 6143 (night)

Owner *The Mothers' Union*
Editor *Margaret Duggan*
Circulation 140,000

FOUNDED 1976. QUARTERLY. Unsolicited mss considered. No fiction or poetry.

Features Family life, social problems, marriage, Christian faith, etc. Maximum 1000 words.
Payment £20–35.

Home Economics & Technology
Forbes Publications Ltd, 2 Drayson Mews, London W8 4LY
☏ 071-938 1035   Fax 071-938 4425

Owner *Forbes Publications Ltd*
Editor *Dilys Wells*
Circulation 4763

TEN ISSUES YEARLY. Contributors should bear in mind that readership tends to be fully qualified home economists or students of the subject.

Features Articles of up to 1200 words welcome on food and nutrition, textile studies, childcare and development, health education, money topics and consumer education.

News Items welcome on the topics listed above. Maximum 500 words.
Payment negotiable.

Home Farm
Broad Leys Publishing Company, Buriton House, Station Road, Newport, Saffron Walden, Essex CB11 3PL
☏ 0799 40922   Fax 0799 41367

Owner *D. & K. Thear*
Editor *Katie Thear*
Circulation 14,000

FOUNDED 1975. BI-MONTHLY journal dealing with practical country living. Unsolicited mss welcome; around 30 are received each week. Articles should be detailed and practical, based on first-hand knowledge about aspects of small farming and country living.

Homebrew Supplier
304 Northridge Way, Hemel Hempstead, Hertfordshire HP1 2AB
☏ 0442 67228   Fax 0442 67228

Owner *Homebrew Publications*
Editor *Evelyn Barrett*
Circulation 2100

FOUNDED 1960. QUARTERLY trade magazine. Unsolicited mss welcome.

Homebrew Today
304 Northridge Way, Hemel Hempstead,
Hertfordshire HP1 2AB
☎0442 67228   Fax 0442 67228

Owner *Homebrew Publications*
Editor *Evelyn Barrett*
Circulation 150,000

FOUNDED 1986. QUARTERLY. Articles on all aspects
of home brewing and the use of homemade wine in
cooking, etc. Unsolicited mss welcome.

Homes and Gardens
King's Reach Tower, Stamford Street,
London SE1 9LS
☎071-261 5678   Fax 071-261 6247

Owner *IPC Magazines Ltd/Reed Publishing*
Editor *Amanda Evans*
Circulation 206,000

FOUNDED 1919. MONTHLY. Almost all published
articles are specially commissioned. No fiction or
poetry. Best to approach in writing with an idea.

Horse and Hound
King's Reach Tower, Stamford Street,
London SE1 9LS
☎071-261 6315   Fax 071-261 5429

Owner *IPC Magazines Ltd*
Editor *Michael Clayton*
Circulation 82,000

WEEKLY. The oldest equestrian magazine on the
market, now re-launched with modern make-up
and colour pictures throughout. Contains regular
veterinary advice and instructional articles, as well
as authoritative news and comment on fox hunting,
international showjumping, horse trials, dressage,
driving and cross-country riding. Also weekly racing and point-to-points, breeding reports and articles. The magazine includes a weekly junior and
young rider section. Regular books and art reviews,
and humorous articles and cartoons are frequently
published. Plenty of opportunities for freelancers.
Unsolicited contributions welcome.
Payment NUJ rates.

Horse & Pony Magazine
Bretton Court, Bretton, Peterborough PE3 8DZ
☎0733 264666   Fax 0733 265515

Owner *EMAP Pursuit Publications*
Editor *Sarah Haw*
Circulation 54,112

Magazine for young (aged 10-16) owners and
'addicts' of the horse. Features include ponycare

and riding articles, and celebrity pieces. Some
interest in freelancers but most feature material is
produced in-house by staff writers.

Horse and Rider
296 Ewell Road, Surbiton, Surrey KT6 7AQ
☎081-390 8547   Fax 081-390 8696

Owner *D. J. Murphy (Publishers) Ltd*
Editor *Alison Bridge*
Circulation 39,000

FOUNDED 1949. MONTHLY. Adult readership, largely
horse-owning. Unsolicited mss are welcome and
should be addressed to the editor. Interested in
fiction and general interest features (particulary
fiction). News and instructional features, which
make up the bulk of the magazine, are almost all
commissioned. Approach in writing with ideas.

Horticulture Week
38-42 Hampton Road, Teddington,
Middlesex TW11 0JE
☎081-943 5000

Owner *Haymarket Magazines Ltd*
Editor *Stovin Hayter*
Circulation 10,000

FOUNDED 1841. WEEKLY. Specialist magazine involved in the supply of business-type information.
No unsolicited mss. Approach in writing in first
instance.

Features *Alison Alford* No submissions without
prior discussion.
Payment negotiable.

News *Fraser Allen* Information about horticultural
businesses — nurseries, garden centres, land-
scapers and parks departments in the various
regions of the UK. No gardening stories.

House Beautiful
National Magazine House, 72 Broadwick Street,
London W1V 2BP
☎071-439 5000   Fax 071-439 5595

Owner *National Magazine Co. Ltd*
Editor *Pat Roberts*
Circulation 271,319

FOUNDED 1989. Lively MONTHLY magazine offering
sound, practical information and plenty of inspiration for those who want to make the most of where
they live. Over one hundred pages of easy reading
editorial. Regular features about decoration, DIY
and home finance. Contact the editor with ideas.

House Buyer

137 George Lane, South Woodford,
London E18 1AJ
☎081–530 7555   Fax 081–530 7609

Owner *Brittain Publications*
Editor *Con Crowley*
Circulation 18,000

MONTHLY magazine with features and articles for house buyers, including features on retirement homes, and mortgage information. Unsolicited mss will not be read or returned.

House & Garden

Vogue House, Hanover Square, London W1R 0AD
☎071–499 9080   Fax 071–493 1345

Owner *Condé Nast Publications Ltd*
Editor *Robert Harling*
Circulation 144,000

Most feature material is produced in-house but a small number of features are commissioned from freelancers, namely in the wine and food sections. Ideas and mss will be considered, particularly from photographers.
Payment varies according to subject, length, rights, etc., particularly in the food section where recipes are involved.

Ice Hockey World and Skating Review

9 Victoria Road, Mundesley-on-Sea,
Norfolk NR11 8JG
☎0263 720038

Editor *Phil Drackett*
Circulation 5000

FOUNDED 1935. MONTHLY during the season. Submissions welcome if preceded by letter/phone but freelance contributions are not generally accepted unless writer has a good knowledge of the sport. Good stories, though, are always considered. All mss to be addressed to the editor. Photographs (colour/b&w) also welcome provided they are of good quality.

Features Maximum 1000 words.
Payment up to £30.

Fiction Rarely, but interested in occasional good short story. Maximum 1000 words.
Payment negotiable.

News Supplied by local stringers, but occasional vacancies.

ID Magazine

5th Floor, Seven Dials Warehouse, 44 Earlham Street, London WC2H 9LA
☎071–240 3282   Fax 071–240 3250

Owner *Levelprint*
Editor *Matthew Collin*
Circulation *c.* 45,000

Fashion magazine for both sexes aged 16–24. Very hip. 'We are always looking for freelance writers with new or unusual ideas.' A different theme each issue — past themes include the Green politics, taste, film, sex, love and loud dance music — means it is advisable to discuss feature ideas in the first instance.

Ideal Home

King's Reach Tower, Stamford Street,
London SE1 9LS
☎071–261 6474   Fax 071–261 6697

Owner *IPC Magazines Ltd*
Editor *Terence Whelan*
Circulation 230,000

FOUNDED 1920. MONTHLY glossy. Unsolicited feature articles are welcome if appropriate to the magazine (one or two are received each week). Prospective contributors wishing to submit ideas should do so in writing to the editor. No fiction.

Features Furnishing and decoration of houses, kitchens or bathrooms; interior design and soft furnishings; furniture in general; home improvements; etc. Length to be discussed with editor.
Payment negotiable.

News Editor *Linda Newman* Suggestions/press releases.
Payment negotiable.

The Illustrated London News

20 Upper Ground, London SE1 9PF
☎071–928 2111   Fax 071–620 1594

Owner *James Sherwood*
Editor-in-Chief *James Bishop*
Circulation 53,970

FOUNDED 1842. SIX ISSUES YEARLY. Covers London and the rest of the UK — travel, wine, restaurants, events, fashion and current affairs. Few opportunities for freelancers but all unsolicited mss are read (receive about 20 a week). The best approach is with an idea in writing. Particularly interested in articles relating to events and developments in contemporary London, and about people working in the capital. All features are illustrated, so ideas with picture opportunities are particularly welcome.

In Britain

Greater London House, Hampstead Road, London NW1 7QQ

☎ 071-388 3171   Fax 071-383 7570

Owner HHL Publishing
Editor Sandra Harris
Circulation 100,000

MONTHLY. Travel and leisure magazine. No unsolicited mss. Approach in writing with ideas. Articles vary from 800-1500 words in length.

The Independent Magazine

See **National Newspapers (The Independent)**

Infusion

16 Trinity Churchyard, Guildford, Surrey GU1 3RR
☎ 0483 62888   Fax 0483 302732
Publisher Bond Clarkson Russell
Editor Fiona Macpherson
Circulation 800,000

FOUNDED 1986. THREE ISSUES YEARLY. Sponsored by the Tea Council. Features women's general interest, health, leisure and all subjects related to tea. All editorial features are commissioned. Approach with ideas only.

InterCity

Redwood Publishing, 20-26 Brunswick Place, London N1 6DJ
☎ 071-490 1444   Fax 071-490 0494

Owner Redwood Publishing
Editor Tony Quinn
Deputy Editor Sarah Openshaw
Circulation 150,000

FOUNDED 1985. TEN ISSUES YEARLY. Sponsored by British Rail. Complimentary business magazine distributed to first-class passengers on InterCity rail routes. Contributions welcome. Approach by phone with idea, and be prepared to follow up by letter, enclosing cuttings if work unknown to the editor.

Interior Design

Incorporated into Designers' Journal in 1991. See **Architectural Review** for details.

Interzone: Science Fiction & Fantasy

217 Preston Drove, Brighton, East Sussex BN1 6FL
☎ 0273 504710

Owner David Pringle
Editor David Pringle
Circulation 10,000

FOUNDED 1982. MONTHLY magazine of science fiction and fantasy. Unsolicited mss are welcome 'only from writers who have a knowledge of the magazine and its contents'. S.a.e. essential for return.

Fiction 2000-6000 words.
Payment £30 per 1000 words.

Features Book/film reviews, interviews with writers, and occasional short articles. Length by arrangement.
Payment negotiable.

Investors Chronicle

Greystoke Place, Fetter Lane, London EC4A 1ND
☎ 071-405 6969   Fax 071-405 5276

Owner Financial Times
Surveys Editor Susan Grayling
Circulation 48,000

FOUNDED 1861. WEEKLY. Opportunities for freelance contributors in the survey section only. All approaches should be made in writing. Over forty surveys are published each year on a wide variety of subjects, generally with a financial, business or investment emphasis. Copies of survey list and synopses of individual surveys are obtainable from the surveys editor.
Payment from £100.

Irish Post

Uxbridge House, 464 Uxbridge Road, Hayes, Middlesex UB4 0SP
☎ 081-561 0059   Fax 081-561 3047

Owner Irish Post Ltd
Editor Donal Mooney
Circulation 75,423

FOUNDED 1970. WEEKLY. News and features relating to the Irish community in Britain. Unsolicited mss welcome. Approach by telephone with ideas.

Jackie

D. C. Thomson, Albert Square, Dundee DD1 9QJ
☎ 0382 23131   Fax 0382 22214

Owner D. C. Thomson & Co. Ltd
Editor Jan Gooderham

Circulation 80,000

FOUNDED 1964. WEEKLY. Scope here for freelance contributors; write in the first instance to the relevant editor.

Features *Jo Ahern* Emotional/fun features dealing with boys, school, friends, parents and growing up. Maximum 2000 words.

Fiction Short Stories: *Paula Craig*; Photostories: *Nikki Gilray Scott* Romantic/humorous stories and serials. Also photostories. Maximum 2000 words. *Payment* £60 minimum.

Jane's Defence Weekly

Sentinel House, 163 Brighton Road, Coulsdon, Surrey CR5 2NH
☎081-763 1030   Fax 081-763 1007

Owner *Jane's Information Group*
Publisher *Paul Beaver*
Editor *Peter Howard*
Circulation 29,000

FOUNDED 1984. WEEKLY. No unsolicited mss. Approach in writing in first instance.

Features Current defence topics (politics, strategy, equipment, industry). Worldwide interest. No history. Maximum 2000 words.
Payment minimum £100 per 1000 words.

Jazz Journal International

113–117 Farringdon Road, London EC1R 3BT
☎071-278 0631   Fax 071-833 5720

Owner *Jazz Journal Ltd*
Editor-in-Chief *Eddie Cook*
Circulation 13,500

FOUNDED 1948. MONTHLY. A specialised jazz magazine, principally using expert contributors whose work is known to the editor. Unsolicited mss not welcome, with the exception of news material (for which no payment is made).

Jewish Chronicle

25 Furnival Street, London EC4A 1JT
☎071-405 9252   Fax 071-405 9040

Owner *Kessler Foundation*
Editor *Edward J. Temko*
Circulation 50,000

Unsolicited mss welcome if 'the specific interests of our readership are borne in mind by writers'. Approach in writing except for urgent current news items. No fiction. Maximum 2000 words for all material. Same policy applies for colour supplement.

Features *Gerald Jacobs*

Leisure/Lifestyle *Angela Kiverstein/Helen Jacobus*

News Home: *Alan Montague*; Foreign: *Joseph Millis*

Colour Magazine/Supplements *Jan Shure/Simon Round*
Payment negotiable.

Jewish Quarterly

PO Box 1148, London NW5 2AZ
☎071-485 4062

Owner *Jewish Literary Trust Ltd*
Editor *Colin Shindler*

FOUNDED 1953. QUARTERLY. Featuring Jewish literature and fiction, politics, art, music, film, poetry, history, dance, community, autobiography, Hebrew, Yiddish, Israel and the Middle East, Judaism, and holocaust studies. Also book reviews. Unsolicited mss welcome but letter or phone call preferred in first instance.

The Journalist

NUJ, Acorn House, 314–320 Gray's Inn Road, London WC1X 8DP
☎071-278 7916   Fax 071-837 8143

Owner *National Union of Journalists*
Editor *Tim Gopsill*
Circulation 30,000

MONTHLY journal of the NUJ. Pieces of interest to journalists, or relevant to the industry, are welcome, but most material is produced in-house and outside contributions are not usually paid for unless submitted by NUJ freelance journalists.

Just Seventeen

15–19 Golderbrock House, Great Titchfield Street, London W1V 7FB
☎071-436 6868   Fax 071-580 4507

Owner *EMAP Metro*
Editor *Morag Prunty*
Circulation 244,000

FOUNDED 1983. WEEKLY. Top of the mid-teen market. News, articles and fiction of interest to girls aged 12–18. Ideas are sought in all areas. Prospective contributors should send ideas to the relevant editorial department, then follow up with phone call.

Beauty *Adelle Lovell*

Acting Features Editor *Lloyd Bradley*

Fiction *Jacqui Deevoy* Maximum 2000 words.

Music *Andrew Fleming*

News *Vici McCarthy*
Payment by arrangement.

Kennel Gazette
Kennel Club, 1-5 Clarges Street, Piccadilly,
London W1Y 8AB
☏ 071-493 6651   Fax 071-495 6162

Owner *Kennel Club*
Editor *Charles Colborn*
Circulation 13,000

FOUNDED 1873. MONTHLY concerning dogs and their breeding. Unsolicited mss welcome.

Features Maximum 2500 words.

News Maximum 500 words.
Payment £70 per 1000 words.

Keyboard Review
Alexander House, Forehill, Ely,
Cambridgeshire CB7 4AF
☏ 0353 665577   Fax 0353 662489

Owner *Music Maker Publications*
Editor *Malcolm Harrison*
Circulation 18,000

FOUNDED 1985. MONTHLY. Broad-based keyboard magazine covering organs, pianos, keyboards, and their players. Unsolicited mss welcome. Approach by phone or in writing with ideas. No general articles on other aspects of the keyboard world.

Features *Malcolm Harrison* Interviews with keyboard players and instrument reviews. Maximum 3000 words.
Payment £45 per 1000 words.

News *Sandra Stafford* Brief items on keyboard world. Maximum 400 words.
Payment up to £20 depending on length.

Labour Party News
150 Walworth Road, London SE17 1JT
☏ 071-701 1234   Fax 071-234 3300

Owner *Labour Party*
Editor *Virginia Gibbons*
Circulation 250,000

FOUNDED 1987. BI-MONTHLY (subject to review). Unsolicited material (with s.a.e.) welcome.

Features Contemporary politics.

News Short items. Maximum 200-250 words.

Reviews Books and films of a directly political interest only.

The Lady
39-40 Bedford Street, Strand, London WC2E 9ER
☏ 071-379 4717   Fax 071-497 2137

Owner *T. G. A. Bowles*
Editor *Arline Usden*
Circulation 66,000

FOUNDED 1885. WEEKLY. Unsolicited mss are welcome; they get about 5000 every year. Nothing is accepted on politics, religion or medicine, or on topics covered by staff writers, i.e. fashion and beauty, household, gardening, finance and shopping.

Features Pieces on British and foreign travel are particularly welcome, and on all other topics except those already mentioned. Maximum 1000 words for illustrated articles; 700 for fillers. All material to the editor.
Payment £55 per 1000 words.
All photographs to support articles should be taken and printed in black and white.
Payment £14-18 per photo used.

Lancashire Magazine
33 Beverley Road, Driffield, Yorkshire YO25 7SD
☏ 0377 43232   Fax 0377 43232

Owner *The Ridings Publishing Co.*
Editor *Winston Halstead*
Circulation 14,500

FOUNDED 1977. BI-MONTHLY. County periodical with a strong Lancashire flavour. Unsolicited mss welcome but few are ever suitable enough to use. Interested only in articles (1000-1500 words), preferably illustrated, with a strong regional slant. No historical articles or poetry.
Payment about £30-35 per printed page.

Liberal Democrat News
4 Cowley Street, London SW1P 3NB
☏ 071-222 7999   Fax 071-222 7904

Owner *Liberal Democrat Party*
Editor *Mike Harskin*

FOUNDED 1988. WEEKLY. As with the political parties, this is the result of the merger of *Liberal News* (1946) and *The Social Democrat* (1981). Political and social topics of interest to party members and supporters. Unsolicited contributions welcome.

Features Maximum 800 words.

News Maximum 350 words.
No payment.

Lifestyle Magazine

The Publishing House, Highbury Station Road,
London N1 1SE
☎ 071-226 2222   Fax 071-226 1255

Owner *Harrington Kilbride*
Editor *Ruth Corbett*
Circulation 50,000

FOUNDED 1989. TWICE-YEARLY. Family guide to
healthy living and Green issues. No unsolicited mss
but good opportunities for freelance writers as
most of the magazine is written by freelancers.
Approach with ideas in writing, including samples
of previous work.

Features Green issues, health, and general family
issues. Maximum 2500 words.
Payment up to £150 per 1000 words.

Lincolnshire Life

PO Box 81, Lincoln LN5 7DY
☎ 0522 77567   Fax 0522 77463

Owner *A. L. Robinson*
Editor *Hilary Hammond*
Circulation 8000

FOUNDED 1961. MONTHLY. Features articles on all
aspects of life in the county: local history, social
issues, tradition, nature and architecture. Interested
in material of both contemporary and historical
nature. Unsolicited mss welcome. Approach in
writing with ideas.
Payment varies.

Literary Review

51 Beak Street, London W1R 3LF
☎ 071-437 9392   Fax 071-734 1844

Owner *Namara Group*
Editor *Auberon Waugh*
Circulation 15,000

FOUNDED 1979. MONTHLY. Publishes book reviews
(commissioned), features and articles on literary
subjects, plus short fiction. Prospective contributors
are best advised to contact the editor in
writing. Unsolicited manuscripts not welcome.
Payment varies.

Living

King's Reach Tower, Stamford Street,
London SE1 9LS
☎ 071-261 5000   Fax 071-261 6892

Owner *IPC Magazines Ltd*
Editor *Olwen Rice*
Circulation 214,104

Women's and family interest glossy magazine sold
at supermarket check-outs and newsagents. Features
are commissioned from outside freelance
writers. Wide-ranging feature needs include family,
education, medical issues, successful women in
small business-type one-offs, and major issues
(divorce, drugs, etc.).
Payment by arrangement.

Logos

Harleyford Estate, Marlow,
Buckinghamshire SL7 2DX
☎ 0628 477577   Fax 0628 477577

Owner *Whurr Publishers Ltd*
Editor *Gordon Graham*
Associate Editor *Betty Cottrell*

LAUNCHED April 1990 as a QUARTERLY. Aims 'to
deal in depth with issues which unite, divide, excite
and concern the world of books,' with an international
perspective. Each issue contains 6–8 articles
of between 3000–5000 words. Hopes to establish
itself as a forum for contrasting views. Suggestions
and ideas for contributions are welcome, and
should be addressed to the editor. Contributors
write from their experience as authors, publishers,
booksellers, librarians, etc. A share of the royalties
goes to a trust fund for causes connected with the
book.

Logos, The Welsh Theological Review

Y Graig, Capel Curig, Gwynedd LL24 0EL
☎ 06904 217   Fax 06904 261

Editors *Fiona Bowie/Oliver Davies*

THRICE-YEARLY A new religious magazine with
articles, book reviews, features, poetry and news of
religious activity in Wales. Unsolicited mss welcome.

London Magazine

30 Thurloe Place, London SW7 2HQ
☎ 071-589 0618

Owner *Alan Ross*
Editor *Alan Ross*
Circulation *c.* 4500

FOUNDED 1954. BI-MONTHLY. Art, memoirs, travel,
poetry, criticism, theatre, music, cinema, book
reviews, photographs. *The Times* was once to say
that '*London Magazine* is far and away the most
readable and level-headed, not to mention best

value for money, of the literary magazines'. About 150–200 unsolicited mss are received weekly.

Fiction Maximum 5000 words. Unsolicited mss welcome; s.a.e. essential.
Payment £100 maximum.

London Review of Books

Tavistock House South, Tavistock Square, London WC1H 9JZ
☎071-388 6751   Fax 071-383 4792

Owner *LRB Ltd*
Editors *Karl Miller/Mary-Kay Wilmers*
Circulation 20,000

FOUNDED 1979. FORTNIGHTLY. News, poems and short stories, plus reviews, essays and articles on political, literary, cultural and scientific subjects. Unsolicited contributions welcome (approximately 35 received each week). Contact the editors in writing.
Payment £60 per 1000 words; poems £50.

Look-in

Floor 27, King's Reach Tower, Stamford Street, London SW1 9LS
☎071-261 6385   Fax 071-261 6032

Owner *IPC Magazines Ltd*
Editor *Frank Hopkinson*
Circulation 100,000

FOUNDED 1971. WEEKLY children's TV, film and pop magazine featuring TV programmes and personalities. Unsolicited mss not generally welcome; prospective contributors are advised to make initial approach in writing.

Features TV, pop, sport, films, general interest, quizzes, etc. — all aimed at children aged 8–13.
Payment negotiable.

Looking Good

Newspaper House, Derngate, Northampton NN1 1NN
☎0604 230000   Fax 0604 31285

Owner *Thomson Regional Newspapers*
Publisher *Alison Panter*
Circulation 27,000

FOUNDED 1984. MONTHLY fashion, beauty and health magazine. Open to ideas in writing. Contact the publisher.

LOOKS

Golderbrock House, 15–19 Great Titchfield Street, London W1P 7FB
☎071-436 6868   Fax 071-580 4507

Owner *EMAP Consumer Magazines Ltd*
Editor *Jenny Tucker*
Circulation 231,000

MONTHLY magazine for young women aged 15–22, which concentrates on fashion, beauty and hair, as well as general interest features, including celebrity news and interviews, fiction, quizzes, etc. Freelance writers are occasionally used in all areas of the magazine. Contact the editor with ideas.
Payment varies.

Love Story

2–4 Leigham Court Road, London SW16 2PD
☎081-769 4444   Fax 081-769 6052

Owner *Argus Consumer Publications*
Editors *Ann Jaloba/Roderick Hudson*
Circulation 40,000

MONTHLY. No opportunities at all for freelance material. Sister magazine to *True Story*, *True Romances* and *Woman's Story*. All stories for all magazines are supplied by American magazine publishers.

Loving

King's Reach Tower, Stamford Street, London SE1 9LS
Fax 071-261 6032

Owner *IPC Magazines Ltd*
Editor *Lorna Read*
Circulation 45,000

MONTHLY. Any good story with a romantic slant considered. Also historical romance. The 'Something Different' section allows authors to experiment with the genre; even crime or science fiction stories might fit the bill. Acceptable story lengths 1000–4000 words. Approach by letter.

Machine Knitting Monthly

3 Bridge Avenue, Maidenhead, Berkshire SL6 1RR
☎0628 770289   Fax 0628 777335

Owner *Anne Smith*
Editor *Sheila Berriff*
Circulation 55,000

FOUNDED 1986. MONTHLY. Unsolicited mss considered 'as long as they are applicable to this specialist publication. We have our own regular contributors each month but I'm always willing to look at new ideas from other writers.' Approach in writing in first instance.

Making Music

20 Bowling Green Lane, London EC1R 0BD
☎ 071–251 1900   Fax 071–251 2619

Owner *Track Record Publishing Ltd*
Editor *Paul Colbert*
Circulation 55,900

FOUNDED 1986. MONTHLY. Approach in writing or by phone with an idea in the first instance.

Features Practical features on playing, being in a band, recording, or getting a record deal. Read and study the magazine prior to approach. Maximum 1500 words.
Payment negotiable.

Management Today

30 Lancaster Gate, London W2 3LP
☎ 071–413 4566   Fax 071–413 4138

Owner *Management Publications Ltd*
Editor *Philip Beresford*
Circulation 103,000

General business topics and features. Ideas welcome. Send brief synopsis to the editor.
Payment about £200 per 1000 words.

Map Collector

48 High Street, Tring, Hertfordshire HP23 5BH
☎ 0442 891004   Fax 0296 623398

Owner *Valerie G. Scott*
Editor *Valerie G. Scott*
Circulation 2500

FOUNDED 1977. QUARTERLY. Articles, book reviews, news, guide to prices — on the history of cartography, i.e. early maps. Not interested in modern mapping.

Features Articles on early maps particularly welcome. Maximum 2500 words.

News Events and exhibitions of early maps. Maximum 300 words.
Payment NUJ rates.

marie claire

195 Knightsbridge, London SW7 1RE
☎ 071–261 5240   Fax 071–261 5277

Owner *European Magazines Ltd*
Editor *Glenda Bailey*
Circulation 222,267

FOUNDED 1988. MONTHLY. An intelligent glossy magazine for women, with strong international features and fashion. No unsolicited mss. Approach with ideas in writing. No fiction.

Features *Michele Lavery* Detailed proposals for feature ideas should be accompanied by samples of previous work.

Marketing Week

St Giles House, 50 Poland Street,
London W1V 4AX
☎ 071–439 4222   Fax 071–439 9669

Owner *Centaur Communications*
Editor *Stuart Smith*
Circulation 41,000

Trade magazine of the marketing industry. Features on all aspects of the business, written in a newsy and up-to-the-minute style. Approach with ideas in the first instance.

Features *Jane Sturges*
Payment negotiable.

Match

Bretton Court, Bretton, Peterborough PE3 8DZ
☎ 0733 260333   Fax 0733 265515

Owner *EMAP Pursuit Publications*
Editor *Paul Stratton*
Circulation 140,296

FOUNDED 1979. WEEKLY football magazine aimed at 8–15-year-olds. Consult the editor or assistant editor before making any submission. Contact may be made either by telephone or in writing. Most material is generated in-house by a strong news and features team. Very little freelance material used, apart from photographs.

Features/News Good and original material is always considered. Maximum 600 words.
Payment negotiable.

Maternity and Mothercraft

Greater London House, Hampstead Road,
London NW1 7QQ
☎ 071–388 3171/822 2275   Fax 071–822 2391

Owner *Maxwell Consumer Publishing*
Editor *Jackie Marsh*
Circulation 130,000

FOUNDED 1965. BI-MONTHLY. Unsolicited mss not welcome. Prospective contributors should make initial contact by telephone or letter.

Features There is a features list and there are occasional opportunities for writers with relevant experience. Being a mother of young children is an added advantage. 850–2000 words.

Matrix

16 Aviary Place, Leeds LS12 2NP
☎ 0532 791264

Owner *British Science Fiction Association*
Editor *Jenny Glover*
Circulation 1300

FOUNDED 1965. BI-MONTHLY newsletter of the BSFA. Features science fiction-orientated news, gossip, pre-publication details of new SF books, details of SF societies, magazines and media, plus occasional author interviews. Initial approach in writing preferred. No fiction or poetry. No literary criticism — this is generally covered by the BSFA sister magazine *Vector*, the critical journal of the BSFA.
No payment.

Mayfair

2 Archer Street, London W1V 7HE
☎ 071-734 9191   Fax 071-734 0614

Owner *Paul Raymond Publications*
Editor *Stephen Bleach*
Circulation 331,760

FOUNDED 1966. MONTHLY. Unsolicited material accepted if suitable to the magazine. Interested in features and humour aimed at men aged 20–30. For style, length, etc., writers are advised to study the magazine.

Mayfair Times

74 South Audley Street, London W1Y 5FF
☎ 071-629 3378   Fax 071-629 9303

Owner *Mayfair Times Ltd*
Editor *Stephen Goringe*
Circulation 20,000

FOUNDED 1985. MONTHLY. Features on Mayfair of interest to both residential and commercial readers. Unsolicited mss welcome.

Me

Elme House, 133 Long Acre, London WC2E 9AD
☎ 071-836 0519   Fax 071-497 2364

Editor *Kay Goddard*
Circulation 600,000

FOUNDED 1989. WEEKLY women's magazine of general interest. No unsolicited mss. Approach in writing with ideas in first instance.

Features/News *Sharon Bexley*
Fiction *June Smith*
Payment varies.

Medal News

Token Publishing Ltd, 84 High Street, Honiton, Devon EX14 8JW
☎ 0404 45414   Fax 0404 45313

Owner *J. W. Mussell*
Editor *Diana Birch*
Circulation 2500

FOUNDED 1989. MONTHLY. Unsolicited material welcome but initial approach by phone or in writing preferred.

Features Only interested in articles from well-informed authors 'who know the subject and do their homework'. Maximum 2500 words.
Payment £20 per 1000 words.

Media Week

33–39 Bowling Green Lane, London EC1R 0DA
☎ 071-837 1212   Fax 071-278 4003

Owner *EMAP Media*

WEEKLY trade magazine. UK and international coverage on all aspects of the media. No unsolicited mss. Approach in writing with ideas.

Melody Maker

26th Floor, King's Reach Tower, Stamford Street, London SE1 9LS
☎ 071-261 5670   Fax 071-261 6706

Owner *IPC Magazines Ltd*
Editor *Allan Jones*
Circulation 71,900

Freelance contributors are used on this tabloid magazine competitor to *NME*. Opportunities exist in reviewing and features.

Features *Ted Mico* A large in-house team plus around six regulars produce most feature material. Send in sample reviews, whether published or not, on pop, rock, soul, funk, etc., to the reviews editor *Andrew Mueller*.
Payment NUJ rates in all cases.

Mensa Magazine

British Mensa Ltd, Mensa House, St John's Square, Wolverhampton WV2 4AH
☎ 0902 772771/2/3   Fax 0902 22327

Owner *British Mensa Ltd*
Editor *Simon Clark*

Circulation 36,500

MONTHLY. Unsolicited mss welcome. Priority is given to members of the Society, but contributions from non-members are also considered. *Payment* negotiable.

Features *Simon Clark* Any general interest topic (e.g. science, travel, education, environment, new technology, etc.). Maximum 2000 words. Feature articles 1500-2000 words. Pieces should be entertaining, informative and concise.

Million: The Magazine About Popular Fiction

217 Preston Drove, Brighton BN1 6FL
☎0273 504710

Owner *Popular Fictions*
Editor *David Pringle*
Circulation 8000 (estimate)

FOUNDED 1990. BI-MONTHLY. The first magazine ever to concentrate exclusively on popular fiction in all its forms. Features criticism and comment on popular and genre fiction. Unsolicited mss welcome (but no fiction!). Approach in writing with ideas, including s.a.e.

Features Any aspect of popular fiction, including some TV, film and comic coverage. Regular interview and review slots also. Maximum 5000 words. *Payment* negotiable.

News Items on popular writers, genres, publishers, etc. Maximum 1000 words. *Payment* negotiable.

Mind Your Own Business

106 Church Road, London SE19 2UB
☎081-771 3614   Fax 081-771 4592

Owner *B. Gledhill/M. Brown*
Editor *Bill Gledhill*
Circulation 48,000

FOUNDED 1978. MONTHLY. Unsolicited material with management appeal welcome. About 12 articles are received each week, of which one or two may be of interest.

Features *Bill Gledhill* Should appeal to management.

Fiction *Sarah Pritchard* Light-hearted, humorous articles with a moral to the story and management-orientated. *Payment* £80-120 per 1000 words approx. Minimum NUJ rates; final fee assessed on quality of finished material.

Mizz

27th Floor, King's Reach Tower, Stamford Street, London SE1 9LS
☎071-261 6319   Fax 071-261 6032

Owner *IPC Magazines Ltd*
Editor *Simon Geller*
Circulation 140,000

FORTNIGHTLY magazine for the 15-19-year-old girl: 'a useful rule of thumb is to write for a 16-year-old'. A wide range of freelance articles welcome on subjects ranging from emotional issues to careers and beauty. Preferred approach varies depending on the nature of material: send ideas in writing, with synopsis, for feature copy; send sample writing with letter for general approach. No fiction.

The Modern Dance

See **Works Publishing** under **Small Presses**

Modern Machine Knitting

3 Bridge Avenue, Maidenhead, Berkshire SL6 1RR
☎0628 770289   Fax 0628 777335

Owner *Modern Knitting Ltd*
Editor *Sue Watson*
Circulation 35,000

FOUNDED 1951. MONTHLY. Anything related to machine knitting and related items. Unsolicited material welcome as is initial approach in writing.

Features Fill 3 pages of magazine including illustrations, diagrams, etc. *Payment* negotiable.

The Modern Review

6 Hopgood Street, London W12 7JU
☎081-749 0593   Fax 081-749 0593

Owner *The Modern Review Ltd*
Editor *Toby Young*
Circulation 15,000

FOUNDED 1991. QUARTERLY. Popular culture magazine - 'low culture for highbrows'. Unsolicited mss considered. Approach by phone or in writing with ideas. Phone calls generally preferred. Not interested in anything which has no connection to popular culture.

Money Week

33-39 Bowling Green Lane, London EC1R 0DA
☎071-837 1212   Fax 071-278 4003

Owner *EMAP Media*
Editor *Nick Morgan*
Circulation 30,000

WEEKLY aimed at the financial services industry. Writers tend to be specialised or experienced financial journalists but 'keen on good freelance writers'. Major part of the magazine is given to features of around 800 words on all aspects of the industry.

Features *Tony McMahon*

News *Amanda Richards*
Payment £150 per 1000 words.

Moneycare
Greater London House, Hampstead Road,
London NW1 7QQ
☎071-377 4633   Fax 071-383 7486

Owner *HHL Publishing*
Editor *Michael Imeson*
Circulation 800,000

The National Westminster Bank magazine. FOUNDED 1983. QUARTERLY on money management. Most articles are commissioned so unsolicited mss are rarely used.

Moneywise
Berkeley Magazines Ltd, 10 Old Bailey,
London EC4M 7NB
☎071-629 8144   Fax 071-409 5261

Owner *Reader's Digest Association*
Editor *Christine Whelan*
Circulation 96,000

FOUNDED 1990. MONTHLY. Unsolicited mss with s.a.e. welcome but initial approach in writing preferred.

More!
42 Great Portland Street, London W1N 5AH
☎071-436 5430   Fax 071-631 0781

Owner *EMAP Metro*
Editor *Fiona Gibson*
Deputy Editor *Tim Fennell*
Circulation 262,000

FOUNDED 1988. FORTNIGHTLY women's magazine aimed at the working woman aged 17–25. News and features plus a lot of 'how-to' articles. Fairly short, snappy style. Maximum 1700 words. Unsolicited material considered but prospective contributors are strongly advised to study the magazine's style before submitting anything.
Payment £150 per 1000 words.

Mosaic
c/o Maureen Richardson, Nottinghamshire County

Council, Leisure Services (Arts & Libraries), Trent Bridge House, Fox Road, West Bridgeford, Nottingham NG2 6BJ
☎0602 608218

Owner *Bay Window Press*
Editors *Sue Thomas/Kevin Fegan*
Circulation 1500

FOUNDED 1992. TWICE-YEARLY. Short stories, poetry and fiction. Locally orientated. Contributors must be resident in Nottinghamshire. Unsolicited mss welcome if original and previously unpublished. No non-fiction. Approach in writing with ideas.

Fiction *Sue Thomas* Showcases — the work of local writers. Maximum 5000 words.

Poetry *Kevin Fegan* Four pages of poetry from local writers. No restriction as such on length.
No payment.

Mother and Baby
Victory House, Leicester Place,
London WC2H 7BP
☎071-437 9011   Fax 071-434 0656

Owner *EMAP Elan Publications*
Editor *Stephanie Neuman*
Circulation 109,061

FOUNDED 1956. MONTHLY. Unsolicited mss welcome, especially personal birth stories and 'Viewpoint' pieces. Approaches may be made by telephone or in writing.

Motor Boat and Yachting
King's Reach Tower, Stamford Street,
London SE1 9LS
☎071-261 5333   Fax 071-261 5419

Owner *IPC Magazines Ltd*
Editor *Alan Harper*
Circulation 31,564

FOUNDED 1904. MONTHLY for those interested in motor boats and motor cruising.

Features *Alan Harper* Cruising features and practical features especially welcome. Illustrations (mostly colour) as important as the text. Maximum 3000 words.
Payment £75 per 1000 words or by arrangement.

News *Alan Harper* Factual pieces. Maximum 200 words.
Payment up to £40 per item.

Motor Caravan World

Andrew House, 2A Granville Road, Sidcup,
Kent DA14 4BN
☏ 081-302 6150   Fax 081-300 2315

Owner *Stone Leisure Group*
Publisher *Bob Griffiths*
Editor *Chris Burlace*

FOUNDED 1975. MONTHLY. Unsolicited mss welcome. Preliminary enquiries by phone or letter are discouraged. Features travel sites, etc. for motor caravans and any news relating to motor caravanning: sites, new sites, rallies, interviews, pictures. Also dealer profiles. Length varies according to subject.
Payment £5–£25 (news); £20–35 (features with pictures/illustrations).

Motor Cycle News

20–22 Station Road, Kettering NN15 7HH
☏ 0536 411111   Fax 0536 411750

Owner *EMAP National Publications*
Contact *The Editor*
Circulation 139,385

WEEKLY, thus relatively news-orientated: particularly keen on motor cycle sport, especially road racing. Some opportunities for freelancers if you can break through the already established network of outside contributors.

Features Most material produced in-house but ideas welcome. Approach the editor in writing. Keen on worldwide motor cycling stories, plus travel or novelty articles supported by good-quality photographs.

Motor Home

Andrew House, 2A Granville Road, Sidcup,
Kent DA14 4BN
☏ 081-302 6150   Fax 081-300 2315

Owner *Stone Leisure Group*
Publisher *Bob Griffiths*
Editor *Chris Burlace*

FOUNDED 1992. QUARTERLY. Features travel sites, etc.,for A-class motor homes and any relevant news: sites, new sites, rallies, interviews. Also dealer profiles. Length varies according to subject.
Payment £5–25 (news); £20–35 (features with pictures/illustrations).

Motorcaravan & Motorhome Monthly (MMM)

8 Swan Meadow, Pewsey, Wiltshire SN9 5HW
☏ 0672 62574   Fax 0980 630770

Owner *Sanglier Publications Ltd*
Editor *Penny Smith*
Circulation 25,000

FOUNDED 1966. MONTHLY. 'There's no money in motorcaravan journalism but for those wishing to cut their first teeth ...' Unsolicited mss welcome if relevant, but ideas in writing preferred in first instance.

Features Caravan site reports — contact the editor for questionnaire. Maximum 1000 words.
Payment £10 with photos.

Travel Motorcaravanning trips (home and overseas). Maximum 3000 words.
Payment £15 per page, with photos.

News Short news items for miscellaneous pages. Maximum 200 words.
No payment.

Fiction 'Never had any but does anyone care to try?' Must be motorcaravan-related and include artwork/photos if possible. Maximum 2000 words.
Payment £15 per page.

Special pages DIY — modifications to motorcaravans. Maximum 1500 words.
Payment £15 per page.

Owner Reports Contributions welcome from motorcaravan owners. Maximum 3000 words.
Payment £15 per page, with photos.

Mountain Biking UK

30 Monmouth Street, Bath BA1 2BW
☏ 0225 442244   Fax 0225 484896

Owner *Future Publishing Ltd*
Editor *Tyn Manley*
Circulation 46,000

FOUNDED 1988. Contributions and new contributors always welcome. Study the magazine's requirements and style in the first instance. Send A5 s.a.e. for free guidelines. Most articles need to be supported by good, dramatic pictures (transparencies only). Contact the editor or his deputy to discuss an idea. Unsolicited mss unlikely to succeed.
Payment negotiable.

Ms London

7–9 Rathbone Street, London W1V 1AF
☏ 071-636 6651   Fax 071-872 0806

Owner *Employment Publications*
Editor-in-Chief *Bill Williamson*
Circulation 127,000

FOUNDED 1968. WEEKLY. Aimed at working women in London, aged 18–35. Unsolicited mss welcome but ideas in writing preferred. Because the magazine is purely London-orientated, there is some bias towards London-based writers who are in touch with the constantly changing trends and attitudes of the capital.

Features Content is varied and ambitious, ranging from stage and film interviews to fashion, careers, relationships, homebuying and furnishing. Always interested to hear from new writers. Approach with ideas. Material should be London-angled, sharp and fairly sophisticated in content. Maximum 1500 words.
Payment about £125 per 1000 words.

News Handled in-house but follow-up feature ideas welcome.

The Music Review

Glyneithin, Burry Port, Dyfed SA16 0TA

Owner *Black Bear Press Ltd (Cambridge)*
Editor *A. F. Leighton Thomas*
Circulation 1000

FOUNDED 1940. QUARTERLY. Academic music journal featuring scholarly articles, book reviews and reviews of new music. Maximum 15,000 words. No real opportunities for writers other than for those who have a highly specialised knowledge of their subject. The majority of contributions come from academics. Unsolicited mss welcome.
Payment negotiable.

Music Week

Spotlight Publications, 8th Floor, Ludgate House, 245 Blackfriars Road, London SE1 9UR
☎071-620 3636   Fax 071-401 8035

Owner *Morgan-Grampian Ltd*
Editor *Steve Redmond*
Circulation 13,280

WEEKLY. Britain's only weekly music business magazine. No unsolicited mss. Approach in writing with ideas.

Features *Selina Webb* Analysis of specific music business events and trends. Maximum 2000 words.

News Music industry news only. Maximum 350 words.

Musical Opinion

2 Princes Road, St Leonards on Sea, East Sussex TN37 6EL
☎0424 715167   Fax 0424 712214

Owner *Musical Opinion Ltd*
Editor *Denby Richards*
Circulation 5000

FOUNDED 1977. MONTHLY. Classical music content, with topical features on music, musicians, festivals, etc., and reviews (concerts, opera, ballet, jazz, CDs, books and music). International readership. No unsolicited mss; commissions only. Ideas always welcome though; approach by phone. It should be noted that topical material has to be submitted six months prior to events. Not interested in review material which is already handled by the magazine's own regular team of contributors.
Payment 'We prefer to negotiate with all writers on all matters.'

Musical Times

4th Floor, Centro House, Mandela Street, London NW1 0DU
☎071-387 3848   Fax 071-388 8532

Owner *Orpheus Publications*
Editor *Basil Ramsey*

Serious-minded journal with a practical approach to its subject. Ideas in writing welcome. No unsolicited mss.
Payment negotiable.

My Guy

27th Floor, King's Reach Tower, Stamford Street, London SE1 9LS
☎071-261 5000   Fax 071-261 6032

Owner *IPC Magazines Ltd*
Editor *Frank Hopkinson*
Circulation 96,000

FOUNDED 1977. WEEKLY teen magazine for girls and boys. No freelance contributions.

My Weekly

80 East Kingsway, Dundee DD4 8SL
☎0382 44276   Fax 0382 462097

Owner *D. C. Thomson & Co. Ltd*
Editor *S. Monks*
Circulation 696,279

A traditional women's WEEKLY which, like others in the D. C. Thomson stable, is currently trying to attract a younger readership, and compete for the young working woman's attention in the marketplace, while not mainating its traditional, loyal readership. D.C. Thomson has long had a policy of encouragement and help to new writers of promise. Ideas welcome. Approach in writing.

Features Particularly interested in humour and human interest pieces (1000–1500 words) which by their very nature appeal to all age groups.

Fiction Three stories a week, ranging in content from the emotional to the off-beat and unexpected. 2000–4000 words. Also serials.
Payment negotiable.

Natural World

20 Upper Ground, London SE1 9PF
☎071–928 2111   Fax 071–620 1594

Owner *Illustrated London News Group/RSNC The Wildlife Trusts Partnership*
Editor *Linda Bennett*
Circulation 160,000

FOUNDED 1981. THRICE-YEARLY. Unsolicited mss welcome if of high quality and relevant to ideals of the magazine. Preferred approach, though, is in writing with an idea. No poetry.

Features Popular but accurate articles on British wildlife and the countryside. Maximum 1500 words.
Payment £100 per 1000 words.

News Interested in national wildlife conservation issues, particularly those involving local nature conservation or wildlife trusts. Maximum 300 words.

The Naturalist

c/o University of Bradford, Bradford BD7 1DP
☎0274 384212   Fax 0274 384231

Owner *Yorkshire Naturalists' Union*
Editor *Prof. M.R.D. Seaward*
Circulation 5000

FOUNDED 1875. QUARTERLY. Natural history, biological and environmental sciences for a professional and amateur readership. Unsolicited mss welcome. Approach with ideas in writing. Particularly interested in material — scientific papers — relating to the north of England.
No payment.

Nature

4 Little Essex Street, London WC2R 3LF
☎071–836 6633   Fax 071–836 9934

Owner *Macmillan Magazines Ltd*
Editor *John Maddox*
Circulation 51,000

Covers all fields of science, with articles and news on science policy only. No features. Little scope for freelance writers. No unsolicited mss. Commissions from specialists within the field generally.

Netball

Netball House, 9 Paynes Park, Hitchin, Hertfordshire SG5 1EH
☎0462 442344   Fax 0462 442343

Owner *All England Netball Association Ltd*
Circulation 5000

FOUNDED 1940. QUARTERLY. No unsolicited mss. No freelance opportunities.

Network

VNU House, 32–34 Broadwick Street, London W1A 2HG
☎071–439 4242   Fax 071–437 8985

Owner *VNU Business Publications*
Editor *Ian Taylor*
Circulation 19,957

MONTHLY. Unsolicited mss never used. Best approach by writing with written synopses.

Features Case studies of user sites, or pieces on the business/ technical issues raised by distributed data processing. Maximum 4000 words.
Payment £130 per 1000 words.

New Beacon

224 Great Portland Street, London W1N 6AA
☎071–388 1266   Fax 071–388 2034

Owner *Royal National Institute for the Blind*
Editor *Ann Lee*
Circulation 5000

FOUNDED 1930. MONTHLY. Published in print, braille and on tape. Unsolicited mss welcome. Approach with ideas in writing. Personal experiences by writers who have a visual impairment (partial sight or blindness), and authoritative items by professionals and volunteers working in the field of visual handicap welcome. Maximum 500 words.
Payment £30 per 1000 words.

New Cyclist

Editorial: Unit 8, Coldstream Workshops, Coldstream, Scotland TD12 4DT
☎0890 3388

Owner *Stonehart Leisure Magazines*
Editor *Jim McGurn*
Circulation 31,000

FOUNDED 1988. MONTHLY general interest cycling magazine. Unsolicited mss welcome (send s.a.e.

for return). Approach by phone with ideas. Not interested in personal accounts like how you began cycling.

Features Almost any cycling subject – green issues, commuting, etc. 'If you are not already a cycling enthusiast it will show in your writing, and we will not be able to use it.' Maximum 2000 words.
Payment rare (£0–80 per 1000 words).

New Humanist

14 Lamb's Conduit Passage, London WC1R 4RH
☏ 071-430 1371   Fax 071-430 1271

Owner *Rationalist Press Association*
Editor *Jim Herrick*
Circulation 3000

FOUNDED 1885. QUARTERLY. Unsolicited mss welcome. No fiction.

Features Articles with a humanist perspective welcome in the following fields: religion (critical), humanism, human rights, philosophy, current events, literature, history and science. 2000–4000 words.
Payment nominal, but negotiable.

Book reviews 750–1000 words, by arrangement with the editor.

New Internationalist

55 Rectory Road, Oxford OX4 1BW
☏ 0865 728181   Fax 0865 793152

Owner *New Internationalist Publications Ltd*
Co-editors *Vanessa Baird/Chris Brazier/David Ransom/Sue Shaw/Troth Wells*
Circulation 75,000

Concerned with world poverty and global issues of peace and politics, with emphasis on the Third World: radical and broadly leftist in approach, but unaligned. Difficult to use unsolicited material as they work to a theme each month, and features are commissioned by the editor on that basis. The way in is to send examples of published or unpublished work; writers of interest are taken up. Unsolicited material for shorter articles (up to 1000 words) could be used in the magazine's regular **Update** and **Endpiece** sections.

New Left Review

6 Meard Street, London W1V 3HR
☏ 071-734 8830   Fax 071-734 0059

Editor *Robin Blackburn*

Magazine of theoretical politics, history and related issues, plus (to a lesser degree) a Marxist reading of the arts and humanities. Material generally provided by academics and expert commentators in the field, rather than by journalists.
No payment.

New Moon Science Fiction

7 Weller Place, High Elms Road, Downe, Orpington, Kent BR6 7JW
☏ 0480 451600

Owner *Trevor Jones*
Editor *George P. Townsend/Trevor Jones*
Circulation 1000

QUARTERLY science fiction magazine providing opportunity for new writers.
Payment £30 per 1000 words.

New Musical Express

King's Reach Tower, Stamford Street, London SE1 9LS
☏ 071-261 5000   Fax 071-261 5185

Owner *IPC Magazines Ltd*
Editor *Danny Kelly*
Circulation 115,000

Britain's best-selling musical WEEKLY. Freelancers used, but always for reviews in the first instance. Specialisation in areas of music (or film, which is also covered) is a help.

Reviews Books *Stephen Dalton* Film *Gavin Martin* LPs *Stuart Bailey* Live *Steve Lamacq*. Send in examples of work, either published or specially written samples.

New Scientist

King's Reach Tower, Stamford Street, London SE1 9LS
☏ 071-261 5000   Fax 071-261 6464

Owner *IPC Magazines Ltd*
Circulation 102,000

FOUNDED 1956. WEEKLY. No unsolicited mss. Approach in writing or by phone with an idea.

Features Commissions only, but good ideas welcome. Maximum 3500 words.

News *Stephanie Pain* Mostly commissions, but ideas for specialist news, particularly from academics and specialist writers, are welcome. Maximum 1000 words.

Reviews/Forum *Richard Fifield* Reviews tend to be commissioned but unsolicited material for Forum is welcome if of general/humorous interest and related to science. Maximum 1000 words. *Payment* £170–190 per 1000 words.

New Statesman and Society

Foundation House, Perseverance Works, 38 Kingsland Road, London E2 8DQ
☏ 071–739 3211   Fax 071–739 9307

Owner *Statesman and Nation Publishing Co.*
Editor *Steve Platt*
Circulation 37,000

WEEKLY magazine of the political left which is the result of a merger in May 1988 of *New Statesman* and *New Society*. Coverage of news, book reviews, arts, current affairs and politics. Unsolicited contributions welcome. New contributors are best advised to contact the editor in the first instance.

Literary/Arts *Boyd Tonkin*

Political *Sarah Baxter*

New Woman

15–19 Great Titchfield Street, London W1P 7FB
☏ 071–436 6868   Fax 071–580 4507

Owner *EMAP Consumer Magazines Ltd*
Editor *Gill Hudson*

MONTHLY. A self-indulgent read on the whole. Main topics of interest: men, sex, love, health, beauty and fashion. Unsolicited contributions welcome but initial approach in writing preferred.

Features/Fiction *Samantha Harrison* Articles must be original and look at subjects or issues from a new or unusual perspective.

News *Suzanna Drew-Edwards*

Beauty *Jan Goodall*

Fashion *Deborah Bee*

19

King's Reach Tower, Stamford Street, London SE1 9LS
☏ 071–261 6410   Fax 071–261 6032

Owner *IPC Magazines Ltd*
Editor *April Joyce*
Circulation 190,000

MONTHLY magazine aimed at the 17–22-year-old girl. A little different from the usual teen magazine mix: *19* are now aiming for a 50/50 balance between fashion/lifestyle aspects and newsier, meatier material, e.g. women in prison, boys,

abortion, etc. Forty per cent of the magazine's feature material is commissioned, ordinarily from established freelancers. 'But we're always keen to see bold, original, vigorous writing from people just starting out ...'

Features *April Joyce* Approach in writing with ideas.

Norfolk Life

Sister magazine to *Suffolk Life* (see entry).

North East Times

Tattler House, Beech Avenue, Fawdon, Newcastle upon Tyne NE3 4LA
☏ 091–284 4495   Fax 091–285 9606

Owner *Chris Robinson*
Editor *Chris Robinson*
Circulation 10,000

MONTHLY county magazine incorporating *Newcastle Life*. No unsolicited mss. Approach with ideas in writing.

The North

51 Byram Arcade, Westgate, Huddersfield HD1 1ND
☏ 0484 434840   Fax 0484 426566

Owner *The Poetry Business*
Editors *Peter Sansom/Janet Fisher*
Circulation 500

FOUNDED 1986. THRICE YEARLY. Unsolicited mss welcome.

Features Critical articles considered on contemporary poetry and poets, but these are usually commissioned. Maximum 1000 words.
Payment nominal.

Fiction No genre fiction. Anything literary or avantgarde, in contemporary style, considered. Maximum 1500–2000 words.
Payment nominal, if at all.

Poetry Contemporary poetry forms the main content of the magazine. Unsolicited mss welcome but contributors are advised to consider the style of the magazine. No particular restrictions on form, length, etc., but 'work must be contemporary, and must speak with the writer's own authentic voice. No traditional poems, echoes of old voices, poems about the death of poet's grandfather, poems which describe how miserable the poet is feeling right now.'
Payment two copies of the magazine.

Northamptonshire Image

Upper Mounts, Northampton NN1 3MR
☏0604 231122   Fax 0604 233000

Owner *Northampton Mercury Co.*
Editor *Peter Hall*
Circulation 18,500

FOUNDED 1905. MONTHLY general interest county magazine. No unsolicited mss. Approach by phone or in writing with ideas. No fiction.

Features Local issues, personalities, businesses, etc., of Northamptonshire interest only. Maximum 500 words.
Payment £60.

News No hard news as such, just monthly diary column.

Other Regulars on motoring, fashion, lifestyle, sport, travel, history, country walks, and picture files. Maximum 500 words.
Payment £60.

Nursing Times

4 Little Essex Street, London WC2R 3LF
☏071-379 0970   Fax 071-497 2664

Owner *Macmillan Magazines Ltd*
Editor *Linda Davidson*

A large proportion of *Nursing Times* feature content is from unsolicited contributions sent on spec. Pieces on all aspects of nursing and health care, both practical and theoretical, written in a lively and contemporary way, are welcome. Commissions also.
Payment varies/NUJ rates apply to commissioned material from union members only.

Observer Magazine

See **National Newspapers (The Observer)**

Office Secretary

Brookmead House, Two Rivers, Station Lane, Witney, Oxon OX8 6BH
☏0993 775545   Fax 0993 778884

Owner *Trade Media Ltd*
Editor *Onay Faiz*
Circulation 113,000

FOUNDED 1986. QUARTERLY. Features articles of interest to secretaries and personal assistants aged 25-60. Unsolicited mss welcome.

Features Chatty but informative pieces on current affairs, health, office and employment-related topics. Maximum 2000 words.
Payment £100 per 1000 words/negotiable.

The Oldie

26 Charlotte Street, London W1P 1HJ
☏071-636 3686   Fax 071-636 3685

Owner *Oldie Publications Ltd*
Editor *Richard Ingrams*
Circulation 100,000

FOUNDED 1992. FORTNIGHTLY general interest magazine with a strong humorous slant for the older person. No unsolicited mss.

On The Edge

PO Box 21, Buxton, Derbyshire SK17 9BR
☏0298 72801   Fax 0298 72839

Owner *Gill Kent*
Editor *Gill Kent*
Circulation 5500

FOUNDED 1987. BI-MONTHLY publication dedicated to climbing and rock climbing. Unsolicited mss welcome. Approach by phone with ideas.

Features Anything to do with rock climbing and climbing. Best to make contact by phone before submissions. Maximum 3000 words.
Payment £20 per 1000 words (photos extra).

News All contributions welcome but no payment. Maximum 300 words.

Opera

1A Mountgrove Road, London N5 2LU
☏071-359 1037   Fax 071-354 2700

Owner *Opera Magazine Ltd*
Editor *Rodney Milnes*
Circulation 12,000

FOUNDED 1950. MONTHLY review of the current opera scene. Almost all articles are commissioned and unsolicited mss are not welcome. All approaches should be made in writing.

Opera Now

241 Shaftesbury Avenue, London WC2H 8EH
☏071-528 8784   Fax 071-528 7991

Owner *Rhinegold Publishing Ltd*
Editor *Graeme Kay*

FOUNDED 1989. MONTHLY. News, features and reviews for those interested in opera. No unsolicited mss. All work is commissioned. Approach with ideas in writing.

Options

King's Reach Tower, Stamford Street,
London SE1 9LS
☏ 071-261 5000   Fax 071-261 6023

Owner *IPC Magazines Ltd*
Editor *Maureen Rice*
Circulation 150,000

Aims to entertain the modern renaissance woman,
worker, mother and wife. Almost all written by a
regular team of freelancers, but new writers are
encouraged: 'commissioned non-commissioned
pieces are requested from new feature writers of
promise'.
Payment about £250 per 1000 words.

Orbis

199 The Long Shoot, Nuneaton,
Warwickshire CV11 6JQ
☏ 0203 327440/385551   Fax 0203 642402

Owner *Mike Shields*
Editor *Mike Shields*
Circulation 1000

FOUNDED 1968. QUARTERLY literary magazine, one
of the few which are completely independent of
any kind of grant aid, and therefore has a high
degree of reader involvement. Unsolicited mss
welcome if accompanied by s.a.e. No initial approach necessary.

Features No critical articles, but short pieces of
about 500 words on topics of current interest are
used. Also reviews (no payment) of recent books.

Fiction Short literary pieces or prose poems of
around 1000 words.

Poetry Forms the main content of each issue.
Wide range of styles from traditional to modern.
One of the best outlets for formal verse, 'but it must
be well executed: pseudo-Tennyson is not required'.
Payment £5 per acceptance plus free copies of the
magazine, plus cash prizes based on readers' votes.

Outlook

87 Kirkstall Road, London SW2 4HE
☏ 081-671 7920

Owner *I. J. Henshall*
Editor *I. J. Henshall*
Circulation 5000

FOUNDED 1988. BI-MONTHLY. Current affairs, film
and indie-pop aimed at 18–30 age group. Unsolicited mss welcome. Approach in writing with ideas.
No poetry or short stories (other than humour).

Features *James Russell* 900–2500 words.

News *David Black* Newsdesk work open to volunteers. Submissions can be of any length up to 1800
words.

Other *James Russell* Humour pieces. 700–1200
words.
No payment.

Paperback Inferno

1 The Flaxyard, Woodfall Lane, Little Neston, South
Wirral L64 4BT
☏ 051-336 3355

Owner *British Science Fiction Association*
Editor *Andy Sawyer*
Circulation 1000

FOUNDED 1977. BI-MONTHLY. Publishes reviews of
science fiction paperbacks and professional SF
magazines. Unsolicited material not welcome as all
reviews are commissioned.

Parents

Victory House, Leicester Place,
London WC2H 7BP
☏ 071-437 9011   Fax 071-434 0656

Owner *EMAP Elan Publications*
Editor *Isobel McKenzie-Price*
Circulation 70,000

FOUNDED 1976. MONTHLY. Unsolicited mss considered, particularly good personal accounts of
pregnancy/birth/parenting, etc., and features commissioned from outside contributors. Approach
with ideas.

PC User

33–39 Bowling Green Lane, London EC1R 0DA
☏ 071-837 1212   Fax 071-278 4003

Owner *EMAP Computing*

FORTNIGHTLY user magazine covering all aspects of
user interest. Advice, reviews, features, market
information, etc. No unsolicited mss. Approach in
writing with ideas.

PCW Plus

30 Monmouth Street, Bath BA1 2BW
☏ 0225 442244   Fax 0225 446019

Owner *Chris Anderson*
Editor *Martin Le Poidevin*
Circulation 27,206

FOUNDED 1986. MONTHLY. Unsolicited contributions welcome but initial approach in writing
preferred.

Features *Martin Le Poidevin* 'We will welcome any interesting feature-length articles on writing but must involve reference to PCW. Good illustrations preferred as well.' Maximum 2000 words. *Payment* about £100/negotiable.

Case in Point Monthly feature on original uses to which people have put their Amstrad PCWs. Good illustrations important. Maximum 1600 words. *Payment* about £100.

Penthouse

Northern & Shell Building, PO Box 381, Millharbour, London E14 9TW
☏ 071-987 5090   Fax 071-987 2160

Owner *Richard Desmond*
Executive Editor *Jonathan Richards*
Managing Editor *Isabel Koprowski*
Circulation *c.*100,000

FOUNDED 1965. 13 ISSUES YEARLY.

Features *Jonathan Richards* Unsolicited mss welcome, 'but most of those we do receive are unsuitable because the authors haven't looked at the magazine'. First approach by phone or in writing with ideas. Maximum 3500 words. *Payment* negotiable 'but generally pretty good'.

News *Zak Jane Kear* Limited opportunities for unsolicited material. No fiction. Must have a fairly long-term appeal.

People Magazine

See **National Newspapers (The People)**

The People's Friend

80 Kingsway East, Dundee DD4 8SL
☏ 0382 462276   Fax 0382 452491

Owner *D. C. Thomson & Co. Ltd*
Editor *Sinclair Matheson*
Circulation 566,000

The *Friend* is basically a fiction magazine, with two serials and several short stories each week. FOUNDED in 1869, it has always prided itself on providing 'a good read for all the family'. All stories should be about ordinary, identifiable characters with the kind of problems the average reader can understand and sympathise with. 'We look for the romantic and emotional developments of characters, rather than an over-complicated or contrived plot. From time to time we can also use a romantic/mystery/adventure/period-type story.

Short Stories Can vary in length from 1000 words or less to as many as 4000.

Serials Long-run serials of 10-15 instalments or more preferred. Occasionally shorter.

Articles Short fillers welcome. *Payment* negotiable.

Pergamon Bridge/Pergamon Chess

See **Bridge Magazine** and **Chess**

Personnel Management

57 Mortimer Street, London W1N 7TD
☏ 071-323 5717   Fax 071-323 5770

Owner *Personnel Publications Ltd*
Editor *Susanne Lawrence*
Circulation 47,014

FOUNDED 1969. MONTHLY specialist magazine for personnel managers. Unsolicited mss welcome only from specialists in the personnel and training fields.

Features *Jane Pickard* Only interested in material written by specialists in their field. Occasional scope for articles by those with experience or knowledge of employment, industrial relations, training, pay areas. Maximum 2500 words. *Payment* NUJ rates.

News *Pauline Crofts* Sometimes interested in reports of relevant events at which a magazine staff member was unable to be present. Length varies. *Payment* NUJ rates.

Picture Postcard Monthly

Reflections of a Bygone Age, 15 Debdale Lane, Keyworth, Nottingham NG12 5HT
☏ 0602 374079

Owner *Brian & Mary Lund*
Editor *Brian Lund*
Circulation 4300

FOUNDED 1978. MONTHLY. News, views, clubs, diary of fairs, sales, auctions, and well researched postcard-related articles. Not interested in general articles supported by postcards. Unsolicited mss welcome. Approach by phone or in writing with ideas.

Pilot

The Clock House, 28 Old Town, Clapham, London SW4 0LB
☏ 071-498 2506   Fax 071-498 6920

Owner *James Gilbert*
Editor *James Gilbert*
Circulation 33,500

FOUNDED 1968. MONTHLY magazine for private plane pilots. No staff writers; the entire magazine is written by freelancers — mostly regulars. Unsolicited mss welcome but ideas in writing preferred. Perusal of any issue of the magazine will reveal the type of material bought.

Features *James Gilbert* Many articles are unsolicited personal experiences/travel accounts from pilots of private planes; good photo coverage is very important. Maximum 3000 words.
Payment £100–700 (first rights).

News *Mike Jerram* Contributions need to be as short as possible. See Pilot Notes in the magazine.

The Pink Paper
77 City Garden Row, London N1 8EZ
☎071–608 2566   Fax 071–608 2544

Owner *Mindmaster Ltd*
Editor *Ben Summerskill*
Circulation 34,600

FOUNDED 1987. WEEKLY. National newspaper for lesbians and gay men covering politics, social issues, health, the arts and all areas of concern to the lesbian/gay community. Unsolicited mss welcome. Initial approach by phone with an idea preferred. Interested in profiles, reviews, in-depth features and short news pieces.

Features *Ben Summerskill* Maximum 800 words.

News *Ben Summerskill* Maximum 200 words.

Arts *James Cary-Parkes* Maximum 200 words.

Community Information *Maggie Davis* Maximum 200 words.
Payment by arrangement.

Platform Magazine
46 Sherbrooke Road, London SW6 7QW
☎071–381 5734   Fax 071–610 1882

Owner *TPN Productions Ltd*
Editor *Robert Winter*
Circulation 5000

FOUNDED 1992. MONTHLY general forum covering career advice, guidance, training workshops, presentation skills, skills training, grievances (particularly financial or legal). No fiction. Mss welcome. Approach in writing with ideas.

News 250–350 words.

Features 750–1500 words.

Specials *Maureen Asser* 1500–3000 words.
Payment by arrangement.

Plays and Players
Pickwick House, 995 High Road,
London N12 8QX
☎081–343 9977   Fax 081–343 7831

Owner *Aaron Gershfield*
Editor *Vera Lustig*
Circulation 8000

Theatre MONTHLY which publishes a mixture of reviews, festival reports and features on all aspects of the theatre. Rarely uses unsolicited material but writers of talent are taken up. Almost all material is commissioned.
Payment under review, but small.

Plus
Revenue Buildings, Chapel Road, Worthing, West Sussex BN11 1BQ
☎0903 214198   Fax 0903 217663

Owner *Challenge Literature Fellowship*
Editor *Virginia Symonds*
Circulation 7000

Highly visual magazine for 9–13-year-olds. Christian-based articles tend to be commissioned but short general interest items provide scope for outside contributions. Prospective contributors should send A4 s.a.e. for sample copy, or submit ideas in writing for consideration.
Payment negotiable.

PM Plus
57 Mortimer Street, London W1N 7TD
☎071–323 5717   Fax 071–323 5770

Owner *Personnel Publications Ltd*
Editor *Susanne Lawrence*
Circulation 47,014

FOUNDED July 1990. MONTHLY magazine for those involved in the personnel scene, and sister publication to **Personnel Management**. Carries the latest news and stories behind the news, plus appointments service.

Poetry Review
22 Betterton Street, London WC2H 9BU
☎071–240 4810   Fax 071–240 4818

Owner *The Poetry Society*
Editor *Peter Forbes*
Circulation 5000

FOUNDED 1909. QUARTERLY poetry magazine. Approximately 5000 unsolicited mss received each year (mostly poetry) and these are welcome, but the odds should be borne in mind by potential contributors. No more than six poems should be sent (s.a.e. essential). Almost all prose is commissioned. A preliminary letter is advisable before submitting reviews or features. Study of the magazine is highly recommended.

Pony
296 Ewell Road, Surbiton, Surrey KT6 7AQ
☎081-390 8547   Fax 081-390 8696

Owner *D. J. Murphy (Publishers) Ltd*
Editor *Kate Austin*
Circulation 38,000

FOUNDED 1948. Lively MONTHLY aimed at 10–16-year-olds. News, instruction on riding, stable management, veterinary care, interviews. Also regular short story slot (maximum 1000 words). Approach in writing with an idea.

Features welcome. Maximum 900 words. *Payment* £65 per 1000 words.
News Written in-house. Photographs and illustrations (serious/ cartoon) welcome. *Payment* £65 per 1000 words.

Popular Crafts
Argus House, Boundary Way, Hemel Hempstead, Hertfordshire HP2 7ST
☎0442 66551   Fax 0442 66998

Owner *Argus Specialist Publications*
Editor *Brenda Ross*
Circulation 30,000

FOUNDED 1980. MONTHLY. The only monthly publication covering crafts of all kinds, and giving full instructions and full-size patterns for craft projects to make. Freelance contributions welcome — copy needs to be lively and interesting. Approach in writing with an outline of idea. Areas of interest: projects to make, with full instructions; profiles of craftspeople; news of craft group activities and successes by individual persons; articles on collecting crafts; personal experiences and anecdotes; general articles on any craft-related subject. *Payment* on publication.

Popular Flying
Norfolk House, 196 Old Bedford Road, Luton, Bedfordshire LU2 7HW
☎0582 37023   Fax 0582 455587

Owner *The Popular Flying Association*
Editor *Peter Underhill*
Circulation 8000

FOUNDED 1956. BI-MONTHLY. Features and articles on all forms of sporting and recreational aviation. Unsolicited mss and ideas in writing welcome. No

payment as the magazine is run entirely by volunteers. Interested in anything related to the magazine's particular branch of light aviation: touring, homebuilding, restoration, etc.

PR Week
22 Lancaster Gate, London W2 3LP
☎071-413 4520   Fax 071-413 4509

Owner *Haymarket Business Publications Ltd*
Editor *Desmond Quigley*
Circulation 20,000

FOUNDED 1984. WEEKLY. Contributions only accepted from experienced journalists. Approach in writing with an idea.

Features *Amanda Hall*

News *Stephen Farish*
Payment £150 per 1000 words.

Practical Boat Owner
c/o IPC Magazines, Westover House, West Quay Road, Poole, Dorset BH15 1JG
☎0202 680593   Fax 0202 674335

Owner *IPC Magazines Ltd*
Editor *George Taylor*
Circulation 70,098

MONTHLY. For the beginner and the experienced owner. Reports on coastal cruising, pleasure sailing, and marine information. Colour supplements: *Cruising*, in June; *Trailer Boating*, in March; *Classic Cruiser*, in October.
Payment negotiable.

Practical Electronics
Intra Press, Intra House, 193 Uxbridge Road, London W12 9RA
☎081-743 8888   Fax 081-743 3062

Owner *Angelo Zgorelec*
Editor *Kenn Garroch*
Circulation 20,000

FOUNDED 1964. MONTHLY. Electronics technology, new products and ideas, plus reviews of hardware. Unsolicited mss and ideas in writing welcome.

Practical Fishkeeping
Bretton Court, Bretton, Peterborough, Cambridgeshire PE3 8DZ
☎0733 264666   Fax 0733 265515

Owner *EMAP Pursuit Publishing Ltd*
Editor *Steve Windsor*
Circulation 41,000

MONTHLY. Practical articles on all aspects of fishkeeping. Unsolicited mss welcome. Approach in writing with ideas.

Practical Gardening

Apex House, Oundle Road, Peterborough,
Cambridgeshire PE2 9NP
☎ 0733 898100   Fax 0733 898433

Owner *EMAP National Publications Ltd*
Editor *Adrienne Wild*
Circulation 107,729

FOUNDED 1960. MONTHLY. Unsolicited mss welcome, but there are few acceptances out of the 150 or so received each year. Submit ideas in writing.

Features Occasional features/photos on gardens (not stately homes) welcome, provided they are in keeping with the magazine's style. Maximum 1200 words.
Payment from £70 per 1000 words.

Practical Householder

Greater London House, Hampstead Road,
London NW1 7QQ
☎ 071-388 3171   Fax 071-387 9518

Owner *Home & Law Magazines Ltd*
Editor *Martyn Hocking*
Circulation 50,000

FOUNDED 1955. MONTHLY. Features on DIY/home improvement subjects. No unsolicited mss. Write to the editor with ideas.

Practical Motorist

Unit 8, Forest Close, Ebblake Industrial Estate,
Verwood, Dorset BH31 6DQ
☎ 0202 823581

Owner *Practical Motorist Ltd*
Editor *Denis Rea*
Circulation 30,000

FOUNDED 1934. MONTHLY. Unsolicited mss welcome. All approaches should be made to the editor. Maximum 1500 words.
Payment 'on merit'. 'Ours is a very specialised field and not many can hope to match our established contributors.'

Practical Photography

Apex House, Oundle Road,
Peterborough PE2 9NP
☎ 0733 898100   Fax 0733 898418

Owner *EMAP Apex Publications Ltd*
Editor *William Cheung*

Circulation 110,041

MONTHLY. All types of photography, particularly technique-orientated pictures. No unsolicited mss. Preliminary approach may be made by telephone. Always interested in new ideas.

Features Anything relevant to the readership, but not 'the sort of feature produced by staff writers'. Bear in mind that there is a three-month lead-in time. Maximum 2000 words.
Payment varies.

News Only 'hot' news applicable to a monthly magazine. Maximum 400 words.
Payment varies.

Practical Wireless

Enefco House, The Quay, Poole,
Dorset BH15 1PP
☎ 0202 678558   Fax 0202 666244
Editor *Rob Mannion*
Circulation 27,000

FOUNDED 1932. MONTHLY. News and features relating to amateur radio, radio construction and radio communications. Unsolicited mss welcome. Approach in writing or by phone with ideas. Copy should be supported where possible by artwork, either illustrations, diagrams or photographs.
Payment £54-70 per page.

Prediction

Link House, Dingwall Avenue, Croydon CR9 2TA
☎ 081-686 2599   Fax 081-760 0973

Owner *Link House Magazines Ltd*
Editor *Jo Logan*
Circulation 35,000

FOUNDED 1936. MONTHLY. Covering astrology and occult-related topics. Unsolicited material in these areas welcome (about 200-300 mss received every year).

Astrology Pieces ranging from 800-2000 words should be practical and of general interest. Charts and astro data should accompany them, especially if profiles.
Payment £25-75.

Features *Jo Logan* Articles on mysteries of the earth, alternative medicine, psychical/occult experiences and phenomena are considered. Maximum 2000 words.
Payment £25-75.

News *Jon Taylor* News items of interest to readership welcome. Maximum 300 words.
No payment.

Prima

Portland House, Stag Place, London SW1E 5AU
☎071-245 8700   Fax 071-630 5509

Owner *G & J*
Editor *Sue James*
Circulation 738,871

FOUNDED 1986. MONTHLY. Top-selling women's magazine.

Features *Jenny Filder* Mostly practical and written by specialists or commissioned from known freelancers. Unsolicited mss not welcome.
Payment About £200 per 1000 words.

Private Eye

6 Carlisle Street, London W1V 5RG
☎071-437 4017   Fax 071-437 0705

Owner *Pressdram*
Editor *Ian Hislop*
Circulation 197,000

FOUNDED 1961. FORTNIGHTLY satirical and investigative magazine. Prospective contributors are best advised to approach the editor in writing. News stories and feature ideas are always welcome, as are cartoons. All jokes written in-house.
Payment in all cases is 'not great', and length of piece varies as appropriate.

Psychic News

2 Tavistock Chambers, Bloomsbury Way,
London WC1A 2SE
☎071-405 3340/3345

Owner *Psychic Press Ltd*
Editor *Tim Haigh*

FOUNDED 1932. *Psychic News* is the world's only WEEKLY spiritualist newspaper. It covers subjects such as psychic research, hauntings, ghosts, poltergeists, spiritual healing, survival after death, and paranormal gifts. No unsolicited mss.

Publishing News

43 Museum Street, London WC1A 1LY
☎071-404 0304   Fax 071-242 0762
Editor *Fred Newman*

WEEKLY newspaper of the book trade. Hardback and paperback reviews and extensive listings of new paperbacks. Interviews with leading personalities in the trade, authors, agents and features on specialist book areas.

Q

42 Great Portland Street, London W1N 5AH
☎071-436 5430   Fax 071-323 0680

Owner *EMAP Metro Publications*
Editor *Paul Du Noyer*
Circulation 166,149

FOUNDED 1986. MONTHLY. Glossy aimed at educated rock music enthusiasts of all ages. Few opportunities for freelance writers. Unsolicited mss are strongly discouraged. Prospective contributors should approach in writing only.

Quartos Magazine

BCM Writer, 27 Old Gloucester Street,
London WC1N 3XX
☎0559 371108

Owner *Suzanne Riley*
Editor *Suzanne Riley*
Circulation 1000

FOUNDED 1987. BI-MONTHLY. Contributions welcome provided they cover writing-related material. Approach by letter with s.a.e.

Features Well-written articles for **Forum** and **Focus** columns welcome. Maximum 800-1000 words.

News All news concerning services, book reviews, competitions, ideas, readers' letters, etc. Maximum 100 words.

Fiction Regular short story competitions with winner printed in future issue. No unsolicited mss; competition entries only. Maximum 1000 words.

A Novel Idea Caters for those interested in novel writing; also regular features on publishing and agency requirements, usually by someone in the business. Maximum 800-1000 words.
Payment £10 per 1000 words (none for news).

RA

Friends of the Royal Academy, Royal Academy of Arts, Burlington House, Piccadilly,
London W1V 0DS
☎071-494 5657   Fax 071-287 9023

Owner *Friends of the Royal Academy*
Editor *Nick Tite*
Circulation 85,000

FOUNDED 1983. QUARTERLY fine art magazine with a controlled circulation. Articles relating to or about the Royal Academy, its members and exhibitions.Unsolicited mss considered but no unsolicited material has yet been published. Make

initial contact in writing. Features should be no longer than 1500 words.
Payment £150.

The Racing Pigeon

Unit 13, 21 Wren Street, London WC1X 0HF
☎ 071-833 5959   Fax 071-833 3151

Owner *The Racing Pigeon Publishing Co. Ltd*
Editor *Rick Osman*
Circulation 25,000

FOUNDED 1898. WEEKLY news magazine for racing pigeon enthusiasts. Only specialist writers considered. Maximum 1000 words. Unsolicited mss welcome.

Radio Communication

RSGB, Lambda House, Cranborne Road, Potters Bar EN6 3JE
☎ 0707 59260   Fax 0707 49503

Owner *Radio Society of Great Britain*
Editor *Mike Dennison*
Circulation 35,000

FOUNDED 1913. MONTHLY. Amateur radio related publication. Features technical articles and anything of interest to the amateur radio world. Unsolicited mss welcome. Approach in writing with ideas.
No payment.

Radio Times

35 Marylebone High Street, London W1M 4AA
☎ 071-580 5577   Fax 071-224 2445

Owner *BBC Enterprises*
Editor *Nicholas Brett*
Circulation 1,932,184

WEEKLY. Best-selling listings journal, having held its position as the market leader among broadcast listings magazines following deregulation in 1992.

Features *Michelle Dickson* Detailed BBC, ITV, Channel 4 and satellite television and radio listings in this magazine are accompanied by interviews and feature material relevant to the week's output. Ninety-five per cent of this is provided by freelance writers, but the topicality of the pieces means close consultation with editors is essential. Unlikely to use unsolicited material, but do take up writers of interest to work on future projects.

RAIL

Apex House, Oundle Road,
Peterborough PE2 9NP
☎ 0733 898100 ext. 6949   Fax 0733 894472

Owner *EMAP Apex Publications*
Editor *Murray Brown*
Circulation 36,476

FOUNDED 1981 FORTNIGHTLY magazine dedicated to modern railway. News and features, and topical newsworthy events. Unsolicited mss welcome. Approach by phone with ideas. Not interested in personal journey reminiscences. No fiction.

Features By arrangement with the editor. Traction-related subjects of interest. Maximum 2000 words.
Payment varies/negotiable.

News Any news item welcomed. Maximum 1000 words.
Payment varies (up to £100 per 1000 words).

The Railway Magazine

King's Reach Tower, Stamford Street,
London SE1 9LS
☎ 071-261 5533/5821   Fax 071-261 5269

Owner *IPC Magazines Ltd*
Editor *Peter Kelly*
Circulation 36,000

FOUNDED 1897. MONTHLY. Articles, photos and short news stories of a topical nature, covering modern railways, steam preservation and railway history welcome. Maximum 2000 words, with sketch maps of routes, etc., where appropriate. Unsolicited mss welcome. Maximum 2000 words.
Payment negotiable.

Rambling Today

1-5 Wandsworth Road, London SW8 2XX
☎ 071-582 6878   Fax 071-587 3799

Owner *Ramblers' Association*
Editor *Linda Hart*
Circulation 89,000

QUARTERLY. Official magazine of the Ramblers' Association, available to members only. Unsolicited mss welcome. S.a.e. required for return.

Features Freelance features are invited on any aspect of walking in Britain and abroad. 900–1300 words, preferably with good photographs.
Payment about £80 per 1000 words.

Reader's Digest

Berkeley Square House, Berkeley Square,
London W1X 6AB
☎071-629 8144   Fax 071-408 0748

Owner *Reader's Digest Association Ltd*
Editor *Russell Twisk*
Circulation 1.6 million

In theory, a good market for general interest features of around 2500 words. However, 'a tiny proportion' comes from freelance writers, all of which are specially commissioned. Currently trying to toughen up its image with a move into investigative journalism. Opportunities exist for short humorous contributions to regular features — 'Life's Like That', 'Humour in Uniform'.
Payment £150.

Record Collector

43–45 St Mary's Road, Ealing, London W5 5RQ
☎081-579 1082   Fax 081-566 2024

Owner *Johnny Dean*
Editor *Peter Doggett*

FOUNDED 1979. MONTHLY. Detailed, well-researched articles welcome on any aspect of record collecting or any collectable artist in the field of popular music (1950s–1990s), with complete discographies where appropriate. Unsolicited mss welcome. Approach with ideas by phone.
Payment negotiable.

Red Rose Magazine

48 Hall Carr Road, Rossendale,
Lancashire BB4 6AW
☎0706 216380

Owner *Millgate Publishing Ltd*
Editor *Nicholas Dunnachie*
Circulation 4000 +

FOUNDED 1989. BI-MONTHLY 'parochial' magazine published by a small publishing company. Interested in articles (maximum 2000 words) on the history and heritage of East Lancashire, particularly the Rossendale Valley.
Payment negotiable.

Report

AMMA, 7 Northumberland Street,
London WC2N 5DA
☎071-930 6441   Fax 071-930 1359

Owner *Assistant Masters and Mistresses Association*
Editor *Julia Hagedorn*
Circulation 131,000

FOUNDED 1978. EIGHT ISSUES YEARLY during academic terms. Contributions welcome. All submissions should go directly to the editor. Articles should be no more than 800 words and must be of practical interest to the classroom teacher.

Resident Abroad

108 Clerkenwell Road, London EC1M 5SA
☎071-251 9321   Fax 071-251 4686

Owner *Financial Times*
Editor *William Essex*
Circulation 17,919

FOUNDED 1979. MONTHLY magazine aimed at British expatriates. Unsolicited mss welcome, if suitable.

Features of up to 1500 words on finance, property, employment opportunities and other topics likely to appeal to readership, such as living conditions in countries with substantial expatriate population.

Fiction Rarely published, but exceptional, relevant stories (no longer than 1000 words) might be considered.
Payment £120 per 1000 words.

The RIBA Journal

39 Moreland Street, London EC1V 8BB
☎071-251 5885   Fax 071-253 1085

Owner *RIBA Magazines Ltd*
Editor *Richard Wilcock*
Circulation 28,322

MONTHLY journal of Royal Institute of British Architects, incorporating *RIBA Interiors*.

Features Specialist articles on architecture, interiors and matters of practice. Maximum 2000 words.
Payment £120 per 1000 words.

Riding

Corner House, Foston, Grantham,
Lincolnshire NG32 3JU
☎0400 82032   Fax 0400 82275

Owner *Scott Publications Ltd*
Editor *Helen Scott*
Circulation 34,000

Aimed at a mostly adult, horse-owning audience, namely the serious leisure rider. Most of the writers on *Riding* are freelance but feature opportunities are limited as regular columnists take up much of the magazine. New and authoritative writers always welcome.
Payment negotiable.

Royal Dempster's

The Publishing House, Highbury Station Road,
London N1 1SE
☎071-226 2222   Fax 071-226 1255

Owner *Harrington Kilbride*
Editor *Nigel Dempster*
Circulation 50,000

FOUNDED 1987. BI-ANNUAL. Royalty and gossip
magazine. Unsolicited mss and ideas in writing
welcome. Send short synopsis of feature ideas with
s.a.e. Interested in anything gossipy/humorous
about 'the season'. Royalty features must be topical, not dated/historical. Maximum 1000 words.
Payment £130 per 1000 words.

Rugby Leaguer

Martland Mill, Martland Mill Lane,
Wigan WN5 0LX
☎0942 214004   Fax 0942 214004

Owner *Lancashire Publications Ltd*
Editor *John Huxley*
Circulation 15,000

FOUNDED 1949. WEEKLY. Complete coverage of all
aspects of rugby league. Unsolicited mss welcome.
Approach in writing with ideas. Not interested in
match coverage reports. Occasional personality
profiles and special issues. Maximum 800 words.
Payment NUJ rates.

Rugby World & Post

Chiltern House, 17 College Avenue,
Maidenhead SL6 6BX
☎0628 776433   Fax 0628 39519

Owner *Rugby Publishing Ltd*
Editor *Nigel Starmer-Smith*
Circulation 46,000

MONTHLY. Features of special rugby interest only.
Unsolicited contributions welcome but s.a.e. essential for return of material. Prior approach by phone
or in writing preferred.

Running Magazine

67-71 Goswell Road, London EC1V 7EN
☎071-410 9410/250 1881   Fax 071-410 9440

Owner *Stonehart Leisure Magazines*
Editor *Nick Troop*
Circulation 45,430

Regular freelance contributors are used. Some
scope perhaps for new outside writers but specialist knowledge is essential for advice features: —
'we would never publish a 'how-to' feature from

someone without expert knowledge'. Personal accounts from readers and personal experience running stories welcome.

Saga Magazine

The Saga Building, Middelburg Square, Folkestone,
Kent CT20 1AZ
☎0303 857523   Fax 0303 220391

Owner *Saga Publishing Ltd*
Editor *Paul Bach*
Circulation 650,000

FOUNDED 1984. TEN ISSUES YEARLY. '*Saga Magazine*
sets out to celebrate the role of older people in
society. It reflects their achievements, promotes
their skills, protects their interests, and campaigns
on their behalf. A warm personal approach, addressing the readership in an up-beat and positive
manner required.' It has a hard core of celebrated
commentators/writers (e.g. Brian Redhead) as
regular contributors and there is limited scope for
well-written features — good-quality, colour transparencies enhance acceptance chances. Subjects
of interest include achievement, hobbies, finance,
food, wine, social comment, motoring, fitness, diet,
etc. Length 1000-1200 words (maximum 1600).
Payment 'very competitive'.

Sailplane and Gliding

281 Queen Edith's Way, Cambridge CB1 4NH
☎0223 247725   Fax 0223 413793

Owner *British Gliding Association*
Editor *Gillian Bryce-Smith*
Circulation 8400

FOUNDED 1930. BI-MONTHLY for gliding enthusiasts.
A specialised magazine with very few opportunities
for freelancers.
No payment.

Sales and Marketing Director

Nat West House, 31 Upper George Street, Luton,
Bedfordshire LU1 2RD
☎0582 456767   Fax 0582 453640

Owner *ISE Publications Ltd*
Editor *Elsa Sharp*
Circulation 12,000

MONTHLY. Unsolicited mss welcome, provided they
are relevant to senior sales and marketing management. Best approach in writing with an idea.

Features Sales techniques, training, technology,
modern management practices, etc. No fiction.
Payment negotiable.

Sales and Marketing Management

Nat West House, 31 Upper George Street, Luton,
Bedfordshire LU1 2RD
☎0582 456767   Fax 0582 453640

Owner *ISE Publications Ltd*
Editor *Elsa Sharp*
Circulation 14,000

MONTHLY. Unsolicited mss welcome on topics
relevant to sales and marketing management. Prospective contributors are best advised to make
initial contact in writing and to present other
published work where possible.

Features Sales techniques, training, technology,
modern management practice, etc. Maximum 2000
words. No fiction.
Payment negotiable.

Sales Direction

Duke House, 37 Duke Street, London W1M 5DF
☎071-486 8591   Fax 071-224 1765

Owner *Sales Direction Magazine Ltd*
Editor *Nigel Ambrose*
Circulation 22,621

FOUNDED 1986. MONTHLY. Unsolicited mss welcome as long as they are relevant to sales
management/business readership. Approach by
phone or in writing with an idea.

Features Lifestyle features up to 1000 words, and
interesting sports pursuits relevant to business
people.

Interviews with top sales directors and business
people in the public eye. Prior discussion essential.
1500–2000 words.

News Maximum 300 words.
Payment £100 per 1000 words.

Salisbury Review

33 Canonbury Park South, London N1 2JW
☎071-226 7791

Owner *Claridge Press*
Editor *Roger Scruton*
Circulation 1500

FOUNDED 1982. QUARTERLY magazine of conservative thought. Editorials and features from a right-
wing viewpoint. Unsolicited material welcome.

Features Maximum 5000 words.

Reviews Maximum 1000 words.
No payment.

Scotland on Sunday Magazine

See **National Newspapers**

Scotland's Runner

113 St George's Road, Glasgow G3 6JA
☎041-332 5738   Fax 041-332 9880

Owner *ScotRun Publications*
Editor *Alan Campbell*
Circulation 10,000

FOUNDED 1986. MONTHLY with features on athletics, fitness, nutrition and health. Unsolicited mss
welcome. Approach in writing with ideas.

The Scots Magazine

D. C. Thomson & Co. Ltd, 2 Albert Square,
Dundee DD1 9QJ
☎0382 23131 ext. 4023   Fax 0382 25511

Owner *D. C. Thomson & Co. Ltd*
Editor *John Rundle*
Circulation 82,000

FOUNDED 1739. MONTHLY. Covers a wide field of
Scottish interests ranging from personalities to
wildlife, climbing, reminiscence, history and folklore. Outside contributions welcome.
Payment by arrangement.

The Scottish Farmer

The Plaza Tower, The Plaza, East
Kilbride G74 1LW
☎03552 46444   Fax 03552 63013

Owner *George Outram & Co. Ltd*
Editor *Angus MacDonald*
Circulation 24,615

FOUNDED 1893. WEEKLY. Farmer's magazine covering most aspects of Scottish agriculture. Unsolicited
mss welcome. Approach with ideas in writing.

Features *Angus MacDonald* Technical articles on
agriculture or farming units. 1000–2000 words.
£8 per 100 words/£20 per photo.

News *John Duckworth* Factual news about farming
developments, political, personal and technological. Maximum 800 words.
Payment £8 per 100 words.

Weekend Family Pages Rural and craft topics.
Payment £8 per 1000 words.

Scottish Field

The Plaza Tower, East Kilbride, Glasgow G74 1LW
☎03552 46444   Fax 03552 63013

Owner *Outram Magazines Ltd*
Editor *Joe Stirling*
Circulation 20,000

FOUNDED 1903. MONTHLY. Unsolicited mss welcome but writers should study the magazine first.

Features *Joe Stirling* Articles of breadth and authority with a Scottish dimension and good visual impact. Maximum 1200 words.
Payment 'above average'.

Fiction *Joe Stirling* One short story monthly by Scottish author, or on well-defined Scottish subject. Maximum 1400 words.
Payment 'above average'.

Scottish Football Today
15 Woodland Terrace, Glasgow G3 6DF
☏ 041-332 8247   Fax 041-331 2652

Owner *Business Information Publications*
Editor *Alan Burnett*
Circulation 20,000

FOUNDED 1985. MONTHLY. General Scottish football news and features. Unsolicited mss welcome but initial approach in writing preferred.

Scottish Golf Magazine
113 St George's Road, Glasgow G3 6JA
☏ 041-332 5738   Fax 041-332 9880

Owner *ScotRun Publications*
Editor *Alan Campbell*
Circulation 10,000

FOUNDED 1986. MONTHLY. Unsolicited mss welcome. Approach in writing with ideas.

Scottish Home & Country
42A Heriot Row, Edinburgh EH3 6ES
☏ 031-225 1934

Owner *Scottish Women's Rural Institutes*
Editor *Stella Roberts*
Circulation 18,000

FOUNDED 1924. MONTHLY. Scottish or rural related issues. Unsolicited mss welcome but reading time may be from 2-3 months. Commissions are rare and tend to go to established contributors only.

Scouting Magazine
Baden Powell House, Queen's Gate,
London SW7 5JS
☏ 071-584 7030   Fax 071-581 9953

Owner *The Scout Association*
Editor *David Easton*

Circulation 36,000

MONTHLY magazine for adults connected to or interested in the Scouting movement. Interested in scouting-related features only. No fiction.
Payment by negotiation.

Screen
The John Logie Baird Centre, University of Glasgow, Glasgow G12 8QQ
☏ 041-330 5035   Fax 041-330 4808

Owner *The John Logie Baird Centre*
Editors *Annette Kuhn/John Caughie/Simon Frith/ Norman King/Sandra Kemp*
Circulation 2500

QUARTERLY academic journal of film and television studies for a readership ranging from undergraduates to media professionals. There are no specific qualifications for acceptance of articles. Freelancers are welcome to send in mss for consideration. Check the magazine's style and market in the first instance.

Screen International
7 Swallow Place, 249-259 Regent Street,
London W1R 7AA
☏ 071-491 9484   Fax 071-355 3337

Owner *International Thomson Business Publishing*
Editor *Oscar Moore*

Trade paper of the film, video and television industries. Expert freelance writers are occasionally used in all areas. No unsolicited mss. Approach with ideas in writing.

Sea Breezes
202 Cotton Exchange Building, Old Hall Street,
Liverpool L3 9LA
☏ 051-236 3935

Owner *Kinglish Ltd*
Editor *Mr C. H. Milsom*
Circulation 18,500

FOUNDED 1919. MONTHLY. Covering virtually everything relating to ships and seamen of a non-technical nature. Unsolicited mss welcome; they should be thoroughly researched and accompanied by relevant photographs. No fiction, poetry, or anything which 'smacks of the romance of the sea'.

Features Factual tales of ships, seamen and the sea, Royal or Merchant Navy, sail or power, nautical history, shipping company histories, epic voyages, etc. Length 1000-4000 words. 'The most readily acceptable work will be that which shows it

is clearly the result of first-hand experience or the product of extensive and accurate research.'
Payment £5 per page (about 640 words).

She Magazine

National Magazine House, 72 Broadwick Street, London W1V 2BP
☎071-439 5000   Fax 071-439 5350

Owner *National Magazine Co. Ltd*
Editor *Linda Kelsey*
Circulation 283,731

Glossy MONTHLY for women, which concentrates on talking to the thirtysomething woman and modern mother, addressing her needs as an individual, a partner and a parent. Talks to its readers in an intelligent, humorous and sympathetic way. Features should be about 1500 words long. Approach with ideas in writing. No unsolicited material.
Payment NUJ rates.

Shoot Magazine

King's Reach Tower, Stamford Street, London SE1 9LS
☎071-261 6287   Fax 071-261 6019

Owner *IPC Magazines Ltd*
Managing Editor *Peter Stewart*
Circulation 170,000

FOUNDED 1969. WEEKLY football magazine. No unsolicited mss. Present ideas for news, features or colour photo-features to the editor in writing.

Features Hard-hitting, topical and off-beat. 450-1500 words.

News Items welcome, especially exclusive gossip and transfer speculation. Maximum 150 words.
Payment NUJ rates (negotiable for exclusive material).

Shooting and Conservation

Marford Mill, Rossett, Wrexham, Clwyd LL11 0HL
☎0244 570881   Fax 0244 571678

Owner *BASC*
Editor *Mike Barnes*
Circulation 110,000

QUARTERLY. Unsolicited mss welcome.

Features/Fiction Good articles and stories on shooting, conservation and related areas are always sought. Maximum 2000 words.
Payment negotiable.

Shooting News & Country Weekly

Yelverton Business Park, Yelverton, Devon PL20 7PE
☎0822 855281   Fax 0822 855372

Owner *Vic Gardner*
Editor *Jayne Willcocks*

FOUNDED 1982. WEEKLY. Unsolicited material welcome. A list of special editions and subjects covered by the magazine is available on request. No fiction.

Features On any field sport topic, and no longer than 1500 words.

News Items considered.
Payment rates available on request.

Shooting Times & Country

10 Sheet Street, Windsor, Berkshire SL4 1BG
☎0753 856061   Fax 0753 859652

Owner *Associated Newspapers Holdings*
Editor *Tim O'Nions*
Circulation 40,623

FOUNDED 1882. WEEKLY. Covers shooting, fishing and related countryside topics. Unsolicited mss considered. Maximum 1100 words.
Payment negotiable.

Shropshire Magazine

77 Wyle Cop, Shrewsbury, Shropshire SY1 1UT
☎0743 362175

Owner *Leopard Press Ltd*
Editor *Pam Green*

FOUNDED 1950. MONTHLY. Unsolicited mss welcome but ideas in writing preferred.

Features Personalities, topical items, historical (e.g. family) of Shropshire, also general interest: homes, weddings, antiques, food, holidays, etc. Maximum 2000 words.
Payment negotiable but modest.

Sight & Sound

British Film Institute, 21 Stephen Street, London W1P 1PL
☎071-255 1444   Fax 071-436 2327

Owner *British Film Institute*
Editor *Philip Dodd*

FOUNDED 1932. MONTHLY. Topical and critical articles on the cinema of any country; book reviews; reviews of every film theatrically released in London; reviews of every video released; regular columns from the USA and Europe. 1000-5000

words. Relevant photographs appreciated. Unsolicited material welcome. Approach in writing with ideas.
Payment by arrangement.

The Sign
St Mary's Works, St Mary's Plain,
Norwich NR3 3BH
☎ 0603 615995   Fax 0603 624483

Owner *Chansitor Publications Ltd*
Editor *Paul Handley*
Circulation 190,000

FOUNDED 1905. MONTHLY inset for Church of England parish magazines. Unsolicited mss welcome.

News/Features Maximum 300 words.
Payment negotiable.

Signature
3rd Floor, Greater London House, Hampstead Road, London NW1 7QQ
☎ 071-388 3171   Fax 071-383 7570

Owner *Maxwell International Contract Publishing*
Editor *Jackie Oliver*
Circulation 150,000

RELAUNCHED 1986. The magazine for Diners Club Cardholders, issued SIX TIMES YEARLY. Unsolicited mss rarely used, but written suggestions welcome.

Features Most of the main features – profiles and travel – are commissioned from regular writers. Maximum 2000 words.
Payment negotiable.

Ski Survey
118 Eaton Square, London SW1W 9AF
☎ 071-245 1033   Fax 071-245 1258

Owner *Ski Club of Great Britain*
Editor *Elisabeth Hussey*
Circulation 26,100

FOUNDED 1903. FIVE ISSUES YEARLY. Commissions only. No unsolicited mss.

The Skier (incl. **Ski Magazine**)
26c London Road, Sevenoaks, Kent TN13 1AP
☎ 0732 743031/2   Fax 0732 743029

Owner *Penfame Ltd*
Editor *Frank Baldwin*
Circulation 30,000

SEASONAL (September–May). SEVEN ISSUES YEARLY. Outside contributions welcome.

Features Various topics covered including race reports, resort reports, fashion, equipment update, dry slope, school news, new products, health and safety. Crisp, tight, informative copy of 1000 words or less preferred.

News All aspects of skiing news covered.
Payment negotiable.

Slimming
Victory House, 14 Leicester Place,
London WC2H 7QP
☎ 071-437 9011   Fax 071-434 0656

Owner *EMAP Elan Publications*
Editor *Kandy Shepherd*
Circulation 250,000

FOUNDED 1969. TEN ISSUES YEARLY. Basically a scientific magazine with most of its material written by staff. Freelance opportunities are very few indeed. There is some scope for first-person experiences of weight control/loss, but only a small number of those received prove suitable. It is best to approach with an idea in writing.
Payment negotiable.

Small Press World
11 Ashburnham Road, Bedford MK40 1DX
☎ 0234 211606

Owner *Small Press Group of Great Britain*
Editor *John Nicholson*

QUARTERLY. Began life in 1987 as the monthly newsletter of the **Small Press Group of Great Britain**. In September 1989 it took on a new format (A3 folded to A4), as a magazine for the general small press world. Its more recent transfiguration into a glossy quarterly magazine, with new title (formerly *Small Press Monthly*) happened in spring 1992. Now the flagship of small presses in Britain and elsewhere. Feature articles, regular department (listings, letters, news from the Group, international small press activity, events affecting small presses, etc.), and mini-magazines: columns on many aspects of small press (mail art, fine press, weird, avantgarde, magic and mystic, local history, etc.). Ideas, news, letters and listings welcome.
No payment.

Smallholder (and Small Farmer)
Hook House, Wimblington March,
Cambridgeshire PE15 0QL
☎ 0354 741182   Fax 0354 741182

Owner *Smallholder Publications*
Editor *Liz Wright*
Circulation 18,000

FOUNDED 1982. MONTHLY. Outside contributions welcome. Send for sample magazine and editorial schedule before submitting anything. Follow up with samples of work to the editor so that style can be assessed for suitability.

Features New writers always welcome, but must have high level of technical expertise — 'not textbook stuff'. 750-900 words (maximum 1500). *Payment* negotiable.

News All agricultural and rural news welcome. 200-300 words (maximum 500). *Payment* £10 per 1000 words.

Smash Hits
52-55 Carnaby Street, London W1V 1PF
☎071-437 8050   Fax 071-494 0851

Owner *EMAP Metro Publications*
Editor *Mike Soutar*
Circulation 391,000

FOUNDED 1979. FORTNIGHTLY. Top of the mid-teen market. Unsolicited mss are not accepted, but prospective contributors may approach in writing with ideas.

Snooker Scene
Cavalier House, 202 Hagley Road, Edgbaston, Birmingham B16 9PQ
☎021-454 2931   Fax 021-452 1822

Owner *Everton's News Agency*
Editor *Clive Everton*
Circulation 16,000

FOUNDED 1971. MONTHLY. No unsolicited mss. Approach in writing with an idea.

Solicitors Journal
21-27 Lamb's Conduit Street, London WC1N 3NJ
☎071-242 2548   Fax 071-430 1729

Owner *Longman Group UK Ltd*
Editor *Marie Staunton*
Circulation 5400

FOUNDED 1856. WEEKLY professional magazine for lawyers. Unsolicited mss welcome. Approach by phone with ideas.

Features Current law or legal practice, and topics of general interest to the profession. *Payment* £50 per 1000 words.

News Mostly commissioned or written in-house but genuine exclusives always welcome. *Payment* negotiable.

Somerset & Avon Life
See **Devon Life**

Somerset Magazine
23 Market Street, Crewkerne, Somerset TA18 7JU
☎0460 78000   Fax 0460 76718

Owner *Smart Print Publications Ltd*
Editor *Jack Rayfield*
Circulation 8000

FOUNDED 1990. MONTHLY magazine with features on any subject of interest (historical, geographical, arts, crafts) to people living in Somerset. Length 1000-1500 words. Unsolicited mss welcome but initial approach in writing preferred. *Payment* negotiable.

The Spectator
56 Doughty Street, London WC1N 2LL
☎071-405 1706   Fax 071-242 0603

Owner *The Spectator (1828) Ltd*
Editor *Dominic Lawson*
Circulation 39,000

FOUNDED 1828. WEEKLY political and literary magazine. Prospective contributors should write in the first instance to the relevant editor. Unsolicited mss welcome, but over 20 are received every week and few are used.

Arts *Jenny Naipaul*

Books *Mark Amory*
Payment 'small'.

Sport and Leisure Magazine
The Sports Council, 16 Upper Woburn Place, London WC1H 0QP
☎071-388 1277   Fax 071-383 5740

Owner *The Sports Council*
Editor *Louise Fyfe*
Circulation 7000

FOUNDED 1949. BI-MONTHLY. Covering sports development, policies and politics, plus new ideas and innovations in the world of sport. Unsolicited mss welcome. Approach by phone with ideas.

News/Features On any of the areas mentioned above. Features should be 750-1000 words. *Payment* £100 per 1000 words.

Reviews Book and video. Maximum 250 words. *Payment* £25.

The Sporting Life
Orbit House, 1 New Fetter Lane,
London EC4A 1AR
☎ 071-822 3291   Fax 071-583 3885

Owner *Mirror Group Newspapers Ltd*
Editor *Mike Gallemore*
Circulation 95,181

DAILY newspaper of the horse-racing world. Always on the look-out for specialised, well-informed racing writers — not necessarily established sports writers. No unsolicited mss. Phone or write with an idea in first instance. 'The talented will be taken up and used again.'

Features *Alastair Down*

Sporting Life Weekender
Orbit House, 1 New Fetter Lane,
London EC4A 1AR
☎ 071-822 2089   Fax 071-583 3885

Owner *Mirror Group Newspapers*
Editor *Phil Lamphee*
Circulation 40,000

FOUNDED 1983. WEEKLY. Prospective contributors should write with ideas in first instance as no articles are published before discussion.
Payment NUJ rates.

Squash Player Magazine
67-71 Goswell Road, London EC1V 7EN
☎ 071-250 1881/410 9410   Fax 071-410 9440

Owner *Stoneheart Leisure Magazines*
Editor *Nick Troop*
Circulation *c.* 10,000

MONTHLY. Unsolicited mss welcome; sample material and synopsis preferred in the first instance.

Features Instructive club and commercial news.

News Tournament reports.

Staffordshire Life
Hourds Publishing Centre, Derby Street,
Stafford ST16 2DT
☎ 0785 57700   Fax 0785 53287

Owner *Hourds Publications Ltd*
Editor *Philip Thurlow-Craig*
Circulation 14,000

FOUNDED 1982. BI-MONTHLY county magazine devoted to Staffordshire, its environs and people. Contributions welcome. Approach in writing with ideas.

Features Maximum 2500 words.

Fashion Copy must be supported by photographs.
Payment NUJ rates.

Stage and Television Today
47 Bermondsey Street, London SE1 3XT
☎ 071-403 1818   Fax 071-403 1418

Owner *Carson and Comerford Ltd*
Editor *Jeremy Jehu*
Circulation 42,000

FOUNDED 1880. WEEKLY. No unsolicited mss. Prospective contributors should write with ideas in the first instance. Occasional feature suggestions from freelancers are considered.

Features Preference is given to material with a business or financial orientation rather than personal pieces or interviews. Maximum 1200 words.
Payment £100 per 1000 words.

News News stories from outside London are always welcome. Maximum 300 words.
Payment £100 per 1000 words.

Stamps
Newspaper House, Tannery Lane, Penketh,
Cheshire WA5 2UD
☎ 0925 724234   Fax 0925 722617

Owner *CGB Publishing*
Consultant Editor *Richard Beith*

MONTHLY. Specialist philately magazine which claims both to encourage the novice and satisfy the expert collector. Outlines of any proposed article to be submitted in the first instance. Articles must have a strong philatelic or postal history content, with appropriate illustrations.

Features All aspects of philately. Maximum 2000 words.
Payment £30 per 1000 words.

Stand Magazine
179 Wingrove Road, Newcastle upon
Tyne NE4 9DA
☎ 091-273 3280

Editors *Jon Silkin/Lorna Tracy*
Circulation 4500

FOUNDED 1952. QUARTERLY. Unsolicited short stories and poetry welcome. Nothing else. Contributions must be accompanied by s.a.e. or international reply coupons, as appropriate.

Fiction *Lorna Tracy* Any previously unpublished work considered. Preferably under 8000 words, but longer also considered.
Payment £30 per 1000 words.

Poetry *Jon Silkin* Unpublished work only. No specification on length. Biennial short story competition (see entry **Prizes**).
Payment £30 per poem.

Staple Magazine

Gilderoy East, Matlock Bath, Derbyshire DE4 3PD
☎0629 583867

Editor *Bob Windsor*

Well-established poetry magazine. Contributions (poetry and fiction) welcome. Runs a biennial open competition (see **Prizes**).
Payment£5–£10 each contribution.

Storm: New Writing from East and West

PO Box 1911, London W11 1SE

Editor *Joanna Labon*

FOUNDED 1990. Distributed by **Jonathan Cape**. QUARTERLY magazine publishing international literary fiction of a high standard in English translation. Unsolicited mss not welcome, but ideas expressed in a short letter will always be considered.
Payment negotiable.

The Strad

4th Floor, Centro House, Mandela Street, London NW1 0DU
☎071-387 3848   Fax 071-388 8532

Owner *Orpheus Publications*
Editor *Helen Wallace*
Circulation 10,000

FOUNDED 1890. MONTHLY for classical string musicians, makers and enthusiasts. Unsolicited mss welcome.

Features Profiles of string players, composers and musical instruments. Maximum 3000 words.

Reviews *Rachel Connolly*
Payment £50 per 1000 words.

Suffolk Life

Barn Acre House, Saxtead Green, Suffolk IP13 9QJ
☎0728 685832   Fax 0728 685842

Owner *Today Magazines Ltd*
Editor *Brenda Davis*
Circulation 40,000

FOUNDED 1989. MONTHLY. General interest, local stories, historical, personalities, wine, travel, food.

Unsolicited mss welcome. Approach by phone or in writing with ideas. Not interested in anything which does not relate specifically to East Anglia. Sister publications run jointly include *Norfolk Life* and *Essex Life*.

Features *Kevin Davis* Maximum 1700 words, with photos.

News *Brenda Davis* Maximum 1000 words, with photos.

Other *Margaret McAlpine* Special pages. Study the magazines for guidelines. Maximum 1700 words.
Payment £20 (news); £25 (other).

Sunday Magazine

See **National Newspapers (News of the World)**

Sunday Express Magazine

See **National Newspapers (Sunday Express)**

Sunday Mail Magazine

See **National Newspapers (Sunday Mail, Glasgow)**

Sunday Mirror Magazine

See **National Newspapers (Sunday Mirror)**

Sunday Post Magazine

See **National Newspapers (Sunday Post, Glasgow)**

Sunday Times Magazine

See **National Newspapers (The Sunday Times)**

Sunk Island Review

PO Box 74, Lincoln LN1 1QG
☎0522 520645

Owner *Sunk Island Publishing*
Editor *Michael Blackburn*
Circulation 1000

FOUNDED 1989. BI-ANNUAL (summer and winter). A pocket-sized paperback of new fiction, poetry, articles, translations, graphics. Some work is commissioned by the editor but unsolicited material is still welcome.

Lives A commissioned piece, written annually, on the effect of a particular place or environment on someone's life and work.

Features Issues of a cultural and social nature considered. No specification on length. *Payment* £10 per 1000 words.

Fiction Short stories and excerpts from novels welcome. No romance or historical fiction, though. Keen to include work of an experimental nature, as well as quality science fiction. *Payment* £10 per 1000 words.

Special Pages Poetry welcome as are short plays for stage or radio, and translations from contemporary writers, particularly from the continent. Monochrome graphics and cartoons considered though these tend to be commissioned. Some scope perhaps for reviews but again these are generally handled in-house. *Payment* £10 per poem or page.

Surrey County Magazine

PO Box 154, South Croydon, Surrey CR2 0XA
☎081–657 8568   Fax 081–657 8568

Owner *Thames Press*
Editor *Theo Spring*
Circulation 8500

FOUNDED 1970. MONTHLY. County matters for Surrey dwellers. News, views, history and comment. No travel, or matters relating outside the county. Unsolicited mss welcome. Approach by phone or in writing with ideas.

Survival and Outdoor Techniques

89 East Hill, Colchester, Essex CO1 2QN
☎0206 865340   Fax 0206 871537

Owner *Aceville Publications Ltd*
Editor *Helen Stuttle*
Assistant Editor *Jerome Smail*

MONTHLY publication on outdoor survival techniques. Unsolicited mss welcome from experienced survival writers. *Payment* £20 per 1000 words; £5 per photograph.

Swimming Times

Harold Fern House, Derby Square,
Loughborough LE11 0AL
☎0509 234433   Fax 0509 235049

Owner *Amateur Swimming Association*
Editor *K. T. Glendenning*
Circulation 16,800

FOUNDED 1923. MONTHLY about competitive swimming and associated subjects. Unsolicited mss welcome.

Features Technical articles on swimming, water polo, diving or synchronised swimming. Length and payment negotiable.

The Tablet

1 King Street Cloisters, Clifton Walk,
London W6 0QZ
☎081–748 8484   Fax 081–748 1550

Owner *The Tablet Publishing Co Ltd*
Editor *John Wilkins*
Circulation 16,500

FOUNDED 1840. WEEKLY. Quality Roman Catholic magazine featuring articles of interest to concerned laity and clergy. Unsolicited material welcome (1500 words) if relevant to magazine's style and market. All approaches should be made in writing. *Payment* from about £50.

Take a Break

Shirley House, 25–27 Camden Road,
London NW1 9LL
☎071–284 0909   Fax 071–284 3778

Owner *H. Bauer*
Editor *John Dale*
Circulation 1.3 million

FOUNDED 1990. WEEKLY. True-life feature magazine. Approach with ideas in writing.

News/Features Always on the look-out for good, true-life stories. Maximum 1200 words. *Payment* negotiable.

Fiction Sharp, succinct stories which are well told and often with a twist at the end. All categories, provided it is relevant to the magazine's style and market. Maximum 1000 words. *Payment* negotiable.

Taste

3rd Floor, 3 Richmond Buildings, off Dean Street,
London W1V 5EA
☎071–734 3430   Fax 071–734 3136

Owner *Drew Smith*
Editor *Drew Smith*

Specialist food and drink magazine which has survived several changes of ownership since its launch in the mid-1980s. Commissions tend to go to established food writers and cooks, except where research of food or cooking styles is seen to be original and breaks new ground. Approach with ideas in writing. No unsolicited mss.

The Tatler
☎ 071-499 9080   Fax 071-409 0451
Owner *Condé Nast Publications Ltd*
Editor *Jane Procter*
Circulation 49,124

Upmarket glossy from the *Vogue* stable. New writers should send in copies of either published work or unpublished material; writers of promise will be taken up. The magazine works largely on a commission basis: they are unlikely to publish unsolicited features, but will ask writers to work to specific projects.

Features *Paul Palmer*

Tees Valley Writer
57 The Avenue, Linthorpe, Middlesbrough,
Cleveland TS5 6QU
☎ 0642 819102
Owner *Management Board of TVW*
Editor *Derek Gregory*
Circulation 2000

FOUNDED 1990. BI-ANNUAL (June and December). Short stories, poetry, articles, graphics, interviews and reviews. Unsolicited mss and ideas in writing welcome. Also features regular competitions (short story, poetry and articles).

Features Articles on Tees Valley region especially welcome but must be of high quality. Maximum 2500 words.
Payment about £20 per article.

Fiction Short stories.
Payment about £20.

Other Poetry, both experimental and traditional.
Payment about £8 per printed page.

Telegraph Magazine
See **National Newspapers (The Daily Telegraph)**

Television Week
33-39 Bowling Green Lane, London EC1R 0DA
☎ 071-837 1212   Fax 071-278 4003
Owner *EMAP Media*
Editor *Richard Gold*
Circulation 13,289

FOUNDED 1988. WEEKLY. No unsolicited mss. Approach in writing in first instance.

Features *Richard Gold* UK and international stories on all aspects of TV broadcast, production, distribution, technology and business. Average

1800 words (maximum 2000). Contact by phone to discuss ideas.
Payment £135 per 1000 words.

The Tennis Times
Ludgate House, 160 Tower Bridge Road,
London SE1 3NB
☎ 071-407 9111   Fax 071-378 1762

Editor *Ryk Richardson*

All matters relating to tennis and its world, plus badminton and squash. Unsolicited contributions welcome. Initial approach in writing preferred.

Features Player profiles, product news and events. Approach the editor with ideas.

News Send factual details — may generate an article.

Fiction occasionally 'if amusing'.

Tennis World
The Spendlove Centre, Enstone Road, Charlbury,
Oxon OX7 3PQ
☎ 0608 811446   Fax 0608 811380

Owner *Presswatch Ltd*
Editor *Alastair McIver*
Circulation 10,502

FOUNDED 1969. MONTHLY. Unsolicited mss welcome.

Features Any ideas on tennis features or tennis personalities are welcome. Maximum 1000 words.
Payment £75-150.

Text
Orchard House, Bollington Cross, Near
Macclesfield, Cheshire SK10 5EG
☎ 0625 573928

Owner *The Textile Society*
Editor *Brenda King*
Circulation 500

FOUNDED 1980. BIANNUAL. The Textile Society's magazine for the study of textile art, design and history. Any textile-related theme, techniques, issues, events and reviews (books and exhibitions). Unsolicited mss welcome. Maximum 3000 words. Approach with ideas in writing.
No payment.

Theologia Cambrensis
Church in Wales Centre, Woodland Place, Penarth,
South Glamorgan
☎ 0222 705278   Fax 0222 387835

Owner *The Church in Wales*
Editor *John Herbert*

FOUNDED 1988. THRICE YEARLY. Concerned exclusively with theology and news of theological interest. Includes religious poetry, letters and book reviews (provided they have a scholarly bias). No secular material. Unsolicited mss welcome. Approach in writing with ideas.

This England

PO Box 52, Cheltenham,
Gloucestershire GL50 1YQ
☎ 0242 577775   Fax 0242 222034

Owner *This England Ltd*
Editor *Roy Faiers*
Circulation 180,000

Published FOUR TIMES YEARLY, with a strong overseas readership. Celebration of England and all things English: famous people, natural beauty, towns and villages, history, traditions, customs and legends, crafts, etc. Generally a rural basis, with the 'Forgetmenots' section publishing readers' recollections and nostalgia. Up to 100 unsolicited pieces received each week. 250–2000 word articles will be considered.
Payment £20 per 1000 words.

Time

Time & Life Building, 153 New Bond Street,
London W1Y 0AA
☎ 071–499 4080   Fax 071–322 1230

Owner *Time Warner, Inc.*
Editor *William Mader* (London Bureau Chief)
Circulation 5.7 million

FOUNDED 1923. WEEKLY current affairs and news magazine. There are no opportunities for freelancers on *Time* as almost all the magazine's content is written by staff members from various bureaux around the world. No unsolicited mss.

Time Out

Tower House, Southampton Street,
London WC2E 7HD
☎ 071–836 4411   Fax 071–836 7118

Publisher *Tony Elliott*
Editor *Simon Mills*
Circulation 90,000

FOUNDED 1968. WEEKLY magazine of news and entertainment in London.

Features *The Editor* 'Usually written by staff writers or commissioned, but it's always worth submitting an idea by phone if particularly apt to the magazine.' Maximum 2500 words.

News *Catherine Pepinster* Despite having a permanent team of staff news writers, sometimes willing to accept contributions from new journalists, 'should their material be relevant to the issue'.

Fiction *Maria Lexton* Occasional creative writing competitions. Details appear in the magazine.
Payment £164 per 1000 words.

The Times Educational Supplement

Priory House, St John's Lane, London EC1M 4BX
☎ 071–253 3000   Fax 071–608 1599

Owner *News International*
Editor *Patricia Rowan*
Circulation 120,000

FOUNDED 1910. WEEKLY. New contributors are welcome, and should phone with ideas for news or features; write for reviews.

Arts and Books *Heather Neill* **Media & Resources** *Gillian Macdonald* Unsolicited reviews are not accepted. Anyone wanting to review should write, sending examples of their work and full details of their academic and professional background to either the literary editor or the media and resources editor. Maximum 1200 words.

Features *Sarah Bayliss* 'Platform': a weekly slot for a well-informed and cogently argued viewpoint, maximum 1200 words; 'Second Opinion': a shorter comment on an issue of the day by somebody well placed to write on the subject, maximum 700 words; 'Features': longer articles on contemporary practical subjects of general interest to the *TES* reader, maximum 1000–1500 words; longer or multi-part features are rarely accepted.
Payment by arrangement.

Special Reports *Joyce Arnold* Subjects covered include: science, travel, music, modern languages, home economics, school visits, primary education, history, geography, mathematics, health, life skills, environmental education, technology, special needs. Articles should relate to current educational practice. Age range covered is primary to sixth form. Maximum 1000–1300 words.
Payment by arrangement.

The Times Educational Supplement Scotland

37 George Street, Edinburgh EH2 2HN
☎ 031–220 1100   Fax 031–220 1616

Owner *Times Newspapers Ltd*
Editor *Willis Pickard*
Circulation 6500

FOUNDED 1965. WEEKLY. Unsolicited mss welcome, but many more are received than can be used.

Features Articles on education in Scotland. Maximum 1500 words.
Payment NUJ rates for NUJ members.

News Items on education in Scotland. Maximum 600 words.

The Times Higher Education Supplement

Priory House, St John's Lane, London EC1M 4BX
☎071-253 3000   Fax 071-608 2349

Owner *Times Supplements Ltd*
Editor *Auriol Stevens*
Circulation 17,845

FOUNDED 1971. WEEKLY. Unsolicited mss are welcome but most articles and *all* book reviews are commissioned. 'In most cases it is better to write, but in the case of news stories it is all right to phone.'
Payment NUJ rates.

Books *Peter Aspden*

Features *Jon Turney* Most articles are commissioned from academics in higher education.

News *David Jobbins* Freelance opportunities very occasionally.

Science *Martin Ince*

Science Books *Robbie Vickers*

The Times Literary Supplement

Priory House, St John's Lane, London EC1M 4BX
☎071-253 3000   Fax 071-251 3424

Owner *News International*
Editor *Ferdinand Mount*
Circulation 30,000

FOUNDED 1902. WEEKLY review of literature. Contributors should approach in writing and be familiar with the general level of writing in the *TLS*.

Literary Discoveries *Alan Jenkins*

Poems *Alan Hollinghurst*

News *Ferdinand Mount* News stories and general articles concerned with literature, publishing and new intellectual developments anywhere in the world. Length by arrangement.
Payment by arrangement.

Titbits

2 Caversham Street, London SW3 4AH
☎071-351 4995   Fax 071-351 4995

Owner *Sport Newspapers Ltd*
Editor *Leonard Holdsworth*
Circulation 150,000

FOUNDED 1895. MONTHLY. Consumer magazine for men covering show business and general interests. Unsolicited mss and ideas in writing welcome. Maximum 3000 words. News, features, particularly photofeatures (colour), and fiction.
Payment negotiable.

Today's Golfer

Bretton Court, Bretton, Peterborough, Cambridgeshire PE3 8DZ
☎0733 264666   Fax 0733 265515

Owner *EMAP Pursuit Publishing*
Editor *Bob Warters*

FOUNDED 1988. MONTHLY. Golf instruction, features, player profiles and news. Unsolicited mss welcome. Approach in writing with ideas. Not interested in instruction material from outside contributors.

Features/News *Martin Vousden* Opinion, player profiles and general golf-related features. Maximum 3000 words. Small interesting news items, oddities and fillers. Maximum 250 words.
Payment £100 per 1000 words.

Today's Runner

Bretton Court, Bretton, Peterborough, Cambridgeshire PE3 8DZ
☎0733 264666   Fax 0733 265515

Owner *EMAP Pursuit Publications*
Editor *Paul Richardson*
Circulation 30,000

FOUNDED 1985. MONTHLY. Instructional articles on running and fitness, plus running-related activities and health.

Features Specialist knowledge an advantage. Opportunities are wide, but approach with idea in first instance.

News Opportunities for people stories, especially if backed up by photographs.

Townswoman

Media Associates, 8 Capitol House, Heigham Street, Norwich NR2 4TE
☎0603 616005   Fax 0603 767397

Owner *Townswomen's Guilds*
Editor *Moira Eagling*
Circulation 34,000

FOUNDED 1933. MONTHLY. No unsolicited mss. Few opportunities as in-house editorial staff are strong.

Traditional Homes

Victory House, 14 Leicester Place,
London WC2H 7BP
☎071-437 9011   Fax 071-434 0656

Owner *EMAP Elan Publications*
Circulation 23,750

FOUNDED 1984. Merged with *Period Homes* in 1988 and with *Traditional Interior Decoration* in 1989. MONTHLY magazine covering conservation, restoration, architecture, antiques and interior design. Unsolicited mss are welcome.
Payment £100 per 1000 words.

Traveller

45–49 Brompton Road, London SW3 1DE
☎071-581 4130   Fax 071-581 1357

Owner *Dr I. M. Wilson*
Editor *Caroline Brandenburger*
Circulation 35,359

FOUNDED 1970. QUARTERLY. Unsolicited mss welcome.

Features Five colour features per issue — copy must be accompanied by good-quality colour transparencies. Contributors' guidelines available with s.a.e., but all articles should be off-beat, independent and travel-based. Maximum 2000 words.
Payment £125 per 1000 words.

Tribune

308 Gray's Inn Road, London WC1X 8DY
☎071-278 0911

Owner *Tribune Publications Ltd*
Editor *Paul Anderson*
Circulation 10,000

Labour's independent WEEKLY. 'We have plenty of opportunities for freelance writers. Miniscule fees may possibly be available for commissioned work only.' Opportunities in features for current affairs pieces with the emphasis on left politics; also reviewing and newswriting. Either send mss in on spec., or ring to discuss an idea.

Reviews *Jeff Lovitt*

Trout Fisherman

Bretton Court, Bretton, Peterborough,
Cambridgeshire PE3 8DZ
☎0733 264666   Fax 0733 265515

Owner *EMAP Pursuit Publications*
Editor *Chris Dawn*
Circulation 44,117

FOUNDED 1977. MONTHLY instructive magazine on trout fishing. Most of the articles are commissioned, but unsolicited mss and quality colour transparencies welcome.

Features Maximum 2500 words.
Payment varies.

True Romances

See **Love Story**

True Story

See **Love Story**

TV Times

King's Reach Tower, Stamford Street,
London SE1 9LS
☎071-261 5000   Fax 071-261 7777

Owner *Reed International*
Editor *Terry Pavey*
Circulation 1,280,505

FOUNDED 1968. WEEKLY magazine of listings and features serving the viewers of independent television, BBC, satellite and radio. Almost no freelance contributions used, except where the writer is known and trusted by the magazine. No unsolicited contributions.

The Universe

1st Floor, St James's Buildings, Oxford Street,
Manchester M1 6FP
☎061-236 8856   Fax 061-236 8530

Owner *Gabriel Communications Ltd*
Editor *Ann Knowles*
Circulation 100,000

Occasional use of new writers, but a substantial network of regular contributors already exists. Interested in a very wide range of material: all subjects which might bear on Christian life. Fiction not normally accepted.
Payment negotiable.

Vector

37 Firs Road, Milnthorpe, Cumbria LA7 7QF
☏05395 62883

Owner *British Science Fiction Association*
Editors *Catie Cary/Kev McVeigh*
Circulation 1300

FOUNDED 1957. BI-MONTHLY. The critical journal of the BSFA about science fiction and its writers. Unsolicited mss welcome, especially if authoritative and well written, but most contributors are either professional science fiction authors or BSFA members. No fiction.

Book Reviews *Chris Maies* Most are submitted by BSFA members. Maximum 800 words.

Features Articles of up to 4000 words welcome, particularly interviews with SF authors, editors, publishers, etc.
No payment.

The Vegan

7 Battle Road, St Leonards-on-Sea, East Sussex TN37 7AA
☏0424 427393   Fax 0424 427393

Owner *Vegan Society*
Editor *Richard Farhall*
Circulation 6000

FOUNDED 1944. QUARTERLY. Deals with the ecological, ethical and health aspects of veganism. Unsolicited mss welcome. Maximum 2000 words.
Payment negotiable.

Vegetarian Living

3rd Floor, 58 High Street, Sutton, Surrey SM1 1EZ
☏081-770 7337   Fax 081-770 7283

Owner *Bob Farrand*
Editor *Nicola Graimes*
Circulation 50,000

MONTHLY. For vegetarians and those interested in a vegetarian lifestyle and philosophy. Unsolicited mss and ideas in writing welcome.

Features Animal welfare, food and recipes, health, nutrition, travel, gardening, environmental issues, and reviews. Maximum 1500 words.
Payment £110 per 1000 words.

News Maximum 500 words.

Verbatim, The Language Quarterly

PO Box 199, Aylesbury, Buckinghamshire HP20 1TQ
☏0296 395880
Editor *Laurence Urdang*

Circulation 25,000

FOUNDED 1974. QUARTERLY. Authors are urged to review a copy of the periodical before submitting anything. Sample available on request. Unsolicited mss welcome. Approach in writing with ideas. No phone calls.

Features Any aspect of language. Maximum 1500 words.
Payment negotiable.

Veteran Car

Jessamine Court, High Street, Ashwell, Hertfordshire SG7 5NL
☏0462 742818   Fax 0462 742997

Owner *The Veteran Car Club of Great Britain*
Contact *The Editor*
Circulation 2000

FOUNDED 1938. BI-MONTHLY magazine which exists primarily for the benefit of members of The Veteran Car Club of Great Britain, although it is available on subscription to non-members. It is concerned with all aspects of the old vehicle hobby — events, restoration, history, current world news, legislation, etc., relating to pre-1919 motor cars. The only professional writers who contribute to the magazine are Club members. No budget for paid contributions.

Video and Satellite Today

Media House, 55 Lower Addiscombe Road, Croydon, Surrey CR0 6PQ
☏081-760 0688   Fax 081-688 9573

Owner *John Payten*
Contact *The Editor*
Circulation 30,000

FOUNDED 1992. MONTHLY. News and reviews of video and satellite listings. Unsolicited mss welcome but approach with idea in writing first.
Payment by agreement.

Video Trade Weekly

20 Bowling Green Lane, London EC1R 0BD
☏071-250 3077   Fax 071-608 0304

Owner *Video Trade Weekly Ltd*
Publisher *Julie Lefebve*
Editor *Jo Jeffery*
Circulation 9586

FOUNDED 1981. WEEKLY. Unsolicited mss and ideas in writing welcome.

Features Approach with ideas. Photos appreciated.

News *Branwell Johnson* Freelance stories on video-related topics welcome.

Video World Magazine

The Northern & Shell Building, PO Box 381, Millharbour, London E14 9TW
☎071-987 5090   Fax 071-987 2160

Owner *Richard Desmond*
Editor *Jane Garner*
Circulation 32,000

FOUNDED 1984. MONTHLY. Features on anything relevant to film and video. Unsolicited contributions welcome, but it is best to ring and discuss ideas with the editor first.

Vogue

Vogue House, Hanover Square, London W1R 0AD
☎071-499 9080   Fax 071-408 0559

Owner *Condé Nast Publications Ltd*
Editor *Alexandra Shulman*
Circulation 181,912

Condé Nast magazines tend to use known writers and commission what's needed, rather than using unsolicited mss. Contacts are useful.

Features *Eve MacSweeney* Upmarket general interest rather than 'women's'. Good proportion of highbrow art and literary articles, as well as travel, gardens, food, home interest and reviews. No fiction.

The Voice

370 Coldharbour Lane, London SW9 8PL
☎071-737 7377   Fax 071-274 8994

Owner *Vee Tee Ay Media Resources*
Editor *Winsome Cornish*
Circulation 47,321

FOUNDED 1982. WEEKLY newspaper, particularly aimed at the black British community. Unsolicited contributions welcome. Initial approach in writing preferred. Few opportunities except in features. Maximum 1000 words.
Payment from £100 per 1000 words/negotiable.

Watch It!

Argus House, Boundary Way, Hemel Hempstead HP2 7ST
☎0442 66551   Fax 0442 66998

Owner *Argus Specialist Publications*
Group Editor *Stuart Cooke*

FOUNDED 1992. The magazine for film fans. FORTNIGHTLY on alternative Thursdays. Up-to-the minute reviews, interviews, competitions, gossip, regular children's page, fan club information, and more.

Video Editor *Jim Bluck*
Film Editor *Dave Reeder*

Waterways World

Kottingham House, Dale Street, Burton-on-Trent, Staffordshire DE14 3TD
☎0283 64290   Fax 0283 61077

Owner *Waterway Productions Ltd*
Editor *Hugh Potter*
Circulation 24,538

FOUNDED 1972. MONTHLY magazine for inland waterway enthusiasts. Unsolicited mss welcome, provided the writer has a good knowledge of the subject. No fiction.

Features *Hugh Potter* Articles (preferably illustrated) are published on all aspects of inland waterways in Britain and abroad, including recreational and commercial boating on rivers and canals.

News *Regan Milnes* Maximum 500 words.
Payment £33 per 1000 words.

Wedding and Home

Greater London House, Hampstead Road, London NW1 7QQ
☎071-388 3171   Fax 071-387 9518

Owner *Maxwell Consumer Magazines*
Editor *Debbie Djordjević*
Circulation 50,000

BI-MONTHLY for women planning their wedding, honeymoon and first home. Most features are written in-house or commissioned from known freelancers. Unsolicited mss are not welcome, but approaches may be made in writing.

Weekly News

Albert Square, Dundee DD1 9QJ
☎0382 23131   Fax 0382 22214

Owner *D. C. Thomson & Co. Ltd*
Editor *W. Kelly*
Circulation 487,606

WEEKLY newsy, family-orientated magazine designed to appeal to the busy housewife. 'We get a lot of unsolicited stuff and there is great loss of life among them.' Usually commission, but writers of

promise will be taken up. Series include showbiz, royals and television. No fiction.
Payment negotiable.

Weight Watchers Magazine

175-179 St John's Street, London EC1V 4RP
☎071-490 1166   Fax 071-490 2518

Owner *GAT Publishing*
Editor *Harriet Cross*
Circulation 152,596

EIGHT ISSUES YEARLY. For slimmers and the health-conscious. Unsolicited mss not normally accepted, but approaches may be made in writing.

Features are usually commissioned by editor or features editor. Length and payment vary depending on subject.

What Car?

38-42 Hampton Road, Teddington,
Middlesex TW11 0JE
☎081-943 5637   Fax 081-943 5659

Owner *Haymarket Publishing Ltd*
Editor-in-Chief *Howard Walker*
Circulation 146,000

Car reports and consumer-based articles to do with motoring generally. No unsolicited mss but some scope for freelancers in both these areas. Testing is only offered to the few, and general articles on aspects of driving are only accepted from writers known and trusted by the magazine as conclusions arrived at can be controversial and need to be scrupulously researched.
Payment NUJ rates.

What Diet & Lifestyle

AIM Publications Ltd, Silver House, 31-35 Beak Street, London W1R 3LD
☎071-437 0796   Fax 071-437 8787

Owner *D. C. Thomson & Co. Ltd*
Editor *Helen Williams*
Circulation 45,000

FOUNDED 1983. BI-MONTHLY. Unsolicited mss not welcome as all news and feature articles are written by in-house or regular commissioned free-lance writers.

What Hi-Fi

38-42 Hampton Road, Teddington,
Middlesex TW11 0JE
☎081-943 5000   Fax 081-943 5098

Owner *Haymarket Magazines Ltd*
Editor *Mark Payton*
Circulation 61,800

FOUNDED 1976. MONTHLY. Features on hi-fi and new technology. No unsolicited contributions. Prior consultation with the editor essential.

Features General or more specific on hi-fi and new technology pertinent to the consumer electronics market. Length 2500-3000 words.
Payment £80 per page.

Reviews Specific product reviews. Generally from an established pool of reviewers but 'willing to look at material from hi-fi enthusiasts who also happen to be journalists'.

What Investment

3rd Floor, 4-8 Tabernacle Street,
London EC2A 4LU
☎071-638 1916   Fax 071-638 3128

Owner *Charterhouse Communications*
Editor *Keiron Root*
Circulation 25,530

FOUNDED 1983. MONTHLY. Features articles on a variety of savings and investment matters. Unsolicited mss welcome. All approaches should be made in writing.

Features 1200-1500 words (maximum 2000).
Payment NUJ rates minimum.

What Mortgage

3rd Floor, 4-8 Tabernacle Street,
London EC2A 4LU
☎071-638 1916   Fax 071-638 3128

Owner *Charterhouse Communications*
Editor *Nia Williams*
Circulation 20,000

FOUNDED 1983. MONTHLY magazine on property purchase, choice and finance. Unsolicited mss welcome; prospective contributors may make initial contact either by telephone or in writing.

Features Up to 1500 words on related topics are considered. Particularly welcome are new angles, new ideas or specialities.
Payment £120 per 1000 words.

What Personal Computer

33-39 Bowling Green Lane, London EC1R 0DA
☎071-837 1212   Fax 071-278 4003

Owner *EMAP Computing*

MONTHLY user magazine. News, features, market information, etc. No unsolicited mss. Approach in writing with ideas.

What Satellite

57–59 Rochester Place, London NW1 9JU
☎071–485 0011   Fax 071–482 6269

Owner *W. V. Publications*
Editor *Geoff Bains*
Circulation 55,000

FOUNDED 1989. MONTHLY. Equipment guide to consumer satellite TV receivers. Comprehensive coverage of all types available, dish system tests, satellite channel listings, installation advice and programming features. Unsolicited mss on technical, programming or user features welcome. Maximum 1000 words.
Payment £85–95 per 1000 words.

What Video

57–59 Rochester Place, London NW1 9JU
☎071–485 0011   Fax 071–284 2145

Owner *W. V. Publications*
Editor *Steve May*
Circulation 43,500

FOUNDED 1980. MONTHLY. Features on video equipment and user features — TVs, VCRs, camcorders, video games and accessories. Unsolicited mss welcome. Particularly interested in application features: outside broadcast video movies and novel trips with video. Maximum 1000 words.
Payment £85–95 per 1000 words.

What's New in Building

Morgan-Grampian House, 30 Calderwood Street, London SE18 6QH
☎081–855 7777   Fax 081–316 3169

Owner *Morgan-Grampian Ltd*
Editor *Derrick Jolley*
Assistant Editor *Wendy Limon*
Circulation 32,500

MONTHLY. Specialist magazine covering new products for building. Unsolicited mss not generally welcome. The only freelance work available is rewriting press release material. This is offered on a monthly basis of 25–50 items of about 150 words each.
Payment £5 per item.

What's new in Farming

Morgan-Grampian House, 30 Calderwood Street, London SE18 6QH
☎081–855 7777 ext. 3420   Fax 081–854 6795

Owner *United Newspapers*
Editor *Jonathan Theobald*
Circulation 68,000

FOUNDED 1977. MONTHLY. The magazine is primarily a guide to new agricultural products, with features covering the application of new technology. Most copy is written in-house or by established freelance contributors.

Features *Clare Cronin/Jonathan Theobald* Articles on relevant agricultural topics. Maximum 2000 words.
Payment negotiable.

What's New in Interiors

Morgan-Grampian House, 30 Calderwood Street, London SE18 6QH
☎081–885 7777   Fax 081–855 2342

Owner *Morgan-Grampian Ltd*
Editor *Anthea Bain*
Circulation 10,600

FOUNDED 1981. TEN ISSUES YEARLY, plus specialist supplements. Aimed at interior designers, architects and specifiers. Unsolicited mss welcome if they are exclusive, well-researched, and specifically targeted at magazine's readership. Make initial contact in writing or by telephone.

Features Good, technical journalists who know the contract interiors market are always sought. Maximum 1500 words. Interested in interiors application stories — CAD, leisure and tourism, and in specialised profiles.
Payment £120 per 1000 words.

What's On in London

182 Pentonville Road, London N1 9LB
☎071–278 4393   Fax 071–837 5838

Owner *E. G. Shaw*
Editor *Michael Darvell*
Circulation 40,000

FOUNDED 1932. WEEKLY guide and information magazine. Features and reviews. Always interested in well thought out and well presented mss. Articles should have London/Home Counties connection, except during the summer when they can be of much wider tourist/historic interest, relating to unusual traditions and events. Approach the editor by telephone in the first instance.
Payment by arrangement.

Art *Ria Higgins*

Cinema *Michael Darvell*

Pop Music *Danny Scott*

Classical Music *Michael Quinn*

Theatre *Clare Bayley*

Which Computer?

33–39 Bowling Green Lane, London EC1R 0DA
☏ 071-837 1212   Fax 071-278 4003

Owner *EMAP Computing*

MONTHLY. News, reports, market information, features, etc. No unsolicted mss. Approach in writing with ideas.

Wiltshire Life

See **Devon Life**

Wine

60 Waldegrave Road, Teddington TW11 8LG
☏ 081-943 5943   Fax 081-943 5871

Owner *The Evro Publishing Co.*
Editor *Ruth Cobb*
Circulation 35,000

FOUNDED 1983. MONTHLY. Unsolicited mss not welcome.

News/Features Wine, food and food/wine-related travel stories. Prospective contributors should approach in writing.

Wisden Cricket Monthly

6 Beech Lane, Guildford, Surrey GU2 5ES
☏ 0483 32573/570358   Fax 0483 33153

Owner *Wisden Cricket Magazines Ltd*
Editor *David Frith*
Circulation c.42,000

FOUNDED 1979. MONTHLY. Very few uncommissioned articles are used, but would-be contributors are not discouraged. Approach in writing.
Payment varies.

Woman

King's Reach Tower, Stamford Street,
London SE1 9LS
☏ 071-261 5000   Fax 071-261 5997

Owner *IPC Magazines Ltd*
Editor *David Durman*
Circulation 860,000

Popular women's magazine which is now in its 53rd year and boasts a readership of over 2.6 million. No unsolicited mss. Most work commissioned. Approach with ideas in writing.

Features *Carole Russell* Maximum 1500 words.

Books *Kate Wright* No unsolicited mss.

Woman and Home

King's Reach Tower, Stamford Street,
London SE1 9LS
☏ 071-261 5423   Fax 071-261 6865

Owner *IPC Magazines Ltd*
Editor *Sue Dobson*
Circulation 453,315

FOUNDED 1926. MONTHLY. Prospective contributors are advised to write with ideas, including photocopies of other published work or details of magazines to which they have contributed. S.a.e. essential for return of material. Most freelance work is specially commissioned.

Features *Jackie Hatton*

Fiction *Kati Nichol* Short stories are usually submitted by agents; serials are always submitted by agents or publishers. No poetry.

Other Fashion, knitting, beauty, home, cookery and travel, all covered by staff writers and specially commissioned freelancers.
Payment about £100 per 1000 words.

Woman's Journal

King's Reach Tower, Stamford Street,
London SE1 9LS
☏ 071-261 6220   Fax 071-261 7061

Owner *IPC Magazines Ltd*
Managing Editor *Sue Price*
Editor *Deirdre Vine*

MONTHLY. Feature ideas welcome with samples of previous work.

Features *Christie Hickman* Major features are generally commissioned, but new ideas on all subjects welcome. Maximum 2000 words.
Payment negotiable.

Fiction *Christie Hickman* No unsolicited material accepted for fiction; stories are mainly bought from agents and publishers direct. Maximum 3000 words.

Design and Homes *Melanie Molesworth*

Fashion *Alex Parnell*

Food *Katie Stewart*

Beauty *Lottie Johansson*

Health *Carolyn Faulder*

Gardening *Elisabeth Jane Howard*

Woman's Own

King's Reach Tower, Stamford Street,
London SE1 9LS
☎071-261 5474   Fax 071-261 5346

Owner *IPC Magazines Ltd*
Editor *Keith McNeill*
Circulation 931,295

WEEKLY. Prospective contributors should contact the features editor in writing in the first instance before making a submission.

Features *Juliet Bell*

Fiction *Jackie Maher* No unsolicited fiction. Annual short story competition. Maximum 3500 words.

Woman's Realm

King's Reach Tower, Stamford Street,
London SE1 9LS
☎071-261 6244   Fax 071-261 5326

Owner *IPC Magazines Ltd*
Editor *Iris Burton*
Deputy Editor *Sally Sheringham*
Circulation 483,000

FOUNDED 1958. WEEKLY. Some scope here for freelancers, who should write in the first instance to the appropriate editor. Unsolicited material will be returned unread.

Features *Liz Prosser* Interested in human interest ideas/articles, dramatic emotional stories, strong adventure and chilling ghost/ supernatural stories. Plus real-life love stories with a difference.
Payment NUJ rates, and £100 for 'wry looks' material.

Fiction *Nick Vermuth* Two short stories used every week, a one-pager (up to 1200 words), plus a longer one (2000-3500). Aimed at a lively-minded woman aged 35 plus, whose horizons are expanding now that family is growing up. Very wide range. A high standard of writing is essential. Some short serials, but these are usually commissioned from regular contributors.
Payment £150 and upwards.

Woman's Story

See **Love Story**

Woman's Weekly

King's Reach Tower, Stamford Street,
London SE1 9LS
☎071-261 6131   Fax 071-261 6322

Owner *IPC Magazines Ltd*
Editor *Judith Hall*
Circulation 905,095

Mass market women's WEEKLY.

Features *Eileen McCarroll* Focus on strong human interest stories, film and television personalities, as well as more traditional homemaking subjects. Freelancers used regularly, but tend to be experienced magazine journalists.

Fiction *Gaynor Davies* Short stories 1500-5000 words; serials 12,000-30,000 words. Guidelines for serials: 'a strong romantic emotional theme with a conflict not resolved until the end'; short stories allow for more variety.

Women's Art Magazine

Fulham Palace, Bishop's Avenue,
London SW6 6EA
☎071-384 1110   Fax 071-384 1110

Owner *Women's Art Slide Library*
Editor *Genevieve Fox*
Circulation 8000

FOUNDED 1985. BI-MONTHLY. Profiles of women artists, interviews, articles of an historical nature (i.e. not 20th-Century artists) related to women's art, international news, exhibition reviews, and theoretical pieces on art history and criticism. Unsolicited mss welcome. Approach in writing with ideas.

News News of women artists in the UK and overseas, including exhibitions and residencies. Also gallery news and women in the art world. Maximum 2000 words.

Features A theme is chosen for each issue, e.g. art and technology; art and health; photography. Contact the editor for details on future themes. Keen to receive international features and historical or theoretical ones. Maximum 3000 words.

Book Reviews 500-1000 words, usually 500. Also publishes relevant cartoons.
Payment by negotiation.

Woodworker

Argus House, Boundary Way, Hemel Hempstead,
Hertfordshire HP2 7ST
☎0442 66551   Fax 0442 66998

Owner *Argus Specialist Publications*
Editor *Zachary Taylor*

Circulation 45,000

FOUNDED 1901. MONTHLY. Contributions welcome; approach with ideas in writing.

Features *Zachary Taylor* Articles on woodworking with good photo support appreciated. Maximum 2000 words. *Payment* £40–60 per page.

News Stories and photos (b&w) welcome. Maximum 300 words. *Payment* £10–25 per story.

Workbox
40 Silver Street, Wiveliscombe, Somerset TA4 2NY
☎0984 24033

Owner *Audrey Babington*
Editor *Audrey Babington*
Circulation 50,000

FOUNDED 1984. QUARTERLY. The magazine caters for the enthusiast and professional in all branches of needlecrafts.

Features Covers a very wide range of needlecrafts, but no 'how-to-make' items.

News Any items welcome, especially about new products, processes, etc., and events. *Payment* by arrangement.

Working Titles
Hall Floor Flat, 80 Hampton Road, Redland, Bristol BS6 2JB
☎0272 237006

Owner *Working Titles Publications*
Editors *Rachel Bentham/Tony Lewis-Jones/Tom Phillips*
Circulation 200

FOUNDED 1988. THRICE-YEARLY. Unsolicited mss (short fiction and poetry) welcome. Features two or three pieces of interesting, sharp fiction plus poetry with contemporary social relevance in each issue. Also poetry reviews. Maximum 2000 words (fiction); 1500 words (poetry reviews).

Works Magazine
See **Works Publishing** under **Small Presses**

World Fishing
Nortide House, Stone Street, Faversham, Kent ME13 8PG
☎0795 536536   Fax 0795 530244

Owner *Nortide Ltd*
Editor *V. Aers*
Circulation 6500

FOUNDED 1952. MONTHLY. Unsolicited mss welcome; approach by phone or in writing with an idea.

News/Features Technical or commercial nature relating to commercial fishing industry worldwide. Maximum 1000 words. *Payment* by arrangement.

The World of Interiors
234 King's Road, London SW3 5UA
☎071-351 5177   Fax 071-351 3709

Owner *Condé Nast Publications Ltd*
Editor *Min Hogg*
Circulation 73,210

FOUNDED 1981. MONTHLY. Best approach by phone or letter with an idea, preferably with reference snaps or guidebooks.

Features *Sarah Howell* Most feature material is commissioned. 'Subjects tend to be found by us, but we are delighted to receive suggestions of houses unpublished elsewhere, and would love to find new writers.'

World Soccer
25th Floor, King's Reach Tower, Stamford Street, London SE1 9LS
☎071-261 5737   Fax 071-261 6019

Owner *IPC Magazines Ltd*
Editor *Keir Radnedge*

FOUNDED 1960. MONTHLY. Unsolicited material welcome but initial approach by phone or in writing preferred. News and features on world soccer.

Writers' Monthly
29 Turnpike Lane, London N8 0EP
☎081-342 8879   Fax 081-347 8847

Owner *The Writer Ltd*
Editor *Shirley Kelly*
Circulation 9000

FOUNDED 1984. MONTHLY magazine (incorporating *The Writer*). Aimed at freelance writers, both beginners and professionals. News and features of interest to writers.

Features 1200–2200 words. 'Always on the lookout for new writers.' Query letter with synopsis in the first instance. 'The main reason for material being rejected is usually because writers have not studied the magazine. Articles should be informative, practical and concise.'

News Compiled in-house; very little scope for outside contributors.

Other Regular short story competitions open to subscribers, plus two major annual ones. The winning story is published in future editions of the magazine, subject to available space.

Writers News
PO Box 4, Nairn, Scotland IV12 4HU
☎0667 54441   Fax 0667 54401

Owner *D. St John Thomas*
Editor *Richard Bell*

FOUNDED 1989. MONTHLY. For writers and aspiring writers, news of all kinds likely to be of interest: market opportunities, courses, grants and competitions, legislation affecting writers, new ways of doing things, opinions of those who matter. Practical and informative articles. 'We want the magazine to belong to its readers and of course hope to publish the best of your work.' Unsolicited mss welcome; ideas should be addressed to the editor in writing. Launched *Writing Magazine* (see below) in 1992.

News *Carol Pope* Press releases of products and events of interest.

Features On how to write and be published. Maximum 1400 words.
Payment negotiable.

The Writers' Rostrum
14 Ardbeg Road, Rothesay, Bute PA20 0NJ
☎0700 502737

Owner *Jenny Chaplin*
Editor *Jenny Chaplin*
Circulation *c.* 1000

FOUNDED 1984. International QUARTERLY magazine for freelance writers. Features poetry, fillers, articles on writing, and short stories. Unsolicited material welcome. Approach in writing with mss or ideas and include s.a.e. for reply. No phone calls. Print-ready submissions need to be on A5 paper with one inch margin all round and typed in single spacing. Most submissions are dealt with quickly (about a month) but publication can take up to 2 years, especially for poetry of which there is a substantial backlog of material on file.

News Success stories re books published by former TWR members and news of poetry/short story competitions.

Features Articles on the craft of writing. General interest/anniversary type material. Positive thought features on health, writing, attitude to life, family problems, etc.

Fiction 15–20 short stories a year (900 words maximum). Nothing controversial, political or obscene.

Specials First-hand experience and comment from published novelists on the craft of writing. Also **Poetry** of seasonal interest, family life, natural beauty.
Payment £1–5 per manuscript. Proceeds go to medical charities.

Writing Magazine
PO Box 4, Nairn, Scotland IV12 4HU
☎0667 54441   Fax 0667 54401

Owner *David St John Thomas*
Editor *Richard Bell*

FOUNDED 1992. News, competitions and articles on all aspects of writing. Unsolicited mss welcome. Approach in writing with ideas.

News *Carol Pope* Press releases of products and events of interest.

Features On how to write and be published; anything of interest to the writer in his work. Maximum 1400 words.
Payment by arrangement.

Xenos
29 Prebend Street, Bedford MK40 1QN
☎0234 349067

Editor *Stephen Copestake*

FOUNDED May 1990. BI-MONTHLY. Science fiction, fantasy, horror, occult, humour, mystery and suspense short story digest. Story lengths flexible, with upper limit of 10,000 words. No purely romantic stories or blood and gore material. All stories printed are evaluated by readers and their comments printed in the Evaluations section of the subsequent issue. All submissions receive free and prompt analysis by the editor, plus suggestions for revision if appropriate. Annual competition.
Payment negotiable.

Yachting Monthly
Room 2209, King's Reach Tower, Stamford Street, London SE1 9LS
☎071-261 6040   Fax 071-261 6704

Owner *IPC Magazines Ltd*
Editor *Andrew Bray*

Circulation 45,000

FOUNDED 1906. MONTHLY magazine for yachting enthusiasts. Unsolicited mss welcome, but many are received and not used. Prospective contributors should make initial contact in writing.

Features *Paul Gelder* A wide range of features concerned with maritime subjects and cruising under sail; well-researched and innovative material always welcome, especially if accompanied by colour transparencies. Maximum 2750 words. *Payment* maximum £113.40 per 1000 words.

Yachts and Yachting

196 Eastern Esplanade, Southend-on-Sea, Essex SS1 3AB
☎0702 582245   Fax 0702 588434

Owner *Yachting Press*
Editor *Frazer Clark*
Circulation 22,500

FOUNDED 1947. FORTNIGHTLY magazine devoted to yacht and dinghy racing. No unsolicited mss. Approach with ideas in writing.

Yorkshire Ridings Magazine

33 Beverley Road, Driffield, Yorkshire YO25 7SD
☎0377 43232   Fax 0377 43232

Owner *Ridings Publishing Co.*
Editor *Winston Halstead*
Circulation 10,500

FOUNDED 1964. BI-MONTHLY county periodical with a strong Yorkshire flavour. Unsolicited mss welcome but only a tiny percentage of those received are ever used.

Features Illustrated articles with strong local interest. Maximum 1500 words. No historical or poetry. *Payment* about £35 per page.

You - The Mail on Sunday Magazine

See **National Newspapers (The Mail on Sunday)**

Young Telegraph

346 Old Street, London EC1V 9NQ
☎071-613 3376   Fax 071-613 3372

Editor *Caroline Clayton*
Circulation 1.4 million

FOUNDED 1990. WEEKLY colour supplement for 8-12-year-olds. Unsolicited mss and ideas in writing welcome.

Features *Damian Kelleher* Usually commissioned. Any youth-orientated material. Maximum 500 words. *Payment* £75 per 500 words.

News *Damian Kelleher* Short, picture-led articles always welcome. Maximum 80 words. *Payment* £90 per 500 words.

Your Horse

Bretton Court, Bretton, Peterborough, Cambridgeshire PE3 8DZ
☎0733 264666   Fax 0733 265515

Owner *EMAP Pursuit Publications*
Editor *Lesley Eccles*
Circulation 40,159

A magazine for all ages which deals with practical horsecare: the skills and problems involved in keeping or riding horses. Gets a lot of unsolicited offerings from knowledgeable readers, some of which are used, but it's best to send ideas to the editor in the first instance. *Payment* negotiable.

Yours Magazine

Apex House, Oundle Road, Peterborough, Cambridgeshire PE2 9NP
☎0733 555123   Fax 0733 312025

Owner *Choice Publications*
Editor *Neil Patrick*
Circulation 127,969

FOUNDED 1973. MONTHLY. Aimed at a readership aged 55 and over.

Features Best approach by letter with outline in first instance. Maximum 1000 words.

News Short newsy items (300–500 words) of interest to readership welcome. *Payment* negotiable.

Fiction One short story used in each issue.

Freelance Rates –
Magazines

Freelance rates vary enormously. The following guidelines, representing an overall increase of 5% on last year's figures, are minimum rates negotiated by the **National Union of Journalists**. Most work can command higher fees from employers whether or not they have NUJ agreements. It is up to freelancers to negotiate the best deal they can.

Group A
Bella, Best, Cosmopolitan, Euromoney, Expression, Management Today, Options, Prima, Smash Hits, Take a Break, Vogue

Group B
Company, Computer Weekly, Elle, Good Housekeeping, Hello!, House & Garden, House Beautiful, Just Seventeen, My Weekly, marie claire, New Woman, She Magazine.

Group C
Accountancy Age, Arena, Country Living, The Face, Harpers & Queen, GQ, Living, Marketing Week, New Scientist, Q.

Group D
Car Mechanics, Gay Times, Parents.

Group E
Bicycle, New Statesman and Society, What Satellite, The Voice.

Words
These figures (rounded off to the nearest £) are the minimum rates which should be paid by magazines in these groups:

	Features (per 1000 words)	News (per 100 words)	Research/ Production/ Reporting/ Sub-Editing/ Picture Research (per day)
Group A	negotiable	negotiable	£115
Group B	£210	£21	£105
Group C	£183	£18	£100
Group D	£131	£12	£89
Group E	£110	£10	£84

Photographic Fees

Commission fees are based on day rates (over 4 hours) and half-day rates (up to 4 hours). Most companies recognise that commission fees are payment for time and will therefore pay reproduction fees on top. Where freelancers are paid over and above the minimum commission fees outlined below this may not apply.

	Commission fees	
	day	half-day
Group A	£220	£136
Group B	£189	£115
Group C	£157	£105
Group D	£136	£ 89
Group E	£126	£ 78

	Reproduction fees			
Up to:	1/4 page	1/2 page	3/4 page	full page
Group A	£81	£105	£141	£241
Group B	£63	£ 94	£126	£178
Group C	£52	£ 78	£105	£157
Group D	£47	£ 63	£ 94	£131
Group E	£42	£ 49	£ 73	£ 99

Colour: Double the above rates.

Cover: 50% extra.

Studio/location work and specialist assignments: £546 per day.

Cartoons

	Group A	Group B & C	Group D & E
Minimum fee	£78	£64	£52
Feature strip	£99	£87	£78

News Agencies

AP Dow Jones
76 Shoe Lane, London EC4A 3JB
☎071-353 8171   Fax 071-353 7866

Associated Press News Agency
12 Norwich Street, London EC4A 1BP
☎071-353 1515/353 6323 (News)/
353 4731 (Photos)   Fax 071-353 8118

Central Office of Information
Hercules Road, London SE1 7DU
☎071-261 8484   Fax 071-928 7652

Extel Financial
Castle House, 37-45 Paul Street,
London EC2A 4DL

☎071-251 3333   Fax 071-490 2444

National News Agency
30 St John's Lane, London EC1M 4BJ
☎071-490 7700   Fax 071-250 1204

Press Association Ltd
85 Fleet Street, London EC4P 4BE
☎071-353 7440   Fax 071-936 2363

Reuters Ltd
85 Fleet Street, London EC4P 4AJ
☎071-250 1122   Fax 071-583 3769

National and Regional Television

BBC Television

BBC Television
Television Centre, Wood Lane, London W12 7RJ
☎081-743 8000

Head of Drama *Mark Shivas*
Head of Light Entertainment *James Moir*
Head of Sports & Events *Jonathan Martin*
Head of Series, Drama *Peter Cregeen*
Head of Serials, Drama *Michael Wearing*
Head of Television Script Unit, Drama *Tony Dinner*
Commissioning Editor, Independent Productions, Drama *Lynda Myles*
Head of Comedy, Light Entertainment *Martin Fisher*
Head of Youth Programmes *Janet Street-Porter*
Head of Documentary Features *Colin Cameron*
Head of Topical Features *John Morrell*
Editor, Community Programmes *Jeremy Gibson*
Head of Science & Features *David Filkin*
Head of Music & Arts *Michael Jackson*
Head of Religious Programmes *Stephen Whittle*
Head of Children's Programmes *Anna Home*
Head of School Broadcasting *Terry Marsh*
Head of Continuing Education *Alan Rogers*
Head of Open University Production Centre *Colin Robinson*
Head of Purchased Programmes *June Morrow*
Controller, BBC1 *Jonathan Powell*
Controller, BBC2 *Alan Yentob*

Throughout its history the BBC has always had a strong regional dimension. Since March 1990, when BBC North East and North West regions were merged into BBC North, there have been seven regions which make up the Regional Directorate under Ronald Neil. The directorate is based on an autonomous management structure and a fully integrated programme output. Of the seven regions, three are national: BBC Scotland, BBC Wales, BBC Northern Ireland. The remaining four English regions, all making local, regional and network programmes, are: BBC Midlands, BBC North, BBC South & East, BBC South & West. (See separate entries for each region below.)

The BBC's Comedy Script Unit, which has discovered people like Carla Lane (*Bread*), has a positive policy towards discovering and encouraging new young talent, and to this end a development unit was established within the Comedy Script Unit in 1991. It has been reported that BBC1 controller, Jonathan Powell, is looking to double the output of a decade ago; and BBC2's controller, Alan Yentob, is keen to output good comedy with an 'edge and narrative'. The BBC's Drama Script Unit was abolished in 1991, but following its demise the BBC, in conjunction with **The Writers' Guild**, has established a series of specifically targeted workshops which are held throughout the year (see **Writers' Guild Workshops** under **Writers' Courses, Circles and Workshops**).

BBC News and Current Affairs
Broadcasting House, London W1A 1AA
☎071-580 4468
BBC Television Centre, Wood Lane, London W12 7RJ
☎081-743 8000

In August 1987 a new directorate was created within the BBC devoted exclusively to news and current affairs. The operation unified News and Current Affairs Radio and the two separate departments of Television News and Television Current Affairs.

Director, News and Current Affairs *Tony Hall*
Deputy Editor, News and Current Affairs, Television *Samir Shah*
Editor, News Programmes *Peter Bell*
Head of News Gathering *Chris Cramer*
Managing Editor, News Programmes *Christopher Graham*
Managing Editor, Weekly Programmes *Peter Kenyatta*
News Editor, Breakfast News *Bob Wheaton*
News Editor, Intake *Mike Robinson*
Editor, Foreign Affairs Unit *John Simpson*
Editor, Business & Economics Unit *Peter Jay*
Editor, Social Affairs Unit *Polly Toynbee*
News Editor, One O'Clock News *Tim Orchard*
News Editor, Six O'Clock News *David Stanford*
News Editor, Nine O'Clock News *Mark Damazer*
News Editor, Daytime Summaries *Diana Morton*

News Editor, Weekend Bulletins *Peter O'Kill*
News Editor, Newsnight *Tim Gardam*
Editor, Public Eye *Nigel Chapman*
News Editor, Panorama *Mark Thompson*

BBC Television Documentary Features

Kensington House, Richmond Way,
London W14 0AX
☎081-895 6161   Fax 081-749 8378

**Acting Head of Documentary Features,
Television** *Peter Pagnamenta*
Manager, Documentary Features *Brendan
Smith*
Editor, BBC1 Single Documentaries *Paul
Hamann*
Editor, 40 Minutes *Caroline Pick*
Editor, Development *Andre Singer*

BBC Television Teletext Services

Television Centre, Wood Lane, London W12 7PJ
☎081-743 8000 ext. 3637/6345
Fax 081-749 6734

Head of Teletext Services *Blair Thomson*

Teletext was invented by BBC and IBA engineers in
the early 1970s. The BBC Teletext Unit was formed
in November 1982 to bring together the different
strands of Teletext broadcasting that developed. In
July 1989 the unit was reorganised within the News
& Current Affairs Directorate. There are two teletext sections: Ceefax and Subtitling (for the deaf
and hard-of-hearing).

Editor, Ceefax *Graham Norwood*
Sports Editor *Annie Briggs*
Ceefax is the main news and information service. It
broadcasts hundreds of pages on both BBC1 and
BBC2, and is on the air at all times when transmit-
ters are broadcasting. Pages include: news, city and
financial news, sport, travel and weather, and
programme-related information.

Manager, Subtitling *Ruth Griffiths*
Manager, Glasgow Unit *Irene Noble*
Subtitling is a rapidly expanding service by which
viewers can call up subtitles for many programmes
by dialling Ceefax page 888. The BBC's aim is to
provide subtitles for all major pre-recorded peak-
time programmes, and a number of live programmes, such as 'Crimewatch' and 'Blue Peter'.
There are presently two units, one in London, one
in Glasgow. Live verbatim subtitling of the 'Nine
O'Clock News', the first in Europe, started in
November 1990, and is being expanded to cover
the one o'clock and six o'clock bulletins, and all
daytime news summaries.

BBC Midlands

Broadcasting Centre, Pebble Mill Road,
Birmingham B5 7QQ
☎021-414 8888   Fax 021-414 8634

Head of Broadcasting *David Waine*
Head of Network Television *Colin Adams*
Head of Drama *Barry Hanson*
News & Current Affairs *Richard Thompson*

Home of the Pebble Mill Studio. Some openings for
well-researched freelance material. Also serves
BBC East Midlands opt-out station, based in Nottingham.

NOTTINGHAM
BBC East Midlands Broadcasting Centre, York
House, Mansfield Road, Nottingham NG1 3JB
☎0602 472395   Fax 0602 475419

News Editor *Roger Protheroe*

Local news only. Served by programmes made in
Birmingham.

BBC North

New Broadcasting House, Oxford Road,
Manchester M60 1SJ
☎061-200 2020   Fax 061-236 1005

Head of Broadcasting *John Shearer*
Head of Network Television *Peter Weil*
Head of Local Programmes, Manchester *Roy
Saatchi*
Editor, Features & Documentaries *David
Taylor*
Editor, Entertainment *Judith Holder*
Editor, Sport *Keith MacKenzie*
Editor, Children's *Richard Simkin*

Manchester is now the headquarters of the newly
formed BBC North region, established in March
1990, incorporating the former North East and
North West divisions which included Leeds and
Newcastle upon Tyne. Leeds and Newcastle continue to make their own programmes and each has
its own Head of Centre. Network production in
Manchester breaks down into seven areas: daytime television; independent productions;
entertainment; youth programmes; features &
documentaries; sport; children's. Independent productions deals with proposals from independent
producers which the BBC is using increasingly.
Direct approaches from writers alone less likely to
succeed.

LEEDS
Broadcasting Centre, Woodhouse Lane,
Leeds LS2 9PX
☎0532 441188   Fax 0532 439387

Head of Centre, Leeds *Martin Brooks*
Editor, News/Look North *Russell Peasgood*

Regional Political Editor *Geoff Talbott*

NEWCASTLE UPON TYNE
Broadcasting Centre, Barrack Road, Newcastle
upon Tyne NE99 2NE
☎ 091-232 1313   Fax 091-221 0112 (News)

Head of Centre *David Seymour*
Editor News/Look North *Ian Cameron*

BBC Northern Ireland

Broadcasting House, 25-27 Ormeau Avenue,
Belfast BT2 8HQ
☎ 0232 338000   Fax 0232 338800

Controller, Northern Ireland *Robin Walsh*
Head of Programmes *Pat Loughrey*
Editor, Current Affairs, TV *Andrew Coleman*
Editor, Television News *Paul Robinson*
Head of Educational Broadcasting *Pat Loughrey*
Editor, Religious Programming *Rev. Dr Robert Tosh*
Head of Sport & Events *Jim Neilly*
Head of Agriculture *John Nicholson*
Features *Harry Adair*
Editor, Music & Arts *Tony McAuley*
Head of Drama *Robert Cooper*
Head of Youth Programmes *Fedelma McVeigh*

BBC Scotland

Broadcasting House, Queen Margaret Drive,
Glasgow G12 8DG
☎ 041-330 2345   Fax 041-334 0614

Controller, Scotland *Patrick Chalmers*
Head of Television, Scotland *Colin Cameron*
Head of News/Current Affairs & Sport
Kenneth Cargill
Head of Music & Arts *John Archer*
Head of Drama *Bill Bryden*
Head of Gaelic *Ken MacQuarrie*
Head of Features *David Martin*
Head of Comedy *Colin Gilbert*
Head of Educational Broadcasting *Allan Jack*
Head of Religious Programmes *Andrew Barr*
Scottish Political Editor *Brian Taylor*

Head office of BBC Scotland with opt-out stations
based in Aberdeen, Dundee and Edinburgh.

ABERDEEN
Broadcasting House, Beechgrove Terrace,
Aberdeen AB9 2ZT
☎ 0224 625233   Fax 0224 642931

Senior Producer, Television *Arthur Anderson*
Chief News Assistant *Sandy Bremner*

News, plus some features, but most programmes
are made in Glasgow.

DUNDEE
Nethergate Centre, 66 Nethergate,
Dundee DD1 4ER
☎ 0382 202481   Fax 0382 202188

News only.

EDINBURGH
Broadcasting House, Queen Street,
Edinburgh EH2 1JF
☎ 031-469 4200   Fax 031-469 4220

Manager, Edinburgh *Mike Shaw*

All programmes made in Glasgow.

BBC South & East

BBC Elstree Centre, Clarendon Road,
Borehamwood, Hertfordshire WD6 1JF
☎ 081-953 6100   Fax 081-953 6267

Head of Broadcasting *Ian Kennedy*
Head of Centre, South East *Colin Stanbridge*
**Head of Network Programmes & Editor,
News, South East** *Guy Pelham*
Managing Editor, Documentaries *Paul Watson*
Managing Editor, History *Roy Davies*
Editor, Entertainment *Dave Ross*

Headquarters of BBC South and East which incorporates Norwich (BBC East), and home of the
history unit. Leisure and one-off programmes, plus
news. No drama.

NORWICH
St Catherine's Close, All Saint's Green, Norwich,
Norfolk NR1 3ND
☎ 0603 619331   Fax 0603 667865

Head of Centre, East *Arnold Miller*
Editor, News *Graham Henshaw*

More of an opt-out station, making its own local
news programmes and occasional network material.

BBC South & West

Broadcasting House, Whiteladies Road,
Bristol BS8 2LR
☎ 0272 732211   Fax 0272 744114

Acting Head of Broadcasting, South & West
Derek Woodcock
Acting Head of Regional & Local Programmes
Roy Corlett
Head of Natural History Unit *Andrew Neal*
Head of Television Features *Peter Salmon*
**Regional TV Manager, West/Topical Unit
Editor** *John Conway*
Editor, News *Sandy Milne*
South & West Political Editor *Paul Cannon*

Regional network centre for the South & West, with opt-out centres in Plymouth (BBC South West) and Southampton (BBC South). Strong features department and home of the BBC's much praised natural history unit. Interested in natural history material from specialist writers only. No drama department.

SOUTHAMPTON
BBC South West, Broadcasting House, Seymour Road, Mannamead, Plymouth PL3 5BD
☎0752 229201   Fax 0752 222058

PLYMOUTH
BBC South West, Broadcasting House, Seymour Road, Mannamead, Plymouth PL3 5BD
☎0752 229201   Fax 0752 222058

Regional Manager & Editor, Features, South West *Phil Speight*
Editor, News *Chris Cook*

Programmes for the South West region are made in the South & West regional headquarters in Bristol. Any material for submission should be sent to Bristol.

SOUTHAMPTON
BBC South, Broadcasting House, Havelock Road, Southampton SO1 0XQ
☎0703 226201   Fax 0703 339931

Regional Manager, South, & Editor, Features *Ian Masters*
Editor, News *Richard Horobin*

Programmes for the South are made in Bristol. Programme ideas and scripts should be sent direct to Bristol.

BBC Wales

Broadcasting House, Llandaff, Cardiff CF5 2YQ
☎0222 572888   Fax 0222 552973

Controller, Wales *Geraint Talfan Davies*
Head of Television *John Stuart Roberts*
Head of News & Current Affairs *Gwilym Owen*
Head of Educational Broadcasting *Keith Jones*
Head of Drama *Ruth Caleb*
Head of Music *Huw Tregelles Williams*
Head of Sport *Gareth Davies*
Head of Features & Documentaries *Barry Lynch*

Headquarters of BBC Wales, with regional television centres in Bangor and Swansea. All Welsh language programmes are transmitted by S4C but produced in Cardiff, which retains full editorial control.

BANGOR
Broadcasting House, Meirion Road, Bangor, Gwynedd LL57 2BY
☎0248 370880   Fax 0248 351443

Head of Production *R. Alun Evans*

News only.

SWANSEA
Broadcasting House, 32 Alexandra Road, Swansea SA1 5DZ
☎0792 654986   Fax 0792 468194

Manager, Swansea *Sulwyn Thomas*

Independent Television

Anglia Television

Anglia House, Norwich NR1 3JG
☎0603 615151   Fax 0603 631032

Managing Director, Anglia Television Films & Drama Ltd *Graeme McDonald*
Executive Director, Survival Anglia Ltd *M. Hay*
Head of Drama, International Television Enterprises Ltd *A. Fletcher*
Director of News *Jim Wilson*
Controller, News *M. Read*
Controller, Current Affairs & Religion *Malcolm Allsop*
Executive Producer, Arts & Features *J. Swinfield*
Sports Editor *Kevin Piper*

Anglia Television is also a major producer of programmes for the ITV network and Channel 4, including drama and the *Survival* wildlife documentaries.

Border Television

Television Centre, Durranhill, Carlisle, Cumbria CA1 3NT
☎0228 25101   Fax 0228 41384

Managing Director/Controller of Programmes *James Graham*
Head of Factual Programmes *Paul Baird*
News Editor *Neil Robinson*

In the last couple of years, Border has greatly increased its programme production, including children's television, with features and documentaries rather than drama. Border also contributes programmes to Channel 4. Most scripts are supplied in-house but occasionally there are commissions. Apart from notes, writers should not submit written work until their ideas have been fully discussed.

Carlton Television

101 St Martin's Lane, London WC2N 4AZ
☎071–240 4000   Fax 071–240 4171

Director of Programmes *Paul Jackson*
Head of Drama *Tracy Hofman*

Head of Current Affairs/Factual Programmes
Paul Corley
Head of Entertainment *John Bishop*

New ITV franchise holder, bound by the ITC guidelines for programming, i.e. it must include news, current affairs, children's and religious programming across a wide range tastes.

Central Independent Television

West Midlands, Central House, Broad Street, Birmingham B1 2JP
☎ 021-643 9898
East Midlands Television Centre, Lenton Lane, Nottingham NG7 2NA
☎ 0602 863322   Fax 0602 435552

Managing Director, Central Productions *Mike Watts*
Controller, Light Entertainment & Daytime *Tony Wolfe*
Controller, Young People/MD FilmFair *Lewis Rudd*
Controller, Features & Documentaries *Roger James*
Controller, Drama/MD Central Films *Ted Childs*

The bulk of the drama output at Central takes the form of series and serials; this and projects already in development means that Central are not actively seeking any drama. The Light Entertainment department makes situation comedy series for which full scripts are welcome and dealt with fairly quickly. Also quiz/game show material welcome. Young People's Programming includes single plays for the *Dramarama* slot, serials and light entertainment. Suitable scripts in this area welcome also.

Channel 4

60 Charlotte Street, London W1P 2AX
☎ 071-631 4444   Fax 071-637 4872

Director of Programmes *Liz Forgan*
Controller of Factual Programmes *John Willis*
Controller of Arts & Entertainment *Andrea Wonfor*

COMMISSIONING EDITORS
Head of Drama *David Aukin*
Drama, Series & Serials *Peter Ansorge*
Talk & Features *Michael Attwell*
Independent Film & Video *Alan Fountain*
Documentaries *Peter Moore*
News & Current Affairs *David Lloyd*
Entertainment *Seamus Cassidy*
Music *Avril MacRory*
Arts *Waldemar Januszczak*
Sport *Mike Miller*
Education *Gwynn Pritchard*

Youth Programmes *Stephen Garrett*
Multicultural Programmes *Farrukh Dhondy*
Finance, Industry & Science *Caroline Thompson*
Religion & Education *Bob Towler*
Chief Film Buyer *Mairi MacDonald*

When Channel 4 started broadcasting as a national TV channel on 2 November 1982, it was the first new TV service to be launched in Britain for 18 years. Under the 1981 Broadcasting Act it was required to cater for tastes and audiences not previously served by the other broadcast channels, and to provide a suitable proportion of educational programmes. Channel 4 does not make any of its own programmes; they are commissioned from the independent production companies, from the ITV sector, or co-produced with other organisations. The role of the commissioning editors is to sift through proposals for programmes and see interesting projects through to broadcast.

Channel 5

Under the 1990 Broadcasting Act, Britain's fifth terrestrial TV channel will have to take on many of the programme obligations of ITV, offering news, current affairs, children's and religious programming across a diverse range of tastes. Channel 5 has the drawback of limited coverage; it will only reach 70% of the country, leaving out sections of the South-east namely. At the time of going to press at least four bids were expected for the franchise. These were from: The Entertainment Channel consortium, funded by Time-Warner and Conrad Black (of *The Daily Telegraph*); Five TV, funded by Canadian entrepreneur Moses Znaimer; Channel S, funded by ex-Channel 4 managing director Justin Dukes; and from Italian television entrepreneur Silvio Berlusconi, in partnership with Mike Bolland of **Channel X**.

Channel Television

The Television Centre, La Pouquelaye, St Helier, Jersey, Channel Isles
☎ 0534 68999   Fax 0534 59446

Director of Programmes *Michael Lucas*

News, current affairs and documentaries provide the bulk of programmes. Makes programmes for the network. Ideas are assessed but only commissioned after sale is made to the network.

GMTV

5th Floor, The Television Centre, Upper Ground, London SE1 9LT
☎ 071-827 7000   Fax 071-827 7001

Managing Director *Christopher Stoddart*
Director of Programmes *Lis Howell*
Editor *Liam Hamilton*

Winner of the national breakfast television franchise with a bid of £34.6 million a year, compared to TV-AM's £14.5 million a year. Initially known as Sunrise Television but changed its name to avoid confusion with **Sky Television**'s breakfast programme of the same name. Jointly owned by **London Weekend Television, Scottish Television, Carlton Television,** *The Guardian, Manchester Evening News* and Disney. GMTV takes over from **TV-AM** on 1 January with live programming from 6 am to 9.25 am. Regular news headlines, current affairs, topical features, showbiz and lifestyle, sports and business, quizzes and competitions, travel and weather reports. *Good Morning,* its main programme, is to be more family-orientated than its predecessor: there will be a section for young children and a women's magazine show. Saturday morning's will be a children's show with news bulletins. There will be a softer approach altogether to news and less time given over to City news. The Sunday morning programme will be a leisure show about family matters. GMTV is hoping to attract a larger audience than TV-AM which at its peak attracted 2.7 million viewers.

Grampian Television

Queen's Cross, Aberdeen AB9 2XJ
☎0224 646464   Fax 0224 635127

Director of Programmes *George W. Mitchell*
Head of News & Current Affairs *Alistair Gracie*
Head of Documentaries & Features *Edward Brocklebank*

Extensive regional news and reports including farming, fishing and sports, interviews and leisure features, various light entertainment, Gaelic and religious programmes, and live coverage of the Scottish political, economic and industrial scene. Serves the area stretching from Fife to Shetland.

Granada Television

Granada TV Centre, Manchester M60 9EA
☎061-832 7211   Fax 061-832 7211 ext. 3405

Director of Programmes *Steve Morrison*
Head of Factual Programming *Rod Caird*
Head of Regional Programming *Stuart Prebble*
Head of Drama *Sally Head*
Head of Entertainment *David Liddiment*
Head of Current Affairs *Ray Fitzwalter*
Head of Sport *Paul Doherty*
Head of Music *Barbara Blyth*
Head of Arts *William Burdett-Coutts*
Head of Feature Film Development *Pippa Cross*
Head of Children's Programmes *Edward Pugh*

Editor, News *John Huntley*
Editor, Regional Features *Charles Tremayne*

Opportunities for freelance writers have decreased of late but mss from professional writers will be considered. All mss should be addressed to the head of scripts.

HTV Cymru/Wales

Culverhouse Cross, Cardiff CF5 6XJ
☎0222 590590   Fax 0222 597183

Director of Programmes *Emyr Daniel*
Controller, Entertainment *Peter Elias Jones*
Controller, Children's & Family (Wales & West) *Peter Murphy*

News and current affairs, parliamentary coverage, the arts, sports, farming, business, education and the community. Productions with an authentic Welsh dimension always sought.

HTV West

Television Centre, Bath Road, Bristol BS4 3HG
☎0272 778366   Fax 0272 722400

Director of Programmes *Derek Clark*

There are no heads of departments as such (unlike its sister company HTV Wales). Interested in original scripts which have a West Country flavour or are written by people who live and work in the region. Strong local programme making in all departments has included series like *Along the Cotswold Way, Looking Back* and *At Home*; links with the community are regularly enhanced through programmes which encourage public response, such as *The Good Neighbour Show, Problems* and *Crimestoppers*. News and current affairs, regional arts, sports, reflections on local life, the region's history and cultural traditions form the backbone of programme coverage through series like *West This Week*. Supplies programmes for Channel 4 and also runs a thriving local junior drama workshop.

Independent Television Association (ITV)

Knighton House, 56 Mortimer Street, London W1N 8AN
☎071-612 8000   Fax 071-580 7892

The ITV Association is the central body representing the 16 independent TV programme companies. It is a non-profit making association whose main task is to determine policy over a wide range of the industry's concerns. Undertakes detailed work for the industry through sub-committees.

Independent Television News

200 Gray's Inn Road, London WC1X 8XZ
☏ 071-833 3000

Editor, ITN Programmes on ITV *David Mannion*
Editor, ITN Programmes on Channel 4 *Richard Tait*
Foreign News Manager *Mary-Ellen Cetra*
Head of Day & Nightime Programmes *Nigel Dacre*
Head of Channel 4 Weekly Programmes *Tony Millett*

ITN provides the main national and international news for the ITV network and Channel 4. ITN's programmes on ITV are *News at 12.30, News at 5.40, News at Ten* and *ITN Morning News*, as well as regular news headlines during the night and morning. There are also three programmes a day at weekends. ITN is contracted by Channel 4 to produce their in-depth news analysis programmes, *Channel 4 News, The Parliament Programme* and *World News* for *Channel 4 Daily*. ITN also provides the news, sport and business news for Oracle, the ITN teletext service, and the first international English language news programme, *ITN's World News*.

London Weekend Television (LWT)

London Television Centre, London SE1 9LT
☏ 071-620 1620

Controller of Entertainment *John Kaye Cooper*
Controller of Drama *Nick Elliott*
Controller of Arts *Melvyn Bragg*
Controller of Features & Current Affairs *Robin Paxton*
Controller of Sport *Stuart McConachie*

Makers of entertainment and drama series like *Surprise Surprise* and *London's Burning*; also *The South Bank Show* and *Aspel & Company*. Provides a large proportion of the network's drama and light entertainment, and is a major supplier to Channel 4.

Meridian Broadcasting

Television Centre, Northam Road,
Southampton SO9 5HZ
☏ 0703 222555   Fax 0703 330050

Head of Broadcasting *Roger Laughton*

New regional ITV franchise winner. It is intended that all network and most regional output will be commissioned from independent producers and programming is bound by the ITC guidelines which insist upon news, current affairs, children's and religious programming across a wide range of tastes.

Oracle Teletext

Craven House, 25-32 Marshall Street,
London W1V 1LL
☏ 071-434 3121   Fax 071-437 8974

News, Sport & City *Peter Hall*
Features *Robbie Burns*

Jointly owned by all the ITV companies operating in Great Britain and Northern Ireland. News, sport and business news services are supplied by Oracle's unit at ITN; national features and service information are provided by the centre in Craven House; regional data service, including TV guides, advertising, local events guide and weather are all produced at Craven House.

Scottish Television

Cowcaddens, Glasgow G2 3PR
☏ 041-332 9999   Fax 041-332 6982

Head of Programming, Scotland *David Scott*
Director of Programmes *Alistair Moffat*
Editor, News & Current Affairs *Blair Jenkins*
Controller of Drama *Robert Love*
Controller of Entertainment *Sandy Ross*
Senior Producer, Education & Features *Erina Rayner*

An increasing number of STV programmes such as *Taggart* and *Take The High Road* are now networked nationally. Programme coverage includes drama, religion, news, sport, outside broadcasts, special features, entertainment and the arts, education and Gaelic programmes. Also produces many one-offs for ITV and Channel 4.

S4C (Welsh 4th Channel)

Parc Ty Glas, Caerdydd CF4 5GG
☏ 0222 747444   Fax 0222 754444

Deputy Programme Controller *Deryk Williams*

The Welsh 4th Channel was established by the Broadcasting Act 1980 with responsibility for a schedule of Welsh and English programmes. The service, known as S4C, consists of about 30 hours per week of Welsh language programmes and more than 85 hours of English language output from Channel 4. Ten hours a week of the Welsh programmes are provided by the BBC; the remainder are purchased from HTV and independent producers. S4C is funded by the IBA/ITC, out of the ITV companies' fourth channel subscriptions. Drama, comedy and documentary.

Thames Television

Thames Television House, 306–316 Euston Road,
London NW1 3BB
☎071-387 9494

Director of Programmes David Elstein
Controller, Network Factual Programmes
Roger Bolton
Controller, Drama Loyd Shirley
Head of Features Mary McAnally
Head of Variety John Fisher
Controller, Light Entertainment John Howard
Davies
Controller, Sport & Outside Broadcasts Bob
Burrows
Controller, Children's/Education Allan Horrox
Head of Music & Arts Ian Martin

Perhaps the strongest of all drama production
departments with *Minder*, *Rumpole of the Bailey*
and *The Bill* to its credit. Light entertainment
output includes: *Give Us a Clue*, *Strike It Lucky*;
documentaries and features: *Unknown Chaplin*,
The Mikado, *Take 6 Cooks*; children's/youth programmes: *Rainbow*, *Sooty*, *The Gemini Factor*.

TSW – Television South West

Derry's Cross, Plymouth PL1 2SP
☎0752 663322   Fax 0752 671970

Director of Programmes Paul Stewart Laing
Head of News & Current Affairs Jon Williams
Head of Documentaries Frank Wintle
Head of Religion/Education Thomas Goodison
News Editor Rod Holmes
Sports Editor Pete Barraclough

Regional news and features, news and sport,
current affairs, consumer affairs, natural history,
arts, regional politics, business, angling, light entertainment, religious and children's.

TV-AM

Breakfast Television Centre, Hawley Crescent,
London NW1 8EF
☎071-267 4300/4377   Fax 071-267 5265

Director of Programmes Bill Ludford
Controller, News & Current Affairs Jeff
Berliner
Political Editor Gerry Foley
Religious Editor Rowanne Pasco
Sports Editor Jim Ferguson
Regional Editor Robert Farrer
Show Business Editor Jason Pollock

Successfully challenged for the ITV national breakfast franchise by Sunrise Television, now **GMTV**.
The franchise will transfer to GMTV on 1 January
1993.

TVS

Television Centre, Southampton SO9 5HZ
☎0703 634211   Fax 0703 211428

Controller, Factual Programmes Peter Williams
Controller, Drama Graham Benson
Controller, Entertainment Gill Stribling-Wright
**Controller, Children's & Family
Programming** Nigel Pickard
Head of Sport Gary Lovejoy
Head of Religion Rev. Stephen Lynas
Head of News David Morris Jones

Full range of regional and ITV network programmes from drama to documentary, children's
and light entertainment. Keen to encourage new
writing as far as possible but only look at mss
which come via literary agents or independent
production companies.

Tyne Tees Television

Television Centre, City Road, Newcastle upon
Tyne NE1 2AL
☎091-261 0181   Fax 091-261 2302

Director of Programmes Adrian Metcalfe
Controller, Regional Programmes Steve Ireland
Head of Education Sheila Browne
News Editor Dave Picken
Sports Editor Roger Tames

Religion, farming, politics, news and current affairs,
documentaries, business, sport and arts.

Ulster Television

Havelock House, Ormeau Road, Belfast BT7 1EB
☎0232 328122   Fax 0232 246695

Controller, Programming A. Bremner
Commissioning Editors Michael Beattie/Andrew
Crockart
News Editor Colm McWilliams
Light Entertainment Will Armstrong
Arts Bob Brien
Outside Broadcasts Alan Hailes
Gardening/Heritage Ruth Johnston/Robert
Lamrock

Regular programmes on news and current affairs,
sport, farming, education, music, light entertainment, arts, politics and industry.

Westcountry Television Ltd

Western Wood Way, Langage Science Park,
Plymouth PL7 5BG
☎0752 333333   Fax 0752 333444

Managing Director *John Prescott Thomas*
Controller, News & Current Affairs *Richard Myers*
Controller, Features *Jane Clarke*

Westcountry Television is one of the new ITV franchise holders and is due to come on the air at the beginning of 1993. Programming is bound by the ITC guidelines and will include news, current affairs, religious and children's programmes, across a wide range of tastes.

Yorkshire Television

Television Centre, Leeds LS3 1JS
☎0532 438283   Fax 0532 445107

Director of Programming *John Fairley*
Controller of Drama *Keith Richardson*
Current Affairs & Documentaries *Grant McKee*
Controller of Entertainment *Vernon Lawrence*
Head of Sport *Robert Charles*
Head of Science & Features *Duncan Dallas*
Head of Local Programmes *Graham Ironside*
Head of Education/Religious *Chris Jelley*

Drama series, film productions, studio plays and long-running series like *Emmerdale*. Always looking for strong writing in these areas, and makes great use of agents to find it. Unknowns should submit at least the first act, ideally the first episode if submitting a series, and synopsis. Documentary/current affairs material tends to be supplied by producers; opportunities in these areas are rare but adaptations of published work as a documentary subject are considered. Light entertainment comes from an already well-established circle of professionals in this area which is difficult to infiltrate. In theory opportunity exists within series/episode material. Best approach is through a good agent.

Cable and Satellite Television

Bravo

United Programming, Twyman House, 16 Bonny Street, London NW1 9PG
☎071-284 1570   Fax 071-284 2042

President *Adam Singer*

Cable programme provider of classic movies 24-hours a day. Delivered to operators on videotape.

British Sky Broadcasting

See **Sky Television**

Cable News Network - CNN

CNN House, 19-22 Rathbone Place,
London W1P 1DF
☎071-637 6800   Fax 071-637 6868

News Editor *Rob Reynolds*

24-hour television news network from the USA, adapted for a European audience. The world's first global television network. All press releases should be sent to Rob Reynolds.

The Children's Channel

9-13 Grape Street, London WC2H 8DR
☎071-240 3422   Fax 071-497 9113

Managing Director *Richard Wolfe*

Cable programme provider of children's programmes between 5 am and 3 pm. Satellite delivered by Intelsat V.

The Discovery Channel

United Programming, Twyman House, 16 Bonny Street, London NW1 9PG
☎071-284 1570   Fax 071-284 2042

Chief Executive *Adam Singer*

Cable programme provider of environmental and ecological films and documentaries. No funds to produce in-house but ideas and treatments welcome.

European Television Networks

The Quadrangle, 180 Wardour Street,
London W1V 4AE
☎071-439 1177   Fax 071-439 1415

Director of Programming *George Black*

Formerly WHSTV but renamed following change of ownership in late 1991. ETN's main subsidiaries are the European Sports Network; Lifestyle; Kindernet, the Dutch language children's channel, and the television facilities group Molinare.

SCREENSPORT
Europe's first sport-dedicated channel, transmitted via Astra satellite. 18 hours a day during the week and 24 hours at weekends. Goes out with 4 simultaneous language tracks (English, French, German and Dutch). A major part of programming is given to live event coverage.

LIFESTYLE
Similar in format to a woman's magazine, Lifestyle is transmitted via Astra satellite from 10 am to 6 pm weekdays, midday to 10 pm weekends. Includes cookery, chat shows, keep-fit, films, dramas, games, health and beauty tips.

Home Video Channel

Unit 11, Canalot Production Studios, 222 Kensal
Road, London W10 5BN
☎ 081-964 1141

Chief Executive *Chris Yates*

Cable programme provider of feature films between 8 pm and 4 am. Delivered to operators on
videotape. Also owns and operates the Adult
Channel via the Astra satellite.

Lifestyle

See **European Television Networks**

MTV Europe

Centro House, 20–23 Mandela Street,
London NW1 0DU
☎ 071-383 4250   Fax 071-383 2064

Managing Director *William Roedy*

Europe's 24-hour youth entertainment channel
available on cable and Astra satellite. Pop and rock
music 24-hours a day.

Screen Sport

See **European Television Networks**

Sky Television (BSkyB)

6 Centaurs Business Park, Grant Way, Syon Lane,
Isleworth, Middlesex TW7 5QD
☎ 081-782 3000   Fax 081-782 3030

The six-channel British Sky Broadcasting group
(owned by News International, Chargeurs, Granada, Pearson and Reed) broadcasts via the Astra
satellite.

SKY ONE
General entertainment channel comprising Sky-
produced and independently commissioned children's, magazine, variety and game shows, plus
drama, comedy, action/adventure, movies and
sport for 16½ hours a day. 'Something for all the
family.'

SKY NEWS
Europe's 24-hour news channel, providing live
coverage of the latest international, national and
business news, current affairs and documentary
programming, plus parliamentary coverage.

SKY MOVIES
24-hours of blockbuster action, comedy, horror
and adventure films plus exclusive live special
events coverage.

MOVIE CHANNEL
Feature film entertainment (24 hours a day), plus
movies for children, classics and the magazine
programme *Spotlight.*

SKY SPORTS
Dedicated to a UK audience, with outstanding live
coverage of major sports events. British and international football, Test cricket, boxing, tennis and
snooker (14 hours a day).

COMEDY CHANNEL
Broad range of comedy including all-time great
British classics, sitcoms from both sides of the
Atlantic and contemporary British humour.

Super Channel

Limeharbour, Melrose House, 14 Lanark Square,
London E14 9QD
☎ 071-418 9418

Managing Director *Marialini Marcucci*

Partly (55%) owned by Beta Television, one of
Europe's fastest growing communications companies, whose interests include the 24-hour music
channel Videomusic (Italy) and Super Channel.
The Virgin Group owns the other 45%. General
entertainment between 5.30 am and 1 am. Satellite
delivered by Entelsat.

Vision Broadcasting

Shaftesbury Centre, Percy Street,
Swindon SN2 2AZ
☎ 0793 511244

Chief Executive *Fran Wildish*

Tape-delivered Christian programming free to operators. Sundays for four hours.

National Radio

BBC and Independent

BBC Radio

Broadcasting House, London W1A 1AA
☎ 071-580 4468
Telex 265781

Controller, Radio 1 *Johnny Beerling*
Controller, Radio 2 *Frances Line*
Controller, Radio 3 *John Drummond*
Controller, Radio 4 *Michael Green*
Controller, Radio 5 *Patricia Ewing*

As we went to press it was reported that Radio 5, launched 1990 to cover live sports events, education and youth programmes, is already under threat for survival; and there is further turbulence at Radio 2 which has seen its audience drop from 11 million to nine million since the loss of its medium wave in 1991. Radio 5's demise is likely to trigger changes throughout BBC radio services. Radio 1, the music-based station, broadcasts occasional series devoted to special areas of music and biographical series. Other special programming includes the summer 'Roadshow' which tours seaside resorts, broadcasting live from a different location each week. Radio 2 is traditionally a popular light entertainment network for the older listener. The network is moving closer to a 'gold' station, specialising in music from the 1960s and '70s, and almost all of its comedy, quizzes and drama slots were to go by the beginning of 1993. All scripted comedy except for *News Huddlines* will disappear, and almost all quiz programmes. Radio 3, devoted mainly to classical and contemporary music, includes drama and talks, with programmes like 'Third Ear'. However, it was announced in April 1992 that the station's drama output was to be halved and one of the first casualties was the Tuesday night play, *Drama Now*. Up to 50 slots for radio drama are to be lost. Radio 4 is the main news and current affairs service with over a third of the channel's airtime devoted to this. Topical output is also covered by analytical/magazine programmes and parliamentary reports, and the station produces a wide range of other material: plays, comedy, quizzes, serials and readings, consumer matters, wildlife, science, phone-ins, gardening, correspondence and specialised information programmes, plus music-based gramophone output, special one-offs and *ad hoc* series.

Principal divisions within BBC Radio are: Drama; Light Entertainment; Sport & Outside Broadcasts; Magazine Programmes; Features, Arts & Education; and Music (Radio 3). News and current affairs come under the aegis of a separate directorate. Religious broadcasting comes under BBC Religious Broadcasting which handles programming for both television and radio.

Head of Light Entertainment *Jonathan James-Moore* Regular programmes include topical comedy weeklies like 'The News Huddlines', 'Week Ending', and many varied quiz and game shows. Contributions welcome to existing series.
Head of Radio Drama *John Tydeman*
Head of Sport/Outside Broadcasts *Larry Hodgson*
Head of Magazine Programmes *Caroline Millington* Regular programmes include 'Woman's Hour', 'Start the Week', 'Call Nick Ross', 'The Food Programme', 'Desert Island Discs', plus programmes for the handicapped, 'Does He Take Sugar', and for the blind, 'In Touch'. Contributions to existing series considered.
Head of Features/Arts/Education *Anne Winder* Written ideas for 20-minute talks or 45-minute documentaries welcome.
Head of School/Children's/Youth Programmes, Radio 5 *David Harding*
Head of Music, Radio 3 *Prof. Adrian Thomas*

BBC Radio Drama

Broadcasting House, London W1A 1AA
☎ 071-580 4468

Head of Drama *John Tydeman*
Editor, Radio 4 Plays *Jeremy Mortimer*
Editor, Series & Serials *Clive Brill*
Editor, Radio 3 Plays *Jeremy Howe*
Producer, Stories *Duncan Minshull*
Editor, Readings *David Benedictus*
Radio 5, Editor, Children/Youth, Drama & Features *Caroline Raphael*

Plays on Radios 3 and 4, plus stories and plays for children on Radio 5. The main drama outlet, Radio

4, broadcasts the following regular programmes: 'Classical Serial'; 'Saturday Playhouse'; 'Sunday Playhouse'; Monday 'Play'/'The Monday Play'; 'Book at Bedtime'; Tuesday 'Play'; Wednesday 'Play'; Thursday 'Play'; 'The Archers'; 'Citizens'.

Short stories should be sent to *Duncan Minshull* at the above address. Drama scripts should be sent to the appropriate editor, but it should be noted that they are normally fully scheduled for the next two years; any incoming mss have to have 'stunning potential'. Probably the best bet for new plays on Radio 4 is 'Afternoon Play'. Its producers are too numerous to list here; scripts should be sent to the *Senior Script Editor*. Programmes vary in their response to new work; some are more sympathetic than others. Writers are advised to familiarise themselves fully with the nature of programmes before submitting scripts.

BBC Radio, News and Current Affairs
Room 3116, Broadcasting House,
London W1A 1AA
☎071–580 4468   Fax 071–636 4295

Editor, News and Current Affairs, Radio *Jenny Abramsky*
Managing Editor, Radio Newsroom *John Williams*
Managing Editor, Current Affairs *Martin Cox*
Managing Editor, Intake *Ray Gowdridge*
Foreign News Editor *Chris Wyld*
General News Service *David Dunford*
Home Affairs *Jon Silverman*
Home News Editor *Phil Longman*

In August 1987 a new directorate was created within the BBC devoted exclusively to news and current affairs. The operation unified News and Current Affairs Radio and the two separate departments of Television News and Television Current Affairs. Radio 4 is the main radio service of news and current affairs with over a third of the channel's airtime devoted to it.

PROGRAMME EDITORS
Today *Phil Harding*
The World at One/The World This Weekend *Roger Mosey*
PM *Kevin Marsh*
The World Tonight *Margaret Budy*
Newsbeat, Radio 1 News *Bob Doran*
News '92, Radio 1 *Mike Gandon*
Editor, Business Programmes *Alan Griffiths*
News Editor, Radio 2 *Steve Mitchell*

Editor, Special Current Affairs Programmes *Anne Sloman*
Commissioning Editor, Weekly Programmes *Brian Walker*

Contributions from outside writers to existing series welcome.

BBC (Radio) Religious Broadcasting
Broadcasting House, London W1A 1AA
☎071–580 4468

Head of Religious Programmes, Radio *Rev. Ernest Rea*

Regular weekday and weekend programmes on Radios 2, 3 and 4, including live broadcast, news and discussion, and a wide variety of single programmes (features and documentaries) on Radios 3 and 4.

BBC World Service
PO Box 76, Bush House, Strand,
London WC2B 4PH
☎071–240 3456   Fax 071–379 6841

Editor, World Service in English *Ernest Warburton*
Editor, World Service News *Bob Jobbins*
Head of Current Affairs *Andrew Joynes*
Head of Central Talks & Features *William Crawley*
Editor, Export Liaison *Sheena Harold*
Sheena Harold is the Liaison Officer to whom all material should be addressed.

The World Service has services in English and 36 other languages. The English service is a round-the-clock service with news and current affairs as the main component. The BBC World Service is financed by a grant-in-aid voted by Parliament and by Foreign and Commonwealth Office contracts for services. In 1991 it was the fourth largest international broadcasting service in the world in numbers of hours of programming per week, with possibly the largest number of regular listeners — somewhere in the region of 120 million.

Other broadcast areas include world business, politics, people/ events & opinions, topical and development issues, the international scene, developments in science, technology and medicine, health matters, farming, sport, religion, music, the media, the arts. Regular Sunday programmes include 'Play of the Week' (classic/contemporary drama) and 'Short Story' (unpublished stories by listeners living outside Britain).

Talks & Features Department: provides scripts in English for translation and broadcast by the 36 foreign language services that make up the BBC World Service. Covers the following areas: (a) analysis of international current affairs; (b) cultural, social and economic affairs in Britain; (c) science, technology and export promotion. Contributors should bear in mind that the target audience cannot be taken to have a ready familiarity with life in this country or with British institutions. Translation skills are not necessary, as this is done exclusively by their own professionals.

BBC Radio Northern Ireland

Broadcasting House, 25–27 Ormeau Avenue, Belfast BT2 8HQ
☎ 0232 338000

Editor, Current Affairs *Rowan Hand*
Editor, Radio News *Eddie Fleming*

Local stations: Radios Foyle and Ulster (see **Local Radio**).

BBC Radio Scotland

Queen Margaret Drive, Glasgow G12 8DG
☎ 041-330 2345   Fax 041-334 0614
5 Queen Street, Edinburgh EH2 1JF
☎ 031-469 4200
Broadcasting House, Beechgrove Terrace, Aberdeen AB9 2ZT
☎ 0224 625233

Head of Radio *Neil Fraser*
Head of News & Current Affairs *Phil Taylor*
Editor, News/Current Affairs *Robin Wyllie*
Editor, Current Affairs *Geoffrey Cameron*
Entertainment Programmes *Robert Noakes*
Topical Programmes *Neil A. Fraser*
Manager, Edinburgh *Mike Shaw*
Senior Producer, Drama, Edinburgh *Stewart Conn*
Editor, Features & Documentaries, Edinburgh *Mike Shaw*

Produces a full range of news and current affairs programmes, plus comedy, documentaries, drama, short stories, talks and features. The emphasis is on speech-based programmes (rather than music, etc.) and programmes reflecting Scottish culture. Scottish BBC Radio has three main roles: to provide a national radio service, primarily from its centres in Glasgow, Edinburgh and Aberdeen; to maintain the local community stations, which take the national programmes and splice these with local material; and to reflect and represent Scottish culture in the UK. Networks (as with plays, for instance, in the recognised Radio 3 and Radio 4 drama slots). Local stations: Radios Aberdeen, Highland, Orkney, Shetland, Solway, and Tweed (see **Local Radio**).

BBC Radio Wales

Broadcasting House, Llandaff, Cardiff CF5 2YQ
☎ 0222 572888   Fax 0222 552973
Broadcasting House, Meirion Road, Bangor LL57 2BY
☎ 0248 370880   Fax 0248 351443
32 Alexandra Road, Swansea SA1 5DZ
☎ 0792 654986   Fax 0792 468194

Head of Radio *Meirion Edwards*
Editor, Radio Wales *Gaynor Shutte*
Editor, Radio Cymru *Lyn Jones*
Head of News/Current Affairs (TV & Radio) *Gwilym Owen*
Editor, Welsh Language Current Affairs *Aled Euris*
Station Manager, Swansea *Sulwyn Thomas*
Head of Production, Bangor *R. Alun Evans*

As with BBC Radio Scotland, there are two aspects to the working of the Welsh network. There are three centres of programme-making (Cardiff, Bangor and Swansea) for the national Welsh BBC network, and two community stations which provide local material for local audiences. These are Radios Clwyd and Gwent (see **Local Radio**).

BFBS (British Forces Broadcasting Service)

PO Box 1234, London W2 1LA
☎ 071-724 1234   Fax 071-706 1582

News Editor *Tony Davis*
Controller of Programmes *Chris Russell*

Classic FM

Academic House, 24–28 Oval Road, London NW1 7DQ
☎ 071-284 3000   Fax 071-284 2835

Chief Executive *John Spearman*
Programme Controller *Michael Bukht*

Winner of the first independent national radio licence regulated by the Radio Authority. (The second has been awarded to **Independent Music Radio**; the third will be a speech-based station and is likely to be awarded some time during 1993). Classic FM, on the air from autumn 1992, is Britain's first independent national radio station specialising in classical music. Features, reviews and talks are expected to be part of the programming, but no details on specific policy were yet available as we went to press.

Independent Music Radio

Breakfast Television Centre, Hawley Crescent, London NW1 8EF
☎ 071-288 4347

Managing Director *John Aumonier*

Winner of the second (of three) independent national radio licences regulated by the Radio Authority, the first of which went to **Classic FM**. Backed by **TV-AM** and Virgin, the station comes on the air early in 1993 (sometime around March) and is essentially a rock/pop station with news bulletins.

Independent Radio News (IRN)

Crown House, 72 Hammersmith Road,
London W14 8YE

☎ 071–371 1515   Fax 071–371 2155

Transmitted from **LBC Newstalk**'s headquarters, IRN supplies national and international news coverage to all independent local radio stations in the UK.

Local Radio

BBC Local Radio

BBC Regional Broadcasting

There are 37 local BBC radio stations transmitting on FM and medium wave. These present local news, information and entertainment to local audiences. They have their own newsroom which supplies local bulletins and national news service. Many have specialist producers. A comprehensive list of programmes for each is unavailable and would soon be out of date. For general information on programming, contact the station manager.

BBC CWR

25 Warwick Road, Coventry CV1 2WR
☎ 0203 559911   Fax 0203 520080

Station Manager *Andy Wright*
Programme Organiser *Charles Hodkinson*

Commenced broadcasting in January 1990. News, current affairs, public service information and community involvement, relevant to its broadcast area: Coventry and Warwickshire. Occasionally uses the work of local writers, though cannot handle large volumes of unsolicited material. Any material commissioned will need to be strong in local interest and properly geared to broadcasting.

BBC Essex

198 New London Road, Chelmsford CM2 9XB
☎ 0245 262393   Fax 0245 490703

Managing Editor *Richard Lucas*
Programme Organiser *Keith Roberts*

Provides no regular outlets for writers but mounts special projects from time to time; these are well publicised on the air.

BBC GLR (Greater London Radio)

PO Box 94.9, 35C Marylebone High Street,
London W1A 4LG
☎ 071-224 2424   Fax 071-487 2908

Managing Editor *Trevor Dann*
Programme Organiser *Kate Marsh*

Greater London Radio was launched in 1988. It broadcasts adult music and local news to Greater London and the Home Counties.

BBC GMR

New Broadcasting House, PO Box 951, Oxford Road, Manchester M60 1SD
☎ 061-200 2000   Fax 061-228 6110

Manager *Martin Henfield*
Programme Editor *Ev Draper*

Formerly Radio Manchester. Very few opportunities apart from 'Write Now', a weekly half-hour regional local writing programme, shared with Radios Merseyside, Lancashire & Cumbria. Contact *Jenny Collins* on 051-708 5500.

BBC Radio Aberdeen

Beechgrove Terrace, Aberdeen AB9 2ZT
☎ 0224 625233   Fax 0224 642931

Editor *Ken Mutch*

News, local only. Midday Thursday programme presented by Robbie Shepherd, called 'Shepherd's Tartan', features books, poetry, etc., of local interest.

BBC Radio Bedfordshire

PO Box 476, Hastings Street, Luton,
Bedfordshire LU1 5BA
☎ 0582 459111   Fax 0582 401467

Station Manager *Mike Gibbons*
Programme Organiser *Jeff Winston*

Encourages freelance contributions from the community across a wide range of radio output, including interview and feature material. The station very occasionally broadcasts drama. Stringent local criteria are applied in selection. Particularly interested in historical topics (five minutes maximum).

BBC Radio Berkshire
42A Portman Road, Reading, Berkshire RG3 1NB
☎ 0734 567056

Editor *Simon Major*

On the air since January 1992.

BBC Radio Bristol
3 Tyndalls Park Road, Bristol BS8 1PP
☎ 0272 741111   Fax 0272 732549

Programme Editor *Malcolm Brammar*

Wide range of feature material.

BBC Radio Cambridgeshire
104 Hills Road, Cambridge CB2 1LD
☎ 0223 315970   Fax 0223 460832

Managing Editor *Margaret Hyde*
Programme Organiser *Gerald Main*

Short stories are broadcast regularly. Scripts from listeners within the county of Cambridgeshire are considered but there is no payment.

BBC Radio Cleveland
Broadcasting House, PO Box 95FM,
Middlesbrough, Cleveland TS1 5DG
☎ 0642 225211   Fax 0642 211356

Programme Organiser *Mick Wormald*

Material used is almost exclusively local to Cleveland, County Durham and North Yorkshire, and written by local writers. Contributions welcome for 'House Call' (Saturdays 1.05–2 pm, presented by Bill Hunter). Poetry and the occasional short story are included.

BBC Radio Clwyd
The Old School House, Glanrafon Road, Mold,
Clwyd CH7 1PA
☎ 0352 700367   Fax 0352 759821

Senior Producer *Tony Todd*

Runs an annual short story competition in conjunction with Wrexham Writers' Workshop. Also regular competitions on 'Memories' and 'Ghoststories' for county residents, plus daily short stories on 'Postbag' though this is restricted to residents of Clwyd only.

BBC Radio Cornwall
Phoenix Wharf, Truro, Cornwall TR1 1UA
☎ 0872 75421   Fax 0872 75045

Programme Editor *Julie Stanton*

Opportunities exist for Cornish poetry and literature on the Sunday afternoon arts programme called 'Seen and Heard'.

BBC Radio Cumbria
Hilltop Heights, London Road, Carlisle CA1 2NA
☎ 0228 31661   Fax 0228 511195

Manager *Michael Marsh*

Few opportunities for writers apart from 'Write Now', a weekly half-hour regional local writing programme, shared with Radios Merseyside, Manchester and Lancashire. Contact *Jenny Collins* on 051-708 5500. Christmas poetry competition in 1991 attracted so many entries that it is likely to be repeated in 1992 and possibly thereafter.

BBC Radio Derby
PO Box 269, Derby DE1 3HL
☎ 0332 361111   Fax 0332 290794

Contact *Station Manager*

BBC Radio Devon
PO Box 100, Exeter EX4 4DB
☎ 0392 215651
Fax 0392 410959   Telex 42440

Station Manager *Roy Corlett*
Programme Organiser *John Lilley*

Short stories — up to 1000 words from local authors only — used weekly on the Sunday afternoon show (2.05–3.30 pm) and on Friday's late-night 'Sou'West' (10.05 pm–midnight).

BBC Radio Foyle
8 Northland Road, Londonderry BT48 7JT
☎ 0504 262244   Fax 0504 260067

Station Manager *Charlie Warmington*
Book Reviews *Stephen Price*

Radio Foyle broadcasts both its own programmes and those for Belfast — for national transmission. Programmes made by Radio Foyle will occasionally be taken up by the national network. Runs a weekly book reviews programme called 'First Impressions'.

BBC Radio Furness
Hartington Street, Barrow-in-Furness,
Cumbria LA14 5FH
☎ 0229 836767   Fax 0229 870008

Senior Producer *Mark Jones*
Producer *Steve Barber*

Community sub-station of Radio Cumbria, to whose 'Write Now' programme unsolicited material will be forwarded. Published authors are welcome as on-air guests.

BBC Radio Gloucestershire
London Road, Gloucester GL1 1SW
☎0452 308585   Fax 0452 306541

Station Manager *Peter Gallimore*
Programme Editor *Mark Hurrell*

News and information covering the large variety of interests and concerns in Gloucestershire. Leisure, sport and music, plus Afro-Caribbean and Asian interests. Unsolicited material is not generally welcome. Competition and twice-yearly short story series encourage local authors. Mss should last 5–6 minutes on air. Send to programme editor.

BBC Radio Guernsey
Commerce House, Les Banques, St Peter Port, Guernsey, Channel Isles
☎0481 728977   Fax 0481 713557

Station Manager *Robert Bufton*
News Editor *Kay Langlois*

BBC Radio Hereford & Worcester
43 Broad Street, Hereford HR4 9HH
☎0432 355252   Fax 0432 356446
Hylton Road, Worcester WR2 5WW
☎0905 748485   Fax 0905 748006

Station Manager *John Pickles*
Programme Organiser *Denzil Dudley*

Interested in short stories, plays or dramatised documentaries with a local flavour.

BBC Radio Highland
Broadcasting House, 7 Culduthel Road, Inverness IV2 4AD
☎0463 221711   Fax 0463 236125

Station Manager *Maggie Cunningham*

BBC Radio Humberside
9 Chapel Street, Hull, North Humberside HU1 3NU
☎0482 23232
Fax 0482 226409   Telex 597031

Station Manager *Geoff Sargieson*
Programme Organiser *Geoff Hibbert*

Broadcasts short stories by local writers each afternoon. Details broadcast.

BBC Radio Jersey
Broadcasting House, Rouge Bouillion, St Helier, Jersey, Channel Isles JE2 3ZA
☎0534 70000   Fax 0534 32569

Station Manager *Robert Bufton*
News Editor *Mike Vibert*

Local news, current affairs and community items.

BBC Radio Kent
Sun Pier, Chatham, Kent ME4 4EZ
☎0634 830505
Fax 0634 830505 ext. 143   Telex 965011

Managing Editor *Jim Latham*
Programme Organiser *Clive Lawrence*

Opportunities exist for writers on the afternoon magazine programme, and on the specialist arts programme, 'Scene and Heard'. Features need to be of strong local interest, as do drama/fiction, for which there are few openings. Occasional commissions are made for local interest documentaries and other one-off programmes. Ten-minute drama competition. An annual event for amateur playwrights with the prize being an opportunity to have their play broadcast on radio.

BBC Radio Lancashire
Darwen Street, Blackburn BB2 2EA
☎0254 262411   Fax 0254 680821

Manager *Chris van Schaick*
Programme Organiser *Mark Thomas*

Not very many opportunities for writers apart from 'Write Now', a weekly half-hour regional local writing programme, shared with Radios Merseyside, Manchester & Cumbria. Contact *Jenny Collins* on 051–708 5500.

BBC Radio Leeds
Broadcasting House, Woodhouse Lane, Leeds LS2 9PN
☎0532 442131   Fax 0532 420652

Station Manager *John Jefferson*
Programme Organiser *Liz Green*

BBC Radio Leicester

Epic House, Charles Street, Leicester LE1 3SH
☎ 0533 516688
Fax 0533 513632 (Management)/511463 (News)

Station Manager *Jeremy Robinson*

BBC Radio Lincolnshire

PO Box 219, Newport, Lincoln LN1 3DF
☎ 0522 511411   Fax 0522 511058

Station Manager *David Wilkinson*
Programme Organiser *Malcolm Swire*
Farming/Features Producer *Alan Stennett*

Unsolicited material only considered if locally
relevant. Maximum 1000 words: straight narrative
preferred, ideally with a topical content.

BBC Radio London

See **BBC Radio GLR**

BBC Radio Manchester

See **BBC Radio GMR**

BBC Radio Merseyside

55 Paradise Street, Liverpool L1 3BP
☎ 051-708 5500   Fax 051-708 5356

Station Manager *Richard Duckenfield*
Senior Producer/Deputy Manager *Barbara Taylor*

No opportunities in news and few, if any, in light
entertainment, drama or fiction. 'Write Now', a
weekly half-hour regional writing programme,
shared with Radios Lancashire, Manchester & Cumbria, features work by local talent from the North
West only. Short stories (maximum 1200 words),
plus poetry and features on writing. Contact *Jenny
Collins* on 051-708 5500.

BBC Radio Newcastle

Broadcasting Centre, Newcastle upon
Tyne NE99 1RN
☎ 091-232 4141   Fax 091-232 5082

Station Manager *Tony Fish*
Programme Organiser *Derm Tanner*

Opportunities for freelance writers are extremely
rare.

BBC Radio Norfolk

Norfolk Tower, Surrey Street, Norwich NR1 3PA
☎ 0603 617411
Fax 0603 622229/633692   Telex 975515

Managing Editor *Keith Salmon*

Good local material welcome for features/
documentaries, but must relate directly to Norfolk.

BBC Radio Northampton

Broadcasting House, Abington Street,
Northampton NN1 2BH
☎ 0604 239100   Fax 0604 230709

Programme Organiser *Nigel Dyson*

Literary outlets limited, but they do occur occasionally in the form of short story competitions/poetry
week, and are trailed accordingly.

BBC Radio Nottingham

York House, Mansfield Road,
Nottingham NG1 3JB
☎ 0602 415161   Fax 0602 481482

Programme Organiser *Nick Brunger*

Interviews with authors form a regular and important part of Radio Nottingham's output.

BBC Radio Oxford

269 Banbury Road, Oxford OX2 7DW
☎ 0865 311444   Fax 0865 311915

Programme Organiser *Stewart Woodcock*

No opportunities at present as the outlet for short
stories has been discontinued for the time being.

BBC Radio Peterborough

PO Box 957, Peterborough PE1 1YT
☎ 0733 312832   Fax 0733 343768

Managing Editor *Margaret Hyde*
Programme Organiser *Gerald Main*
Senior Producer (Peterborough) *Steve Somers*

Sister service, launched May 1990, to Radio Cambridgeshire. Mid-morning programme called 'Peterborough Today' (9 am-midday), with Jo Pinnock
on the Peterborough arts scene.

BBC Radio Sheffield

60 Westbourne Road, Sheffield S10 2QU
☎ 0742 686185   Fax 0742 664375

Station Manager *Nigel Kay*
Programme Organiser *Everard Davy*

Radio Sheffield does not broadcast any short stories or poetry. Radio 4's producer for network features and drama, however, is based at Radio Sheffield and is interested in local writing.

BBC Radio Shropshire
2-4 Boscobel Drive, Shrewsbury, Shropshire SY1 3TT
☏0743 248484
Fax 0743 271702   Telex 35187

Station Manager *Lawrie Bloomfield*
Programme Organiser *Eric Smith*

Unsolicited literary material very rarely used, and then only if locally relevant.

BBC Radio Solent
Broadcasting House, Havelock Road, Southampton SO1 0XR
☏0703 631311
Fax 0703 339648   Telex 47420

Station Manager *Steve Panton*
Acting Programme Editor *Mike Hapgood*

Occasional short story competitions.

BBC Radio Solway
Lovers Walk, Dumfries DG1 1NZ
☏0387 68008
Fax 0387 52568   Telex 776671

Editor *Willie Johnston*

The lunchtime arts programme 'Spotlight' features a writers' workshop slot in which established authors read and assess amateur submissions. Locally relevant mss should be addressed to *Lindsay Cannon*.

BBC Radio Stoke
Cheapside, Hanley, Stoke on Trent ST1 1JJ
☏0782 208080   Fax 0782 289115

Station Manager *John Collard*
Programme Organiser *Mervyn Gamage*

Emphasis on news, current affairs and local topics. Music represents one third of total output. Unsolicited material of local interest is welcome. Send to the programme organiser.

BBC Radio Suffolk
Broadcasting House, St Matthews Street, Ipswich IP1 3EP
☏0473 250000   Fax 0473 210887

Managing Editor *Ivan Howlett*
Programme Organiser *Jim Ensom*

Strongly speech-based, dealing with news, current affairs, community issues, the arts, agriculture, commerce, travel, sport and leisure. Three programmes frequently carry interviews with writers. These are: 'Suffolk Daily'; 'John Eley in the Afternoon'; and the arts programme 'Preview'.

BBC Radio Surrey
Broadcasting House, University of Surrey, Guildford GU2 5AP
☏0483 306113   Fax 0483 304952

Editor *Claire Paul*

BBC Radio Sussex
Marlborough Place, Brighton, East Sussex BN1 1TU
☏0273 680231   Fax 0273 571754/601241

Programme Organiser *Jim Beaman*

BBC Radio Tweed
Municipal Buildings, High Street, Selkirk TD7 4BU
☏0750 21884   Fax 0750 22400

Senior Producer *Geoff Webster*

BBC (Radio) Wiltshire Sound
Broadcasting House, Prospect Place, Swindon, Wiltshire SN1 3RW
☏0793 513626   Fax 0793 513650

Station Manager *Tony Talmage*
Programme Organiser *Mike Gray*

BBC Radio WM
PO Box 206, Birmingham B5 7SD
☏021-414 8484   Fax 021-472 3174

Station Manager *Tony Inchley*
Programme Organiser *Tony Wadsworth*

BBC Radio York
20 Bootham Row, York YO3 7BR
☏0904 641351   Fax 0904 610937

Station Manager *Barry Stockdale*
Programme Organiser *Andy Jones*

A limited outlet for short stories and features, provided they are either set locally or have some other local relevance.

Greater London Radio
See **BBC GLR**

Independent Local Radio

Aire FM/Magic 828
PO Box 2000, Leeds LS3 1LR
☎ 0532 452299   Fax 0532 421830

Programme Controller *Paul Fairburn*

Beacon Radio/WABC
267 Tettenhall Road, Wolverhampton WV6 0DQ
☎ 0902 757211   Fax 0902 745456

Programme Director *Peter Wagstaff*

No outlets for unsolicited literary material at present.

Radio Borders
Tweedside Park, Tweedbank, Galashiels TD1 3TD
☎ 0896 59444   Fax 0896 59494

Programme Controller *Rod Webster*
Head of News *Jill McPherson*

Breeze AM
See **Essex Radio**

BRMB FM/XTRA AM
Radio House, Aston Road North,
Birmingham B6 4BX
☎ 021-359 4481
Fax 021-359 1117   Telex 339707

Head of Programmes *Ian Rufus*
Head of News *Colin Palmer*

Occasional drama, plus an annual short story competition; and some demand for comedy material. Opportunities for writers in the various feature series which the station puts out.

Radio Broadland
St Georges Plain, 47–49 Colegate,
Norwich NR3 1DB
☎ 0603 630621   Fax 0603 666353

Programme Director *Mike Stewart*
Head of Features *Dick Hutchinson*

Contact head of features for feature material.

Brunel Classic Gold
See **GWR FM**

Capital FM/Capital Gold
PO Box 958, Euston Tower, London NW1 3DR
☎ 071-608 6080   Fax 071-387 2345

Head of News & Talks *Nicholas Wheeler*

Britain's largest commercial radio station, with a large interest in a number of other independent local radio stations, including the Monte Carlo-based Riviera Radio. Main outlet is news and showbiz programme each weekday evening at 7 pm called 'The Way It Is'. This covers current affairs, features and pop news, aimed at a young audience. The vast majority of material is generated in-house.

Chiltern Radio
Chiltern Road, Dunstable, Bedfordshire LU6 1HQ
☎ 0582 666001   Fax 0582 605139

News Editor *Paul Chantler*

Part of the Chiltern Radio Network. Opportunities for radio drama only, but these are rare. If a script is of exceptional local interest, it has a fair chance of being considered.

Radio City/City FM/Radio City Gold
PO Box 194, 8–10 Stanley Street,
Liverpool L1 6AF
☎ 051-227 5100   Fax 051-471 0330

Managing Director *Dave Lincoln*
Programme Controller *Tony McKenzie*

Opportunities for writers are very few and far between. However, some poetry and short narrative fiction is broadcast. This tends to be listeners' contributions and there is no payment.

Radio Clyde
Clydebank Business Park, Clydebank G81 2RX
☎ 041-306 2272
Fax 041-306 2265   Telex 779537

Programme Director *Alex Dickson*

Radio Clyde and the IBA, together with the Society of Authors and **The Writers' Guild**, launched a major new commissioning scheme for radio drama in 1989. The aim was to create a regular strand of specially produced plays for independent radio stations. Members of the Society or Guild were asked to submit outlines for previously unsubmitted work towards a one-hour production for radio — preference for contemporary themes, and no special emphasis on Scottish works. Accepted outlines led to full-length script commissions for production at Radio Clyde's drama department. Few opportunities outside of this now as programmes usually originate in-house or by commission. All documentary material is made in-house. Good local news items always considered.

CN.FM 103

PO Box 1000, Vision Park, Chivers Way, Histon, Cambridge CB4 4WW
☎ 0223 235255   Fax 0223 235161

Managing Director *David Cocks*

Sister station of Hereward Radio. Not usually any openings as all material is compiled and presented by in-house staff.

Cool FM

See **Downtown Radio**

County Sound Radio

Broadfield House, Brighton Road, Crawley, West Sussex RH11 9TT
☎ 0293 519161   Fax 0293 560927

Group Programme Controller *John Wellington*
Deputy Programme Controller *Andrew Marshall*
Head of News *Martin Campbell*

Regional AM service which together with **Radio Mercury** is now under the new management of Allied Radio. Local programming continues, however, in both transmission areas. Predominantly speech-based station. Local interest items welcome. Send to deputy programme controller. The group's programme controller is based at Radio Mercury.

DevonAir Radio/South West One

35–37 St David's Hill, Exeter EX4 4DA
☎ 0392 430703   Fax 0392 411893

Programme Controller *Michael Holloway*

Owned by West Country Broadcasting. No opportunities for freelancers.

Downtown Radio/Cool FM

Newtownards, Co. Down, Northern Ireland BT23 4ES
☎ 0247 815555   Fax 0247 815252

Programme Head *John Rosborough*

Downtown Radio first ran a highly successful short story competition in 1988, attracting over 400 stories. The competition became an annual event and writers are asked to submit material during the winter and early spring. The competition is promoted in association with Eason & Co. For further information, write to *Derek Ray* at the station.

Essex Radio/Breeze AM

Radio House, Clifftown Road, Southend on Sea, Essex SS1 1SX
☎ 0702 333711   Fax 0702 345224

Programme Controllers *Peter Holmes* (Essex Radio)/*Keith Rogers* (Breeze AM)

No real opportunities for writers' work as such, but will often interview local authors of published books. Contact *Carol Walker* (Programming Secretary) in the first instance.

Radio Forth RFM/Max AM

Forth House, Forth Street, Edinburgh EH1 3LF
☎ 031–556 9255   Fax 031–558 3277

Programme Director *Tom Steele*

Arts *Alec Shuttleworth* Opportunities in the two-minute feature series 'The Story of...'.

Light Entertainment *Tom Steele* Sixty-second 'Radio Cartoons'.

News Editor *David Johnston* News stories welcome from freelancers.

Max AM, launched 1990, is aimed at the 40+ age group. Although music-based, it includes a wide range of specialist general interest programmes.

Fox FM

Brush House, Pony Road, Cowley, Oxfordshire OX4 2XR
☎ 0865 748787   Fax 0865 748721/
748736 (news)

Programme Controller *Steve Ellis*
Head of News *Abi Donald*

Backed by an impressive list of shareholders including the Blackwell Group of Companies. No outlet for creative writing; however, authors soliciting book reviews should contact *David Freeman* at the station.

GEM-AM

29–31 Castle Gate, Nottingham NG1 7AP
☎ 0602 581731
Fax 0602 588614   Telex 37463

Managing Director/Programme Controller
Chris Hughes

Part of the Midlands Radio Group. Also transmits from Derby and Leicester, and runs the same short story series/competition as Trent FM (see entry).

Great North Radio (GNR)
See **Metro FM**

Great Yorkshire Radio
PO Box 777, Sheffield
☎0742 766766/721021   Fax 0742 853159
Also PO Box 777, Bradford/Hull/Leeds

Programme Controller *Dean Pepall*

Little opportunity for writers, although phone-in programmes may consider interviewing relevant authors.

GWR FM/Brunel Classic Gold
PO Box 2000, Watershed, Canon's Road,
Bristol BS99 7SN
☎0272 279900/Brunel 258600
Fax 0272 279900 ext. 303

**Station Director/Programme Controller,
GWR** *Steve Orchard*
Station Director, Brunel *Simon Cooper*
Programme Director, Brunel *Trevor Fry*

Both stations also transmit from Swindon. Very few opportunities. Almost all material originates in-house. GWR is targeted at the under 40s, while Brunel is aimed at the more mature (35/40+) listener.

Hallam FM
900 Herries Road, Hillsborough, Sheffield S6 1RH
☎0742 853333   Fax 0742 853159

Programme Controller *Steve King*

Hereward FM
PO Box 225, Queensgate Centre,
Peterborough PE1 1XJ
☎0733 346225   Fax 0733 896400 (news)

Programme Controller *Adrian Crookes*

Not usually any openings offered to writers as all material is compiled and presented by in-house staff.

Horizon Radio
Broadcast Centre, Crownhill, Milton Keynes,
Buckinghamshire MK8 0AB
☎0908 269111   Fax 0908 564893

Programme Controller *Paul Chantler*

Part of the Chiltern Radio Network.

Invicta FM/Invicta Supergold
PO Box 100, Whitstable, Kent CT5 3QX
☎0227 772004   Fax 0227 771558

Programme Controller *John Lewis*

Music-based station, serving listeners in the South East. 'Always on the look-out for creative, innovative programming ideas of any kind.'

IRN (Independent Radio News)
See **National Radio**

LBC Newstalk FM/London Talkback Radio/IRN
Crown House, 72 Hammersmith Road,
London W14 8YE
☎071-371 1515   Fax 071-371 2166

Director of Programmes (London Talkback)
Robin Malcolm

LBC Newstalk FM combines extensive local, national and international news, with informative, thought-provoking programmes. London Talkback Radio features news, views and phone-ins. New ideas welcome, preferably preceded by an explanatory letter.

Leicester Sound FM
Granville House, Granville Road,
Leicester LE1 7RW
☎0533 551616   Fax 0533 550869

Managing Director/Programme Controller
Stuart Linnell
Operations Manager *Tim Dickens*
News Editor *Peter Butler*

Predominantly a music station. Occasionally runs short story competitions. Very occasionally, unsolicited material of local interest — 'targeted at our particular audience' — may be broadcast.

Magic 828
See **Aire FM**

Marcher Sound

The Studios, Mold Road, Wrexham LL11 4AF
☎0978 752202   Fax 0978 759701

Programme Controller *Paul Mewies*

Occasional features and advisory programmes.
Welsh language broadcasts weekdays at 6.00 pm.

Max AM

See **Radio Forth RFM**

Mercia FM

Hertford Place, Coventry CV1 3TT
☎0203 633933   Fax 0203 258206

Programme Controller *Stuart Linnell*

Weekly arts programme called 'Centre Stage'.
Producers *Clive Skelhon/Sue White*

Radio Mercury

Broadfield House, Brighton Road, Crawley, West
Sussex RH11 9TT
☎0293 519161
Fax 0293 560927   Telex 87503

Group Programme Controller *John Wellington*

From 1992 Radio Mercury will be merged under
the management of Allied Radio, together with
County Sound. Local programming will, however,
continue in both transmission areas. Predominantly
music-based station operating on FM. Very little
opportunity for unsolicited material.

Metro FM/Great North Radio (GNR)

Swalwell, Newcastle upon Tyne NE99 1BB
☎091–488 3131/496 0337   Fax 091–488 9222

Programme Controller, Metro *Giles Squire*
Programme Controller, GNR *Steve Martin*

Very few opportunities for writers, but phone-in
programmes may interview relevant authors. Some
interest in short comedy for the Metro FM station.

Moray Firth Radio

PO Box 271, Scourgurie Place, Inverness IV3 6SF
☎0463 224433
Fax 0463 243224   Telex 75643

Programme Controller *Thomas Prag*
Book Reviews *May Marshall*

Book reviews every Monday afternoon at 3.15 pm
and every Sunday evening at 10.15 pm. Also
fortnightly arts programme called 'The North Bank

Show' which features interviews with authors, etc.
Runs an annual competition for amateur dramatists
called 'Playsearch'.

Northants Radio

Broadcast Centre, Enterprise Park, Boughton
Green, Northampton NN2 7AH
☎0604 29811   Fax 0604 250666

Programme Controller *Paul Chantler*

Part of the Chiltern Radio Network. Little scope for
creative writing but runs book reviews and author
interviews.

NorthSound Radio

45 King's Gate, Aberdeen AB2 6BL
☎0224 632234   Fax 0224 633282

Station Manager *John Martin*
Programme Controller *John Trousdale*

Produces a regular series on books and authors
called 'Book Ends'; Scottish authors are of particular interest. Keen to promote new work. Contact
Michael Mappin, Production Department.

Ocean Sound/South Coast Radio

Whittle Avenue, Segensworth West, Fareham,
Hampshire PO15 5PA
☎0489 589911   Fax 0489 589453

Programme Director *Jeremy Scott*
Programme Controller *Guy Hornsby*
News Editor *Karen Woods*

For economic reasons, Ocean Sound rarely considers commissioning an external writer to produce
drama/short stories for the station. All submissions
are, however, considered, but only those with a
special local connection are likely to be taken
further. There are plans to run a short story
competition on South Coast Radio.

Orchard FM

Haygrove House, Shoreditch, Taunton,
Somerset TA3 7BT
☎0823 338448   Fax 0823 321044

Programme Controller *David Rodgers*
News Editor *Charles Eden*

Summaries for music programming welcome. Send
ideas in the first instance.

Radio Orwell

See **SGR FM**

Pennine FM
See **Pulse FM**

Piccadilly Gold/Key 103
127–131 The Piazza, Piccadilly Plaza,
Manchester M1 4AW
☎061-236 9913   Fax 061-228 1503

Programme Director *Mark Story*

Music-based station. Very occasional author interviews.

Plymouth Sound
Earl's Acre, Alma Road, Plymouth PL3 4HX
☎0752 227272   .   Fax 0752 670730

Programme Controller *Louise Churchill*

Owned by West Country Broadcasting.

Pulse FM
PO Box 3000, Bradford BD1 5NE
☎0274 731521   Fax 0274 307774

Programme Controller *Alan Ross*

Formerly traded as Pennine FM.

Red Dragon FM/Touch AM
Radio House, West Canal Wharf, Cardiff CF1 5XJ
☎0222 384041/237878   Fax 0222 384014

Programme Controller *Jon Gripton*

Red Rose Gold/Rock FM
PO Box 301, St Paul's Square, Preston PR1 1YE
☎0772 556301   Fax 0772 201917

Programme Director *John Myers*

Music-based station. No outlets for writers.

Saxon Radio
See **SGR FM**

Severn Sound/Severn Sound Supergold
67 Southgate Street, Gloucester GL1 2DQ
☎0452 423791   Fax 0452 529446

Programme Controller *Paul Chantler*
Head of News *Richard Franklin*

Independently owned station, not part of any larger group.

SGR FM 97.1/96.4
Electric House, Lloyds Avenue, Ipswich IP1 3HZ
☎0473 216971   Fax 0473 230350
Long Brackland, Bury St Edmunds, Suffolk, IP33 1JY
☎0284 701511   Fax 0284 706446

Programme Director *Mike Stewart*
Station Manager (Bury St Edmunds) *Nigel Rennie*

Incorporates the former Radio Orwell and Saxon Radio stations. Few openings here, and 'even fewer' in drama and light entertainment.

Signal Cheshire
Regent House, Heaton Lane, Stockport,
Cheshire SK4 1BX
☎061-480 5445   Fax 061-474 1806

Programme Controller *John Evington*
Head of News *Paul Sheldon*

Signal Radio
Studio 257, Stoke Road, Stoke on Trent ST4 2SR
☎0782 747047
Fax 0782 744110   Telex 367444

Programme Controller *John Evington*
Head of News *Paul Sheldon*

South Coast Radio
See **Ocean Sound/South Coast Radio**

South West One
See **DevonAir Radio**

South West Sound FM
See **West Sound**

Southern Sound Classic Hits
PO Box 2000, Brighton, East Sussex BN41 2SS
☎0273 430111   Fax 0273 430098

Programme Manager *Mark Flanagan*
News Manager *Phil Bell*

Spectrum Radio
Endeavour House, Brent Cross, London NW2 1JT
☎081-905 5000   Fax 081-209 1029

Station & Programme Controller *Wolfgang Bucci*

Minority community programmes across a broad spectrum of groups: Afro-Caribbean, Asian, Arabic,

Chinese, Greek, Italian, Jewish, Persian, Spanish. Appropriately targeted news/magazine items and book reviews will receive consideration.

Swansea Sound
Victoria Road, Gowerton, Swansea SA4 3AB
☎0792 893751   Fax 0792 898841

Head of Programmes *Andrew Armitage*

Interested in a wide variety of material, though news items must be of local relevance. An explanatory letter, in the first instance, is advisable.

Radio Tay
PO Box 123, Dundee DD1 9UF
☎0382 200800
Fax 0382 24549   Telex 76412

Station Manager/Director *Sandy Wilkie*
Programme Controller *Ally Ballingall*

Wholly-owned subsidiary of Radio Forth. All unsolicited material is assessed. Short stories and book reviews of local interest are welcome. Send to the programme controller.

TFM Radio
Yale Crescent, Stockton on Tees TS17 6AA
☎0642 615111   Fax 0642 674402

Director of Programmes & Resources *Brian Lister*

Limited opportunities but always willing to consider new ideas.

Touch AM
See **Red Dragon FM**

Trent FM
29–31 Castlegate, Nottingham NG1 7AP
☎0602 581731   Fax 0602 588614
Market Place, Derby DE1 3AA
☎0332 292945   Fax 0332 292229

Managing Director/Programme Controller
Chris Hughes

Part of the Midlands Radio Group. Few opportunities, but runs a short story series/competition annually.

Documentaries '... perhaps if locally orientated and discussed up-front'.

Features *John Shaw* Rarely used.

Light Entertainment Christmas material only.

2CR (Two Counties Radio)
5 Southcote Road, Bournemouth BH1 3LR
☎0202 294881
Fax 0202 299314   Telex 418362

Programme Controller *Phil Coope*

Wholly owned subsidiary of the GWR Group. Serves Dorset and Hampshire.

210 FM
PO Box 210, Reading RG3 5RZ
☎0734 413131   Fax 0734 431216

Programme Controller *Phil Coope*

John Baish produces and presents a weekly 2-hour entertainment programme called *Entertainment 91*. Authors interviewed, with particular emphasis on music/film/video-related books. Subsidiary of GWR Group.

Viking FM
Commercial Road, Hull HU1 2SA
☎0482 25141
Fax 0482 218650/587067   Telex 597572

Programme Controller *Roy Leonard*
News Editor *Claire Dalton*

WABC (Nice 'n' Easy Radio)
See **Beacon Radio**

Wear FM, 103.4
Foster Building, Chester Road, Sunderland, Tyne & Wear SR1 3SD
☎091–515 2103   Fax 091–515 2270

Station Manager *Pieta O'Shaughnessy*

Came on the air toward the end of 1990 and was named 'Station of the Year' for its 'life, verve, style and wit' in the Sony Radio Awards 1992 . Music, community-based programmes, talks, etc. 24 hours a day, seven days a week.

WEMS
PO Box 225, Queensgate Centre,
Peterborough PE1 1XJ
☎0733 346225   Fax 0733 896400

Programme Controller *Andy Gillies*

West Sound Radio/South West Sound FM

Radio House, 54 Holmston Road, Ayr KA7 3BE
☎ 0292 283662   Fax 0292 283665

Programme Controller *Gordon McArthur*

Radio Wyvern

PO Box 22, 5–6 Barbourne Terrace,
Worcester WR1 3JZ
☎ 0905 612212

Managing Director *Norman Bilton*
Programme Controller *Stephanie Denham*

Independent company, not part of any larger group. Very occasionally, a local writer may be commissioned to produce something of interest to the Wyvern audience.

Xtra AM

See **BRMB FM**

Freelance Rates – Broadcasting

Freelance rates vary enormously. The following should be treated as guidelines. Minimum rates recommended by the **National Union of Journalists** represent an overall increase of 5% on last year's rates. Most work can command higher fees from employers whether or not they have NUJ agreements. It is up to freelancers to negotiate the best deal they can.

BBC

Radio News Reports (excluding local radio, including External Services): £34.36 for up to two minutes (domestic news broadcasts) and up to three minutes; £7.77 for each minute thereafter.

Television News Reports (including regional): £42.34 for up to two minutes; £10.50 for each minute thereafter.

Radio (excluding local): £63.97 for up to two minutes; £13.24 for each minute thereafter.

Radio (local): £17.58 for up to two minutes; £6.32 for each minute thereafter.

News Copy: £10.43 (network); £7.77 non-network.

Commissioned Sports Results: £2.81 per result.

Still Photographers (commission rates): £45.48 (half-day); £90.95 full day.

Still Fees (black and white or colour): £33.90 for a single picture or first picture in a series: second use £16.95; third and subsequent use £11.35. Where a series is provided on the same event: £16.95 for first use of the second picture; £11.35 for first use of third and subsequent use.

Day and half-day rates: Category one (reporters in network regional television and radio): £94.21 a day; £47.10 half-day. Category two (freelancers who work regularly as regional journalists/sub-editors, or primarily as news reporters on local radio): £74.68 a day; £37.13 half-day. Category three (reporters in local radio): £64.32 a day; £32.16 half-day.

Radio Talks and Features

Interviews
Up to five minutes: £40
Five to eight minutes: £46
Eight to twelve minutes: £56
Twelve minutes and over: negotiable
Script and read: £16.30 per minute
Script only: £12 per minute
Illustrated talks: £13.30 per minute
Linked interviews: 1 interview: £72; 2 interviews: £93.

Features/documentaries

Up to 7 minutes: £151.90 ; £21.70 per minute thereafter.

Talks

Contributions for one national region (Scotland, Wales or Northern Ireland) may be contracted at two-thirds of the rates above.

Association of Independent Radio Contractors (excluding LBC/IRN)

News Copy Ordered or submitted, and broadcast by the station; £6.68 per item.

News Reports (Voice) For a report or talk on tape or broadcast by a freelancer: £17.99 for the first two minutes; £6 per minute thereafter.

Day Rates £62.67 a day (over 4 hours and up to 8); £31.33 half-day (up to 4 hours).

Sports Ordered match coverage, including previews, flashes and summaries: £32.68; ordered calls for running reports and additional telephone fee: £12.34; result only service: £2.67. Travelling and out-of-pocket expenses are generally paid.

ITV Association

News

Report or Talk Recorded on tape/film, or broadcast: not less than £44.60.

Sports Reports As above, not less than £47.40.

Sports Copy Not recorded or broadcast: not less than £10.40, with payment for results only £4.64.

News Copy Not recorded or broadcast: not less than £9.

Ordered Assignments Ordered reports or talks shall be paid for even if not used; in such cases the minimum rate shall be paid.

Daily engagements Day rate £93; half-day £52.

Commission fee for photographers to take still photographs Day assignment £93; half-day £52.

The above items do not include travelling and out-of-pocket expenses.

Stills

Black and white and colour: first use £28.84; second use £14.87; third and subsequent use £8.39.

For a series of pictures first use: £62.50; second use: £27.88; third and subsequent use: £18.60. Travel and out-of-pocket expenses shall be paid in addition.

Research

TV organisations which hire freelancers to research programme items should pay on a day rate which reflects the value of the work and the importance of the programme concerned. Research or reporting for a national programme networked by either BBC, ITV or Channel 4 should pay freelancers at least £136.50 a day.

Presentation

In all broadcast media, presenters command higher fees than news journalists. There is considerable variation in what is paid for presenting programmes and videos, according to their audience and importance. Day rates with London television companies are usually about £136.50 a day.

Radio Drama

A beginner in radio drama should receive at least £34.61 per minute for a sixty-minute script. For an established writer – one who has three or more plays to his credit – the minimum rate per minute is £52.70.

Fees for dramatisations range from 65-85% of the full drama rate, depending on the degree of original material and dialogue.

An attendance payment of £31 per production paid to established writers is currently under negotiation.

Television Drama

For a sixty-minute teleplay, the BBC will pay an established writer £6660 and a beginner £4230. The corresponding figures for ITV are £7751 for the established writer, £5507 for a writer new to television but with a solid reputation in other literary areas.

Day rates for attendance at read-throughs and rehearsals is £60.40 for the BBC and £62.40 for ITV.

Feature Films

An agreement between **The Writers' Guild**, **PACT** and **IPPA** allows for a minimum guaranteed payment to the writer of £31,200 on a feature film with a budget in excess of £2 million; £19,000 on a budget from £750,000 to £2 million; £14,000 on a budget below £750,000.

Look First, Read Later

Forget the bestseller lists. The hottest title of the year and the biggest single earner for many a bookshop did not even register in the literary league. That's because it was not a book at all. It was a video.

Disney's *Fantasia* sold over 3.5 million copies. And this for a cartoon whimsy produced over fifty years ago.

It's enough to make Jeffrey Archer wince with envy.

Fantasia was backed by a huge television and press advertising campaign and released just before Christmas – which makes it unlikely that its sales record will be beaten before the next orgy of present buying. But the *Fantasia* phenomenon should not be judged in isolation. It is one of many indicators of a shift in the pattern of consumer spending towards film and video and away from books.

To begin with what we know for a fact, the sell-through video market has grown prodigiously in the last six years. In 1985, turnover was in the region of £15 million. Estimates for 1991 range from £350 to £400 million. At this rate, sell-through will overtake the video rental market, currently valued at £564 million, within two years. More to the point, while rental tends to cater for the lower social strata, sell-through appeals more to the ABCs,the middle-class, middle-aged and middle of the road punters who up till now have filled their drawing rooms with books.

Publishers and booksellers deny emphatically that books are at risk. Every year, the trade registers an expansion of output – up to 68,000 new titles and new editions in 1991, a 70% increase on a decade ago. But this staggering total disguises a plethora of desk-top guides and manuals, abstruse reflections of academe, small press specialities and large press aberrations which never reach the bookshop let alone attract reviews or other recognition.

For a more accurate assessment of the state of the trade, look at sales per title (down) and sales per new title (seriously down). Even in the late eighties, a first novel could be expected to make a modest return on a run of 2–3000 copies. Now, according to Dan Franklin of Secker & Warburg, the average sale of a new hardback novel has fallen below 600.

Indeed, the whole future of the hardback has been put at risk by W. H. Smith's decision to stop placing orders for high-priced books by newcomers, however attractive the subject or beguiling the reviews. Henceforth, it will be only the proven bestsellers (authors with five blockbusters to their credit) who will qualify for hardback display. Such is the marketing power of Smith's that publishers are already cutting back on their hardback list in favour of paperback originals.

And not before time. A hardback novel of unknown quality at £14.99 must compare unfavourably with, say, a full-length video feature at £9.99 or less. Nobody, as far as I know, has researched the connection between the decline of hardback sales and growing popularity of video but the circumstantial evidence for a link is very strong.

This is not to argue that the book is in terminal decline. It *is* to argue that publishers and booksellers need to get their act together if they want to keep their share of the leisure market. To linger for a moment over the expiring hardback; it survived for so long because there was little in the way of competition. Prices leapt ahead of inflation on the assumption that book buyers and, most particularly, the libraries, would somehow bear the financial strain. Essential to the equation was the popular conviction – in no way discouraged by the book trade – that high prices were justified by high costs. But not a bit of it. In reality the hardback is not much more expensive to produce than the paperback. Printing and binding account for just 15% of a £15 hardback – a mere £2.25 against £6.75 which goes to the bookseller and £3.75 to the publisher. It will surprise no one that the author is left with a measly 10 per cent or £1.50.

In other words, hardbacks were a safe racket until videos came along to spice up the competition. The revolution has even extended to the libraries which are giving over an ever higher proportion of shelf space to video and audio tapes. The purists might protest but on any objective criteria it is hard to establish that popular fiction (by far the largest category of library borrowing) has any inherent virtue in its written form.

So where do we go from here? As befits an essentially conservative trade, booksellers have reacted cautiously to the video revolution. They cashed in on *Fantasia* but then so did every petrol station, newsagent and corner shop in the land. When it comes to a steady bestseller like John Wayne's *The Quiet Man*, a distinctly old-fashioned feature which sells a thousand copies a day with a back sale logging close on 700,000, the bookshops barely get a look in.

In all, there are four thousand outlets for videos with the largest slice of the market held by Woolworths, which started the sell-through phenomenon with the launch of its Video Collection in 1985, and Our Price Video set up by W.H. Smith as the first retail chain to sell video only. Currently, Our Price has 34 branches and a turnover of £20 million. Conventional bookshops with their motley collection of safe cassettes have a long way to catch up. But at least they are capable of adapting quickly – a couple of telephone calls will replace a stack of slow-selling books with a faster line of merchandise.

It's harder for publishers to come to terms with commercial reality. The creative and technical skills needed to produce three hundred pages of readable text are not easily transferable to film making. This was made clear as early as the mid-60s when the more adventurous types burned their fingers on the marketing of education packs incorporating what were then known quaintly as 'audio and visual aids'. The products did not match the promise.

But, like any other business people, publishers should be capable of learning new tricks. A few like Longmans and Nelson have led the way with special divisions to commission videos, mostly for adult education. Why have they not moved ahead further and faster and why are their rivals so reluctant to engage in similar ventures? It all comes down to a simple question of economics. Even with the extravagant author advances of recent years, books have just about the lowest production costs in the media catalogue. Videos are in the higher bracket. Even a straightforward language-learning video absorbs a production budget of £30–£50,000, while for a 90-minute feature of the type favoured by Channel Four's *Film on Four*, there is not much change out of £500,000.

Publishers worry about committing this level of investment, the more so because they know that the BBC and the independent production companies are already doing a creditable job in feeding the video outlets with newish products. They know, too, that the leading players are gearing themselves up to increase output, using cinema and television as marketing tools to exploit the more profitable sell-through market. It is no coincidence that Carlton, the star turn in last year's battle for the television franchises, describes itself as a publisher broadcaster.

The question for book publishers to answer is whether they can afford to stand aside. That they are not entirely convinced of the continuing pre-eminence of the written word is suggested by their fast-growing interest in audio cassettes. This sector is growing as quickly as video but has the great virtue of lower production costs. Random Century, with its Audiobooks label, and HarperCollins are among those taking up the challenge of beating the BBC at its own game. A pattern for development is suggested by Random Century's simultaneous release of hardback and audio versions of Martin Amis' *Time's Arrow* and Julian Barnes' *Talking it Over*. Both did well.

The next tentative step forward is the production of illustrated books which make use of film techniques to create realistic pictorial mock-ups of historical events. The book packager, Roxby Press, has actually used a professional film director to oversee the making of its *I Was There* series. Meanwhile, Thames and Hudson have come out with its spectacular *New Horizons*, six books which grabbed the attention of one critic with 'their succession of stunning images'. Interestingly, this series is a buy-in from France where there is much greater willingness to see books and videos as complementary products.

What next? Mills and Boon are planning to raid their romance list for video spin-offs; other publishers will move forward tentatively as they spot sectors of the market where production companies are under-represented (education is the obvious example) or where they can see the chance of cutting costs by attracting sponsors. But for the breakthrough we must wait for one of the conglomerates to show its mettle. The best guess is that News International will be first to flex its multi-media muscle in the video market. For the moment, the company's heavy debt load is inhibiting expansion but as soon as Sky Television breaks even, the incentive to open up another profit centre will prove irresistible.

What all this means for the writer is harder to predict. Every visual product is dependent on the Hitchcock rule: 'To make a fine film, you need three things: a great script, a great script and a great script.' But increased opportunities for screenwriters is likely to be offset by a fall in demand for the printed word. First-time writers take note. The successful novel of the future could well be the book of the video.

Film, TV and Video Production Companies

Acacia Productions Ltd
80 Weston Park, London N8 9TB
☎081-341 9392   Fax 081-341 4879

Contact *J. Edward Milner/Nikki Milner*

Video and television: documentary and corporate, plus training. OUTPUT *Vietnam After the Fire* (feature documentary); *Fragile Earth* (several); news reports on Third World environment for Channel 4 News. Unsolicited mss not generally welcome. Very interested in new writing for TV, 'especially if it is related to current environmental concerns, or North-South issues'.

Action Time
Wrendal House, 2 Whitworth Street West,
Manchester M1 5WX
☎061-236 8999   Fax 061-236 8845

Chief Executive *Steven Leahy*
Controller of Entertainment *Trish Kinane*
Head of Production *Malcolm Quiggin*

Major producers and licensers of TV quiz, game and entertainment shows such as *You've Been Framed, Catchphrase, Busman's Holiday, Joker in the Pack, One to Win, Love at First Sight.* In 1991/2 410 hours were screened on UK networks. All original material is processed through the UK office. Action Time has production bases in the Germany and Australia, with co-production partners in France, Holland, Ireland, Canada, Russia, Spain, Norway, Sweden, South America and the US.

Adam Video Productions
21 Dungarvan Avenue, Roehampton,
London SW15 5QU
☎081-876 3333

Contact *John McAdam*

Audio video — corporate identity, staff training and safety at work. *Specialises* in marketing support and corporate identity productions to industry, commerce and education. *Special areas* optical/opthalmic. No unsolicited mss but welcomes any

new creative work: 'any collection of works that will sell the product or message'.

Alan Afriat Associates
24 Combemartin Road, London SW18 5PR
☎081-789 2663   Fax 081-780 2787

Contact *Alan Afriat*

Film, video and television: drama, documentary, corporate and interactive video-disc material. OUTPUT drama, documentary and educational programmes for Thames TV. Unsolicited scripts welcome. Interested in new writing.

After Image Ltd
32 Acre Lane, London SW2 5SG
☎071-737 7300   Fax 071-326 1850

Contact *Jane Thorburn*

Makers of television, with a particular interest in the arts, unusual people or events and drama. OUTPUT includes *Alter Image; Tales of Faith* and *Foxes,* both short operas; *Camera,* a new opera for television; *Les Ballets Africains* and *Outrage!.* Concentrate much on the visual aspects of television and interested in new material, specifically for television. Send unsolicited treatments rather than complete mss.

Aisling Films Ltd
Lynden House, 112-114 Lisburn Road,
Belfast BT9 6AH
☎0232 661638   Fax 0232 661614

Film and television drama and documentary. No unsolicited mss. Interested in all new work, but 'don't have the time to comment on unsolicited scripts'. OUTPUT *The End of the World Man* (children's feature film); *The Schooner* (TV drama).

Amber Films
5-9 The Side (rear), Newcastle upon
Tyne NE1 3JE
☎091-232 2000   Fax 091-230 3217

Contact *Murray Martin*

Television programmes, documentaries, cinema and animation. OUTPUT with a drama/scripted content has included *Keeping Time; Byker; In Fading Light; Seacoal; Dream On; Writing in the Sand.* Unsolicited scripts/ ideas considered but 'we exist primarily to produce our own ideas'.

Greg Angel (Film and Television)

5 Westmorland Close, Woosehill, Wokingham, Berkshire RG11 9AZ
☎ 0734 794607   Fax 0734 794607

Film, video and TV: drama, documentary and corporate. Interactive video (drama) for corporate training; multi-media distance learning packages; documentaries for corporate and broadcast markets; live business television via satellite (Pan European/USA). No unsolicited scripts. No particular policy towards new writing as yet, but always interested in 'good' new writing.

Antelope Films Ltd

3 Fitzroy Square, London W1P 5AH
☎ 071-387 4454
Fax 071-388 9935   Telex 266205 AFLG

Managing Director *Mick Csaky*

Drama and documentaries for film, video and TV. Unsolicited mss welcome. OUTPUT has included *Heart of the Dragon* (12-part series on China for Channel 4); *Testament* (7-part series for Channel 4); *The Midas Touch* (6-part series for BBC); *Nureyev* (90-minute biography for the South Bank Show); *Terror* (3-part documentary series for Channel 4).

ANV Productions

47A Kendal Street, London W2 2BU
☎ 071-262 3074   Fax 071-723 1479

Contact *Antony Norris*

Specialises in business television: training videos, commercials and documentaries. CLIENTS include British Telecom, House of Fraser, Gateway Food Markets.

Apple Television

A2, Connaught Business Centre, Hyde Estate Road, Hendon, London NW9 6JL
☎ 081-205 6687   Fax 081-205 0430

Contact *Ronnie Cairnduff*

Video — corporate, educational, training and promotional. Unsolicited scripts considered.

Artifax Ltd

118 Addison Gardens, London W14 0DS
☎ 071-602 5666   Fax 071-603 7154

Contact *Elizabeth Queenan*

Film and video — music, arts, drama, light entertainment and documentary. OUTPUT includes *The Secret Life of Machines* (Channel 4), and *Not Mozart* (BBC).

Artts International

Highfield Grange, Bubwith, North Yorkshire YO8 7DP
☎ 0757 288088   Fax 0757 288253

Contact *Carolyn Graham*

Commercial video production company. A complete service from initial idea through scripting, casting, production and post-production. CLIENTS Boothferry Borough Council, British Telecom, Making Space — Schizophrenia Society, York Guitar Quartet. No unsolicited scripts.

Aspect Film and Television Productions Ltd

36 Percy Street, London W1P 9FG
☎ 071-636 5303   Fax 071-436 0666

Contact *Paul Sommers*

Drama, documentary and corporate television. Unsolicited scripts and ideas welcome.

Aspen Business Communications

Christ Church, Cosway Street, London NW1 5NJ
☎ 071-262 2622   Fax 071-706 4811

Contact *Amanda Thompson/Bernard Morris*

Corporate film and video production for corporate communications, company and product promotion. OUTPUT has included training films, promotional videos and investor relations videos.

Aurora Sound and Vision

05 Hellesdon Park Road, Norwich NR6 5DR
☎ 0603 789509   Fax 0603 402844

Contact *Steve Bloomfield*

Video marketing and training programmes; radio commercials. Commissions only, but interested in seeing unsolicited mss as examples of work.

AVC Group

Walters Farm Road, Tonbridge, Kent TN9 1QT
☎ 0732 365107   Fax 0732 362600

Contact *Brian Adams*

A specialist business communication company who
work as consultants for corporate clients.
Specialises in corporate videos, conferences, PR
events and award ceremonies, safety, sales and
marketing, and training.

Humphrey Barclay Productions/First Choice

5 Anglers Lane, London NW5 3DG
☎ 071-482 1992   Fax 071-485 4287

Contact *Al Mitchell/Tony Humphreys*

TV — situation comedy and drama. First Choice,
run by producer/writer Moira Williams, makes
drama for film and TV. Both HBP and First Choice
have a joint administrative base with Barclay, ex-
LWT, as director of both. HBP will continue to
concentrate on fully commissioned projects, while
First Choice plans to acquire and develop scripts
through a development fund financed by the parent
company. OUTPUT (Humphrey Barclay) *That's Love*
(TVS); *Up the Garden Path* (Granada); *Desmonds*
(Channel 4); (First Choice) *Behaving Badly*
(Channel 4); *A Masculine Ending* (BBC); *A Fine
Blue Day* (Columbia Pictures); *Death of a
Doormouse* (NB/ YTV).

Barony Film and Television Productions Limited

4 Picardy Place, Edinburgh EH1 3JT
☎ 031-558 3275   Fax 031-557 8498

Contact *Barbara McKissack*

Broadcast and non-broadcast documentary, drama
and current affairs. OUTPUT *Living with AIDS*
(health documentary for Scottish Health Education
Group); *Dear Mr Gorbachev* (Viewpoint '90 feature
documentary for Central TV); *Submarine* (arts
documentary for Channel 4); *The Italian Connection* (unemployment initiatives programme for the
BBC and European Commission); *Heavenly*
(fantasy documentary for Channel 4). Currently
developing short and feature-length drama. Unsolicited scripts welcome.

Michael Barratt Ltd

5-7 Forlease Road, Maidenhead,
Berkshire SL6 1RP
☎ 0628 770800   Fax 0628 770144

Contact *Michael Barratt*

Corporate and educational video, and television
programmes. Also a wide range of publishing work
including company newspapers, brochures and
training manuals.

Peter Batty Productions

Claremont House, Renfrew Road, Kingston,
Surrey KT2 7NT
☎ 081-942 6304
Fax 081-336 1661 Telex 262433 MONREF G 2685

Contact *Peter Batty*

Television programmes and commercials, primarily
broadcast documentaries. Recent OUTPUT has included *A Time for Remembrance* and *Swastika
Over British Soil.*

Behr Cinematography

22 Redington Road, London NW3 7RG
☎ 071-794 2535   Fax 071-794 2535

Contact *Arnold Behr/Betty Burghes*

Documentary, educational, corporate film and/or
video, usually for volunteer organisations. No actors, except voice-overs. No unsolicited mss.

Paul Berriff Productions Ltd

The Chestnuts, Woodfield Lane, Hessle, North
Humberside HU13 0EW
☎ 0482 641158   Fax 0482 641158

Contact *Paul Berriff/Janice Kearns*

Television documentary. OUTPUT has included
Lakeland Rock for Channel 4, *Lifeboat* series for
BBC1, *Fire* for BBC's 'Forty Minutes', *Animal Squad*
for BBC1. More recent achievements include
Rescue — a 13-part documentary for ITV; *M25:
The Magic Roundabout* for 'First Tuesday'; *Animal
Squad Undercover* — series for Channel 4; *Child
Abuse Case 152* for BBC1 'Inside Story'; *Lessons of
Darkness* for BBC2's 'Fine Cut'.

Bevanfield Films

2A Duke Street, Manchester Square,
London W1M 5AA
☎ 071-487 4920   Fax 071-487 5472

Contact *Mary Swindale*

Television programmes, cinema and animation.
Most adaptations are generated in-house, and
unsolicited scripts are not generally accepted.

BFV Ltd

Rear of 149 High Street, Ebury Road,
Rickmansworth, Hertfordshire WD3 1AR
☎0923 771222   Fax 0923 896059

Contact *Robert Evans*

Programmes for industry, commerce and television. Film and video documentaries; commercial, industrial, medical and scientific films; children's television. Unsolicited mss considered but 'as our output is so specialised, we feel it may be a wasted effort by writers'. Mostly use staff writers.

Martin Bird Productions

Saucelands Barn, Coolham, Horsham, West
Sussex RH13 8QG
☎0403 741620   Fax 0403 741647

Contact *Alastair Martin-Bird*

Makers of film and video specialising predominantly in programmes covering equestrianism and the countryside. No unsolicited scripts, but always looking for new writers who are fully acquainted with the subject.

Stuart Black Productions

79 Charlbert Court, Eamont Street,
London NW8 7DB
☎071-722 7636

Contact *Stuart Black*

Film, video and television: general documentaries and corporate work, including work for transport and charity organisations. No unsolicited scripts. Send synopsis in the first instance. Policy is to encourage new writing 'if there's talent there'.

Black Tulip

12 Winchester Place, London N6 5HJ
☎081-341 7966

Contact *Mr Lorne Magory*

Feature films and television — children's drama and comedy. New writers and unsolicited material welcome. No documentaries.

Blackbird Productions

Suite 115, The Plaza, 535 King's Road,
London SW10 0SZ
☎071-352 4882   Fax 071-351 3728

Contact *Sally Bell/John Coxall*

Video and television: drama, documentary and corporate. OUTPUT *The Wild Bunch* (children's comedy); *The DJ Kat Show* (children's comedy); plus lots of corporate, training and educational material. Scripts welcome provided they are accompanied by return s.a.e. and synopsis. Very open to new writing, particularly comedy, for television only.

Blackrod

The Chrysalis Building, 13 Bramley Road,
London W10 6SP
☎071-221 2213   Fax 071-221 6337

Contact *Nigel Ward*

Corporate television — drama and documentary. One of the biggest corporate video makers, with a fistful of awards for excellence in the field. 'Since we make bespoke programmes for corporate clients, we have no use for unsolicited material.'

Blossom Productions Ltd

Suite 10, 91 St Martin's Lane, London WC2H 0DG
☎071-497 3740   Fax 071-497 3740

Contact *Ms S. R. M. Sutton*

Film and television: drama and documentary. OUTPUT *Closed Circuit* (cinema short released by Rank); *World of Herbs* (documentary series for Channel 4). Send treatments only. No scripts. 'If it's good we like it.'

Matt Boney Associates

'Woodside', Holdfast Lane, Grayswood,
Haslemere, Surrey GU27 2EU
☎0428 656178

Contact *Matt Boney*

Writer/director for video and television — commercials, documentaries, skiing and travel. No unsolicited mss.

Penny Bould Media

Media House, Bishops Itchington, Near Leamington Spa, Warwickshire CV33 0SP
☎0926 614131/613090   Fax 0926 613199

Contact *Penny Bould*

Corporate and training videos; radio, TV and corporate audio broadcast. Also produce newsletters, brochures, technical reports, marketing and promotional literature, press releases and feature scripts for press, radio and TV, both in the UK and abroad. Most material is produced in-house. No unsolicited scripts. Interested only in writers with proven commercial writing experience. Approach in writing.

Box Clever

25 Bewdley Street, Islington, London N1 1HB
☏071-607 5766   Fax 071-700 2248

Contact *Claire Walmsley*

Film, video and TV. Documentary, commercials and training. OUTPUT includes BBC documentaries, and programmes for Channel 4, the European Commission and a number of charity organisations. No unsolicited mss. Outlines and proposals only. New writing encouraged but opportunities in the present climate are very limited.

Brilliant Ideas Productions

45 Muswell Road, London N10 2BS
☏081-444 9574   Fax 081-365 3664

Contact *Annie Moore*

Video and television documentary programming for family audience. OUTPUT includes *Cats* (series for YTV). 'Always interested' in new writing. Unsolicited mss welcome for factual programming only.

British Film Institute Production

29 Rathbone Street, London W1P
☏071-636 5587

British Lion Screen Entertainment Ltd

Pinewood Studios, Iver,
Buckinghamshire SL0 0NH
☏0753 651700
Fax 0753 656391   Telex 847505

Contact *Peter R.E. Snell* (Chief Executive)

Film production. OUTPUT has included *A Man for All Seasons, Treasure Island, Turtle Diary, Lady Jane* and *The Crucifer of Blood.* No unsolicited mss.

Broadcast Communications

14 King Street, London WC2E 8HN
☏071-240 6941   Fax 071-379 5808

Contact *Michael Braham/Susan Lowery*

One of the first independents to be set up and now producing over 250 hours of television a year, including Channel 4's morning and lunchtime business programmes. Recently benefited from a huge injection of capital from *The Guardian* and *Manchester Evening News,* who bought a 90% stake at the end of 1989. Factual/current affairs/business programmes and corporate video. OUTPUT Television: *The Business Programme, Business Daily;* Corporate: training, customer care, safety at work and financial matters such as pensions. 'All

material has a tendency towards the financial sector where most of our clients come from'. No unsolicited mss.

Broadsword Television

Anglia House, Norwich NR1 3JG
☏0603 615151   Fax 0603 661593

Contact *Tim Child*

Film and video — children's, documentary, light entertainment and television.

Broadwick Productions

78 Romilly Road, London N4 2QX
☏071-226 7157   Fax 071-354 5875

Contact *Sarah Wickham/Simon Lethbridge*

Wide range of corporate productions including documentary, educational, financial, point-of-sale, training and pop promos. Unsolicited mss welcome. 'Always attempt to use at least two new writers each year for corporate production. Opportunity varies according to quantity and quality of incoming work.'

Brook Productions

21-24 Bruges Place, Randolph Street,
London NW1 0TF
☏071-482 6111   Fax 071-284 0626

Contact *Anne Lapping*

Makers of arts, drama, current affairs and documentary television. OUTPUT *A Week in Politics; A Vote for Hitler; The Thatcher Factor; A Strike out of Time; Against My Nature; Three of a Kind; Incident in Judaea; Madness.*

John Burder (Films)

7 Saltcoats Road, London W4 1AR
☏081-995 0547   Fax 081-995 3376

Contact *John Burder*

Producer of television programmes and corporate videos. OUTPUT *Peter Ustinov, Looking Back* (TV); *In Breach* (medical corporate); *The Common Sense Guides* (training series). No unsolicited mss; all work is commissioned.

Burrill Productions

19 Cranbury Road, London SW6 2NS
☏071-736 8673   Fax 071-731 3921

Contact *Timothy Burrill*

Feature films. OUTPUT *Tess* (Roman Polanski); *Pirates of Penzance; Supergirl; The Fourth Protocol.* No unsolicited mss.

Cadenza
57 Great Cumberland Place, London W1H 7LJ
☎071-402 8858   Fax 071-262 4143

Contact *Ann Zahl*

TV/film — drama, classical music, arts, comedy and documentary.

Camden Productions
20 Jeffreys Street, London NW1 9PR
☎071-482 0527

Contact *Theresa FitzGerald/Philip Kemp*

Two writers who develop their own work exclusively. No unsolicited mss.

Camerson Television
Unit 8A, Intec 2, Wade Road, Basingstoke, Hampshire RG24 0NE
☎0256 460457   Fax 0256 817378

Contact *Richard Wilson*

Corporate and television broadcast production company.

Caravel Film Techniques Limited
The Great Barn Studios, Cippenham Lane, Slough, Berkshire SL1 5AU
☎0753 821218   Fax 0753 571383

Contact *Nick See*

Film, video and television — documentary and commercials. No unsolicited mss. 'We keep a file on writers' details and always welcome any new information.'

Carnival Films & Theatre Ltd
12 Raddington Road, Ladbroke Grove, London W10 5TG
☎081-968 0968/1818/1717   Fax 081-968 0155/0177

Contact *Brian Eastman* (Film)/*Andrew Welch* (Theatre)

Film and television producers, plus theatre productions. Formerly traded as Picture Partnership Productions Ltd which was founded in 1978. OUTPUT Films: *Under Suspicion* (Columbia/Rank/LWT); *Whoops Apocalypse* (ITC). Television: *Father's Day*

(Channel 4); *Blott on the Landscape* (BBC); *Porterhouse Blue* (Channel 4); *Agatha Christie's Poirot* (LWT); *Jeeves & Wooster* (Granada); *Forever Green* (LWT); *The Big Battalions* (Channel 4); *Traffik* (Channel 4). Theatre productions include: *Up on the Roof; Shadowlands* and *Map of the Heart.*

Cartwn Cymru
Model House, Bull Ring, Llantrisant CF7 8EB
☎0443 222316   Fax 0443 229242

Contact *Naomi Jones*

Animation production company. Producers of *Toucan 'Tecs* (YTV/ S4C) for ITV children's network. Currently working on *Funnybones* (SAC/BBC Enterprises).

Pearl Catlin Associates
Production Centre, The Clock House, Summersbury Drive, Shalford, Guildford GU4 8JQ
☎0483 67932   Fax 0483 302646

Contact *Pearl Catlin/Peter Yolland/Paul Bernard*

Film and video — drama, documentary, children's factual, corporate and commercials. Interested in creative ideas for all kinds of programmes.

Celador Productions Ltd
39 Long Acre, London WC2E 9JT
☎071-240 8101   Fax 071-836 1117

Contact *Paul Smith/Nic Phillips*

Primarily light entertainment programming for all broadcast channels, including game shows, variety, factual and selected documentary projects. OUTPUT *Everybody's Equal* and *Crazy Comparisons* for ITV; *Canned Carrott, Carrott's Commercial Breakdown* and *Auntie's Bloomers* for BBC; *Classic Country* for BSB. Also Sky TV's London link for the Oscar Awards.

Chameleon Television Ltd
The Magistretti Building, 1 Harcourt Place, West Street, Leeds LS1 4RB
☎0532 434017   Fax 0532 431267

Contact *Chris Lister*

Drama, light entertainment and documentaries for Channel 4, ITV and BBC.

Channel X

Middlesex House, 34–42 Cleveland Street,
London W1P 5SB
☎071-436 2200   Fax 071-436 1475

Contact *Alan Marke/Mike Bolland*

FOUNDED 1986 by Jonathan Ross to develop his
first series *The Last Resort*. The large production
fees generated by the long runs of the show fund a
number of shorter series. Channel X turns over
£2–3 million a year now and Katie Lander believes
a key priority for independents should be staff
training. OUTPUT *The Last Resort; One Hour with
Jonathan Ross; Tonight with Jonathan Ross; Vic
Reeves Big Night Out; The Sean Hughes Show.*

Chapel Broadcast Productions Ltd

Stonehill Studios, Shields Road, Pelaw, Gateshead,
Tyne & Wear NA10 0HW
☎091-495 0925   Fax 091-438 5508

Contact *Ian Farnworth*

Corporate videos: biotechnology; civil, mechanical,
electrical and chemical engineering; automotive
and defence industry; financial; motorsport (speed-
way racing). Sports programmes for cable and
satellite (ice hockey, basketball, indoor cricket);
plus sports newsgathering for regional terrestrial
broadcast stations. Power generation; health and
safety; also TV programmes (light entertainment
such as *Today's Comedians*) for satellite and cable
broadcasting; and video sell-through products. No
unsolicited mss. All scriptwriting done in-house.

Chapman Clarke Television

59 Cotham Hill, Bristol BS6 6JR
☎0272 239270   Fax 0272 745287
Lee International Studios, Administration Block,
Studios Road, Shepperton, Middlesex TW17 02D

Contact *Dr Jane Chapman*

Film and video — documentary, docu-drama and
feature film development, particularly for the European market. OUTPUT has included *Women — The
Way Ahead* (Channel 4 series); *Showreel* (BBC
series); *Europe by Design* (BBC1 series). 'The
company seeks to break down the barriers between entertainment and education television with
programme formats of wide appeal for all UK
channels. We encourage unsolicited scripts and
read everything that is submitted, especially children's drama.'

Chatsworth Television Ltd

97–99 Dean Street, London W1V 5RA
☎071-734 4302   Fax 071-437 3301

Contact *Malcolm Heyworth*

Well-established drama and light entertainment
television producers with 18 years of experience
behind them. All unsolicited scripts are read.

Cheerleader Productions

62 Chiswick High Road, London W4 1SY
☎081-995 7778   Fax 081-995 7779

Contact *Charles Balchin/Mike Milne/Piers Croton*

Sports programme makers. OUTPUT has included
American football, sumo wrestling, power-sprint
racing, tennis, golf, 3-day eventing, Grand Prix
motor racing and martial arts. CLIENTS include BBC,
ITV, Channel 4 and foreign broadcasters.

Chess Valley Films and Video Ltd

Film House, Little Chalfont,
Buckinghamshire HP7 9PY
☎0494 762222   Fax 0494 763333

Contact *Heather M. Davies* (Producer/Director)/
Ron Haddock (Director)

Corporate television including training, promotion-
al, marketing, PR, sales, education, documentary.
CLIENTS European Commission, Glaxo, National
Grid, Unilever, South Yorks Passenger Transport
Executive, Taylor Woodrow, National Remote
Sensing Centre, GEC Corporate, and many others.
No unsolicited mss.

CHG Communications

108 Clarendon Road, London W11 2HR
☎071-727 4269   Fax 071-727 3918

Contact *Jeremy Hamp*

Television drama; corporate film and video.
OUTPUT has included a 3-part drama for Ford
Motors on customer care (with 'lip sync' into
twelve languages), technical service training video
programmes, and a one-hour television play. Commissioned work only. No unsolicited mss but
always keen to meet scriptwriters.

Childsplay Productions Ltd

8 Lonsdale Road, London NW6 6RD
☎071-328 1429   Fax 071-328 1416

Contact *Kim Burke/Peter Tabern*

Broadcast: drama, features, children's (not pre-
school) and educational. OUTPUT includes
Streetwise, All Change, Picture Box and *Miles is
Better.* Send treatments rather than full scripts.
'Always happy to work with new, enthusiastic

writers with interesting ideas, or those willing to collaborate on an idea.'

Chrysalis Television Productions Ltd

The Chrysalis Building, Bramley Road, London W10 6SP
☎071-221 2213   Fax 071-221 6455

Contact *Tony Orsten/Linda McDougall/Neil Duncanson* (CTV Productions)/ *Linda James/ Stephen Bayley/Jenny Reeks* (Red Rooster Films & TV)

Part of the Media and Communications Division of the Chrysalis Group. FOUNDED four years ago as a broadcast television arm to the well-known independent music company. CTV has recently merged with the highly rated and successful drama and children's entertainment company, Red Rooster. Produces programmes for all broadcast channels, with particular expertise in drama. Currently developing projects for both the international and domestic markets. Proposals welcome.

Cinecosse Video

Riversfield, Ellon, Aberdeenshire AB41 9EY
☎0358 22150   Fax 0358 20053

Contact *Michael Marshall*

Video and television production for corporate and documentary material. Also promotional, sales and training presentations. OUTPUT *Scotland's Larder* (documentary series for GTV). CLIENTS InterCity, IBM, BP Exploration, Total Oil. No unsolicited mss. 'We commission scripts from specialist writers according to type of production in hand.'

Cinexsa Film Productions Limited

33 Gresse Street, London W1P 2AH
☎071-436 8781   Fax 071-436 6327

Contact *Robert Davies/Jimmy Wright*

Film, video and TV — documentary and commercials. No unsolicited mss but 'new writing is encouraged'. Off-line editing facilities and full post-production available.

Cirrus Films

186 Amyand Park Road, St Margarets, Twickenham, Middlesex TW1 3HY
☎081-892 3195   Fax 081-892 5850

Contact *Phil Warren*

Film, video and television — drama and documentary. Always interested in new writing but prefers to receive an introduction by letter first.

Clark Production

Kenilworth House, 79–80 Margaret Street, London W1N 7HB
☎071-636 4448   Fax 071-636 4448

Contact *Bernard Clark*

FOUNDED 1985. *Specialises* in current affairs, news and documentary series. OUTPUT has included *Hard News, Opinions, Levin* (series for Channel 4); *Moneywise* and *This Way Out* (TVS). Unsolicited mss welcome, send introductory letter in the first instance.

The Clear Picture Company

Folds Head Farm, Calver, Nr Sheffield S30 1XJ
☎0433 631086   Fax 0433 631069

Contact *Shaun Gilmartin/Judy Laybourn*

Film, video and television: documentary and corporate work. OUTPUT documentaries on a deaf musician, on Hull City play, Radon Gas and prison officer training programmes; corporate work for the Army. No drama. 'We use in-house writers on most projects. However, we do occasionally use freelance talent from across a range of skills.'

Cleveland Productions

5 Rainbow Court, Oxhey, Hertfordshire WD1 4RP
☎0923 254000   Fax 0923 254000

Contact *Michael Gosling*

Communications in sound and vision. Film and video — documentary and commercials. Tape slide and multi-track recording facilities available.

Commercial Facilities Ltd (Colstar International)

11 Wythburn Place, London W1H 5WL
☎071-437 5725   Fax 071-706 1704

International distributors and producers of broadcast programming for all media: documentaries, short films, drama programme specials and series. Library includes films and series on the arts, science, history, social concerns and natural history. OUTPUT includes *In Search of Wildlife; Antarctic Challenge*; also various biographies of international artists like James Ensor, Alex Colville, David Shepherd and Eugene Ionesco.

Compass Film Productions Ltd

6 Newburgh Street, London W1V 1LH
☎071-734 8115   Fax 071-434 9256

Contact *Simon Heaven*

Specialists since 1974 in documentary, educational and promotional programmes for television and corporate clients. Recent OUTPUT has included *Another Way of Life; Music of the Outsiders; Concerning Cancer; Violent Lives*; and *A Door to Understanding*, for Channel 4. No unsolicited mss.

Component Television Productions Ltd

5 Woodstock Road, London W4 1DS
✆081-747 0069

Contact *Gaby Bedford*

Corporate videos, documentary, drama, retail videos and television. Welcomes unsolicited mss. 'Most of our work is commissioned but we are open to ideas, particularly for Channel 4 programming.'

Convergent Communications Ltd

17 Alfred Place, London WC1E 7EB
✆071-436 6643   Fax 071-436 6640

Contact *Philip Day*

Corporate video and training films. CLIENTS include Bradford & Bingley Building Society, Unisys, Shell, IBM and British Telecom. Unsolicited mss welcome.

Corporate Communication Consultants Ltd

47 Dean Street, London W1V 5HL
✆071-287 0833   Fax 071-434 4278

Contact *Nick Crean/Johnny Forshall*

Film and video — corporate and commercials. CLIENTS include Andersen Consulting; Beefeater Gin; Del Monte Foods International; Eurotunnel; The General Council for British Shipping; ICI Fibres; P&O; The Rural Development Commission; The Samaritans; Saatchi & Saatchi; The Stock Exchange; Tambrands. 'We are very keen to hear from new writers, but please send CVs rather than scripts.'

Creative Channel Ltd

Channel TV, Television Centre, La Pouquelaye, St Helier, Jersey JE2 3ZD
✆0534 68999   Fax 0534 59446

Managing Director *Gordon de Ste Croix*

Part of the Channel Television Group. Producers of TV commercials and corporate material — information, promotional, sales, training and events coverage. OUTPUT *This is Jersey* and *This is Guernsey* (video souvenir travel guides); promotional videos for Jersey and Guernsey; plus over 200 commercials a year. No unsolicited mss; new writing/scripts commissioned as required. Interested in hearing from local writers resident in the Channel Islands.

Creative Film Makers Ltd

Pottery Lane House, 34A Pottery Lane, London W11 4LZ
✆071-229 5131   Fax 071-229 4999

Contact *Michael Seligman/Julian Roberts*

Corporate and sports documentaries, commercials and television programmes. OUTPUT *The World's Greatest Golfers*, plus various corporate and sports programmes for clients like Nestlé, Benson & Hedges, Wimpey, Bouygues. Always open to suggestions but have hardly ever received unsolicited material of any value. Keen nevertheless to encourage new writers.

Creative Television Workshops Ltd

21 D'Arblay Street, London W1V 3FN
✆071-437 7333   Fax 071-734 3571

Contact *W. D. Young*

Commercials, corporate, educational, promotional and documentary.

Crew Green Associates Ltd

Mytton Mill, Mondford Bridge, Shrewsbury, Shropshire SY4 1AH
✆0743 850058   Fax 0743 850182

Contact *Simon Rea*

Film and video makers — in-house communications, training, sales, corporate and PR, marketing and below-the-line advertising. Unsolicited mss welcome.

Cricket Ltd

1 Lower James Street, London W1R 3PN
✆071-287 4848   Fax 071-413 0654

Director *Andrew Davies*
Creative Director (Film & Video) *Mark Johnson*
Producer (Film & Video) *Judy Wild*

Communications solutions for business clients wishing to influence a key audience. Film and video backed up by printed support and live coverage of events such as product launches, exhibitions and conferences. In addition, consultancy work, particularly for clients managing organisational change.

Cromdale Films Ltd

12 St Paul's Road, London N1 2QN
☏ 071-226 0178 Fax 081-871 2158

Contact *Ian Lloyd*

Film, video and TV — drama and documentary. OUTPUT *The Face of Darkness* (feature film); *Drift to Dawn* (rock music drama); *The Overdue Treatment* (documentary); *Russia, The Last Red Summer* (documentary). Initial phone call advised before submission of scripts.

Crown Business Communications Ltd

Crown House, 72 Hammersmith Road,
London W14 8YE
☏ 071-371 2500 Fax 071-371 1600

Contact *Marc Wright*

Part of the Crown Communications Group. Film and video — corporate, documentary, drama, educational, and television. CLIENTS include British Telecom, RTZ, Sainsbury, European Parliament, National Power, Birds Eye, Walls, DTI.

Crystalvision Ltd

Communications House, Blue Riband Estate,
Roman Way, Croydon CR9 3RA
☏ 081-781 6444 Fax 081-681 2340

Contact *Frazer Ashford* (Executive Producer)

Video, TV and cable/satellite programming — children's, documentary, drama, music, sports. No mss; send treatments/outlines only in the first instance. 'Each project is studied on merit; if the story/idea is good we would work with new writers.'

CTR Productions

31 Lismore Crescent, Broadfield, Crawley, West Sussex RH11 9DA
☏ 0293 548475

Contact *Ian Cunningham/Roseanna Coils*

Radio — drama, children's, specialist music programmes and commercials; also television documentary, game shows, children's and music programmes.

Cwmni'r Castell Cyf

12 Carlton Road, Colwyn Bay, Clwyd LL29 8RS
☏ 0492 533148 Fax 0492 531126

Contact *Elwyn Vaughan Williams*

Light entertainment television programmes. OUTPUT has included *Fe Hoffwn I; Galw Gari; Rargian Fawr*, plus comedy sketches for S4C.

Dane Productions

23 Trapham Road, Maidstone, Kent ME16 0EL
☏ 0622 756238 Fax 0622 690914

Contact *John Reynolds*

Film and video — corporate and commercials. CLIENTS include Mars, ICI, Glaxo, Bank of America, Kimberly-Clark, Van Leer. Unsolicited mss welcome.

Dareks Production House

58 Wickham Road, Beckenham, Kent BR3 2RQ
☏ 081-658 2012 Fax 081-658 2012

Contact *David Crossman*

Independent producers of corporate and broadcast television.

Daring Deeds Ltd

17-18 Alphabet Square, Hawgood Street,
London E3 3RT
☏ 071-538 9194 Fax 071-987 6054

Contact *Stephen Brown/Suzy Rowe*

Film and video producers: commercials, corporate work, promotional and training. Videos, conferences and PR brochures. Unsolicited mss welcome but time is not always available to read them. 'More interested in writers with proven experience in relevant market sector' than in new writers.

Dateline Productions Ltd

79 Dean Street, London W1V 5HA
☏ 071-437 4510/1834 Fax 071-287 6544

Contact *Miranda Watts*

Film and video — documentary and corporate. Unsolicited mss welcome. 'We are always interested in widening our list of possible writers.'

DBA Television

21 Ormeau Avenue, Belfast BT2 8HD
☏ 0232 231197 Fax 0232 333302

Contact *David Barker*

Long-established makers of documentary. OUTPUT has included *Power in the Blood* for Arena BBC2; *Heart on the Line* for Channel 4; *Hobo* (feature documentary) for the BBC; and *Drink Talking*, a series on alcoholism. In production: a six-part documentary series on County Fermanagh in Northern Ireland, with Carlo Gebler; and a four-part series, *The Heart of Man*, with Damian Gorman. Freelancers are encouraged to present summaries in writing first.

DBI Communication

21 Congreve Close, Warwick CV34 5RQ
☎0926 497695   Fax 0926 490512
Edit Studio: 131 Warwick Road, Kenilworth, Warwickshire CV8 1HY
☎0926 58901

Contact *David B. Impey*

Video — corporate, promotional, safety, training and sales. No unsolicited mss as most programmes are 'customised'. OUTPUT has included *Play Safe* with Keith Chegwin about the dangers of children entering quarries, shown in schools nationwide; *Guide Dog Training* (series); *Restoration of Wellesbourne Watermill; Restoration of Warwick Castle Watermill;* a programme about the construction of gas pipelines from Rugby to Coventry for British Gas.

Deptford Beach Productions Ltd

79 Wardour Street, London W1V 3TH
☎071-734 8508   Fax 071-287 2112

Contact *Tony Kirkhope*

FOUNDED 1985 to make independent productions for Channel 4. OUTPUT includes a documentary about Jean-Luc Godard which was written and directed by him. Unsolicited material considered.

Dibgate Productions Ltd

Studio 4, Parkstead Lodge, 31 Upper Park Road, London NW3 2UL
☎071-722 5634

Contact *Nicholas Parsons*

Documentary and travel films; plus comedy shorts for cinema and television. OUTPUT has included *A Fair Way to Play, Mad Dogs and Cricketers, Relatively Greek, Viva Menorca* and *Terribly British.*

Directors Video Company

89A Victoria Road, Aldershot,
Hampshire GU11 1JE
☎0252 316429   Fax 0252 344362

Contact *Sarah Rouse*

Corporate video; drama and documentary. OUTPUT Mostly corporate identity programmes, recruitment and new product launches. Unsolicited mss welcome. Writers 'with new ideas and showreels of video scripts' are particularly welcome.

Diverse Productions Ltd

6 Gorleston Street, London W14 8XS
☎071-603 4567   Fax 071-603 2148

Contact *Rita Shamia*

Corporate video, and television — current affairs, satellite business news, and educational programmes; all produced in-house. Recent OUTPUT has included *Rough Guide to Careers; Europe Express; Checkout; Uncertainties; Not on Sunday* and *New Age* for Channel 4.

Dragon Communications Ltd

Centre Heights, 137 Finchley Road,
London NW3 6JH
☎071-722 4494   Fax 071-722 2232

Contact *Tom Huish*

Medical and scientific films and corporate video.

Drake A-V Video Ltd

89 St Fagans Road, Fairwater, Cardiff CF5 3AE
☎0222 560333   Fax 0222 554909

Contact *Ian Lewis*

Corporate A-V film and video — mostly promotional, training or educational. Scripts in these fields welcome.

Ronald Dunkley Associates Ltd

13-14 Bateman Street, London W1V 6EB
☎071-734 7600   Fax 071-734 7143

Contact *Barry Palin/Ronald Dunkley*

Film and video — drama, documentary, PR, training, educational, recruitment and sales. CLIENTS include British Telecom, Post Office, British Red Cross Society, Calor Gas. No unsolicited mss.

Eagle and Eagle Ltd

15 Marlborough Road, London W4 4EU
☎081-995 1884   Fax 081-995 5648

Contact *Robert Eagle/Catharine Alen-Buckley*

Film, video and television: drama, documentary and corporate work. OUTPUT broadcast programmes on aviation, psychology, medicine, education; plus children's drama. No unsolicited scripts. No policy on new writing.

Edinburgh Film & Video Productions

Nine Mile Burn, by Penicuik, Midlothian EH26 9LT
☎ 0968 672131   Fax 0968 672685

Contact *R. Crichton*

Film, TV drama and documentary. OUTPUT *Torch; Silent Mouse; The Curious Case of Santa Claus; The Stamp of Greatness.* No unsolicited scripts at present.

Edric Audio Visual Ltd

34–36 Oak End Way, Gerrards Cross, Buckinghamshire SL9 8BR
☎ 0753 884646   Fax 0753 887163

Contact *Ivor Congdon* (Managing Director)

Makers of corporate, training, promotional and educational videos.

Electric Picture Machine

Production Office, 8B St Vincent Street, Edinburgh EH3 6SH
☎ 031–557 4609   Fax 031–557 4365

Contact *Kenneth B. Andrew/Avis Moore*

Film and video — corporate, documentary, drama, educational, light entertainment, music, arts, promotional and television. CLIENTS include British Gas Scotland, National Trust, London Underground, John Menzies, General Accident, Pittencrieff. Unsolicited scripts welcome.

Elstree (Production) Co. Ltd

Elstree Studios, Shenley Road, Borehamwood, Hertfordshire WD6 1JG
☎ 081–953 1600   Fax 081–953 9697

Produces feature films and television drama/ situation comedy. OUTPUT *Prospects* for Euston Films/Channel 4; *Rude Health* for Channel 4; *Othello* for the BBC; *Great Expectations* for Disney Channel. In development: *Old Curiosity Shop* for Disney Channel and *Buddy* (international co-production — London/New York/Australia). No unsolicited scripts at present.

Enigma Productions Ltd

13–15 Queen's Gate Place Mews, London SW7 5BG
☎ 071–581 0238   Fax 071–584 1799

Contact *David Puttnam/Colin Vaines*

Underwent a major relaunch in 1988 following David Puttnam's resignation from Columbia Pictures Hollywood. Backed by Warner Brothers, NatWest, Fujisankei Communications and British Satellite Broadcasting and 'could provide the model for a new beginning for British cinema' (David Puttnam). 'We shall use British crews but with writers, actors and directors from around the world.' First production: *Memphis Belle* (true story of an American B-17 bomber crew in Second World War). OUTPUT includes *Meeting Venus* (a comedy about a multinational opera company). In development: *Being Human; Fade Out* (drama set in Prague in the 1940s); *Shackleton* (true story of the Antarctic Explorer); *Chico Mendes* (true story of the Brazilian rainforest campaigner).

Enlightenment AV & Video

17–18 Diss Business Centre, Frenzehall Lane, Diss, Norfolk IP21 4EW
☎ 0379 640755   Fax 0379 640855

Contact *Adrian Tayler*

Video productions for training and industrial marketing. All scripts currently produced in-house or commissioned by a client for a specific project, but will consider unsolicited mss if it has market potential, e.g. industrial training material.

Epic Interactive Media Company

VPS House, 22 Brighton Square, Brighton, East Sussex BN1 1HD
☎ 0273 728686   Fax 0273 821567

Contact *Jim Brathwaite*

Producers of computer-based training and interactive video, and compact disc-based programmes. Training, information and point-of-sale material. CLIENTS include Bradford & Bingley Building Society, HMSO, ICI, Shell, North West Water, and many others.

Espresso TV

109 Canalot Production Studios, 222 Kensal Road, London W10 5BN
☎ 081–960 5525   Fax 081–960 4054

Contact *David Hooper*

Film and video production — corporate, documentaries, commercials and live events. Unsolicited scripts welcome.

Ettinger Brothers Productions

3 Church Road, Penny Lane, Liverpool L15 9EA
☏ 051-734 2240   Fax 051-733 2468

Contact *Philip Ettinger/Robert Ettinger*

TV documentary, general interest television and sports/general interest video production. Always interested in new writing. Unsolicited mss welcome.

Euston Films

365 Euston Road, London NW1 3AR
☏ 071-387 0911   Fax 071-388 2122

Contact *Victoria Blunden*

Feature films; television series and serials. OUTPUT has included *Selling Hitler, Anglo-Saxon Attitudes, Minder.* No unsolicited mss.

Eyewitness Ltd

The Drove, Sherfield English Road, Romsey,
Hampshire SO51 6EF
☏ 0794 22500   Fax 0794 23601

Contact *Slim MacDonnell/Sandra James*

Film and video: documentaries, commercials, pop promos and drama — all with hazardous shooting content in common. OUTPUT *The Chief* (Anglia TV); *Split Second* (feature film); plus commercials (specialised segments) for Eagle Star, Radio Rentals, Impulse, Pepsi Cola, and others. Unsolicited mss welcome.

Farnham Film Company Ltd

34 Burnt Hill Road, Lower Bourne, Farnham,
Surrey GU10 3LZ
☏ 0252 710313
Fax 0252 725855   Telex 9312110463 (FF) G

Contact *Ian Lewis*

Television and film — drama and documentaries. Unsolicited mss welcome. 'We would rather do something good and new than something mediocre and well known — but resent time-wasters.'

Fast Forward Productions

Crescent Studio, 18 High Street, Holywood, Co.
Down, Northern Ireland BT18 9AD
☏ 02317 7697   Fax 02317 2289

Contact *John Nicholson/Moya Neeson*

Video and television for documentary and corporate material. OUTPUT *Farming Ulster,* the company's first broadcast commission, for Ulster TV. Currently working on the RTE/BBC Northern Ireland co-production series on gardening, *Greenfingers,* and in negotiation with other British, Irish, American and Canadian networks. No unsolicited scripts. 'We would prefer to chat to someone first by telephone to see if there was a project of mutual interest.'

Filmfair Ltd

1-4 Jacobs Well Mews, London W1H 5PD
☏ 071-935 1596   Fax 071-935 0229

Contact *Gary Smith*

FOUNDED 1966. Makers of model and cel animation. OUTPUT *The Wombles; Paddington Bear; Bangers and Mash; Huxley Pig; Rod 'n' Emu; Dream Stone; Brown Bear's Wedding; White Bear's Secret; Astro Farm.* Unsolicited mss welcome.

FilmIt Productions Ltd

2 Tunstall Road, London SW9 8BN
☏ 071-738 4175   Fax 071-738 3787

Contact *John Samson/Susan Honeyford*

Film, video and television drama, documentary, and corporate work. OUTPUT *Free for All* (viewer-led current affairs, Channel 4); *A Polite Enquiry* and *Gulf Between Us* (documentaries for Channel 4). No unsolicited scripts. Send letter with 1-2-page synopsis in the first instance.

Filmnova

Portman House, Portland Road, Jesmond,
Newcastle upon Tyne NE2 1AQ
☏ 091-222 0733   Fax 091-222 1897

Contact *Peter Brown*

Film and video production company for broadcast and corporate clients.

Filmworks

65 Brackenbury Road, London W6 0BG
☏ 081-741 5631   Fax 081-748 3198

Contact *Geraldine Easter/Jonathan Bohm*

Television, documentary and corporate programmes. OUTPUT *Captain Star Inventing the Universe* (animation series); *In the Footsteps of Scott* (travel/adventure); *On the Trail of the Chinese Wildman* (travel/adventure). Unsolicited mss welcome. No specific policy as such towards new writing.

First Choice
See **Humphrey Barclay Productions**

First Creative Group Ltd
Unit 8, Chorley West Business Park, Ackhurst Road, Chorley, Lancashire PR7 1LH
☎ 02572 66411/3   Fax 02572 68490

Contact *Andy Dakin/Martin Hollingworth*

Film, video and A-V production. Varied output including medical, corporate training, promotional and conference. Unsolicited ideas and approaches from established scriptwriters welcome.

First Freedom Productions Ltd
15 Rochester Square, London NW1 9SA
☎ 071–482 7307   Fax 071–485 4692

Contact *Graham Addicott/Paul O'Dell/Ken Craig*

Television documentary and corporate work. OUTPUT *This Week* (ITV); *The World This Week/ Dispatches* (Channel 4). More interested in treatments than in full scripts, particularly for series ideas across the range, i.e. factual, light entertainment, etc. No specific policy towards new writing.

First House Productions Ltd
First House, Sutton Street, Birmingham B1 1PE
☎ 021–622 3065   Fax 021–666 6488

Contact *David Wilkins/Julie Farrington*

Video — commercials, corporate, educational and television. CLIENTS ITV Sport, the BBC, and many commercials: Rank, Stuart Crystal, Tarmac, Royal Doulton, CAA, Leeds Permanent Building Society, Ford Motor Co.

Fitting Images Ltd
Alfred House, 127A Oatlands Drive, Weybridge, Surrey KT13 9LB
☎ 0932 840056   Fax 0932 858075

Managing Director *Sue Fleetwood*

Film and video: point-of-sale; health and safety; corporate; induction; team building; customer relations; keyboard skills; security. Unsolicited mss welcome.

Five Lamps Group
Five Lamps Studio, West Avenue, Derby DE1 3HR
☎ 0332 383322   Fax 0332 291268

Contact *Mollie Kirkland/David Regan*

Producers of industrial videos, conferences, audio visual and interactive training. Total in-house facilities, including writing. No unsolicited mss.

Flamingo Pictures
47 Londsdale Square, London N1 1EW
☎ 071–607 9958   Fax 071–609 7669

Contact *Christine Oestreicher*

Producers of mostly cinema, plus TV.

Flashback Television Ltd
2–3 Cowcross Street, London EC1M 6DR
☎ 071–490 8996   Fax 071–490 5610

Contact *Taylor Downing/Linda Stradling*

Television producers: drama and drama-documentaries. OUTPUT *Divorce - Who Gets the Children?*; *Adoption - All for the Sake of the Children* (drama-documentaries for Thames TV). No unsolicited scripts, but policy is to encourage new writing.

Flying Pig Productions Ltd
13 High Street, Thornbury, Bristol BS12 2AE
☎ 0454 281898   Fax 0454 281868

Contact *Rob Champion/Anthony Boyle*

Film: documentary and drama; TV: children's and educational; video: promotional, training and educational. CLIENTS include Royal Mail and British Rail. Many projects in development and under consideration by Channel 4, ITV and the BBC. No unsolicited mss; send treatments/ 2-page synopses. Interested in new writing.

Flying Tiger Film and TV Productions
13–15 Northgate, Heptonstall, West Yorkshire HX7 7ND
☎ 0422 844595

Contact *Jay Jones*

Corporate programmes, documentary and commercials. No unsolicited mss; ideas/concepts welcome.

FM Television Ltd

92 Water Lane, Wilmslow, Cheshire SK9 5BB
☎0625 533580　　　　　　Fax 0625 531992

Contact *Hilary Pinnock*

Sports programmes for international broadcasters; corporate videos for industry. OUTPUT includes *Formula One World Grand Prix Powerboat* series. General motorsport and watersport programming. No unsolicited mss.

Formula Communications

Avebury Court Studios, 3 Avebury Court, Maylands Industrial Estate, Hemel Hempstead, Hertfordshire HP2 7TA
☎0442 250247　　　　　　Fax 0442 61358

Contact *Colleen Bending/Steve Arnold*

Video — commercials, corporate and training; A-V multi-image production, conferences, presentations, live events and shows. No unsolicited scripts.

Mark Forstater Productions Ltd

Suite 60, 124-128 Barlby Road, London W10 6BL
☎081-964 1888　　　　　　Fax 071-960 9819

Contact *Nicola Lund*

Active in the selection, development and production of material for film and television. OUTPUT *Monty Python and the Holy Grail; The Odd Job; The Grass is Singing; Xtro; Forbidden; Separation; The Fantasist; Shalom Joan Collins; The Touch.* Unsolicited mss considered but synopses preferred in the first instance.

Fourth Wall Productions

1 Little Argyll Street, London W1R 5DB
☎071-437 2222　　　　　　Fax 071-734 0663

Contact *Lino Ferrari/Bob Marsland*

Television programmes, current affairs, documentary, light entertainment and corporate. Initial approaches should be made on only one or two sides of A4 paper. Day-time contact number should be supplied whenever possible.

Fox Television

10-12 Fitzroy Mews, London W1P 5DQ
☎071-387 3308　　　　　　Fax 071-388 6265

Contact *Derek Shepherd*

Corporate, documentary and television.

Freeway Films

67 George Street, Edinburgh EH2 2JG
☎031-225 3200　　　　　　Fax 031-225 3667

Contact *John McGrath/Susie Brown*

Film outlet for John McGrath's work. OUTPUT has included *Blood Red Roses* and *There is a Happy Land* for Channel 4; *The Dressmaker* for Film on 4 International and British Screen; *John Brown's Body* for Channel 4 — a 3-part history of the industrial working classes in Scotland; *Border Warfare,* also for Channel 4 — a 3-part history of the relations between Scotland and England. Currently developing several feature films.

Frontroom Films Ltd

1 The Barton, Mill Road, Countess Wear, Exeter, Devon EX2 6LJ
☎0392 70985　　　　　　Fax 0392 431405

Television and cinema, both shorts and full-length features. OUTPUT has included *Acceptable Levels, Ursula Glenys, Intimate Strangers, The Love Child* and *Wild Flowers.*

Ian Gall Television

The Syms Building, Bumpers Farm Industrial Estate, Chippenham, Wiltshire SN14 6NQ
☎0249 443493　　　　　　Fax 0249 443569

Contact *Rosie Britton*

Video — corporate, documentary, educational and television. 'Since most of our output is bespoke programming, we have no use for unsolicited material.'

Ken Gamble Productions

Suite 4, Hazeldine House, Telford TF3 4JL
☎0952 291445　　　　　　Fax 0952 291093

Contact *Christine Gamble*

Film and TV programme producers for industry and broadcast. Translations, systems transfer, and TV production facilities.

Gateway Audio Visual and Video

472 Green Lanes, London N13 5XF
☎081-882 0177　　　　　　Fax 081-882 4161

Contact *Graham L. Smart*

Producers of video and film for sponsors. OUTPUT has included marketing, training and corporate programmes for various clients; also TV commercials. No unsolicited mss but 'always on the lookout for new scriptwriters'.

John Gau Productions

Burston House, 1 Burston Road, Putney,
London SW15 6AR
☎081-788 8811   Fax 081-789 0903

Contact *John Gau*

Documentaries and series for television, plus corporate video. OUTPUT has included *Assignment Adventure, Moneyspinner* and *Sputniks, Bleeps and Mr Perry* for Channel 4; the *Korea* series for BBC1; *Reaching for the Skies* for BBC2; *Voyager* for Central; and *The Power and The Glory* for BBC2.

Noel Gay Television

6th Floor, 76 Oxford Street, London W1R 1RB
☎071-412 0400   Fax 071-412 0300

Contact *Charles Armitage/Nick Symons*

The association with Noel Gay (theatrical agency/production company) makes this one of the most securely financed independents in the business. OUTPUT includes *The Last Laugh; The Happening; Into the Groove; Red Dwarf; Ruby Wax; Merlin; Pallas.*

GCP

5 Drayton Gardens, London W13 0LG
☎081-997 3513   Fax 081-840 7842

Contact *Geoff Cotton*

Video and television: comedy, drama and corporate work. OUTPUT includes sitcom and drama for broadcast stations and corporate videos. No unsolicited scripts. Not interested in new writing except by recommendation.

Gibb Rose Organisation Ltd

Pinewood Studios, Iver Heath,
Buckinghamshire SL0 0NH
☎0753 651700   Fax 0753 630372

Contact *Sydney Rose* (Managing Director)/*Keith Belcher* (Creative Director)

Feature films, TV (music, film, documentary), video (including corporate). Unsolicited mss not welcome unless at full screenplay level. 'We will examine ideas and scripts after initial discussion with the author.' However, story outlines/treatments will be considered if submitted by bona fide persons/organisations in the publishing/media sectors of the entertainment industry.

Adrian Gilpin Television

Penshurst Place, Penshurst, Tonbridge,
Kent TN11 8DG
☎0892 870307

Contact *Adrian Gilpin*

TV/film production. Particularly interested in TV comedy scripts and drama at the moment.

Goldcrest Films and Television Ltd

36–44 Brewer Street, London W1R 3HP
☎071-437 8696
Fax 071-437 4448   Telex 267458 GOLDCR

Chief Executive Officer *John Quested*
Director of Acquisitions *Jo Deakin*

Goldcrest Films and Television was established in the late Seventies and rapidly grew into a leading independent production company involved in the funding, production and distribution of quality feature films and television programmes. In November 1990, Goldcrest's management team, led by John Quested, achieved a buy-out from the Brent Walker Leisure Group of the company's film and television operation. With a current library of over 75 film and TV titles, Goldcrest is an independent and fully integrated entertainment company focusing on the core activities of film production and worldwide distribution. Feature film scripts are accepted through agents only. Goldcrest is geared towards producing two medium-budgeted features a year.

The Good Film Company

2nd Floor, 14–15 D'Arblay Street,
London W1V 3FP
☎071-734 1331   Fax 071-734 2997

Contact *Yanina Barry*

Commercials, pop videos and corporate. OUTPUT has included a Style Council pop video; *Water Safety* and *Hypothermia in the Elderly* (for the C.O.I). CLIENTS include National Express Coaches, Camel Cigarettes, Tunisian Tourist Board. Unsolicited mss welcome.

Gower Training

Gower House, Crost Road, Aldershot,
Hampshire GU11 3HR
☎0252 330021/331551   Fax 0252 317446

Contact *Claire Leebrook*

General management training films. Part of Gower Publishing.

Grapevine TV

Hebron House, Sion Road, Bristol BS3 3BD
☎0272 637973   Fax 0272 631770

Contact *Adrian Mack*

Corporate videos, plus art videos. OUTPUT *Right From the Start* on using professional land surveyors; programmes for local authorities such as Avon Equal Opportunities Unit; *Working with Clive*, a case study of a man with multiple disabilities. No unsolicited scripts. Will commission as production demands. Adrian Mack has run several scriptwriting courses.

Grasshopper Productions Ltd

50 Peel Street, London W8 7PD
☎071-229 1181   Fax 071-229 2070

Contact *Joy Whitby*

Children's programmes and adult drama. No unsolicited mss.

Greenpark Productions Ltd

St Wilfrids, 101 Honor Oak Park,
London SE23 3LB
☎081-699 7234   Fax 081-699 1223

Contact *David Morphet*

Film, video and television — shorts, documentary, specialised and corporate. Unsolicited mss welcome.

Greenpoint Films

5A Noel Street, London W1V 3RB
☎071-437 6492   Fax 071-437 0644

Contact *Ann Scott/Patrick Cassavetti*

A small company whose members act as individual producers and directors. Check before sending unsolicited material.

Colin Gregg Films Ltd

11 Compton Terrace, London NW1
☎071-704 9398

Contact *Colin Gregg*

Feature films for Channel 4 and BBC2. OUTPUT *Remembrance; To The Lighthouse; Lamb; Hard Travelling; We Think The World of You; Drowning in the Shallow End*. Unsolicited mss not welcome.

Griffin Productions

Balfour House, 46–54 Great Titchfield Street,
London W1P 7AE
☎071-636 5066   Fax 071-436 3232

Contact *Adam Clapham*

Documentary and TV drama. OUTPUT has included *Painting With Light* for BBC; *Odyssey* for Channel 4; *Act of Betrayal* (mini-series) and *Secret Weapon* (TV film) for ITV; *Not A Penny More, Not a Penny Less* (TV mini-series) with the BBC).

Reg Grundy Productions (GB) Ltd

Enterprise House, 59–65 Upper Ground,
London SE1 9PQ
☎071-928 8942   Fax 071-928 8417

Television — drama and light entertainment. OUTPUT includes *Going For Gold, Jeopardy, Keynotes* and *Press Your Luck*.

David Hall Productions

19 The Drive, Leeds LS8 1JF
☎0532 661207

Contact *David Hall*

Makers of television drama, documentaries and film; also corporate video. Unsolicited mss welcome. New writing encouraged and supported but 'unfortunately I do not have the financial resources to provide development funding for speculative projects'. OUTPUT *Maggie's Children; All of You Out There* (both documentaries for Channel 4); *To Everything A Season* (feature film in development); and various regional documentaries for Yorkshire Television.

Hammer Film Productions

Elstree Studios, Shenley Road, Borehamwood,
Hertfordshire WD6 1JG
☎081-953 1600   Fax 081-905 1127

Contact *Roy Skeggs/Richelle Wilder*

HandMade Films

26 Cadogan Square, London SW1X 0JP
☎071-581 1265   Fax 071-584 7338

Feature films. OUTPUT has included *Mona Lisa; The Missionary; Time Bandits; Withnail and I; The Lonely Passion of Judith Hearne; The Raggedy Rawney; Checking Out; How To Get Ahead in Advertising; Nuns on the Run*. Company policy is not to accept unsolicited mss direct from writers, 'though we do consider submissions from literary agents, publishers and producers'.

Haraco Ltd

48 Hylton Street, Hockley, Birmingham B18 6HN
☎ 021-523 3341   Fax 021-523 8064

Contact *Paul Rabone*

Commercials and corporate videos. CLIENTS include Rolls Royce, Goodyear, Yamaha Keyboard, Britvic, Pepsi.

Harnett Milan Ltd

53 Cavendish Road, London SW12 0BL
☎ 081-675 6778   Fax 081-673 1959

Contact *Angie Milan/Phil Harnett/Ian Watson*

Corporate and industrial videos for sales, training, recruitment, product launches and promotion. Unsolicited mss in these fields welcome. Writing commissioned generally from writers with specialist knowledge in a given field such as science, engineering, information technology.

Hat Trick Productions Ltd

10 Livonia Street, London W1V 3PH
☎ 071-434 2451   Fax 071-287 9791

Contact *Denise O'Donoghue*

Television programmes. OUTPUT *Norbert Smith - A Life; Whose Line is it Anyway?; Newsroom; Drop the Dead Donkey; Harry Enfield's Television Programme; Have I Got News For You; Clive Anderson Talks Back; S & M; Paul Merton Series; Round the Bend; The Big One.* Various projects in development.

Hawkshead Ltd

3 Fitzroy Square, London W1P 5AH
☎ 071-388 1234   Fax 071-387 5789

Contact *Nigel Houghton/Carol Haslam/Angela Law/Jane Mitchell*

Film and video — broadcast: documentary, educational and factual entertainment. Corporate: training, promotional and employee communications. OUTPUT includes *Fat Man in Argentina* (Channel 4, S4C, WGBH, Channel 7 Australia); *Remember, Remember* (BBC2); *Roux Brothers* (BBC2); *The Manager* (Channel 4); *Heading for the Top End* (Channel 4, WNET); *Yo! Mrs Askew - Think of England* (BBC2); *South Bank Show - Douglas Adams* (LWT); *A Taste of Japan* (BBC2). CLIENTS include Brittany Ferries, Boots, Department of Employment, Equitable Life, London Underground, Metropolitan Police, PowerGen, CFI, Learning International.

Hawthornden Films

Cambridge Court, Cambridge Road, Frinton-on-Sea, Essex CO13 9HN
☎ 0255 676381   Fax 0255 679275

Contact *Timothy Foster*

Very active in European film co-production in the Netherlands, France and Italy. At present developing *Winter in Zima* and *The Flying Dutchman.* Only interested in original European-based feature material.

Head to Head Communication Ltd

The Hook, Fiveways Business Centre, Plane Tree Crescent, Feltham, Middlesex TW13 7AQ
☎ 081-893 7766   Fax 081-893 2777

Contact *Bob Carson*

Business and corporate communication.

Head-On Productions Ltd

235 Goswell Road, London EC2 7JD
☎ 071-837 3388   Fax 071-837 8211

Contact *Peter Stevenson*

Corporate video. CLIENTS SAS (inflight programmes); First National Finance Corporation (investor relations), and Prudential Corporation (marketing). No unsolicited mss but contact from writers with samples of work welcome. 'Always interested in good writers with requisite visual sense and commercial acumen.'

John Hemson

Heatherbank Studios, 3 Silverbirches Lane, Aspley Heath, Woburn Sands, Milton Keynes MK17 8TL
☎ 0908 583002   Fax 0908 281035

Contact *John Hemson*

Film and television — training, sales and documentary.

Jim Henson Productions Ltd

1B Downshire Hill, London NW3 1NR
☎ 071-431 2818   Fax 071-431 3737

Contact *Duncan Kenworthy*

Feature films and television — family entertainment and children's. OUTPUT *Labyrinth* (film); *The Witches* (film); *The Muppet Show* (ITV); *The Storyteller* (Channel 4); *Mother Goose Stories* (ITV); *Jim Henson's Greek Myths* (Channel 4). No unsolicited mss read except when offered by a literary agent.

Highgate Films

41B Hornsey Lane Gardens, Milton Park,
London N6 5NY
☏ 081–348 7298   Fax 081–341 6334

Contact *Peter Bloore* (Artistic Director)

TV documentary and drama, and feature films.
Screenplay writers needed to develop projects and
write dialogue but 'we have very little funding to
develop many scripts... More interested in writers'
ability than in completed manuscripts. Keen to see
well thought out feature film storyline/synopses.
Plot-driven storytelling is very poor in most of the
material we receive.' No unsolicited faxes.

Hines Communications Ltd

3rd Floor, Stephen House, Bethesda Street,
Burnley, Lancashire BB11 1PR
☏ 0282 52521   Fax 0282 30297

Contact *David E. Hines/Jackie Rodgers*

Television — broadcast and corporate. Moving
towards more drama this year. Unsolicited mss
welcome.

Holmes Associates

17 Rathbone Street, London W1P 1AF
☏ 071–637 8251   Fax 071–637 9024

Contact *Andrew Holmes*

Prolific originators, producers and packagers of
documentary, drama and music television. OUTPUT
has included *The House of Bernarda Alba* (Channel
4/WNET/Amaya); *Piece of Cake* (drama mini-series
for LWT); *Well Being* and *Signals* (Channel 4);
Chish 'n' Fips (Central); *Video & Chips* (HTV); *Four
Up Two Down* and *Rock Steady* (Channel 4);
Timeline (with MPT, TVE Spain & TRT Turkey).

Holmes & Moriarty

Mincloon, Rahoon, Co. Galway, Republic of Ireland
☏ 010 353 91 22855   Fax 010 353 91 22514

Contact *Antony Sellers*

Drama and documentary for film and television.
Currently focusing on development of contemporary fiction. Will review appropriate script material.

Horntvedt Television

The Power House, Alpha Place, Flood Street,
London SW3 5SZ
☏ 071–376 7611   Fax 071–351 2951

Contact *Kit Horntvedt/Howard Webster/Miles
Millar*

Television producers. Recent OUTPUT includes the
one-hour documentary *Classic Racing*. 'We encourage and use new writing but require c.v. in the first
instance, preferably through an agent.' No unsolicited mss.

Hourglass Pictures Ltd

117 Merton Road, Wimbledon,
London SW19 1ED
☏ 081–540 8786   Fax 081–542 6598

Contact *Martin Chilcott* (Director)

Film and video; documentary, drama and commercials. OUTPUT public relations material for government and industrial bodies; health and social issues
for the World Health Organisation; product promotion for pharmaceutical companies. Open to new
writing.

Michael Howes Productions Ltd

6 Theed Street, Waterloo, London SE1 8ST
☏ 071–928 7851

Contact *Mike Howes*

Film, video and television: documentary and corporate work. OUTPUT *Sinfonietta* (music documentary series); *Uncertain Truth* (humanities series);
The Singing Voice (music documentary); *The Listening* (music documentary). No unsolicited
scripts.

HPICM

53 Frith Street, London W1V 5TE
☏ 071–434 0929   Fax 071–434 1204

Contact *Nigel Lloyd-Jones*

Face to face business communications.

Hubner Films Ltd

77 Dean Street, London W1V 5MA
☏ 071–439 4060/437 6082   Fax 071–287 1072

Contact *Martin Hubner/Sarah McGee*

Film commercials, corporate videos and documentaries, and feature film scripts. CLIENTS Associated
Newspapers, Gateway Supermarkets, De Beers Diamonds, Bentalls, British Gas, IBM, Nat West, Audi,
Parkfield/Ford (USA). Unsolicited scripts or outlines for feature films and documentaries welcome.
Material is read and discussed before being forwarded if promising to TV/film companies or
agents for production packaging.

ICE International Video Films Ltd

31 King Street West, Manchester M3 2PN
☎061-834 3992 Fax 061-834 3993

Contact David Kent-Watson

TV and video — film and drama. OUTPUT *Into the Darkness; Firestar; Eye of Satan; GBH II; Assassinator; Kill.* Unsolicited mss welcome; always looking for new writers. Currently setting up a production facility in Malta.

The Ideas Factory

Maxron House, Green Lane, Romiley,
Stockport SK6 3JG
☎061-406 6685 Fax 061-406 6672

Contact Martin Duffy

TV, film and video production. *Special interests* adventure, travel, disability, and investing in projects which already have part finance guaranteed. Producers of *The Big 8* wheelchair basketball sports series for Channel 4.

Illuminations

19-20 Rheidol Mews, Rheidol Terrace,
London N1 8NU
☎071-226 0266 Fax 071-359 1151

Contact Linda Zuck

Primarily a documentary production company making cultural programmes for a Channel 4 and BBC audience. OUTPUT has included *State of the Art* (6-part documentary series); *Ghosts in the Machine* (6-part video compilation series); *The A–Z of TV* and *1001 Nights TV; TV Heaven; Bookmark* programmes — *Amis K. and Writers' Day Jobs; Arena — Chi Chi the Panda*; plus various other documentaries about art, science and television. No unsolicited mss.

Illustra Communications Ltd

13-14 Bateman Street, London W1V 6EB
☎071-437 9611 Fax 071-734 7143

Contact Douglas Kentish/Barry Palin

Film and video — television, cinema, commercials and corporate. Unsolicited mss from known writers are always welcome.

Imagicians Ltd

34 Fouberts Place, London W1V 2BH
☎071-287 5211 Fax 071-734 6813

Contact Alan Scales

Diverse range of productions from television documentary features to in-flight videos and corporate production. OUTPUT has included *The Great Palace — The Story of Parliament; Mary Wesley — Not That Sort of Girl* and *Princess of Wales at 30* for the BBC; *Street Hockey* sports series for Channel 4; various corporate videos for clients like ICI, IBM, WH Smith and British Telecom. Also programme producers for **European Television Networks (ETN)**.

In Video Productions Ltd

16 York Place, Edinburgh EH1 3EP
☎031-557 2151 Fax 031-557 5465

Contact Sheila Williamson/Sam Docherty

Film and video — commercials, corporate, educational, promotional and broadcast programmes.

In-House Corporate Video

The Boundary House, Old Warwick Road,
Lapworth, Warwickshire B94 6LU
☎0564 783958 Fax 0564 783619

Contact John Pluck (Senior Producer)

Corporate films and videos for training, marketing and public relations. No unsolicited mss but interested in hearing from writers with corporate experience. Send sample of writing in this area.

Inca Video & Film Productions

Park House Studios, PO Box 111,
London SE26 5DB
☎081-778 7318 Fax 081-659 5048

Contact Peter Ashton

Video and film — travel, commercials, promotional and sales. No unsolicited mss.

Input Video Ltd

Woodger Road, Shepherds Bush Green,
London W12 8QP
☎081-740 5222 Fax 081-746 0811

Contact Alex Leche/Dave Simpson (Editor)

Video and TV — broadcast and corporate production and post-production. OUTPUT About 50 'sell-through' videos. No unsolicited material. Freelance scriptwriters used occasionally.

Insight Productions Ltd

Gidleigh Studio, Gidleigh, Chagford, Newton Abbot, Devon TQ13 8HP
☎0647 432686 Fax 0647 433141

Contact *Brian Skilton*

TV and film — drama, documentary and light entertainment. OUTPUT has included *Taming the Flood, Streets Ahead, Dartmoor The Threatened Wilderness* and *Camargue* (all for Channel 4); also *Playing Away* (feature film for Film on 4). No unsolicited mss. 'We welcome new ideas/film scripts for cinema or TV but prefer to discuss the subject before accepting a script to read or comment upon.'

Interesting Television Ltd

The Boundary House, Old Warwick Road, Lapworth, Warwickshire B94 6LU
☎0564 783958   Fax 0564 783619

Contact *John Pluck* (Senior Producer)

Producers of broadcast television documentaries and feature series on film and video for ITV and BBC TV. Currently looking towards cable, satellite and home video to broaden its output. Ideas for television documentaries particularly welcome. Send a treatment in the first instance, particularly if the subject is 'outside our area of current interest'. OUTPUT has included television programmes on heritage, antiques, gardening, science and industry; also projects on heritage, health and sports for the home video front.

International Broadcasting Trust

2 Ferdinand Place, London NW1 8EE
☎071-482 2847   Fax 071-284 3374

Contact *Paddy Coulter*

Television programmes on Third World, development and environmental issues. New ideas welcome, but send outlines in writing in the first instance.

Peter Isaac Medical Information Services

Peckover House, North Brink, Wisbech, Cambridgeshire PE13 1JR
☎0945 474008   Fax 0945 474009

Contact *Peter Isaac*

Film, video and TV — medical and zoological documentaries. *Special interest* in medical and animal husbandry. Open to new writing but no unsolicited mss. OUTPUT has included BMA award-winning *Understanding Chemotherapy*; also *Living with Lymphomas; Early Detection of Breast Cancer; Understanding Cystic Fibrosis* and *A Kind Goodbye* (Pedigree petfoods); *Chernobyl: A Challenge to Haematologists*.

Isolde Films Ltd

4 Kensington Park Gardens, London W11 3HB
☎071-727 3541   Fax 071-727 3632

Contact *Clare Lewthwaite*

Film and television — drama and documentary. OUTPUT *Menuhin; Maria Callas; Testimony; In From the Cold; Pushkin*. Unsolicited material is read, but please send a written outline first.

Jacaranda Productions Ltd

J House, 6 Studland Street, Hammersmith, London W6 0JS
☎081-741 9088   Fax 081-748 5670

Contact *Katy Eyre/Hamish Adam*

Educational, training and corporate.

Brian Jenkinson Film & Television Productions Ltd

12 Beech Grove, Whitley Bay, Northumberland NE26 3PJ
☎091-252 7354   Fax 091-252 7354

Contact *Brian Jenkinson*

Commercials, documentary and corporate. Freelance scriptwriting used in all categories.

Jericho Productions Ltd

29 Cholmeley Park, Highgate, London N6 5EL
☎081-341 1834   Fax 081-348 6851

Managing Director *Bernard Krichefski*

Television and video producers: drama, corporate and commercials. OUTPUT includes *Family* Andrew Kazamia; and *Finding Sarah* Julia Kearsley, for Channel 4's *4 Play* slot. CLIENTS Barratt Homes, Jersey Tourism, British Midland Airways.

Michael Kann Associates Ltd

6-10 Lexington Street, London W1R 3HS
☎071-439 9882   Fax 071-734 8574

Contact *Michael Kann*

Corporate films, including documentary and drama. CLIENTS include Ford Motor Co., British Council, Bank of England, Post Office, Foreign & Commonwealth Office. No unsolicited mss but always looking for fresh new writing.

Kay Communications Ltd

Gauntley Court Studios, Gauntley Court,
Nottingham NG7 5HD
☏ 0602 781333   Fax 0602 783734

Contact *John Alexander*

Makers of industrial video programmes and training
programmes. Scripts written in-house. No unsolicited mss.

Kingfisher Television Productions Ltd

Line House Barnstone, Nottingham NG13 9JN
☏ 0949 60101   Fax 0949 60139

Contact *Alan Jones*

Knaves Acre Productions

Pinewood Studios, Pinewood Road, Iver,
Buckinghamshire SL0 0NH
☏ 0753 651700   Fax 0753 656087

Contact *Bryan Izzard/Annie Bridges*

Part of Bryan Izzard Television Group. Makers of
broadcast television, easy listening music, unusual
biographies of unusual composers, comedy (particularly sit-com), popular video drama. OUTPUT
Tonight at 8.30 (Noel Coward comedy series
starring Joan Collins for BBC1); *An Actor's Life for
Me* (BBC1); *A Land of Smiley* (operetta for Channel
4); *Holding the Baby* (sit-com for Central).

Lagan Pictures Ltd

7 Rugby Court, Agincourt Avenue,
Belfast BT7 1PN
☏ 0232 326125   Fax 0846 689587

Contact *Stephen Butcher*

Film, video, television: drama, documentary and
corporate work. 'We welcome unsolicited manuscripts from writers living in or originating from
Northern Ireland irrespective of subject matter, and
from other writers if of relevance to Northern
Ireland.' Encourages new writers in Northern Ireland.

Landseer Film and Television Productions Ltd

140 Royal College Street, London NW1 0TA
☏ 071-485 7333   Fax 071-485 7573

Contact *Derek Bailey*

Film and video production: documentary, drama,
music and arts, children's and current affairs.
Recent productions: *Not Pots* (Channel 4);
Kenneth MacMillan at 60 (BBC); *The Russians Are*

Coming (Channel 4); *Biosphere II* (Central); *Hakan
Hardenberger* (South Bank Show); *La Stupenda*
(BBC Omnibus).

Lawson Productions Ltd

2 Clarendon Close, London W2 2NS
☏ 071-706 3111   Fax 071-706 3035

Contact *Sarah Lawson*

Film & TV — drama and comedy. OUTPUT has
included *That's Love* (UK and US); *Home to Roost*
(US version); *The Dawning* with Anthony Hopkins;
Life After Life with George Cole; *Natural Lies*
(BBC). No unsolicited mss unless via agents, but
always interested in new talent.

Lifetime Group

Suffolk House, 1–8 Whitfield Place,
London W1P 5SF
☏ 071-387 9808   Fax 071-387 9106

Director, Research & Development *Lucy
Wagner*

Film, video and television: drama, documentary,
children's and corporate work. OUTPUT includes:
The Animal Contract (documentaries with
Desmond Morris); *Runaway Bay* (children's action
adventure); *Floyd on Spain*; plus sell-through video
programmes. Unsolicited scripts welcome. Always
interested in new writing.

Lodestar Productions Ltd

15 Eyot Gardens, London W6 9TN
☏ 081-748 8517

Contact *Peter Coulson*

Film and TV — drama and documentary. Documentaries include *Odyssey* (Channel 4); *Nature*
(PBS) and *Natural World* (BBC). Drama in development: *Plant Hunters; Unflinching* (NFDF); *Anna's
Story* (Channel 4 Film on Four). Projects tend to
have 'a world about us nature: a wilderness/
exploring bias'. Commissions from new writers but
these tend to come by way of recommendation.

Lombard Productions Ltd

22 Poland Street, London W1V 3DD
☏ 071-434 0251   Fax 071-734 0859

Contact *Peter Hort*

Film and television drama, commercials and documentary. OUTPUT *Magic* (TV drama series);
Supercar (documentary on Panther sports car);
various cinema and TV commercials. No unsolicited material without prior phone call outlining

project. On the look-out for good original scripts for television and feature films.

London Film Productions Ltd

Kent House, 14-17 Market Place, Great Titchfield Street, London W1N 8AR
☏071-323 5241   Fax 071-436 2834
Contact *Tom Donald*

Makers of a wide range of international television and film. OUTPUT has included *The Scarlet Pimpernel; Kim; Country Girls; Poldark; I Claudius.* No unsolicited material considered.

London Scientific Films

12 Newburgh Street, London W1V 5LG
☏071-734 7589   Fax 071-287 0355
Contact *Mike Cockburn*

Film, video and TV documentaries. OUTPUT includes *A Brush with The Greens* (for Channel 4, about the making of a green toothpaste); plus various documentaries on the latest in medical developments for a medical audience. Unsolicited material welcome but not returned unless accompanied by s.a.e. Interested in hearing from new writers in the science documentary field.

Longman Training

Longman House, Burnt Mill, Harlow, Essex CM20 2JE
☏0279 623850   Fax 0279 623795
Contact *Maxine Morse*

Providers of corporate training and interactive training videos. No unsolicited mss.

LTV Productions

53 Kirkgate, Shipley, Bradford BD18 3LU
☏0274 585289   Fax 0274 531698
Contact *Simon Allison*

Video — drama and documentary; company training and sales promotion. No unsolicited mss.

Lucida Productions

1st Floor, 53 Greek Street, London W1V 5LR
☏071-437 1140/439 8234   Fax 071-287 5335
Contact *Paul Joyce/Chris Rodley*

Television and cinema: arts, adventure, current affairs, documentary, drama and music. OUTPUT has included *Motion and Emotion: The Films of*

Wim Wenders 1989; Dirk Bogarde - By Myself; Sam Peckinpah - Man of Iron; Naked Making Lunch. Unsolicited scripts welcome.

Mac Films

The Old School, Charlton, Malmesbury, Wiltshire SN16 9DL
☏0666 822072   Fax 0666 824958
Contact *Ian McArthur*

Film, commercials, drama and documentary. OUTPUT includes *Off the Hook* (drama); *Krumnagel* (film); *Portrait of Evan S. Connel & Cancer Relief* (documentary); *Pink Floyd Carrera Panamericana* (film). Unsolicited scripts welcome.

Maiden Films Ltd

Quarry Bank, Quarry Wood, Marlow, Buckinghamshire SL7 1RF
☏0628 890999   Fax 0628 890090
Contact *Mila Rocho*

Film and video; commercials, point-of-sale and information on topics such as pension legislation with a drama-based approach. No unsolicited mss. Interested in new material though.

Main Communications

City House, 16 City Road, Winchester SO23 8SD
☏0962 870680   Fax 0962 870699
Contact *Eben Wilson*

Multimedia marketing and communications company — film, video, and TV; drama, documentary and commercials. OUTPUT marketing communications, educational, professional and managerial distance learning, documentary programmes for broadcast TV, and children's material. Interested in proposals for television programmes, and in ideas for video sell-throughs, interactive multimedia and business information texts and programming.

Malachite Ltd

East Kirkby House, Spilsby, Lincolnshire PE23 4BX
☏07903 538   Fax 07903 409
Contact *Charles Mapleston*

Producers of film, video and television for documentary and corporate material. OUTPUT *John Clare's Journey; Filming the Fens; Fiore - Sculpting Tuscany.* Unsolicited mss not generally welcome. Send simple 1-page outline in first instance. 'We generally only work with people who have special experience and expertise in their chosen subject, and are usually too busy to read new writing.'

Malone Gill Productions Ltd

Canaletto House, 39 Beak Street,
London W1R 3LD
☎071-287 3970
Fax 071-287 8146   Telex 262433 Ref W6701

Contact *Georgina Denison*

Mainly documentary but also some drama. Previous projects include: *Levy's Christmas* (five programmes for Channel 4); *The Buried Mirror: Reflections on Spain and the New World* (five hours written and presented by Carlos Fuentes) for BBC2/Discovery Channel; *Nomads* (four hours on the people of the marginal lands of mountain, snow and desert) for Channel 4 and ITEL; *Nature Perfected* (six half-hours on the cultural history of the garden) for Channel 4 and Io Corporation, Japan. Approach by letter with proposal in the first instance.

Mike Mansfield Television Ltd

5-7 Carnaby Street, London W1V 1PG
☎071-494 3061   Fax 071-494 3057

Contact *Hilary Stewart/Hilary McLaren, Esq/Lucy Dickson*

Television for BBC, ITV network and Channel 4. OUTPUT includes *Animal Tales; Shady Tales; Jean Michel Jarre - Paris, La Défense; Cue the Music; The Music Game.*

Maritz Communications

Globe Park, Marlow, Buckinghamshire SL7 1YW
☎0628 486011   Fax 0628 475737

Contact *Paul Corrick*

A-V and video production, and conferences.

Marking Inc Productions

5 Mercer Street, Covent Garden,
London WC2H 9QP
☎071-240 2345   Fax 071-836 9461

Contact *Stacy Marking*

Film and TV — drama and documentary. OUTPUT *Guide to Genius* series for Channel 4 (ACE). Query letter in the first instance.

Matawa

See **Palace Productions**

Mayhew Business Communication Ltd

63 White Lion Street, London N1 9PP
☎071-837 0012   Fax 071-278 1632

Contact *John Mayhew*

Corporate communications, face-to-face presentations and corporate video makers in the areas of training, marketing and internal communications. Household-name clients.

MCEG Virgin Vision

Atlantic House, 1 Rockley Road, Shepherd's Bush,
London W14 0DL
☎081-740 5500
Fax 081-967 1360/1361   Telex 892890

Contact *Angus Margerison* (Managing Director)/ *Colin Higgs* (Acquisitions Manager)

Worldwide distributor of feature films and video on all media. Video programming — comedy, education, children's, music and feature film. OUTPUT 1991 releases: *Salute of the Jugger; Beverly Hills Brats; The Handmaid's Tale; Stepfather 2; Teenage Mutant Ninja Turtles; RoboCop 2.*

Medialab Ltd

Chelsea Wharf, 15 Lots Road, London SW10 0QH
☎071-351 5814   Fax 071-351 7898

Contact *John Gaydon* (Chairman)

FOUNDED 1982. Film and video production: music videos, TV commercials and TV programming.

Medical & Scientific Productions

Spoke Grange, Fir Tree Avenue, Stoke Poges,
Buckinghamshire SL2 4NN
☎0753 516644   Fax 0753 516965

Contact *Peter Fogarty*

Corporate — medical programmes for health care professionals. Health care ideas welcome. No unsolicited mss.

Meditel Productions Ltd

Bedford Chambers, The Piazza, Covent Garden,
London WC2E 8HA
☎071-836 9216/9364   Fax 071-836 9461

Contact *Joan Shenton/Felicity Milton*

Investigative documentaries: science, medicine and health, education and social issues; daytime magazine programmes factually based with an element of fun; drama and animation. OUTPUT *Dispatches:*

AZT - Cause for Concern; The Power to Change (education project for deprived children in Colombia). No unsolicited mss; writers should submit programme ideas on factual/drama/documentary ideas. Either previous experience is essential or new writers will work closely with a producer appointed by the company.

Melendez Films

33 Gresse Street, London W1P 2AH
☎071-323 2311   Fax 071-323 2331

Contact *Steven Melendez/Graeme Spurway*

Independent producers working with TV stations. Animated films aimed mainly at a family audience, produced largely for the American market, and prime-time network broadcasting. Also develops and produces feature films (eight so far). OUTPUT has included *Peanuts* (half-hour TV specials); *The Lion, The Witch and The Wardrobe; Babar the Elephant* (TV specials); *Dick Deadeye or Duty Done*, a rock musical based on Gilbert & Sullivan operettas, and a video of fairytales *Happily Everafter.* Always interested in new ideas. 'Three of the above walked in through the door.'

Melrose Film Productions

16 Bromells Road, London SW4 0BL
☎071-627 8404   Fax 071-622 0421

Contact *Alison Roux*

Management training films.

Mentorn Films

138-140 Wardour Street, London W1V 3AD
☎071-287 4545   Fax 071-287 3728

Contact *Tom Gutteridge*

FOUNDED in 1985 by ex-BBC arts producer Tom Gutteridge. Producer of *Challenge Anneka*, the most successful peak-time show produced by an independent, regularly attracting 12 million viewers. Film and video — cinema, documentary, drama, music, arts, and television. Now diversifying into non-broadcast corporate videos also.

Mersey Television Company Ltd

Campus Manor, Childwall Abbey Road,
Liverpool L16 0JP
☎051-722 9122   Fax 051-722 1969

Contact *Margaret Seiga*

The best-known of the independents, based in the North of England. Makers of television programmes

— drama and fiction serials for popular consumption only. OUTPUT *Brookside* and *What Now?* for Channel 4; *Waterfront Beat* for BBC.

Midnight Films Ltd

4th Floor, Ramillies House, 1-2 Ramillies Street,
London W1V 1DF
☎071-494 0926   Fax 071-494 2676

Contact *Michael Hamlyn*

FOUNDED 1976. Became active in 1981 when Julien Temple and Michael Hamlyn formed a partnership to produce *The Secret Policeman's Other Ball.* Developed *Absolute Beginners* until Julien Temple left to set up his own company. OUTPUT includes *White City* (1985), a music feature starring Pete Townshend; *U2 Rattle and Hum*, a full-length feature film — part concert film/part cinema verité documentary directed by Phil Joanou; and numerous pop promos for major international artists. Michael Hamlyn is currently working on a six-picture comedy deal with **Polygram** and **Working Title Films.**

John Mills Film and Television

4 Effingham Road, Surbiton, Surrey KT6 5JY
☎081-398 8084   Fax 081-339 0760

Contact *John Mills*

Documentary, music videos, concert films. OUTPUT *Anthrax Live; Julian Cope Live; Aswad Live; Womack and Womack Live*; plus numerous music videos, conference videos and television commercials.

Mills Video Company

11 Hope Street, Liverpool L1 9BJ
☎051-709 9822   Fax 051-709 6585

Contact *Andrew Mills*

Corporate and training videos. No unsolicited mss.

Mirus Productions

86 Adelaide Grove, London W12 0JL
☎081-673 4550

Contact *Mike Wallington/Howard Johnson*

Documentary, music and arts television. OUTPUT includes many programmes for Channel 4: *This Joint is Jumpin; Colonial Madness; One Love; Art Tatum; Black Faith; Us.*

MJW Productions

13 Carlisle Road, London NW6 6TL
☎081-968 6542   Fax 081-968 0038

Contact *Margaret Williams*

Makers of music and arts documentaries, opera and dance films. Credits include: *Bodystyles; Flesh and Blood* and *Different Trains* (for Channel 4); *Noël A Paris* (Antenne 2); *Living by Design* (for the Design Council); *A Love Divided* (Channel 4/WDR); *Scipio's Dream - Not Mozart; Cross Channel* (both for BBC2).

MNV

Dove Barn, Lambs Lane, Wootton, by Woodstock, Oxon OX20 1DG
☎0993 812670   Fax 0993 812670

Contact *Michael Norman*

Video production — corporate, training and communications. Also video publishing and conference television. OUTPUT includes special interest videos for Reader's Digest Home Video Library and much big-screen television work for conferences. No unsolicited mss but interested in new writers.

The Morrison Company

110-112 Parkway, London NW1 7AN
☎071-267 7746   Fax 071-267 7746

Contact *Don Morrison*

Film and video — drama, documentary and commercials. Unsolicited mss welcome.

Mosaic Film & Video Productions

68 Clarence Road, Teddington,
Middlesex TW11 0BW
☎081-977 6514/3769   Fax 081-494 0595

Contact *Adrian Antrum*

Film and video: TV and corporate documentaries. Areas of interest: social, spiritual/religious, metaphysical, paranormal and environmental. No unsolicited mss. All new writing is commissioned or self-generated.

Mosaic Pictures Ltd

3rd Floor, 8-12 Broadwick Street,
London W1V 1FH
☎071-437 4526   Fax 071-434 4178

Contact *Colin Luke*

Film — television programmes.

Mother Films

60A Yukon Road, London SW12 9PX
☎081-675 2931

Contact *Nick O'Hagan*

Film and television — drama, comedy and documentary. Keen to work with new writers. Approach by letter for update on current interest. No unsolicited scripts.

Moving Direction

Ground Floor, 97 Strawberry Vale, Twickenham, Middlesex TW1 4SJ
☎081-891 2604   Fax 081-892 1544

Contact *Shaun Gale* (Director/Producer)

Makers of documentary and fictional productions on video/film. OUTPUT *Hard as Nails* (adult comedy); *The Executive PA* (promotional programme for a new magazine for the *Daily Mail* group); *Thriving On Steam* (documentary on the future of steam); *'Presenting' in an Ideal World* (corporate production for Panasonic UK).

Mulberry Ltd

6 Upper Tachbrook Street, London SW1V 1SH
☎071-828 5254

Contact *Tim Megaw*

Film and video — corporate. CLIENTS Hanson, Melody Radio, Houbigant Perfume, Marathon Oil.

New Decade Productions

49 Kings Drive, Wembley Park,
Middlesex HA9 9HN
☎081-904 9100   Fax 081-202 6199

Contact *Stanley Marks*

Film, video and TV documentary; corporate video. Produces mainly advertising, public relations, training and recruiting programmes. No unsolicited mss.

New Media

12 Oval Road, Camden Town, London NW1 7DH
☎071-482 5258   Fax 071-482 4957

Contact *Susie Barratt* (Marketing Executive)

Multimedia design and production company producing film, video, laservision, CD-I, CDTV and DVI.

Newgate Company
See **Theatre Producers**

Normandy Film Productions
The Old Green School, 1A Park Road, Old Isleworth, Middlesex TW7 6AZ
☎081-568 6025

Contact *David Turnbull*

Producers of drama-documentaries and children's programmes for broadcast TV and sell-through videos. Particular expertise and wide experience in music, arts, children's, agriculture, countryside and equestrian subjects. Also corporate material for clients like Norwich Union and DEC.

Open Mind Productions
6 Newburgh Street, London W1V 1LH
☎071-437 0624   Fax 071-434 9256

Video and television production, including documentary and educational. OUTPUT For BBC Schools TV *Zig Zag: Water; The Geography Programme: Images of the Earth*. No unsolicited material. 'We are a small company interested in expanding into drama, probably initially into children's TV.' Interested in ideas in this area. Chris Ellis, director of the company, is a guest lecturer to the Writing for BBC TV training programme and the London Media Workshop.

Original Film & Video Productions Ltd
13 Bateman Street, London W1V 6EB
☎071-734 9721/9804   Fax 071-734 7143

Contact *Boyd Catling*

Corporate film and video; commercials; broadcast TV; video publishing. Unsolicited mss welcome. Most writing is commissioned by clients themselves and some is originated in-house.

Orion Picture Corporation
5-8 Warwick Street, London W1R 5RA
☎071-753 8753

London office of an American giant.

Ovation Productions Ltd
Osprey House, 10 Little Portland Street, London W1N 5DF
☎071-637 8575   Fax 071-580 5686

Contact *John Plews*

Corporate video and conference scripts. Unsolicited mss not welcome. 'We talk to new writers from time to time.'

Oxford Film & Video Makers
The Stables, North Place, Headington, Oxford OX3 9HY
☎0865 60074   Fax 0865 742901

Contact *Mark Ginsburg*

Makers of film and video for community, art, educational, trade union and broadcast audiences. OUTPUT *Amazon Sisters; Swords into Ploughshares; Futures on the Line*. Productions involve new writing which is mostly done in-house. Brief drama scripts for trainee projects welcome.

Pace Productions Ltd
12 The Green, Newport Pagnell, Buckinghamshire MK16 0JW
☎0908 618767   Fax 0908 617641

Contact *Chris Pettit/Aileen Spankie*

Film and video — drama, documentary, corporate and commercials.

Palace Productions
16-17 Wardour Mews, London W1V 3FF
☎071-734 7060   Fax 071-437 3248

Contact *Stephen Woolley/Nik Powell/Elisabeth Karlsen*

An impressive list of credits which includes *Company of Wolves, Absolute Beginners* and *Mona Lisa*, but future uncertain as we went to press. It was reported that Nik Powell and Steve Woolley were to set up a new production company, **Matawa**, for the various film projects they had in development with 'troubled' Palace Productions. The new company, backed by Polygram, is likely to move to new premises to continue development on such projects as *Backbeat, Galatea* and *Jonathan Wild*.

Palace TV
16-17 Wardour Mews, London W1V 3FF
☎071-734 7060   Fax 071-437 3248

Contact *Valery Ryan*

FOUNDED 1989. Television only. OUTPUT *Lenny Live & Unleashed; Beyond the Groove; A Woman at War*. Summaries of ideas, in writing, are welcome.

Panoptic Productions

296A Latimer Road, London W10 6QW
☎081-960 5588   Fax 081-964 0616

Contact *Jean Newington*

Documentary film makers.

Paper Moon Productions

The Production House, 5 Wynnstay Gardens,
Marlow Bottom, Marlow,
Buckinghamshire SL7 3NR
☎0628 890537   Fax 0628 475872

Contact *David Haggas*

Television and video — medical and health education documentaries. OUTPUT includes: *Shamans and Science*, a medical documentary examining the balance between drugs discovered in nature and those synthesised in laboratories. Unsolicited scripts welcome. Interested in new writing from people who really understand television programme-making.

Parallax Pictures Ltd

7 Denmark Street, London WC2H 8LS
☎071-836 1478   Fax 071-497 8062

Contact *Sally Hibbin*

Documentaries and drama, including Channel 4 projects like *Riff-Raff*, and *Great Britain United*, for the 'Critical Eye' documentary series.

Paramount Pictures (UK) Ltd

Paramount House, 162-170 Wardour Street,
London W1V 4AB
☎071-287 6767   Fax 071-734 0387

No unsolicited scripts.

Paramount Revcom

Balfour House, 46-54 Great Titchfield Street,
London W1P 7AE
☎071-636 5066   Fax 071-436 3232

Contact *Michael Deakin*

Drama mini-series. OUTPUT includes *Not a Penny More, Not a Penny Less* with the BBC.

PCP - Production Centre Productions

3 Ways House, 40-44 Clipstone Street,
London W1P 7EA
☎071-323 3220   Fax 071-637 2590

Contact *Michael Darlow*

Television programmes: drama, documentary and light entertainment.

Peake Productions

141 Victor Road, London SE20 7JU
☎081-659 4122

Contact *Andrew Peake*

TV news and documentary; drama and comedy. Scripting and producing promotional and training video for foreign markets. Unsolicited mss welcome. Always interested in good writing.

Pelicula Films

7 Queen Margaret Road, Glasgow G20 6DP
☎041-945 3333   Fax 041-946 8345

Contact *Mike Alexander*

Television producers. Makers of drama documentaries and music programmes for Channel 4 and the BBC. OUTPUT *Gramsci; Down Home; Scapa Flow - 1919; The Jazz Apple; The Land of Europe; Aly Meets the Cajuns; The Shetland Sessions*. New ideas welcome, but make initial contact by phone.

Pentagon Communications

Anchor House, The Maltings, Hull HU1 3HA
☎0482 226298   Fax 0482 226245

Contact *Jon Levy*

Mainly corporate, plus TV documentary, drama and commercials. Unsolicited mss welcome.

PGP Films

33 Berwick Street, London W1V 3RF
☎071-494 2101   Fax 071-287 5268

Contact *Kristy Jell*

Film and video: commercials and corporate. No unsolicited material.

Picture Base International

13-14 Golden Square, London W1R 3AG
☎071-287 5800   Fax 071-287 3779

Contact *Michael Custance*

Television drama and films. OUTPUT *The Little Matchgirl* (HTV); *Child of Love* (Film on Four for S4C/Channel 4); *Passion and Paradise* (HTV/ABC, USA/CTV, Canada); *Small Stages* (Channel 4); *The Trial of George Washington* (BBC); *Voices in the Garden* (BBC/Antenne 2/La Sept).

Picture Palace Productions

5-10 Lexington Street, London W1R 3HS
☎071-439 9882   Fax 071-734 8574

Contact *Malcolm Craddock*

Well-established production company specialising
in drama and documentaries. OUTPUT includes *The
Orchid House* (4-part drama for Channel 4); *Firing
the Bullets, Hunting the Squirrel* and *Pushed* (UK
episodes of *Eurocops* for European Co-Production
Association); *When Love Dies* (Channel 4 '4 Play'
series). Also TV commercials and sponsored films.

Picturehead Productions

34 Wardour Street, London W1V 3LF
☎071-734 3110/439 6643

Contact *Tony Fish/Peter Hearn*

Film and video — children's, cinema, documen-
ary, drama and television. No unsolicited material.

Phil Pilley Productions

Lee International Studios, Studios Road,
Shepperton, Middlesex TW17 0QD
☎0932 562611   Fax 0932 568989

Contact *Phil Pilley/Julie Bailey*

Film and video for TV. Mainly sports, including
documentaries for the BBC, ITV, Channel 4 and the
United States. Unsolicited ideas and synopses welcome. Also books, mainly on sport.

Polygram Filmed Entertainment

30 Berkeley Square, London W1X 5HA
☎071-493 8800   Fax 071-499 2596

Contact *Stewart Till*

Films, TV drama and music programming. Unsolicted material will be forwarded as appropriate, but
written summaries of ideas are preferred in the first
instance.

Portman Entertainment

Pinewood Studios, Iver Heath,
Buckinghamshire SL0 0NH
☎0753 630366   Fax 0753 630332

Contact *Victor Glynn/Andrew Warren*

Feature films and mini-series for television. OUTPUT
includes *Gravy Train; Act of Will; Hostage; And a
Nightingale Sang; Friday On My Mind.* Receives a
great many unsolicited scripts, all of them so far
unsuitable for production. Letters with treatments/

outlines are read in hope: send these before
submitting a finished script.

Poseidon Productions Ltd

113 Wardour Street, London W1V 3TD
☎071-734 4441/5140
Fax 071-437 0638   Telex 22347 POSFILM

Contact *Frixos Constantine*

Television and film makers/distributors for educated art-loving film audience. OUTPUT includes documentaries for Channel 4 and TV commercials.
Specialises in supplying film facilities and co-
productions in Soviet Union. Office in Moscow.
Unsolicited scripts welcome.

Pretty Clever Pictures Ltd

Post 59, Shepperton Studios, Studios Road,
Shepperton, Middlesex TW17 0QD
☎0932 562611   Fax 0932 568989

Contact *Geraldine Morgan*

Broadcast programmes, commercials, corporate
communication, promos, special projects and titles, and media training. Unsolicited mss welcome.

Primetime Television Ltd

Seymour Mews House, Seymour Mews, Wigmore
Street, London W1H 9PE
☎071-935 9000   Fax 071-487 3975

Contact *Ian Gordon/Richard Price*

Family drama, including children's documentary
series, music specials and adult drama series.
Recent OUTPUT has included *Re: Joyce* (BBC); *José
Carreras - A Life* (LWT); *The CIA* (BBC/A&E/NRK);
Peter Ustinov on the Orient Express (Primedia). No
unsolicited scripts.

The Principal Film Company Ltd

3rd Floor, Arlette House, 143 Wardour Street,
London W1V 3TB
☎071-494 4348
Fax 071-437 3830   Telex 298343 X PRESX G

Contact *Richard Sattin/Mike Slee/Sarah Claxton*

Film, video and television — documentary, light
entertainment and drama. OUTPUT includes *Horst
P. Horst* (BBC); *The Visible Difference* (WGBH/
Nova); *Hob's Grave* (Children's Foundation);
Echoes of America (Channel 4); *Nowhere To Play*
(Channel 4); *After the Warming* (PBS). 'We are
happy to receive scripts direct but a recommenda-
tion tends to galvanise the reader's attention?'

Priory Film Productions

36 Etheldene Avenue, London N10 3QH
☏ 081-444 3018

Contact *Richard Hill/Anna Evans*

Film and video — broadcast, corporate and promotional; plus documentaries specialising in tourism and travel, but now looking to broaden treatment range. OUTPUT includes training and recruitment films for corporate sector clients; productions for local and regional authorities; television commercials; and promotional material for British Tourist Authority and British Waterways Board. No unsolicited material. Writing generally commissioned for specific projects.

The Production Pool Ltd

52 Tottenham Street, London W1P 9PG
☏ 071-323 0691   Fax 071-436 6287

Contact *Ann Wingate*

Film and television drama. OUTPUT includes *Making Waves* (short film for British screen and Channel 4). No unsolicited scripts.

Purchasepoint Video

14-16 Peterborough Road, London SW6 3BN
☏ 071-731 1377   Fax 071-731 2506

Contact *Ian Maddison*

Film and video — corporate, documentary, educational and commercials.

Purkis Neale Productions Ltd

4 Dunstable Mews, London W1N 1RQ
☏ 071-486 8166   Fax 071-486 2094

Contact *David Neale* (Producer)/*Chris Purkis* (Writer/Director)

Video producers: commercials and corporate material. CLIENTS Britain's Petite, Crown & Andrews, ScreenSport, Yorkshire Bank, Varig Airlines, London Metropole Hotel, Saudi Bank. No unsolicited scripts. 'We write all our own work.' May occasionally consider scripts submitted by an agent.

Quad Production Co.

Lincoln House, The Paddocks, Cherry Hinton Road, Cambridge CB1 4DH
☏ 0223 413711   Fax 0223 416125

Contact *Andy Dean*

Conferences, events and video production mainly for corporate clients. *Specialises* in programmes with an element of entertainment, especially comedy. Unsolicited mss welcome if appropriate.

Quanta Ltd

Production Centre, Threeways House, 40-44 Clipstone Street, London W1P 7EA
☏ 071-323 3220   Fax 071-637 2590
Old Forge House, Rodbourne Road, Corston, Malmesbury, Wiltshire SN16 0HA
☏ 0666 824871   Fax 0666 824871

Contact *Nicholas Jones*

FOUNDED 1982. Documentary makers, now developing TV fiction as well. TV OUTPUT includes science programmes for *Horizon* (BBC2); *Equinox* (Channel 4); and others. Scripts are written in-house or commissioned. Unsolicited mss for TV drama will be read.

Quay Productions Ltd

17-21 Dean Street, Newcastle upon Tyne NE1 1PQ
☏ 091-221 0087   Fax 091-261 0160

Contact *Richard Johns*

Video — publishing and corporate. Television commercials. Do not welcome unsolicited mss. 'We need to see writer's c.v. first, then discuss any work.'

Ragdoll Productions

49 High Street, Henley-in-Arden, West Midlands B95 5AA
☏ 0564 794076   Fax 0564 794461

Contact *Anne Wood*

Maker of children's television programmes. OUTPUT *Magic Mirror* (ITV); *Storytime; Brum* (BBC); *Boom!; Pob's Programme; Pob's Playtime* (Channel 4); *Rosie & Jim; Playbox* (Central).

Alvin Rakoff Productions Ltd

1 The Orchard, Chiswick, London W4 1JZ
☏ 081-994 1269   Fax 081-995 3191

Contact *Alvin Rakoff*

TV and film. OUTPUT *Paradise Postponed* (TV miniseries); *A Voyage Round My Father; The First Olympics - 1896; Dirty Tricks.* No unsolicited mss.

Rank Production

127 Wardour Street, London W1V 4AD
☏ 071-439 9531   Fax 071-439 2395

Contact *Russell Turner*

Film and video — television, cinema, commercials, educational and animation.

Red Lion Communications Ltd
76 Cleveland Street, London W1P 5DS
☎071-323 4540

Contact *Mike Kilcooley*

Video producers: commercials, training and corporate work, including product launch videos, in-house training, open learning, multi-media programmes, etc. 'We work on commissioned projects which are funded by clients and do not speculate - hence we do not welcome unsolicited scripts.'

Red Rooster Film & Entertainment Ltd
See **Chrysalis Television Production Ltd**

Renaissance Vision
9 Capitol House, Heigham Street,
Norwich NR2 4TE
☎0603 767272   Fax 0603 768163

Contact *B. Gardner*

Video — full range of corporate work (training, sales, promotional, etc.). Production of educational and special interest video publications. Willing to consider good ideas and proposals.

Riverfront Pictures Ltd
Dock Cottages, Peartree Lane, Glamis Road,
Wapping, London E1 9SR
☎071-481 2939   Fax 071-480 5520

Contact *Jeff Perks/Carole Crouch*

Arts, comedy, documentary, drama, music, and young people's programmes. Production of broadcast programmes, specialising in cultural subjects. OUTPUT *Our Lives; A Wee Bit Cheeky; Everyone a Special Kind of Artist; Breaking Through; The New Eastenders; Cola Cowboys; Raag Rung; Chorus Theatre of Manipur; Just Like That* (all for Channel 4); *Night Moves; The Year '89; Glen Parva* (BBC).

David & Kathy Rose Partnership
159 Earlsfield Road, London SW18 3DD
☎081-874 0744   Fax 081-870 8765

Contact *Kathy Rose/David Rose*

Television and film production.

Roymark Ltd
Unit 224, Canalot Production Studios, 222 Kensal Road, London W10 5BN
☎081-968 6063   Fax 081-968 0714

Contact *Andrew G. B. Kerr*

Film, video and television — drama and documentary. OUTPUT includes programmes for government bodies, public and private companies, and for broadcasting. No unsolicited mss.

Schonfeld Productions International/ SPI 80 Ltd
BCM-Summer, 27 Old Gloucester Street,
London WC1N 3XX
☎071-435 1007

Contact *Victor Schonfeld*

Drama, arts, current affairs, documentary, films for television and cinema. OUTPUT includes *MoneyLove; Shattered Dreams; The Animals Film; Courage Along the Divide; And I Don't Have To Do the Dishes.*

Scope Picture Productions Ltd
123 Blythswood Street, Glasgow G2 4EN
☎041-248 3123   Fax 041-248 3423

Contact *Alison Bye* (TV commercials)/*Bill Gordon* (corporate)

Corporate film and video; broadcast documentaries and sport; TV commercials. OUTPUT has included *Waste Without Wasteland; Locate in Scotland; Scottish Eye*; also Scottish football coverage weekly. Unsolicited mss, realistic scripts and ideas welcome.

Sevenday Productions
Queen Elizabeth II Conference Centre, Broad Sanctuary, London SW1P 3EE
☎071-798 4499   Fax 071-799 1066

Contact *Ivor Gaber/Suzanne Franks*

TV news, current affairs and documentary; non-broadcast information and educational programmes. OUTPUT *Skynews* political coverage; House of Commons Select/Standing Committee sessions; training films in rural areas for the Department of Employment; computing information programming for primary schools. Documentary material welcome.

Seventh House Films
83 Park Lane, Norwich, Norfolk NR2 3EL
☎0603 762401   Fax 0603 768298

Contact *Clive Dunn/Angela Rule*

Film, video and television: documentary only. OUTPUT *A Drift of Angels* (three women and the price of art); *Bare Heaven* (the life and fiction of L. P. Hartley); *A Swell of the Soil* (life of Alfred Munnings); *Light Out of the Sky* (the art and life of Edward Seago). 'We welcome programme proposals with a view to collaborative co-production. Always interested in original and refreshing expressions for visual media.

Shooting Picture Co. Ltd

44 Lexington Street, London W1R 3LH
☎ 071–734 9566   Fax 071–734 9303

Contact *Jillo Waddington*

Film and video — commercials. CLIENTS include Coca-Cola, Adams Childrenswear, Procter & Gamble, Flora, Marmite, National & Provincial, Eurotunnel, De Veers Diamonds. Unsolicited mss welcome.

The Short Film Company

57 Water Lane, Wilmslow, Cheshire SK9 5BQ
☎ 0625 549922   Fax 0625 549982

Contact *Clive Chapman*

Film and video; TV commercials. Unsolicited material welcome.

Signals, Essex Media Centre

21 St Peter's Street, Colchester CO1 1EW
☎ 0206 560255

Contact *Caroline Norbury* (Co-ordinator)/*Mike Ribbans* (Education & Development Officer)

Promotion and documentary work for the voluntary and arts sectors. Specialists in media education projects. No unsolicited mss.

Siren Film & Video Co-op

6 Harris Street, Middlesbrough,
Cleveland TS1 5EF
☎ 0642 221298

Contact *David Eadington*

Local distribution to community groups, etc.; local TV production and work for Channel 4. Unsolicited material welcome.

Siriol Productions

3 Mount Stuart Square, Butetown,
Cardiff CF1 6RW
☎ 0222 488400   Fax 0222 485962

Contact *Robin Lyons*

Animated films aimed at a family audience, both short and full-length. OUTPUT TV specials: *A Winter Story; Space Baby; Under Milk Wood; Santa and the Tooth Fairies;* Serials: *Super Ted; Wil Cwac Cwac;* also *The Easter Egg; The Princess and The Goblin; Gerald of Wales.* Ideas and scripts for animated programmes are welcome (though no unsolicited mss have so far been produced). Most writing presently done by Robin Lyons but new blood will be needed in the future. Interested in hearing from writers with experience in writing half-hour animated programme series.

Skippon Video Associates

183 Drury Lane, London WC2B 5QF
☎ 071–240 8777   Fax 071–240 8779

Contact *Jennifer Skippon*

Training and corporate videos; health and safety. No unsolicited mss.

Skyline Film & TV Productions Ltd

126 Rusthall Avenue, London W4 1BS
☎ 071–224 2440

Contact *Mairi Bett*

Television programmes, educational, corporate, drama and feature films. Supplier of programmes to all major broadcasters. Always interested in new ideas/talent, but a preliminary phone call is advisable.

SMI Business Television

Station Road, Gerrards Cross,
Buckinghamshire SL9 8ES
☎ 0753 889011   Fax 0753 880233

Contact *John Groves/Nick Thompson*

Video and television for corporate clients. Live, interactive business television for private company networks only. No policy on new writing.

Smith & Watson Productions

Brooking Place, Brooking, Dartington,
Devon TQ9 6DW
☎ 0803 863033   Fax 0803 863033

Contact *Chris Watson/Nick Smith*

Film, video and TV — documentaries, drama, party political broadcasts (for the Liberal Democrats), and commercials. Unsolicited mss welcome. Interested in new writing.

Solo Vision Ltd
49-53 Kensington High Street, London W8 5ED
☎071-376 2166   Fax 071-938 3165
Contact *Don Short*

Video and television: documentary, game shows, and corporate work. OUTPUT *Starmate* (the astrology game); *Surrogate Grandmother* (documentary, LWT/Cable USA); plus video packaging. No unsolicited scripts, but 'opportunity exists for talented newcomers'.

Sonoptics Communications Group
Rosier Farm, Billingshurst, West Sussex RH14 9DE
☎0403 782386   Fax 0403 784949
Contact *Nigel Fraser*

Video — training, promotional, educational, commercials. No unsolicited mss but always interested in new writers.

Spectel Productions Limited
121 Church Hill Road, Hansworth,
Birmingham B20 3PY
☎021-554 5074   Fax 021-554 5074
Contact *David Webster*

Film and video — documentary and corporate; also video publishing. No unsolicited scripts.

Spectrum Communications Ltd
16-18 Acton Park Estate, Stanley Gardens,
London W3 7QE
☎081-740 4444   Fax 081-749 5361
Contact *Kenneth Moon*

Film and video: corporate work only, mainly for large blue-chip clients like Vauxhall or IBM. Wide range of programmes. No unsolicited scripts. 'We like to meet new writers, but they must have clear understanding of the corporate market.'

Tom Steel Productions
56 Sutherland Square, London SE17 3EL
☎071-701 6695   Fax 071-703 7425
Contact *Tom Steel*

Corporate and broadcast. The company writes and develops its own material always. CLIENTS include Omega and Hilton International. OUTPUT *Touch and Go - the Battle for Crete* and *Scotland's Story* (24 half-hour episodes for Channel 4).

Strawberry Productions Ltd
36 Priory Avenue, London W4 1TY
☎081-994 4494
Contact *John Black*

Film, video and TV — drama and documentary; corporate and video publishing. Unsolicited mss welcome.

Swanlind Ltd
The Wharf, Bridge Street, Birmingham B1 2JR
☎021-616 1701   Fax 021-616 1520
Contact *Mike Davies*

Business television and corporate communications.

Tabard Productions
15 Wadham Gardens, London NW3 3DN
☎071-586 6474   Fax 071-722 4685
Contact *Vance Chapman*

Film and video — corporate and commercials. Unsolicited mss welcome.

Talbot Television Ltd
Greendon House, 7C/D Bayham Street,
London NW1 0EY
☎071-380 1189   Fax 071-383 5369
Contact *Anthony S. Gruner*

Animation, children, documentary, drama, educational, light entertainment, music, arts, television and game shows.

Talisman Films Ltd
5 Addison Place, London W11 4RJ
☎071-603 7474   Fax 071-602 7422
Contact *Allan Shallcross/Neil Richards*

Film and television for drama: developing the full range of drama — TV series, serials and single films, as well as theatre features. 'We will only consider material submitted via literary agents.' Interested in supporting and encouraging new writing.

Talkback Productions

33 Percy Street, London W1P 9FG
☏071-631 3940　　　　　Fax 071-631 4273

Contact *Chris Langham/Peter Fincham/Sioned William*

Set up in 1981 by comedians Mel Smith and Griff Rhys Jones to make radio commercials. Corporate videos followed. Now concentrating on building up broadcast work, in particular comedy drama.

Team Two Ltd

11 Bessborough Street, London SW1V 2JD
☏071-834 1361　　　　　Fax 071-834 1361

Contact *Richard Collin*

Video and television production company. Documentaries and corporate work. OUTPUT *Timewatch* (BBC); *Tomorrow's World* (1968-73); *Sporting Chance* (for Channel 4/repeated BBC2). CLIENTS BBC, HTV, TSW, Channel 4, ITN, IBA, Royal Navy, Royal Marines, NATO, ICL, and many more including various universities. No unsolicited scripts. Works primarily to produce own material.

Television in Business Ltd

Suite 9, 50 Sullivan Road, London SW6 3DX
☏071-371 0771　　　　　Fax 071-736 9669

Contact *J. Peter Kinkead/Melanie May*

Corporate films and television documentaries. CLIENTS British Airways, Visa, Digital Equipment Corporation, BAT Industries, Eagle Star. No unsolicited mss. Open to new writing depending on project. TV documentary series currently in development, plus TV drama.

Television Visualeyes

East Royd House, Woodlands Drive, Apperley Bridge, West Yorkshire BD10 0PA
☏0532 503467

Contact *Alan Hydes*

Film, video and television: drama and corporate work. Children's TV programmes, promotional, recruitment and security films for the Halifax Building Society. No unsolicited scripts. Interested in new ideas for conversion to drama.

Teliesyn

3 Mount Stuart Square, The Docks,
Cardiff CF1 6EE
☏0222 480911　　　　　Fax 0222 481552

Contact *Mary Simmonds/Carmel Gahan*

Film and video — broadcast TV drama, documentary, music and social action. Will consider unsolicited mss only if accompanied by synopsis. Encourages new writing wherever possible, often with a script editor on hand. Involved in the Celtic Film Festival and Cyfle (Welsh Language Film Training course). OUTPUT *Which Side Are You On?* (drama documentary S4C/Channel 4); *Christmas Story/Chwedl Nadolig* (drama co-production S4C/ HTV); *Yr Enwog Wmffre Hargwyn* (children's adventure series for Channel 4); *Living Proof* (social action series for HTV); *Hughesovka and the New Russia* (documentary series for BBC2/S4C).

Tern Television Productions Ltd

303 King Street, Aberdeen AB2 3AP
☏0224 631000　　　　　Fax 0224 644601

Contact *David Strachan/Gwyneth Hardy*

Video — broadcast, corporate and training. *Specialises* in religious and factual programmes. Unsolicited mss welcome.

Theatre of Comedy Co.
See **Theatre Producers**

Third Eye Productions Ltd

Unit 210, Canalot Studios, 222 Kensal Road,
London W10 5BN
☏081-969 8211　　　　　Fax 081-960 8790

Contact *Lynda Wright*

Makers of television and film documentary programmes for the BBC and Channel 4. OUTPUT *The Encircled Sea; Lest We Forget; Yo Yo Ma — A Month in Tanglewood; Now Then; Cine-Memo; Violent Disorder; Black Bag.*

Tiger Television Ltd

47 Dean Street, London W1V 5HL
☏071-434 0672　　　　　Fax 071-287 1448

Contact *Sue Hancock*

Television producers for documentary programmes and comedy — variety, sitcom and comedy drama. OUTPUT *Mr Bean; Just for Laughs; Monty Python Omnibus; Dead at Thirty.* Unsolicited mss read but a higher priority is given to work submitted through agents. Writers submitting work on spec should bear in mind that when the volume of material is heavy, it can take up to three months to respond. Writers are advised to submit a brief CV with scripts.

Tomahawk Films Ltd

East Wing, Clevedale, The Avenue, Twyford,
Winchester, Hampshire SO21 1NJ
☏0962 714989   Fax 0962 714989

Contact *Brian Matthews/Paul Stelb*

Film and video. OUTPUT specialist military and
sporting projects for release on home video;
Channel Islands Occupied (50-minute TV production later released on video). No unsolicited mss.
Interested in new writing but do not have the
finances to fund other people's work.

Topaz Productions Ltd

Manchester House, 46 Wormholt Road,
London W12 0LS
☏081-749 2619   Fax 081-749 0358

Contact *Malcolm Taylor*

Film and video — corporate and broadcast.
OUTPUT *The Poetry Book* (Channel 4). CLIENTS
Lloyds Bank, Alliance & Leicester, NatWest, Stand-
ard Chartered Bank, B & Q, Phillips Petroleum.

Touch Productions

2nd Floor, 25 Beak Street, London W1R 3LB
☏071-287 5520   Fax 071-437 3675

Contact *Jacqui Loton*

Human-interest documentaries for broadcast only.
OUTPUT includes *Watching the Detectives* (Channel
4); *Coast of Dreams* (Channel 4); several films for
*Everyman, QED, Cutting Edge, Dispatches, Short
Stories* and *Facing Up to Aids*. Intending to move
into drama. 'We prefer people to call with ideas
first rather than send unsolicited mss.'

Town House Productions Ltd

45 Islington Park Street, London N1 1QB
☏071-226 7450   Fax 071-359 6026

Contact *Mike Raggett/Olivia Slot*

Film and video — corporate and publishing.

Triangle Two Ltd

33 Rathbone Place, London W1P 1AD
☏071-637 0667   Fax 071-436 4410

Contact *Vincent Joyce*

Film and video for non-broadcast use: museums,
exhibitions, companies. OUTPUT has included *The
Cinema Goes to War* for the Museum of the Moving
Image and interactive videos for the Imperial War
Museum; also marketing multi-image and video

productions for Broadgate, Ludgate and Stockley
Park developments. No unsolicited mss. Prefers to
meet writers direct, not via agencies. Writers must
be experienced in writing for screen and should be
involved in visualisation.

Turners Film & Video Productions

7 Pink Lane, Newcastle upon Tyne NE1 5HT
☏091-232 1809   Fax 091-232 9823

Contact *John Grant* (Production Director)

Film and video development and production. Unsolicited mss for factual programmes welcome.
Policy on new writing: 'to seek out and encourage!'

Twentieth Century Fox Productions Ltd

Twentieth Century House, 31-32 Soho Square,
London W1V 6AP
☏071-437 7766   Fax 071-437 1625

Contact *Company Secretary*

London office of the American giant.

Twin Continental Films Ltd

119 Totteridge Lane, London N20
☏081-445 6677   Fax 081-445 0483

Contact *Mr V. Pattel*

Television programmes, cinema, commercials,
documentary and fiction, feature films. Most scripts
are commissioned, though unsolicited material is
welcome.

Ty Gwyn Films Ltd

Y Ty Gwyn, Llanllyfni, Caernarfon,
Gwynnedd LL54 6DG
☏0286 881235

Contact *Gareth Wynn Jones*

Makers of situation comedy, contemporary gritty
Welsh subjects and spy thrillers (spies are the
current vogue). Primary role is to provide output
for the Welsh fourth channel S4C. Bilingual
(English/Welsh) productions. New writing welcome in English as well as Welsh.

Tyburn Productions Ltd

Pinewood Studios, Iver Heath,
Buckinghamshire SL0 0NH
☏0753 651700
Fax 0753 656844   Telex 847505

Contact *Gillian Garrow* (Director of Research & Development)

Television producers specialising in popular drama. OUTPUT TV movies: *The Masks of Death; Murder Elite; Courier; The Abbot's Cry; Peter Cushing: A One-Way Ticket to Hollywood.*

UBA Ltd

Pinewood Studios, Pinewood Road, Iver Heath, Buckinghamshire SL0 0NH
☎ 0753 656699   Fax 0753 656844

Contact *Marina Gratsos* (Creative Affairs Executive)

Quality feature films and television for an international market. OUTPUT *Windprints; The Lonely Passion of Judith Hearne; Taffin; Castaway; Turtle Diary.* In development: *Dancing with the Devil; A Witch in New York; Duke and Duchess of Beverly Hills; Imagine; Love's Executioner.* Other projects: *Horses of War; Mediterranean; The Starving Rich; The Kindergarten; Ghost Hunter* (pilot programme for Granada TV). Prepared to commission new writing whether adapted from another medium or based on a short outline/treatment. Concerned with the quality of the script (*Turtle Diary* was written by Harold Pinter) and breadth of appeal. 'Exploitation material' not welcome.

Uden Associates Ltd

Unit 3, Chelsea Wharf, Lots Road,
London SW10 0QJ
☎ 071-351 1255/7601   Fax 071-376 3937

Contact *Fiona Reid*

Film and television production. CLIENTS include the BBC, Channel 4, Guinness, RAC, Post Office, Nuclear Electric. Initial contact should be made by phone.

United Television Artists Ltd

1 Little Argyll Street, London W1R 5DB
☎ 071-437 2222   Fax 071-287 5053

Contact *David Rowley*

Film and video — corporate, documentary, educational, promotional and television. CLIENTS include Channel 4, BBC, British Aerospace, Department of the Environment, British Telecom, Royal Ordnance, MoD.

Upstream

Ridings House, 66 Alma Road, Windsor,
Berkshire SL4 3EZ
☎ 0753 858895   Fax 0753 864123

Contact *Peter Wrigglesworth*

Film, video, multi-image and live events. Contact from established freelance writers outlining previous experience welcome.

VATV

60–62 Margaret Street, London W1N 7FJ
☎ 071-636 9421   Fax 071-436 7426

Contact *Jane Lighting*

No longer a production company. Now concentrating its efforts as an international distribution company specialising in factual programming for broadcast, cable, satellite, home-video, non-theatrical and educational markets. A Channel 4, BBC and ITN distributor, also representing 60 other independent production companies for international sales.

Vera Productions

30–38 Dock Street, Leeds LS10 1JF
☎ 0532 428646   Fax 0532 426937

Contact *Alison Garthwaite/Catherine Mitchell*

Producers of video for drama, documentary, corporate, promotional, training and campaigning material. OUTPUT *Children Who Foster; I Want to be an Astronaut; Video 28* (celebration and record of lesbians' response to Clause 28 of the Local Government Bill); *International Women's Day* (exploration of day's history and how celebrated). Unsolicited mss welcome from women only. New writers welcome.

Verronmead Ltd

30 Swinton Street, London WC1X 9NX
☎ 071-609 3290   Fax 071-609 3290

Contact *Maureen Harter/David Wood*

Children's programmes, documentaries, drama and women's. Many for Channel 4. Recent OUTPUT includes *Back Home* (TVS). Unsolicited mss and new writing welcome.

Video Arts (Production) Ltd

Dumbarton House, 68 Oxford Street,
London W1N 9LA
☎ 071-637 7288   Fax 071-580 8103

Contact *Margaret Tree*

Film and video — corporate, educational and training. CLIENTS include Lloyds of London, Department of Trade and Industry, The Performing Right Society.

Video At Work

High Ground, Finchampstead,
Berkshire RG11 3SE
☎ 0734 730909   Fax 0734 731811

Contact Gerry Clarke

Corporate video production: sales and training. OUTPUT has included staff training videos for British Airways and Midland Bank. Unsolicited mss welcome.

Video Enterprises

12 Barbers Wood Road, High Wycombe,
Buckinghamshire HP12 4EP
☎ 0494 534144   Fax 0494 534144

Contact Maurice R. Fleisher

Video and television, mainly corporate. OUTPUT Business and industrial training, promotional material and conferences. No unsolicited material 'but always ready to try out good new writers'.

Video Presentations

PO Box 281, Wimbledon, London SW19 3DD
☎ 081-542 7721   Fax 081-542 7721

Contact John Holloway

Corporate video. CLIENTS include the Post Office, IBM, British Gas, Bally, Lloyds Bank.

Video Production Associates

2 Dalmally Close, Acomb Park, York YO2 2XS
☎ 0904 705030

Contact David Pritchard

Producer of corporate, promotional, educational and training videos, documentaries and AV slide presentations. Also full back-up and support including PR, promotion and marketing, scriptwriting, media training and general PR services.

Videoplus Productions Ltd

34 Northbrook Street, Newbury,
Berkshire RG13 1DJ
☎ 0635 522727   Fax 0635 582121

Contact Mike Spencer

Video — corporate, sales, training, promotional and documentary. CLIENTS include Castrol UK, Radio Rentals, Hewlett Packard and Dana.

Videotel Productions/Living Tape Productions

Ramillies House, 1-2 Ramillies Street,
London W1V 1DF
☎ 071-439 6301
Fax 071-437 0731   Telex 298596

Contact Nick Freethy/Di Burgess

Film, video and TV of a broadly educational nature but not exclusively so. Unsolicited mss welcome in the education and training fields only. 'We would like to support new writers who can put up with the ego-bashing they are likely to get from industrial and commercial sponsors.' OUTPUT has included Oceans of Wealth (British Gas, DTI & Channel 4); Response to Marine Chemical Spills (for industrial consortium); Dealing with Violence and Aggression at Work (NHS, THF); Defence against Drug Traffikers (SKULK); Alcohol with Care (Mobil); Responsible Chemical Manufacturing (consortium of chemical companies).

Vidox Video Productions Ltd

Milton House, Roper Close, Canterbury,
Kent CT2 7EP
☎ 0227 763888   Fax 0227 450744

Contact Mary Bekes

Makers of corporate and training videos and TV commercials. Unsolicited mss welcome.

Viewpoint Group Ltd

145-157 St John Street, London EC1V 4QJ
☎ 071-253 4483   Fax 071-253 5653

Contact Vincent Hanna

Television, documentary, corporate and training. CLIENTS BBC TV, Channel 4, British Airways, Sony, the Metropolitan Police, Department of Health. Unsolicited mss welcome.

Visionventures International Ltd

12 Neal's Yard, London WC2H 9DP
☎ 071-379 0733   Fax 071-379 0117

Contact Joe McCann

Distributors and producers of film and television. Unsolicited mss welcome but 80% of those received are usually rejected. In production: Tightrope Men; Chekhov's Two Sisters (feature films); The Driving Force (documentary series).

The Visual Connection (TVC) Ltd

1 Rostrevor Mews, London SW6 5AZ
☏ 071-731 6300   Fax 071-736 9462

Contact *Hugh Price*

Business television: corporate and training, with specialisation in the pharmaceutical and construction industries. CLIENTS include British Airways, Smithkline Beecham, Grand Met, Glaxo, British Museum.

Wadlow Grosvenor

19-20 Grosvenor Street, London W1X 9FD
☏ 071-409 1225   Fax 071-491 8135

Contact *Ron Appleton*

Film and video — corporate, documentary, educational and broadcast.

Wall to Wall Television

8-9 Spring Place, Kentish Town,
London NW5 3ER
☏ 071-485 7424   Fax 071-267 5292

Contact *Andy Lipman/Jane Root/Alex Graham*

Documentary and entertainment series, features, and more recently drama. OUTPUT *For Love or Money* and *The Media Show* (Channel 4); *Verdict; The Thing Is; The Human Face; Style Trial* (all for BBC). Material is produced either in-house or by direct commission. Rarely uses agents. Happy to consider new documentary ideas: write in the first instance with outline. Intended expansion means 'there should be more opportunities for writers'.

The Walnut Partnership

Film & Television Production, Crown House,
Armley Road, Leeds LS12 2EJ
☏ 0532 456913   Fax 0532 439614

Contact *Geoff Penn*

Producers of corporate and independent film and video. Freelance writers used for corporate work.

Warner Sisters

21 Russell Street, London WC2B 5HP
☏ 071-836 0134   Fax 071-836 6559

Contact *Lavinia Warner/Jane Wellesley* (Chief Executives)

FOUNDED 1984. Film and video — drama, documentary, television and feature films. OUTPUT includes *GI Brides; Selling Hitler; Rides; Life's a Gas; She-Play; That's Entertaining;* documentaries about

Tristan da Cunha, Madagascar and Sarawak. Developing dramas and documentaries with various companies including Carlton, Meridian and CTE.

Waterfront Productions

17-21 Dean Street, Newcastle upon
Tyne NE1 1PQ
☏ 091-261 0162   Fax 091-261 0160

Contact *Chris Potter*

Agricultural, environment, countryside, natural history, farming and business specialists — documentary and broadcast. OUTPUT includes *Landmark, Up Country* and *Northern Business Awards* for Tyne Tees Television.

Watershed Television Ltd

53 Queen Square, Bristol BS1 4LH
☏ 0272 276864   Fax 0272 252093

Contact *Liz Keynes/Chris James*

Film and video — broadcast, corporate, training and educational programmes. No unsolicited mss. 'We know that we only produce good programmes on the basis of good scripts. Can you work to tight deadlines, tight budgets and still be good?'

Wheelbase Films Video and Television (CMR Productions Ltd)

55 Elm Park Gardens, London SW10 9PA
☏ 071-352 1729   Fax 071-352 2850

Contact *Brian Robins/Joanna Bond*

Film and video — corporate and documentary. Specialists in motoring and motor sport. CLIENTS include Ford, Goodyear, Jaguar, Mercedes-Benz and Pirelli. Commissioned scripts only.

White City Films

79 Sutton Court Road, Chiswick, London W4 3EQ
☏ 081-994 6795/4856   Fax 081-995 9379

Contact *Aubrey Singer*

Films. No unsolicited mss. OUTPUT has included *The Restoration of the Sistine Chapel* (NTV); *The Witness of the Long March* (Channel 4); *Return to Saigon; Return to Peking; Joseph Needham, FRS FBA.*

Michael White Productions Ltd

13 Duke Street, St James's, London SW1Y 6DB
☏ 071-839 3971   Fax 071-839 3836

Contact *Michael White*

High-output company whose credits include *White Mischief, Nuns on the Run, The Comic Strip Series,* and (theatre) *Bus Stop.* Contributions are passed by Michael White to a script reader for consideration.

David Wickes Productions Ltd

169 Queen's Gate, London SW7 5HE
☎071-225 1382   Fax 071-589 8847

Contact *David Wickes/Sue Davies*

Television programmes and cinema.

Maurice Winnick Associates Ltd

66 Melbourne Way, Bush Hill Park,
London EN1 1XQ
☎081-366 2978   Fax 081-363 7127

Producer of quiz panel game shows for TV and theatre. No unsolicited material but always interested in new ideas/writing.

Working Title Films Ltd/WTTV Ltd

1 Water Lane, Kentish Town Road,
London NW1 8NZ
☎071-911 6100   Fax 071-911 6150

Contact *Tim Bevan/Sarah Radclyffe/Alison Owen/ Debra Hayward* (Films); *Antony Root/Gary Shoefield/Grainne Marmion/Simon Wright* (Television)

Feature films and television drama. OUTPUT Films: *My Beautiful Laundrette; Caravaggio* (with the BFI); *Personal Services* (with Zenith); *Sammy and Rosie Get Laid; A World Apart; Paperhouse; The Tall Guy; Diamond Skulls; Chicago Joe and the Showgirl; Fools of Fortune; Drop Dead Fred; Rubin and Ed; Robin Hood* (for 20th Century Fox); *London Kills Me; Map of the Human Heart; Bob Roberts.* Television: *Echoes; Smack and Thistle; News Hounds; Lorna Doone; Edward II, Squash.*

World Wide International Television

21–25 St Anne's Court, London W1V 3AW
☎071-434 1121
Fax 071-734 0619   Telex 269271 WWPICS

Contact *Nicole Cauverien*

Television drama, factual, entertainment and children's programming.

Worldview Pictures

35 Inkerman Road, London NW5 3BT
☎071-267 3633   Fax 071-284 0477

Contact *Stephen Trombley*

Documentaries and series for television, plus corporate video. Synopses welcome from writers. OUTPUT 1992: *Padesi* (YTV/La Sept); *The Execution Party* (Discovery Channel).

Worldwide Television News

The Interchange, Oval Road, London NW1 7EP
☎071-410 5200   Fax 071-410 8302

Contact *Gerry O'Reilly*

Video and TV documentary, news, features, sport and entertainment. OUTPUT *Earthfile* (weekly documentary on environment); *Roving Report* (weekly documentary on current affairs), general news and features weekly services; *Healthfile* (13-part series on global health topics); *Hands Across the World* (children's news, environmental and entertainment programme series), *Marine Mammals,* plus many one-off specials. Unsolicited material welcome.

WSTV Productions Ltd

Abbotswood House, Monkmead Lane, West Chiltington, West Sussex RH20 2PF
☎0798 813961   Fax 0798 813811

Contact *Bill Stewart*

Corporate video producers working mainly in the retail store and building sectors. CLIENTS British Home Stores, British Nuclear Fuels, CBI, DHSS, Esso, Marks & Spencer, Midland Bank, National Westminster Bank, J. Sainsbury, Toshiba (UK), Wimpey Homes, among many.

Greg Younger Associates

Baron's Croft, Hare Lane, Blindley Heath,
Surrey RH7 6JA
☎0342 832515   Fax 0342 833768

Contact *Greg Younger*

Film, video, TV — drama, documentary and commercials. Unsolicited mss welcome.

Yo-Yo Films

197 Camberwell New Road, London SE5 0TJ
☎071-735 3711   Fax 071-735 0795

Contact *Philip Bartlett/Laurens Postma*

Film, video and television — drama, documentary and commercials. Unsolicited mss welcome.

ZED Ltd

2nd Floor, 29 Heddon Street, London W1R 7LL
☎071-494 3181   Fax 071-434 1203

Contact *Glenn Wilhide/Sophie Balhetchet*

Television drama. OUTPUT includes *The Manageress; The Camomile Lawn; The Missing Reel* (co-production), all for Channel 4.

Zenith Productions Ltd

43-45 Dorset Street, London W1H 4AB
☎071-224 2440   Fax 071-224 3194

Contact *Archie Tait* (Head of Development)/*Sarah Golding* (Development Manager)

Co-owned by leading independent communications company Carlton, and Paramount Television. Feature films and television. OUTPUT Films: *Prick Up Your Ears; The Wolves of Willoughby Chase; The Reflecting Skin; Trust; Just Like A Woman;* *Simple Men*. Television: *Inspector Morse; Paradise Club; Shoot to Kill; Chimera; Firm Friends; Children of the Dragon*. No unsolicited scripts.

The Zoom Production Co. Ltd

102 Dean Street, London W1V 5RA
☎071-434 3895   Fax 071-734 2751

Contact *Tom Coates* (Producer)

Film and video — documentary, drama, promotional, training, marketing, educational and medical. Unsolicited mss welcome 'if there is a likelihood of attracting sponsorship or financial backing. Always willing to meet new talent, time permitting'.

Theatre Producers

Aba Daba

30 Upper Park Road, London NW3 2UT
☎071-722 5395

Plays and satirical pantomimes performed at venues like the Water Rats, Underneath the Arches and the Canal Café in London. The company writes all its own material but would be happy to consider some of the great piles of unsolicited mss they receive, were it not for the fact that there is absolutely no money available for outsiders.

Actors Touring Company

Alford House, Aveline Street, London SE11 5DQ
☎071-735 8311   Fax 071-735 1031 attn ATC

Contact *Nicholas Bone* (Production Manager)

ATC are well known for producing lively new versions of classic works. They take classics by major European writers, and work with writers in adapting them for ATC use. Only unsolicited mss with classic/ epic features or intentions are welcome. Intending to work more with writers in this way in the future. Interested in small casts of under eight.

Albany Empire

Douglas Way, London SE8 4AG
☎081-691 8016   Fax 081-691 4426

Contact *Gary Saward*

FOUNDED 1968. Plays to an Afro-Caribbean and white working class audience. Previous productions have included: *Mass Carib* Felix Cross; *Gut Girls* Sarah Daniels; *Gaslight* Patrick Hamilton. No unsolicited mss as no way of handling them. Generally produces a mixture of new writing and re-interpreted classics.

Albemarle of London

74 Mortimer Street, London W1N 7DF
☎071-631 0135   Fax 071-323 3074

Pantomimes only, and Albemarle write their own scripts.

Aldersgate Productions

12 Palace Street, London SW1E 5JF
☎071-828 6591   Fax 071-821 5819

Contact *Ronald Mann* (Secretary)

Plays of a broadly Christian nature for the West End and for the main theatre touring circuit. Previous productions have included: *Ride, Ride* (a musical about John Wesley); *Sentenced to Life* (a play about euthanasia by Malcolm Muggeridge); *Song of the Lion* (a one-man show about C.S. Lewis). Co-producers of *The Lion, The Witch and The Wardrobe*, and other Narnia plays.

Almeida Theatre Company

Almeida Street, Islington, London N1 1TA
☎071-226 7432   Fax 071-704 9581

Contact *Ian McDiarmid/Jonathan Kent* (Artistic Directors)

FOUNDED 1980. The Almeida, under the artistic leadership of Ian McDiarmid and Jonathan Kent, is now in its third year as a full-time producing theatre, presenting a year-round theatre and music programme in which international writers, composers, performers, directors and designers are invited to work with British artists on challenging new and classical works. Previous productions: *The Rehearsal; Bajazet; Betrayal; The Lulu Plays; All For Love; Party Time; The Gigli Concert.* No unsolicited mss: 'our producing programme is very limited and linked to individual directors and actors'.

Alternative Theatre Company Ltd

(trading as the Bush Theatre)
Bush Theatre, Shepherds Bush Green,
London W12 8QD
☎071-602 3703   Fax 071-602 7614

Contact *Nick Drake*

FOUNDED 1972. Produces about five new plays a year (principally British, some foreign) and hosts up to four visiting companies also producing new work: 'we are a writer's theatre'. Scripts are read by a team of associates, then discussed with the management, a process which takes three months.

The theatre offers commissions, recommissions to ensure further drafts on promising plays, and a guarantee against royalties so writers are not financially penalised even though the plays are produced in a small house. New plays at the Bush have included: *Kiss of the Spiderwoman* Manuel Puig; *More Light* Snoo Wilson; *Raping the Gold* Lucy Gannon; *Handful of Stars, Poor Beast in the Rain, Belfry* Billy Roche; *The Fatherland* Murray Watts; *Boys Mean Business* Catherine Johnson; *The Pitchfork Disney* Philip Ridley; *Our Own Kind* Roy MacGregor.

Yvonne Arnaud Theatre

Millbrook, Guildford, Surrey GU1 3UX
☎0483 64571   Fax 0483 64071

Contact *James Barber*

New work always considered. Credits include: *Sweet William* Bernard Slade; *Groucho* Arthur Marx & Robert Fisher; *It Runs in the Family* Ray Cooney; *Married Love* Peter Luke; *The Secret of Sherlock Holmes* Jeremy Paul; *Over My Dead Body* Michael Sutton & Anthony Fingleton; *Hidden Laughter* Simon Grey; *Map of the Heart* William Nicholson.

Belgrade Theatre, Coventry

Belgrade Square, Coventry CV1 1GS
☎0203 256431   Fax 0203 550680

Contact *Robert Hamlin* (Director)

Main house productions include a significant number of first and second productions with most new plays commissioned by the theatre. The studio theatre is dedicated to new writing, first and second productions. The theatre has recently launched a regional writers' workshop scheme in conjunction with West Midlands TWU.

Birmingham Repertory Theatre

Broad Street, Birmingham B1 2EP
☎021-236 6771   Fax 021-236 7883

Contact *Tony Clark/Gwenda Hughes* (Associate Directors)

Main house and studio forum. In the main theatre, plays are chosen because they fully exploit the epic size of the stage (with its 60-foot proscenium) and auditorium (900 seats in a single curved rake). This applies to new plays as much as to established ones. In the studio theatre, the Rep intends to present a mix of touring and in-house productions throughout the year, and priority is given to the work of local writers. 'We have a panel of readers who assess all new plays sent in to us. We run a writers' group in association with our local theatre

writers union, for writers based in the West Midlands, who meet to read and discuss scripts and work in progress.'

Bootleg Theatre Company

Sherborne House, 20 Greyfriars Close, Salisbury, Wiltshire SP1 2LR

Contact *Colin Burden*

FOUNDED 1984. Tries to encompass as wide an audience as possible but generally plays to an audience aged 15–30 and has a tendency towards plays with socially relevant themes. A good bet for new writing since unsolicited mss are very welcome. 'Our policy is to produce new and/or rarely seen plays and anything received is given the most serious consideration for inclusion in our schedule.' Actively seeks to obtain grants to specifically commission writers to produce material for the company. Keeps a close eye on relevant competitions in their search for material. Playwrights whose work has been performed include Barrie Keeffe, Tony Marchant and Sam Snape. In 1991, the company performed a successful tour of Philip Goulding's award-winning one-man play *Different Animal*.

Borderline Theatre Company

Darlington New Church, North Harbour Street, Ayr KA8 8AA
☎0292 281010

Contact *John Murtagh* (Artistic Director)

FOUNDED 1974. A touring company taking shows to main house theatres in city centres and small venues in outlying districts, plus the Edinburgh Festival, Mayfest and, occasionally, London. Mainly new and contemporary work, plus revivals: *George's Marvellous Medicine* Roald Dahl (a spectacular children's show); *Misterio Buffo* Dario Fo (one-man show with Robbie Coltrane); *A Night in the Ukraine* Voxburgh & Laxarus; *Four in a Million* Les Blair; *Shanghied* Liz Lochhead; plus pantomime and children's plays. Synopsis with cast size preferred in the first instance. Borderline try to include one new work every season. 'We are looking for writing which is stimulating, relevant and, above all, entertaining, which will lend itself to dynamic physical presentation.'

Bristol Express Theatre Company

20 Mocatta House, Brady Street, Whitechapel, London E1 5DL
☎071-247 4156/7965

Contact *Andy Jordan* (Director)

Bristol Express, a non-funded, professional middle-scale, national touring company, has a continuing commitment to the discovery, development and encouragement of new writing, principally through a research and development programme called *The Play's The Thing!* This consists of public/private staged and rehearsed readings; workshops and full-scale productions. 'We look for plays that are socially/emotionally/theatrically/politically significant, analytical and challenging. The company is concerned to produce work which attempts to mix genres (and create new ones!), is eloquent and honest, while remaining accessible and entertaining... It's unusual for a play sent to (or not commissioned by) the company to be accepted on its receipt.' Previous productions have included: *Child's Play* Jonathan Wolfman; *Winter Darkness* Allan Cubitt; *Prophets in the Black Sky* John Matshikiza; *Lunatic & Lover* Michael Meyer.

Bristol Old Vic Company

Theatre Royal, King Street, Bristol BS1 4ED
☎0272 277466   Fax 0272 225055

Contact *Les Smith (Dramaturg)*

The Bristol Old Vic has a serious commitment to new writing, both for the Theatre Royal (capacity 650) and the New Vic (capacity 150). The company commissions a number of plays each year and attempts to respond to unsolicited scripts with intelligence, speed and sympathy. There is a readers' panel which meets regularly. Readers produce a report for the company and for the author. 'We are looking for serious plays, funny plays and, above all, plays with something important to say.'

Bush Theatre

See **Alternative Theatre Company**

Cambridge Theatre Company

8 Market Passage, Cambridge CB2 3PF
☎0223 357134   Fax 0223 467335

Contact *James Williams* (Administrator)

Limited script reading facilities. Unsolicited mss may not be read. Letters and synopses welcome.

Carnival Films & Theatre Ltd

See **Film, TV and Video Producers** section

Century Theatre Touring

New Century Building, Hill Street,
Crewe CW1 1BX
☎0270 501800   Fax 0270 501888

Contact *Artistic Director*

FOUNDED 1948. National touring company visiting middle-scale receiving houses and arts centres in provincial towns throughout England. Mostly mainstream for mildly conservative audiences. Recent productions have included: *She Stoops to Conquer; Playboy of the Western World; Company; Double Double; The Importance of Being Earnest; Bitter Sweet; Hapgood; Barnstormers.* No unsolicited mss; send synopsis in the first instance. Has developed a strong house style by producing established work — more often than not with a strong musical content. Interested in new work. Runs writers' workshops on request, as part of a week's performing residency at a given venue, and charges a small fee for this.

Channel Theatre Trust Ltd

Granville Theatre, Victoria Parade, Ramsgate,
Kent CT11 8DG
☎0843 588280

Contact *Philip Dart*

A middle-scale national touring company based at the Granville Theatre. Theatre-in-Education and community theatre company attached. Previous productions have included national tours of *The Woman in Black; Lettice and Lovage,* Tom Stoppard's *Rough Crossing* and a production of Shaw's *Arms and the Man* for the Malvern Festival 1991. Community tours include new adaptations of *The Ingoldsby Legends* and *The Shadow of Dr Syn,* and a production of the melodrama *Black Ey'd Susan.* Interested in new writing, particularly Theatre-in-Education and small-scale work of quality, but financial restraints make full-scale production of new work unlikely.

Cherub Company London Ltd

Arches 5 & 6, Midland Road, St Pancras,
London NW1
☎071-383 0947

Contact *Vi Marriott/Andrew Visnevski*

FOUNDED 1978. Plays to a young, mixed audience, and to schools. Other than repertoire, mostly classics. Previous productions have included: British Council tour of *Twelfth Night;* Alan Bennett's *The Old Country; The Duchess of Malfi* (St George's Theatre, London). No unsolicited mss: 'we have no opportunity of producing new plays because we are unfunded'. On very rare occasions, if funding is available, a play on a specific theme will be commissioned.

Chichester Festival Theatre

Festival Theatre Productions Co. Ltd, Oaklands Park, Chichester, West Sussex PO19 4AP
☎0243 784437 Fax 0243 787288

Contact *Artistic Director*

Main house and studio (the Minerva). New work considered but 'we only have resources to read scripts that have been recommended by known practitioners and recognised literary agents.'

Churchill Theatre

High Street, Bromley, Kent BR1 1HA
☎081-464 7131 Fax 081-290 6968

Contact *John Wallbank*

Produces a broad variety of popular plays, both new and revivals. Previous productions have included: Ken Hill's *Phantom of the Opera; Some Like It Hot; Don't Dress for Dinner* Marc Camoletti (adap. Robin Hawdon); *High Flyers* Paul Kember; *A Slight Hangover* Ian Ogilvy; *Intent to Kill* Ted Willis; *The Heiress* Henry James. Most productions go on either to tour or into the West End. New scripts welcome.

Citizens Theatre

Gorbals, Glasgow G5 9DS
☎041-429 5561 Fax 041-429 7374

Contact *Giles Havergal* (Artistic Director)

Over the last few years the Citizens Theatre has found it increasingly difficult to do new work. They do not have a formal reading panel so unsolicited scripts are returned straight away. Productions tend to be mostly classic revivals, or adaptations/ translations by resident dramatist Robert David MacDonald.

Alan Clements Productions

27 Station Road, March,
Cambridgeshire PE15 8LE
☎0354 52961

Contact *Alan Clements*

Small-scale operation, producing pantomimes and only one or two plays a year. Of these, very little is new — *Sweeney Todd* being a recent exception. There is generally little hope for new writers here.

Ron Coburn International Productions

Vaudevilla, Elliot Road, Dundee DD2 1SY
☎0382 69025

Contact *Ron Coburn*

Ron Coburn writes and produces internationally touring musical variety shows like *A Breath of Scotland* and *The Waggle o' the Kilt.* Venues range from Carnegie Hall to Mablethorpe and Skegness. As the material needs to travel to North America and is usually of a topical nature, it's not feasible to use outside writers.

Michael Codron Ltd

Aldwych Theatre Offices, Aldwych,
London WC2B 4DF
☎071-240 8291 Fax 071-240 8467

Contact *Joe Scott Parkinson* (General Manager)

Michael Codron Ltd manage the Aldwych and Adelphi theatres, and own the Vaudeville Theatre in London's West End. The plays they produce don't necessarily go into these theatres, but always tend to be big-time West End fare like *Woman in Mind* with Julia McKenzie. Previous productions have included: *Hapgood; Look Look; Uncle Vanya; The Sneeze.* No particular rule of thumb on subject matter or treatment. The acid test is whether 'something appeals to Michael'. Straight plays rather than musicals.

The Coliseum, Oldham

Fairbottom Street, Oldham OL1 3SW
☎061-624 1731 Fax 061-624 5318

Contact *Artistic Director*

Considered a good bet for new playwrights, the Coliseum is besieged by more scripts than it can read. 'We like to do new writing that's popular and relevant to our audience.' No unsolicited scripts. Approach with letter and synopsis. Previous productions have included: *A Night on the Tiles* Frank Vickery; *Girlfriends* Howard Goodall; *Stage Fright* Peter Fieldson; *The Steamie* Tony Roper; *Clowns on a School Outing* Ken Campbell; *Hotstuff.* Plays often come by way of contacts or commissions but good unsolicited scripts still stand a chance. Just don't expect a swift decision.

Communicado Theatre Company

Royal Lyceum Theatre, Grindlay Street,
Edinburgh EH3 9AX
☎031-229 7404/228 5465 Fax 031-228 3955

Contact *Gerard Mulgrew* (Artistic Director)

FOUNDED 1982. Touring company which 'aims to entertain the widest range of audience' and encourages new writing, especially Scottish. Unfortunately there are no facilities for dealing with unsolicited scripts. Productions have included:

Danton's Death (adap. by Gerard Mulgrew); *The Creature from the Mermaid's Purse* Anne Downie; *Mary Queen of Scots Got Her Head Chopped Off* Liz Lochhead.

Contact Theatre Company

Oxford Road, Manchester M15 6JA
☎061-274 3434   Fax 061-273 6286

Contact *Brigid Larmour* (Artistic Director)

FOUNDED 1972. Plays predominantly to a young audience (15–35), with a particular interest in contemporary work, especially from the North-west, and in non-naturalistic writing. Definitely not interested in naturalistic plays. Work by black, female and young writers, and work which creates opportunities for black and female performers, is particulary welcome. Commissions up to three plays a year. Recent productions have included: *The Singing Ringing Tree* Charlotte Keatley (première); *Mary Queen of Scots Got Her Head Chopped Off* Liz Lochhead (second production); *Safe Sex* Harvey Fierstein (UK première).

Crucible Theatre

55 Norfolk Street, Sheffield S1 1DA
☎0742 760621   Fax 0742 701532

Contact *Director's secretary*

Unsolicited scripts are seen by a reader and a small number may go on to a rehearsed reading/workshop. Finished scripts are always preferred to synopses or ideas. Scripts sent by a recognised theatre agent, director or actor are given more attention.

Cumbernauld Theatre Company

Kildrum, Cumbernauld G67 2BN
☎0236 737235   Fax 0236 738408

Contact *Liz Carruthers*

FOUNDED 1979. Popular community entertainment. Productions have included children's shows, new plays, Scottish material, educational/community plays, and popular theatre. New plays commissioned but unsolicited mss not welcome.

Cwmni Theatr Gwynedd

Deiniol Road, Bangor, Gwynedd LL57 2TL
☎0248 351707   Fax 0248 351915

Contact *Graham Laker* (Artistic Director)

FOUNDED 1984. Welsh language work only at present. Classic Welsh plays, translations of European repertoire and new work, including adaptations from novels. A mainstream theatre, performing in major theatres on the Welsh circuit. New Welsh work always welcome; English work considered only if it deals with issues strictly relevant to North Wales. 'We are keen to discuss projects with established writers and offer commissions where possible.' Recent productions have included adaptations from Welsh novels, Brecht and Chekhov translations, and new comedy. Other activities include the hosting of an annual new writing festival in February.

Derby Playhouse

Eagle Centre, Derby DE1 2NF
☎0332 363271   Fax 0332 294412

Contact *Mark Clements* (Artistic Director)

FOUNDED 1948. Plays to a mixed audience. Unsolicited mss welcome. 'We read all plays submitted, and have a small budget for commissioning.' Currently developing a younger audience so particularly interested in work suitable for them. OUTPUT has included *And A Nightingale Sang* C. P. Taylor; *On the Piste* John Godber; *The Innocents* William Archibald; *Far from the Madding Crowd* (adap. Sally Hedges).

Dramatis Personae Ltd

19 Regency Street, London SW1P 4BY
☎071-834 9300

Contact *Nathan Silver*

Run by Nathan Silver and Maria Aitken, the company turns its hand to a variety of production projects and is currently co-producing with the BBC on arts documentary subjects. Interested in new plays but most come by way of contacts in the business. No unsolicited scripts. Approach by letter in the first instance.

The Dukes

Moor Lane, Lancaster LA1 1QE
☎0524 67461   Fax 0524 67461

Contact *Jon Pope* (Artistic Director)

FOUNDED 1971. Plays to an extremely mixed audience which is difficult to target. Recent productions have included: *Twelfth Night* and *Treasure Island* (both outdoor promenades); *Teechers* John Godber; *Turn of the Screw* (adap. Jon Pope) *Stevie* Hugh Whitemore. No unsolicited scripts. Also hosts two workshops by the North-West Playwrights' Group in February each year.

Durham Theatre Company

The Arts Centre, Vane Terrace, Darlington, County Durham DL3 7AX

☎0325 469861

Contact *Artistic Director*

FOUNDED 1977. Audience defined by the range of community venues that the theatre visits throughout County Durham and the North-East. Produces an annual pantomime, a popular autumn show and a spring tour. Prefers to receive brief synopsis and c.v. rather than complete mss. New writing considered only if appropriate to programme demands.

Eastern Angles Theatre Company

Sir John Mills Theatre, Gatacre Road, Ipswich, Suffolk IP1 2LQ

☎0473 218202　　　　　Fax 0473 250954

Contact *Ivan Cutting*

FOUNDED 1982. Plays to a rural audience for the most part. All productions are new: some commissioned, some devised, some researched documentaries. Unsolicited mss welcome. 'We are always keen to develop and produce new writing, especially that which is germane to a rural area.' Involved in Eastern Arts' Write Lines project.

E&B Productions Ltd

Suite 3, Waldorf Chambers, 11 Aldwych, London WC2B 4DA

☎071-836 2795　　　　　Fax 071-379 4892

Contact *Paul Elliott/Brian Hewitt-Jones*

Interested in seeing new scripts but may take some time to read them. Previous productions: *Buddy* (West End and US); *Pirates of Penzance; Kiss Me Kate; Rick's Bar in Casablanca*, and major pantomimes (West End and provinces).

English Stage Company Ltd

See **Royal Court Theatre**

Farnham Repertory Company Ltd

Redgrave Theatre, Brightwells, Farnham, Surrey GU9 7SB

☎0252 727000　　　　　Fax 0252 712350

Contact *Graham Watkins* (Artistic Director)

Plays to a middle-class, middle-aged audience in the main, despite efforts to attract a younger audience. Classics, new plays, 20th-century dramas, comedies, thrillers. Unsolicited mss welcome. New writing produced 'as often as we can'. Not interested in plays with large casts.

Field Day Theatre Company

Foyle Arts Centre, Old Foyle College, Lawrence Hill, Derry BT48 7NJ

☎0504 360196　　　　　Fax 0504 365419

Contact *Gary McKeone (Administrator)*

A touring company which tends to commission its plays from Irish writers. Previous productions have included: *Pentecost* Stewart Parker; *The Cure at Troy* Seamus Heaney.

Vanessa Ford Productions Ltd

Upper House Farm, Upper House Lane, Shamley Green, Guildford, Surrey GU5 0SX

☎0483 268530　　　　　Fax 0483 278203

Contact *Vanessa Ford*

Touring and West End. Recent productions have included: *A Christmas Carol; The Horse and His Boy; The Magician's Nephew; Noddy; Winnie the Pooh; The Lion, The Witch and The Wardrobe; Tales of Toad Hall; The Voyage of the Dawn Treader*. Also classical seasons touring and in London. Keen to see new work: finished scripts, ideas or synopses but do much of their own writing and in-house adaptations.

Clare Fox Associates

9 Plympton Road, London NW6 7EH

☎071-372 2301　　　　　Fax 071-372 2301

Contact *Clare Fox*

Producers and general managers from the commercial West End. Very interested in new writing. Credits include *Bent* Martin Sherman; *Mr & Mrs Nobody* Hugh Whitemore; *Of Mice and Men* John Steinbeck; *The Amen Corner* James Baldwin; *Never the Sinner* John Logan; *Dancing at Lughnasa* Brian Friel.

Robert Fox Ltd

6 Beauchamp Place, London SW3 1NG

☎071-584 6855　　　　　Fax 071-225 1638

Contact *Robert Fox*

Usually concerned only with work suitable for West End production. Credits, including co-productions, include: *Another Country; Chess; Lettice and Lovage; Madhouse in Goa; Burn This; When She Danced; The Ride Down Mount Morgan*. Scripts, while usually by established playwrights, are always read.

Mark Furness Ltd

10 Garrick Street, London WC2E 9BH
☎071-836 7373   Fax 071-379 3539
Contact *Mark Furness*

Comedies, drama and thrillers. Recent West End productions have included: *'Allo 'Allo; Peter Pan* (the musical); *The Boys Next Door; Unseeded; Don't Dress for Dinner; Revenge; Reflected Glory; The Blue Angel.* Productions on tour and overseas: *Doctor Who; Forsyte Saga; Jamaica Inn; Some Like it Hot.* Unsolicited scripts welcome.

Gate Theatre Company Ltd

11 Pembridge Road, London W11 3HQ
☎071-229 5387

Contact *Simon Reade* (Literary Manager)

FOUNDED 1979. Plays to a mixed, London-wide audience, depending on production. Aims to produce British premières of plays which originate from abroad and translations of neglected classics. Most work is with translators. Recent productions have included: *Dear Elena Sergeevna* Ludmilla Razumovskaya (trans. Cathy Porter); *The Ingolstadt Plays* Marieluise Fleisser (trans. Tinch Minter & Elisabeth Bond-Pable); *Anowa* Ama Ata Aidoo; *Damned For Despair* Tirso de Molina (trans. Laurence Boswell). Unsolicited scripts welcome. Enclose s.a.e.

Gay Sweatshop

Interchange Studios, Dalby Street,
London NW5 3NQ
☎071-485 5799
Fax 071-482 5292 (attn Gay Sweatshop)

Contact *James Neal-Kennerley/Lois Weaver* (Artistic Directors)

FOUNDED 1975. Plays to a wide audience, particularly those interested in lesbian/gay theatre and sexual politics. OUTPUT Script-based plays: *The Last Enemy* Carl Miller; *Twice Over* Jackie Kay; *Paradise Now and Then* Noel Greig & Richard Coles; *Kitchen Matters* Bryony Lavery; *Raising the Wreck* Sue Frumin; *Compromised Immunity* Andy Kirby; *This Island's Mine* Philip Osment. Also festivals of new work presented as staged rehearsed readings: *Gay Sweatshop x 10; G S x 12*. Committed to encouraging new work by lesbian, black and disabled playwrights. Work submitted generally includes representation of those sections of the community which are under-represented in mainstream theatre. Unsolicited scripts welcome.

Globe Players Theatre Company

36 St James's Avenue, Hampton Hill,
Middlesex TW12 1HH
☎081-979 5497

Touring, mostly schools in London and the Home Counties. An established repertoire of plays for younger children and classics for secondary schools. Not open to any applications at all.

Gloucestershire Everyman Theatre Company Ltd

Regent Street, Cheltenham GL50 1HQ
☎0242 512515   Fax 0242 224305

Contact *Martin Houghton* (Artistic Director)

FOUNDED 1891. Describes its audience as broad, and is in the process of developing a younger audience. Revivals of both classic and contemporary plays; musicals, new plays with particular emphasis on the life of the region; Christmas shows for children and families. Unsolicited mss welcome but approach in writing with brief synopsis in the first instance is preferred. Priority is given to local writers and plays need to be relevant to the region.

Derek Glynne (London) Pty Ltd

25 Haymarket, London SW1Y 4EN
☎071-930 1981/235 3046   Fax 071-839 2977

Contact *Mrs Denise Parkhurst* (Administrator)

Derek Glynne is a producer in partnership with American and Australian producers. There are two aspects of the company's work: taking international companies like the **Royal Shakespeare Company** and Marcel Marceau abroad; producing plays largely for Australian and American audiences. Most of these originate abroad so there is little hope for playwrights here. However, they have recently commissioned a new play (to be produced in 1992), and unsolicited mss/ideas of promise are passed on for consideration.

Graeae Theatre Company

25 Bayham Street, London NW1 0EY
☎071-383 7541/7492 (Voice/Minicom)
Fax 071-383 5479

Contact *Steve Mannix* (Administrative Director)

Graeae remains Britain's only full-time professional theatre company of disabled performers. Programme includes national and international small scale touring productions, arts development programmes and training events. Unsolicited scripts welcome. New work based around the issues of disability commissioned. Graeae also runs the

Graeae Writers Project aimed at encouraging disabled writers to develop their skills and write for theatre, film, television and radio. Formed the Graeae Youth Theatre in May 1992.

Great Eastern Stage

Witham Park, Waterside South, Lincoln LN5 7JN
☎ 0522 534924   Fax 0522 560216

Contact *Maurice Raphael (Administrator)*

Small-scale regional (plus national) touring company. Primarily classically-based, but presents one or two new plays each year. Unsolicited scripts welcome.

Greenwich Theatre Ltd

Crooms Hill, London SE10 8ES
☎ 081-858 4447   Fax 081-858 8042

Contact *Artistic Director*

Strong policy here to encourage new writing which must, by necessity, be reduced to one, sometimes two, productions per year. Bearing this in mind, 'we do positively encourage writers to send in scripts; we are always on the look-out for new writing which is accessible to our mixed audience. Less keen on initial approach with ideas, preferring to read a finished script'.

Hampstead Theatre

Swiss Cottage Centre, London NW3 3EX
☎ 071-722 9224   Fax 071-722 3860

Contact *Anna Koutelieri*

Produces mainly new plays. Scripts are initially assessed by a team of script readers and their responses are shared with management in monthly script meetings. The literary manager and/or artistic director then read and consider many submissions in more detail. It can therefore take 2–3 months to reach a decision. Writers recently produced at Hampstead include Martin Allen, Stephen Bill, Terry Eagleton, Brian Friel, Julian Garner, Jean-Claude Grumberg, Catherine Hayes, Beth Henley, Dusty Hughes, Stephen Jeffreys, Terry Johnson, Tom Kempinski, Wendy Kesselman, Hanif Kureishi, Mike Leigh, Frank McGuinness, Mustapha Matura, Anthony Minghella, Rona Munro, Jennifer Phillips, Dennis Potter, Philip Ridley, James Saunders, Martin Sherman, Mel Smith and Michael Wall.

Harrogate Theatre Company

Oxford Street, Harrogate, North Yorkshire HG1 1QF
☎ 0423 502710

Contact *Andrew Manley* (Artistic Director)

FOUNDED 1950. Describes its audience as 'eclectic, all ages and looking for innovation'. Past productions have included: *Serious Money; Nora* (British première of Ibsens's *Doll's House*, adap. Ingmar Bergman); *The Cherry Orchard* and *Uncle Vanya* (both British premières, adap. David Mamet); *My Children! My Africa!; The Marriage of Figaro* (a commissioned translation and adaptation combining Beaumarchais, Mozart and Da Ponte); *School for Wives*. Unsolicited scripts welcome. Tries to do one new play or adaptation a year but 'it's a struggle'.

Hazemead Ltd

1st Floor, 235–241 Regent Street, London W1R 5DD
☎ 071-629 4817   Fax 071-629 5668

Contact *Anne Chudleigh*

Producers of summer seasons and pantomimes all over the country. Interested in sitcoms, sketches and children's programmes. New writers and scripts come to them principally through recommendation, but unsolicited mss and letters are always welcome.

Philip Hindin

66 Melbourne Way, Bush Hill Park, Enfield, Middlesex EN1 1XQ
☎ 081-366 2978   Fax 081-363 7127

Contact *P. Hindin*

Producer of quiz panel game shows for TV and theatre. No unsolicited material but always interested in new ideas/writing.

The Hiss & Boo Company

24 West Grove, Walton on Thames, Surrey KT12 5NX
☎ 0932 248931   Fax 0932 248946

Contact *Ian Liston*

Keen to see and read as much new work as possible, provided a synopsis and introductory letter is offered in the first instance. Particularly interested in new thrillers, comedy thrillers, black comedies and melodrama. Unsolicited mss not welcome. Any material submitted must be accompanied by s.a.e. if return is desired. Previous productions have included: *Double Act; An Ideal Husband; Fertility Dance; Mr Men's Magical Island; Mr Men and the Space Pirates; Nunsense; Corpse!; Groucho: A Life in Revue; See How They Run.*

Horseshoe Theatre Company
The Shrubbery, Cliddesden Road, Basingstoke,
Hampshire RG21 3ER
☎ 0256 55844 Fax 0256 57130

Contact *Adrian Reynolds* (Artistic Director)

Productions in the main house for the 1991/92 season included: *Tess of the d'Urbervilles* (adap. Michael Fry); *Absurd Person Singular* Alan Ayckbourn; *Beauty and the Beast* (adap. Malcolm Sircom); *A Streetcar Named Desire* Tennessee Williams; *Blithe Spirit* Nöel Coward; *Monday After the Miracle* William Gibson; *Little Tramp* (book, lyrics and music by David Pomeranz – world première). Recent Central Studio productions have included: *The Complete Casanova* John Constable (world première in association with the Proteus Theatre Company); *Not About Heroes* Stephen Macdonald.

Hull Truck Theatre Company
Spring Street, Hull HU2 8RW
☎ 0482 224800 Fax 0482 228546

Contact *Barry Nettleton* (Administrator)

John Godber, the artistic director of this high-profile Northern company since 1984, has very much dominated the scene with his own successful plays. However, a change of direction means that the company now does at least one of John's plays a year, with new emphasis on outside writers. Most of the new plays have been commissioned. Previous productions have included: *Catwalk* Jane Thornton; *On The Piste* John Godber; *Sweet Sorrow* Alan Plater; *Can't Stand Up for Falling Down* Richard Cameron. The company admits it doesn't always get around to reading unsolicited mss. Synopses and letters are preferred. Bear in mind the artistic policy of Hull Truck, which is 'accessibility and popularity'. In general they are not interested in musicals, or in plays with many more than 8 characters.

Humberside Theatre in Education
Humberside Cultural Enterprise Centre, Middleton Street, Springbank, Hull HU3 1NB
☎ 0482 24256

Contact *Amanda J. Smith*

FOUNDED 1983. Full-time company playing to Humberside schools, with a strong tradition of devising its own work. Recent productions have included: *Thicker Than Water* Julie Wilkinson (for 8-10-year-olds); *Frog and Toad* (adap. by Bill Morrison from Arnold Lobel stories); *Tent of Blue* (devised by the company itself for 11-13-year-olds). No unsolicited mss unless specific to this area of work. Interested in developments in new writing and in working with new writers but funding does not often allow this.

Richard Jackson
59 Knightsbridge, London SW1X 7RA
☎ 071-235 3671

Independent-minded producer who only does 'plays which appeal to me'. Besieged by mss and tends to go out for what he wants (particularly European material). Works mainly in smaller-scale London fringe theatres where he can take risks the West End can no longer afford. Credits include bringing *Quentin Crisp* to a theatre audience. Recent productions have included: *Pasolini* Michael Azama; *I Ought to Be in Pictures* Neil Simon; *Eden Cinema* Marguerite Duras; *Noonbreak* Paul Claudel.

Pola Jones Associates Ltd
5 Dean Street, London W1V 5RN
☎ 071-439 1165 Fax 071-437 3994

Contact *Andre Ptaszynski/Andrew Fell*

FOUNDED 1982. Unsolicited scripts welcome. Comedy and musicals preferred. Previous productions have included: *The Nerd*, with Rowan Atkinson; *Progress* Doug Lucie; *The Gambler*, with Mel Smith; *Return to the Forbidden Planet; Show Boat; Evita; My Fair Lady*. Also produces comedy for TV: *Tygo Road; Joking Apart*.

Stephen Joseph Theatre
Valley Bridge Parade, Scarborough YO11 2PL
☎ 0723 370540 Fax 0723 360506

Contact *Alan Ayckbourn* (Artistic Director)/ *Gordon Townsend* (Script Assistant)

A small theatre-in-the-round seating 307 people, with additional studio theatre seating 75-90. Positive policy on new work. For obvious reasons, Alan Ayckbourn's work is featured heavily in the repertoire, but plays from other sources are encouraged. Past productions have included: *Woman in Black* (adap. Stephen Mallatratt); *The Ballroom* Peter King; *The Parasol* Frank Dunai; *Wolf at the Door* Henry Becque; *One Over the Eight* Peter Robert Scott. Plays should have a strong narrative and be accessible. Minimum three-month reading period 'but, sadly, it can take longer'.

Bill Kenwright Ltd
55-59 Shaftesbury Avenue, London W1V 7AA
☎ 071-439 4466 Fax 071-437 8370

Contact *Bill Kenwright*

Presents both revivals and new shows for West End and touring theatres. Although new work tends to be by established playwrights, this does not preclude or prejudice new plays from new playwrights. Scripts should be addressed to Bill Kenwright with a covering letter. 'We have enormous amounts of scripts sent to us. They are read systematically. Please do not phone; the return of your script or contact with you will take place in time.'

King's Head Theatre

115 Upper Street, London N1 1QN
☎071-226 8561/1916

Contact *Donal O'Mathuna* (Literary Manager)

New scripts are welcome and are farmed out to consultants for reading and evaluation. An unpretentious little café theatre, the King's Head nevertheless produces some strong work, notably *Diary of a Somebody* by John Lahr, about the life and death of Joe Orton. Other productions have included *Artist Descending A Staircase* Tom Stoppard; *Heyday* Herbert Appleman; *This Savage Parade* Anthony Shaffer; *The Fling* Asher; Noël Coward's *Easy Virtue* and *A Slice of Saturday Night* The Heather Brothers (both of which transferred to the West End) and *Kvetch* Steven Berkoff.

Brian Kirk Associates

7 Wigton Place, Kennington, London SE11 5AN
☎071-820 0077   Fax 071-820 1237

Contact *Brian Kirk*

Commercial West End producers and general managers. Scripts by recommendation only.

David Kirk Productions

12 Panmuir Road, London SW20 0PZ
☎081-947 0130

Contact *David Kirk*

Commercially managed, bringing post-London tours, revivals and some new plays to provincial and suburban theatres. Productions usually have two or three TV names in them, but 'we will listen to suggestions of scripts strong enough not to need these'. Not interested in verse plays, rock musicals or scripts more suited to the Fringe. No unsolicited mss. Send preliminary letter, outlining proposal in the first instance, and include return postage. Recent productions have included post-London tours of Alan Ayckbourn's *Taking Steps;* Peter Terson's *Strippers;* Bob Larbey's *A Month of Sundays;* and a revival of Alan Bennett's *The Old Country.* New plays have included *Local Murder*

Peter Whalley; *Mr Fothergill's Murder* Peter O'Donnell; *Agenda for Murder* Denis Cleary & Joseph Boyer; *Dead of Night* Peter Whalley.

Knightsbridge Theatrical Productions

15 Fetter Lane, London EC4A 1JJ
☎071-583 8687   Fax 071-583 0046

Contact *Mrs S. Gray*

Straight plays and musicals suitable for production in the West End only. Occasionally plays on tour. New writing welcome; unsolicited mss will always be considered.

Leeds Playhouse

See **West Yorkshire Playhouse**

Leicester Haymarket Theatre

Belgrave Gate, Leicester LE1 3YQ
☎0533 530021   Fax 0533 513310

Joint Artistic Directors *Paul Kerryson/Julia Bardsley*

'We aim for a balanced programme of original and established works.' Recent productions have included: an adaptation of *Thérèse Raquin; Dead Soil* (British première); and a new version of *Merrily We Roll Along.* A script reading panel has been established, and new writing is welcome.

Library Theatre Company

St Peter's Square, Manchester M2 5PD
☎061-234 1913   Fax 061-228 6481
Forum Theatre, Leningrad Square, Manchester M22 5RT
☎061-437 8211

Contact *Christopher Honer* (Artistic Director)

Produces new and contemporary work, as well as occasional classics; also musicals, broad-appeal plays, and popular classics at the Forum Theatre. No unsolicited mss. Send outline of the nature of the script first. Encourages new writing through the commissioning of new plays and through a programme of staged readings to help writers' development.

Live Theatre Company

7-8 Trinity Chare, Newcastle upon Tyne NE1 3DF
☎091-261 2694

Contact *Max Roberts* (Artistic Director)

FOUNDED 1973. Tours to non-theatre venues in an attempt to play to people who might not normally frequent the theatre. Plays reflect the lives and concerns of working class people. The company's home theatre is currently developing plays to a varied audience from Newcastle and surrounding areas. Recent productions have included: *Hair in the Gate* Mike Chaplin; *Rockin' The Cradle* Pauline Hadaway, Karen Hope & Anne Orwin; *Greenfingers* Mike Wilcox; *Some Like it Cold* Steve Chambers. Occasional plays, while still for a general adult audience, target particular sections of that audience, e.g. *Cradle* for women; *Some Like it Cold* for 15–25-year-olds. Unsolicited scripts welcome. 'We are a new writing company but have a particular commitment to writers from the North-east who can write from that perspective. However, our work is never parochial but universal.' Also runs writers' workshops and rehearsed readings of new plays in short seasons. Committed to young people interested in writing, performing, etc.

Liverpool Playhouse

Williamson Square, Liverpool L1 1EL
☎051-709 8478   Fax 051-709 7113

Contact *Ian Kellgren* (Artistic Director)

Regional theatre very active in promoting new writing, with an impressive record on first plays. Past productions: *An Awfully Big Adventure* Beryl Bainbridge; *Journeymen Jack* Phil Wood; *Fears and Miseries of the Third Term* by twelve acclaimed writers, such as Catherine Hayes and Frank McGuinness; *A Brusque Affair* Shaun Duggan; *Dead of Night* Peter Whalley; *Double Take* Deborah Moggach; *The Little Sister* Bill Morrison. Finished scripts preferred to synopses and ideas. Committed to developing new work in both its auditoria.

London Actors Theatre Company

Battersea District Library, 265 Lavender Hill, London SW11 1JB
☎071-223 3108

Contact *Chris Fisher*

FOUNDED 1985. Plays to a varied audience, with new plays normally targeted at young people. First revivals of important British plays considered. Productions have included: *The Screamer* (a musical for 5-year-olds upwards); *Jekyll & Bumble* (likewise); *Frankenstein* (new adaptation). Unlikely to read unsolicited plays quickly and very unlikely to produce them. 'We normally commission writers directly and work with them closely in developing ideas and projects.'

London Bubble Theatre Company

3–5 Elephant Lane, London SE16 4JD
☎071-237 4434   Fax 071-231 2366

Contact *Jonathan Petherbridge* (Artistic Director)

Produces workshops, plays and events for a mixed audience of theatregoers and non-theatregoers, wide-ranging in terms of age, culture and class. Unsolicited mss welcome but 'our reading service is extremely limited and there can be a considerable wait before we can give a response'. Produces at least one new show a year which is invariably commissioned. Recent productions: *Measure for Measure; The Good Person of Sezuan; Brainpower* Nona Shepherd.

Lyric Theatre Hammersmith

King Street, London W6 0QL
☎081-741 0824   Fax 081-741 7694

Contact *Peter James* (Director)

Theatre with a long tradition of putting on new work, and always keen to receive scripts. Currently the main house is concentrating on modern European drama, plus revivals and new plays by British playwrights. Productions have included *State of Affairs* Graham Swannell (trans. Duchess); *Mumbo Jumbo* Robin Glendinning (Mobil prizewinner); *Atonement* Barry Collins; *Asylum* Paul Kember; *Madhouse in Goa* Martin Sherman; *Prin* Andrew Davies (trans. Lyric); *La Bête* David Hirson. Finished scripts only — they take at least 6 weeks to process, but a report is made to the director on every manuscript received. No longer able to produce in its 110-seat studio owing to reduced funding but the studio continues to host work, including new, by some of the best touring companies in the country.

MAC - The Centre for Birmingham

Cannon Hill Park, Birmingham B12 9QH
☎021-440 4221   Fax 021-446 4372

Contact *Dorothy Wilson* (Programme Director)

Home of Birmingham Readers and Writers Festival, Cannon Hill Puppet Theatre, Birmingham Film and TV Festival, Birmingham Art Trust, Photo Call, Birmingham Dance Agency, Sampad (South Asian Arts Development Agency) and the Big Brum TIE Company.

Cameron Mackintosh

1 Bedford Square, London WC1B 3RA
☎071-637 8866   Fax 071-436 2683

Producer of *Cats, Les Misérables, Phantom of the Opera, Little Shop of Horrors, Follies, Miss Saigon, Moby Dick, Five Guys Named Moe*. One of the most important producers in London's West End. Unsolicited scripts are read and considered (there is no literary manager, however) but chances of success are slim. Produces musicals only, and never more than one a year which tends to come by way of contacts. Not currently producing for the stage (until 1994 at the earliest) as Mackintosh is tied up with the film production of *Les Misérables* and *Miss Saigon*, and is working with the National Theatre on revivals of great musicals, the first one of which, *Carousel*, opens in December 1992.

Marianne Macnaghten
Dundarave, Bushmills, Co. Antrim BT57 8ST
☎02657 31215

Contact *Marianne Macnaghten*

Freelance director and producer. 'Regrettably cannot always acknowledge scripts.'

The Made in Wales Stage Company
Mount Stuart House, Mount Stuart Square,
Cardiff CF1 6DQ
☎0222 484017   Fax 0222 490104

Contact *Gilly Adams* (Artistic Director)

Varied audience. Works with Welsh and Wales-based writers and actors to create new and exciting plays which reflect the authentic Anglo-Welsh voice, whilst not being parochially Welsh. Formed in 1982, since when it has premièred and toured 22 new plays. Productions have included: *On the Black Hill* Charles Way (adap. from Bruce Chatwin's novel); *Branwen* Tony Conran; *The Scam* Peter Lloyd; *The Fourth World* Dick Edwards; *The Best Years of Our Lives* Laurence Allan. In addition, the company mounts an annual festival of new writing called Write On, and runs workshops, rehearsed readings and a script-reading service throughout the year.

Marcellus Productions Ltd
11 Chelverton Road, London SW15 1RN
☎081-788 5663

Contact *Jimmy Thompson*

Jimmy Thompson acts more as a director than producer, but is always on the look-out for new plays. Recent productions have included: *Don't Misunderstand Me* Patrick Cargill; *The Quiz Kid* (written by the Thompsons); *Wind in the Willows; My Giddy Aunt*, with Molly Sugden; *Touch and Go*, with Ruth Madoc. Not really in the market for avant

garde or social plays, but will consider thrillers, revue, farce and romantic comedy.

Lee Menzies Ltd
20 Rupert Street, London W1V 7FN
☎071-437 0127   Fax 071-734 3495

Contact *Lee Menzies*

Commercial West End producer. Will consider 'good, original and commercial scripts'.

Merseyside Everyman Theatre Company
5-9 Hope Street, Liverpool L1 9BH
☎051-708 0338   Fax 051-709 0398

Contact *John Doyle* (Artistic Director)

FOUNDED 1964. Of about eight shows a year, at least one, hopefully more, are new plays. Tends to produce new versions of old classics, idiosyncratic Shakespeares, Willy Russell and Brecht — a very catholic repertoire; the common ingredient is an up-front bold style. Productions are designed to appeal to non-traditional audiences. Recent productions have included: *The White Devil* Webster; *School for Scandal* Sheridan. 'In theory we welcome unsolicited mss, but in practice we find we don't have the staff to do a proper reading job on them.' Writer-in-residence *Jeff Young*.

Midland Arts Centre
See **MAC - The Centre for Birmingham**

Midnight Theatre Company
103 Redston Road, London N8 7HG
☎081-341 6607

Contact *Derek Wax*

FOUNDED 1989. Classic and contemporary plays by new or neglected writers from Britain and around the world, suitable for production at leading London fringe venues. Interested in new writing of promise, particularly 'in plays which are ambitious in scope, which offer fresh insights, and explore relationships in an authentic and striking way'. Send synopsis with s.a.e. in first instance. 'We do not have the resources to read unsolicited scripts.'

Monstrous Regiment Ltd
Ground Floor Studio, 78 Luke Street,
London EC2A 4PY
☎071-613 0651   Fax 071-613 0652

Contact *Clare Venables* (Artistic Director)

FOUNDED 1976. Committed particularly to inventive and innovative ways of looking at scripts, and interested in women's experiences. Policy of encouraging new writing whenever possible, and will read unsolicited mss if they can handle them. Previous productions have included: *The Colony* Marivaux (trans. Byg Hanna); *Waving* Carol Bunyan; *Island Life* Jenny McLeod; *Medea* Euripides.

Kenneth More Theatre

Oakfield Road, Ilford, Essex IG1 1BT
☎081-553 4464   Fax 081-553 5476

Contact *Vivyan Ellacott*

Productions range from rock musicals to grand opera, gay theatre to Shakespeare, for an audience of both local senior citizens and young upwardly mobile East-Enders. Unsolicited mss are not welcome as there aren't the resources to cope with them. Studio plays (about 30 minutes long) welcome, but there's already a long backlog in line. Send synopses, not scripts.

Norman Murray & Anne Chudleigh Ltd

1st Floor, 235–241 Regent Street,
London W1R 5DD
☎071-629 4817   Fax 071-629 5668

Contact *Anne Chudleigh*

More agents than producers, handling light entertainment performers as well as comedy writers. 'We are always looking for new ideas in respect of comedy material, situation comedy TV plays.' Also pantomimes.

New Shakespeare Company

Open Air Theatre, Regent's Park,
London NW1 4NP
☎071-935 5884   Fax 071-487 4562

Contact *Ian Talbot* (Artistic Director)

Mainly Shakespeare and revivals, except for summer lunchtime children's theatre which is usually specially commissioned. Very occasional new work.

New Victoria Theatre

Etruria Road, Newcastle under Lyme,
Staffordshire ST5 0JG
☎0782 717954   Fax 0782 712885

Contact *Peter Cheeseman* (Theatre Director)

FOUNDED 1967. Plays to a fairly broad-based audience which tends to vary from production to production. A high proportion are not regular theatre-goers and new writing is one of the theatre's main ways of contacting new audiences. Unsolicited scripts welcome provided they are accompanied by s.a.e. for return. Commissions about four new plays each year and is determined to increase the number. Previous productions have included: *Good Golly Miss Molly!* Bob Eaton; *The Moonstone* (adap. Chris Martin); *Merlin and the Sleeping King* Nigel Bryant; *The Barber of Seville* (trans. Henry Livings); *The Pretty Lady* Joyce Holliday (from Arnold Bennett).

Newgate Company

13 Dafford Street, Larkhall, Bath, Avon BA1 6SW
☎0225 318335

Contact *Jo Anderson*

A commonwealth of established actors, directors and playwrights, Newgate originally concerned itself solely with theatre writing (at the Bush, Stratford, Roundhouse, etc.). Previous productions have included: *Hitler's Whistle* (Orchard Theatre Co.); *Solstice* (Bristol Express Co.). However, in the course of development, several productions fed into a list of ongoing historically-based drama for BBC Radio 4: *Russian Connection; Dhobey Boys;* and for screen: *Immortal Beloved*, for Ken Russell/BBC TV/Channel 4. Recent productions for TV include *Stray Cat* with Little Bird Productions. Now looking to develop this co-production strand for film and television projects.

Newpalm Productions

26 Cavendish Avenue, London N3 3QN
☎081-349 0802   Fax 081-346 8257

Contact *Phil Compton*

Rarely produces new plays (*As Is* by William M. Hoffman, which came from Broadway to the Half Moon Theatre, was an exception to this). National tours of productions such as *Noises Off, Seven Brides for Seven Brothers* and *Rebecca*, at regional repertory theatres, are more typical examples of Newpalm's work. Unsolicited mss, both plays and musicals are, however, welcome; scripts are preferable to synopses.

Northampton Repertory Players Ltd

See **Royal Theatre**

Northcott Theatre

Stocker Road, Exeter, Devon EX4 4QB
☎0392 56182
Fax 0392 263108 attn Northcott Theatre

Contact *John Durnin* (Artistic Director)

FOUNDED 1967. The Northcott is the South-west's principal subsidised repertory theatre, situated on the University of Exeter campus. Describes its audience as 'geographically diverse, financially comfortable, conservative in taste, with a core audience of AB1s (40–60 age range)'. Currently looking to broaden the base of its audience profile, targeting younger and/or non-mainstream theatre-goers in the 16–35 age range. Aims to develop, promote and produce quality new writing which reflects the life of the region and addresses the audience it serves. Unsolicited mss welcome but turnaround is necessarily slow and the script reading service tends to be locally orientated. Not interested in 'pastiche drawing-room comedy, imitation Ayckbourn, farce from the Ray Cooney school of theatre, murder-mysteries or thrillers, or anything that employs TV naturalism'. Recent OUTPUT has included: *Wild Oats* John O'Keefe; *Inventing a New Colour* Paul Godfrey; *Merlin's Dream* Karoline Leach; *One for the Road* Willy Russell. During 1991–92, severe financial pressures on the theatre resulted in only one new writing commission (*Merlin's Dream*). It is hoped that during the 1992–93 season the company will be able to return to its previous target of a minimum of two new pieces each season, one for the main house, the other for the studio theatre in Emmanuel Hall. The Northcott is a founder-member of the South West Theatre Consortium which actively supports and participates in a variety of new writing projects, showcases, workshops, rehearsed readings and competitions.

Northern Stage Company

67A Westgate Road, Newcastle upon Tyne NE1 1SG
☎091-232 3366   Fax 091-261 9699

Contact *Alan Lyddiard* (Artistic Director)

A newly formed production company based in Newcastle. As there is no literary manager, the reading of scripts is likely to be a fairly lengthy process. The company plans to involve itself in the production of new work, including co-productions with other local companies. Writers' workshops are likely to be arranged.

Northumberland Theatre Company

The Playhouse, Bondgate Without, Alnwick, Northumberland NE66 1PQ
☎0665 602586

Contact *Gillian Hambleton*

FOUNDED 1978. Predominantly rural, playing to village halls and community centres throughout Northumberland and the Scottish borders; also to schools (YPT/TIE). Productions range from established classics to new work and popular comedies, but must be appropriate to their audience. Unsolicited scripts welcome provided they are suitable for production tours. The company encourages new writing and commissions when possible. Financial constraints restrict casting to a maximum of five.

Norwich Puppet Theatre

St James, Whitefriars, Norwich, Norfolk NR3 1TN
☎0603 615564

Contact *Pat Holtom/Christine Willison*

Plays to a young audience (aged 4–16), with occasional shows for adult audiences interested in puppetry. Christmas/summer season shows, plus school tours. Unsolicited mss welcome if relevant. Send to *Luis Boy* (artistic director).

Nottingham Playhouse

Nottingham Theatre Trust, Wellington Circus, Nottingham NG1 5AF
☎0602 474361   Fax 0602 475759

Contact *Ruth Mackenzie* (Executive Director)

Aims to make innovation popular, and present the best of world theatre, working closely with the communities of Nottingham and Nottinghamshire. Unsolicited mss will be read. It normally takes about six months, however, and 'we have never yet produced an unsolicited script. All our plays have to achieve a minimum of sixty per cent audiences in a 732-seat theatre. We have no studio.'

Nuffield Theatre

University Road, Southampton SO2 1TR
☎0703 671871
Fax 0703 593939 attn Nuffield Theatre

Contact *Patrick Sandford* (Artistic Director)/*Penny Gold* (Script Executive)

Well known as a good bet for new playwrights, the Nuffield gets an awful lot of scripts. They tend to do a couple of new plays every season, often by established playwrights, though not as a matter of policy. Previous productions have included *Exchange* by Yri Trifonov (trans. Michael Frayn) which transferred to the Vaudeville Theatre; *The Floating Light Bulb* Woody Allen (British première); new plays by Claire Luckham: *The Dramatic Attitudes of Miss Fanny Kemble,* and by Claire Tomalin: *The Winter Wife.* Open-minded about subject and style, producing musicals as well as straight plays. Scripts preferred to synopses in the case of writers new to theatre. All will, eventually, be read 'but please be patient. We do not have a large team of paid readers. We read everything ourselves.'

The Old Vic

Waterloo Road, London SE1 8NB
☎071-928 2651   Fax 071-261 9161

Contact *Andrew Leigh* (General Manager)

The Old Vic is owned by Ed and David Mirvish, who after three years of presenting seasons of European classics, now operate as a West End theatre. Intend to return to producing three or four plays a year, with star casts. No unsolicited scripts.

Orange Tree Theatre

1 Clarence Street, Richmond, Surrey TW9 2SA
☎081-940 3633

Contact *Sam Walters* (Artistic Director)

One of those just-out-of-London theatre venues which are good for new writing, both full-scale productions and rehearsed readings, although these usually take place in the room above the Orange Tree pub. The first season in the new premises included *Cat with Green Violin* Jane Coles; *Stars in the Morning Sky* Alexander Galin; *The Pool of Bethseda* Allan Cubitt; *Self Portrait* Sheila Yeger; *Cerceau* Viktor Slavkin (trans. Adrian Brine). Prospective playwrights should bear in mind that unsolicited mss are read but patience (and s.a.e.) are required.

Orchard Theatre

108 Newport Road, Barnstaple, Devon EX32 9BA
☎0271 71475   Fax 0271 71825

Contact *Bill Buffery* (Artistic Director)

FOUNDED 1969. Plays appealing to a wide age range, which tour some 60 or 70 cities, towns and villages throughout Devon, Cornwall, Dorset, Somerset, Avon and Gloucestershire. Programme includes classics, new adaptations, outstanding modern work and newly commissioned plays on West Country themes. OUTPUT *The Tempest; Frankenstein; The Dream Maker; The Little Mermaid.* 'A large proportion of our work is concerned with the history, literary traditions and present-day life of the region. Unsolicited mss are usually unsuccessful simply because the theatre is committed to several commissioned new plays at any one time.'

Oxford Stage Company

3rd Floor, 15-19 George Street, Oxford OX1 2AU
☎0865 723238   Fax 0865 790625

Contact *John Retallack* (Artistic Director)

A middle-scale touring company producing established and new plays. Unsolicited mss welcome. At least one new play or new adaptation a year.

Paines Plough – The Writers Company

Interchange Studios, Dalby Street,
London NW5 3NQ
☎071-284 4483   Fax 071-284 4506

Contact *Robin Hooper* (Literary Manager)

Produces new writing. Recent plays have included *Abolition* Gabriel Gbadamosi; *Art of Success* Nick Dear; *Crux* April de Angelis; *The Clink* Stephen Jeffreys; *Augustine* Anna Furse; and George Orwell's *Down and Out* (adap. Nigel Gearing). Receives around five unsolicited scripts a week and reports are made on all plays received. Writers' workshops held in London. Accompanies productions on tour.

Palace Theatre, Watford

Clarendon Road, Watford WD1 1JZ
☎0923 35455   Fax 0923 819664

Contact *Lou Stein* (Artistic Director)

An important point of policy is the active commissioning of new plays. Previous productions have included: Stein's own adaptation of *The Adventures of Pinocchio*; Adrian Mitchell's *Woman Overboard*; Louise Page's *Diplomatic Wives*; Stephen Bill's *Over A Barrel*; Ranjit Bolt's new adaptation of *The Marriage of Figaro.* More recently: an entire season of new and commissioned work, including Bolt's *The Barber of Seville,* and Jon Carter's *The Baby.*

Pentameters

Three Horseshoes, 28 Heath Street,
London NW3 6TE
☎071-435 6757

Contact *Leonie Scott-Matthews*

Plays and poetry readings. Very interested in new plays ('we've been a new writing theatre since

1968') but no resources to deal with an influx of scripts, so send letters and synopses first. Broadminded in terms of subject matter and style.

James Perry Productions Ltd

1F Morpeth Terrace, London SW1P 1EW
☎071–828 2203

Contact *Jimmy Perry*

FOUNDED 1956. James Perry Productions is a small company which exists solely to handle the work of Jimmy Perry, creator of, among others, *Dad's Army, Turns, You Rang My Lord, It Ain't Half Hot Mum* and *Hi De Hi.*

Plantagenet Productions

Westridge Open Centre, Highclere, Near Newbury, Berkshire RG15 9PJ
☎0635 253322

Contact *Dorothy Rose Gribble (Miss)*

Recorded library of the spoken word (classical), with short list of drawing-room recitals. Based at Westridge Open Centre, a showcase for visiting recitals of music mainly. Also a venue for small seminars, healing studies and holidays. No unsolicited scripts.

Players' Theatre

The Arches, Villiers Street, Strand, London WC2N 6NG
☎071–839 1134   Fax 071–839 8067

Contact *Reginald Woolley/Geoffrey Brawn*

Produces Victorian music hall entertainment, researched largely from sources like the British Library.

Polka Children's Theatre

240 The Broadway, London SW19 1SB
☎081–542 4258   Fax 081–542 7723

Contact *Artistic Director*

This Wimbledon theatre is interested in receiving scripts suitable for children of all ages, but principally 3–5, 5–8 and 9–12. 'Our overall writing policy is to present excellent theatre for children which is both educational and entertaining'. Main house productions include original plays connected to school project work, Christmas plays, summer musical-plays, adaptations of classic stories, novels, folk tales and puppet plays. Particularly interested in plays that need a cast of no more than five to seven people.

Prestige Plays

83 George Street, London W1H 5PL
☎071–486 1732   Fax 071–224 2215

Contact *Charles Vance/Jill Streatfeild*

In the market for medium-scale touring productions and summer season plays. Hardly any new work and no commissions but writing of promise stands a good chance of being passed on to someone who might be interested in it. Occasional try-outs for new work in the Sidmouth repertory theatre. Send s.a.e. for return of mss.

Q20 Theatre Company

Ivy Lea, Fyfe Lane, Baildon, Shipley, West Yorkshire BD17 6DP
☎0274 591417/581316

Contact *John Lambert*

Produces shows mainly for school and community venues. Particularly interested in plays for children. Q20 writes a lot of its own material and rarely has the resources to pay outside professional contributors. Write initially with ideas.

Queen's Theatre Hornchurch

Billet Lane, Hornchurch, Essex RM11 1QT
☎04024 56118   Fax 04024 52348

Contact *Marina Caldarone* (Artistic Director)/*Sean O'Connor*

FOUNDED 1953. Nothing too adventurous for this mainly white, middle-class audience. Modern work, translations or classics are difficult to sell without a household name in the production. New artistic director Marina Caldarone, however, wishes to broaden the company's repertoire. Committed to producing at least one new work per season (two a year), and keen to set up a complementary studio company which would develop new work. 'We try to offer as broad a repertoire as we can within our economic limitations.' Eight shows a year, including one musical and one Christmas/panto slot. Always interested in 'the well-made play' and now encouraging the submission of more experimental work as well as translations, adaptations, and classics. Has an established tradition of successful comedies and musicals which have transferred to the West End, e.g. *Blood Brothers.* Unsolicited mss welcome; all are assessed but this can take some considerable time.

Quill Theatre Productions

247 Norwood Road, London SE24 9AG
☎081–674 1050

Contact *Ann Parnell McGarry* (Artistic Director)

Quill exists to produce new work and suffers enormous gaps in its production schedule when, as is often the case, decent new work can't be found. Writing can be set in any time or dimension imaginable, as long as it offers a fresh insight. 'Originality of approach is the most important thing.' In the market for serious work and fast witty comedies. Finished scripts are preferred unless someone wants to try out 'a truly brilliant idea which we can develop together. We have no preconceptions on size of cast. It is a lengthy process.'

The Really Useful Group Ltd
20 Tower Street, London WC2H 9NS
☎071-240 0880   Fax 071-240 1204

Contact *Alistair Smith*

Commercial/West End theatre producers whose output has included *Joseph and the Amazing Technicolor Dreamcoat, Cats, Phantom of the Opera, Starlight Express, Daisy Pulls It Off, Lend Me a Tenor, Arturo Ui* and *Aspects of Love.*

Red Shift Theatre Company
Battersea Arts Centre, Lavender Hill,
London SW11 5TF
☎071-223 3256   Fax 071-978 5207

Contact *Artistic Director*

FOUNDED 1982. Nationwide audience, aged 16+. Classic and new plays, written or adapted to suit small to middle-scale national touring. Most work is commissioned. Unlikely that unsolicited material would be considered for production. Work in close liaison with new writers so as to evolve the work to suit the audience.

Redgrave Theatre
See **Farnham Repertory Company Ltd**

Michael Redington
10 Maunsel Street, London SW1P 2QL
☎071-834 5119   Fax 071-828 6947

Contact *Michael Redington*

Interested only in new work but unsolicited mss are not welcome; new plays generally come by way of contacts in the business. Plays for the West End.

Redroofs Associates
Redroofs, Littlewick Green, Maidenhead,
Berkshire SL6 3QY
☎0628 822982   Fax 0628 822461

Contact *June Rose* (Executive Director)

Only interested in full-scale children's musicals based on classic titles, and in potted versions of Shakespeare for schools. Only welcome mss if they meet these exact requirements. Previous productions have included: *Charlie and the Chocolate Factory; The Lion, The Witch and The Wardrobe* (musical); *Once Upon a Time; The Princess and the Goblin.*

Roundabout Theatre Productions
139A New Bond Street, London W1Y 9FB
☎071-499 0162   Fax 071-491 0047

Contact *Carl Lewis*

No facilities for reading mss, and no interest in new work.

Roundabout Theatre in Education
College Street Centre for Performing Arts, College Street, Nottingham NG1 5AQ
☎0602 476202

Contact *Kitty Parker*

FOUNDED 1973. Theatre in Education company of the Nottingham Playhouse. Plays to a young audience aged 5-18 years of age. Some programmes are devised or adapted in-house, some are commissioned. Unable to resource the adequate response required for unsolicited scripts. 'We are committed to the encouragement of new writing as and when resources permit.'

Royal Court Theatre (English Stage Company Ltd)
Sloane Square, London SW1W 8AS
☎071-730 5174   Fax 071-730 4705

Contact *Mel Kenyon* (Literary Manager)

The English Stage Company was founded by George Devine in 1956 to put on new plays. John Osborne, John Arden and Arnold Wesker, Edward Bond and Caryl Churchill, Howard Barker and Michael Hastings are all among the writers this theatre has discovered. Other writers such as Christopher Hampton and David Hare have worked here in the literary department. The aim of the Royal Court is to develop and perform the best in new writing for the theatre, encouraging writers from all sections of society to address the problems and possibilities of our times.

Royal Exchange Theatre Company

St Ann's Square, Manchester M2 7DH
☎061-833 9333   Fax 061-832 0881

Contact *Alan Pollock* (Literary Manager)

FOUNDED 1976. The Royal Exchange has developed a new writing policy, which they find is attracting a younger audience to the theatre. The company produces plays by young dramatists like Iain Heggie, Michael Wall, Alex Finlayson, Rod Wooden and Randhi McWilliams; also English and foreign classics, modern classics, adaptations and new musicals. The Royal Exchange receives anything from 500–2000 scripts a year. These are read by Alan Pollock and a team of readers. Only a tiny percentage is suitable, but opportunities also exist for rehearsed readings, workshops and consultation on new work of promise. Currently there is one writer-in-residence, and a number of plays are commissioned each year. Runs the **Mobil Playwriting Competition**.

Royal National Theatre

South Bank, London SE1 9PX
☎071-928 2033
Fax 071-620 1197   Telex 297306

Contact *John Burgess*

Unsolicited mss are read, but the majority of The National's new plays come about as a result of a direct commission or from existing contacts with playwrights. There is no quota for new work, though so far more than a third of plays presented have been the work of living playwrights. Writers new to the theatre would need to be of exceptional talent to be successful with a script here, though the NT Studio acts as a bridge between the theatre and a limited number of playwrights, through readings, workshops and discussion. In some cases a new play is presented for a shorter-than-usual run in the Cottesloe Theatre.

Royal Shakespeare Company

Barbican Centre, London EC2Y 8BQ
☎071-628 3351   Fax 071-374 0818

Contact *Colin Chambers* (Literary Manager)

The literary department, headed by Colin Chambers, receives around 500 unsolicited mss a year of which ninety-eight per cent are totally unsuitable for the RSC. But the RSC is committed to new plays and roughly a third of the company's total output is new work. This is generally commissioned and unsolicited offerings from unknowns are rarely successful. Bear in mind that the RSC is *not* interested in straightforwardly biographical plays (they get an awful lot of Lives of Elizabeth I) or singlemindedly topical writing, and have no use for reworkings of Shakespeare. Musicals, particularly rewritings of *Kiss Me Kate* or *Les Misérables* (these used to arrive by the sackful) are not generally welcome. 'There is a tendency among playwrights to assume that because the RSC have done a play once, they're in the market for more of the same. Usually the reverse is true, and it's wise to check whether a subject has been covered previously before submitting mss.' The RSC organises festivals in which new work is often a prominent feature but has little, if any, involvement with rehearsed readings and workshops.

Royal Theatre

15 Guildhall Road, Northampton NN1 1EA
☎0604 38343   Fax 0604 602408

Contact *Michael Napier Brown* (Artistic Director)

FOUNDED 1927. Describes its audience as 'wide-ranging in terms of taste; 50% middle-class of all ages; and fairly conservative'. Produces at least two new works each year. Unsolicited scripts welcome and always read. New work tends to be produced for the studio theatre, theatre-in-education, community touring and youth theatre, rather than for the main house. Previous productions have included: *Below the Belt; The Fancy Man; Mrs Klein* and *Martin Chuzzlewit*. Also produces Schools Showcase: a week of performances from schools across the county.

Salisbury Playhouse

Malthouse Lane, Salisbury, Wiltshire SP2 7RA
☎0722 320117

Contact *Mary Gould* (Administrator)/*Deborah Paige* (Artistic Director)

A survey made in 1987 established that seventy-three per cent of the Playhouse's audience was over 35 years of age. New work is encouraged. The company tries to build new writing into its programme where possible, and to encourage an understanding of the need for new plays, both through the work of its writer-in-residence and by establishing professional writers support groups and monitoring rehearsed readings of new work. The artistic director and readers' panel will not necessarily read unsolicited material unless there is a likelihood of production. In the first instance a letter and synopsis, not script, should be sent. Include s.a.e. for return of material.

Shared Experience Theatre

Soho Laundry, 9 Dufours Place, London W1V 1FE
☎071-434 9248   Fax 071-287 8763

Contact *Nancy Meckler* (Artistic Director)

FOUNDED 1975. Varied audience depending on venue, since this is a touring company. Recent productions have included: *The Bacchae* Euripides; *True West* Sam Shepard; *Abingdon Square* Maria Irene Fornes; *Heartbreak House* George Bernard Shaw. No unsolicited mss. Primarily not a new writing company but 'we are interested in innovative new scripts'.

Stanley Sher Enterprises Ltd
28 Oakhampton Court, Park Avenue, Roundhay, Leeds LS8 2JF
☎ 0532 731348

Contact *Stanley Sher*

FOUNDED 1962. Plays for a family audience: pantomime and popular theatre, plus children's productions. Unsolicited mss welcome.

Sherman Theatre Ltd
Senghennydd Road, Cardiff CF2 4YE
☎ 0222 396844   Fax 0222 665581

Contact *Phil Clark* (Artistic Director)

FOUNDED 1973. Young people's theatre, with main house and studio. Recent productions of new plays have included: *A Kiss on the Bottom* and *Sleeping with Mickey Mouse* Frank Vickery; *Dracula* Sion Eirian; *Y Plentyn Coll* and *The Pathway Home* Mike Kenny. Unsolicited material welcome but priority will be given to production of new local talent.

Snap People's Theatre Trust
Millars One House, Southmill Road, Bishop's Stortford, Hertfordshire CM23 3DH
☎ 0279 504095

Contact *Andy Graham*

FOUNDED 1979. Plays to young people in four age groups (5-7; 7-11; 11-14; 15-21), and to the thirty-something age group. Classic adaptations and new writing. Writers should make an appointment to discuss possibilities rather than submit unsolicited material. New writing encouraged. 'Projects should reflect the writer's own beliefs, be thought-provoking, challenging and accessible.'

Soho Theatre Company
The Cockpit Theatre, Gateforth Street, London NW8 8EH
☎ 071-262 7907   Fax 071-723 8146

Contact *Abigail Morris* (Artistic Director)

A new writing theatre company. The system for dealing with unsolicited mss is as follows: scripts go out to a team of readers; those they find interesting are passed on to the artistic director, who invites writers of promise to join the workshop series. The company produces around four shows a year. Recent productions have included: *Caving In* Ayshe Raif; *Me and My Friend* Gillian Plowman; *Emisori Rites* Sila Kamyua. Following the closure of the Soho Poly Theatre in January 1991, the Company has taken over the management of the Cockpit Theatre, and the first in-house production was held in September 1992. Presents the **Verity Bargate Award** annually.

The Sphinx (formerly Women's Theatre Group)
Sadler's Wells, Rosebery Avenue, London EC1R 4TN
☎ 071-713 0991/2

Contact *Sue Parrish* (Artistic Director)/*Janet Waugh* (General Manager)

FOUNDED 1974. Tours new plays nationally to studio theatres and arts centres. Commissions two new plays a year by women.

Barrie Stacey Productions/Santa Fe Productions Ltd
Flat 8, 132 Charing Cross Road, London WC2H 0LA
☎ 071-836 6220/4128   Fax 071-836 2949

Contact *Barrie Stacey*

Currently setting up tours of various plays, some Barrie Stacey's, some by other writers. Always interested in two/three-handers for production, and in film synopses. Fast and experienced script writers in-house.

Stoll Moss Theatres Ltd
Manor House, 21 Soho Square, London W1V 5FD
☎ 071-437 2274   Fax 071-434 1217

Contact *Roger Filer*

One of the most influential theatrical empires, with eleven theatres to its credit: Apollo; Cambridge; Duchess; Garrick; Globe; Her Majesty's; London Palladium; Lyric Shaftesbury Avenue; Queen's; Royalty and Theatre Royal Drury Lane.

Swan Theatre
The Moors, Worcester WR1 3EF
☎ 0905 726969   Fax 0905 723738

Contact *Pat Trueman* (Artistic Director)

Produces one new play each season in the main house, and is looking towards developing more new work.

Swansea Little Theatre Ltd

Dylan Thomas Theatre, Maritime Quarter, 7 Gloucester Place, Swansea SA1 1TY
☎0792 473238

Contact *Dylan Thomas Theatre*

Anglo-Welsh plays, with regular production of Dylan Thomas' *Under Milkwood*. Repertoire ranges from Shakespeare to family comedies. New writing encouraged: one new play each season as a matter of policy. New scripts are considered by a panel of readers/producers.

Tabard Theatre

2 Bath Road, Chiswick, London W4 1LW
☎081-995 6035

Contact *Kate Bone*

FOUNDED 1985. Hosts theatre workshops and play readings, and has a theatre-letting policy. The company produces about six shows a year, ranging from new writing to classic works. These play to a wide audience in the Hounslow and Greater London area. Scripts (preferably preceded by a letter and accompanied by s.a.e) are assessed by a panel of readers and returned with comments. Runs West London Playwriting Competition (details from address above).

Temba Theatre Company Ltd

The Blackfriars Foundry, 156 Blackfriars Road, London SE1 8EN
☎071-721 7161   Fax 071-721 7232

Contact *Alby James* (Director)

FOUNDED 1972 by Alton Kumalo, a Black South African actor, primarily to give expression to Black cultures in Britain. Alby James became director in 1984. He focused the company on establishing a Black theatre aesthetic as opposed to making a political statement. The unique characteristics of this work is the dominant presence of Black actors, an innovative music-theatre approach, the influence of Black theatrical forms and its promotion of an integrated and multi-cultural theatre. Temba is the very model of a modern theatre company. It tramps the land in search of fresh audiences, with a repertoire which embraces the classics, revivals and plenty of new work. Committed to producing distinctive productions of classical dramas, adaptations of classic novels and modern classics aimed at a wide and varied audience. Recent productions: *Glory!* Felix Cross (first prizewinner of the 1988 **LWT Plays on Stage** competition); *Mamma Decemba* Nigel Moffatt; *Streetwise* Benjamin Zephaniah; *Ghosts* Henrik Ibsen; *A Killing Passion* Alby James & Sheena Wrigley (based on the novella, *The Transposed Heads*, by Thomas Mann).

Theatr Clwyd

County Civic Centre, Mold, Clwyd CH7 1YA
☎0352 756331   Fax 0352 758323

Contact *Artistic Director*

Lively theatre company with a policy of genuine encouragement as far as new writing is concerned. All scripts are passed on to an in-house reader — scripts are preferred to synopses and ideas. Open-minded on subjects — musicals and children's are considered. New work has included *Barnaby and the Old Boys* Keith Baxter; *Self Portrait* Sheila Yeger.

Theatr Powys

Drama Centre, Tremont Road, Llandrindod Wells, Powys LD1 5EB
☎0597 824444   Fax 0597 826230

Contact *The Writer-in-Residence*

FOUNDED 1972. Plays to a predominantly rural audience with community targeted plays. Repertoire includes: Theatre in Education projects in both primary and secondary school sectors; small to middle-scale community tours; middle-scale Christmas tours; youth theatre shows; and community arts residencies — the majority of which is new writing. Projects are mostly commissioned and full support is given to new writers: 'we hold the only writer-in-residence post of its kind in Wales.'

Theatre of Comedy Company

210 Shaftesbury Avenue, London WC2H 8DP
☎071-379 3345   Fax 071-836 0466

Contact *Alan Strachan* (Artistic Director)

FOUNDED 1983 to produce new work, and regard themselves as a good bet for new plays. Interested in strong comedy in the widest sense — Chekov comes under the definition as does farce. Also has a light entertainment division, developing new scripts for television, namely situation comedy and series.

Theatre Foundry

Theatre Foundry Ltd, The Multi-Purpose Centre,

Victoria Road, Darlaston, West
Midlands WS10 8AP
☎021-526 6947   Fax 021-568 6852
Contact *Artistic Director*

FOUNDED 1982. Small-scale touring company
which performs in the West Midlands area. Closely
identified with the Black Country. Some work
tightly targeted to particular community groups,
some for more general audiences. Limited opportunities for new writing — most commissions based
on very tight brief. Unsolicited mss not encouraged, but ideas or treatments for projects with
particular relevance to local communities are always welcome.

Theatre Royal Stratford East
Gerry Raffles Square, London E15 1BN
☎081-534 7374   Fax 081-534 8381
Contact *Jeff Teare* (Associate Director)

Lively East London theatre, catering for a very
mixed audience, both local and London-wide.
Produces new plays, musicals, classics, youth theatre and local community plays/events. Special
interest in Asian work. A good bet for new work.
Unsolicited scripts are welcome: 'we do read them
eventually!'

Theatre Royal Windsor
Windsor, Berkshire SL4 1PS
☎0753 863444   Fax 0753 831673
Contact *Mark Piper* (Artistic Director)

FOUNDED 1938. Plays to a middle-class, West End-
type audience. Produces 13 plays a year and
'would be disappointed to do fewer than two new
plays in a year; always hope to do half a dozen'.
1991 productions included: three thrillers; five
modern classics; four comedies; and one farce.
Only interested in scripts along these lines.

Theatre Workshop Edinburgh
34 Hamilton Place, Edinburgh EH3 5AX
☎031-225 7942   Fax 031-220 0112
Contact *Adrian Harris* (Artistic Director)

Plays to a young, broad-based audience with much
of the work targeted towards particular groups or
communities. OUTPUT has included adaptations of
Radclyffe Hall's *The Well of Loneliness* and Aharon
Appelfeld's *Badenheim 1939* — two community
performance projects — and *The Last Colony*, a
Theatre in Education programme touring to secondary schools in Scotland. Unsolicited mss welcome. Enclose s.a.e. Particularly interested in new

work for children and young people. Scripts are
read by the director and one other staff member
and take about 8–10 weeks to be processed for
response. Frequently engages writers for
collaborative/devised projects. Commissions a significant amount of new writing for a wide range of
contexts, from large-cast community plays to small-
scale professional tours. Favours writers based in
Scotland, producing material relevant to a contemporary Scottish audience. Runs playwright's workshop, plus other courses and classes.

Thorndike Theatre (Leatherhead) Ltd
Church Street, Leatherhead, Surrey KT22 8DF
☎0372 376211   Fax 0372 362595
Contact *Bridget Guymer* (Production Coordinator)

West End and touring — seventy per cent of the
company's work goes out on tour; children's and
family plays. Fairly conservative audience. Out of a
total of ten in-house productions each year, five
new plays are sought. Unsolicited mss welcome
(send s.a.e. for return). OUTPUT has included *Déjà
Vu* John Osborne; *Travels with My Aunt* Graham
Greene.

Tigerwise Theatrical Management
71 St Georges Square, London SW1V 3QN
☎071-828 3349   Fax 071-630 8454
Contact *Anthony Smee*

The company rarely produces drama, but could do
in the future. No unsolicited mss at present; send
letters and synopses only in the first instance.

Traverse Theatre
Cambridge Street, Edinburgh EH1 2ED
☎031-228 1404
Contact *Jane Ellis*

The Traverse is the most well-known theatre in
Scotland for new writing; indeed it has a policy of
putting on nothing but new work by new writers.
Also has a strong international programme of work
in translation and visiting companies. Recent productions have included: *Bondagers* Sue Glover and
The Bench Aleksandr Gelman. Unsolicited mss
welcome. Jane Ellis heads a reading panel which
reads and comments upon every script received.

Trends Management
54 Lisson Street, London NW1 6ST
☎071-723 8001   Fax 071-258 3591

Theatre production is just one facet of this company's work (also acts as an agency and has an extensive wardrobe department for the designing, making and hiring of costumes). Productions are on the light entertainment side, namely revues and pantomimes. No unsolicited mss. Most material is self-generated.

Tricycle Theatre

269 Kilburn High Road, London NW6 7JR
☎071-372 6611

Contact *Nicolas Kent* (Artistic Director)

FOUNDED 1980 but was destroyed by fire in 1987 and re-opened at the end of 1989. Plays to a very mixed audience, in terms of both culture and class. Previous productions have included: *Nativity* Nigel Williams; *Boots for the Footless* Brian Behan; *Joe Turner's Come and Gone* August Wilson; *Grumberg: A Long Way From Home* Yemi Ajibade; *A Free Country* Jean-Claude Grubey (trans. Tom Kempinski). Encourages new writing from women and ethnic minorities (particularly black and Irish). Looks for a strong narrative drive with popular appeal, not 'studio' plays. Also runs workshops for writers.

Tron Theatre Company

63 Trongate, Glasgow G1 5HB
☎041-552 3748   Fax 041-552 6657

Contact *Michael Boyd* (Artistic Director)

FOUNDED 1981. Plays to a very broad cross-section of Glasgow and beyond, including international tours (Toronto 1990; New York 1991; Montreal 1992). Recent productions have included: *Hosanna* Michel Tremblay (trans. Bowman & Findlay); *Cinzano* Petrushevskaya (trans. Mulrine); *The Offski Variations* Marcella Evaristi; *Crow* Hughes & Boyd; *Salvation* Peter Arnott; *The Baby* Chris Hannan; *Good* C. P. Taylor; *The Bloody Chamber* Angela Carter & Hall. Interested in premières of ambitious plays by experienced Scottish writers, and in new Irish work. Unsolicited mss welcome.

Umbrella Theatre

26 Lancaster Road, Brighton, East Sussex BN1 5DG
☎0273 562090   Fax 0273 563515

Contact *Colin Granger*

Stages productions of plays and other original work from abroad — in English. Particularly interested in new writing from Europe, both translations and scripts in their original language. Past productions have included: *Komiker Kaberett*, based on the work of Karl Valentin (Germany); *Cabaret Camique*, based on the writings of French humourist Pierre Henri Cami; *Angel Knife* Jean Sigrid (Belgium) and *Gloomy Sunday* Peter Muller (Hungary). Unsolicited mss welcome.

Umoja Theatre Company

The Base, 59 Bethwin Road, London SE5 0XY
☎071-701 6396   Fax 071-703 3796

Contact *Artistic Directors*

FOUNDED June 1983. Plays to a predominantly black audience. Produces two adult plays and one for children each year. Unsolicited mss welcome. New writers encouraged. Own venue: *The Base*, taking incoming shows, workshops and training. Rehearsal space available.

Unicorn Theatre for Children

Arts Theatre, 6–7 Great Newport Street, London WC2H 7JB
☎071-379 3280   Fax 071-836 5366

Contact *Dorothy Wooder*

FOUNDED 1947 as a touring company, and took up residence in the Arts Theatre in 1967. Plays mainly to children between the ages of 4–12. Recent productions have included: *Chalk Circle* Diane Samuels, and *Hans Christian Anderstories* — a recreation by Ken Campbell, Charles Causley, Claire Luckham, Adrian Mitchell and Fay Weldon of some of the famous tales. Unsolicited scripts welcome. Runs the **Unicorn Theatre Young Playwrights' Competition** annually.

John Wallbank Associates Ltd

St Martin's Theatre, West Street, London WC2H 9NH
☎071-379 5665   Fax 071-836 1375

Contact *John Wallbank*

Plays and musicals suitable for West End production and touring. New writing welcome.

Michael Ward Theatre Productions

Radnors, 39 Thames Street, Windsor, Berkshire SL4 1PR
☎0753 863982

Contact *Michael Ward*

FOUNDED 1984. New writing encouraged (non-political preferred). Interested in quality new work that could be used for touring or London. Send synopsis with script, including s.a.e. for return. Close association with leading literary agent and with two West End management companies.

Warehouse Theatre, Croydon

Dingwall Road, Croydon CR0 2NF
☎081-681 1257   Fax 081-681 8186

Contact *Ted Craig* (Artistic Director)/*Sheila Dewey* (resident playwright)

South London's new writing theatre, seating 120. Produces six new plays a year and co-produces with companies who share a commitment to new work. Continually building upon a tradition of discovering and nurturing new writers, with activities including a monthly writers' workshop and the annual South London Playwriting Festival (see entry **Festivals**), which is held in the autumn. Recent productions have included: *The Mysterie of Maria Marten* Chris Bond; *Playing Sinatra* Bernard Kops; *Fighting for the Dunghill* Guy Jenkins; *Turners Crossing* Sheila Dewey. Unsolicited scripts welcome but writers should bear in mind that the theatre is committed to productions at least nine months in advance.

Watermill Theatre

Bagnor, Newbury, Berkshire RG16 8AE
☎0635 45834   Fax 0635 45834

Contact *Jill Fraser*

The Watermill tries to put on one new piece of work each year. Past productions: a new musical by George Stiles & Anthony Drewe entitled *Just So*; *Hindsight* Richard Everett; a musical adventure story for 5-12 year-olds entitled *King Rollo – Space Crusader*, and *King Rollo's Stolen Christmas*.

West Yorkshire Playhouse

Quarry Hill Mount, Leeds LS9 8AW
☎0532 442141   Fax 0532 448252

Contact *Jude Kelly*

Committed to programming new writing as part of its overall policy. Puts on play readings and works with Yorkshire Writers' Group on writers' surgeries, etc. Past productions, many of which have been world premières, have included: *Safe in Our Hands* Andy de la Tour; *Sunsets and Glories* Peter Barnes; *Lifelines* — six contemporary plays in repertoire.

Whirligig Theatre

14 Belvedere Drive, Wimbledon,
London SW19 7BY
☎081-947 1732   Fax 081-879 7648

Contact *David Wood*

One play a year in a major theatre venue, usually a musical for primary school audiences and weekend family groups. Interested in scripts which exploit the theatrical nature of children's tastes. Previous productions have included: *The See-Saw Tree*, *The Selfish Shellfish*, *The Gingerbread Man*, *The Old Man of Lochnagar*, *The Ideal Gnome Expedition*, and *Save the Human*.

Winged Horse Touring Productions

The Old Athenaeum Theatre Building, 179 Buchanan Street, Glasgow G1 2JZ
☎041-556 2494   Fax 041-333 1021

Contact *Hamish Glen* (Artistic Director)

FOUNDED 1979. Touring company which plays to a wide variety of diverse audiences in urban and rural venues throughout Scotland and northern England. New plays are the core of their output and are by Scottish-based writers (both established and new) and narrative-based. Most work is commissioned. Recent productions have included: *Elizabeth Gordon Quinn* Chris Hannan; *Bailegangaire* Tom Murphy; *American Buffalo* David Mamet; *The Evil Doers* Chris Hannan.

W & J Theatrical Enterprises Ltd

51A Oakwood Road, London NW11 6RJ
☎081-458 1608   Fax 081-458 1608

Contact *Bill Roberton*

Theatrical agents for actors and comedians; also directors and writers of farce and pantomime. No scripts.

Wolsey Theatre Company

Civic Drive, Ipswich IP1 2AS
☎0473 218911   Fax 0473 212946

Contact *Antony Tuckey* (Artistic Director)/ *Margaret Fisher* (Submissions)

FOUNDED 1979. Tries to do one new play a year in the main house, and has a Theatre in Education programme which commissions two new plays a year. Unsolicited mss welcome. Recent productions include *Three Sisters; Within the Fortress* (new play); *The Scarlet Pimpernel; Into the Woods; Who's Afraid of Virginia Woolf; Absent Friends; A Midsummer Night's Dream.*

Women's Theatre Group

See **The Sphinx**

York Theatre Royal

St Leonard's Place, York YO1 2HD
☎0904 658162   Fax 0904 611534

Contact *Derek Nicholls* (Artistic Director)

Recent productions have included: *One for the Road; Private Lives; A Chorus of Disapproval; To Kill a Mockingbird.* 'We regret that unsolicited scripts cannot be accepted.'

The Young Vic

66 The Cut, London SE1 8LZ
☎071-633 0133   Fax 071-928 1585

Contact *David Thacker* (Artistic Director)

FOUNDED 1970. Aims for an audience of all ages and from all class backgrounds, with a priority for attracting teenagers and young adults. Contemporary classics and classics, especially Shakespeare, and plays for families; plus busy Youth Theatre programme. Unsolicited mss welcome but turn-round may be very slow. Not a new writing theatre but tries to programme one new production a year, which tends to be by an established writer.

Playwrights' Minimum Terms

The Writers' Guild and the **Theatre Writers' Union** achieved something of a breakthrough with their negotiation of a minimum terms agreement with the **Independent Theatre Council**, the representative body of small to middle-scale professional theatre companies, national and regional touring companies and producing venues.

The two sides settled for a *minimum* fee of £3244 for a full-length play and £2168.40 for a shorter play, these figures being the equivalent of 20.8 weeks and 13.9 weeks of the ITC minimum company rate of pay. The following are extracts from the agreement. Full copies can be obtained from The Writers' Guild.

'The Copyright of the play shall remain vested in the Writer and no rights in the play shall be granted to the Manager other than those specifically stated.

'The Writer grants the Manager the exclusive right to present the Play in its original production . . . for one year from the decision to produce . . . in the United Kingdom other than West End . . . except for periods of 4 consecutive weeks or less at the Arts Theatre, Donmar Warehouse, and Royal Court (Downstairs) . . . and abroad so long as these are named in the tour schedule . . .

'If the Manager wishes to include a West End Option clause in the contract, then he/she must state this at the time of signing the agreement and make an additional payment of £150 above the minimum fee . . . Provided that the payment has been made then the Manager may exercise her/his option to buy the West End rights in the Play for a period of one year.

'The option must be exercised within three months of the last scheduled performance of the Play by the Manager, or by the end of the period of exclusive rights whichever is the later . . .

'The Manager shall pay for the West End rights a fee of 50% of the original fee. This 50% option fee shall be a non-returnable advance against future royalties from the West End run.

'At the end of the first year of the West End rights, the Manager can choose to extend the rights for another year for a further option fee of 50% of the original fee.

'The initial fee entitles the Manager to present the Play for a total of 21 weeks (not necessarily consecutive) . . . without payment for performance or royalties.

'If the Manager wishes to present the Play for longer than 21 weeks or during a period of additional non-exclusive rights then the performing rights for these weeks can be bought at a weekly fee . . . of 2% of the original fee.

'From the date of delivery of the script the Manager shall have 6 weeks in which to discuss the Play with the Writer.

'If the Manager does not require rewrites then by the end of a further 3 weeks (i.e. 9 weeks following delivery of the script) the Manager will inform the Writer in writing of the decision whether or not to produce. If the Manager requires rewrites, then the Writer shall be asked to produce such rewrites by the end of a further 6 week period . . .

'Following delivery of the rewrites, the Manager shall have a further 6 weeks in which to decide whether to produce the Play. By the end of this 6 week period the Manager will inform the Writer in writing of the decision whether or not to produce.

'If the Manager decides not to produce the Play, then the last instalment of the fee shall not be payable and the rights of the Play shall revert to the Writer.

'The Manager shall not change the text of the Play without the Writer's permission.

'Any changes or alterations agreed by the Writer of any kind whatsoever automatically become the sole copyright of the Writer.

'The choice of director, designer and actors of the Play shall be subject to mutual agreement between the Manager and the Writer . . .

'The Writer shall be accorded credit at least of equal prominence to that accorded directors and leading actors in posters, programmes, leaflets, and all paid advertising . . .

'The Writer shall have the right to attend rehearsals . . .

'Any rewrites during rehearsal agreed between the Writer and the Manager shall be covered by the Writer's duties of this contract and no additional payment shall be due.'

Festivals

The following list of festivals includes a number of arts festivals with literature-related events.

Aldeburgh Poetry Festival

Goldings, Goldings Lane, Leiston,
Suffolk IP16 4EB
☎0728 830631   Fax 0728 452715

Contact *Michael Laskey*

Now in its fourth year, an annual international festival held over one weekend each November in Aldeburgh, and remarkable for its large audiences and friendly atmosphere. Events, usually eight in total, vary each year. Regular features include a residency, poetry readings, a children's event, a lecture, cabaret, performance-poetry spots and the festival prize for a first collection (see entry **Prizes**).

Arundel Festival

The Arundel Festival Society Ltd, The Mary Gate, Arundel, West Sussex BN18 9AT
☎0903 883690   Fax 0903 884276

Contact *Mrs R. J. Buckland*

Annual festival held at the end of August/beginning of September for eleven days. Events include poetry, prose readings and lectures, open-air Shakespeare in Arundel Castle, concerts with internationally known artists, jazz, visual arts and active fringe.

Avon Poetry Festival

c/o Clifton Library, Princess Victoria Street, Clifton, Bristol BS8 4BX
☎0761 32546

Co-ordinator *Sandra Stevens*

FOUNDED 1986, this unique festival was acclaimed by the Literature Festivals Committee as the 'biggest and best poetry festival in the country'. Since 1988 it has been a through-the-year festival, 'with equal emphasis on community involvement and poetry as a fine art'. Correspondence on poetry issues welcome whether local, general, mainstream or radical. As well as special events, APF coordinates community poetry-in-performance each month (on the 2nd Tuesday of the month in Bristol, 3rd Wednesday in Bath); also workshops, mixed media activities and long-term projects. Publishes the quarterly *Avon Literary Intelligencer.*

Bath Fringe Festival

The Bell, 103 Walcot Street, Bath BA1 5BW
☎0225 427441

Administrator *Morag Deyes*

FOUNDED 1981. Annual festival held in May/June. A wide range of events including poetry, prose readings, traditional storytelling and lectures, jazz, comedy, kites and children's events.

BBC Radio Drama Young Playwright's Festival

Room 6114, Broadcasting House,
London W1A 1AA

Contact *Claire Grove*

FOUNDED 1988. Second festival broadcast autumn 1991. Open to writers aged 15–30. Scripts should be original radio plays or adaptations of the writer's own work for radio. The Festival is likely to become a biennial event with drama slots given over to young writers for one or two weeks. Contact above for precise details.

Belfast Festival at Queen's

Festival House, 25 College Gardens,
Belfast BT9 6BS
☎0232 667687   Fax 0232 663733

Director *Michael Barnes*

FOUNDED 1964. Annual two-and-a-half week festival held in November. Organised by Queen's University in association with the Arts Council of Northern Ireland, the festival covers a wide variety of events, including literature. Programme available in September.

Berkshire Literary Festival

See **Word For Word**

Birmingham Readers and Writers Festival

MAC, The Centre for Birmingham, Cannon Hill Park, Birmingham B12 9QH

☎021–440 4221   Fax 021–446 4372

Festival Director *Kate Organ*
Festival Associate *David Lodge*

FOUNDED 1983. Annual two-week festival held in May. Concerned with all aspects of contemporary reading and writing, with visiting authors, workshops, performances, cabaret, conferences and special programmes for young people.

Brighton Festival

Festival Office, Marlborough House, 54 Old Steine, Brighton BN1 1EQ

☎0273 29801 ext. 2380/1   Fax 0273 822095

Contact *General Administrator*

FOUNDED 1967. One of the largest arts festivals in the country. Now in its 25th year. Annual May festival with a wide variety of events including concerts, dance, film, humour, jazz, literature, theatre, opera and exhibitions.

Bury St Edmunds Arts Festival

Festival Office, Borough Offices, Angel Hill, Bury St Edmunds IP33 1XB

☎0284 763233

Festival Manager *Paul Gudgin*

FOUNDED 1984. Annual 17-day arts festival held in May. Literature, recitals, dance and films. 1992 programme included the BBC Philharmonic Orchestra, Javanese and Balinese dance and the Oxford Poets.

Buxton International Festival

1 Crescent View, Hall Bank, Buxton, Derbyshire SK17 6EN

☎0298 70395   Fax 0298 72289

Contact *General Manager*

FOUNDED 1979. Annual three-week opera festival held in July/August. Rarely performed operas are staged by an international company and the programme is complemented by a wide variety of other musical events.

Cambridge Festival

c/o Philips Telecom, St Andrew's Road, Cambridge CB4 1DP

☎0223 62770   Fax 0223 356411

Contact *Festival Administrator*

FOUNDED 1963. Annual two-week festival held at the end of July. A wide variety of events includes music, theatre, dance, exhibitions, film and literature.

Canterbury Festival

59 Ivy Lane, Canterbury, Kent CT1 1TU

☎0227 452853   Fax 0227 781830

Contact *Festival Office*

FOUNDED 1984. Annual two-week festival held in October. A mixed programme of events including talks by visiting authors, readings and storytelling, concerts in the cathedral, jazz, master classes, drama, visual arts, opera, film, cabaret and dance.

Cardiff Literature Festival

The Welsh Academy, 3rd Floor, Mount Stuart House, Mount Stuart Square, Cardiff CF1 6DQ

☎0222 492025   Fax 0222 492930

Director *Kevin Thomas*

FOUNDED 1986. Annual week-long festival held in the autumn. Readings, workshops, discussions, children's events, science fiction and fantasy conventions, and prize-givings. 1991 festival guests included Sorley MacLean, John Julius Norwich, Tony Benn and Labi Siffre.

Cheltenham Festival

See **The Daily Telegraph Cheltenham Festival of Literature**

Chester Literature Festival

34 Hamilton Place, Chester CH2 3JQ

☎0244 310212   Fax 0244 317277

Chairman *Stephen Whitaker*

FOUNDED 1989. Annual festival organised by local bookshops, writers' groups and Chester Arts Association. Major events sponsored by publishers. Usually held during the second week of July but was held in October in 1992.

Cleveland Festival

See **Write Around — A Celebration of Cleveland Writing**

Cley Little Festival of Poetry

5 East Cliff Flats, Tucker Street, Cromer,
Norfolk NR27 9HA
☏0263 513077

Festival Organiser *Megan Allan*

FOUNDED 1950. Annual village festival of great age,
to which distinguished poets are invited to read
and discuss their work. Usually held in May and
September/October.

Colchester–Essex Festival

Department of Literature, University of Essex,
Colchester CO4 3SQ
☏0206 872636
Fax 0206 873598 (Gps 3/2 Auto)

Contact *Joseph Allard*

Began life as a literature festival but later expanded
to include a variety of other events. Held annually:
Festival '92 held 12–28 November.

Contact Young Playwrights' Festival

Oxford Road, Manchester M15 6JA
☏061-274 3434

Contact *Community Team*

FOUNDED 1986. Annual summer festival open to
young people aged between 11 and 25 living in the
North-west of England. From the entries, which
need to be in by the January of the festival year,
twenty are selected for workshops and from these,
seven plays are produced by a professional company in Contact's Brickhouse Studio theatre before a
two-week tour of three of the plays to schools in
the region. All of the seven finalists are taken on a
residential writing course in the Lake District with
professional writers and directors who help them
to develop their work. All scripts submitted to the
festival receive a critical analysis.

Coventry Festival

Belgrade Theatre, Belgrade Square,
Coventry CV1 1GS
☏0203 256431   Fax 0203 550680

Contact *Festival Organiser*

FOUNDED 1982. Annual two-week festival held in
the summer, usually June. Temporarily suspended
in 1992, but 'we hope to resume in 1994'.

The Daily Telegraph Cheltenham Festival of Literature

Town Hall, Imperial Square,
Cheltenham GL50 1QA
☏0242 521621   Fax 0242 573902

Contact *Festival Organiser*

FOUNDED 1949. Sponsored by *The Daily Telegraph*.
Annual festival held in October. The first purely
literary festival of its kind, this festival has over the
past decade developed from an essentially local
event into the largest and most popular in Europe.
A wide range of events including talks and lectures,
poetry readings, novelists in conversation, exhibitions, discussions, cabaret and a large bookfair.

Dartington Literary Festival (Ways with Words)

Droridge Farm, Dartington, Totnes,
Devon TQ9 6JQ
☏0803 867311

Contact *Kay Dunbar*

Ways with Words, the Dartington Literary Festival
sponsored by *The Observer*, was initiated in August
1992. Guest authors included Anthony Burgess,
Andrew Motion, Fiona MacCarthy, Malcolm
Bradbury and Melvyn Bragg. Readings, discussions,
workshops and children's events cover a wide
range of subjects including (in 1992) romance,
biography, poetry, sex, childhood, science and
religion. Day and weekend participants also welcome.

Doncaster Literature Festival

Doncaster Central Library, Waterdale,
Doncaster DN1 3JE
☏0302 734305/852389   Fax 0302 369749

Contact *Festival Organiser*

FOUNDED 1988. Annual festival (4–5 days) at the
end of September/ beginning October, covering a
wide range of events for adults and children.
Readings, cabaret, drama, music and creative writ-
ing workshops. Visiting authors have included
Andrea Newman, Stan Barstow, Michael
Hardcastle, Simon Armitage, Carol Ann Duffy, Pete
Morgan, Maura Dooley, Elean Thomas, Ian
McMillan, Martyn Wiley, Margaret Drabble, Alun
Ereira, Berlie Doherty. Also features the Doncaster
Writers' Handicap Race held at the town's race-
course.

The Festival of Dover

Festival Office, Dover Town Hall, Biggin Street, Deal, Kent CT14 6BB
☏ 0304 375192

Contact *Festival Organiser*

First festival held in May 1992 with plans to make it an annual event. A two-week festival, with 1992 events including concerts, exhibitions, a creative writing workshop, and PD James talking about her crime novels.

Durham Literary Festival

c/o Durham City Library, South Street, Durham
☏ 091-384 7719

Contact *The Secretary/Paul Rubinstein*

FOUNDED 1989. Annual event held over 7–8 days at various locations in the city. Workshops, plus performances, cabaret, and other events.

Edinburgh Book Festival

Scottish Book Centre, 137 Dundee Street, Edinburgh EH11 1BG
☏ 031-228 5444   Fax 031-228 4333

Director *Shona Munro*
Children's Fair Organiser *Valerie Bierman*

FOUNDED 1983. Biennial book festival held during the first fortnight of the Edinburgh International Festival. Now established as Britain's biggest book event, the programme includes discussions, readings and lectures by writers of national and international reputation. The next festival will be held in August 1993.

Exeter Festival

Festival Office, Civic Centre, Exeter EX1 1JN
☏ 0392 265200   Fax 0392 265265

Festival Organiser *Lesley Maynard*

FOUNDED 1974. Annual two-and-a-half-week festival with a variety of events including concerts, theatre, dance and exhibitions.

Glasgow Mayfest

18 Albion Street, Glasgow G1 1LH
☏ 041-552 8000   Fax 041-552 6611

Director *Robert Robson*

FOUNDED 1982. Annual three-week festival in May. The second largest arts festival (after Edinburgh), with a wide range of events from community groups to major international performers. Theatre,

dance, music, comedy and literature events which in 1992 included a symposium organised by the Scottish **PEN** organisation on writing for children.

Greenwich Festival

151 Powis Street, London SE18 6JL
☏ 081-317 8687   Fax 081-316 5009

Contact *Festival Office*

FOUNDED 1970. Annual festival presented by the London Borough of Greenwich, held in June. The 1991 programme featured a wide variety of events including world music, drama, a poetry course and readings, jazz, comedy and rock.

Hay-on-Wye Festival of Literature

Festival Office, Hay-on-Wye HR3 5BX
☏ 0497 821217   Fax 0497 821066

Festival Director *Peter Florence*

FOUNDED 1988. Annual spring festival which is sponsored by *The Sunday Times.* 1992 guests included Vaclav Havel giving the PEN lecture, Simon Schama giving the TLS lecture, Joseph Brodsky, Amos Oz, Ismail Kadare, Martin Amis, David Grossman and Joseph Heller. The climax of the festival, perhaps, is the presentation of the **John Edeyrn Hughes** prize.

Hull Festival

Festival Office, 5 Humber Place, Hull HU1 1UD
☏ 0482 587776

Director *Rowena Swallow*

1992 saw the first 8-month festival running from early April to late November. A wide range of events including a literature festival in November featuring, amongst others, Miroslav Holub, Caryl Phillips, Nina Cassian and a major celebration of Philip Larkin.

Ilkley Literature Festival

Festival Office, 9A Leeds Road, Ilkley, West Yorkshire LS29 8DH
☏ 0943 601210

Director/Administrator *Jonathan Davidson*

FOUNDED 1973. Three festivals a year of 4–5 days' duration. Past writers have included Tony Harrison, Sarah Dunnant, Irina Ratushinskaya, Colin Thubron. Also presents children's events, storytellers, theatre and music, and creative writing workshops. Runs the **Yorkshire Open Poetry Competition**. Phone to join mailing list.

Kent Literature Festival

The Metropole Arts Centre, The Leas, Folkestone,
Kent CT20 2LS
☎ 0303 255070

Festival Director *David Stone*
Festival Administrator *Ann Fearey*

FOUNDED 1980. Annual week-long festival held at
the end of October which aims to bring the best in
modern writing to a large audience. Visiting
authors are a regular feature along with creative
writing workshops, discussions and children's/
family events. Also runs the **Kent Young Writers
of the Year Award**.

King's Lynn, The Drama Festival

19 Tuesday Market Place, King's Lynn,
Norfolk PE30 1JW
☎ 0553 691661   Fax 0553 691779

Contact *Anthony Ellis*

FOUNDED 1990 — the first festival was held in
December over a three-day period. Guests included
Malcolm Bradbury, Sheridan Morley and Snoo
Wilson among others. As with the Fiction and
Poetry Festivals in King's Lynn (see entries below),
this takes the form of an annual residential week-
end.

King's Lynn, The Fiction Festival

19 Tuesday Market Place, King's Lynn,
Norfolk PE30 1JW
☎ 0553 691661   Fax 0553 691779

Contact *Anthony Ellis*

FOUNDED 1989. An annual residential weekend
festival which generally takes place around
February/March. Over the weekend there are read-
ings and discussions, attended usually by guest
writers of which there are eight. 1992 guests were
Beryl Bainbridge, Elspeth Barker, Malcolm
Bradbury, Esther Freud, John Fuller, George Mac-
Beth, Deborah Moggach, Marina Warner.

King's Lynn, The Poetry Festival

19 Tuesday Market Place, King's Lynn,
Norfolk PE30 1JW
☎ 0553 691661   Fax 0553 691779

Contact *Anthony Ellis*

FOUNDED 1985. An annual residential weekend
festival held on one of the last two weekends of
September. Attended by eight guest poets who in
1991 were Carol Ann Duffy, Gavin Ewart, George
MacBeth, Sir William Golding, Glyn Maxwell,

Medbh McGuckian, Peter Orr, Carol Rumens, Matthew Sweeney. Events include readings and discussion panels.

Lancaster Literature Festival

67 Church Street, Lancaster LA1 1ET
☎ 0524 62166

Director *Zosia Koc*

FOUNDED 1978. Annual festival held in October,
covering a wide range of events including readings,
workshops, theatre, dance, cabaret, music and
children's.

Liverpool Festival

Bluecoats Chambers, School Lane,
Liverpool L1 3BX
☎ 051-709 8151

Director *Jayne Casey*

FOUNDED 1986. Originally biennial, now an annual
festival held in June. A broad range of events
including literature.

City of London Festival

St Paul's Churchyard, London EC4M 8BU
☎ 071-248 4260

FOUNDED 1962. Annual 17-day festival with a
musical emphasis held in July. 1992 events included the City of London Carl Flesch International
Violin Competition, The Dubliners, The Nash En-
semble, Natural Theatre Company and 'Poems on
the Underground'.

London New Play Festival

30 Brownlow Road, London N11 2DE
☎ 071-281 4690

Contact *Phil Setren*

Full production of fifteen new plays each year in
the spring. The festival committee reviews about
300 submissions a year and selects fifteen of these
for production. Organises staged readings and
workshops also. Deadline for submissions is the
end of January each year. Productions have included new writing by Claire Booker, Katie Campbell
and Julie Balloo.

Ludlow Festival

Castle Square, Ludlow, Shropshire SY8 1AY
☎ 0584 875070

Contact *Festival Organiser*

FOUNDED 1959. Annual two-week festival held in the last week of June and first week of July with an open-air Shakespearean production held in Ludlow Castle (1992 - *As You Like It*) and a varied programme of events including recitals, opera and talks (Simon Brett spoke on crime writing in 1992).

New London Radio Playwrights Festival

LAB/LBC New London Radio Playwrights' Festival, Independent Radio Drama Productions, PO Box 518, Manningtree, Essex CO11 1XD

FOUNDED 1990 for writers working, studying or living in Greater London and attracted over 300 scripts in 1991. The festival, which falls into two parts (workshops and script competition) offers an opportunity to learn about radio writing. Part one (workshop) begins with an open discussion on radio drama led by **LBC**'s resident drama directors at various venues throughout London in June and July, followed by a recording day at LBC. Participants (by application only) will be invited to submit a five-minute pilot script for selection and subsequent recording by a professional cast at LBC. Writers will be involved at every stage of production. Phase two of the festival invites anyone living, working or studying in London to submit scripts to the competition. Five plays will be chosen to go into production and will be broadcast on LBC the following year. Scripts should be no more than 45 minutes in length and writers should bear in mind that plays will be broadcast daily in five-minute episodes. Deadline for entries is 31 December each year. Scripts should be sent to the address above. Sponsored by the **London Arts Board**. **Writer's Guild** rates paid for transmission. Festival brochure available from LBC.

Norfolk and Norwich Festival

St Andrew's Hall, Norwich NR3 1AU
℡ 0603 614921

Director *Heather Newill*

FOUNDED 1824. The second oldest festival in the UK. Annual two-week festival on a theme held in October. 1992's theme was 'New Horizons', celebrating the European Community and commemorating the 500th anniversary of Columbus' discovery of America.

Royal Court Young Writers' Festival

Royal Court Young People's Theatre, 309 Portobello Road, London W10 5TD
℡ 081-960 4641   Fax 081-960 1434

Contact *Festival Organiser*

Open to young people up to the age of 25 who live in the regions targeted by each particular festival. Focuses on the process of playwriting: writers and directors from the Royal Court visit three regions with five centres in each region, leading a workshop on playwriting. A second visit extends this process to the point at which young people attending are invited to submit work for the festival. Intensive work on the final draft of plays precedes production at the Royal Court Theatre Upstairs before going on tour in the participating regions.

Rye Festival

Arling House, Rye Hill, East Sussex TN31 7NH
℡ 0797 222123

Contact *Tony Neville*

Annual festival held during the first week of September, featuring a wide variety of literary, musical and artistic events. Music, drama, poetry, literature, comedy, visual arts, children's events (and sometimes cinema) at various venues in the historic town of Rye.

Salisbury Festival

Festival Office, The King's House, 65 The Close, Salisbury, Wiltshire SP1 2EN
℡ 0722 323883   Fax 0722 323883

Director *Simon Halsey*

FOUNDED 1972. Annual festival held in the first two weeks of September. The theme of the 1992 festival was 'The English Abroad' and events included a Literature Day featuring Max Hastings, Victoria Glendinning, Joanna Trollope, Colin Thubron, Bernice Rubens, Howard Jacobson, Paul Bailey, Dr Tom McArthur and Leslie Thomas. Other literature events consisted of John Julius Norwich on Osbert Lancaster, an 'Original Writing Showcase' and 'Poetry Please!'.

South London Playwrighting Festival

Warehouse Theatre, Dingwall Road, Croydon Surrey CR0 2NF
℡ 081-681 1257

FOUNDED 1985. Annual autumn festival of full-length and unperformed plays, judged by a panel of theatre professionals. Finalists given rehearsed readings during the festival. Entries welcomed from all parts of the UK. Scripts, plus two stamped addressed envelopes (one script-sized), should reach the Warehouse Theatre by the end of July. Previous winners produced at the theatre include: Kevin Hood *Beached;* Anne Aylor *Children of the Dust;* Mark Bunyan *Dinner;* Ellen Fox *Conversations with George Sandburgh After a Solo*

Flight Across the Atlantic; Guy Jenkin *Fighting for the Dunghill.*

Stratford-upon-Avon Poetry Festival

The Shakespeare Centre, Henley Street, Stratford-upon-Avon, Warwickshire CV37 6QW
☏0789 204016   Fax 0789 296083

Festival Director *Roger Pringle*

FOUNDED 1953. Annual festival held on Sunday evenings during July and August. Readings by poets and professional actors.

Ways with Words, the Dartington Literary Festival

See **Dartington Literary Festival**

Windsor Festival

Dial House, Englefield Green, Surrey TW20 0DU
☏0784 432618

Contact *Laurence West*

FOUNDED 1969. Annual two-week autumn festival held in Windsor Castle State Rooms, St George's Chapel and Eton College. A wide range of events including ballet, poetry and prose readings.

Worcester Festival of Literature

Waterstone's Booksellers, 95 High Street, Worcester WR1 2HL
☏0905 723397

Secretary *Pat Davidson*

FOUNDED 1988. Autumn festival with poetry readings and workshops, readings by authors, drama and some music.

Word For Word, Berkshire Literature Festival

Library & Information Service, Shire Hall, Shinfield Park, Reading, Berkshire RG2 9XD
☏0734 233255   Fax 0734 233203

Contact *Linda Barlow*

FOUNDED 1989 and incorporates the former Berkshire Poetry Festival. Aims to present the idea of literature as fun, not elitist, and involves people in creative writing in every form. Held in the spring.

Write Around — A Celebration of Cleveland Writing

Berwick Hills Library, Ormesby Road, Berwick Hills, Middlesbrough, Cleveland TS3 7RP
☏0642 246947

Contact *Alyson Perry*

FOUNDED 1989. Annual 2-week festival with a commitment to local writers. Held (1992) in the last two weeks of October, featuring competitions for poetry (no line limit), short stories (2500 words), non-fiction/ magazine articles (1000 words), and stage drama (apply for details). Publishes anthologies of poetry and short stories compiled from competition entries and other submissions. Contact above for copies or further information.

York Festival

5/6 King's Court, York YO1 2LD
☏0904 679700

Director *Julia Veall*

FOUNDED 1951, when it was selected to be part of the Festival of Britain. Quadrennial festival held in June. Events include poetry readings, drama, dance, music, opera and (in 1992) The York Cycle of Mystery Plays held at the Theatre Royal.

European Publishers

Amalthea-Verlag Gesellschaft mbH
Am Heumarkt 19, A-1030 Vienna
☎010 43 222 723560

FOUNDED 1917. *Publishes* art, belles lettres, fiction, music.

Bölau Verlag Gesellschaft mbH & Co KG
Dr Karl Lueger-Ring 12, A-1014 Vienna
☎010 43 222 638735 Fax 010 43 222 638158

FOUNDED 1624. *Publishes* art, history, history of civilisation, humanities.

Bohmann Druck und Verlag GmbH & Co
Leberstrasse 122, A-1110 Vienna
☎010 43 222 741595
Fax 010 43 222 741595183

FOUNDED 1936. *Publishes* business, computers, travel, periodicals.

W. Braumüller, Universitäts-Verlagsbuchhandlung GmbH
Servitengasse 5, A-1092 Vienna
☎010 43 222 348124
Fax 010 43 222 3702805

FOUNDED 1783. *Publishes* agriculture, economics, education, history, general non-fiction, literature, philosophy, psychology, periodicals.

Carinthia, Universitätsverlag
Völkermarkter Ring 25, A-9020 Klagenfurt
☎010 43 463 5880210
Fax 010 43 463 5880105

FOUNDED 1893. *Publishes* art, fiction and religion.

Wilhelm Ennsthaler Verlag
Stadtplatz 26, A-4400 Steyr
☎010 43 7252 22053 Fax 010 43 7252 27089

FOUNDED 1880. *Publishes* belles lettres, history, natural health and poetry.

Europa Verlag GmbH
Altmannsdorfer Strasse 154-156, A-1232 Vienna
☎010 43 222 672622
Fax 010 43 222 672511300

FOUNDED 1946. *Publishes* belles lettres, literature, philosophy, social and political sciences, current affairs

hptH Verlagsgesellschaft mbH & Co KG
Frankgasse 4, A-1096 Vienna
☎010 43 222 437203
Fax 010 43 222 43720326

FOUNDED 1985. *Publishes* children's.

Landesverlag Buchverlag
Hafenstrasse 1-3, A-4020 Linz
☎010 43 732 276451/276236

FOUNDED 1872. *Publishes* art, biography, cookery, countryside, gift books, history, literature.

Leykam Buchverlagsgesellschaft mbH
Stempfergasse 3, A-8010 Graz
☎010 43 316 8166760
Fax 010 43 316 81667639

FOUNDED 1585. *Publishes* art, general fiction and textbooks.

Paul Neff, Verlag
Hackinger Strasse 52, A-1140 Vienna
☎010 43 222 940611
Fax 010 43 222 947641288

FOUNDED 1829. *Publishes* art, biography, general fiction, music.

Niederösterreichisches Pressehaus, Verlag
Gutenbergstrasse 12, A-3100 St Pölten
☎010 43 2742 61561

FOUNDED 1889. *Publishes* architecture, art, history, literature.

Orac Verlag Gesellschaft mbH
Schönbrunner Strasse 59-61, A-1050 Vienna
☎010 43 222 534520
Fax 010 43 222 53452227

FOUNDED 1946. *Publishes* cooking, economics, environment, general non-fiction, health, law, management, politics, sports.

Österreichischer Bundesverlag Gesellschaft mbH
Schwarzenbergstrasse 5, A-1010 Vienna 1
☎010 43 222 5122963

FOUNDED 1772. *Publishes* art, belles lettres, education materials, general fiction, general science, history, military history, music, reference, textbooks, children's.

Pinguin-Verlag Pawlowski GmbH
Lindenbühelweg 2, A-6021 Innsbruck
☎010 43 512 811830 Fax 010 43 512 893243

FOUNDED 1945. *Publishes* art, calendars, non-fiction, reference, children's.

Springer-Verlag
Mölkerbastei 5, A-1011 Vienna
☎010 43 222 5339614/18
Fax 010 43 222 638158

FOUNDED 1924. *Publishes* engineering, fundamental and natural sciences, law, medicine and textbooks (university).

Verlag Styria
Schönaugasse 64, A-8011 Graz
☎010 43 316 80630 Fax 010 43 316 8063-709

FOUNDED 1869. *Publishes* belles lettres, biography, current affairs, education, history, philosophy, reference, religion.

Rudolf Trauner, Verlag
Köglstrasse 14, A-4021 Linz
☎010 43 732 278241 Fax 010 43 732 283516

FOUNDED 1946. *Publishes* cookery, illustrated books, popular medicine, science, textbooks.

Verlagsanstalt Tyrolia Gesellschaft mbH
Exlgasse 20, A-6010 Innsbruck
☎010 43 512 81541 Fax 010 43 512 8154126

FOUNDED 1888. *Publishes* general non-fiction, illustrated books, schoolbooks, theology, tour guides, children's.

Paul Zsolnay Verlag GmbH
Prinz Eugen-Strasse 30, A-1040 Vienna
☎010 43 222 50576610
Fax 010 43 222 505766110

FOUNDED 1923. *Publishes* belles lettres, biography, general fiction, non-fiction, history, poetry.

Belgium

Editions Casterman
28 rue des Soeurs Noires, B-7500 Tournai
☎010 32 69 254211   Fax 010 32 69 254229

FOUNDED 1780. *Publishes* art, history, children's, comics.

Davidsfonds VZW
Blijde Inkomststr 79, B-3000 Leuven
☎010 32 16 221801   Fax 010 32 16 223532

FOUNDED 1875. *Publishes* arts, education, law, literature, philosophy, politics, religion, social sciences, children's.

Editions Delta SA
55 rue Scailquin, B-1030 Brussels
☎010 32 2 217 5555 Fax 010 32 2 217 9393

FOUNDED 1976. *Publishes* art, directories and yearbooks for EC and other European organisations, general literature, restaurant guides, who's whos.

Elsevier Librico NV
Leuvensesteenweg 325, B-1940 Woluwe Zauentem
☎010 32 2 7209090

FOUNDED 1960. *Publishes* art, biography, children's, documentaries, history, literature, nature, practical guides, reference, travel.

Facet NV
Wetstraat 63, B-2060 Antwerp 6
☎010 32 3 235 8183   Fax 010 32 3 236 6146

FOUNDED 1976. *Publishes* miscellaneous subjects, specialising in children's books.

Drukkerij Uitgeverij Lannoo
Kasteelstr 97, B-8880 Tielt
☎010 32 51 424211   Fax 010 32 51 401152

FOUNDED 1909. *Publishes* art, children's current affairs, biography, economics, general non-fiction, guide books, history, management, photography, poetry, politics, religion.

Uitgeversmaatschappij A Manteau NV
Isabellalei 76, B-2018 Antwerp
☎010 32 3 2301264   Fax 010 32 3 2301225

FOUNDED 1932. *Publishes* belles lettres, biography, general fiction, poetry, textbooks (secondary), literary periodicals.

Uitgeverij De Sikkel NV
Nijverheidsstr 8, B-2150 Malle
☎010 32 3 3124761   Fax 010 32 3 312586

FOUNDED 1919. *Publishes* education, music, sports, periodicals, software.

Standaard Uitgeverij
Belgielei 147a, B-2018 Antwerp
☎010 32 3 2395900   Fax 010 32 3 2308550

FOUNDED 1924. *Publishes* dictionaries, encyclopedias, economics, general fiction, general science, how-to, politics, textbooks, children's, comics.

Librairie Vanderlinden SA
17 rue des Grands-Carmes, B-1000 Brussels
☎010 32 2 5116140

FOUNDED 1897. *Publishes* art, general fiction, science, textbooks, children's.

Denmark

Amanda
49 Nörre Sögade, DK-1370 Copenhagen K
☎010 45 33 330121   Fax 010 45 33 150720

Publishes   handbooks,   non-fiction   and schoolbooks.

Carit Andersens Forlag A/S
Skudehavnsvej 27, DK-2100 Copenhagen Ø
☎010 45 31 291980   Fax 010 45 31 296090

Publishes fiction, illustrated books, limited editions, non-fiction, travel.

Forlaget Apostrof ApS
24 Berggreensgade, DK-2100 Copenhagen Ø
☎010 45 31 208420   Fax 010 45 31 208453

FOUNDED 1980. *Publishes* children's picture books, fiction, literature, humour, non-fiction, psychology.

Aschehoug Dansk Forlag A/S
7 Klosterrisvej, DK-2100 Copenhagen Ø
☎010 45 31 294422   Fax 010 45 39 271010

FOUNDED 1914. *Publishes* textbooks.

Bogans Forlag
8 Kastaniebakken, DK-3540 Lynge
☎010 45 42 188055   Fax 010 45 42 188769

FOUNDED 1974. *Publishes* general non-fiction paperbacks, occult, popular science.

Bonniers Bøger A/S
130 Strandboulevarden, DK-2100 Copenhagen Ø
☎010 45 31 295500   Fax 010 45 31 184366

FOUNDED 1989. *Publishes* book series, general fiction and non-fiction.

Borgens Forlag A/S
33 Valbygaardsvej, DK-2500 Valby
☎010 45 31 462100   Fax 010 45 36 441488

FOUNDED 1948. *Publishes* art, children's computers, crafts and leisure, education, general fiction and non-fiction, handbooks, health and social science, religion, textbooks.

Forlaget Forum A/S
4 Snaregade, DK-1205 Copenhagen K
☎010 45 33 147714   Fax 010 45 33 147791

FOUNDED 1940. *Publishes* fiction, general, history, mysteries, children's.

Forlaget Fremad A/S
1 Kronprinsengade, PO Box 2252, DK-1019
Copenhagen K
☏010 45 33 934340

FOUNDED 1912. *Publishes* general fiction, textbooks, children's and periodicals.

FSRs Forlag
8 Kronprinsessegade, DK-1306 Copenhagen K
☏010 45 33 939191   Fax 010 45 33 110913

Publishes economics, law, accountancy and taxation, management, textbooks (university).

G.E.C. Gad Publishers
32 Vimmelskaftet, DK-1161 Copenhagen K
☏010 45 33 150558   Fax 010 45 33 123825

FOUNDED 1855. *Publishes* art, education, general science, law, management, psychology, reference, religion and textbooks.

Gjellerup & Gad Publishers Ltd
32 Vimmelskaftet, DK-1161 Copenhagen K
☏010 45 33 150558

FOUNDED 1884. *Publishes* educational, reference and textbooks (all levels).

Grafisk Forlag A/S
7 Klosterrisvej, DK-2100 Copenhagen Ø
☏010 45 39 272744   Fax 010 45 39 271010

FOUNDED 1941. *Publishes* children's, easy readers and textbooks.

Gyldendalske Boghandel, Nordisk Forlag A/S
3 Klareboderne, DK-1001 Copenhagen K
☏010 45 33 110775   Fax 010 45 33 110323

FOUNDED 1770. *Publishes* general fiction, belles lettres, poetry, biography, history, how-to, music, art, philosophy, reference, medicine, psychology, general and social sciences, textbooks (all levels) and educational materials, audiovisual software and children's.

P. Haase & Søns Forlag A/S
8 Løvstraede, DK-1152 Copenhagen K
☏010 45 33 115999   Fax 010 45 33 115959

FOUNDED 1877. *Publishes* alternative health, audiovisual aids, children's, fiction, education, humour, non-fiction and occult.

Hekla Forlag
61A & B Store Kongensgade, PO Box 9011, DK-1022 Copenhagen K
☏010 45 33 911933   Fax 010 45 33 911949

FOUNDED 1979. *Publishes* general fiction and non-fiction.

Hernovs Forlag
14-16 Bredgade, DK-1260 Copenhagen K
☏010 45 33 156284   Fax 010 45 33 156209

FOUNDED 1941. *Publishes* general fiction, non-fiction and children's.

Holkenfeldts Forlag A/S
28 C Emdrupvej, DK-2100 Copenhagen Ø
☏010 45 31 184590

Publishes general fiction, non-fiction and reference.

Høst & Søns Forlag A/S
35 Nørre Søgade, PO Box 2212, DK-1018
Copenhagen K
☏010 45 33 153031   Fax 010 45 33 155155

FOUNDED 1836. *Publishes* Danish guidebooks, hobbies and crafts, languages, nature, travel, reference, children's.

Forlaget Hovedland
19 Stenvej, DK-8270 Højbjerg
☏010 45 86 276500   Fax 010 45 86 272928

Publishes fiction, non-fiction, ecology, social sciences.

Forlaget Per Kofod ApS
7 Krystalgade, DK-1172 Copenhagen K
☏010 45 33 150347   Fax 010 45 33 931493

Publishes fiction, non-fiction, children's illustrated art.

Komma & Clausen
28 C Emdrupvej, DK-2100 Copenhagen Ø
☏010 45 31 183477   Fax 010 45 31 202075

Publishes popular reference.

Morten A. Korch's Forlag
2 Aurehøjvej, DK-2900 Hellerup
☏010 45 31 620859

Publishes fiction and children's.

Det Ny Lademann A/S
37 Gerdasgade, DK-2500 Valby
☎010 45 36 441120   Fax 010 45 36 442236

FOUNDED 1954. *Publishes* general non-fiction and encyclopedias.

Lindhardt and Ringhof
14 Kristianiagade, DK-2100 Copenhagen K
☎010 45 35 434455   Fax 010 45 35 436520

FOUNDED 1971. *Publishes* general fiction & non-fiction.

Lohses Forlag
25 Korskaervej, DK-7000 Fredericia
☎010 45 75 934455   Fax 010 45 75 5926146

FOUNDED 1868. *Publishes* religion and children's.

Mallings ApS
638 Strandvesen, DK-2930 Klampenborg
☎010 45 31 643555

FOUNDED 1975. *Publishes* education, children's, picture books.

Munksgaard International Publishers Ltd
35 Nørre Søgade, PO Box 2148, DK-1016 Copenhagen K
☎010 45 33 127030   Fax 010 45 33 129387

FOUNDED 1917. *Publishes* fiction, medicine, nursing, dentistry, psychology, schoolbooks, scientific journals and software.

Rasmus Navers Forlag A/S
8 Løvstraede, DK-1152 Copenhagen K
☎010 45 33 115999   Fax 010 45 33 115959

Publishes fiction and humour.

Nyt Nordisk Forlag Arnold Busck A/S
49 Købmagergade, DK-1150 Copenhagen K
☎010 45 33 111103   Fax 010 45 33 934490

FOUNDED 1896. *Publishes* general fiction, biography, history, how-to, music, art, philosophy, reference, religion, medicine, psychology, general and social sciences, textbooks (university, secondary and primary).

Jörgen Paludans Forlag ApS
10 Fiolstraede, DK-1171 Copenhagen K
☎010 45 33 150675   Fax 010 45 33 150676

Publishes economics, education, history, non-fiction, political science, psychology, reference.

Politikens Forlag A/S
26 Vestergade, DK-1456 Copenhagen K
☎010 45 33 112122   Fax 010 45 33 932152

FOUNDED 1946. *Publishes* art, games, general non-fiction, how-to, history and documentary, hobbies, maps and atlases, music, nature study, sports, travel.

Hans Reitzels Forlag A/S
35 Nørre Søgade, PO Box 1073, DK-1008 Copenhagen K
☎010 45 33 140451   Fax 010 45 33 155155

FOUNDED 1949. *Publishes* Hans Christian Andersen, philosophy, psychology and sexology.

Rhodos, International Science and Art Publishers
Niels Brocks Gård, 36 Strandgade, DK-1401 Copenhagen K
☎010 45 31 543080   Fax 010 45 31 954742

FOUNDED 1959. *Publishes* art, fiction, general and social sciences and handbooks.

Rosinante/Munksgaard
35 Nørre Søgade, PO Box 2148, DK-1016 Copenhagen K
☎010 45 33 127030   Fax 010 45 33 936569

FOUNDED 1982. *Publishes* cookery, economics, fiction (Danish and translated), general non-fiction and politics, including immigration.

Samlerens Forlag A/S
4 Snaregade, DK-1205 Copenhagen K
☎010 45 33 131023   Fax 010 45 33 144314

FOUNDED 1942. *Publishes* biography, contemporary history and politics, general fiction.

Det Schönbergske Forlag A/S
5 Landemaerket, DK-1119 Copenhagen K
☎010 45 33 113066   Fax 010 45 33 330045

FOUNDED 1857. *Publishes* art, belles lettres, poetry, biography, general fiction and non-fiction, history, philosophy, textbooks (all levels).

Spektrum Forlagsaktieselskab
14 Skindergade, DK-1159 Copenhagen K
☎010 45 33 326322   Fax 010 45 33 326454
FOUNDED 1990. *Publishes* non fiction only.

Strandbergs Forlag ApS
475 Vedbaek Strandvej, DK-2950 Vedbaek
☎010 45 42 894760   Fax 010 45 42 894701
FOUNDED 1861. *Publishes* computer science, cultural history, humour, travel.

Tiderne Skifter
14 Skindergade, DK-1159 Copenhagen K
☎010 45 33 124284   Fax 010 45 33 144205
FOUNDED 1979. *Publishes* criticism, fiction, photography and arts, sexual and cultural politics.

Forlaget Vindrose A/S
33 Valbygaardsvej, DK-2500 Valby
☎010 45 31 462100   Fax 010 45 36 441488
FOUNDED 1980. *Publishes* belles lettres, general fiction, poetry, science and social science.

Forlaget Wøldike K/S
13 Staegers Alle, DK-2000 Frederiksberg
☎010 45 31 863954   Fax 010 45 38 337080
FOUNDED 1969. *Publishes* fiction and non-fiction.

France

Editions Actes Sud
Passage du Mejan, F-13200 Arles
☎010 33 9049 8691   Fax 010 33 9096 9525
FOUNDED 1978. *Publishes* biography, essays, literature, poetry, theatre.

Editions Arthaud SA
20 rue Monsieur le Prince, F-75006 Paris
☎010 33 1 4329 1220
Fax 010 33 1 4329 2148
FOUNDED 1890. *Publishes* arts, history, literature, mountaineering, sailing, sports and travel.

Editions Aubier-Montaigne SA
13 quai Conti, F-75006 Paris
☎010 33 1 4326 5559

Fax 010 33 1 4329 2148
FOUNDED 1924. *Publishes* belles lettres, history, languages, philosophy, poetry, psychology, reference, religion, sociology, textbooks (university).

André Balland
33 rue St-André-des-Arts, F-75006 Paris
☎010 33 1 4325 7440
Fax 010 33 1 4633 5621
FOUNDED 1966. *Publishes* biography, documentary, fiction, humour.

Editions Pierre Belfond
216 blvd St-Germain, F-75007 Paris
☎010 33 1 4544 3823
Fax 010 33 1 4544 9804
FOUNDED 1963. *Publishes* art, belles lettres, bibliography, biography, general fiction, history, music and poetry.

Editions Belin
8 rue Férou, F-75278 Paris 06
☎010 33 1 4634 2142
Fax 010 33 1 4325 1829
FOUNDED 1777. *Publishes* educational material, children's, general science, textbooks (secondary and primary), literary and scientific periodicals.

Editions Bordas
17 rue Rémy-Dumoncel, F-75661 Paris
☎010 33 1 4279 6200
Fax 010 33 1 4322 8518
FOUNDED 1946. *Publishes* dictionaries, encyclopedias, education, general non-fiction and reference.

Editions Calmann-Lévy SA
3 rue Auber, F-75009 Paris
☎010 33 1 4742 3833
Fax 010 33 1 4742 7781
FOUNDED 1836. *Publishes* biography, economics, general fiction, history, humour, memoirs, philosophy, psychology, how-to, science fiction, social sciences, sports.

Editions Casterman
66 rue Bonaparte, F-75006 Paris
☎010 33 1 4325 2005
Fax 010 33 1 4354 5424

FOUNDED 1780. *Publishes* architecture, children's books and albums, diaries, economics, fiction, music, cartoons, strips, painting, photography, cinema, politics, practical living, poetry, religion, urban questions, records.

La Découverte
1 pl Paul-Painlevé, F-75005 Paris
☎010 33 1 4633 4116
Fax 010 33 1 4633 4677

FOUNDED 1959. *Publishes* belles lettres, poetry, history, philosophy, political economy.

Librairie Delagrave Sàrl
15 rue Soufflot, F-75240 Paris 05
☎010 33 1 4325 8866
Fax 010 33 1 4634 1133

FOUNDED 1865. *Publishes* education, children's, general science, technical and textbooks.

Editions Denoël Sàrl
30 rue de l'Université, F-75007 Paris
☎010 33 1 4261 5085
Fax 010 33 1 4261 1490

Publishes art, deluxe editions, documents, economics, general and science fiction, history, philosophy, political science, psychology, reference, sports, thrillers.

La Différence
103 rue la Fayette, F-75010 Paris
☎010 33 1 4285 4311
Fax 010 33 1 4874 2043

FOUNDED 1976. *Publishes* art, essays, French and foreign literature, poetry.

Librairie Arthème Fayard
75 rue des Sts-Pères, F-75006 Paris
☎010 33 1 4544 3845
Fax 010 33 1 4222 4017

FOUNDED 1854. *Publishes* atlases, biography, general fiction, history, general human and social sciences, music, religion, spirituality, reference, technology.

Flammarion et Cie
26 rue de Racine, F-75278 Paris 06
☎010 33 1 4051 3100
Fax 010 33 1 4329 2148

FOUNDED 1875. *Publishes* general fiction and non-fiction, belles lettres, poetry, biography, history, how-to, photography, art, philosophy, reference, economics, general and social science, textbooks (university), education, medicine, children's.

Editions Gallimard
5 rue Sébastien-Bottin, F-75007 Paris
☎010 33 1 4544 3919
Fax 010 33 1 4544 9919

FOUNDED 1911. *Publishes* art, belles lettres, poetry, biography, general fiction, history, music, philosophy, children's.

Les Editions Gautier-Languereau SA
44 rue La Boëtie, F-75008 Paris
☎010 33 1 4562 1052
Fax 010 33 1 4561 0792

FOUNDED 1885. *Publishes* general fiction, how-to and children's.

Editions J Glenat SA
6 rue Lieutenant Chanaron, BP 177, F-38008 Grenoble
☎010 33 7687 3758   Fax 010 33 7687 8210

FOUNDED 1974. *Publishes* cookery, sport, travel, cartoons strips (adventure, erotica, children's humour, science fiction, thrillers).

Société des Editions Grasset et Fasquelle
61 rue des Sts-Pères, F-75006 Paris
☎010 33 1 4544 3814
Fax 010 33 1 4222 6418

FOUNDED 1907. *Publishes* belles lettres, general fiction and non-fiction, philosophy and children's.

Librairie Gründ
60 rue Mazarine, F-75006 Paris 6
☎010 33 1 4329 8740
Fax 010 33 1 4329 4986

FOUNDED 1880. *Publishes* arts and art reference, gift books, how-to, nature, animals, travel, children's.

Hachette
79 blvd St-Germain, F-75288 Paris 06
☎010 33 1 4634 8634

FOUNDED 1826. *Publishes* general fiction, nonfiction, history, how-to, architecture, art, music, travel, reference, education, science, textbooks, bibliography, engineering, music, politics, economics, social science, philosophy, sports, languages, children's.

Editions Hatier SA
8 rue d'Assas, F-75006 Paris
☎010 33 1 4954 4883
Fax 010 33 1 4049 0045

FOUNDED 1880. *Publishes* art, chess, children's fiction, cinema, history, humanities, literature, nature, tour guides.

Pierre Horay Editeur
22 bis passage Dauphine, F-75006 Paris
☎010 33 1 4354 5390
Fax 010 33 1 4051 0637

FOUNDED 1946. *Publishes* art, music, belles lettres, biography, general fiction, history, how-to, children's.

Editions Klincksieck
11 rue de Lille, F-75007 Paris
☎010 33 1 4260 3825
Fax 010 33 1 4296 4063

FOUNDED 1842. *Publishes* archaeology, belles lettres, literature, music, general and social sciences, history, linguistics and philology.

Editions Robert Laffont
6 pl St-Sulpice, F-75279 Paris 06
☎010 33 1 4329 1233
Fax 010 33 1 4327 1412

FOUNDED 1941. *Publishes* general fiction, history, documentary, philosophy, religion, art, music, biography, medicine, general and social sciences, psychology, textbooks, translations.

Librairie Larousse
17 rue du Montparnasse, F-75298 Paris
☎010 33 1 4544 3817
Fax 010 33 1 4544 1524

FOUNDED 1852. *Publishes* dictionaries, encyclopedias, general and social sciences, linguistics, reference, technical, textbooks, children's.

Editions Jean-Claude Lattès
17 rue Jacob, F-75006 Paris
☎010 33 1 4634 0310
Fax 010 33 1 4325 3047

FOUNDED 1968. *Publishes* biography, documents, general fiction and non-fiction, how-to, music.

Les Editions Magnard Sàrl
122 blvd St-Germain, F-75006 Paris
☎010 33 1 4326 3952
Fax 010 33 1 4633 9604

FOUNDED 1933. *Publishes* textbooks, educational, international series in basic French and children's.

Masson Editeur
120 blvd St-Germain, F-75280 Paris 06
☎010 33 1 4634 2160
Fax 010 33 1 4329 5718

FOUNDED 1804. *Publishes* economics, law, medicine, scientific and technical and social science.

Michel de Maule
3 rue Honoré-Chevalier, F-75006 Paris
☎010 33 1 4544 1765
Fax 010 33 1 4548 6537

FOUNDED 1986. *Publishes* fine arts, general literature in French and foreign languages, music, musical reviews, musical scores and philosophy.

Mercure de France SA
26 rue de Condé, F-75006 Paris
☎010 33 1 4329 2113

FOUNDED 1891. *Publishes* belles lettres, general fiction, poetry, history, philosophy, psychology, social science.

A M Métaillié
5 rue de Savoie, F-75006 Paris
☎010 33 1 4326 6010
Fax 010 33 1 4337 0234

FOUNDED 1979. *Publishes* ethnology, sociology and foreign literature.

Michelin et Cie (Services de Tourisme)
46 ave de Breteuil, F-75324 Paris 07
☎010 33 1 4566 1234
Fax 010 33 1 4566 1163

FOUNDED 1900. *Publishes* atlases, maps, travel and tourist guides in various languages.

Les Editions de Minuit SA
7 rue Bernard-Palissy, F-75006 Paris
☏010 33 1 4222 3794

FOUNDED 1942. *Publishes* general fiction, literature, philosophy, social science.

Fernand Nathan
9 rue Méchain, F-75014 Paris
☏010 33 1 4587 5000
Fax 010 33 1 4331 2169

FOUNDED 1881. *Publishes* reference, dictionaries, art, philosophy, textbooks, psychology, general and social sciences, guidebooks, nature, history, education and children's paperbacks.

Paris Musées
31 rue des Francs-Bourgeois, F-75004 Paris
☏010 33 1 4276 6795
Fax 010 33 1 4276 6622

FOUNDED 1985. *Publishes* architecture, decorative and fine arts, furniture, fashion and costume, history of Paris and photography.

Les Presses de la Cité
12 Ave d'Italie, F-75013 Paris
☏010 33 1 4416 0500
Fax 010 33 1 4416 0511

FOUNDED 1947. *Publishes* French and foreign literature, history, biography, anthropology, essays, science fiction, popular fiction, war, how-to, travel, children's.

Presses Universitaires de France (PUF)
108 blvd St-Germain, F-75006 Paris 06
☏010 33 1 4634 1201
Fax 010 33 1 4634 6540

FOUNDED 1921. *Publishes* biography, history, geography, music, art, philosophy, reference, religion, engineering, psychology, medicine, general, social and political science, textbooks (university).

Editions du Seuil
27 rue Jacob, F-75261 Paris 06
☏010 33 1 4046 5050
Fax 010 33 1 4329 0829

FOUNDED 1935. *Publishes* general fiction, literature, poetry, biography, history, how-to, music, art, philosophy, religion, psychology, general and social sciences, textbooks (university), politics, illustrated books and children's.

Les Editions de la Table Ronde
9 rue Huysmans, F-75006 Paris
☏010 33 1 4222 2891
Fax 010 33 1 4222 0342

FOUNDED 1944. *Publishes* belles lettres, biography, general fiction and non-fiction, history, psychology, religion, social science.

Librairie Vuibert SA
63 blvd St-Germain, F-75005 Paris
☏010 33 1 4325 6100
Fax 010 33 1 4325 7586

FOUNDED 1877. *Publishes* children's, sciences, economics, law, mathematics, physics and schoolbooks.

Germany

Bauverlag GmbH
Postfach 1460, D-6200 Wiesbaden 1
☏010 49 611 791030   Fax 010 49 611 791285

FOUNDED 1929. *Publishes* architecture, building and surveying, engineering, energy and environment, dictionaries, periodicals.

Verlag C H Beck
Postfach 400340, D-8000 Munich 40
☏010 49 89 381890   Fax 010 49 89 38189402

FOUNDED 1763. *Publishes* archaeology, history, literary history, social sciences, philosophy, theology, economics, law, art, music, linguistics, illustrated books, classics, popular non-fiction, anthropology.

Bertelsmann AG
Carl-Bertelsmann-Str 270, D-4830 Gütersloh 1
☏010 49 5241 801   Fax 010 49 89 4318908

FOUNDED 1835. *Publishes* general fiction and non-fiction, children's biography, current affairs, arts, foreign works in translation.

B L V Verlagsgesellschaft mbH
Postfach 400320, D-8000 Munich 40
☎010 49 89 127050 Fax 010 49 89 12705354

FOUNDED 1946. *Publishes* nature guides, gardening, biology, agricultural textbooks, horses, sport and fitness, cars and motorcycles, mountaineering, hiking, cookery, health, education.

Verlag G Braun GmbH
Postfach 1709, D-7500 Karlsruhe
☎010 49 721 1650 Fax 010 49 721 165227

Publishes general science, medicine, textbooks (secondary) and periodicals.

F A Brockhaus
Dudenstr 6, D-6800 Mannheim 1
☎010 49 621 390101 Fax 010 49 621 3901389

FOUNDED 1805 *Publishes* dictionaries, encyclopedias, biography, history, fiction, nature, general science, music, travel.

Cornelsen und Oxford University Press GmbH
Mecklenburgische Str 53, D-1000 Berlin 33
☎010 49 30 829960 Fax 010 49 30 82996299

FOUNDED 1971. *Publishes* English language teaching (all levels).

Verlag Harri Deutsch
Gräfstr 47, D-6000 Frankfurt am Main 90
☎010 49 69 775021 Fax 010 49 69 7073739

FOUNDED 1960. *Publishes* agriculture and natural sciences, technical, reference, mathematics, economics, textbooks, language dictionaries and chess.

Verlag Moritz Diesterweg
Postfach 110651, D-6000 Frankfurt am Main 1
☎010 49 69 420810 Fax 010 49 69 42081100

FOUNDED 1860. *Publishes* education, textbooks (all levels), social science and psychology.

Droemersche Verlagsanstalt Th Knaur Nachf
Postfach 800480, D-8000 Munich 80
☎010 49 89 92710 Fax 010 49 89 9271168

FOUNDED 1901. *Publishes* general fiction, nonfiction, children's, reference, dictionaries, current

affairs, popular science, how-to, self-help and atlases.

D T V Deutscher Taschenbuch Verlag GmbH & Co KG
Postfach 400422, D-800 Munich 40
☎010 49 89 3817060 Fax 010 49 89 346428

FOUNDED 1961. *Publishes* general fiction, biography, belles lettres, art, music, poetry, history, philosophy, religion, medicine, psychology, general and social sciences, classical literature, children's cartoons, postcard books, maps and travel guides, two-language editions.

DuMont Buchverlag GmbH & Co KG
Postfach 100468, D-5000 Cologne 1
☎010 49 221 20531 Fax 010 49 221 2053281

FOUNDED 1956. *Publishes* archaeology, art, illustrated books, games, guidebooks and travel.

Econ-Verlag GmbH
Postfach 300321, D-4000 Düsseldorf 30
☎010 49 211 439060 Fax 010 49 211 4390668

Publishes general fiction, biography, history, politics, reference, religion, music, psychology, medicine, general and social sciences, art, archeology, travel, audiovisual teaching aids.

Falken-Verlag GmbH
Postfach 1120, D-6272 Niedernhausen-Ts
☎010 49 6127 7020 Fax 010 49 6127 702133

FOUNDED 1923. *Publishes* herbalism, popular health, natural history, cookery, gardening, how-to, photography, popular computing, motorcycles, travel, videos.

S Fischer Verlag GmbH
Postfach 700355, D-6000 Frankfurt am Main 70
☎010 49 69 60620 Fax 010 49 69 6062214

FOUNDED 1886. *Publishes* general fiction, nonfiction, biography, history, philosophy, social science, psychology, poetry, belles lettres, music, art, popular reference.

Walter de Gruyter & Co
Genthiner Str 13, D-1000 Berlin 30
☎010 49 30 260050 Fax 010 49 30 26005222

FOUNDED 1919. *Publishes* anthropology, natural science, philosophy, theology, law, history, medicine, classical studies, literary criticism, business studies, technology, works in English and French.

Carl Hanser Verlag

Kolbergerstr 22, Postfach 860420, D-8000 Munich 86

☏010 49 89 926940   Fax 010 49 89 984809

FOUNDED 1928. *Publishes* general fiction, biography, belles lettres, poetry, general science, philosophy, chemistry computer science, biotechnology, dentistry, business management.

Rudolf Haufe Verlag GmbH & Co KG

Postfach 740, D-7800 Freiburg im Breisgau

☏010 49 761 36830 Fax 010 49 761 3683236

FOUNDED 1934. *Publishes* business management, finance, law, social science, textbooks (university)

Verlag Herder GmbH & Co KG

Hermann-Herder-Str 4, Postfach, D-7800 Freiburg im Breisgau

☏010 49 761 27171   Fax 010 49 761 2717520

FOUNDED 1801. *Publishes* biography, belles lettres, photography, history, philosophy, psychology, theology, art, reference, education, children's.

Wilhelm Heyne Verlag

Postfach 201204, D-8000 Munich

☏010 49 89 2317170 Fax 010 49 89 2800943

FOUNDED 1934. *Publishes* general fiction, mystery, romance, westerns, science fiction, biography, history, occult, psychology, how-to, film, cookery, cartoons, poetry.

Hoffmann und Campe Verlag

Harvestehuder Weg 45, D-2000 Hamburg 13

☏010 49 40 441881 Fax 010 49 40 27173164

FOUNDED 1781. *Publishes* general fiction, biography, belles lettres, poetry, history, art, illustrated books, philosophy, psychology, music, general and social sciences, marine history.

S Karger GmbH

Postfach 1724, D-8034 Germering, Munich

☏010 49 89 843035   Fax 010 49 89 8418083

FOUNDED 1890. *Publishes* natural science, medicine and psychology.

Klett-Cotta Verlag

Postfach 809, D-7000 Stuttgart 1

☏010 49 711 66720   Fax 010 49 711 628053

FOUNDED 1977. *Publishes* fiction, history, art, psychology and related fields, education, ecology, history, sociology.

Knorr und Hirth Verlag GmbH

Hannoversche Str 41, Postfach 52, D-3016 Seelze

☏010 49 5137 70370 Fax 010 49 5137 703799

FOUNDED 1894. *Publishes* almanacs, arts, geography and travel guides in major European languages and Japanese.

Verlag W Kohlhammer GmbH

Postfach 800430, D-7000 Stuttgart 80

☏010 49 711 78631   Fax 010 49 711 7863263

FOUNDED 1866. *Publishes* art, architecture, history, literary history, economics, law, theology, medicine, electronics, engineering, natural science, humanities, public administration, travel.

Langenscheidt KG

Postfach 401120, D-8000 Munich 40

☏010 49 89 360960   Fax 010 49 89 363862

FOUNDED 1856. *Publishes* language phrase books and textbooks, bilingual dictionaries (including electronic format) German as a foreign language and audiovisual materials.

Gustav Lübbe Verlag GmbH

Postfach 200127, D-5060 Bergisch Gladbach 2

☏010 49 2202 1210

FOUNDED 1856. *Publishes* general fiction and non-fiction, thrillers, fantasy, biography, archaeology, history and how-to.

Mairs Geographischer Verlag

Marco-Polo-Str 1, D-7302 Ostfildern 4

☏010 49 711 45020 Fax 010 49 711 4502201

FOUNDED 1948. *Publishes* atlases, maps and tour guides (Baedeker/Marco Polo).

Verlag Moderne Industrie AG & Co

Postfach 1761, D-8910 Landsberg am Lech

☏010 49 8191 1251 Fax 010 49 8191 125309

FOUNDED 1952. *Publishes* advertising, marketing, management and data processing.

Mosaik Verlag

Postfach 800360, D-8000 Munich 80
☎010 49 89 431890 Fax 010 49 89 43189555

Publishes cookery, gardening, crafts, health and medicine, field guides, sports, reference

R Oldenbourg Verlag GmbH

Postfach 801360, D-8000 Munich 80
☎010 49 89 4112248 Fax 010 49 89 4112207

FOUNDED 1858. *Publishes* science and technology, social science, school textbooks, reference, history, liberal arts, psychology, periodicals.

Verlag Paul Parey

Postfach 106304, D-2000 Hamburg 1
☎010 49 40 339690/30
Fax 010 49 40 33969198/9

FOUNDED 1848. *Publishes* biology, animal husbandry, veterinary medicine, horticulture, natural medicine, water management and environment, hunting and fishing, riding, technical and scientific journals.

Prisma-Verlag

Postfach 1461, D-7010 Leipzig
☎010 49 41 281411

FOUNDED 1957. *Publishes* archaeology, art and culture, illustrated books (many in English and Russian) and historical fiction.

Rowohlt Tashenbuch

Hamburger Strasse 17, Postfach 1349, W-2057 Reinbeck
☎010 49 40 72720   Fax 010 49 40 7272319

FOUNDED 1953. *Publishes* fiction and non-fiction including popular non-fiction works, plus children's and foreign literature in translation.

K G Saur Verlag GmbH & Co KG

Postfach 711009, D-8000 Munich 7
☎010 49 89 769020 Fax 010 49 89 76902150

FOUNDED 1948. *Publishes* reference, documentation and information science, data processing.

Schroedel Schulbuchverlag GmbH

Postfach 810760, D-3000 Hanover 81
☎010 49 511 838880 Fax 010 49 511 8388343

FOUNDED 1981. *Publishes* school textbooks.

Edition Helmut Sigloch GmbH & Co

Zeppelinstrasse 35A, D-7118 Kunzelsau
☎010 49 7940 140100
Fax 010 49 7940 140108

FOUNDED 1972. *Publishes* illustrated non-fiction, including cookery, in three languages.

Springer-Verlag GmbH & Co KG

Tiergartenstr 17, D-6900 Heidelberg
☎010 49 30 82070   Fax 010 49 30 8214091

FOUNDED 1842. *Publishes* biology, chemistry, medicine, psychology, physics, mathematics, computers, engineering, economics, philosophy, law, reference, scientific periodicals (German and English).

Suhrkamp Verlag

Postfach 101945, D-6000 Frankfurt am Main
☎010 49 69 756010 Fax 010 49 69 75601522

FOUNDED 1950. *Publishes* general fiction, biography, belles lettres, poetry, philosophy, German–Jewish writing, children's general science, education, psychology.

Georg Thieme Verlag

Postfach 104853, D-7000 Stuttgart 30
☎010 49 711 89310 Fax 010 49 711 8931298

FOUNDED 1886. *Publishes* (many in English) earth and biosciences, chemistry, medicine, dentistry, veterinary periodicals.

K. Thienemanns Verlag

Blumenstrasse 36, D-7000 Stuttgart
☎010 49 711 210550 Fax 010 49 711 2105539

FOUNDED 1849. *Publishes* fiction, non-fiction and children's, including picture books.

Buchverlage Ullstein GmbH

Thomas-Wimmer-Ring 11, D-8000 Munich 22
☎010 49 30 25913570
Fax 010 49 30 25913523

FOUNDED 1903. *Publishes* fiction, biography, belles lettres, poetry, music, art, history, ethnology, politics, militaria, travel, popular science, social sciences, education.

Urban und Schwarzenberg GmbH

Postfach 202440, D-8000 Munich 2
☎010 49 89 53830   Fax 010 49 89 5383221

FOUNDED 1866. *Publishes* medicine and university textbooks.

V C H Verlagsgesellschaft mbH
Postfach 101161, D-6940 Weinheim
℡010 49 6201 6020   Fax 010 49 6201 602328

FOUNDED 1921. *Publishes* medicine and biomedicine, biotechnology, chemistry, physics, computer science, civil engineering, architecture, industrial property law, history, art, monographs, university textbooks, periodicals.

VEB Verlag Enzyklopädie Leipzig
Postfach 130, DDR-7010 Leipzig
℡010 49 41 7801

FOUNDED 1956. *Publishes* foreign language textbooks and dictionaries.

Vogel-Verlag KG
Postfach 6740, D-8700 Würzburg 1
℡010 49 931 4180   Fax 010 49 931 4182100

FOUNDED 1891. *Publishes* agriculture, electronic, mechanical engineering, metalworking, cars, management, foreign language publications (in 14 languages) and periodicals.

Georg Westermann Verlag GmbH
Postfach 5367, D-3300 Brunswick
℡010 49 531 7080   Fax 010 49 531 796569

FOUNDED 1838. *Publishes* non-fiction and periodicals.

Italy

Adelphi Edizioni SpA
Via S. Giovanni sul Muro 14, I-20121 Milan
℡010 39 2 72000975 Fax 010 39 2 89010337

FOUNDED 1962. *Publishes* general fiction, biography, belles lettres, art, philosophy, religion, psychology, general science, music.

Editore Armando Armando SRL
Piazza Sidney Sonnino 13, I-00153 Rome
℡010 39 6 5894525   Fax 010 39 6 5818564

FOUNDED 1963. *Publishes* social sciences, philosophy, psychology, education, linguistics, nursing, politics, textbooks, children's.

Verlagsanstalt Athesia
Postfach 417, I-39100 Bolzano-Bozen
℡010 39 471 925111 Fax 010 39 471 925229

FOUNDED 1907. *Publishes* guidebooks, maps, travel, mountaineering (also in German), history, cookery, art, law, poetry, periodicals, textbooks.

Bompiana
Via Mecenate 91, I-20138 Milan
℡010 39 2 50951   Fax 010 39 2 5065361

FOUNDED 1929. *Publishes* fiction, children's, nonfiction, art, theatre, science, dictionaries, encyclopedias.

Bulzoni Editore SRL (Le Edizioni Universitarie d'Italia)
Via De Liburni 14, I-00185 Rome
℡010 39 6 4455207   Fax 010 39 6 4450355

FOUNDED 1969. *Publishes* fiction, literature, essays, philosophy, arts, theatre, cinema, science, sociology, engineering, law, linguistics, textbooks (university)

Edizioni Calderini
Emilia Lev 31, I-40139 Bologna
℡010 39 51 492211   Fax 010 39 51 490200

FOUNDED 1952. *Publishes* arts, crafts, sport, cookery, travel guides, architecture, natural sciences, computer science, mechanics, electrical engineering, textbooks (university and secondary).

Capitol Editrice Dischi CEB
Via Minghetti 17/19, I-40057 Cadriano di Granarolo Emilia (Bologna)
℡010 39 51 766612/766421/2

FOUNDED 1956. *Publishes* general fiction, biography, children's, textbooks (secondary and primary), reference, medicine, educational materials, audiovisual aids.

Nuova Casa Editrice Licinio Cappelli SpA
Via Marsili 9, I-40124 Bologna
℡010 39 51 239060   Fax 010 39 51 239286

FOUNDED 1851. *Publishes* general fiction, film scripts, drama, music, biography, belles lettres, poetry, art, history, philosophy, religion, children's, reference, textbooks (all levels).

CEDAM (Casa Editrice Dr A Milani)
Via Jappelli 5/6, I-35121 Padua
☎010 39 49 656677   Fax 010 39 49 8752900

FOUNDED 1902. *Publishes* arts, literature, belles lettres, philosophy, medicine, law, general and social sciences, philosophy, politics, engineering, textbooks and languages.

Città Nuova Editrice
Via degli Scipioni 265, I-00192 Rome
☎010 39 6 3216212   Fax 010 39 6 3207185

FOUNDED 1959. *Publishes* education, textbooks (secondary), religion, philosophy, psychology, sociology, children's.

CLEUP (Cooperative Libraria Editrice dell'Università di Padova)
Via G Prati 19, I-35122 Padua
☎010 39 49 650261   Fax 010 39 49 8753496

FOUNDED 1962. *Publishes* engineering, linguistics, statistics, psychology, psychoanalysis, science, medicine, political science, textbooks (university).

De Agostini Ragazzi SpA
Via Decembrio 30, I-20137 Milan
☎010 39 2 55012236 Fax 010 39 2 55018050

FOUNDED 1955. *Publishes* children's fiction and non-fiction.

Edizioni E – Elle SRL
Via San Francesco 62, I-34133 Trieste
☎010 39 40 772376   Fax 010 39 40 772214

FOUNDED 1984. *Publishes* books for children.

E C I G (Edizioni Culturali Internazionali Genova)
Via Caffaro 19/10, I-16124 Genoa
☎010 39 10 208800   Fax 010 39 10 208664

FOUNDED 1971. *Publishes* literature, essays, philosophy, psychology, textbooks (university).

Gruppo Editoriale Fabbri SpA
Via Mecenate 91, I-20138 Milan
☎010 39 2 50951 Fax 010 39 2 5065361

FOUNDED 1945. *Publishes* general encyclopedias, textbooks (secondary and primary), reference, arts, music, medicine, science, history, nature, leisure, children's.

Aldo Francisci Editore
Via Puccini 27, I-35031 Abano Terme (PD)
☎010 39 49 810956   Fax 010 39 49 810956

FOUNDED 1977. *Publishes* literature, poetry, history, philosophy, psychiatry, sociology, politics, economics, health, art, archaeology, local guidebooks, library science, periodicals.

Garzanti Editore
Via Senato 25, I-20121 Milan
☎010 39 2 77871   Fax 010 39 2 76009233

FOUNDED 1861. *Publishes* general fiction, crime, literature, biography, poetry, art, history, children's reference, textbooks (secondary and primary), encyclopedias and dictionaries.

Giunti Publishing Group
Via V Gioberti 34, I-50121 Florence
☎010 39 55 66791   Fax 010 39 55 268312

FOUNDED 1840. *Publishes* fiction, essays, art, history, guidebooks, handbooks, popular science, mathematics, psychology, chemistry, linguistics, textbooks, dictionaries, children's. Italian publishers of National Geographical Society books.

Grafis Edizioni
Via 11 Giugno 4, I-40033 Casalecchio di Reno (Bologna)
☎010 39 51 758235   Fax 010 39 51 758236

FOUNDED 1965. *Publishes* art, photography, architecture, local history.

Gremese Editore SRL
Via Virginia Agnelli 88, I-00151 Rome
☎010 39 6 6814001   Fax 010 39 6 6812978

FOUNDED 1978. *Publishes* theatre, cinema, music, dance, art, photography, fashion, cookery, travel, literary reference, sport, hobbies, astrology.

Guida Editori SpA
Via D Morelli 16/B, I-80121 Naples
☎010 39 81 7644414   Fax 010 39 81 764414

FOUNDED 1973. *Publishes* art, essays, history, philosophy and fiction.

Istituto Geografico de Agostini SpA
Via Giovanni da Verrazano 15, I-28100 Novara
☎010 39 321 4241   Fax 010 39 321 471286

FOUNDED 1901. *Publishes* art, literature, belles lettres, history, religion, reference, geography, maps and partworks.

Istituto per l'Enciclopedia del Friuli Venezia Giulia

Via Marco Volpe 17/B, I-33100 Udine
☎010 39 432 208055

FOUNDED 1969. *Publishes* history, art, encyclopedias, essays, guidebooks, linguistics, fiction and children's.

Editoriale Jaca Book

Via Aurelio Saffi 19, I-20123 Milan
☎010 39 2 4982341   Fax 010 39 2 48193361

FOUNDED 1966. *Publishes* human and social sciences, philosophy, religion, history, archaeology, natural sciences, anthropology, art, architecture, photography, literature, children's and facsimiles.

Gruppo Editoriale Jackson SpA

Via Pola 9, I-20124 Milan
☎010 39 2 69481 Fax 010 39 2 6948238

FOUNDED 1975. *Publishes* information science only.

Antonio Lalli Editore

Via Fiume 60, I-53036 Poggibonsi (Siena)
☎010 39 577 933305

FOUNDED 1965. *Publishes* fiction, thrillers, mystery, humour, biography, memoirs, poetry, drama, cinema, art, bibliography, current affairs, philosophy, sociology, education, politics, religion, culture (including local interest and dialect), children's and comics.

Luciano Landi Editore SRL

CP 80, I-52027 San Giovanni Caldarno (FI)
☎010 39 55 92112/93075

FOUNDED 1960. *Publishes* folklore and local interest, literature, art, history, essays, sport, encyclopedias.

Giuseppe Laterza e Figli SpA

Via di Villa Sacchetti 17, I-00197 Rome
☎010 39 6 803693   Fax 010 39 6 878053

FOUNDED 1885. *Publishes* art, architecture, archaeology, history, social science, textbooks (university and secondary), reference, religion, science, biography, belles lettres and classics.

Il Lavoro Editoriale

Via Tommasi 15, 1-60124 Ancona
☎010 39 71 205355/202088

FOUNDED 1981. *Publishes* literature, humanities, medicine, history and periodicals.

Levrotto e Bella Libreria Editrice Universitaria SAS

Corso Vittorio Emanuele II 26, I-10123 Turin
☎010 39 11 832535

FOUNDED 1942. *Publishes* technology, science and textbooks (university).

Liguori Editore SRL

Via Mezzocannone 19, I-80134 Naples
☎010 39 81 206077   Fax 010 39 81 5527139

FOUNDED 1949. *Publishes* literary criticism, philosophy, history, linguistics, sociology, economics, mathematics, astronomy, natural sciences, anthropology, medicine, technology, periodicals.

Liviana Editrice SpA

Via Luigi Dottesio 1, I-35138 Padua
☎010 39 49 8710099 Fax 010 39 49 8710261

FOUNDED 1948. *Publishes* textbooks and manuals (university and school).

Longanesi & C

Via Salvini 3, I-20122 Milan
☎010 39 2 782551/5   Fax 010 39 2 781422

FOUNDED 1946. *Publishes* general fiction, biography, belles lettres, art, music, history, philosophy, religion, psychology, general and social sciences, medicine, how-to.

Cartiere Binda de Medici SpA Divisione Editoriale Piccoli

Via S Sofia 10, I-20122 Milan
☎010 39 2 86 18 47

FOUNDED 1943. *Publishes* children's books.

Arnoldo Mondadori Editore SpA

PBO 1824, I-20101 Milan
☎010 39 2 75421   Fax 010 39 2 75422302

FOUNDED 1907. *Publishes* general fiction, romance, mystery, classics, biography, art, music, poetry, philosophy, religion, history, how-to, reference, medicine, psychology, general science, textbooks (secondary), educational materials and children's.

Società Editrice Il Mulino
Str Maggiore 37, I-40125 Bologna
☎010 39 51 256011   Fax 010 39 51 256034

FOUNDED 1954. *Publishes* linguistics, literary criticism, music, theature, history, philosophy, law, political science, economics, social science, psychology, textbooks (university) and journals.

Gruppo Ugo Mursia Editore SpA
Via Tadino 29, I-20124 Milan
☎010 39 2 29403030   Fax 010 39 2 2041557

FOUNDED 1922. *Publishes* general fiction, poetry, belles lettres, art, history, biography, philosophy, religion, reference, textbooks, educational material, general and social science, nautical, children's.

Dall'Oglio Editore SRL
Via Santa Croce 20-2, I-20122 Milan
☎010 39 2 58101575   Fax 010 39 2 58106083

FOUNDED 1925. *Publishes* general fiction, poetry, belles lettres, biography, history.

Edizioni Paoline SRL
Piazza Soncino 5, I-20092 Cinisello Balsamo (Milan)
☎010 39 2 6600621   Fax 010 39 2 66015332

FOUNDED 1914. *Publishes* dictionaries, encyclopedias, how-to, reference, medicine, psychology, art, music, belles lettres, biography, philosophy, history, general fiction.

RCS Rizzoli Libri SpA
Via Scarsellini 13/17, 20161 Milan
☎010 39 2 6406/1   Fax 010 39 2 6469155

FOUNDED 1909. *Publishes* art, belles lettres, biography, children's history, hobbies, medicine, music, religion, social science and economics, textbooks and reference.

S A I E Editrice SRL
Corso Regina Margherita 2, I-10153 Turin
☎010 39 11 871022

FOUNDED 1954. *Publishes* encyclopedias, dictionaries, reference, economics, history, earth sciences, medicine, philosophy, religion, education, art, literary criticism, children's.

S E I (Società Editrice Internationale)
Corso Regina Margherita 176, I-10152 Turin
☎010 39 11 571   Fax 010 39 11 511320

FOUNDED 1908. *Publishes* general fiction, biography, belles lettres, art, history, philosophy, religion, general and social sciences, psychology, educational materials (textbooks and software for PCs/language laboratories) and children's.

Sonzogno
Via Mecenate 91, I-20138 Milan
☎010 39 2 50951   Fax 010 39 2 5065361

FOUNDED 1818. *Publishes* fiction: adventure, mystery and romance, and general non-fiction.

Sperling e Kupfer Editori SpA
Via Monte di Pietà 24, I-20121 Milan
☎010 39 2 876614   Fax 010 39 2 8053882

FOUNDED 1899. *Publishes* general fiction and non-fiction, biography, health, travel, sport, how-to, management, economics.

Todariana Editrice
Via Lazzaro Papi 15, I-20135 Milan
☎010 39 2 5460353   Fax 010 39 2 5460353

FOUNDED 1967. *Publishes* fiction, poetry, fantasy and science fiction, essays, sociology, psychology, dialect studies.

Edizioni Scolastiche Unicopli SpA
Via Verona 9, I-20135 Milan
☎010 39 2 5459675/5459721

FOUNDED 1985. *Publishes* essays and textbooks (university).

The Netherlands

Uitgeverij Ambo BV
Pr Marielaan 8, Postbus 308, 3740 AH Baarn
☎010 31 2154 22141   Fax 010 31 2154 23855

FOUNDED 1963. *Publishes* philosophy, religion, sociology, history, psychology and literature.

Ark Boeken Publishing House
Donauweg 4, 1043 AJ Amsterdam
☎010 31 20 114847

FOUNDED 1913. *Publishes* children's material, picture books and religion.

A A Balkema

Postbus 1675, 3000 BR Rotterdam
☎010 31 10 4145822 Fax 010 31 10 4135947

FOUNDED 1932. *Publishes* (in English, specialising in South Africa) Africa, mining and soil mechanics, palaeontology, marine biology and aquaculture, botany, zoology and history.

Born NV Uitgeversmaatschappij

Postbus 22, 9400AA Assen
☎010 31 59 2011641

FOUNDED 1885. A member of the Kluwer Group. *Publishes* general fiction, children's engineering, how-to, philosophy, social science, medicine, reference and textbooks.

A J Brill

Postbus 9000, 2300 PA Leiden
☎010 31 71 312624 Fax 010 31 71 317532

FOUNDED 1683. *Publishes* earth/life sciences and humanities.

Elsevier

Postbus 470, 1061 AL Amsterdam
☎010 31 20 5152371 Fax 010 31 20 832617

FOUNDED 1880. *Publishes* sciences (all fields), management and professional, medicine, finance, engineering, history, law, literature, linguistics, education (languages), trade journals, newspapers, periodicals, electronic databases.

Frank Fehmers Productions

Singel 512, 1017 AX Amsterdam
☎010 31 20 238766 Fax 010 31 20 246262

Publishes international books and film co-productions (including merchandising and licensing), plus television and children's.

Keesing Uitgeversmaatschappij BV

Postbus 1118, 1000 BC Amsterdam
☎010 31 20 5641111 Fax 010 31 20 970305

FOUNDED 1977. *Publishes* general fiction and non-fiction, education and Assimil language courses.

Kluwer Academic Publishers BV

Postbus 17, 3300 AA Dordrecht
☎010 31 78 334911 Fax 010 31 78 33454

Publishes astronomy and earth sciences, ecology, energy, humanities, philosophy, linguistics, mathematics, chemistry.

Kluwer Group

Houtweg 16, 4014 AA Culemboug
☎010 3 3450 71300 Fax 010 3 3450 18970

FOUNDED 1889. *Publishes* education, technical encyclopedias, trade books and journals, law and taxation, newspapers and periodicals.

Uitgeversmaatschappij J H Kok BV

Gildestr 5, 8263 AH Kampen
☎010 31 5202 92555 Fax 010 31 5202 27331

FOUNDED 1894. *Publishes* general fiction, poetry, biography, belles lettres, history, art, psychology, philosophy, religion, general and social sciences, alternative medicine, nature, crafts, how-to, textbooks and educational material, calendars and children's.

M & P Publishing House

Schoutlaan 4, 6002 EA Weert
☎010 31 4950 36880 Fax 010 31 4950 21145

FOUNDED 1974. *Publishes* general non-fiction only.

Meulenhoff International

Herengracht 507, PO Box 100, 1000 AC Amsterdam
☎010 31 20 267555 Fax 010 31 20 205516

Publishes international co-productions, art and general non-fiction. Meulenhoff Nederland specialises in Dutch and translated literature, science fiction and non-fiction.

Uitgeverij H Nelissen BV

Parkstr 47, 3743 ED Baarn
☎010 31 2154 12386 Fax 010 31 2154 23877

FOUNDED 1922. *Publishes* sociology and social sciences, politics, education, religion, philosophy and textbooks.

Servire BV Uitgevers

Secr Varkevisserstr 52, 2225 Le Katwijk aan Zee
☎010 31 1718 16741

FOUNDED 1921. *Publishes* (in Dutch and English) human endeavour and creativity, alternative living, mysticism, psychology, education.

Uitgeverij Het Spectrum BV

Montalbaendreef 2, 3562 LC Utrecht
☎010 31 30 650683   Fax 010 31 30 620850

FOUNDED 1935. *Publishes* science fiction, mystery, crime, illustrated non-fiction, encyclopedias, science, New Age, nature, history, travel, management.

Swets en Zeitlinger BV

Heereweg 347, 2161 CA Lisse
☎010 31 2521 35111   Fax 010 31 2521 15888

FOUNDED 1901. *Publishes* music, education, psychology and psychological tests, life sciences, medicine, engineering.

Time-Life Books BV

Ottho Heldringstr 5, 1066 AZ Amsterdam
☎010 31 20 5104911   Fax 010 31 20 175077

Publishes photography, art, cookery, gardening, how-to, general, social and political sciences, and history.

Uitgeverij De Toorts

Nijverheidsweg 1, Postbus 9585, 2003 LN Haarlem
☎010 31 23 154500   Fax 010 31 23 154501

FOUNDED 1936. *Publishes* health and medicine, psychology and psychotherapy, humanities, music, literature, management, children's.

Uniboek BV

Postbus 97, 3 990 DB Houten
☎010 31 3403 77660
Fax 010 31 3403 77600

FOUNDED 1891. *Publishes* thrillers and general fiction, children's, literature, cookery, design, lifestyle, archaeology, politics, multi-volume reference.

Uniepers BV

Postbus 8082, 1005 AB Amsterdam
☎010 31 20 112397   Fax 010 31 20 119972

FOUNDED 1961. *Publishes* (mostly in co-editions) art, music, cookery, wine and history.

V N U Business Press Group BV

Rijnsburgstr 11, 1059 AT Amsterdam
☎010 31 20 5102911

Publishes business and marketing, computers, information sciences and data management, career guidance.

V U Boekhandel/Uitgeverij BV

PO Box 7161, 1007 MC Amsterdam
☎010 31 20 6444355 Fax 010 31 20 6462719

FOUNDED 1980. *Publishes* medicine, biology, psychology, philosophy, theology, science, politics, history, sociology, economics, law, languages.

Uit-Mij West-Friesland

Kleine Noord 7-9, 1621 JD Hoorn
☎010 31 2290 18941 Fax 010 31 2290 16949

FOUNDED 1944. *Publishes* general fiction, children's and general science.

Wolters-Noordhoff-Longman BV

Postbus 58, 9700 MB Groningen
☎010 31 50 226922

Publishes English language teaching material and books.

Norway

Ansgar Forlag A/S

Storgt 39, 0182 Oslo 1
☎010 47 2 362800   Fax 010 47 2 362000

FOUNDED 1934. *Publishes* general fiction, art, biography, children's, religion.

H. Aschehoug & Co (W. Nygaard)

PO Box 363 Sentrum, 0102 Oslo 1
☎010 47 2 429490   Fax 010 47 2 206395

FOUNDED 1872. *Publishes* general fiction and non-fiction, children's, textbooks (primary and secondary), reference, handbooks.

Aventura Forlag

PO Box 404 Sentrum, 0103 Oslo 1
☎010 47 2 335360   Fax 010 47 2 335985

FOUNDED 1982. *Publishes* general fiction and non-fiction, children's and practical handbooks.

Bladkompaniet A/S

PO Box 148, Kalbakken, 0902 Oslo 9
☎010 47 2 257190   Fax 010 47 2 165059

FOUNDED 1915. *Publishes* general fiction and non-fiction.

J W Cappelens Forlag A/S

PO Box 71 Ankertorget, N-0133 Oslo 1
☎010 47 2 429440   Fax 010 47 2 422776

FOUNDED 1829. *Publishes* fiction, general non-fiction, children's, maps and atlases, handbooks, encyclopedias and schoolbooks.

N W Damm & Søn A/S

PO Box 1755 Vika, 0122 Oslo 1
☎010 47 2 429165   Fax 010 47 2 114707

FOUNDED 1843. *Publishes* children's, handbooks, reference, encyclopedias and general fiction.

Dreyers Forlag A/S

PO Box 1153 Sentrum, 0107 Oslo 1
☎01 47 2 335850   Fax 010 47 2 335805

FOUNDED 1942. *Publishes* fiction, handbooks, art and music.

Ex Libris Forlag A/S

PO Box 2130 Grünerløkka, 0505 Oslo 5
☎010 47 2 384450   Fax 010 47 2 385160

FOUNDED 1982. *Publishes* thrillers and general fiction, non-fiction, art, children's, calendars and stationery.

Gyldendal Norsk Forlag

PO Box 6860 St Olavs Plass, 0130 Oslo 1
☎010 47 2 200710   Fax 010 47 2 425953

FOUNDED 1925. *Publishes* fiction and non-fiction, art, music, illustrated books, textbooks (all levels), children's.

Kunnskapsforlaget I/S

PO Box 6736 St Olavs Plass, 0130 Oslo 1
☎010 47 2 205215   Fax 010 47 2 333443

FOUNDED 1975. *Publishes* encyclopedias and dictionaries.

NKI Forlaget

PO Box 111, N-1341 Bekkestua
☎010 47 2 122950   Fax 010 47 2 581902

FOUNDED 1967. *Publishes* textbooks (secondary), engineering, vocational training.

NKS-Forlaget (Ernst G. Mortensens stiftelse)

PO Box 5853 Hegdehaugen, 0308 Oslo 3
☎010 47 2 568500   Fax 010 47 2 566820

FOUNDED 1971. *Publishes* education, textbooks, handbooks and travel.

Det Norske Samlaget

PO Box 4672 Sofienberg, 0506 Oslo 5
☎010 47 2 687600   Fax 010 47 2 687502

FOUNDED 1868. *Publishes* general fiction, biography, belles lettres, history, philosophy, religion, reference, children's periodicals.

Chr. Schibsteds Forlag A/S

PO Box 1178 Sentrum, 0107 Oslo 1
☎010 47 2 863000   Fax 010 47 2 425492

FOUNDED 1839. *Publishes* biography, handbooks, crafts, travel, reference and children's.

Solum Forlag A/S

PO Box 140 Skøyen, 0212 Oslo 2
☎010 47 2 500400   Fax 010 47 2 501453

FOUNDED 1973. *Publishes* general fiction and non-fiction, human sciences, textbooks, children's.

Tano AS

Kristian Augustsgt. 7A, 0164 Oslo 1
☎010 47 2 110260   Fax 010 47 2 204583

FOUNDED 1976. *Publishes* general non-fiction, education, textbooks, computing.

Tiden Norsk Forlag

PO Box 8813 Youngstorget, 0028 Oslo 1
☎010 47 2 429520   Fax 010 47 2 426458

FOUNDED 1933. *Publishes* general fiction and non-fiction, plus children's.

Universitetsforlaget

PO Box 2959 Tøyen, 0608 Oslo 6
☎010 47 2 677600   Fax 010 47 2 677575

FOUNDED 1950. *Publishes* textbooks (all levels), medicine, journals, scientific research publications (in English).

Yrkesopplaering I/S
PO Box 6767 St Olavs Plass, 0130 Oslo 1
☎010 47 2 205230   Fax 010 47 2 336873

FOUNDED 1979. *Publishes* textbooks (secondary and adult), technical and vocational training.

Portugal

Armenio Amado, Editoria de Simoes, Beirao & Cia Lda
Ceira, 3000 Coimbra
☎010 351 39 26980

FOUNDED 1929. *Publishes* religion, philosophy, history, politics, social science, psychology, law, languages.

Bertrand Editora Lda
Rua Anchieta 29 – 1, 1200 Lisbon
☎010 351 1 3420084/5 Fax 01 351 1 3468286

FOUNDED 1727. *Publishes* literature (Portuguese and foreign), art, essays, children's social sciences, dictionaries.

Editorial Caminho SARL
Alameda de Santo António dos Capuchos 6B, 1100 Lisbon
☎010 351 1 542683   Fax 010 351 1 534346

FOUNDED 1977. *Publishes* general fiction, children's sociology and politics.

Livraria Civilizacão (Americo Fraga Lamares & Ca Lda)
Rua Alberto Aires de Gouveia 27, Oporto 1
☎010 351 2 22286/7   Fax 010 351 2 312382

FOUNDED 1921. *Publishes* fiction, children's, history, social and political science, economics.

Didactica Editora
Av Ilha da Madeira 26-A, 1400 Lisbon
☎010 351 1 3011731 Fax 010 351 1 3014887

FOUNDED 1944. *Publishes* Portuguese, French and English language, mathematics, science, biology, physical education.

D I F E L – Difusao Editorial Lda
Rua D. Estefania 46B, 1000 Lisbon
☎010 351 1 537677   Fax 010 351 1 545886

FOUNDED 1983. *Publishes* fiction (Portuguese and foreign), general non-fiction, belles lettres.

Publicacoes Dom Quixote Lda
Rua Luciano Cordeiro 116-2, 1098 Lisbon codex
☎010 351 1 3158079/81
Fax 010 351 1 574595

FOUNDED 1965. *Publishes* general fiction, poetry, belles lettres, philosophy, general and social science, history, education, reference, children's cartoons, humour.

Publicacoes Europa-America Lda
Apdo 8, Estrada Lisbon-Sintra km 14, 2726 Mem Martins
☎010 351 1 9211461/2/3
Fax 010 351 1 9217940

FOUNDED 1945. *Publishes* general fiction, belles lettres, poetry, biography, art, music, history, philosophy, general and social science, how-to, medicine, psychology, children's (including nursery), textbooks (university), technical, engineering.

Gradiva – Publicacoes Lda
Rua Almeida e Sousa 21 r/c Esq, 1300 Lisbon
☎010 351 1 674067   Fax 010 351 1 674068

FOUNDED 1981. *Publishes* science including human sciences, philosphy, history, education, fiction and science fiction, illustrated books, children's.

Livros Horizonte Lda
Rua das Chagas 17, 1 Dto, 1121 Lisbon codex
☎010 351 1 3466917 Fax 010 351 1 3426921

FOUNDED 1953. *Publishes* sociology, psychology, textbooks (university), arts, children's.

Lello e Irmão
Rua das Carmelitas 144, 4000 Oporto
☎010 351 2 2002037   Fax 010 351 2 318511

FOUNDED 1881. *Publishes* general fiction, children's history, dictionaries.

Porto Editora Lda
Rua da Restauracao 365, 4099 Oporto codex
☎010 351 2 2005813   Fax 010 351 2 313072

FOUNDED 1944. *Publishes* textbooks (all levels), educational materials, dictionaries, foreign language teaching, maps, law, general non-fiction.

Edições 70 Lda
Ave. Elias Garcia 81, P-1000 Lisbon
☎010 351 1 8599936 Fax 010 55 1 2842942

FOUNDED 1970. *Publishes* fiction (thrillers and science fiction), African literature, human and social sciences, music, belles lettres, essays, science, children's, comics.

Texto Editora
Apdo 4081, 10502 Lisbon
☎010 351 1 7165308 Fax 010 351 1 7150403

FOUNDED 1977. *Publishes* textbooks (nursery, primary, secondary), education, management, cookery, health, children's and general fiction.

Editorial Verbo SA
Rua Carlos Testa 1, Lisbon
☎010 351 1 562131   Fax 010 351 1 562139

FOUNDED 1949. *Publishes* encyclopedias, educational material, general science, history, children's.

Spain

Publicaciones de l'Abadia de Montserrat
Abadia de Montserrat, Barcelona
☎010 34 3 2450303   Fax 010 34 3 4473594

FOUNDED 1915. *Publishes* (mostly in Catalan) religion, literature, biography, children's history, geography and travel.

Editorial Alhambra SA
Claudio Coello 76, 28001 Madrid
☎010 34 1 4316460   Fax 010 34 1 4314563

FOUNDED 1942. *Publishes* medicine and nursing, general science, psychology, philosophy, history, literature, children's, languages, textbooks (all levels) audiovisual aids.

Alianza Editorial SA
Milan 28, 28043 Madrid
☎010 34 1 2000045   Fax 010 34 1 3811810

FOUNDED 1965. *Publishes* general fiction, poetry, belles lettres, art, music, philosophy, political and social sciences, history, mathematics and general science.

Ediciones Anaya SA
Josefa Valcárcel 27, 28027 Madrid
☎010 34 1 3200119   Fax 010 34 1 7426473

FOUNDED 1959. *Publishes* textbooks (all levels) and educational materials.

Bosch Casa Editorial SA
Calle Compte d'Urgell 51 bis, 08011 Barcelona
☎010 34 3 4548437   Fax 010 34 3 3236736

FOUNDED 1934. *Publishes* science, technology, law, philology, literature.

Editorial Casals SA
Calle Caspe 79, 08013 Barcelona
☎010 34 3 2323713   Fax 010 34 3 2456895

FOUNDED 1870. *Publishes* children's (fiction, preschool and primary).

Ediciones Ceac SA
Apdo 926, 08020 Barcelona
☎010 34 3 3073004   Fax 010 34 3 3084392

FOUNDED 1957. *Publishes* children's, education, arts and crafts, domestic science, technical and psychology.

Debate SA
Calle Zurbano 92-5, 28003 Madrid
☎010 34 1 5765582   Fax 010 34 1 4351498

FOUNDED 1977. *Publishes* fiction, essays, children's, encyclopedias, textbooks (university) and large print.

Destino SL
Concejo de Ciento 425, 08009 Barcelona
☎010 34 3 2652305   Fax 010 34 3 2657537

FOUNDED 1942. *Publishes* general fiction, children's, art and history.

Editorial Don Quijote
Calle Horno de Haza 21, Edificio La Purissima local 9, 18002 Granada
☎010 34 58 278789

FOUNDED 1981. *Publishes* fiction, poetry, essays, theatre, history, textbooks (university).

E D H A S A
Diagonal 519-521, 08029 Barcelona
☎010 34 3 2395105   Fax 010 34 3 4194584

FOUNDED 1946. *Publishes* historical and general fiction, literature and essays.

Editoria Empeño
14 Plaza Marques de Camarines 7, Aravaca, 28023 Madrid
☎010 34 1 2079386

FOUNDED 1980. *Publishes* fiction, poetry, science and technology, sociology and English language (including children's).

Eumo Editorial
Carrer de Miramarges s/n, 08500 Vic (Barcelona)
☎010 34 3 8860794   Fax 010 34 3 8891063

FOUNDED 1979. *Publishes* education, history and literature.

E U N S A (Ediciones Universidad de Navarra SA)
Apdo 396, 31080 Pamplona
☎010 34 48 256850   Fax 010 34 48 256854

FOUNDED 1967. *Publishes* journalism, business administration and economics, law, engineering, architecture, education, medicine and nursing, philosophy, theology, bibliography, encyclopedias, periodicals.

Editorial Fundamentos
Caracas 15, 28010 Madrid
☎010 34 1 3199619   Fax 010 34 1 3195584

FOUNDED 1970. *Publishes* fiction, literature, cinema and theatre, criticism, songs, social science and psychology.

Editorial Gedisa SA
Muntaner 460, entresuelo 1A, 08006 Barcelona
☎010 34 3 20160000   Fax 010 34 3 2019665

FOUNDED 1977. *Publishes* psychology and psychoanalysis, social and human sciences, education, philosophy, general non-fiction, biography, sport.

Gustavo Gili SA
Rosellon 87-89, 08029 Barcelona
☎010 34 3 3228161   Fax 010 34 3 3229205

FOUNDED 1902. *Publishes* art and design, architecture, communication and general technology.

Grijalbo SA
Aragón 385, 08013 Barcelona
☎010 34 3 2587000   Fax 010 34 3 2580495

FOUNDED 1942. *Publishes* general fiction and non-fiction, biography, history, politics, philosophy, religion, psychology, social sciences, technology, reference, art.

Ediciones Hiperión SL
Salustiano Olózaga 14, 28001 Madrid
☎010 34 3 1 5776015
Fax (*via* Camara de Comercio) 010 34 1 4355523

FOUNDED 1976. *Publishes* fiction, poetry, literary criticism, essays, philosophy, history, Arabic studies.

Editorial Incafo SA
Castello 59, 28001 Madrid
☎010 34 1 4313460   Fax 010 34 1 4313589

FOUNDED 1973. *Publishes* (some titles in English) art, natural history, ecology and exploration in Spain and Latin America.

Ediciones Jover SA
San Pedro Martir 18, 08012 Barcelona
☎010 34 3 2185662   Fax 010 34 3 4154291

FOUNDED 1946. *Publishes* education and science.

Laertes SA de Ediciones
Calle Montseny 43 bajos, 08012 Barcelona
☎010 34 3 2376869   Fax 010 34 3 2376944

FOUNDED 1975. *Publishes* fiction (modern Spanish and foreign), classics, children's adventure, gay literature, cinema and travel.

Editorial Laia SA
Guitard 43-5, 08014 Barcelona
☎010 34 3 3215562   Fax 010 34 3 3217975

FOUNDED 1972. *Publishes* literature, essays, social sciences, psychology, general non-fiction.

LaSal (Edicions de les Dones)
Riereta 13, 0800 Barcelona
☎010 34 3 3231798/3298450

FOUNDED 1978. *Publishes* women only – fiction and non-fiction.

McGraw-Hill Interamericana de España SA
Basauri s/n, Aravaca, 28023 Madrid
☏010 34 1 3728193

FOUNDED 1984. Formerly Emalsa SA. *Publishes* biology and health studies.

Miraguano SA Ediciones
Calle Hermosilla 104, 28009 Madrid
☏010 34 1 4016990   Fax 010 34 1 4021843

FOUNDED 1979. *Publishes* literature, alternative medicine, zen, ecology and science fiction.

Mondadori Espana SA
Avda Alfonso XIII50, 28016 Madrid
☏010 34 1 4136111   Fax 010 34 1 4159033

FOUNDED 1987. *Publishes* fiction, essays, biography, illustrated books, history, science and general non-fiction.

Planeta SA
Corcega 273-277, 08008 Barcelona
☏010 34 3 2175050   Fax 010 34 3 2177140

FOUNDED 1952. *Publishes* general fiction and non-fiction.

Plaza Y Janés SA
Virgen de Guadalupe 21-23, 08950 Esplugas de Llobregat
☏010 34 3 3710200   Fax 010 34 3 3715343

FOUNDED 1959. *Publishes* general fiction, classics and general non-fiction.

Santillana SA
Juan Bravo 38, 28006 Madrid
☏010 34 1 5783159   Fax 010 34 1 5783220

FOUNDED 1964. Formerly Ediciones Alfaguara. *Publishes* general fiction, world classics, and children's books.

Seix Barral SA
Córcega 270, 08008 Barcelona
☏010 34 3 2186400/66 Fax 010 34 3 2184773

FOUNDED 1945. *Publishes* fiction (including classics) from Europe, the Americas and the Far East, plus poetry and drama.

Editorial Teide SA
Calle Viladomat 291, 08029 Barcelona
☏010 34 3 4104507   Fax 010 34 3 3224192

FOUNDED 1940. *Publishes* textbooks (all levels), educational materials, dictionaries, languages, sailing, geography, history, philosophy, art.

Editorial Timun Mas SA
Calle Castillejos 294/296-1, 08025 Barcelona
☏010 34 3 3477233   Fax 010 34 3 2357470

Publishes teaching handbooks and children's.

Tusquets Editores
Calle Iradier 24 bajos, 08017 Barcelona
☏010 34 3 4174170   Fax 010 34 3 4176703

FOUNDED 1969. *Publishes* fiction, biography, art, cookery, erotica, philsophy, history, general and social sciences.

Ediciones Versal SA
Plaza Lesseps 33, 08023 Barcelona
☏010 34 3 3257404   Fax 010 34 3 436898

FOUNDED 1984. *Publishes* literature, general non-fiction, biography and essays.

Editorial Luis Vives (Edelvives)
Apdo 387, 50080 Zaragoza
☏010 34 76 347000   Fax 010 34 76 345979

FOUNDED 1932. *Publishes* textbooks (all levels), educational material and children's.

Sweden

Almqvist och Wiksell International
Sundbybergsvagen 1, S-171 Solna
☏010 46 8 237990   Fax 010 46 8 7912335

Publishes science, technology and periodicals.

Bonnier Fakta Bokforlag AB
Box 3159, S-103 63 Stockholm
☏010 46 8 29120   Fax 010 46 8 217125

FOUNDED 1981. *Publishes* general non-fiction, textbooks (university), encyclopedias, dictionaries, handbooks, field guides, art, cookery and co-editions.

Albert Bonniers Forlag AB
Box 3159, S-103 63 Stockholm
☏010 46 8 229120   Fax 010 46 8 208451

FOUNDED 1837. *Publishes* general fiction, teenage, reference, general non-fiction and periodicals.

Bonniers Juniorforlag AB
Kammakargatan OA, Box 3159, S-103 63
Stockholm
☏010 46 8 229120   Fax 010 46 8 6760105

FOUNDED 1979. *Publishes* children's books.

Bokforlaget Bra Bocker AB
Sodra Vagen, S-263 80 Hoganas
☏010 46 42 339000   Fax 010 46 42 330504

FOUNDED 1965. *Publishes* general fiction, illustrated books, history, geography, encyclopedias.

Brombergs Bokförlag AB
Box 45151, S-104 30 Stockholm
☏010 46 8 329050   Fax 010 46 8 348701

FOUNDED 1973. *Publishes* general fiction and non-fiction, popular and political science.

Bokförlaget Forum AB
Box 14115, S-104 41 Stockholm
☏010 46 8 6604122   Fax 010 46 8 6676439

FOUNDED 1944. *Publishes* general fiction, biography and memoirs, art, natural history, travel, how-to, reference, general non-fiction.

L Ts Forlag AB (Lantbrukarnas Riksforbund och Studieforbundet Vuxenskolan)
Ynglingsgatan 2-4, S-105 33 Stockholm
☏010 46 8 78752001   Fax 010 46 8 322085

FOUNDED 1935. *Publishes* general fiction, crafts and pattern books, gardening, farming, social history, politics, economics, adult education, popular science (illustrated).

Liber AB
Box 3071, S-103 61 Stockholm
☏010 46 8 7399000   Fax 010 46 8 320851

FOUNDED 1973. *Publishes* textbooks (all levels), dictionaries, business management, economics, law, technology, nursing, social sciences, correspondence courses, maps, general fiction.

Bokförlaget Natur och Kultur
Box 27323, S-102 54 Stockholm
☏010 46 8 6668600   Fax 010 46 8 6607299

FOUNDED 1922. *Publishes* general non-fiction, general science, biography, history, psychology, textbooks and audiovisual material (primary and secondary), and children's.

Norstedts Forlag AB
Box 2052, S-103 12 Stockholm 2
☏010 46 8 7893000   Fax 010 46 8 214006

FOUNDED 1823. *Publishes* general fiction and non-fiction, dictionaries and children's.

Rabēn och Sjögren Bokforlag AB
Box 45022, S-104 30 Stockholm
☏010 46 8 349960   Fax 010 46 8 302899

FOUNDED 1942. *Publishes* general fiction and non-fiction, children's, how-to, nature, outdoor pursuits, music, art, history and social science, economics and psychology.

Richters Fölag AB
Ostra Förstadsgatan 46, S-205 Malmö
☏010 46 40 380600   Fax 010 46 40 930820

FOUNDED 1942. *Publishes* fiction, handbooks, children's, international co-productions.

Bokförlags AB Tiden
Box 30184, S-104 25 Stockholm
☏010 46 8 130130   Fax 010 46 8 569344

FOUNDED 1912. *Publishes* general fiction and non-fiction, children's, illustrated books, memoirs, history, politics, social sciences, psychology.

Wahlströms Bokfölag AB
Warfvinges vag 30, S-112 51 Stockholm
☏010 46 8 244600   Fax 010 46 8 509761

FOUNDED 1911. *Publishes* general fiction and non-fiction, and children's.

Switzerland

Editions L'Age d'Homme – La Cîté
PO Box 67, CH-1000 Lausanne
☏010 41 21 3120095   Fax 010 41 21 208440

FOUNDED 1966. *Publishes* general and science fiction, poetry, belles lettres, literary criticism, biography, philosophy, exotica, art, music, cinema, social sciences.

Arche Verlag AG
Raabe und Vitali, Hoelderlinstr 14, CH-8030 Zurich
☎010 41 1 2522410   Fax 010 41 1 2611115
FOUNDED 1944. *Publishes* belles lettres and modern literature.

Artemis Verlags AG
Munstergasse 9, CH-8024 Zurich
☎010 41 1 2521100 Fax 010 41 1 2624792
FOUNDED 1943. *Publishes* art, architecture, travel guides, philosophy, history and current affairs, biography, classical fiction, textbooks and children's.

Benteli Verlag
Bumplizstrasse 101, CH-3018 Berne
☎010 41 31 554433   Fax 010 41 31 551776
FOUNDED 1899. *Publishes* general fiction, poetry, belles lettres, art, history, reference, textbooks.

Benziger AG
Bellerivestr 3, CH-8008 Zurich
☎010 41 1 3837052   Fax 010 41 1 3837416
FOUNDED 1792. *Publishes* general fiction and non-fiction, children's and religion.

Diogenes Verlag AG
Sprecherstr 8, CH-8032 Zurich
☎010 41 1 2548511   Fax 010 41 1 2528407
FOUNDED 1953. *Publishes* fiction, children's and art.

Librairie Droz SA
PO Box 389, CH-1211 Geneva 12
☎010 41 22 466666   Fax 010 41 22 472391
FOUNDED 1924. *Publishes* literature, poetry, belles lettres, history and social science, religion, reference, textbooks (university).

Hallwag Verlag AG
Nordring 4, CH-3001 Berne
☎010 41 31 423131   Fax 010 41 31 414133

FOUNDED 1912. *Publishes* general non-fiction, how-to, cookery, wine-growing, horses, travel and maps, history, general science.

Kummerly und Frey (Geographischer Verlag)
Hallerstr 6-10, CH-3001 Berne
☎010 41 31 235111
FOUNDED 185. *Publishes* geography, maps and town plans, illustrated books.

Langenscheidt AG
PO Box 326, CH-8021 Zurich
☎010 41 42 232300   Fax 010 41 1 2122149
Publishes linguistics.

Larousse (Suisse) SA
PO Box 502, CH-1211 Geneva 6
☎010 41 22 369140
Publishes dictionaries, reference and textbooks.

Manesse Verlag GmbH
Badergasse 9, CH-8001 Zurich
☎010 41 1 2525551   Fax 010 41 1 2625347
FOUNDED 1944. *Publishes* classical literature (worldwide), essays and history.

Nebelspalter Verlag
Pestalozzistrasse 5, 9400 Rorschach
☎010 41 71 414341   Fax 010 41 71 414313
FOUNDED 1946. *Publishes* humour, cartoons and periodicals.

Neptun-Verlag
PO Box 307, CH-8280 Kreuzlingen 1
☎010 41 72 727262   Fax 010 41 72 727243
FOUNDED 1946. *Publishes* modern history, travel and children's.

Neue Zurcher Zeitung AG Buchverlag
Postfach, CH-8021 Zurich
☎010 41 1 2581505   Fax 010 41 1 2581399
Publishes illustrated books and textbooks.

Orell Füssli Verlag
Postfach, CH-8022 Zurich
☎010 41 1 2113630　　Fax 010 41 1 2113411

FOUNDED 1519. *Publishes* children's, educational material, illustrated books, art, how-to, transport, history, geography, economics, biography.

Editions Payot Lausanne
33 ave de la Gare, CH-1001 Lausanne
☎010 41 21 3413331　　Fax 010 41 21 494648

FOUNDED 1875. *Publishes* art, music, poetry, belles lettres, history, general and natural sciences, law, business, psychology, philosophy, agriculture, sport.

Verlag Rot-Weiss AG
Postfach 1308, Baelliz 56, CH-3600 Thun
☎010 41 33 229803　　Fax 010 41 33 229810

FOUNDED 1988. *Publishes* restaurant, hotel and general tourist guides, in German and English.

Sauerlander AG
Postfach, CH-5001 Aarau
☎010 41 64 221264　　Fax 010 41 64 245780

FOUNDED 1807. *Publishes* children's, textbooks and educational materials (all levels), belles lettres,

poetry, biography, natural and social sciences, medicine, history.

Scherz Verlag AG
Marktgasse 25, CH-3000 Berne 7
☎010 41 31 226831　　Fax 010 41 31 210375

FOUNDED 1939. *Publishes* general fiction, crime thrillers, biography, history, psychology, philosophy, general non-fiction.

Editions D'Art Albert Skira SA
89 route de Chêne, CH-1208 Geneva
☎010 41 22 495533　　Fax 010 41 22 495535

FOUNDED 1928. *Publishes* art, art history and educational materials.

Zytglogge Verlag
PO Box 12, CH-3073 Gumligen
☎010 41 31 522030/40 Fax 010 41 31 522524

FOUNDED 1965. *Publishes* literature, belles lettres, art, politics and children's.

US Publishers

International Reply Coupons

For return postage, send International Reply Coupons (IRCs), available from the Post Office. Letters 60 pence; mss according to weight. Check with the Post Office.

ABC–Clio, Inc.

Suite 805, 50 South Steele Street,
Denver CO 80209
☏ 0101 303 333 3003 Fax 0101 303 333 4037

Vice President *Heather Cameron*

FOUNDED 1955. *Publishes* non-fiction: how-to and reference, including art and architecture, education, government and politics, history, military and war, women's studies/issues, current world issues. About 35–40 titles a year. No unsolicited mss; synopses and ideas welcome. *Royalties* paid annually. *UK subsidiary* **Clio Press Ltd**, Oxford.

Abingdon Press

201 Eighth Avenue South, Box 801,
Nashville TN 37202
☏ 0101 615 749 6404 Fax 0101 615 749 6512

Editorial Director *Neil M. Alexander*

Publishes non-fiction: religious (lay and professional), children's religious and academic texts. About 80 titles a year. Approach in writing only with synopsis and samples. S.a.e. essential.

Harry N. Abrams, Inc.

100 Fifth Avenue, New York NY 10011
☏ 0101 212 206 7715 Fax 0101 212 645 8437

Publisher/Editor-in-chief *Paul Gottlieb*

Subsidiary of Times Mirror Co. *Publishes* illustrated books: art, design, nature, outdoor recreation. No fiction. About 90 titles a year. Submit completed mss (no dot matrix), together with sample illustrations.

Academy Chicago Publishers

213 West Institute Place, Chicago IL 60610
☏ 0101 312 751 7302 Fax 0101 312 751 7306

Editorial Director *Anita Miller*

FOUNDED 1985. *Publishes* fiction: mystery and mainstream; and non-fiction: biography, sociology, travel, true crime and historical. No romance,

children's, young adult, religious, sexist or avant-garde. About 25 titles a year. Unsolicited mss welcome if accompanied by IRCs. No synopses or ideas.

IMPRINTS
Cassandra Editions ('Lost' Women Writers) TITLES *Memoirs of an Ex-Prom Queen* Alix Kates Shulman; *A Mirror for Witches* Esther Forbes. *Royalties* paid twice yearly. *Distributed* in the UK and Europe by Gazelle, Lancaster.

Ace Science Fiction
See **Berkley Publishing Group**

Bob Adams, Publishers, Inc.

260 Center Street, Holbrook MA 02343
☏ 0101 617 767 8100 Fax 0101 617 767 0994

Publishes general non-fiction: careers, business, personal finance, relationships, parenting and maternity, self improvement, reference, cooking, sports, games and humour. Ideas welcome. TITLES *2002 Things to Do on a Date; America's Growth Stocks; Your Executive Image; The Job Bank Series; Baseball's All-time Goats.*

Addison-Wesley Publishing Co., Inc.

General Books Division, Jacob Way,
Reading MA 01867
☏ 0101 617 944 3700 Fax 0101 617 944 8243

Publisher *David Miller*

Publishes biography, business/economics, health, history, how-to, politics, psychology, computers and science. No fiction. About 125 titles a year. Approach in writing or by phone in first instance, then submit synopsis and one sample chapter. *Royalties* paid.

Aegina Press, Inc.

59 Oak Lane, Spring Valley,
Huntington WV 25704
☏ 0101 304 429 7204

Managing Director *Ira Herman*

FOUNDED 1984. *Publishes* all types of fiction, non-fiction and poetry. Currently expanding its lists, with an emphasis on fiction. TITLES *Water Dancing; The Zhivago Poems; Caught Up in Time.* Unsolicited mss, synopses and ideas for books welcome, provided they are accompanied by return postage. Keen to encourage new authors.

IMPRINTS
University Editions *Ira Herman* TITLES *The Book of the Son; On the Edge; Remember Us.*
Royalties paid annually or twice yearly depending on the book; publishes on both a royalty and subsidy basis.

Aero Books
See **TAB Books**

University of Alabama Press
Box 870380, Tuscaloosa AL 35487
☎0101 265 348 5180   Fax 0101 265 348 9201

Director *Malcolm MacDonald*

Publishes academic books only. 40 titles a year.

Aladdin Books
See **Macmillan Children's Book Group**

University of Alaska Press
1st Floor, Gruening Building, University of Alaska, Fairbanks, Alaska 99775-1580
☎0101 907 474 6389   Fax 0101 907 474 7225

Manager *Debbie Van Stone*
Managing Editor *Carla Helfferich*

Traces its origins back to 1927 but was relatively dormant until the early 1980s. *Publishes* scholarly works about Alaska and the North Pacific rim, with a special emphasis on circumpolar regions. 5–10 titles a year. Unsolicited mss, synopses and ideas welcome. No fiction or poetry.

DIVISIONS
Ramuson Library/Historical Translation Series *Marvin Falk* TITLES *Bering's Voyages: The Reports from Russia; Tlingit Indians of Alaska* **Oral Biography Series** *William Schneider* TITLES *The Life I've Been Living; Kusiq: An Eskimo Life History from the Arctic Coast of Alaska* **Monograph Series** *Carla Helfferich* TITLES *Intertidal Bivalves: A Guide to the Common Marine Bivalves of Alaska* **Classic Reprint Series** *Terrence Cole* TITLES *Arctic Village: A 1930s Portrait of Wiseman, Alaska.*

Alyson Publications, Inc.
40 Plympton Street, Boston MA 02118
☎0101 617 542 5679

Publisher *Sasha Alyson*

FOUNDED 1979. *Publishes* lesbian and gay fiction and non-fiction. No unsolicited mss. Send a 1-2 page synopsis with return postage included. About 15 titles a year.

IMPRINTS
Alyson Wonderland Books for children of lesbian and gay parents. Mss welcome if accompanied by s.a.e.
Royalties paid annually.

AMACOM
135 West 50th Avenue, New York NY 10020
☎0101 212 903 8081   Fax 0101 212 903 8168

Director/Submissions *Weldon P. Rackley*

Owned by American Management Association. *Publishes* business books only, including general management, business communications, sales and marketing, small business, finance, computers and information systems, human resource management and training, career/personal growth skills, research development, project management and manufacturing, quality/customer service titles. 60–65 titles a year. Proposals welcome.
Royalties paid twice yearly.

American Mensa Press
See **Gardner Press, Inc.**

Anchor Books
See **Bantam Doubleday Dell Publishing Group**

Anvil
See **Krieger Publishing Co., Inc.**

Archway
See **Simon & Schuster**

University of Arizona Press
1230 North Park Avenue, 102, Tucson AZ 85719
☎0101 602 621 1441   Fax 0101 602 621 8899

Director *Stephen Cox*
Senior Editor *Joanne O'Hare*

FOUNDED 1959. Academic non-fiction, particularly with a regional/ cultural link. About 45 titles a year.

University of Arkansas Press
McIlroy House, 201 Ozark Avenue,
Fayetteville AR 72701
☎0101 501 575 3246 Fax 0101 501 575 6044

Director *Miller Williams*

FOUNDED 1981. *Publishes* scholarly monographs, fiction, poetry and general trade including travel, cookery, etc. Particularly interested at present in scholarly works in history, politics, sociology and literary criticism. About 35–40 titles a year. *Royalties* paid annually.

Athena
See **Paragon House Publishers**

Atheneum Books
See **Macmillan Children's Book Group**

Atlantic Monthly Press
19 Union Square West, New York NY 10003
☎0101 212 645 4462 Fax 0101 212 727 0180

Publisher *Morgan Entrekin*

Publishes general non-fiction including gardening, and some fiction. About 90 titles a year. Approach in writing, submitting sample chapter. S.a.e. essential.

Avalon Books
401 Lafayette Street, New York NY 10003
☎0101 212 598 0222 Fax 0101 212 979 1862

Publisher *Barbara J. Brett*

Publishes wholesome romance, mystery romance and westerns. Also hardcover books for the library market. No 'old-fashioned, predictable, formula-type books. We are looking for contemporary characters and fresh contemporary plots'. Unsolicited mss, synopses and ideas welcome. Send first chapter and complete outline. About 60 titles a year.

Avery Publishing Group, Inc.
120 Old Broadway, Garden City Park, New York NY 11040
☎0101 516 741 2155 Fax 0101 516 742 1892

Managing Editor *Rudy Shur*

FOUNDED 1976. *Publishes* adult trade non-fiction, specialising in childbirth, childcare, alternative health, self-help, New Age, military history and natural cooking, plus college textbooks. About 30

titles a year. No unsolicited mss; synopses and ideas welcome if accompanied by s.a.e.

DIVISIONS
Avery Trade TITLES *The Macrobiotic Way; Prescription for Nutritional Healing.* **Avery College** TITLES *The Power of Colour; The Family Bed; Cooking with the Right Side of the Brain.* *Royalties* paid twice yearly.

Avon Books
1350 Avenue of the Americas, New York NY 10019
☎0101 212 481 5602 Fax 0101 212 532 2172

Publisher *Carolyn Reidy*

FOUNDED 1941. A division of the Hearst Corporation. *Publishes* mass market and trade paperbacks, adult, young adult and children's. Fiction: contemporary and historical romance, science fiction and fantasy, action and adventure, suspense and thrillers, mystery and westerns. Non-fiction (all types): how-to, popular psychology, self-help, health, history, war, sports, business and economics, biography and politics. No textbooks. Over 400 titles a year. Submit query letter only.

DIVISIONS
Avon *Mark Gompertz* Trade paperbacks; **Avon Camelot Books** *Ellen Krieger* Children's books; **Avon Flare** *Ellen Krieger* Young adult readers; **Avon Books** *Robert Mecoy* Adult mass market paperbacks.

Baen Books
PO Box 1403, Riverdale NY 10471
☎0101 212 548 3100

Publisher/Editor-in-Chief *James Baen*

Publishes science fiction and fantasy only. Unsolicited mss and synopses welcome provided they are accompanied by s.a.e. or International Reply Coupons.
Royalties paid twice yearly.

Ballantine/Del Rey/Fawcett/Ivy Books
See **Random House, Inc.**

Bantam Doubleday Dell Publishing Group
666 Fifth Avenue, New York NY 10103
☎0101 212 765 6500 Fax 0101 212 492 9700

President/Publisher *Linda Grey*
Vice-President/Publisher *Lou Aronica* (Mass market)
Vice-President/Publisher *Matthew Shear* (Hardcover/Trade)

Publishes general fiction: mysteries, westerns, romance, war, science fiction and fantasy, crime and thrillers, adventure; also non-fiction, including New Age and computers, plus children's. Most work comes through agents. No unsolicited mss. Synopses with IRCs to appropriate editor may be considered.

DIVISIONS/IMPRINTS
Bantam Books IMPRINTS **Spectra** (science fiction), **New Age, New Sciences, Bantam New Fiction** (original fiction in trade paperback), **Bantam Non-Fiction, Domain** (historical), **Fanfare** (women's fiction/romance), **Falcon** (men's adventure), **Crime Line, Computer Books. Dell Books. Doubleday** IMPRINTS **Anchor Books, Currency, Image, Nan A. Talese, Perfect Crime, Dolphin Books, Spy Books, Zephyr Books**.

Barron's Educational Series
250 Wireless Boulevard, Hauppauge NY 11788
☎0101 516 434 3311   Fax 0101 516 434 3723

Chairman/President *Manuel Barron*

FOUNDED 1942. *Publishes* adult non-fiction, children's fiction and non-fiction, test preparation materials and language materials/tapes. No adult fiction. 200 titles a year.

Editorial Head *Grace Freedson* TITLES *Indoor Plants; Pet Care Manual; Biz Kids Guide to Success.* Unsolicited mss, synopses and ideas for books welcome.
Royalties paid twice yearly.

Basic Books
See **HarperCollins Publishers Inc.**

Beacon Press
25 Beacon Street, Boston MA 02108
☎0101 617 742 2110   Fax 0101 617 723 3097

Director *Wendy J. Strothman*

Publishes general non-fiction. About 60 titles a year. Approach in writing, or submit synopsis and sample chapters (with International Reply Coupons) to the editorial department.

Beech Tree Books
See **William Morrow & Co., Inc.**

Bell Books
See **Boyds Mills Press**

Bergh Publishing, Inc.
276 Fifth Avenue, Suite 715, New York NY 10001
☎0101 212 686 8551   Fax 0101 212 779 2290

Chairman/Managing Director *Sven-Erik Bergh*

Part of Bergh & Bergh Publishers, Switzerland. FOUNDED 1966. *Publishes* non-fiction mostly, including memoirs and cookery; also crime/thriller stories and yearbooks. 10 titles in 1991. Synopses and ideas for books welcome if accompanied by return postage. Query first. No unsolicited material. *Royalties* annually.

Berkley Publishing Group
200 Madison Avenue, New York NY 10016
☎0101 212 951 8848   Fax 0101 212 213 6706

Editor-in-Chief *Leslie Gelbman*

Publishes general fiction and non-fiction: business, how-to and nutrition. About 900 titles a year. No unsolicited mss. Submit synopsis and first three chapters for Ace Science Fiction.

IMPRINTS
Berkley, Berkley Trade Paperbacks, Jove, Diamond, Pacer, Ace Science Fiction.

Bowling Green State University Popular Press
Bowling Green OH 43403
☎0101 419 372 7867   Fax 0101 419 372 8095

Managing Director *Pat Browne*

FOUNDED 1970. *Publishes* non-fiction for libraries as reference or textbooks. 25 titles a year. Unsolicited mss, synopses and ideas welcome. No fiction. *Royalties* paid twice yearly.

Boyds Mills Press
910 Church Street, Honesdale PA 18431
☎0101 717 253 1164   Fax 0101 717 253 0179

Chairman *Kent Brown Jr*
Managing Director *Larry Rosler*

A subsidiary of Highlights for Children, Inc. FOUNDED 1990 as a publisher of children's trade books. *Publishes* children's fiction, non-fiction and poetry. 29 titles in 1991. Unsolicited mss, synopses and ideas for books welcome. No romance.

IMPRINTS

Caroline House *Kent Brown* TITLES *Two Badd Babies; Hudson River.* **Bell Books** *Kent Brown* TITLES *Barnyard Tracks; Muriel & Ruth.* **Wordsong** *Bernice Cullinan* TITLES *Street Rhymes Around the World; Creatures of Earth, Sea and Sky.*
Royalties paid twice yearly.

Bradbury Press
See **Macmillan's Children's Book Group**

British American Publishing
19 British American Boulevard, Latham NY 12110
☎0101 518 786 6000   Fax 0101 518 786 1134

Chairman *Bernard F. Conners*
Managing Director *Kathleen A. Murphy*

Publishes general fiction and non-fiction. No romance, science fiction, gothic or horror. 10–15 titles a year. Unsolicited mss, synopses and ideas welcome.

IMPRINTS

Paris Review Editions, BAP (trade paperback list). TITLES *Portable People; Looking Back; Frog.*
Royalties paid twice yearly.

University of California Press
2120 Berkeley Way, Berkeley CA 94720
☎0101 415 642 4247   Fax 0101 415 643 7127

Director *James H. Clark*

Publishes academic non-fiction, fiction and poetry in translation. About 275 titles a year. Preliminary letter with outline preferred.

Carol Publishing
600 Madison Avenue, New York NY 10022
☎0101 212 486 2200   Fax 0101 212 486 2231

Publishes some fiction but mostly non-fiction: biography and autobiography, history, science, humour, how-to, illustrated and self-help. About 100 titles a year. No unsolicited mss.

Caroline House
See **Boyds Mills Press**

Carolrhoda Books, Inc.
241 First Avenue North, Minneapolis MN 55401
☎0101 612 332 3344   Fax 0101 612 332 7615

Publishes children's: nature, biography, history, beginners' readers, world cultures, photo essays.

Carroll & Graf Publishers, Inc.
260 Fifth Avenue, New York NY 10001
☎0101 212 889 8772   Fax 0101 212 545 7909

Contact *Kent Carroll*

FOUNDED 1983. General trade publisher. *Publishes* fiction: literary, mainstream, mystery, science fiction, erotica, fantasy and suspense. No genre romance. Also non-fiction: history, biography, psychology and current affairs. Query with synopsis and s.a.e. in the first instance. About 125 titles a year.
Royalties paid twice yearly.

Cassandra Editions
See **Academy Chicago Publishers**

Charlesbridge Publishing
85 Main Street, Watertown, MA 02172
☎0101 617 926 0329   Fax 0101 617 926 5720

Chairman *Brent Farmer*
Managing Director *Elena Wright*

FOUNDED 1980 as an educational publisher focusing on thinking and teaching processes. *Publishes* children's educational programmes (pre-kindergarten through to grade 8) and non-fiction picture books for 3–8 year-olds. 8 titles in 1991. TITLES *Going to a Horse Farm; Will We Miss Them? Endangered Species; Cheetah, Fast as Lightning.* Unsolicited mss, synopses and ideas welcome. Mss must be paged, with suggested illustrations described for each page. No fiction or topics other than those related to nature/science. 'No talking animals.'
Royalties paid yearly.

University of Chicago Press
5801 South Ellis Avenue, Chicago IL 60637–1496
☎0101 312 702 7700   Fax 0101 312 702 9756

Publishes academic non-fiction only.

Chronicle Books
275 Fifth Street, San Francisco CA 94103
☎0101 415 777 7240   Fax 0101 415 777 8887

Executive Editor *Nion McEvoy*

Division of Chronicle Publishing. *Publishes* food and cookery, gardening, art and design, health and medicine, nature, photography, leisure and travel, children's, adult fiction and short stories. About 100 titles a year. Query or submit outline/synopsis and sample chapters.

DIVISIONS
Children's *Victoria Rock;* **Cooking/Gardening** *Bill LeBlond;* **Art** *Nion McEvoy;* **Fiction** *Jay Schaefer.*
Royalties paid twice yearly.

Clarion Books

215 Park Avenue South, New York NY 10003
☎0101 212 420 5800 Fax 0101 212 420 5855

Publisher *Dorothy Briley*

Clarion Books began in 1965 as an imprint of Seabury Press. The Clarion name was inaugurated in 1974 and acquired by **Houghton Mifflin Co.** in 1979. *Publishes* children's books. TITLES *Tuesday* David Wiesner; *Our Teacher's Having a Baby* Eve Bunting; *Itchy Richard* Jamie Gilson; *The Ancient Cliff Dwellers of Mesa Verde* Caroline Arnold. About 50 titles a year. No novelty, series or genre fiction. Unsolicited mss, synopses and ideas welcome. Synopses should be accompanied by sample chapter(s).
Royalties paid twice yearly.

Clarkson N. Potter

See **Random House, Inc.**

Collier Books

See **Macmillan Children's Book Group**

Computer Books

See **Bantam Doubleday Dell Publishing Group**

Contemporary Books

180 North Michigan Avenue, Chicago IL 60601
☎0101 312 782 9181 Fax 0101 312 782 2157

Editorial Director *Nancy Crossman*

Publishes general adult non-fiction only.

Crestwood House

See **Macmillan's Children's Book Group**

Crime Line

See **Bantam Doubleday Dell Publishing Group**

Crown Publishing Group

See **Random House, Inc.**

CSS Publishing Co.

628 South Main Street, Lima OH 45804
☎0101 419 227 1818 Fax 0101 419 228 9184

Chairman *Wesley Rank*
Managing Director *Fred Steiner*

FOUNDED 1970. *Publishes* religious books only, focusing on lectionary-based sermons and worship aids for clergy. 50 titles in 1991. TITLES *A Season of Saints; The Vine and The Branches; The Roads Jesus Travelled.* Unsolicited mss, synopses and ideas welcome.

IMPRINTS
Fairway Press *Ellen Shockey* TITLES *Whither Thou Goest; His Truth Keeps Marching On; Love in a Manger.*
Royalties paid twice yearly.

DAW Books, Inc.

375 Hudson Street, 3rd Floor, New York NY 10014-3658
☎0101 212 366 2096/Submissions 366 2095 Fax 0101 212 366 2090

Publishers *Betsy Wollheim/Sheila Gilbert*
Submissions Editor *Peter Stampfel*

FOUNDED 1971 by Donald and Elsie Wollheim as the first mass market publisher devoted to science fiction and fantasy. One of the very few family-run companies still surviving as such after the buy-out shake-ups of the last decade. 'We have a very personal and hands-on approach to what we do.' *Publishes* science fiction/fantasy, and some horror. No short stories, anthology ideas or non-fiction. Unsolicited mss, synopses and ideas for books welcome. About 36 titles a year.
Royalties paid twice yearly.

Del Rey Books

See **Random House, Inc.**

Dell Books

See **Bantam Doubleday Dell Publishing Group**

Dial Books for Young Readers

375 Hudson Street, New York NY 10014
☎0101 212 366 2800 Fax 0101 212 366 2020

Submissions *Phyllis J. Fogelman*

Part of NAL Penguin, Inc. *Publishes* children's books, including picture books, beginners' readers, fiction and non-fiction for junior and young adults. 80 titles a year. Unsolicited mss welcome.

IMPRINTS
Dial Easy-to-Read Hardback and softcover editions, **Puffin Pied Piper/Puffin Pied Piper Giant** Softcover only.
Royalties paid twice yearly.

Dimensions for Living

201 Eighth Avenue South, Box 801,
Nashville TN 37202
☎0101 615 749 6404 Fax 0101 615 749 6512

Publishes non-fiction books for laity (inspirational, Bible study, Christian living and self-help).

Dolphin Books

See **Bantam Doubleday Dell Publishing Group**

Domain Books

See **Bantam Doubleday Dell Publishing Group**

Dorchester Publishing Co., Inc.

Suite 1008, 276 Fifth Avenue, New York NY 10001
☎0101 212 725 8811 Fax 0101 212 532 1054

President/Publisher *Gerard Brisman*

Publishes historical romance, time-travel romance, futuristic romance, horror and westerns. About 150 titles a year.

DIVISIONS/IMPRINTS
Leisure Books *Frank Walgren* TITLES *Midnight Fire* Madeline Baker; *Terms of Love* Shirl Henke. No unsolicited mss; send query or synopsis with first three chapters. No submissions returned without IRCs., and no simultaneous submissions.

Doubleday

See **Bantam Doubleday Dell Publishing Group**

William B. Eerdmans Publishing Co.

255 Jefferson Avenue, SE, Grand Rapids,
Michigan 49503
☎0101 616 459 4591 Fax 0101 616 459 6540

President *William B. Eerdmans Jr*
Editor-in-Chief *Jon Pott*

FOUNDED 1915 as a theological and reference publisher. Gradually began publishing in other genres with authors like C. S. Lewis, Dorothy Sayers and Malcolm Muggeridge on its lists. *Publishes* religious: theology, biblical studies, ethical and social concern, the arts, children's, history and biography; also social criticism, politics, literature and current affairs. 75 titles in 1991. Unsolicited mss, synopses and ideas welcome.

DIVISIONS
Children's *Amy Eerdmans* **Other** *Charles van Hof* TITLES *Dictionary of Biblical Tradition in English Literature; Systematic Theology; The Divine Dramatist: George Whitfield and the Rise of Modern Evangelicalism.*
Royalties paid twice yearly.

M. Evans & Co., Inc.

216 East 49th Street, New York NY 10017
☎0101 212 688 2810 Fax 0101 212 486 4544

Chairman *George C. de Kay*

FOUNDED 1954 as a packager. Began publishing in 1962. Best known for its popular psychology and medicine books, with titles like *Body Language, Open Marriage, Pain Erasure* and *Aerobics. Publishes* general non-fiction and popular fiction (romance, westerns). No unsolicited mss; query first. Unsolicited ideas and synopses welcome. TITLES *What Smart Women Know* S. Carter & J. Sokol; *Total Concentration* Harold Levinson; *The Seashell People: Growing Up in Adulthood* Martha Horton; *Safe Eating* Patrick Quillin. About 40 titles a year.
Royalties paid twice yearly.

Facts on File, Inc.

460 Park Avenue South, New York NY 10016
☎0101 212 683 2244 Fax 0101 212 683 3633

President *Tom Conoscenti*
Publisher *Martin Greenwald*

Started life in the early 1940s with News Digest subscription series to libraries. Began publishing on specific subjects with the Checkmark Books series and developed its current reference and trade book programme in the 1970s. *Publishes* general trade and academic reference only. 155 titles in 1991, but there are plans to trim this down to about 125 a year. No fiction, cookery or popular non-fiction. Unsolicited synopses and ideas welcome; no mss. Send query letter in the first instance.

DIVISIONS
General Reference *Susan Schwartz* TITLES *Shakespeare A–Z; Eyewitness History Series.* **Academic Reference** *Eleanora Von Deksen* TITLES *Maps on File; Encyclopedia of the Third World.* **Young Adult** *James Warren* TITLES *Straight*

Talk Series; Discovering Science Series; Fashions of the Decade Series.
Royalties paid twice yearly. *Overseas subsidiary* **Facts on File**, Oxford, England.

Fairway Press
See **CSS Publishing Co.**

Falcon
See **Bantam Doubleday Dell Publishing Group**

Fanfare
See **Bantam Doubleday Dell Publishing Group**

Farrar, Straus & Giroux, Inc.
19 Union Square West, New York NY 10003
☏0101 212 741 6900

Children's Editors *Stephen Roxburgh/Margaret Ferguson*

Publishes fiction and non-fiction, picture books and novels for children and young adults. Approximately 100 titles a year. Submit synopsis and sample chapters (copies of artwork/photographs as part of package).

Fawcett Juniper
See **Random House, Inc.**

Fielding Travel Books
See **William Morrow and Co., Inc.**

Fodor's Travel Publications
See **Random House, Inc.**

Four Winds Press
See **Macmillan's Children's Books**

Samuel French, Inc.
45 West 25th Street, New York NY 10010
☏0101 212 206 8990   Fax 0101 212 206 1429

Editor *Lawrence Harbison*

FOUNDED 1830. *Publishes* plays in paperback: Broadway and off-Broadway hits, light comedies, mysteries, one-act plays and plays for young audiences. Unsolicited mss welcome. No synopses. About 80–90 titles a year.

Editor *Lawrence Harbison*
Royalties paid annually (books); twice yearly (amateur productions); monthly (professional productions). *Overseas associates* in London, Toronto and Sydney.

Gardner Press, Inc.
19 Union Square West, New York NY 10003
☏0101 212 924 8293   Fax 0101 212 242 6339

Chairman *Gardner Spungin*
Managing Director *Maral Boyadjian*

FOUNDED 1975 as a publisher of professional, reference and textbooks in the helping/care professions. *Publishes* books on family therapy, alcohol and drug abuse, clinical social work, psychotherapy, psychiatry, psychoanalysis, criminal behaviour and child development; also university-level textbooks in these professions. A trade book division was later added in 1985 publishing self-help titles. Plans to expand its trade list and to enter fields connected with environmental sciences. Unsolicited material welcome provided it is accompanied by return postage.

DIVISIONS/IMPRINTS
Gestalt Institute of Cleveland Press, American Mensa Press, Gardner Trade Books, Gardner Professional.
Royalties paid twice yearly.

Gestalt Institute of Cleveland Press
See **Gardner Press, Inc.**

Greenwillow Books
See **William Morrow and Co., Inc.**

Harcourt Brace Jovanovich
Children's Division, 1250 Sixth Avenue, San Diego CA 92101
☏0101 619 699 6810   Fax 0101 619 699 6777

Publishes fiction, poetry and non-fiction: biography, travel, children's, science, current affairs, history. No unsolicited mss except for children's.

Harmony
See **Random House, Inc.**

HarperCollins Publishers, Inc.
10 East 53rd Street, New York NY 10022
☏0101 212 207 7000   Fax 0101 212 207 7797

Chief Executive *George Craig*

Owned by News Corporation. *Publishes* general fiction, non-fiction and college textbooks in hardcover, trade paperback and mass market formats.

DIVISIONS

Harper Paperbacks *Geoff Hannell;* **Adult Trade** *William Shinker;* **Children's** *Marilyn Kriney;* **College** *Susan Katz;* **Basic Books** *Martin Kessler;* **Scott Feresman** *Richard Peterson;* **Zondervan** *James Buick.*

Harvard University Press
79 Garden Street, Cambridge MA 02138
☏0101 617 495 2600   Fax 0101 617 495 5898

Editor-in-chief *Aida D. Donald*

Publishes scholarly non-fiction only. About 120 titles a year. Free book catalogue and mss guidelines available.

Harvest House Publishers
1075 Arrowsmith, Eugene OR 97402
☏0101 503 343 0123   Fax 0101 503 342 6410

President *R. C. Hawkins Jr*
Vice President, Editorial *Eileen L. Mason*

Publishes Christian living, counselling, fiction, children's and contemporary issues. TITLES *Chosen for Blessing* H. Norman Wright; *Getting the Best Out of Your Kids* Dr Kevin Leman; *Pathways to Armageddon* Betty Lynn. Unsolicited mss, synopses and ideas for books welcome, with IRCs.
Royalties paid annually.

Hearst Books
See **William Morrow & Co., Inc.**

Heartland
See **NorthWord Press**

Hippocrene Books, Inc.
171 Madison Avenue, New York NY 10016
☏0101 212 685 4371   Fax 0101 212 779 9338

Editorial Director *George Blagowidow*

Publishes general non-fiction and reference books. Particularly strong on dictionaries, language studies, maps and travel guides. No fiction. No unsolicited mss. Send brief summary, table of contents and one chapter for appraisal.

Holiday House, Inc.
425 Madison Avenue, New York NY 10017
☏0101 212 688 0085   Fax 0101 212 421 6134

Vice President/Editor-in-Chief *Margery Cuyler*

Publishes children's general fiction and non-fiction (pre-school to secondary). About 35–40 titles a year. Submit synopsis and three sample chapters for novels and chapter books; complete mss (without artwork) for picture books.

Houghton Mifflin Co.
2 Park Street, Boston MA 02108
☏0101 617 725 5000   Fax 0101 617 573 4916

Submissions Editor *Janice Harvey*

Publishes literary fiction and general non-fiction, including natural history, biography, health, history, current affairs, psychology and science. Also children's fiction and non-fiction. Average 100 titles a year. Queries only for adult material; synopses, outline and sample chapters for children's non-fiction; complete mss for children's fiction. IRCs required with all submissions/queries.

IMPRINTS
Clarion Books Children's fiction and non-fiction (see entry).

Human Services Institute
See **TAB Books**

University of Illinois Press
54 E. Gregory, Champaign IL 61820
☏0101 217 333 0950   Fax 0101 217 244 8082

Editorial Director *Richard L. Wentworth*

Publishes fiction: ethnic, experimental, mainstream, short story collections and thematic anthologies; no novels. Also non-fiction: scholarly and general — particularly in the humanities and Americana. About 100 titles a year. Send query letter first.

Indiana University Press
10th & Morton Streets, Bloomington IN 47405
☏0101 812 855 4203   Fax 0101 812 855 7931

Director *John Gallman*

Publishes scholarly non-fiction in specific subject areas. List available. Query in writing in first instance.

University of Iowa Press
Kuhl House, 119 West Park Road, Iowa City IA 52242
☏0101 319 335 2000   Fax 0101 319 335 2055

Director *Paul Zimmer*

FOUNDED 1969 as a small scholarly press publishing about 5 books a year. Now publishing about 30 a year in a variety of scholarly fields. Also local interest, short stories, fiction and poetry. No unsolicited mss; query first. Unsolicited ideas and synopses welcome.
Royalties paid annually.

Iowa State University Press
2121 South State Avenue, Ames IA 50010
☏0101 515 292 0140   Fax 0101 515 292 3348

FOUNDED 1924 as an offshoot of the university's journalism department. *Publishes* agriculture, archaeology and anthropology, art and design, architecture, aviation, biography and autobiography, biological science, business, economics, education, engineering, film, geography, geology, history, home economics, journalism and mass communication, language, mathematics and statistics, medical, music, philosophy, psychology, physics, politics, law, recreation, sociology and veterinary. 58 titles in 1991. Unsolicited proposals for books welcome.

IMPRINTS

Iowa Heritage Collection, Great Plains Environmental Design Series *Herbert Gottfried;* **Henry A. Wallace Series on Agricultural History and Rural Studies** *Richard Kirkendall;* **History of Science and Technology Reprint Series** *Stephen G. Brush;* **History of Technology and Science Reprint Series** *Alan I. Marcus;* **Women in Science and Technology** *Diane Calbrese;* **Venture Series in Veterinary Medicine** *Joe Morgan.*
Royalties paid annually; sometimes twice yearly.

Ivy Books
See **Random House, Inc.**

University Press of Kansas
2501 West 15th Street, Lawrence, Kansas 66049
☏0101 913 864 4154   Fax 0101 913 864 4586

Managing Director *Fred M. Woodward*

FOUNDED 1946. Became the publishing arm for all six state universities in Kansas in 1976. *Publishes* scholarly books in American history, women's studies, presidential studies, social and political

philosophy, political science, military history, environmental and sociology. About 35 titles a year. Proposals welcome.
Royalties paid annually.

Kent State University Press
Kent, Ohio 44242-0001
☏0101 216 672 7913   Fax 0101 216 672 3104

Director *John T. Hubbell*
Editor *Julia Morton*

FOUNDED 1965. *Publishes* scholarly works in history and biography, literary studies, archaeological research, arts and general non-fiction. 20–25 titles a year. Queries welcome; no mss.
Royalties paid twice yearly.

Alfred A. Knopf Inc.
See **Random House, Inc.**

Krieger Publishing Co., Inc.
PO Box 9542, Melbourne, Florida 32902
☏0101 407 724 9542   Fax 0101 407 951 3671

Chairman *Robert E. Krieger*
President *Donald E. Krieger*

Publishes business science and economics, education and communication, history, mathematics and computer science, medical science, psychology, chemistry, physical and natural sciences, reference, technology and engineering. 75 titles in 1991.

Editorial Head *Mary Roberts* Unsolicited mss welcome. Not interested in synopses/ideas.

IMPRINTS
Anvil, Orbit.
Royalties paid yearly.

Lerner Publications Co.
241 First Avenue North, Minneapolis MN 55401
☏0101 612 332 3344   Fax 0101 612 332 7615

Contact *Jennifer Martin*

Publishes books for children and young adults: geography, social issues, biographies, history, economics, ethnic studies, science, nature, activities, hi-lo, sports, some fiction.

Little, Brown & Co., Inc.
34 Beacon Street, Boston MA 02108
☏0101 617 227 0730
Trade Editorial Office: 1271 Avenue of the Americas, New York NY 10020

Division of Time Warner, Inc. FOUNDED 1877. *Publishes* contemporary popular fiction and literary fiction. Also non-fiction: how-to, distinctive cookbooks, biographies, history, nature, science and sports. About 100 titles a year. No unsolicited mss. Query letter in the first instance.

Llewellyn Publications

PO Box 64383, St Paul MN 55164
☎0101 612 291 1970   Fax 0101 612 291 1908

President/Publisher *Carl L. Weschcke*
Acquisitions Manager *Nancy J. Mostad*

Division of Llewellyn Worldwide Ltd. FOUNDED 1902. *Publishes* self-help and how-to: astrology, alternative health, tantra, Fortean studies, tarot, yoga, santeria, dream studies, metaphysics, magic, witchcraft, herbalism, Shamanism (religion of Siberian origin), organic gardening, women's spirituality, graphology, palmistry, parapsychology. About 60 titles a year. Unsolicited mss welcome; proposals preferred. IRCs. essential in all cases. Books are distributed in the UK by Foulsham.

Longman Publishing Group

95 Church Street, White Plains NY 10601
☎0101 914 993 5000   Fax 0101 914 997 8115

FOUNDED 1974. *Publishes* textbooks: primary, secondary, college and adult education, tertiary and professional. World history, politics, economics, communications, social sciences, sociology, education, English, Latin, foreign languages and EFL. No trade, art or children's. About 200 titles a year.

Lothrop, Lee & Shepard

See **William Morrow and Co., Inc.**

Louisiana State University Press

Baton Rouge LA 70893
☎0101 504 388 6294   Fax 0101 504 388 6461

Director *L. E. Phillabaum*

Publishes fiction: two novels, two short story collections and six volumes of poetry a year; plus non-fiction: Southern history, American history, French history, Southern literary criticism, American literary criticism, biography, political science, music (jazz) and Latin American studies. About 70 titles a year. Send International Reply Coupons for mss guidelines.

Lyons & Burford, Publishers

31 West 21st Street, New York NY 10010
☎0101 212 620 9580   Fax 0101 212 929 1836

Chairman *Nick Lyons*
Managing Director *Peter Burford*

Publishes outdoor, nature, gardening and angling titles, plus cookery. 45 titles in 1991. No unsolicited mss; synopses and ideas welcome. *Royalties* paid twice yearly.

Macmillan Children's Book Group

866 Third Avenue, New York NY 10022
☎0101 212 702 2000   Fax 0101 212 605 3068

Publishes children's picture books, fiction and non-fiction. About 160 titles a year.

IMPRINTS
Aladdin Books, Bradbury Press, Collier Books (young adults only)**, Crestwood House, Four Winds Press, McElderry Books. Atheneum Books** *Jonathan J. Lanman* Hardcover fiction and non-fiction, including picture books, from pre-school age through to young adult. No textbooks, activity books, pamphlets, magazines or religious. **Charles Scribner's Sons** *Clare Costello* Fiction and non-fiction. Unsolicited mss not welcome except in the case of picture books. Send synopsis and sample chapters (fiction); query letters only (non-fiction). Include return postage with all submissions.

McElderry Books

See **Macmillan's Children's Book Group**

McFarland & Company, Inc., Publishers

PO Box 611, Jefferson NC 28640
☎0101 919 246 4460   Fax 0101 919 246 5018

President/Editor-in-Chief *Robert Franklin*
Vice-President *Rhonda Herman*
Editor *Lisa Camp*

FOUNDED 1979. A library-orientated press, publishing reference books and scholarly monographs in many fields: East Asian studies, performing arts, sports, women's studies, music and fine arts, business, history and librarianship. *Specialises* in general reference. No unsolicited mss; send query letter first. Synopses and ideas welcome. No fiction, poetry, children's, New Age, inspirational or autobiographical works. About 110 titles a year. TITLES *African States and Rulers; Ballparks of North America; The Presidents' Last Years; Homophones and Homographs; Peace Organizations: A*

Directory; Mythological and Classical World Art Index; Surnames for Women.
Royalties paid annually. *Overseas associates* **Shelwing Ltd.**

University of Massachusetts Press

PO Box 429, Amherst MA 01004
☎0101 413 545 2217 Fax 0101 413 545 1226

Managing Director *Bruce Wilcox*

FOUNDED 1964. *Publishes* scholarly, general interest, black, ethnic, women's studies, cultural criticism, architecture and environmental design, literary criticism, poetry, philosophy, political science, sociology. Unsolicited mss considered but query letter preferred in the first instance. Synopses and ideas welcome. About 30 titles a year.
Royalties paid annually.

Minstrel

See **Simon & Schuster**

University of Missouri Press

2910 LeMone Boulevard, Columbia MO 65201-8227
☎0101 314 882 7641 Fax 0101 314 884 4498

Director/Editor-in-Chief *Beverly Jarrett*

Publishes academic: history, literary criticism, intellectual thought and related humanities disciplines; plus poetry and short stories — usually two volumes of each a year. Best approach is by letter. Send brief samples of poetry/short stories for consideration, and synopses for academic work. About 45–50 titles a year.

MIT Press

55 Hayward Street, Cambridge MA 02142
☎0101 617 253 1558 Fax 0101 617 258 6779

Acquisitions Co-ordinator *Lise Solomon*

Publishes non-fiction: technologically sophisticated books including computer science and artificial intelligence, economics, architecture, cognitive science, linguistics and philosophy. Average 200 titles a year. Submit synopsis or proposal, academic resumé and sample chapters.

William Morrow and Co., Inc.

1350 Avenue of the Americas, New York NY 10019
☎0101 212 261 6500 Fax 0101 212 261 6595

Editorial Director *Adrian Zackheim*

Publishes fiction, poetry and general non-fiction. Approach in writing only. No unsolicited mss or proposals. Proposals read only if submitted through a literary agent (50,000–100,000 words).

IMPRINTS
Hearst Books/Hearst Marine Books *Ann Bramson;* **Fielding Travel Books** *Randy Ladenheim-Gil;* **Quill Trade Paperbacks** *Andy Dutter.* Children's imprints: **Morrow Junior Books** *David Reuther;* **Lothrop, Lee & Shepard** *Susan Pearson;* **Greenwillow Books** *Susan Hirschman;* **Tambourine Books** *Paulette Kaufmann;* **Mulberry Books/Beech Tree Books** (trade paperbacks) *Amy Cohn.*

Mulberry Books

See **William Morrow and Co., Inc.**

Nan A. Talese Books

See **Bantam Doubleday Dell Publishing Group**

NavPress Publishing Group

PO Box 35001, Colorado Springs CO 80935
☎0101 719 548 9222 Fax 0101 719 260 7223

Publisher *John Eames*
Editorial Director *Bruce Nygren*
Submissions *Debby Weaver*

FOUNDED 1975 as a publisher of bible studies (the publishing branch of the Navigators). *Publishes* bible studies, marriage and parenting, Christian living, singles issues, ethics in the workplace, church growth. About 60 titles a year. TITLES *Parenting Adolescents; Church Without Walls; Rocking the Roles.* No children's, picture books, secular fiction or poetry. No unsolicited mss; synopses and ideas welcome.

IMPRINTS
NavPress, Piñon Press.
Royalties paid quarterly. *Overseas associates* worldwide.

University of Nevada Press

MS 166, Reno NV 89557-0076
☎0101 702 784 6573 Fax 0101 702 784 6200

Director *Thomas Radko*
Editor-in-Chief *Nicholas Cady*

FOUNDED 1960. *Publishes* natural history, Basque studies and regional studies mostly. 20 titles in 1991. Unsolicited material welcome if it fits in with areas published, or offers a 'new and exciting' direction.
Royalties paid twice yearly.

New Age/New Sciences
See **Bantam Doubleday Dell Publishing Group**

University Press of New England
17½ Lebanon Street, Hanover NH 03755
✆0101 603 643 7100 Fax 0101 603 643 1540
Chair/Director *Thomas L. McFarland*

FOUNDED 1970. A scholarly book publisher sponsored by eleven institutions of higher education in the region: Brandeis, Brown, Clark, Dartmouth, Middlebury, Tufts, Wesleyan and the universities of Connecticut, New Hampshire, Rhode Island and Vermont. *Publishes* general and scholarly non-fiction: American and European history, literature and literary criticism, cultural theory, art history, philosophy, psychology, education, regional interest and natural sciences. Plus poetry, essays and short stories through the Wesleyan Poetry Series and Bread Loaf Writers Conference. Lead title for 1991/2: *Writers on Writing* ed. Bob Pack & Jay Parini. Also publishers of various journals: *Anthrozoos: A Multi-disciplinary Journal on the Interactions of People, Animals and Environment; International Environmental Affairs; New England Review: Middlebury Series.* About 55 titles a year. Unsolicited material welcome.

IMPRINTS

Wesleyan University Press Interdisciplinary studies, history, literature, women's studies, government and public issues, biography, poetry, social and natural sciences.
Royalties paid annually. *Overseas associates* Trevor Brown Associates, London.

University of New Mexico Press
1720 Lomas NE, Albuquerque NM 87131-1591
✆0101 505 277 2346 Fax 0101 505 277 9270
Editor *Jeffrey Grathwohl*

Publishes scholarly non-fiction across a wide range of fields, plus illustrated and biography. No fiction, how-to, children's, humour, self-help, technical or textbooks. About 60 titles a year.

NorthWord Press, Inc.
PO Box 1360, Minocqua WI 54548
✆0101 715 356 9800 Fax 0101 715 356 9762
Publisher *Tom Klein*
Editor-in-Chief *Greg Linder*

FOUNDED 1985 with the publication of publisher Tom Klein's book, *Loon Magic* and has since expanded rapidly to become America's principal nature publisher. Non-fiction only: nature, wildlife,

environmental, natural history, outdoor and sporting titles for adults; nature and wildlife titles for children. About 20 titles a year. TITLES *America's Rainforest; Moose Country; Elk Country; Canoe Country; Wild Wisconsin; White Wolf.* Unsolicited synopses/ideas welcome; send proposal, outline and sample chapter or two. Include international reply coupons for return.

IMPRINTS
Heartland TITLES *The Land Remembers; Northern Retreats; Prairie Visions.* **Willow Creek Press** TITLES *Wingshooters Autumn; Wild Harvest Cookbook; Those of the Forest; Trout on a Stick; Bass Fever.*
Royalties paid twice yearly.

W.W. Norton & Company
500 Fifth Avenue, New York NY 10110
✆0101 212 354 5500
Editor *Liz Malcolm*

Publishes quality fiction and non-fiction. No occult, paranormal, religious, cookbooks, arts and crafts, genre fiction (formula romances, science fiction or westerns), children's books or young adult. About 300 titles a year. Query letters should include brief description of submission, of writing credentials and experience relevant to submissions. Submissions should consist of several sample chapters including the first; non-fiction submissions should also include a detailed outline of content. Return postage essential for response.

University of Oklahoma Press
1005 Asp Avenue, Norman OK 73019-0445
✆0101 405 325 5111 Fax 0101 405 325 4000
Editor-in-Chief *John Drayton*

Publishes non-fiction only: American Indian studies, Western American history, classical studies, literary theory and criticism, women's studies. About 70 titles a year.

Open Court Publishing Co.
Box 599, Peru IL 61354
✆0101 815 223 2520 Fax 0101 815 223 1350
Publisher *M. Blouke Carus*

FOUNDED 1987. *Publishes* scholarly non-fiction: philosophy, Jungian analysis, psychology, comparative religion, science, mathematics, public policy, education, Oriental studies. About 15 titles a year. Write or submit synopsis and two or three sample chapters.

Orbit
See **Krieger Publishing Co., Inc.**

Orion Books
See **Random House, Inc.**

Pantheon Books
See **Random House, Inc.**

Paragon House Publishers
90 Fifth Avenue, New York NY 10011
☏0101 212 620 2820   Fax 0101 212 633 0518

Editor-in-Chief *Ken Stuart*

FOUNDED 1983. *Publishes* non-fiction: biography, reference and textbooks. Subjects include Americana, history, philosophy, politics and religion. Also poetry from established writers only. About 100 titles a year. Send query or outline with table of contents in the first instance.

DIVISIONS/IMPRINTS
Trade *P. J. Dempsey* **College** *Evelyn Fazio* TITLES *Spying for America* Miller; *The Vision of Buddhism* Corless; **Athena** *P. J. Dempsey* TITLES *Don Fernando* Maugham; *Bombs Away* Steinbeck.
Royalties paid twice yearly.

Paris Review Editions
See **British American Publishing**

Pelican Publishing Company
1101 Monroe Street, Box 189, Gretna LA 70053
☏0101 504 368 1175

Editor *Nina Kooij*

Publishes fiction: very limited requirement (including children's books) and non-fiction: general (especially cookbooks, travel, art, architecture and inspirational). About 45 titles a year. Initial enquiries required for all submissions.

Pelion Press
See **Rosen Publishing Group, Inc.**

University of Pennsylvania Press
418 Service Drive, Philadelphia PA 19104
☏0101 215 898 1671   Fax 0101 215 898 0404

Managing Director *Thomas M. Rotell*

FOUNDED 1896. *Publishes* scholarly, reference, professional, textbooks and trade. No fiction or poetry.

TITLES include *Women at War, Love Sickness in the Middle Ages.* No unsolicited mss but synopses and ideas for books welcome. 91 titles in 1991.
Royalties paid annually.

Perfect Crime
See **Bantam Doubleday Dell Publishing Group**

Piñon Press
See **NavPress Publishing Group**

Players Press
PO Box 1132, Studio City CA 91614-0132
☏0101 818 789 4980

Chairman *William-Alan Landes*
Managing Director *Sharon Gorrell Hoffman*

FOUNDED 1965 as a publisher of plays; now publishes across the entire range of performing arts. Plays, musicals, theatre, film, cinema, television, costume, puppetry, plus technical theatre and cinema material. 36 titles in 1991.

Editorial Head *Robert W. Gordon* TITLES *Performance One; Scenes for Acting and Directing; The New Competitor, Shakespeare's Characters; How to Break into the Film Business.* No unsolicited mss; synopses/ideas welcome. Send query letter.
Royalties paid twice yearly. *Overseas subsidiaries* in Canada, Australia and the UK.

Plenum Publishing
233 Spring Street, New York NY 10013
☏0101 212 620 8000   Fax 0101 212 463 0742

Senior Editor, Trade Books *Linda Greenspan Regan*

FOUNDED 1946. *Publishes* quality non-fiction for the intelligent layman and the professional: trade science, social sciences, health, psychology and criminology. Queries only. About 350 titles a year.

Pocket Books
See **Simon & Schuster**

Prentice Hall
See **Simon & Schuster**

Prima Publishing and Communications

PO Box 1260, Rocklin CA 95677
☎0101 916 786 0426 Fax 0101 916 786 0488

Chairman *Ben Dominitz*

FOUNDED 1984. *Publishes* general non-fiction: cookbooks, business, health, psychology, parenting, etc. No unsolicited mss; send 2–3 page proposal with IRCs. Unsolicited synopses and ideas for books welcome. 54 titles in 1991; 120 projected for 1992.

IMPRINTS
Secrets of the Games Video and computer game books; **Prima** Computer application books.
Royalties paid twice yearly.

Princeton University Press

41 William Street, Princeton NJ 08540
☎0101 609 258 4900 Fax 0101 609 258 6305

Editor-in-Chief *Emily Wilkinson*

Publishes non-fiction: art and architecture, anthropology, history, philosophy, religion, political science, music, biological and physical sciences, biography, computer science, language and literature, translation and women's studies. About 265 titles a year. Queries only.

Putnam Publishing Group

200 Madison Avenue, New York NY 10016
☎0101 212 951 8400 Fax 0101 212 213 6706

Editorial *Gene Brissie/Patty Gauch/Neil Nyren*

Publishes general fiction and non-fiction, including children's. Major fiction publisher.

Quill Trade Paperbacks

See **William Morrow and Co., Inc.**

Rand McNally & Co.

PO Box 7600, Chicago IL 60680
☎0101 708 673 9100 Fax 0101 708 673 1985

Editor *Jon Leverenz*

Publishes world atlases and maps, road atlases of North America and Europe, city and state maps of the United States and Canada, educational wall maps, atlases and globes.

Random House, Inc.

Trade Division: 201 East 50th Street, New York NY 10022
☎0101 212 572 2600 Fax 0101 212 572 0158/2593
Children's Division: 225 Park Avenue South, New York NY10003
☎0101 212 254 1600

Owned by Advance Publications. FOUNDED 1925. *Publishes* trade fiction: adventure, confessional, experimental, fantasy, historical, horror, humour, mainstream, mystery and suspense; and non-fiction: biography, history, economics, politics, health, business, sports, humour, food and cookery, self-help, Americana, nature and environment, psychology, religion, sociology. About 180 titles a year. Plus children's fiction: adventure, confessional (young adult), fantasy, historical, horror, humour, mystery, picture books, science fiction, suspense, young adult; and children's non-fiction: biography, humour, illustrated, nature and the environment, leisure, science and sport. About 300 titles a year. Submissions via agents preferred.

DIVISIONS/IMPRINTS
Children's Send synopsis and three sample chapters.
Crown Publishing (Tel: 572 6190). Popular trade non-fiction. IMPRINTS **Clarkson N. Potter, Orion Books, Harmony**. Preliminary letter essential.
Ballantine/Del Rey/Fawcett/Ivy Books (Tel: 751 2600). IMPRINTS **Del Rey** Science fiction and fantasy. Submit complete mss (not less than 50,000 words) or detailed outline with first three chapters. Pay particular attention to plotting and satisfactory conclusion. **Fawcett Juniper** Non-fiction (adult) and fiction (mainstream, children's and young adult). Query first.
Alfred A. Knopf, Inc. *Ashbel Green* Literary fiction and non-fiction, including scholarly. Submit complete mss for fiction (30,000–150,000 words); approach in writing for non-fiction (40,000–150,000 words). **Pantheon** (Tel: 751 2600). Fiction and non-fiction. Query first. **Vintage Books, Random House Reference, Fodor's Travel Publications**.
Royalties paid twice yearly.

The Rosen Publishing Group, Inc.

29 East 21st Street, New York NY 10010
☎0101 212 777 3017 Fax 0101 212 777 0277

President *Roger Rosen*
Editor *Patra McShary*

Publishes non-fiction books (reference, self-help and textbooks) for a young adult audience on careers and personal guidance, and high-lo books for reluctant readers. Areas of interest include art, health (coping), music, biography, geography, self-esteem, drug abuse prevention. Also publishes *Icarus*, a quarterly magazine of new writing from around the world. About 70 titles a year. Write with outline and sample chapters.

IMPRINT
Pelion Press Music titles.

Rutgers University Press

109 Church Street, New Brunswick NJ 08901
☎0101 908 932 7762 Fax 0101 908 932 7039

Director *Kenneth Arnold*
Editor-in-Chief *Marlie Wasserman*

FOUNDED 1936. *Publishes* scholarly books and fiction. Unsolicited mss, synopses and ideas for books welcome. About 70 titles a year. *Royalties* paid annually.

St Martin's Press, Inc.

175 Fifth Avenue, New York NY 10010
☎0101 212 674 5151 Fax 0101 212 420 9314

FOUNDED 1952. *Publishes* general fiction, especially crime; and adult non-fiction: history, self-help, political science, biography, scholarly, popular reference. About 1100 titles a year. Unsolicited mss considered; enquiry letter preferred in the first instance.

Scarecrow Press, Inc.

52 Liberty Street, PO Box 4167,
Metuchen NJ 08840
☎0101 908 548 8600 Fax 0101 908 548 5767

President *Albert W. Daub*
Vice-President *Norman Horrocks*

FOUNDED 1950 as a short-run publisher of library reference books. Acquired by Grolier, Inc., Connecticut, in 1970. *Publishes* reference, scholarly and monographs (all levels) for libraries. About 100 titles a year. Expansion planned. Unsolicited mss welcome but material will not be returned unless requested, and accompanied by return postage. Unsolicited synopses and ideas for books welcome. Possible change of address late 1993.

Senior Editor *Barbara A. Lee* TITLES *American Artists: Signatures and Monograms, 1800–1989; Latin American Studies: A Basic Guide to Sources; Directory of Blacks in the Performing Arts.* *Royalties* paid annually.

Schocken Books, Inc.

201 East 50th Street, New York NY 10022
☎0101 212 572 2559 Fax 0101 212 572 6030

Senior Editor *Bonny Fetterman*

Publishes serious non-fiction (including reprints): Jewish studies, women's studies, history, social science, psychology and education.

Scholastic, Inc.

730 Broadway, New York NY 10003
☎0101 212 505 3000 Fax 0101 212 505 3217

Executive Editor *Ann Reit*

Publishes fiction for middle grade (8–12-year-olds) and young adults: family stories, friendship, mysteries and school, and adult romance. Also non-fiction: biography and multicultural subjects. Mss with outlines and three sample chapters welcome.

Scott Feresman

See **HarperCollins Publishers, Inc.**

Charles Scribner's Sons

See **Macmillan Children's Book Group**

Silver Burdett Press

See **Simon & Schuster**

Simon & Schuster

Trade Books Division, 1230 Avenue of the Americas, New York NY 10020
☎0101 212 698 7000

Fiction and non-fiction through agents only. Fiction: mystery and suspense, thrillers, science fiction, romance, westerns. Non-fiction: history, biography, science and technology, philosophy, arts, popular culture, reference, cookery, humour and general. No textbooks, specialised, poetry or plays. No unsolicited mss or queries.

DIVISIONS/IMPRINTS
Pocket Books Fiction and non-fiction, including young adult and children's. IMPRINTS **Archway, Minstrel, Pocket Star, Washington Square Press**. Also **Prentice Hall, Silver Burdett Press**.

Spectra

See **Bantam Books, Inc.**

Spy Books

See **Bantam Doubleday Dell Publishing Group**

Stanford University Press

Stanford CA 94305-2235

☏ 0101 415 723 9598 Fax 0101 415 725 3457

Editor *Norris Pope*

Publishes non-fiction: scholarly works in all areas of the humanities, social sciences and natural sciences, plus a few general interest titles and academic books. About 75 titles a year. No unsolicited mss; query in writing first.

Sterling Publishing

387 Park Avenue South, New York NY 10016

☏ 0101 212 532 7160 Fax 0101 212 213 2495

Contact *Sheila Anne Barry*

FOUNDED 1949. *Publishes* non-fiction only: alternative lifestyle, games/ puzzles, how-to, health, home medical, business, cookery, hobbies, children's humour and science, pets, recreation, sports, military, New Age, nature, wine, woodworking, technical and reference. About 80 titles a year. Query or submit chapter list, outline and two sample chapters.

Gareth Stevens Children's Books

1555 North River Center Drive, Suite 201,
Milwaukee WI 53212

☏ 0101 414 225 0333 Fax 0101 414 225 0377

President *Gareth Stevens*

Publishes children's books only. About 80 titles a year. No unsolicited material at present as schedule is full for some time to come.
Royalties paid annually.

TAB Books

Blue Ridge Summit PA 17214

☏ 0101 717 794 2191

Fax 0101 717 794 5344   Telex 820562

Publisher *Stephen Fitzgerald*
Director of Acquisitions *Ron Powers*

Part of **McGraw-Hill, Inc**. *Publishes* computer hardware and software, marine and nautical, aviation, automotive, electronics, electrical and electronics repair, woodworking, home improvement, arts and crafts, science fair projects, self-help, substance abuse treatment, business, graphic design, model railways, etc. Unsolicited mss, synopses and ideas for books welcome.

DIVISIONS/IMPRINTS

TAB Books *Ron Powers* TITLES *Science Magic for Kids; Basic Digital Electronics*; **Design Press** *Nancy Green* TITLES *Graphic Design*;

International Marine *Jon Eaton*; **Windcrest Books** *Ron Powers* TITLES *D Base IV Programming*; **Human Services Institute** *Kim Tabor* TITLES *Abused No More*; **Aero Books** *Jeff Worsinger* TITLES *A-7 Corsair II*.
Royalties paid twice yearly.

Tambourine Books

See **William Morrow and Co., Inc.**

Temple University Press

Broad and Oxford Streets, Philadelphia PA 19122

☏ 0101 215 787 8787 Fax 0101 215 787 4719

Editor-in-Chief *Michael Ames*

Publishes scholarly non-fiction: American history, Latin American studies, law, cultural studies, sociology, women's studies, health care, philosophy, public policy, labour studies, urban studies, photography and black studies. About 70 titles a year. Authors generally academics. Write in first instance.

University of Tennessee Press

293 Communications Building,
Knoxville TN 37996-0325

☏ 0101 615 974 3321 Fax 0101 615 974 3724

FOUNDED in the late 1800s. Began full-time publication of scholarly works in 1947. *Publishes* non-fiction: anthropology, folklore, literature, American history, Southern studies, feminist literary criticism, women's studies, American religious history and African-American studies. Unsolicited material/ outlines welcome in these areas. About 25–30 titles a year.
Royalties paid twice yearly.

University of Texas Press

PO Box 7819, Austin TX 78713-7819

☏ 0101 512 471 7233/Editorial: 471 4278

Fax 0101 512 320 0668

Director *Joanna Hitchcock*
Assistant Director/Executive Editor *Theresa J. May*

Publishes scholarly non-fiction: anthropology, archaeology, cultural geography, Latin/Mexican/ native American studies, politics, sociology, biology and earth sciences, environmental, American/ Soviet/Texan urban studies, women's, film, medieval, literary studies, Middle Eastern studies, regional cookbooks, natural history, Latin American literature in translation, art and architecture, classics. Unsolicited material welcome in above subject areas only. About 70 titles a year. *Royalties* paid annually.

Time-Life Books, Inc.

777 Duke Street, Alexandria VA 22314
☎0101 703 838 7000   Fax 0101 703 838 7474

Publishes non-fiction general interest books, usually heavily illustrated, and originated in-house. No unsolicited mss. About 45 titles a year.

Times Books

201 East 50th Street, New York NY 10022
☎0101 212 872 8094   Fax 0101 212 872 8244

Editorial Director *Steve Wasserman*

Publishes non-fiction only: business, economics, science and medical, biography, history, women's issues, cookery, current affairs, language and education. Unsolicited mss not considered. Letter essential. About 45 titles a year.

Trinity Press International

3725 Chestnut Street, Philadelphia PA 19104
☎0101 215 387 8757   Fax 0101 215 387 8805

Managing Director *Dr Harold Rast*

FOUNDED 1989. *Publishes* religion and theology. Acts as distributor for **SCM Press** and **Epworth Press**, London.

Universe Publishing, Inc.

300 Park Avenue South, New York NY 10010
☎0101 212 387 3400   Fax 0101 212 387 3644

Editorial Director *Adele J. Ursone*

Publishes non-fiction only: art history and criticism, with an emphasis on women's studies and the 20th century, and illustrated gift books on popular subjects. About 20 titles a year. Send synopsis with two to three sample chapters and sample illustrative material.

University Editions

See **Aegina Press, Inc.**

University Press of America, Inc.

4720 Boston Way, Lanham, Maryland 20706
☎0101 301 459 3366   Fax 0101 301 459 2118

Publisher *James E. Lyons*

FOUNDED 1975. *Publishes* scholarly monographs, college and graduate level textbooks. No children's, elementary or high school. About 450 titles a year. Submit outline or request proposal questionnaire.
Royalties paid annually. *Distributed* by Eurospan Ltd, London.

Van Nostrand Reinhold

115 Fifth Avenue, New York NY 10003
☎0101 212 254 3232   Fax 0101 212 254 9499

Publishes professional, technical, scientific reference and texts in the following fields: occupational health and industrial safety; electrical, mechanical, civil and industrial engineering; computer science and data processing; architecture, graphic arts and interior design; food/fish science and technology, cooking and tourism, chemistry and chemical engineering; environmental science, gemology and earth science; mathematics and statistics; biomedical science; building construction.

Vintage Books

See **Random House, Inc.**

Walker & Co

720 Fifth Avenue, New York NY 10019
☎0101 212 265 3632   Fax 0101 212 307 1764

Contact *Submissions Editor*

Publishes fiction: thriller and adventure, mystery and suspense, regency romance, westerns and children's. Also non-fiction: Americana, art, biography, business histories, how-to books, children's, science, history, media, psychiatric, music, nature, sports, parenting, psychology, recreation, reference, popular science, self-help. About 100 titles a year. All submissions should be accompanied by s.a.e.

Warner Books

666 Fifth Avenue, New York NY 10103
☎0101 212 484 2900   Fax 0101 212 484 2713

Senior Editor *Fredda Isaacson*

Publishes non-fiction: celebrity biography, cookery, how-to, humour, illustrated reference, self-help, true crime, business. Query or submit outline with sample chapters and letter.

Washington Square Press

See **Simon & Schuster**

Washington State University Press

Cooper Publications Building, Pullman,
Washington 99164-5910
☏0101 509 335 3518   Fax 0101 509 335 8568

Director *Thomas H. Sanders*

FOUNDED 1928. Revitalised in 1984 to publish
hardcover originals, trade paperbacks and reprints.
Publishes mainly on the history, prehistory and
culture of the Northwest United States (Washington, Idaho, Oregon, Montana) and British Columbia, but works that focus on national topics or
other regions may also be considered. No fiction,
historical fiction, how-to or gardening material.
8–10 titles a year. TITLES *The Washington High
Bench: A Biographical History of the State Supreme
Court, 1889–1991; Asian Americans: Comparative
and Global Perspectives.* Unsolicited mss welcome.
No synopses or ideas.
Royalties paid annually.

Willow Creek Press

See **NorthWord Press**

Windcrest Books

See **TAB Books**

Wordsong

See **Boyds Mills Press**

Zephyr Books

See **Bantam Doubleday Dell Publishing Group**

Zondervan

See **HarperCollins Publishers, Inc.**

US Agents

International Reply Coupons

For return postage, send International Reply Coupons (IRCs), available from the Post Office. Letters 60 pence; mss according to weight. Check with the Post Office.

Dominick Abel Literary Agency, Inc.
146 West 82nd Street, Suite 1B, New York NY 10024
☎0101 212 877 0710   Fax 0101 212 595 3133

President *Dominick Abel*

FOUNDED 1975. *Handles* non-fiction and fiction. No scripts. Works mostly with established/published writers. No unsolicited mss. Send query letter with International Reply Coupons for response. No reading fee. *Commission* Home 10%; Dramatic 15%; Foreign 20%. *Overseas associates* **David Grossman Literary Agency.**

Acton & Dystel
928 Broadway, New York NY 10010
☎0101 212 473 1700   Fax 0101 212 505 0278

Contact *Jane Dystel*

FOUNDED 1975. *Handles* non-fiction and fiction. *Specialises* in politics, history, biography, current affairs, celebrities, sport, commercial (mystery and historical romance in particular) and literary fiction. No reading fee. CLIENTS include Lorene Cary, Jason Miller, Tip O'Neill, Jennifer Wilde. *Commission* Home 15%; Dramatic 15%; Foreign 19%.

Marcia Amsterdam Agency
Suite 9A, 41 West 82nd Street, New York NY 10024
☎0101 212 873 4945   Fax 0101 212 873 4945

Contact *Marcia Amsterdam*

FOUNDED 1969. *Specialises* in mainstream fiction, horror, suspense, humour, young adult, TV and film scripts. No poetry, books for the 8–10 age group or how-to. No unsolicited mss. First approach by letter only and enclose International Reply Coupons. No reading fee for outlines and synopses. CLIENTS include Kristopher Franklin, Ruby Jean Jensen, Robert Leininger, William H. Lovejoy, Joyce Sweeney. *Commission* Home 15%; Dramatic 10%; Foreign 20%.

Bart Andrews & Associates
7510 Sunset Boulevard 100, Los Angeles CA 90046
☎0101 213 851 8158   Fax 0101 310 271 5952

Contact *Bart Andrews*

FOUNDED 1982. General non-fiction: show business, biography and autobiography, film books, trivia, TV and nostalgia. No scripts. No fiction, poetry, children's or science. No books of less than major commercial potential. *Specialises* in working with celebrities on autobiographies. No unsolicited mss. 'Send a brilliant letter (with IRCs for response) extolling your manuscript's virtues. Sell me!' CLIENTS include J. Randy Taraborrelli, Wayne Newton, Dick Maurice, Bart Andrews, Bill Givens. No reading fee. *Commission* Home 15%; Translation 15%. *Overseas associates* **Abner Stein**, London.

Joseph Anthony Agency
8 Locust Court Road, 20 Mays Landing, New Jersey NJ 08330
☎0101 609 625 7608

Contact *Joseph Anthony*

FOUNDED 1964. *Handles* all types of novel and scripts for TV: 2-hour mini-series, screenplays and ½-hour sitcoms. No poetry, short stories or pornography. *Specialises* in action, romance and detective novels. Unsolicited mss welcome. Return postage essential. Reading fee charged to new writers: novels £75; screenplays £100. CLIENTS include Robert Long, Sandi Wether. *Commission* Home 15%; Dramatic 20%; Translation 20%.

Appleseeds Management
200 East 30th Street, Suite 302, San Bernardino CA 92404
☎0101 909 882 1667
Hollywood: 1870 North Vermont Avenue, Suite 560, Hollywood CA 90027

Contact *S. James Foiles/Tommy Caldwell* (Hollywood)

FOUNDED 1988. Signatory to the Writers Guild of America Agreement. *Handles* action/adventure, mystery, science fiction, horror/occult, general non-fiction, biography, true crime and self-help. Also screenplays and teleplays (no series). Query with full mss and IRCs. Screenplays to *Tommy Caldwell* in Hollywood. No reading fee. *Commission* Home 10–20%; Dramatic 10–20%.

The Artists Group

1930 Century Park West, Suite 403, Los Angeles CA 90067
☎0101 213 552 1100 Fax 0101 213 277 9513

Contact *Robert Malcolm/Hal Stalmaster/Nancy Moon-Broadstreet/Art Rutter*

FOUNDED 1978. Screenplays and plays for film/TV/ theatre and radio. No unsolicited mss. Write with list of credits, if any. No reading fee. *Commission* Home 10%; Dramatic 10%; Translation 10%.

Author Aid Associates

340 East 52nd Street, New York NY 10022
☎0101 212 758 4213/980 9179

Editorial Director *Arthur Orrmont*

FOUNDED 1967. *Handles* fiction and non-fiction, both children's and adult, verse collections and scripts for film, television and theatre. No cookbooks, computing. *Specialises* in war, aviation, cults, New Age, occult, history, literary/commercial fiction, biography and autobiography. TITLES include *A Guide to Literary Agents of North America* (4th ed.). No unsolicited mss. Advance query essential. Reading fee charged to new/ unpublished authors. Short queries answered by return mail. CLIENTS include Eddie Ensley, Maurice Rowden, Igor Yefimov. *Commission* Home 10-15%; Dramatic 20%; Translation 20%.

The Authors Resource Center & Tarc Literary Agency

PO Box 64785, Tucson AZ 85728-1785
☎0101 602 325 4733

Contact *Martha R. Gore*

FOUNDED 1984. *Handles* mainstream adult fiction and non-fiction. No scripts unless a book contract has already been signed. No biography or autobiography (unless celebrity). No poetry, essays, short stories, romance, science fiction or children's (except from established authors). *Specialises* in self-help, pop psychology, new science, business self-help, military, true/fiction crime, modern westerns, contemporary novels, books with Jewish themes, both fiction and non-fiction, crafts and hobbies. All self-help material must be written or co-authored by professionals. Not handling any work from authors based outside the US at present. No unsolicited mss. No response without IRCs. No reading fee. Critiques, editing and ghostwriting service available. CLIENTS Jim Christ, Sherry Sedgwick, Mary McConnell, J. M. Hayes. *Commission* Home 15%; Foreign 20%.

Julian Bach Literary Agency

747 Third Avenue, New York NY 10017
☎0101 212 753 2605 Fax 0101 212 688 8297

Contact *Julian Bach*

FOUNDED 1959. *Handles* non-fiction and fiction. No children's, young adult, science fiction, fantasy, futuristic, poetry or photography. No scripts. Unsolicited mss welcome but query first. Submissions should include brief synopsis (typed), sample chapters (50 pp maximum), publishing history, etc. Send photocopies which do not need returning or postal coupons for return. CLIENTS Jerry Baker, Pat Conroy, Jan Morris, Hedrick Smith, Nancy Thayer, Adam Ulam, Robin Winks. *Commission* Home 15%; Dramatic 15%; Foreign 20%. *Overseas associates* worldwide.

Malaga Baldi Literary Agency

PO Box 591, Radio City Station, New York NY 10101
☎0101 212 222 1221

Contact *Malaga Baldi*

FOUNDED 1986. *Handles* quality fiction and non-fiction. No scripts. No westerns, men's adventure, science fiction/fantasy, romance, how-to, young adult or children's. Writers of fiction should send mss with covering letter, including IRCs for return of mss and stamped addressed postcard for notification of receipt. Allow ten weeks minimum for response. For non-fiction, approach in writing with a proposal, table of contents and two sample chapters. No reading fee. CLIENTS include Margaret Erhart, Bettina Berch, Maud Farrell, David J. Skal. *Commission* Home 15%; Dramatic 15%; Translation 15–20%. *Overseas associates* **Abner Stein**, **Marsh & Sheil Ltd**, Japan Uni.

The Balkin Agency, Inc.

PO Box 222, Amherst MA 01004
☎0101 413 256 1934 Fax 0101 413 256 1935

Contact *Richard Balkin*

FOUNDED 1973. *Handles* adult non-fiction only. No reading fee for outlines and synopses. *Commission* Home 15%; Foreign 20%.

Lois Berman

The Little Theatre Building, 240 West 44th Street,
New York NY 10036
☏0101 212 575 5114   Fax 0101 212 575 5176

Contact *Lois Berman*

FOUNDED 1972. Dramatic writing only, by referral.

Meredith Bernstein Literary Agency, Inc.

2112 Broadway, Suite 503A, New York NY 10023
☏0101 212 799 1007   Fax 0101 212 799 1145

Contact *Meredith Bernstein/Elizabeth Cavanaugh/ Patrick LoBrutto*

FOUNDED 1981. Fiction and non-fiction of all types. No children's. Send query letter first; unpublished authors welcome. IRCs essential for response. Nominal reading fee for unpublished writers. CLIENTS include Georgina Gentry, Shirl Henke, David Jacobs, Kay Nolte Smith, Nancy Picard. *Commission* Home 15%; Dramatic 15%; Translation 20%. *Overseas associates* **Abner Stein**, Lennart Sane, Thomas Schluck.

Reid Boates Literary Agency

PO Box 328, 274 Cooks Crossroad,
Pittstown NJ 08867-0328
☏0101 908 730 8523   Fax 0101 908 730 8931

Contact *Reid Boates*

FOUNDED 1985. *Handles* general fiction and non-fiction. *Specialises* in journalism and media, serious self-help, biography and autobiography, true crime and adventure, popular science, current affairs, trade reference and quality fiction. No scripts. No science fiction, fantasy, romance, western, gothic, children's or young adult. Enquire by letter with IRCs in first instance. No reading fee. CLIENTS include James Sterngold, Dr Donald Johanson, Jon Winokur, estate of Ava Gardner. *Commission* Home 15%; Dramatic 15%; Translation 20%. *Overseas associates* **David Grossman Literary Agency; Marsh & Sheil**; Japan Uni.

Georges Borchardt, Inc.

136 East 57th Street, New York NY 10022
☏0101 212 753 5785   Fax 0101 212 838 6518

FOUNDED 1967. Works mostly with established/ published authors. *Specialises* in fiction, biography, and general non-fiction of unusual interest. Unsolicited mss not read. *Commission* Home 10%; Dramatic 10%; UK 15%; Translation 20%. *UK associates* **Richard Scott Simon Ltd**, London.

Brandenburgh & Associates Literary Agency

24555 Corte Jaramillo, Murrieta CA 92562
☏0101 714 698 5200

Contact *Don Brandenburgh*

FOUNDED 1986. *Specialises* in non-fiction for the evangelical Christian market, including inspirational, Christian living and education, social issues, Christian ministry/missions, theology/doctrine, evangelism, marriage and family, fiction (limited), devotional (limited). Some general trade material, namely education and psychology. No poetry, children's, young adult, occult or metaphysical. No unsolicited mss; send query letter with IRCs. No reading fee. CLIENTS John Desjarlais, Bill Hand, Terry Hershey, Evelyn Minshull. *Commission* Home 10%; Dramatic 20%; Translation 20%.

Brandt & Brandt Literary Agents, Inc.

1501 Broadway, New York NY 10036
☏0101 212 840 5760   Fax 0101 212 840 5776

Contact *Carl D. Brandt/Gail Hochman/Charles Schlessiger*

FOUNDED 1914. *Handles* non-fiction amd fiction. No poetry or children's books. No unsolicited mss. Approach by letter describing background and ambitions. No reading fee. *Commission* Home 10%; Dramatic 10%; Foreign 20%. *UK associates* **A. M. Heath & Co. Ltd.**

Pema Browne Ltd

Pine Road, HCR Box 104B, Neversink NY 12765
☏0101 914 985 2936   Fax 0101 914 985 7635

Contact *Pema Browne/Perry Browne*

FOUNDED 1966. *Handles* mass market mainstream and hardcover fiction: romance, men's adventure, horror, humour, westerns, children's picture books and young adult. Non-fiction: how-to, politics, religion and reference. Also scripts for film. No unsolicited mss; send query letter with IRCs. Reading fee charged according to length of mss. Also handles illustrators' work. CLIENTS Valerie Mangrum, Catherine Toothman. *Commission* Home 15%; Dramatic 10%; Translation 15%.

Maria Carvainis Agency, Inc.

235 West End Avenue, New York NY 10023
☏0101 212 580 1559   Fax 0101 212 877 3486

Contact *Maria Carvainis*

FOUNDED 1977. *Handles* fiction: general mainstream, contemporary women's, mystery, suspense, fantasy, historical and young adult. Non-fiction: business, finance, women's issues, political biography, medicine, psychology and popular science. No film scripts unless from writers with established credits. No science fiction. No unsolicited mss; they will be returned unread. Queries only, with IRCs for response. No reading fee. CLIENTS Mary Balogh, David Bottoms, Joseph H. Boyett, Sandra Brown, Neil F. Comins, Pam Conrad, Jose Yglesias. Represents over 60 authors. Maria Carvainis is a member of the Association of Authors Representatives and Chair of its Contracts Committee. She is also a member of the Writers Guild of America, Mystery Writers of America, and Romance Writers of America. *Commission* Home 15%; Dramatic 15%; Translation 20%.

Martha Casselman, Literary Agent

PO Box 342, Calistoga CA 94515-0342
☎0101 707 942 4341

Contact *Martha Casselman/Sue Farley*

FOUNDED 1979. *Handles* all types of fiction and non-fiction. Main interests: food/cookery, biography, current affairs, popular sociology and children's. No scripts, textbooks, poetry, coming-of-age fiction or science fiction. Especially interested in cookery with an appeal to the American market for possible co-publication in UK. Send queries and brief summary, with return postage; 40–60 sample pages for fiction. If you do not wish return of material, please state so. Also include, where applicable, any material on previous publications, reviews, brief biography. No proposals via fax. No reading fee. *Commission* Home 15%.

The Catalog Literary Agency

PO Box 2964, Vancouver WA 98668
☎0101 206 694 8531

Contact *Douglas Storey*

FOUNDED 1986. *Handles* popular, professional and textbook material in all subjects, especially business, health, money, science, technology, computers, electronics and women's interests; also how-to, self-help, mainstream fiction and children's non-fiction. No genre fiction. No scripts, articles, screenplays, plays, poetry or short stories. No reading fee. No unsolicited mss. Query with an outline and sample chapters and include IRCs. CLIENTS include Malcolm S. Foster, Isaac O. Olaleye, Deborah Wallace. *Commission* Home 15%; Dramatic 20%; Translation 20%.

Linda Chester Literary Agency

265 Coast, La Jolla CA 92037
☎0101 619 454 3966   Fax 0101 619 454 7338

Contact *Laurie Fox*

FOUNDED 1978. *Handles* literary fiction and non-fiction: biography, business, psychology and self-help, history, popular culture, fine and performing arts, science and health. No scripts, children's or textbooks. No unsolicited mss; send query letter with IRCs for reply. No reading fee for solicited material. Evaluation/critique service available (£350). *Commission* Home 15%; Dramatic 15%; Translation 25%.

Connie Clausen Associates

Suite 16H, 250 East 87th Street, New York NY 10128
☎0101 212 427 6135   Fax 0101 212 996 7111

Contact *Connie Clausen/Andra Brill*

FOUNDED 1976. Works mostly with established/published authors. *Specialises* in trade non-fiction of all kinds. Unsolicited mss not read. CLIENTS include Quentin Crisp, Robert Haas, David Letterman, Cher, Dr Ray Guarendi, Dr Sonya Friedman. *Commission* Home 15%; Dramatic 15%; Foreign 20%. *UK associates* **David Grossman Literary Agency**.

Diane Cleaver, Inc.

55 Fifth Avenue, New York NY 10003
☎0101 212 206 5606   Fax 0101 212 463 8718

FOUNDED 1983. Fiction and non-fiction. No scripts. No how-to, science fiction or illustrated. No unsolicited mss. Query first. No reading fee. CLIENTS include Jerry Oster, Kim Chernin, James Lardner. *Commission* Home 15%; Translation 19%. *Overseas associates* **Abner Stein**, London.

Hy Cohen Literary Agency Ltd

111 West 57th Street, New York NY 10019
☎0101 212 757 5237   Fax 0101 212 397 1580

President *Hy Cohen*

FOUNDED 1975. Fiction and non-fiction. No scripts. Unsolicited mss welcome, but synopsis with sample 100 pp preferred. International Reply Coupons essential. No reading fee. CLIENTS include Alex Ayres, John Drummen, Gary Friedman, Ann Gabriel, Daniel Hayes, Victoria Houseman, Elaine Long, Tom Lorenz, Thomas O'Donnell. *Commission* Home 10%; Dramatic 10%; Foreign 20%. *Overseas associates* **Abner Stein**, London.

Ruth Cohen, Inc.

Box 7626, Menlo Park CA 94025
☎0101 415 854 2054

President *Ruth Cohen*

FOUNDED 1982. Works mostly with established/ published authors but will consider new writers. *Specialises* in high-quality children's, young adult and women's fiction, plus genre fiction: mystery and historical romance. No poetry, short stories or film scripts. Send opening 10 pp, plus synopsis. No reading fee. International Reply Coupons for correct postage essential. *Commission* Home 15%; Dramatic 15%; Foreign 20%.

Frances Collin Literary Agency

110 West 40th Street, Suite 1403, New York NY 10018
☎0101 212 840 8664

Contact *Frances Collin*

FOUNDED 1948. No scripts. No unsolicited material. Submissions only accepted via agents. *Overseas associates* **Abner Stein**, London.

Connor Literary Agency

640 West 153rd Street, D2, New York NY 10031
☎0101 212 491 5233   Fax 0101 212 491 5233

Contact *Marlene Connor/Mina Kumar*

FOUNDED 1985. *Handles* general non-fiction, contemporary women's fiction, popular fiction, black fiction and non-fiction, how-to, mysteries and crafts. Also film and TV scripts. Particularly interested in illustrated books. No unsolicited mss; send query letter in the first instance. Reading fee (£100 full mss, with reader's report). CLIENTS Lenore Carroll, Sindiwe Magona, Nadezda Obradovic, Randy Russell, Nina Tassi. *Commission* Home 15%; UK 25%; Translation 25%. *Overseas associates* in England and Spain.

Creative Concepts Literary Agency

PO Box 10261, Harrisburg PA 17105
☎0101 717 432 5054

Contact *Michele Glance Serwach*

FOUNDED 1987. *Handles* non-fiction, literary fiction and commercial fiction, including romance, mystery, science fiction and horror. Also scripts for film, TV, theatre and radio. No autobiographies (unless celebrity) or poetry collections which do not have universal appeal. *Specialises* in romance, mystery and informative self-help. Send synopsis (250–500 words) together with list of credits. Reading fee £95. CLIENTS Doc & Katy Abraham, Donald Dahl, Renee Harmon, Bill Simpson. *Commission* Home 10%; Dramatic 15%; Translation 15%.

Richard Curtis Associates, Inc.

171 East 74th Street, Second Floor, New York NY 10021
☎0101 212 772 7363

Contact *Richard Henshaw/Rob Cohen/Richard Curtis*

FOUNDED 1969. *Handles* genre and mainstream fiction, plus some commercial non-fiction. Scripts rarely.

Curtis Brown Ltd

10 Astor Place, New York NY 10003
☎0101 212 473 5400
606 North Larchmont, LA 90004

Contact *Perry Knowlton/Peter L. Ginsberg/Emilie Jacobson/Maureen Walters/ Marilyn Marlow/Clyde Taylor/Irene Skolnick/Laura Blake/Ginger Knowlton/* Film, TV, Audio rights (Los Angeles): *Timothy Knowlton/Jess Taylor/*Screenplays and teleplays: *Jeannine Edmunds*

FOUNDED 1914. *Handles* general fiction and nonfiction. Also scripts for film, TV, theatre and radio. No unsolicited mss; queries only, with IRCs for reply. No reading fee. *Commission* Home 15%; Dramatic 15% (options)/ 10% (when exercised); Translation 20%.

Joan Daves Agency

21 West 26th Street, New York NY 10010-1083
☎0101 212 685 2663   Fax 0101 212 685 1781

Contact *Joan Daves/Jennifer Lyons*

FOUNDED 1952. Tradebooks: fiction, non-fiction and children's. No science fiction, romance or textbooks. No scripts. No unsolicited mss. Send query letter in the first instance. 'A detailed synopsis seems valuable only for non-fiction work. Material submitted should specify the author's background, publishing credits and similar pertinent information.' No reading fee. CLIENTS Frederick Franck, Elizabeth Marshall Thomas, estates of Martin Luther King Jr, Isaac Babel and Heinrich Böll. *Commission* Home 15%; Dramatic 10–25%; Foreign 20%.

Elaine Davie Literary Agency

Village Gate Square, 274 North Goodman Street, Rochester NY 14607
☎0101 716 442 0830

President *Elaine Davie*

FOUNDED 1986. *Handles* all types of adult fiction and non-fiction, specialising in books by and for women. Particularly interested in commercial genre fiction. No scripts. No short stories, anthologies, poetry or children's. Approach with an idea by letter in first instance, enclosing synopsis, sample chapters and IRCs. No reading fee. CLIENTS include Paul Bagdon, Marcia Evanich, Christina Skye. All submissions to *Elaine Davie. Commission* Home 15%; Dramatic 20%; Translation 20%.

The Deering Literary Agency

1507 Oakmont Drive, Acworth GA 30101
☎0101 404 591 2051 Fax 0101 404 591 0369
Director *Charles F. Deering*

FOUNDED 1989. *Handles* non-fiction (all subjects) and fiction: historical, mystery, romance, literary, religious, horror, science fiction and fantasy. Unsolicited mss welcome. *Specialises* in new authors. Reading fee of £125 (up to 100,000 words); £150 (over 100,000). CLIENTS include Theodore J. Nottingham, Jack Ruby, Michael Staudinger, Dutchess Wagner. *Commission* Home 12%; Dramatic 18%; Translation 15%.

Anita Diamant Literary Agency

Suite 1508, 310 Madison Avenue, New York NY 10017
☎0101 212 687 1122
Contact *Anita Diamant/Robin Rue*

FOUNDED 1917. *Handles* fiction and non-fiction. No academic, children's, science fiction and fantasy, poetry, articles, short stories, screenplays or teleplays. Works in association with Hollywood film agent. No unsolicited mss. Write with description of work, short synopsis and details of publishing background. No reading fee. CLIENTS include V. C. Andrews, Pat Hagan, Linda Howard, Richard Lederer, Mark McGarrity, Andrew Neiderman, R & K Petraz. *Commission* Home 15%; Dramatic 15%; Translation 20%. *Overseas associates* **A. M. Heath & Co**, London.

Sandra Dijkstra Literary Agency

1155 Camino del Mar, Suite 515, Del Mar CA 92014
☎0101 619 755 3115 Fax 0101 619 792 1494
Contact *Katherine Goodwin*

FOUNDED 1981. *Handles* quality non-fiction, contemporary and genre fiction: crime, horror, historical, science fiction and fantasy. No scripts. No westerns, contemporary romance or poetry. Willing to look at children's projects. *Specialises* in psychology, self-help, science, health, business, memoirs, biography, mystery/thrillers. Dedicated to

promoting new and original voices and ideas. For fiction: send the first 50 pp and synopsis; for non-fiction: a proposal with overview, chapter outline, biography and preferably sample chapters. All submissions should be accompanied by IRCs. No reading fee. CLIENTS include Amy Tan, Max DePree, Robert Ferrigno, Le Ly Hayslip, Susan Faludi. *Commission* Home 15%; Translation 20%. *Overseas associates* **Abner Stein**, London; Agence Hoffman, Germany.

Robert Ducas Literary Agency

See **Caroline Davidson and Robert Ducas (UK Agents)**

Dupree/Miller & Associates, Inc., Literary Agency

5518 Dyer Street, Suite 3, Dallas TX 75206
☎0101 214 692 1388 Fax 0101 214 987 9654
Contact *Jan Miller/David Smith/Sunita Batra*

FOUNDED 1984. *Handles* fiction, non-fiction and film/TV mini-series scripts. No poetry, short stories, literary criticism or genre romance. Unsolicited mss welcome. Send sample proposal rather than query, with overall synopsis, biographical material and 1–3 sample chapters. Include a return envelope with reply coupons if material is to be returned. Reading fee £10. CLIENTS Dr Ravi Batra, Dr Stephen Covey, Jose Eber, Payne Harrison, Tony Robbins. *Commission* Home 15%; Dramatic 15%; Translation 20%.

Dykeman Associates, Inc.

4115 Rawlins, Dallas TX 75219-3661
☎0101 214 528 2991 Fax 0101 214 528 0241
Contact *Alice Dykeman*

FOUNDED 1974. *Handles* non-fiction, namely celebrity profiles and biographies, and some movie scripts. No unsolicited mss; send outline or synopsis. Reading fee of £250 charged. *Commission* Home 15%.

Educational Design Services, Inc.

PO Box 253, Wantagh NY 11793
☎0101 718 539 4107/516 221 0995
President *Bertram Linder*
Vice President *Edwin Selzer*

FOUNDED 1979. *Specialises* in educational material and textbooks for sale to school markets. IRCs must accompany submissions. *Commission* Home 15%; Foreign 25%.

Vicki Eisenberg Literary Agency

929 Fernwood, Richardson TX 75080
☏0101 214 918 9062　Fax 0101 214 918 9976

Contact *Vicki Eisenberg*

FOUNDED 1985. *Handles* commercial fiction and non-fiction, literary and dramatic rights. No children's, short stories or poetry. No unsolicited mss will be read; unsolicited queries welcome. Query first with detailed synopsis of work. No reading fee. *Commission* 15%. *Overseas associates* **Barbara Levy Literary Agency**, London.

Peter Elek Associates

PO Box 223, Canal Street Station, New York NY 10013
☏0101 212 431 9368　Fax 0101 212 966 5768

Contact *Michelle Roberts*

FOUNDED 1979. *Handles* adult non-fiction and children's picture books. No scripts, novels, psychology, New Age, poetry, short stories or autobiography. No unsolicited mss; send letter of enquiry with IRCs for reply; include resumé, credentials, brief synopsis. No reading fee. CLIENTS Tedd Arnold, Nava Atlas, Dr Robert Ballard, Patrick Brogan, Robert Bateman, Chris Dodd, Leah Komaiko. *Commission* Home 15%; Dramatic/ Foreign 20%. *Overseas associates* **Vardey & Brunton Associates**, London.

Ellen Lively Steele & Associates

PO Drawer 447, Organ NM 88052-0447
☏0101 505 382 5440　Fax 0101 505 382 9821

Contact *Vincent M. Lockhart/Dale & Lisa York*

FOUNDED 1980. *Handles* adventure, mystery, suspense, horror, metaphysical, children's, cookbooks, mainstream, etc. However, 'a sound idea and proficient writing precludes genre consideration'. Also handles film, television, radio and theatre scripts. No romance. No unsolicited mss; send query letter with outline only in first instance. No reading fee. CLIENTS Ching Yun Bezine, John Broussard, Don Murray, John Riley, Sandra Woodruff. Signatory to the Writer's Guild of America. *Commission* 10%, plus copyright.

The Ethan Ellenberg Literary Agency

548 Broadway, Suite 5E, New York NY 10012
☏0101 212 431 4554　Fax 0101 212 941 4652

Contact *Ethan Ellenberg/Liana De Feo*

FOUNDED 1983. *Handles* commercial and literary fiction and non-fiction, plus film and TV rights for published authors only. *Specialises* in category

fiction, including thrillers, science fiction, fantasy and horror, mystery, crime, historical and other romance, first novels and narrative literary novels. Non-fiction: biography, health, popular science and history. Eager to work with talented novelists in all categories for development of long-term top-selling success. 'Editorial work without charge for authors we believe in.' Unsolicited mss accepted but must be accompanied by International Reply Coupons to cover cost of return or reply. Query letter preferred in the first instance and/or outline and first three sample chapters. IRCs essential in all cases. No reading fee. CLIENTS include Mark Berent, Bob Mayer, Clay Reynolds, Steve Vance. *Commission* Home 15%; Dramatic 15%; Translation 10%.

Ann Elmo Agency, Inc.

60 East 42nd Street, New York NY 10165
☏0101 212 661 2880/1/2
Fax 0101 212 661 2883

Contact *Lettie Lee/Mari Cronin/Ann Elmo*

FOUNDED in the 1940s. *Handles* literary and romantic fiction, mysteries and mainstream; also non-fiction in all subjects, including biography and self-help. Some children's (8–12-year-olds) and young adult. Query letter with outline of project in the first instance. No reading fee. *Commission* Home 15–20%. *Overseas associates* **John Johnson Ltd**, London.

Evans & Associates

14330 Caves Road, Novelty OH 44072-9503
☏0101 216 338 3264

Contact *Clyde Evans*

FOUNDED 1987. Fiction: mystery, suspense, spy, westerns, science fiction and general commercial fiction. No scripts. Approach in writing with synopsis and sample chapters, together with IRCs. No reading fee. CLIENTS include Mirian Study Giles, Sophia Zufa. *Commission* 15%.

John Farquharson Ltd

Suite 1007, 250 West 57th Street, New York NY 10107
☏0101 212 245 1993　Fax 0101 212 245 8678

Contact *Deborah Schneider*

FOUNDED 1919 (London), 1980 (New York). Works mostly with established/published authors. *Specialises* in general trade fiction and non-fiction. No poetry, short stories or screenplays. No reading fee for outlines. Submissions must be accompanied by IRCs. *Commission* Home 15%; Dramatic 10%; Foreign 20%. *Overseas associates* **John**

Farquharson (Curtis Brown Group Ltd), London.

Florence Feiler Literary Agency

1524 Sunset Plaza Drive, Los Angeles CA 90069
☏ 0101 310 652 6920/659 0945

Contact *Florence Feiler*

FOUNDED 1967. *Specialises* in fiction, non-fiction, how-to, textbooks, translations, TV and film scripts/tapes. No short stories or pornography. No unsolicited mss. First approach by letter. No reading fee. CLIENTS include literary estates of Isak Dinesen (*Out of Africa* and *Babette's Feast*) and Bess Streeter Aldrich. Member of PEN American Center; PEN USA West Center; Academy Television Arts & Sciences; Mystery Writers of America; California Writers Association; Women In Film. *Commission* Home 10%; Foreign 20%.

Marje Fields/Rita Scott

165 West 46th Street, 909, New York NY 10036
☏ 0101 212 764 5740

Contact *Ray Powers*

FOUNDED 1971. *Handles* fiction, non-fiction and plays. Film scripts rarely. No children's or poetry. Send query letter first; no unsolicited mss. Reading fee charged occasionally. CLIENTS include John Westermann, Nicole Jeffords, Patrick Dennis estate. *Commission* Home 15%; Dramatic 15%; Translation 20%. *Overseas associates* **A. M. Heath & Co**, London.

Frieda Fishbein Ltd

2556 Hubbard Street, Brooklyn NY 11235
☏ 0101 212 247 4398

President *Janice Fishbein*

FOUNDED 1925. Eager to work with new/unpublished writers. *Specialises* in historical romance, historical adventure, male adventure, mysteries, thrillers, family sagas, 'non-reporting' and how-to. Also books on the environment, nursing and medicine, plus plays and screenplays. No poetry, magazine articles, short stories or young children's. First approach with query letter. No reading fee for outlines at our request; otherwise charged (enquire in writing for details). CLIENTS Gary Bohlke, Herbert Fisher, Jeanne Mackin, Thomas Millstead, Roy Schroeder, Robert Simpson, Alicen White. *Commission* Home 10%; Dramatic 10%; Foreign 20%.

Flannery, White & Stone

180 Cook, Suite 404, Denver CO 80206
☏ 0101 303 399 2264   Fax 0101 303 399 3006

Contact *Connie Solowiej/Robert FitzGerald/ Barbara Schroichet*

FOUNDED 1987. *Handles* literary and mainstream fiction, children's, general non-fiction and business. Also screenplays for motion pictures. No theatre or radio. No pornography. Call or write with query in first instance. No unsolicited mss. CLIENTS include Reginald McKnight, Maxine Schur, David Seals. *Commission* Home 15%; Dramatic 15%; Translation 20%.

ForthWrite Literary Agency

PO Box 922101, Sylmar CA 91392
☏ 0101 818 365 3400

Contact *Wendy L. Zhorne*

FOUNDED 1988. *Handles* all types of fiction and non-fiction. *Specialises* in children's books and non-fiction, especially history (English and Scottish), also self-help, business, home and health, crafts and animal care. Send query letter with IRCs. Reading fee charged in some cases. 'A dedicated, zealous agency' which only represents 'quality material we are enthusiastic about'. *Commission* Home/Dramatic 15%; Translation 20%.

Robert A. Freedman Dramatic Agency, Inc.

Suite 2310, 1501 Broadway, New York NY 10036
☏ 0101 212 840 5760

President *Robert A. Freedman*

FOUNDED 1928 as Brandt & Brandt Dramatic Department, Inc. Took its present name in 1984. Works mostly with established authors. *Specialises* in plays, film and TV scripts. Unsolicited mss not read. *Commission* Dramatic 10%.

Candice Fuhrman Literary Agency

PO Box F, Forest Knolls CA 94933
☏ 0101 415 488 0161   Fax 0101 415 488 4335

Contact *Candice Fuhrman*

FOUNDED 1987. *Handles* commercial adult fiction and serious non-fiction. *Specialises* in biography, self-help and how-to. Keen to work with new/unpublished writers. No scripts. No children's or genre fiction. Unsolicited mss welcome but query letter preferred first. No reading fee. *Commission* Home 15%; Translation 10%; Foreign 10%.

Jay Garon-Brooke Associates, Inc.

415 Central Park West, 17th Floor, New York NY 10025
☎0101 212 866 3654 Fax 0101 212 666 6016

President *Jay Garon*
Vice Presidents *Jean Free/Nancy Coffey*

FOUNDED 1951. Fiction and non-fiction: history and historical romance, suspense/thrillers, political intrigue, horror/occult, self-help. No category romance, westerns or mysteries. No unsolicited mss. First approach by query letter. No reading fee. CLIENTS include Mary Cahill, Virginia Coffman, Elizabeth Gage, James Leo Herlihy, Burt Hirschfeld, Patricia Matthews, Daoma Winston, John Grisham, Cherokee P. McDonald. *Commission* Home 15%; Dramatic 10–15%; Foreign 30%. *Overseas associates* **Abner Stein**, London.

Max Gartenberg, Literary Agent

521 Fifth Avenue, Suite 1700, New York NY 10175
☎0101 212 860 8451 Fax 0101 201 535 5033

Contact *Max Gartenberg*

FOUNDED 1954. Works mostly with established/published authors. *Specialises* in non-fiction and trade fiction. No reading fee for outlines. CLIENTS include William Ashworth, Linda Davis, Ralph Hickok, Charles Little, David Roberts. *Commission* Home 10%; Dramatic 10%; Foreign 15%.

Gelles-Cole Literary Enterprises

Woodstock Towers, 320 East 42nd Street, New York NY 10017
☎0101 212 573 9857

President *Sandi Gelles-Cole*

FOUNDED 1983. *Specialises* in general commercial fiction and women's business books. No scripts. No science fiction and fantasy. No unsolicited mss; query first. Reading fee charged. Editorial service available, including mss evaluation, character and plot development.

Gladden Unlimited

PO Box 7912, San Diego CA 92701
☎0101 619 224 5051

Contact *Carolan Gladden*

FOUNDED 1987. Signatory to the Writers Guild of America Agreement. *Handles* fiction including mainstream: action/adventure, science fiction and fantasy, horror and thrillers. Also general non-fiction, movie and TV screenplays. No romance, westerns, mystery, poetry, children's, short stories or religion. Dedicated to assisting new writers

achieve publication. No unsolicited mss. Query with postage and IRCs. answered in 3 weeks. Fee of £100 charged for marketability evaluation which is refunded if material is placed. *Commission* Home 15%; Dramatic 10%; Translation 20%.

Sanford J. Greenburger Associates

55 Fifth Avenue, New York NY 10003
☎0101 212 206 5600 Fax 0101 212 463 8718

Contact *Heide Lange/Diane Cleaver/Faith Hamlin/ Beth Vesel*

Handles fiction and non-fiction. No scripts. No unsolicited mss. First approach with query letter and synopsis. No reading fee.

The Charlotte Gusay Literary Agency

10532 Blythe Avenue, Los Angeles CA 90064
☎0101 310 559 0831 Fax 0101 310 559 2639

Contact *Charlotte Gusay*

FOUNDED 1988. *Handles* fiction, non-fiction and children's for the commercial trade market. Some scripts, but very selective about them. Particularly keen to take books to film. Always looking for good children's illustrators, good humour/cartoonists, outstanding ethnic, non-sexist children's writers, quirky off-beat fiction, and strong non-fiction. No science fiction, horror, short pieces or collections of stories. No unsolicited mss; send query letter first with succinct outline of project. No response without IRCs. CLIENTS Ken Grissom, Miriam Marx Allen, Annie Reiner, Barry Yourgrau. *Commission* Home 15%; Dramatic 10%; Translation/ Foreign 25%.

John Hawkins & Associates, Inc.

71 West 23rd Street, Suite 1600, New York NY 10010
☎0101 212 807 7040 Fax 0101 212 807 9555

Contact *John Hawkins/William Reiss/Sharon Friedman*

FOUNDED 1893. *Handles* fiction, non-fiction, children's, science fiction, psychology, politics, biography. No scripts or romance. No unsolicited mss; send queries with synopsis and IRCs for response. No reading fee. CLIENTS Gail Godwin, John Katzenbach, Joyce Carol Oates, Alex Haley, Tom Wicker. *Commission* Apply for rates. *UK associates* **Murray Pollinger**.

Heacock Literary Agency, Inc.
1523 Sixth Street, Suite 14, Santa
Monica CA 90401
☎0101 213 393 6227/213 451 8523/4

President *James B. Heacock*
Vice President *Rosalie G. Heacock*

FOUNDED 1978. Works with a small number of new/unpublished authors. *Specialises* in non-fiction on a wide variety of subjects: health, nutrition, exercise, beauty, women's studies, popular psychology, crafts, business expertise, pregnancy, parenting, alternative health concepts, contemporary celebrity biographies. Also novels by established authors and film/TV scripts by full-time professionals and members of the Writer's Guild. No unsolicited mss. Queries with International Reply Coupons only. No reading fee. CLIENTS include Dr Joseph Bark, Dr Arnold Fox & Barry Fox, Don & Audrey Wood, Paul Horn, Larry D. Brimner. *Commission* Home 15% on first £50,000 each year, 10% thereafter; Foreign 15% if sold direct, 25% if agent used.

The Jeff Herman Agency, Inc.
500 Greenwich Street, Suite 501C, New York NY 10013
☎0101 212 941 0540   Fax 0101 212 941 0614

Contact *Jeffrey H. Herman*

Handles non-fiction, textbooks and reference. No scripts. No unsolicited mss. Query letter with IRCs in the first instance. No reading fee. CLIENTS include Robert Shook, George Gallup. Jeff Herman publishes a useful reference guide to the book trade called *The Insider's Guide to Book Editors, Publishers & Literary Agents* (Prima/St Martin's Press). *Commission* Home 15%; Translation 10%.

Susan Herner Rights Agency, Inc.
PO Box 303, Scarsdale NY 10583
☎0101 914 725 8967   Fax 0101 914 725 8969

Contact *Susan N. Herner/Sue P. Yuen*

FOUNDED 1987. Adult non-fiction and fiction, both literary and commercial: thrillers, science fiction, romance and horror. No screenplays, teleplays or children's. Approach by letter with sample chapters and outline. No postage coupons. No reading fee. CLIENTS include Hara Marano, Jonathan Littel, Libby Sydes, Tim Underwood. *Commission* Home 15%; Dramatic 20%; Translation 20%. *Overseas associates* **David Grossman Literary Agency**.

Frederick Hill Associates
1842 Union Street, San Francisco CA 94123
☎0101 415 921 2910   Fax 0101 415 921 2802

Contact *Fred Hill/Bonnie Nadell*

FOUNDED 1979. General fiction and non-fiction. No scripts. Send query letter detailing past publishing history if any. International Reply Coupons required. CLIENTS include Katherine Neville, Randy Shilts. *Commission* Home 15%; Dramatic 15%; Foreign 20%. *Overseas associates* **Abner Stein Agency**, London.

Hull House Literary Agency
240 East 82nd Street, New York NY 10028
☎0101 212 988 0725   Fax 0101 212 794 8758

President *David Stewart Hull*
Associate *Lydia Mortimer*

FOUNDED 1987. *Handles* commercial fiction, mystery, biography, military history and true crime. No scripts, poetry, short stories, romance, science fiction and fantasy, children's or young adult. No unsolicited mss; send single page letter describing project briefly, together with short biographical note and list of previous publications if any. IRCs essential. No reading fee. *Commission* Home 15%; Translation 20%.

International Publisher Associates, Inc.
746 West Shore, Sparta NJ 07871
☎0101 201 729 9321

Executive Vice President *Joe DeRogatis*

FOUNDED 1982. *Specialises* in all types of non-fiction, plus books for the US movie industry. No reading fee for outlines but IRCs essential for return. Eager to work with new/unpublished writers. *Commission* Home 15%; Foreign 20%.

Sharon Jarvis and Co., Inc.
260 Willard Avenue, Staten Island NY 10314
☎0101 718 720 2120

President *Sharon Jarvis*

FOUNDED 1985. *Handles* genre/commercial fiction and general non-fiction. Works mostly with established/published authors but will consider new writers. No unsolicited mss; query in the first instance. *Commission* Home 15%; Foreign 25%.

Natasha Kern Literary Agency, Inc.
PO Box 2908, Portland OR 97208-2908
☎0101 503 297 6190   Fax 0101 503 297 8241

Contact *Natasha Kern*

FOUNDED 1986. *Handles* non-fiction, commercial and scholarly, both adult and children's: current affairs, science, cookery, health, psychology, business, true crime, celebrity biography, self-help and how-to, controversial and women's issues. Also fiction: romance, historicals, westerns, high-tech, medical thrillers, action and adventure. No horror or fantasy. Also handles film and TV rights. No unsolicited mss; queries welcome. Send IRCs with description of project, information on how complete it is and brief autobiography. £35 reading fee for unpublished authors. CLIENTS include Robin Lee Hatcher, Douglas Bloch, Anne Hinds, Barney Leeson, Carole McKelvey. *Commission* Home 15%; Dramatic 15%; Translation 20%.

Kidde, Hoyt & Picard Literary Agency

333 East 51st Street, New York NY 10022
☎0101 212 755 9461 Fax 0101 212 593 4688

Chief Associate *Katharine Kidde*
Associate *Mary Nichols*

FOUNDED 1981. *Specialises* in mainstream and literary fiction, romantic fiction (historical and contemporary), and general non-fiction. No reading fee. Query first. CLIENTS include Michael Cadnum, Jim Oliver, Patricia Robinson, Frank Sherry. *Commission* 10%.

Daniel P. King

5125 North Cumberland Boulevard, Whitefish Bay WI 53217
☎0101 414 964 2903 Fax 0101 414 964 6860

President *Daniel P. King*

FOUNDED 1974. *Specialises* in mystery and non-fiction books on crime and espionage. Also handles mainstream fiction including crime/mystery and science fiction. Scripts handled by representative office in Beverly Hills, California. No unsolicited mss. Send synopsis or sample chapter first or (and preferably) a concise letter (1–2 pages) describing the book. No reading fee unless an author wants a critique on his material. CLIENTS include John Bonnet, Ella Griffiths, Cyril Joyce. *Commission* Home 10%; Dramatic 10%; Foreign 20%.

Paul Kohner, Inc.

9169 Sunset Boulevard, Los Angeles CA 90069
☎0101 213 550 1060 Fax 0101 213 276 1083

Contact *Gary Salt*

FOUNDED 1938. *Handles* a broad range of books for subsidiary rights sales to film and TV. Few direct placements with publishers as film and TV scripts are the major part of the business. *Specialises* in true crime, biography and history. Non-fiction preferred to fiction for the TV market but anything 'we feel has strong potential' will be considered. No short stories, poetry, science fiction or gothic. Unsolicited material will be returned unread. Approach via a third-party reference or send query letter with professional resumé. No reading fee. CLIENTS include Evan Hunter, Tony Huston, John Katzenbach, Charles Marowitz, Alan Sharp, Donald Westlake. *Commission* Home 10%; Publishing 15%; Dramatic 10%.

Barbara S. Kouts, Literary Agent

PO Box 558, Bellport NY 11713
☎0101 516 286 1278 Fax 0101 516 286 1538

FOUNDED 1980. *Handles* fiction, non-fiction and children's. No romance, science fiction or scripts. No unsolicited mss. Query letter in the first instance. No reading fee. CLIENTS include Hal Gieseking, Nancy Mairs, Robert San Souci. *Commission* Home 10%; Foreign 20%. *Overseas associates* **Murray Pollinger**, London.

Lucy Kroll Agency

390 West End Avenue, New York NY 10024
☎0101 212 877 0556 Fax 0101 212 769 2832

Contact *Lucy Kroll/Barbara Hogenson*

FOUNDED in 1949. *Handles* fiction, non-fiction, including style and design, and scripts for film, TV, theatre and radio. No unsolicited mss. Recommendations from clients are preferred but unsolicitied queries welcome and should be accompanied by IRCs. No reading fee. CLIENTS include Horton Foote, Nan Robertson, O. Carl Simonton, E. Kubler-Ross, the estate of James Thurber. *Commission* Home 10%; Dramatic 10%; Translation 20%.

Peter Lampack Agency, Inc.

551 Fifth Avenue, Suite 2015, New York NY 10017
☎0101 212 687 9106 Fax 0101 212 687 9109

Contact *Peter Lampack/Anthony Gardner/Sandra Blanton*

FOUNDED in 1977. *Handles* commercial fiction: male action and adventure, contemporary relationships, historical, mysteries and horror, literary fiction. Also non-fiction from recognised experts in a given field, plus biographies, autobiographies, theatrical motion picture screenplays and teleplays. No series or episodic material. No category novels, particularly science fiction and historical romance. Best approach by letter in first instance. 'We will respond within two weeks and invite the submission of manuscripts which we would like to examine.' Not in the business of 'poaching' other agents' clients. No reading fee. CLIENTS include J. M. Coetzee, Clive Cussler, Johanna Kingsley, David Osborn, Warren Adler, Doris Mortman, Judith Kelman, Jessica March, Fred Mustard Stewart. *Commission* Home 15%; Dramatic 15%; Translation/UK 20%.

Robert Lantz-Joy Harris Literary Agency

888 Seventh Avenue, New York NY 10106
☏0101 212 262 8177 Fax 0101 212 262 8707

Contact *Joy Harris*

Handles adult non-fiction and fiction. No unsolicited mss. Query letter in the first instance. No reading fee. *Commission* Home 15%; Dramatic 10%; Foreign 20%. *Overseas associates* Michael Meller, Germany; **Abner Stein**, London; Tuttle Mori, Japan/China; Rosemarie Buchman, Scandinavia/Spain; Eliane Benisti, France. Film sub-agent: Antonella Antonelli, Italy.

The Lazear Agency, Inc.

430 First Avenue North, Suite 416,
Minneapolis MN 55401
☏0101 612 332 8640 Fax 0101 612 332 4648

Contact *Wendy Lazear/Jonathon Lazear*

FOUNDED 1984. *Handles* fiction: mysteries, suspense, young adult and literary; also true crime, addiction recovery, biography, memoirs, travel, children's picture books, business, and scripts for film and TV. No poetry or stage plays. Approach by letter, with description of mss, short autobiography and IRCs. No reading fee. CLIENTS include Noah Adams, Melody Beattie, Andrei Codrescu, Al Franken, Merrill Lynch, Harvey Mackay, Gary Paulsen, J. Pillsbury, Will Weaver. *Commission* Home 15%; Dramatic 15%; Translation 10%.

The Lee Allan Agency

P.O. Box 18617, Milwaukee WI 53218
☏0101 414 357 7708 Fax 0101 414 357 7708

Contact *Andrea Knickerbocker/Lee Matthias*

FOUNDED 1983. *Specialises* in mystery, techno-thrillers, suspense/thriller, horror, westerns, war, science fiction and fantasy, commercial fiction, including young adult and mainstream. Some non-fiction, including self-help, cookbooks, humour, true crime and occult. Also handles feature film screenplays properly formatted to the Writer's Guild of America guidelines; no TV, stage plays,

radio or joke routines. No autobiographies (except for celebrities), scholarly works, articles, short pieces, technical or how-to books. No unsolicited mss. Send query letters first, with IRCs, giving length/word count. Novels — min. 50,000 words; scripts — min. 90 pp, max. 140 pp. No reading fee. CLIENTS include John Deakins, Franklin Allen Leib, David North and John Randall. *Commission* Home 15%; Dramatic 10%; Foreign up to 20%.

L. Harry Lee Literary Agency

PO Box 203, Rocky Point NY 11778
☏0101 516 744 1188

Contact *Ken Copel* (science fiction); *Sue Hollister Barr* (adventure/ humour/westerns); *Patti Roenbeck* (romance/mainstream/mystery/ suspense); *Lisa Judd* (historical/fantasy); *Cami Callirgos* (horror/erotica); *Colin James* (mainstream/military/war); *Katie Polk* (mystery/ detective); *Mary Lee Gaylor* (mainstream/ contemporary); *James Kingston* (motion pictures); *Stacy Parker* (TV).

FOUNDED 1979. *Handles* adventure, westerns, horror, romance, mainstream/ contemporary, science fiction, humour, detective, military, war, historical, erotica, fantasy, occult, suspense, plays, literature. Also scripts for film, TV and theatre: handles a lot of material which goes into motion pictures/TV. No gay, lesbian, feminist, confessional, religious, poetry, how-to, children's, biographies, cookery, picture or textbooks. Strictly fiction. Keen on comedy and currently looking for comedy screenplays. No unsolicited mss; query letter first with IRCs, details, a page or two, on project and 1 pp autobiography. Response time 2 weeks. Reading fee charged in two parts depending on appraisal (total £180–250). CLIENTS include Luis Anguilar, James Colaneri, Ken Copel, Anastassia Evereaux, Edward Feit, Dennis Glover, James G. Kingston, Charlie Purpura. *Commission* Novels 15%; Film/Drama 10%.

Adele Leone Agency, Inc.

26 Nantucket Place, Scarsdale NY 10583
☏0101 914 961 2965 Fax 0101 914 337 0361

Contact *Adele Leone/Ralph Leone/Richard James Monaco*

FOUNDED 1979. Works mostly with established/ published authors. *Specialises* in historical, gothic, regency and contemporary romance, science fiction and fantasy, westerns, horror, men's adventure, thrillers, mystery, general women's and mainstream fiction. Non-fiction: speciality and general non-fiction, biography, military, dictionaries, health, nutrition, science, New Age. No scripts. No poetry, young adult or children's. Unsolicited material welcome; send three chapters and outline in the first instance. International Reply Coupons required. No reading fee. CLIENTS include David Bohm, Diane Chamberlain, Phoebe Conn, Simon Hawke, Clifford Linedecker, Constance O'Day Flannery, David Peat & John Briggs, John Skipp & Craig Spector, Janelle Taylor. *Commission* Home 15%; Dramatic 15%; Foreign 10% (if shared). *Overseas associates* **MBA Literary Agents Ltd**, London.

Levant & Wales, Literary Agency, Inc.

108 Hayes Street, Seattle WA 98109
☏0101 206 284 7114   Fax 0101 206 284 1025

Contact *Dan Levant/Elizabeth Wales*

FOUNDED 1988. *Handles* quality fiction and nonfiction. No scripts except via sub-agents. No genre fiction, westerns, romance, science fiction or horror. Special interest in local (Pacific Northwest) clients. No unsolicited mss; send query letter with publication list and writing sample. No reading fee. *Commission* Home 15%; Dramatic/Translation 20%.

Ellen Levine, Literary Agency, Inc.

Suite 1801, 15 East 26th Street, New York NY 10010-1505
☏0101 212 899 0620

Contact *Diana Finch/Anne Dubuisson*

FOUNDED 1980. *Handles* all types of books. No scripts. No unsolicited mss. First approach by letter. No material unless requested. Send International Reply Coupons for reply, and for return of material if required. No telephone calls. No reading fee. *Commission* Home 15%; Dramatic 10%; Foreign 20%. *Overseas associates* **A.P. Watt**, London.

Lighthouse Literary Agency

711 Hillcrest Street East, Altamonte Springs FL 32701
☏0101 407 831 3813
All correspondence to: PO Box 2105, Winter Park, FL32790

Contact *Sandra Kangas*

FOUNDED 1988. *Handles* fiction, non-fiction, film scripts and children's. Currently accepting new writers. Send query letter first, including brief synopsis and background information/experience. Include return postage with all correspondence. 'If we want to see more, we will ask.' Reading fee for entire mss (£60). CLIENTS include Galen C. Dukes, Dennis Cole Hill, Laura Happel. *Commission* Home

15%; Dramatic 15%; Screenplays 10%; Translation 20%.

Ray Lincoln Literary Agency

Elkins Park House, Suite 107-B, 7900 Old York Road, Elkins Park PA 19117
☏0101 215 635 0827

Contact *Mrs Ray Lincoln*

FOUNDED 1974. *Handles* adult and children's fiction and non-fiction: biography, science, nature, popular medicine, psychology and psychiatry, history. Scripts as spin-offs from book mss only. No poetry or plays unless adaptations from published book. Keenly interested in adult biography, in all types of children's books (age 5 and upwards, not illustrated), in fine adult fiction, science and nature. No unsolicited mss; send query letter first, including International Reply Coupons for response. If interested, material will then be requested. No reading fee. *Commission* Home/Dramatic 15%; Translation 20%.

Literary/Business Associates

2000 North Ivan Avenue 3, Hollywood CA 90068
Correspondence: PO Box 2415, Hollywood, CA 90078
☏0101 213 465 2630

Contact *Shelley Gross*

FOUNDED 1979. *Handles* non-fiction trade books: New Age, health and fitness, philosophy, psychology, trends, humour, business, mysticism. Also fiction: thrillers, romance, suspense, action and adventure, mystery and occult. No scripts. No Christian evangelical, travel, sleazy sex or children's. *Specialises* in health, how-to, mainstream fiction, healing and women's issues. Query by letter with brief outline of contents and background (plus IRCs). Fee charged (£90 for up to 75,000 words) for detailed analysis of mss. Professional editing also available (rates per page or hour). *Commission* Home 15%; Translation 20%; Film rights 15%.

Literary & Creative Artists Agency

3539 Albemarle Street NW, Washington DC 20008
☏0101 202 362 4688   Fax 0101 202 362 4688

Contact *Muriel Nellis/Jane Roberts*

FOUNDED 1981. *Handles* health and human potential, politics, public policy, true crime, history, biography, culture, lifestyle and entertainment, how-to, real life and human drama. Scripts also welcome for TV and film but most tend to be derivative from books already handled. No poetry, pornographic, academic or educational textbooks.

Particulary interested in 'insider' books: 'derived from the author's authoritative position, with implications or usefulness for general rather than discrete audiences'. No unsolicited mss; approach by letter with précis of proposed work, chapter outline, biographical sketch and any other information relating to the book's commercial potential. Include IRCs for response. Response time 2 weeks. No reading fee. *Commission* Home 15%; Dramatic 20%; Translation 20–25%.

Living Faith Literary Agency
PO Box 566397, Atlanta GA 30356
☎0101 404 751 1917

Contact *M. L. Jones*

FOUNDED 1983. *Handles* fiction, children's, devotional, self-help, biography, bible stories, autobiography, some poetry, prophecy, and books of family interest. No scripts. No erotic or vulgar. Unsolicited mss welcome; preferred approach though is by letter enclosing first three chapters, chapter synopses and IRCs for return of material/response. No reading fee. CLIENTS Joyce Price, Will Lester, Dr L. G. Stevin. *Commission* Home 10%; UK 15%.

Sterling Lord Literistic, Inc.
One Madison Avenue, New York NY 10010
☎0101 212 696 2800   Fax 0101 212 686 6976

Contact *Peter Matson/Sterling Lord*

FOUNDED 1979. *Handles* all genres, fiction and non-fiction, plus scripts for TV, radio, film and theatre. *Specialises* in literary fiction. Unsolicited mss welcome but preferred approach is by letter outlining proposal. No reading fee. *Commission* Home 15%; UK 20%; Translation 20%. *Overseas associates* **Peters, Fraser & Dunlop Ltd**, London.

Margret McBride Literary Agency
4350 Executive Drive, Suite 225, San Diego CA 92121
☎0101 619 457 0550   Fax 0101 619 457 2315

Contact *Winifred Golden/Susan Travis*

FOUNDED 1980. Mainstream fiction, non-fiction and biography, true crime, thrillers and suspense, political memoirs, science fiction. No scripts, children's, poetry or technical. No unsolicited mss. Query first. No reading fee. CLIENTS Spencer Johnson, Kenneth Blanchard, Noel Riley Fitch, Jeanne Jones, Charles Garfield, Lawrence Miller. *Commission* Home 15%; Audio/ Film rights/Translation 25%. *Overseas associates* Michael Meller, Munich; Kiyoshi Asano,

Japan; Licht & Licht, Denmark; Eliane Benisti; France; Raquel de la Concha, Spain.

Donald MacCampbell, Inc.
12 East 41st Street, New York NY 10017
☎0101 212 683 5580

President *Donald MacCampbell*
Editor *Maureen Moran*

FOUNDED 1940. *Handles* women's fiction only. No scripts, non-fiction, science fiction, westerns or suspense. *Specialises* in romance. No unsolicited mss; approach by letter. No reading fee. *Commission* US Book Sales 10%; First Novels US 15%.

Richard P. McDonough, Literary Agent
812 Centre Street, Boston MA 02130
☎0101 617 522 6388

Contact *Richard P. McDonough*

FOUNDED 1986. General non-fiction and literary fiction. No scripts. No genre fiction except mysteries and thrillers. No unsolicited mss; query first with three sample chapters and include IRCs. No reading fee. CLIENTS Jess Brallier, M. R. Montgomery, Jane Holtz Kay, Peter Guralnick. *Commission* 15%.

McIntosh & Otis, Inc.
310 Madison Avenue, New York NY 10017
☎0101 212 687 7400   Fax 0101 212 687 6894

Contact *Julie Fallowfield* (Adult books)/*Dorothy Markinko* (Juvenile)

FOUNDED 1928. Adult and children's general trade books, fiction and non-fiction. No textbooks or scripts. No unsolicited mss. Approach first with a letter indicating nature of the work plus details of background. No reading fee. CLIENTS include Mary Higgins Clark, Shirley Hazzard, Victoria Holt, Harper Lee. *Commission* Home 15%; Dramatic 15%; Foreign 20%. *UK associates* **A.M. Heath & Co. Ltd**.

Carol Mann Agency
55 Fifth Avenue, New York NY 10003
☎0101 212 206 5635   Fax 0101 212 463 8718

Contact *Victoria Sanders/Carol Mann*

FOUNDED 1977. *Handles* general trade fiction and non-fiction, plus some film and television. *Specialises* in psychology, popular culture, history and social policy. No unsolicited mss; queries with

IRCs. No reading fee. CLIENTS Paul Auster, Marita Golden, Dr Judith Wallerstein, Helen Washington, Terry Williams, Professor William Julius Wilson. *Commission* Home/Dramatic 15%; Translation 20%. *UK associates* **Abner Stein**, London.

Denise Marcil Literary Agency, Inc.
685 West End Avenue, Suite 9C, New York NY 10025
☎0101 212 932 3110

President *Denise Marcil*

FOUNDED 1977. *Specialises* in non-fiction: money, business, health, childcare, parenting, self-help and how-to; and commercial fiction, especially women's, mysteries and psychological suspense. Query letters only, with IRCs. CLIENTS include Rosanne Bittner, Carol Kane, Fayrene Preston. *Commission* Home 15%; Dramatic 15%; Foreign 20%.

Betty Marks
Suite 9F, 176 East 77th Street, New York NY 10021
☎0101 212 535 8388

Contact *Betty Marks*

FOUNDED 1969. Works mostly with established/published authors. *Specialises* in journalists' non-fiction and novels. No reading fee for outlines. *Commission* Home 15%; Foreign 20%. *Overseas associates* **Abner Stein**, London; Mohrbooks, Germany; International Editor, Spain; and Rosemary Buchman.

The Evan Marshall Agency
22 South Park Street, Suite 216, Montclair NJ 07042-2744
☎0101 201 744 1661   Fax 0101 201 744 6312

Contact *Evan Marshall/Lisa Healy*

FOUNDED 1987. *Handles* general adult fiction and non-fiction, and scripts for film and television. No unsolicited mss; send query letter first. Reading fee charged (£28) to unpublished authors. *Commission* Home 15%; UK 20%; Translation 20%.

Marshall Cameron Agency
Rt 1, Box 125, Lawtey FL 32058
☎0101 904 964 7013   Fax 0101 904 964 6905

Contact *Margo Prescott*

FOUNDED 1984. Non-fiction, fiction, TV movies and feature films. *Specialises* in screenplays and teleplays. Open to new talent. No reading fee for outlines; fee charged for mss. Critiques and in-

depth evaluations on writer's request. 95% of material represented is scripts. *Commission* Home 15%; Dramatic 15%; Foreign 20%.

Claudia Menza Literary Agency
1170 Broadway, Room 807, New York NY 10001
☎0101 212 889 6850   Fax 0101 212 889 6850

President *Claudia Menza*

FOUNDED 1983. *Specialises* in fiction and non-fiction dealing with serious subjects (i.e. political and medical issues). No reading fee. No unsolicited mss; queries and synopses only. *Commission* Home 15%; Dramatic 15%; Foreign 20%.

Mews Books Ltd
c/o Sidney B. Kramer, 20 Bluewater Hill, Westport CT 06880
☎0101 203 227 1836   Fax 0101 203 227 1144

Contact *Sidney B. Kramer/Fran Pollak*

FOUNDED 1970. *Handles* adult fiction and non-fiction, children's, pre-school and young adult. No scripts, short stories or novellas (unless by established authors). *Specialises* in cookery, medical, health and nutrition, scientific non-fiction and children's. Unsolicited material welcome. Presentation must be professional. Partial submissions should include summary of plot/characters, one or two sample chapters, personal credentials and brief on target market. No reading fee. *Commission* Home 15%; Film 20%; Translation 20%. *UK associates* **Abner Stein**, London.

The Peter Miller Agency, Inc.
Office: 220 West 19th Street, Suite 501, New York NY 10011
☎0101 212 929 1222   Fax 0101 212 206 0238
Packages: PO Box 1817, Old Chelsea Station, New York NY 10011
☎0101 212 929 1222   Fax 0101 212 206 0238

President *Peter Miller*
Associates *Giselle Dean Miller/Blake Herron/ David Weaver/Anthony Schneider*
Consultant *John Stryder*

FOUNDED 1976. Commercial fiction and non-fiction. *Specialises* in true crime, Hollywood history and biographies. All books with film and television potential. No poetry, pornography, non-commercial or academic. No unsolicited mss. Approach by letter with one-page synopsis. Reading fee for unpublished authors. Fee recoupable out of first monies earned. CLIENTS include Vincent T. Bugliosi, Martin Caidin, Christopher Cook Gilmore, Michael Peak, Brigette Roux-Lough, Jean

Sasson, Ted Sennett, Gene Walden. *Commission* Home 15%; Dramatic 10–15%; Foreign 20–25%.

Miller & Associates Inc.

See **Dupree/Miller & Associates, Inc., Literary Agency**

Robert P. Mills

c/o Richard Curtis Associates, 171 East 74th Street, New York NY 10021
☏ 0101 212 772 7363   Fax 0101 212 772 7393

Contact *Richard Curtis*

Henry Morrison, Inc.

PO Box 235, 320 McLain Street, Bedford Hills NY 10507
☏ 0101 914 666 3500   Fax 0101 914 241 7846

Contact *Henry Morrison/Joan Gurgold*

FOUNDED 1965. *Handles* general fiction, crime and science fiction, and non-fiction. No scripts unless by established writers. Unsolicited material welcome; send query letter with outline of proposal (1–5 pp). No reading fee. CLIENTS Beverly Byrne, Joe Gores, Robert Ludlum. *Commission* Home 15%; UK 20%; Translation 20%.

Multimedia Product Development, Inc.

410 South Michigan Avenue, Suite 724, Chicago IL 60605
☏ 0101 312 922 3063   Fax 0101 312 922 1905

Contact *Jane Jordan Browne*

FOUNDED 1971. Biography, history, current affairs, mainstream fiction, genre novels, science, psychology, social science, how-to. No autobiography (except celebrities). No poetry or scripts. No unsolicited mss. Send query letter with International Reply Coupons only. No reading fee. CLIENTS include Helen Hooven Santmyer, Jackie Hyman, James Kahn, Axel Madsen, Donald A. Stanwood, Susan Sussman, J. Patrick Wright. *Commission* Home 15%; Dramatic 15%; Foreign 15–20%. *Overseas associates* **A.M. Heath & Co. Ltd**, London.

Ruth Nathan Agency

c/o Van Horn Co., 80 Fifth Avenue, New York NY 10011
☏ 0101 212 675 6063   Fax 0101 212 691 1561

FOUNDED 1984. *Handles* art books, biography and showbiz. No romance, humour, self-help or political. No unsolicited mss. Query first. No reading fee. CLIENTS include Robert Emmet Long, Foster Hirsch, Harrice Miller, Jeannie Sakol, Max Wilk. *Commission* 15%.

B.K. Nelson Literary Agency

84 Woodland Road, Pleasantville NY 10570–1322
☏ 0101 914 741 1322/212 889 0637
Fax 0101 914 741 1324

President *Bonita K. Nelson*

FOUNDED 1979. *Specialises* in non-fiction: how-to, self-help, biography, textbooks (elementary, high tech and college levels), business and sport. Some fiction, plus film/TV and stage scripts. No unsolicited mss. First approach with letter. Reading fee charged. *Commission* Home 15%; Dramatic 15%; Foreign 15%.

New Age World Services & Books

62091 Valley View Circle, Joshua Tree CA 92252
☏ 0101 619 366 2833

Contact *Victoria E. Vandertuin*

FOUNDED 1957. New Age fiction and non-fiction, young adult fiction and non-fiction, and poetry. No scripts, drama, missionary, biography, sports, erotica, humour, travel or cookbooks. *Specialises* in New Age, self-help, health and beauty, meditation, yoga, channelling, how-to, metaphysical, occult, psychology, religion, lost continents, time travel. Unsolicited mss and queries welcome. Reading fee charged. *Commission* Home 15%; Foreign 20%.

New England Publishing Associates, Inc.

Box 5, Chester CT 06412
☏ 0101 203 345 4976   Fax 0101 203 345 3660

Contact *Elizabeth Frost Knappman/Edward W. Knappman*

FOUNDED 1983. Mainly non-fiction. *Specialises* in current affairs, history, science, women's studies, reference, psychology, biography, true crime. No textbooks, children's, collections/anthologies. No scripts. Unsolicited mss considered but query letter or phone call preferred first. No reading fee. CLIENTS include Lary Bloom, Philip Ginsburg, William Packard, Carl Rollyson. *Commission* Home 15%. *Overseas associates* Scott-Ferris Agency; **Marsh & Sheil Ltd**, London. *Representation* throughout Europe and Japan.

Regula Noetzli Literary Agency
444 East 85th Street, New York NY 10028
☎0101 212 628 1537 Fax 0101 212 744 3145
Contact *Regula Noetzli*

FOUNDED 1989. *Handles* adult fiction (literary and mystery) and non-fiction including psychology, popular science, biography, history, true crime. No scripts, how-to, science fiction, romance, poetry or children's. No unsolicited mss. Send query letter and sample chapter/outline. No reading fee. CLIENTS Dr E. Golamb, Dr M. Weissberg, Wendy Williams. *Commission* Home 15%; UK 20%; Tranlation 20%. *Overseas associates* **Shelley Power**, UK.

The Betsy Nolan Literary Agency
50 West 29th Street, Suite 9 West, New York NY 10001
☎0101 212 799 0700 Fax 0101 212 689 0376
Contact *Betsy Nolan/Carla Glasser/Donald Lehr*

FOUNDED 1980. Novels and non-fiction including health, popular culture, music, business, gardening, cooking and lifestyle. No reading fee. *Commission* Home 15%; Foreign 20%.

Nugent Literary
170 10th Street North, Naples FL 33940
☎0101 813 262 3683/7562
Contact *Ray E. Nugent*

FOUNDED 1976. *Specialises* in adult non-fiction. Send query with synopsis, resumé, sample chapters and at least 50 pp of text. No reading fee for outlines. IRCs. with International Reply Coupons essential. *Commission* Home 15%; Dramatic 15%; Translation 20%.

The Otte Company
9 Goden Street, Belmont MA 02178
☎0101 617 484 8505
Contact *Jane H. Otte*

FOUNDED 1973. *Specialises* in adult trade books. *Handles* non-fiction and fiction. No scripts. No unsolicited mss. Approach by letter. No reading fee for outlines. *Commission* Home 15%; Dramatic 7½%; Foreign 20%. *Overseas associates* **Aitken & Stone Ltd**, London.

The Panettieri Agency
142 Marcella Road, Hampton VA 23666
☎0101 804 825 1708

Contact *Eugenia Panettieri*

FOUNDED 1988. *Handles* historical romance, contemporary romance, women's fiction, general mainstream fiction, suspense, mystery and regency. No scripts, children's, picture books, poetry or short stories. Particulary interested at present in women's fiction. Send query letter in first instance, but unsolicited mss also welcome. Reading fee charged (£25 partial submissions; £75 complete mss). CLIENTS Anita Gordon, Steven Linder, Sarah Temple. *Commission* Home 15%; UK 15%; Translation 20%.

The Ray Peekner Literary Agency, Inc.
PO Box 3308, Bethlehem PA 18017
☎0101 215 974 9158 Fax 0101 215 974 8228
Contact *Barbara Puechner*

FOUNDED 1973. Works mostly with established/published authors. *Specialises* in mysteries, westerns and mainstream suspense. No romance or scripts. No unsolicited mss; queries only. Most new clients are referred by existing clients. No reading fee. CLIENTS include Bill Crider, Loren D. Estleman, G. Clifton Wisler, Don Coldsmith, Joe R. Lansdale. *Commission* Home 10%; Dramatic 10%; Foreign 20%. *Overseas associates* The English Agency; Thomas Schluck; Bookman; Agenzia Letteraria; La Nouvelle.

Pegasus International, Inc.
PO Box 5470, Winter Park FL 32795-5470
☎0101 407 831 1008

Director *Gene Lovitz*
Contact *Carole Morling*

FOUNDED 1987. 'We work with unpublished authors. Once an author comes aboard we work together to accomplish a marketable work, and never abandon the author once she or he is accepted as a client. Accordingly, we are rather selective in whom we represent.' *Handles* non-fiction and fiction: children's, regency and historical romances, horror, New Age, fantasy and magic, gothic, science fiction, war, mystery, plus film/TV scripts. *Specialises* in science fiction, the 'intellectual novel', and translations into English. No hardcore pornography or verse. 'We will accept erotica done on the level of Anais Nin, making a distinction between pornography and erotica.' Approach in writing with proposal. Reading fee charged but reimbursed upon publication. *Commission* 10%.

Penmarin Books

2171 East Francisco Boulevard, Suite L, San Rafael CA 94901
☎0101 415 457 7746   Fax 0101 415 454 0426

Contact *Hal Lockwood*

FOUNDED 1987. *Handles* projects for popular trade publication, both fiction and non-fiction. No poetry or children's; no school, scholarly or academic books. Unsolicited mss welcome; initial approach in writing preferred: send professional/personal background details, project outline or synopsis (2-3 pp), sample of past or current writing (5-8 pp) and pre-paid return postage. No reading fee for initial reading. *Commission* 15%.

Perkins Literary Agency

PO Box 48, Childs MD 21916-0048
☎0101 410 398 2647

Contact *Esther R. Perkins*

FOUNDED 1979. *Handles* fiction only: men's interest, mysteries, regencies and historical romance. No scripts, non-fiction, children's or poetry. No unsolicited mss. Send query letter. Reading fee charged. CLIENTS William Bervhardt, Karla Hocker, Vivan Vaughan. *Commission* Home 15%; UK 20%; Translation 20%. *Overseas associates* Lennart Sane.

James Peter Associates, Inc.

PO Box 772, Tenafly NJ 07670
☎0101 201 568 2002   Fax 0101 201 568 2959

Contact *Bert Holtje*

FOUNDED 1971. Non-fiction only. 'Many of our authors are historians, psychologists, physicians — all are writing trade books for general readers.' No scripts. No fiction or children's books. *Specialises* in history, popular culture, health, biography and politics. No unsolicited mss. Send query letter first, with brief project outline, samples and biographical information. No reading fee. CLIENTS include Alan Axelrod, Marc Dorio, Elizabeth Judd, Ron Pasquariello, Carol Turkington, and many more. A member of the Association of Author's Representatives. *Commission* 15%.

Alison J. Picard, Literary Agent

PO Box 2000, Cotuit MA 02635
☎0101 508 477 7192   Fax 0101 508 420 0762

Contact *Alison Picard*

FOUNDED 1985. *Handles* mainstream and literary fiction, contemporary and historical romance, children's and young adult, mysteries and thrillers; plus non-fiction. No short stories unless suitable for major national publications, and no poetry. Rarely any science fiction and fantasy. Particularly interested in expanding non-fiction titles. Approach with written query. No reading fee. *Commission* 15%. *Overseas associates* **A. M. Heath & Co. Ltd**, London.

Arthur Pine Associates, Inc.

250 West 57th Street, New York NY 10019
☎0101 212 265 7330   Fax 0101 212 265 4650

Contact *Richard Pine/Lori Andiman*

FOUNDED 1970. *Handles* fiction and non-fiction (adult only). No scripts, children's, autobiographical (unless celebrity), textbooks or scientific. No unsolicited mss. Send query letter with synopsis, including IRCs in first instance. Reading fee charged. *Commission* 15%.

Popkin/Cooke

15340 Albright Street, Suite 204, Pacific Palisades CA 90272
☎0101 310 459 2834   Fax 0101 310 459 4128
236 East Davie Street, Raleigh, NC 27601
☎0101 919 834 1456

FOUNDED 1989. Fiction: mystery, contemporary, historical, and non-fiction. Interested in social issues. Approach with outline/ synopsis, plus three chapters, accompanied by IRCs. No reading fee for initial reading. *Commission* Home 15%; Foreign 20%.

Aaron M. Priest Literary Agency

Suite 3902, 122 East 42nd Street, New York NY 10168
☎0101 212 818 0344   Fax 0101 212 573 9417

Contact *Aaron Priest/Molly Freidrich*

Fiction and non-fiction. No unsolicited mss; queries only. No reading fee. IRCs essential. *Commission* Home 15%.

Susan Ann Protter Literary Agent

Suite 1408, 110 West 40th Street, New York NY 10018
☎0101 212 840 0480

Contact *Susan Protter*

FOUNDED 1971. General fiction, mysteries, thrillers, science fiction and fantasy. Also non-fiction: history, general reference, auto/biography, science, health. No romantic fiction, poetry, religious, children's or sport manuals. No scripts. First approach with letter, including International Reply Coupons.

No reading fee. CLIENTS include Terry Bisson, David G. Hartwell, Anthony S. Mercatante, Robert Edwin Herzstein, Rudy Rucker, Frank King and Michael D. Weaver. *Commission* Home 15%; Dramatic 15%; Foreign 25%. *Overseas associates* **Abner Stein**, London.

Quicksilver Books, Literary Agents
50 Wilson Street, Hartsdale NY 10530
✆0101 914 946 8748

President *Bob Silverstein*

FOUNDED 1987. *Handles* literary fiction and mainstream commercial fiction: suspense, thriller, contemporary, mystery and historical. Also general non-fiction including self-help, psychology, holistic healing, ecology, environmental, biography, fact crime, New Age, health, nutrition, enlightened wisdom and spirituality. No scripts, science fiction and fantasy, pornographic, children's or romance. UK material being submitted must have universal appeal for the US market. Unsolicited material welcome but must be accompanied by IRCs for response, together with biographical details, covering letter, etc. No reading fee. CLIENTS John Harricharan, Susan S. Lang, Katrina Raphaell, Brad Steiger, W. J. Weatherby. *Commission* Home/ Dramatic 15%; Translation 20%.

D. Radley-Regan & Associates
PO Box 243, Jamestown NC 27282
✆0101 919 454 5040

Contact *D. Radley-Regan*

FOUNDED 1987. Eager to work with new/ unpublished authors. *Specialises* in fiction (mystery and thriller) and non-fiction. Also handles scripts for film and TV. No reading fee for queries; charge for full mss. Expect 6 weeks' response time on queries, 12–18 weeks on mss. *Commission* 25%.

Helen Rees Literary Agency
308 Commonwealth Avenue, Boston MA 02116
✆0101 617 262 2401 Fax 0101 617 262 2401

Contact *Joan Mazmanian*

FOUNDED 1982. *Specialises* in books on health and business; and also handles biography, autobiography and history. No scholarly, academic or technical books. No scripts. No unsolicited mss. Send query letter with International Reply Coupons. No reading fee. CLIENTS include Joan Borysenko, Donna Carpenter, Senator Barry Goldwater, Sandra Mackey, Price Waterhouse, Alan Dershowitz. *Commission* Home 15%; Foreign 20%.

Rights Unlimited, Inc.
101 West 55th Street, New York NY 10019
✆0101 212 246 0900 Fax 0101 212 246 2114

Contact *Bernard Kurman*

FOUNDED 1985. *Handles* fiction, non-fiction, business and children's picture books. No scripts, poetry, short stories, educational or literary works. Unsolicited mss welcome; query letter with synopsis preferred in the first instance. Reading fee £50. CLIENTS Charles Berlitz, Gyo Fujikawa, Norman Lang. *Commission* Home 15%; Translation 20%.

Richard H. Roffman Associates
697 West End Avenue, Suite 6A, New York NY 10025
✆0101 212 749 3647/8

President *Richard Roffman*

FOUNDED 1967. Richard Roffman, mayor of Times Square since 1960, has spent most of his life in and around Times Square — his main interest in life being 'to make Times Square greater than ever before in every possible way'. He is a publicist, radio/TV broadcaster, journalist, lawyer, talent representative and teacher. *Handles* a varied range of material, primarily non-fiction, the only criterion being quality. No unsolicited mss or synopses. Send query letter with biographical outline and short concise summary of project for consideration. No returns made unless requested and accompanied by IRCs. No pornography or subversive material. *Commission* 10%.

Rosenstone/Wender
3 East 48th Street, 4th Floor, New York NY 10017
✆0101 212 832 8330 Fax 0101 212 759 4524

Contact *Phyllis Wender/Susan Perlman Cohen*

FOUNDED 1981. *Handles* fiction, non-fiction, children's, young adult and scripts for film, TV and theatre. No material for radio. No unsolicited mss. Send letter outlining the project, credits, etc. No reading fee. *Commission* Home 15%; Dramatic 10%; Foreign 20%. *Overseas associates* **A.P. Watt Ltd**, London; La Nouvelle Agence, France; Andrew Nurnberg, Netherlands; The English Agency, Japan; Mohrbooks, Germany; Ole Licht, Scandinavia.

Jean Rosenthal Literary Agency
28 East 11th Street, New York NY 10003
✆0101 212 677 4248

Contact *Jean Rosenthal*

FOUNDED 1980. *Handles* non-fiction: travel, encyclopedias and children's. Series and co-productions very much preferred. No scripts. 'No bad first novels' but will take on 'anything I think I can sell'. Send query letter with return postage. Synopses should be accompanied by international money order to the value of £25.00. *Commission* Home 15%; Translation 20%.

Jane Rotrosen Agency
318 East 51st Street, New York NY 10022
☎0101 212 593 4330   Fax 0101 212 935 6985

Contact *Stephanie Laidman/Meg Ruley/Andrea Cirillo*

Handles general trade fiction: romance, horror, mysteries, thrillers and fantasy; and popular non-fiction. No scripts, educational, professional or belles lettres. *Specialises* in commercial fiction. No unsolicited mss; send query letter in the first instance. No reading fee. CLIENTS Peter Abrahams, Julie Garwood, Judith Michael, Michael Palmer, John Saul, Norman Spinrad. *Commission* Home 15%; UK 20%; Translation 20%. *Overseas associates* in Italy and Holland.

Sagalyn Literary Agency
8000 B Maple Ridge Road, Bethesda, MD 20814

FOUNDED 1980. *Handles* quality fiction and non-fiction. CLIENTS include Rick Atkinson, David Ignatius, Jean Carper, Peter Kurth. *UK associates* Carolyn Brunton.

Sandum & Associates
144 East 84th Street, New York NY 10028
☎0101 212 737 2011

Contact *Howard E. Sandum*

FOUNDED 1987. *Handles* general adult non-fiction — all categories; plus commercial and literary fiction. No scripts. No children's, poetry or short stories. No unsolicited mss. Third-party referral preferred but direct approach by letter, with synopsis, brief biography and IRCs is accepted. No reading fee. CLIENTS include James Cowan, Martha Horton, Ward Morehouse III, Silvia Sanza. *Commission* Home 15%; Dramatic 15%; Translation/Foreign 20%. *UK associates* Scott Ferris Associates.

SBC Enterprises, Inc.
11 Mabro Drive, Denville NJ 07834–9607
☎0101 201 366 3622

Contact *Alec Bernard/Eugenia Cohen*

FOUNDED 1979. *Handles* trade fiction, non-fiction, theatrical scripts, plus film and telemovies. No unsolicited mss; send query letter with IRCs. and International Reply Coupons in first instance. No reading fee. Works with new/unpublished writers as well as with established ones. *Commission* varies.

Jack Scagnetti Literary Agency
Suite 210, 5330 Lankershim Boulevard, North Hollywood CA 91601
☎0101 818 762 3871/761 0580
Fax 0101 818 760 1382

Contact *Jack Scagnetti*

FOUNDED 1974. Works mostly with established/published authors. *Handles* non-fiction, fiction, film and TV scripts. No reading fee for outlines. *Commission* Home 10%; Dramatic 10%; Foreign 15%.

Schaffner Agency, Inc.
6625 Casas Adobes Road, Tucson, Arizona 85704
☎0101 602 797 8000   Fax 0101 602 797 8271

Contact *Timothy Schaffner*

FOUNDED 1948. *Specialises* in literary fiction, biographies, travel and general non-fiction. Query letter in first instance. No reading fee for outlines. International Reply Coupons required. CLIENTS include Maxine Hong Kingston, Rick Bass, Robley Wilson. *Commission* Home 15%; Dramatic 20%; Foreign 20%. *Overseas associates* **A.M. Heath & Co. Ltd**, London.

Schlessinger–Van Dyck Agency
2814 PSFS Building, 12 South 12th Street, Philadelphia PA 19107
☎0101 215 627 4665   Fax 0101 215 627 0488

Contact *Blanche Schlessinger/Barrie Van Dyck*

FOUNDED 1987. *Handles* general non-fiction, commercial fiction and children's. No scripts, textbooks, science fiction, horror, fantasy, New Age, or first fiction. *Specialises* in true crime and mysteries, children's and cookbooks. No unsolicited mss; send query with outline, table of contents, 40–50 sample pp and biographical details. IRCs. with International Reply Coupons essential for response. No reading fee. CLIENTS Neil Albert, Jack Engelhard, Gene Hart, Susan Lieberman, Robin Moore, William Woys Weaver. *Commission* Home/Dramatic 15%; Translation 20–30%. *Overseas associates* **June Hall Literary Agency**, London.

Susan Schulman Literary Agency

454 West 44th Street, New York NY 10036
☏0101 212 713 1633/4/5
Fax 0101 212 581 8830

Contact *Susan Schulman/Thereas Gotti* (Film)/
William C. Fecke (Theatre)/*Amelia Blanquerra*
(Editorial)

FOUNDED 1979. *Handles* fiction: literary, contemporary women's, mysteries, contemporary romance, light horror, topical thrillers, historical romance, gothic and regency. Also non-fiction: science and the social sciences, health and nutrition, pyschology, child care, family and child rearing, art history and military. No unsolicited mss. Query first including outline and three sample chapters with IRCs. No reading fee. Represents properties for film and television, and works with agents in appropriate territories for translation rights. *Commission* Home/Dramatic 15%; Translation 20%. *Overseas associates* **Serafina Clarke**, London.

Laurens R. Schwartz

5 East 22nd Street, Suite 15D, New
York NY 10010-5315
☏0101 212 228 2614   Fax 0101 212 228 2614

Contact *Laurens R. Schwartz*

FOUNDED 1984. Works mostly with established authors. *Handles* 80% non-fiction, from scholarly to how-to; also fiction, children's and adult, and scripts for film, TV, radio and theatre. *Specialises* in entertainment, technology, politics, sociology, mathematics, anthropology, history, biography, New Age, etc. No pornography. No unsolicited mss. Send query letter including c.v./resumé, 1–3 pp synopsis of project, table of contents (for non-fiction) or 1 non-returnable chapter (for fiction). No reading fee. Represents a number of European authors. *Commission* Home 15%; Foreign 25%.

Rita Scott

See **Marje Fields/Rita Scott**

Sebastian Agency

PO Box 1369, San Carlos CA 94070
☏0101 415 598 0310   Fax 0101 415 637 9615

Contact *Jan Johnson*

FOUNDED 1985. *Handles* adult fiction: mainstream, literary and genre (mystery, suspense, historical) and non-fiction: psychology and self-help, business and careers, computers, current affairs and journalism, popular history, science, politics, sport and women's issues. No scripts. No romance, fantasy,

science fiction or horror. No unsolicited mss; send query first with brief biography, outline, synopsis (no more than 50 pp) and IRCs. No reading fee. *Commission* Home 15%; Dramatic 20%; Translation 20%. Agency fee charged (£100) for previously unpublished authors. *Overseas associates* Michael Meller Literary Agency.

Shapiro-Lichtman Talent Agency

8827 Beverly Boulevard, Los Angeles CA 90048
☏0101 310 859 8877   Fax 0101 310 859 7153

FOUNDED 1969. Works mostly with established/published authors. *Handles* film and TV scripts. Unsolicited mss will not be read. *Commission* Home 10%; Dramatic 10%; Foreign 20%.

The Shepard Agency

73 Kingswood Drive, Bethel CT 06801
☏0101 203 790 4230/1780
Fax 0101 203 743 1879

Contact *Jean Shepard/Lance Shepard*

FOUNDED 1987. *Handles* non-fiction: business, food, self-help and travel, and some fiction: adult, children's and young adult. Some scripts also. No pornography. *Specialises* in business. Send query letter, table of contents, sample chapters and IRCs for response. No reading fee. *Commission* Home 15%; Dramatic 15%; Translation 20%.

Lee Shore Agency

440 Friday Road, Pittsburgh PA 15209
☏0101 412 821 0440   Fax 0101 412 821 6099

Contact *Cynthia Sterling/Alice Stock/Anna Aivaliotis*

FOUNDED 1988. *Handles* non-fiction, including textbooks, and mass market fiction: horror, romance, mystery, westerns, science fiction. Also some young adult and, more recently, screenplays. *Specialises* in New Age, self-help, how-to and quality fiction. No children's. No unsolicited mss. Send IRCs. with International Reply Coupons for guidelines before submitting work. Reading fee charged. CLIENTS include Mel Blount, Jeff Coe, Dr Lynn Hawker, Kenneth Schatz, Susan Sheppard. *Commission* Home 15%; Dramatic 20%.

Bobbe Siegel, Literary Agency

41 West 83rd Street, New York NY 10024
☏0101 212 877 4985   Fax 0101 212 877 4985

Contact *Bobbe Siegel*

FOUNDED 1975. Works mostly with established/ published authors. *Specialises* in literary fiction, detective, suspense, historical, science fiction, biography, how-to, women's interest, fitness, health, beauty, sports, pop psychology. No scripts. No cookbooks, crafts, children's, short stories or humour. First approach with letter including International Reply Coupons for response. No reading fee. Critiques given if the writer is taken on for representation. CLIENTS include Frank Bianco, John De Santis, Nina Herrmann Donnelley, Margaret Mitchell Dukore, Fred Hatfield, Primo Levi. *Commission* Home 15%; Dramatic 20%; Foreign 20%. (Foreign/ Dramatic split 50/50 with subagent.) *Overseas associates* **John Pawsey**, Worthing, West Sussex.

Sierra Literary Agency

PO Box 1090, Janesville CA 96114
☎0101 916 253 3250

Contact *Mary Barr*

FOUNDED 1988. *Handles* fiction: mainstream, adventure, contemporary, romantic. Also a variety of non-fiction, primarily self-help. No scripts, children's or poetry. Eager to work with new writers. Reluctant to read unsolicited mss; send query with synopsis and sample chapters. No reading fee. *Commission* 10%.

The Evelyn Singer Literary Agency, Inc.

PO Box 594, White Plains NY 10602
☎0101 914 949 1147/914 631 5160

Contact *Evelyn Singer*

FOUNDED 1951. Works mostly with established/ published authors. *Handles* fiction and non-fiction, both adult and children's. Adult: health, medicine, how-to, diet, biography, celebrity, conservation, political, serious novels, suspense and mystery. Children's: educational non-fiction for all ages and fiction for the middle/teen levels. No picture books unless the author is or has an experienced book illustrator. No formula romance, poetry, sex, occult, textbooks or specialised material unsuitable for trade market. No scripts. No unsolicited mss. First approach with letter giving writing background, credits, publications, including date of publication and publisher. IRCs. or International Reply Coupons essential. No phone calls. No reading fee. CLIENTS include William Beechcroft, Mary Elting, Franklin Folsom, William F. Hallstead, Rose Wyler. *Commission* Home 15%; Dramatic 20%; Foreign 25%. *Overseas associates* **Laurence Pollinger Ltd**, London.

Singer Media Corporation

Seaview Business Park, 1030 Calle Cordillera, Unit 106, San Clemente CA 92672
☎0101 714 498 7227 Fax 0101 714 498 2162

Contact *Helen J. Lee*

FOUNDED 1940. *Handles* contemporary romance, non-fiction and biographies. *Specialises* in business books and psychological self-help. No scripts or personal adventure novels. No unsolicited mss. Letter first. Reading fee for unpublished authors of $300 for a complete critique and suggestions. Fee deducted from advance if publisher found. Worldwide newspaper syndicate. CLIENTS include Dr Frank S. Caprio, Dr Muriel Oberleder, C. Northcote Parkinson, W.E.D. Ross. *Commission* Home 15%; Foreign 20%.

Michael Snell Literary Agency

Bridge and Castle Road, Truro MA 02666
☎0101 508 349 3718

President *Michael Snell*
Vice President *Patricia Smith*

FOUNDED 1980. Eager to work with new/ unpublished writers. *Specialises* in business and computer books (professional and reference to popular trade how-to); general how-to and self-help on all topics, from diet and exercise to sex, psychology and personal finance; plus literary and suspense fiction. No unsolicited mss. Send outline and sample chapter with return postage for reply. No reading fee for outlines. Brochure available on how to write a book proposal. Send IRCs. *Commission* Home 15%.

Southern Writers

635 Gravier Street, Suite 1020, New Orleans LA 70130
☎0101 504 525 6390 Fax 0101 504 524 7349

Contact *Pamela G. Ahearn*

FOUNDED 1979. *Handles* fiction and non-fiction. Particularly interested in books about the deep South and in romantic fiction. Also handles mainstream general non-fiction, mysteries, thrillers, horror, historical romance and young adult. No scripts, short stories, poetry, autobiography or articles. Approach in writing with query. Reading fee charged to authors unpublished in the field. CLIENTS include John Edward Ames, Rexanne Becnel, Jim Garrison, Marie Goodwin, John McCormack, Meagan McKinney, Keith Miller, Mary Lou Widmer, Lynette Vinet. *Commission* Home 15%; Dramatic 20%; Translation 20%. *Overseas associates* **Abner Stein**, London; Uwe Luserke, Europe.

Spieler Literary Agency

154 West 57th Street, Room 135, New York NY 10019
☎0101 212 757 4439 Fax 0101 212 333 2019

Contact *Joseph Spieler/Lisa M. Ross*

FOUNDED 1980. *Handles* literary fiction and non-fiction. No how-to or genre romance. *Specialises* in history, science, ecology, social issues and business. No scripts. Approach in writing with IRCs. No reading fee. CLIENTS include James Chace, Susan Chace, Amy Ehrlich, Paul Hawken, Joe Kane, Walter Laqueur, Catherine Maccoun, Akio Morita, Marc Reisner. *Commission* Home 15%; Dramatic 15%; Translation 20%. *Overseas associates* **Abner Stein**, London; **Marsh & Sheil Ltd**, London.

Philip G. Spitzer Literary Agency

788 Ninth Avenue, New York NY 10019
☎0101 212 265 6003 Fax 0101 212 765 0953

Contact *Philip Spitzer*

FOUNDED 1969. Works mostly with established/published authors. *Specialises* in general non-fiction (politics, current events, sport, biography) and fiction (mystery and suspense). No reading fee for outlines. CLIENTS include Thomas Allen, James Lee Burke, Andre Dubus, Sonny Kleinfield, Robert Mayer, Norman Polmar, Ralph Wiley. *Commission* Home 15%; Dramatic 15%; Foreign 20%. *Overseas associates* **Murray Pollinger**, London.

Lyle Steele & Co. Ltd

511 East 73rd Street, Suite 7, New York NY 10021
☎0101 212 288 2981 Fax 0101 212 288 1196

President *Lyle Steele*
Vice President *Stan Sitarski*
Project Editor, Chicago *James Kepler*

FOUNDED 1985. *Handles* general non-fiction and category fiction, including mysteries (anxious to see good British mysteries), thrillers, horror and occult. Also North American rights to titles published by major English publishers. *Specialises* in history, true crime, social and political issues, health, self-help, New Age and business. No scripts unless derived from books already being handled. No romance. No unsolicited mss: query with IRCs in first instance. No reading fee. CLIENTS include Eileen Fulton, Jane Gillespie, Valerie Gray. *Commission* 10%. *Overseas associates* worldwide.

Gloria Stern Agency (Hollywood)

12535 Chandler Boulevard, Suite 3, North Hollywood CA 91607
☎0101 818 508 6296

Contact *Gloria Stern*

FOUNDED 1984. *Handles* film scripts and mainstream fiction. 'No books containing gratuitous violence'. Approach with letter, biography and synopsis. Reading fee charged by the hour. *Commission* Home 10–15%; Foreign 18%.

Gloria Stern Agency (New York)

1230 Park Avenue, New York NY 10128
☎0101 212 289 7698

Contact *Gloria Stern*

FOUNDED 1976. 85% non-fiction, including biography, social issues, philosophy and history; 15% mainstream fiction. *Specialises* in education, women's issues, biography, serious fiction, mystery and cookery. No scripts, how-to, poetry, short stories or first fiction from unpublished authors. First approach by letter stating content of book, including one chapter, list of competing books, qualifications as author and International Reply Coupons. No reading fee. *Commission* Home 10–15%; Dramatic 10%; Foreign UK 15% shared; Translation 20% shared. *Overseas associates* **A.M. Heath & Co. Ltd**, London.

Jo Stewart Agency

201 East 66th Street, Suite 184, New York NY 10021
☎0101 212 879 1301

Contact *Jo Stewart*

FOUNDED 1978. *Handles* fiction and non-fiction, young adult and adult. No scripts. No unsolicited mss; send query letter first. No reading fee. *Commission* Home 10%; Foreign 20%; Unpublished 15%. *Overseas associates* **Murray Pollinger**, London.

Gunther Stuhlmann Author's Representative

PO Box 276, Becket MA 01223
☎0101 413 623 5170

Contact *Gunther Stuhlmann/Barbara Ward*

FOUNDED 1954. *Handles* literary fiction, biography and serious non-fiction. No film/TV scripts unless from established clients. No short stories, detective, romance, adventure, poetry, technical or computers. *Specialises* in 20th-century literature, translations of Japanese literature and modern American writers. Query first with IRCs, including sample chapters and synopsis of project. 'We take on few new clients.' No reading fee. CLIENTS include B. H. Friedman, Anais Nin, Richard Powers, Otto Rank. *Commission* Home 10%; Foreign 15%; Translation 20%.

H.N. Swanson, Inc.

8523 Sunset Boulevard, Los Angeles CA 90069
☎0101 310 652 5385 Fax 0101 310 652 3690

Contact *Thomas Shanks* (Managing Director)/ *Annette van Duren/Steve Fisher/Michele Wallerstein/Adam Fierro* (Literary)

FOUNDED 1934. Fiction (thrillers, adventure, plays), radio, audio cassettes and TV. No scientific, medical or sexploitation. No unsolicited mss. Send a letter with International Reply Coupons in the first instance. No reading fee. *Commission* Home 10%; Dramatic 10%; Foreign 20%. *UK associates* various.

The Tantleff Office

375 Greenwich Street, Suite 700, New York NY 10013
☎0101 212 941 3939 Fax 0101 212 941 3948

Contact *Jack Tantleff/John B. Santoianni/Jill Bock*

FOUNDED 1986. *Handles* scripts for TV, film, theatre and radio. No books. No unsolicited mss; queries only. No reading fee. CLIENTS Marsha Norman, David Rabe, Mark O'Donnell, Howard Korder. *Commission* 10%.

2M Communications Ltd

121 West 27th Street, Suite 601, New York NY 10001
☎0101 212 741 1509 Fax 0101 212 691 4460

Contact *Madeleine Morel*

FOUNDED 1982. *Handles* non-fiction only: everything from pop psychology and health to cookery books, biographies and pop culture. No scripts. No fiction, children's, computers or science. No unsolicited mss; send letter with sample pages and IRCs. No reading fee. CLIENTS include David Steinman, Janet Wolfe, Donald Woods. *Commission* Home 15%; Dramatic 15%; Translation 20%. *Overseas associates* **Jane Gregory Agency**, London; Thomas Schluck Agency, Germany; Asano Agency, Japan; Bengt Nordin Agency, Scandinavia; EAIS, France; Living Literary Agency, Italy; Nueva Agencia Literaria Internacional, Spain.

Susan P. Urstadt, Inc.

PO Box 1676, New Canaan CT 06840
☎0101 203 966 6111 Fax 0101 203 966 2249

President *Susan P. Urstadt*

FOUNDED 1975. *Specialises* in decorative arts, antiques, architecture, gardening, cookery, biography, performing arts, sports, current affairs, natural history and environment, lifestyle, current living trends and popular reference. Query with outline, sample chapter, author biography and IRCs. CLIENTS include Emyl Jenkins, Elizabeth Stillinger, Thomas Powers. *Commission* Home 15%; Dramatic 20%; Foreign 20%.

Van der Leun & Associates

464 Mill Hill Drive, Southport CT 06490
☎0101 203 259 4897

Contact *Patricia Van der Leun*

FOUNDED 1984. *Handles* fiction and non-fiction. No scripts. No science fiction or fantasy romance. *Specialises* in art and architecture, science, biography and fiction. No unsolicited mss; query first, with proposal and short biography. No reading fee. CLIENTS include David Darling, Liu Binyan, Robert Fulghum, Christopher Manes. *Commission* 15%. *Overseas associates* **Abner Stein**, London; Michelle LePautre; English Agency, Japan; Carmen Balcells, Spain; T & L Literary Agents, The Netherlands; Karin Schindler, South America; Susanno Zesi, Italy.

Carlson Wade

49 Bokee Court, Room K-4, Brooklyn NY 11223
☎0101 718 743 6983

Contact *Carlson Wade*

FOUNDED 1949. All types of fiction and non-fiction. No poetry, textbooks or scripts. Unsolicited mss considered but letter of description with International Reply Coupons preferred. Reading fee of £50 for books; £10 for short scripts. *Commission* 10%.

Wallace Literary Agency

177 East 70th Street, New York NY 10021
☎0101 212 570 9090 Fax 0101 212 772 8979

FOUNDED 1988. Unsolicited mss not welcome. *Commission* Rates upon applications. *UK associates* **A. M. Heath & Co.**, London.

Bess Wallace Literary Agency

PO Box 972, Duchesne UT 84021
☎0101 801 738 2317
6733 West Carol Ann Way, Peoria AZ 85345
☎0101 602 486 2389

Contact *Bess Wallace* (Utah)/Penni Wallace (Arizona)

FOUNDED 1977. *Handles* non-fiction. No romance, eroticism or poetry. No scripts. Unsolicited mss welcome but query first. No reading fee. *Commission* Home 15%; Dramatic 10%; Translation 10%.

Gerry B. Wallerstein Agency

2315 Powell Avenue, Suite 12, Erie PA 16506
℡0101 814 833 5511 Fax 0101 814 833 6260

Contact *Gerry B. Wallerstein*

FOUNDED 1984. Adult fiction and non-fiction. No scripts unless by established clients. No children's, textbooks, esoteric or autobiographical (unless celebrity). Broad range of clients, main interest being marketability of material. No unsolicited mss. Send IRCs. with International Reply Coupons for information regarding submissions. Reading fee charged for non-established authors. CLIENTS include Carl Caiati, Jack D. Coombe, Nan DeVincentis-Hayes, Gregory Janicki, Charlotte White. *Commission* Home 15%; Dramatic 15%; Translation 20%.

John A. Ware Literary Agency

392 Central Park West, New York NY 10025
℡0101 212 866 4733 Fax 0101 212 866 4734

Contact *John Ware*

FOUNDED 1978. *Specialises* in biography, history, current affairs, investigative journalism, science, inside looks, health and psychology (academic credentials required). Also handles literary fiction, sport, oral history, Americana and folklore. No category fiction except mysteries/thrillers. Unsolicited mss not read. Send query letter first with IRCs. No reading fee. CLIENTS include Dr Stephen E. Ambrose, John Casti, Jennifer Johnston. *Commission* Home 10%; Dramatic 10%; Foreign 20%.

Waterside Productions, Inc.

2191 San Elijo Avenue, Cardiff-by-the-Sea CA 92007-1839
℡0101 619 632 9190 Fax 0101 619 632 9295

Contact *Julie Castiglia*

FOUNDED 1982. *Handles* mainstream and category fiction, psychology, science, women's issues, business, all trade and general non-fiction. No science fiction or horror. No unsolicited mss; send query letter. No reading fee. *Commission* Home 15%; Dramatic 20%; Translation 25%. *Overseas associates* **Radala & Associates**, England; Asano Agency, Japan; Von Sydow, Sweden; Ruth Liepman,

Germany; Elias Vera Lemarie, France; Tuttle-Mori Agency, Inc., China; Lawrence Smith, Argentina.

Wecksler-Incomco

170 West End Avenue, New York NY 10023
℡0101 212 787 2239 Fax 0101 212 496 7035

Contact *Sally Wecksler/Joann Amparan*

FOUNDED 1971. *Handles* mostly illustrated non-fiction, including nature, plus some literary fiction. No scripts, romance, violence, graphic sex or self-help. No unsolicited mss; queries only. No reading fee. CLIENTS Roger Axtell, Loren Singer, Ethel Blacker. *Commission* Home 15%; Translation 20%.

Cherry Weiner Literary Agency

28 Kipling Way, Manalapan NJ 07726
℡0101 908 446 2096

Contact *Cherry Weiner*

FOUNDED 1977. *Handles* more or less all types of genre fiction: science fiction and fantasy, romance, mystery, westerns. No scripts. No non-fiction. No unsolicited mss. No submissions except through referral. No reading fee. CLIENTS include Victoria Thompson, Jean Lorrah, Gael Baudino. *Commission* 15%. *Overseas associates* **Abner Stein**, London; Thomas Schluck, Germany.

Wieser & Wieser, Inc.

118 East 25th Street, New York NY 10010
℡0101 212 260 0860 Fax 0101 212 505 7186

Contact *Olga B. Wieser/George J. Wieser/Jake Elwell*

FOUNDED 1976. Works mostly with established/published authors. *Specialises* in literary and mainstream fiction, serious and popular historical fiction, and general non-fiction: business, finance, aviation, sports, photography, cookbooks, travel and popular medicine. No poetry, children's, science fiction or religious. No unsolicited mss. First approach by letter with International Reply Coupons. No reading fee for outlines. CLIENTS include the Bettmann Archive, Dale Brown, William Goyen estate, Richard Herman Jr, Douglas C. Jones, Edith Layton, John Nance. *Commission* Home 15%; Dramatic 15%; Foreign 20%.

Ruth Wreschner, Authors' Representative

10 West 74th Street, New York NY 10023
℡0101 212 877 2605 Fax 0101 212 595 5843

Contact *Ruth Wreschner*

FOUNDED 1981. Works mostly with established/ published authors but 'will consider very good first novels, both mainstream and genre, particularly British mystery writers'. *Specialises* in popular medicine, health, how-to and fiction. No screenplays or dramatic plays. First approach with query letter and International Reply Coupons. For fiction, send a synopsis and first 100 pp; for non-fiction, an outline and two sample chapters. No reading fee. CLIENTS include Mary Ann Bartusis, Reed E. Bunzel, Dennis Florig, Charles Salter. *Commission* Home 15%; Foreign 20%.

Ann Wright Representatives, Inc.

136 East 56th Street, Suite 2C, New York NY 10022
☏0101 212 832 0110 Fax 0101 212 750 9686

Contact *Dan Wright*

FOUNDED 1961. Signatory to the Writers Guild of America Agreement. *Specialises* in screenplays for film and TV. Also handles 'faction' drama and fiction. No academic, scientific or scholarly. Approach by letter; no reply without IRCs. Include outline and credits only. Encourages new film and TV writers, and has something of a reputation in this field. No reading fee. CLIENTS include Theodore Bonnet, Tom Dempsey, Donald Dewey, Kerry Kiernan, Taber McMordie, Edmund Naughton, John Peer Nugent, Richard Rees, Brian Reich, Bill Skirrow, Eric Van Hoffman. *Commission* Home varies according to current trend (between 10–20%); Dramatic 10% of gross.

Stephen Wright, Authors' Representative

PO Box 1341, FDR Station, New York NY 10150
☏0101 212 213 4382

Contact *Stephen Wright*

FOUNDED 1984. *Handles* fiction and non-fiction including mystery, spy/ thriller, crime, suspense, mainstream, biographies and children's. Also scripts for film and TV. No unsolicited mss; query first with brief synopsis of mss, biographical details and IRCs for response. Reading fee for writers not established in their field. CLIENTS Jack Lynch, Walter Oleksy, Jonathan Goodman, William J. Lambert. *Commission* 10% for professional writers; 15% for unpublished/new writers.

Writer's Consulting Group

PO Box 492, Burbank CA 91503
☏0101 818 841 9294

Contact *Jim Barmeier*

FOUNDED 1985. *Handles* unusual true stories, true crime, health, how-to, contemporary fiction, educational and scripts for film, TV, theatre and radio. No historical or romance novels. Unsolicited mss welcome; query letter with outline and summary preferred. No reading fee. *Commission* 10%.

Writers House, Inc.

21 West 26th Street, New York NY 10010
☏0101 212 685 2400 Fax 0101 212 685 1781

Contact *Albert Zuckerman/Amy Berkower/ Merrilee Heifetz/Susan Cohen/Susan Ginsburg*

FOUNDED 1974. *Handles* all types of fiction, including children's and young adult, plus narrative non-fiction: history, biography, popular science, pop and rock culture. No scripts. *Specialises* in popular fiction, women's novels, thrillers and children's. No professional or scholarly. For consideration of unsolicited mss, send letter of enquiry, 'explaining why your book is wonderful and outlining your writing background'. No reading fee. CLIENTS include Ken Follett, Craig Shaw Gardner, Eileen Goudge, Stephen Hawking, Robin McKinley, Ann Martin, Francine Pascal, Cynthia Voigt, F. Paul Wilson. *Commission* Home 15%; Dramatic 15%; Foreign 20%. *Overseas associates* **Blake Friedmann Literary Agency Ltd**, London.

Writers' Productions

Box 630, Westport CT 06881
☏0101 203 227 8199

Contact *David L. Meth*

FOUNDED 1981. Eager to work with new/ unpublished writers. *Handles* literary fiction and non-fiction. *Special interests* Asia and Asian Americans, especially Japan and Korea; and serious nonfiction 'that will have some influence on society'. Send sample (30 pp), together with IRCs. and International Reply Coupons. No reading fee. CLIENTS include Junghyo Ahn, Kathleen Barnes, Seicho Matsumoto, Kenji Miyazawa, John Nance. *Commission* Home 15%; Dramatic 25%; Foreign 25%.

Writers' Representatives

25 West 19th Street, New York NY 10011–4202
☏0101 212 620 9009 Fax 0101 212 620 9010

Contact *Glen Hartley/Lynn Chu*

FOUNDED 1985. *Handles* fiction, non-fiction and scripts for books already sold. Non-fiction submissions should include book proposal, detailed table of contents and sample chapters. Fiction submissions should include sample chapters, not synopses. All must be accompanied by biography, reviews, if any, and IRCs. No reading fee. CLIENTS include Harold Bloom, Steven Ozment, Roger Kimball, David Lehman Tama Starr, Melanie Thernstrom. *Commission* 15/20%.

James N. Frey, Una-Mary Parker, Jerry E. Patterson, Boyce Rensberger. *Commission* Home 15%; Dramatic 15%; Foreign 20%. *Overseas associates* **Abner Stein**, London; and most countries worldwide.

Susan Zeckendorf Associates
171 West 57th Street, Suite 11B, New York NY 10019
☏0101 212 245 2928   Fax 0101 212 977 2643

President *Susan Zeckendorf*

FOUNDED 1979. Works with new/unpublished writers. *Specialises* in literary fiction, commercial women's fiction, international espionage and mysteries; and in non-fiction: namely illustrated and science. No category romance, science fiction or scripts. No unsolicited mss. Send query letter describing mss. No reading fee. CLIENTS include Doris Jean Austin,

Tom Zelasky Literary Agency
3138 Parkridge Crescent, Chamblee GA 30341
☏0101 404 458 0391

Contact *Tom Zelasky*

FOUNDED 1982. *Handles* detective fiction, mystery and suspense, westerns, adventure, romance, and all manner of mainstream fiction. No unsolicited mss. Call or write outlining proposal. Reading fee of £100 for first 450 pp double-spaced. *Commission* Home 10-15%; Foreign 25%.

US Press, Journals and Broadcasting

ABC News
8 Carburton Street, London W1P 7DT
☎ 071-637 9222   Fax 071-631 5084

Director, News Coverage, Europe, Middle East & Africa *Ned Warwick*
Senior Editor, Europe *Pierre Salinger*

The Associated Press
See **News Agencies**

Baltimore Sun
10 Bolt Court, Fleet Street, London EC4A 3DB
☎ 071-353 3531   Fax 071-493 9896

Bureau Chief *Richard O'Mara*

Bloomberg Business News
City Gate House, 39-45 Finsbury Square,
London EC2A 1PX
☎ 071-256 9010   Fax 071-374 6138/256 5326

Bureau Chief *David Keefe*

Business Week
34 Dover Street, London W1X 4BR
☎ 071-491 8985

Bureau Manager *Richard Melcher*

Cable News International
CNN House, 19-22 Rathbone Place,
London W1P 1DF
☎ 071-637 6800   Fax 071-637 6868

Bureau Chief *David Feingold*

CBS News
68 Knightsbridge, London SW1X 7LL
☎ 071-581 4801   Fax 071-581 4431

Bureau Chief *Peter Bluff*

Chicago Tribune Press
85 Fleet Street, London EC4Y 1EE
☎ 071-353 6126   Fax 071-583 4388

Chief European Correspondent *Ray Moseley*

Forbes Magazine
Berkeley Square House, Berkeley Square,
London W1X 5PE
☎ 071-465 0120   Fax 071-465 0121

European Bureau Manager *Peter Fuhrman*

Fortune Magazine
Time & Life Building, New Bond Street,
London W1Y 0AA
☎ 071-499 4080   Fax 071-322 1269

Bureau Chief *Carla Rapoport*

International Herald Tribune
63 Long Acre, London WC2E 9JH
☎ 071-836 4802   Fax 071-240 2254

London Correspondent *Erik Ipsen*

Journal of Commerce
18-20 Laystall Street, London EC1R 4PA
☎ 071-278 2727   Fax 071-837 2168

Chief European Correspondent *Janet Porter*

Life Magazine
Time & Life Building, 153 New Bond Street,
London W1Y 0AA
☎ 071-499 4080   Fax 071-322 1182

Bureau Chief *Gail Ridgwell*

Los Angeles Times
150 Brompton Road, London SW3 1HX
☎ 071-823 7315   Fax 071-823 7308

Bureau Chief *Dan Fisher*

National Public Radio
Room 230, CB, Bush House, Aldwych,
London WC2B 4PH
☎071-257 2752   Fax 071-379 6846
Bureau Chief *John Ydstie*

NBC News
8 Bedford Avenue, London WC1B 2NQ
☎071-637 8655   Fax 071-636 2628
Bureau Chief *Karen Curry*

The New York Times
76 Shoe Lane, London EC4A 3JB
☎071-353 8181   Fax 071-583 1458
Chief Correspondent *Craig R. Whitney*

Newsweek
18 Park Street, London W1Y 4HH
☎071-629 8361   Fax 071-408 1403
Bureau Chief *Daniel Pedersen*

Coverage of news, politics, issues and current
affairs, for 'an intelligent adult readership'.

People Magazine
Time & Life Building, 153 New Bond Street,
London W1Y 0AA
☎071-499 4080   Fax 071-322 1125
Special Correspondent *Jerene Jones*

Philadelphia Inquirer
7 The Ridgeway, London NW11 8TD
☎081-455 6877

Correspondent *Larry Eichel*

Reader's Digest Association
Berkeley Square House, London W1X 6AB
☎071-629 8144   Fax 071-408 0748
Editor-in-Chief, British Edition *Russell Twisk*

San Francisco Examiner
53 Devonshire Road, London W5
☎081-567 9444
London Correspondent *Dan Ehrlich*

Time Magazine
Time & Life Building, 153 New Bond Street,
London W1Y 0AA
☎071-499 4080   Fax 071-322 1230
Bureau Chief *B. William Mader*

US News and World Report
169 Piccadilly, London W1V 9DD
☎071-493 4643   Fax 071-493 8308
Senior European Editor *Robin Knight*

USA Today
27 Rochester Road, London NW1 9JJ
☎071-482 1019   Fax 071-482 6348
London Correspondent *Allen F. Richardson*

Voice of America
76 Shoe Lane, London EC4A 3JB
☎071-410 0960   Fax 071-410 0966
Senior Editor *Phil Haynes*

Wall Street Journal
76 Shoe Lane, London EC4A 3JB
☎071-334 0006   Fax 071-353 4893
Bureau Chief *Glynn Mapes*

Washington Post
18 Park Street, London W1Y 4HH
☎071-629 8958   Fax 071-629 0050
London Correspondent *Glenn Frankel*

I Quote, You Plagiarise

The Law of Copyright

The overview on copyright is contained in the 1988 Act, a weighty volume of legalese which restates the basic rules and adds some new ones.

Copyright protection lasts for fifty years from the end of the calendar year in which the author dies. The rule now applies to unpublished, as well as published, works. No longer will unpublished works remain in copyright until they are published and for fifty years thereafter.

For a published work of joint authorship, protection runs from the end of the year of the death of the author who dies last. The fifty-year rule applies to all written work including letters.

As a general principle, the author is the first owner of copyright except when he is working for someone else. In this case, the copyright will belong to the employer unless otherwise agreed. For journalists this is a backward step – under the 1956 Act the rights automatically granted to an employer were limited to publication in newspapers and magazines. This protection is missing from the 1988 Act.

It is different for freelancers. Or, rather, it can be different for freelancers if they bother to read *and* amend the small print in their contracts. In principle, freelancers own the copyright of all written, commissioned material, handing over to an editor only those rights agreed at the time of commissioning. At issue here is not simply the right to have a say on how material is used after its first publication but also the more sensitive matter of supplementary fees.

In practice, most editors are under pressure from their masters to negotiate contracts which cancel out a freelancer's rights. The journalists' unions are urging freelancers to resist blatant attempts to undermine the 1988 Act but the need to make a living in a highly competitive market may weaken the resolve of all but the top-flight contenders who are able to dictate their own terms.

The problem of starting from a weak bargaining position is shared by contributors to academic and specialist journals. Michael Ryder, writing in the spring edition of *The Author*, reports on an increasing tendency of editors to make the signature on a copyright assignment form a condition of publication.

'It is explained on the form (somewhat patronisingly for naïve academics) that the reasons for assignment are: (a) that items lacking the copyright symbol in the USA automatically fall into the Public Domain (which I am told is no longer true); and (b) to regularise applications to reproduce. It is stated that 50 per cent of any fees to reproduce material will be passed on to the author – I say, Why not 100 per cent? The key point is that there is no mention on the form of photocopying and fees for it, although permission might be given on the cover of the journal for photocopying, with a request that in the USA the requisite fees be sent to the appropriate agency – no mention of the ALCS in Britain.'

He continues:

'Publishers of multi-author volumes also take copyright. I have a chapter in a book just published by a supposedly very reputable academic publisher and I discovered that it takes copyright unless you write to say otherwise. I wrote back to say that it could not do so without a written assignment but I am the only person to have retained the copyright in his chapter, my name being specifically listed on the appropriate prelim page!'

The only remedy, says Michael Ryder, is to mark assignment forms 'signed under protest' but he knows very well that most academics never even think about copyright, a human weakness long ago discovered by Robert Maxwell, among others, to their great profit.

Another problem area is film and television. **The Writers' Guild** has this to say:

'Under the 1988 Act, the author of a film "shall be taken to be . . . the person by whom the arrangements necessary for the making of the film are undertaken" and this is a phrase that is generally understood to refer to the producer. It is this idiosyncratic abuse of the word "author" that causes so much heartache to writers and directors, for of course the function of the film producer is akin to a book's publisher, not its author.'

At the very least, creative authors and entrepreneurs should be treated even-handedly.

Copyright on Ideas

Writers trying to sell ideas should start on the assumption that it is almost impossible to stake an exclusive claim. So much unsolicited material comes the way of script departments, duplication of ideas is inevitable.

Frequent complaints of plagiarism have led major production companies to point out the risks whenever they acknowledge an unsolicited synopsis or script, warning correspondents, 'it is often the case that we are currently considering or have already considered ideas that may be similar to your own'.

That this is not a complete defence is suggested by the case brought by a London schoolteacher, Keith Wooldridge, against Radio 4. Mr Wooldridge asserted that the BBC had purloined his idea for a series about pets and their owners. A district judge at Bromley Crown Court agreed with him and ordered the BBC to pay damages and costs. One of the interesting features of the case is that it was brought under the small claims procedure. This limits damages to £1000 but avoids the heavy legal fees associated with a High Court action.

The rash of cases that may follow Mr Wooldridge's triumph will be of little comfort to those who have suffered the attention of unscrupulous rivals. In a highly competitive, fast-moving business, manuscripts can end up in the wrong hands. If there are worries on this score, a useful precaution is to copy a manuscript, send it to yourself by registered post, then deposit the package and dated receipt at a bank or other safe place. At least then no one can fault memory on essential detail.

And resist the urge to give out all your best ideas at an expensive lunch or in a brain-storming session with an ever-so-friendly producer who just might be able to slot your programme into his overcrowded schedule. It is flattering to be invited to hold forth but the experience can be costly unless there is an up-front fee. No less a writer than Frederic Raphael has been caught out in this way. Invited to develop a 'major series', he soon discovered that:

> 'I had been swindled into spending time and energy, without fee, on a project to which no one was committed at all. My ideas were now on file; my garrulous suggestions were lodged in the minds of those who might later, without acknowledgement, make use of them. I was not wholly shattered to be told eventually, on the telephone, by the senior producer (who said that he had "learned a lot" from "our" experience), that the Department Head had decided to put the whole thing on ice.'

The lesson was plain.

> 'The way I feel about executives, the time is approaching when I shall charge a consultancy fee for saying hello. And another for goodbye.'

Copyright on Characters

Even when a script is accepted for broadcasting, problems of copyright can still occur. A frequent source of dispute is the lifting of characters from one series to another when there are two or more writers involved.

'TV people like to believe that the character becomes their own,' writes Kenneth Royce, creator of *The XYY Man* and *Bulman*, 'forgetting that without the author's original, there would be no such character.' As a minimum precaution he urges a writer approaching a TV deal 'to resist strongly any attempt to change the names of his characters. Why make stealing easier than it already is?'

Copyright in Titles

If copyright over characters is difficult to establish, it is nearly impossible with titles. Only when a title is distinctive and clearly identified with the work of a particular author is there any chance of gaining an injunction against its use, or something very close to it, by another writer.

Copyright in Lectures and Speeches

A change introduced by the 1988 Act is the ownership of copyright in a lecture.

The old rule was unnecessarily complicated and depended, for example, on whether the lecturer was speaking from prepared notes. Now, even if a speaker talks without notes, copyright exists in a lecture as soon as it is recorded (in writing or otherwise) but not until then. The copyright belongs to the person who spoke the words, whether or not the recording was made by, or with the permission of, the speaker.

This means that nobody may make substantial use of a transcript of a lecture without permission. The Act does, however, make one important exception: where a record of spoken words is made to report current events, it is not an infringement of copyright to use or copy the record for that purpose provided that:

(a) the record is a direct record of the spoken words

(b) the making of the record was not prohibited by the speaker.

Fair Dealing

Under the 'fair-dealing' rule, a writer has the undisputed right to quote another writer for 'purposes of criticism or review', as long as 'sufficient acknowledgement' is given. There are limits of course. It is not the done thing to lift 'a substantial part' of a copyright work without permission. Unfortunately, there is little agreement on what constitutes 'a substantial part'. Legal precedents suggest that the quality of the 'part' and its value to the user must be taken into account as well as its length in determining whether it is 'substantial'. This explains how, in one case, four lines from a thirty-two line poem were held to amount to 'a substantial part'. On the other hand, even a 'substantial' quotation from a copyright work may be acceptable if a student or critic is engaged in 'fair dealing with a literary work for the purposes of research or music study'.

Common sense suggests basing the assessment on the length and importance of the quotation; the amount quoted in relation to the text as a whole; the extent to which the work competes with the work quoted and the extent to which the words quoted are saving a writer time and trouble.

Some years ago the **Society of Authors** and the **Publishers' Association** stated that they would usually regard as 'fair dealing' the use of a single extract of up to 400 words, or a series of extracts (of which none exceeds 300 words) to a total of 800 words from a prose work, or of extracts to a total of 40 lines from a poem, provided that this did not exceed a quarter of the poem.

Permission

For the quotation of a 'substantial' extract from a copyright work or for any quotation of copyright material, however short, for an anthology, application should be made to the publishers of the original work.

It is much in the author's interest to deal with permissions as early as possible. Last minute requests just before a book goes to press can lead to embarrassing difficulties if fees charged are too high or if permission is refused.

The **Society of Authors** and the **Publishers' Association** have recently revised their recommendation for 'basic *minimum* fees' for quotation and anthology use of copyright material.

Prose: The suggested rate is £82–£96 per 1000 words for world rights. The rate for the UK and Commonwealth or the USA alone is usually half of the world rate. For an individual country (e.g. Canada, Australia or New Zealand): one quarter of the world rate.

Where an extract is complete in itself (e.g. a chapter or short story) publishers sometimes charge an additional fee at half the rate applicable for 1000 words.

This scale generally covers one edition only. An additional fee may be payable if the material is used in a reset or offset edition or in a new format or new binding (e.g. a paperback edition) and will certainly be required if the publisher of an anthology sub-licenses publication rights to another publisher.

Fees vary according to the importance of the author quoted, the proportion of the original work that the user intends to quote and its value to the author/publisher requesting permission. The expected size of the print-run should also be taken into consideration and may affect the fee. It is usual to halve the fees for quotations to be used in scholarly works with print-runs of under 1000 copies.·

Poetry: For anthology publication in the UK and Commonwealth a minimum fee of £30 should be charged for the first ten lines; thereafter £1.50 per line for the next twenty lines and £1 a line subsequently. This rate may be reduced by one-third if the poem appears in a literary or scholarly journal or an anthology that contains more than forty poems in copyright or in a book with a print-run of less than 1500 copies. The rates for established poets may well be significantly higher.

For any subsequent edition or for separate publication elsewhere (e.g. in the USA, Australia, Europe, Canada) it is recommended that a further fee be charged and that this could be reduced to not less than half the original fee – in order to encourage the wide sale of anthologies containing the work of new poets. Anthology fees for publication in the USA of established poets may well match the fees for anthology use in the UK.

For quotation in a work of criticism or review (e.g. a biography) over the limit of 'fair dealing' some discount from these anthology fees is normally given.

Wider Interests

Further changes in copyright law may soon wing their way across from Brussels. If a European Commission proposal goes through, Britain's term of copyright could be extended by 20 years to bring it into line with Germany. Authors' descendants will benefit. So, too, will agents and publishers with valuable properties to protect. But a new generation of writers who want access to existing work may have cause to complain. As Mark Le Fanu of the **Society of Authors** points out, 'Historians and biographers prefer to be able to draw on material freely as soon as possible'.

Whatever happens, copyright law will remain a minefield. Tread warily.

Professional Associations and Societies

Alliance of Literary Societies

Birmingham and Midland Institute, Margaret Street,
Birmingham B3 3BS
☎ 021–236 3591

President *Gabriel Woolf*
Honorary Secretary *Kenneth N. Oultram*
Secretary *P. A. Fisher*

FOUNDED 1974. Acts as a liaison body between member societies and, when necessary, as a pressure group. Deals with enquiries and assists in preserving buildings and places with literary connections. Over eighty societies are involved, including the Francis Bacon Society, the **Chesterton Society**, the Sherlock Holmes Society, the D. H. Lawrence Society, the Jules Verne Circle and the Friends of Alfred Williams. A directory of literary societies is maintained. The ALS produces an annual fanzine, *Chapter One*, which is distributed to affiliated societies. Details from the editor, Kenneth Oultram (0606 891 303).

Arvon Foundation

Totleigh Barton, Sheepwash, Beaworthy,
Devon EX21 5NS
☎ 040 923338
Lumb Bank, Heptonstall, Hebden Bridge, West Yorkshire HX7 6DF
☎ 0422 843714

Co-Presidents *Terry Hands/Ted Hughes OBE*
Chairman *Lawrence Sail*

FOUNDED 1968. Offers people of any age (over 16) and any background the opportunity to live and work with professional writers. Five-day residential courses are held throughout the year at Arvon's two centres, covering poetry, narrative, drama, writing for children, songwriting and the performing arts. A number of bursaries towards the cost of course fees are available for those on low incomes, the unemployed, students and pensioners. Runs a biennial poetry competition (see entry **Prizes**).

Association of American Correspondents in London

12 Norwich Street, London EC4A 1BP
☎ 071–353 1515   Fax 071–353 8118

Contact *Sandra Marshall*

Subscription £80 for each organisation, plus £25 each department of an organisation desiring separate listing in the Association's handbook

FOUNDED 1919 to serve the professional interests of its member organisations, promote social cooperation among them, and maintain the ethical standards of the profession.

Association of Authors' Agents

c/o 2nd Floor, 79 St Martin's Lane,
London WC2N 4AA
☎ 071–836 4271   Fax 071–497 2561

Secretary *Sara Fisher*

Membership £50 p.a.

FOUNDED 1974. Membership voluntary. The AAA maintains a code of practice, provides a forum for discussion, and represents its members in issues affecting the profession.

Association of British Editors

8-16 Great New Street, London EC4P 4ER
☎ 0480 492133   Fax 0480 492805

Executive Director *Jock Gallagher*
Honorary Secretary *Nicholas Herbert*

Subscription £40 p.a.

FOUNDED 1985. Independent organisation for the study and enhancement of journalism worldwide. Established to protect and promote the freedom of the Press. Members are expected to 'maintain the dignity and rights of the profession; consider and sustain standards of professional conduct; exchange ideas for the advancement of professional ideals; work for the solution of common problems.' Membership is limited, but open to persons who have immediate charge of editorial or news policies.

Association of British Science Writers (ABSW)

c/o British Association for the Advancement of

Science, Fortress House, 23 Savile Row,
London W1X 1AB
☎071-494 3326   Fax 071-734 1658
Secretary *Peter Briggs*

Membership £15 p.a.; £12 (Associate)

ABSW has played a central role in improving the standards of science journalism in the UK over the last forty years. The Association seeks to improve standards by means of networking, lectures and organised visits to institutional laboratories and industrial research centres. Puts members in touch with major projects in the field and with experts worldwide. A member of the European Union of Science Journalists' Associations, ABSW is able to offer heavily subsidised places on visits to research centres in most other European countries and hosts reciprocal visits to Britain by European journalists. Membership open to those who are considered to be *bona fide* science writers/ editors, or their film/ TV/radio equivalents, who earn a substantial part of their income by promoting public interest in and understanding of science. Assists in the administration and judging of the **Glaxo Science Writers' Fellowships**, a series of awards for outstanding science journalism in newspapers, journals and broadcasting.

Association for Business Sponsorship of the Arts (ABSA)
Nutmeg House, 60 Gainsford Street, Butlers Wharf,
London SE1 2NY
☎071-378 8143   Fax 071-407 7527

A national independent organisation which was established by the business community, concerned with both the concept and practical details of business sponsorship of the arts and representation of sponsors' interests. Those seeking sponsorship can join ABSA's arts mailing list (£7) to receive copies of specialist publications including a sponsorship manual.

Association of Comics Enthusiasts
80 Silverdale, London SE26 4SJ
☎081-699 7725

Contact *Denis Gifford*

Subscription £6 p.a.; £12 overseas

FOUNDED 1978. The only society for all those interested in the history and development of British comics. Subscribers receive six issues of the association's newsletter, *Comic Cuts*.

Association of Independent Libraries
Portico Library, 57 Mosley Street,
Manchester M2 3HY
☎061-236 6785

Secretary *Mrs Janet Allan*

Established to 'further the advancement, conservation and restoration of a little known but important living portion of our cultural heritage'. Membership is open to libraries founded between 1768-1841, before the creation of the public library service, and includes the **Devon & Exeter Institution, Linen Hall Library** and **Plymouth Proprietary Library**.

Association of Independent Radio Companies
Radio House, 46 Westbourne Grove,
London W2 5SH
☎071-727 2646   Fax 071-229 0352

Company Secretary *Don Edgerton*

The AIRC is the trade association of the independent radio companies. It represents members' interests to Government, the Radio Authority, trade unions, copyright organisations and other bodies.

Association of Learned and Professional Society Publishers
48 Kelsey Lane, Beckenham, Kent BR3 3NE
☎081-658 0459

Secretary *Bernard Donovan*

FOUNDED 1972 to foster the publishing activities of learned societies and academic and professional bodies. Membership is limited to such organisations and those publishing on behalf of member organisations.

Association of Little Presses
89A Petherton Road, London N5 2QT
☎071-226 2657

Coordinator *Bob Cobbing*
Secretary *Stan Trevor*

Subscription £10 p.a.

FOUNDED 1966 as a loosely knit association of individuals running little presses, who grouped together for mutual self-help and encouragement. First acted as a pressure group to extend the availability of grant aid to small presses and later became more of an information exchange, advice centre and general promoter of small press publishing. Currently represents over 300 publishers and associates throughout Britain. Membership is open to presses and magazines as well as to individuals and institutions. ALP publishes a thrice-yearly magazine, *Poetry and Little Press Information* (PALPI); information booklets such as *Getting Your Poetry Published* (over 35,000 copies sold since 1973) and *Publishing Yourself: Not Too Difficult After All* which advises those who are thinking of self-publishing; the annual *Catalogue of Small Press Books in Print*; and a regular newsletter. A full list of little presses (some of which, like **Bloodaxe Books**, are now sufficiently established and successful to be considered in the mainstream of the business) is available from ALP, or from the **Welsh Arts Council** Oriel Bookshop (£5.55 incl. p&p). ALP also organises bookfairs, exhibitions and gatherings around the country. Its main focus, that of supporting members' presses, brings it into contact with organisations worldwide. Over 80% of all new poetry in Britain is published by small presses and magazines but the Association is by no means solely devoted to publishers of poetry; its members produce everything from comics to cookery, novels and naval history.

The Authors' Club

40 Dover Street, London W1X 3RB
☏ 071-499 8581

Secretary *Mrs Ridgway*

Entry Fee £125 (Town/Country); £105 (Young Members up to 35/ Retired Members)

Annual Subscription £375 p.a. (Town); £188 (Country); £125 (Young Members); £140 (Retired Members)

FOUNDED 1891 by Sir Walter Besant. For men and women writers and those with literary interests.

Authors' Licensing and Collecting Society

33-34 Alfred Place, London WC1E 7DP
☏ 071-255 2034   Fax 071-323 0486

President *Lord Willis*

Secretary General *Janet Hurrell*

Subscription £5.88 incl. VAT (free to members of **The Society of Authors** and the **Writers' Guild**); £7 (Overseas)

A non-profit making society collecting and distributing payment to writers in areas where they are unable to administer the rights themselves, such as reprography, certain lending rights, private and off-air recording and simultaneous cabling. Open to writers and their heirs.

BAFTA (British Academy of Film and Television Arts)
195 Piccadilly, London W1V 9LG
☏ 071-734 0022   Fax 071-734 1792

Director *A. J. Byrne*

Subscription £115 p.a.; £60 (Country)

FOUNDED 1947. Membership limited to 'those who have contributed to the industry' over a minimum period of three years. Provides facilities for screening and discussions; encourages research and experimentation; lobbies Parliament; and makes annual awards.

BAPLA (British Association of Picture Libraries and Agencies)
13 Woodberry Crescent, London N10 1PJ
☏ 081-444 7913   Fax 081-883 9215

Administrator *Sal Shuel*

An association of more than 275 picture libraries and agencies, who between them handle more than 300 million images: 'black and white, colour, very old, very new, scientific, absurd, news, kittens in furry slippers, aardvarks, Zulus, and almost everything in between'. *The Directory* (obtainable from the above address) is a guide to who has what and where they are. The Association also offers advice on costs, etc., and publishes an entertaining journal.

BASCA (British Academy of Songwriters, Composers and Authors)
34 Hanway Street, London W1P 9DE
☏ 071-436 2261   Fax 071-436 1913

Contact *Eileen Stow*

Subscription from £16 p.a.

FOUNDED 1947. The Academy offers advice and support for songwriters and represents members' interests to the music industry. It also issues a standard contract between publishers and writers and a collaborators' agreement. Members receive the Academy's quarterly magazine.

The Bibliographical Society

Collections & Preservation, British Library, Great Russell Street, London WC1B 3DG
☏ 071-323 7567   Fax 071-323 7771

President *B. C. Bloomfield*
Honorary Secretary *Mrs M. Foot*

Subscription £23 p.a.

Aims to promote and encourage the study and research of historical, analytical, descriptive and textual bibliography, and the history of printing, publishing, bookselling, bookbinding and collecting; to hold meetings at which papers are read and discussed; to print and publish works concerned with bibliography; to form a bibliographical library. Publishes a quarterly magazine called *The Library*.

Book House Ireland

65 Middle Abbey Street, Dublin 1
Republic of Ireland
☏ 010 353 1 730108   Fax 010 353 1 735919

Administrator *Cecily Golden*

FOUNDED 1983 by CLE: the Irish Book Publishers Association and the Booksellers' Association of Great Britain and Ireland. Its purpose is to draw together, to represent and further the interests of these two organisations and to provide a joint secretariat. Provides an information and resource centre, booktrade information, meeting facilities, training courses and seminars on all aspects of the booktrade, regular newsletters and a weekly bestseller list. Both CLE and the BA are housed in the same offices as BHI.

Book Packagers Association

93A Blenheim Crescent, London W11 2EQ
☏ 071-221 9089

Chairman *Bruce Marshall*
Secretary *Rosemary Pettit*

Subscription £150 p.a.

Aims to provide members with a forum for the exchange of information, to improve the image of packaging and to represent the interests of members. Activities include meetings, dinners, the provision of standard contracts and a joint stand at London Book Fair.

Book Trust

Book House, 45 East Hill, London SW18 2QZ
☏ 081-870 9055   Fax 081-874 4790

Chief Executive *Keith McWilliams*

Subscription £25 p.a.

FOUNDED 1925. The Trust offers a free book information service to the public (written enquiries only) and a trade service on subscription. The Children's Book Foundation acts as a source of advice and information on all aspects of children's literature, with a comprehensive collection of every book published in the last 24 months; and Children's Book Week is run by the Book Trust. Other aspects of its work include organising touring exhibitions, administering 14 literary prizes including the **Booker**, and carrying out surveys for publication. Publications include books about books, writers, prizes and education (a free list with order form is available from Book House).

Book Trust Scotland

The Scottish Book Centre, 137 Dundee Street,
Edinburgh EH11 1BG
☏ 031-229 3663   Fax 031-228 4293

Contact *Lindsey Fraser*

FOUNDED 1945. Book Trust Scotland works with schools, libraries, writers, artists, publishers, bookshops and individuals to promote the pleasures of reading to people of all ages. It provides a book information service which draws on the children's reference library (a copy of every children's book published in the previous twelve months), the Scottish children's book collection, a range of press cuttings on Scottish literary themes and a number of smaller collections of Scottish books. Book Trust Scotland administers the **Kathleen Fidler Award**, and publishes guides to Scottish books and writers, both adult and children's.

Booksellers Association

272 Vauxhall Bridge Road, London SW1V 1BA
☏ 071-834 5477   Fax 071-834 8812

Director *Tim Godfray*

FOUNDED 1895 to promote and protect the interests of 3400 bookselling businesses including independent, chain and multiple. The BA helps members to sell more books and reduce costs. It represents members' interests to publishers, Government, authors and others in the trade as well as offering marketing assistance, running training courses, conferences, seminars and exhibitions. Publishes directories, catalogues, surveys and various other publications connected with the book trade and administers the **Whitbread Prize**.

The Booksellers' Association of Great Britain and Ireland (Irish Branch)

British Amateur Press Association

Michaelmas, Cimarron Close, South Woodham Ferrers, Essex CM3 5PB
☏ 0245 324059

Subscription £5 p.a.

A non-profit making, non-sectarian society founded in 1890 to 'promote the fellowship of writers, artists, editors, printers, publishers and other craftsmen/women. To encourage them to edit, print and publish, as a hobby, magazines, books and other literary works' by letterpress and other processes. Not an outlet for writing, except between other members in their private publications, but a fraternity providing contacts between amateur writers, journalists, artists, etc. Postal enquiries only.

British American Arts Association

116 Commercial Street, London E1 6NF
☎071-247 5385   Fax 071-247 5256

Director *Jennifer Williams*

The BAAA addresses the problems of transatlantic cultural exchange. It offers advice and counselling in all arts disciplines, runs a conference programme and takes on special projects. Emphasis is on the non-profit sector. The BAAA is not a grant-giving organisation.

British Association of Industrial Editors

3 Locks Yard, High Street, Sevenoaks, Kent TN13 1LT
☎0732 459331

FOUNDED 1949 and incorporated in 1963. The professional association for people in corporate internal communication and related functions. Provides a wide range of services to its members, including workshops, seminars and courses, conferences and publications.

British Copyright Council

Copyright House, 29–33 Berners Street, London W1P 4AA
☎071-359 1895   Fax 071-359 1895

Contact *Geoffrey Adams* (Secretary)

Works for the international acceptance of copyright and acts as a lobby/watchdog organisation on behalf of the trade on legal and professional matters. An umbrella organisation which does not deal with individual enquiries.

The British Council

10 Spring Gardens, London SW1A 2BN
☎071-930 8466   Fax 071-839 6347

Contact *Press Office* (071-389 4878)/*Literature Department* (071-389 4069)

The British Council promotes Britain abroad. It provides access to British ideas, talents, expertise and experience in education and training, books and periodicals, the English language, literature and the arts, sciences and technology. It is an independent, non-political organisation represented in 92 countries, where it runs 162 offices, 127 libraries and 62 English teaching centres in 33 countries.

The British Film Commission

70 Baker Street, London W1M 1DT
☎071-224 5000   Fax 071-224 1013

Chief Executive *Andrew Patrick*

FOUNDED 1991. The BFC is a new, government-funded body whose aim is to promote the United Kingdom as the preferred European location for film-makers throughout the world.

British Film Institute

21 Stephen Street, London W1P 1PL
☎071-255 1444   Fax 071-436 7950

Membership £13.50/£28.50 p.a. (Concessions £8)

FOUNDED 1933. Exists to encourage the development of film, television and video in the UK. Its divisions include: the National Film Archive; National Film Theatre (NFT); Museum of the Moving Image; **British Film Institute Production; British Film Institute Library and Information Services**; and Sight and Sound (**BFI Stills, Posters and Designs**). It also funds film theatres in the regions and has an education unit.

British Guild of Travel Writers

Bolts Cross Cottage, Peppard, Henley on Thames, Oxon RG9 5LG
☎04917 411   Fax 04917 669

Chairman *Robin Neillands*
Honorary Secretary *Penny Visman*

Subscription £50 p.a.

The professional association of travel writers, broadcasters, photographers and editors which aims to serve its membership's interest professionally and acts as a forum for debate and discussion, with monthly meetings. Members (c.135) are required to earn the majority of their income from travel reporting. The Guild represents its members to the BTA.

British Science Fiction Association

29 Thornville Road, Hartlepool,
Cleveland TS26 8EW

Membership Secretary *Jo Raine*

Subscription £12 p.a.

For both writers and readers of science fiction and fantasy. Publishes *Matrix* (news), *Focus* (writing tips and market information), *Vector* (criticism) and *Paperback Inferno* (paperback and magazine reviews). Also offers creative writing groups, a magazine chain and an information service.

British Screen Finance

14–17 Wells Mews, London W1P 3FL
☎071–323 9080   Fax 071–323 0092

Contact *Tessa Ross/Simon Perry*

A private company aided by government grant and backed by a consortium which includes Rank, Channel 4, Granada and Pathé. Exists to invest in British films or films co-produced with other countries. Divided into two functions: British Screen Development for script development (contact *Tessa Ross*), and production investment (contact *Simon Perry*). Develops around 18 projects per year, and has invested in 68 British feature films in the last six years.

Campaign for Press and Broadcasting Freedom

96 Dalston Lane, London E8 1NG
☎071–923 3671   Fax 071–923 3672

Subscription £10 p.a. (concessions available); £20 p.a. (Institutions); £15 p.a. (Organisations)

Broadly-based pressure group working for more accountable and accessible media in Britain. Advises on right of reply and takes up the issue of the portrayal of minorities. Members receive *Free Press* (bi-monthly), discounts on publications and news of campaign progress.

Chartered Institute of Journalists

2 Dock Offices, Surrey Quays, Lower Road,
London SE16 2XL
☎071–252 1187   Fax 071–232 2302

Director *Bill Tadd*
National Secretary *Christopher Underwood*
Subscription £75–160 (by assessment)

FOUNDED 1884. The Chartered Institute is concerned with professional journalistic standards and with safeguarding the freedom of the media. It is open to writers, broadcasters and journalists (including self-employed) in all media. Affiliation is available to part-time or occasional practitioners and to overseas journalists who can join the Institute's International Division. Members also belong to the IOJ (Institute of Journalists), an independent trade union which protects, advises and represents them in their employment or freelance work; negotiates on their behalf and provides legal assistance and support. The IOJ (TU) is part of the Federation of Professional Associations, a group of small, independent unions with regional officers throughout the country.

Children's Book Foundation

See **Book Trust**

Circle of Wine Writers

The White House, Lowgate, Lutton, Near Spalding,
Lincolnshire PE12 9HP
☎0406 364006

Honorary Secretary *Robert W. Layton*

Membership £25 p.a.

FOUNDED 1962. Open to all *bona fide* authors, broadcasters, journalists, lecturers and tutors who are engaged in, or earn a significant part of their income from, communicating about wine and spirits. Aims to improve the standard of writing, broadcasting and lecturing about wine; to contribute to the growth of knowledge and interest in wine; to promote wine of quality in the UK and to comment adversely on faulty products or dubious practices which could lead to a fall in consumption; to establish and maintain good relations between the Circle and the wine trade in the best interests of the consumer.

CLE: The Irish Book Publishers' Association

See **Book House Ireland**

Comedy Writers' Association of Great Britain

61 Parry Road, Ashmore Park,
Wolverhampton WV11 2PS
☎0902 722729

Contact *Ken Rock*

FOUNDED 1981 to assist and promote the work of comedy writers. The Association is a self-help group designed to encourage and advise its members to sell their work. It is an international organisation with representatives in Britain, Germany, Cyprus, Sweden, Belgium, Luxembourg, Czechoslovakia, Denmark, Finland and Canada. International seminar with videos of foreign TV comedy programmes, bookshop and business club where members can discuss opportunities. Members often come together to work jointly on a variety of comedy projects for British and overseas productions. Publishes regular magazines and monthly market information.

Coventry Writers' Association
10 Ridgethorpe, Willenhall Wood,
Coventry CV3 3GP
☎0203 304647

Membership Secretary *Julie Moseley*

Subscription £5 p.a.

FOUNDED 1986. Represents a network of writers throughout the Coventry and Warwickshire area. Acts as an information exchange; organises events; and generally seeks to promote the interests of writers in the region. Operates via an annually elected organising committee and is wholly dependent on subscriptions from members.

Crime Writers' Association (CWA)
PO Box 172, Tring, Hertfordshire HP23 5LP
☎044 282 8496

Secretary *Anthea Fraser*

Membership £35 (Town); £30 (Country)

Full membership is limited to professional crime writers, but publishers, literary agents, booksellers, etc., who specialise in crime are eligible for Associate membership. Meetings are held monthly in Soho, with informative talks frequently given by police, scenes of crime officers, lawyers, etc., and a weekend conference is held annually in different parts of the country. Produces a monthly newssheet called *Red Herrings* and presents various annual awards (see **CWA** entries under **Prizes**).

The Critics' Circle
c/o The Stage & Television Today, 47 Bermondsey Street, London SE1 3XT
☎071-403 1818   Fax 071-403 1418

President *William Hall*
Honorary General Secretary *Peter Hepple*

Subscription £12 p.a.

Membership by invitation only. Aims to uphold and promote the art of criticism (and the commercial rates of pay thereof) and preserve the interests of its members: professionals involved in criticism of film, drama, music and ballet.

Directory Publishers Association
93A Blenheim Crescent, London W11 2EQ
☎071-221 9089

Contact *Rosemary Pettit*

Subscription £104-624 p.a.

FOUNDED 1970 to promote the interests of *bona fide* directory publishers and protect the public from disreputable and fraudulent practices. The objectives of the Association are to maintain a code of professional practice to safeguard public interest; to raise the standard and status of directory publishing throughout the UK; to promote business directories as a medium for advertising; to protect the legal and statutory interests of directory publishers; to foster bonds of common interest among responsible directory publishers and provide for the exchange of technical, commercial and management information between members. Meetings, seminars, conference and representation at book fairs.

Edinburgh Bibliographical Society
New College Library, Mound Place,
Edinburgh EH1 2LU
☎031-225 8400 ext. 256   Fax 031-220 0952

Honorary Secretary *Dr M. Simpson*

Subscription £7; £5 (Students)

FOUNDED 1890. Organises lectures on bibliographical topics and visits to libraries. Publishes a biennial magazine called *Transactions*, which is free to members, and other occasional publications.

Educational Television Association
The King's Manor, Exhibition Square,
York YO1 2EP
☎0904 433929

An umbrella organisation for individuals and organisations using television for education and training. Annual awards scheme, and annual conferences. School membership now available. New members always welcome. 1992 European Conference held in Strasbourg.

The English Association
The Vicarage, Priory Gardens, Bedford Park,
London W4 1TT
☎081-995 4236

Secretary *Ruth Fairbanks-Joseph*

FOUNDED 1906 to promote understanding and appreciation of the English language and its literature. Activities include sponsoring a number of publications and organising lectures and conferences for teachers, plus annual sixth-form conferences. Publications include *English, Use of English, Primary English, Year's Work in English Studies* and *Essays and Studies.*

Federation of Entertainment Unions
79 Redhill Wood, New Ash Green, Longfield, Kent DA3 8QP
☎0474 874606   Fax 0474 874277
Secretary *John Morton*

Consists of two committees: one concerned with media; the other with live entertainment. Represents the following unions: British Actors' Equity Association; Broadcasting Entertainment Cinematograph and Theatre Union; Film Artistes' Association; Musicians' Union; **National Union of Journalists**; **Writers' Guild of Great Britain**.

Federation of Worker Writers and Community Publishers (FWWCP)
c/o 68 Grand Parade, Brighton, East Sussex BN2 2JY
☎0273 571916
Contact *The FWWCP Worker*

FOUNDED 1976, the FWWCP grew out of a need for working class writers to be united and acknowledged. The Federation is a collective national voice comprising around fifty member groups, including writing workshops, local history projects, community publishers and literacy-based writing and publishing groups. Many of the FWWCP's member groups, including Bristol Broadsides, Centreprise and Commonword, have a strong interest in poetry. All the groups are committed to writing based on working class experience, and include a strong contribution from women, Black, Asian and gay writers. Produces a thrice-yearly magazine and occasional anthologies as well as promoting the many publications of member groups via bookstalls and a mail order facility. Organises regular training days on all aspects of community writing and publishing, conferences, poetry competitions; and produces community publishing information packs.

Foreign Press Association in London
11 Carlton House Terrace, London SW1Y 5AJ
☎071-930 0445   Fax 071-925 0469
Contact *Davina Crole/Catherine Flury*

Membership (not incl. VAT) £76 p.a. (Full); £71 (Associate Journalists); £84 (Associate Non-Journalists)

FOUNDED 1888. Non-profit making service association for foreign correspondents based in London, providing a variety of press-related services.

Gaelic Books Council (An Comann Leabhraichean)
Department of Celtic, University of Glasgow, Glasgow G12 8QQ
☎041-330 5190

Chairman *Professor Donald MacAulay*
Executive/Editorial Officer *Ian MacDonald*

FOUNDED 1968. Encourages and promotes Gaelic publishing by offering publication grants, commissioning authors, organising competitions, advising readers and providing practical help for writers.

Gay Authors Workshop
See **Writers' Courses, Circles and Workshops**

General Practitioner Writers Association
Jasmine Cottage, Hampton Lucy, Warwick
☎0789 840509

Contact *Dr F. M. Hull*

Subscription £15 p.a.

FOUNDED 1986 to promote and improve writing activities within and for general practices. Open to general practitioners, practice managers, nurses, etc. and professional journalists writing on anything pertaining to general practices. Publishes a twice-yearly journal; holds three meetings yearly, generally discussions on a particular theme. Very keen to develop input from interested parties who work mainly outside of the profession. Workshops also organised on a regular basis.

Guild of Agricultural Journalists
The Farmers Club, 3 Whitehall Court, London SW1A 2EL
☎071-930 3557   Fax 071-839 7864

Honorary General Secretary *Don Gomery*

Subscription £25 p.a.

FOUNDED 1944 to promote a high professional standard among journalists who specialise in agriculture, horticulture and allied subjects. Represents members' interests with representative bodies in the industry; provides a forum through meetings and social activities for members to meet eminent people in the industry; maintains contact with associations of agricultural journalists overseas; promotes schemes for the education of members and for the provision of suitable entrants into agricultural journalism.

Guild of British Newspaper Editors
See **The Newspaper Society**

Guild of Motoring Writers
30 The Cravens, Smallfield, Surrey RH6 9QS
☎0342 843294   Fax 0342 843294

General Secretary Sharon Scott-Fairweather

FOUNDED 1944. Represents members' interests and provides a forum for members to exchange information.

Humberside Writers' Association (HWA)
14 Danesway, Woodhall Park, Beverley HU17 7JQ
☎0482 868801

Chairman Robert Freeman

Annual membership fee £1.50

FOUNDED 1987 by local writers, would-be writers and people interested in new writing, who gathered together with the backing of their regional arts association to create a platform for local scribblers, published or otherwise. Organises and promotes writing-related events and workshops within the Humberside area. Publishes information about events, competitions, workshops, publications and any other news, local or national, about opportunities of interest to members. Regular meetings (last Wednesday of the month), to which writers, publishers and agents are invited; plus dayschools, readings, newsletter and library/resource unit.

Independent Publishers Guild
25 Cambridge Road, Hampton,
Middlesex TW12 2JL
☎081-979 0250

Secretary Yvonne Messenger

Subscription £54 p.a.

FOUNDED 1962. Membership open to independent publishers, packagers and suppliers, i.e. professionals in allied fields. Regular meetings, conferences, seminars, a bulletin and regional groups.

Independent Theatre Council
4 Baden Place, Crosby Row, London SE1 1YW
☎071-403 1727   Fax 071-403 1745

Contact Gavin Palmer

The management association and representative body for small/ middle-scale theatres (up to around 250 seats) and touring theatre companies. Negotiates contracts and has established standard agreements with Equity on behalf of all professionals working in the theatre. Negotiations with the **Theatre Writers' Union** and **The Writers' Guild** for a contractual agreement covering rights and fee structure for playwrights reached their conclusion in 1991. Copies of the minimum terms agreement can be obtained from The Writers' Guild. Extracts from the agreement can be seen under *Playwrights' Minimum Terms* following the listing of Theatre Producers (see Contents).

Institute for Social Inventions
See **Small Presses**

Institute of Translation and Interpreting
377 City Road, London EC1V 1NA
☎071-713 7600

Membership is open to those who satisfy stringent admission criteria and can provide evidence of adequate professional translation or interpreting experience. Offers affiliation and student membership. Benefits include listing in an index which specifies the skills and languages of each member. Publishes a bimonthly bulletin, a quarterly journal called *Professional Translator & Interpreter* (published jointly with **The Translators Association**) and a *Directory of Translators & Interpreters* listing qualified members of both the ITI and the TA.

IPPA (Independent Programme Producers' Association)
See **PACT (Producers Alliance for Cinema and Television)**

IVCA Writers Group
Bolsover House, 5-6 Clipstone Street,
London W1P 7EB
☎071-580 0962   Fax 071-436 2606

Contact Liz Lydiate

The special interest group within the IVCA (International Visual Communications Association) which represents scriptwriters in the corporate and nonbroadcast television industry.

Lancashire Authors' Association

Heatherslade, 5 Quakerfields, Westhoughton,
Bolton, Lancashire BL5 2BJ
☎ 0942 816785

General Secretary *Eric Holt*

Membership £7 p.a.; £10 (Couples); £1 (Juniors)

FOUNDED 1909 for writers and lovers of Lancashire literature and history. Aims to foster and stimulate interest in Lancashire history and literature as well as in the preservation of the Lancashire dialect. Meets four times a year on Saturday at various locations. Publishes a quarterly journal called *The Record* which is issued free to members and holds eight annual competitions (open to members only) for both verse and prose. Also produces an annual magazine, *Red Rose*, which is a collation of members' work. Comprehensive library with access for research to members.

The Library Association

7 Ridgmount Street, London WC1E 7AE
☎ 071-636 7543   Fax 071-436 7218

Chief Executive *Ross Shimmon*

The professional body for librarians and information managers, with 25,000 individual and institutional members. **Library Association Publishing** produces 25 new titles each year and has over 200 in print. The *LA Record* is the monthly magazine for members.

London Screenwriters' Workshop

See **Writers' Courses, Circles and Workshops**

Medical Journalists' Association

Old Barley Mow, 185 High Street, Stony Stratford,
Milton Keynes MK11 1AP
☎ 0908 564623

Chairman *Pat Blair*
Secretary *Gwen Yates*

Subscription £20 p.a. (under review)

FOUNDED 1966-67. Aims to improve the quality and practice of medical journalism and to improve relationships and understanding between medical journalists and the medical profession. Regular meetings with senior figures in medicine and medico politics; teach-ins on particular subjects to help journalists with background information; sponsorship of courses in medical journalism; weekend symposium for an invited audience of members and people with newsworthy stories in the field; awards for medical journalists offered by various commercial sponsors, plus MJA's own

award financed by members. Publishes a detailed directory of members and freelancers with their speciality areas.

Medical Writers Group

84 Drayton Gardens, London SW10 9SB
☎ 071-373 6642   Fax 071-373 5768

Contact *Jacqueline Granger-Taylor*

FOUNDED 1980. A specialist group within **The Society of Authors** offering advice and help to authors of medical books. Administers the **Glaxo Prizes for Medical Writing and Illustration**.

The Montpelier Society

47 Old Steine, Brighton BN1 1NW

Contact *Honorary Secretary*

A non-profit making body which provides a forum where members of the literary worlds can meet. Arranges meetings on all matters relating to writers and writing. Aims to support and encourage writers of all categories. Regular discussion groups. Strong connections with **Brighton Festival** and the University of Sussex. Supported by **South East Arts**.

National Union of Journalists

Acorn House, 314 Gray's Inn Road,
London WC1X 8DP
☎ 071-278 7916
Fax 071-837 8143   Telex 892384

Acting General Secretary *Jacob Ecclestone*

Subscription £123 p.a. (freelance)

Responsible for wages and conditions agreements which apply throughout the industry. Provides advice and representation for its members, as well as administering disputes, unemployment and other benefits. Publishes *Freelance Directory, Fees Guide, The Journalist* and *The Freelance* (see **Magazines).**

New Playwrights Trust

Interchange Studios, 15 Dalby Street,
London NW5 3NQ
☎ 071-284 2818/267 9421   Fax 071-482 5292

Director *Polly Thomas*
Administrator *Ben Payne*

Subscription Telephone for details (group rates available)

Membership open to playwrights at all stages of their careers, and to actors and directors. Organises projects and joint projects including rehearsed readings, workshops and discussions. Runs a script-reading service, bulletin and library service, and a link service between writers and theatre companies. Projects have included *Wordplay '88, The Play's the Thing!* — a development programme organised by the **Bristol Express Theatre Company**, *Changing Directions* — intensive workshops on non-naturalism in writing, and *Script Forum* — monthly development workshops. Forthcoming projects include the publication of a *Black Playwrights Directory*.

Newspaper Conference
See **The Newspaper Society**

The Newspaper Society
Bloomsbury House, Bloomsbury Square, 74–77 Great Russell Street, London WC1B 3DA
☎071-636 7014   Fax 071-631 5119

Director *Dugal Nisbet-Smith*

Organisation for the provincial/London suburban morning, evening and weekly newspapers. At the same address: Guild of British Newspaper Editors (President *Colin Mailer*); Newspaper Conference (a newspaper society organisation concerned primarily with newsgathering facilities in London for the regional press); and the Young Newspapermen's Association for young newspaper executives (Honorary Secretary *Joanne Butcher*).

NUJ
See **National Union of Journalists**

Office of Arts and Libraries
Horse Guards Road, London SW1P 3AL
☎071-270 3000   Fax 071-270 5776

Among its more routine responsibilities, the OAL funds the British Library, and is responsible for the new library project at St Pancras. It is also responsible for funding to **The Arts Council** and **Regional Arts Boards**, the national museums and galleries, the Public Lending Right and the Royal Commission on Historical Manuscripts. It is responsible within government for the public library service in England and for library and information matters generally, where they are not the responsibility of other departments.

Outdoor Writers Guild
86 Burford Gardens, London N13 4LP
☎081-886 1957   Fax 081-886 1957

Honorary Secretary *Hugh Westacott*

Subscription £15 p.a.

FOUNDED 1980 to promote a high professional standard among writers who specialise in outdoor activities; to represent members' interests with representatives of the outdoor leisure industry; to circulate members with news of writing opportunities. Presents awards for excellence to members.

PACT (Producers Alliance for Cinema and Television)
Gordon House, Greencoat Place, London SW1P 1PH
☎071-233 6000   Fax 071-233 8935

Chief Executive *John Woodward*
Membership Officer *Martin Hart*

FOUNDED 1992. Incorporates the Producers Association and the Independent Programme Producers Association. PACT exists to serve the film and independent television production sector and is the UK contact point for co-production, co-finance partners and distributors. Membership services include a dedicated industrial relations unit; a varied calendar of seminars and events; business and legal advice; representation at international film and television markets; a comprehensive research programme; various publications: monthly newsletter, *Fact*, journal, *Impact*, annual members' directory and a number of specialist guidebooks; a members' regional network; affiliation with European and international producers' organisations; extensive information and production advice. PACT also lobbies actively with broadcasters, financiers and governments to ensure that the producer's voice is heard and understood in Britain and Europe.

PEN
7 Dilke Street, London SW3 4JE
☎071-352 6303   Fax 071-351 0220

General Secretary *Josephine Pullein-Thompson*

Membership £25 (Town); £20 (members living over 50 miles from London/Overseas)

English PEN is part of International PEN, a worldwide association of writers which fights for freedom of expression and speaks out for writers who are imprisoned or harassed for having criticised their governments, or for publishing other unpopular views. FOUNDED in London in 1921, International PEN now consists of 107 centres in 68 countries. PEN originally stood for poets, essayists and novelists, but membership is now open to poets, playwrights, essayists, editors and novelists, plus translators and a wide range of published or performed writers. A programme of talks and discussions is supplemented by the publication of a twice-yearly magazine.

The Penman Literary Club

175 Pall Mall, Leigh on Sea, Essex SS9 1RE
☎ 0702 74438

Subscription £11.25 in the first year; £8.25 thereafter

FOUNDED 1950. International writers' society offering criticism of members' work, general advice and use of writers' library.

Performing Right Society

29–33 Berners Street, London W1P 4AA
☎ 071-580 5544   Fax 071-631 4138

Collects and distributes royalties arising from performances and broadcasts of copyright music on behalf of its composer, lyricist and music publisher members and members of affiliated societies worldwide.

Periodical Publishers Association (PPA)

Imperial House, 15–19 Kingsway,
London WC2B 6UN
☎ 071-379 6268   Fax 071-379 5661

Contact *Nicholas Mazur*

FOUNDED 1913 to promote and protect the interests of magazine publishers in the UK.

The Personal Managers' Association Ltd

1 Summer Road, East Molesey, Surrey KT8 9LX
☎ 081-398 9796

Co-chairs *Jane Annakin/Marc Berlin/David Wilkinson*
Secretary *Angela Adler*

Subscription £200 p.a.

An association of artists' and dramatists' agents (membership not open to individuals). Monthly meetings for exchange of information and discussion. Maintains a code of conduct and acts as a lobby when necessary. Applicants screened. A high proportion of play agents are members of the PMA.

Player–Playwrights

St Augustine's Church Hall, Queen's Gate,
London SW7

Contact *Peter Thompson*
at 9 Hillfield Park, London N10 3QT
☎ 081-883 0371

Subscription £5 p.a., plus £1 per attendance

FOUNDED 1948. A society for newcomers to play and television writing. Membership includes established writers and actors. Meets on Monday evenings; members' scripts are read or performed and a discussion follows.

Playwrights Co-operative

117 Waterloo Road, London SE1
☎ 071-633 9811

Contact *Vivienne Cottrell*

FOUNDED 1981. For writers of a professional standard based in London. Has evolved a process of script development involving a sequence of readings, discussions and workshops. Holds story conferences, rehearsed readings and workshops in central London; offers critical and professional advice, and help in getting the final script produced. Since its inception, an average of 34% of the scripts which have been through the Co-op have ended in production.

Playwrights' Workshop

22 Brown Street, Altrincham, Cheshire WA14 2EU
☎ 061-928 3095

Honorary Secretary *Robert Coupland*

Subscription £2 p.a.

FOUNDED 1949. The Society meets monthly in Manchester and aims to support playwrights of all kinds who are interested in furthering their work. Guest speakers on all aspects of the theatre. Past members include Michael Dines and Harry Kershaw. Provides reading service with report by private reader (reasonable terms).

Poetry Book Society

See **Organisations of Interest to Poets**

The Poetry Society

See **Organisations of Interest to Poets**

Private Libraries Association

Ravelston, South View Road, Pinner,
Middlesex HA5 3YD

Honorary Secretary *Frank Broomhead*

Membership £20 p.a.

FOUNDED 1956. An international society of book collectors. The Association's objectives are to promote and encourage the awareness of the benefits of book ownership, and the study of books, their production, and ownership; to publish works concerned with this, particularly those which are not commercially profitable, to hold meetings at which papers on cognate subjects can be read and discussed. Lectures and exhibitions are open to non-members.

Producers Association
See **PACT (Producers Alliance for Cinema and Television)**

The Publishers Association
19 Bedford Square, London WC1B 3HJ
☏071-580 6321-5/580 7761/323 1548
Fax 071-636 5375   Telex 267160 PUBASS G

Chief Executive *Clive Bradley*

The national UK trade association with over 350 member companies in the industry. Very much a trade body representing the industry to Government and the European Commission, and providing services to publishers. Writers with queries are referred on to **The Society of Authors** or **The Writers' Guild**. Publishes the *Directory of Publishing* in association with **Cassell**. Also home of the Book Development Council (the PA's international division), the Educational Publishers Council (School books) and the Council of Academic and Professional Publishers. For Scotland, see the **Scottish Publishers Association**.

The Romantic Novelists' Association
9 Hillside Road, Southport, Merseyside PR8 4QB
☏0704 60945

Secretary *Marie Murray*

Subscription £12 p.a. (Town); £10 p.a. (Country)

Membership is open to published writers of romantic novels or two or more full-length serials, and to publishers, literary agents, booksellers and librarians. Meetings are held in London and guest speakers are often invited. *RNA News* is published quarterly and issued free to members. Administers annual awards (see **Prizes**).

Royal Society of Literature
1 Hyde Park Gardens, London W2 2LT
☏071-723 5104

President *Lord Jenkins of Hillhead*

Subscription £20 p.a.

FOUNDED 1823. Membership by application to the secretary. Fellowships are conferred by the Society on the proposal of two Fellows. Membership benefits include lectures and poetry readings in the Society's rooms. Lecturers have included Muriel Spark, John Mortimer, Victoria Glendinning and Alan Massie. Presents the **Royal Heinemann Award** and the **Winifred Holtby Memorial Prize**.

Royal Television Society
Tavistock House East, Tavistock Square, London WC1H 9HR
☏071-387 1970   Fax 071-387 0358

Editor *Peter Fiddick*

Subscription £60; £72 surface/£90 airmail (Overseas)

FOUNDED 1927. Covers all disciplines involved in the television industry. Provides a forum for debate and conferences on technical, social and cultural aspects of the medium. Presents various journalism and programme awards and runs a wide range of training courses.

Science Fiction Foundation
Polytechnic of East London, Longbridge Road, Dagenham, Essex RM8 2AS
☏081-590 7722   Fax 081-590 7799

Contact *Joyce Day*

A national academic body for the furtherance of science fiction studies. Publishes *Foundation*, a thrice-yearly magazine containing academic articles about science fiction, and reviews of new fiction. Research library open to the public by appointment.

Scottish Library Association
Motherwell Business Centre, Coursington Road, Motherwell ML1 1PW
☏0698 52526   Fax 0698 52057

Executive Secretary *Robert Craig*

FOUNDED 1908 to bring together everyone engaged in or interested in library work in Scotland. The Association has over 2300 members, covering all aspects of library and information work. Its main aims are the promotion of library services and the qualifications and status of librarians.

Scottish Newspaper Publishers' Association

48 Palmerston Place, Edinburgh EH12 5DE
☎031-220 4353   Fax 031-220 4344

Director *J. B. Raeburn*

FOUNDED around 1905. The representative body for the publishers of paid-for weekly and associated free newspapers in Scotland. Represents the interests of the industry to Government, public and other bodies and provides a range of services including industrial relations, education and training, and advertising. It is an active supporter of the Press Complaints Commission.

Scottish Print Employers' Federation

48 Palmerston Place, Edinburgh EH12 5DE
☎031-220 4353   Fax 031-220 4344

Director *J. B. Raeburn*

FOUNDED 1910. Employers' organisation and trade association for the Scottish printing industry. Represents the interests of the industry to Government, public and other bodies and provides a range of services including industrial relations. Negotiates a national wages and conditions agreement with the Graphical, Paper and Media Union, as well as education, training and commercial activities. The Federation is a member of Intergraf, the international confederation for employers' associations in the printing industry. In this capacity its views are channelled on the increasing number of matters affecting print businesses emanating from the European Community.

The Scottish Publishers Association

Scottish Book Centre, Fountainbridge Library, 137 Dundee Street, Edinburgh EH11 1BG
☎031-228 6866   Fax 031-228 3220

Director *Lorraine Fannin*
Promotion Manager *Anna Fenge*
Administrator *Helen Kemp*

The Association represents over 60 Scottish publishers, from multinationals to very small presses, in a number of capacities, but primarily in the co-operative promotion and marketing of their books. The SPA also acts as an information and advice centre for both the trade and general public. It publishes seasonal catalogues, membership lists, a detailed *Directory of Publishing in Scotland*, and provides its membership with a regular newsletter. The SPA represents its members at international bookfairs, provides opportunities for publishers' training, carries out market research, and encourages export initiatives.

Small Press Group of Britain (SPG)

BM Bozo, London WC1N 3XX
☎0234 211606

Subscription £15 p.a.

FOUNDED 1988. Provides information and news from the world of independent publishing. Aims to increase public awareness of the valuable role of small presses throughout the UK. A forum for small presses of all kinds. Publishes the *SPG Yearbook* giving information on over 300 small presses, with an A–Z of books, pamphlets, magazines, comics and booklets currently in print, plus advice on making and marketing small press publications. Members receive a monthly magazine called *Small Press Monthly*. Organises an annual international Small Press Fair in London as well as regional fairs and jointly exhibits at fairs in London, Frankfurt, the USA and Europe.

The Society of Authors

84 Drayton Gardens, London SW10 9SB
☎071-373 6642   Fax 071-373 5768

General Secretary *Mark Le Fanu*

Subscription £60/65 p.a.

FOUNDED 1884. The Society of Authors is an independent trade union with some 5500 members. It advises on negotiations with publishers, broadcasting organisations, theatre managers and film companies; takes up complaints and pursues legal action for breach of contract, copyright infringement, etc. Together with **The Writers' Guild**, the Society has played a major role in advancing the Minimum Terms Agreement for authors. Among the Society's publications are *The Author* (a quarterly journal) and the *Quick Guides* series to various aspects of writing. Other services include a pension fund and a group medical insurance scheme. Authors under 35, who are not yet earning a significant income from their writing, may apply for membership at a lower subscription of £47. Contact the Society for a free booklet giving further information.

Society of Civil Service Authors

8 Bawtree Close, Sutton, Surrey SM2 5LQ
☎081-661 9169

Honorary Secretary *Mrs Joan Hykin*

Subscription £10 p.a.

FOUNDED 1935. Aims to encourage authorship by present and past members of the Civil Service and to provide opportunities for social and cultural relationships between civil servants who are authors or who aspire to be authors. Annual competitions, open to members only, are held for short stories, poetry, sonnets, travel articles, humour, etc. Members receive *The Civil Service Author*, a bi-monthly newsletter.

Society of Freelance Editors and Proofreaders

c/o The Secretary, 16 Brenthouse Road,
London E9 6QG
☎081-986 4868

Chair *Norma Whitcombe*
Vice-Chair *Eric Smith*
Secretary *Jane Sugarman*

Subscription £24 p.a. (Individuals); £6 p.a. (Students); £60 p.a. (Corporate); £6 registration fee for new members

FOUNDED 1988 in response to the growing number of editorial freelancers and their increasing importance to the publishing industry. Aims to promote high editorial standards by disseminating information and through advice and training, and to achieve recognition of the professional status of its members. The Society also supports moves towards recognised standards of training and qualifications.

Society of Indexers

16 Green Road, Birchington, Kent CT7 9JZ
☎0843 41115

Secretary *Claire Troughton*

Subscription £20 p.a.; £25 (Institutions)

FOUNDED 1957. Publishes *The Indexer* (bi-annual, April and October); *Micro-Indexer* (bi-annual dealing with computer indexing) and a quarterly newsletter. Issues an annual list of members and the *(IA) Indexers Available*, which lists members and their subject expertise. In addition the Society runs an open-learning course entitled *Training in Indexing*. Recommends rates of pay — currently £9.75 per hour.

Society of Women Writers and Journalists

110 Whitehall Road, London E4 6DW
☎081-529 0886

Honorary Secretary *Jean Hawkes*

Subscription £18 (Town); £15 (Country); £10 (Overseas)

FOUNDED 1894. The first of its kind to be run as an association of women engaged in journalism. Aims

to encourage literary achievement, uphold professional standards and social contact with other writers. Lectures given at monthly lunchtime meetings. Offers advice to members and has regular seminars, etc. Publishes *The Woman Journalist* three times a year.

Society of Young Publishers

12 Dyott Street, London WC1A 1DF

Chairman *Iain Brown*
Secretary *Andrew Conway*

Subscription £20 p.a.

Provides facilities whereby members can increase their knowledge and widen their experience of all aspects of publishing. Open to those in related occupations, with an overall age limit of 35. Publishes a monthly magazine called *Inprint* and holds meetings on the last Wednesday of each month at **The Publishers Association**.

South Bank Board: Literature Office

Artistic Projects Department, Royal Festival Hall,
South Bank Centre, London SE1 8XX
☎071-921 0906   Fax 071-928 0063

Literature Officer *Maura Dooley*

Maura Dooley's aims were to 'create a strong presence for literature on the South Bank'. Her brief covered all aspects of writing, and a venue within the Royal Festival Hall, called The Voice Box, has now been established to house a variety of literature events. Plans include the appointment of a writer-in-residence.

South Eastern Writers' Association

7 Kent View Avenue, Leigh on Sea,
Essex SS9 1HE
☎0702 78637/77083   Fax 0702 77083

Chairman *Marion Hough*
Secretary *Adele Ramet*

FOUNDED 1989 to bring together writers, both experienced and novice, in an informative but informal atmosphere. The Association holds a weekend residential conference at Ye Olde Plough House Motel in Bulphan, Essex, in March each year as well as a one-day seminar in September at the same venue. It is a non-profit making organisation. Recent guest speakers include Maureen Lipman, Jack Rosenthal, George Layton, Simon Brett and Terry Pratchett.

Sports Writers' Association of Great Britain

43 Lime Grove, New Malden, Surrey KT3 3TP
☎081-942 1930   Fax 081-942 1930

Secretary *Alan Hughes*

Subscription £15 p.a.

FOUNDED 1948 to promote and maintain a high professional standard among journalists who specialise in sport in all its branches and to serve members' interests.

Television History Centre

42 Queen Square, London WC1N 3AJ
☎071-405 6627   Fax 071-242 1426

Contact *Sharon Goulds/Marilyn Wheatcroft*

Home of the television history workshop. Provides a range of resources (including a catalogue of videos available for sale or hire), materials, information and assistance to help people record their own history.

Theatre Writers' Union

c/o The Actors' Centre, 4 Chenies Street,
London WC1E 7EP
☎071-631 3619

Contact *Laurence Scott*

Formed in the mid 1970s. Specialises in the concerns of all who write for live performance. Has national branch network. Actively seeks a membership which represents the rich cultural diversity of playwriting today. Responsible for the very first standard agreements on minimum pay and conditions for playwrights working in British theatre. Founder members include Caryl Churchill and David Edgar. Any playwright who has written a play is eligible to join. Annual subscription is related to income from playwriting. Members may receive legal and professional advice, copies of standard contracts and regular newsletters.

The Translators' Association

84 Drayton Gardens, London SW10 9SB
☎071-373 6642   Fax 071-373 5768

Contact *Gordon Fielden*

FOUNDED 1958 as a subsidiary group within the **The Society of Authors** to deal exclusively with the special problems of literary translators into the English language. Members are entitled to all the benefits and services of the parent Society without extra charge. The Association offers free legal and general advice and assistance on all matters relating to translators' work, including the vetting of contracts and information about improvements in fees. Membership is normally confined to translators who have had their work published in volume or serial form or produced in this country for stage, television or radio. Translators of technical work for industrial firms or government departments are in certain cases admitted to membership if their work, though not on general sale, is published by the organisation commissioning the work.

The Union of Welsh Writers (Undeb Awduron Cymru)

Cynfelin, Lôn Talwrn, Llangefni, Anglesey,
Gwynedd LL77 7RP
☎0248 724155

Secretary *M. P. Jones*

Membership £5 p.a.

FOUNDED 1974. Aims to provide a comprehensive service and support for members: mainly authors who publish a wide variety of material written predominantly in Welsh. Members include novelists, poets, short story writers and children's authors.

Ver Poets

Haycroft, 61–63 Chiswell Green Lane, St Albans,
Hertfordshire AL2 3AL
☎0727 867005

Chairman *Ray Badman*
Organiser/Contact *May Badman*

Membership £8 p.a.; £10 (Overseas)

FOUNDED 1966 to promote poetry and to help poets. Has a postal membership of several hundred. Holds meetings in St Albans, runs a poetry bookstall for members' books and publications from other groups, publishes members' work in magazines, organises poetry competitions. Gives help and advice whenever they are sought, makes available to members information about other poetry groups, events and opportunities for publication.

Welsh Academy

3rd Floor, Mount Stuart House, Mount Stuart Square, Cardiff CF1 6DQ
☎0222 492025   Fax 0222 492930

Director *Kevin Thomas*

FOUNDED 1968. The Welsh Academy is the English Language section of **Yr Academi Gymreig**, the national society of Welsh writers. The Academy exists to promote English literature in Wales. Organises readings, an annual conference (generally held in May) and general literary events such as the **Cardiff Literature Festival**. There are three tiers of membership: Fellow (Maximum 12. An honorary position offered to those who have made an outstanding contribution to the literature of Wales over a number of years); Member (Open to all who are deemed to have made a contribution to the literature of Wales whether writers, editors or critics); Associate Member (Open to all who are interested in the Academy's work). Publications include: *BWA*, the Academy's newsletter; *The Oxford Companion to the Literature of Wales; Writing in Wales; The Literature of Wales in Secondary Schools; How the Earth Was Formed Quiz And Other Poems and Stories by Children; The New Welsh Review; A Bibliography of Anglo-Welsh Literature; Interweave*.

Welsh Books Council (Cyngor Llyfrau Cymraeg)

Castell Brychan, Aberystwyth, Dyfed SY23 2JB
☎ 0970 624151   Fax 0970 625385

Director *Gwerfyl Pierce Jones*
Head of Editorial Department *Dewi Morris Jones*

FOUNDED 1961 to stimulate interest in Welsh literature and to support authors. The Council distributes the government grant for Welsh language publications and promotes and fosters all aspects of both Welsh and Welsh interest book production. Its Editorial, Design, Marketing and Children's Books departments and wholesale distribution centre offer central services to publishers in Wales. Writers in Welsh and English are welcome to approach the Editorial Department for advice on how to get their manuscripts published. *Book News From Wales/ Llais Llyfrau*, quarterly, includes book lists, reviews and articles on various aspects of Welsh writing and publishing.

West Country Writers' Association

Malvern View, Garway Hill, Hereford HR2 8EZ
☎ 09818 495

President *Christopher Fry*
Honorary Secretary *Mrs Anne Double*

Subscription £5 p.a. (under review)

FOUNDED 1951. Of interest to published authors. Meets to discuss news and views and to listen to talks. Conference and newsletters.

Women in Publishing

c/o The Bookseller, 12 Dyott Street, London WC1A 1DF

Contact *Information Officer*

Membership £15 p.a. (Individuals); £10 (Unwaged); £20 (if paid for by company)

Aims to promote the status of women working within the publishing industry and related trades, to encourage networking, and to provide training for career and personal development. Monthly meetings held on the second Wednesday of the month at **The Publishers Association** at 6.30 pm. Monthly newsletter.

Women Writers Network (WWN)

23 Prospect Road, London NW2 2JU
☎ 071-794 5861

Membership Secretary *Cathy Smith*

Subscription £20 p.a.; £30 p.a. (Overseas)

FOUNDED 1985. Provides a forum for the exchange of information, support, career and networking opportunities for working women writers. Meetings, seminars, excursions, newsletter and directory.

The Writers' Guild of Great Britain

430 Edgware Road, London W2 1EH
☎ 071-723 8074   Fax 071-706 2413

General Secretary *Walter J. Jeffrey*

Annual subscription 1% of that part of the author's income earned in the areas in which the Guild operates, with a minimum of £60 and a maximum of £910.

FOUNDED 1959. The Writers' Guild is the writers' trade union, affiliated to the TUC. It represents professional writers in film, radio, television, theatre and publishing. The Guild has negotiated agreements on which writers' contracts are based with the BBC, Independent Television companies, and **PACT** (the Producers' Alliance for Cinema and Television). Those agreements are regularly renegotiated, both in terms of finance and conditions. In 1979, together with the **Theatre Writers' Union**, the Guild negotiated the first ever industrial agreement for theatre writers. Further agreements followed with the Theatre National Committee (the Royal National Theatre, the RSC, and the English Stage Company) and with the **Independent Theatre Council**, the organisation which covers small theatres and ` the Fringe. The Guild initiated a campaign in the early Eighties which achieved the first ever publishing agreement for writers with the publisher **W H Allen**. Jointly with **The Society of**

Authors, that campaign has continued and each year sees new agreements with more publishers. Perhaps the most important breakthrough came with **Penguin** in July 1990.

The Guild regularly provides individual help and advice to members on contracts, conditions of work, and matters which affect a member's life as a professional writer. Members are given the opportunity of meeting at craft meetings, which are held on a regular basis throughout the year. Following the demise of the BBC's Drama Script Unit last year, The Writers' Guild, in conjunction with the BBC, has established a series of specifically targeted workshops held throughout the year (see **Writers' Guild Workshops** under **Writers' Courses, Circles and Workshops**). Membership to the Guild is by a points system. One major piece of work (a full-length book, an hour-long television or radio play, a feature film, etc.) entitles the author to full membership; writers who do not qualify for full membership may apply for temporary membership, paying the basic subscription of £60.

Yachting Journalists' Association

Paradise, Church Lane, Yealmpton, Plymouth, Devon PL8 2HG
☎ 0752 881435   Fax 0752 881435

Honorary Secretary *Roger Lean-Vercoe*

Subscription £15 p.a.

To further the interest of yachting, sail and power, and to provide support and assistance to journalists in the field.

Yorkshire Dialect Society

Farfields, Weeton Lane, Weeton, Near Leeds LS17 0AN
☎ 0423 734377

Secretary *Stanley Ellis*

Subscription £5.50

FOUNDED 1897. To promote interest in and preserve a record of the Yorkshire dialect. Publishes dialect verse and prose writing. Two journals to members annually. Details of publications are available from the librarian, YDS, School of English, University of Leeds, LS2 9JT.

Young Newspapermen's Association

See **The Newspaper Society**

Yr Academi Gymreig

3rd Floor, Mount Stuart House, Mount Stuart Square, Cardiff CF1 6DQ
☎ 0222 492064   Fax 0222 492930

Co-ordinator *Dafydd Rogers*

FOUNDED 1959. National society of Welsh writers. Aims to encourage writing in Welsh. Publishes *Taliesin*, plus books on Welsh literature and an English/Welsh dictionary. Organises readings, conferences and general literary events. Various tiers of membership available.

Literary Societies

William Barnes Society

65A Buxton Road, Weymouth, Dorset DT4 9PL

☎ 0305 771954

Contact *F. M. Langford*

Subscription £4 p.a.

FOUNDED 1983 to provide a forum in which admirers of the Dorset poet could share fellowship and pleasure in his work. William Barnes (1801–86) is best known as the writer of Dorset dialect poetry. His interest in dialect prompted him to become a learned philologist and he published many papers in defence of native English against the incursions of French and Latin. Quarterly meetings and newsletter.

E. F. Benson Society

88 Tollington Park, London N4 3RA

☎ 071-272 3375

Secretary *Allan Downend*

Subscription £7.50 (UK/Europe); £12.50 (Overseas)

FOUNDED 1985 to promote the life and work of E. F. Benson and the Benson family. Organises social and literary events, exhibitions and talks. Publishes a quarterly newsletter and annual journal, *The Dodo*; and holds an archive which includes the Seckersen Collection (transcriptions of the Benson collection at the Bodleian Library).

The Betjeman Society

14 The Precincts, Canterbury, Kent CT1 2EH

☎ 0227 454200

Contact *Membership Secretary*

Subscription £7 (Individual); £9 (Family); £3 (Student); £2 extra each category for overseas members

Aims to promote the study and appreciation of the work and life of Sir John Betjeman. Annual programme includes poetry reading, lectures, discussions, visits to places associated with Betjeman, and various social events. Meetings are held in London and other centres. Regular newsletter and annual journal, *The Betjemanian*.

The Bewick Society

The Old Vicarage, Ovingham, Prudhoe, Northumberland NE42 6BW

☎ 0661 835445   Fax 0661 835882

Contact *Dr Frank Atkinson*

Subscription £7 p.a.

FOUNDED 1988 to promote an interest in the life and work of Thomas Bewick, wood-engraver and naturalist (1753–1828). Organises related events and meetings and runs the Bewick birthplace museum.

British Fantasy Society

15 Stanley Road, Morden, Surrey SM4 5DE

☎ 081-540 9443

President *Ramsay Campbell*
Vice-President/Secretary *Di Wathen*

Subscription from £12 p.a.

FOUNDED 1971 for devotees of fantasy, horror and related fields in literature, art and the cinema. Publishes a regular newsletter with information and reviews of new books and films, plus related fiction and non-fiction magazines. Annual conference at which the **British Fantasy Awards** are presented.

The Bronte Society

Bronte Parsonage Museum, Haworth, Keighley, West Yorkshire BD22 8DR

☎ 0535 642323   Fax 0535 647131

Contact *Membership Secretary*

Subscription £6 p.a. (UK/Europe); £10 (Overseas); joint subscriptions and life membership also available

FOUNDED 1893. Aims and activities include the preservation of manuscripts and other objects related to or connected with the Bronte family, and the maintenance and development of the museum and library at Haworth. The society holds regular meetings, lectures and exhibitions; and publishes information relating to the family, and a bi-annual society journal.

The Browning Society

10 Pembridge Square, London W2 4ED
☎071-221 5748 Fax 071-792 0730

Contact *Dr Mairi Calcraft*

Subscription £10 p.a.

FOUNDED 1969 to promote an interest in the lives and poetry of Robert and Elizabeth Barret Browning. The society's journal, *Browning Society Notes*, is published twice yearly and meetings are arranged in the London area.

The Byron Society/International Byron Society

The Byron Society, Byron House, 6 Gertrude Street, London SW10 0TN
☎071-352 5112
International Byron Society, Newstead Abbey, Newstead Abbey Park, Nottingham NG15 8GE
☎0623 797392

Joint Honorary Director, Byron Society *Mrs Elma Dangerfield*
Joint International Secretary *Mrs Maureen Crisp*

Subscription £15 p.a.

FOUNDED 1876, and revived in 1971. Aims to promote knowledge and discussion of Lord Byron's life and works, and those of his contemporaries, through lectures, readings, concerts, performance and international conferences.

Randolph Caldecott Society

Clatterwick Hall, Little Leigh, Northwich, Cheshire CW8 4RJ
☎0606 891303

Honorary Secretary *Kenneth N. Outram*

Subscription £5-8 p.a.

FOUNDED 1983. To promote the life and work of artist/book illustrator Randolph Caldecott. Meetings held in the spring and autumn in Caldecott's birthplace, Chester. Guest speakers, outings, newsletter, exchanges with the society's American counterpart. Caldecott died and was buried in St Augustine, Florida. A medal in his memory is awarded annually in the US for children's book illustration.

The Carlyle Society, Edinburgh

20 Grange Crescent, Edinburgh EH9 2EH
☎031-667 6661

Honarary Secretary *Jean R. Guild*

Subscription £2 p.a.; £10/£20 (life/US)

FOUNDED 1929. To examine the lives of Thomas Carlyle and his wife Jane, his writings, contemporaries, and influences. Meetings are held about six times a year, and an annual members' journal is published.

Lewis Carroll Society (Daresbury)

Clatterwick Hall, Little Leigh, Northwich, Cheshire CW8 4RJ
☎0606 891303

Honorary Secretary *Kenneth N. Oultram*

Subscription £5 p.a.

FOUNDED 1970. To promote the life and work of the author of the world-famous *Alice's Adventures*. Holds regular meetings in the spring and autumn in Carroll's birthplace, Daresbury, in Cheshire. Guest speakers, theatre visits and a newsletter.

The Chesterton Society

11 Lawrence Leys, Bloxham, Near Banbury, Oxon OX15 4NU
☎0295 720869

Secretary *Robert Hughes*

Subscription £15 p.a.

FOUNDED 1964 to promote the ideas and writings of G. K. Chesterton.

The John Clare Society

The Stables, 1A West Street, Helpston, Peterborough PE6 7DU
☎0733 252678

Honorary Secretary *Mrs J. Mary Moyse*

Subscription £7.50 (Individual); £10 (Joint); £6/£7.50 (Retired/Joint Retired); £10 (Group/Library); £3 (Student); apply for overseas rates

FOUNDED 1981. Promotes a wider appreciation of the life and works of the poet John Clare (1793-1864). Organises the annual Clare Festival in Helpston in July; arranges exhibitions, poetry readings and conferences; and produces an annual society journal and quarterly newsletter.

William Cobbett Society

Combe Wood, 12 Burnt Hill Way, Boundstone,
Farnham, Surrey GU10 4RN
☎025125 3543

Contact *Reg Hatt*

Subscription £5 p.a.

FOUNDED 1976. To promote the life and works of
William Cobbett — farmer, soldier, MP, political
journalist, writer. Annual memorial lecture, informal meetings, and twice-yearly publication of the
society journal. Also an annual rural re-ride, based
on one of the famous *Rural Rides*.

The Arthur Conan Doyle Society

Grasmere, 35 Penfold Way, Dodleston,
Chester CH4 9ML
☎0244 660988

Contact *Christopher Roden*

Subscription £12 (UK/Europe); £14 (Overseas)

FOUNDED 1989. To promote the study and discussion of the life and works of Sir Arthur Conan
Doyle. Occasional meetings, functions and visits.
Publishes an annual journal and twice-yearly newsletter.

Joseph Conrad Society

c/o POSK, 238–246 King Street, London W6 0RF

Secretary *Hugh Epstein*

Subscription £12 (UK); £15 (Europe); £17 (Elsewhere)

FOUNDED 1974. To promote the knowledge and
study of the works and life of Joseph Conrad. The
society has a permanent study centre, associated
with the **Polish Library**, which contains a substantial collection of first and later editions and
critical works on Conrad. Holds an international
conference over 4 days in July each year. Also
administers the Dan Holliday Prize, an annual essay
competition which offers a substantial prize for
essays on Conrad and Henry James. Write for
details.

The Dickens Fellowship

48 Doughty Street, London WC1N 2LF
☎071–405 2127   Fax 071–831 5175

Contact *Edward G. Preston*

FOUNDED 1902. The society's particular aims and
objectives are: to bring together lovers of Charles
Dickens; to spread the message of Dickens which
the society believes to be love of humanity ('the
keynote of all his work'); to remedy social injustice
for the poor and oppressed; to assist in the
preservation of material and buildings associated
with Dickens. Annual conference and journal
called *The Dickensian*.

The George Eliot Fellowship

71 Stepping Stones Road, Coventry,
Warwickshire CV5 8JT
☎0203 592231

Contact *Mrs Kathleen Adams*

Subscription £7 p.a.; £75 (Life); concessions for
pensioners

FOUNDED 1930. Exists to honour George Eliot and
promote interest in her life and works. Readings,
memorial lecture, birthday luncheon and functions.

The Gaskell Society

Far Yew Tree House, Over Tabley, Knutsford,
Cheshire WA16 0HN
☎0565 634668

Honorary Secretary *Joan Leach*

Subscription £5 p.a.; £10 (Overseas)

FOUNDED 1985 to promote and encourage the
study and appreciation of the life and works of
Elizabeth Cleghorn Gaskell. Meetings held in
Knutsford, Manchester and London; residential
study weekends and visits; annual journal and bi-
annual newsletter.

The Gatty Society

40 Shirley Gardens, Rusthall, Tunbridge Wells,
Kent TN4 8JH
☎0892 546972   Fax 0892 864371

Contact *Alan W. Hooker*

Subscription £5 p.a.

FOUNDED 1990 to foster an interest in the works of
Mrs Margaret Gatty, Mrs Juliana Horatia Ewing (née
Gatty), and the other literary members of the Gatty
family.

The Ghost Story Society

2 Looe Road, Croxteth, Liverpool L11 6LJ

Secretary *Jeffrey Dempsey*

Subscription £7 p.a.; £8 (Overseas); £16 (USA)

FOUNDED 1988 to promote and celebrate the work
of past and present writers of ghost stories and
supernatural fiction. Publishes new fiction in its

annual journal called *All Hallows* and keeps members up to date with new publications by means of regular newsletters. Runs short story competitions at intervals and winning stories are published in the Society's journal.

The Gothic Society

Chatham House, Gosshill Road, Chislehurst, Kent BR7 5NS

☎081-467 8475   Fax 081-295 1967

Contact *Jennie Gray*

Subscription £17 p.a.; £19.50 (Overseas)

FOUNDED 1990 for the amusement of those who delight in morbid, macabre and black-hued themes. Society suppers in unusual places, social events. Publishes a newsletter five times a year as well as other books and studies related specifically to the society's interests.

Rider Haggard Appreciation Society

27 Deneholm, Whitley Bay NE25 9AU

☎091-252 4516

Contact *Roger Allen*

Subscription £7 p.a.

FOUNDED 1985. To promote appreciation of the life and works of Sir Henry Rider Haggard, English novelist, 1856-1925. News/books exchange, and meetings every two years.

The Thomas Hardy Society

PO Box 1438, Dorchester, Dorset DT1 1YH

Honorary Secretary *Mrs Helen Taylor*

Subscription £12; £20 (Corporate); £15 (Individual Overseas); £25 (Corporate Overseas)

FOUNDED 1967. To promote the reading and study of the works and life of Thomas Hardy. Thrice-yearly journal, events and a biennial conference.

The Henty Society

Fox Hall, Kelshall, Royston, Hertfordshire SG8 9SE

☎076387 208

Honorary Secretary *Mrs Ann J. King*

Subscription £10 p.a.; £12 (Overseas)

FOUNDED 1977 to study the life and work of George Alfred Henty, and to publish research, bibliographical data and lesser known works, namely short stories. Organises conferences and social gatherings in the UK and Canada, and publishes quarterly bulletins to members.

The Sherlock Holmes Society of London

3 Outram Road, Southsea, Hampshire PO5 1QP

☎0705 812104

Honorary Secretary *Cdr G. S. Stavert*

Subscription £6 p.a. (Associate); £10 (Full)

FOUNDED 1951. The study of the life and work of Sherlock Holmes and Dr Watson, and their creator, Sir Arthur Conan Doyle. Offers correspondence and liaison with international societies, plus a bi-annual society journal.

Hopkins Society

Daniel Owen Centre, Earl Road, Mold, Clwyd, Wales CH7 1AP

☎0352 758403   Fax 0352 700236

Contact *Sandra Wynne*

Subscription £5 p.a.

FOUNDED 1990 to celebrate the life and work of Gerard Manley Hopkins; to inform members of any publications, courses or events about the poet. Holds an annual lecture on Hopkins in the spring; produces two newsletters a year; sponsors and organises educational projects based on Hopkins' life and works.

W. W. Jacobs Appreciation Society

3 Roman Road, Southwick, West Sussex BN42 4TP

☎0273 596217   Fax 081-879 7317 attn ARJ

Contact *A. R. James*

FOUNDED 1988 to encourage and promote the enjoyment of the works of W. W. Jacobs, and stimulate research into his life and works. Publishes a quarterly newsletter free to those who send s.a.e. (9in x 4in). No subscription charge. Biography, bibliography, directories of plays and films are available for purchase.

The Kipling Society

2nd Floor, Schomberg House, 80–82 Pall Mall, London SW1Y 5HG

☎0428 652709

Secretary *Norman Entract*

Subscription £20 p.a.

FOUNDED 1927. The Society's main activities are: maintaining a specialised library; answering enquiries from the public (schools, publishers, writers and the media); arranging a regular programme of lectures and an annual luncheon with guest speaker; and publishing a quarterly journal. Open to anyone interested in the prose and verse, life and times of Rudyard Kipling (1865-1936).

The T. E. Lawrence Society
44 Sandown Road, Stevenage,
Hertfordshire SG1 5SF
☎ 0438 353174

Secretary *Mr P. C. Metcalfe*

Subscription £12.50 p.a.

FOUNDED 1985 to advance the education of the public in the life and works of T. E. Lawrence, and to promote and publish research into both areas.

Arthur Machen Literary Society
19 Cross Street, Caerleon, Gwent NP6 1AF
☎ 0633 422520

Contact *Rita Tait*

Subscription £12 (UK); overseas rates available

Exists to honour the life and work of writer Arthur Machen (1863-1947). Publishes a twice-yearly newsletter and journal; plus hardback books by and about Machen and his circle under its publishing arm, the Green Round Press. Gives assistance to researchers on the 1890s mystery and imagination genre of which Machen was part.

New Canterbury Literary Society
Malthouse Cottage, Padworth, Reading,
Berkshire RG7 4JT
☎ 0734 713206   Fax 0734 713206

English Correspondent *David Wilkinson*

Membership by recommendation

FOUNDED 1963. Aims to promote knowledge and understanding of the life and work of Richard Aldington. The society is a small group of people who exchange information by means of a quarterly newssheet issued and edited by Professor Norman Gates from Haddonfield, New Jersey. It is based on the mock literary society, the CLS (Canterbury Literary Society) initiated by Richard Aldington in the late 1920s. The original CLS gathered together a group of Aldington's closest friends — including D. H. Lawrence. Members were deemed by Aldington to have been rejected by the literary milieu.

Northern Musgraves Sherlock Holmes Society
Overdale, 69 Greenhead Road, Huddersfield, West Yorkshire HD1 4ER
☎ 0484 426957

Contact *David Stuart Davies*

Subscription £10 p.a. (UK)

FOUNDED 1988 to promote enjoyment and study of Sir Arthur Conan Doyle's *Sherlock Holmes* through publications and meetings. The second largest Sherlock Holmes society in Great Britain. Open membership.

The Beatrix Potter Society
120 Aldwick Road, Bognor Regis, West Sussex PO21 2PB
☎ 0243 823058

Contact *Mrs Anne M. Poulter*

Subscription £7 p.a.

FOUNDED 1980 to promote the study of Beatrix Potter (1866-1943). Potter was not only the author of *The Tale of Peter Rabbit* and other classics of children's literature; she was also a landscape and natural history artist, diarist, farmer and conservationist, and was responsible for the preservation of large areas of the Lake District through her gifts to the National Trust. The Society upholds and protects the integrity of the inimitable and unique work of the lady, her aims and bequests.

The Dorothy L. Sayers Society
Rose Cottage, Malthouse Lane, Hurstpierpoint,
West Sussex BN6 9JY
☎ 0273 833444

Contact *Christopher Dean*

Subscription £6 p.a.

FOUNDED 1976 to promote the study of the life, works and thoughts of Dorothy Sayers; to encourage the performance of her plays and publication of her books and books about her; to preserve original material and provide assistance to researchers. Acts as a forum and information centre, providing material for study purposes which would otherwise be unavailable. Annual seminars.

The Trollope Society
9A North Street, Clapham, London SW4 9HY
☎ 071-720 6789/2123

Contact *John Letts/Anthony Juckes*

FOUNDED 1987. The study and promotion of Anthony Trollope's works, allied to the publication of the first complete edition of his novels.

Edgar Wallace Society

7 Devonshire Close, Amersham, Buckinghamshire HP6 5JG
☎ 0494 725398

Organiser *John A. Hogan*

Subscription £8 p.a.; £10 (Overseas); £5.50 (Senior Citizens)

FOUNDED 1969 by Edgar's daughter, Penelope, to bring together all who have an interest in Edgar Wallace. Members receive a brief biography of her father by Penelope Wallace, with a complete list of all published book titles. A 24-page quarterly newsletter, *Crimson Circle*, is issued in February, May, August and November.

The Walmsley Society

Sherbrook, Newlands Drive, Leominster HR6 8PR
☎ 0568 611733

Joint Secretary *Jack L. W. Hazell*

Subscription £6 p.a.; £7 (Family); £5 (Students/Senior Citizens)

FOUNDED 1985 to promote interest in the art and writings of Ulric and Leo Walmsley. Two annual meetings, one held in Robin Hood's Bay on the East Yorkshire coast, spiritual home of the author Leo Walmsley. The society also seeks to foster appreciation of the work of his father, Ulric Walmsley, RA.

Mary Webb Society

4 Lythwood Road, Bayston Hill, Shrewsbury SY3 0LU
☎ 074372 2766

Contact *Mrs A. Parry*

Subscription £5 p.a.

FOUNDED 1972 to further the reading and apprecia-tion of the works of Mary Webb; to foster apprecia-tion of the countryside about which she wrote; and to liaise with other organisations in encouraging scholarship and education in the spirit of Mary Webb. Talks, lectures, events, summer school. For information contact Mrs Parry above, or Mrs H. M. Dormer at 6 Ragleth Road, Church Stretton, Shrop-shire SY6 7BN. Tel: 0694 722755.

H. G. Wells Society

English Department, Nene College, Moulton Park, Northampton NN2 7AL
☎ 0604 715000   Fax 0604 720636

Hon. General Secretary *Dr Sylvia Hardy*

Subscription £6.50 (UK); £8.00 (Overseas); £12.00 (Corporate)

FOUNDED 1960 to promote an interest in and appreciation of the life, work and thought of Herbert George Wells.

The Charles Williams Society

26 Village Road, London N3 1TL

Contact *Honorary Secretary*

FOUNDED 1975 to promote interest in, and provide a means for, the exchange of views and informa-tion on the life and work of Charles Williams.

The Henry Williamson Society

16 Doran Drive, Redhill, Surrey RH1 6AX
☎ 0737 763228

Membership Secretary *P. F. Murphy*

Subscription £8 p.a.; £10 (Family); £4 (Students)

FOUNDED 1980 to encourage, by all appropriate means, a wider readership and deeper understand-ing of the literary heritage left by the 20th-century English writer Henry Williamson (1895–1977). Twice-yearly journal.

Arts Councils and Regional Arts Boards

Arts Councils

The Arts Council of Great Britain

14 Great Peter Street, London SW1P 3NQ
☎071-333 0100   Fax 071-973 6590

Chairman *Lord Palumbo*
Secretary General *Anthony Everitt*

The 1992/93 grant dispensed by the Arts Council stands at c.£221.2 million. From this fund the Arts Council supports arts organisations, artists, performers and others: grants can also be made for particular productions, exhibitions and projects. Grants available to individuals are detailed in the free Arts Council folder: *Awards & Schemes 1992/93*. The total amount set aside for literature for 1992/93 is £1,300,000, an increase on last year's figure of over 10%.

Drama Director *Ian Brown* New writing is supported through *Theatre Writing Allocations* (contact the Drama Department for more details).
Literature Director *Alastair Niven* The Literature Department has defined support for writers, education, access to literature including the touring of authors and literary exhibitions, cultural diversity, and an international view of writing including more translation into English among its top priorities. P. D. James (Baroness James of Holland Park) recently completed her term as Chair of the Literature Advisory Panel and the new Chair will be announced by the Minister for the National Heritage. This year the Arts Council will be giving at least twelve grants of £6000 each to individual writers. Applicants must have at least one published book. Details available from the Literature Department from July 1992.

Arts Council of Northern Ireland

181A Stranmillis Road, Belfast BT9 5DU
☎0232 381591   Fax 0232 661715

Literature Officer *Ciaran Carson*
Drama Director *Denis Smyth*

Funds book production by established publishers, programmes of readings, literary festivals, writers-in-residence schemes and literary magazines and periodicals. Occasional schools programmes and anthologies of children's writing are produced. Annual awards and bursaries for writers are available. Financial assistance is also provided for the commissioning of new theatre writing. The presentation of new work is supported through project grants. Further information available on this from the Drama Department. Holds information also on various groups associated with local arts, workshops and courses.

Scottish Arts Council

12 Manor Place, Edinburgh EH3 7DD
☎031-226 6051   Fax 031-225 9833

Literature Director *Walter Cairns*

The Council's work for Scottish-based professional writers, who have a track record of publication, includes: bursaries (considered twice yearly); travel and research grants (considered three times yearly); writing fellowships (posts usually advertised) and an international writing fellowship (organised reciprocally with the Canada Council); and two schemes: *Writers in Schools* and *Writers in Public* — a list of writers willing to participate in the schemes is published. Also publishes lists of Scottish writers' groups, workshops, circles, awards and literary agents.

Welsh Arts Council

Museum Place, Cardiff CF1 3NX
☎0222 394711   Fax 0222 221447

Literature Director *Tony Bianchi*

Funds literary magazines and book production, *Writers on Tour* and bursary schemes, the **Welsh Academy, Welsh Books Council, Hay-on-Wye Literature Festival, Cardiff Literature Festival** and the **Tŷ Newydd Writers' Residential Centre**; also children's literature, annual prizes, competitions, and readings at the Council's bookshop, Oriel.

Drama Director *Michael Baker* Of particular interest to writers is the new WAC Drama Committee theatre writing policy and programmes, which aim to develop theatrical experience among Wales-based writers through a variety of schemes — in particular, by funding writers on year-long attachments.

Regional Arts Boards

Council of Regional Arts Associations
See **Regional Arts Bureau**

Regional Arts Bureau
5 City Road, Winchester, Hampshire SO23 8SD
☎0962 851063   Fax 0962 842033

Executive Director *Christopher Gordon*
Assistant *Carolyn Nixson*

The newly formed Regional Arts Bureau (now a company limted by guarantee) is retained by the ten regional arts boards (RABs) in England, as their joint mechanism, and to provide services and information for them on an economy of scale. It takes over from the former Council of Regional Arts Associations. (Scotland, Northern Ireland and Wales have their own Arts Councils; and Wales has three regional arts associations.) RABs are support and development agencies for the arts in the regions, and policies develop not only in response to regional demand but also to assist new initiatives in areas of perceived need and these, aside from the broad objectives of all RABs, will vary from region to region.

DIRECT GRANTS FOR WRITERS
While most of the RABs designate part of their budget for allocation direct to writers, this is often a minor proportion, which new or aspiring playwrights stand little chance of receiving. Money is more readily available for the professional, though because of the emphasis on community access to the arts in many of the boards, this is often allocated to writers' appearances in schools and community settings, theatre workshops, etc., rather than to support the writer at the typewriter. New writing is also encouraged through the funding of small presses and grants to theatre companies for play commissions. Details of their schemes can be obtained from individual RABs.

Cleveland Arts
PO Box 12, Marton House, Borough Road, Middlesbrough TS4 2YP
☎0642 211347   Fax 0642 251209

Cleveland Arts is an *independent* arts development agency working in the county of Cleveland. Works in partnership with local authorities, public agencies, the business sector, schools, colleges, individuals and organisations to coordinate, promote and develop the arts — crafts, film, video, photography, music, drama, dance, literature, public arts, disability, black arts, community arts.

East Midlands Arts
Mountfields House, Forest Road, Loughborough, Leicestershire LE11 3HU
☎0509 218292   Fax 0509 262214

Literature Officer *Debbie Hicks*
Drama Officer *Helen Flach*

Covers Leicestershire, Nottinghamshire, Derbyshire (excluding the High Peak district) and Northamptonshire. A comprehensive information service for regional writers includes an extensive *Writers' Information Pack*, with details of local groups, workshops, residential writing retreats, publishers and publishing information, regional magazines which offer a market for work, advice on approaching the media, on unions, courses and grants. Also available is a directory of writers, primarily to aid people using the *Artists At Your Service* scheme and to establish *Writers' Attachments*. Writers' bursaries are granted for work on a specific project — all forms of writing are eligible except for local history and biography. Writing for the theatre can come under the aegis of both Literature and Drama. A list of writers' groups is available, plus *Foreword*, the literature newsletter.

Leicester Sound in collaboration with East Midlands Arts is offering a local writer the opportunity to gain professional radio training and learn all about writing for broadcast. The trainee will at the same time be opening up the airwaves to lively arts and literature coverage. Part of a recognised training programme covering the region, this is the first placement of its kind to a commercial radio station. East Midlands Arts provide a trainee with a bursary of £3360 to support the writer for two days a week over six months while Leicester Sound provide full training and support plus studio and production facilities. The trainee will be involved in assessing the broadcast potential of the local literary scene, producing features for broadcast and developing opportunities for local writing and arts coverage. Closing date for applications last year was 12 December. Applicants should contact the Media and Publishing Arts Department at East Midlands Arts (0509 218292) for further information on the scheme.

Eastern Arts Board
Cherry Hinton Hall, Cambridge CB1 4DW
☎0223 215355   Fax 0223 248075

Literature Officer *Don Watson*
Assistant Director (Performing Arts) *Sandy Bailey*

Covers Bedfordshire, Cambridgeshire, Essex, Hertfordshire, Norfolk, Suffolk and (from October 1991) Lincolnshire. Policy emphasises quality and access. As a self-styled arts development agency, great stress is placed upon work with publishers within the region and on literature in performance. On the drama side, greater emphasis is placed on the creation of a structure to support the playwright — by means of adequate workshops and performance opportunities, rather than direct grants, though a small fund exists for the commissioning of work. In literature, support is given to education, festivals and performances, and publishing. The Board runs a critical reading service and offers a range of bursaries annually for individual writers. Supplies a list of literary groups, workshops and local writing courses.

London Arts Board

Elme House, 3rd Floor, 133 Long Acre,
London WC2E 9AF
☎071–240 1313/Helpline: 071–240 4578
Fax 071–240 4580

Literature Officer *Lavinia Greenlaw*

The London Arts Board replaced Greater London Arts with effect from October 1991. New policies are determined by the new Board. Potential applicants for support for literature and other arts projects should contact the Board for information.

North Wales Arts

10 Wellfield House, Bangor, Gwynedd LL57 1ER
☎0248 353248   Fax 0248 351077

Deputy Director/Literature Officer *J. Clifford Jones*
Regional Officer *Sandra Wynne* at Canolfan Daniel Owen, Earls Road, Mold, Clwyd CH7 1AP (Tel: 0352 758403; Fax 0352 700236)

Covers Gwynedd, Clwyd and the Montgomeryshire district of Powys. The Association's role in the field of literature is fourfold: to highlight all aspects of the literary heritage in both English and Welsh; to foster an understanding and appreciation of this tradition; to stimulate others to develop these traditions; to encourage promising new initiatives. Priorities include the *Authors in Residence, Authors on Video* and *Authors on Tour* schemes, and the support of literary circles, Eisteddfodau and community newspapers. Can supply list of names and addresses of regional groups, circles, workshops and courses in the region. Contact the Literature Officer.

North West Arts Board

4th Floor, 12 Harter Street, Manchester M1 6HY
☎061–228 3062   Fax 061–236 5361

Arts Development Officer (Literature) *Christine Bridgwood*
Arts Development Officer (Theatre) *Sue Williams*

Restructured October 1991 to cover Cheshire, Greater Manchester, Merseyside, Lancashire (except West Lancs) and the High Peak district of Derbyshire. Gives financial assistance to a great variety of projects and schemes, including **Lancaster Literature Festival** and creative writing courses. The *Write Around* scheme subsidises writers' placements in schools, community organisations, etc. The *Live Writing* scheme assists literature promoters with the cost of organising readings and performance. For information sheets and further details of what is available, contact the Literature Assistant. NWAB publishes a directory of local groups, with details of over forty organisations ranging from groups like Chester Poets to Elders and Betters (for those over 60).

Northern Arts Board

9–10 Osborne Terrace, Jesmond, Newcastle upon Tyne NE2 1NZ
☎091–281 6334   Fax 091–281 3276

Head of Published and Broadcast Arts *John Bradshaw*

Covers Cleveland, Cumbria, Durham, Northumberland and Tyne and Wear, and was the first regional arts association in the country to be set up by local authorities. It supports both organisations and writers and aims to stimulate public interest in artistic events. Offers Writers Awards for published writers to release them from work or other commitments for short periods of time to enable them to concentrate on specific literary projects. A separate scheme for playwrights is operated by the Northern Playwrights Society. Northern Arts makes drama awards to producers only. Also funds writers' residencies, and has a fund for publications. Contact list of regional groups and workshops available.

South East Arts

10 Mount Ephraim, Tunbridge Wells,
Kent TN4 8AS
☎0892 515210   Fax 0892 549383

Literature Officer *Celia Hunt*
Drama Officer *Linda Lewis*

Covers Kent, Surrey and Sussex (excluding the London boroughs). The Literature panel 'aims to create a high public profile for contemporary writing; and to encourage aspiring writers to develop their skills'. Priorities include writers' residencies and the *Writers in Education* and *Live Literature* schemes; also the continued support of literature festivals in the region. For a small fee, South East Arts offers a reader service under which a writer can submit work to professional readers for critical comment. A regular newsletter is available, as well as a Writers' Information Pack, with names and addresses of groups and workshops throughout the area.

South East Wales Arts

Victoria Street, Cwmbran Gwent NP44 3YT
☎ 0633 875075   Fax 0633 875389

Literature Officer *Bob Mole*

Can supply names and addresses of local groups, workshops and writing courses, and information on local writing schemes.

South West Arts

Bradninch Place, Gandy Street, Exeter EX4 3LS
☎ 0392 218188   Fax 0392 413554

Literature Officer *Ingrid Squirrell*
Theatre Officer *Hilary Garnham*

Covers Avon, Cornwall, Devon, much of Dorset, Gloucestershire and Somerset. 'The central theme running through the Association's constitution is development ... increasing, improving, encouraging, advancing and co-ordinating.' The literature policy aims to promote a healthy environment for writers of all kinds and to encourage a high standard of new writing. The programme includes residential courses, residencies and a *Writers in Education* scheme. There is also direct investment in small presses, publishers and community groups. Literary festivals, societies and arts centres are encouraged. Also available from SWA is a service called *Second Opinion* which is a free manuscript reading service, covering poetry, plays, fiction and film scripts. In addition, the theatre department aims to support the development of theatre writing by funding writers' workshops, seasons of new plays, and a theatre script reading service. List of regional groups and workshops available from the Literature Officer.

Southern Arts

13 St Clement Street, Winchester,
Hampshire SO23 9DQ
☎ 0962 855099   Fax 0962 861186

Literature Officer *Jane Spiers*
Marketing & Information Officer *Venice Marriott*
Theatre Officer *Allanah Lucas*

Covers Berkshire, Buckinghamshire, Hampshire, the Isle of Wight, Oxfordshire, Wiltshire and parts of Dorset. The literature panel funds fiction and poetry readings, festivals, magazines, bursaries, a literature prize, a manuscript appraisal service, publications, residencies and two schemes: *Write Connections*, which subsidises writers working in education and the community, and *Write Reactions*, a new scheme aimed at helping new and unpublished writers within the region. For a fee of £10, manuscripts from interested writers will be placed with a specially selected professional writer who will give 'a friendly, constructive and unbiased appraisal' of the work. The service covers all types of writing: novels, poems, plays, TV, film and radio scripts, feature articles and short stories. Holds a list of over 30 writers' workshops and groups in the region. Contact the Literature Officer.

West Midlands Arts

82 Granville Street, Birmingham B1 2LH
☎ 021-631 3121   Fax 021-643 7239

Literature Officer *David Hart*

Under the *Support for Writers* projects are community and new work schemes which respectively offer support towards residency-type work and new writing in context, including publishing. Holds a list of writing groups and workshops throughout its region. Contact the Literature Officer.

West Wales Arts

3 Red Street, Carmarthen, Dyfed SA31 1QL
☎ 0267 234248   Fax 0267 233084

Literature Officer *Emyr Williams*

West Wales Arts covers Dyfed and West Glamorgan. It supports a network of writers' groups through the West Wales Arts/Welsh Arts Council *Writers on Tour* scheme and organises an ongoing series of community writing projects under the banner of its *In Black and White* initiative. Writers receive additional support through their participation in residencies and other activities in the education and health care sectors. In conjunction with the Welsh Office, the Association also supports a network of Welsh language community newspapers. Publishing ventures are referred to other agencies. Supplies a list of names and addresses of over 20 groups in Dyfed and West Glamorgan, including groups like Carmarthen Writers' Circle (see **Writers' Courses Circles and Workshops**).

Yorkshire & Humberside Arts

21 Bond Street, Dewsbury, West
Yorkshire WF13 1AY
☏ 0924 455555   Fax 0924 466522

Literature Officer *Steve Dearden*
Drama Officer *Shea Connolly*

Following the restructure (October 1991) Yorkshire Arts now covers the Humberside region also. 'Libraries, publishing houses and the education service all make major contributions to the support of literature. Recognising the resources these agencies command, Yorkshire & Humberside Arts actively seeks ways of acting in partnership with them, whilst at the same time retaining its particular responsibility for the living writer and the promotion of activities currently outside the scope of these agencies.' Funding goes to the **Arvon Foundation** at Lumb Bank; the Yorkshire Art Circus for community publishing; the *Live Writing* scheme, which subsidises projects involving professional writers and students at all levels; and to awards for local independent publishers. Also offers support for literature in performance, namely for live poetry events and the **Ilkley Literature Festival**, Huddersfield Poetry Festival, Bête Noire readings. Holds a list of workshops and writers' groups throughout the region. Contact the Literature Officer.

The Postal Workshop

What is a Postal Workshop?

A workshop group, or folio, usually consists of six to eight members, with the rules varying according to each editor's requirements. They work on the principle of a round robin bringing in helpful suggestions and unbiased criticism of your work which can be put aside until such time as you are ready to use it in your writing, while you in turn read and advise on the writing of others in the folio – an arrangement with the added advantage over local circles that you can therefore give and receive your comments within the comfort of your own home.

The postal workshop/folio system has something for everyone, with a selection of specific or mixed genres for the serious novelist and short story writers. Articles and letters to editors are also catered for, or simply letters with a theme outside the writing field – a particular English county, for instance, hobbies and even a club for those who are housebound or phobic.

Receiving a folio is really like having a host of friends call on you at once, all bubbling with news and views on any manner of subjects. The days of the lonely writer are long gone and help is only a letter away. Because members are not graded by ability, newcomers can and do receive the help and guidance from experienced writers.

The normal length of time for dealing with the folio/workshop is seven days per member and so each circulation should take roughly between six and eight weeks. When it arrives, you read through each member's contribution and write your comments on the sheet provided. Most groups include a letter, which can evoke some excellent topics both in and out of the writing field, and sometimes add new ideas. Once your own letter and chapter are added, you merely parcel up securely and send to the next recipient.

Where do you find out about these workshops?

There is a number of publications, large and small, specifically aimed at the writer, and these magazines often publicise and/or advertise the various postal workshops/folios with the aim of assisting their regular readership.

I approached several last year when setting up my own workshop for crime writers and was pleasantly surprised by their helpful response. One editor telephoned to say when she would be including the item, and not one refused to give the free publicity which has helped to produce sufficient members for three groups – so far.

Many of these writer's magazines and some postal workshops can be found listed within *The Writer's Handbook* or from your local Arts Council (also listed). In addition you can purchase a pocket-sized directory of postal workshops and folios, priced £1 post-free, from Cathie Gill, Drakemyre Croft, Cairnorrie, Methlick, Ellon, Aberdeenshire, AB41 0JN.

Why not join a workshop and discover the benefits for yourself? You might be delighted by the results.

Stella A. Milner

Independent Postal Workshops

Adult Modern Romance Novel Folio
41 Ingleside Road, Kingswood, Bristol BS15 1HJ
Contact *Sheila Ackerman*
Designed for serious writers in the romance field. Send s.a.e. for details.

Article Folio
1 Foxley Drive, Bishop's Stortford, Hertfordshire CM23 2EB
Contact *Ruth Bagnall*
Easy-going but enthusiastic group. Send s.a.e. for details.

Book Folio
17 Andrews Crescent, Peterborough, Cambridgeshire PE4 7XL
Contact *Kate Dean*
For writers who have a complete draft of a book which needs revision.
Maximum number on the rota is six and each member receives one mss per
week, to be read, criticised and passed on by first post the following Monday.
The system demands dedicated writers who will guarantee to deal with one
mss per week for as long as it takes. It allows for more in-depth criticism than a
Manuscript Folio, which arrives with six–eight mss. Kate Dean says she is willing to act as liaison for other genres, i.e. put interested novelists of the same
genre in touch with each other. Send s.a.e., plus two second-class stamps for
further details.

Concordant Poets
87 Brookhouse Road, Farnborough, Hampshire GU14 0BU
Six folios who welcome and encourage newcomers of either sex into their fold
of accomplished poets.

The Anna Owens Dragons – Fantasy Folio
17 Andrews Crescent, Peterborough, Cambridgeshire PE4 7XL
Contact *Kate Dean*
For novels or short stories. Started as a children's folio but has been extended
to include adult. Send s.a.e. for details.

Historical Novel Folio
17 Purbeck Heights, Mount Road, Parkstone, Poole, Dorset BH14 0QP
Contact *Doris Myall-Harris*
A single folio dealing with any period before the Second World War. Send s.a.e.
for details.

Partners in Crime
17 Eton Road, Burton-on-Trent, Staffordshire DE14 2SP
Contact *Stella A Milner*
For serious novelists, a folio which specialises in the entire spectrum of crime, including **murder, mystery, suspense** and **thrillers**. Each member includes a chapter of their novel for the rest of the group to read, the contents regulated by the restriction of pages: 10 double sided sheets of heavy duty paper or 20 flimsy, thus keeping postal costs to a minimum.

Scribo
Flat 1, 31 Hamilton Road, Boscombe, Bournemouth, Dorset BH1 4EQ
Contact *K. Sylvester/P. A. Sylvester*
Established over 20 years ago, Scribo circulates folios to members who currently number about 30, some published and bestselling, others unpublished. The only criteria for joining Scribo is that members must be actively engaged in writing novels. **Forum** folios discuss everything of interest to novelists; problems are shared and information exchanged; and **Manuscript** folios offer friendly criticisms and advice. Three specialist folios: **Crime**, **Romance** and **Fantasy/Science Fiction** have recently been added.

Women's Magazine Short Story Folio
37 Darrell Charles Court, 100 Park Road, Uxbridge, Middlesex UB8 1JQ
Contact *Mrs Rita Kerr*
Designed for serious writers in the romance field. Send s.a.e. for details.

Writers' Courses, Circles and Workshops

Courses

Aberdeen
University of Aberdeen, Centre for Continuing Education, Regent Building, Regent Walk, Aberdeen, AB9 1FX (Tel 0224 272448). Practical writing class/workshop, held weekly.

Belfast
University of Ulster, Continuing Education, BT37 0QB (Tel 0232 365131). Creative writing course/workshop of ten sessions. Aims to develop and provoke thought about creative skills, looking at characterisation, viewpoint, dialogue and imagery. Open to all forms and genres. Fee £15 (concessions available). Contact the Administrative Officer.

Birmingham
Sandwell College, High Street, West Bromwich, B70 8DW (Tel 021–556 6000, ext. 8633). Creative writing courses held Wednesday afternoons and evenings, from September to July. Script writing, poetry, etc. Contact Dave Richmond.
The **University of Birmingham**, School of Continuing Studies, Edgbaston, Birmingham B15 2TT (Tel 021–414 5606/7/8). Day and weekend classes. Courses are held at locations throughout Birmingham, the West Midlands, Hereford & Worcester and Shropshire. Detailed course brochure available from the above address. The University also offers an MA course in Playwriting Studies.

Bristol
The **University of Bristol**, Department for Continuing Education, Wills Memorial Building, Queen's Road, Bristol BS8 1HR (Tel 0272 303629). Courses in Bristol and throughout the surrounding counties (Avon, Dorset, Gloucestershire, Somerset, Wiltshire). Examples: *Women and Writing*, for women who write or would like to begin to write (poetry, fiction, non-fiction, journals); *Writing Creative Non-Fiction*, for all those interested in journalism, features, travel writing, local history or biography. Detailed brochure available.

Cornwall
Magic Words, Coach House, Rashleigh Vale, Truro, Cornwall TR1 1TJ (Tel 0872 78885). Non-residential courses (weekend, long weekend and one week) Workshops, tutorials and writing exercises. The course is run by D. M. Thomas, full-time writer/poet. Courses take place in the author's study and are open to anyone who writes or would like to write. Groups are kept small

for personal attention. Brochure available. Contact D. M. Thomas/Denise Aldred.

The **School of Creative Writing**, Weavers Press Publishing, Tregeraint House, Zennor, St Ives, Cornwall TR26 3DB (Tel 0736 797061). A correspondence course for beginners, covering all the basics of writing articles, features, short stories, novels, non-fiction, marketing and writing for publication. Assignments are assessed and advice is given by an experienced writer. Contact John T. Wilson. Residential courses of one week's duration are also available.

Derbyshire
Writers' Summer School, The Hayes, Swanwick, Derbyshire. A week-long, residential summer school: lectures, informal talks and discussion groups, forums, panels, quizzes and competitions, and 'a lot of fun'. Open to everyone, from absolute beginners to published authors. Held in August from late Saturday to Friday morning. Cost (1992) £158 all inclusive. Contact Philippa Boland at The Red House, Mardens Hill, Crowborough, East Sussex, TN6 1XN (Tel 0892 653943).

Devon
The Arvon Foundation, see **Professional Associations and Societies**.

Durham
Residential creative writing course offered at **Beamish Hall College**, Stanley, Co. Durham, DH9 0RG (Tel 0207 233147). Details available in the autumn but usually held over the summer. The 1992 writing summer school featured Arthur Appleton as one of the guest speakers.

Edinburgh
Edinburgh University, Centre for Continuing Education, 11 Buccleuch Place, Edinburgh EH8 9LW (Tel 031–650 1000). Several writing-orientated courses. Beginners welcome. Course brochure available.

Glasgow
University of Glasgow, Department of Adult and Continuing Education, 59 Oakfield Avenue, Glasgow G12 8LW (Tel 041–330 4394). Evening writing classes spread over a period of ten weeks, with classes once a week. Examples: *Women's Writing, Masters of the Short Story, The Writers' Group*. Fees are in the region of £25, with concessions available for elderly or unemployed applicants.

Gwynedd
Taliesin, Tŷ Newydd, Llanystumdwy, Criccieth, Gwynedd, LL52 0LW (Tel 0766 522811). Residential writers' centre set up by the Taliesin Trust with the support of the Welsh Arts Council to encourage and promote writing in both English and Welsh. Courses run from Monday evening to Saturday morning. Each course has two tutors and takes a maximum of 16 participants. The centre offers a wide range of specific courses including a general beginners' course called *Starting to Write*. Early booking essential. Fees £196 inclusive; weekend courses available £96 inclusive. People on low incomes may be eligible for a grant or bursary. Course leaflet available.

Hull
Hull College of Further Education, Queen's Garden Centre, Hull, North Humberside HU1 3DG (Tel 0482 29943). Offers part-time day/evening writing courses, including *Creative Writing, Reading & Writing Poetry, Selling Words, Writing and Devising Plays, Fiction Writing, Short Story Writing*, at various centres within the city. Most courses begin in September and last for a period of ten weeks. Contact Ed Strauss on ext. 226.

Kent
University of Kent at Canterbury, School of Continuing Education, Rutherford College, The University, Canterbury, Kent CT2 7NX (Tel 0227 764000). Contact Jean Field ext. 7647. Creative writing day class, and evening workshop, at which members are encouraged to develop their faculties of self-criticism and an appreciation of the technicalities of literature and literary expression.
International Forum, The Oast House, Plaxtol, Sevenoaks, Kent TN15 0QG (Tel 0732 810925). Wide range of courses (one, two or three-day), on screenwriting and other key creative roles in film and television. Courses run throughout the year and concessions are available for members of certain trade organisations. Contact Joan Harrison.

Leeds
University of Leeds, Adult Education Centre, 37 Harrow Road, Middlesbrough, Cleveland TS5 5NT (Tel 0642 814987). Creative writing courses held in the autumn and spring terms in Cleveland. Contact Andy Croft.

Lincolnshire
The Hen House, Hawerby Hall, North Thoresby, Lincolnshire DN36 5QL (Tel 0472 840278). Women's holiday and study centre offering courses and workshops. Looks at imagery, characterisation, dialogue, analysis of the short story format, and much more. Group writing exercises, in-depth discussion and *fun*. Fees range from about £115 plus VAT for a weekend course to £220 for the week. Contact Pearlie McNeill; enclose s. a. e. for course details.

Liverpool/Merseyside
South Mersey College, Adult & Community Education, Riversdale Road, Liverpool, L19 3QR (Tel 051–427 1227). *Media Script Writing* course which explores techniques, forms of news presentation, documentary, bulletins, etc. Also creative writing courses designed to suit the individual needs of students.
University of Liverpool, Centre for Continuing Education, 19 Abercromby Square, PO Box 147, Liverpool L69 3BX (Tel 051–794 6900). Several writing courses, including *Creative Writing, Writing for the Media, Black Writing for Performance, Imaginative Writing*. Most are held in the evenings. Fees vary; some courses are free. Contact the Director; enclose s. a. e. for details.
Wirral Metropolitan College, Faculty of Arts, Design & Creative Studies, Withens Lane, Wallasey, Merseyside (Tel 051–639 8371). Freelance journalism courses. Initial training in writing for newspapers, radio and television; instruction in writing, layout, research, marketing, shorthand and interviewing; use of word processors and DTP facilities. 20 weeks (20 hours per week). Contact Sandy Felton or Dave Dunn.

Writing in Merseyside, c/o Toxteth Branch Library, Windsor Street, Liverpool L8 1XF (Tel 051–709 7489) is a mini-directory which lists facilities, resources and opportunities in the Merseyside area. Excellent publication for putting writers in touch with what's available in their area. Everything from workshops and courses to competitions, research and library facilities, plus tips. Comprehensive course information on all areas of writing is provided.

London

City University, Northampton Square, London EC1V 0HB (Tel 071–477 8000 ext. 3268/3179/3253). Creative writing classes include: *Writer's Workshop, Poetry Writing, Writing Freelance Articles for Newspapers, Creative Writing, Story Telling, Women Writer's Workshop.* Contact the Secretary, Courses for Adults.

London College of Printing, School of Media & Management Studies, Elephant & Castle, London SE1 6SB (Tel 071–820 9226). Part-time and full-time courses in journalism. Courses vary from year to year but previous programmes have included *Writing for Magazines, English for Journalists, Sub-editing.*

London School of Journalism, Hillgate Village, 37 Uxbridge Street, London W8 7TQ (Tel 071–727 7241). Correspondence courses with an individual approach to each student; students remain with the same tutor throughout their programme. Course options include writing for television, radio, children, articles, short stories, fiction, poetry and journalism, and can be started at any time of the year. Fees vary but range from £99 for *Prose Writing (Grammar)* to £325 for *Journalism.* Contact Patricia Butler.

National Council for the Training of Journalists, Carlton House, Hemnall Street, Epping, Essex CM16 4NL. For details of full-time courses in journalism, write to the NCTJ, enclosing a 9in x 4in s. a. e.

National Film & Television School, Beaconsfield Studios, Station Road, Beaconsfield, Buckinghamshire, HP9 1LG (Tel 0494 671234). Writers' course designed for students who already have experience of writing in other fields. The course is divided into two parts: a self-contained intensive one-month course concentrating on the fundamentals of screenwriting, and a one-year course for 6–8 students selected from the one-month course: intensive programme of writing and analysis combined with an understanding of the practical stages involved in the making of a film.

Periodicals Training Council, 15–19 Kingsway, London WC2B 6UN (Tel 071–836 8798). Courses for those interested in writing for magazines. Options: *Introduction to Magazine Journalism*, a course for beginners covering news reporting, feature writing and interviewing, as well as subbing, layout, etc.; *Researching & Interviewing*, for journalists with some experience of news/feature writing; *Better Feature Writing, Sharper News Stories; Editing News.* Fees vary: £750/ 825 plus VAT for the beginners' courses; £365 plus VAT for *Better Feature Writing.*

pma Training, The Old Anchor, Church Street, Hemingford Grey, Cambridgeshire PE18 9DF (Tel 0480 300653). One, two or three-day editorial, PR and publishing courses held in central London. High-powered, intensive courses run by Keith Elliott, former Fleet Street journalist and magazine editor. Writers course include: *News Writing, Journalistic Style, Feature Writing, Writing Better Headlines, Sharpening Your Style, Investigate Reporting, Writing as A Freelance.* Fees range from about £180–400 plus VAT.

Polytechnic of Central London, Room 104, 35 Marylebone Road, London NW1 5LS (Tel 071–911 5000 ext. 3261). Various short courses in writing, including *Script Writing for Radio and Television*, a 10-week evening class which provides an introduction to writing techniques and related production processes. Students are required to do a scriptwriting exercise for sound production.

Screenwise International, 9 Chester Mews, Belgravia, London SW1X 7AJ (Tel 071–582 7998). Short courses in screenwriting. Applicants are required to submit a 1–3 pp sample of their creative or non-fiction writing. Contact the Course Administrator for details of fees.

Screenwriters Studio, c/o PACT, Gordon House, 10 Greencoat Place, London SW1P 1PH. High-powered, intensive, residential course for 12 professional screenwriters selected from nominations from within the industry. A non-profit making venture sponsored by industry organisations.

Scriptwriters Tutorials offers professional tuition to small numbers of writers who wish to learn scriptwriting for film/television/radio and stage. Group beginner, intermediate and advanced courses are available as well as individual tuition, script evaluation service and correspondence courses. Also weekend seminars and an annual writers' retreat in Gascony. For details send s. a. e. to, Stuart Browne, Director, Scriptwriters Tutorials, 65 Lancaster Road, London N4 4PL (Tel 071–272 2335).

The Writing School, 29 Turnpike Lane, London N8 0EP (Tel 081–342 8980). Correspondence course covering writing for articles, short stories, books, plays and scripts, with a strong emphasis on writing to sell. Fee (1992) £269. Contact the Director of Studies for enrolment details.

Manchester
The Writers Bureau, Sevendale House, 7 Dale Street, Manchester M1 1JB (Tel 061–228 2362). Comprehensive home-study writing course with personal tuition service from professional writers. Fee (1992) £219.

Newcastle upon Tyne
University of Newcastle upon Tyne, Centre for Continuing Education, Newcastle upon Tyne, NE1 7RU (Tel 091–222 6000). Writing-related courses include: *The Write Bite, Writing From the Inside Out, Word Processes: An Advanced Creative Course*. Courses run over 10 weeks and cost about £18. Contact the Secretary, Adult Education Programme.

Portsmouth
Higbury College of Technology, Dovercourt Road, Cosham, Portsmouth PO6 2SA (Tel 0705 383131). Radio and television journalism training. 1 year full-time course with various attachments to radio stations. Contact John Kendrick for full details.

Reading
University of Reading, Department of Extended Education, London Road, Reading RG1 5AQ (Tel 0734 318347). Evening courses over several weeks. The creative writing course, *Life into Fiction*, aims to encourage writing from participants' observation of life going on around them. Beginners welcome. Also two

further creative writing courses: *Coming out with it,* aimed at anyone who wants to write and needs feedback and encouragement from a group; and *Getting on with it,* designed for those who are already writing. Fees £49 (concessions available).

Sheffield

University of Sheffield, Division of Continuing Education, 85 Wilkinson Street, Sheffield, S10 2GJ (Tel 0742 768555, ext. 4920/1). Creative writing courses and workshops: fiction, writing for the media. Day and evening classes, residential courses.

Southampton

University of Southampton, Department of Adult Education, SO9 5NH (Tel 0703 595000). Creative writing course and writers' workshop, both morning classes lasting 10 weeks. Courses are held in local/regional centres.

Staffordshire

Keele University, Department of Adult and Continuing Education, Staffordshire ST5 5BG (Tel 0782 625116). Writing-related courses have included *Short Story Writing* and *Poetry Writing.*

Stirling

University of Stirling, Continuing Education, Airthrey Castle, Stirling FK9 4LA (Tel 0786 3171). Writers' workshop at Airthrey Castle on Monday mornings for 8 weeks. Covers writing for all media.

Suffolk

Fen Farm, 10 Angel Hill, Bury St Edmunds, Suffolk IP33 1UZ (Tel 0284 753110). Five-day residential courses from late afternoon Monday to Saturday morning. Courses have included *The Techniques of Writing Drama; Beginning to Write; Radio Plays; Poetry; Writing for Children.* Open to all over 16 who have a desire to write. Fee (including food, tuition and accommodation) £195. Funded by **Eastern Arts Board.** Grants may be available for those on low incomes.

Surrey

University of Surrey, Department of Educational Studies, Guildford Institute, Ward Street, Guildford, Surrey, GU1 4LH (Tel 0483 62142). Creative writing workshops held on Tuesday mornings for 20 weeks. Fee £69 (concessions available). Contact Louise Bray, Extra Mural Courses.

Sussex

University of Sussex, Centre for Continuing Education Centre, Education Development Building, Falmer, Brighton, BN1 9RG (Tel 0273 678040). Runs two day schools in *Writing for Radio.* Participants have use of the university's recording facilities. Scripts are read, recorded and then discussed on air. Fee about £20 for one day; £36 for two (concessions available).

Warwick

University of Warwick, Open Studies, Continuing Education Department, Coventry CV4 7AL (Tel 0203 523523). Creative writing courses held at the university or in regional centres. Beginners welcome. Five evening courses of 10 weeks and Saturday morning workshops at the university.

Worcester
Loch Ryan Writers, Loch Ryan Hotel, 119 Sidbury, Worcester, WR5 2DH (Tel 0905 351143). Weekend residential writing workshops commencing October 1992. Emphasis on poetry, but also prose and drama (contact Gwynneth Royce).

Yorkshire
ARTTS International, Highfield Grange, Bubwith, North Yorkshire YO8 7DP (Tel 0757 288088). Theatre, radio and screenwriting courses (initial concept through to script development). Contact Carolyn Graham, Promotions Manager.
The Arvon Foundation see **Professional Associations and Societies**.
Open College of the Arts, Houndhill, Worsbrough, Barnsley S70 6TU (Tel 0226 730495). The OCA correspondence course, *Starting to Write*, offers help and stimulus, without an emphasis on commercial success, from experienced writers/tutors. Contact Jennifer Barraclough.

Circles and Workshops

Regional Arts Boards
A nationwide network of writers' circles (hundreds of them, too many to list here) exists, designed to provide an informal atmosphere of mutual help and constructive criticism for writers of all grades. Your regional arts board can usually provide a comprehensive list of those in your area, and may also offer courses within its region. Some may offer training grants or bursaries to writers wishing to attend a residential course outside the region. See **Arts Councils and Regional Arts Boards** for listings.

Aireings Workshops, Headingley Hyde Park, Leeds. Regular monthly workshops on the second Monday of the month. Organised by Aireings Publications, 24 Brudenell Road, Leeds LS6 1BD (Tel 0532 785893).
BBC Writers' Workshops Following the demise of the BBC's Drama Script Unit last year, the BBC has established a series of specifically targeted workshops which are held throughout the year. Participants are selected on a competitive basis and number no more than six for any one event. Workshops, which are sponsored by various organisations, are presented by BBC script editors and producers. 1992 workshops included one for black women writers, plus writing for series and the writer-producer relationship. Workshops that are open to the public are advertised in the 'Noticeboard' section of the *Radio Times*. Contact the BBC Script Unit (Tel 081-743 8000).
Carmarthen Writers' Circle, Penpedwar, Llanllwni, Pencader, Dyfed SA39 9DW (Tel 055935 302). Contact Maggie Rothwell. Runs annual short story competition (see entry **Prizes**).
Chiltern Writers' Group invites writers, publishers, editors and agents to its monthly meetings. Contact Marina Oliver, Half Hidden, West Lane, Bledlow, Near Princes Risborough (Tel 0844 5973).

Directory of Writers' Circles, Oldacre, Horderns Park Road, Chapel en le Frith, Derbyshire SK12 6SY (Tel 0298 812305). Comprehensive directory of writers' circles, containing contacts and addresses of hundreds of groups and circles including postal circles, meeting throughout the country. Some overseas entries too. Published by **Laurence Pollinger Ltd** and available from editor Jill Dick at the above address (price £3. 00, post free).

The **Exeter & Devon Arts Centre**, Bradninch Place, Gandy Street, Exeter EX4 3LS (Tel 0392 219741) regularly hold workshops for writers. A copy of their quarterly programme of events is available from the Centre.

Gay Authors Workshop, BM Box 5700, London WC1N 3XX (Tel 071–520 5223). Established 1978 to encourage and support lesbian/gay writers. Regular meetings and a newsletter. Contact Kathryn Byrd. Membership £4; £2 unwaged.

Humberside Writer's Association Workshop see **Professional Associations and Societies**.

Liverpool Women Writers, The Old Police Station, Lark Lane, Liverpool 17. Established 1987. An informal, 'non-hierarchical' creative writing group. Meetings are held fortnightly on Tuesdays from 8.00 pm to 9.30 pm. Contact: Elspeth on 051–734 2069; Shirley or Suzanne on 051–727 2739.

London Screenwriters' Workshop, 1 Greek Street, London W1V 6NQ (Tel 071–434 0942/ 081–551 5570). Established by writers in 1983 as a forum for contact, information and tuition. LSW helps new and established writers in the film, TV and video industries. Organises a continuous programme of workshops, events with industry figures, seminars and courses. Contact Ray Frensham. Membership £18 p. a.

Merseyside Association of Writers Workshops, 12 Aspinall Street, Prescot, Merseyside. Member organisation for many writers' workshops in the region. Contact Michael Kirkland on 051–426 0188 for listing.

Merseyside Trade Union Community and Unemployed Resource Centre Playwrights' Workshop, MTUCURC, 24 Hardman Street, Liverpool, L1 9AX (Tel 051–709 3995 ext. 250). Workshops for theatre held at the University of Liverpool on Wednesdays for 20 weeks.

Outwrite — South Humberside Writing Project, Scunthorpe Central Library, Carlton Street, Scunthorpe, South Humberside, DN15 7LU (Tel 0724860161). Regular creative writing workshops run jointly with the **Workers' Educational Association** (see below) in Grimsby, Barton upon Humber (both fortnightly) and Scunthorpe (monthly). Groups are tutor-led and run for one year. Also day/weekend workshops; performance tours by visiting writers and poets; open days with local creative writing magazines; and schools creative writing workshops. Contact Jonathan Davidson.

Playwrights' Workshop, 22 Brown Street, Altrincham, Cheshire, WA14 2EU (Tel 061–928 3095). Monthly meetings see **Small Presses**. Readings, Guest speakers, etc.

Southport Writers' Circle, 53 Richmond Road, Birkdale, Southport, Merseyside PR8 4SB. Contact Alison Chisholm. Runs poetry competition (see entry **Prizes**).

Speakeasy invites poets and writers to Milton Keynes most months (contact Carol Bara, Speakeasy, 19 Carwardon, Stantonbury, Milton Keynes, MK14 6AH (Tel 0908 310066 evenings).

Workers' Educational Association National Office: Temple House, 9 Upper Berkeley Street, London W1H 8BY. London regional office (covering London, Middlesex, Surrey, part of Essex and part of Hertfordshire): 32 Tavistock

Square, London, WC1H 9EZ (Tel 071–387 8966). The WEA is a nationwide voluntary body with members drawn from all walks of life. It was founded in 1903 to bring higher education to more people. It runs writing courses and workshops throughout the country and all courses are open to everyone. Branches in most towns and many villages, with 19 district offices covering the whole of the UK. WEA districts appoint and pay their own tutors and are responsible for the quality of the education in their classes. Contact your district WEA office for courses in your region.

Editorial, Research and other Services

Lesley & Roy Adkins
Longstone Lodge, Aller, Langport,
Somerset TA10 0QT
☎ 0458 250075   Fax 0458 250858

Contact *Lesley Adkins/Roy Adkins*

Offers indexing, research, editing, manuscript criticism/advice, contract writing for publishers, proofreading, book reviews and feature writing. *Special interests* archaeology (worldwide), history and heritage.

Arioma Editorial Services
Gloucester House, High Street, Borth,
Dyfed SY24 5HZ
☎ 0970 871296

Contact *Moira Smith*

FOUNDED 1987. Staffed by ex-London journalists, who work mainly with authors wanting to self-publish. Editing, indexing, ghost writing, cover design, plus initial help with marketing and publicity. Sample chapter and synopsis required. All types of book welcome, but work must be of a 'sufficiently high standard'. No reading fee. Rates on application.

Astron Appointments Ltd
20–24 Uxbridge Street, London W8 7TA
☎ 071–229 6423/9171   Fax 071–221 7594

Contact *Nicole Brenchley/John Broom/Deborah Rea/Roger Stacey*

In addition to a long-standing register of permanent job-seekers within publishing, Astron now have a freelance register with details of a large number of people available to undertake all types of freelance assignments within the publishing field.

Authors' Research Services (ARS)
32 Oak Village, London NW5 4QN
☎ 071–284 4316   Fax 071–284 4316

Contact *Richard Wright*

Research and document supply service, particularly to authors, academics and others without easy access to London libraries and sources of information. Also indexing of books and journals. Rates negotiable.

Booksprint
252 Goswell Road, London EC1V 7EB
☎ 081–341 7650   Fax 081–490 1344

Contact *Ann Kritzinger*

Print production service to self-publishers. Recently acquired an electronic printing machine which offers a quick print service with lower production costs. Keen to work with self publishers. Associated editing and reading service called **Scriptmate** (see entry this section).

Bucks Literary Services
73 Vicarage Road, Marsworth, Near Tring,
Hertfordshire HP23 4LU
☎ 0296 668630

Contact *Anne Stobbs*

Offers editing, advisory and secretarial assistance to authors. Reasonable terms and a speedy service.

Graham Burn Productions
9–13 Soulbury Road, Linslade, Leighton Buzzard,
Bedfordshire LU7 2RL
☎ 0525 377963/376390   Fax 0525 382498

Offers complete production services to writers wishing to publish their own material, and pre-press services to other publishers.

Carter Rae Communications
15 Moray Place, Edinburgh EH3 6DT
☎ 031–225 9979   Fax 031–220 2895

Contact *Jenny Carter/Janet Rae*

Specialises in the production of newspapers and magazines for commerce and industry. Full editorial service: writing, editing, proof-reading, etc. Rates on application.

Deeson Editorial Services

100 Grove Vale, London SE22 8DR
☏081-693 3383   Fax 081-299 0862
Also at: Ewell House, Faversham, Kent ME13 8UP
☏0795 535468   Fax 0795 535469

Contacts *Dr Tony Deeson/Tracey Inge/Dominic Deeson*

ESTABLISHED 1959. A comprehensive research/ writing/editing service for books, magazines, newspapers, articles, annual reports, submissions, presentations. Design and production facilities. Specialists in scientific, technical, industrial and business-to-business subjects.

Fern House Publications

19 High Street, Haddenham, Ely,
Cambridgeshire CB6 3XA
☏0353 741229   Fax 0353 741601

Partners *Rodney Dale/Henry Dale*

Rodney Dale is a widely published author and producer of published matter, and series editor for *Discoveries & Inventions* for the British Library. Fern House deals mainly with scientific and technical material, but has also handled biography, jazz and folklore. Offers consultancy and practical help at all stages — editorial and artistic — of the publishing chain.

Gordon Jarvie Editorial

81 Comiston Drive, Edinburgh EH10 5QT
☏031-447 3417

Contact *Gordon Jarvie*

Full range of editorial and research services, including authorship, editing, proofreading, blurb writing, indexing, market analyses, etc. Also literary agency (see **UK Agents**).

Deborah Manley

57 Plantation Road, Oxford OX2 6JE
☏0865 310284   Fax 0865 59671

Contact *Deborah Manley*

Specialises in book publishing, mainly educational, children's, reference and travel. Offers project management, editorial reports, copy-editing, writing, rewriting, research, indexing, proof-reading, and caption copy. NUJ rates.

Northern Writers Advisory Services (NWAS)

77 Marford Crescent, Sale, Cheshire M33 4DN
☏061-969 1573

Contact *Jill Groves*

Offers publishing services such as copy-editing, proof-reading, word-processing and desktop publishing (with laser printing). Does much of its work with societies (mainly local history), and small presses. NWAS's specialist subject is history of all types, but especially local and family history; also take on biographies, books on computer software, and leisure books. Rates on application, but very reasonable.

Out of Print Book Service

13 Pantbach Road, Birchgrove, Cardiff CF4 1TU
☏0222 627703

Contact *L. A. Foulkes*

FOUNDED 1971. Covers all subjects including fiction and non-fiction. No charge for search. Write for details.

Plain Words (Business Writers)

96 Wellmeadow Road, London SE6 1HW
☏081-698 5269/697 3227   Fax 081-461 5705

Contact *Henry Galgut/Judy Byrne*

Offers writing, editing, design and printing services for industrial, commercial, public and other organisations: newsletters, brochures, handbooks, publicity material, press releases, etc., plus in-house business letter-writing workshops tailored to clients' needs. Fees depend on the nature and extent of the work.

David Pritchard Editorial

2 Dalmally Close, Acomb Park, York YO2 2XS
☏0904 705030

Contact *David Pritchard*

Editor, writer, researcher and advice service. Trained journalist; academic and creative writer with experience in newspapers, TV, radio, conference reports, newsletter, PR, etc.

Readers

46 Fordyce Road, Hartlepool,
Cleveland TS25 4DD

Contact *Preston Ward/Marc Capetian*

FOUNDED 1992. Reading/editing service in contact with London agents for writers of fiction. Offers constructive and objective reading/editing for beginners and intermediate writers. Service includes: detailed chapter analysis; hints on character building and plot construction; advice on grammar, spelling and punctuation. Provides reading list for writers wishing to study 'the cream' of a particular genre, and will suggest/contact publishers/agents for clients. Strictly one-to-one relationship, with regular correspondence to assist writers. £55 fee per mss (postage extra). All enquiries must be accompanied by s.a.e. for prompt reply.

Reading & Righting (Robert Lambolle Services)

618B Finchley Road, London NW11 7RR
☎081-455 4564   Fax 081-209 1231

Reader/literary editor, with agency, publisher and theatre experience. Offers detailed manuscript evaluation, analysis of prospects and next-step guidelines. Fiction, non-fiction, drama and screenplays. Also editorial services. Write with s.a.e. for further information and terms.

Scriptmate

252 Goswell Road, London EC1V 7EB
☎081-341 7650   Fax 081-490 1344

Contact *Ann Kritzinger*

Writers' advisory service. Professional editing and readers-for-writers service. Associated with **Booksprint** print production service (see entry this section), and publishes under the imprint Scriptmate Editions which, in 1989, held the *Guinness Book of Records* world title for fastest publisher.

Howard Seddon Associates

BM Box 1129, London WC1N 3XX
☎0923 229784

Contact *Dr Keith Seddon*

FOUNDED 1988. Editorial, general advice and writing service for authors, publishers and businesses. Editing, copy-editing, proofreading, blurb copy, ghostwriting, copy-writing, indexing, for books,

journals, reports, brochures and promotional leaflets. Reading and appraisal service for authors who require objective assessment. Report service for publishers. Rates negotiable. Affiliated to HSA Authors' Agents.

Strand Editorial Services

16 Mitchley View, South Croydon,
Surrey CR2 9HQ
☎081-657 1247

Contact *Derek Bradley*

All stages of editorial production of house journals, magazines, newsletters, publicity material, etc. Short-term, long-term, and emergency projects. Sub-editing and proof-reading, and book reviews (educational, training and business). Reasonable rates (negotiable).

Writerlink

5 Clipstone Street, London W1P 7EB
☎071-323 4323   Fax 071-323 0286

Contact *Richard Paine/Charles Dawes/John Hare/ Keiren Phelan*

Offers professional reading and report service, plus information on editing. Rates on application.

The Writers' Exchange

14 Yewdale, Clifton Green, Swinton M27 2GN

Contact *The Secretary*

FOUNDED 1978. Reading and appraisal service for writers preparing to submit material to, or having had material rejected by, literary agents and/or publishers. Offers 'constructive, objective evaluation service, particularly for those who can't get past the standard rejection slip barrier, or who have had mss rejected by publishers and need an impartial view of why it did not sell.' Novels, short stories, film, TV, radio, and stage plays. Reading fee £3.25 per 1000 words; Initial Appraisal £35. Send s.a.e. for details.

Press Cuttings Agencies

Durrant's Press Cuttings

103 Whitecross Street, London EC1Y 8QT
☎ 071-588 3671   Fax 071-374 8171

Covers national/London dailies; London/Greater London weeklies; provincial dailies, weeklies and Sundays; Scottish/Welsh/Channel Isles papers; free sheets; consumer magazines; specialised and trade publications; foreign press in association with agencies abroad. Cuttings are posted twice weekly by first class mail. Rates are fully comprehensive; no additional charges such as reading fee. Minimum rate (about £125 plus VAT) covers 100 cuttings or lasts 6 months, whichever is sooner.

International Press-Cutting Bureau

224-236 Walworth Road, London SE17 1JE
☎ 071-708 2113   Fax 071-701 4489

Contact *Robert Podro*

Covers national, provincial, trade, technical and magazine press. Cuttings are normally sent twice weekly by first class post and there are no additional service charges or reading fees. Subscriptions for 100 and 250 cuttings are valid for six months. Larger subscriptions expire after one year even if the total number of cuttings subscribed for has not been reached. 100 cuttings (£136, plus VAT); 200 (£260, plus VAT).

Lincoln Hannah Ltd MediaScan

89½ Worship Street, London EC2A 2BE
☎ 071-377 1742/247 5513   Fax 071-377 6103

Overnight press cutting service, covering dailies, regionals, Sundays, and trade press, plus Scottish regionals, dailies and Sundays, and European press. Monthly reading fee (£29.15), delivery fee, plus cost per cutting (UK material: 81p unmounted, £1.04 mounted). European rates on application.

Premium Monitoring Ltd

139 Tooley Street, London SE1 2HZ
☎ 071-403 6033   Fax 071-407 5857

Contact *Sandra Appleyard/Christopher Banner/ Sarah Wait*

Press cuttings service — overnight monitoring, same-day service, early morning delivery. National and regional dailies, plus business and consumer publications covered. Rates on application.

Romeike & Curtice

Hale House, 290-296 Green Lanes,
London N13 5TP
☎ 081-882 0155   Fax 081-882 6716

Contact *Angela Webb*

Covers national and international dailies and Sundays, provincial papers, consumer magazines, trade and technical journals, national radio/TV logs and teletext services. Back research and advertising checking services are also available.

Timms Premium

139 Tooley Street, London EC4A 2DQ
☎ 071-403 6033   Fax 071-407 5857

Contact *Sarah Wait*

National, international, and provincial papers, plus weekly and monthly trade magazines. Rates on application.

We Find It (Press Clippings)

103 South Parade, Belfast BT7 2GN
☎ 0232 646008

Contact *Avril Forsythe-Clarke*

Specialises in Northern Ireland press and magazines, both national and provincial. Rates on application.

Bursaries, Fellowships and Grants

Aosdàna Scheme

The Arts Council (An Chomhairle Ealaíon), 70 Merrion Square, Dublin 2, Republic of Ireland
☎010 353 1 611840   Fax 010 353 1 761302

Contact *Literature Officer*

Aosdàna is an affiliation of creative artists engaged in literature, music and the visual arts, and consists of not more than 150 artists who have gained a reputation for achievement and distinction. Membership is by competitive sponsored selection and is open to Irish citizens or residents only. Members are eligible to receive an annuity for a five-year term to assist them in pursuing their art full-time.
Award IR£6000 (annuity)

Arts Council Theatre Writing Bursaries

14 Great Peter Street, London SW1P 3NQ
☎071-333 0100   Fax 071-973 6590

Contact *Drama Director*

Intended to provide experienced playwrights with an opportunity to research and develop a play for the theatre independently of financial pressures and free from the need to write for a particular market. Writers must be resident in England. Writers resident in Wales, Scotland or Northern Ireland should approach their own Arts Council. Closing date for applications mid-January 1993.
Award £3000.

Arts Council Writers' Bursaries

14 Great Peter Street, London SW1P 3NQ
☎071-333 0100   Fax 071-973 6590

Contact *Literature Department*

The Arts Council now offers twelve bursaries a year to the value of £6000 each. Applications need to be in by 31 September and should be accompanied by a c.v., description and sample of work in progress, statement of annual income and three copies of a previously published creative work. Judges will make their choices principally on the grounds of artistic quality, basing that judgment on their reading of work in progress and evidence

before them of the writer's past achievement. Previous award winners include: Biyi Bandele-Thomas, Deborah Levy, Mary Scott, Atima Srivastava, Harry Tait, Ruel White, Michael Donaghy, Carol Ann Duffy, Sean O'Brien, Peter Sansom, Matthew Sweeney, Meirion & Susan Harries (jointly).
Award up to £6000.

The Authors' Contingency Fund

The Society of Authors, 84 Drayton Gardens, London SW10 9SB
☎071-373 6642   Fax 071-373 5768

This fund makes modest grants to published authors who find themselves in sudden financial difficulties.

The Authors' Foundation

The Society of Authors, 84 Drayton Gardens, London SW10 9SB
☎071-373 6642   Fax 071-373 5768

Annual grants to writers whose publisher's advance is insufficient to cover the costs of research involved. Application by letter to The Authors' Foundation giving details, in confidence, of the advance and royalties, together with the reasons for needing additional funding. Final entry date each year is 30 June. Total of £35,000 available.

The K. Blundell Trust

The Society of Authors, 84 Drayton Gardens, London SW10 9SB
☎071-373 6642   Fax 071-373 5768

Annual grants to writers whose publisher's advance is insufficient to cover the costs of research. Author must be under 40, has to submit copy of his/her previous book and the work must 'contribute to the greater understanding of existing social and economic organisation'. Application by letter. Final entry date each year is 30 June. Total of £15,000 available.

British Academy Publication Subventions

20–21 Cornwall Terrace, London NW1 4QP
☏ 071–487 5966   Fax 071–224 3807

Contact *Assistant Secretary, Research Grants*

Thrice-yearly award to help defray production costs of scholarly publications which might otherwise not succeed in finding a publisher. Work to be published must be a serious contribution to scholarship and the applicant must have secured a publisher prior to application. Subventions do not normally exceed 25% (up to a maximum of £2000) of the direct costs of production, excluding any element of publisher's overheads. Awards are made either in the form of an interest-free loan, repayable from the proceeds of sales, or in certain circumstances, in the form of an outright grant. Final entry dates: 1 September; 30 November; 28 February.

British Academy Small Personal Research Grants

20–21 Cornwall Terrace, London NW1 4QP
☏ 071–487 5966   Fax 071–224 3807

Contact *Assistant Secretary, Research Grants*

Quarterly award to further original creative research at postdoctoral level in the humanities and social sciences. Entrants must no longer be registered for postgraduate study, and must be resident in the UK. Final entry dates end of September, November, February and April.
Award maximum £5000.

Bursaries in Literature

The Arts Council (An Chomhairle Ealaíon), 70 Merrion Square, Dublin 2, Republic of Ireland
☏ 010 353 1 611840   Fax 010 353 1 761302

Contact *Literature Officer*

Annual competition awarded to creative writers (fiction, poetry, drama) to enable concentration on, or completion of, specific projects. Final entry date each year is 15 April. Open to Irish citizens or residents only.
Award £2000–£7000.

Cholmondeley Awards

The Society of Authors, 84 Drayton Gardens, London SW10 9SB
☏ 071–373 6642   Fax 071–373 5768

FOUNDED 1965 by the late Dowager Marchioness of Cholmondeley. Annual non-competitive awards for the benefit and encouragement of poets of any age,

sex or nationality, for which submissions are not required. Presentation date June. 1992 winners: Allen Curnow, Donald Davie, Carol Ann Duffy, Roger Woddis.
Award (total) £8000, usually shared.

The Economist/Richard Casement Internship

The Economist, 25 St James's Street, London SW1A 1HG
☏ 071–839 7000

Contact *Business Affairs Editor* (re Casement Internship)

For a journalist under 24 to spend three months in the summer writing for *The Economist* about science and technology. Applicants should write a letter of introduction along with an article of approximately 600 words suitable for inclusion in the Science and Technology Section. Competition details normally announced in the magazine late January and 5–6 weeks allowed for application.

European Cultural Foundation

Jan van Goyenkade 5, Amsterdam, Netherlands 1075 HN
☏ 010 31 20 760222   Fax 010 31 20 752231

Contact *James Took MBE*, Director, UK National Committee, Pilgrims, Appledore, Near Ashford, Kent TN26 2AE
☏ 023383 215

Grants programme supporting multinational European projects that involve the active participation of non-profit making bodies from at least three, preferably more, European countries. Endeavours to increase awareness of the European dimension of our societies. Concerned primarily with basic values, culture, education, environment, the media, and the problems of European society in general (including East–West relations). Grants awarded for one year as part of total cost of forthcoming projects (not given retrospectively). Application direct to General Secretariat in Amsterdam, after consultation with James Took (see Contact above).

E. M. Forster Award

American Academy & Institute of Arts & Letters, 633 West 155 Street, New York NY 10032-7599, USA

An award given from time to time to an English writer to enable the writer to spend time in the United States. The award is funded by American publication rights of E. M. Forster's posthumously published novel, *Maurice*, transferred to the Academy-Institute by Christopher Isherwood.

Timothy Mo was awarded £12,500 in 1992, in return for which he will visit the US in the next two years and report on his visit.
Award varies.

Fulbright-Chandler Arts Fellowship Award

The Fulbright Commission, 6 Porter Street, London W1M 2HR
☎ 071-486 7697   Fax 071-224 4567

Contact *Programme Director*

Award for detective and spy fiction writing to an American writer to study and research in the UK. Offered by the Fulbright Commission in association with the Raymond Chandler Estate to commemorate the centenary of Raymond Chandler. Candidates need to demonstrate that a period of work or study in the UK can be expected to contribute significantly to his or her future work and to an enhancement of Anglo-American cultural understanding. Closing date 1 March. 1992 winner: Ian Rankin.
Award air travel and grant (£10,000 in 91/92).

Funding for Script Development

39C Highbury Place, Highbury, London N5 1QP
☎ 071-226 9903   Fax 071-354 2706

Contact *Philip Hughes*

ESTABLISHED 1989. Triennial award to provide financial support for the writing of screenplays and for pre-production in the area of fiction intended for the cinema or TV. Open to members of the European Community, Austria, Switzerland, and EFTA countries.

Glaxo Science Writers' Fellowships

Association of British Science Writers, c/o British Association for the Advancement of Science, Fortress House, 23 Savile Row, London W1X 1AB
☎ 071-494 3326   Fax 071-734 1658

Contact *Sue Lowell*

A series of annual awards for outstanding science journalism in newspapers, journals and broadcasting.

Eric Gregory Trust Fund

The Society of Authors, 84 Drayton Gardens, London SW10 9SB
☎ 071-373 6642   Fax 071-373 5768

Annual competitive awards of varying amounts are made each year for the encouragement of young poets under the age of 30 who can show that they are likely to benefit from an opportunity to give more time to writing. Open only to British-born subjects resident in the UK. Final entry date 31 October. Presentation date June. 1992 winners: Jill Dawson, Hugh Dunkerley, Christopher Greenhalgh, Marita Maddah, Stuart Paterson, Stuart Pickford.
Award (total) £31,000.

The Guardian Research Fellowship

Nuffield College, Oxford OX1 1NF
☎ 0865 278520   Fax 0865 278621

Contact *Warden's Secretary*

One-year Fellowship endowed by the Scott Trust, owner of *The Guardian*, to give someone working in the media the chance to put their experience into a new perspective, publish the outcome and give a *Guardian* lecture. Applications welcomed from journalists and management members, in newspapers, periodicals or broadcasting. Research or study proposals should be directly related to experience of working in the media. Accommodation and meals in college will be provided, and a 'modest' supplementary stipend might be arranged to ensure the Fellow does not lose out from the stay. Advertised annually in November.

Francis Head Bequest

The Society of Authors, 84 Drayton Gardens, London SW10 9SB
☎ 071-373 6642   Fax 071-373 5768

Designed to provide grants to established British authors over the age of 35 who need financial help during a period of illness, disablement or temporary financial crisis.

The Independent Student Journalist Bursary

40 City Road, London EC1Y 2DB
☎ 071-253 1222   Fax 071-956 1435

Contact *Head of Personnel*

A number of bursaries are available for graduate trainee journalists to join the nine-month Newspaper Journalism Diploma Course at the City University Graduate Centre for Journalism, starting September. Bursaries will cover the course fee, plus £3500 living expenses. The course will include a period of attachment to an editorial department at *The Independent*. Applicants must be recent graduates or in the final year of a course leading to a degree or equivalent qualification. Details on how to apply are available from the Head of Personnel. Enquiries should be marked 'Graduate Trainee'.

Closing date February. Advertisement inviting applications is published in the paper from the beginning of January.

Ralph Lewis Award

University of Sussex Library, Brighton BN1 9QL
☎ 0273 678158   Fax 0273 678441

ESTABLISHED 1985. Triennial award set up by Ralph Lewis, a Brighton author and art collector who left money to fund awards for promising manuscripts which would not otherwise be published. The award is given in the form of a grant to a UK-based publisher in respect of an agreed 3-year programme of publication of literary works by new authors or by established authors using new styles or forms. No direct applications from writers. Next award 1995. Previous winners: **Peterloo Poets** (1989-91); **Serpent's Tail** (1992-94).

Macaulay Fellowship

The Arts Council (An Chomhairle Ealaíon), 70 Merrion Square, Dublin 2, Republic of Ireland
☎ 010 353 1 611840   Fax 010 353 1 761302

Contact *Literature Officer*

To further the liberal education of a young creative artist. Candidates for this triennial award must be under 30 on 30 June, or 35 in exceptional circumstances, and must be Irish citizens or residents. Last awarded 1990.
Award £3500.

McColl Arts Foundation Bursaries

McColl Arts Foundation, London W1M 5FM
☎ 071-935 4788

Contact *Alastair Creamer* (Managing Director)

The McColl Arts Foundation is offering 26 grants to those pursuing careers in all areas of the arts. The aim is to encourage artists to create work inspired by their 'residence' in another country. Bursaries are open to all students, postgraduates and other artists living in the British Isles.

The John Masefield Memorial Trust

The Society of Authors, 84 Drayton Gardens, London SW10 9SB
☎ 071-373 6642   Fax 071-373 5768

This trust makes occasional grants to professional poets (or their immediate dependents) who are faced with sudden financial problems.

Somerset Maugham Trust Fund

The Society of Authors, 84 Drayton Gardens, London SW10 9SB
☎ 071-373 6642   Fax 071-373 5768

The annual awards arising from this Fund are designed to encourage young writers to travel and to acquaint themselves with the manners and customs of other countries. Candidates must be under 35 and submit a published literary work in volume form in English. They must be British subjects by birth. Final entry date 31 December. Presentation in June. 1992 winners: Geoff Dyer *But Beautiful*; Lawrence Norfolk *Lemprière's Dictionary*; Gerard Woodward *Householder*. *Award* £5000 each.

Mobil Bursary

Royal Exchange Theatre, St Ann's Square, Manchester M2 7DH
☎ 061-833 9333   Fax 061-832 0881

Contact *Mobil Bursary*

A bursary of £10,000 to fund a writer-in-residence for one year at the **Royal Exchange Theatre**. The bursary may be awarded to one of the winners of the **Mobil Playwriting Competition** or to any entrant who shows potential through fresh and vivid writing.

National Poetry Foundation Grants

(Registered charity no: 283032)
27 Mill Road, Fareham, Hampshire PO16 0TH
☎ 0329 822218

Contact *Johnathon Clifford*

The **National Poetry Foundation** considers applications for grant aid of up to £1000 where other funding is not available and the product will benefit poetry in general. Send details together with s.a.e. to NPF (Grants) at the above address.

The Airey Neave Trust

The Airey Neave Trust, 40 Bernard Street, London WC1N 1LG
☎ 071-837 0460   Fax 071-833 4102

Contact *Hannah Scott*

INITIATED 1989. Annual research fellowships for up to three years — towards a book or paper — for serious research connected with national and international law, and human freedom. Attached to a particular university — those involved include the universities of: London, Cambridge and Oxford, plus The Queen's University, Belfast. Interested applicants should come forward with ideas at the beginning of the year, preferably before March.

New Horizons

The Calouste Gulbenkian Foundation, 98 Portland Place, London W1N 4ET

Contact *Administrator, New Horizons*

New Horizons is a new bursary scheme designed to help established artists work in a new art form. It is open to writers and artists across all media forms. Applicants must be established in their own art form, resident in the UK and have a strong desire to work in a new art form. If you are a novelist, for example, and want to write plays or an opera libretto, you are eligible for New Horizons, but the intention to change art forms must amount to more than just a one-off project. Applications particularly welcome from women and minority ethnic groups. Successful applicants will be expected to undertake a period of research in the new area of work and will be required to write a report for the Foundation on completion. About 6–7 awards a year are envisaged. Final entry date in April.
Award about £2000–3000 (maximum £5000).

Newspaper Press Fund

Dickens House, 35 Wathen Road, Dorking, Surrey RH4 1JY
☎0306 887511 Fax 0306 76104

Director/Secretary *Peter Evans*

Aims to relieve distress among journalists and their dependants. Limited help available to non-member journalists. Continuous and/or occasional financial grants; also retirement homes for eligible beneficiaries. Information and subscription details available from The Secretary.

Northern Arts Literary Fellowship

Northern Arts, 10 Osborne Terrace, Jesmond, Newcastle upon Tyne NE2 1NZ
☎091-281 6334 Fax 091-281 3276

Contact *Published & Broadcast Arts Department*

A competitive fellowship tenable at and co-sponsored by the universities of Durham and Newcastle upon Tyne for a period of two academic years.
Award £12,000 p.a.

Northern Arts Writers Awards

Northern Arts, 10 Osborne Terrace, Jesmond, Newcastle upon Tyne NE2 1NZ
☎091-281 6334 Fax 091-281 3276

Contact *Published & Broadcast Arts Department*

Awards are offered to established authors resident in the **Northern Arts** area on basis of literary merit. Application spring/ summer. Also available, one-month residencies at Tyrone Guthrie Centre, Ireland.
Award variable.

Oppenheim John Downes Memorial Trust

36 Whitefriars Street, London EC4Y 8BH

Grants to writers and artists of all descriptions who are over the age of 30 and unable to pursue their vocation by reason of their poverty. Applicants must be British by birth and of British parents and grandparents. Awards made annually in December. Final application date 1 November.
Grant variable, but usually between £50 and £1500.

Prometheus Award

British Museum Press, 46 Bloomsbury Street, London WC1B 3QQ
☎071-323 1234

Contact *Alasdair Macleod*

FOUNDED 1991. Annual award for the most outstanding synopsis for a first book by a young author in the field of archaeology, ethnography or ancient history. The aim of the award is to counter the tendency to specialisation among young writers and encourage them to think across disciplinary boundaries or a wide historical time-scale. 1991 winner: Richard Rudgley for his synopsis of *The Alchemy of Culture: Intoxicants in Society* which entails a worldwide historical and geographical study of intoxicant use, drawing on ethnographic and archaeological data. Due for publication by **British Museum Press** in spring 1993. Requests for submissions for the 1993 award will be made early in the year. Entrants must be under 35 on or before 31 July each year, and must be citizens of the UK, with resident status. Final entry date end July.
Prize Bursary of £2000 towards completion of the work, plus publishing contract.

The Margaret Rhondda Award

The Society of Authors, 84 Drayton Gardens, London SW10 9SB
☎071-373 6642 Fax 071-373 5768

Competitive award given to a woman writer as a grant-in-aid towards the expenses of a research project in journalism. Triennial, next award 1993. Final entry date 31 December. Presentation date

June. 1990 awards: Mary Loudon (£500); Clare Jenkins (£250).

Award (total) £750.

The Royal Literary Fund

144 Temple Chambers, Temple Avenue, London EC4Y 0DT
☎ 071-353 7150

Secretary *Mrs Fiona Clark*

Makes grants to published authors of approved literary merit on the basis of financial need. For further details and application form, write to the above address.

Scottish Arts Council Bursaries and Awards

See **Regional and Other Arts Associations**

Southern Arts Literature Bursaries

13 St Clement Street, Winchester, Hampshire SO23 9DQ
☎ 0962 855099   Fax 0962 861186

Contact *Literature Officer*

Southern Arts Literature Panel offers three bursaries of £1000 annually to writers living in the region to enable them at an early or critical stage in their career to set aside time to work on a specific project. Awards can be used to cover a period of unpaid leave while writing from home, to finance necessary research and travel, or to purchase equipment.

Laurence Stern Fellowship

Graduate Centre for Journalism, City University, Northampton Square, London EC1V 0HB
☎ 071-477 8000

Contact *Robert Jones*

Awarded to a young journalist experienced enough to work on national stories. It gives them the chance to work on the national desk of the *Washington Post*. Benjamin Bradlee, the *Post's* Vice-President, selects from a shortlist drawn up in March/April.

The Sunday Times Fellowship

1 Pennington Street, London E1 9XW

Contact *Michael Williams* (Managing Editor, News)

For anyone from an African, Asian or Caribbean background, *The Sunday Times* is offering a fellowship to help develop journalistic skills. Applications are sought from young people who have already started on a journalistic career or from graduates leaving university with experience of student newspapers. Formal training and practical experience alongside staff journalists will be given.

Thames Television Theatre Writers' Scheme

Teddington Lock, Teddington, Middlesex TW11 9NT
☎ 081-948 1154

Contact *Jack Andrews*

Awards bursaries to playwrights. Applicants must be sponsored by a theatre which then submits the play for consideration by a panel. 1991 winners: James Stock (RSC); Paul Sirett (Theatre Royal Stratford); Roy MacGregor (Bush Theatre); Martin Sadofski (Royal National); Yasmin Judd (Talawa Theatre). Each award allows the playwright a twelve-month attachment but following the recent reallocation of television franchises, the scheme is currently under review. For up-to-date information, contact Jack Andrews, the Administrator, on the above telephone number.

David Thomas Prize

The Financial Times, 1 Southwark Bridge, London SE1 9HL
☎ 081-873 3000

Deputy Managing Editor *Robin Pauley*

FOUNDED 1991. Annual award in memory of David Thomas, FT journalist killed on assignment in Kuwait in April 1991, 'whose life was characterised by original and radical thinking coupled with a search for new subjects and orthodoxies to challenge'. The award will provide an annual study/travel grant to enable the recipient to take a career break to explore a theme in the fields of industrial policy, Third World development or the environment. Entrants may be aged 21–30, of any nationality, and must not be engaged in full-time education. A given theme which changes from year to year is announced in the early autumn. 1992 theme: 'What will the collapse of communism do to the environment?'. Entrants should submit 500 words on the theme, together with a brief c.v. and proposal outlining how the award could be used to explore the theme further. Award winners will be required to write an essay of 1500–2000 words at the end of the study period; the essay will be considered for

publication in the newspaper. Final entry date (1992) 31 December.
Prize £2000 travel grant.

Tom-Gallon Trust

The Society of Authors, 84 Drayton Gardens, London SW10 9SB
☏ 071-373 6642 Fax 071-373 5768

A biennial award is made from this Trust Fund to fiction writers of limited means who have had at least one short story accepted. Authors wishing to enter should send a list of their already published fiction, giving the name of the publisher or periodical in each case and the approximate date of publication; one published short story; a brief statement of their financial position; an undertaking that they intend to devote a substantial amount of time to the writing of fiction as soon as they are financially able to do so; and an s.a.e. for the return of work submitted. Next entry date 20 September 1994. Presentation date June.
Award £500.

The Betty Trask Awards

The Society of Authors, 84 Drayton Gardens, London SW10 9SB
☏ 071-373 6642 Fax 071-373 5768

These annual awards are for authors who are under 35 and Commonwealth citizens, awarded on the strength of a first novel (published or unpublished) of a traditional or romantic (rather than experimental) nature. The awards must be used for a period or periods of foreign travel. Final entry date 31 January. Presentation June. 1992 winners: Liane Jones *The Dream Stone;* Peter Rosenberg *Kissing Through a Pane of Glass;* Edward St Aubyn *Never Mind;* Tibor Fishcher *Under the Frog;* Eugene Mullan *The Last of his Line.*
Award (total) £25,000.

The Travelling Scholarships

The Society of Authors, 84 Drayton Gardens, London SW10 9SB
☏ 071-373 6642 Fax 071-373 5768

Annual, non-competitive awards for the benefit of British authors, to enable them to travel abroad. 1992 winners: Anne Devlin, Elaine Feinstein, Iain Sinclair, Emma Tennant.
Award (total) £6000.

UEA Writing Fellowship

University of East Anglia, University Plain, Norwich NR4 7JT
☏ 0603 592810

Contact *Lorna Sage* (English & American Studies)

Awarded to a writer of established reputation in any field, usually for the period of the Summer term. The duties of the Fellowship are discussed at an interview. It is assumed that one activity will be the pursuit of the Fellow's own writing. In addition the Fellow will be expected to (a) offer an undergraduate creative writing course in the School of English and American Studies during the Summer term, and to read and grade work received; (b) offer fifteen less formal sessions of 1 hour or more made up of readings, workshops, tutorials, and/or visits to seminars; (c) arrange, with help from UEA and Eastern Arts, additional visits and readings by other writers from outside the University. It is hoped that (b) and (c) above will involve students from the University as a whole; and in some cases participants from the city and the region. Applications for the Fellowship should be lodged with the Administrative Secretary by 15 November each year.
Award £2500 (under review).

Arthur Welton Scholarship

Society of Authors, 84 Drayton Gardens, London SW10 9SB
☏ 071-373 6642 Fax 071-373 5768

Contact *The Secretary*

Funded by the Canadian author Arthur Welton, the Arthur Welton Foundation is offering a scholarship worth up to £10,000 to a talented creative writer to enable the writer to concentrate for a certain period on writing without having to earn a living. Applicants must be a permanent UK or Irish resident, have been commissioned by a British publisher to write a full-length work of fiction (including short stories), poetry, biography, autobiography or play. No crime stories or thrillers. Application by letter to the Society of Authors giving an outline and schedule of project, indication of their family and financial circumstances (including information on publisher's advance), c.v., professional reference(s), sample of work or reviews in the case of previously published work. Closing date 30 June.

Prizes

J. R. Ackerley Prize

English Centre of International PEN, 7 Dilke Street, London SW3 4JE
☎071-352 6303   Fax 071-351 0220

Commemorating the novelist/autobiographer, J. R. Ackerley, this prize is awarded for a literary autobiography, written in English and published in the year preceding the award. Previous winners include: Paul Binding *St Martin's Ride*; Anthony Burgess *Little Wilson and Big God;* John Healy *The Grass Arena;* Germaine Greer *Daddy, We Hardly Knew You.*
Prize £2000.

The Acorn Award

See **Nottinghamshire Children's Book Award**

Aldeburgh Poetry Festival Prize

Goldings, Goldings Lane, Leiston, Suffolk IP16 4EB
☎0728 830631   Fax 0728 452715

Festival Coordinator *Michael Laskey*

FOUNDED 1989 by the Aldeburgh Poetry Trust. Sponsored jointly by Waterstone's and the Aldeburgh Bookshop for the best first collection published in Britain or the Republic of Ireland in the preceding twelve months. Open to any first collection of poetry of at least 40 pp. Final entry date 1 October. 1991 winner: Mark Roper *The Hen Ark.*
Prize £500, plus an invitation to read at the following year's festival.

Alexander Prize

Royal Historical Society, University College London, Gower Street, London WC1E 6BT
☎071-387 7532   Fax 071-387 7532

Contact *Literary Director*

Awarded for an historical essay of not more than 8000 words. Competitors may choose their own subject for their essay, but must submit their choice for approval in the first instance to the Literary Director of the Royal Historical Society.
Prize Medal, plus £250.

An Duais don bhFilíocht i nGaelige

(Prize for Poetry in Irish)
The Arts Council (An Chomhairle Ealaíon), 70 Merrion Square, Dublin 2, Republic of Ireland
☎010 353 1 611840   Fax 010 353 1 761302

Contact *Literature Officer*

Triennial award for the best book of poetry in the Irish language published in the preceding three years. Last awarded 1992.
Prize £1000.

Hans Christian Andersen Awards

IBBY (International Board of Books for Young People), Nonnenweg 12, Postfach CH-4003, Basle, Switzerland
☎010 41 61 272 2917

Contact *Leena Maissen* (Executive Director)

The highest international prizes for children's literature. Candidates are nominated by national boards of the IBBY. Two biennial prizes are awarded to the author and illustrator whose body of work has made a lasting contribution to children's literature. Awarded in even-numbered years. Next award 1994.
Award Gold medals.

Eileen Anderson Central Television Drama Award

Central Television, Central House, Broad Street, Birmingham B1 2JP
☎021-643 9898   Fax 021-616 4766

Contact *John Palmer*

INITIATED in 1987, with money left by the late Dr Eileen Anderson and contributed to by Central, this is an annual award to encourage new theatre writing in the Midlands. Open to all new plays or an adaptation commissioned or premièred by a building-based theatre company in the Central

Television region. Previous winners include: Vilma Hollingbery & Michael Napier Brown *Is This The Day?* (premièred at the Royal Theatre Northampton; Lucy Gannon *Wicked Old Nellie* (Derby Playhouse); Timberlake Wertenbaker *The Love of The Nightingale* (commissioned by the Royal Shakespeare Company's The Other Place in Stratford).
Prize: £1500, plus a unique trophy worth an additional £500, designed each year by a local college of education. A plaque is awarded to the theatre which commissioned the work.

Angel Literary Award

The Angel Hotel, Angel Hill, Bury St Edmunds, Suffolk IP33 1LT
☎ 0284 753926   Fax 0284 750092

Contact *Caroline Gough*

This award is intended to stimulate interest in, and support for, writers in East Anglia. Two prizes are given, one for a work of fiction and one for a work of non-fiction. Books must have been published between October 1991 and September 1993 and written by authors living and working in East Anglia (Norfolk, Suffolk, Essex and Cambridgeshire). Entries must be submitted by 31 August. 1991 winner: Fiction: Elspeth Barker *O Caledonia;* Non-fiction: Sir Robert Rhodes James *Bob Boothby.*
Prize £1000 & £500, awarded as judged appropriate.

Rosemary Arthur Award

National Poetry Foundation, 27 Mill Road, Fareham, Hampshire PO16 0TH

Contact *Johnathon Clifford*

FOUNDED 1990. Annual award to get unknown poets of merit published in book form. Anyone who has not previously had a book published may submit between 20 and 40 poems together with s.a.e. and £5 reading fee at any time during the year. Winners are announced in February.
Award Complete funding for a book of the poet's work, plus £100 and an engraved carriage clock.

Arvon Foundation International Poetry Competition

Kilnhurst, Kilnhurst Road, Todmorden, Lancashire OL14 6AX
☎ 0706 816582   Fax 0706 816359

Contact *David Pease*

FOUNDED 1980. Biennial competition (odd years) for poems written in English and not previously broadcast or published. There are no restrictions

on the number of lines, themes, age of entrants or nationality. No limit to the number of entries. Entry fee: £3.50 per poem.
Prize (1st) £5000.

Authors' Club First Novel Award

The Authors' Club, 40 Dover Street, London W1X 3RB
☎ 071-373 5244

INSTITUTED 1954. This award is made for the most promising work published in Britain and is presented at a dinner held at the Authors' Club. Entries for the award are accepted from publishers and must be full-length — short stories are not eligible.
Award £500.

Baal Book Prize

BAAL Publications Secretary, CLAC, School of Education, Open University, Milton Keynes MK7 6AA
☎ 0908 653383

Contact *David Graddol*

Annual award by the British Association for Applied Linguistics to an outstanding book in the field of applied linguistics. Final entry date April. Previous winner: Susan Berk-Seligson *The Bilingual Courtroom.*
Cash prize.

Verity Bargate Award

The Soho Theatre Company, The Cockpit Theatre, Gateforth Street, London NW8 8EH
☎ 071-262 7907   Fax 071-723 8146

Contact *Jack Bradley*

To commemorate the late Verity Bargate, founder and director of the **Soho Theatre Company**. This award is presented annually for a new and unperformed play. Send s.a.e. for details; if submitting scripts, enclose one s.a.e. script-size and one standard-size. The Soho Theatre Company also runs many courses for new writers. Previous winners: David Spencer, Melissa Murray, Mick Maloney, Gillian Plowman, Lyndon Morgans.
Award £1000, plus production by the Soho Theatre Company.

H. E. Bates Short Story Competition

Events Team, Directorate of Environment Services, Northampton Borough Council, Cliftonville House, Bedford Road, Northampton NN4 0NW
☎ 0604 233500   Fax 0604 29571

Contact *Liz Carroll*

Named after the late H. E. Bates, one of the masters of the short story form, this competition is for short stories of 2000 words maximum. Any writer resident in Great Britain is eligible, and there are categories for children under 11 and under 16. *Prize* (1st) £100.

BBC WILDLIFE Magazine Awards for Nature Writing

Broadcasting House, Whiteladies Road, Bristol BS8 2LR
☎0272 732211   Fax 0272 467075

Contact *Rosamund Kidman Cox* (Editor of *BBC WILDLIFE Magazine*)

Annual competition for professional and amateur writers. Entries should be a single essay, either on personal observations of or thoughts about nature — general or specific — or about reflections on human relationships with nature. Entry forms published usually in the March and April issues of the magazine.
Prizes £1000 for best essay by a professional or amateur writer; £400 for best essay by an amateur writer (only if a professional writer wins the top award); £200 for best essay by a young writer aged between 13 and 17; £100 for best essay by a young writer aged 12 or under.

Samuel Beckett Award

c/o Faber & Faber, 3 Queen Square, London WC1N 3AU
☎071-465 0045   Fax 071-465 0034

Contact *Editorial Department*

Jointly sponsored by Channel 4, the Royal Court Theatre and Faber & Faber, this award aims to give support and encouragement to new playwrights at a crucial stage of their careers. Two prizes are given, one for a first play for the stage and another for a first play for television, both to have been professionally performed or transmitted during the calendar year.
Prize £1500 (each category).

Adolphe Bentinck Prize

D. den Hertog, 22 place du Général, Catroux, Paris 75017
☎0101 33 1 4763 5454
Fax 0101 33 1 4267 0326

Contact *D. den Hertog*

FOUNDED 1972. Annual award established by Baroness Bentinck in memory of her husband, the Dutch diplomat who devoted his life to his country,

to the defence of liberty and international cooperation. Awarded for an important contribution either to European unity or to the cause of peace and the fight against fanaticism. Final entry date August. Previous winners: Paul Nitze *From Hiroshima to Glasnost;* Jean-Baptiste Duroselle *Europe & History of its Peoples.*
Prize £15,000.

David Berry Prize

Royal Historical Society, University College London, Gower Street, London WC1E 6BT
☎071-387 7532

Triennial award (next in 1994) for an essay of not more than 10,000 words on Scottish history within the period of James I to James VI. Candidates may select subject from the relevant period, providing it has been submitted to and approved by the Council of the Royal Historical Society.
Prize £250.

James Tait Black Memorial Prizes

University of Edinburgh, David Hume Tower, George Square, Edinburgh EH8 9JX
☎031-650 3619   Fax 031-662 0772

Contact *Department of English Literature*

Two prizes, one for biography and one for fiction, instituted in 1918 in memory of a partner of the publishing firm of **A. & C. Black Ltd** and supported since 1979 by the **Scottish Arts Council**. Each prize is awarded for a book published in Britain in the previous twelve months. Prize winners are announced in February each year. Previous winners include: Claire Tomalin *The Invisible Woman*; William Boyd *Brazzaville Beach*; Adrian Desmond & James Moor *Darwin;* Iain Sinclair *Downriver.*
Prize £1500 each.

Boardman Tasker Memorial Award

14 Pine Lodge, Dairyground Road, Bramhall, Stockport, Cheshire SK7 2HS
☎061-439 4624

INSTITUTED 1983, this award is given for a work of fiction, non-fiction or poetry, whose central theme is concerned with the mountain environment and which can be said to have made an outstanding contribution to mountain literature. Authors of any nationality are eligible, but the book must have been published or distributed in the UK for the first time between 1 November 1992 and 31 October 1993. Entries from publishers only. 1991 winners: Alison Fell *Mer de Glace;* Dave Brown & Ian Mitchell *A View from the Ridge.*
Prize £1500 (may vary at Trustees' discretion).

Booker Prize for Fiction

Book Trust, Book House, 45 East Hill,
London SW18 2QZ
☎081-870 9055   Fax 081-874 4790

Contact *Christine Shaw*

The leading British literary prize, set up in 1968 by Booker McConnell Ltd, with the intention of rewarding merit, raising the stature of the author in the eyes of the public and increasing the sale of the books. The announcement of the winner has been televised live since 1981, and all books on the shortlist experience a substantial increase in sales. Eligible novels must be written in English by a citizen of Britain, the Commonwealth, the Republic of Ireland or South Africa, and must be published in the UK for the first time between 1 October and 30 September of the year of the prize. Entries are accepted from UK publishers who may each submit not more than 3 novels within the appropriate scheduled publication dates. The judges may also ask for certain other eligible novels to be submitted to them. Annual award. Previous winners include: Ben Okri *The Famished Road* (1991); A. S. Byatt *Possession* (1990); Kazuo Ishiguro *The Remains of the Day* (1989).
Prize £20,000.

BP Arts Journalism Awards

Arts Council, 14 Great Peter Street,
London SW1P 3NQ
☎071-973 6458   Fax 071-973 6560

Contact *Arts Council Press Office*

First presented in 1986 in recognition of the contribution made by journalists throughout the UK towards the understanding and appreciation of the arts. Sponsored by British Petroleum. Four main categories: (a) best news story or feature article about the arts or heritage in a newspaper or periodical (not including reviews); (b) best radio programme on the arts or heritage; (c) best television programme on the arts or heritage; (d) a picture or series of pictures published in a newspaper or periodical which best illustrates an event in the arts or heritage. Winners announced in March. Previous winners include: Fiona Maddocks (press); Mike Greenwood (radio); Andy Lipman (TV); Sue Adler (photography).
Prize (1st) £1500; £500 for runner-up in each category.

Bridport Arts Centre Creative Writing Competition

Arts Centre, South Street, Bridport,
Dorset DT6 3NR
☎0308 27183

Contact *The Administrator*

A competition for poetry and short story writing. Unpublished work only, written in English. Send s.a.e. for entry form. Also runs a separate competition for young writers. Final entry date early April. Send s.a.e for entry form.
Prizes normally £1000, £500 & £250 in each category, plus runners-up prizes.

Katharine Briggs Folklore Award

The Folklore Society, University College London,
Gower Street, London WC1E 6BT
☎071-387 5894

Contact *The Convener*

An annual award in November for a book, published in Britain between 1 June and 30 May in the previous calendar year, which has made the most distinguished non-fiction contribution to folklore studies. Intended to encourage serious research in the field which Katharine Briggs did so much to establish. The term folklore studies is interpreted broadly to include all aspects of traditional and popular culture, narrative, belief, custom and folk arts. Previous winners include: Simon Charley *Rites of Marrying, The Wedding in Scotland.*
Prize £50, plus engraved goblet.

British Book Awards

Publishing News, 43 Museum Street,
London WC1A 1LY
☎071-404 0304   Fax 071-242 0762

A mixed bag of trade awards which includes: Book Jacket of the Year; Travel Writer of the Year; Children's Author of the Year; Illustrated Children's Book of the Year; Chain Bookseller of the Year; Independent Bookseller of the Year; Author of the Year; Distributor of the Year; Publisher of the Year; Book Promotion of the Year; Editor of the Year; Bestseller of the Year. The top author prize is not necessarily for work of great literary merit but it is awarded to an author who has made the biggest impact. Winners will receive mounted brass pen nibs to be known as Nibbies — 'the equivalent of Oscars'. 1991 winners: Headline (Publisher of the Year); Roddy Doyle *The Van* (Book Jacket of the Year); Mark Shand (Travel Writer of the Year); Dick King-Smith (Children's Author of the Year); Helen Oxenbury *Farmer Duck* (Illustrated Children's Book of the Year); Pan Macmillan *Scarlett* (Book Promotion of the Year); Penguin Distribution (Distributor of the Year); Michael Fishwick, HarperCollins (Editor of the Year); Peter Mayle (Author of the Year); Kaydal, Clitheroe (Independent Bookseller of the Year); Waterstone's, Bournemouth (Chain Bookseller of the Year).
Award Mounted brass pen nibs.

British Comparative Literature Association Translation Prizes

St John's College, Oxford OX1 3JP
☎0865 277381   Fax 0865 277435

Contact *Dr Nicholas Crowe*

FOUNDED 1983. Annual competition, open to literary translations from all languages. Special prizes for translations from Hebrew, Yiddish and other languages on a Jewish theme; Chinese (annual/biennial); and Swedish (biennial). Final entry date 15 December.
Prizes (1st) £350; (2nd) £150; plus publication for all winning entries in the Association's annual journal *Comparative Criticism*.

British Fantasy Awards

15 Stanley Road, Morden, Surrey SM4 5DE
☎081-540 9443

Secretary *Di Wathen*

Awarded by the **British Fantasy Society** at its annual conference for Best Novel and Best Short Story categories, among others. Previous winners include: Piers Anthony, Clive Barker, Ken Bulmer, Ramsey Campbell, Stephen King, Dean R. Koontz, Michael Moorcock, Lisa Tuttle, Gene Wolfe.

British Literature Prize

See **David Cohen British Literature Prize**

British Science Fiction Award

275 Londsdale Avenue, Intake,
Doncaster DN2 6HJ
☎0302 367556

Contact *Nicholas Mahoney* (Award Administrator)

Annual awards for work first published or presented in Britain during the preceding year, given in four categories: Best Novel; Best Short Fiction; Best Media Presentation; Best Artwork. The award is given by the **British Science Fiction Association**. A shortlist of five in each category is arrived at by a nominating ballot voted on by British Science Fiction Association members. A final ballot by BSFA members and members of the Easter Science Fiction Convention determines the winners.
Award Trophy.

James Cameron Award

City University, Department of Journalism,
Northampton Square, London EC1V 0HB
☎071-477 8221   Fax 071-477 8574

Contact *The Administrator*

Annual award for journalism to a reporter of any nationality, working for the British media, whose work is judged to have contributed most during the year to the continuance of the Cameron tradition. Administered by the City University, Department of Journalism.

The City of Cardiff International Poetry Competition

The Welsh Academy, 3rd Floor, Mount Stuart House, Mount Stuart Square, Cardiff CF1 6DQ
☎0222 492025   Fax 0222 492930

Contact *Kevin Thomas*

FOUNDED 1986. An annual competition for unpublished poems in English of up to 50 lines. Launched in the spring with a summer closing date.
Prize (total) £4000.

Carey Award

Society of Indexers, 16 Green Road, Birchington, Kent CT7 9JZ
☎0843 41115

Secretary *Claire Troughton*

A private award made by the Society to a member who has given outstanding services to indexing. The recipient is selected by Council with no recommendations considered from elsewhere.

Carmarthen Writers' Circle Short Story Competition

Penpedwar, Llanllwni, Pencader,
Dyfed SA39 9DW
☎055935 302

Contact *Maggie Rothwell*

FOUNDED 1990. Annual. All stories must be unpublished and not yet accepted for publication. Entries must be anonymous and an entry form, giving titles of all stories, must be attached to submissions. Any number may be submitted; entry fee £3 per story. Stories must be typed in double-spacing on one side of A4 paper.
Prize (1st) £100; (2nd) £60; (3rd) £30. All prize winners will be put on tape for the Talking Newspaper.

Cheltenham Prize

The Daily Telegraph Cheltenham Festival of Literature, c/o Town Hall, Cheltenham, Gloucestershire GL50 1QA
☎0242 521621   Fax 0242 573902

Contact *Nicola Bennett*

The Cheltenham Prize is awarded annually and is given to the author of a work of literature, who is deemed in the opinion of an independent judge to have made an outstanding contribution to the previous year's literature, but which has not yet received the critical attention it deserves. *Prize* £500.

Children's Book Award

The Federation of Children's Book Groups, 30 Senneleys Park Road, Northfield, Birmingham B31 1AL
☎ 021-427 4860

Contact *Jenny Blanch*

FOUNDED 1980. Awarded annually for best book of fiction suitable for children. Unique in that it is judged by the children themselves. Previous winners include: Mick Inkpen *Threadbear*; Robert Swindells *Room 13*; Roald Dahl & Quentin Blake *Matilda*. In 1992 there were three category prizes also: Picture Books; Short Novels; Longer Novels. *Award* A splendid silver and oak sculpture made by Graham Stewart & Tim Stead, plus portfolio of letters, drawings and comments from the children who took part in the judging; category winners received silver bowls designed by the same artist.

Children's Book Circle Eleanor Farjeon Award

c/o Naia Bray-Moffat, Penguin Books Ltd, 27 Wright's Lane, London W8 5TZ
☎ 071-938 2200   Fax 071-937 8704

This award, named in memory of the much loved children's writer, is for distinguished services to children's books either in this country or overseas, and may be given to a librarian, teacher, publisher, bookseller, author, artist, reviewer, television producer, etc. at the discretion of the Children's Book Circle. Previous winners include: Jill Bennett (1990), deputy headteacher who pioneered the use of 'real books' in the classroom and author of *Learning to Read with Picture Books*. *Award* £500.

Arthur C. Clarke Award for Science Fiction

Science Fiction Foundation, Polytechnic of East London, Longbridge Road, Dagenham, Essex RM8 2AS
☎ 081-590 7722   Fax 081-590 7799

Contact *Joyce Day*

ESTABLISHED 1986. The Arthur C. Clarke Award is given yearly to the best science fiction novel first published in the UK in the previous calendar year. Both hardcover and paperback books qualify. Made possible by a generous donation from Arthur C. Clarke, this award is selected by a rotating panel of six judges nominated by the **British Science Fiction Association**, the International Science Policy Foundation and the **Science Fiction Foundation**. Previous winners include: Margaret Atwood *The Handmaid's Tale*; George Turner *The Sea and Summer*; Rachel Pollack *Unquenchable Fire*; Geoff Ryman *The Child Garden*; Colin Greenland *Take Back Plenty*. *Award* £1000.

Cleveland Festival Competitions

See **Write Around - A Celebration of Cleveland Writing** in **Festivals** section

David Cohen British Literature Prize

Arts Council of Great Britain, 14 Great Peter Street, London SW1P 3NQ
☎ 071-333 0100

Contact *Literature Officer*

By far the most valuable literature prize in Britain, the British Literature Prize, launched by the **Arts Council** in 1992, will be awarded biennially. Anyone is eligible to nominate candidates and the award will be for writings in either English, Welsh or Gaelic, encompassing dramatists as well as novelists, poets and essayists. The main prize will be for a body of work rather than a single play or book and is being donated by the David Cohen Family Charitable Trust in association with Coutts Bank. The David Cohen trust was set up in 1980 by David Cohen, general practitioner son of a property developer. The trust has helped composers, choreographers, dancers, poets, playwrights and actors. The Council is providing a further £10,000 to enable the winner to commission new work, with the dual aim of encouraging young writers and readers. Lord Palumbo, Arts Council chairman, has said: 'We hope the award will come to be regarded as the supreme accolade for a living British author'. First prize awarded spring 1993. *Award* £30,000, plus £10,000 towards new work.

Collins Biennial Religious Book Award

HarperCollins Publishers, 77-85 Fulham Palace Road, London W6 8JB
☎ 081-741 7070   Fax 081-307 4064

Contact *Lesley Walmsley*

Biennial award given for a book which has made the most distinguished contribution to the relevance of Christianity in the modern world, written by a living citizen of the Commonwealth, the Republic of Ireland or South Africa. 1991 winner: John MacQuarrie *Jesus Christ in Modern Thought*. *Award* £5000.

Commonwealth Writers Prize

The Chairman, CACLALS, University of Guelph, Dept of English, Guelph, Ontario, Canada N1G 2W1
☎ 0101 519 824 4120 ext. 8391
Fax 0101 519 837 1315

Contact *Professor Diana Brydon*

ESTABLISHED 1987. Eligible books (novel or short stories) must be in English and written by a Commonwealth citizen. Entries must be submitted by publishers. The 1993 prize will be administered from a new address but enquiries can still be sent to the above. Previous winners: David Malouf *The Great World*; Pauline Melville *Shape-Shifter*.
Prizes Best Book £10,000; Best First Book £2000; eight prizes of £500 given at regional level.

The Constable Trophy

Constable Publishers Ltd, 3 The Lanchesters, 162 Fulham Palace Road, London W6 9ER
☎ 081-741 3663   Fax 081-748 7562

Contact *Caroline Sanderson* at
Book Trust, Book House, 45 East Hill, London SW18 2QZ
☎ 081-870 9055

Biennial competition, supported by the northern-based regional arts associations, for a previously unpublished novel by a writer living in the North of England. Winning entry may be considered for publication by **Constable**. Next award 1994.
Prize (1st) £1000, and £1000 in advance of royalties on acceptance for publication by Constable.

Thomas Cook Travel Book Awards

c/o Edmund Swinglehurst, Thomas Cook, 45 Berkeley Street, London W1A 1EB
☎ 071-408 4175   Fax 071-408 4299

The annual awards are given to encourage the art of travel writing in three categories: (a) best narrative travel book, (b) best guidebook published in the current year, (c) best illustrated guide book. 1992 winners: Norman Lewis *A Goddess in the Stones* & Gavin Young *In Search of Conrad* (joint narrative); Fran Hazelton *London's American Past*

(guidebook); Gordon Stainforth *Eyes to the Hills* (illustrated).
Awards (a) £7500 (b) £2500 (c) £1500.

Catherine Cookson Fiction Prize

Transworld Publishers Ltd, 61–63 Uxbridge Road, London W5 5SA
☎ 081-579 2652

Contact *Catherine Cookson Fiction Prize Administrator*

A new (1992) annual prize from Transworld Publishers, in celebration of the achievement of Catherine Cookson. Awarded to a novel, of at least 70,000 words, which possesses strong characterisation, authentic background and storytelling quality, which are the mark of Cookson's work. The work may be contemporary or historical. Submissions must be in English and original (no translations), and must not have been previously published in any form. Final entry date 31 May; winner announced in October.
Award £10,000, plus publication by **Transworld**. Publishing contract will include advance and royalties. Runners-up may be offered publication on terms to be negotiated.

The Duff Cooper Prize

54 St Maur Road, London SW6 4DP
☎ 071-736 3729   Fax 071-731 7638

Contact *Artemis Cooper*

An annual award for a literary work in the fields of biography, history, politics or poetry, published by a recognised publisher (member of the **Publishers' Association**) during the previous 24 months. Financed by the interest from a trust fund commemorating Duff Cooper, first Viscount Norwich (1890–1954).
Prize c.£250.

The Giles Cooper Awards

BBC Broadcasting House, London W1A 1AA
☎ 071-580 4468   Fax 071-636 9786

Contact *Alan Drury*

INITIATED 1979. Awarded annually by a panel of judges to the writers of what they consider to have been the best scripts written for radio in the year. Set up by the **BBC** and **Methuen** to recognise, and to perpetuate in tangible form, examples of good radio writing. Nomination is restricted to the producers and editors of the works in question. Previous winners include: David Cregan *A Butler Did It*; Richard Nelson *Eating Words*; Anthony Minghella *Cigarettes and Chocolate*; Nigel D.

Moffat *Lifetime*; Christina Reid *The Last of a Dyin' Race*; Caryl Phillips *The Wasted Years*.

Crabbe Memorial Poetry Competition

Lower Mead, Alphamstone, Near Bures,
Suffolk CO8 5HS
☎0787 227105

Honorary Competition Secretary *Mrs Gill Phillips*

ESTABLISHED 1954 on the bicentenary of the birth of George Crabbe by the Suffolk Poetry Society. Open to 'those who by birth, education or residence are Suffolk people'. Annual award presented at Aldeburgh in October. Send s.a.e. for details, rules and entry form. Final entry date 31 May.
Prize (1st) Crabbe Memorial Silver Challenge Rose Bowl engraved with winner's name plus £100; (2nd) £60; (3rd) £40.

Rose Mary Crawshay Prize

The British Academy, 20–21 Cornwall Terrace,
London NW1 4QP
☎071-487 5966   Fax 071-224 3807

Contact *The Secretary of the British Academy*

FOUNDED 1882 by Rose Mary Crawshay, this prize is given for a historical or critical work by a woman of any nationality on English literature, with particular preference for a work on Keats, Byron or Shelley. The work must have been published in the preceding three years.
Prize normally two prizes of £300 each.

John Creasey Memorial Award

Crime Writers' Association, PO Box 172, Tring,
Hertfordshire HP23 5LP

Contact *The Secretary*

FOUNDED 1973, following the death of crime writer John Creasey, founder of the **Crime Writers' Association**. This award is given annually for the best crime novel by a previously unpublished author. Nominations from publishers only. Previous winners include: Walter Mosley *Devil in a Blue Dress*.
Award Cheque (sum varies), plus magnifying glass.

Crime Writers' Association Awards

See **Gold Dagger Award for Non-Fiction; Gold, Silver & Diamond Dagger Awards for Fiction; John Creasey Memorial Award; Last Laugh Award; New Law Journal Rumpole Award**

Daily Telegraph/British Association Young Science Writer Awards

British Association, Fortress House, 23 Savile Row,
London W1X 1AB
☎071-494 3326   Fax 071-734 1658

Contact *Lynn Milsom*

FOUNDED 1986. The awards are open to anyone aged between 16–28 for a short article (no more than 800 words) on an exciting scientific discovery. The piece should be written as a newspaper article (some entries will be published in *The Daily Telegraph*) and should therefore be punchy and free of jargon — without compromising the science. Substantial prizes include a trip to the US for the annual meeting of the American Association for the Advancement of Science.

Rhys Davies Award

Welsh Academy, 3rd Floor, Mount Stuart House,
Mount Stuart Square, Cardiff CF1 6DQ
☎0222 492025   Fax 0222 492930

Contact *Kevin Thomas*

FOUNDED 1991. Annual award for a Welsh short story in English, from writers born in Wales or currently living in Wales. Launched in the spring with closing date in summer.
Prize (total) £4500.

Deo Gloria Award

Book Trust, Book House, 45 East Hill,
London SW18 2QZ
☎081-870 9055   Fax 081-874 4790

ESTABLISHED 1990. Sponsored by the Deo Gloria Trust which was founded in 1965 by Kenneth Frampton to share the Christian faith in popular ways which reach people untouched by more traditional church methods. The award is given for a full-length novel published in the preceding twelve months and written from a positive Christian standpoint by an author of British or Commonwealth nationality. Final entry date end September. 1991 winner: Tim Winton *Cloudstreet*.
Award £5000.

Isaac & Tamara Deutscher Memorial Prize

c/o Gerhard Wilkie, 75 St Gabriels Road,
London NW2 4DU
☎081-450 0469

An annual award in recognition of, and as encouragement to, outstanding research in the Marxist tradition of Isaac Deutscher. Made to the author of

an essay or full-scale work published or in manuscript. Entries should be submitted by 1 May each year.
Award £500.

George Devine Award

17A South Villas, London NW1 9BS
☎ 071-267 9793 (eves)

Contact *Christine Smith*

Annual award for a promising new playwright writing for the stage in memory of George Devine, artistic director of the **Royal Court Theatre**, who died in 1965. Send two copies of the script to Christine Smith by 1 March. Information leaflet available.
Prize £3500.

Denis Devlin Award

The Arts Council (An Chomhairle Ealaíon), 70 Merrion Square, Dublin 2, Republic of Ireland
☎ 010 353 1 611840   Fax 010 353 1 761302

Contact *Literature Officer*

Triennial award for the best book of poetry in English by an Irish poet, published in the preceding three years. Last awarded 1992.
Award £1200.

Pierre Dreyfus Award

Guild of Motoring Writers, 30 The Cravens, Smallfield, Surrey RH6 9QS
☎ 0342 843294

Contact *Sharon Scott-Fairweather*

FOUNDED 1977. Awarded annually by Renault UK Ltd in honour of Pierre Dreyfus, President Director General of the Regie Renault from 1955–75 to a member of the Guild of Motoring Writers who is judged to have made the most outstanding journalistic effort during the year. 1991 winner: Brian Laban.
Prize £1000, plus trophy.

Earthworm Award

Friends of the Earth, 26–28 Underwood Street, London N1 7JQ
☎ 071-490 4734   Fax 071-490 0881

Contact *The Earthworm Award Administrator, Events Dept*

Set up in 1987 by Friends of the Earth and the first children's book prize of its kind. Sponsored by Save & Prosper. Aims to promote and reward environmental awareness and sensitivity in literature for children of all ages. Looking for books of every kind, fact and fiction, which promote an awareness and appreciation of the natural world; encourage an overall sense of environmental responsibility; present concepts and facts accurately and clearly where appropriate. Entries need to express a sympathetic and positive approach and need not present an explicit Green message. Applications are invited from publishers for books published or distributed between 1 May and 31 April of the previous year. Closing date end April. 1991 winner: *The Last Rabbit* ed. Jennifer Curry.
Prize (1st) £2500; two runners-up £500.

The Encore Award

The Society of Authors, 84 Drayton Gardens, London SW10 9SB
☎ 071-373 6642   Fax 071-373 5768

FOUNDED 1990. Awarded to an author who has had one (and only one) novel previously published. 1991 winner: Carey Harrison *Richard's Feet.*
Prize (total) £7500.

Envoi Poetry Competition

Envoi, 44 Rudyard Road, Biddulph Moor, Stoke on Trent, Staffordshire ST8 7JN

Contact *Roger Elkin*

Run by *Envoi* poetry magazine, published thrice yearly. Competitions are featured regularly, with prizes of £135 each issue. Winning poems are published. Send s.a.e. to Competition Editor, David Bowes, 17 Millcroft, Bishop's Stortford, Herts CM23 2BP.

European Literary and Translation Prizes

Commission of the European Communities, 8 Storey's Gate, London SW1P 3AT
☎ 071-973 1992   Fax 071-973 1900

FOUNDED 1990 to bring knowledge and appreciation of European literature to a wider public and to celebrate the strength and diversity of the European literary tradition. Member countries of the EC nominate their best works of literature and translation from the last three years. Sponsored by the Commission. 1991 winners: Mario Luzi *Frasi e Encisi di un Canto Salutare* (literature); Frans Van Woerden *De Brug van Londen* (translation).
Prize 20,000 ecus (about £14,000).

European Prize for the Translation of Poetry

European Poetry Library, P. Coutereelstraat 76,
Leuven, Belgium B-3000
☎010 32 16 23 53 51
Fax 010 32 16 23 49 49

Triennial prize offered by the European Commission in Brussels for translations of poetry, written by living poets from other Community countries. Both poems and translations must be in one of the nine official Community languages and the translations must have been published in book form in the previous four years. Next prize 1993. Submit five copies of the translation before the end of 1992, marking envelope: 'European Prize for Translation of Poetry'.
Prize £6000.

Geoffrey Faber Memorial Prize

Faber & Faber Ltd, 3 Queen Square,
London WC1N 3AU
☎071-465 0045   Fax 071-465 0034

ESTABLISHED 1963 as a memorial to the founder and first chairman of **Faber & Faber**, this prize is awarded in alternate years for the volume of verse and the volume of prose fiction judged to be of greatest literary merit published in the UK in the preceding two years. Authors must be under 40 at the time of publication and citizens of the UK, Commonwealth, Republic of Ireland or South Africa. 1991 winner: Carol Birch *The Fog Line*.
Prize £1000.

Prudence Farmer Award

New Statesman and Society, Foundation House,
Perseverance Works, 38 Kingsland Road,
London E2 8DQ
☎071-739 3211   Fax 071-739 9307

Contact *Hugo Williams*

For the best poem to have been published in the *New Statesman and Society* during the previous year (Jan–July).
Award £100.

Fawcett Society Book Prize

46 Harleyford Road, London SE11 5AY
☎071-587 1287   Fax 071-587 1287

Contact *Charlotte Burt*

An annual award to the author of a book (alternately fiction and non-fiction) which has made a substantial contribution to the understanding of women's concerns, attitudes or roles. All works submitted for the prize are placed in the **Fawcett** Library at City of London Polytechnic. 1992 winners include: Lucy Hughes-Hallett *Cleopatra: Histories, Dreams and Distortions*; Jacqueline Rose *The Haunting of Sylvia Plath*.
Prize £500.

The Kathleen Fidler Award

c/o Book Trust Scotland, The Scottish Book Centre,
Fountainbridge Library, 137 Dundee Street,
Edinburgh EH11 1BG
☎031-229 3663   Fax 031-228 4293

For an unpublished novel for children aged 8–12, to encourage authors new to writing for this age group. The work must be the author's first attempt to write for this age range. Final entry date end October. 1991 winner: George Hendry *Greg's Revenge*.
Award £1000, plus publication.

Sir Banister Fletcher Award

The Authors' Club, 40 Dover Street,
London W1X 3RB
☎071-373 5244

This award is financed by the income from a trust left by the late Sir Banister Fletcher, who was president of the Authors' Club for many years. It is presented annually for the best book on architecture or the fine arts published in the preceding year. Submissions: Fletcher Award Committee, RIBA, 66 Portland Place, London W1N 4AD. Previous winners: John Onians *Bearers of Meaning: Classical Orders in Antiquity*; Sir Michael Levey *Giambattista Tiepolo: His Life and Art*.
Award £500.

The John Florio Prize

The Translators' Association, 84 Drayton Gardens,
London SW10 9SB
☎071-373 6642

Contact *Kate Pool*

ESTABLISHED 1963 under the auspices of the Italian Institute and the British-Italian Society, this prize is awarded biennially for the best translation into English of a twentieth-century Italian work of literary merit and general interest, published by a British publisher in the two years preceding the prize. Next award 1994; closing date 31 December 1993. Previous winners: Patrick Creagh for *Danube* Claudio Magris and *Blind Argus* Gesualdo Bufalino.
Prize £1000.

Anne Frankel Prize

c/o Peter Hepple, Critics' Circle, 47 Bermondsey
Street, London SE1 3XT
☎ 071-403 1818   Fax 071-403 1418

FOUNDED 1991. Annual prize for young film critics
in memory of the late Anne Frankel, who wrote on
film. Set up by her father William Frankel, former
editor and now chairman of the *Jewish Chronicle*.
Age limit for entrants is 25. Entries should be self-
submitted and have been published in a local/
national/student newspaper or periodical. Submit
three examples of work, sending four copies of
each to the above address. Previous closing date
end August. Check submission details for 1993.
Prize £500.

David Gemmell Cup

Hastings Writers Group, c/o W. H. Johnson
9 White Court, King's Ride, Alfriston
East Sussex BN26 5XP

Contact *W. H. Johnson*

ESTABLISHED 1988. Annual award to encourage
writers of short fiction resident in Sussex. From
1992 it has been open to entrants resident in East
and West Sussex, Kent and Surrey. Final entry date
end August. The competition is organised by
Hastings Writers' Group and is presented by its
donor David Gemmell. The top ten entrants receive
a written critique of their work. 1991 winner: Ralph
Hill.
(1st) David Gemmell Cup plus £125; (2nd) £75;
(3rd) £30; (4th) £20.

Glaxo Prize for Medical Writing & Illustration

The Society of Authors, 84 Drayton Gardens,
London SW10 9SB
☎ 071-373 6642   Fax 071-373 5768

Contact *Secretary of the Medical Writers Group*

Annual award in two categories (medical textbook
and illustrated medical book) written and pub-
lished in the UK in the year preceding the award.
Final date 21 April 1993. Previous winners: Michael
Hutson *Sports Injuries;* Kenneth R. Maravilla &
Wendy A. Cohen *MRI Atlas of the Spine;* John D.
Williams, A. William Asscher, David B. Moffat &
Eric Sanders *Clinical Atlas of the Kidney.*
Prize £1000 (each category).

Glenfiddich Awards

W. Grant & Sons Ltd, Independence House, 84
Lower Mortlake Road, Richmond,
Surrey TW9 2HS
☎ 081-332 1188   Fax 081-332 1695

A series of awards to writers and broadcasters who
have contributed most to the civilised appreciation
of food and drink through articles, books, illustration and photography published in the UK. Also
covers TV and radio programmes, as well as a
Special Award for outstanding work or event. 1991
winners: Food Book of the Year: *The Flavours of
Andalucia* Elisabeth Luard; Drink Book of the Year:
Oz Clarke's New Classic Wines; Food Writer of the
Year: Claudia Roden for articles in *The Daily
Telegraph* and *Observer Magazine*; Drink Writer of
the Year: Joanna Simon for articles in *The Sunday
Times*; Cookery Writer of the Year: Lynda Brown
for articles in *The Observer* and *Taste*; Restaurant
Writer of the Year: Matthew Fort for articles in *The
Guardian* and *Country Homes & Interiors;* Whisky
Writer of the Year: Jim Murray for articles in *The
Observer;* Trade Writer of the Year: John Harvey &
Richard Wilson for articles in *Farmers Weekly*;
Radio Programme of the Year: 'Designer Genes' in
the series 'One Step Beyond' produced by Sue
Broom and presented by Chris Serle for BBC Radio
4; Television Programme of the Year: 'Matters of
Taste' produced by Jancis Robinson and Nicholas
Lander of Eden Productions for Channel 4; Visual
Award Winner: writer and stylist Joy Davies, pho-
tographer Robin Broadbent and art director Robin
Harvey for 'A Palatable Pastiche' in *Harpers &
Queen*; Special Award: Arabella Boxer, Adnams
Wine Merchants, CAMRA; Overall and Glenfiddich
Trophy Winner: Claudia Roden.
Award Overall winner (chosen from the category
winners) £3000, plus the Glenfiddich Trophy (held
for one year); category winners £800 each, plus a
case of Glenfiddich Pure Malt Scotch Whisky and
an engraved commemorative quaich.

Gold Dagger Award for Non-Fiction

Crime Writers' Association, PO Box 172, Tring,
Hertfordshire HP23 5LP

Contact *The Secretary*

Annual award administered by the **Crime Writ-
ers' Association** for the best non-fiction crime
book published during the year. Previous winner:
John Bossy *Giordano Bruno and the Embassy
Affair.*
Award Dagger, plus cheque (sum varies).

Gold, Silver & Diamond Dagger Awards for Fiction

Crime Writers' Association, PO Box 172, Tring,
Hertfordshire HP23 5LP

Contact *The Secretary*

Annual awards (Gold and Silver) administered by
the **Crime Writers' Association** for the best

crime fiction published during the year; Diamond Dagger Award for a lifetime's achievement in the world of crime fiction. Nominations from publishers only. Previous winners: Leslie Charteris (Diamond); Barbara Vine *King Solomon's Carpet* (Gold); Frances Fyfield *Deep Sleep* (Silver). *Award* Dagger, plus cheque (sum varies).

GPA Book Award

GPA House, Shannon, County Clare
Republic of Ireland
☎ 010 353 61 360000 Fax 010 353 61 360888

Contact *Ann White*

Triennial award (1992/95) established in 1989 to celebrate and identify the best in contemporary Irish writing. Books in the categories of fiction, poetry and general (autobiography, biography, history, essays, belles lettres and criticism) will be considered. Authors must be born in Ireland, or resident there for three years. Previous winner: John Banville *The Book of Evidence*. *Prize* IR£50,000.

Edgar Graham Book Prize

School of Oriental and African Studies, Thornhaugh Street, Russell Square, London WC1H 0XG
☎ 071-637 2388 ext. 2336/436 3844

Contact *Sue-Anne Mayne*

ESTABLISHED 1984. Biennial award in memory of Edgar Graham. Aims to encourage research work in Third World agricultural and industrial development. Open to published works of original scholarship on modern agricultural and/or industrial development in Asia and/or Africa. Final entry date 30 April of the year preceding the award, for books published in the preceding two calendar years. *Prize* £1000.

The Guardian Children's Fiction Award

The Guardian, 119 Farringdon Road,
London EC1R 3ER
☎ 071-278 2332   Fax 071-837 2114

Contact *Children's Book Editor*

Annual award for an outstanding work of fiction for children by a British or Commonwealth author, first published in the UK in the preceding year, excluding picture books and previous winners. Final entry date end December. Previous winners: Rachel Anderson *Paper Faces*; Hilary McKay *The Exiles*. *Award* £1000.

The Guardian Fiction Prize

The Guardian, 119 Farringdon Road,
London EC1R 3ER
☎ 071-278 2332   Fax 071-837 2114

Contact *Literary Editor*

ESTABLISHED 1965. An annual award for a novel published by a British or Commonwealth writer, which is chosen by the literary editor in conjunction with the paper's regular reviewers of fiction. 1991 winner: Alan Judd *The Devil's Own Work*. *Prize* £2000.

Guinness Peat Aviation Literary Award

See **GPA Book Award**

Thomas Hardy Society Prize

21 Abbot's Walk, Cerne Abbas,
Dorchester DT2 7JN
☎ 0300 341434

Contact *Dr James Gibson*

FOUNDED 1985. Awarded to the writer or editor of a book which, in the opinion of the panel, contributes most to the appreciation of Hardy's writings and/or life and background. Any book published in the UK, US or Commonwealth before 31 December each year. Previous winners: Prof. Lennart Bjork for his edition of *Hardy: Notebooks*; Prof. Michael Millgate for his *Collective Letters of Thomas Hardy*. *Prize* £200.

The Hawthornden Prize

42A Hays Mews, Berkeley Square,
London W1X 7RU

An annual award for a work of imaginative literature by a British subject published during the previous year. Previous winners: Robert Shaw, V. S. Naipaul. *Prize* £2000.

Heinemann Fiction Award

East Midlands Arts, Mountfields House, Forest Road, Loughborough, Leicestershire LE11 3HU
☎ 0509 218292   Fax 0509 262214

Contact *Debbie Hicks*

FOUNDED 1990 by **East Midlands Arts** and **Heinemann** to promote new writing in the East Midlands. A biennial award (next award 1994). Work in any genre may be submitted. Authors must be resident in the East Midlands Arts region. Entries must be unpublished and not less than 40,000

words, and cannot be under consideration by a publisher. Entry forms (£5 entry fee) and presentation details from the above address. Final entry date May 1994. Judges will be looking for a work of outstanding literary excellence making a major contribution to the field of new fiction. 1990 winner: Alison Anthony *Strange Malady.*
Prize (1st) £2000; regional winner from shortlist £1000. Winner also receives a specially commissioned tropy made a local craftsperson and the possibility of publication by Heinemann.

Felicia Hemans Prize for Lyrical Poetry

University of Liverpool, PO Box 147
Liverpool, L69 3BX
☎051-794 2458   Fax 051-708 6502

Contact *The Registrar*

FOUNDED 1899. Annual award for published or unpublished verse. Open to past or present members and students of the University of Liverpool. One poem per entrant only. Closing date 1 May. *Prize* £30.

David Higham Prize for Fiction

c/o Book Trust, Book House, 45 East Hill, London SW18 2QZ
☎081-870 9055   Fax 081-874 4790

Contact *Caroline Sanderson*

An annual award for a first novel or book of short stories published in the UK in the year of the award by an author who is a citizen of Britain, the Commonwealth, the Republic of Ireland or South Africa. 1991 winner: Elspeth Barker *O Caledonia. Award* £1000.

William Hill Sports Book of the Year

c/o Lay & Partners, Citybridge House, 235-245 Goswell Road, London EC1V 7JD
☎071-365 7646 (Graham Sharpe)/
837 1475 (Tim Moss)
Fax 071-889 0472 (Graham Sharpe)/
833 4615 (Tim Moss)

Contact *Graham Sharpe/Tim Moss*

FOUNDED 1989. Annual award introduced by Graham Sharpe of bookmakers William Hill. Sponsored by William Hill and thus dubbed the 'bookie' prize, it is the first Sports Book of the Year award. Final entry date September. 1991 winner: Thomas Hauser *Mohammad Ali: His Life and Times.*
Prize £3000 (reviewed annually), plus £500 free bet and a day at the races.

Calvin & Rose G. Hoffman Prize

c/o The Headmaster, King's School, Canterbury, Kent CT1 2ES
☎0227 475501

Contact *The Headmaster*

Annual award for distinguished publication on Christopher Marlowe, established by the late Calvin Hoffman, author of *The Man Who was Shakespeare* (1955) as a memorial to himself and his wife. For essays of at least 5000 words written in English for their scholarly contribution to the study of Christopher Marlowe and his relationship to William Shakespeare. Final entry date September. Previous winners: Prof. Dr Kurt Tetzeli von Rosador, Dr R. Dutton, Prof. R. Danson, Prof. T. Cartelli.
Prize not less than £7500.

Dan Holliday Prize

See **Joseph Conrad Society (Literary Societies)**

Winifred Holtby Memorial Prize

Royal Society of Literature, 1 Hyde Park Gardens, London W2 2LT
☎071-723 5104

An annual award for the best regional work of fiction written in English by a living citizen of the UK, Republic of Ireland or the Commonwealth, published in the year of the prize. Previous winners: Nino Ricci *Lives of the Saints*; Shusha Guppy *The Blindfold Horse*; Maggie Hemingway *The Bridge*; Hilary Mantel *Fludd.*
Prize £750.

John Edeyrn Hughes Prize

Development Board for Rural Wales, Ladywell House, Newtown, Powys SY16 1JB
☎0686 626965

Contact *Geraint Davies*

FOUNDED 1990. Annual award by the Development Board for Rural Wales for a published work of fiction or non-fiction with a rural theme or setting — poetry, travel, biography, autobiography or fiction. Presented at the **Hay-on-Wye Festival of Literature** in the spring.
Prize £5000.

The Independent Award for Foreign Fiction

The Independent, 40 City Road, London EC1Y 2DB
☎071-253 1222   Fax 071-962 0016

Contact *Philippa Baker*

FOUNDED 1990. Full-length novel or collection of short stories, translated into English and published in the UK in the year preceding the award. 'To reward and promote the best fiction from abroad translated into English for the first time.' Twelve monthly awards to produce a shortlist of 12 books for the annual award announced in July. No cash prize for monthly awards. 1991 winners: Milan Kundera *Immortality* (trans. Peter Kussi); Saiichi Maruya *Rain in the Wind* (trans. Dennis Keene). *Award* £10,000.

International Reading Association Literacy Award

International Reading Association, 800 Barksdale Road, PO Box 8139, Newark Delaware 19714-8139, USA
☎0101 302 731 1600 Fax 0101 302 731 1057

Contact *Wendy L. Russ*

The International Reading Association is a non-profit education organisation devoted to improving reading instruction and promoting literacy worldwide. In addition to the US £5000 award presented each year on International Literacy Day (September 8), the organisation gives more than 25 awards in recognition of achievement in reading research, writing for children, media coverage of literacy, and literacy instruction.

Irish Times Aer Lingus Irish Literature Prizes

Irish Times Ltd, 11-15 D'Olier Street, Dublin 2
☎010 353 1 679 2022 Fax 010 353 1 773 282

Contact *Gerard Cavanagh* (Administrator, Book Prizes)

Two prizes, one awarded for a book of non-fiction prose (history, biography, autobiography, criticism, politics, sociological interest, travel and current affairs) and one for a first book of creative literature (a novel, collection of short stories or volume of poetry) in English or Gaelic. Previous winners: J. J. Lee *Ireland* (non-fiction); Colm Toibin *The South* (fiction).
Prize IR£10,000 each category.

Irish Times-Aer Lingus International Fiction Prize

Irish Times Ltd, 11-15 D'Olier Street, Dublin 2
☎010 353 1 679 2022 Fax 010 353 1 773 282

Contact *Gerard Cavanagh* (Administrator, Book Prizes)

Prizes are awarded in four categories which alternate — two per year. 1993 and 1995 award categories are for non-fiction prose (history, biography, autobiography, criticism, politics, sociological interest, travel and current affairs) and for a first book of creative literature (novel, collection of short stories or volume of poetry). Entries can be written either in English or Irish and must be published (in Ireland, the UK or USA). In 1994 (then 1996) the two categories will be fiction and poetry. Previous winner: Louise Begley *Wartime Lies*.
Prize IR £10,000 (each category).

Mary Vaughan Jones Award

Welsh Books Council, Castell Brychan, Aberystwyth, Dyfed SY23 2JB
☎0970 624151 Fax 0970 625385

Contact *The Administrator*

Triennial award for distinguished services in the field of children's literature in Wales over a considerable period of time. Next award 1994.
Award Silver trophy to the value of £600.

Kelpie Competition

Canongate Press, 14 Frederick Street, Edinburgh EH2 2HB
☎031-220 3800 Fax 031-220 3888

Contact *Mary Neat*

Biennial award for a new novel for the 8-13 age range. Co-sponsored by **Canongate Press, BBC Scotland** and the **Scottish Library Association**. Next award 1993.

The Sir Peter Kent Conservation Book Prize

Book Trust, Book House, 45 East Hill, London SW18 2QZ
☎081-870 9055 Fax 081-874 4790

Contact *Christine Shaw*

ESTABLISHED by BP Exploration for a book on creative conservation of the environment. Entries from UK publishers only. Previous winners: Philip Wayne *Operation Otter*, Jonathan Kingdon *Island Africa*; George Monbiot *Amazon Watershed*.
Prize (1st) £5000; £2000 prize for book on conservation for 8-16 year olds.

Kent & Sussex Poetry Society Open Competition

c/o Clive Eastwood, 8 Edward Street, Southborough, Tunbridge Wells, Kent

Contact *Clive Eastwood*

Open poetry competition. Entry fee £2 per poem. Poems should be in English, unpublished and not accepted for publication elsewhere, and should not have been entered for any other current poetry competition. Maximum 40 lines on any subject, in any form and style. Presentation details should be checked before submitting anything.
Prize (1st) £200; (2nd) £100; (3rd) £50.

Kent Young Writers of the Year Award

Kent Literature Festival, The Metropole Arts Centre, The Leas, Folkestone, Kent CT20 2LS
☎ 0303 255070

Contact *David Stone/Ann Fearey*

FOUNDED 1990. Funded by TVS Artswork, British Telecom, **South East Arts** and Kent County Council. Annual award for nine young writers aged between 5–18 years, whereby their writing will be brought to the attention of the public at the **Kent Literature Festival** in October.

The Martin Luther King Memorial Prize

National Westminster Bank Ltd, 7 Fore Street, Chard, Somerset TA20 1PJ

Contact *John Brunner*

An annual award for a literary work (including poetry, plays, TV or film scripts) reflecting the ideals to which Dr King dedicated his life. Work must have been published or performed in the UK during the previous calendar year. No enquiries answered without s.a.e.
Prize £100.

Lakeland Book of the Year

Cumbria Tourist Board, Ashleigh, Holly Road, Windermere LA23 2AQ
☎ 05394 44444   Fax 05394 44041

Contact *Regional Publicity Officer*

INITIATED 1984. An annual award, funded by Cumbrian author Hunter Davies, for the best book or booklet on any aspect of Cumbria and the Lake District published in the previous calendar year. Entry date mid-February. 1991 winner: David Clifford *The Diaries of Lady Anne Clifford*.
Award £100.

Last Laugh Award

Crime Writers' Association, PO Box 172, Tring, Hertfordshire HP23 5LP

Contact *The Secretary*

Annual award administered by the **Crime Writers' Association** for the funniest crime novel published during the year. Nominations from publishers only. Previous winner: Mike Ripley *Angels in Arms*.
Award Gold-plated fountain pen.

Leek Arts Festival International Poetry Competition

44 Rudyard Road, Biddulph Moor, Stoke on Trent ST8 7JN
☎ 0782 517892

Contact *Roger Elkin*

Any number of unpublished poems in English of up to 40 lines. Entry fee of £2 per poem. Final entry date April. 1991 winners: Rose Flint, Caroline Price, John Sewell & Maureen Wilkinson.
Prize (1st) £1000; (2nd) £600; (3rd) £400; plus 5 runner-up prizes of £100 each and 3 annual subscriptions to *Envoi* magazine.

The Library Association Besterman Medal

7 Ridgmount Street, London WC1E 7AE
☎ 071–636 7543   Fax 071–436 7218

Awarded annually for an outstanding bibliography or guide to literature first published in the UK during the preceding year. Recommendations for the award are invited from members of **The Library Association**. Among criteria taken into consideration in making the award are: authority of the work and quality of articles or entries; accessibility and arrangement of the information; scope and coverage; quality of indexing; adequacy of references; accuracy of information; physical presentation; and the originality of the work. Previous winners include: William Ringler *Bibliography and Index of English Verse Printed 1476–1558*; Philip H. Bolton *Dickens Dramatized;* Philip O'Brien *T. E. Lawrence: A Bibliography*.
Award Medal.

The Library Association Carnegie Medal

7 Ridgmount Street, London WC1E 7AE
☎ 071–636 7543   Fax 071–436 7218

First awarded in 1936. Presented for an outstanding book for children written in English and first published in the UK during the preceding year. This

award is not necessarily restricted to books of an imaginative nature. Previous winners include: Susan Price *The Ghost Drum*; Geraldine McCaughrean *A Pack of Lies*; Anne Fine *Goggle-Eyes*. 1991 winner: Gillian Cross *Wolf*.
Award Medal.

The Library Association Kate Greenaway Medal

7 Ridgmount Street, London WC1E 7AE
☎071-636 7543　　　　　Fax 071-436 7218

First awarded in 1955. Presented annually for the most distinguished work in the illustration of children's books first published in the UK during the preceding year. Previous winners include: Adrienne Kennaway *Crafty Chameleon*; Barbara Firth *Can't You Sleep, Little Bear?*; Michael Foreman *War Boy*. 1991 winner: Gary Blythe *The Whale's Song*.
Award Medal.

The Library Association McColvin Medal

7 Ridgmount Street, London WC1E 7AE
☎071-636 7543　　　　　Fax 071-436 7218

Annual award for an outstanding reference book first published in the UK during the preceding year. Books eligible for consideration include: encyclopedias, general and special; dictionaries, general and special; biographical dictionaries; annuals, yearbooks and directories; handbooks and compendia of data; atlases. Recommendations invited from members of **The Library Association**. Previous winners include: Geoffrey Campbell-Platt *Fermented Foods of the World: A Dictionary and Guide*; Christopher Hibbert, ed. *The Encyclopaedia of Oxford*; *The Oxford English Dictionary*, 2nd ed.
Award Medal.

The Library Association Wheatley Medal

7 Ridgmount Street, London WC1E 7AE
☎071-636 7543　　　　　Fax 071-436 7218

Annual award for an outstanding index first published in the UK during the preceding three years. Whole work must have originated in the UK and recommendations for the award are invited from members of **The Library Association**, the **Society of Indexers**, publishers and others. Previous winners include: Neil R. Fisk *Short History of Wilson's School*, 3rd ed.; Bobby Burke *Halsbury's Laws of England*, 4th ed; Richard Raper *The Works of Charles Darwin*.
Award Medal.

Lichfield Prize

Lichfield Prize, Tourist Information Centre, Donegal House, Bore Street, Lichfield, Staffordshire WS13 6NE
☎0543 252109

Contact *Mrs D. Broach/Mr S. Smith* at Lichfield District Council on 0543 414000 ext 2027

FOUNDED 1988. Biennial award initiated by Lichfield District Council to coincide with the Lichfield Festival. Run in conjunction with James Redshaw Books Ltd. Awarded for a previously unpublished novel based upon the geographical area of the Lichfield district, contemporary or historical, but not futuristic. 1991 winner: John Caine *A Nest of Singing Birds*. Next award 1993. Final entry date 31 May.
Prize £5000, plus possible publication.

Literary Review Grand Poetry Competition

51 Beak Street, London W1R 3LF
☎071-437 9392　　　　　Fax 071-734 1844

Monthly competition on a given theme. All poems entered must not exceed 40 lines; 'they must rhyme, scan and make sense'. See magazine for further details.
Prize (1st) usually £400; (2nd) £150; plus £10 for poems printed.

LWT Plays on Stage

The London Television Centre, London SE1 9LT
☎071-261 3688　　　　　Fax 071-928 6948

Contact *Michael Hallifax/Suzy Stoyel*

FOUNDED 1990. A competition for professional UK drama companies to help three winning companies stage a play of their choice. The judging panel consists of an actress, an actor, a director, a playwright and either a designer or an impresario. 1990 winners: The Traverse Theatre, Edinburgh, with *The Bondagers* by Sue Glover; The Gate Theatre, London, with *Damned for Despair* by Tirso de Molina; Northumberland Theatre Company, Alnwick, with *These Things Do Happen* by Stewart Howson. Suspended 1991. Details for 1992 were available from May 1992; check for 1993 requirements.
Prizes: (1st) £18,000; (2nd) £16,000; (3rd) £14,000.

Sir William Lyons Award

The Guild of Motoring Writers, 30 The Cravens, Smallfield, Surrey RH6 9QS
☎0342 843294　　　　　Fax 0342 843294

Contact *Sharon Scott-Fairweather*

An annual competitive award to encourage young people in automotive journalism and foster interests in motoring and the motor industry. Entrance by two essays and interview with Awards Committee. Applicants must be British, aged 17–23 and resident in UK. Final entry date 1 October. Presentation date December.
Award £500.

Agnes Mure Mackenzie Award

The Saltire Society, 9 Fountain Close, 22 High Street, Edinburgh EH1 1TF
☎ 031-556 1836   Fax 031-557 1675

Contact *Kathleen Austin*

ESTABLISHED 1965. Triennial award in memory of the late Dr Agnes Mure Mackenzie to promote a published work of Scottish historical research (including intellectual history and the history of science). Open to books published between September 1990 and September 1993. Previous winners: Professor T. C. Smout *A Century of the Scottish People 1830–1950*. Editions of texts not eligible; originals only.
Prize Bound and inscribed copy of the winning publication.

W. J. M. Mackenzie Book Prize

Political Studies Association, Dept of Politics, Salford University, Salford M5 4NT
☎ 061-745 5945   Fax 061-745 5945

Contact *Davina Miller* (PSA Administrative Secretary)

FOUNDED 1987. Annual award to best work of political science published in the UK during the previous year. Submissions from publishers only. Final entry date in May. Previous winners: James Mayall *Nationalism and International Society*; Brian Barry *Theories of Justice;* Avi Shlaim *Collusion Across the Jordan.*
Prize £100, plus travel/attendance at three-day annual conference.

McKitterick Prize

Society of Authors, 84 Drayton Gardens, London SW10 9SB
☎ 071-373 6642

Contact *Awards Secretary*

Annual award for a full-length work in the English language, first published in the UK or unpublished. Open to writers over 40 who have not had any

adult novel published other than the one submitted. Closing date 20 December. 1992 winner: Alberto Manguel *News from a Foreign Country.*
Prize £5000.

Enid McLeod Prize

Franco-British Society, Room 636, Linen Hall, 162–168 Regent Street, London W1R 5TB
☎ 071-734 0815

Executive Secretary *Mrs Marian Clarke*

FOUNDED 1982. Annual award to the author of a work of literature published in the UK which, in the opinion of the judges, has contributed most to Franco-British understanding. Any full-length work written in English by a citizen of the UK, Commonwealth, Republic of Ireland, Pakistan, Bangladesh and South Africa. Nominations from publishers for books published between 1 January and 31 December of the year of the prize. Previous winners: Allan Massie *A Question of Loyalties*; Frank Giles *The Locust Years.*
Prize Copy of Enid McLeod's memoirs, plus cheque.

Macmillan Prize for a Children's Picture Book

18–21 Cavaye Place, London SW10 9PG
☎ 071-373 6070   Fax 071-370 0746

Contact *Publicity Manager* (Macmillan Children's Books)

Established in order to stimulate new work from young illustrators in art schools, and to help them start their professional lives. Fiction or non-fiction. Macmillan Children's Books have the option to publish any of the prize winners.
Prize (1st) £750; (2nd) £400; (3rd) £150.

Macmillan Silver Pen Award

The English Centre of International PEN, 7 Dilke Street, London SW3 4JE
☎ 071-352 6303   Fax 071-351 0220

An annual award for a volume of short stories written in English by a British author and published in the UK in the year preceding the prize. Nominations by the PEN Executive Committee only. Previous winner: Pauline Melville *Shape-Shifter.*
Prize £500, plus silver pen.

McVitie's Prize for Scottish Writer of the Year

Michael Kelly Associates, Scottish Legal Building, 95 Bothwell Street, Glasgow G2 7HY
☎041-204 2580 Fax 041-204 0245
Contact *Deborah Watson*

FOUNDED 1987. Sponsored by United Biscuits (Holdings) plc for imaginative published works, including TV and film scripts, by Scottish writers. Entries accepted in English, Scots or Gaelic. Previous winners: Alan Bold *MacDiarmid*; Sorley Maclean *From Wood to Ridge*; William Boyd *Brazzaville Beach.*
Prize £10,000, plus £500 each to four shortlisted writers.

The Mail on Sunday Novel Competition

The Mail on Sunday, PO Box 2, Central Way, Feltham, Middlesex TW14 0TG
☎071-938 6000

Annual award, now in its ninth year. Judges look for a story/ character that springs to life in the 'tantalising opening 150 words of a novel'. 1991 winners: Jeff Phelps, Emma Cochrane, Shane Adams, Erin Anderson, Angela Lewis, Pat Simpson.
Award (1st) £400 book tokens and a weekend writing course at the **Arvon Foundation**; (2nd) £300 tokens; (3rd) £200 tokens; three runners-up receive £150 tokens each.

The Mail on Sunday/John Llewellyn Rhys Prize

Book Trust, Book House, 45 East Hill, London SW18 2QZ
☎081-870 9055 Fax 081-874 4790
Contact *Caroline Sanderson*

An annual young writer's award for a memorable work of any kind. Entrants must be under the age of 35 at the time of publication; books must have been published in the UK in the year of the award. The author must be a citizen of Britain or the Commonwealth, writing in English. Previous winners: Ray Monk *Wittgenstein*; A. L. Kennedy *Night Geometry and the Garscadden Trains.*
Prize £5000.

Arthur Markham Memorial Prize

University of Sheffield, PO Box 594, Firth Court, Sheffield S10 2UH
☎0742 768555 Fax 0742 728014
Contact *Academic Registrar's Office*

There are six categories for work specially written for this annual prize: short story, essay, single poem, group of poems, one-act play, first chapter of a novel on a given subject announced annually. Candidates must be manual workers at a coal mine or have previously worked as miners.
Prize £350.

Marsh Christian Trust Award

The Authors' Club, 40 Dover Street, London W1X 3RB
☎071-499 8581

A biennial award for the most significant biography published over a two year period by a British publisher. 1991 winner: Hugh & Mirabel Cecil *Clever Hearts.* Next entry date 1993.
Award £3000, plus silver trophy presented at a dinner.

Kurt Maschler Award (Emil)

Book Trust, Book House, 45 East Hill, London SW18 2QZ
☎081-870 9055 Fax 081-874 4790
Contact *Celia Parry-Jones*

For 'a work of imagination in the children's field in which text and illustration are of excellence and so presented that each enhances, yet balances the other'. Books published in the current year in the UK by a British author and/or artist, or by someone resident for ten years, are eligible. 1991 winner: Colin McNaughton *Have You Seen Who's Just Moved in Next Door to Us?.*
Award £1000.

Dorothy Maugher National Trophy Short Story Competition

Havant & District Writers' Circle, 41 Keydell Avenue, Horndean, Waterlooville, Hampshire PO8 9TD
☎0705 594250
Contact *The Secretary*

For original short stories up to 2000 words. Entry fee £2 per story. Several entries may be sent (s.a.e. essential for reply). Full details and entry form from above. Twelve prizes in all. Final entry date 31 October 1992.

Michelin Award

Guild of Motoring Writers, 30 The Cravens, Smallfield, Surrey RH6 9QS
☎0342 843294
Contact *Sharon Scott-Fairweather*

Abandoned due to lack of support in 1987, this award was reintroduced in 1990 for articles written by Guild members on transport and the environment. 1991 winner: Anthony Gould.
Prize £1000.

MIND Book of the Year – The Allen Lane Award

MIND, 22 Harley Street, London W1N 2ED
☏ 071–637 0741   Fax 071–323 0061

INAUGURATED 1981, this annual award in memory of Sir Allen Lane, is given to the author of the book, fiction or non-fiction, published in the current year, which furthers public understanding of mental health problems.
Award £1000.

Mobil Playwriting Competition for the Royal Exchange Theatre Company

Royal Exchange Theatre, St Ann's Square, Manchester M2 7DH
☏ 061–833 9333   Fax 061–832 0881

Contact *The Mobil Playwriting Competition*

FOUNDED 1984. Awarded to an original full-length play in English, representing an important source of new theatre writing. Leading international contest - it has attracted nearly 5000 entries from 25 different countries. Entries must be submitted under a pseudonym. Closing date for 1991/2 competition was August 1992; check requirements for 1993/4. Previous winners include: Robin Glendinning *Mumbo Jumbo;* Iain Heggie *A Wholly Healthy Glasgow;* Michele Celeste *Hanging the President;* Rod Wooden *Your Home in the West;* Randhi McWilliams *Sidewalk Sidney;* and the late Michael Wall's *Amongst Barbarians.* From the three competitions to date, over thirty plays have received exposure; several have been published; and several playwrights have become Writers-in-Residence at the Royal Exchange. Entrants to the competition are also eligible for the **Mobil Bursary** (£10,000), which funds the post of Writer-in-Residence at the theatre for one year.
Prizes (1st) £15,000, plus performance by **Royal Exchange Theatre Company** and possible publication, circumstances permitting; four special prizes of £1000 each to writers judged worthy of recognition.

Scott Moncrieff Prize

The Translators' Association, 84 Drayton Gardens, London SW10 9SB
☏ 071–373 6642

An annual award for the best translation published by a British publisher during the previous year of French twentieth-century work of literary merit and general interest. 1991 winner: Brian Pearce for his translation of *Bread and Circuses* Paul Veyne.
Prize £900.

Montagu Trophy

Guild of Motoring Writers, 30 The Cravens, Smallfield, Surrey RH6 9QS
☏ 0342 843294

Contact *Sharon Scott-Fairweather*

First presented by Lord Montagu on the occasion of the opening of the National Motor Museum at Beaulieu in 1972. Awarded annually to a member of the Guild who, in the opinion of the nominated jury, has made the greatest contribution to recording in the English language the history of motoring or motor cycling in a published book or article, film, television or radio script, or research manuscript available to the public. Previous winner: Adriano Cimarosti *The Camel Complete History of Grand Prix Racing.* Suspended for a year in 1991. Contact above for details 1993.

The Mother Goose Award

Books for Children, Whiteway Court, The Whiteway, Cirencester, Gloucestershire GL7 7BA
☏ 0285 657081   Fax 0285 657086

Contact *Sally Grindley*

For the most exciting newcomer to British children's book illustration. 1991 winner: Amanda Harvey *A Close Call.*
Prize £1000, plus a bronze goose egg.

Shiva Naipaul Memorial Prize

The Spectator, 56 Doughty Street, London WC1N 2LL
☏ 071–405 1706   Fax 071–242 0603

Contact *Virginia Utley*

An annual competition for the writer best able to describe a visit to a foreign place or people; for the most acute and profound observation of cultures and/or scenes evidently alien to the writer. Submissions must be unpublished and no more than 4000 words. Recent winners: Vanessa Letts, William T. Vollmann and Sousa Jamba.
Prize £1000, plus publication in *The Spectator.*

National Poetry Competition

The Poetry Society, 22 Betterton Street,
London WC2H 9BU
☎071-240 4810   Fax 071-240 4818

Competition Organiser *Betty Redpath*

The major annual open poetry competition in Britain. Prizes are awarded for an unpublished poem of 40 lines or less by anyone over the age of 16. There is an entry fee per poem, and a maximum entry of 15 poems per writer. Further details and entry form available on receipt of an s.a.e.
Prizes (1st) £2000, plus publication in a special anthology produced by **The Poetry Society**; (2nd) £1000; (3rd) £500; plus smaller prizes.

Natural World Book of the Year Award

Sea Containers House, 20 Upper Ground,
London SE1 9PF
☎071-928 2111

Contact *Linda Bennett*

ESTABLISHED 1987. Annual award to encourage the publication of high-quality natural history books. Open to books published between 1 October and 30 September about British wildlife or countryside. Final entry date end of August. Previous winner: Jeremy Thomas *The Butterflies of Britain & Ireland.* Administered by *Natural World* magazine.
Prize £500, plus magazine promotion feature of book.

NCR Book Award for Non-Fiction

NCR Book Award, 206 Marylebone Road,
London NW1 6LY
☎071-725 8271   Fax 071-724 6519

Contact *The Administrator*

ESTABLISHED 1987 (first award made 1988), the NCR Book Award is for a book written in English by a living writer from Britain, the Commonwealth or Republic of Ireland, and first published in the UK. One of the UK's single most valuable annual book prizes, with a total prize money of £29,500, and the only major prize specifically for non-fiction. Publishers only may submit titles, limited to three per imprint. The award will cover all areas of non-fiction except academic, guidebooks and practical listings (such as cookery books). Titles must be published in the twelve months between 1 April and 31 March. A shortlist of four books will be announced in mid-April and the winning book in mid-May. The aim of the award is to stimulate interest in non-fiction writing, reading and publishing in the UK. 1992 winner: Jung Chang *Wild Swans: Three Daughters of China.*

Prizes (1st) £25,000; three runners-up shortlisted £1500.

New Law Journal Rumpole Award

Crime Writers' Association, PO Box 172, Tring,
Hertfordshire HP23 5LP

Contact *The Secretary*

Administered by the **Crime Writers' Association** and sponsored by the *New Law Journal*, this is a biennial award for the book which best portrays legal procedure. Submissions should be made to James Morton, Editor, The New Law Journal, 9-12 Bell Yard, Temple Bar, London WC2A 2JR. Previous winner: Frances Fyfield *Trial By Fire.*
Prize £250.

Nobel Prize

Box 5232/Sturegatan 14, S-102 45 Stockholm,
Sweden
☎010 46 8 663 0920   Fax 010 46 8 660 3847

Contact *Information Section*

Awarded yearly for outstanding achievement in physics, chemistry, physiology or medicine, literature and peace. FOUNDED by Alfred Nobel, a chemist who proved his creative ability by inventing dynamite. In general, individuals cannot nominate someone for a Nobel Prize. The rules vary from prize to prize but the following are eligible to do so for Literature: members of the Swedish Academy and of other academies, institutions and societies similar to it in membership and aims; professors of history of literature or of languages at universities or colleges; Nobel Laureates in Literature; presidents of authors' organisations which are representative of the literary activities of their respective countries. British winners of the literature prize, first granted in 1901, include Rudyard Kipling, John Galsworthy and Winston Churchill. Recent winners: Wole Soyinka (Nigeria); Joseph Brodsky (USA); Naguib Mahfouz (Egypt); Camilio Jose Cela (Spain); Octavio Paz (Mexico); Nadine Gordimer (South Africa).
Prize in the region SEKr 6,000,000 (around £1,000,000) - increasing each year to cover inflation.

Northern Poetry Award

Littlewood Arc, Nanholme Centre, Shaw Wood
Road, Todmorden, Lancashire OL14 6DA
☎0706 818419   Fax 0706 818948

Contact *John Killick*

ESTABLISHED 1989. Biennial award set up to stimulate the writing and reading of quality new poetry in the North of England. Open to all who live in the area covered by the Northern regional arts boards (see **Arts Councils and Regional Arts Boards**). Final entry date June. Previous winners: Peter Bond, David Craig, Ian Duhig, Stephen Edwards, Leah Fleetwood, Adele Geras, Meg Peacocke, M. A. Portch, Irene Rawnsley, Copland Smith, John Ward.

Prize Publication, plus small cash prize.

Northern Stories Award

Littlewood Arc, Nanholme Centre, Shaw Wood Road, Todmorden, Lancashire OL14 6DA
☎0706 818419   Fax 0706 818948

Contact *John Killick*

ESTABLISHED 1988. Biennial award set up to stimulate the writing and reading of quality short fiction in the North of England. Open to all living in the area covered by the Northern regional arts boards (see **Arts Councils and Regional Arts Boards**). Final entry date in July. Previous winners: John Latham, Adele Geras, David Almond, Alison Leonard, Ian McMillan, Ray Brown.

Prize Publication, plus small cash prize.

Nottinghamshire Children's Book Award

Nottinghamshire Children's Book Award, Nottinghamshire County Council, Education Library Service, Glaisdale Parkway, Nottingham NG8 4GP
☎0602 854200

Contact *Ann Fairbairn* (Library)

FOUNDED 1989. Annual award jointly organised and promoted by Nottingham Libraries and Dillons Bookstore, who sponsor the award. The aim is to encourage reading and draw attention to the exciting range of children's books available. The award is given in two categories: The Acorn Award, for an outstanding book written and illustrated for the 0–7 age group; and The Oak Tree Award, for an outstanding book written and illustrated for the 8–12 age group. Books must have been published for the first time in the UK in the preceding year. Final entry date end March. 1991 winner: Mick Inkpen *Threadbear* (Acorn); Annie Dalton *The After-Dark Princess* (Oak Tree).

Award £250 (each category).

Oak Tree Award

See **Nottinghamshire Children's Book Award**

Odd Fellows (Manchester Unity) Social Concern Book Award

Book Trust, Book House, 45 East Hill, London SW18 2QZ
☎081-870 9055   Fax 081-874 4790

Contact *Caroline Sanderson*

An annual award for a book whch makes a significant contribution to highlighting an issue of social concern. Entries must have been published in the UK in the current year in English and been written by citizens of the Commonwealth, Republic of Ireland or South Africa. Previous winner: David Cook *Second Best.*

Award £2000.

C. B. Oldman Prize

Aberdeen University Library, Queen Mother Library, Meston Walk, Aberdeen AB9 2UE
☎0224 272592   Fax 0224 487048

Contact *Richard Turbet*

ESTABLISHED 1989 by the International Association of Music Libraries, UK Branch. Annual award for best book of music bibliography, librarianship or reference published the year before last (i.e. books published in 1991 considered for the 1993 prize). Previous winners: Andrew Ashbee, Michael Talbot, Donald Clarke, John Parkinson.

Prize £150.

Outposts Poetry Competition

Hippopotamus Press, 22 Whitewell Road, Frome, Somerset BA11 4El
☎0373 66653

Contact *Roland John*

Annual competition for an unpublished poem of not more than 40 lines run by **Hippopotamus Press**.

Prize c.£1000.

OWG/COLA Awards for Excellence

Outdoor Writers' Guild, 86 Burford Gardens, London N13 4LP
☎081-886 1957

Contact *Hugh Westacott*

FOUNDED 1990. Annual award by the Outdoor Writers' Guild and the Camping & Outdoor Leisure Association to raise the standard of outdoor writing, journalism and broadcasting. Winning categories include best book, best guidebook, best feature, best news round-up, best technical report. Open to OWG members only. Closing date April. Previous winners include: Leigh Hatts, Nick Crane,

Steve Venables, Hazel Constance, Catherine Moore.
Prize (total) £1000.

Catherine Pakenham Award

The Sunday Telegraph, 1 Canada Square, Canary Wharf, London E14 5DT
☎071-538 5000

Contact *Joanne Henwood*

FOUNDED 1970, this is an annual award in memory of Lady Catherine Pakenham, and is given for a published article (750-2000 words) by women aged between 18 and 25 resident in Britain and involved in or intending to take up a career in journalism.
Award £1000, plus five runner-up prizes of £100 each.

The People's Prize

Scottish Library Association, Motherwell Business Centre, Coursington Road, Motherwell ML1 1PW
☎0698 52526

Contact *Robert Craig*

FOUNDED 1989. Annual fiction prize set up by the **Scottish Library Association** and *The Herald*, Glasgow. Nominations from libraries; selection from six shortlisted books by public vote through forms published in the newspaper and available in libraries. Awarded to a work of fiction by a Scottish writer or writer resident in Scotland, published during the previous year. 1991 winner: Alan Spence *The Magic Flute*.
Prize £5000.

Peterloo Poets Open Poetry Competition

2 Kelly Gardens, Calstock, Cornwall PL18 9SA
☎0822 833473

Contact *Lynn Chambers*

FOUNDED 1986. Annual competition sponsored by Marks & Spencer for unpublished English language poems of not more than 40 lines. Final entry date end January. Previous winners: David Craig, Rodney Pybus, Debjani Chatterjee, Donald Atkinson, Romesh Gunesekera.
Prize £2000.

Poetry Business Competition

51 Byram Arcade, Westgate, Huddersfield HD1 1ND
☎0484 434840   Fax 0484 426566

Contact *Duncan Curry*

FOUNDED 1987. Annual award which aims to discover and publish new writers. Entrants should submit 16 pp of poems. Entry fee £10. There are two winners who share in having their work published together, produced by the **Poetry Business** under the **Smith/Doorstop** imprint. There is also an anthology published of the 'Best of the Rest'. Final entry date in the autumn. Previous winners: Michael Lasky & Steven Waling, Mimi Khalvati & David Morley, Liz Cashdan & Julia Casterton, Moniza Alvi & Peter Daniels.
No cash prize.

The Portico Prize

The Portico Library, 57 Mosley Street, Manchester M2 3HY
☎061-236 6785

Contact *Mrs Jo Francis*

FOUNDED 1985. Administered by the Portico Library in Manchester. Biennial award (odd-numbered years) for a work of fiction or non-fiction set wholly or mainly in the North West/ Cumbria. Next award 1993. 1991 winner: Alan Hankinson *Coleridge Walks the Fells*.
Prize £1500.

Michael Powell Book Award

British Film Institute, 21 Stephen Street, London W1P 1PL
☎071-255 1444   Fax 071-436 7950

Contact *Wayne Drew*

Annual award given by the British Film Institute for a book by a British author on film or television which is both innovative and accessible, with a lively approach to the media. Previous winners include: Kevin Brownlow *Behind the Mask of Innocence*; Roger Bolton *Death on the Rock and other stories*; Joel Finler *The Hollywood Story*.
Award varies.

Pulitzer Prizes

The Pulitzer Prize Board, 702 Journalism, Columbia University, New York NY 10027
☎0101 212 854 3841/2

Contact *The Secretary*

Awards for journalism in US newspapers, and for literature, drama and music by American nationals. Deadline February 1 (journalism); March 14 (music); March 1 (drama); July 1 for books published between Jan 1-June 30, amd Nov 1 for books published between July 1–Dec 31 (literature). 1992 winners: Fiction: Jane Smiley *A Thousand Acres*; Non-fiction: Daniel Yergin *The Prize*.

Quartos Magazine Short Story Competitions
See **Magazines**

Questors Theatre Student Playwright Competition
12 Mattock Lane, Ealing, London W5 5BQ
☎ 081-567 0011

Contact *Elaine Orchard* (Theatre Manager)

Annual award, now in its sixth year. The winning play is performed at Questors Theatre. Closing date October.
Prize £1000.

Radio Times Drama & Comedy Awards
BBC Magazines, 35 Marylebone High Street, London W1M 4AA
☎ 071-580 5577   Fax 071-486 7764

Contact *Alison Gundry*

Annual awards for an original work for either radio or television not previously performed in public. Each entry to be supported by a sponsor experienced in production. Details of awards are announced in *Radio Times* in March.
Award £5000 (each category).

Trevor Reese Memorial Prize
Institute of Commonwealth Studies, University of London, 28 Russell Square, London WC1B 5DS
☎ 071-580 5876   Fax 071-255 2160

Contact *Director's Secretary*

ESTABLISHED 1980 with the proceeds of contributions to a memorial fund to Dr Trevor Reese, reader in Commonwealth Studies at the Institute and a distinguished scholar of imperial history (d. 1976). Biennial award (next award 1994/5) for a scholarly work by a single author in the field of Imperial and Commonwealth history published in the preceding two years. Final entry date March 1994.
Prize £1000.

Regional Press Awards
1st Floor, Post Office Headquarters, 130 Old Street, London EC1V 9PQ
☎ 071-320 7133   Fax 071-320 7437

A mixed bag of awards including Campaigning Journalist of the Year; Feature Writer of the Year; Columnist of the Year; Young Journalist of the Year (not older than 23 on 31 December); Sports Writer of the Year; Specialist Writer of the Year. Open to all journalists, whether freelance or staff, who do not work on national newspapers. Final entry date 31 January. Run by the *UK Press Gazette* and sponsored by the Post Office. Presentation details and entry form from address above.
Prize £250, plus certificate. Newspaper of the Year wins £1000 to donate to a local community project.

Rhône Poulenc Prize
See **Science Book Prizes**

Rhyme International Prize
c/o Orbis Magazine, 199 The Long Shoot, Nuneaton, Warwickshire CV11 6JQ
☎ 0203 327440/385551   Fax 0203 642402

Contact *Mike Shields*

ESTABLISHED 1982. Annual competition aimed at promoting rhyming poetry. Entry fee £2.50 per poem. Entries may fall into two categories: rhymed poems of less than 50 lines; or formal: sonnet, villanelle, etc. Final entry date end September.
Prize (total) £1000.

Rogers Prize
Scholarships Section, Room 21A, Senate House, Malet Street, London WC1E 7HU
☎ 071-636 8000 ext. 3042

Contact *Mrs M. Praulins*

Annual award for an essay or dissertation on alternately a medical or surgical subject, which is named and appointed by the University of London on the advice of the relevant Board of Studies. Essays and dissertations must be in English and shall be typewritten or printed.
Prize £250.

Romantic Novelists' Association Major Award
38 Stanhope Road, Reading RG2 7HN
☎ 0734 871154

Contact *Betty O'Rourke* (The Organiser)

Annual award now sponsored by Boots the Chemist for the best romantic novel of the year, open to non-members as well as members of the **Romantic Novelists' Association**. Novels must be published between 1 December of previous year and 30 November of the year of entry. Authors must be based in the UK. Previous winners include: Susan Kay *Phantom* (1991); Reay Tannahill *Passing Glory* (1990); Sarah Woodhouse *The Peacock's Feather* (1989). The organiser for the award changes every two years. There will probably be a new organiser for 1993 but enquiries can be directed to the above. *Award* £5000.

Romantic Novelists' Association/ Netta Muskett Award
9 Hillside Road, Southport, Merseyside PR8 4QB
☎0704 60945

Contact *Marie Murray*

Also known as the New Writers Award. The award is for unpublished writers in the field of the romantic novel. Entrants are required to join the Association as probationary members. Mss entered for this award must be specifically written for it.

Rooney Prize for Irish Literature
Rooney Prize, Strathin, Templecarrig, Delgany, Co. Wicklow, Republic of Ireland
☎010 353 1 287 4769

Contact *Jim Sherwin*

FOUNDED 1976. Annual award to encourage young Irish writing to develop and continue. Writer must be Irish, under 40 and published. A non-competitive award with no application procedure. *Prize* IR £3500 (tax free).

Routledge Ancient History Prize
c/o Richard Stoneman, Senior Editor, Routledge, 11 New Fetter Lane, London EC4P 4EE
☎071-583 9855   Fax 071-583 0701

Annual award presented to the author of the best contribution in English to the understanding of the history of the classical world. Typescripts (70,000–120,000 words) should be submitted by 31 August each year. No editions or commentaries. Works submitted should not normally be such as to require extensive photographic illustration or extensive typesetting in foreign alphabets. Funded by **Routledge** who will also publish the winning title. No restriction on age, nationality or status of candidates. 1992 winners: (joint) Thomas Wiedemann *Emperors and Gladiators* and Hagith Sivan *Ausonius of Bordeaux*. Both books will be published by Routledge in 1992/3. *Prize* £500, plus publication.

Rover Group Award
Guild of Motoring Writers, 30 The Cravens, Smallfield, Surrey RH6 9QS
☎0342 843294

Contact *Sharon Scott-Fairweather*

Awarded annually to the Guild member judged to have done most towards improving reader understanding of the issues affecting the vehicle industry. 1991 winner: Geoffrey Howard. *Prize* £1000.

Royal Economic Society Prize
Royal Economic Society, University of York, York YO1 5DD
☎0904 433575

Contact *Prof. John D. Hey*

Biennial award for the best article published in *The Economic Journal.* Open to members of the Royal Economic Society only. Final entry date for 1992/3 competition is December 1993. Previous winners: Drs O. P. Attanasio & Guilielmo Weber. *Prize* £1000.

Royal Heinemann Award
Royal Society of Literature, 1 Hyde Park Gardens, London W2 2LT
☎071-723 5104

Works of any kind of literature may be submitted by their publishers for consideration under this award, but only living authors are considered. Genuine contributions to literature originally written in English are sought, but preference will be given to publications which are unlikely to command large sales: poetry, biography, criticism, etc. 1991 winner: Alan Judd *Ford Maddox Ford.* *Award* £5000 (1992), but varies.

The RTZ David Watt Memorial Prize
RTZ Corporation plc, 6 St James's Square, London SW1Y 4LD
☎071-930 2399   Fax 071-930 3249

INITIATED 1987 to commemorate the life and work of David Watt. Annual award, open to writers currently engaged in writing for newspapers and journals, in the English language, on international and political affairs. The winners are judged as having made 'outstanding contributions towards the clarification of international and political issues and the promotion of a greater understanding of such issues'. Closing date March. Previous winners include: Edward Mortimer, for a discussion of socialism in Western Europe in the *Financial Times;* Timothy Garton Ash, for an article on European

integration in *The Spectator*, Ian Davidson, for an article on communist regimes in Eastern Europe; Neal Ascherson of *The Independent on Sunday*.
Prize £5000.

Sagittarius Prize

Society of Authors, 84 Drayton Gardens, London SW10 9SB
☏ 071-373 6642   Fax 071-373 5768

FOUNDED 1990. For first published novel by an author over the age of 60. Closing date mid-late December. 1992 winner: Hugh Leonard *Parnell and the Englishwoman*.
Prize £2000.

Ian St James Awards

c/o The Merric Davidson Consultancy, Oakwood, Ashley Park, Tunbridge Wells, Kent TN4 8UA
☏ 0892 514282   Fax 0892 514282

INITIATED 1989. Administered by the Ian St James Trust. Presented to twelve previously unpublished authors for short stories of between 5–10,000 words. These awards are 'an opportunity for talented and as yet unpublished writers to achieve recognition'. Ian St James is a successful novelist who hopes to attract both literary and commercial fiction from aspiring writers. The competition rules state: 'Copyright in the 12 award winning manuscripts will become the property of the Ian St James Trust upon payment of the appropriate prize money (a minimum of £1000 to each writer).' Winning entries are published in a paperback anthology by **HarperCollins** in the autumn. Final entry date 31 January 1993. 1991 winners: Faith Addis *Small Beginnings*; Alan Dunn *French Kisses*; Stephanie Ellyne *Me and Renate*. Entry forms available from bookshops from October usually.
Award (total) £33,000.

Schlegel-Tieck Prize

The Translators' Association, 84 Drayton Gardens, London SW10 9SB
☏ 071-373 6642

Contact *Kate Pool*

An annual award for the best translation of a German 20th-century work of literary merit and interest published by a British publisher during the preceding year. 1991 winners: John Woods, Christoph Ransmayr, Hugh Young, Edgar Hilsenrath.
Prize £2200.

Science Book Prizes

Copus, c/o The Royal Society, 6 Carlton House Terrace, London SW1Y 5AG
☏ 071-839 5561 ext. 266   Fax 071-930 2170

Contact *Jill A. Nelson*

FOUNDED 1987 by COPUS (Committee on the Public Understanding of Science). Sponsored by Rhône Poulenc. Annual awards for popular nonfiction science and technology books judged to contribute most to the public understanding of science. Books must be published during the previous calendar year in their first English edition in the UK. The prizes, totalling £25,000, are awarded in two categories: the Rhône Poulenc prize awarded for a book for general readership; and the Science Book Junior Prize, shared cash prize for books written primarily for young people. This may be divided for different age categories (under 14 and under 8) and for discretionary awards (e.g. for illustration). Final entry date January. 1992 winners: Jared Diamond *The Rise and Fall of the Chimpanzee*; Peter Rowan *The Amazing Voyage of the Cucumber Sandwich*; David Burne *How Nature Works*.
Prizes The Rhône-Poulenc Prize £10,000; Science Book Junior Prize £10,000 shared.

Scottish Arts Council Book Awards

Scottish Arts Council, 12 Manor Place, Edinburgh EH3 7DD
☏ 031-226 6051   Fax 031-225 9833

Contact *Literature Officer*

A number of awards are given biannually to authors of published books in recognition of high standards in new writing from new and established writers. Authors should be Scottish, resident in Scotland or have published books of Scottish interest. Applications from publishers only. Previous winners include: G. F. Dutton *Squaring the Waves*; James Kelman *Greyhound for Breakfast*; Andro Linklater *Compton Mackenzie: A Life*; Brian McCabe *One Atom to Another*.
Award £1000 each.

Scottish Book of the Year

Saltire Society, 9 Fountain Close, 22 High Street, Edinburgh EH1 1TF
☏ 031-556 1836

Contact *Paul H. Scott* (Convener)/*Kathleen Austin* (Administrator)

ESTABLISHED 1982. Annual award open to any author of Scottish descent or living in Scotland, or to anyone who has written a book which deals with either the work and life of a Scot or with a Scottish

problem, event or situation. Nominations are invited from editors of leading newspapers, magazines and periodicals. 1992 winner: Duncan Macmillan *Scottish Art 1460-1990*. There is also an additional prize for the best first book by an author publishing for the first time.
Cash prize.

SCSE Book Prizes

Faculty of Education, Bristol Polytechnic, Redland Hill, Bristol BS6 6UZ
☎ 0272 741251   Fax 0272 732251
Contact *Professor P. Croll*

Annual awards given by the Standing Conference on Studies in Education for the best book on education published during the preceding year and for the best book by a new author. Nomination by members of the Standing Conference and publishers.
Prizes £1000 and £500.

Signal Poetry for Children Award

Thimble Press, Lockwood, Station Road, South Woodchester, Stroud GL5 5EQ
☎ 0453 873716/872208   Fax 0453 878599
Contact *Nancy Chambers*

This award is given annually for particular excellence in one of the following areas: single-poet collections published for children; poetry anthologies published for children; the body of work of a contemporary poet; critical or educational activity promoting poetry for children. All books for children published in Britain are eligible regardless of the original country of publication. Unpublished work is not eligible. Previous winners include: Allan Ahlberg *Heard it in the Playground;* James Berry *When I Dance;* John Mole *Boo to a Goose*, illus. by Mary Norman.
Award £100.

André Simon Memorial Fund Book Awards

61 Church Street, Isleworth, Middlesex TW7 6BE
☎ 081-560 6662   Fax 081-847 0660
Contact *Tessa Hayward*

Three awards given annually for the best book on drink, best on food and special commendation in either.
Award £2000 (best books); £1000 (special commendation); £200 to shortlisted books.

Smarties Prize for Children's Books

Book Trust, Book House, 45 East Hill,
London SW18 2QZ
☎ 081-870 9055   Fax 081-874 4790
Contact *Celia Parry-Jones*

ESTABLISHED 1985 to encourage high standards and stimulate interest in books for children, this prize is given for a children's book (fiction), written in English by a citizen of the UK or an author resident in the UK, and published in the UK in the year ending 31 October. There are three age-group categories: under 5, 6-8 and 9-11. An overall winner from these categories is chosen for the Smarties Book Prize. 1991 winners: Martin Waddell & Helen Oxenbury *Farmer Duck* (0-5 yrs); category winners: Magdalen Nabb & Pirkko Vainio *Josie Smith and Eileen* (6-8 yrs); Philip Ridley *Krindlekrax* (9-11 yrs). Non-fiction previously eligible, but no longer, due to lack of resources.
Prizes £8000 (overall winner); £2000 (other categories).

Smith Corona Prize

3A High Street, Rickmansworth,
Hertfordshire WD3 1HP
☎ 0923 777111   Fax 0923 896370
Contact *Debra Simpson*

Quarterly competition sponsored by Smith Corona (UK) Ltd and featured in *Writers Monthly* magazine (see **Magazines**) for a short story or piece of writing on a selected topic.
Prize Personal word processor or electronic typewriter.

W. H. Smith Literary Award

W. H. Smith, 7 Holbein Place,
London SW1W 8NR
☎ 071-730 1200 ext. 5458   Fax 071-730 0195
Contact *Michael Mackenzie*

Annual prize awarded to a UK, Republic of Ireland or Commonwealth citizen for the most outstanding contribution to English literature, published in English in UK in the preceding year. Previous winners include: Thomas Pakenham *The Scramble for Africa;* Derek Walcott *Omeros;* Christopher Hill *A Turbulent, Seditious, and Fractious People: John Bunyan and His Church.*
Prize £10,000.

W. H. Smith Young Writers' Competition

W. H. Smith, 7 Holbein Place,
London SW1W 8NR
☏ 071-730 1200 ext. 5456   Fax 071-730 0195

Contact Lois Beeson

Annual awards for poems or prose by anyone in the UK under the age of 17. There are three age groups. Over sixty individual winners have their work included in a paperback every year.
Prize (total) more than £6500.

Southern Arts Literature Prize

Southern Arts, 13 St Clement Street, Winchester, Hampshire SO23 9DQ
☏ 0962 855099   Fax 0962 861186

Contact Literature Officer

This prize is awarded annually to an author living in the **Southern Arts** region for the most promising work of prose or poetry published during the year. 1991 winner: Bernard O'Donoghue The Weakness. Final entry date late October.
Prize £1000, plus a craft commission to the value of £500.

Southport Writers' Circle Poetry Competition

c/o Mrs Alison Chisholm, 53 Richmond Road, Birkdale, Southport, Merseyside PR8 4SB

For previously unpublished work which has not been entered in any other current competition. Entry fee £1.50 first poem, plus £1 for each subsequent entry. Maximum 40 lines on any subject and in any form. Closing date end April. Poems must be entered under a pseudonym, accompanied by a sealed envelope marked with the pseudonym and title of poem, containing a stamped addressed envelope. Entries must be typed on A4 paper and be accompanied by the appropriate fee payable to Southport Writers' Circle. No application form is required. Envelopes should be marked 'Poetry Competition'. Postal enquiries only. No calls.
Prize (1st) £100; (2nd) £50; (3rd) £25.

Stand Magazine Short Story Competition

Stand Magazine, 179 Wingrove Road, Newcastle upon Tyne NE4 9DA
☏ 091-273 3280

Contact The Administrator

Biennial award for a short story written in English and not yet published, broadcast or under consideration elsewhere. Final entry date 31 March 1993. Send s.a.e. for entry form.
Prize (total) £2250.

The Winifred Mary Stanford Prize

Hodder & Stoughton, 47 Bedford Square,
London WC1B 3DP
☏ 071-636 9851   Fax 071-631 5248

This biennial award (even years) is open to any book published in the UK in English which has been in some way inspired by the Christian faith, and written by a man or woman who is under 50 years of age at the time of publication. Literary merit is a prime factor in consideration for the award, but the form may be from a wide range including poetry, fiction, biography, autobiography, biblical exposition, religious experience and witness. Submission is invited, from publishers only, of books published in the two years prior to the award which is presented at Easter. 1992 winner: Susan Howatch Scandalous Risks.
Prize £1000.

Staple Open Poetry Competition

Tor Cottage, 81 Cavendish Road, Matlock, Derbyshire DE4 3HD
☏ 0629 582764

Contact Don Measham

Biennial open competition run by Staple magazine. Final entry date for 1993 competition: 31 December 1992. Next award 1995 with final entry date end December 1994.
Prize (total) £500.

Sunday Express Book of the Year Award

Ludgate House, 245 Blackfriars Road,
London SE1 9UX
☏ 071-928 8000   Fax 071-922 7964

INITIATED 1987. An award for a work of fiction published in the current year. Books are nominated by a panel of judges. No entries from publishers. Previous winners: Michael Frayn A Landing on the Sun; J. M. Coetzee Age of Iron; Rose Tremain Restoration.
Prize £20,000.

Sunday Times Award for Small Publishers

c/o Book Trust, Book House, 45 East Hill,
London SW18 2QZ
☎081-870 9055   Fax 081-874 4790

Contact *Caroline Sanderson*

Open to any publisher producing between five and forty titles a year, which must primarily be original titles, not reprints. Takes place at the beginning of the year when entrants are invited to submit their catalogues for the last twelve months, together with two representative titles. INITIATED in 1988, the first winner was **Fourth Estate**. 1992 winner: **Blackstaff Press Ltd**.

Sunday Times Special Award for Excellence in Writing

The Sunday Times, 1 Pennington Street,
London E1 9XN
☎071-782 7000   Fax 071-782 5120

Contact *Penny Perrick*

INITIATED 1987. Annual award to fiction and non-fiction writers who have not received sufficient recognition. The panel consists of *Sunday Times* journalists, publishers and other figures from the book world. Previous winners: Anthony Burgess, Seamus Heaney, Stephen Hawking, Ruth Rendell, Muriel Spark.
Award Silver trophy, in the shape of a book, inscribed with the winner's name.

Sunday Times Young British Writer of the Year Award

Society of Authors, 84 Drayton Gardens,
London SW10 9SB
☎071-373 6642   Fax 071-373 5768

Contact *Diana Shine*

FOUNDED 1991. Open to published writers under the age of 35 for a work of fiction, non-fiction and poetry. Entries from publishers only. 1991 winner: Helen Simpson *Four Bare Legs in a Bed*.
Prize £5000.

Edith & Joseph Sunlight Award

Balfour Diamond Jubilee Trust, Balfour House, 741 High Road, London N12 0BQ
☎081-446 1477   Fax 081-446 1180

The award, which is given in Manchester, takes the form of an inscribed crystal glass bowl which is awarded for literary works, the content of which enhances cultural relations between the United Kingdom and the state of Israel. Previous winners:

Martin Gilbert, Dr Conor Cruise O'Brien, Paul Johnson, Lord Weidenfeld, David Pryce Jones, The Chief Rabbi Dr Jonathan Sacks.

E. Reginald Taylor Essay Competition

Journal of the British Archaeological Association,
Institute of Archaeology, 36 Beaumont Street,
Oxford OX1 2PG

Contact *Dr Martin Henig* (by post only)

A biennial prize, in memory of the late E. Reginald Taylor, for the best unpublished essay, not exceeding 7500 words, on a subject of archaeological, art history or antiquarian interest within the period from the Roman era to AD 1830. The essay should show *original* research on its chosen subject, and the author will be invited to read the essay before the Association. In addition, the essay may be published in the Journal of the Association if approved by the Editorial Committee. Next entry date 31 October 1994.
Prize £100.

Tees Valley Writer Competitions

See **Tees Valley Writer (Magazines)**

Anne Tibble Poetry Competition

Events Team, Directorate of Environment Services,
Northampton Borough Council, Cliftonville House,
Bedford Road, Northampton NN4 0NW
☎0604 233500   Fax 0604 29571

Contact *Liz Carroll*

Entries should preferably be typed on one side of paper only and must not exceed 20 lines. Any writer resident in Great Britain is eligible, and there are categories for children: under 11; under 16.
Prize (1st) £100.

Time-Life Silver PEN Award

English Centre of International PEN, 7 Dilke Street,
London SW3 4JE
☎071-352 6303   Fax 071-351 0220

An annual award, the winner being nominated by the PEN Executive Committee, for an outstanding work of non-fiction written in English and published in England in the year preceding the prize. Previous winners: Susan Richards *Epics of Everyday Life*; William St Clair *The Godwins and the Shelleys*.
Prize £1000, plus silver pen.

Times Educational Supplement Information Book Awards

Times Educational Supplement, Priory House, St John's Lane, London EC1M 4BX
☎071-253 3000 Fax 071-608 1599

Contact *Literary Editor*

ESTABLISHED 1986. Two annual awards made for Best Information Books: one for the age range 10–16, the second for children up to the age of 10. Books must have been published in Britain or the Commonwealth in the year preceding the award. Final entry date usually 31 August. Also, a third award for Best Schoolbook, with age and subject range varying from year to year. 1991 winners: Junior Information Book Award: *Ian & Fred's Big Green Book* Fred Pearce & Ian Winton; Senior Information Book Award: *An Egyptian Pyramid* Jacqueline Morley, Mark Bergin & John James; Schoolbook, Primary Award: no prize awarded; Schoolbook, Secondary Award (joint) *After the Bomb: Brother in the Land* English & Media Centre and *Thin Ice* (OUP).
Award £500 (each category).

The Tir Na N-Og Award

Welsh Books Council, Castell Brychan, Aberystwyth, Dyfed SY23 2JB
☎0970 624151 Fax 0970 625385

An annual award given to the best original book published for children in the year prior to the announcement. There are three categories: Best Welsh Fiction; Best Welsh Non-fiction; Best English Book with an authentic Welsh background.
Award minimum £350; maximum £500.

Marten Toonder Award

The Arts Council (An Chomhairle Ealaíon), 70 Merrion Square, Dublin 2, Republic of Ireland
☎010 353 1 611840 Fax 010 353 1 761302

Contact *Literature Officer*

A triennial award for creative writing. Next award 1995. Open to Irish citizens or residents only.
Award £3000.

John Tripp Award

The Welsh Academy, 3rd Floor, Mount Stuart House, Mount Stuart Square, Cardiff CF1 6DQ
☎0222 492025 Fax 0222 492930

Contact *Kevin Thomas*

FOUNDED 1990. Themes and rules may vary from year to year. The 1992 award was for spoken poetry. Open to Welsh nationals or residents only.

Usually launched in the spring with closing date in summer.
Prize (total) £1400.

Dorothy Tutin Award

National Poetry Foundation, 27 Mill Road, Fareham, Hampshire PO16 0TH

Contact *Johnathon Clifford*

FOUNDED 1979. Biannual award to the person whom it is felt has done the most to encourage the writing of poetry throughout the UK. By recommendation only.
Award Engraved carriage clock.

Unicorn Theatre Young Playwrights' Competition

Unicorn Theatre for Children, Arts Theatre, Great Newport Street, London WC2H 7JB
☎071-379 3280 Fax 071-836 5366

Contact *Dorothy Wooder*

Annual awards to young playwrights aged 4–12 for plays on a theme decided by the theatre. Entries by the end of December. Three age groups: 4–6; 7–9; 10–12. The plays are judged by a committee of writers. The winners take part in workshops on the plays with members of the **Unicorn Theatre for Children Club** in preparation for performances on stage the following spring.

T. E. Utley Award

The Secretary, T. E. Utley Memorial Fund 38 Aldridge Road Villas, London W11 1BR
☎071-792 3501

Contact *The Secretary*

Open to writers under 35 years of age for a work of originality in political thought of any colour. Closing date end May. Applicants should contact the Secretary in the first instance for details of presentation.
Award £5000.

Vauxhall Trophy

Guild of Motoring Writers, 30 The Cravens, Smallfield, Surrey RH6 9QS
☎0342 843294

Contact *Sharon Scott-Fairweather*

Awarded annually to the Guild member judged to have written the best article(s) explaining any aspect of automotive design or technology. 1991 winner: Anthony Curtis.
Prize Trophy, plus £750.

Ver Poets Poetry Competitions

Haycroft, 61–63 Chiswell Green Lane, St Albans,
Hertfordshire AL2 3AL
☏ 0727 867005

Contact *May Badman*

Various competitions organised by **Ver Poets**, the main one being the annual Open Poetry Competition for unpublished poems of no more than 30 lines written in English. Final entry date 30 April. Entry fee £2 per poem. Entries must be made under a pseudonym, with name and address on form or separate sheet. An anthology of winning and selected poems as well as the adjudicators' report is normally available from mid-June. The society also runs two member competitions, one in the autumn, closing 30 September, with publication in an anthology for winning and selected entries. Entry fee £2 per poem. The other, known as Ver Poets Mini-Comps, are run every six months, with an entry fee of 50p per poem. *Prizes* Open: (1st) £500; (2nd) £300; plus two runner-up prizes of £100. Autumn Competition: (1st) £100; (2nd) £50; plus two runner-up prizes of £25. Mini-Comps: total of entry fees divided and publication in the society's magazine, *Poetry Post*.

Vogue Talent Contest

Vogue, Vogue House, Hanover Square,
London W1R 0AD
☏ 071-499 9080   Fax 071-408 0559

Contact *Georgina Boosey*

ESTABLISHED 1951. Annual award for young writers and journalists (under 25 on 1 January in the year of the contest). Final entry date beginning April. Entrants must write three pieces of journalism on given subjects. *Prize* £1000, plus a month's work experience with *Vogue*; (2nd) £500.

Wadsworth Prize for Business History

Business Archives Council, 185 Tower Bridge Road, London SE1 2UF
☏ 071-407 6110

Annual award for scholarly contribution to the history of British business and commercial affairs. Previous winner: Sir Peter Thompson *Sharing the Success: The Story of NFC*. *Prize* £200.

Wandsworth Writers London Competition

Town Hall, Wandsworth High Street,
London SW18 2PU
☏ 081-871 6364

Contact *Assistant Director of Leisure and Amenity Services (Libraries, Museum & Arts)*

An annual competition, open to all writers of 16 and over who live, work or study in the Greater London Area. There are three categories, all for previously unpublished work, in poetry, plays and the short story. *Prize* £800 for each class, divided between the top three in each category; plus two runner-up prizes in each class.

Welsh Arts Council Book of the Year Awards

Welsh Arts Council, Museum Place,
Cardiff CF1 3NX
☏ 0222 394711   Fax 0222 221447

Contact *Tony Bianchi*

Annual non-competitive prizes awarded for works of exceptional literary merit written by Welsh authors (by birth or residence), published in Welsh or English during the previous calendar year. There is one major prize in English, the Book of the Year Award, and one major prize in Welsh, Gwobr Llyfr y Flwyddyn. Shortlists of three titles in each language are announced in April; winners announced in May. *Prizes* £3000 (each); £1000 to each of four runners-up.

Whitbread Book of the Year and Literary Awards

Minster House, 272 Vauxhall Bridge Road,
London SW1V 1BA
☏ 071-834 5477   Fax 071-834 8812

Contact *Lorna Peppiatt*

Publishers are invited to submit books for this annual competition designed for writers who have been resident in Great Britain or the Republic of Ireland for three years or more. The awards are made in two stages. First, nominations are selected in five categories: novel, first novel, biography, children's novel and poetry. One of these is then voted by the panel of judges as Whitbread Book of the Year. 1991 winners: Jane Gardam *Queen of the Tambourine* (novel); Gordon Burn *Alma Cogan* (first novel); Michael Longley *Gorse Fires* (poetry); John Richardson *A Life of Picasso* (biography and Book of the Year); Diana Hendry *Harvey Angell* (children's novel).

Awards £20,500 (Book of the Year); £2000 (all nominees).

Whitfield Prize

Royal Historical Society, University College London, Gower Street, London WC1E 6BT
☎ 071-387 7532

Contact *Literary Director*

An annual award for the best new work within a field of British history, published in the UK in the preceding calendar year. The book must be the author's first (solely written) history book and be an original and scholarly work of historical research. Final entry date end December.
Prize £1000.

John Whiting Award

Arts Council of Great Britain, 14 Great Peter Street, London SW1P 3NQ
☎ 071-333 0100   Fax 071-973 6590

Contact *The Drama Director*

FOUNDED 1965. Annual award to commemorate the life and work of the playwright John Whiting (*The Devils, A Penny for a Song*). Any writer who has received during the previous two calendar years an award through the **Arts Council's Theatre Writing Schemes** or who has had a première production by a theatre company in receipt of annual subsidy is eligible to apply. Awarded to the writer whose play most nearly satisfies the following: a play in which the writing is of special quality; a play of relevance and importance to contemporary life; a play of potential value to the British theatre. Closing date mid January 1992. 1992 winner: Roy MacGregor *Our Own Kind.*
Prize £6000.

Alfred and Mary Wilkins Memorial Poetry Competition

Birmingham & Midland Institute, 9 Margaret Street, Birmingham B3 3BS
☎ 021-236 3591

Contact *J. Hunt* (Administrator)

An annual competition for an unpublished poem not exceeding 40 lines, written in English by an author over the age of 15 and living, working or studying in the UK. The poem should not have been entered for any other poetry competition. Six prizes awarded in all.
Prize (total) £475.

Griffith John Williams Memorial Prize

3 Llawr Ty Mount Stuart, Sgwar Mount Stuart, Cardiff CF1 6DQ
☎ 0222 492064

Contact *Dafydd Rogers*

FOUNDED 1965. Biennial award in honour of the first President of the **Welsh Academy** which aims to promote writing in Welsh. Entries must be the first published work of authors or poets writing in Welsh. Work must have been published in the two-year period preceding the award.
Award £400.

Raymond Williams Community Publishing Prize

Literature Dept, Arts Council, 14 Great Peter Street, London SW1P 3NQ
☎ 071-973 6442   Fax 071-973 6590

ESTABLISHED 1990. Award for unpublished/published work which exemplifies the values of ordinary people and their lives — a matter embodied in Williams' own work. Final entry date April.

H. H. Wingate Prize

PO Box 1148, London NW5 2AZ
☎ 071-485 4062   Fax 071-485 2329

Contact *Michael Lazarus*

Annual awards (one for fiction, one for non-fiction and one for poetry) for works which best stimulate an interest in and awareness of themes of Jewish interest. Books must have been published in the UK in the year of the award and be written in English by an author resident in Britain, Commonwealth, Israel, Republic of Ireland or South Africa. Previous winners: Amos Oz *Black Box* ; Anton Gill *The Journey Back from Hell* ; Bernice Rubens *Kingdom Come.*
Prize Fiction: £4000; Non-fiction: £3000; Poetry: £1000.

Wolfson History Awards

Wolfson Foundation, 18–22 The Haymarket, London SW1Y 4DQ
☎ 071-930 1057   Fax 071-930 1036

Contact *The Director*

FOUNDED 1972. Two awards made annually to authors of published historical works, with the object of encouraging historians to communicate with general readers as well as with their professional colleagues. Previous winners include: Prof. Paul Kennedy *The Rise and Fall of the Great*

Powers, Lord Bullock *Hitler and Stalin, Parallel Lives*.
Award (total) £25,000.

Woman's Own Short Story Competition
See **Magazines** section

Writers Monthly Short Story Competitions
See **Magazines** section

Yorkshire Open Poetry Competition
c/o Ilkley Literature Festival, 9A Leeds Road, Ilkley, West Yorkshire LS29 8DH
☎0943 601210

Contact *Jonathan Davidson*

Annual open poetry competition run by the Ilkley Literature Festival. Final entry date beginning of August each year. 1991 winner: John Sewell.
Prize (total) £500.

Yorkshire Post Art and Music Awards
Yorkshire Post, PO Box 168, Wellington Street, Leeds LS1 1RF
☎0532 432701 ext. 1512   Fax 0532 443430

Contact *Margaret Brown*

Two annual awards made to authors whose work has contributed most to the understanding and appreciation of art and music. Books should have been published in the preceding year in the UK. Previous winners: Charles Hemming *British Landscape Painters: A History and Gazetteer;* David Cairns *Berlioz: The Making of An Artist.*
Award £1000 each.

Yorkshire Post Best First Work Awards
Yorkshire Post, PO Box 168, Wellington Street, Leeds LS1 1RF
☎0532 432701 ext. 1512   Fax 0532 443430

Contact *Margaret Brown*

An annual award for a work by a new author published during the preceding year. 1991 winner: Harriet O'Brien *Forgotten Land.*
Prize £1000.

Yorkshire Post Book of the Year Award
Yorkshire Post, PO Box 168, Wellington Street, Leeds LS1 1RF
☎0532 432701 ext. 1512   Fax 0532 443430

Contact *Margaret Brown*

An annual award for the book (either fiction or non-fiction) which, in the opinion of the judges, is the best work published in the preceding year. 1991 winner: Corelli Barnett *Engage the Enemy More Closely.*
Prize £1200.

Young Playwright of the Year Award
Scottish Youth Theatre, Old Athenaeum Theatre, 179 Buchanan Street, Glasgow G1 2JZ
☎041-332 5127   Fax 041-333 1021

Contact *Mary McCluskey* (Artistic Director)

Part of the Young Playwright of the Year Festival run by the Scottish Youth Theatre in association with the Royal Scottish Academy of Music and Drama. Scripts can be sent in at any time of the year and will be read by a professional writer who will comment on the work. Precise details of entry requirements from above. Festival applications are open to all young writers who are native Scots and/ or resident in Scotland, aged between 15–25. During the festival, held over ten days in Glasgow in December, selected young playwrights will work with professional writers, directors and actors to present a workshop performance — a short piece of work by each playwright. Of these one will be selected for the award. Closing date usually in October.

Young Science Writer Awards
See **Daily Telegraph/British Association Young Science Writer Awards**

Young Writers' Competition
Young Writers' Competition, PO Box 328, Cardiff CF1 6YA
☎0222 492025

Contact *Administrator*

Launched in the spring; final entry date July. Open to anyone aged 18 and under. The 1992 competition was the Blackwood Miners Institute Young Writers' Competition. There were six prize categories: poetry up to age 11; 12–15; and 16–18; plus prose from each of the same three age groups. Seven winners are selected from each of the six different categories. Schools with the highest overall standard of entry will be awarded a tropy.
£1000 (total) shared between 42 prizewinners.

Mellor, Can you Spare a Dime?

The Libraries and PLR

It was a nice try. Throughout the year and particularly during the build-up to the general election, the libraries made a strong pitch for a larger share of public funds. Elderly intellectuals were wheeled out to declare that in their day libraries were temples of reason, founts of knowledge, bastions against the philistines and many other worthy clichés besides. Now, with ever more books being published at ever-rising prices, the libraries are so strapped for cash that they can no longer afford to supply a chap with the book he wants on the day he wants it.

This much is true. But it is pushing it a bit far to argue that boosting the injection of taxpayers' money would work a miracle cure. For one thing, no government in its right mind will agree to link public expenditure to book prices imposed by the publishing conglomerates. That book prices have rushed ahead of inflation nobody denies. But when asked why this should be so, publishers have little to say. The truth, of course, is that until recently publishers felt able to charge whatever they wanted for their product, reasoning that libraries had no choice but to pay the asking price. Greediness brought retribution. The government clamped down on the libraries and the libraries were forced to clamp down on the publishers. Squeals of anguish all round.

But whichever way this conflict is eventually reconciled, the horror stories put about by the Library Association (a narrower choice of books, staff laid off, early closing of premises) should not be allowed to hide the fact that libraries are big business.

We take out 565 million books a year at a collective cost of around £594 million or over £10 per head for every man, woman and child in the United Kingdom. This puts us far ahead of most other developed coutries with the exception in Europe only of the Netherlands and Denmark.

For yet more startling revelations, look how the figures break down. Close on 80 per cent of expenditure is allocated to labour – not of writing the books, of course, but of handing them back and forth across the counter. After other administrative costs, a mere £100 million is spent on acquisitions and of this, averaging out royalty payments, just £9 million goes to authors.

If there was ever a convincing example of exploitation of the workers, this is it. But take heart. A white knight can be seen charging towards us, his standard emblazoned with the glorious legend – PLR.

Public Lending Right allows for a modest payment to authors (writers, translators and illustrators) whose books are lent out from public libraries. The amount they receive is proportional to the number of borrowings credited to their titles over a year.

PLR has been in operation for nine years and while there are still vociferous complaints that payments are derisory (the latest rate per loan is 1.81 pence, up from 1.37 pence last year) the principle is at least established that authors should make some return, other than royalties, on library services.

These are the ground rules for PLR:

To qualify, an author must be resident in the United Kingdom or Germany (the latter as part of a reciprocal deal). For a book to be eligible it must be printed, bound and put on sale. It must not be mistaken for a newspaper or periodical, or be a musical score. Crown copyright is excluded, also books where authorship is attributed to a company or association. But – and this is where mistakes often occur – the author does not have to own copyright to be eligible for PLR. Anyone who has disclaimed copyright as part of a flat fee commission, for instance, will still have a claim if his name is on the title page.

Under PLR, the sole writer of a book may not be its sole author. Others named on the title page, such as illustrators, translators, compilers, editors and revisers, may have a claim to authorship. Where there are joint authors – two writers say, or a writer and illustrator – they can strike their own bargain on how their entitlement is to be split. But translators may apply, without reference to other authors, for a 30% fixed share (to be divided equally between joint translators). Similarly, an editor or compiler may register a 20% share provided he has written 10% of the book or at least ten pages of text. Joint editors or compilers must divide the 20% share equally.

Authors and books can be registered for PLR only when application is made during the author's lifetime. However, once an author is registered, the PLR on his books continues for 50 years after his death. If he wishes, he can assign PLR to other people and bequeath it by will.

If a co-author is dead or untraceable, the remaining co-author can still register for a share of PLR so long as he provides supporting evidence as to why he alone is making application.

As from 1992, the criteria for eligibility have been amended slightly to allow for cases where an author's name is not given on the title page, or where a book lacks a conventional title page. In these instances, it will now be possible for a writer to register if he is named elsewhere in the book and can show that his contribution would normally have merited a title page credit. Alternatively, proof of a royalty payment is equally acceptable. Where there are several writers, one of whom cannot prove eligibility, the co-authors can provide a signed statement testifying to their colleague's right to a share of the PLR payment.

The other significant change to eligibility concerns the former rule that books were disqualified if more than three authors were named on the title page. This has been abolished and there is now no maximum limit on the number of authors who can apply for part-shares.

One limiting factor has been introduced. Authors can no longer register books that do not have an ISBN. Tracing them was simply too expensive.

The maximum an author can earn from PLR is £6000, a jackpot hit in 1990–91 by 81 big names in popular fiction. A further 16,783 writers qualified for some sort of payment but the majority (11,653) earned less than £100. A sad 3339 registered authors received nothing at all from PLR.

Among the various ideas for extending PLR is for the system to embrace reference books consulted on library premises (they do this in Sweden) and books borrowed from academic and specialist libraries. At present, loans of books in schools do not qualify, which seems a little unjust and titles published annually (like *Writer's Handbook*) rarely figure in public library lending. More seriously, the system favours multiple copies of 'easy reads' against larger books which are liable to be kept out for the whole of a borrowing period and in some cases, far beyond.

But the most serious objection to PLR as currently practised is its narrow sampling base. Just thirty libraries are involved and while they are chosen to maintain a balance of relevant factors such as size, stock, proportion of children's issues, location and socio-economic status of the borrowers, it is clear that injustices do creep in.

A recent correspondent in *The Bookseller* spoke forcefully on one of the more obvious drawbacks to the present sample.

'I am loaned in a local rather than national or countrywide area; and loaned like crazy at that, I happen to know. Yet not one penny will ever come from lendings unless a library within, say, six or seven miles is sampled.'

PLR is moving towards 'whole authority' sampling, allowing for the collection of data from all computerised service points in an authority. This will provide a larger and more comprehensive sample at little extra cost. But to extend the sample still further will eat into the PLR grant which means spending more on operating costs and less on payments to authors.

It seems that we can't win. Unless, of course, David Mellor writes out a large cheque. Then again, pigs might fly.

PLR application forms and details can be obtained from: The Registrar, PLR Office, Bayheath House, Prince Regent Street, Stockton on Tees, Cleveland TS18 1DF (Tel 0642 604699).

Library Services

Armitt Trust & Library

Ambleside, Cumbria LA22 0BZ
☎ 05394 33949

Open 10.00 am to 12.30 pm & 1.30 pm to 4.00 pm
Monday, Tuesday, Wednesday and Friday

Access By arrangement (phone or write)

Books relating to the history and topography of the Lakes and its counties; major antiquarian/modern guidebook collections; collection of Victorian photographs by Herbert Bell and others; fine art collection including work by J. B. Pine, John Harden, William Green, Sir George Beaumont and others, including a large holding of Beatrix Potter's scientific drawings/paintings; large document and manuscript archive with papers relating to Wordsworth, De Quincey, Hartley, Coleridge, Ruskin, Harriet Martineau, Arthur Ransome and Hugh Walpole.

Art & Design Library (Westminster)

2nd Floor, Westminster Reference Library, St Martin's Street, London WC2H 7HP
☎ 071-798 2038   Fax 071-798 2040

Open 10.00 am to 7.00 pm Monday to Friday; 10.00 am to 5.00 pm Saturday

Access For reference only, otherwise closed

Located on the second floor of the City of Westminster's main reference library. An excellent reference source for fine and applied arts, including antiques, architecture, ceramics, coins, costume, crafts, design, furniture, garden history, interior decoration, painting, sculpture, textiles. Complete runs of major English Language periodicals such as *Studio*; exhibition catalogues; guidebooks to historic houses, castles, gardens and churches. Some older books and most periodicals earlier than 1970 are in storage and at least three days' notice is required before they can be obtained.

The Athenaeum, Liverpool

Church Alley, Liverpool L1 3DD
☎ 051-709 7770

Open 10.00 am to 5.00 pm Monday to Friday

Access To club members; researchers by application only

General collection, with books dating from the 15th century, now concentrated mainly on local history with a long run of Liverpool directories and guides. *Special collections* Liverpool playbills; William Roscoe; Blanco White; Robert Gladstone; 18th-century plays; 19th-century economic pamphlets; the Norris books; bibles; Yorkshire and other genealogy. Some original drawings, portraits and topographical material.

Bank of England Reference Library

Threadneedle Street, London EC2R 8AH
☎ 071-601 4715   Fax 071-601 5460

Open 9.30 am to 5.00 pm Monday to Friday

Access For research workers by prior arrangement only, when material is not readily available elsewhere

50,000 volumes of books and periodicals. 3000 periodicals taken. UK and overseas coverage of banking, finance and economics. *Special collections* Central bank reports; UK 17th–19th century economic tracts; Government reports in the field of banking.

Barbican Library

Barbican Centre, London EC2Y 8DS
☎ 071-638 0569

Open 9.30 am to 5.30 pm Monday, Wednesday, Thursday and Friday; 9.30 am to 7.30 pm Tuesday; 9.30 am to 12.30 pm Saturday

Open access

Situated on Level 7 of the Barbican Centre, this is the City of London's largest lending library. Limited study facilities are available. The library seeks to reflect the Centre's emphasis on the arts and includes strong collections on painting, sculpture, theatre, cinema and ballet, as well as a large music library with books, scores, cassettes and CDs (sound recording loans available at a small charge). Also houses the City's main children's library and has special collections on finance, natural resources, conservation, socialism and the history of London. Service available for house-bound readers.

Barnsley Public Library

Central Library, Shambles Street, Barnsley S70 2JF
☎ 0226 733241   Fax 0226 285458

Librarian *C. Vickers*

Open 9.30 am to 8.00 pm Monday and Wednesday; 9.30 am to 6.00 pm Tuesday, Thursday and Friday; 9.30 am to 5.00 pm Saturday (but specialist departments closed on certain weekday evenings and Saturday afternoon)

Open access

General library, lending and reference. Archive collection of family history and local firms; local studies: coalmining, local authors, Yorkshire and Barnsley; music library (books, records, tapes); large junior library.

BBC Data Enquiry Service

Room 7, 1 Portland Place, London W1A 1AA
☎ 071–927 5998   Fax 071–637 0398

Contact *Carol Tierney*

Open 9.30 am to 5.30 pm Monday to Friday

Access Telephone or written enquiries only

The Enquiry Service is a fee-based information broker. It was set up in 1981 to draw on the extensive information resources of the BBC and works solely for clients from outside the Corporation. The resources include press cuttings and reference libraries whose main strengths are arts and entertainment; biographical information; industrial information; political affairs; political, economic, social events; and world affairs.

BBC Written Archives Centre

Peppard Road, Caversham Park, Reading RG4 8TZ
☎ 0734 472742 ext. 280/1/2/3 Fax 0734 461145

Contact *Written Archives Officer*

Open 9.45 am to 5.15 pm Tuesday to Friday

Access For reference, by appointment only

Holds the written records of the BBC, including internal papers from 1922 to 1962 and published material to date. Certain services carry a charge.

Belfast Public Libraries: Central Library

Royal Avenue, Belfast, Northern Ireland BT1 1EA
☎ 0232 243233   Fax 0232 332819

Senior Reference Librarian *Hugh Russell*

Open 9.30 am to 8.00 pm Monday and Thursday; 9.30 am to 5.30 pm Tuesday, Wednesday and Friday; 9.30 am to 1.00 pm Saturday

Open access To lending libraries; reference libraries by application only

Over 2 million volumes for lending and reference. *Special collections* United Nations/Unesco depository; complete British Patent Collection; Northern Ireland Newspaper Library; British and Irish government publications. The Central Library offers the following reference departments: Humanities and General Reference; Irish and Local Studies; Business and Law; Science and Technology; Fine Arts, Language and Literature; Music and Recorded Sound. The lending library, supported by twenty branch libraries and two mobile libraries, offers special services to hospitals, prisons and housebound readers.

Birmingham and Midland Institute

Margaret Street, Birmingham B3 3BS
☎ 021–236 3591

Administrator/Librarian *J. Hunt*

Access For research, to students (loans restricted to members)

ESTABLISHED 1855. Later merged with the Birmingham Library (now renamed the Priestley Library) which was founded in 1779. The Priestley Library specialises in the humanities, with over 130,000 volumes in stock. Headquarters of the **Alliance of Literary Societies**; founder member of the **Association of Independent Libraries**. Meeting-place of 42 affiliated societies including many devoted to poetry and literature.

Bishopsgate Library

230 Bishopsgate, London EC2M 4QH
☎ 071–247 8895

Open 9.30 am to 5.30 pm Monday to Friday

Open access

City of London lending library, housed in the newly refurbished Bishopsgate Institute. Wide range of fiction and non-fiction, language courses on cassette, foreign fiction, paperbacks, maps and guides for travel at home and abroad, some children's books, and a selection of large print. A fully stocked reference library is provided by the Institute in an adjoining area and is available to all.

Bradford Central Library

Princes Way, Bradford BD1 1NN
☎0274 753600   Fax 0274 395108

Open 9.00 am to 7.30 pm Monday to Friday; 9.00 am to 5.00 pm Saturday

Open access

Wide range of books and media loan services, including major local history collections. Comprehensive reference and information facilities. Specialised business information service. Study facilities and publishing programme. Involved in local creative writing scheme, In Your Own Write.

British Architectural Library

Royal Institute of British Architects, 66 Portland Place, London W1N 4AD
☎071-580 5533   Fax 071-631 1802

Open 1.30 pm to 5.00 pm Monday; 10.00 am to 8.00 pm Tuesday; 10.00 am to 5.00 pm Wednesday, Thursday and Friday; 10.00 am to 1.30 pm Saturday

Open access For reference (loans restricted to RIBA members)

Collection of drawings, manuscripts, photographs and 400 indexed periodicals. All aspects of architecture, current and historical. Material both technical and aesthetic, covering related fields including: interior design, landscape architecture, topography, the construction industry and applied arts. Brochure available; queries by telephone, letter or in person.

British Film Institute Library and Information Services

21 Stephen Street, London W1P 1PL
☎071-255 1444   Fax 071-436 7950

Open 10.30 am to 5.00 pm Monday, Tuesday, Thursday, Friday; 1.30 pm to 8.00 pm Wednesday (under review); telephone enquiry service operates from 10.00 am to 5.00 pm

Access Reading library only; daily, weekly and annual membership available

The world's largest collection of information on film and television including periodicals, cuttings, scripts, related documentation, personal papers. Information available on-line through SIFT (Summary of Information on Film and Television).

British Library Business Information Service

25 Southampton Buildings, Chancery Lane, London WC2A 1AW
☎071-323 7454 (Free) 071-323 7457 (Priced Enquiry Service) Fax 071-323 7453

Open 9.30 am to 9.00 pm Monday to Friday; 10.00 am to 1.00 pm Saturday

Open access

Priced Enquiry Service 10.00 am to 5.00 pm Monday to Friday

Free Enquiry Service 9.30 am to 5.00 pm Monday to Friday

A resource facility for those engaged in all aspects of business.

British Library Information Sciences Service

7 Ridgmount Street, London WC1E 7AE
☎071-323 7688   Fax 071-323 7691

Open 9.00 am to 6.00 pm Monday, Wednesday, Friday; 9.00 am to 8.00 pm Tuesday and Thursday (mid July–September 9.00 am to 6.00 pm Monday to Friday)

Access For reference only (loans restricted to members of the Library Association or by British Library form)

Provides British and foreign material on librarianship, information science and related subjects. *Special collections* theses on librarianship.

British Library Manuscripts Department

Great Russell Street, London WC1B 3DG
☎071-323 7513/14   Fax 071-323 7745

Open 10.00 am to 4.45 pm Monday to Saturday (closed second week of November)

Access Reading facilities only, by reader's pass

A useful publication, *The British Library: Guide to the catalogues and indexes of the Department of Manuscripts* by M.A.E. Nickson, is available (£1.95) to guide the researcher through this vast collection of manuscripts dating from Ancient Greece to the present day. Approximately 85,000 volumes are housed here.

British Library Map Library

Great Russell Street, London WC1B 3DG
☎071-323 7700   Fax 071-323 7736

Open 10.00 am to 4.30 pm Monday to Saturday

Access By reader's pass or Map Library day pass

A collection of 1.7 million maps, charts and globes with particular reference to the history of British cartography. Maps for all parts of the world in wide range of scales and dates, including the most comprehensive collection of Ordnance Survey maps and plans. *Special collections* King George III Topographical Collection and Maritime Collection, and the Crace Collection of maps and plans of London. Also satellite imagery, microfiche, catalogue and browse film.

British Library Music Library

Great Russell Street, London WC1B 3DG
☎071-323 7527   Fax 071-323 7751

Open 9.30 am to 4.45 pm Monday to Friday; on Saturday material is made available 10.00 am to 4.45 pm in the Manuscripts students room

Access By reader's pass

Special collections The Royal Music Library (containing almost all Handel's surviving autographed scores) and the Paul Hirsch Music Library. Also a large collection (about one and a quarter million items) of printed music, both British and foreign.

British Library National Sound Archive

29 Exhibition Road, London SW7 2AS
☎071-589 6603   Fax 071-823 8970

Open 10.00 am to 5.00 pm Monday to Friday (Thursday till 9.00 pm)

Open access

Listening service (by appointment) 10.00 am to 5.00 pm Monday to Friday (Thursday till 9.00 pm)

Northern Listening Service
British Library Document Supply Centre, Boston Spa, West Yorkshire: 9.15 am to 4.30 pm Monday to Friday
☎0937 843434

An archive of over three quarters of a million discs and more than 60,000 hours of tape recordings, including all types of music, oral history, drama, wildlife, selected BBC broadcasts and BBC Sound Archive material. Produces a thrice-yearly newsletter, *Playback*.

British Library Newspaper Library

Colindale Avenue, London NW9 5HE
☎071-323 7353   Fax 071-323 7379

Open 10.00 am to 4.45 pm Monday to Saturday (last newspaper issue 4.15 pm)

Access By reader's pass or Newspaper Library day pass (available from and valid only for Colindale Avenue)

English provincial, Scottish, Irish, Commonwealth and foreign newspapers from *c*.1700 are housed here. London newspapers from 1801 and most large weekly periodicals are also in stock. (London newspapers pre-dating this are housed in Great Russell Street.) Readers are advised to check availability of newspapers in advance as the library is very popular.

British Library Official Publications and Social Sciences Service

Great Russell Street, London WC1B 3DG
☎071-323 7536/7   Fax 071-323 7039

Open 9.30 am to 4.45 pm Monday to Friday

Access By reader's pass

Provides access to current and historical official publications from all countries, plus publications of intergovernmental bodies. Also House of Commons sessional papers from 1715; UK legislation; current and back numbers of UK electoral registers; and up-to-date reference books on the social sciences.

British Library Oriental and India Office Collections

Orbit House, 197 Blackfriars Road,
London SE1 8NG
☎071-412 7873   Fax 071-412 7870

Open 9.30 am to 5.45 pm Monday to Friday; 9.30 am to 12.45 pm Saturday

Open access Reading pass required for reading room (loans restricted to members)

A comprehensive collection of printed volumes and manuscripts in the languages of North Africa, the Near and Middle East and all of Asia, plus official records of the East India Company and British government in India until 1948. Also prints, drawings and painting by British artists of India.

British Library Reading Room

Great Russell Street, London WC1B 3DG
☎071-636 1544 (Switchboard);
071-323 7678 (Admissions); 071-323 7676
(Bibliographical/holdings' enquiries)
Fax 071-323 7736

Open 9.00 am to 5.00 pm Monday, Friday and Saturday; 9.00 am to 9.00 pm Tuesday, Wednesday, Thursday (closed week following the last complete week in October)

Access By reader's pass

Large and comprehensive stock of books and periodicals relating to the humanities and social sciences for reference and research which cannot easily be done elsewhere. Also exhibitions on literary and historical figures and a permanent exhibition on the history of printing and binding. Telephone enquiries welcome. Leaflet *Applying for a Reader's Pass* available for guidance.

British Library Science Reference and Information Service

Holborn Reading Room, 25 Southampton Buildings, London WC2A 1AW
☎ 071-323 7494/7496 Fax 071-323 7495

Open 9.30 am to 9.00 pm Monday to Friday; 10.00 am to 1.00 pm Saturday

Chancery House Reading Room, Chancery Lane, London WC2A 1AW
☎ 071-323 7902 Fax 071-323 7906

Open 9.30 am to 5.30 pm Monday to Friday

Aldwych Reading Room, 9 Kean Street, London WC2B 4AT
☎ 071-323 7288 Fax 071-323 7217 (enquiries)/ 071-323 7290 (photocopy requests)

Open 9.30 am to 5.30 pm Monday to Friday

Open access

A division of the The British Library, SRIS is the national library for modern science and technology providing an invaluable resource facility for technical journalists. Telephone enquiries welcome.

British Psychological Society Library

c/o Psychology Library, University of London, Senate House, Malet Street, London WC1E 7HU
☎ 071-636 8000 ext. 5060 Fax 071-436 1494

Open Term-time: 9.30 am to 9.00 pm Monday to Thursday; 9.30 am to 6.30 pm Friday; 9.30 am to 5.30 pm Saturday (holidays: 9.30 am to 5.30 pm Monday to Saturday)

Access Members only

Reference library, containing the British Psychological Society collection of periodicals — over 140 current titles housed alongside the University of London's collection of books and journals. Largely for academic research. General queries

referred to Swiss Cottage Public Library which has a very good psychology collection.

Cardiff Central Library

Frederick Street, St David's Link, Cardiff
South Glamorgan CF1 4DT
☎ 0222 382116 Fax 0222 238642

Open 9.00 am to 6.00 pm Monday, Tuesday and Friday; 9.00 am to 8.00 pm Wednesday and Thursday; 9.00 am to 5.30 pm Saturday

General lending library with the following departments: leisure, music, children's, local studies, information, science and humanities. Kurzweil reader available for those with visual handicap.

Catholic Central Library

47 Francis Street, London SW1P 1QR
☎ 071-834 6128

Librarian *J. Bond*

Open 10.00 am to 5.00 pm Monday to Friday; 10.00 am to 1.30 pm Saturday

Open access For reference (non-members must sign in; loans restricted to members)

Contains books, many not readily available elsewhere, on theology, religions worldwide, scripture and the history of churches of all denominations.

Central Music Library (Westminster)

Victoria Library, 160 Buckingham Palace Road, London SW1W 9UD
☎ 071-798 2192 Fax 071-798 2181

Open 9.30 am to 7.00 pm Monday to Friday; 9.30 am to 5.00 pm Saturday

Open access

Located at Victoria Library, this is the largest public music library in the South of England, with extensive coverage of all aspects of music, including books, periodicals and printed scores. No recorded material, notated only. Lending library includes a small collection of CDs and cassettes.

Children's Book Foundation Reference Library

Book House, 45 East Hill, London SW18 2QZ
☎ 081-870 9055 Fax 081-874 4790

Open 9.00 am to 5.00 pm Monday to Friday

Access For reference only

A comprehensive collection of children's literature, related books and periodicals. Aims to have all children's titles published within the last two years. An information service covers all aspects of children's literature, including profiles of authors and illustrators.

City Business Library
1 Brewers Hall Garden, London EC2V 5BX
☎071-638 8215

Open 9.30 am to 5.00 pm Monday to Friday

Open access For reference

Books, pamphlets, periodicals and newspapers of current business interest, mostly financial. Aims to satisfy the day-to-day information needs of the City's business community, and in so doing has become one of the leading public resource centres in Britain in its field. Strong collection of directories for both the UK and overseas, plus companies information, market research sources, management, law, banking, insurance, statistics and investment.

City of London Libraries
See **Barbican Library; Bishopsgate Library; City Business Library; Guildhall Library; St Bride Printing Library; Shoe Lane Library.**

Commission of the European Communities Information Office
Jean Monnet House, 8 Storey's Gate,
London SW1P 3AT
☎071-973 1992   Fax 071-973 1900/10

Open 10.00 am to 1.00 pm Monday to Friday; Phone calls: 2.00 pm to 5.00 pm Monday to Friday; Information Point: 10.00 am to 1.00 pm & 2.00 pm to 5.00 pm Monday to Friday

Open access For reference

Reference works on the European Community, plus copies of all non-technical EEC publications. Runs the **European Literary & Translation Prizes**.

Commonwealth Resource Centre
Kensington High Street, London W8 6NQ
☎071-603 4535   Fax 071-602 7374

Librarian *Karen Peters*

Open 10.00 am to 4.45 pm Monday to Saturday

Access For reference

Special collection Books and periodicals on Commonwealth countries. Also a large collection of directories and reference books on the Commonwealth and information on political, social and economic affairs, art, cultural organisations and bibliography.

Commonwealth Secretariat Library
10 Carlton House Terrace, Pall Mall,
London SW1Y 5AH
☎071-839 3411 ext. 5013   Fax 071-930 0827

Open 9.15 am to 5.15 pm Monday to Friday

Access For reference only, by appointment

Extensive reference source concerned with economy, development, trade, production and industry of Commonwealth countries; also sub-library specialising in human resources including women, youth, health, management and education.

Coventry Central Library
Smithford Way, Coventry CV1 1FY
☎0203 832315   Fax 0203 832440

Open 9.00 am to 8.00 pm Monday, Tuesday, Thursday and Friday; 9.30 am to 8.00 pm Wednesday; 9.00 am to 4.30 pm Saturday

Open access

Located in the middle of the city's main shopping centre. Approximately 120,000 items (books, records, cassettes and CDs) for loan; plus reference collection of business information and local history. *Special collections* Cycling and motor industries; George Eliot collection; Angela Brazil collection; local newspapers on microfilm from 1740 onwards. Over 600 periodicals taken. Kurzweil reader and CCTV available for people with visual handicap.

Derby Central Library
Wardwick, Derby DE1 1HS
☎0332 255389   Fax 0332 369570

Open 9.30 am to 7.00 pm (Wednesday till 1.00 pm; Saturday till 4.00 pm)

General public lending library including local studies library: the largest collection of resources in existence (multi-media) relating to Derby and Derbyshire.

Devon & Exeter Institution Library
7 Cathedral Close, Exeter, Devon EX1 1EZ
☎0392 74727

Librarian *Sheila Stirling*

Open 9.00 am to 5.00 pm Monday to Friday

Access Members only

FOUNDED 1813. Contains over 36,000 volumes, including long runs of 19th-century journals, theology, history, topography, early science, biography and literature. A large and growing collection of books, journals, newspapers, prints and maps relating to the South-West.

English Folk Dance and Song Society Library

Vaughan Williams Memorial Library, Cecil Sharp House, 2 Regent's Park Road, London NW1 7AY
℡ 071-284 0523   Fax 071-284 0523

Open 9.30 am to 5.30 pm Monday to Friday

Access For reference to the general public, on payment of a daily fee; members may borrow books and use the library free of charge

A multi-media collection: books, periodicals, manuscripts, tapes, records, CDs, films, videos. Mostly British folk culture and how this has developed around the world. Some foreign language material, and some books in English about foreign cultures. Also, the history of the English Folk Dance and Song Society.

Equal Opportunities Commission Library

Overseas House, Quay Street, Manchester M3 3HN
℡ 061-833 9244   Fax 061-835 1657

Open 9.00 am to 5.00 pm Monday to Friday

Access For reference (loans available)

Books and pamplets on equal opportunities and gender issues. Non-sexist children's books and Equal Opportunities Commission publications. Also an information service with periodicals and press cuttings.

Farming Information Centre

National Farmers' Union, Agriculture House, London SW1X 7NJ
℡ 071-235 5077   Fax 071-235 3526

Open 10.00 am to 4.30 pm Monday to Thursday

Access For reference only (telephone first)

The politics of agriculture rather than technical aspects, and union affairs. Houses a picture library of farmland and machines.

Fawcett Library

City of London Polytechnic, Old Castle Street, London E1 7NT
℡ 071-247 5826/320 1189

Open Term-time: 11.00 am to 8.30 pm Monday; 10.00 am to 5.00 pm Wednesday to Friday (holidays: 10.00 am to 5.00 pm Monday to Friday)

Open access to non-polytechnic members on payment either of annual membership fee: £10 (students/unwaged £5); or one-day fee: £2 (students/ unwaged £1)

The leading library for feminist studies and research into all other aspects of women's history with emphasis on social sciences and the humanities. Contains extensive stocks of books, pamphlets, photographs and archive materials. Limited loans to members. The **Mary Evans Picture Library** (see entry **Picture Libraries**) acts as agent for the Fawcett Library's pictorial material.

Foreign and Commonwealth Office Library

King Charles Street, London SW1A 2AH
℡ 071-270 3017   Fax 071-930 2364

Access For reference only

An extensive stock of books, pamphlets and other reference material on all aspects of historical, socio-economic and political subjects relating to countries covered by the Foreign and Commonwealth Office. Particularly strong on official Commonwealth publications and Commonwealth/ Dependent Territories legislation. The library is undergoing a period of considerable change during 1992 and will not be open to the public. Staff will endeavour to answer written or telephone enquiries, and it is hoped that by 1993 access will be restored to *bonafide* researchers.

French Institute Library

17 Queensberry Place, London SW7 2DT
℡ 071-589 6211   Fax 071-581 5127

Contact *Claire Fons*

Open 11.00 am to 7.00 pm Monday, Tuesday, Wednesday and Friday

Open access For reference (loans restricted to members)

Annual membership £15; students and OAPs £10

A collection of over 81,000 volumes mainly centred on cultural interests with special emphasis on the French language, literature and history. Video library and children's library (5000 books); plus 3500 press cuttings.

Greater London History Library

40 Northampton Road, London EC1R 0HB
☎071-606 3030 ext. 3822   Fax 071-833 9136

Open 9.30 am to 4.45 pm Tuesday to Friday

Access For reference only

Covers all aspects of the life and development of London, specialising in the history and organisation of local government in general, and London in particular. Books on London history and topography, covering many subjects. Also London directories dating back to 1677, plus other source material including Acts of Parliament, Hansard reports, statistical returns, atlases, yearbooks and many complete sets of newspapers and magazines.

Guildford Institute of University of Surrey Library

Ward Street, Guildford, Surrey GU1 4LH
☎0483 62142

Librarian *Mrs Patricia Chapman*

Open 10.00 am to 3.00 pm Monday to Friday (under review and occasionally closed at lunchtime)

Open access To members only

FOUNDED 1834. Some 10,000 volumes of which 7500 were printed before the First World War. The remaining stock consists of recently published works of fiction, biography and travel. Newspapers and periodicals also available. *Special collections* include an almost complete run of the *Illustrated London News* from 1843-1906, the Institute's Minute Books, a collection of Victorian scrapbooks, and about 400 photos and other pictures relating to the Institute's history and the town of Guildford.

Guildhall Library

Aldermanbury, London EC2P 2EJ
☎071-606 3030 (for direct dial, see below)

Access For reference (but much of the material is kept in storage areas and is supplied to readers on request; proof of identity is required for consultation of certain categories of stock)

Part of the Corporation of London libraries. Seeks to provide a basic general reference service but its major strength, acknowledged worldwide, is in its historical collections. The library is divided into three sections, each with its own catalogues and enquiry desks. These are: Printed Books; Manuscripts; the Print Room.

PRINTED BOOKS

Open 9.30 am to 5 pm Monday to Saturday
☎071-260 1868/1870

Strong on all aspects of London history, with wide holdings of English history, topography and genealogy, including local directories, poll books and parish register transcripts. Also good collections of English statutes, law reports, parliamentary debates and journals, and House of Commons papers. Home of several important collections deposited by London institutions: the Marine collection of the Corporation of Lloyd's, the Stock Exchange's historical files of reports and prospectuses, the Clockmakers' Company library and museum, the Gardeners' Company, Fletchers' Company, the Institute of Masters of Wine and Gresham College.

MANUSCRIPTS

Open 9.30 am to 4.45 pm Monday to Saturday (closed 1.00 pm to 2.00 pm on Saturday; no requests for records after 4.30 pm)
☎071-260 1863

The official repository for historical records relating to the City of London (except those of the Corporation of London itself which are housed at the Corporation Records Office). Records date from the 11th century to the present day. They include archives of most of the City's parishes, wards and livery companies, and of many individuals, families, estates, businesses, schools, societies and other institutions, notably the Diocese of London and St Paul's Cathedral. Although mainly of City interest, holdings include material for the London area as a whole and beyond.

PRINT ROOM

Open 9.30 am to 5.00 pm Monday to Friday
☎071-260 1839

An unrivalled collection of prints and drawings relating to London and the adjacent counties. The emphasis is on topography, but there are strong collections of portraits and satirical prints. The map collection includes maps from the capital from the mid-16th century to the present day and various classes of Ordnance Survey maps. Other material includes photographs, theatre bills and programmes, trade cards, book plates and playing cards as well as a sizeable collection of Old Master prints.

Hatfield Polytechnic Library

College Lane, Hatfield, Hertfordshire AL10 9AD
☎0707 279678   Fax 0707 279670

Open Term-time: 8.45 am to 9.30 pm Monday to Thursday; 8.45 am to 7.00 pm Friday; 2.00 pm to 5.00 pm Saturday; 2.00 pm to 7.00 pm Sunday (holidays: 9.00 am to 5.00 pm Monday to Friday)

Access For reference (loans available to non-Polytechnic members on external borrowers scheme at £25 p.a.)

280,000 volumes and 2000 journals in science technology and social science, including law, across all three of the polytechnic's campuses. There are two other site libraries, one at Hertford (business), the other at Wall Hall, near Radlett (education and humanities). Desk research, postal interlibrary loans and consultancy undertaken by HERTIS Information and Research Unit which is based at Hatfield and has capacity for up to 300 subscribing companies and organisations.

Health Information Library (Westminster)
Marylebone Library, Marylebone Road, London NW1 5PS
☎071-798 1039   Fax 071-798 1044

Open 10.00 am to 7.00 pm Monday; 9.30 am to 7.00 pm Tuesday to Friday; 9.30 am to 5.00 pm Saturday

Open access

Located in Westminster's Marylebone public library. Books, pamphlets and periodicals covering all aspects of medicine and the health services.

HERTIS
See **Hatfield Polytechnic Library**

Highgate Literary and Scientific Institution Library
11 South Grove, London N6 6BS
☎081-340 3343

Open 10.00 am to 5.00 pm Tuesday to Friday; 10.00 am to 4.00 pm Saturday (closed Monday)

Access For reference only

Annual membership £26 single; £40 family

35,000 volumes of general fiction and non-fiction, with a children's section, and special collection on local history, London, and the local poets, Coleridge and Betjeman.

Holborn Library
32-38 Theobalds Road, London WC1X 8PA
☎071-413 6343/4/5/6

Open 10.00 am to 7.00 pm Monday and Thursday; 10.00 am to 6.00 pm Tuesday and Friday; 10.00 am to 5.00 pm Saturday (closed all day Wednesday)

Open access

London Borough of Camden public library, specialising in law, with over 35,000 items in stock.

Sherlock Holmes Collection (Westminster)
Marylebone Library, Marylebone Road, London NW1 5PS
☎071-798 1206   Fax 071-798 1019

Open 9.30 am to 7.00 pm Monday to Friday; 9.30 am to 5.00 pm Saturday

Access For reference only (telephone first)

Located in Westminster's Marylebone Library. An extensive collection of material from all over the world, covering Sherlock Holmes and Sir Arthur Conan Doyle. Books, pamphlets, journals, newspaper cuttings and photos, much of which is otherwise unavailable in this country. Some background material.

Imperial War Museum
Department of Printed Books, Lambeth Road, London SE1 6HZ
☎071-416 5000   Fax 071-416 5374

Open 10.00 am to 5.00 pm Monday to Saturday (restricted service Saturday)

Access For reference (but at least 24 hours notice must be given for intended visits)

A large collection of material on 20th-century life with detailed coverage of the two world wars and other conflicts. Books, pamphlets and periodicals, including many produced for short periods in unlikely wartime settings; also maps, biographies and privately printed memoirs, and foreign language material. Research material available in the following departments: Art, Documents, Exhibits and Firearms, Film, Sound & Records, Photographs.

Italian Institute Library
39 Belgrave Square, London SW1X 8NX
☎071-235 1461   Fax 071-235 4618

Open 9.30 am to 5.00 pm Monday to Friday

Open access For reference

A collection of over 25,000 volumes relating to all aspects of Italian culture. Texts are mostly in Italian, with some in English.

Kent County Central Lending Library

Springfield, Maidstone, Kent ME14 2LH
☏0622 696511   Fax 0622 690897

Open 10.00 am to 6.00 pm Monday, Tuesday, Wednesday and Friday; 10.00 am to 7.00 pm Thursday; 9.00 am to 4.00 pm Saturday

Open access

300,000 volumes of non-fiction, mostly academic. English literature, poetry, classical literature, drama (including playsets), music (including music sets). Strong, too, in sociology, art and history. Loans to all who live or work in Kent; those who do not may consult stock for reference or arrange loans via their own local library service.

Leeds Library

18 Commercial Street, Leeds LS1 6AL
☏0532 453071

Open 9.00 am to 5.00 pm Monday to Friday

Access To members; research use upon application to the librarian

FOUNDED 1768. Contains over 120,000 books and periodicals from the 15th century to the present day. *Special collections* include reformation pamphlets, civil war tracts, Victorian and Edwardian children's books and fiction, European language material, spiritualism and psychical research, plus local material.

Linen Hall Library

17 Donegall Square North, Belfast BT1 5GD
☏0232 321707   Fax 0232 438586

Librarian *John Gray*

Open Monday to Saturday from 9.30 am (closing time varies)

Open access For reference (loans restricted to members)

FOUNDED 1788. Contains about 200,000 books. As well as general stock, there is a substantial Irish and Local Studies collection, with over 80,000 items.

Liverpool City Libraries

William Brown Street, Liverpool LE3 8EW
☏051-225 5429   Fax 051-207 1342

Open 9.00 am to 7.30 pm Monday to Thursday; 9.00 am to 5.00 pm Friday and Saturday

Open access

Arts and Recreations Library 50,000 volumes covering all subjects in arts and recreation.

Commercial and Social Sciences Library Business and trade directories, plus all UK statutes and law reports. Serves as a depository library for UNO and EEC reports.

General, Religion and Philosophy Library/ Hornby Library Contains stock of 68,000 volumes and 24,000 maps, plus book plates, prints and autographed letters. *Special collections* Walter Crane and Edward Lear illustrations.

International Library Open shelf and reserve stocks on language, literature, geography and history. *Special collection* British history, with much on politicians and statesmen. 20,000 copies of British, American and European plays, plus language tapes in twenty languages.

Music Library Extensive stock relating to all aspects of music. Includes 128,000 volumes and music scores, 18,500 records and over 3000 cassettes. *Special collections* Carl Rosa Opera Company Collection and Earl of Sefton's early printed piano music.

Record Office and Local History Department Printed and audiovisual material relating to Liverpool, Merseyside, Lancashire and Cheshire, together with archive material mainly on Liverpool. Some restrictions on access, with 30-year rule applying to archives.

Science and Technology Library Extensive stock dealing with all aspects of science and technology, including British and European standards and patents.

London Borough of Camden Information and Reference Services

Swiss Cottage Library, 88 Avenue Road,
London NW3 3HA
☏071-413 6533/4

Open 10.00 am to 7.00 pm Monday and Thursday; 10.00 am to 6.00 pm Tuesday and Friday; 10.00 am to 5.00 pm Saturday (closed all day Wednesday)

Open access

Over 60,000 volumes and 400 periodical titles.

London College of Printing and Distributive Trades: Department of Learning Resources

Elephant and Castle, London SE1 6SB
☏071-735 9100 ext. 2043   Fax 071-582 5700

Open Term-time: 9.30 am to 7.15 pm Monday to Thursday; 9.30 am to 5.45 pm Friday (holidays: 9.00 am to 4.30 pm Monday to Friday; closed August)

Access By subscription (£25 p.a.)

Books, periodicals, slides, videos and computer software on all aspects of the art of the book: printing, management, film/photograph, graphic arts. *Special collections* Private press books and the history and development of printing and books. The London College of Printing merged with the College for the Distributive Trades in 1990 and is a constituent college of the London Institute. The Department of Learning Resources now operates across the three sites of the new college at: Elephant & Castle; Leicester Square; Back Hill, Clerkenwell.

The London Library

14 St James's Square, London SW1Y 4LG
☎071-930 7705/6   Fax 071-930 0436

Librarian *Douglas Matthews*

Open 9.30 am to 5.30 pm Monday to Saturday (Thursday till 7.30 pm)

Access For members only (£100 p.a.)

The London Library Trust was founded in 1952 with the object of making the resources of the library accessible to scholars and students who cannot afford the full annual membership fee; making grants for original research work at the Library; and purchasing works of scholarship for the Library which it might not otherwise acquire. Last year's grants totalled over £6000.

With over a million books and 8300 members, The London Library 'is the most distinguished private library in the world; probably the largest, certainly the best loved'. Founded in 1841, it is wholly independent of public funding. There are few restrictions on membership; anybody can apply and at present there is no waiting list. Members can take home up to ten books; fifteen if the member lives more than twenty miles from St James's Square. Particularly strong in European languages. The library specialises in the humanities. Science and technology, medicine and law are excluded. A computer-based system of cataloguing and book circulation has recently been introduced, and a compact disc edition of *The Times* and *The Sunday Times*, together with all the necessary viewing equipment, is being installed to help preserve the library's printed copies of the papers which, however, will continue to be available and kept up-to-date. (1990 and 1991 disc editions are already on line.) The system will provide a comprehensive and rapid search facility for specific news/feature items, and even illustrations.

Some disruption is likely through 1992 and into 1993 while the new extension above the north bay of the reading room is completed. The removal of certain books/periodicals for the duration of the contract, including bound volumes of *The Times* (but not the *Index* or *Obituaries*), and relocation of other material is inevitable.

Lord Louis Library

Orchard Street, Newport, Isle of Wight PO30 1LL
☎0983 527655/823800 (reference library)

Open 9.30 am to 5.30 pm Monday to Friday (Saturday till 5.00 pm)

Open access

General adult and junior fiction and non-fiction collections; local history collection and periodicals. Also the county's main reference library.

Manchester Central Library

St Peters Square, Manchester M2 5PD
☎061-234 1900   Fax 061-234 1963

Open 10.00 am to 8.00 pm Monday, Tuesday, Wednesday and Friday; 10.00 am to 5.00 pm Saturday

Open access

One of the country's leading reference libraries with extensive collections covering all subjects. Subject departments include: Commercial, Technical, Social Sciences, Arts, Music, Local Studies, Chinese, General Readers, Language & Literature, Visually Impaired People's Service. Large lending stock.

Marylebone Library (Westminster)

See **Health Information Library; Sherlock Holmes Collection; Westminster Archives & Local History Collection.**

Ministry of Agriculture, Fisheries and Food

Main Library, 3 Whitehall Place,
London SW1A 2HH
☎071-270 8420/8421   Fax 071-270 8125

Open 9.30 am to 5.00 pm Monday to Friday

Access For reference (but at least 24 hours notice must be given for intended visits)

Large stock of volumes on temperate agriculture, horticulture and fisheries.

National Library of Scotland

George IV Bridge, Edinburgh EH1 1EW
☎031-226 4531/459 4531   Fax 031-220 6662

Open *Main Reading Room* 9.30 am to 8.30 pm
Monday, Tuesday, Thursday and Friday; 10.00 am
to 8.30 pm Wednesday; 9.30 am to 1.00 pm
Saturday. *Map Library* 9.30 am to 5.00 pm Monday,
Tuesday, Thursday and Friday; 10.00 am to 5.00
pm Wednesday; 9.30 am to 1.00 pm Saturday.
Scottish Science Library 9.30 am to 5.00 pm
Monday, Tuesday, Thursday and Friday; 9.30 am to
8.30 pm Wednesday.

Access To reading rooms and Map Library, for
research not easily done elsewhere, by reader's
ticket

Collection of over 6 million volumes. The library
receives all British and Irish publications. Large
stock of newspapers and periodicals. Many special
collections, including early Scottish books, theology, polar studies, baking, phrenology and liturgies.
Also large collections of maps, music and manuscripts including personal archives of notable Scottish persons.

National Library of Wales
Aberystwyth, Dyfed SY23 3BU
☎ 0970 623816   Fax 0970 615709

Open 9.30 am to 6.00 pm Monday to Friday; 9.30
am to 5.00 pm Saturday (closed Bank Holidays and
first week of October)

Access To reading room and map room by
reader's ticket, available on application

Collection of over 3 million books including large
collections of periodicals, maps and manuscripts.
Particular emphasis on humanities in foreign material, and on Wales and other Celtic areas in all
collections.

Natural History Museum Library
Cromwell Road, London SW7 5BD
☎ 071-938 9191   Fax 071-938 9290

Open 10.00 am to 4.30 pm Monday to Friday

Access To *bona fide* researchers, by reader's
ticket (telephone first to make an appointment)

The library is in five sections: general; botany;
zoology; entomology; palaeontology/mineralogy.
The sub-department of ornithology is housed at
Zoological Museum, Akeman Street, Tring, Herts
HP23 6AP (Tel 0442 834181). Resources available
include books, journals, maps, manuscripts, drawings and photographs covering all aspects of
natural history, including palaeontology and miner-
alogy, from the 14th century to the present day.
Also archives and an historical collection on the
museum itself.

Newcastle Literary and Philosophical Society Library
Westgate Road, Newcastle upon Tyne NE1 1SE
☎ 091-232 0192

Librarian *Margaret Norwell*

Open 9.30 am to 7.00 pm (Tuesdays till 8.00 pm;
Saturdays till 1.00 pm)

Access To members; scholars on application only

Over 140,000 volumes, many of them old and rare.
Special collections include 19th-century science
and technology, history, exploration and travel,
biography, music, and local history.

Newcastle upon Tyne Central Library
Princess Square, Newcastle upon Tyne NE99 1DX
☎ 091-261 0691   Fax 091-261 1435

Open 9.30 am to 8.00 pm Monday and Thursday;
9.30 am to 5.00 pm Tuesday, Wednesday and
Friday; 9.00 am to 5.00 pm Saturday

Open access

Extensive local studies collection, including newspapers, illustrations and genealogy. Also business,
science, humanities and arts, educational guidance
unit, open learning resource centre, marketing
advice centre.

Northumberland County Library
The Willows, Morpeth,
Northumberland NE61 1TA
☎ 0670 512385   Fax 0670 518012

Open 10.00 am to 8.00 pm Monday, Tuesday,
Wednesday and Friday; 9.30 am to 12.30 pm
Saturday (closed Thursday)

Open access

Books, periodicals, newspapers, records, cassettes,
CDs, video, microcomputers, CD-ROM, prints,
microforms, vocal scores, playsets, community
resource equipment. *Special collections* Northern
Arts Poetry Library: 12,000 volumes of modern
poetry; cinema: comprehensive collection of about
5000 volumes covering all aspects of the cinema;
family history: extensive collections of genealogical
materials including census returns, the International Genealogical Index, OPCS index of births, deaths
and marriages, local pedigrees and marriage indexes.

Nottingham Central Library
Angel Row, Nottingham NG1 6HP
☎ 0602 412121   Fax 0602 504207

Open 9.30 am to 8.00 pm Monday to Friday; 9.00 am to 1.00 pm Saturday

Open access

General public lending library: business information, the arts, local history, religion, literature. Videos, periodicals, spoken word, recorded music. Extensive back-up reserve stocks. Drama and music sets for loan to groups.

Nottingham Subscription Library Ltd

Bromley House, Angel Row,
Nottingham NG1 6HL
☏ 0602 473134

Librarian *Jane Corbett*

Open 9.30 am to 5.00 pm Monday to Friday; also first Saturday of each month from 10.00 am to 12.30 pm for members only

FOUNDED 1816. Collection of 30,000 books including local history, topography, biography, travel and fiction.

Office of Population Censuses & Surveys Library

St Catherine's House, 10 Kingsway,
London WC2B 6JP
☏ 071-242 0262 ext. 2235-8 Fax 071-340 1779

Open 9.30 am to 4.00 pm Monday to Friday

Access By appointment only

Population censuses and vital statistics reports from most countries. Law and administration of birth, marriage and death registration, demography, epidemiology, psychology, survey methodology.

Oxford Central Library

Westgate, Oxford OX1 1DJ
☏ 0865 815549

Open 9.15 am to 7.00 pm Monday, Tuesday, Thursday and Friday (Wednesday and Saturday till 5.00 pm)

General lending and reference library including the Centre for Oxfordshire Studies. Also periodicals, music library and children's library.

Penzance Library

Morrab House, Morrab Gardens, Penzance,
Cornwall TR18 4DQ
☏ 0736 64474

Librarian *L. Lowdon*

Open Tuesday to Saturday (hours vary)

Access Non-members may use the library for a small daily fee, but may not borrow books

A private subscription lending library of over 60,000 volumes covering virtually all subjects except modern science and technology, with large collections on history, literature and religion. There is a comprehensive Cornish collection of books, newspapers and manuscripts including the Borlase letters; a West Cornwall photographic archive; many runs of 18th and 19th-century periodicals; a collection of over 2000 books published before 1800.

Plymouth Proprietary Library

Alton Terrace, 111 North Hill, Plymouth,
Devon PL4 8JY
☏ 0752 660515

Librarian *Camilla M. Blackman*

Open Monday to Saturday from 9.30 am (closing time varies)

Access Members only

FOUNDED 1810. The library contains approximately 17,000 volumes of mainly 20th-century work.

Poetry Library

South Bank Centre, Royal Festival Hall (Level 5, Red Side), London SE1 8XX
☏ 071-921 0943/0664/0940   Fax 071-928 0063

Open 11.00 am to 8.00 pm 7 days a week

Open access Membership free and open to all on production of proof of identity and permanent address. Members may borrow up to four books for up to four weeks at a time. Non-members welcome to browse.

FOUNDED by the Arts Council in 1953. A collection of 45,000 titles of modern poetry since 1912, from Georgian poetry to Rap, representing all English-speaking countries and including translations into English by contemporary poets. Two copies of each title are kept, one for loan and one for reference. A wide range of poetry magazines and periodicals from all over the world are kept; also cassettes, records and videos for consultation, with some available for loan. Plus children's poetry section — school visits welcome. An information service compiles lists of poetry magazines, competitions, publishers, bookshops, groups and workshops, which are available from the library on receipt of a large s.a.e. It also has a noticeboard for lost quotations, through which it tries to identify lines or fragments of poetry which have been sent in by other readers. General enquiry service also available.

Polish Library

238-246 King Street, London W6 0RF
☎081-741 0474

Open 10.00 am to 8.00 pm Monday and Wednesday; 10.00 am to 5.00 pm Tuesday and Friday; 10.00 am to 1.00 pm Thursday and Saturday (lending library closed Tuesday and Thursday)

Access For reference (loans to scholars and those interested in Polish affairs only)

Books, pamphlets, periodicals, maps, music, photographs on all aspects of Polish history and culture. *Special collections* Emigré publications; Joseph Conrad and related works; Polish underground publications.

Press Association Library

85 Fleet Street, London EC4P 4BE
☎071-353 7440
Fax 071-583 6082 (Photo Library)

Open News Library: 9.00 am to 11.00 pm seven days a week; Photo Library: 9.30 am to 5.00 pm

The national news agency offers public access to over 14 million news cuttings on every subject from 1926 onwards, and over 5 million colour and b&w photographs from 1902 to the present day. *Pictures* Personal callers welcome. *Cuttings* Contact the librarian on ext. 3160.

Harry Price Library of Magical Literature

University of London Library, Senate House, Malet Street, London WC1E 7HU
☎071-636 4514   Fax 071-636 5841

Open Term-time: 10.00 am to 6.30 pm Monday to Friday; 10.00 am to 5.30 pm Saturday (holidays: 10.00 am to 5.30 pm Monday to Saturday)

Open access For reference only, restricted to members of the University and accredited research students (apply in writing)

Over 14,000 volumes and pamphlets on psychic phenomena and pseudo-phenomena; books relating to spiritualism and its history, to hypnotism, telepathy, astrology, conjuring and quackery.

Public Record Office

Ruskin Avenue, Kew, Richmond, Surrey TW9 4DU
☎081-876 3444   Fax 081-878 8905

Open 9.30 am to 5.00 pm Monday to Friday

Access For reference, by reader's ticket, available free of charge on production of proof of identity

Also at Chancery Lane, London WC2A 1LR

Over 90 miles of shelving house the national repository of records of central Government in the UK and law courts of England and Wales, which extend in time from the 11th-20th century. Medieval records and the records of the State Paper Office from the early 16th-late 18th century, plus the records of the Privy Council Office and the Lord Chamberlain's and Lord Steward's departments, together with the records of the decennial censuses, 1841-1891, are held at Chancery Lane. Modern government department records, together with those of the Copyright Office, are held at Kew; these date mostly from the late 18th century. Under the Public Records Act, records are normally only open to inspection when they are 30 years old. Chancery Lane also houses a small permanent exhibition of records (open 10.00 am to 5.00 pm Monday to Friday).

Library of the Religious Society of Friends

Friends House, Euston Road, London NW1 2BJ
☎071-387 3601   Fax 071-388 1977

Open 10.00 am to 5.00 pm Tuesday to Friday (closed last full week November and week preceding Spring Bank Holiday)

Access For reference, to members of the Society of Friends and to *bona fide* researchers on introduction or letter of recommendation

Quaker history, thought and activities from the 17th century onwards. Supporting collections on peace, anti-slavery and other subjects in which Quakers have maintained long-standing interest. Also archives and manuscripts relating to the Society of Friends.

Royal Geographical Society Library

1 Kensington Gore, London SW7 2AR
☎071-589 5466   Fax 071-584 4447

Open 10.00 am to 5.00 pm Monday to Friday (Map Room closed 1.00 pm to 2.00 pm)

Access To map room and picture library; library and reading rooms restricted for use by Fellows and members

Books and periodicals on geography, topography, cartography, voyages and travels. Map Room houses map sheets, atlases and expedition reports.

Photographs on travel and exploration are housed in the picture library.

Royal Society Library

6 Carlton House Terrace, London SW1Y 5AG
☎071-839 5561   Fax 071-930 2170

Open 10.00 am to 5.00 pm Monday to Friday

Access For research only, to *bona fide* researchers on application to the librarian

Science, history of science, scientists' biographies, science policy reports, and publications of international scientific unions and national academies from all over the world.

Royal Society of Medicine Library

1 Wimpole Street, London W1M 8AE
☎071-408 2119   Fax 071-408 0062

Open 9.00 am to 9.30 pm Monday to Friday; 10.00 am to 5.00 pm Saturday

Access For reference only, on introduction by Fellow of the Society (temporary membership may also be granted)

Books and periodicals on general medicine, biochemistry and biomedical science. Extensive historical material.

St Bride Printing Library

Bride Lane, London EC4Y 8EQ
☎071-353 4660   Fax 071-583 7073

Open 9.30 am to 5.30 pm Monday to Friday

Open access

City of London public reference library. Appointments advisable for consultation of special collections. Every aspect of printing and related matters: publishing and bookselling, newspapers and magazines, graphic design, calligraphy and type, papermaking and bookbinding. One of the world's largest specialist collections in its field, with over 40,000 volumes, over 2000 periodicals (200 current titles), and extensive collection of volumes, drawings, manuscripts, prospectuses, patents and materials for printing and typefounding. Noted for its comprehensive holdings of historical and early technical literature.

Science Fiction Foundation Research Library

Polytechnic of East London, Longbridge Road, Dagenham, Essex RM8 2AS
☎081-590 7722 ext. 2177   Fax 081-590 7799

Access For research, by appointment only (telephone first)

The largest collection outside the USA of science fiction and related material — including autobiographies and critical works. *Special collection* Runs of 'pulp' magazines dating back to the 1920s. Foreign language material — large Russian collection, plus Flat Earth Society papers.

Science Museum Library

Imperial Insitute Road, off Exhibition Road, London SW7 5NH
☎071-938 8234   Fax 071-938 8213

Open 10.00 am to 5.30 pm Monday to Saturday

Open access Reference only; no loans

National reference library for the history and public understanding of science and technology, with a large collection of source material.

Scottish Poetry Library

Tweeddale Court, 14 High Street, Edinburgh EH1 1TE
☎031-557 2876

Librarian *Dr Tom Hubbard*

Open access Membership (£10 p.a.)

A comprehensive collection of work by Scottish poets in Gaelic, Scots and English, plus the work of international poets, including books, tapes, videos and magazines. Borrowing is free to all. Services include a postal lending service, for which there is a small fee (catalogues of the lending collection for sale) and a mobile library which can visit schools and other centres by arrangement. Members receive a newsletter and support the library, whose work includes exhibitions, bibliographies, information and promotion in the field of poetry. Also available is an on-line catalogue and computer index to poetry.

Sheffield Libraries and Information Services

Central Library, Surrey Street, Sheffield S1 1XZ
☎0742 734711   Fax 0742 735009

Sheffield Archives
52 Shoreham Street, Sheffield S1 4SP
☎0742 734756

Open 9.30 am to 5.30 pm Monday to Thursday; 9.00 am to 1.00 pm & 2.00 pm to 4.30 pm Saturday (documents should be ordered by 5.00 pm Thursday for Saturday)

Access By reader's pass

Holds documents relating to Sheffield and South Yorkshire, dating from the 12th century to present day, including records of the City Council, churches, businesses, landed estates, families and individuals, institutions and societies.

Arts and Social Sciences Reference Library
☎ 0742 734747/8/9

Open 10.00 am to 8.00 pm Monday; 10.00 am to 5.30 pm Tuesday, Thursday and Friday; 1.00 pm to 8.00 pm Wednesday; 9.30 am to 4.30 pm Saturday

Access For reference only

A comprehensive collection of books, periodicals and newspapers covering all aspects of arts (excluding music) and social sciences.

Music and Video Library
☎ 0742 734733

Open As for Arts and Social Services above

Access For reference (loans to ticket holders only)

An extensive range of books, records, CDs, cassettes, scores, etc. related to music. Also a video cassette loan service.

Local Studies Library
☎ 0742 734753

Open As for Arts & Social Sciences above

Access For reference (but advance notice advisable)

Extensive material covering all aspects of Sheffield and its population, including maps, photos and taped oral histories.

Business, Science and Technology Reference Library
☎ 0742 734736/7 (Business); 734742/3 (Science & Technology)

Open As for Arts & Social Sciences above

Access For reference only

Extensive coverage of science and technology as well as commerce and commercial law. British patents and British and European standards with emphasis on metals. Hosts the World Metal Index. The business section holds a large stock of business and trade directories, plus overseas telephone directories and reference works with business emphasis.

Sheffield Information Service
☎ 0742 734760/1

Open 10.00 am to 1.00 pm & 2.00 pm to 5.30 pm Monday, Tuesday and Friday; 1.00 pm to 5.30 pm Wednesday and Thursday; 9.30 am to 1.00 pm Saturday

Full local information service covering all aspects of the Sheffield community.

Shoe Lane Library
Hill House, Little New Street, London EC4A 3JR
☎ 071-583 7178

Open 9.30 am to 5.30 pm Monday, Wednesday, Thursday and Friday; 9.30 am to 6.30 pm Tuesday

Open access

City of London general lending library, with a comprehensive stock of 48,000 volumes, more than half of which are on display. Some specialisation in graphics, advertising and illustrated works.

Spanish Institute Library
102 Eaton Square, London SW1W 9AN
☎ 071-235 1484/5   Fax 071-235 4115

Open 9.30 am to 1.00 pm and 2.30 pm to 6.00 pm Monday to Thursday; 9.30 am to 2.00 pm Friday

Open access For reference

Spanish literature, history, art, philosophy. Books, slides, tapes, records and films.

Sunderland Central Library
Borough Road, Sunderland SR1 1PP
☎ 091-514 1235   Fax 091-510 0675

9.30 am to 7.30 pm Monday and Wednesday; 9.30 am to 5.00 pm Tuesday, Thursday and Friday; 9.30 am to 4.00 pm Saturday

The city's main lending and reference library. Local studies and children's sections, plus sound and vision department (CDs, cassettes, videos, talking books). The City of Sunderland maintains a further nineteen branch libraries. Special services available to housebound readers, hospitals and schools, plus two mobile libraries and an open learning library van.

Swiss Cottage Library
See **London Borough of Camden Information and Reference Services**

Theatre Museum Library & Archive
1e Tavistock Street, London WC2E 7PA
☎ 071-836 7891   Fax 071-836 5148

Open 10.30 am to 4.30 pm Tuesday to Friday (closed 1.00 pm to 2.00 pm)

Access By appointment only

The Theatre Museum was founded as a separate department of the Victoria & Albert Museum in 1974 and moved to its own building in Covent Garden in 1987. The museum (open Tuesday to Friday 11.00 am to 7.00 pm) houses permanent displays, temporary exhibitions, a studio theatre, and organises a programme of special events, performances, lectures and guided visits. The library houses the UK's largest performing arts research collections, including books, photographs, designs, engravings, programmes, press cuttings, etc. All the performing arts are covered but strengths are in the areas of theatre history, ballet, circus and stage design. The Theatre Museum has recently acquired much of the British Theatre Association's library and is providing reference access to its collections of play texts and critical works.

Trades Union Congress Library

Congress House, Great Russell Street, London WC1B 3LS
☎ 071-636 4030 ext. 220/1/2
Fax 071-636 0632

Librarian *Christine Coates*

Open 10.00 am to 5.00 pm Monday to Friday

Access For research, by appointment only

Industrial relations, wages and conditions of employment, trade unions, economics, occupational health, international trade union activities and other areas covered by TUC policy. Also a small collection of photographs.

United Nations London Information Centre

20 Buckingham Gate, London SW1E 6LB
☎ 071-630 1981   Fax 071-976 6478

Open 10.00 am to 1.00 pm and 2.00 pm to 5.00 pm Monday, Wednesday and Thursday; Information Centre: 9.30 am to 1.00 pm and 2.00 pm to 5.30 pm Monday to Friday

Open access For reference only

A full stock of official publications and documentation from the United Nations.

Victoria Library (Westminster)

See **Central Music Library; Westminster Archives & Local History Collection.**

Western Isles Libraries

Public Library, Keith Street, Stornoway, Isle of Lewis PA87 2QG
☎ 0851 703064   Fax 0851 705657

Open 10.00 am to 5.00 pm Monday to Thursday; 10.00 am to 7.00 pm Friday; 10.00 am to 1.00 pm Saturday

Open access

General public library stock, plus local history and Gaelic collections including maps, printed music and cassettes; census records and Council minutes; music collection (records and cassettes). Branch libraries on the isles of Barra, Benbecula, Harris and Lewis.

Westminster Archives & Local History Collection

Victoria Library, 160 Buckingham Palace Road, London SW1W 9UD
☎ 071-798 2180   Fax 071-798 2181

Open 9.30 am to 7.00 pm Monday to Friday; 9.30 am to 1.00 pm and 2.00 pm to 5.00 pm Saturday

Marylebone Library, Marylebone Road, London NW1 5PS
☎ 071-798 1206   Fax 071-798 1019

Open 10.00 am to 7.00 pm Monday; 9.30 am to 5.00 pm Tuesday, Wednesday and Friday; 9.30 am to 7.00 pm Thursday; 9.30 am to 1.00 pm and 2.00 pm to 5.00 pm Saturday

Access For reference

Comprehensive coverage of the history of Westminster and selective coverage of general London history. 22,000 books, together with a large stock of maps, prints, photographs, and theatre programmes. Victoria Library deals with the area south of Oxford Street/Bayswater Road; Marylebone Library houses archives relating to the area north of that line.

Westminster (City of) Reference Libraries

See **Westminster Reference Library; Marylebone Library; Victoria Library.**

Westminster Reference Library

35 St Martin's Street, London WC2H 7HP
☎ General & Performing Arts 071-798 2036/
Publications 071-798 2034/1285
Fax 071-798 2040

Librarian *Judith Russell*

Open 10.00 am to 7.00 pm Monday to Friday; 10.00 am to 5.00 pm Saturday

Access For reference only

A general reference library with emphasis on the following: Art & Design (see separate entry); Performing Arts: theatre, cinema, radio, television and dance; Official Publications: major collection of HMSO publications from 1947, plus parliamentary papers dating back to 1906, and a ten-year file of key statistical publications from OECD, UN, UNESCO, EC, etc.; Maps: an excellent map and town plan collection for Britain, plus international material; Business: UK directories, trade directories, company and market data; Periodicals: long files of many titles. Two working days' notice is required for some monographs and most older periodicals. Information for Business service available (charged).

The Wiener Library

4 Devonshire Street, London W1N 2BH
☎071–636 7247   Fax 071–436 6428

Open 10.00 am to 5.30 pm Monday to Friday

Access By letter of introduction (readers needing to use the Library for any length of time should become members)

Private library — one of the leading research centres on European history since the First World War, with special reference to the era of totalitarianism and to Jewish affairs. Founded by Dr Wiener in Amsterdam in 1933, it holds material that is not available elsewhere. Books, periodicals, press archives, documents, pamphlets, leaflets and brochures. Much of the material can be consulted on microfilm.

Dr Williams's Library

14 Gordon Square, London WC1H 0AG
☎071–387 3727

Open 10.00 am to 5.00 pm Monday, Wednesday, Friday; 10.00 am to 6.30 pm Tuesday, Thursday

Open access To reading room (loans restricted to subscribers)

Annual subscription £10; ministers of religion and certain students £5

Primarily a library of theology, religion and ecclesiastical history. Also philosophy, history (English and Byzantine). Particularly important for the study of English Nonconformity.

Wolverhampton Central Library

Snow Hill, Wolverhampton WV1 3AX
☎0902 312025   Fax 0902 714579

Open 10.00 am to 7.00 pm Monday to Thursday; 10.00 am to 5.00 pm Friday and Saturday

Archives & Local Studies Collection 10.00 am to 1.00 pm & 2.00 pm to 5.00 pm Monday, Tuesday, Thursday and Friday (Wednesday and Saturday by appointment)

General lending and reference libraries, plus children's library and the Archives & Local Studies library. Also audio visual library holding records, cassettes, CDs, videos and music scores.

York Central Library

Museum Street, York YO1 2DS
☎0904 655631/654144 (reference library)
Fax 0904 611025

Open 9.30 am to 8.00 pm Monday, Tuesday and Friday; 9.30 am to 1.00 pm Wednesday; 9.30 am to 5.30 pm Thursday; 9.30 am to 4.00 pm Saturday

Reference Library 9.00 am to 8.00 pm Monday, Tuesday, Wednesday and Friday; 9.00 am to 5.30 pm Thursday; 9.00 am to 1.00 pm Saturday

General lending library plus reference library incorporating local organisations database; local studies library for York and surrounding area; business information service; microfilm/fiche readers for national and local newspapers; census returns and family history resource; general reference collection. Maintains strong links with other local history resource centres, namely the Borthwick Institute, York City Archive and York Minster Library. Audio books service and music library.

Words with Pictures

A curator from the Ashmolean once told me that no book could be remotely worthwhile if it had coloured plates, and furthermore he thought that people and publishers who bothered museums for such colour photography wasted valuable museum time. Despite having spent an embarrassingly long time finding pictures for books, I sometimes agree and wish that the trees still grew. Does anyone really need 150 colour illustrations (often quaintly described as 'full') of Great Train Disasters or Patio Gardens for Microwave Cooks? Those apart, it goes without saying that for many books pictures are an illumination. How to achieve the best for the least amount of money is the general aim.

If your publisher supplies you with a picture researcher and asks you merely to make a few suggestions, your life will be easier. You must devoutly hope that she (and it usually is a she) is an imaginative, intelligent and experienced being who will astound and delight you with images that you never dreamt existed, let alone have seen in tens of other books. If you are offered the research services of either the editor's girlfriend looking for some amusing work while waiting for a place on a flower-arranging course, or the chairman's niece recovering from a nervous breakdown, beware. Do ask to see whatever pictures have been collected before the book is designed and try to make a case for eliminating any illustration that you believe to be too hackneyed or inaccurate. You may need to be quite persuasive: picture researchers feel emotionally attached to some pictures. Those tracked down in the album of an old colonel in Leamington Spa, or chanced upon among the 19,000 items of printed and engraved ephemera bequeathed to the British Museum by Miss Sarah Sophia Banks are precisely those that they will defend until the last tube home has run. They will often equate the degree of difficulty in finding the picture with excellence. Authors should also beware the obstinate designer and his (for it is often a he) single-minded determination to blow up full-page the most irrelevant picture in the pile. This may be equalled by his fierce determination to drop the most interesting. 'Quality,' he will mutter, 'such bad quality,' and then, with appalling finality 'It won't *reproduce*.' This is the time to get the picture researcher on your side but sometimes the depressing fact has to be accepted.

Caption writing is a chore and often has to be completed between lunch and tea on a Friday afternoon. However, authors generally write them best. Those knocked off by editors and picture researchers have a way of occasionally contradicting the text: figures who should be safely running a mission station in Africa make simultaneous ghostly appearances at a Sandringham shooting party, or artists mysteriously paint large portraits after their deaths.

To the author who is to provide his own illustrations I offer a few tips. Having agreed to do the work, you should try to get the publisher to agree to pay for all the expenses incurred in including illustrations in a book. These can mount up with surprising speed: (1) the cost of new photography; (2) the cost of the actual photographs to send to the printers; (3) the cost of using photographic agencies – this might be a 'research fee' (even though you might have spent all day looking through their files yourself), a 'facility fee', a 'loan fee'; (4) the reproduction fee payable on publication; and (5) the cost of copies of the book to the colonel in Leamington Spa who lent you his album.

It used to be the case that if you did your research carefully in museums and archives, you could find pictures cheaply or even for free. This is no longer the case. The Public Record Office will charge something approaching £60 for UK and Commonwealth rights for a black and white illustration even for a scholarly book and the museums are out there in the market place fighting to be enterprising.

It may seem to be stating the obvious, but pictures can take an unconscionable time to materialise and you are by and large powerless to speed the process. Allow at least three months if possible. The following scenes are depressingly familiar to me. You find in the National Buildings Record the perfect photograph of an old archbishop's tomb, joyfully order a print – and then are told of the eight-week wait. The wrong negative number (never mind if the fault is theirs or yours): you rip open your packet from the British Library eagerly awaiting a photograph of Nelson's handwriting done with his left hand – and your eye falls on a photograph of what you can only assume is a folio from the Anglo Saxon Chronicle. American museums hardly ever write replies and when they do they invariably want extraordinarily complicated pre-payment of invoices in dollars with much mention of bank account numbers. In each of these cases you need the picture for the printer in two weeks' time . . .

Don't ever imagine, or hope, that a photograph taken by anyone other than a professional will be any good for reproducing. There is a 98% chance that if it is a black and white it will be small and fuzzy and that if it is in colour it will have half a Ford Sierra or a fat lady in a red anorak in the foreground, quite spoiling the view of Schinkel's greatest building. Try to get hold of large format black and white prints, approximately 10×8 in, with a glossy finish. Check colour transparencies with a magnifying glass to see that they are sharply in focus.

There are guides to help you through the maze. Picture agencies have proliferated in the last twenty years and it is no longer a toss-up between the Mansell Collection, Paul Popper or the Radio Times Hulton Picture Library. The best and most recent guidebok is *The Picture Researcher's Handbook* by Hilary and Mary Evans. The 5th edition, published in autumn 1992, is from Blueprint and has worldwide coverage. For purely British sources, the annual directory produced by BAPLA (British Association of Picture Libraries and Agencies, 13 Woodberry Crescent, London N10 1PJ, Tel 081-444 7913) is cheap and provides a good index of specialities.

Of course, an author can employ a picture researcher directly. An experienced freelance will currently charge £12–14 per hour and should do the work far quicker than a novice charging less. There will also be expenses: travel phone and postage. The advantage is that such a researcher will work to a budget and produce the goods within the time limit. Clearly, you should find someone with a knowledge of the subject; a researcher who has mainly worked on interior design books will not necessarily be aware of the best source for photographs of the Korean war. A personal recommendation is always easiest but SPRED, the Society of Picture Researchers and Editors, runs a very efficient (free) Freelance Register Service. Ruth Smith at 14 Stanhope Road, St Albans Herts AL1 5BL (Tel 0727 833676) will put you in touch with a researcher who she thinks will be right for the job and who she knows is free to do the work. It is almost true that a picture researcher is only as good as her or his address book – you could try taking one out for a drink and asking their advice.

Philippa Lewis

Philippa Lewis is a picture researcher and writer and runs Edifice, a picture library for architectural subjects.

Picture Libraries

Ace Photo Agency
22 Maddox Street, London W1R 9PG
☎071-629 0303   Fax 071-495 6100

Colour files include lifestyles, business, industry, sports, celebrities, glamour, skies and sunsets, still life, special effects, art, natural history, illustration and much more. Visitors welcome. Catalogues available. Commissions undertaken.

Action Images Ltd
74 Willoughby Lane, London N17 0SP
☎081-885 3000   Fax 081-808 6167

Contact *John Sibley/David Jacobs*

Half a million colour and 100,000 b&w images of sport. Commissions undertaken.

Action Plus
54-58 Tanner Street, London SE1 3LL
☎071-403 1558   Fax 071-403 1526

Sports photographic agency, providing international coverage of over 120 sports and leisure activities worldwide. Media and commercial markets supplied.

Adams Picture Library
156 New Cavendish Street, London W1M 7FJ
☎071-636 1468   Fax 071-436 7131

Over half a million transparencies of selected work from more than 400 photographers from all over the world. Many subjects are stocked in great depth and the library is constantly being updated with new material. Brochure available.

Lesley & Roy Adkins Picture Library
Longstone Lodge, Aller, Langport,
Somerset TA10 0QT
☎0458 250075   Fax 0458 250858

Colour coverage of archaeology, heritage and related subjects (UK, some Europe), prehistoric, Roman, medieval sites and monuments, landscapes and countryside, housing, architecture, towns, villages and religious monuments.

Adlib Specialist Picture Source
33 Albury Avenue, Isleworth, Middlesex TW7 5HY
☎081-847 3777   Fax 081-568 2402

Specialist collections include cars, children, girls, landscapes, nature, the ocean and travel.

AFP (Agence France Presse)
See **Popperfoto**

Malcolm Aird Associates
18A Upper Park Road, London NW3 2UP
☎0787 210111

Rural and urban Britain, landscapes, people at work, industry.

Alba Pictures
The Sutors, 28 Broadstone Park,
Inverness IV2 3LA
☎0463 233717

Contact *Ken MacTaggart*

Scottish landscapes, Highlands and Islands, mountaineering in Britain and around the world, world travel, general landscape, volcanoes, glaciers, geological studies.

Bryan & Cherry Alexander Photography
Higher Cottage, Manston, Sturminster Newton,
Dorset DT10 1EZ
☎0258 73006   Fax 0747 51474

Contact *Cherry Alexander*

70,000 colour transparencies, specialising in polar regions, with emphasis on the wildlife and native peoples of the Arctic.

All-Action Picture Library

32 Great Sutton Street, London EC1V 0DX
☎071-608 2988/9   Fax 071-250 3376

Comprehensive colour library comprising material on all fields of pop celebrities, entertainment and acting, plus some royalty, sport and politics. Commissions undertaken.

Chris Allan Aviation Library

AV Distributors (London) Ltd, 21-22 St Albans Place, Upper Street, London N1 0NX
☎071-226 1508   Fax 071-359 8523

Contact *Anna Kafetz*

About 10,000 transparencies (35 mm, 6x6 cm colour) on military and commercial aircraft.

Allsport (UK) Ltd

Allsport House, 3 Greenlea Park, Prince George's Road, London SW19 2JD
☎081-685 1010   Fax 081-648 5240

A large specialist library with 4 million colour transparencies, covering 130 different sports and top sports personalities. Represented in 27 countries worldwide. Large studio and digital wiring facilities through Hasselblad picture desk.

Ancient Art and Architecture Collection

6 Kenton Road, Harrow-on-the-Hill, Middlesex HA1 2BL
☎081-422 1214   Fax 081-426 9479

Colour and b&w coverage of civilisations of the world: arts, cities, architecture, landscapes, peoples and religions.

Andes Press Agency

26 Padbury Court, London E2 7EH
☎071-739 3159   Fax 071-739 3159

Contact *Val Baker/Carlos Reyes*

80,000 colour transparencies and 300,000 b&w, specialising in social documentary, world religions and theologians, Latin America and Britain.

Heather Angel/Biofotos

Highways, 6 Vicarage Hill, Farnham,   .
Surrey GU9 8HJ
☎0252 716700
Fax 0252 727464 FAO Heather Angel

Worldwide natural history, wildlife and landscapes: polar regions, tropical rain forest flora and fauna, all species of plants and animals in natural habitats from Africa, Asia (notably China), Australasia, South America and USA, urban wildlife, pollution, global warming. Catalogue available. Commissions undertaken.

Animal Photography

4 Marylebone Mews, New Cavendish Street, London W1M 7LF
☎071-935 0503   Fax 071-487 3038

Colour and b&w coverage of horses, dogs, cats, zoos, the Galapagos Islands, East Africa. Commissions undertaken.

Museum of Antiquities Picture Library

University and Society of Antiquaries of Newcastle upon Tyne, Newcastle upon Tyne NE1 7RU
☎091-222 7844   Fax 091-261 1182

Contact *Lindsay Allason-Jones/Sue Purvis*

25,000 images, mostly b&w, of special collections including: Hadrian's Wall Archive (b&ws taken over the last 100 years); Gertrude Bell Archive (during her travels in the Near East, 1900-26); and aerial photographs of archaeological sites in the North of England. Visitors welcome by appointment.

Aquarius Picture Library

See **UK Agents**

Aquila Photographics

PO Box 1, Studley, Warwickshire B80 7AN
☎052785 2357   Fax 052785 7507

Colour and b&w natural history library specialising in birds, British and European wildlife, North America, Africa and Australia, environmental subjects, farming, habitats and related subjects, domestic animals and pets.

Arcaid

The Factory, 2 Acre Road, Kingston upon Thames, Surrey KT2 6EF
☎081-546 4352   Fax 081-541 5230

Historic and contemporary architecture and interior design by leading architectural photographers. Covers international and British subjects, single images and series, with background information.

Visitors welcome by appointment. Commissions undertaken.

Architectural Association Slide Library
36 Bedford Square, London WC1B 3ES
☎071-636 0974   Fax 071-414 0782

Contact *Valerie Bennett*

80,000 35 mm slides, 5000 large format b&w negatives on architecture from the 1920s to 1930s.

Ardea London Ltd
35 Brodrick Road, London SW17 7DX
☎081-672 2067   Fax 081-672 8787

Wildlife, natural history and conservation topics in colour and b&w. Animals, birds, plants and fish in their natural habitat worldwide.

Art Directors Photo Library
Image House, 86 Haverstock Hill, London NW3 2BD
☎071-485 9325/267 6930   Fax 071-485 7776

Work from international photographers which includes computer graphics, hi-tech, industry, business, space, personalities, lifestyles, travel, skies, still life, entertainment, fashion, cars (vintage and modern), the USA, Europe, Asia, Africa and the Tropics. Catalogue available.

Art Resource Illustration Library
28 Shelton Street, London WC2H 9JN
☎071-240 1447   Fax 071-836 0199

Contact *Ruth Wood*

Constantly updated illustration library ranging in style from photo-realistic to impressionistic. 'Everything from industry to sport, from abstracts to science fiction'. Commissions undertaken.

Artbank International
8 Woodcroft Avenue, London NW7 2AG
☎081-906 2288   Fax 081-906 2289

Illustration and art library holding thousands of images by many renowned artists. Large format transparencies. Catalogue available on request. Represents a diverse group of UK and American illustrators for commissioned work. Portfolios available for viewing.

Aspect Picture Library Ltd
40 Rostrevor Road, London SW6 5AD
☎071-736 1998/731 7362   Fax 071-731 7362

Colour and b&w worldwide coverage of countries, events, industry and travel, with large files on art, namely paintings, space, China and the Middle East.

Associated Sports Photography
21-25 Green Walk, Leicester LE3 6SE
☎0533 320310   Fax 0533 311123

Colour and b&w coverage of all sports including major international events and personalities.

Audio Visual Services
St Mary's Hospital Medical School, London W2 1PG
☎071-725 1739   Fax 071-724 7349

Contact *B. Tallon/E. R. Sparks*

Colour and b&w, mostly 35 mm colour. Clinical medicine, contemporary and historical, including HIV-AIDS material and history of penicillin. Member of **BAPLA**. Commissions undertaken.

Aviation Photographs International
15 Downs View Road, Swindon, Wiltshire SN3 1NS
☎0793 497179   Fax 0793 497179

200,000 colour photos covering all aspects of modern military hardware. Extensive coverage of military and civil aviation, both current and vintage/warbird types. Commissions undertaken for both photography and research.

Aviation Picture Library
35 Kingsley Avenue, London W13 0EQ
☎081-566 7712   Fax 081-566 7714

Contact *Austin John Brown*

Specialists in the aviation field but also a general library which includes travel, architecture, transport, landscapes and skyscapes. Special collections: aircraft and all aspects of the aviation industry; aerial obliques of Europe, USA, Caribbean and West Africa; architectural and town planning. Commissions undertaken on the ground and in the air.

Aviemore Photographic Scotland
Main Road, Aviemore, Highland PH22 1RH
☎0479 810371   Fax 0479 811351

Colour and b&w coverage of Scotland: sports, tourism, landscapes.

Axel Poignant Archive

115 Bedford Mansions, Bedford Avenue,
London WC1B 3AG
☎071-636 2555   Fax 071-636 2555

Anthropological and ethnographic subjects, especially Australia and the South Pacific. Also Scandinavia (early history and mythology), Sicily and England.

A-Z Botanical Collection Ltd

Bedwell Lodge, Cucumber Lane, Essendon,
Hatfield, Hertfordshire AL9 6JB
☎0707 49091   Fax 0707 46613

Contact *Jeremy Finlay*

150,000 transparencies, specialising in plants and related subjects.

Clive Barda

See **Performing Arts Library**

Barnaby's Picture Library

Barnaby House, 19 Rathbone Street,
London W1P 1AF
☎071-636 6128   Fax 071-637 4317

Colour and b&w coverage of a wide range of subjects: nature, transport, industry and historical, including a collection on Hitler. Commissions undertaken.

Barts Medical Picture Library

Dept of Medical Illustration, St Bartholomew's
Hospital, West Smithfield, London EC1A 7BE
☎071-601 8080/1   Fax 071-796 3753

Contact *The Photo Librarian*

Clinical manifestations of the majority of known diseases and conditions; X-rays, scans and illustrations, including historical material; plus some aspects of hospital activities. Visitors welcome by appointment only.

Colin Baxter Photography Ltd

Unit 2/3, Block 6, Caldmellside Industrial Estate,
Lanark ML11 6SR
☎0555 65022   Fax 0555 4775

Contact *A. Russell/M. Rensner*

Over 50,000 images specialising in Scotland. Also the Lake District, Yorkshire, Cotswolds, France, Iceland and a special collection on Charles Rennie Mackintosh's work.

Beken of Cowes Ltd

16 Birmingham Road, Cowes, Isle of
Wight PO31 7BH
☎0983 297311   Fax 0983 291059

Maritime subjects from 1888 to the present day. Marine photographers to HRH The Duke of Edinburgh. Commissions undertaken.

Ivan J. Belcher Colour Picture Library

34 Berry Croft, Abingdon, Oxfordshire OX14 1JL
☎0235 521524

Extensive colour library specialising in top-quality transparencies (6x6cm) depicting the British scene, and constantly updated. Particular emphasis on tourist, holiday and heritage locations, including famous cities, towns, picturesque harbours, rivers, canals, villages, cottages, castles, rural scenes and traditions photographed throughout the seasons.

Andrew Besley PhotoLibrary

The Cross, Levant, St Ives, Cornwall TR26 3LJ
☎0736 756756   Fax 0736 756555

Contact *Andrew Besley*

Specialist library of 20,000 images of West Country faces and places.

BFI Stills, Posters and Designs

British Film Institute, 21 Stephen Street,
London W1P 1PL
☎071-255 1444   Fax 071-323 9260

Contact *Bridget Kinally*

Holds images from more than 60,000 films and TV programmes on 5 million b&w prints and over 500,000 colour transparencies. A further 20,000 files hold portraits of film and TV personalities and cover related general subjects such as studios, equipment, awards. Also holds original posters and set and costume designs. Visitors welcome by appointment only.

John Birdsall Photographic Library

75 Raleigh Street, Nottingham NG7 4DL
☎0602 782645   Fax 0602 785546

Contact *John Birdsall/Clare Marsh*

Thousands of b&w images of social documentary with a non-sexist, non-racist bias. Also extensive colour collection of children, youth, old age, health and disability. Catalogue available on request.

Anthony Blake

54 Hill Rise, Richmond, Surrey TW10 6UB
☏081-940 7583   Fax 081-948 1224

Colour coverage of all aspects of food and wine: cooking, restaurants, farming, vineyards, fishing. Catalogue available. Commissions undertaken.

John Blake Picture Library

The Georgian House, 6 The Plain, Thornbury, Bristol, Avon BS12 2AG
☏0454 418321/413240   Fax 0454 416636

Colour and b&w worldwide coverage. Commissions undertaken.

BMV Picturebank International

79 Farringdon Road, London EC1M 3JY
☏071-405 5021   Fax 071-831 2982

General file and specialists in world travel. Commissions undertaken.

Chris Bonington Library

Badger Hill, Nether Row, Hesket Newmarket, Wigton, Cumbria CA7 8LA
☏069 98286   Fax 069 98238

Contact Frances Daltrey

Thousands of 35 mm colour images (some larger format, plus b&w) on mountaineering: climbers, mountains, travel, expeditions, local people and customs in many mountain regions.

Janet and Colin Bord

See **Fortean Picture Library**

Boys Syndication

Red House, Newbourn, Woodbridge, Suffolk IP12 4PX
☏0473 36333   Fax 0394 380483

Contact Pam Boys

Colour collections: Michael Boys and Jacqui Hurst on gardening; also interiors, food, wine and travel.

Bridgeman Art Library

19 Chepstow Road, London W2 5BP
☏071-727 4065/229 7420   Fax 071-792 8509

Colour transparency library of paintings and works of art from antiquity to the present day, including furniture, glass, ceramics, silver and needlework. Catalogue available. Agents for many UK museums and overseas collections. Commissions undertaken and same-day service available.

Hamish Brown Scottish Photographic

21 Carlin Craig, Kinghorn, Fife KY3 9RX
☏0592 890422

Colour and b&w library: Scottish sites, topography, buildings, historical, mountains, Ireland, Morocco and world travel. Book illustrations. Maps drawn. Commissions undertaken.

Bubbles Photolibrary

23A Benwell Road, London N7 7BL
☏071-609 4547   Fax 071-607 1410

Babies, children, pregnancy and women's health. Commissions undertaken.

Cable & Wireless Visual Resource

New Mercury House, 26 Red Lion Square, London WC1R 4UQ
☏071-315 4885   Fax 071-315 5052

Contact Lesley A. Wood

Telecommunications collection, plus worldwide scenics, street scenes, the Far East, Caribbean, USA and Pacific. Over 30,000 transparencies on 35 mm. Visitors by appointment.

Calendar Concepts & Design

33 Albury Avenue, Isleworth, Middlesex TW7 5HY
☏081-847 3777   Fax 081-568 2402

Contact Michael A. Brown

10,000 colour transparencies organised under calendar themes: scenic, animals and wildlife, florals, cars, glamour, ocean, travel.

Camera Press

Russell Court, Coram Street, London WC1H 0NB
☏071-837 4488   Fax 071-278 5126

High-quality photofeatures and up-to-date coverage of international events, celebrities and royals.

Camera Ways Ltd Picture Library

Court View, Egerton, Near Ashford,
Kent TN27 9BD
☎023376 454

Contact *Caryl & Derek Budd*

Expanding collection of over 15,000 colour slides covering traditional country crafts, country people, village scenes, landscapes, natural history, nature reserves, environmental issues, habitats, rivers and ponds, storm damage, trees, angling entomology, European flora and fauna, Falkland Islands, and aerial views of Southern England. Special collections include scenes from ITV's *Country Ways* series and Derek Budd's wildlife/nature programmes, plus a new bird collection from international ornithologist Dr Jim Flegg.

Camerapix Picture Library

8 Ruston Mews, London W11 1RB
☎071-221 0077/0249   Fax 071-792 8105

Colour coverage of assignments and expeditions in Africa, Asia and the Middle East: indigenous cultures, industry, landscapes, political leaders, African wildlife, and an outstanding Islamic portfolio. Material not available in London may be accessed from the Nairobi collection.

The Casement Collection

2 Frobisher Crescent, Stanwell, Staines,
Middlesex TW19 7DX
☎0784 254918

Colour and b&w travel library, particularly strong on North America and the Gulf. Not just beaches and palm trees. Based on Jack Casement's collection, with additions by other photographers.

J. Allan Cash Ltd

74 South Ealing Road, London W5 4QB
☎081-840 4141   Fax 081-566 2568

Colour and b&w coverage of travel, natural history, people, space, sport, industry, agriculture and many other subjects. New material regularly contributed by 300 plus photographers.

Celtic Picture Library

5 Llys Llannerch, St Asaph, Clwyd LL17 0AZ
☎0745 730395   Fax 0745 730395

Coverage of Wales, including environment, conservation, tourism, landscapes, farming and historic sites. Commissions undertaken.

Central Press Photos Ltd

See **Hulton Picture Company**

Cephas Picture Library

20 Bedster Gardens, West Molesey,
Surrey KT8 1SZ
☎081-979 8647   Fax 081-979 8647

The wine industry and vineyards of the world is the subject on which Cephas has made its reputation. The collection is probably the most comprehensive in the world (6x7 mainly, and supported by detailed captions). Strong collection, increasingly, of the spirit and beer industries, and a general library, including Europe, UK, USA, and the Far East. No search charge if pictures are used. Visitors by appointment.

The Children's Library

2 Devonshire Mews West, London W1N 1FP
☎071-935 2626   Fax 071-935 7557

Children, ranging from babies to teenagers, both on location and in the studio.

Christel Clear Marine Photography

Roselea, Church Lane, Awbridge, Near Romsey,
Hampshire SO51 0HN
☎0794 41081   Fax 0794 40890

Contact *Nigel Dowden/Christel Dowden*

Over 50,000 images on 35 mm and 645 transparency: yachting and boating from Grand Prix sailing to small dinghies, cruising locations and harbours. Visitors by appointment.

Christian Aid Photo Library

PO Box 100, London SE1 7RT
☎071-620 4444   Fax 071-620 0719

Pictures from Africa, Asia and Latin America, relating to small-scale community based programmes. Mostly development themes: agriculture, health, education, urban and rural life.

The Cinema Museum

The Old Fire Station, 46 Renfrew Road,
London SE11 4NA
☎071-820 9991   Fax 071-793 0849

Colour and b&w coverage (including stills) of the motion picture industry throughout its history, including the Ronald Grant Archive. Small collections on theatre, variety, television and popular music.

Circa Photo Library

c/o Icorec, Didsbury College, Wilmslow Road,
Manchester M20 8RR
☎061-434 0828   Fax 061-434 8374

Contact *Joanne O'Brien*

Specialist library covering environment issues and world religions, including festivals, worship, prayer and celebration at home and in the community.

John Cleare/Mountain Camera

Hill Cottage, Fonthill Gifford, Salisbury,
Wiltshire SP3 6QW
☎0747 89320   Fax 0747 89320

Colour and b&w coverage of mountains and wilderness, expeditions, landscapes from all continents, geographical features and cities. Consultancy work undertaken for mountains, mountaineering and wilderness travel.

Stephanie Colasanti

38 Hillside Court, 409 Finchley Road,
London NW3 6HQ
☎071-435 3695   Fax 071-435 9995

Colour coverage of Europe, Africa, Asia, United Arab Emirates, the Caribbean, USA, Australia, New Zealand, the Pacific Islands and South America: people, animals, towns, agriculture, landscapes, carnivals, markets, archaeology, religion and ancient civilisations. Travel assignments undertaken. Medium format transparencies (2¼ square).

Bruce Coleman Wildlife & Travel Photo Library

Unit 16, Chiltern Business Village, Arundel Road,
Uxbridge, Middlesex UB8 2SN
☎0895 257094   Fax 0895 272357

Colour coverage of natural history, ecology, archaeology, anthropology, horticulture, agriculture, science, social documentary and historical illustration.

Collections

13 Woodberry Crescent, London N10 1PJ
☎081-883 0083   Fax 081-883 9215

Contact *Laura Boswell/Brian Shuel*

100,000 colour; 50,000 b&w images in a collection of collections. Collections is confined to the British Isles only by specialist photographers: *Family Life* by Anthea Sieveking; *Raw Food* by David Burch; *Horticulture* by Patrick Johns; *British Steam Railway Lines* by Alain le Garsmeur; *British Castles* by Roy Stedall-Humphryes; *British Customs, British Bridges* and b&w fun by Brian Shuel. Family life, horticulture, British customs, bridges, castles, railways, fungi, potters, hill farming and the North Sea. Visitors welcome by appointment.

Colorsport

44 St Peter's Street, London N1 8JT
☎071-359 2714   Fax 071-226 4328

Colour and b&w coverage of sport, sports personalities throughout the world, football from 1881, cricket from 1920s. Visitors welcome.

Compix

Commonwealth Institute, Kensington High Street,
London W8 6NQ
☎071-603 4535 ext. 237
Fax 071-602 7374   Telex 8955822

Colour coverage of the lives and people of the Commonwealth. Information leaflet available.

Comstock Photofile Ltd

28 Chelsea Wharf, 15 Lots Road,
London SW10 0QQ
☎071-351 4448   Fax 071-352 8414

Comprehensive coverage of people, industry, science, travel, natural history and the Susan Griggs collection of editorial photography (scenes, cities, lifestyles, peoples worldwide). Also desktop photography products. Free catalogue on request.

Conway Picture Library

See **The Victory Archive**

Sylvia Cordaiy Photo Library

72 East Ham Road, Littlehampton, West
Sussex BN17 7BQ
☎0903 715297   Fax 0903 731605

Contact *Sylvia Cordaiy*

Colour and b&w coverage of a wide range of subjects: architecture, worldwide travel, wildlife, global environmental topics, landscapes, cities and villages, UK counties, the RSPCA at work with both wild and domestic animals, veterinary work, the Pony Drift, ocean racing and tall ships, plus a large selection of card/calendar market work. Visitors welcome.

Country Life Library

King's Reach Tower, Stamford Street,
London SE1 9LS
℡071-261 6337   Fax 071-261 5139

Contact *Camilla Costello*

Over 150,000 b&w negatives and 15,000 colour transparencies dating back to 1897. Country houses, stately homes, churches and town houses in Britain and abroad, interiors of architectural interest (ceilings, fireplaces, furniture, paintings, sculpture), and exteriors showing many landscaped gardens. Visitors by appointment.

County Visuals

Planning Dept, Kent County Council, Springfield,
Maidstone, Kent ME14 2LX
℡0622 696171   Fax 0622 687620

Contact *Tony Hemsted*

Scenes across the county of Kent: attractions, activities, general countryside, villages, coastline and developments such as the Channel Tunnel and high-speed rail link.

Philip Craven Worldwide Photo-Library

Surrey Studios, 21 Nork Way, Nork, Banstead,
Surrey SM7 1PB
℡0737 373737

Contact *Philip Craven*

Extensive coverage of worldwide subjects on 6x7 cm and 5x4 sheet. Travel, wildlife, British scenes, cities, villages, countryside, gardens, historic buildings.

Sue Cunningham Photographic

56 Chatham Road, Kingston upon Thames,
Surrey KT1 3AA
℡081-541 3024   Fax 081-541 5388

Member of **BAPLA**. Specialist collection of over 35,000 shots (mainly colour, some b&w) on Brazil. Other subjects include Chile, Portugal, Spain, Peru, the UK, and children.

James Davis Travel Photography

30 Hengistbury Road, New Milton,
Hampshire BH25 7LU
℡0425 610328   Fax 0425 638402

Travel collection: people, places, emotive scenes and tourism. Constantly updated by James Davis and a team of photographers, both at home and abroad. Same-day service available.

Peter Dazeley Photography

The Studios, 5 Heathmans Road, Parsons Green,
London SW6 4TJ
℡071-736 3171   Fax 071-371 8876

Extensive golf library dating from 1970: colour and b&w coverage of major tournaments. Constantly updated, with thousands of images of players (male and female), courses worldwide and miscellaneous images: clubs, teaching shots, balls, etc.

Design Council Picture Library

28 Haymarket, London SW1Y 4SU
℡071-839 8000   Fax 071-925 2130

Colour coverage of all aspects of design. No loans; no reproduction — educational resources only, for use in lectures — talks, etc. The Young Designers Centre is located on the upper floor of the Design Centre and provides a slide loan service to schools and colleges. The aim of the Design Council — a Government-sponsored organisation — is to help manufacturers use design effectively to improve their products and their profits. It works closely with both industry and education.

Douglas Dickins Photo Library

2 Wessex Gardens, Golders Green,
London NW11 9RT
℡081-455 6221

Worldwide colour and b&w coverage, specialising in Asia, particularly India, Indonesia and Japan. Meeting educational requirements on landscape, archaeology, history, religions, customs, people and folklore.

C M Dixon

The Orchard, Marley Lane, Kingston, Canterbury,
Kent CT4 6HJ
℡0227 830075   Fax 0227 830075

Colour coverage of ancient civilisations, archaeology and art, ethnology, mythology, world religion, museum objects, geography, geology, meteorology, landscapes, people and places from many countries including most of Europe, USSR, Ethiopia, Iceland, Morocco, Sri Lanka, Tunisia, Turkey, Egypt, Uzbekistan.

Dominic Photography

9A Netherton Grove, London SW10 9TQ
℡071-352 6118   Fax 071-351 0058

Contact *Zoë Dominic/Catherine Ashmore*

Colour and b&w coverage of the entertainment world from 1957 onwards: dance, opera, theatre, ballet, musicals and personalities.

Patrick Eagar Photography

5 Ennerdale Road, Kew Gardens, Surrey TW9 3PG
☎081-940 9269   Fax 081-332 1229

Colour and b&w coverage of cricket from 1965. Test matches, overseas tours and all aspects of the sport. Also a wine collection, mostly in colour, of vineyards, grapes, cellars and winemakers of France, other European countries, Australia and New Zealand.

Ecoscene

4 Heatherview Cotts, Shortfield, Frensham, Surrey GU10 3BH
☎025125 4395   Fax 025125 5695

Contact *Sally Morgan*

Colour library specialising in environment, ecology, natural history, wilderness, pollution and related topics. Member of **BAPLA**.

Edifice

14 Doughty Street, London WC1N 2PL
☎071-405 9395   Fax 071-267 3632

Contact *Philippa Lewis/Gillian Darley*

Colour coverage of architecture and buildings of all possible descriptions; also gardens, urban and rural landscape, ornament and period features. No search fee. Visitors by appointment.

Edinburgh Photographic Library

54 Great King Street, Edinburgh EH3 6QY
☎031-557 3405

Contact *Helen Henderson*

Colour coverage of everything and anything to do with Scotland.

Empics Ltd

26 Musters Road, West Bridgford, Nottingham NG2 7PL
☎0602 455885   Fax 0602 455243

Contact *Colin Panter*

Colour and b&w coverage of international and national news and sport, especially football. Transmission available by electronic picture desk. Commissions undertaken.

English Heritage Photographic Library

517 Fortress House, 23 Savile Row, London W1X 1AB
☎071-973 3338   Fax 071-973 3001

Contact *Lucy Bunning/Celia Bell*

Coverage of all English Heritage properties: castles, abbeys, mills, Roman ruins, standing stones, churches, gardens, paintings, elegant interiors to industrial architecture. Also English Civil War and tournament re-enactments. Contemporary and archive photographs.

EPA (European Pressphoto Agency)

See **Popperfoto**

Robert Estall Photographs

Falcon House, 12–14 Swan Street, Boxford, Colchester, Essex CO6 5NZ
☎0787 210111   Fax 0787 211440

Extensive colour coverage (75,000 transparencies) of Britain and France: countryside, villages, standing stones and circles, Roman roads, walls and villas, castles and haunted sites. Also comprehensive files on Canada, plus all the colour photos from Angela Fisher, Carol Beckwith and David Coulson's books on tribal Africa. Interested in co-operative publishing ventures with authors.

E. T. Archive

19 Albany Street, London NW1 4DX
☎071-584 3137   Fax 071-823 8996

Contact *Anne-Marie Ehrlich/Fiona Purvis*

Fine art and historical subjects from archaeology to zoology. Special collections on music, militaria and Australia. Visitors by appointment.

Greg Evans International Photo Library

91 Charlotte Street, London W1P 1LB
☎071-636 8238 (4 lines)   Fax 071-637 1439

Colour coverage of a wide range of subjects including travel, winter skiing, UK scenery, families, industry, business, sport, abstracts, natural history. Visitors welcome. Commissions undertaken. No search fee. Colour catalogue available.

Mary Evans Picture Library

59 Tranquil Vale, Blackheath, London SE3 0BS
☎081-318 0034   Fax 081-852 7211

General, international, historical collection from ancient times to recent past. Prints, photographs, periodicals and ephemera. *Special collections* Sigmund Freud; Psychical Research; Fawcett Library (women's rights); Bruce Castle Museum (London daily life); Ernst Dryden illustration archive; Roger Mayne, Thurston Hopkins & Grace Robertson (1950s and 1960s documentation); Ida Kar & Jeffrey Morgan (portraits); Institution of Civil Engineers: Town & Country Planning; Meledin Collection (Russian history). Holds reciprocal arrangement with Explorer Archives in Paris.

Express Newspapers Picture Library

Ludgate House, 245 Blackfriars Road,
London SE1 9UX
☎071-922 7902/3/4/5/6   Fax 071-922 7966

Contact *Dennis Hart/Robert Warway/Terry Norman*

One and a half million images updated daily, with strong collections on personalities, royalty, showbiz, sport, fashion, nostalgia and events. Wire facility available.

Eye Ubiquitous

1 Brunswick Road, Hove, East Sussex BN3 1DG
☎0273 26135   Fax 0273 820775

Contact *Paul Seheult*

General stock specialising in social documentary worldwide.

Eyeline Photography

5 Royal Crescent, Cheltenham,
Gloucestershire GL50 3DA
☎0242 513567   Fax 0242 250280

Colour and b&w coverage of sport, with emphasis on sailing and powerboating. Also various watersports, equestrian events and pigeon racing. Commissions undertaken.

Chris Fairclough Colour Library

Studio 65, Smithbrook Kilns, Cranleigh,
Surrey GU6 8JJ
☎0483 277992   Fax 0483 267984

Contact *Chris Fairclough/Bridget Sherlock*

General colour library with special collections on religion, education, travel, children, people and places. Commissions undertaken and studio facility.

Falklands Pictorial

Vision House, 16 Broadfield Road, Heeley,
Sheffield S8 0XJ
☎0742 589299   Fax 0742 550113

Colour and b&w photographs showing all aspects of Falklands life from 1880 to the present day.

Farmers Publishing Group Picture Library

The Quadrant, Quadrant House, Sutton,
Surrey SM2 5AS
☎081-652 4914   Fax 081-652 8901

Large agricultural collection. B&w coverage of all aspects of farming and country life. Also colour transparencies.

Paul Felix

Hornbeam House, Robinson Lane, Woodmancote,
Near Cirencester, Gloucestershire GL7 7EW
☎0285 831703

Small, specialised library covering all aspects of modern country life, including craftsmen, traditional and modern crafts (from charcoal burning and stonewalling to baskets for hot air balloons and acrylic jewellery), plus large number of landscapes and gardens, including the Cotswolds, Thames Valley, Chilterns and other parts of Great Britain.

Financial Times Picture Collection

Number One, Southwark Bridge, London SE1 9HL
☎071-873 3484/3671   Fax 071-873 3697

Contact *Tricia Lee/Susan Kew*

Known for its large collection of key statesmen, politicians and business personalities. Photographers tour the globe covering major financial centres, industry, agriculture and many other aspects of daily life both in the industrialised and developing worlds. Material is mainly b&w; colour is gradually being extended. Subjects: accidents, advertising, agriculture, animals/pets, archaeology, art, ceremonies, construction and property, crime, defence, education, energy, entertainment, environment, finance, health and medical, disability, industry, industrial disputes, people, politics, demonstrations, religion, retailing, science and technology, social welfare, homelessness, poverty, unemployment, housing, sport and leisure, telecommunications, transport.

Michael & Patricia Fogden

Mid Cambushinnie Cottage, Kinbuck, Dunblane, Perthshire FK15 9JU
☎0786 822069   Fax 0786 822069

Contact *Susan Fogden*

Natural history collection, with special reference to rain forests and deserts. Emphasis on quality rather than quantity; growing collection of around 10,000 images.

Ron & Christine Foord Colour Picture Library

155B City Way, Rochester, Kent ME1 2BE
☎0634 847348

Small specialist library with over 1000 species of British and European wild flowers, plus garden flowers, trees, indoor plants, pests and diseases, mosses, lichen, cacti and the majority of larger British insects.

Footprints Colour Picture Library

PO Box 251, Wadhurst, East Sussex TN5 6YA
☎0892 782043   Fax 0892 783406

Contact *Paula Leaver*

Tropical beaches, holiday destinations and general travel coverage, underwater photography including marine life, tropical fish, reef invertebrates, marine conservation topics and scuba diving, watersports, food and flowers, and country images. Commissions undertaken.

Werner Forman Archive Ltd

36 Camden Square, London NW1 9XA
☎071-267 1034   Fax 071-267 6026

Colour and b&w coverage of ancient civilisations, the Near and Far East and primitive societies around the world. A number of rare collections. Subject lists available.

Format Partners Photo Library

19 Arlington Way, London EC1R 1UY
☎071-833 0292

Contact *Maggie Murray*

All-women social documentary photographic library with worldwide cover in colour and b&w: women's issues, work, health, education, disability, Asian and Black community culture, the elderly and the very young.

Robert Forsythe Picture Library

16 Lime Grove, Prudhoe, Northumberland NE42 6PR
☎0661 834511

Contact *Robert & Fiona Forsythe*

25,000 transparencies of post-war transport publicity and ephemera. Robert Forsythe is a transport and industrial heritage historian and consultant. Subjects include transport and industry nationwide and transport heritage in Northern Britain. Ephemera collection is highly unusual offering much potential for illustrations.

Fortean Picture Library

Melysfan, Llangwm, Corwen, Clwyd LL21 0RD
☎049082 472   Fax 049082 321

Mysteries and strange phenomena worldwide; British prehistoric sites and folklore; Welsh countryside.

FotoFlite

Littlestone Road, New Romney, Kent TN28 8LN
☎0679 64891   Fax 0679 63534

Aerial photography of 75,000 ships of all types, naval and private. Constantly updated.

The Fotomas Index

5 Highland Croft, Beckenham, Kent BR3 1TB
☎081-663 6628   Fax 081-650 7429

Contact *Arthur Allan*

General historical collection including pre-1900. Subjects include London, topography, art, satirical, social and political history.

Fox Photos Ltd
See **Hulton Picture Company**

Francis Frith Collection

Charlton Road, Andover, Hants SP10 3LE
☎0264 353113   Fax 0264 332811

Member of **BAPLA**. Over a third of a million images of 4000 towns and villages throughout the UK, taken between 1860 and 1970. Largely topographical in nature, showing the changing face of locations over the period. Also royalty, railways, harvesting, blacksmiths, fashion, and more. Catalogue available.

Galaxy Picture Library
1 Milverton Drive, Ickenham, Uxbridge,
Middlesex UB10 8PP
☏ 0895 637463

Contact *Robin Scagell*

Small but growing library specialising in astronomy, space, the sky, clouds and sunsets. Composites of foregrounds, stars, moon and planets prepared to commission.

The Garden Picture Library
15 Ransome's Dock, 35 Parkgate Road,
London SW11 4NP
☏ 071-228 4332   Fax 071-924 3267

Contact *Sally Wood*

Gardens, plants, patios, indoor planting, outdoor living, decorative and structural work, water features, swimming pools, seasonal aspects, conservatories, people in gardens.

Leslie Garland Picture Library
69 Fern Avenue, Jesmond, Newcastle upon
Tyne NE2 2QU
☏ 091-281 3442   Fax 091-281 3442

Contact *Leslie Garland*

Member of **BAPLA**. Architecture, bridges, castles, cities, civil engineering and construction, countryside, ecology and environment, geography and geology, farming, heritage, industry, landscapes, leisure, mountains, natural history, people, seas and skies, tourism and travel, towns and villages, transport, weather, wild flowers. Covering Northumberland, Durham, Cumbria, Tyne & Wear, Cleveland, Yorkshire and Lancashire, Scotland, Europe and the Far East. Mostly medium format colour transparencies, with other formats and b&w also available. Commissions undertaken.

Genesis Space Photo Library
Peppercombe Lodge, Horns Cross,
Devon EX39 5DH
☏ 0237 451 756   Fax 0237 451 600

Contact *Tim Furniss*

Colour and b&w spaceflight collection including rockets, spacecraft, spacemen, Earth, moon and planets.

Geonex UK Ltd
92–94 Church Road, Mitcham, Surrey CR4 3TD
☏ 081-685 9393   Fax 081-685 9479

Colour and b&w aerial photographs of most parts of UK, with very detailed urban work in some cases; also architectural. Commissions undertaken.

GeoScience Features
6 Orchard Drive, Wye, Kent TN25 5AU
☏ 0233 812707   Fax 0233 812707

Fully computerised and comprehensive library containing the world's principal source of volcanic phenomena. Extensive collections, providing scientific detail with technical quality, of rocks, minerals, fossils, microsections of botanical and animal tissues, animals, biology, birds, botany, chemistry, earth science, ecology, environment, geology, geography, habitats, landscapes, macro/microbiology, peoples, sky, weather, wildlife and zoology. Over 140,000 original colour transparencies in medium and 35 mm format. Subject lists available on application.

Glamour International
16 Broadfield Road, Sheffield S8 0XJ
☏ 0742 589299   Fax 0742 550113

Contact *Dave Muscroft/Bob Twigg*

The UK's only specialist glamour library: dressed glamour, head shots, boy-girl, beauty, lifestyle and Page 3 models.

Martin and Dorothy Grace
40 Clipstone Avenue, Mapperley,
Nottingham NG3 5JZ
☏ 0602 208248   Fax 0602 626802

Member of **BAPLA**. Colour coverage of Britain's natural history, specialising in trees, shrubs and wild flowers. Also birds and butterflies, habitats, landscapes, ecology. Subject lists available.

Ronald Grant Archive
See **The Cinema Museum**

Greater London Photograph Library
Greater London Record Office & History Library,
40 Northampton Road, London EC1R 0HB
☏ 071-606 3030 ext. 3823   Fax 071-833 9136

A large collection on London, mostly topographical and architectural. Subjects include education, local authority housing, transport, the Thames, parks, churches, hospitals, war damage, pubs, theatres and cinemas. Also major redevelopments: The South Bank, The City, Covent Garden and Docklands.

Sally and Richard Greenhill

357A Liverpool Road, London N1 1NL
☎071-607 8549   Fax 071-607 7151

Colour and b&w photos of a social documentary
nature: child development, pregnancy and birth,
education and urban scenes in London and Northern England. Also Modern China 1971–89, Hong
Kong, USA, longhouse life in Sarawak, and other
material from around the world.

Greenpeace Communications Ltd

5 Bakers Row, London EC1R 3DB
☎071-833 0600   Fax 071-837 6606

Colour and b&w stills and video coverage of global
environmental issues, Greenpeace campaigns and
direct actions: whales, seals, dolphins, pollution,
acid rain, Antarctica, military and civil nuclear, the
Mediterranean, Baltic, Pacific, coral reefs, global
warming, ozone depletion and much more.

Susan Griggs Agency Ltd

See **Comstock Photofile Ltd**

V. K. Guy Ltd

Silver Birches, Troutbeck, Windermere,
Cumbria LA23 1PN
☎05394 33519   Fax 05394 32971

Contact *Vic Guy/Pauline Guy/Mike Guy/Paul Guy*

British landscapes and architectural heritage. Colour brochure available. 20,000 5x4 transparencies,
suitable for tourism brochures.

Sonia Halliday Photographs

22 Bates Lane, Weston Turville,
Buckinghamshire HP22 5SL
☎029 661 2266   Fax 029 661 2266

Stained glass, biblical subjects in all media, Middle
Eastern archaeology, architecture, ethnology and
industry, Turkish illuminated manuscripts, mosaics,
murals, tapestries, cave paintings, African bush-
men, mythology, landscapes and cloudscapes from
around the world.

Tom Hanley

61 Stephendale Road, London SW6 2LT
☎071-731 3525

Colour and b&w coverage of London, England,
Europe, Canada, India, the Philippines, Brazil,
China, Japan, Korea, Taiwan, the Seychelles, Cay-
man Islands, USA. Also pop artists of the '60s,
Atlantic sailing by Blyth & Ridgeway, First World

War trenches, removal of London Bridge to America, and much more. Current preoccupation with
Greece, ancient and modern.

Robert Harding Picture Library

58–59 Great Marlborough Street,
London W1V 1DD
☎071-287 5414   Fax 071-631 1070

Colour coverage of a wide range of subjects
including children, beauty, art, architecture, cities,
computer graphics, women, fashion, landscapes,
space, sport, technology, transport, travel. Specialist collections include: Tutankhamun, The Chinese
Exhibition, Alistair Cowin's Beauty Bank, The Equinox Picture Library, IPC Magazine's Syndication
and the *Financial Times* colour material.

Harpur Garden Library

44 Roxwell Road, Chelmsford, Essex CM1 2NB
☎0245 257527   Fax 0245 344101

Jerry Harpur's personal collection of gardens in
Britain, France, Australia, South Africa, the US and
Morocco (35 mm and 6x7, mainly colour but some
b&w). Inspired partly by contemporary designers
and horticulturalists but also includes historic gardens: front and back gardens, formal, plant associations, all four seasons, formal, containers,
fences, hedges, herbs, hillsides, seaside, lawns,
paths, paving, rock, arbours, scented, fruit and
vegetables, ornaments, water and integrated gardens.

Jim Henderson Photographer

Crooktree, Kincardine O'Neill, Aboyne,
Aberdeenshire AB34 4JD
☎0339 882149

Contact *Jim Henderson*

Scenic and general activity coverage of NE
Scotland-Grampian region for tourist, holiday and
activity illustration. Also special collection covering
80 Aurora Borealis displays from 1989 to 1992.
Commissions undertaken.

John Heseltine Picture Library

Overden, Watledge, Nailsworth,
Gloucestershire GL6 0AZ
☎0453 835792   Fax 0453 835792

Contact *John Heseltine*

40,000 colour transparencies of landscapes, food
and travel.

Hobbs Golf Collection

5 Winston Way, New Ridley, Stocksfield,
Northumberland NE43 7RF
☎0661 842933

Contact *Michael Hobbs*

Specialist golf collection: players, courses, art, memorabilia and historical topics (1300-1992). Commissions undertaken.

David Hoffman Photo Library

21 Norman Grove, London E3 5EG
☎081-981 5041   Fax 081-980 2041

David Hoffman

Social documentary library covering drugs, policing, riots, strikes, racism, homelessness, ecology, pollution and related social issues. Colour and b&w images since the late 1970s, with recent pictures from Europe and Thailand on ecology, environmental and pollution issues. Also odd specialist files covering various subjects from cycling to local authority services.

Michael Holford

PO Box 39, Loughton, Essex IG10 1RF
☎081-508 4358   Fax 081-508 3359

Colour coverage of art history from pre-history to the 19th century: architecture, objects, coins, ceramics, tapestries, glass, ivories, jewellery, miniatures, early scientific instruments, the Bayeux tapestry, Sumerian, Babylonian, Assyrian, Egyptian, Greek, Roman, Indian, Chinese, Japanese, Mayan, Inca, Viking, Anglo-Saxon and medieval art.

Holt Studios International Ltd

The Courtyard, 24 High Street, Hungerford,
Berkshire RG17 0NF
☎0488 683523   Fax 0488 683511

Library Manager *Andy Morant*

World agriculture and horticulture both from a pictorial and a technical point of view. Commissions undertaken worldwide.

Houses & Interiors Photographic Features Agency

2D The Colonnade, Rye Road, Hawkhurst,
Kent TN18 4ES
☎0580 754078   Fax 0580 754197

Contact *Richard Wiles/Liz Strutt*

House interiors, exteriors, interior design, architectural details, gardens, house plants, DIY and renovations. Commissions undertaken.

The Hulton Picture Company

Unique House, 21-31 Woodfield Road,
London W9 2BA
☎071-266 2662   Fax 071-266 6392

The Hulton Picture Company, the largest picture resource in Europe, holds images (over 20 million) from ancient history through the early years of photography up to present day. News events, sport, royalty, war, social history, people and places — photos, lithographs, etchings, engravings, woodcuts. A unique source of visual and reference material. Includes the Keystone, Three Lions, Fox Photos and Central Press collections. Catalogue available. UK agent for Syndication International, Reuters and the Bettmann Archive in New York. Electronic catalogues of 10,000 images available on CD-ROM.

The Robert Hunt Library

2nd Floor, 19 Phipp Street, London EC2A 4NP
☎071-739 3536   Fax 071-729 7871

Colour and b&w coverage of warfare, arts, film stars, animals, sport, crime, disasters and royalty (British, European, Middle Eastern, Asian and tribal). Visitors welcome. Subject list available.

Jacqui Hurst

219 Felsham Road, London SW15 1BD
☎081-789 5008   Fax 081-780 2427

Contact *Jacqui Hurst*

Approximately 3000 colour transparencies of regional foods and crafts, and India. Fishsmokers, mussel gatherers, millers and bakers, chocolatiers, markets, fruit picking, salmon netting, farmhouse cheeses, soft cheeses, goats and ewes cheese, cheese shops, woven fabrics, smocking and quilting, paper crafts, pottery, thatching, blockmaking and printing, rugmaking, tie & dye, screen printing, Rajasthan villages, sarees, Indian wall painting, camel fairs, markets, and much more.

The Hutchison Library

118B Holland Park Avenue, London W11 4UA
☎071-229 2743/727 6410   Fax 071-792 0259

Colour and b&w worldwide coverage of agriculture, architecture, industry, landscape, transport, ecology, energy, environment, families, festivals, human relationships, pregnancy, birth, leisure, modern life, peoples and religions, technology, lifestyles, travel, urban and country life, weather, wildlife. Collections include: Disappearing World (ethnic minorities); Puttkamer (Amazon Indians); Long Search (world religions); Felix Greene (China, North Vietnam, Tibet); Tribal Eye; Shogun Experience; Spirit of Asia; New Pacific.

Hylton Warner Photography/Barry Webb Associates

89 St Fagans Road, Fairwater, Cardiff CF5 3AE
☎0222 560333   Fax 0222 554909

Contact *Barry Webb*

Extensive and growing library of pictures of South Wales from the ground and air. Photo-illustration commissions for education and general publications undertaken.

Illustrated London News Picture Library

20 Upper Ground, London SE1 9PF
☎071-928 2111 ext. 4141/2 Fax 071-928 1469

Engravings, photographs and illustrations from 1842 to the present day, taken from magazines published by Illustrated Newspapers: *Illustrated London News; Graphic; Sphere; Tatler; Sketch; Illustrated Sporting and Dramatic News; Illustrated War News 1914-18; Bystander; Britannia & Eve.* Social history, London, Industrial Revolution, wars, travel.

The Image Bank

7 Langley Street, London WC2H 9JA
☎071-240 9621   Fax 071-831 1489
55 Spring Gardens, Manchester M2 2BX
☎061-236 9226   Fax 061-236 8723

Contact *Karen Osborne* (London)/*Rowan Sykes* (Manchester)

Stock photography and illustration. Over 1 million constantly updated images from 450 photographers and 337 illustrators. Free catalogue available. Creative advertising, editorial and corporate commissions undertaken. For magazines, partworks and books, contact the publishing department. Visitors welcome.

Images of Africa Photo Bank

11 The Windings, Lichfield,
Staffordshire WS13 6AN
☎0543 262898   Fax 0543 417154

Contact *David Keith Jones*

Africa: its people, wildlife, landscapes, birds, towns and cities, from Alexandria to South Africa.

Images Colour Library

Kingswood House, 180 Hunslet Road,
Leeds LS10 1AF
☎0532 433389   Fax 0532 425605
9 Rosemont Road, London NW3 6NG
☎071-435 8175   Fax 071-794 8853

A general contemporary library specialising in top-quality advertising, editorial and travel photography. Catalogues available. Visitors welcome.

Impact Photos

26-27 Great Sutton Street, London EC1V 0DX
☎071-251 5091   Fax 071-608 0114

Colour and b&w editorial material, specialising in people and places around the world, with an emphasis on reportage. Subjects include: environment, religion, sports, politicians, agriculture, landscapes, personalities, current affairs, industry, horticulture. Commissions undertaken. Free colour brochure available.

Imperial War Museum Department of Photographs

Lambeth Road, London SE1 6HZ
☎071-416 5333/5330   Fax 071-416 5379

A national archive of photographs of war in this century. Mostly the two world wars but also other conflicts involving Britain and the Commonwealth. Mostly b&w. Visitors welcome. Appointments preferred.

The Independent Newspaper Picture Library

40 City Road, London EC1Y 2DB
☎071-956 1777   Fax 071-956 1500

Contact *Elizabeth Lynch*

Widespread coverage of major news events in the last six years, plus business, sport, personalities and overseas events. Mostly b&w; some colour now available.

Innes Photographic Library

11-13 The Square, Hessle, North
Humberside HU13 0AF
☎0482 649271   Fax 0482 647189

In-depth coverage of Humberside and the Yorkshire/Lincolnshire Wolds. Special collections include the construction of the Humber Bridge and b&w coverage of the Hull fishing fleet. Commissions undertaken. Visitors welcome.

The Insight Picture Library

49 Bleaswood Road, Oxenholme, Kendal,
Cumbria LA9 7EZ
☎ 0539 740240/723391   Fax 0539 730203

Specialist collection of the English Lake District and its people.

International Centre for Conservation Education Photo Library

Greenfield House, Guiting Power, Cheltenham,
Gloucestershire GL54 5TZ
☎ 0451 850777   Fax 0451 850705

Contact *Kathleen Collier*

Colour and b&w coverage of conservation, environmental issues, scenery and wildlife in Britain, Africa, South East Asia and the Middle East. Income from the library supports the Centre's work in conservation education in developing countries.

International Photobank

Loscombe Barn Farmhouse, West Knighton,
Dorchester, Dorset DT2 8LS
☎ 0305 854145   Fax 0305 853065

Colour and b&w coverage of travel subjects: places, people, folklore, events.

Camilla Jessel Photo Library

Riverside House, Riverside, Twickenham,
Middlesex TW1 3DJ
☎ 081-892 1470   Fax 081-744 1217

Colour and b&w coverage of babies and children, specialising in pre-school children, pregnancy, childbirth, newborns, children in hospital, race relations, baby and child development.

Joel Photographic Library

Unit 105, Blackfriars Foundry Annexe, 65 Glasshill
Street, London SE1 0QR
☎ 071-721 7274   Fax 071-721 7276

Contact *Patrick Skinner/Chris Parker*

85,000 images of travel and the sky. Commissions undertaken worldwide.

Trevor Jones Thoroughbred Photography

55 Ashridge Way, Morden, Surrey SM4 4ED
☎ 081-542 3584   Fax 081-395 4054

Contact *Trevor Jones/Gillian Jones*

Extensive library of high-quality colour photographs depicting all aspects of thoroughbred horse racing dating from 1987. Major group races, English classics, studs, stallions, mares and foals, early morning scenes, personalities, jockeys, trainers and prominent owners. Also international work: USA Breeders Cup, Arc de Triomphe, French Derby, Laytown racing on sands at low tide and on frozen lake.

The Kennel Club Library

1–5 Clarges Street, London W1Y 8AB
☎ 071-499 0844   Fax 071-495 6162

Multi-media collection relating to the dog and its world. Printed material dating back to the 17th Century. Photographic material, mostly b&w, some dating back to 1870.

The Keystone Collection

See **Hulton Picture Company**

The Kobal Collection

4th Floor, 184 Drummond Street,
London NW1 3HP
☎ 071-383 0011   Fax 071-383 0044

Colour and b&w coverage of Hollywood films: portraits, stills, publicity shots, posters, ephemera. Visitors by appointment.

Kos Image Library

11 Talina Centre, Bagleys Lane, London SW6 1XX
☎ 071-371 5287   Fax 071-371 8691

Contact *Ciara Collins*

Worldwide marine subjects from yachting to seascapes. Constantly updated, covering all aspects of water-based subjects.

Landscape Only

14A Dufours Place, Broadwick Street,
London W1V 1FE
☎ 071-437 2655/734 7344   Fax 071-287 0126

Colour and b&w worldwide coverage of landscapes, cityscapes and related subjects.

Frank Lane Picture Agency Ltd

Pages Green House, Wetheringsett, Stowmarket, Suffolk IP14 5QA

☏ 0728 860789   Fax 0728 860222

Colour and b&w coverage of natural history and weather. Represents Silvestris Fotoservice, Germany and works closely with Eric and David Hosking.

André Laubier Picture Library

4 St James Park, Bath, Avon BA1 2SS

☏ 0225 420688

Photographs, maps, stereographs, posters and greeting cards from 1935 to the present day. Travel, natural history, architecture, art, industry, people, transport, sport, customs, crafts, abstracts, special effects, World War II, and much more. 35 mm medium format. Photo assignments, artwork, design, and line drawings undertaken. Stock lists on request. Visitors by appointment only. Correspondence welcome in English, French or German.

The Erich Lessing Archive of Fine Art & Culture

c/o Magnum Photos, Moreland Building, 2nd Floor, 23–25 Old Street, London EC1V 9HL

☏ 071-490 1771   Fax 071-608 0020

Computerised archive of large format transparencies depicting the contents of many of the world's finest art galleries as well as ancient archaeological and biblical sites. Over 70,000 pictures can be viewed on microfiche. Represented by **Magnum Photos Ltd**.

London Features International Ltd

3 Boscobel Street, London NW8 8PS

☏ 071-723 4204   Fax 071-723 9201

Colour and b&w coverage of international showbusiness, pop, royalty, sport, politics, personalities.

Museum of London Picture Library

London Wall, London EC2Y 5HN

☏ 071-600 3699 ext. 254   Fax 071-600 1058

Contact *Gavin Morgan*

Comprehensive coverage of the history and archaeology of London represented in painting, photographs and historic artefacts. Special files include Roman and medieval archaeology, costume, suffragettes and Port of London.

Lupe Cunha Photos

843–845 Green Lanes, Winchmore Hill, London N21 2RX

☏ 081-360 0144   Fax 081-886 6812

Children, health, pregnancy and general women's interest. Also special collection on Brazil. Commissions undertaken.

MacQuitty International Photographic Collection

7 Elm Lodge, River Gardens, Stevenage Road, London SW6 6NZ

☏ 071-385 6031/384 1781   Fax 071-384 1781

Contact *Dr Miranda MacQuitty*

Colour and b&w collection on aspects of life in over 70 countries: dancing, music, religion, death, archaeology, buildings, transport, food, drink, nature. Visitors by appointment.

Magnum Photos Ltd

Moreland Buildings, 2nd Floor, 23–25 Old Street, London EC1V 9HL

☏ 071-490 1771   Fax 071-608 0020

Head of Library *John Easterby*

FOUNDED 1947 by Cartier Bresson, George Rodger, Robert Capa and David 'Chim' Seymour. Represents over 50 of the world's leading photo journalists. Coverage of all major world events from the Spanish Civil War to the present day. Also a large collection of personalities.

The Raymond Mander & Joe Mitchenson Theatre Collection

The Mansion, Beckenham Place Park, Beckenham, Kent BR3 2BP

☏ 081-658 7725

Contact *Richard Mangan*

Enormous collection covering all aspects of the theatre: plays, actors, dramatists, music hall, theatres, singers, composers, etc. Visitors welcome by appointment.

The Martin Library

45 Stainforth Road, Newbury Park, Ilford, Essex IG2 7EL

☏ 081-590 4144

Wildlife photography by Frank Martin.

S & O Mathews Photography

Stitches Farm House, Eridge, East Sussex TN3 9JB
☎0892 852848   Fax 0892 853314

Country life, landscapes, gardens and flowers.

Milepost 92½

See **Railways & Steam Locomotives of the World Photo Library**

Lee Miller Archives

Burgh Hill House, Chiddingly, Near Lewes, East Sussex BN8 6JF
☎0825 872691   Fax 0825 872733

The work of Lee Miller (1907–77). Includes portraits of prominent surrealist artists: Ernst, Eluard, Miró, Picasso, Penrose, Carrington, Tanning, and others. Surrealist and contemporary art, poets and writers, fashion, the Middle East, Egypt, the Balkans in the 1930s, London during the Blitz, war in Europe and the liberation of Dachau.

Monitor Syndication

17 Old Street, London EC1V 9HL
☎071-253 7071   Fax 071-250 0966

Picture Editor *David Willis*

Colour and b&w coverage of leading international personalities. Politics, entertainment, royals, judicial, commerce, religion, trade unions, well-known buildings. Syndication to international, national and local media.

Mountain Camera

See **John Cleare**

Moving Image Research & Library Services

21-25 Goldhawk Road, London W12 8QQ
☎081-740 4604   Fax 081-749 6142

Contact *Jason Anstey*

British Airways collection: inflight stills of aircraft including Concorde, 747s-400s, inflight service and worldwide destinations.

David Muscroft Photography and Picture Library

Vision House, 16 Broadfield Road, Heeley, Sheffield S8 0XJ
☎0742 589299   Fax 0742 550113

Colour and b&w coverage of snooker: all aspects of the game from the 19th Century onwards. Also other sporting subjects, an extensive glamour library and general file.

National Maritime Museum Picture Library

Greenwich, London SE10 9NF
☎081-312 6631/6667   Fax 081-312 6632

Manager *Keith Percival*

Over three million maritime-related images and artefacts, including oil paintings from the 16th Century to present day, prints and drawings, historic photographs, plans of ships built in the UK since the beginning of the 18th Century, models, rare maps and charts, instruments, etc. Over 50,000 items within the collection are now photographed and with the Historic Photographs Collection form the basis of the picture library's stock.

National Medical Slide Bank

Graves Educational Resources, 220 New London Road, Chelmsford, Essex CM2 9BJ
☎0245 283351   Fax 0245 354710

Colour coverage of clinical/general medicine and pathology drawn from the collections of hospitals and medical schools. Many images available on NMSB videodisc.

National Monuments Record

Fortress House, 23 Savile Row, London W1X 2JQ
☎Architecture: 071-973 3091;
Archaeology:'071-973'3148   Fax 071-494 3998
Alexander House, 19 Fleming Way, Swindon SN1 2NG
☎0793 414100   Fax 0793 414101

Contact *Anne Woodward/Mhairi Handley*
(Fortress House)/*Roger Harris* Alexander House

The National Monuments Record picture collection is divided into three parts. Fortress House holds the Historic English Architecture collection managed by Anne Woodward and the Archaeology in England collection handled by Mhairi Handley. The third part of the collection, over four million photographs, is the Air Photographs of England archive. Published archive guide available for all three collections.

National Railway Museum Picture Library

Leeman Road, York YO2 4XJ
☎0904 621261   Fax 0904 611112

250,000 images, mainly b&w, covering every aspect of railways from 1866 to the present day. Visitors by appointment.

The National Trust Photographic Library

36 Queen Anne's Gate, London SW1H 9AS
☎071-222 9251/7690   Fax 071-222 5097

Collection of mixed format transparencies covering landscape and coastline throughout England, Wales and Northern Ireland; also architecture, interiors, gardens, painting and conservation. Brochure available on request.

Natural History Museum Picture Library

Cromwell Road, London SW7 5BD
☎071-938 9122/9035   Fax 071-938 8709/8881

Contact *Martin Pulsford/Lodvina Mascarenhas*

5000 large format transparencies on natural history and related subjects: extinct animals, dinosaurs, fossils, anthropology, minerals, gemstones, fauna and flora. Commissions of museum specimens undertaken.

Natural History Photographic Agency (NHPA)

See **NHPA**

Natural Science Photos

33 Woodland Drive, Watford,
Hertfordshire WD1 3BY
☎0923 245265   Fax 0923 246067

Colour coverage of natural history subjects worldwide. The work of some 100 photographers including animals, birds, reptiles, amphibia, fish, insects and other invertebrates, habitats, plants, fungi, geography, weather, scenics, horticulture, agriculture, farm animals and registered dog breeds. Researched by experienced scientists Peter and Sondra Ward. Visits by appointment. Commissions undertaken.

Network Photographers

3-4 Kirby Street, London EC1N 8TS
☎071-831 3633   Fax 071-831 4468

Colour and b&w coverage of UK and international affairs, social and political issues. Also industry, agriculture, arts, politics, news, sport, leisure and science. Foreign material available. Commissions undertaken. List available.

Newsfocus Press Photograph Agency Ltd

18 Rosebery Avenue, London EC1R 4TD
☎071-833 8691   Fax 071-278 9180

Contact *David Fowler*

Portrait photography of leading British and international personalities. Subjects include politics, entertainment, royalty and media. Also a collection on well-known London buildings. No search fee. Commissions and studio work undertaken.

NHPA (Natural History Photographic Agency)

Little Tye, 57 High Street, Ardingly, West Sussex RH17 6TB
☎0444 892514   Fax 0444 892168

High-quality colour and b&w coverage of natural history worldwide. Specialist files include: Bushman culture; high-speed subjects (flying and leaping creatures, splashes, explosions, etc.); extensive files on African and North/South American wildlife; the ANT collection of Australasian subjects.

David Noble Photography

Longleigh, 28 Coolinge Lane, Folkestone,
Kent CT20 3QT
☎0303 254263   Fax 0303 850714

Contact *David & Jenny Noble*

Landscapes and cityscapes of the UK, USA, France, Holland and Vienna, and a good selection on the SE and county of Kent.

The Northern Picture Library

Unit 2, Bentinck Industrial Estate, Ellesmere Street, Chester Road, Manchester M15 4LN
☎061-834 1255   Fax 061-832 6270

Colour coverage of landscapes and topography of Britain and the world. Trees, animals, industry, farming, sport, flowers. Commissions undertaken.

Observer Colour Library

PO Box 33, Edenbridge, Kent TN8 5PB
☎0342 850313   Fax 0342 850244

Half a million pictures from the *Observer* magazine.

Only Horses Picture Agency

27 Greenway Gardens, Greenford,
Middlesex UB6 9AF
☎081-578 9047   Fax 081-575 7531

Colour and b&w coverage of all aspects of the horse. Foaling, retirement, racing, show jumping, eventing, veterinary, polo, breeds, personalities.

George Outram Picture Library

195 Albion Street, Glasgow G1 1QP
☎041-552 6255/305 3209   Fax 041-553 1355

Over 6 million images: b&w and colour photographs from c.1900 from the *Herald* (Glasgow) and *Evening Times*. Current affairs, Scotland, Glasgow, Clydeside shipbuilding and engineering, personalities, World Wars I and II, sport.

Oxford Picture Library

1 North Minksey Village, Oxford OX2 0NA
☎0865 723404   Fax 0865 725294

Contact *Annabel Webb/Chris Andrews*

Specialist collection on Oxford: the city, university and colleges, events, people, scenic. Also scenic views of Cambridge, Shatford, Henley, Bath and the Cotswolds, and a wildlife collection from the Channel Islands. Commissions undertaken.

Oxford Scientific Films Photo Library

Long Hanborough, Witney, Oxon OX8 8LL
☎0993 881881   Fax 0993 882808

Natural history subjects photographed by Oxford Scientific Films: animals, plants, histology, embryology, landscapes, conservation, pollution, high speed and time lapse. Commissions undertaken. Visits by appointment.

Hugh Palmer

Knapp House, Shenington, Near Banbury, Oxon OX15 6NE
☎0295 87433   Fax 0295 87709

Library Administrator *Carolyn Ley*

Extensive coverage of gardens from Britain and Europe, stately homes, conservatories and garden buildings. Medium format transparencies from numerous specialist commissions for books and magazines.

Panos Pictures

9 White Lion Street, London N1 9PD
☎071-278 1111/837 7505   Fax 071-278 0345

Documentary colour and b&w library specialising in Third World and Eastern Europe, with emphasis on environment and development issues. A leaflet is available. All profits from this library go to the

Panos Institute to further its work in international sustainable development.

David Paterson Library

88 Cavendish Road, London SW12 0DF
☎081-673 2414

Travel, landscapes, nature, mountains from the UK, Europe, North Africa, the Himalayas, Japan and Scotland.

Performing Arts Library

52 Agate Road, London W6 0AH
☎081-748 2002   Fax 081-563 0538

Colour and b&w pictures of all aspects of the performing arts, including classical music, opera, theatre, ballet and contemporary dance, musicals, concert halls, opera houses and festivals.

Photo Flora

46 Jacoby Place, Priory Road, Edgbaston, Birmingham B5 7UN
☎021-471 3300

Specialist in British and European wild plants, with colour coverage of most British species (rare and common) and habitats; also travel in North India, Nepal, Egypt, China and Tibet.

Photo Library International Ltd

PO Box 75, Leeds LS7 3NZ
☎0532 623005   Fax 0532 625366

Contemporary colour coverage of most subjects, including industry.

Photo Resources

The Orchard, Marley Lane, Kingston, Canterbury, Kent CT4 6JH
☎0227 830075   Fax 0227 830075

Colour and b&w coverage of archaeology, art, ancient art, ethnology, mythology, world religion, museum objects.

Photofusion

17A Electric Lane, London SW9 8LA
☎071-738 5774   Fax 071-738 5509

Contact *Janis Austin*

Colour and b&w coverage of contemporary social issues including babies and children, disablement, education, the elderly, environment, family, health, housing, homelessness, people general and work. List available.

The Photographers' Library

81A Endell Street, London WC2H 9AJ
☏071-836 5591/240 5554   Fax 071-379 4650

Covers principal European, North American, African and Far Eastern centres. Industry, transport, sport, families, landscapes, skyscapes and seascapes. Brochure available.

Photos Horticultural

169 Valley Road, Ipswich, Suffolk IP1 4PJ
☏0473 257329   Fax 0473 233974

Colour coverage of all aspects of gardening in Britain and abroad, including extensive files on plants in cultivation and growing wild.

PictureBank Photo Library Ltd

Parman House, 30–36 Fife Road, Kingston upon Thames, London KT1 1SY
☏081-547 2344   Fax 081-974 5652

Member of **BAPLA**. 250,000 colour transparencies covering people (girls, couples, families, children), travel and scenic (UK and world), moods (sunsets, seascapes, deserts, etc.), industry and technology, environments and general. Commissions undertaken. Visitors welcome.

Pictures Colour Library

10A Neal's Yard, London WC2H 9DP
☏071-497 2034   Fax 071-497 3070

Landscapes, travel, people, children, food, interiors, architecture, industry, glamour and still life. Visitors welcome.

Planet Earth Pictures/Seaphot

4 Harcourt Street, London W1H 1DS
☏071-262 4427   Fax 071-706 4042

Marine and natural history photographs, including underwater. Wildlife and landscapes around the world, conservation and pollution. Commissions undertaken, especially underwater.

Popperfoto

Paul Popper Ltd, The Old Mill, Overstone Farm,
Overstone, Northampton NN6 0AB
☏0604 670670   Fax 0604 670635

Includes early colour from 1940s and b&w from 1870 to the present day. Subjects include Scott's 1910–12 Antarctic expedition, wars, royalty, sport, politics, transport, crime, topography, history and social conditions worldwide. Houses the EPA (European Pressphoto Agency), AFP (Agence France Presse), Reuter and UPI collections: worldwide news events, European politics and news in depth. The UPI collection commences 1932; Reuter from its start in 1985 to the present day.

Premaphotos Wildlife

2 Willoughby Close, Kings Coughton, Alcester,
Warwickshire B49 5QJ
☏0789 762938   Fax 0789 762938

Natural history worldwide. Subjects include flowering and non-flowering plants, fungi, slime moulds, fruits and seeds, galls, leaf mines, seashore life, mammals, birds, reptiles, amphibians, insects, spiders, habitats, scenery and cultivated cacti. Commissions undertaken. Visitors welcome.

Press Association Ltd

See **Library Services**

Press-tige Pictures

3 Newmarket Road, Cringleford,
Norwich NR4 6UE
☏0603 54345   Fax 0603 259250

Colour and b&w photographs of natural history subjects. Some high-speed and scientific. Commissions undertaken.

Professional Sport

8 Apollo Studios, Charlton Kings Mews,
London NW5 2SA
☏071-482 2311   Fax 071-482 2441

Colour and b&w coverage of tennis, golf, soccer, athletics, boxing, winter sports and many minor sports. News and feature material supplied worldwide. Computerised library with in-house processing and studio facilities; photo transmission services available for editorial and advertising.

QA Photos

8 Stade Street, Hythe, Kent CT21 6BD
☏0303 268233   Fax 0303 266273

All aspects relating to the Channel Tunnel since 1986, plus other tunnel and construction shots.

Quadrant Picture Library

Quadrant House, The Quadrant, Sutton,
Surrey SM2 5AS
☎081-652 3427/8   Fax 081-652 8933

Colour and b&w coverage of transport and motor sport from early 1900s to the present day. Also motoring artwork from the '20s and '30s.

Railfotos

Millbrook House Ltd, 90 Hagley Road, Edgbaston,
Birmingham B16 8YH
☎021-454 1308
Fax 021-454 4224 quote Millbrook House

One of the largest specialist libraries dealing comprehensively with railway subjects worldwide. Colour and b&w dating from the turn of the century to present day. Up-to-date material on UK, South America and Far East (except Japan), especially China: cities, rivers, bridges and general travel, England 1950s and '60s, and a maritime collection of the same period. Visitors by appointment.

Railways and Steam Locomotives of the World Photo Library

Milepost, 92½, Newton Harcourt,
Leicestershire LE8 0FH
☎0533 592068   Fax 0533 593001

Colour coverage of the last steam locomotives in the world, taken on expeditions over the last 20 years; modern railways, British preserved and tourist lines; dramatic locations and situations.

Raleigh International Picture & Features Library

4th Floor, The Power House, Alpha Place, Flood Street, London SW3 5SZ
☎071-351 7541   Fax 071-351 9372

Contact *Mark Bainbridge/Steve Benbow*

Incorporating *The Directory of International Travel and Location Photographers.* Colour coverage of worldwide locations and subjects. Commissions undertaken worldwide.

Redferns

7 Bramley Road, London W10 6SZ
☎071-792 9914   Fax 071-792 0921

Colour and b&w coverage of pop, jazz, easy listening, heavy metal, country and folk music. Includes over 5000 artists and an early American jazz collection. List and brochure available.

Reflections PhotoLibrary

The Bath Brewery, Toll Bridge Road, Bath,
Avon BA1 7DE
☎0225 852554   Fax 0225 852528

Contact *Colin Bowers/Jennie Woodcock*

Family life, maternity, babies and childcare, teenagers, health and education, world wildlife, environmental, pollution, flora and fauna, world tribes and landscapes (UK/worldwide).

Relay Photos Ltd

10 Vale Royal, London N7 9AP
☎071-700 0771   Fax 071-700 6842

Contact *Andre Csillag*

Colour and b&w coverage of pop personalities since 1965. Constantly updated from work undertaken worldwide.

Remote Source

The Royal Geographical Society, 1 Kensington Gore, London SW7 2AR
☎071-589 5466   Fax 071-584 4447

Travel, exploration, expeditions, places and cultures worldwide. Commissions undertaken.

Repfoto London

74 Creffield Road, London W3 9PS
☎081-992 2936   Fax 081-992 9641

Contact *Robert Ellis*

A specialist service for the rock music industry. Incorporates the Rock Library: colour and b&w photographs from 1965 to the present day.

Retna Pictures Ltd

1 Fitzroy Mews, Cleveland Street,
London W1P 5DQ
☎071-388 3444   Fax 071-383 7151

Colour and b&w coverage of international rock and pop performers, actors, actresses, entertainers and celebrities. Also a general stock library covering a wide range of subjects, including travel, people, sport and leisure, flora and fauna, and the environment.

Retrograph Archive Ltd

164 Kensington Park Road, London W11 2ER
☎071-727 9378/9426   Fax 071-229 3395

Contact *J. Ranicar-Breese*

A vast archive of commercial and decorative art (1860–1960). Worldwide labels and packaging for food, wine, chocolate, soap, perfume, cigars and cigarettes; fine art and commercial art journals, fashion magazines, posters, Victorian greeting cards, wallpaper and gift wrap sample books, music sheets, folios of decorative design and ornament — Art Nouveau and Deco; hotel, airline and shipping labels; memorabilia, tourism, leisure, poster art, postcards, food and drink, transport and entertainment. Originals viewed then photographed to order. Lasers for book dummies, packaging, mock-ups, film/TV action props. Colour brochure on request. Medium format. Colour, b&w and illustration.

Reuter and UPI
See **Popperfoto**

Rex Features Ltd
18 Vine Hill, London EC1R 5DX
☎071–278 7294/3362
Fax 071–837 4812   Telex 25491 A/B REXPHO G

Established in the 1950s. Colour and b&w coverage of news, politics, personalities, show business, glamour, humour, art, medicine, science, landscapes, royalty, etc.

RIDA Photo Library
21 Victoria Road, Surbiton, Surrey KT6 4JZ
☎081–399 0810   Fax 081–390 5400

Contact *David Bayliss*

Geological and geographical collection: fossils, rocks, minerals, field and economic geology and geography.

Ann Ronan Picture Library
Wheel Cottage, Bishops Hull, Taunton,
Somerset TA1 5EP
☎0823 252737   Fax 0823 336785

History of science and technology in the form of 150,000 illustrations from printed sources AD 1500–1900. Personalities, scientific experiments, manufacturing, mining, agriculture, transport, child labour, cookery, communications, medicine.

RoSPA (Royal Society for the Prevention of Accidents)
Cannon House, The Priory, Queensway,
Birmingham B4 6BS
☎021–200 2461
Fax 021–200 1254   Telex 336546

Colour and b&w coverage of all aspects of safety: road, occupational, home, water, education.

Royal Geographical Society Picture Library
1 Kensington Gore, London SW7 2AR
☎071–584 4447   Fax 071–584 4447

Contact *Rachel Duncan*

Historical monochrome and modern colour collection dating from the 1860s to present day: travel, exploration, expeditions, places and their culture worldwide.

The Royal Photographic Society
The Octagon, Milsom Street, Bath BA1 1DN
☎0225 462841   Fax 0225 448688

Contact *Debbie Ireland*

History of photography, with an emphasis on pictorial photography as an art rather than a documentary record. Photographic processes and cameras, landscape, portraiture, architecture, India, Victorian and Edwardian life.

RSPB Picture Library
The Lodge, Sandy, Bedfordshire SH19 2DL
☎0767 680551   Fax 0767 692365

Contact *Chris Sargeant*

Colour and b&w images of birds, butterflies, moths, mammals, reptiles and their habitats.

Peter Sanders Photography
9 Meades Lane, Chesham,
Buckinghamshire HP5 1ND
☎0494 773674

Contact *Peter Sanders/Hafsa Garwatik*

The world of Islam past and present: people, mosques, calligraphy, celebrations, agriculture, historic material, prayer, Ka'aba, etc., Egypt, India, Saudi Arabia, Morocco, Sudan, Mauritania, Mali, Senegal, UK, USA and more.

Science Photo Library
112 Westbourne Grove, London W2 5RU
☎071–727 4712/229 9847   Fax 071–727 6041

Research Manager *Venita Paul*

Colour and b&w coverage of all aspects of science, technology and medicine. Subjects include laboratories, industry, hospitals, astronomy, biology, botany, chemistry, computers, earth sciences, genetics, landscapes, physics, satellite imagery, space, zoology.

The Scottish Highland Photo Library
Croft Roy, Crammond Brae, Tain,
Ross-shire IV19 1JG
☎0862 892298

Contact *Hugh Webster*

10,000 colour transparencies of the Scottish Highlands and Islands. Not just a travel library though; images cover industry, agriculture, fisheries and many other subjects of the Highlands and Islands.

Screen Ventures
49 Goodge Street, London W1P 1FB
☎071-580 7448   Fax 071-631 1265

Colour and b&w coverage of Asia, Middle East and Northern Africa. All aspects of life in these areas. Commissions undertaken.

Sealand Aerial Photography
Goodwood Airfield, Chichester, West
Sussex PO18 0PH
☎0243 781025   Fax 0243 531422

Colour coverage of subjects throughout the UK. Operations carried out throughout the year.

Sefton Photo Library
30-30A Mason Street, Manchester M4 5EY
☎061-832 7670/834 9423   Fax 061-834 9423

Wide selection of subjects from the UK and abroad. Mostly colour, some b&w. Industry, business, sport, farming, scenic, personalities, jazz musicians (and some classical), space, and many more. Special collections on the North of England and Victorian/Edwardian scenes. Commissions undertaken.

Select Photos
N5 Studios, Metropolitan Wharf, Wapping Wall,
London E1 9SS
☎071-265 1422   Fax 071-265 1421

Contact *Shirley Berry*

Colour and b&w coverage of environmental issues, current affairs and politics. Commissions undertaken.

Phil Sheldon Golf Picture Library
3 Grimsdyke Crescent, Arkley, Barnet,
Hertfordshire EN5 4AH
☎081-440 1986   Fax 081-440 9348

Over 100,000 colour and b&w photos dating from 1976 including detailed coverage of 42 major championships, 8 Ryder Cup matches and over 300 other tournaments. Expanding collection which includes player action, portraits, instruction material, trophies and over 200 courses from around the world. Also classic 1960s collection by photographer Sidney Harris.

Skishoot Offshoot
62 Roupell Street, London SE1 8SS
☎071-620 0882   Fax 071-928 7075

Contact *Jo Hiles/John Pakington*

Predominantly skiing and ski-related subjects, but also an expanding travel library. Commissions undertaken.

Skyscan Balloon Photography
Oak House, Toddington, Cheltenham,
Gloucestershire GL54 5BY
☎0242 621357   Fax 0242 621343

Colour and b&w aerial views taken from a camera platform suspended beneath a tethered helium balloon, remotely controlled by a ground operator and flown at heights of 60-600 feet. Unique low-level views of Britain, heritage sites, London, general city and landscapes. All material to 6x6 cm format. Commissions undertaken.

South American Pictures
48 Station Road, Woodbridge, Suffolk IP12 4AT
☎0394 383963/383279   Fax 0394 380176

Colour and b&w images of South/Central America and Mexico, including archaeology and the Amazon. Frequently updated. There is an archival section, with pictures and documents from most countries.

Spectrum Colour Library
41-42 Berners Street, London W1
☎071-637 1587   Fax 071-637 3681

A large collection including travel, sport, people, pets, scenery, industry, British and European cities, etc. Visitors welcome by appointment.

Split Second

1A Doughty Street, Gray's Inn Road,
London WC1N 2PH
☎ 071-831 4316   Fax 071-831 4322

Contact *Leo Mason*

Sports and live action.

Frank Spooner Pictures Ltd

Unit B7, Hatton Square, 16-16A Baldwin's
Gardens, London EC1N 7US
☎ 071-405 9943   Fax 071-831 2483

Handles UK distribution of GLMR, Harry Benson,
Stills Press Agency and Gamma Presse Images of
Paris. Subjects include current affairs, show busi-
ness, fashion, politics, travel, adventure, sport,
personalities, films, animals and the Middle East.
Represented in more than 30 countries.

Sporting Pictures (UK) Ltd

7A Lamb's Conduit Passage, London WC1R 4RG
☎ 071-405 4500
Fax 071-831 7991   Telex 27924

Colour and b&w coverage of professional, amateur
and leisure sports, including coverage of major
names and events of the last 20 years. Visitors
welcome. Commissions undertaken.

The Still Moving Picture Library

67A Logie Green Road, Edinburgh EH7 4HF
☎ 031-557 9697   Fax 031-557 9699

Contact *John Hutchinson/Sue Hall*

Colour, b&w and 16 mm film coverage of Scotland
and sport. The largest photo and film library in
Scotland, holding the Scottish Tourist Board's
library.

Still Pictures Environmental Agency

199A Shooters Hill Road, Blackheath,
London SE3 8UL
☎ 081-858 8307   Fax 081-858 2049

Contact *Mark Edwards/Chris Suckling*

Environment and Third World development issues
from over 60 countries.

Stock Shot

Mirefoot, Burneside, Kendal, Cumbria LA8 9AB
☎ 0539 740770   Fax 0539 731546

Contact *Jess Stock*

Skiing, mountains and mountaineering, Alpine
landscapes, mountain bikes, expeditions and travel.

Stockfile

PO Box 605, Virginia Water, Surrey GU25 4SS
☎ 0344 844395   Fax 0344 843513

Contact *Jill Daun/Steven Behr*

Principally a mountain biking and skiing collection
covering all aspects of these activities and related
topics. Expanding travel section also.

Stockphotos

7 Langley Street, London WC2H 9JA
☎ 071-240 7361   Fax 071-831 1489
55 Spring Gardens, Manchester M2 2BX
☎ 061-236 9226   Fax 061-236 8723

Contact *Karen Osborne* (London)/*Rowan Sykes*
(Manchester)

People, families, couples, executives, scenic, food
& drink, medical, travel, sport, leisure, industry,
special effects. Free catalogue available. Visitors
welcome.

Tony Stone Worldwide

Worldwide House, 116 Bayham Street,
London NW1 0BA
☎ 071-267 7166   Fax 071-722 9305

Travel, wildlife, industry, sports and people. Catalogue available.

Jessica Strang Library

86 Cambridge Gardens, London W10 6HS
☎ 081-969 7292

Interiors and design, the vanishing architecture of
London and specialist idiosyncratic collections,
gardens, sculpture, current architecture, local colour and markets. Also America, Bali, Burma, Corsi-
ca, Egypt, France, Holland, Japan, Kenya, Malaysia,
Singapore, Spain, and many more countries.

Survival Anglia Photo Library

48 Leicester Square, London WC2H 7FB
☎ 071-321 0101   Fax 071-493 2598

Colour and b&w coverage of all aspects of natural
history. Catalogue available.

Swift Picture Library Ltd

Claremont, Redwood Close, Ringwood,
Hampshire BH24 1PR
☎0425 478333   Fax 0425 471525

Contact *Mike Read*

Specialists in wildlife, landscape and travel photography. Comprehensive coverage of British locations and species, with increasing numbers of countries abroad. Also rural activities, conservation, gardens, environmental and many other subjects.

Sygma

Wheatsheaf House, 4 Carmelite Steet,
London EC4Y 0BN
☎071-353 4551   Fax 071-583 4239

Contact *Claire Gouldstone*

World events, news, personalities, famous stars, and many other subjects.

Syndication International

4-12 Dorrington Street, London EC1N 7TB
☎071-404 0004   Fax 071-430 2437

Extensive world travel pictures from Berlitz, the British Tourist Authority and English Tourist Board. Major photo library specialising in pop, royalty and personalities. Agents for Mirror Group Newspapers, BBC News and Current Affairs and for the *Financial Times* photos and computer generated graphics.

The Telegraph Colour Library

Visual House, 1 Mastmaker Road,
London E14 9WT
☎071-987 1212   Fax 071-538 3309

Contact *Colin James*

Leading stock photography agency covering a wide subject range: business, sport, people, industry, animals, medical, nature, space, travel and graphics. Free catalogue available. Same-day service to UK clients.

Three Lions

See **Hulton Picture Company**

Patrick Thurston PhotoLibrary

10 Willis Road, Cambridge CB1 2AQ
☎0223 352547   Fax 0223 66274

Colour photography of Britain: scenery, people, museums, churches, coastline. Also various countries abroad: Australia, Sweden and Bulgaria. Commissions undertaken.

Topham Picture Source

PO Box 33, Edenbridge, Kent TN8 5PB
☎0342 850313   Fax 0342 850244

Colour and b&w coverage of news, personalities, war, royalty, topography, natural history.

B. M. Totterdell Photography

Constable Cottage, Burlings Lane, Knockholt,
Kent TN14 7PE
☎0959 32001

Contact *Barbara Totterdell*

12,000 colour and b&w images of volleyball and all aspects of the sport.

Trades Union Congress

See **Library Services**

Tessa Traeger

7 Rossetti Studios, 72 Flood Street,
London SW3 5TF
☎071-352 3641   Fax 071-352 4846

Food, gardens, travel and artists. Visitors welcome.

The Travel Library

Freshfields, 29 Swan Way, Crookham Village, Fleet,
Hampshire GU13 0TU
☎0252 627233   Fax 0252 812399

Contact *Philip Enticknap*

About 7000 6x7 transparencies of people and places worldwide. Large collection on Malta, Galicia and Asturias.

Peter Trenchard's Image Store Ltd

The Studio, West Hill, St Helier, Jersey, Channel
Islands JE2 3HB
☎0534 69933   Fax 0534 89191

Colour coverage of the Channel Islands. Commissions undertaken.

Tropix Photographic Library

156 Meols Parade, Meols, Wirral,
Merseyside L47 6AN
☎051-632 1698   Fax 051-632 1698

Contact *Veronica Birley*

Leading specialists on the developing world in all its aspects. Environmental topics widely covered. Assignment photography undertaken at home and overseas. New collections welcome, especially West African, Central American and environmental; please write for details.

Universal Pictorial Press & Agency Ltd

30–34 New Bridge Street, London EC4V 6BN
☎071–248 6730   Fax 071–489 8982

News Editor *Peter Dare*

Colour and b&w coverage of news, royalty, politics, sport, arts, and many other subjects. Commissions undertaken for press and public relations.

UPI

See **Popperfoto**

USSR Photo Library

Conifers House, Cheapside Lane, Denham, Uxbridge UB9 5AE
☎0895 834814   Fax 0895 834028

Images of Russia and the Republics: cities, museums, cathedrals, resorts, traditional costumes and dances, craftsmen at work.

V&A Picture Library

Victoria and Albert Museum, South Kensington, London SW7 2RL
☎071–938 8352/8354   Fax 071–938 8353

30,000 colour and half a million b&w photos of decorative and applied arts, including ceramics, ivories, furniture, costumes, textiles, stage, musical instruments, toys, Indian, Far Eastern and Islamic objects.

The Venice Picture Library

2 Peter's Court, Porchester Road, London W2 5DR
☎071–229 9808   Fax 071–221 7884

Contact *Sarah Quill*

12,000 colour and 5000 b&w photos of most aspects of the city of Venice, islands and lagoon. Commissions undertaken.

The Victory Archive

c/o Popperfoto, The Old Mill, Overstone Farm, Northampton NN6 0AB
☎0604 670670   Fax 0604 670635

Formerly the Conway Picture Library. Magazine photo collections from women's journals 1940s–1960s. Colour and b&w coverage of personalities, fashion and features, plus a transport section, which includes naval shipping from the 19th century. Excellent World War Two material.

Viewfinder Colour Photo Library

The Production House, 147A St Michael's Hill, Cotham, Bristol BS2 8DB
☎0272 237268/239449   Fax 0272 239198

Quality colour coverage of occupations, industry, leisure, people, scenics, transport, travel, British Isles, agriculture, sport.

The Vintage Magazine Company Ltd

203–213 Mare Street, London E8 3QE
☎081–533 7588   Fax 081–533 7283

A large collection of movie stills and photographs covering music, glamour, social history, theatre posters, ephemera, postcards.

Visionbank Library/England Scene

Suite 212, Business Design Centre, Islington Green, London N1 0QH
☎071–288 6080   Fax 071–288 6094

Extensive worldwide coverage of many subjects. 'The world's largest collection of pictures of England and, we like to think, the best.'

Visnews Still Service

Cumberland Avenue, Park Royal, London NW10 7EH
☎081–453 4233/4227
Fax 081–695 0620   Telex 22678 VIS LDN G

Colour coverage of international political leaders, personalities and locations. Stills service available from Visnews' international coverage, clients' own video or Aston caption generator.

The Charles Walker Collection

9 Rosemont Road, London NW3 6NG
☎071–435 8175   Fax 071–794 8853

One of the foremost collections in the world on subjects popularly listed as 'Mystery, myth and magic'. The collection includes astrology, occultism, witchcraft and many other related areas. Catalogue available.

John Walmsley Picture Library

27 Wyeths Road, Epsom, Surrey KT17 4EB
✆0372 743374

Specialist library covering all aspects of work and education from pre-school to adult. Photos are indexed by subject and age. Wide selection of people at work and in learning environments such as playgroups, schools, colleges, universities and skill centres. Images reflect a multi-racial Britain. Recently added a new complementary medicine collection to its lists: over 30 therapies from acupuncture and yoga to more obscure treatments like moxibustion and metamorphic technique. Commissions undertaken. Subject list available on request.

Waterways Photo Library

39 Manor Court Road, Hanwell, London W7 3EJ
✆081-840 1659   Fax 081-567 0605

Colour and b&w coverage of rivers, canals, bridges, locks, aqueducts, tunnels, waterway holidays, canal art, fishing, wildlife, town and country, with growing collection of recent, non-waterway material in both England and Wales. Many off the beaten track shots. Commissions undertaken.

Weimar Archive

8-9 The Incline, Coalport, Telford,
Shropshire TF8 7HR
✆0952 680050   Fax 0952 587184

Contact *Dr Simon Taylor*

Pre-1945 Germany, central European royalty, Soviet posters & cartoons (1917-45), and German art (pre-1945).

West Air Photography

40 Alexandra Parade, Weston super
Mare BS23 1QZ
✆0860 710233 (24-hour)/0934 621333
Fax 0934 635421

750,000 aerial shots of England and Wales, particularly the South-West. No search fee. Commissioned aerial photography undertaken all year round. Specialists in oblique stereoscopic surveys.

Eric Whitehead Picture Library and Agency

PO Box 33, Kendal, Cumbria LA9 4SU
✆05396 21002

Snooker, outdoor pursuits, Cumbria: events, places and people. Commissions undertaken.

Elizabeth Whiting & Associates

Basement, 21 Albert Street, London NW1 7LU
✆071-388 2828   Fax 071-387 1615

Specialist library covering all aspects of interior decoration, architecture and home interest, plus extensive selection of plants and gardens.

Janine Wiedel

6 Stirling Road, London SW9 9EE
✆071-737 0007

Social documentary over the last 20 years. Education, industry, women's issues, childbirth, ethnic groups (Eskimos, Gypsies, Asian and Black communities in UK), Arctic, Iceland, Galapagos Islands, Iran, Europe, USA. Commissions undertaken. Leaflets available. Visitors welcome by appointment.

Wilderness Photographic Library

Mill Barn, Broad Raine, Sedbergh,
Cumbria LA10 5ED
✆05396 20196   Fax 05396 21293

Contact *John Noble*

Striking colour images from around the world, from polar wastes to the Himalayas and Amazon jungle. Subjects: mountains, Arctic, deserts, icebergs, wildlife, rainforests, glaciers, geysers, exploration, caves, rivers, eco-tourism, people and cultures, canyons, seascapes, marine life, weather, volcanoes, mountaineering, skiing, geology, conservation, adventure sports, national parks, the Antarctic and Amazonia.

Andy Williams Photo Library

3 Levylsdene, Merrow, Guildford, Surrey GU1 2RS
✆0483 572778   Fax 0483 304829

Colour coverage of the British Isles and Near Continent. London, castles, cathedrals, scenic moods, old world inns, historic houses, gardens, cottages, golf, waterfalls, windmills, lighthouses. Commissions undertaken. Visitors welcome.

David Williams Picture Library

50 Burlington Avenue, Glasgow G12 0LH
☏ 041-339 7823   Fax 041-337 3031

Colour coverage of Scotland, Iceland and the Faroes. Landscapes, historical sites, buildings, geology and physical geography. Medium format and 35 mm.

S&I Williams Power Pix International Picture Library

Castle Lodge, Wenvoe, Cardiff CF5 6AD
☏ 0222 595163
Fax 0222 593905   Telex 995411

Colour coverage of a wide range of subjects including abstracts, agriculture, aviation, glamour, landscapes, natural history, people, sport, sub-aqua, yachting, America, Australia, Canada, Europe, India, Japan and Great Britain. Commissions undertaken. Catalogue available.

Vaughan Williams Memorial Library

English Folk Dance and Song Society, Cecil Sharp House, 2 Regent's Park Road, London NW1 7AY
☏ 071-284 0523   Fax 071-284 0523

Colour and b&w coverage of traditional/folk music, dance and customs worldwide, focusing on Britain and other English-speaking nations. Photographs date from the late 19th Century to the present day.

The Wingfield Sporting Art Library

35 Sibella Road, London SW4 6JA
☏ 071-622 6301   Fax 071-622 6301

Contact *Mary Ann Wingfield*

Sporting works of art, both historical and contemporary, covering 50 different sports. Commissions undertaken.

Roger Wood Library

45 Victoria Road, Deal, Kent CT14 7AY
☏ 0304 372786   Fax 0304 368910

Colour and b&w archive of the Middle East, especially antiquities. Egypt, North Africa, Iran, some Gulf States, Greece, Turkey, Ethiopia, Pakistan, Bangladesh. Member of **BAPLA**.

Woodmansterne Ltd

Watford Business Park, Watford WD1 8RD
☏ 0923 228236/816734   Fax 0923 245788

Colour coverage of Britain, Europe and the Holy Land. Architecture, cathedrals, interiors, painting, sculpture, natural history, butterflies, volcanoes, transport, space exploration, opera and ballet, sunsets, state occasions.

Michael Woodward Licensing

Parlington Hall, Aberford, West Yorkshire LS25 3EG
☏ 0532 813913   Fax 0532 813911

Represents over 100 illustrators, artists and photographers, with extensive files on most subjects. New artists should forward samples. Brochure on request. See also **UK Agents**.

Woolverton Colour Library

Hatters End, Lawton Cross, Kingsland, Leominster, Herefordshire HR6 9AU
☏ 05447 584

Colour coverage of UK, France, Germany, Austria, Switzerland, Belgium, Sicily, Yugoslavia and Greece; most of Europe and Egypt. Landscapes and architecture, Alpine and British wild flowers. Visitors welcome.

World Pictures/Feature-Pix Colour Library

85A Great Portland Street, London W1N 5RA
☏ 071-437 2121   Fax 071-439 1307

Colour collection aimed at the travel and holiday market. Popular resort areas updated regularly. Commissions undertaken.

George Wright

Mountover Farm, Rampisham, Dorchester, Dorset DT2 0PL
☏ 0935 83333   Fax 0935 83326

English gardens, landscapes, people and events, British and European regional cooking, India, Nepal and a large collection on Barcelona. Portraits as featured in the *Observer* and *Independent* magazines, plus general European travel and life.

York Archaeological Trust for Excavation and Research Ltd

1 Pavement, York YO1 2NA
☏ 0904 643211   Fax 0904 640029

Colour and b&w coverage of the antiquities, archaeology and architecture of the City of York and surrounding area.

John Robert Young Collection

61 De Montfort Road, Lewes, East
Sussex BN7 1SS
☎0273 475216

Contact *Jennifer Barrett*

50,000 transparencies on travel, religion and military subjects.

Tax and the Writer

'No man in this country is under the smallest obligation, moral or other, to arrange his affairs as to enable the Inland Revenue to put the largest possible shovel in his stores.

'The Inland Revenue is not slow, and quite rightly, to take every advantage which is open to it . . . for the purpose of depleting the taxpayer's pockets. And the taxpayer is, in like manner, entitled to be astute to prevent as far as he honestly can the depletion of his means by the Inland Revenue.'

Lord Clyde, *Ayrshire Pullman v Inland Revenue Commissioners, 1929.*

Income Tax

What is a professional writer for tax purposes?

Writers are professionals while they are writing regularly with the intention of making a profit; or while they are gathering material, researching or otherwise preparing a publication.

A professional freelance writer is taxed under Case II of Schedule D of the *Income and Corporation Taxes Act 1988*. The taxable income is the amount received, either directly or by an agent, on his behalf, less expenses wholly and exclusively laid out for the purposes of the profession. If expenses exceed income, the loss can either be carried forward and set against future income from writing or set against other income which is subject to tax in the same year. If tax has been paid on that other income, a repayment can be obtained, or the sum can be offset against other tax liabilities. Special loss relief can apply in the opening year of the profession. Losses made in the first four years can be set against income of up to five earlier years.

Where a writer receives very occasional payments for isolated articles, it may not be possible to establish that these are profits arising from carrying on a continuing profession. In such circumstances these 'isolated transactions' may be assessed under Case VI of Schedule D of the *Income and Corporation Taxes Act 1970*. Again, expenses may be deducted in arriving at the taxable income, but, if expenses exceed income, the loss can only be set against the profits from future isolated transactions, or other income assessable under Case VI.

Expenses

A writer can normally claim the following expenses:

(a) Secretarial, typing, proofreading, research. Where payments for these are made to the author's wife or husband, they should be recorded and entered in the author's tax return, or (in the case of a married woman her husband's tax return) as earned income which is subject to the usual personal allowances.

(b) Telephone, telegrams, postage, stationery, printing, maintenance, insurance, dictation tapes, batteries, any equipment or office requisites used for the profession.

(c) Periodicals, books (including presentation copies and reference books) and other publications necessary for the profession, but amounts received from the sale of books should be deducted.

(d) Hotels, fares, car running expenses (including repairs, petrol, oil, garaging, parking, cleaning, insurance, licence, road fund tax, depreciation), hire of cars or taxis in connection with:
  (i) business discussions with agents, publishers, co-authors, collaborators, researchers, illustrators, etc.
  (ii) travel at home and abroad to collect background material.

(e) Publishing and advertising expenses, including costs of proof corrections, indexing, photographs, etc.

(f) Subscriptions to societies and associations, press cutting agencies, libraries, etc., incurred wholly for the purpose of the profession.

(g) Premiums to pension schemes such as the *Society of Authors Retirement Benefits Scheme*. Depending on age, up to 40% of net earned income can be paid into a personal pension plan.

(h) Rent, and water rates, etc., the proportion being determined by the ratio which the number of rooms are used exclusively for the profession bears to the total number of rooms in the residence. But see note on *Capital Gains Tax* below.

(i) Lighting, heating and cleaning. A carefully estimated figure of the business use of these costs can be claimed as a proportion of the total.

(j) Accountancy charges and legal charges incurred wholly in the course of the profession including cost of defending libel actions, damages in so far as they are not covered by insurance and libel insurance premiums. However, where in a libel case, damages are awarded to punish the author for having acted maliciously the action becomes quasi-criminal and costs and damages may not be allowed.

(k) TV and video rental (which may be apportioned for private use), and cinema or theatre tickets, if wholly for the purpose of the profession, e.g. playwriting.

(l) Capital allowances for equipment, e.g. car, TV, radio, hi-fi sets, tape and video recorders, dictaphones, typewriters, desks, bookshelves, filing cabinets, photographic equipment. Allowances vary in the Finance Acts depending upon political and economic views prevailing. At present they are set at 25%. On motor cars the allowance is 25% in the first year and 25% of the reduced balance in each successive year limited to £2000 each year. The total allowances in the case of all assets must not exceed the difference between cost and eventual sale price. Allowances will be reduced to exclude personal (non-professional) use where necessary.

(m) Lease rent. The cost of lease rent of equipment is allowable; also on cars, subject to restrictions for private use and for expensive cars.

(n) Gifts to charitable bodies are allowed, subject to certain conditions, provided they are reasonable in amount and for a cause connected with the donor's professional activities. Tax relief is also available for three-year (minimum) covenants to charities. With effect from 1 October 1990 individuals can obtain tax relief on one-off charitable gifts subject to certain generous limits.

NB It is always advisable to keep detailed records. Diary entries of appointments, notes of fares and receipted bills are much more convincing to the Inland Revenue than round figure estimates.

Capital Gains Tax

The exemption from Capital Gains Tax which applies to an individual's main residence does not apply to any part of that residence which is used exclusively for business purposes. The effect of this is that the appropriate proportion of any increase in value of the residence since 31 March 1982 can be taxed, when the residence is sold, at the maximum rate of 40% (at present).

Writers who own their houses should bear this in mind before claiming expenses for the use of a room for writing purposes. Arguments in favour of making such claims are that they afford some relief now, while Capital Gains Tax in its present form may not stay for ever. Also, where a new house is bought in place of an old one, the gain made on the sale of the first study may be set off against the cost of the study in the new house, thus postponing the tax payment until the final sale. For this relief to apply, each house must have a study, and the author must continue his profession throughout. On death there is an exemption of the total Capital Gains of the estate. No relief from tax will be given on community charge.

NB Writers can claim that their use is non-exclusive and restrict their claim to the cost of extra lighting, heating and cleaning to avoid Capital Gains Tax liability.

Can a writer average out his income over a number of years for tax purposes?

Under Section 534 of the *Income and Corporation Taxes Act 1988*, a writer may in certain circumstances spread over two or three fiscal years lump sum payments, whenever received, and royalties received during two years from the date of first publication or performance of work. Points to note are:

(a) The relief can only be claimed if the writer has been engaged in preparing and collecting material and writing the book for more than twelve months.

(b) If the period of preparing and writing the work exceeds twelve months but does not exceed twenty-four months, one-half of the advances and/or royalties will be regarded as income from the year preceding that of receipt. If the period of preparing and writing exceeds twenty-four months, one-third of the amount received would be regarded as income from each of the two years preceding that of receipt.

(c) For a writer on a very large income, who otherwise fulfils the conditions required, a claim under these sections could result in a tax saving. If his income is not large he should consider the implication, in the various fiscal years concerned, of possible loss of benefit from personal and other allowances and changes in the standard rate of income tax.

It is also possible to average out income within the terms of publishers' contracts, but professional advice should be taken before signature. Where a husband and wife collaborate as writers, advice should be taken as to whether a formal partnership agreement should be made or whether the publishing agreement should be in joint names.

Is a lump sum paid for an outright sale of the copyright or part of the copyright exempt from tax?
No. All the money received from the marketing of literary work, by whatever means, is taxable. Some writers, in spite of clear judicial decisions to the contrary, still seem to think that an outright sale of, for instance, the film rights in a book, is not subject to tax.

Is there any relief where old copyrights are sold?
Section 535 of the *Income and Corporation Taxes Act 1988* gives relief where not less than ten years after the first publication of the work the author of a literary, dramatic, musical or artistic work assigns the copyright therein wholly or partially, or grants any interest in the copyright by licence, and:

(a) the consideration for the assignment or grant consists wholly or partially of a lump sum payment, the whole amount of which would, but for this section, be included in computing the amount of his/her profits or gains for a single year of assessment, and

(b) the copyright or interest is not assigned or granted for a period of less than two years.

In such cases, the amount received may be spread forward in equal yearly instalments for a maximum of six years, or, where the copyright or interest is assigned or granted for a period of less than six years, for the number of whole years in that period. A 'lump sum payment' is defined to include a non-returnable advance on account of royalties.

It should be noted that a claim may not be made under this section in respect of a payment if a prior claim has been made under Section 534 of the *Income and Corporation Taxes Act 1988* (see section on spreading lump sum payments over two or three years) or vice versa.

Are royalties payable on publication of a book abroad subject to both foreign tax as well as UK tax?
Where there is a Double Taxation Agreement between the country concerned and the UK, then on the completion of certain formalities no tax is deductible at source by the foreign payer, but such income is taxable in the UK in the ordinary way. When there is no Double Taxation agreement, credit will be given against UK tax for overseas tax paid. A complete list of countries with which the UK has conventions for the avoidance of double taxation may be obtained from the Inspector of Foreign Dividends, Lynwood Road, Thames Ditton, Surrey KT7 0DP, or the local tax office.

Residence Abroad
Writers residing abroad will, of course, be subject to the tax laws ruling in their country of residence, and as a general rule royalty income paid from the United Kingdom can be exempted from deduction of UK tax at source, providing the author is carrying on his profession abroad. A writer who is intending to go and live abroad should make early application for future royalties to be paid without deduction of tax to HM Inspector of Taxes, Claims Branch, Magdalen House, Stanley Precinct, Bootle, Merseyside L69 9BB. In certain circumstances writers resident in the Irish Republic are exempt from Irish Income Tax on their authorship earnings.

Are grants or prizes taxable?
The law is uncertain. Some Arts Council grants are now deemed to be taxable, whereas most prizes and awards are not, though it depends on the conditions in each case. When submitting a statement of income and expenses, such items should be excluded, but reference made to them in a covering letter to the Inspector of Taxes.

What if I disagree with a tax assessment?
Income Tax law requires the Inspector of Taxes to make an assessment each year calculating the amount of income tax payable on the 'profits' of the profession. Even though accounts may have already been submitted the assessment can quite possibly be estimated and overstated.

The taxpayer has the right of appeal within 30 days of receipt of the assessment and can request that the tax payable should be reduced to the correct liability which he must estimate as accurately as possible. However, if he underestimates the amount, interest can become payable on the amount by which he underpays when the correct liability is known.

What is the item 'Class 4 N.I.C.' which appears on my tax assessment?
All taxpayers who are self-employed pay an additional national insurance contribution if their earned income exceeds a figure which is varied each year. This contribution is described as Class 4 and is calculated in the tax assessment. It is additional to the self-employed Class 2 (stamp) contribution but confers no additional benefits and is a form of levy. It applies to men aged under 65 and women under 60. Tax relief is given on half the Class 4 contributions.

Value Added Tax

Value Added Tax (VAT) is a tax currently levied at $17^1/2\%$ on:
(a) the total value of taxable goods and services supplied to consumers,
(b) the importation of goods into the UK,
(c) certain services from abroad if a taxable person receives them in the UK for the purpose of their business.

Who is Taxable?
A writer resident in the UK whose turnover from writing and any other business, craft or art on a self-employed basis is greater than £36,600 annually, before deducting agent's commission, must register with HM Customs & Excise as a taxable person. A business is required to register:
– at the end of any month if the value of taxable supplies in the past 12 months has exceeded the annual threshold; or
– at any time, if there are reasonable grounds for believing that the value of taxable supplies in the next 30 days will exceed the annual threshold.

Penalties will be claimed in the case of late registration. A writer whose turnover is below these limits is exempt from the requirements to register for VAT, but may apply for voluntary registration, and this will be allowed at the discretion of HM Customs & Excise.

A taxable person collects VAT on outputs (turnover) and deducts VAT paid on inputs (taxable expenses) and where VAT collected exceeds VAT paid, must remit the difference to HM Customs & Excise. In the event that input exceeds output, the difference will be repaid by HM Customs & Excise.

Outputs (Turnover)

A writer's outputs are taxable services supplied to publishers, broadcasting organisations, theatre managements, film companies, educational institutions, etc. A taxable writer must invoice, i.e. collect from, all the persons (either individuals or organisations) in the UK for whom supplies have been made, for fees, royalties or other considerations plus VAT. An unregistered writer cannot and must not invoice for VAT. A taxable writer is not obliged to collect VAT on royalties or other fees paid by publishers or others overseas. In practice, agents usually collect VAT for the registered author.

Taxable at the standard rate	*Taxable at the zero rate*	*Exempt*
Rent of certain commercial premises	Books	Rent of non-commercial premises
	Periodicals	
Advertisements in newspapers, magazines, journals and periodicals	Lighting	Community charge
		Postage
	Heating	Services supplied by unregistered persons
Agent's commission (unless it relates to monies from overseas, when it is zero-rated)	Coach, rail, and air travel	Subscriptions to the Society of Authors, PEN, NUJ, etc.
Accountant's fees		Wages and salaries
Solicitor's fees re business matters		Insurance
Agency services (typing, copying, etc.)		Taxicab fares
Word processors, typewriters and stationery		
Artists' materials		
Photographic equipment		*Outside the scope of VAT*
Tape recorders and tapes		PLR (Public Lending Rights)
Hotel accommodation		Profit shares
Motor-car expenses		Theatres and concerts
Telephone		Dividend income

NB This list is not exhaustive.

VAT on Gas and Electricity
Under recent legislation, VAT is to be charged on gas and electricity supplied for business use. VAT will be charged on quarterly gas bills of over 455 therms and electricity bills of over 3010 kw hours, if more than 40% of this is used for business. As very few, if any, authors use anything like 40% of their gas and electricity for business purposes, bills should generally not be subject to VAT.

Remit to Customs
The taxable writer adds up the VAT which has been paid on taxable inputs, deducts it from the VAT received and remits the balance to Customs. Business with HM Customs is conducted through the local VAT Offices of HM Customs which are listed in local telephone directories, except for tax returns which are sent direct to the Customs and Excise VAT Central Unit, Alexander House, 21 Victoria Avenue, Southend on Sea, Essex SS99 1AA.

Accounting
A taxable writer is obliged to account to HM Customs & Excise at quarterly intervals. Accounts must be completed and sent to VAT Central Unit within 28 days of the accounting date. It should be noted that only invoices are necessary to complete a VAT return, not receipts.

It is possible to account for the VAT liability under the Cash Accounting Scheme (Note 731), whereby the author accounts for the output tax when the invoice is paid or royalties, etc., are received. The same applies to the input tax, but as most purchases are probably on a 'cash basis', this will not make a considerable difference to the author's input tax. This scheme is only applicable to those with a taxable turnover of less than £300,000 and, therefore, is available to the majority of authors. The advantage of this scheme is that the author does not have to account for VAT before receiving payment, thereby relieving the author of a cash flow problem. To join or transfer to this scheme, application must be made to the VAT office to which the author is assigned.

It is also possible to pay VAT by nine estimated direct debits, with a final balance at the end of the year (see leaflet 732).

Registration
A writer will be given a VAT registration number which must be quoted on all VAT correspondence. It is the responsibility of those registered to inform those to whom they make supplies of their registration number. A writer who would not normally be required to register as taxable may, on receipt of a single large payment, for example in respect of film rights or a paperback edition, find that the quarterly or annual turnover has risen above the limits and is liable to register. If the local VAT Office is satisfied that the turnover will not exceed £36,600 in the next 12 months, they may not insist on registration.

Voluntary Registration
A writer whose turnover is below the limits may apply to register. If the writer is paying a relatively large amount of VAT on taxable inputs – agent's commissions, accountant's fees, equipment, materials, or agency services, etc. – it may make a significant improvement in the net income to be able to offset the VAT on these inputs. An author who pays relatively little VAT may find it easier, and no more expensive, to remain unregistered.

Fees and Royalties

A taxable writer must notify those to whom he makes supplies of the Tax Registration Number at the first opportunity. One method of accounting for and paying VAT on fees and royalties is the use of multiple stationery for 'self-billing', one copy of the royalty statement being used by the author as the VAT invoice. A second method is for the recipient of taxable outputs to pay fees, including authors' royalties, without VAT. The taxable author then renders a tax invoice for the VAT element and a second payment, of the VAT element, will be made. This scheme is cumbersome but will involve only taxable authors. Fees and royalties from abroad will count as payments for exported services and will accordingly be zero-rated.

Agents and Accountants

A writer is responsible to HM Customs for making VAT returns and payments. Neither an agent nor an accountant nor a solicitor can take this over, although they can be helpful in preparing and keeping VAT returns and accounts. Their professional fees or commission will, except in rare cases where the adviser or agent is himself unregistered, be taxable at the standard rate and will represent some of a writer's taxable inputs. An agent's commission in respect of zero-rated fees and royalties from abroad is not liable for VAT.

Income Tax – Schedule D

An unregistered writer can claim some of the VAT paid on taxable inputs as a business expense allowable against income tax. However, certain taxable inputs fall into categories which cannot be claimed under the income tax regulations. A taxable writer, who has already offset VAT on inputs, cannot charge it as a business expense for the purposes of income tax.

Certain Services From Abroad

A taxable author who resides in the United Kingdom and who receives certain services from abroad must account for VAT on those services at the appropriate tax rate on the sum paid for them. Examples of the type of services concerned include: services of lawyers, accountants, consultants, provisions of information and copyright permissions.

Inheritance Tax

Inheritance Tax was introduced in 1984 to replace Capital Transfer Tax, which had in turn replaced Estate Duty, the first of the death taxes of recent times. Paradoxically, Inheritance Tax has reintroduced a number of principles present under the old Estate Duty.

The general principle now is that all legacies on death are chargeable to tax (currently 40%), except for legacies between spouses which are exempt, as are the first £147,000 of legacies to others. Gifts made more than seven years before death are exempt, but those made within this period are taxed on a sliding scale. No tax is payable at the time of making the gift.

In addition, each individual may currently make gifts of up to £3000 in any year and these will be considered to be exempt. A further exemption covers any number of annual gifts not exceeding £250 to any one person.

If the £3000 is not utilised in one year it, or the unused balance, can be given in the following year (but no later), plus that year's exemptions. Gifts out of income, which means those which do not reduce one's capital or one's living standards, are also exempt if they are part of one's normal expenditure.

At death all assets are valued: they will include any property, investments, life policies, furniture and personal possessions, bank balances and, in the case of authors, the value of their copyrights. All, with the sole exception of copyrights are capable (as assets) of accurate valuation, and, if necessary, can be turned into cash. The valuation of copyright is, of course, complicated, and frequently gives rise to difficulty. Except where they are bequeathed to the owner's husband or wife, very real problems can be left behind by the author.

Experience has shown that a figure based on two to three years' past royalties may be proposed by the Inland Revenue in their valuation of copyright. However, it all depends. If a book is running out of print or if, as in the case of educational books, it may need revision at the next reprint, these factors must be taken into account. In many cases the fact that the author is no longer alive and able to make personal appearances, or provide publicity, or write further works, will result in lower or slower sales. Obviously this is an area in which help can be given by the publishers, and in particular one needs to know what their future intentions are, what stocks of the books remain, and what likelihood there will be of reprinting.

There is a further relief available to authors who have established that they have been carrying on a business, normally assessable under case II of Schedule D, for at least two years prior to death. Copyright can be treated as 'business property' and in these circumstances 'business property relief' is available. This relief represents a 50% reduction in the valuation of copyright so the tax saving can be quite substantial. At the time of going to press it seems possible that relief will be given at 100%.

If the author has sufficient income, consideration should be given to building up a fund to cover future liabilities. One of a number of ways would be to take out a whole life assurance policy which is assigned to the children, or other beneficiaries, the premiums on which are within the annual exemption of £3000. The capital sum payable on the death of the assured is exempt from inheritance tax.

Anyone wondering how best to order his affairs for tax purposes, should consult an accountant with specialised knowledge in this field. Experience shows that a good accountant is well worth his fee which, incidentally, so far as it relates to matters other than personal tax work, is an allowable expense.

The information contained in this section is adapted from **The Society of Authors** *Quick Guides to Taxation* (Nos 4 and 7), with the kind help of A.P. Kernon, FCA.

Companies Index

The following codes have been used to classify the index entries:

AA	European Publishers	**M**	Theatre Producers
AB	Writers' Workshops	**N**	US Publishers
A	UK Publishers	**O**	US Agents
B	The Specialists/Small Presses (Poetry)	**P**	US Press & Journals
C	Little Magazines (Poetry)	**Q**	Professional Associations & Societies
D	Organisations of Interest to Poets	**R**	Regional and Other Arts Associations
E	UK Packagers	**S**	Bursaries, Fellowships & Grants
F	UK Agents	**T**	Prizes
G	National Newspapers	**U**	Library Services
H	Regional Newspapers	**V**	Picture Libraries
HH	News Agencies	**W**	Small Presses
I	Magazines	**X**	Festivals
J	Television	**Y**	Editorial Services
K	Radio	**YY**	Press Cuttings Agencies
L	Film, TV & Video Companies	**Z**	Literary Societies

AA Publishing **A** 9
Aard Press **W** 133
Abacus **A** 9
Abacus Literary Agency **F** 159
Aba Daba **M** 377
Abadia de Montserrat
(Publicaciones de l') **AA** 430
ABC - All Books For Children **A** 9
ABC News **P** 482
ABC–Clio, Inc. **N** 436
Abel (Dominick) Literary Agency
Inc. **O** 455
Aberdeen University Press **A** 9
Abingdon Press **N** 436
Abington Publishing **A** 9
Abrams (Harry N.), Inc. **N** 436
Absolute Press **A** 9
Abson Books **A** 9
Acacia Productions Ltd **L** 337
Academic Press **A** 10
Academy Books **A** 10
Academy Chicago Publishers **N** 436
Academy Editions **A** 10
Acair Ltd **A** 10
A. & C. Black Ltd **A** 17
Accent Educational Publishers Ltd **A** 10
Accountancy **I** 217
Accountancy Age **I** 217
Ace Photo Agency **V** 598
Ace Science Fiction **N** 436
Ackerley (J.R.) Prize **T** 542

Acorn Award, The **T** 542
Actes Sud (Editions) **AA** 415
Actinic Press **A** 10
Action Images Ltd **V** 598
Action Plus **V** 598
Action Time **L** 337
Active Life **I** 217
Acton & Dystel **O** 455
Actors Touring Company **M** 377
Acumen **I** 217
Adams (Bob) Publishers, Inc. **N** 436
Adams Picture Library **V** 598
Adam Video Productions **L** 337
Ada Press, The **B** 119
Addison-Wesley Publishing Co., Inc. **N** 436
Addison–Wesley Publishers Ltd **A** 10
Adelphi Edizioni SpA **AA** 422
Adelphi Press **B** 119
Adkins (Lesley & Roy) **Y** 531
Adkins (Lesley & Roy) Picture Library **V** 598
Adlard Coles Ltd **A** 10
Adlib Paperbacks **A** 11
Adlib Specialist Picture Source **V** 598
ADviser **I** 217
Aegina Press, Inc. **N** 436
Aero Books **N** 437
AFP (Agence France Presse) **V** 598

African Affairs **I** 217
After Image Ltd **L** 337
Age d'Homme – La Cité (Editions L') **AA** 433
Agenda **B** 124
Agenda Editions **C** 119
Agneau 2 **A** 11
Agog **B** 124
Aird (Malcolm) Associates **V** 598
Aire FM/Magic 828 **K** 324
Aireings **B** 124
Aireings Workshops **AB** 528
Airforces Monthly **I** 218
Air International **I** 218
Airlife Publishing Ltd **A** 11
Aisling Films Ltd **L** 337
Aitken & Stone Ltd **F** 159
AK Press/AKA Books **W** 133
Alabama (University of) Press **N** 437
Aladdin Books **N** 437
Alan Afriat Associates **L** 337
Alan (Richard) Publications **W** 133
Alaska (University of) Press **N** 437
Alban Press, The **A** 11
Albany Empire **M** 377
Alba Pictures **V** 598
Albemarle of London **M** 377
Albion Press Ltd, The **E** 148
Aldeburgh Poetry Festival **X** 403
Aldeburgh Poetry Festival Prize **T** 542

Aldersgate Productions **M** 377
Alembic Press, The **W** 133
Alexander (Bryan & Cherry) Photography **V** 598
Alexander (Jacintha) Associates **F** 159
Alexander Prize **T** 542
Alhambra (Editorial) SA **AA** 430
Alianza Editorial SA **AA** 430
All-Action Picture Library **V** 599
Allan (Chris) Aviation Library **V** 599
Allan (Ian) Ltd **A** 11
Allardyce, Barnett, Publishers **A** 11
Allen (J.A.) & Co. Ltd **A** 11
Allen Lane The Penguin Press **A** 57
Alliance of Literary Societies **Q** 489
Allison & Busby **A** 11
Allsport (UK) Ltd **V** 599
Almeida Theatre Company **M** 377
Almqvist och Wiksell International **AA** 432
Aloes **B** 119
Alphabet & Image Ltd **E** 148
Alphabooks **A** 11
Alternative Theatre Company Ltd **M** 377
Alun Books **B** 119
Alvin Rakoff Productions Ltd **L** 366
Alyson Publications, Inc. **N** 437
AMACOM **N** 437
Amalthea-Verlag Gesellschaft mbH **AA** 410
Amanda **AA** 412
Amateur Film and Video Maker **I** 218
Amateur Gardening **I** 218
Amateur Golf **I** 218
Amateur Photographer **I** 218
Amateur Stage **I** 218
Amber Films **L** 337
Amber Lane Press Ltd **A** 11
Ambit **I** 219
Ambo (Uitgeverij) BV **AA** 425
American Mensa Press **N** 437
American, The **I** 219
America (University of) Press **N** 453
Amra Imprint **W** 133
Amsco **A** 12
Amsterdam (Marcia) Agency **O** 455
Anaya (Ediciones) SA **AA** 430
Anaya Publishers Ltd **A** 12
Anchor Books **N** 437

Ancient Art and Architecture Collection **V** 599
Andersen (Hans Christian) Awards **T** 542
Andersen Press Ltd **A** 12
Andersens (Carit) Forlag A/S **AA** 412
Anderson (Darley) Books **F** 159
Anderson (Eileen) Central Television Drama Award **T** 542
Andes Press Agency **V** 599
Andrews (Bart) & Associates **O** 455
Andromeda Oxford Ltd **E** 148
An Duais don bhFiliocht i nGaeilge **T** 542
Angel (Greg) (Film and Television) **L** 338
Angel (Heather)/Biofotos **V** 599
Angel Literary Award **T** 543
Anglia Television **J** 308
Angling Times **I** 219
Angus & Robertson (UK) **A** 12
Animal Photography **V** 599
Animal World **I** 219
Annabel **I** 219
Ansgar Forlag A/S **AA** 427
Antelope Films Ltd **L** 338
Anthony (Joseph) Agency **O** 455
Antique and New Art **I** 219
Antique Collectors' Club **A** 12
Antique Collector, The **I** 219
Antique Dealer and Collectors' Guide, The **I** 220
Antiquities (Museum of) Picture Library **V** 599
Anvil **N** 437
Anvil Press Poetry Ltd **A** 12
ANV Productions **L** 338
Aosdàna Scheme **S** 535
AP Dow Jones **HH** 304
Apostrof (Forlaget) ApS **AA** 412
Apparition Press **W** 133
Apples & Snakes **D** 128
Appleseeds Management **O** 455
Apple Television **L** 338
Appletree Press Ltd **A** 12
Aquarian Press **A** 13
Aquarist & Pondkeeper **I** 220
Aquarius **C** 124
Aquarius Literary Agency & Picture Library **F** 159
Aquarius Picture Library **V** 599
Aquila Photographics **V** 599
Arcaid **V** 599
Arche Verlag AG **AA** 434
Architects' Journal/The Architectural Review **I** 220
Architectural Association Slide Library **V** 600

Architectural Design **I** 220
Archival Facsimiles Ltd **E** 148
Archway **N** 437
Ardea London Ltd **V** 600
Arena **I** 220
Argus Books **A** 13
Arioma Editorial Services **Y** 531
Aris & Phillips Ltd **A** 13
Arizona (University of) Press **N** 437
Arkana **A** 13
Arkansas (University of) Press **N** 438
Ark Boeken Publishing House **AA** 425
Ark **A** 13
Armada **A** 13
Armado (Armenio), Editore de Simoes, Belrao & Cia Lda **AA** 429
Armando Armando (Editore) SRl **AA** 422
Armitt Trust & Library **U** 577
Arms & Armour Press **A** 13
Arnaud (Yvonne) Theatre **M** 378
Arnold (Edward) **A** 13
Arrow Books Ltd **A** 13
Artbank International **V** 600
Art & Craft **I** 220
Art & Design **I** 221
Art & Design Library (Westminster) **U** 577
Art Directors Photo Library **V** 600
Artech House **A** 13
Artemis Press **A** 13
Artemis Verlags AG **AA** 434
Arthaud (Editions) SA **AA** 415
Arthur (Rosemary) Award **T** 543
Artifax Ltd **L** 338
Artists Group, The **O** 456
Artist, The **I** 221
Art Monthly **I** 221
Art Newspaper, The **I** 221
Art Resource Illustration Library 600
Arts Council of Great Britain **R** 513
Arts Council of Northern Ireland **R** 513
Arts Council Theatre Writing Bursaries **S** 535
Arts Council Writers' Bursaries **S** 535
Artts International **L** 338
Artts International **AB** 528
Arundel Festival **X** 403
Arvon Foundation **Q** 489
Arvon Foundation International Poetry Competition **T** 543

Aschehoug Dansk Forlag A/S **AA** 412
Aschehoug (H) & Co **AA** 427
Ashford, Buchan & Enright **A** 13
Ashgate Publishing Co. Ltd **A** 13
Aspect **E** 149
Aspect **F** 160
Aspect Film and Television Productions Ltd **L** 338
Aspect Picture Library Ltd **V** 600
Aspen Business Communications **L** 338
AS Publishing **E** 148
Associated Press News Agency **HH** 304
Associated Press, The **P** 482
Associated Publicity Holdings **A** 14
Associated Sports Photography **V** 600
Associated University Presses (AUP) **A** 14
Association for Business Sponsorship of the Arts (ABSA) **Q** 490
Association of American Correspondents in London **Q** 489
Association of Authors' Agents **Q** 489
Association of British Editors **Q** 489
Association of British Science Writers (ABSW) **Q** 489
Association of Comics Enthusiasts **Q** 490
Association of Independent Libraries **Q** 490
Association of Independent Radio Companies **Q** 490
Association of Learned and Professional Society Publishers **Q** 490
Association of Little Presses **Q** 490
Aston Publications **A** 14
Astron Appointments Ltd **Y** 531
Athena **N** 438
Athenaeum, Liverpool **U** 577
Atheneum Books **N** 438
Athesia (Verlagsanstalt) **AA** 422
Athletics Weekly **I** 221
Athlone Press, The **A** 14
Atlantic Europe Publishing Co. Ltd **A** 14
Atlantic Large Print **A** 14
Atlantic Monthly Press **N** 438
Atlas Press **W** 133
Attic Books **A** 14

Aubier-Montaigne (Editions) SA **AA** 415
Audio Books **A** 15
Audio Visual Services **V** 600
Aurora Sound and Vision **L** 338
Aurum Press Ltd **A** 15
Aussteiger Publications **W** 134
Austen Cornish **A** 15
Author Aid Associates **O** 456
Authors' Club First Novel Award **T** 543
Authors' Club, The **Q** 491
Authors' Contingency Fund, The **S** 535
Authors' Foundation, The **S** 535
Authors' Licensing and Collecting Society **Q** 491
Authors' Research Services (ARS) **Y** 531
Authors Resource Center & Tarc Literary Agency, The **O** 456
Author, The **I** 221
Autocar & Motor **I** 221
Autolycus Press **A** 15
Autumn Publishing Ltd **E** 149
Avalon Books **N** 438
AVC Group **L** 339
Avebury **A** 15
Aventura Forlag **AA** 427
Avery Publishing Group, Inc. **N** 438
Aviation Photographs International **V** 600
Aviation Picture Library **V** 600
Aviemore Photographic Scotland **V** 600
Avon Books **N** 438
Avon Poetry Festival **X** 403
Axel Poignant Archive **V** 601
A–Z Botanical Collection **V** 601
Baal Book Prize **T** 543
Baby Magazine **I** 222
Bach (Julian) Literary Agency **O** 456
Back Brain Recluse (BBR) **I** 222
Baen Books **N** 438
BAFTA (British Academy of Film and Television Arts) **Q** 491
Baillière Tindall **A** 15
Baker (Yvonne) Associates **F** 160
Balance **I** 222
Baldi (Malaga) Literary Agency **O** 456
Baldwin (M. & M.) **W** 134
Balkema (A A) **AA** 426
Balkin Agency, Inc., The **O** 456
Balland (André) **AA** 415
Ballantine/Del Rey/Fawcett/Ivy Books **N** 438
Baltimore Sun **P** 482

Banker, The **I** 222
Bank of England Reference Library **U** 577
Bantam/Bantam Press **A** 15
Bantam Doubleday Dell Publishing Group **N** 438
BAPLA (British Association of Picture Libraries and Agencies **Q** 491
Barbican Library **U** 577
Barclaycard Magazine **I** 222
Barclay (Humphrey) Productions/First Choice **L** 339
Barda (Clive) **V** 601
Bare Wires **B** 124
Bargate (Verity) Award **T** 543
Barker (Arthur) Ltd **A** 15
Barnaby's Picture Library **V** 601
Barnes (William) Society **Z** 507
Barnsley Public Library **U** 578
Barny Books **A** 15
Baron Birch **A** 15
Barony Film and Television Productions Limited **L** 339
Barracuda Books Ltd/Quotes Ltd **A** 15
Barratt (Michael) Ltd **L** 339
Barrie & Jenkins Ltd **A** 15
Barron's Educational Series **N** 439
Bartholomew **A** 15
Barton House Publishing **W** 134
Barts Medical Picture Library **V** 601
BASCA (British Academy of Songwriters, Composers and Authors) **Q** 491
Basic Books **N** 439
Bates (H. E.) Short Story Competition **T** 543
Bath Fringe Festival **X** 403
Batsford (B.T.) Ltd **A** 16
Batty (Peter) Productions **L** 339
Bauverlag GmbH **AA** 418
Baxter (Colin) Photography **V** 601
Bay View Books Ltd **A** 16
BB Books **W** 134
BBC Books **A** 16
BBC CWR **K** 319
BBC Data Enquiry Service **U** 578
BBC Essex **K** 319
BBC Gardeners' World Magazine **I** 222
BBC GLR (Greater London Radio) **K** 319
BBC GMR **K** 319
BBC Good Food **I** 222
BBC Midlands **J** 306
BBC News and Current Affairs **J** 305
BBC North **J** 306

BBC Northern Ireland **J** 307
BBC Radio **K** 315
BBC Radio Aberdeen **K** 319
BBC Radio Bedfordshire **K** 319
BBC Radio Berkshire **K** 320
BBC Radio Bristol **K** 320
BBC Radio Cambridgeshire **K** 320
BBC Radio Cleveland **K** 320
BBC Radio Clwyd **K** 320
BBC Radio Cornwall **K** 320
BBC Radio Cumbria **K** 320
BBC Radio Derby **K** 320
BBC Radio Devon **K** 320
BBC Radio Drama **K** 315
BBC Radio Drama Young
  Playwright's Festival **X** 403
BBC Radio Foyle **K** 320
BBC Radio Furness **K** 320
BBC Radio Gloucestershire **K** 321
BBC Radio Guernsey **K** 321
BBC Radio Hereford & Worcester
  K 321
BBC Radio Highland **K** 321
BBC Radio Humberside **K** 321
BBC Radio Jersey **K** 321
BBC Radio Kent **K** 321
BBC Radio Lancashire **K** 321
BBC Radio Leeds **K** 321
BBC Radio Leicester **K** 322
BBC Radio Lincolnshire **K** 322
BBC Radio London **K** 322
BBC Radio Manchester **K** 322
BBC Radio Merseyside **K** 322
BBC Radio Newcastle **K** 322
BBC Radio, News and Current
  Affairs **K** 316
BBC Radio Norfolk **K** 322
BBC Radio Northampton **K** 322
BBC Radio Northern Ireland **K**
  317
BBC Radio Nottingham **K** 322
BBC Radio Oxford **K** 322
BBC Radio Peterborough **K** 322
BBC (Radio) Religious
  Broadcasting **K** 316
BBC Radio Scotland **K** 317
BBC Radio Sheffield **K** 322
BBC Radio Shropshire **K** 323
BBC Radio Solent **K** 323
BBC Radio Solway **K** 323
BBC Radio Stoke **K** 323
BBC Radio Suffolk **K** 323
BBC Radio Surrey **K** 323
BBC Radio Sussex **K** 323
BBC Radio Tweed **K** 323
BBC Radio Wales **K** 317
BBC (Radio) Wiltshire Sound **K**
  323
BBC Radio WM **K** 323
BBC Radio York **K** 323

BBC Regional Broadcasting **K** 319
BBC Scotland **J** 307
BBC South & East **J** 307
BBC South & West **J** 307
BBC Television **J** 305
BBC Television Documentary
  Features **J** 306
BBC Television Teletext Services
  J 306
BBC Wales **J** 308
BBC WILDLIFE Magazine **I** 223
BBC WILDLIFE Magazine Awards
  for Nature Writing **T** 544
BBC World Service **K** 316
BBC Written Archives Centre **U**
  578
Beacon Press **N** 439
Beacon Radio/WABC **K** 324
Beanstalk Books Ltd **E** 149
Beckett (Samuel) Award **T** 544
Beck (Verlag C H) **AA** 418
Bedfordshire Magazine **I** 223
Bedford Square Press **A** 16
Bedlam Press **B** 120
Beech Tree Books **N** 439
Bee World **I** 223
Behr Cinematography **L** 339
Beken of Cowes Ltd **V** 601
Belcher (Ivan J.) Colour Picture
  Library **V** 601
Belfast Festival at Queen's **X** 403
Belfast Public Libraries **U** 578
Belfast Telegraph **H** 196
Belfond (Editions Pierre) **AA** 415
Belgrade Theatre, Coventry **M** 378
Belhaven Press **A** 16
Belin (Editions) **AA** 415
Belitha Press Ltd **E** 149
Bella **I** 223
Bell Books **N** 439
Bellevue Books **A** 16
Bellew Publishing Co. Ltd **A** 17
Bennett Books **A** 17
Bennett (David) Books Ltd **E** 149
Benson (E. F.) Society **Z** 507
Benteli Verlag **AA** 434
Bentinck (Adolphe) Prize **T** 544
Benziger AG **AA** 434
Bergh Publishing, Inc. **N** 439
Berg Publishers Ltd **A** 17
Berkley Publishing Group **N** 439
Berkshire Literary Festival **X** 403
Berkswell Publishing Co. Ltd **A** 17
Berkswell Publishing Co. Ltd **E**
  149
Berman (Lois) **O** 457
Bernstein (Meredith) Literary
  Agency, Inc. **O** 457
Berriff (Paul) Productions Ltd **L**
  339

Berry (David) Prize **T** 544
Bertelsmann AG **AA** 418
Bertrand Editora Lda **AA** 429
Besley (Andrew) PhotoLibrary **V**
  601
Best **I** 223
Bête Noire **C** 124
Betjeman Society, The **Z** 507
Bevanfield Films **L** 339
Bewick Society, The **Z** 507
BFBS (British Forces Broadcasting
  Service) **K** 317
BFI Publishing **A** 17
BFI Stills, Posters and Designs **V**
  601
BFV Ltd **L** 340
Bible Society Publishing **A** 17
Bibliographical Society, The **Q**
  491
Bicycle **I** 223
Big Little Poem Books **B** 120
Big Paper, The **I** 224
Bingley (Clive) Books **A** 17
Biofotos/Heather Angel **V** 599
Bird (Martin) Productions **L** 340
Birds **I** 224
Birdsall (John) Photographic
  Library **V** 601
Birmingham and Midland Institute
  U 578
Birmingham Evening Mail **H** 197
Birmingham Post **H** 197
Birmingham Readers and Writers
  Festival **X** 404
Birmingham Repertory Theatre **M**
  378
Bishopsgate Library **U** 578
Bison Books Ltd **E** 149
Black (A. & C.) Ltd **A** 17
Black Beauty & Hair **I** 224
Blackbird Productions **L** 340
Blackie & Son Ltd **A** 18
Black (James Tait) Memorial
  Prizes **T** 544
Blackrod **L** 340
Black Spring Press Ltd **A** 18
Blackstaff Press Ltd **A** 18
Black (Stuart) Productions **L** 340
Black Swan **A** 18
Black Tulip **L** 340
Blackwell Publishers **A** 18
Blackwell Scientific Publications
  Ltd **A** 18
Bladkompaniet A/S **AA** 428
Blake (Anthony) **V** 602
Blake Friedmann Literary Agency
  Ltd* **F** 160
Blake (John) Picture Library **V**
  602
Blake Publishing **A** 19

Blandford Publishing Ltd **A** 19
BLA Publishing Ltd **E** 150
Bloodaxe Books Ltd **A** 19
Bloomberg Business News **P** 482
Bloomsbury Books **A** 19
Bloomsbury Publishing Ltd **A** 19
Blossom Productions Ltd **L** 340
Blue Bridge Press **B** 120
Blueprint **I** 224
Blueprint Monographs **A** 19
Blundell (K.) Trust, The **S** 535
B L V Verlagsgesellschaft mbH **AA** 418
BMV Picturebank International **V** 602
Boardman Tasker Memorial Award **T** 544
Boates (Reid) Literary Agency **O** 457
Boat International **I** 224
Bobcat **A** 19
Bodley Head Childrens **A** 20
Bogans Forlag **AA** 412
Bogg **B** 124
Bohmann Druck und Verlag Gesellschaft **AA** 410
Bölau Verlag Gesellschaft **AA** 410
Bolt (David) Associates **F** 160
Bolton Evening News **H** 197
Bompiana **AA** 422
Boney (Matt) Associates **L** 340
Bonington (Chris) Library **V** 602
Bonnier Fakta Bokforlag AB **AA** 432
Bonniers (Albert) Forlag AB **AA** 433
Bonniers Böger A/S **AA** 412
Bonniers Juniorforlag AB **AA** 433
Book and Magazine Collector **I** 224
Book Castle, The **W** 134
Bookdealer **I** 225
Booker Prize for Fiction **T** 545
Book Guild, The **A** 20
Book House Ireland **Q** 492
Bookmarks Publications **A** 20
Book Packagers Association **Q** 492
Book Packaging and Marketing **E** 150
Books **I** 225
Booksellers Association **Q** 492
Bookseller, The **I** 225
Booksprint **Y** 531
Book Trust **Q** 492
Book Trust Scotland **Q** 492
Bookworms Literary Agency **F** 160
Bootleg Theatre Company **M** 378
Borchardt (Georges), Inc. **O** 457

Bordas (Editions) **AA** 415
Borderlines **C** 124
Borderline Theatre Company **M** 378
Border Television **J** 308
Borgens Forlag A/S **AA** 412
Born NV Uitgeversmaatschappij **AA** 426
Bosch Casa Editorial SA **AA** 430
Bould (Penny) Media **L** 340
Bound Spiral, The **C** 124
Bounty Books **A** 20
Bowker-Saur Ltd **A** 20
Bowling Green State University Popular Press **N** 439
Box Clever **L** 341
Boxtree **A** 20
Boyars (Marion) Publishers Ltd **A** 20
Boydell & Brewer Ltd **A** 21
Boyds Mills Press **N** 439
Boys Syndication **V** 602
Bozo **W** 134
BP Arts Journalism Awards **T** 545
BPS Books **A** 21
Bra Bocker (Bokforlaget) AB **AA** 433
Bracken Books **A** 21
Bracken Press **W** 135
Bradbury Press **N** 440
Bradford Central Library **U** 579
Bradford Poetry Quarterly **B** 124
Bradgate Press **B** 120
Brainwave Communications **B** 120
Brampton Publications **A** 21
Brandenburgh & Associates Literary Agency **O** 457
Brandt & Brandt Literary Agents, Inc. **O** 457
Braumüller (W.), Universitäts-verlagsbuchhandlung GmbH **AA** 410
Braun (Verlag G) GmbH **AA** 419
Bravo **J** 313
Brealey (Nicholas) Publishing Ltd **A** 21
Breese (Martin) Publishing **A** 21
Breeze AM **K** 324
Brentham Press **W** 135
Breslich & Foss **E** 150
Brian (Martin) & O'Keeffe Ltd **A** 21
Bridge, The **C** 124
Brides and Setting Up Home **I** 225
Bridge Magazine **I** 225
Bridgeman Art Library **V** 602
Bridge Studios **A** 22
Bridport Arts Centre Creative Writing Competition **T** 545

Briggistane **C** 124
Briggs (Katharine) Folklore Award **T** 545
Brighton Festival **X** 404
Brill (A J) **AA** 426
Brilliant Ideas Productions **L** 341
Brimax Books **A** 22
Bristol Express Theatre Company **M** 378
Bristol Old Vic Company **M** 379
British Academic Press **A** 22
British Academy Publication Subventions **S** 536
British Academy Small Personal Research Grants **S** 536
British Academy, The **A** 22
British Amateur Press Association **Q** 493
British American Arts Association **Q** 493
British American Publishing **N** 440
British Architectural Library **U** 579
British Association of Industrial Editors **Q** 493
British Bandsman, The **I** 225
British Birds **I** 225
British Book Awards **T** 545
British Book News **I** 225
British Chess Magazine **I** 226
British Comparative Literature Association Translation Prizes **T** 546
British Copyright Council **Q** 493
British Council, The **Q** 493
British Fantasy Awards **T** 546
British Fantasy Society **Z** 507
British Film Commission, The **Q** 493
British Film Institute **Q** 493
British Film Institute Library and Information Services **U** 579
British Film Institute Production **L** 341
British Guild of Travel Writers **Q** 493
British Haiku Society **D** 129
British Journalism Review **I** 226
British Library Business Information Service **U** 579
British Library Information Sciences Service **U** 579
British Library Manuscripts Department **U** 579
British Library Map Library **U** 579
British Library Music Library **U** 580
British Library National Sound Archive **U** 580
British Library Newspaper Library **U** 580

British Library Official Publications and Social Sciences Service **U** 580

British Library Oriental and India Office Collections **U** 580

British Library Reading Room **U** 580

British Library Science Reference and Information Service **U** 581

British Library, The **A** 22

British Lion Screen Entertainment Ltd **L** 341

British Literature Prize **T** 546

British Medical Journal **I** 226

British Museum Press **A** 22

British Psychological Society Library **U** 581

British Science Fiction Association **Q** 494

British Science Fiction Award **T** 546

British Screen Finance **Q** 494

British Sky Broadcasting **J** 313

BRMB FM/XTRA AM **K** 324

Broadcast **I** 226

Broadcast Communications **L** 341

Broadside **W** 135

Broadsword Television **L** 341

Broadwick Productions **L** 341

Brockhaus (F A) **AA** 419

Brokers' Monthly & Insurance Adviser **I** 226

Bromley (Rosemary) Literary Agency **F** 160

Bronte Society, The **Z** 507

Brooke Associates (Manchester) Ltd **E** 150

Brook Productions **L** 341

Brooks Books **A** 22

Browne (Pema) Ltd **O** 457

Brown (Hamish) Scottish Photographic **V** 602

Brownie, The **I** 226

Browning Society, The **Z** 508

Brown, Son & Ferguson, Ltd **A** 23

Brown Watson Ltd **A** 23

Brown Wells and Jacobs Ltd **E** 150

Brunel Classic Gold **K** 324

Bryan (Felicity) **F** 160

Bryant (Peter) (Writers) **F** 161

Bubbles Photolibrary **V** 602

Bucks Literary Services **Y** 531

Budgerigar World **I** 227

Building **I** 227

Bulzoni Editore SRL **AA** 422

Burder (John) (Films) **L** 341

Burlington Magazine, The **I** 227

Burn (Graham) Productions **Y** 531

Burns & Oates Ltd **A** 23

Burrill Productions **L** 341

Bursaries in Literature **S** 536

Burston (Diane) Literary Agency **F** 161

Burton Mail **H** 198

Bury St Edmunds Arts Festival **X** 404

Bush Theatre **M** 379

Business Education Publishers Ltd **A** 23

Business Life **I** 227

Businesslike Publishing **W** 135

Business Traveller **I** 227

Business Week **P** 482

Butterworth & Co. (Publishers) Ltd/Butterworth Tax Publishers **A** 23

Butterworth–Heinemann **A** 23

Buxton International Festival **X** 404

Bycornute Books **F** 161

Byron Society, The/International Byron Society **Z** 508

Byway Books **A** 23

Cable News International **P** 482

Cable News Network - CNN **J** 313

Cable & Wireless Visual Resource **V** 602

Cadenza **L** 342

Cadogan Books Ltd **A** 23

Caldecott (Randolph) Society **Z** 508

Calderini (Edizioni) **AA** 422

Calder Publications Ltd **A** 23

Calendar Concepts & Design **V** 602

California (University of) Press **N** 440

California University Press **A** 24

Calliope Women's Writing **C** 124

Calmann & King Ltd **E** 150

Calmann-Lévy SA **AA** 415

Calvin & Rose G. Hoffman Prize **T** 554

Cambridge Evening News **H** 199

Cambridge Festival **X** 404

Cambridgeshire Life **I** 227

Cambridge Theatre Company **M** 379

Cambridge University Press **A** 24

Camcorder User **I** 227

Camden Productions **L** 342

Camerapix Picture Library **V** 603

Camera Press **V** 602

Camera Ways Ltd Picture Library **V** 603

Cameron Books (Production) Ltd **E** 150

Cameron (James) Award **T** 546

Camerson Television **L** 342

Caminho (Editorial) SARL **AA** 4?

Campaign **I** 228

Campaign for Press and Broadcasting Freedom **Q** 494

Campbell (David) Publishers Ltd **A** 24

Campbell Thomson & McLaughl Ltd* **F** 161

Camping and Caravanning **I** 228

Camping Magazine **I** 228

Canal and Riverboat **I** 228

Canongate Press **A** 24

Canongate Publishing Ltd **B** 000

Canterbury Festival **X** 404

Cape (Jonathan) Ltd **A** 25

Capital FM/Capital Gold **K** 324

Capital Gay **I** 228

Capitol Editrice Dischi CEB **AA** 422

Cappelens (J W) Forlag A/S **AA** 428

Cappelli (Nuova Casa Editrice Licinio) SpA **AA** 422

Caravan Magazine **I** 229

Caravel Film Techniques Limited **L** 342

Carcanet Press Ltd **A** 25

Cardiff Central Library **U** 581

Cardiff Literature Festival **X** 404

Cardiff (The City of) Internationa Poetry Competition **T** 546

Carey Award **T** 546

Carinthia, Universitätsverlag **AA** 410

Carlton Books Ltd **A** 25

Carlton Television **J** 308

Carlyle Society, Edinburgh, The ? 508

Carmarthen Writers' Circle **AB** 528

Carmarthen Writers' Circle Short Story Competition **T** 546

Car Mechanics **I** 229

Carnell Literary Agency* **F** 161

Carnival **A** 25

Carnival Films & Theatre Ltd **L** 342

Carnival Films & Theatre Ltd **M** 379

Caroline House **N** 440

Carol Publishing **N** 440

Carolrhoda Books, Inc. **N** 440

Carroll & Graf Publishers, Inc. **N** 440

Carroll (Lewis) Society **Z** 508

Cars and Car Conversions Magazine **I** 229

Carter Rae Communications **Y** 531

Cartwn Cymru **L** 342
Carvainis (Maria) Agency, Inc. **O** 457
Car **I** 228
Casals (Editorial) SA **AA** 430
Casarotto Ramsay Ltd **F** 161
Casement Collection, The **V** 603
Cash (J. Allan) Ltd **V** 603
Cassandra Editions **N** 440
Cassell **A** 25
Casselman (Martha), Literary Agent **O** 458
Cass (Frank) **A** 25
Casterman (Editions) **AA** 411
Casterman (Editions) **AA** 415
Castleden Publications **W** 135
Catalog Literary Agency, The **O** 458
Catch **I** 229
Cathie (Kyle) Ltd **A** 26
Catholic Central Library **U** 581
Catholic Herald **I** 229
Catlin (Pearl) Associates **L** 342
Cat World **I** 229
Caves & Caving **I** 230
CBD Research Ltd **A** 26
CBS News **P** 482
Ceac (Ediciones) SA **AA** 430
CEDAM (Casa Editrice Dr A Milani) **AA** 423
Celador Productions Ltd **L** 342
Celtic Picture Library **V** 603
Cencrastus **C** 124
Centaur Press Ltd **A** 26
Central Books Ltd **A** 26
Central Independent Television **J** 309
Central Music Library (Westminster) **U** 581
Central Office of Information **HH** 304
Central Press Photos Ltd **V** 603
Century Publishing **A** 26
Century Theatre Touring **M** 379
Cephas Picture Library **V** 603
Certified Accountant **I** 230
Chacom **I** 230
Chadwyck-Healey Ltd **A** 26
Challenge **I** 230
Chambers (W & R) **A** 27
Chameleon Television Ltd **L** 342
Chancerel Publishers Ltd **E** 151
Channel Television **J** 309
Channel Theatre Trust Ltd **M** 379
Channel X **L** 343
Channel 4 **J** 309
Channel 5 **J** 309
Chapel Broadcast Productions Ltd **L** 343
Chapman **A** 27

Chapman **C** 124
Chapman **I** 230
Chapman Clarke Television **L** 343
Chapman (Geoffrey) **A** 27
Chapman & Hall Ltd **A** 27
Chapman (Paul) Publishing Ltd **A** 27
Chapmans Publishers **A** 27
Chapter Two **W** 135
Charlesbridge Publishing **N** 440
Chartered Institute of Journalists **Q** 494
Chatsworth Library **A** 27
Chatsworth Television Ltd **L** 343
Chatto & Windus Ltd **A** 27
Chat **I** 230
Cheerleader Productions **L** 343
Cheltenham Festival **X** 404
Cheltenham Prize **T** 546
Cherrytree Press Children's Books **A** 28
Cherub Company London Ltd **M** 379
Cheshire Life **I** 231
Chess **I** 231
Chess Valley Films and Video Ltd **L** 343
Chester Chronicle **H** 200
Chester (Linda) Literary Agency **O** 458
Chester Literature Festival **X** 404
Chester Poets **C** 124
Chesterton Society, The **Z** 508
Cheverell Press, The **W** 135
CHG Communications **L** 343
Chicago Tribune Press **P** 482
Chicago (University of) Press **N** 440
Chichester Festival Theatre **M** 380
Chilcote (Judith) Agency **F** 161
Child Education **I** 231
Children's Book Award **T** 547
Children's Book Circle Eleanor Farjeon Award **T** 547
Children's Book Foundation **Q** 494
Children's Book Foundation Reference Library **U** 581
Children's Channel, The **J** 313
Children's Library, The **V** 603
Child's Play (International) Ltd **A** 28
Childsplay Productions Ltd **L** 343
Chiltern Radio **K** 324
Chiltern Writers' Group **AB** 528
Chivers Press (Publishers) **A** 28
Choice **I** 231
Cholmondeley Awards **S** 536
Christel Clear Marine Photography **V** 603

Chris (Teresa) Literary Agency **F** 162
Christian Aid Photo Library **V** 603
Christian Focus Publications **A** 28
Christian Herald **I** 231
Chronicle and Echo **H** 207
Chronicle Books **N** 440
Chrysalis Books **B** 120
Chrysalis Television Productions Ltd **L** 344
Churchill Livingstone **A** 28
Churchill Theatre **M** 380
Church Music Quarterly **I** 232
Church of England Newspaper **I** 231
Church Times **I** 232
C. Hurst & Co. **A** 53
Cicerone Press **A** 28
Cinecosse Video **L** 344
Cinema Museum, The **V** 603
Cinexsa Film Productions Limited **L** 344
Circa Photo Library **V** 604
Circle of Wine Writers **Q** 494
Cirrus Films **L** 344
Citizens Theatre **M** 380
Citizen, The (Gloucester) **H** 202
Città Nuova Editrice **AA** 423
City Business Library **U** 582
City Limits **I** 232
City of London Libraries **U** 582
Civilizacao (Americo Fraga Lamares & Cia Lda) **AA** 429
Clanjam Frie **C** 124
Clare (John) Books **A** 28
Clare (John) Society, The **Z** 508
Clarendon Press **A** 29
Claridge Press **A** 29
Clarion Books **N** 441
Clarke (Arthur C.) Award for Science Fiction **T** 547
Clarke (Serafina) **F** 162
Clark (Philip) Ltd **E** 151
Clark Production **L** 344
Clark (Robin) **A** 29
Clarkson N. Potter **N** 441
Clark (T. & T.) **A** 29
Clarson-Leach (Robert) **F** 162
Classical Guitar **I** 232
Classical Music **I** 232
Classic FM **K** 317
Classic Words & Image **A** 29
Clausen (Connie) Associates **O** 458
Cleare (John)/Mountain Camera **V** 604
Clear Picture Company, The **L** 344
Cleaver (Diane), Inc. **O** 458
Clematis Press Ltd **A** 29

Clements (Alan) Productions **M** 380

CLE: The Irish Book Publishers' Association **Q** 494

CLEUP (Cooperative Libraria Editrice dell'Università di Padova) **AA** 423

Cleveland Arts **R** 514

Cleveland Festival **X** 404

Cleveland Festival Competitions **T** 547

Cleveland Productions **L** 344

Cley Little Festival of Poetry **X** 405

Climber and Hill Walker **I** 232

Clio Press Ltd **A** 29

Clowes (Jonathan) Ltd **F** 162

Club International **I** 232

CN.FM 103 **K** 325

CNP Publications/Lyfrow Trelyspen **W** 136

Cobbett (William) Society **Z** 509

Coburn (Ron) International Productions **M** 380

Cobweb **B** 124

Cochrane (Elspeth) Agency **F** 162

Codron (Michael) Ltd **M** 380

Cohen (David) British Literature Prize **T** 547

Cohen (Hy) Literary Agency Ltd **O** 458

Cohen (Ruth), Inc. **O** 458

Coin Monthly **I** 233

Coin News **I** 233

Colasanti (Stephanie) **V** 604

Colchester–Essex Festival **X** 405

Coleman (Bruce) Wildlife & Travel Photo Library **V** 604

Coleman (Frank) Publishing **A** 29

Coles (Dianne) Agency **F** 162

Colin (Rosica) Ltd **F** 162

Coliseum Oldham, The **M** 380

Collections **V** 604

Collier Books **N** 441

Collin (Frances) Literary Agency **O** 459

Collins **A** 29

Collins Biennial Religious Book Award **T** 547

Collins & Brown **A** 29

Colorsport **V** 604

Columbia University Press **A** 30

Comedy Writers' Association of Great Britain **Q** 494

Commerce Magazine **I** 233

Commercial Facilities Ltd (Colstar International) **L** 344

Commission of the European Communities Information Office **U** 582

Commonwealth Resource Centre **U** 582

Commonwealth Secretariat Library **U** 582

Commonwealth Writers Prize **T** 548

Commonword Ltd **A** 30

Communicado Theatre Company **M** 380

Company **I** 233

Compass Film Productions Ltd **L** 344

Compix **V** 604

Component Television Productions Ltd **L** 345

Computer Books **N** 441

Computer Weekly **I** 233

Computing **I** 233

Comstock Photofile Ltd **V** 604

Comstock-Smith Literary Agency **F** 163

Conan Doyle (Arthur) Society, The **Z** 509

Condé Nast Books **A** 30

Condor **A** 30

Connor Literary Agency **O** 459

Conrad (Joseph) Society **Z** 509

Conran Octopus **A** 30

Constable & Co. Ltd **A** 30

Constable Trophy, The **T** 548

Consumers' Association **A** 30

Contact Theatre Company **M** 381

Contact Young Playwrights' Festival **X** 405

Contemporary Books **N** 441

Contemporary Review **I** 233

Convergent Communications Ltd **L** 345

Conway-Gordon (Jane) **F** 163

Conway Picture Library **V** 604

Conway (Vernon) Ltd **F** 163

Cookson (Catherine) Fiction Prize **T** 548

Cook (Thomas) Travel Book Awards **T** 548

Cool FM **K** 325

Cooper (Duff) Prize, The **T** 548

Cooper (Giles) Awards, The **T** 548

Cooper (Leo) **A** 31

Cordaiy (Sylvia) Photo Library **V** 604

Core **C** 124

Corgi **A** 31

Cornelsen und Oxford University Press GmbH **AA** 419

Cornerhouse Publications **A** 31

Cornish Life **I** 234

Cornwall Books **A** 31

Coronet Books **A** 31

Corporate Clothing & Textile Ca **I** 234

Corporate Communication Consultants Ltd **L** 345

Cosmopolitan **I** 234

Cotswold Life **I** 234

Council for British Archaeology 31

Council of Regional Arts Associations **R** 514

Country Homes and Interiors **I** 234

Country Life **I** 234

Country Life Library **V** 605

Country Living **I** 235

Countryman, The **I** 235

Country Quest **I** 235

Country-Side **I** 235

Countryside Books **A** 31

Country Sports **I** 235

County Sound Radio **K** 325

County Visuals **V** 605

Courier and Advertiser, The (Dundee) **H** 201

Coventry Central Library **U** 582

Coventry Evening Telegraph **H** 200

Coventry Festival **X** 405

Coventry Writers' Association **Q** 495

Crabbe Memorial Poetry Competition **T** 549

Crabtree Publishing **A** 31

Craven (Philip) Worldwide Phot Library **V** 605

Crawshay (Rose Mary) Prize **T** 549

Creasey (John) Memorial Awar **T** 549

Creative Camera **I** 235

Creative Channel Ltd **L** 345

Creative Comics **E** 151

Creative Concepts Literary Agency **O** 459

Creative Film Makers Ltd **L** 345

Creative Review **I** 235

Creative Television Workshops Ltd **L** 345

Creative Tone Ltd **F** 163

Crescendo & Jazz Music **I** 235

Crescent Moon Publishing **W** 13

Cresrelles Publishing Co. **A** 31

Crestwood House **N** 441

Crew Green Associates Ltd **L** 34

Crew (Rupert) Ltd **F** 163

Cricketer International, The **I** 23

Cricket Ltd **L** 345

Crime Club **A** 32

Crime Line **N** 441

Crime Writers' Association Awards **T** 549
Crime Writers' Association (CWA) **Q** 495
Critics' Circle, The **Q** 495
Crocus **A** 32
Cromdale Films Ltd **L** 346
Crown Business Communications Ltd **L** 346
Crown Publishing Group **N** 441
Crowood Press Ltd, The **A** 32
Crucible **A** 32
Crucible Theatre **M** 381
Cruickshank Cazenove Ltd **F** 163
Crystalvision Ltd **L** 346
CSS Publishing Co. **N** 441
CTR Productions **L** 346
Cumbernauld Theatre Company **M** 381
Cumbria **I** 236
Cunningham (Sue) **V** 605
Curlew Press **B** 120
Currey (James) Publishers **A** 32
Curtis Brown Group Ltd **F** 163
Curtis Brown Ltd **O** 459
Curtis Garratt Ltd **E** 151
Curtis (Richard) Associates, Inc. **O** 459
Curzon Press Ltd **A** 32
C. W. Daniel Co. Ltd, The **A** 32
Cwmni'r Castell Cyf **L** 346
Cwmni Theatr Gwynedd **M** 381
Cycling Weekly **I** 236
Cyphers **B** 124
Daily Express **G** 187
Daily Mail **G** 187
Daily Mirror **G** 187
Daily Post (Liverpool) **H** 205
Daily Record (Glasgow) **H** 209
Daily Sport (Manchester) **G** 187
Daily Star **G** 188
Daily Telegraph/British Association Young Science Writer Awards **T** 549
Daily Telegraph Cheltenham Festival of Literature **X** 405
Daily Telegraph, The **G** 188
Daish (Judy) Associates Ltd **F** 164
Dalesman Publishing Co. Ltd **A** 32
Dalesman, The **I** 236
Dalton (Terence) Ltd **A** 32
Damm (N W) & Son A/S **AA** 428
Dance & Dancers **I** 236
Dance Theatre Journal **I** 236
Dancing Times, The **I** 236
Dane Productions **L** 346
Dangaroo Books **B** 120
Daniel (C. W.) Co. Ltd, The **A** 32
Daniels Publishing **W** 136
Dareks Production House **L** 346

Darf Publishers Ltd **A** 33
Daring Deeds Ltd **L** 346
Dark Diamonds Publications **W** 136
Dartington Literary Festival (Ways with Words) **X** 405
Dartmouth Publishing Co. **A** 33
Darton, Longman & Todd **A** 33
Darts World **I** 237
Dateline Magazine **I** 237
Dateline Productions Ltd **L** 346
Daves (Joan) Agency **O** 459
David & Charles Publishers **A** 33
David Hall's Coarse Fishing Magazine **I** 237
David Hall's Match Fishing Magazine **I** 237
Davidsfonds VZW **AA** 411
Davidson (Caroline) and Robert Ducas Literary Agency **F** 164
Davidson (Merric) Literary Agency **F** 164
Davie (Elaine) Literary Agency **O** 459
Davies (Christopher) Publishers Ltd **A** 33
Davies (Rhys) Award **T** 549
Davis (James) Travel Photography **V** 605
Davis-Poynter (Reg) **F** 164
DAW Books, Inc. **N** 441
Daybreak **A** 34
Day by Day **I** 237
Dazeley (Peter) Photography **V** 605
DBA Television **L** 346
DBI Communication **L** 347
De Agostini Ragazzi SpA **AA** 423
Debate SA **AA** 430
Debrett's Peerage Ltd **A** 34
Decanter **I** 237
Découverte, La **AA** 416
Dedalus Ltd **A** 34
Deering Literary Agency **O** 460
Deeson Editorial Services **Y** 532
Delacorte Press **A** 34
Delagrave Sàrl (Librairie) **AA** 416
Dell Books **N** 441
Del Rey Books **N** 441
Delta (Editions) SA **AA** 411
Denniston & Lownie **F** 164
Denoël (Editions) Sàrl **AA** 416
Dent (J. M.) **A** 34
Deo Gloria Award **T** 549
Deptford Beach Productions **L** 347
Derby Central Library **U** 582
Derby Evening Telegraph **H** 200
Derby Playhouse **M** 381

Derbyshire Life and Countryside **I** 238
Descent **I** 238
Design **I** 238
Design Council Picture Library **V** 605
Designers' Journal **I** 238
DESIGNING **I** 238
Destino SL **AA** 430
Det Norske Samlaget **AA** 428
Deutsch (André) Ltd **A** 34
Deutscher (Isaac & Tamara) Memorial Prize **T** 549
Deutsch (Verlag Harri) **AA** 419
Devine (George) Award **T** 550
Devlin (Denis) Award **T** 550
DevonAir Radio/South West One **K** 325
Devon & Exeter Institution Library **U** 582
Devon Life **I** 238
De Wolfe (Felix) **F** 164
Diadem **A** 34
Diagram Visual Information **E** 151
Dial Books for Young Readers **N** 441
Diamant (Anita) Literary Agency **O** 460
Diamond Press **W** 136
Dibgate Productions Ltd **L** 347
Dickins (Douglas) Photo Library **V** 605
Didactica Editora **AA** 429
Diesterweg (Verlag Moritz) **AA** 419
D I F E L **AA** 429
Différence, La **AA** 416
Dijkstra (Sandra) Literary Agency **O** 460
Dimensions **I** 238
Dimensions for Living **N** 442
Dinosaur **A** 34
Diogenes Verlag AG **AA** 434
Director **I** 239
Directors Video Company **L** 347
Directory of Writers' Circles **AB** 528
Directory Publishers Association **Q** 495
Dirt Bike Rider (DBR) **I** 239
Disability Now **I** 239
Disabled Driver **I** 239
Discovery Channel, The **J** 313
Distaff **C** 124
Diverse Productions Ltd **L** 347
Dixon (C M) **V** 605
Doctor's Dilemma **C** 125
Dog and Bone Publishers **B** 120
Dog World **I** 239

Dollar of Soul/Chicken Sigh Press **B** 120
Dolphin Book Co. Ltd **A** 35
Dolphin Books **N** 442
Domain Books **N** 442
Dominic Photography **V** 605
Dom Quixote (Publicacoes) Lda **AA** 429
Donald (John) Publishers Ltd **A** 35
Doncaster Literature Festival **X** 405
Doncaster Star, The **H** 200
Don Quijote (Editorial) **AA** 430
Dorchester Publishing Co., Inc. **N** 442
Dorian Literary Agency **F** 164
Dorling Kindersley Ltd **A** 35
Dorset Evening Echo **H** 212
Dorset Life **I** 239
Doubleday **A** 35
Doubleday **N** 442
Dover, The Festival of **X** 406
Downlander Publishing **B** 000
Downtown Radio/Cool FM **K** 325
Doyle (Colleen) **F** 165
D. P. Publications Ltd **A** 35
Dragonby Press, The **W** 136
Dragon Communications **L** 347
Dragonfly Press **W** 136
Dragon's World **A** 35
Drake A-V Video Ltd **L** 347
Drake Educational Associates **A** 35
Dramatis Personae Ltd **M** 381
Drew (Richard) Publishing **A** 35
Drexl (Anne) **F** 165
Dreyers Forlag A/S **AA** 428
Dreyfus (Pierre) Award **T** 550
Droemersche Verlagsanstalt Th Knaur Nachf **AA** 419
Droz (Librairie) SA **AA** 434
D T V Deutscher Taschenbuch Verlag GmbH & Co KG **AA** 419
Duckworth (Gerald) & Co. **A** 36
Dukes, The **M** 381
DuMont Buchverlag GmbH & Co KG **AA** 419
Dunitz (Martin) Ltd **A** 36
Dunkley (Robert) Associates Ltd **L** 347
Dunrod Press **A** 36
Dupree/Miller & Associates, Inc., Literary Agency **O** 460
Durham Literary Festival **X** 406
Durham Theatre Company **M** 382
Durrant's Press Cuttings **YY** 534
Duty Free Magazine **I** 240
Dykeman Associates, Inc. **O** 460
Eady (Toby) Associates Ltd **F** 165

Eager (Patrick) Photography **V** 606
Eagle **A** 36
Eagle and Eagle Ltd **L** 347
Early Music **I** 240
Early Times **I** 240
Earthscan Publications Ltd **A** 36
Earthworm Award **T** 550
East Anglian Daily Times **H** 203
Eastern Angles Theatre Company **M** 382
Eastern Arts Board **R** 514
Eastern Daily Press **H** 201
Eastern Daily Press **H** 207
East Midlands Arts **R** 514
East-West Publications **A** 36
E&B Productions Ltd **M** 382
Ebury Press **A** 36
Echo Room Press **B** 120
Echo Room, The **C** 125
E C I G **AA** 423
Ecologist, The **I** 240
Economist Books **A** 36
Economist/Richard Casement Internship, The **S** 536
Economist, The **I** 240
Econ-Verlag GmbH **AA** 419
Ecoscene **V** 606
Ecuatorial **B** 125
Eddison Sadd Editions **E** 151
Eden Centre Books **B** 120
E D H A S A **AA** 430
Edifice **V** 606
Edinburgh Bibliographical Society **Q** 495
Edinburgh Book Festival **X** 406
Edinburgh Film & Video Productions **L** 348
Edinburgh Photographic Library **V** 606
Edinburgh Review **I** 240
Edinburgh University **AB** 523
Edinburgh University Press **A** 37
Edric Audio Visual Ltd **L** 348
Education **I** 240
Educational Design Services, Inc. **O** 460
Educational Television Association **Q** 495
Education Now Publishing Cooperative Ltd **W** 137
Education & Training **I** 241
Eerdmans (William B.) Publishing Co. **N** 442
Egotist Press **W** 137
Eisenberg (Vicki) Literary Agency **O** 461
Electrical Times **I** 241
Electric Picture Machine **L** 348
Elek (Peter) Associates **O** 461

Elgar (Edward) Publishing Ltd **A** 37
Eliot (George) Fellowship **Z** 509
Elite Words & Image **A** 37
Ellenbank Press **W** 137
Ellenberg (Ethan), Literary Agency, The **O** 461
Ellen Lively Steele & Associates 461
Elle **I** 241
Elliot Right Way Books **A** 37
Ellis (Aidan) Publishing **A** 37
Elmo (Ann) Agency, Inc. **O** 461
Elm Publications **A** 37
Elsevier **AA** 426
Elsevier Librico NV **AA** 411
Elsevier Science Publishers **A** 38
Elstree (Production) Co. **L** 348
Elvendon Press **A** 38
Emap Business Publishing **A** 38
Embroidery **I** 241
Empeño (Editoria) **AA** 431
Empics Ltd **V** 606
Empire **I** 241
Encore Award, The **T** 550
Engineering **I** 242
Engineer, The **I** 241
English Association, The **Q** 496
English Folk Dance and Song Society Library **U** 583
English Heritage Magazine **I** 242
English Heritage Photographic Library **V** 606
English Stage Company Ltd **M** 3
Enigma Productions Ltd **L** 348
Enitharmon Press **A** 38
Enlightenment AV & Video **L** 34
Ennsthaler (Wilhelm) **AA** 410
Ensign Publications **A** 38
Envoi **B** 120
Envoi Poetry Competition **T** 550
Envoi Poets **C** 125
EPA (European Pressphoto Agency) **V** 606
Epic Interactive Media Company **L** 348
Epworth Press **A** 38
Equal Opportunities Commission Library **U** 583
Equofinality **B** 120
Erskine Press/Bluntisham Books 39
Escape: The Career Change Magazine **I** 242
ES **I** 242
Espresso TV **L** 348
Esquire **I** 242
Essentials **I** 242
Essex Countryside **I** 243
Essex Life **I** 243

Essex Radio/Breeze AM **K** 325
Estall (Robert) Photographs **V** 606
E. T. Archive **V** 606
Ettinger Brothers Productions **L** 349
Eumo Editorial **AA** 431
E U N S A (Ediciones Universidad de Navarra SA) **AA** 431
Euromoney **I** 243
Euromonitor **A** 39
Europa-America (Publicaoes) Lda **AA** 429
Europa Publications Ltd **A** 39
Europa Verlag Gesellschaft mbH **AA** 410
European Association for the Promotion of Poetry **D29**
European Cultural Foundation **S** 536
European Literary and Translation Prizes **T** 550
European Medical Journal **I** 243
European Prize for the Translation of Poetry **T** 551
European Television Networks **J** 313
European, The **G** 188
Europe 1992 **A** 40
Euston Films **L** 349
Evans & Associates **O** 461
Evans Brothers Ltd **A** 39
Evans (Faith) Associates **F** 165
Evans (Greg) International Photo Library **V** 606
Evans (Mary) Picture Library **V** 606
Evans (M.) & Co., Inc. **N** 442
Evening Advertiser **H** 211
Evening Argus (Brighton) **H** 198
Evening Chronicle (Bath) **H** 196
Evening Chronicle (Newcastle upon Tyne) **H** 206
Evening Chronicle (Oldham) **H** 207
Evening Courier (Halifax) **H** 202
Evening Echo (Basildon) **H** 196
Evening Echo (Bournemouth) **H** 198
Evening Express **H** 195
Evening Gazette (Blackpool) **H** 197
Evening Gazette (Colchester) **H** 200
Evening Gazette (Middlesbrough) **H** 206
Evening Herald (Plymouth) **H** 208
Evening Leader (Mold) **H** 206
Evening News (Edinburgh) **H** 201
Evening News (Norwich) **H** 207

Evening News & Star **H** 199
Evening News (Worcester) **H** 212
Evening Post (Bristol) **H** 198
Evening Post Nottingham **H** 207
Evening Post (Reading) **H** 209
Evening Sentinel **H** 210
Evening Standard **H** 205
Evening Star (Ipswich) **H** 203
Evening Telegraph (Kettering) **H** 204
Evening Telegraph (Peterborough) **H** 208
Evening Telegraph & Post **H** 201
Evening Times (Glasgow) **H** 201
Evergreen **I** 243
Everyman **A** 40
Everyman's Library **A** 40
Everywoman **I** 243
Executive Strategy **I** 243
Executive Travel **I** 243
Exeter & Devon Arts Centre **AB** 528
Exeter Festival **X** 406
Exeter Life **I** 243
Exeter (University of) Press **A** 40
Exile **B** 125
Exley Publications Ltd **A** 40
Ex Libris Forlag A/S **AA** 428
Expatriate, The **I** 243
Export Sales and Marketing **I** 244
Express & Echo (Exeter) **H** 201
Expression **I** 244
Express Newspapers Picture Library **V** 607
Express & Star **H** 212
Extel Financial **H** 304
Eyeline Photography **V** 607
Eye Ubiquitous **V** 607
Eyewitness Ltd **L** 349
Eyre & Spottiswoode **A** 40
E – Elle (Edizioni) SRL **AA** 423
Fabbri (Gruppo Editoriale) SpA **AA** 423
Faber & Faber Ltd **A** 40
Faber (Geoffrey) Memorial Prize **T** 551
Face, The **I** 244
Facet NV **AA** 411
Facts On File **A** 40
Facts on File, Inc. **N** 442
Fairclough (Chris) Colour Library **V** 607
Fairway Press **N** 443
Falcon **N** 443
Falken-Verlag GmbH **AA** 419
Falklands Pictorial **V** 607
Falmer Press **A** 41
Family Circle **I** 244
Family Tree Magazine **I** 244
Fanfare **N** 443

Farmer (Prudence) Award **T** 551
Farmers Publishing Group Picture Library **V** 607
Farmers Weekly **I** 245
Farming Information Centre **U** 583
Farming News **I** 245
Farming Press Books **A** 41
FarmWatch **I** 245
Farnham Film Company Ltd **L** 349
Farnham Repertory Company Ltd **M** 382
Farquharson (John) **F** 165
Farquharson (John) Ltd **O** 461
Farrar, Straus & Giroux, Inc. **N** 443
Fast Car **I** 245
Fast Forward Productions **L** 349
Fast Lane **I** 245
Fawcett Juniper **N** 443
Fawcett Library **U** 583
Fawcett Society Book Prize **T** 551
Fayard (Librarie Arthème) **AA** 416
Feather Books **W** 137
Federation of Entertainment Unions **Q** 496
Federation of Worker Writers and Community Publishers **Q** 496
Fehmers (Frank) Productions **AA** 426
Feiler (Florence) Literary Agency **O** 462
Felix (Paul) **V** 607
Fen Farm **AB** 527
Fern House Publications **Y** 532
Fernhurst Books **A** 41
Ferry Press **B** 120
Ferry Publications **W** 137
Fidler (Kathleen) Award **T** 551
Field Day Theatre Company **M** 382
Fielding Travel Books **N** 443
Fields (Marje)/Rita Scott **O** 462
Field, The **I** 245
Fifty Plus **I** 245
Figs **B** 125
Filmfair Ltd **L** 349
FilmIt Productions Ltd **L** 349
Film Link Literary Agency **F** 165
Film Monthly **I** 246
Filmnova **L** 349
Film Review **I** 246
Filmworks **L** 349
Financial Times **G** 188
Financial Times Picture Collection **V** 607
First Choice **I** 246
First Choice **L** 350
First Creative Group Ltd **L** 350
First Down **I** 246

First Freedom Productions **L** 350
First House Productions Ltd **L** 350
First Offense **B** 125
First Time **C** 125
Fischer (S) Verlag GmbH **AA** 419
Fishbein (Frieda) Ltd **O** 462
Fitch (Laurence) Ltd **F** 165
Fitting Images Ltd **L** 350
Fitzgerald Publishing **W** 137
Five Lamps Group **L** 350
Five Leaves Left **C** 125
Flambard Press **B** 120
Flamingo **A** 41
Flamingo Pictures **L** 350
Flammarion et Cie **AA** 416
Flannery, White & Stone **O** 462
Flashback Television Ltd **L** 350
Fletcher Award, Sir Banister **T** 551
Flight International **I** 246
Flora **I** 246
Florio (John) Prize **T** 551
Floris Books **A** 41
Flying Pig Productions Ltd **L** 350
Flying Tiger Film and TV
   Productions **L** 350
FlyPast **I** 247
FM Television Ltd **L** 351
Fodor **A** 41
Fodor's Travel Publications **N** 443
Folk Roots **I** 247
Fontana **A** 41
Foolscap **B** 125
Foord (Ron & Christine) Colour
   Picture Library **V** 608
Football Monthly **I** 247
Footmark Publications **W** 138
Footprints Colour Picture Library
   V 608
Forbes Magazine **P** 482
Ford (Vanessa) Productions Ltd
   M 382
Foreign and Commonwealth
   Office Library **U** 583
Foreign Press Association in
   London **Q** 496
Forest Books **A** 41
Forest Books **B** 120
Forman (Werner) Archive **V** 608
Format Partners Photo Library **V**
   608
Formula Communications **L** 351
Forstater (Mark) Productions Ltd
   L 351
Forster (E. M.) Award **S** 536
Forsythe (Robert) Picture Library
   V 608
Fortean Picture Library **V** 608
*Fortean Times: The Journal of
   Strange Phenomena* **I** 247

Forth Naturalist & Historian **W**
   138
ForthWrite Literary Agency **O** 462
Fortress Books **W** 138
Fortune Magazine **P** 482
Forum (Bokforlaget) AB **AA** 433
Forum (Forlaget) A/S **AA** 412
Foster (Jill) Ltd **F** 165
FotoFlite **V** 608
Fotomas Index, The **V** 608
Foulsham (W.) & Co. **A** 42
*Foundation: The Review of
   Science Fiction* **I** 247
Fount **A** 42
Fountain Press Ltd **A** 42
Fourth Estate Ltd **A** 42
Fourth Wall Productions **L** 351
Four Winds Press **N** 443
Foxbury Press **A** 42
Fox (Clare) Associates **M** 382
Fox FM **K** 325
Fox & Howard Literary Agency **F**
   166
Fox Photos Ltd **V** 608
Fox Press **W** 138
Fox (Robert) Ltd **M** 382
Fox Television **L** 351
Fragmente **B** 125
Francisci (Aldo) Editore **AA** 423
Frankel (Anne) Prize **T** 552
Franklin Watts **A** 42
Frederick Warne **A** 95
Free Association Books **A** 42
Freedman (Robert A.) Dramatic
   Agency, Inc. **O** 462
Freelance Market News **I** 247
Freelance, The **I** 247
Freelance Writing & Photography
   I 247
Freeman (W. H.) & Co. Ltd **A** 42
Freeway Films **L** 351
Fremad (Forlaget) A/S **AA** 412
French Institute Library **U** 583
French's **F** 166
French (Samuel), Inc. **N** 443
French (Samuel) Ltd **A** 43
Frith (Francis) Collection **V** 608
Frogmore Papers, The **B** 125
Frontier Publishing **W** 138
Frontroom Films Ltd **L** 351
FSRs Forlag **AA** 413
Fuhrman (Candice) Literary
   Agency **O** 462
Fulbright-Chandler Arts
   Fellowship Award **S** 537
Fulton (David) (Publishers) **A** 43
Fundamentos (Editorial) **AA** 431
Funding for Script Development **S**
   537
Funfax/Junior Funfax **A** 43

Furness (Mark) Ltd **M** 383
Futerman (Vernon) Associates
   166
Gabriel (Jüri) **F** 166
Gaelic Books Council **Q** 496
Gaia Books Ltd **A** 43
Gairfish **B** 125
Gairm Publications **A** 43
Galactic Central Publications **W**
   138
Galaxy Picture Library **V** 609
Galdragon Press **B** 120
Gallery **C** 120
Gallery Children's Books **A** 43
Gallery Press **B** 120
Gall (Ian) Television **L** 351
Gallimard (Editions) **AA** 416
Gamble (Ken) Productions **L** 3 [
Garden Answers **I** 248
Gardenhouse Editions Ltd **E** 15 [
Garden News **I** 248
Garden Picture Library, The **V** [
Gardiner (Julia) Books **A** 43
Gardner (Kerry) Management **F**
   166
Gardner Press, Inc. **N** 443
Garland (Leslie) Picture Library
   609
Garnet Miller (J.) Ltd **A** 43
Garon-Brooke (Jay) Associates,
   Inc. **O** 463
Gartenberg (Max), Literary Age [
   O 463
Garzanti Editore **AA** 423
Gaskell Society, The **Z** 509
Gate Theatre Company Ltd **M** 3 [
Gateway Audio Visual and Vide [
   L 351
Gateway Books **A** 45
Gatty Society, The **Z** 509
Gau (John) Productions **L** 352
Gauthier-Languereau (Les
   Editions) SA **AA** 416
Gavarnie Publications **B** 121
Gay Authors Workshop **Q** 496
Gay Authors Workshop **AB** 529 [
Gay Men's Press (GMP Publishe [
   Ltd), The **A** 44
Gay (Noel) Television **L** 352
Gay Sweatshop **M** 383
Gay Times **I** 248
Gazette (South Shields) **H** 210
GCP **L** 352
G.E.C. Gad Publishers **AA** 413
Gedisa (Editorial) SA **AA** 431
Gelles-Cole Literary Enterprises [
   463
GEM-AM **K** 325
Gemmell (David) Cup **T** 552
Genera Editions **B** 121

General Practitioner Writers Association **Q** 496
Genesis Space Photo Library **V** 609
Geographia **A** 44
Geological Society Publishing House **W** 138
Geonex UK Ltd **V** 609
GeoScience Features **V** 609
Gestalt Institute of Cleveland Press **N** 443
Ghost Story Society, The **Z** 509
Gibbons Stamp Monthly **I** 248
Gibb Rose Organisation Ltd **L** 352
Gibson (Robert) & Sons **A** 44
Gild of St George **B** 121
Gili (Gustavo) SA **AA** 431
Gillis (Pamela) Management **F** 166
Gilpin (Adrian) Television **L** 352
Ginn **A** 44
Girl About Town **I** 248
Giroscope **I** 248
Giunti Publishing Group **AA** 423
Gjellerup & Gad Publishers Ltd **AA** 413
Gladden Unlimited **O** 463
Glamour International **V** 609
Glasgow (Mary) Publications **A** 44
Glasgow Mayfest **X** 406
Glass (Eric) Ltd **F** 166
Glaxo Prize for Medical Writing & Illustration **T** 552
Glaxo Science Writers' Fellowships **S** 537
Glenat (Editions J.) SA **AA** 416
Glenfiddich Awards **T** 552
Global Tapestry Journal **C** 125
Globe Players Theatre Company **M** 383
Glosa **W** 138
Gloucestershire Echo **H** 199
Gloucestershire Everyman Theatre Company Ltd **M** 383
Glynne (Derek) (London) Pty Ltd **M** 383
GMTV **J** 309
Godfrey Cave Holdings Ltd **A** 44
Goldcrest Films and Television Ltd **L** 352
Gold Dagger Award for Non-Fiction **T** 552
Golden Cockerel Press Ltd **A** 44
Gold, Silver & Diamond Dagger Awards for Fiction **T** 552
Golf Monthly **I** 249
Golf Weekly **I** 249
Golf World **I** 249
Gollancz (Victor) Ltd **A** 45
Gomer Press **A** 45

Gomer Press **B** 121
Good Film Company, The **L** 352
Good Food Retailing **I** 249
Good Holiday Magazine **I** 249
Good Housekeeping **I** 249
Good Ski Guide **I** 249
Good Stories **I** 250
Gordon & Breach Science Publishers **A** 45
Gothic Press **W** 139
Gothic Society, The **Z** 510
Gower Publishing Ltd **A** 45
Gower Training **L** 352
GPA Book Award **T** 553
GPC Books **A** 46
GQ **I** 250
Grace (Martin and Dorothy) **V** 609
Gradiva – Publicacoes Lda **AA** 429
Graeae Theatre Company **M** 383
Grafis Edizioni **AA** 423
Grafisk Forlag A/S **AA** 413
Grafton Books Ltd **A** 46
Graham-Cameron Publishing **A** 46
Graham (Edgar) Book Prize **T** 553
Graham & Trotman Ltd **A** 45
Gramophone **I** 250
Grampian Television **J** 310
Granada Television **J** 310
Granta **I** 250
Granta Publications **A** 46
Grant Books **W** 139
Grant (Ronald) Archive **V** 609
Granville Publishing **A** 46
Grapevine TV **L** 353
Grasset et Farquelle (Société des Editions) **AA** 416
Grasshopper Productions Ltd **L** 353
Great Eastern Stage **M** 384
Greater London History Library **U** 584
Greater London Photograph Library **V** 609
Greater London Radio **K** 324
Great North Radio (GNR) **K** 326
Great Outdoors, The **I** 250
Great Yorkshire Radio **K** 326
Green Books **A** 46
Green Book, The **C** 125
Greenburger (Sanford J.) Associates **O** 463
Green (Christine) (Authors' Agent) Ltd **F** 167
Greene (Elaine) Ltd **F** 167
Greenhill Books/Lionel Leventhal Ltd **A** 46
Greenhill (Sally and Richard) **V** 610

Green Magazine **I** 250
Greenock Telegraph **H** 202
Greenpark Productions Ltd **L** 353
Greenpeace Books **E** 152
Greenpeace Communications Ltd **V** 610
Greenpoint Films **L** 353
Green Print **A** 46
Greenscene **I** 251
Greenwich Festival **X** 406
Greenwich Theatre Ltd **M** 384
Greenwillow Books **N** 443
Gregg (Colin) Films Ltd **L** 353
Gregory (Eric) Trust Fund **S** 537
Gregory & Radice Authors' Agents* **F** 167
Gremese Editore SRL **AA** 423
Gresham Books **A** 46
Grevatt & Grevatt **A** 46
Greville Press **B** 121
Greylag Press **B** 121
Grey Seal Books **A** 47
Gridiron **I** 251
Griffin Productions **L** 353
Griggs (Susan) Agency Ltd **V** 610
Grijalbo SA **AA** 431
Grimsby Evening Telegraph **H** 202
Grisewood & Dempsey **A** 47
Grisewood & Dempsey Ltd **E** 152
Grossman (David) Literary Agency Ltd **F** 167
Grosvenor Books **A** 47
Grotius Publications **A** 47
Grub Street **A** 47
Grub Street **E** 152
Gründ (Librairie) **AA** 416
Grundy (Reg) Productions (GB) Ltd **L** 353
Grune & Stratton **A** 47
Gruyter (Walter de) & Co **AA** 419
Gryphon Press **B** 121
G. T. Foulis & Co Ltd **A** 42
Guardian Books **A** 47
Guardian Children's Fiction Award, The **T** 553
Guardian Fiction Prize, The **T** 553
Guardian Research Fellowship, The **S** 537
Guardian, The **G** 189
Guernsey Evening Press & Star **H** 202
Guida Editori SpA **AA** 423
Guide Patrol **I** 251
Guiding **I** 251
Guildford Institute of University of Surrey Library **U** 584
Guildhall Library **U** 584
Guild of Agricultural Journalists **Q** 496

Guild of British Newspaper Editors Q 497
Guild of Motoring Writers Q 497
Guinness Peat Aviation Literary Award T 553
Guinness Publishing Ltd A 47
Gunsmoke Westerns A 48
Gusay (Charlotte) Literary Agency, The O 463
Guy (V. K.) Ltd V 610
GWR FM/Brunel Classic Gold K 326
Gyldendal Norsk Forlag AA 428
Gyldendalske Boghandel, Nordisk Forlag A/S AA 413
Haase (P.) & Söns Forlag A/S AA 413
Hachette AA 416
Haddock (Peter) Ltd A 48
Haggard (Rider) Appreciation Society Z 510
Haiku Quarterly C 125
Hairflair I 251
Hair I 251
Halban (Peter) Publishers A 48
Hale (Robert) Ltd A 48
Halifax Building Society Magazine I 252
Hallam FM K 326
Hall (David) Productions L 353
Halliday (Sonia) Photographs V 610
Hall (June) Literary Agency F 167
Hallwag Verlag AG AA 434
Hambledon Press, The A 48
Hamilton House Mailings E 152
Hamish Hamilton Ltd A 48
Hamlyn A 48
Hammer Film Productions L 353
Hampshire, The County Magazine I 252
Hampstead Theatre M 384
Hanbury (Maggie) F 167
Hancock (Roger) Ltd F 167
Handgunner I 252
HandMade Films L 353
Hangman Books B 121
Hanley (Tom) V 610
Hanser (Carl) Verlag AA 420
Haraco Ltd L 354
Harcourt Brace Jovanovich A 48
Harcourt Brace Jovanovich N 443
Hardie (Xandra) Literary Agency F 167
Harding (Robert) Picture Library V 610
Hard Pressed Poetry B 121
Hardy (Thomas) Society Prize T 553
Hardy (Thomas) Society Z 510

Harley Books A 48
Harmony N 443
Harnett Milan Ltd L 354
HarperCollins Publishers N 443
HarperCollins Publishers Ltd A 49
Harpers & Queen I 252
Harpur Garden Library V 610
Harrap Publishing Group Ltd A 50
Harrogate Theatre Company M 384
Harvard University Press A 50
Harvard University Press N 444
Harvest House Publishers N 444
Harvill A 50
Hastings Arts Pocket Press B 121
Hatfield Polytechnic Library U 584
Hatier (Librarie) SA AA 417
Hat Trick Productions Ltd L 354
Hat C 125
Haufe (Rudolf) Verlag GmbH & Co KG AA 420
Haunted Library W 139
Hawkins (John) & Associates, Inc. O 463
Hawkshead Ltd L 354
Hawthornden Films L 354
Hawthornden Prize, The T 553
Haynes Publishing Group A 50
Hay-on-Wye Festival of Literature X 406
Hazemead Ltd M 384
Hazleton Publishing A 50
Heacock Literary Agency, Inc. O 464
Head (Francis) Bequest S 537
Headland Publications B 121
Headline Book Publishing A 50
Head-On Productions Ltd L 354
Head to Head Communication Ltd L 354
Headway A 51
Health and Efficiency I 252
Health & Fitness I 252
Health Information Library (Westminster) U 585
Health Now I 252
Hearing Eye B 121
Hearst Books N 444
Heartland N 444
Heart of Albion Press W 139
Heath (A. M.) & Co Ltd F 167
Heinemann Fiction Award T 553
Hekla Forlag AA 413
Helicon Publishing A 51
Hello! I 252
Helm (Christopher) Publishers A 51
Hemans (Felicia) Prize for Lyrical Poetry T 554

Hemson (John) L 354
Henderson (Jim) Photographer 610
Henderson Publishing Ltd A 51
Hen House AB 524
Henry (Ian) Publications Ltd A
Henson (Jim) Productions L 35
Henty Society, The Z 510
Herald Express (Torquay) H 21
Herald, The (Glasgow) G 189
Herbert Press, The A 51
Herder (Verlag) GmbH & Co K(AA 420
Here's Health I 253
Hereward FM K 326
Herman (Jeff) Agency, Inc., The O 464
Hermitage Publishing W 139
Herner (Susan) Rights Agency, Inc. O 464
Hern (Nick) Books A 52
Hernovs Forlag AA 413
Hertfordshire Countryside I 253
HERTIS U 585
Heseltine (John) Picture Library 610
Heyne (Wilhelm) Verlag AA 42
Hi-Fi News & Record Review I 253
Higbury College of Technology AB 526
Higham (David) Associates Ltd 168
Higham (David) Prize for Fictio T 554
Highgate Films L 355
Highgate Literary and Scientific Institution Library U 585
Highland Books A 52
High Life I 253
Hill (Frederick) Associates O 4(
Hilltop Press W 139
Hill (William) Sports Book of th Year T 554
HIM I 253
Hindin (Philip) M 384
Hines Communications Ltd L 3
Hiperion (Ediciones) SL AA 43
Hippo Books A 52
Hippocrene Books, Inc. N 444
Hippopotamus Press B 21
Hisarlik Press W 139
Hiss & Boo Company, The M 3
History Today I 253
HMSO Books A 52
Hobbs Golf Collection V 611
Hobsons Publishing A 52
Hodder & Stoughton Ltd A 52
Hodgson (Pamela) Writers' Agency F 168

Hoffman (David) Photo Library **V** 611
Hoffmann und Campe Verlag **AA** 420
Hogarth Press Ltd, The **A** 53
Holborn Library **U** 585
Holford (Michael) **V** 611
Holiday House, Inc. **N** 444
Holiday Which? **I** 254
Holkenfeldts Forlag A/S **AA** 413
Holliday (Dan) Prize **T** 554
Holmes Associates **L** 355
Holmes McDougall **A** 53
Holmes & Moriarty **L** 355
Holmes (Sherlock) Society of London, The **Z** 510
Holtby (Winifred) Memorial Prize **T** 554
Holtkamp and Whitlam Ltd **E** 152
Holt Rinehart & Winston **A** 53
Holt Studios International **V** 611
Holt (Vanessa) Associates **F** 168
Home and Country **I** 254
Homebrew Supplier **I** 254
Homebrew Today **I** 255
Home Economics & Technology **I** 254
Home & Family **I** 254
Home Farm **I** 254
Homes and Gardens **I** 255
Home Video Channel **J** 314
Honest Ulsterman, The **C** 125
Honno **B** 121
Hopkins Society **Z** 510
Horay (Pierre) Editeur **AA** 417
Horizon Books **A** 53
Horizon Radio **K** 326
Horizonte (Livros) Lda **AA** 429
Horntvedt Television **L** 355
Horse and Hound **I** 255
Horse and Rider **I** 255
Horse & Pony Magazine **I** 255
Horseshoe Theatre Company **M** 385
Horticulture Week **I** 255
Hoskins (Valerie) **F** 168
Höst & Söns Forlag A/S **AA** 413
Houghton Mifflin Co. **N** 444
Hourglass Pictures Ltd **L** 355
House Beautiful **I** 255
House Buyer **I** 256
House & Garden **I** 256
Houses & Interiors Photographic Features Agency **V** 611
Hovedland (Forlaget) **AA** 413
Howard Seddon Associates **F** 168
Howarth (Tanja) **F** 168
Howes (Michael) Productions Ltd **L** 355
How To Books Ltd **A** 53

HPICM **L** 355
Hpt Verlagsgesellschaft mbH & Co KG **AA** 410
HTV Cymru/Wales **J** 310
HTV West **J** 310
Hub Editions **B** 000
Hubner Films Ltd **L** 355
Huddersfield Daily Examiner **H** 203
Hughes (John Edeyrn) Prize **T** 554
Hull College of Further Education **AB** 523
Hull Daily Mail **H** 203
Hull Festival **X** 406
Hull House Literary Agency **O** 464
Hull Truck Theatre Company **M** 385
Hulton Educational **A** 53
Hulton Picture Company **V** 611
Human Horizons **A** 53
Human Services Institute **N** 444
Humberside Theatre in Education **M** 385
Humberside Writers' Association (HWA) **Q** 497
Humberside Writer's Association Workshops **AB** 528
Hunt (Robert) Library, The **V** 611
Hunt & Thorpe **A** 53
Hurst (C.) & Co. **A** 53
Hurst (Jacqui) **V** 611
Hutchinson Books **A** 53
Hutchinson Reference **A** 53
Hutchison Library, The **V** 611
Hylton Warner Photography/Barry Webb Associates **V** 612
Ian Allan Ltd **A** 11
IBC Publishing **A** 53
Ice Hockey World and Skating Review **I** 256
ICE International Video Films Ltd **L** 356
ICM **F** 168
Ideal Home **I** 256
Ideas Factory, The **L** 356
ID Magazine **I** 256
Ilex Publishers Ltd **E** 152
Ilkley Literature Festival **X** 406
Illinois (University of) Press **N** 444
Illuminations **L** 356
Illuminations **C** 125
Illustra Communications **L** 356
Illustrated London News Picture Library **V** 612
Illustrated London News **I** 256
Image Bank, The **V** 612
Images Colour Library **V** 612
Images of Africa Photo Bank **V** 612

Imagicians Ltd **L** 356
Imison (Michael) Playwrights **F** 168
Impact Photos **V** 612
Imperial War Museum **U** 585
Imperial War Museum Department of Photographs **V** 612
Impressions **C** 125
In Britain **I** 257
Incafo (Editorial) SA **AA** 431
Inca Video & Film Productions **L** 356
Indelible Inc **W** 140
Independent Award for Foreign Fiction, The **T** 554
Independent Magazine, The **I** 257
Independent Music Radio **K** 317
Independent Newspaper Picture Library, The **V** 612
Independent on Sunday **G** 190
Independent Publishers Guild **Q** 497
Independent Radio News (IRN) **K** 318
Independent Student Journalist Bursary, The **S** 537
Independent Television Association (ITV) **J** 310
Independent Television News **J** 311
Independent, The **G** 189
Independent Theatre Council **Q** 497
Indiana University Press **N** 444
Infusion **I** 257
In-House Corporate Video **L** 356
Ink Inc. Ltd **E** 152
Inkshed **B** 125
Innes Photographic Library **V** 612
Input Video Ltd **L** 356
Insight Picture Library, The **V** 613
Insight Productions Ltd **L** 356
Institute For Social Inventions **W** 140
Institute for Social Inventions **Q** 497
Institute of Translation and Interpreting **Q** 497
Intellect Books **W** 140
InterCity **I** 257
Interesting Television Ltd **L** 357
Interim Press **B** 121
Interior Design **I** 257
International Broadcasting Trust **L** 357
International Centre for Conservation Education Photo Library **V** 613

International Concrete Poetry Archive **B** 121
International Copyright Bureau Ltd **F** 169
International Herald Tribune **G** 190
International Herald Tribune **P** 482
International Photobank **V** 613
International Press-Cutting Bureau **YY** 534
International Publisher Associates, Inc. **O** 464
International Reading Association Literacy Award **T** 555
International Scripts **F** 169
Inter Publishing Ltd **A** 55
Interzone: Science Fiction & Fantasy **I** 257
Inverse **B** 125
Investors Chronicle **I** 257
Invicta FM/Invicta Supergold **K** 326
In Video Productions Ltd **L** 356
Invincible Press **A** 54
Iolo **W** 140
Iota **B** 125
Iowa State University Press **N** 445
Iowa (University of) Press **N** 445
IPPA **Q** 497
Irish News, The **H** 196
Irish Post **I** 257
Irish Review **B** 125
Irish Times-Aer Lingus International Fiction Prize **T** 555
Irish Times Aer Lingus Irish Literature Prizes **T** 555
Iron **B** 125
Iron Press **C** 121
Isaac (Peter) Ltd **L** 357
Isis Large Print/Isis Audio Books **A** 54
Isolde Films Ltd **L** 357
Issue One **C** 125
Istituto Geografico de Agostini SpA **AA** 423
Istituto per l'Enciclopedia del Friuli Venezia Giulia **AA** 424
Italian Institute Library **U** 585
IVCA Writers Group **Q** 497
Ivy Books **N** 445
J. A. Allen & Co. Ltd **A** 11
Jaca Book (Editoriale) **AA** 424
Jacaranda Productions Ltd **L** 357
Jackie **I** 257
Jackson (Gruppo Editoriale) SpA **AA** 424
Jackson (Richard) **M** 385
Jackson's Arm Press **B** 121

Jacobs (W. W.) Appreciation Society **Z** 510
Jai Press Ltd **A** 54
J. Allan Cash Ltd **V** 603
James (Arthur) Ltd **A** 54
James Currey Publishers **A** 32
Jane Publishing **B** 121
Jane Rotrosen Agency **O** 474
Jane's Defence Weekly **I** 258
Jane's Information Group **A** 54
Janet and Colin Bord **V** 602
Jarrold Publishing **A** 54
Jarvie (Gordon) Editorial **Y** 532
Jarvie (Gordon), Literary Agent **F** 169
Jarvis (Sharon) and Co. **O** 464
Jazz Journal International **I** 258
Jenkinson (Brian) Film & Television Productions Ltd **L** 357
Jericho Productions Ltd **L** 357
Jersey Evening Post **H** 203
Jessel (Camilla) Photo Library **V** 613
Jets **A** 55
Jewish Chronicle **I** 258
Jewish Quarterly **I** 258
Joel Photographic Library **V** 613
Joe Soap's Canoe **C** 125
Jonathan Cape Ltd **A** 25
Jones (Mary Vaughan) Award **T** 555
Jones (Pola) Associates **M** 385
Jones (Trevor) Thoroughbred Photography **V** 613
Joseph (Stephen) Theatre **M** 385
Journalist, The **I** 258
Journal of Commerce **P** 482
Journal, The **H** 206
Jover (Ediciones) SA **AA** 431
Judd (Jane) Literary Agency **F** 169
Just Seventeen **I** 258
Juvenilia **F** 169
Kahn & Averill **A** 54
Kann (Michael) Associates Ltd **L** 357
Kansas (University of) Press **N** 445
Karger (S) GmbH **AA** 420
Karnak House **A** 55
Katabasis **B** 121
Kay Communications Ltd **L** 358
Keele University **AB** 527
Keesing Uitgeversmaatschappij BV **AA** 426
Kelly (Frances) **F** 170
Kelpie Competition **T** 555
Kenilworth Press Ltd **A** 55
Kennel Club Library, The **V** 613
Kennel Gazette **I** 259
Kenneth More Theatre **M** 389
Kensal Press, The **A** 55

Kent County Central Lending Library **U** 586
Kent Evening Post **H** 199
Kent Literature Festival **X** 407
Kent Messenger **H** 205
Kent (Sir Peter) Conservation Book Prize, The **T** 555
Kent State University Press **N** 445
Kent & Sussex Courier **H** 211
Kent & Sussex Poetry Society Open Competition **T** 555
Kent Young Writers of the Year Award **T** 556
Kenwright (Bill) Ltd **M** 385
Kenyon-Deane **A** 55
Kern (Natasha) Literary Agency, Inc. **O** 464
Keyboard Review **I** 259
Kidde, Hoyt & Picard Literary Agency **O** 465
Kime Publishing **A** 55
King (Daniel P.) **O** 465
Kingfisher Books **A** 55
Kingfisher Television Productions Ltd **L** 358
King (Laurence) **A** 55
King (Martin Luther) Memorial Prize, The **T** 556
King's Head Theatre **M** 386
Kingsley (Jessica) Publishers Ltd **A** 56
King's Lynn, The Drama, Fiction and Poetry Festival **X** 407
Kingsway Publications **A** 56
Kingswood Press **A** 56
Kipling Society, The **Z** 510
Kirk (Brian) Associates **M** 386
Kirk (David) Productions **M** 386
Kittiwake Press **W** 140
Klett-Cotta Verlag **AA** 420
Klincksieck (Editions) **AA** 417
Kluwer Academic Publishers **A** 56
Kluwer Academic Publishers BV **AA** 426
Kluwer Group **AA** 426
Knaves Acre Productions **L** 358
Knight Books **A** 56
Knight Features **F** 170
Knightsbridge Theatrical Productions **M** 386
Knopf (Alfred A.) Inc. **N** 445
Knorr und Hirth Verlag **AA** 420
Kobal Collection, The **V** 613
Kofod (Forlaget Per) ApS **AA** 413
Kogan Page Ltd **A** 56
Kohlhammer (Verlag W) **AA** 420
Kohner (Paul), Inc. **O** 465
Kok (Uitgeversmaatschappij J H) BV **AA** 426
Komma & Clausen **AA** 413

Korch's (Morten A.) Forlag **AA** 413

Korvet Publishing and Distribution **W** 140

Kos Image Library **V** 613

Kouts (Barbara S.), Literary Agent **O** 465

KQBX **B** 121

Krax **C** 125

KRAX **B** 121

Krieger Publishing Co., Inc. **N** 445

Krino **C** 125

Kroll (Lucy) Agency **O** 465

K.T. Publications **B** 121

Kummerly und Frey (Geographischer Verlag) **AA** 434

Kunapipi **C** 125

Kunnskapsforlaget I/S **AA** 428

Kwemarabak Publications **B** 121

Label **C** 126

Labour Party News **I** 259

Lademann (Det Ny) A/S **AA** 414

Ladybird Books Ltd **A** 57

Lady, The **I** 259

Laertes SA de Ediciones **AA** 431

Laffont (Editions Robert) **AA** 417

Lagan Pictures Ltd **L** 358

Laia (Editorial) SA **AA** 431

Lakeland Book of the Year **T** 556

Lalli (Antonio) Editore **AA** 424

Lampack (Peter) Agency, Inc. **O** 465

Lancashire Authors' Association **Q** 498

Lancashire Evening Post **H** 209

Lancashire Evening Telegraph **H** 197

Lancashire Magazine **I** 259

Lancaster Literature Festival **X** 407

Landesverlag Buchverlag **AA** 410

Landi (Luciano) Editore SRL **AA** 424

Landscape Only **V** 613

Landseer Film and Television Productions Ltd **L** 358

Lane (Frank) Picture Agency Ltd **V** 614

Langenscheidt AG **AA** 434

Langenscheidt KG **AA** 420

Lannoo (Uitgeverij) **AA** 412

Lantz (Robert)-Joy Harris Literary Agency **O** 467

Larklane Poetry Books **B** 000

Larousse (Librairie) **AA** 417

Larousse (Suisse) SA **AA** 434

LaSal (Edicions de les Dones) **AA** 431

Last Laugh Award **T** 556

Laterza (Giuseppe) e Figli **AA** 424

Lattes (Editions Jean-Claude) **AA** 417

Laubier (André) Picture Library **V** 614

Lavoro Editoriale, Il **AA** 424

Lawrence (T. E.) Society **Z** 511

Lawrence & Wishart Ltd **A** 57

Lawson Productions Ltd **L** 358

Lazear Agency, Inc., The **O** 466

LBC Newstalk FM/London Talkback Radio/IRN **K** 326

Leading Edge Press & Publishing Ltd **E** 153

Leamington Courier **H** 204

Leaves/Scales **B** 121

Lee Allan Agency, The **O** 466

Leeds Library **U** 586

Leeds Playhouse **M** 386

Leek Arts Festival International Poetry Competition **T** 556

Lee (L. Harry) Literary Agency **O** 466

Leicester Haymarket Theatre **M** 386

Leicester Mercury **H** 204

Leicester Sound FM **K** 326

Leicester University Press **A** 57

Lello e Irmao **AA** 429

Lemon, Unna and Durbridge Ltd **F** 170

Lennard Books **E** 153

Lennard Publishing **A** 55

Leone (Adele) Agency, Inc. **O** 466

L'Epine Smith & Carney Associates **F** 170

Lerner Publications Co. **N** 445

Lessing (Erich) Archive of Fine Art & Culture, The **V** 614

Letts (Charles) & Co. Ltd **A** 58

Levant & Wales, Literary Agency, Inc. **O** 467

Leventhal (Lionel) Ltd **A** 58

Levine (Ellen), Literary Agency, Inc. **O** 467

Levrotto e Bella Libreria Editrice Universitaria SAS **AA** 424

Levy (Barbara) Literary Agency **F** 170

Lewis (Ralph) Award **S** 538

Lexus Ltd **E** 153

Leykam Buchverlagsgesellschaft mbH **AA** 410

Libbey (John) & Co. Ltd **A** 58

Liber AB **AA** 433

Liberal Democrat News **I** 259

Liber Press **A** 58

Library Association Besterman Medal, The **T** 556

Library Association Carnegie Medal, The **T** 556

Library Association Kate Greenaway Medal, The **T** 557

Library Association McColvin Medal, The **T** 557

Library Association Publishing **A** 58

Library Association, The **Q** 498

Library Association Wheatley Medal, The **T** 557

Library of the Religious Society of Friends **U** 590

Library Theatre Company **M** 386

Lichfield Prize **T** 557

Life Magazine **P** 482

Lifestyle **J** 314

Lifestyle Magazine **I** 260

Lifetime Group **L** 358

Lighthouse Literary Agency **O** 467

Liguori Editore SRL **AA** 424

Lime Tree **A** 58

Lincoln (Frances) Ltd **A** 58

Lincoln Hannah Ltd MediaScan **YY** 534

Lincoln (Ray) Literary Agency **O** 467

Lincolnshire Echo **H** 205

Lincolnshire Life **I** 260

Linden Press **A** 59

Lindhardt and Ringhof **AA** 414

Linen Hall Library **U** 586

Lines Review **C** 126

Lionheart Books **E** 153

Lion Publishing **A** 58

Lions/Picture Lions/Young Lions **A** 59

Literary/Business Associates **O** 467

Literary & Creative Artists Agency **O** 467

Literary Review **I** 260

Literary Review Grand Poetry Competition **T** 557

Little, Brown & Co., Inc. **N** 445

Little, Brown & Co. (UK) Ltd **A** 59

Little (Christopher) **F** 170

Little Magazine Collection and Poetry Store **D** 129

Littlewood Arc **W** 141

Liverpool City Libraries **U** 586

Liverpool Echo **H** 205

Liverpool Festival **X** 407

Liverpool Playhouse **M** 387

Liverpool University Press **A** 59

Liverpool Women Writers **AB** 529

Live Theatre Company **M** 386

Livewire Books for Teenagers **A** 60

Liviana Editrice SpA **AA** 424

Living **I** 260
Living Faith Literary Agency **O** 468
Llewellyn Publications **N** 446
Lobby Press **B** 121
Lochar Publishing Ltd **A** 59
Loch Ryan Writers **AB** 528
Lodestar Productions Ltd **L** 358
Logaston Press **W** 141
Logos **I** 260
Logos, The Welsh Theological Review **I** 260
Lohses Forlag **AA** 414
Lombard Productions Ltd **L** 358
Lomond Press **B** 121
London Actors Theatre Company **M** 387
London Arts Board **R** 515
London Borough of Camden Information and Reference Services **U** 586
London Bubble Theatre Company **M** 387
London (City of) Festival **X** 407
London College of Printing **AB** 525
London Features International Ltd **V** 614
London Film Productions **L** 359
London Independent Books **F** 170
London Library, The **U** 587
London Magazine **I** 260
London (Museum of) Picture Library **V** 614
London New Play Festival **X** 407
London Review of Books **I** 261
London School of Journalism **AB** 525
London Scientific Films **L** 359
London Screenwriters' Workshop **Q** 498
London Screenwriters' Workshop **AB** 529
London Weekend Television (LWT) **J** 311
Longanesi & C **AA** 424
Longman Group Ltd **A** 60
Longman Publishing Group **N** 446
Longman Training **L** 359
Look-in **I** 261
Looking Good **I** 261
LOOKS **I** 261
Loony Balloonies **A** 60
Lord Louis Library **U** 587
Lord (Sterling) Literistic **O** 468
Los Angeles Times **P** 482
Lothrop, Lee & Shepard **N** 446
Louisiana State University Press **N** 446
Love Story **I** 261

Loving **I** 261
L Ts Forlag AB **AA** 433
LTV Productions **L** 359
Luath Press Ltd **W** 141
Lübbe (Gustav) Verlag **AA** 420
Lucida Productions **L** 359
Ludlow Festival **X** 407
Lund Humphries Publishers **A** 60
Lupe Cunha Photos **V** 614
Lutterworth Press, The **A** 60
LWT Plays on Stage **T** 557
Lyfrow Trelyspen **W** 141
Lymes Press **B** 122
Lyons & Burford, Publishers **N** 446
Lyons (Sir William) Award **T** 557
Lyric Theatre Hammersmith **M** 387
Lythway Large/Children's Large Print **A** 61
Macaulay Fellowship **S** 538
MacCampbell (Donald), Inc. **O** 468
Macdonald & Co. Ltd **A** 61
Mac Films **L** 359
Machen (Arthur) Literary Society **Z** 511
Machine Knitting Monthly **I** 261
Mackenzie (Agnes Mure) Award **T** 558
Mackenzie (W. J. M.) Book Prize **T** 558
Mackintosh (Cameron) **M** 387
Macmillan Children's Book Group **N** 446
Macmillan Prize for a Children's Picture Book **T** 558
Macmillan Publishers Ltd **A** 61
Macmillan Silver Pen Award **T** 558
Macnaghten (Marianne) **M** 388
MacQuitty International Photographic Collection **V** 614
MacRae (Julia) Books **A** 62
MAC - The Centre for Birmingham **M** 387
Made in Wales Stage Company, The **M** 388
Magenta Press **B** 122
Magic Words **AB** 522
Magic 828 **K** 326
Magi Publications **A** 62
Magnard Sàrl (Les Editions) **AA** 417
Magnum Photos Ltd **V** 614
Maiden Films Ltd **L** 359
Mail (Hartlepool) **H** 203
Mail on Sunday/John Llewellyn Rhys Prize, The **T** 559

Mail on Sunday Novel Competition, The **T** 559
Mail on Sunday, The **G** 190
Main Communications **L** 359
Mainstream Publishing Co. (Edinburgh) Ltd **A** 62
Mairs Geographischer **AA** 420
Making Music **I** 262
Malachite Ltd **L** 359
mallings **AA** 414
Malone Gill Productions Ltd **L** 36■
Mammon Press **B** 122
Mammoth **A** 62
Management Today **I** 262
Manchester Central Library **U** 587
Manchester Evening News **H** 205
Manchester Poets **B** 122
Manchester University Press **A** 62
Mandala **A** 62
Mandarin **A** 62
Mander (Raymond) & Joe Mitchenson Theatre Collection The **V** 614
Manderville Press **B** 122
Mandrake **W** 141
Manesse Verlag GmbH **AA** 434
Manley (Deborah) **Y** 532
Mannamead Press **B** 122
Mann (Andrew) Ltd **F** 171
Mann (Carol) Agency **O** 468
Mann (George) Books **A** 62
Mansell **A** 63
Mansfield (Mike) Television Ltd **L** 360
Manteau (Uitgeversmaatschappij A) NV **AA** 412
Manuscript ReSearch **F** 171
Many Press, The **B** 122
Map Collector **I** 262
Mar **C** 126
Marcellus Productions Ltd **M** 388
Marcher Sound **K** 327
Marcil (Denise) Literary Agency, Inc. **O** 469
Marc **A** 63
Margaret Ramsay Ltd **F** 175
marie claire **I** 262
Marine Day Publishers **W** 141
Mariner's Library **A** 63
Mariscat Press **B** 122
Maritz Communications **L** 360
Marjacq Scripts Ltd **F** 171
Market House Books Ltd **E** 153
Marketing Week **I** 262
Markham (Arthur) Memorial Prize **T** 559
Marking Inc Productions **L** 360
Marks (Betty) **O** 469
Marshall Cameron Agency **O** 469
Marshall Cavendish Books **E** 153

Marshall Editions Ltd **E** 153
Marshall (Evan) Agency **O** 469
Marshall Pickering **A** 63
Marsh Christian Trust Award **T** 559
Marsh & Sheil Ltd **F** 171
Martinez (M. C.) Literary Agency **F** 171
Martin (Judy) **F** 171
Martin Library, The **V** 614
Marvin (Blanche) **F** 172
Marylebone Library **U** 587
Maschler (Kurt) Award (Emil) **T** 559
Masefield (John) Memorial Trust, The **S** 538
Masks/Masks Noir **A** 63
Mason (Kenneth) Publications Ltd **A** 63
Massachusetts (University of) Press **N** 447
Masson Editeur **AA** 417
Matawa **L** 360
Match **I** 262
Maternity and Mothercraft **I** 262
Mathews (S & O) Photography **V** 615
Matrix **I** 263
Maugham (Somerset) Trust Fund **S** 538
Maugher (Dorothy) National Trophy Short Story Competition **T** 559
Maule (Michel de) **AA** 417
Max AM **K** 327
Mayfair **I** 263
Mayfair Times **I** 263
Mayhew Business Communication Ltd **L** 360
Maypole Editions **W** 141
MBA Literary Agents Ltd* **F** 172
McBride (Margret) Literary Agency **O** 468
McColl Arts Foundation Bursaries **S** 538
McDonough (Richard P.), Literary Agent **O** 468
MCEG Virgin Vision **L** 360
McElderry Books **N** 446
McFarland & Company, Inc., Publishers **N** 446
McGraw-Hill Book Co. Europe **A** 60
McGraw-Hill Interamericana de Espana SA **AA** 432
McIntosh & Otis, Inc. **O** 468
McKitterick Prize **T** 558
McLean (Bill) Personal Management **F** 171
McLeod (Enid) Prize **T** 558

MCM Publishing **A** 61
McMullen (Eunice) Children's Literary Agent Ltd **F** 171
McVitie's Prize for Scottish Writer of the Year **T** 559
Meadow Books **A** 63
Medal News **I** 263
Medialab Ltd **L** 360
Media Week **I** 263
Medical Journalists' Association **Q** 498
Medical & Scientific Productions **L** 360
Medical Writers Group **Q** 498
Medici (Cartiere Binda de) SpA **AA** 424
Medici Society Ltd, The **A** 63
Meditel Productions Ltd **L** 360
Melendez Films **L** 361
Melody Maker **I** 263
Melrose Film Productions **L** 361
Melrose Press Ltd **A** 63
Memes **C** 126
Menard Press **B** 122
Mensa Magazine **I** 263
Mentorn Films **L** 361
Menza (Claudia) Literary Agency **O** 469
Menzies (Lee) Ltd **M** 388
Mercat Press **A** 63
Mercia FM **K** 327
Mercure de France SA **AA** 417
Mercury Business Books **A** 65
Merehurst Ltd **A** 64
Meridian Books **W** 141
Meridian Broadcasting **J** 311
Merlin Press Ltd **A** 64
Mermaid Books **A** 64
Merseyside Association of Writers Workshops **AB** 529
Merseyside Everyman Theatre Company **M** 388
Merseyside Poetry Circuit **B** 122
Mersey Television Company Ltd **L** 361
Métaillié (A.M.) **AA** 417
Methuen/Methuen Children's Books **A** 64
Metro FM/Great North Radio (GNR) **K** 327
Metro News (Birmingham) **H** 197
Meulenhoff International **AA** 426
Mews Books Ltd **O** 469
Me **I** 263
Michael Barratt Ltd **L** 339
Michael Joseph Ltd **A** 55
Michael & Patricia Fogden **V** 608
Michelin Award **T** 559
Michelin et Cie (Services de Tourisme) **AA** 417

Microbridgade **B** 122
Midland Arts Centre **M** 388
Midland Publishing Ltd **A** 64
Midnag Publications **B** 122
Midnight Films Ltd **L** 361
Midnight Theatre Company **M** 388
Milepost 92$81 **V** 615
Milestone Publications **A** 64
Millenium **A** 64
Miller & Associates Inc. **O** 470
Miller (Lee) Archives **V** 615
Miller (Peter) Agency The **O** 469
Miller's Publications **A** 64
Million: The Magazine About Popular Fiction **I** 264
Mills & Boon Ltd **A** 64
MIlls (John) Film and Television **L** 361
Mills (Robert P.) **O** 470
Millstone Lit **F** 172
Mills Video Company **L** 361
Milne (Richard) Ltd **F** 172
MIND Book of the Year – The Allen Lane Award **T** 560
Mind Your Own Business **I** 264
Minerva **A** 65
Ministry of Agriculture, Fisheries and Food **U** 587
Minority Rights Group **W** 142
Minstrel **A** 65
Minstrel **N** 447
Minuit (Les Editions de) SA **AA** 418
Miraguano SA Ediciones **AA** 432
Mirus Productions **L** 361
Missouri (University of) Press **N** 447
Mitchell Beazley Ltd **A** 65
MIT Press **N** 447
MIT Press Ltd, The **A** 65
Mitre **A** 65
Mizz **I** 264
MJW Productions **L** 362
MM Productions Ltd **E** 154
MNV **L** 362
Mobil Bursary **S** 538
Mobil Playwriting Competition for the Royal Exchange Theatre Company **T** 560
Modern Dance **I** 264
Moderne Industrie (Verlag) AG & Co **AA** 420
Modern Machine Knitting **I** 264
Modern Review, The **I** 264
Momentum **C** 126
Monarch Publications **A** 65
Moncrieff (Scott) Prize **T** 560
Mondadori (Arnoldo) Editore SpA **AA** 424
Mondadori Espana SA **AA** 432

Moneycare I 265
Money Week I 264
Moneywise I 265
Monitor Syndication V 615
Monstrous Regiment Ltd M 388
Montagu Trophy T 560
Montpelier Society, The Q 498
Moonstone B 126
Moorland Publishing Co Ltd A 65
Moray Firth Radio K 327
More! I 265
More (Kenneth) Theatre M 389
Morgan Samuel Editions E 154
Morning Star G 190
Morning Star Publications B 122
Morris (Neil & Ting) E 154
Morrison Company, The L 362
Morrison (Henry) Inc. O 470
Morris (William) Agency UK F 172
Morrow (William) and Co. N 447
Mosaic I 265
Mosaic Film & Video Productions L 362
Mosaic Pictures Ltd L 362
Mosaik Verlag AA 421
Mosby Year Book Europe A 65
Mother and Baby I 265
Mother Films L 362
Mother Goose Award, The T 560
Mother Tongue Publishing Co-Op B 122
Motley (Michael) Ltd F 172
Motor Boat and Yachting I 265
Motorcaravan & Motorhome Monthly (MMM) I 266
Motor Caravan World I 266
Motor Cycle News I 266
Motor Home I 266
Motor Racing Publications A 66
Mountain Biking UK I 266
Mountain Camera V 615
Moving Direction L 362
Moving Image Research & Library Services V 615
Moving Picture Library, The V 622
Mowbray A 66
M & P Publishing House AA 426
Ms London I 266
MTV Europe J 314
Mulberry Books N 447
Mulberry Ltd L 362
Mulino (Societe Editrice Il) AA 425
Muller A 66
Multimedia Product Development, Inc. O 470
Munksgaard International Publishers Ltd AA 414
Murray (John) (Publishers) A 66

Murray (Norman) & Anne Chudleigh Ltd M 389
Mursia (Ugo) Editore SpA AA 425
Muscroft (David) Photography and Picture Library V 615
Musical Opinion I 267
Musical Times I 267
Music Review, The I 267
Music Week I 267
My Guy I 267
My Weekly I 267
Naipaul (Shiva) Memorial Prize T 560
Naked City C 126
Nan A. Talese Books N 447
Nathan (Fernand) AA 418
Nathan (Ruth) Agency O 470
National Convention of Press and Small Presses D 129
National Council for the Training of Journalists AB 525
National Film & Television School AB 525
National Library of Scotland U 587
National Library of Wales U 588
National Maritime Museum Picture Library V 615
National Medical Slide Bank V 615
National Monuments Record V 615
National News Agency HH 304
National Poetry Competition T 561
National Poetry Foundation W 130
National Poetry Foundation Grants S 538
National Public Radio P 483
National Railway Museum Picture Library V 615
National Trust Photographic Library, The V 616
National Union of Journalists Q 498
Natural History Museum Library U 588
Natural History Museum Picture Library V 616
Natural History Photographic Agency (NHPA) V 616
Naturalist, The I 268
Natural Science Photos V 616
Natural World I 268
Natural World Book of the Year Award T 561
Nature I 268
Natur och Kultur (Bokforlaget) AA 433

Nautical A 66
Navers (Rasmus) Forlag A/S AA 414
NavPress Publishing Group N 44
NBC News P 483
NCR Book Award for Non-Fictio T 561
NCVO Publications A 66
Neave (Airey) Trust, The S 538
Nebelspalter Verlag AA 434
Neff (Paul), Verlag AA 410
Nelissen (Uitgeverij H) BV AA 426
Nelson (B.K.) Literary Agency O 470
Nelson (Thomas) & Sons Ltd A 6
Neptun-Verlag AA 434
Netball I 268
Network I 268
Network Photographers V 616
Neue Zurcher Zeitung AG Buchverlag AA 434
Nevada (University of) Press N 447
New Age/New Sciences N 448
New Age World Services & Book O 470
New Arcadian Press W 142
New Beacon I 268
New Beacon Books B 122
New Broom Private Press B 122
New Canterbury Literary Society 511
Newcastle Literary and Philosop ical Society Library U 588
Newcastle upon Tyne Central Library U 588
New Cyclist I 268
New Decade Productions L 362
New Departures C 126
New England Editions Ltd E 154
New England Publishing Associates, Inc. O 470
New England (University Press o N 448
New English Library A 67
Newgate Company M 389
New Holland (Publishers) A 67
New Hope International C 126
New Horizons S 539
New Humanist I 269
New Internationalist I 269
New Law Journal Rumpole Awar T 561
New Left Review I 269
New London Radio Playwrights Festival X 408
New Media L 362
New Mexico (University of) Press N 448

New Moon Science Fiction **I** 269
New Musical Express **I** 269
New Orchard Editions **A** 67
Newpalm Productions **M** 389
New Playwrights Trust **Q** 498
New Portway Large Print **A** 67
New River Project **B** 122
New Scientist **I** 269
Newsfocus Press Photograph
  Agency Ltd **V** 616
New Shakespeare Company **M**
  389
News of the World, The **G** 190
Newspaper Conference **Q** 499
Newspaper Press Fund **S** 539
Newspaper Society, The **Q** 499
New Statesman and Society **I** 270
News, The (Portsmouth) **H** 209
Newsweek **P** 483
New Victoria Theatre **M** 389
New Welsh Review **C** 126
New Woman **I** 270
New York Times, The **P** 483
Nexus **A** 67
NFER-NELSON Publishing Co **A**
  67
NHPA (Natural History
  Photographic Agency) **V** 616
Nicholson **A** 67
Niederösterreichisches
  Pressehaus, Verlag **AA** 411
  191 270
90s **A** 67
NKI Forlaget **AA** 428
NKS-Forlaget (Ernst G.
  Mortensens stiftelse) **AA** 428
Noach (Maggie) Literary Agency,
  The **F** 172
Nobel Prize **T** 561
Noble (David) Photography **V** 616
Noetzli (Regula) Literary Agency
  O 471
Nolan (Betsy) Literary Agency,
  The **O** 471
Nonesuch Press **A** 67
Norfolk and Norwich Festival **X**
  408
Norfolk Life **I** 270
Normandy Film Productions **L**
  363
Norstedts Forlag AB **AA** 433
Northampton Repertory Players
  Ltd **M** 389
*Northamptonshire Evening
  Telegraph* **H** 207
Northamptonshire Image **I** 271
North and South **B** 122
Northants Radio **K** 327
Northcliffe Newspapers Group Ltd
  H 195

Northcote House Publishers **A** 67
Northcott Theatre **M** 390
North East Times **I** 270
Northern Arts Board **R** 515
Northern Arts Literary Fellowship
  S 539
Northern Arts Poetry Library **D**
  129
Northern Arts Writers Awards **S**
  539
Northern Echo, The **H** 200
Northern House **B** 122
Northern Musgraves Sherlock
  Holmes Society **Z** 511
Northern Picture Library **V** 616
Northern Poetry Award **T** 561
Northern Stage Company **M** 390
Northern Stories Award **T** 562
Northern Writers Advisory
  Services (NWAS) **Y** 532
Northlight **C** 126
NorthSound Radio **K** 327
North, The **I** 270
North, The **C** 126
Northumberland County Library **U**
  588
Northumberland Theatre
  Company **M** 390
North Wales Arts **R** 515
North West Arts Board **R** 515
North West Evening Mail **H** 195
NorthWord Press, Inc. **N** 448
Norton (W. W.) & Company **N**
  448
Norvik Press Ltd **W** 142
Norwich Puppet Theatre **M** 390
Nottingham Central Library **U** 588
Nottingham Playhouse **M** 390
Nottinghamshire Children's Book
  Award **T** 562
Nottingham Subscription Library
  Ltd **U** 589
NRB Publications **W** 142
Nuffield Theatre **M** 390
Nugent Literary **O** 471
NUJ **Q** 499
Nurnberg (Andrew) Associates
  Ltd **F** 173
Nursing Times **I** 271
Nutshell **C** 126
Nye (Alexandra) **F** 173
Nyt Nordisk Forlag Arnold Busck
  A/S **AA** 414
Oak Tree Award **T** 562
Oak **A** 68
Oasis **C** 126
Oasis Books **B** 122
Oberon Books **A** 68
Observer Colour Library **V** 616
Observer Magazine **I** 271

Observer, The **G** 191
Ocean Sound/South Coast Radio
  K 327
Octagon Press Ltd **A** 68
Octopus Publishing **A** 68
Odd Fellows (Manchester Unity)
  Social Concern Book Award **T**
  562
Odyssey **C** 126
Office of Arts and Libraries **Q** 499
Office Secretary **I** 271
Oglio (Dall') Editore SRL **AA** 425
Oklahoma (University of) Press **N**
  448
Oldenbourg (R) Verlag GmbH **AA**
  421
Oldie, The **I** 271
Oldman (C.B.) Prize **T** 562
Old Vic, The **M** 391
O'Leary (David) Literary Agents **F**
  173
Oliver & Boyd **A** 68
O'Mara (Michael) Books **A** 68
Omega Books **A** 68
Omnibus Press **A** 68
Only Horses Picture Agency **V**
  616
On The Edge **I** 271
Open Books Publishing Ltd **A** 68
Open College of the Arts **AB** 528
Open Court Publishing Co. **N** 448
Open Gate Press **A** 68
Open Letters **A** 68
Open Mind Productions **L** 363
Open University Press **A** 69
Opera **I** 271
Opera Now **I** 271
Oppenheim John Downes
  Memorial Trust **S** 539
Optima **A** 69
Options **I** 272
Oracle Teletext **J** 311
Orac Verlag Gesellschaft mbH **AA**
  411
Orange Tree Theatre **M** 391
Orbis **I** 272
Orbit **A** 69
Orbit **N** 449
Orchard Books **A** 69
Orchard FM **K** 327
Orchard Theatre **M** 391
Orell Fussli Verlag **AA** 434
Ore **C** 126
Oriel Bookshop **D** 130
Oriflamme Publishing **W** 142
Original Film & Video Productions
  Ltd **L** 363
Orion Books **A** 69
Orion Books **N** 449
Orion Picture Corporation **L** 363

Orion Publishing Group **A** 69
Oscars Press **B** 122
Osprey **A** 69
Österreichischer Bundesverlag Gesellschaft mbH **AA** 411
Ostinato **B** 126
Oswald Wolff Books **A** 96
Otte Company, The **O** 471
Otter **C** 126
Outdoor Writers Guild **Q** 499
Outlook **I** 272
Out of Print Book Service **Y** 532
Outposts **B** 126
Outposts Poetry Competition **T** 562
Outram (George) Picture Library **V** 617
Outwrite **AB** 529
Ovation Productions Ltd **L** 363
Overdrawn Books **B** 122
Overdue Books **B** 122
Owen (Deborah) Ltd **F** 173
Owen (Peter) Ltd **A** 69
OWG/COLA Awards for Excellence **T** 562
Owl Press **A** 70
Oxford Central Library **U** 589
Oxford Film & Video Makers **L** 363
Oxford Illustrated Press/Oxford Publishing Co. **A** 70
Oxford Mail **H** 208
Oxford Picture Library **V** 617
Oxford Poetry **C** 126
Oxford Scientific Films Photo Library **V** 617
Oxford Stage Company **M** 391
Oxford University Press **A** 70
Oyster Books Ltd **E** 154
Pace Productions Ltd **L** 363
PACT (Producers Alliance for Cinema and Television) **Q** 499
Paines Plough – The Writers Company **M** 391
Paisley Daily Express **H** 208
Pakenham (Catherine) Award **T** 563
Palace Productions **L** 363
Palace Theatre, Watford **M** 391
Palace TV **L** 363
Paladin **A** 70
Palmer (Hugh) **V** 617
Paludans (Jörgen) Forlag ApS **AA** 414
Pan Books Ltd **A** 70
Panda Books **A** 70
Pandora Press **A** 70
Panettieri Agency, The **O** 471
Panoptic Productions **L** 364
Panos Pictures **V** 617

Pantheon Books **N** 449
Paoline (Edizioni) SRL **AA** 425
Paperback Inferno **I** 272
Paperduck **A** 71
Paperfronts **A** 71
Paper Moon Productions **L** 364
Paper Tiger Books **A** 70
Paragon House Publishers **N** 449
Paragon Softcover Large Print **A** 71
Parallax Pictures Ltd **L** 364
Paramount Pictures (UK) **L** 364
Paramount Revcom **L** 364
Paranoia Press (Teesside) **W** 142
Paraphernalia **C** 126
Parents **I** 272
Parey (Verlag Paul) **AA** 421
Paris Musées **AA** 418
Paris Review Editions **N** 449
Parke Sutton Publishing Ltd **E** 154
Partizan Press **W** 143
Partridge Press **A** 71
Paternoster Press Ltd **A** 70
Paterson (David) Library **V** 617
Paterson (Mark) & Associates **F** 173
Patrick Stephens Ltd **A** 88
Paupers' Press **W** 143
Pavilion Books Ltd **A** 71
Pawsey (John) **F** 173
Payot Lausanne (Editions) **AA** 435
P.B.B. **B** 122
PBI Publications **A** 71
PCP - Production Centre Productions **L** 364
PC User **I** 272
PCW Plus **I** 272
Peake Productions **L** 364
Pearl Catlin Associates **L** 342
Pearlstine (Maggie) **F** 174
Peekner (Ray) Literary Agency, Inc., The **O** 471
Peepal Tree Books **W** 143
Pegasus International, Inc. **O** 471
Pelham Books **A** 71
Pelican Publishing Company **N** 449
Pelicula Films **L** 364
Pelion Press **N** 449
Penguin Books Ltd **A** 71
Penman Literary Agency **F** 174
Penman Literary Club, The **Q** 500
Penmarin Books **O** 472
Pennine FM **K** 328
Pennine Ink **C** 126
Pennine Platform **C** 126
Pennsylvania (University of) Press **N** 449
Penny Press **A** 73

Pen & Sword Books Ltd **A** 71
Pentagon Communications **L** 36▮
Pentameters **M** 391
Penthouse **I** 273
Pen: umbra **C** 126
Penzance Library **U** 589
PEN **Q** 499
People Magazine **I** 273
People Magazine **P** 483
People's Friend, The **I** 273
People's Poetry, The **C** 126
People's Prize, The **T** 563
People, The **G** 191
People to People **C** 126
Perfect Crime **N** 449
Performing Arts Library **V** 617
Performing Right Society **Q** 500
Pergamon Bridge/Pergamon Chess **I** 273
Pergamon Press **A** 73
Periodical Publishers Associatio▮ (PPA) **Q** 500
Periodicals Training Council **AB** 525
Perkins Literary Agency **O** 472
Permanent Press **B** 122
Perry (James) Productions **M** 39▮
Personal Managers' Association Ltd, The **Q** 500
Personnel Management **I** 273
Peter Batty Productions **L** 339
Peter (James) Associates, Inc. **O** 472
Peterloo Poets **W** 143
Peterloo Poets Open Poetry Competition **T** 563
Peters Fraser & Dunlop Group Ltd* **F** 174
PGP Films **L** 364
Phaidon Press Ltd **A** 73
Philadelphia Inquirer **P** 483
Philip (George) **A** 73
Phillimore & Co. Ltd **A** 73
Phoenix **A** 73
Phoenix (Kingsway) **A** 73
Phoenix Press **B** 122
Photo Flora **V** 617
Photofusion **V** 617
Photographers' Library, The **V** 618
Photo Library International Ltd **▮** 617
Photo Resources **V** 617
Photos Horticultural **V** 618
Piatkus Books **A** 73
Picador **A** 74
Picard (Alison J.) Literary Agent **O** 472
Piccadilly Gold/Key 103 **K** 328
Piccadilly Press **A** 74

Piccolo **A** 74
Pictorial **A** 74
PictureBank Photo Library Ltd **V** 618
Picture Base International **L** 364
Picturehead Productions **L** 365
Picture Palace Productions **L** 365
Picture Postcard Monthly **I** 273
Picture Publishing Company Ltd **A** 74
Pictures Colour Library **V** 618
Pig Press **B** 122
Pilley (Phil) Productions **L** 365
Pilot **I** 273
Pimlico **A** 74
Pine (Arthur) Associates **O** 472
Pinguin-Verlag Pawlowski KG **AA** 411
Pink Paper, The **I** 274
Piṇon Press **N** 449
Pinter Publishers Ltd **A** 74
Piper **A** 74
Pitkin Pictorials **A** 74
Pitman Publishing **A** 74
Plain Words (Business Writers) **Y** 532
Planet **C** 126
Planeta SA **AA** 432
Planet Earth Pictures/Seaphot **V** 618
Plantagenet Productions **M** 392
Platform Magazine **I** 274
Players Press **N** 449
Players' Theatre **M** 392
Player–Playwrights **Q** 500
Playne Books **E** 154
Plays and Players **I** 274
Playwrights Co-operative **Q** 500
Playwrights' Workshop **Q** 500
Plaza Y Janes SA **AA** 432
Plenum Publishing **N** 449
Plenum Publishing Ltd **A** 74
Plexus Publishing Ltd **A** 75
Plus **I** 274
Pluto Press Ltd **A** 75
Plymouth Proprietary Library **U** 589
Plymouth Sound **K** 328
pma Training **AB** 525
PM Plus **I** 274
PN Review **C** 127
Pocket Books **N** 449
Poetica **C** 127
Poetical Histories **B** 122
Poetry and Audience **C** 127
Poetry Book Society **Q** 500
Poetry Business **B** 122
Poetry Business Competition **T** 563
Poetry Business, The **W** 143

Poetry Durham **C** 127
Poetry Ireland Review **C** 127
Poetry Library **U** 589
Poetry Listing **D** 131
Poetry London Newletter **D** 131
Poetry Nottingham **C** 127
Poetry Now **C** 123
Poetry Review **I** 274
Poetry Society, The **Q** 501
Poetry World **C** 127
Poets Voice **C** 127
Polish Library **U** 590
Politikens Forlag A/S **AA** 414
Polity Press **A** 75
Polka Children's Theatre **M** 392
Pollinger (Laurence) Ltd **F** 174
Pollinger (Murray) **F** 174
Polygon **A** 75
Polygram Filmed Entertainment **L** 365
Polytechnic of Central London **AB** 526
Pony **I** 275
Popkin/Cooke **O** 472
Popperfoto **V** 618
Popular Crafts **I** 275
Popular Dogs **A** 75
Popular Flying **I** 275
Population Censuses & Surveys Library, Office of **U** 589
Pop Universal **A** 75
Portico Prize, The **T** 563
Portlight Press **B** 123
Portman Entertainment **L** 365
Porto Editora Lda **AA** 429
Poseidon Productions Ltd **L** 365
Potter (Beatrix) Society **Z** 511
Powell (Michael) Book Award **T** 563
Power Publications **W** 143
Power (Shelley) Literary Agency Ltd **F** 174
Practical Boat Owner **I** 275
Practical Electronics **I** 275
Practical Fishkeeping **I** 275
Practical Gardening **I** 276
Practical Householder **I** 276
Practical Motorist **I** 276
Practical Photography **I** 276
Practical Wireless **I** 276
Prebendal Press **B** 123
Prediction **I** 276
Premaphotos Wildlife **V** 618
Premium Monitoring Ltd **YY** 534
Prentice Hall **N** 449
Presentations **A** 75
Press Association Library **U** 590
Press Association Ltd **HH** 304
Press Association Ltd **V** 618
Presses de la Cité, Les **AA** 418

Presses Universitaires de France (PUF) **AA** 418
Press & Journal, The **H** 195
Press-tige Pictures **V** 618
Prestige Plays **M** 392
Prest Roots Press **B** 123
Pretty Clever Pictures Ltd **L** 365
Previous Parrot Press **W** 143
Previous Parrot Press **B** 123
Price (Harry) Library of Magical Literature **U** 590
Price (Mathew) Ltd **E** 155
Priest (Aaron M.) Literary Agency **O** 472
Prima **I** 277
Prima Publishing and Communications **N** 450
Primetime Television Ltd **L** 365
Primitive Poetry Press **B** 123
Princess House **A** 75
Princeton University Press **A** 75
Princeton University Press **N** 450
Principal Film Company Ltd **L** 365
Printer's Devil **B** 000
Priory Film Productions **L** 366
Prisma-Verlag Zenner und Gürchott **AA** 421
Prism Press Book Publishers **A** 75
Pritchard (David) Editorial **Y** 532
Private Eye **I** 277
Private Libraries Association **Q** 501
Producers Alliance for Cinema and Television (PACT) **Q** 499
Producers Association **Q** 501
Production Pool Ltd, The **L** 366
Professional Sport **V** 618
Prometheus Award **S** 539
Proteus **A** 76
Protter (Susan Ann) Literary Agent **O** 472
PR Week **I** 275
Psychic News **I** 277
Psychopoetica **C** 127
Public Record Office **U** 590
Publishers Association, The **Q** 501
Publishing News **I** 277
Puffin **A** 76
Pulitzer Prizes **T** 563
Pulse FM **K** 328
Purchasepoint Video **L** 366
Purkis Neale Productions Ltd **L** 366
Purple Heather Publications **B** 123
Putnam Publishing Group **N** 450
PVA Management Ltd **F** 175
Pythia Press **W** 143
QA Photos **V** 618
QED Books **W** 144

Quad Production Co. **L** 366
Quadrant Picture Library **V** 619
Quanta Ltd **L** 366
Quartet Books **A** 76
Quarto Publishing **E** 155
Quartos Magazine **I** 277
Quartos Magazine Short Story Competitions **T** 564
Quay Books Exeter **W** 144
Quay Productions Ltd **L** 366
Queen Anne Press **A** 76
QueenSpark Books **W** 144
Queen's Theatre Hornchurch **M** 392
Quest **C** 127
Questors Theatre Student Playwright Competition **T** 564
Quicksilver Books, Literary Agents **O** 473
Quiller Press **A** 76
Quilliam Press Ltd **W** 144
Quill Theatre Productions **M** 392
Quill Trade Paperbacks **N** 450
Quotes Ltd **A** 76
Q **I** 277
Q20 Theatre Company **M** 392
RA **I** 277
Raben och Sjogren Bokforlag AB **AA** 433
Racing Pigeon, The **I** 278
RAC Publishing **A** 76
Radala & Associates **F** 175
Radio Borders **K** 324
Radio Broadland **K** 324
Radio City/City FM/Radio City Gold **K** 324
Radio Clyde **K** 324
Radio Communication **I** 278
Radio Forth RFM/Max AM **K** 325
Radio Mercury **K** 327
Radio Orwell **K** 327
Radio Tay **K** 329
Radio Times **I** 278
Radio Times Drama & Comedy Awards **T** 564
Radio Wyvern **K** 330
Radius **A** 76
Radley-Regan (D.) & Associates **O** 473
Ragdoll Productions **L** 366
Railfotos **V** 619
Railway Magazine, The **I** 278
Railways and Steam Locomotives of the World Photo Library **V** 619
RAIL **I** 278
Rakoff (Alvin) Productions **L** 366
Raleigh International Picture & Features Library **V** 619
Rambling Today **I** 278

Ramsay Head Press, The **A** 76
Rand McNally & Co. **N** 450
Random House, Inc. **N** 450
Random House Publishing Group Ltd **A** 76
Rank Production **L** 366
Raven Arts **B** 123
R & B Publishing **A** 77
RCS Rizzoli Libri SpA **AA** 425
Readers **Y** 532
Reader's Digest **I** 279
Reader's Digest Association **P** 483
Reader's Digest Association Ltd **A** 78
Reading & Righting (Robert Lambolle Services) **Y** 533
Reality Studios **B** 123
Really Useful Group Ltd, The **M** 393
Reaper Books **W** 144
Record Collector **I** 279
Redbeck Press **B** 123
Red Dragon FM/Touch AM **K** 328
Red Earth Publications **W** 144
Redferns **V** 619
Red Fox **A** 78
Redgrave Theatre **M** 393
Redington (Michael) **M** 393
Redlake Press, The **W** 144
Red Lion Communications Ltd **L** 367
Redroofs Associates **M** 393
Red Rooster Film & Entertainment Ltd **L** 367
Red Rose Gold/Rock FM **K** 328
Red Rose Magazine **I** 279
Red Sharks Press **B** 123
Red Shift Theatre Company **M** 393
Redstone Press **W** 145
Reed International Books **A** 78
Reese (Trevor) Memorial Prize **T** 564
Rees (Helen) Literary Agency **O** 473
Reflections PhotoLibrary **V** 619
Regional Arts Bureau **R** 514
Regional Press Awards **T** 564
Reinhardt Books Ltd **A** 80
Reitzels (Hans) Forlag A/S **AA** 414
Relay Photos Ltd **V** 619
Remote Source **V** 619
Renaissance **B** 127
Renaissance Vision **L** 367
Repfoto London **V** 619
Report **I** 279
Resident Abroad **I** 279
Retna Pictures Ltd **V** 619
Retrograph Archive Ltd **V** 619
Reuter and UPI **V** 620

Reuters Ltd **HH** 304
Re-Verb **B** 123
Rex Features Ltd **V** 620
Reynolds (Jim) Associates **F** 17⬛
Rhinoceros **C** 127
Rhodos, International Science and Art Publishers **AA** 414
Rhondda (Margaret) Award, Th⬛ **S** 539
Rhône Poulenc Prize **T** 564
Rhyme International Prize **T** 564
Rialto, The **C** 127
RIBA Journal, The **I** 279
Richters Forlag AB **AA** 433
RIDA Photo Library **V** 620
Rider **A** 80
Riding **I** 279
Rights Unlimited, Inc. **O** 473
Rivelin Grapheme Press **B** 000
Riverfront Pictures Ltd **L** 367
Roads **C** 127
Robert Ducas Literary Agency **C** 460
Robertson (Patricia) **F** 175
Robinson Publishing **A** 80
Robinswood Press, The **W** 145
Robson Books Ltd **A** 81
Rockingham Press **B** 123
Roffman (Richard H.) Associate⬛ **O** 473
Rogers, Coleridge & White Ltd* 175
Rogers Prize **T** 564
Romantic Novelists' Association Major Award **T** 564
Romantic Novelists' Association/Netta Muskett Award **T** 565
Romantic Novelists' Association The **Q** 501
Romeike & Curtice **YY** 534
Romer Publications **W** 145
Ronan (Ann) Picture Library **V** 620
Rooney Prize for Irish Literature 565
Rosendale Press Ltd **A** 81
Rosen Publishing Group, Inc., T⬛ **N** 450
Rosenstone/Wender **O** 473
Rosenthal (Jean) Literary Agenc⬛ **O** 473
Rose Partnership (David & Kath⬛ **L** 367
Rosinante/Munksgaard **AA** 414
RoSPA (Royal Society for the Prevention of Accidents) **V** ⬛
Rot-Weiss (Verlag) AG **AA** 435
Roundabout Theatre in Educati⬛ **M** 393

Roundabout Theatre Productions **M** 393
Roundhouse Publishing Ltd **A** 81
Routledge Ancient History Prize **T** 565
Routledge, Chapman & Hall **A** 81
Rover Group Award **T** 565
Rowohlt Tashenbuch **AA** 421
Roxby Press Ltd **E** 155
Royal Court Theatre (English Stage Company Ltd) **M** 393
Royal Court Young Writers' Festival **X** 408
Royal Dempster's **I** 280
Royal Economic Society Prize **T** 565
Royal Exchange Theatre Company **M** 394
Royal Geographical Society Library **U** 590
Royal Geographical Society Picture Library **V** 620
Royal Heinemann Award **T** 565
Royal Literary Fund, The **S** 540
Royal National Theatre **M** 394
Royal Photographic Society, The **V** 620
Royal Shakespeare Company **M** 394
Royal Society Library **U** 591
Royal Society of Literature **Q** 501
Royal Society of Medicine Library **U** 591
Royal Television Society **Q** 501
Royal Theatre **M** 394
Roymark Ltd **L** 367
RSPB Picture Library **V** 620
RTZ David Watt Memorial Prize, The **T** 565
Rugby Leaguer **I** 280
Rugby World & Post **I** 280
Running Magazine **I** 280
Rutgers University Press **N** 451
Ryder (Herta) **F** 176
Rye Festival **X** 408
Sadie Fields Productions **E** 155
Sagalyn Literary Agency **O** 474
Saga Magazine **I** 280
Saga **A** 82
Sage Publications Ltd **A** 82
Sagittarius Prize **T** 566
S A I E Editrice SRL **AA** 425
Sailplane and Gliding **I** 280
St Bride Printing Library **U** 591
St James (Ian) Awards **T** 566
St Martin's Press, Inc. **N** 451
St Paul Publications **A** 82
St Paul's Bibliographies **A** 82
Salamander Books Ltd **A** 82
Salariya Book Company Ltd **E** 155

Sales and Marketing Director **I** 280
Sales and Marketing Management **I** 281
Sales Direction **I** 281
Sales (Ian) Associates **F** 176
Salisbury Festival **X** 408
Salisbury Playhouse **M** 394
Salisbury Review **I** 281
Salmon Literary Magazine **B** 127
Salopoet **C** 127
Samlerens Forlag A/S **AA** 414
Sanders (Peter) Photography **V** 620
Sandum & Associates **O** 474
Sandwell College **AB** 522
San Francisco Examiner **P** 483
Sangam Books Ltd **A** 82
Santillana SA **AA** 432
Satis **B** 123
Satori Books **B** 123
Satori Press **B** 123
Sauerlander AG **AA** 435
Saur (KG) Verlag GmbH & Co KG **AA** 421
Savitri Books Ltd **E** 155
Saxon Radio **K** 328
Sayers (Dorothy L.) Society **Z** 511
Sayle (Tessa) Agency **F** 176
SBC Enterprises, Inc. **O** 474
S. B. Publications **A** 82
Scagnetti (Jack) Literary Agency **O** 474
Scarborough Evening News **H** 209
Scarecrow Press, Inc. **N** 451
Scarlett Press **A** 83
Sceptre Books **A** 83
Schaffner Agency, Inc. **O** 474
Scherz Verlag AG **AA** 435
Schibsteds (Chr.) Forlag A/S **AA** 428
Schlegel-Tieck Prize **T** 566
Schlesinger–Van Dyck Agency **O** 474
Schocken Books, Inc. **N** 451
Scholastic, Inc. **N** 451
Scholastic Publications Ltd **A** 83
Schönbergske (Det) Forlag A/S **AA** 414
Schonfeld Productions International/SPI 80 Ltd **L** 367
School of Creative Writing **AB** 523
Schroedel Schulbuchverlag GmbH **AA** 421
Schulman (Susan) Literary Agency **O** 475
Schwartz (Laurens R.) **O** 475
Science Book Prizes **T** 566
Science Fiction Foundation **Q** 501

Science Fiction Foundation Research Library **U** 591
Science Museum Library **U** 591
Science Photo Library **V** 620
SCM Press Ltd **A** 83
Scolar Press **A** 83
Scope International Ltd **A** 83
Scope Picture Productions **L** 367
Scorpion Publishing Ltd **A** 84
Scotland on Sunday **H** 209
Scotland on Sunday Magazine **I** 281
Scotland's Runner **I** 281
Scots Magazine, The **I** 281
Scotsman, The **G** 191
Scott Feresman **N** 451
Scottish Academic Press **A** 84
Scottish Arts Council **R** 513
Scottish Arts Council Book Awards **T** 566
Scottish Arts Council Bursaries and Awards **S** 540
Scottish Book of the Year **T** 566
Scottish Farmer, The **I** 281
Scottish Field **I** 281
Scottish Football Today **I** 282
Scottish Golf Magazine **I** 282
Scottish Highland Photo Library, The **V** 621
Scottish Home & Country **I** 282
Scottish Library Association **Q** 501
Scottish Newspaper Publishers' Association **Q** 502
Scottish Poetry Library **U** 591
Scottish Print Employers' Federation **Q** 502
Scottish Publishers Association, The **Q** 502
Scottish Television **J** 311
Scott (Rita) **O** 475
Scouting Magazine **I** 282
Scratch **C** 127
Screen **I** 282
Screen International **I** 282
Screen Sport **J** 314
Screen Ventures **V** 621
Screenwise International **AB** 526
Screenwriters Studio **AB** 526
Scribner's (Charles) Sons **N** 451
Scriptmate **Y** 533
Scriptwriters Tutorials **AB** 000
SCSE Book Prizes **T** 567
Scunthorpe Evening Telegraph **H** 210
Sea Breezes **I** 282
Seaby (B. A.) Ltd **A** 84
Seafarer **A** 84
Seagull Books **A** 84
Sealand Aerial Photography **V** 621

Search Press Ltd/Burns & Oates Ltd **A** 84
Sebastian Agency **O** 475
Secker & Warburg **A** 84
Seddon (Howard) Associates **Y** 533
Sefton Photo Library **V** 621
Seifert Dench Associates **F** 176
S E I (Società Editrice Internationale) **AA** 425
Seix Barral SA **AA** 432
Select Photos **V** 621
Seren Books **W** 145
Serpent's Tail **A** 84
Servire BV Uitgevers **AA** 426
Settle Press **A** 85
Seuil (Editions du) **AA** 418
Sevenday Productions **L** 367
70 (Edicoes) Lda **AA** 430
Seventh House Films **L** 367
Severn House Publishers **A** 85
Severn Sound/Severn Sound Supergold **K** 328
SGR FM 97.1/96.4 **K** 328
Shakespeare Head Press **A** 85
Shanbhala **A** 85
Shapiro-Lichtman Talent Agency **O** 475
Shared Experience Theatre **M** 394
Sharkey (James) Associates **F** 176
Sharland Organisation Ltd **F** 176
Shaw (Vincent) Associates **F** 176
Shearsman **B** 127
Sheba Feminist Press **A** 85
Sheffield Libraries and Information Services **U** 591
Sheil Land Associates Ltd* **F** 177
Sheldon (Caroline) Literary Agency **F** 177
Sheldon (Phil) Golf Picture Library **V** 621
Sheldon Press **A** 85
Sheldrake Press Ltd **E** 155
She Magazine **I** 283
Shepard Agency, The **O** 475
Shepheard-Walwyn (Publishers) Ltd **A** 85
Sherlock Holmes Collection (Westminster) **U** 585
Sherlock Publications **W** 145
Sherman Theatre Ltd **M** 395
Sher (Stanley) Enterprises **M** 395
Ship of Fools **B** 123
Ship Pictorial Publications **A** 85
Shire Publications Ltd **A** 85
Shoe Lane Library **U** 592
Shooting and Conservation **I** 283
Shooting News & Country Weekly **I** 283
Shooting Picture Co. Ltd **L** 368

Shooting Times & Country **I** 283
Shoot Magazine **I** 283
Shore (Lee) Agency **O** 475
Short Film Company, The **L** 368
Shropshire Magazine **I** 283
Shropshire Star (Telford) **H** 211
Sidgwick & Jackson Ltd **A** 86
Siegel (Bobbe), Literary Agency **O** 475
Sierra Literary Agency **O** 476
Sight & Sound **I** 283
Sigloch (Edition Helmut) GmbH & Co **AA** 421
Signal Cheshire **K** 328
Signal Poetry for Children Award **T** 567
Signal Radio **K** 328
Signals, Essex Media Centre **L** 368
Signature **I** 284
Signet **A** 86
Sign, The **I** 284
Sikkel (Uitgeverij De) NV **AA** 412
Silent Books **A** 86
Silver Burdett Press **N** 451
Simmons (Jeffrey) **F** 177
Simon André Memorial Fund Book Awards **T** 567
Simon (Richard Scott) Agency **F** 177
Simon & Schuster **N** 451
Simon & Schuster Ltd **A** 86
Sinclair-Stevenson **A** 86
Singer (Evelyn) Literary Agency, Inc., The **O** 476
Singer Media Corporation **O** 476
Siren Film & Video Co-op **L** 368
Siriol Productions **L** 368
Skier, The **I** 284
Skippon Video Associates **L** 368
Skira (Editions d'Art Albert) SA **AA** 435
Skishoot Offshoot **V** 621
Ski Survey **I** 284
Skoob Books Publishing Ltd **A** 86
Skyline Film & TV Productions Ltd **L** 368
Skyscan Balloon Photography **V** 621
Sky Television (BSkyB) **J** 314
Slimming **I** 284
Slow Dancer **C** 127
Slow Dancer Press **B** 123
Smallholder (and Small Farmer) **I** 284
Small Press Group of Britain (SPG) **Q** 502
Small Press World **I** 284
Smarties Prize for Children's Books **T** 567
Smash Hits **I** 285

SMI Business Television **L** 368
Smith (Carol) Literary Agency **F** 177
Smith Corona Prize **T** 567
Smith/Doorstop **W** 145
Smith Gryphon Ltd **A** 86
Smiths Knoll **C** 127
Smith & Watson Productions **L** 368
Smith (W. H.) Literary Award **T** 567
Smith (W. H.) Young Writers' Competition **T** 568
Smoke **C** 127
Smythe (Colin) Ltd **A** 86
Snap People's Theatre Trust **M** 395
Snell (Michael) Literary Agency **O** 476
Snooker Scene **I** 285
Society for Promoting Christian Knowledge (SPCK) **A** 86
Society of Authors, The **Q** 502
Society of Civil Service Authors **Q** 502
Society of Freelance Editors an Proofreaders **Q** 503
Society of Indexers **Q** 503
Society of Women Writers and Journalists **Q** 503
Society of Young Publishers **Q** 503
Soho Theatre Company **M** 395
Solaris **B** 123
Solicitors Journal **I** 285
Solo Books Ltd **A** 87
Solo Syndication & Literary Agency Ltd **F** 177
Solo Vision Ltd **L** 369
Solum Forlag A/S **AA** 428
Sol **B** 127
Somerset & Avon Life **I** 285
Somerset Magazine **I** 285
Sonoptics Communications Grc **L** 369
Sonzogno **AA** 425
South **B** 000
South American Pictures **V** 621
South Bank Board: Literature Office **Q** 503
South Coast Radio **K** 328
South East Arts **R** 515
South Eastern Writers' Associat **Q** 503
South East Wales Arts **R** 516
Southern Arts **R** 516
Southern Arts Literature Bursar **S** 540
Southern Arts Literature Prize **T** 568

Southern Sound Classic Hits **K** 328
Southern Writers **O** 476
South London Playwrighting Festival **X** 408
South Mersey College **AB** 524
Southover Press **W** 145
Southport Writers' Circle **AB** 529
Southport Writers' Circle Poetry Competition **T** 568
South Wales Argus **H** 206
South Wales Echo **H** 199
South Wales Evening Post **H** 211
South West Arts **R** 516
South West One **K** 328
South West Sound FM **K** 328
Souvenir Press Ltd **A** 87
Spacelink Books **W** 145
Spanish Institute Library **U** 592
Spanner **B** 123
SPCK **A** 87
Speakeasy **AB** 529
Spectacular Diseases **B** 123
Spectator, The **I** 285
Spectel Productions Limited **L** 369
Spectra **N** 451
Spectrum Colour Library **V** 621
Spectrum Communications Ltd **L** 369
Spectrum Radio **K** 328
Spectrum (Uitgeverij Het) BV **AA** 427
Spektrum Forlagsaktieselskab **AA** 415
Spellmount Ltd **A** 87
Sperling e Kupfer Editori SpA **AA** 425
Sphinx, The **M** 395
Spieler Literary Agency **O** 477
Spindlewood **A** 87
Spitzer (Philip G.) Literary Agency **O** 477
Split Second **V** 622
Spokes **B** 127
Spon (E&FN) **A** 88
Spooner (Frank) Pictures **V** 622
Sport and Leisure Magazine **I** 285
Sporting & Leisure Press **A** 88
Sporting Life, The **I** 286
Sporting Life Weekender **I** 286
Sporting Pictures (UK) Ltd **V** 622
Sports Writers' Association of Great Britain **Q** 504
Springer-Verlag **AA** 411
Springer-Verlag GmbH & Co KG **AA** 421
Springfield Books Ltd **A** 88
Spy Books **N** 451
Squash Player Magazine **I** 286

Stacey (Barrie) Productions/Santa Fe Productions Ltd **M** 395
Staffordshire Life **I** 286
Stage and Television Today **I** 286
Stainer & Bell Ltd **A** 88
Stam Press **A** 88
Stamps **I** 286
Standaard Uitgeverij **AA** 412
Stand Magazine **I** 286
Stand Magazine Short Story Competition **T** 568
Stanford University Press **N** 452
Stanford (Winifred Mary) Prize, The **T** 568
Stanley Paul **A** 88
Staple Magazine **I** 287
Staple Magazine **C** 127
Staple Open Poetry Competition **T** 568
Starke Publishers (Harold) Ltd **A** 88
Star (Sheffield) **H** 210
Steel (Elaine) **F** 178
Steele (Lyle) & Co. Ltd **O** 477
Steel (Tom) Productions **L** 369
Stein (Abner) **F** 178
Steinberg (Micheline) Playwrights' Agent **F** 178
Stephens (Patrick) Ltd **A** 88
Stepney Books Publications **W** 145
Sterling Publishing **N** 452
Stern (Gloria) Agency (Hollywood & New York) **O** 477
Stern (Lawrence) Fellowship **S** 540
Stevens (Gareth) Children's Books **N** 452
Stewart (Jo) Agency **O** 477
Still Pictures Environmental Agency **V** 622
Stingy Artist/Last Straw Press **B** 123
St John Thomas (David) Publisher **A** 82
Stockfile **V** 622
Stockphotos **V** 622
Stock Shot **V** 622
Stoll Moss Theatres Ltd **M** 395
Stone Flower Ltd **A** 88
Stone (Tony) Worldwide **V** 622
Storm: New Writing from East and West **I** 287
Strad, The **I** 287
Strandbergs Forlag ApS **AA** 415
Strand Editorial Services **Y** 533
Strang (Jessica) Library **V** 622
Stratford-upon-Avon Poetry Festival **X** 409

Strawberry Productions Ltd **L** 369
Stride **W** 146
Studio Editions Ltd **A** 88
Studio Vista **A** 89
Stuhlmann (Gunther) Author's Representative **O** 477
Styria (Verlag) **AA** 411
Suffolk Life **I** 287
Sugg (Belinda) Literary Agency **F** 178
Suhrkamp Verlag **AA** 421
Sumach Press, The **A** 88
Summersdale Publishers **A** 89
Sunday Express **G** 192
Sunday Express Book of the Year Award **T** 568
Sunday Express Magazine **I** 287
Sunday Independent **H** 208
Sunday Life (Belfast) **H** 196
Sunday Magazine **I** 287
Sunday Mail (Glasgow) **H** 209
Sunday Mail Magazine **I** 287
Sunday Mercury **H** 197
Sunday Mirror **G** 192
Sunday Mirror Magazine **I** 287
Sunday News (Belfast) **H** 196
Sunday Post (Glasgow) **H** 209
Sunday Post Magazine **I** 287
Sunday Sport **G** 192
Sunday Sun **H** 206
Sunday Telegraph **G** 193
Sunday Times Award for Small Publishers **T** 569
Sunday Times Fellowship, The **S** 540
Sunday Times Magazine **I** 287
Sunday Times Special Award for Excellence in Writing **T** 569
Sunday Times, The **G** 193
Sunday Times Young British Writer of the Year Award **T** 569
Sunderland Central Library **U** 592
Sunderland Echo **H** 210
Sunflower Books **A** 89
Sunk Island Review **I** 287
Sunk Island Review **C** 127
Sunlight (Edith & Joseph) Award **T** 569
Sun, The **G** 191
Super Channel **J** 314
Surrey County Magazine **I** 288
Surrey University Press **A** 89
Survival and Outdoor Techniques **I** 288
Survival Anglia Photo Library **V** 622
Sussex University Press **A** 89
Sutton (Alan) Publishing Ltd **A** 89
Swan Hill Press **A** 89
Swanlind Ltd **L** 369

Swansea Little Theatre Ltd **M** 396
Swansea Poetry Workshop **B** 123
Swansea Review **C** 128
Swansea Sound **K** 329
Swanson (H. N.), Inc. **O** 478
Swan Theatre **M** 395
Sweet & Maxwell Ltd **A** 89
Swets en Zeitlinger BV **AA** 427
Swift Children's Books **A** 90
Swift Picture Library Ltd **V** 623
Swimming Times **I** 288
Swiss Cottage Library **U** 592
Sygma **V** 623
Syndication International **V** 623
S4C (Welsh 4th Channel) **J** 311
Tabard Productions **L** 369
Tabard Theatre **M** 396
Tabb House **A** 89
TAB Books **N** 452
Table Ronde (Les Editions de la) **AA** 418
Tablet, The **I** 288
Take a Break **I** 288
Tak Tak Tak **C** 128
Talbot Television Ltd **L** 369
Taliesin **AB** 523
Talisman Films Ltd **L** 369
Talkback Productions **L** 370
Tamarind Ltd **W** 146
Tambourine Books **N** 452
Tano AS **AA** 428
Tantleff Office, The **O** 478
Tarragon Press **A** 90
Taste **I** 288
Tatler, The **I** 289
Tauber (Peter) Press Agency **F** 178
Tauris (I.B.) & Co. Ltd **A** 90
Taurus Press of Willow Dene **B** 123
Taxus Press **W** 146
Taylor (E. Reginald) Essay Competition **T** 569
Teach Yourself Books **A** 90
Team Two Ltd **L** 370
Tears in the Fence **C** 128
Tees Valley Writer **I** 289
Tees Valley Writer Competitions **T** 569
Teide (Editorial) SA **AA** 432
Telegraph & Argus **H** 198
Telegraph Colour Library **V** 623
Telegraph Magazine **I** 289
Television History Centre **Q** 504
Television in Business Ltd **L** 370
Television Visualeyes **L** 370
Television Week **I** 289
Teliesyn **L** 370
Temba Theatre Company Ltd **M** 396

Templar Company **E** 156
Temple House Books **A** 90
Temple Press Ltd **W** 146
Temple University Press **N** 452
Tennessee (University of) Press **N** 452
Tennis Times, The **I** 289
Tennis World **I** 289
10th Muse **C** 128
Tenth Decade **C** 128
Terminus Publications **W** 146
Tern Television Productions Ltd **L** 370
T. E. Utley Award **T** 570
Texas (University of) Press **N** 452
Texto Editora **AA** 430
Text **I** 289
TFM Radio **K** 329
Thames and Hudson Ltd **A** 90
Thames Head **E** 156
Thames Publishing/Autolycus Press **A** 90
Thames Television **J** 312
Thames Television Theatre Writers' Scheme **S** 540
Theatr Clwyd **M** 396
Theatre Foundry **M** 396
Theatre Museum Library & Archive **U** 592
Theatre of Comedy Co. **L** 370
Theatre of Comedy Company **M** 396
Theatre Royal Stratford East **M** 397
Theatre Royal Windsor **M** 397
Theatre Workshop Edinburgh **M** 397
Theatre Writers' Union **Q** 504
Theatr Powys **M** 396
Dickens Fellowship, The **Z** 509
Echo (Southampton), The **H** 210
Hogarth Press Ltd, The **A** 53
Keystone Collection, The **V** 613
Northern Echo, The **H** 207
Theologia Cambrensis **I** 290
Thieme (Georg) Verlag **AA** 421
Thienemanns (K.) Verlag **AA** 421
Third Eye Productions Ltd **L** 370
Third Half, The **C** 128
Third House (Publishers) **W** 146
This England **I** 290
Thomas Cook Travel Book Awards **T** 548
Thomas (David) Prize **S** 540
Thomson Regional Newspapers Ltd **H** 195
Thorndike Theatre (Leatherhead) Ltd **M** 397
Thornes (Stanley) (Publishers) **A** 90

Thornhill Press **A** 91
Thorsons Publishing Group **A** 91
Three Hills Books **A** 91
Three Lions **V** 623
Threshold Books **A** 91
Thurley (J. M.) **F** 178
Thurston (Patrick) PhotoLibrary 623
Tibble (Ann) Poetry Competition **T** 569
Tiden (Bokforlags) AB **AA** 433
Tiden Norsk Forlag **AA** 428
Tiderne Skifter **AA** 415
Tiger Television Ltd **L** 370
Tigerwise Theatrical Management **M** 397
Time-Life Books BV **AA** 427
Time-Life Books, Inc. **N** 453
Time-Life Silver PEN Award **T** 568
Time Magazine **P** 483
Time Out **I** 290
Times Books **A** 91
Times Books **N** 453
Times Educational Supplement Information Book Awards **T** 570
Times Educational Supplement Scotland, The **I** 291
Times Educational Supplement, The **I** 290
Times Higher Education Supplement, The **I** 291
Times Literary Supplement **I** 291
Times, The **G** 193
Time **I** 290
Timms Premium **YY** 534
Timun Mas (Editorial) SA **AA** 432
Tir Na N-Og Award, The **T** 570
Titan Books **A** 91
Titbits **I** 291
Todariana Editrice **AA** 425
Today **G** 193
Today's Golfer **I** 291
Today's Runner **I** 291
Tolkein **A** 91
Tolley Publishing Co. Ltd **A** 91
Tomahawk Films Ltd **L** 371
Tom-Gallon Trust **S** 541
Toonder (Marten) Award **T** 570
Toorts (Uitgeverij De) **AA** 427
Topaz Productions Ltd **L** 371
Topham Picture Source **V** 623
Torque Press **B** 123
Totterdell (B.M.) Photography **V** 623
Toucan Books Ltd **E** 156
Touch AM **K** 329
Touch Productions **L** 371
Town House Productions Ltd **L** 371

Townswoman **I** 292
Tracks **A** 91
Trades Union Congress **V** 623
Trades Union Congress Library **U** 593
Traditional Homes **I** 292
Traeger (Tessa) **V** 623
Translators' Association, The **Q** 504
Transworld Publishers Ltd **A** 92
Trask (Betty) Awards, The **S** 541
Trauner (Rudolf), Verlag **AA** 411
Traveller **I** 292
Travel Library, The **V** 623
Travelling Scholarships, The **S** 541
Traverse Theatre **M** 397
Trenchard's (Peter) Image Store Ltd **V** 623
Trends Management **M** 397
Trent FM **K** 329
Trentham Books Ltd **A** 92
Triangle **A** 92
Triangle Two Ltd **L** 371
Tribune **I** 292
Tricycle Theatre **M** 398
Trinity Press International **N** 453
Tripp (John) Award **T** 570
Trollope Society, The **Z** 511
Trombone Press **W** 146
Tron Theatre Company **M** 398
Tropix Photographic Library **V** 623
Trotman & Co. Ltd **A** 92
Trout Fisherman **I** 292
True Romances **I** 292
True Story **I** 292
TSW – Television South West **J** 312
T. & T. Clark **A** 29
Tuba Press **B** 123
Tufnell Press, The **W** 146
Turners Film & Video Productions **L** 371
Turret Books **B** 124
Tusquets Editores **AA** 432
Tutin (Dorothy) Award **T** 570
TV-AM **J** 312
TVS **J** 312
TV Times **I** 292
Twentieth Century Fox Productions Ltd **L** 371
Twin Books UK Ltd **E** 156
Twin Continental Films Ltd **L** 371
2CR (Two Counties Radio) **K** 329
Two-Can Publishing Ltd **A** 92
2M Communications Ltd **O** 478
210 FM **K** 329
Tyburn Productions Ltd **L** 371
Ty Gwyn Films Ltd **L** 371
Tyne Tees Television **J** 312

Tyrannosaurus Rex Press **W** 147
Tyrolia (Verlagsanstalt) Gesellschaft mbH **AA** 411
Ty New ydd **D** 132
UBA Ltd **L** 372
Uden Associates Ltd **L** 372
UEA Writing Fellowship **S** 541
Ullstein (Buchverlage) GmbH **AA** 421
Ulster News Letter **H** 196
Ulster Television **J** 312
Umbrella Theatre **M** 398
Umoja Theatre Company **M** 398
Underground Press **B** 124
Understanding **C** 128
Uniboek BV **AA** 427
Unicopli (Edizione Scolastiche) SpA **AA** 425
Unicorn Books **A** 92
Unicorn Theatre for Children **M** 398
Unicorn Theatre Young Playwrights' Competition **T** 570
Uniepers BV **AA** 427
Union of Welsh Writers, The **Q** 504
United Nations London Information Centre **U** 593
United Television Artists Ltd **L** 372
Universal Pictorial Press & Agency Ltd **V** 624
Universe Publishing, Inc. **N** 453
Universe, The **I** 292
Universitetsforlaget **AA** 428
University Editions **N** 453
University of Aberdeen **AB** 522
University of Birmingham **AB** 522
University of Bristol **AB** 522
University of Glasgow **AB** 523
University of Kent at Canterbury **AB** 524
University of Leeds **AB** 524
University of Newcastle upon Tyne **AB** 526
University of Reading **AB** 526
University of Sheffield **AB** 527
University of Southampton **AB** 528
University of Stirling **AB** 527
University of Surrey **AB** 527
University of Sussex **AB** 527
University of Ulster **AB** 522
University of Warwick **AB** 527
Unwin Hyman **A** 93
UPI **V** 624
Upstream **L** 372
Urban und Schwarzenberg GmbH **AA** 421
Urstadt (Susan P.), Inc. **O** 478

USA Today **P** 483
Usborne Publishing Ltd **A** 93
US News and World Report **P** 483
USSR Photo Library **V** 624
Utley (T. E.) Award **T** 570
Vallentine, Mitchell **A** 93
Van der Leun & Associates **O** 478
Vanderlinden (Librairie) SA **AA** 412
Van Nostrand Reinhold **N** 453
V&A Picture Library **V** 624
Vardey & Brunton Associates* **F** 178
Variorum **A** 93
VATV **L** 372
Vauxhall Trophy **T** 570
V C H Verlagsgesellschaft mbH **AA** 422
VEB Verlag Enzyklopädie Leipzig **AA** 422
Vector **I** 293
Vegan, The **I** 293
Vegetarian Living **I** 293
Venice Picture Library, The **V** 624
Ventura Publishing Ltd **A** 93
Vera Productions **L** 372
Verbatim, The Language Quarterly **I** 293
Verbo (Editorial) SA **AA** 430
Vermilion **A** 93
Ver Poets **Q** 504
Ver Poets Poetry Competitions **T** 571
Verronmead Ltd **L** 372
Versal (Ediciones) SA **AA** 432
Verse **C** 128
Verso Ltd **A** 93
Veteran Car **I** 293
Victor (Ed) Ltd **F** 179
Victoria House Publishing Ltd **E** 156
Victoria Library (Westminster) **U** 593
Victory Archive, The **V** 624
Video and Satellite Today **I** 293
Video Arts (Production) Ltd **L** 372
Video At Work **L** 373
Video Enterprises **L** 373
Videoplus Productions Ltd **L** 373
Video Presentations **L** 373
Video Production Associates **L** 373
Videotel Productions/Living Tape Productions **L** 373
Video Trade Weekly **I** 293
Video World Magazine **I** 294
Vidox Video Productions **L** 373
Viewfinder Colour Photo Library **V** 624
Viewpoint Group Ltd **L** 373

Vigil Publications **B** 124
Viking **A** 93
Viking FM **K** 329
Vindrose (Forlaget) A/S **AA** 415
Vintage **A** 93
Vintage Books **N** 453
Vintage Magazine Company Ltd, The **V** 624
Virago Press Ltd **A** 93
Virgin Publishing **A** 93
Vision **C** 123
Visionbank Library/England Scene **V** 624
Vision Broadcasting **J** 314
Vision Press Ltd **A** 94
Visionventures International **L** 373
Visnews Still Service **V** 624
Visual Connection (TVC) **L** 374
Vives (Editorial Luis) (Edelvives) **AA** 432
V N U Business Press Group BV **AA** 427
Vogel-Verlag KG **AA** 422
Vogue **I** 294
Vogue Talent Contest **T** 571
Voice of America **P** 483
Voice, The **I** 294
Volcano Press **A** 94
V U Boekhandel/Uitgeverij BV **AA** 427
Vuibert (Librairie) SA **AA** 418
WABC (Nice 'n' Easy Radio) **K** 329
Wade (Carlson) **O** 478
Wadlow Grosvenor **L** 374
Wadsworth Prize for Business History **T** 571
Wahlstroms Bokforlag AB **AA** 433
Wakefield Historical Publications **W** 147
Wales on Sunday **G** 194
Wales (University of) Press **A** 94
Walker Books Ltd **A** 94
Walker (Charles) Collection, The **V** 624
Walker & Co **N** 453
Walker (S.) Literary Agency **F** 179
Wallace (Bess) Associates **O** 478
Wallace (Edgar) Society **Z** 512
Wallace Literary Agency **O** 478
Wallbank (John) Associates **M** 398
Wallerstein (Gerry B.) Agency **O** 479
Wall Street Journal **P** 483
Wall to Wall Television **L** 374
Walmsley (John) Picture Library **V** 625
Walmsley Society, The **Z** 512
Walnut Partnership, The **L** 374

Wandsworth Writers London Competition **T** 571
Ward Lock Ltd **A** 94
Ward (Michael) Theatre Productions **M** 398
Ware (Cecily) Literary Agents **F** 179
Warehouse Theatre, Croydon **M** 399
Ware (John A.) Literary Agency **O** 479
Warner Books **N** 453
Warner Chappell Plays Ltd **A** 95
Warner Chappell Plays Ltd **F** 179
Warner Sisters **L** 374
Warner/Warner-Futura **A** 95
Washington Post **P** 483
Washington Square Press **N** 453
Washington State University Press **N** 454
Watch It! **I** 294
Waterfront Productions **L** 374
Waterline Books **A** 95
Watermill Theatre **M** 399
Watershed Television Ltd **L** 374
Waterside Productions, Inc. **O** 479
Waterways Photo Library **V** 625
Waterways World **I** 294
Watson, Little Ltd* **F** 179
Watt (A. P.) Ltd **F** 179
Watts Group, The **A** 95
Wayland (Publishers) Ltd **A** 95
Ways with Words, the Dartington Literary Festival **X** 409
W. B. Saunders/Saunders Scientific Publications **A** 82
Wear FM, 103.4 **K** 329
Weavers Press Publishing **A** 95
Webb & Bower (Publishers) **A** 95
Webb (Mary) Society **Z** 512
Wecksler-Incomco **O** 479
Wedding and Home **I** 294
Weekly News **I** 294
We Find It (Press Clippings) **YY** 534
Weidenfeld & Nicolson Ltd **A** 95
Weight Watchers Magazine **I** 295
Weimar Archive **V** 625
Weiner (Cherry) Literary Agency **O** 479
Wells (H.G.) Society **Z** 512
Wellsweep Press **B** 124
Welsh Academy **Q** 504
Welsh Arts Council **R** 513
Welsh Arts Council Book of the Year Awards **T** 571
Welsh Books Council $51(Cyngor Llyfrau Cymraeg) **Q** 505

Welton (Arthur) Scholarship **S** 541
WEMS **K** 329
West Air Photography **V** 625
West Coast Magazine **B** 128
Westcountry Television Ltd **J** 31
West Country Writers' Associati **Q** 505
Westermann (Georg) Verlag GmbH **AA** 422
Western Daily Press **H** 198
Western Isles Libraries **U** 593
Western Mail (Cardiff) **H** 199
Western Morning News **H** 208
West-Friesland (Uit-Mij) **AA** 42°
West Midlands Arts **R** 516
Westminster Archives & Local History Collection **U** 593
Westminster (City of) Reference Libraries **U** 593
Westminster Reference Library 593
West Sound Radio/South West Sound FM **K** 330
West Wales Arts **R** 516
Westwords **C** 128
West Yorkshire Playhouse **M** 39
Weyfarers **C** 128
W. Foulsham & Co. **A** 42
Wharncliffe Publishing Ltd **A** 95
What Car? **I** 295
What Diet & Lifestyle **I** 295
What Hi-Fi **I** 295
What Investment **I** 295
What Mortgage **I** 295
What Personal Computer **I** 296
What Satellite **I** 296
What's New in Building **I** 296
What's New in Farming **I** 296
What's New in Interiors **I** 296
What's On in London **I** 296
What Video **I** 296
Wheelbase Films Video and Television (CMR Productions Ltd) **L** 374
W. H. Freeman & Co. Ltd **A** 43
Which? Books **A** 96
Which Computer? **I** 297
Whirligig Theatre **M** 399
White City Films **L** 374
Whitehead (Eric) Picture Librar and Agency **V** 625
White (Michael) Productions L **L** 374
White Rose Literary Magazine, The **C** 128
Whitfield Prize **T** 572

Whiting (Elizabeth) & Associates **V** 625
Whiting (John) Award **T** 572
Whittet Books Ltd **A** 96
W. H. Smith Literary Award **T** 567
W. H. Smith Young Writers' Competition **T** 568
Whyld Publishing Co-op **W** 147
Wickes (David) Productions Ltd **L** 375
Wide Skirt Press, The **B** 124
Wide Skirt, The **C** 128
Wiedel (Janine) **V** 625
Wiener (Dinah) Ltd **F** 180
Wiener Library, The **U** 594
Wieser & Wieser, Inc. **O** 479
Wilderness Photographic Library **V** 625
Wiley (John) & Sons Ltd **A** 96
Wilkins (Alfred & Mary) Memorial Poetry Competition, The **T** 572
Williams (Andy) Photo Library **V** 625
Williams (Charles) Society **Z** 512
Williams (David) Picture Library **V** 626
Williams (Griffith John) Memorial Prize **T** 572
Williamson (Henry) Society, The **Z** 512
Williams (Raymond) Community Publishing Prize **T** 572
Williams's (Dr) Library **U** 594
Williams (S & I) Power Pix International Picture Library **V** 626
Williams (Vaughan) Memorial Library **V** 626
Willow Creek Press **N** 454
Wiltshire Life **I** 297
Windcrest Books **N** 454
Windrush Press, The **A** 96
Windsor Festival **X** 409
Windsor Large Print **A** 96
Wine **I** 297
Wingate (H. H.) Prize **T** 572
Winged Horse Touring Productions **M** 399
Wingfield Sporting Art Library, The **V** 626
Winnick (Maurice) Associates Ltd **L** 375
Wirral Metropolitan College **AB** 524
Wisden Cricket Monthly **I** 297
Wise **A** 96
Wisley Handbooks **A** 96
Witherby (H. F. & G.) Ltd **A** 96
W & J Theatrical Enterprises Ltd **M** 399

Woburn Press **A** 96
Wøldike (Forlaget) K/S **AA** 415
Wolfe Publishing **A** 96
Wolff (Oswald) Books **A** 96
Wolfson History Awards **T** 572
Wolsey Theatre Company **M** 399
Wolters-Noordhoff-Longman BV **AA** 427
Wolverhampton Central Library **U** 594
Woman **I** 297
Woman and Home **I** 297
Woman's Journal **I** 297
Woman's Own **I** 298
Woman's Own Short Story Competition **T** 573
Woman's Realm **I** 298
Woman's Story **I** 298
Woman's Weekly **I** 298
Women in Publishing **Q** 505
Women's Art Magazine **I** 298
Women's Press, The **A** 96
Women's Theatre Group **M** 399
Women Writers Network (WWN) **Q** 505
Woodhead Publishing Ltd **A** 97
Woodmansterne Ltd **V** 626
Wood (Roger) Library **V** 626
Woodward (Michael) Creations Ltd **F** 180
Woodward (Michael) Licensing **V** 626
Woodworker **I** 298
Woolverton Colour Library **V** 626
Worcester Festival of Literature **X** 409
Word and Action (Dorset) **B** 124
Word For Word, Berkshire Literature Festival **X** 409
Wordsong **N** 454
Wordwright Books **A** 97
Wordwright Books **E** 156
Workbox **I** 299
Workers' Educational Association **AB** 529
Working Title Films Ltd/WTTV Ltd **L** 375
Working Titles **I** 299
Works Magazine **I** 299
Works Publishing **W** 147
World Fishing **I** 299
World International Publishing Ltd **A** 97
World of Interiors, The **I** 299
World Pictures/Feature-Pix Colour Library **V** 626
World Soccer **I** 299
Worldview Pictures **L** 375
World Wide International Television **L** 375

Worldwide Television News **L** 375
W & R Chambers **A** 27
Wreschner (Ruth), Authors' Representative **O** 479
Wright (Ann) Representatives, Inc. **O** 480
Wright (George) **V** 626
Wright (Stephen) Authors' Representative **O** 480
Write Around - A Celebration of Cleveland Writing **X** 409
Writerlink **Y** 533
Writers Bureau, The **AB** 526
Writer's Consulting Group **O** 480
Writers' Exchange, The **Y** 533
Writers Forum **B** 124
Writers' Guild, The **AB** 526
Writers' Guild of Great Britain, The **Q** 505
Writers' Guild Workshops **AB** 529
Writers House, Inc. **O** 480
Writers' Monthly **I** 299
Writers Monthly Short Story Competitions **T** 573
Writers News **I** 300
Writers' Own Magazine **C** 128
Writers' Productions **O** 480
Writers' Representatives **O** 480
Writers' Rostrum, The **I** 300
Writers' Summer School **AB** 523
Write Stuff, The **F** 180
Writing in Merseyside **AB** 525
Writing Magazine **I** 300
Writing School, The **AB** 526
Writing Women **C** 128
WSTV Productions Ltd **L** 375
Xenos **I** 300
Xtra AM **K** 330
Yachting Journalists' Association **Q** 506
Yachting Monthly **I** 300
Yachts and Yachting **I** 301
Yale University Press (London) **A** 97
Yates (Roy) Books **A** 97
Yearling **A** 97
Yoffroy Publications **W** 147
York Archaeological Trust for Excavation and Research **V** 626
York Central Library **U** 594
York Festival **X** 409
Yorkshire Arts Circus Ltd **A** 97
Yorkshire Dialect Society **Q** 506
Yorkshire Evening Post **H** 204
Yorkshire & Humberside Arts **R** 517
Yorkshire Open Poetry Competition **T** 573
Yorkshire Post **H** 204

Yorkshire Post Art and Music Awards **T** 573
Yorkshire Post Best First Work Awards **T** 573
Yorkshire Post Book of the Year Award **T** 573
Yorkshire Ridings Magazine **I** 301
Yorkshire Television **J** 313
York Theatre Royal **M** 399
Younger (Greg) Associates **L** 375
Young (John Robert) Collection **V** 627
Young Library Ltd **A** 98
Young Newspapermen's Association **Q** 506
Young Playwright of the Year Award **T** 573
Young Science Writer Awards **T**

573
Young Telegraph **I** 301
Young Vic, The **M** 400
Young Writers' Competition **T** 573
Your Horse **I** 301
Yours Magazine **I** 301
You - The Mail on Sunday Magazine **I** 301
Yo-Yo Films **L** 375
Yr Academi Gymreig **Q** 506
Yrkesopplaering I/S **AA** 429
Zeckendorf (Susan) Associates **O** 481
Zed Books Ltd **A** 98
ZED Ltd **L** 376
Zelasky (Tom) Literary Agency **O** 481
Zena Publications **B** 124

Zenith Productions Ltd **L** 376
Zephyr Books **N** 454
Zoe Books Ltd **E** 156
Zomba **A** 98
Zondervan **N** 454
Zoom Production Co. Ltd, The **L** 376
Zora Press **B** 124
Zsolnay (Paul), Verlag GmbH **AA** 411
Zytglogge Verlag **AA** 435
Zzero Books **W** 147

Subject Index

Academic: Publishers (UK)
Aberdeen University Press 9
Acair Ltd 10
Addison-Wesley Publishers Ltd
    10
Aris & Phillips Ltd 13
Ashgate Publishing Co. Ltd 13
Batsford (B.T.) Ltd 16
Berg Publishers Ltd 17
Blackwell Publishers 18
Book Guild, The 20
California University Press 24
Cambridge University Press 24
Carcanet Press Ltd 25
Cassell 25
Columbia University Press 30
Curzon Press Ltd 32
Donald (John) Publishers Ltd 35
Duckworth (Gerald) & Co. Ltd 36
Edinburgh University Press 37
Exeter (University of) Press 40
Freeman (W. H.) & Co. Ltd 42
Golden Cockerel Press Ltd 44
Grevatt & Grevatt 46
Harcourt Brace Jovanovich Ltd 48
Harvard University Press 50
Hodder & Stoughton Ltd 52
Jai Press Ltd 54
Leicester University Press 57
Library Association Publishing 58
Liverpool University Press 59
Macmillan Publishers Ltd 61
Manchester University Press 62
MIT Press Ltd, The 65
Octagon Press Ltd 68
Open Books Publishing Ltd 68
Open University Press 69
Oxford University Press 70
Penguin Books Ltd 71
Pergamon Press 73
Plenum Publishing Ltd 74
Pluto Press Ltd 75
Princeton University Press 75
Routledge, Chapman & Hall Ltd
    81
Sage Publications Ltd 82
Scottish Academic Press 84
Search Press Ltd/Burns & Oates
    Ltd 84
Souvenir Press Ltd 87

Sutton (Alan) Publishing Ltd 89
Tauris (I.B.) & Co. Ltd 90
Vision Press Ltd 94
Wales (University of) Press 94
Yale University Press (London) 97

Academic: Packagers
Archival Facsimiles Ltd 148
Diagram Visual Information Ltd
    151

Academic: Agents (UK)
Futerman (Vernon) Associates
    166
Howard Seddon Associates 168
Kelly (Frances) 169

Academic: Publishers (US)
Alabama (University of) Press 437
Arizona (University of) Press 437
Arkansas (University of) Press 438
Arkansas (University of) Press 438
California (University of) Press
    440
Chicago (University of) Press 440
Facts on File, Inc. 442
Harvard University Press 444
Illinois (University of) Press 444
Indiana University Press 444
Iowa (University of) Press 445
Kansas (University of) Press 445
Kent State University Press 445
Massachusetts (University of)
    Press 447
McFarland & Company, Inc.,
    Publishers 446
Missouri (University of) Press 447
New England (University Press of)
    448
New Mexico (University of) Press
    448
Open Court Publishing Co. 448
Pennsylvania (University of) Press
    449
Rutgers University Press 451
St Martin's Press, Inc. 451
Scarecrow Press, Inc. 451
Stanford University Press 452
Temple University Press 452

Tennessee (University of) Press
    452
Texas (University of) Press 452
University Press of America 453

Academic: Agents (US)
Schwartz (Laurens R.) 475

**Academic:
Bursaries/Fellowships**
British Academy Publication
    Subventions 536

Academic: Small Presses
Hisarlik Press 139
Peepal Tree Books 143
Romer Publications 145

**Accounting/Taxation:
Publishers (UK)**
Chapman (Paul) Publishing Ltd 27
D. P. Publications Ltd 35
Harcourt Brace Jovanovich Ltd 48
Longman Group Ltd 60
Reed International Books 78
Tolley Publishing Co. Ltd 91

**Accounting/Taxation:
Magazines**
Accountancy 217
Accountancy Age 217
Certified Accountant 230

**Adventure & Exploration:
Publishers (UK)**
Airlife Publishing Ltd 11
Hodder & Stoughton Ltd 52
Mann (George) Books 62

**Adventure & Exploration:
Packagers**
MM Productions Ltd 154

**Adventure & Exploration:
Agents (UK)**
Solo Syndication & Literary
    Agency Ltd 177

Adventure & Exploration: Film, TV and video producers
Ideas Factory, The 356
Lucida Productions 359

Adventure & Exploration: Publishers (US)
Avalon Books 438
Avon Books 438
Bantam Doubleday Dell Publishing Group 438
Random House, Inc. 450
Walker & Co 453

Adventure & Exploration: Agents (US)
Appleseeds Management 455
Boates (Reid) Literary Agency 457
Browne (Pema) Ltd 457
Ellen Lively Steele & Associates 461
Fishbein (Frieda) Ltd 462
Gladden Unlimited 463
Kern (Natasha) Literary Agency, Inc. 464
Lampack (Peter) Agency, Inc. 465
Lee (L. Harry) Literary Agency 466
Leone (Adele) Agency, Inc. 466
Literary/Business Associates 467
Sierra Literary Agency 476
Swanson (H. N.), Inc. 478
Zelasky (Tom) Literary Agency 481

Adventure & Exploration: Picture Libraries
Cleare (John)/Mountain Camera 604
Popperfoto 618
Remote Source 619
Royal Geographical Society Picture Library 620
Spooner (Frank) Pictures 622
Wilderness Photographic Library 625

Advertising: Magazines
Campaign 228
Creative Review 235

Advertising: Film, TV and video producers
ANV Productions 338
Aurora Sound and Vision 338
Batty (Peter) Productions 339
BFV Ltd 340
Boney (Matt) Associates 340
Box Clever 341

Caravel Film Techniques Limited 342
Catlin (Pearl) Associates 342
Cinexsa Film Productions Limited 344
Cleveland Productions 344
Corporate Communication Consultants Ltd 345
Creative Channel Ltd 345
Creative Film Makers Ltd 345
Creative Television Workshops Ltd 345
Crew Green Associates Ltd 345
Dane Productions 346
Daring Deeds Ltd 346
DBI Communication 347
Espresso TV 348
Eyewitness Ltd 349
First House Productions Ltd 350
Flying Tiger Film and TV Productions 350
Formula Communications 351
Gateway Audio Visual and Video 351
Gibb Rose Organisation Ltd 352
Good Film Company, The 352
Haraco Ltd 354
Hemson (John) 354
Hourglass Pictures Ltd 355
Illustra Communications Ltd 356
Inca Video & Film Productions 356
In Video Productions Ltd 356
Jenkinson (Brian) Film & Television Productions Ltd 357
Jericho Productions Ltd 357
Lombard Productions Ltd 358
Mac Films 359
Maiden Films Ltd 359
Main Communications 359
Medialab Ltd 360
MIlls (John) Film and Television 361
Morrison Company, The 362
New Decade Productions 362
Original Film & Video Productions Ltd 363
Pace Productions Ltd 363
Pentagon Communications 364
PGP Films 364
Poseidon Productions Ltd 365
Pretty Clever Pictures 365
Priory Film Productions 366
Purchasepoint Video 366
Purkis Neale Productions Ltd 366
Quay Productions Ltd 366
Rank Production 366
Red Lion Communications Ltd 367

Scope Picture Productions Ltd 367
Shooting Picture Co. Ltd 368
Short Film Company, The 368
Smith & Watson Productions 368
Sonoptics Communications Grou 369
Tabard Productions 369
Twin Continental Films Ltd 371
Vidox Video Productions Ltd 37.
Watershed Television Ltd 374
Younger (Greg) Associates 375
Yo-Yo Films 375

Advertising: Libraries
Shoe Lane Library 592

Advertising: Picture Librarie
Financial Times Picture Collectio 607
Retrograph Archive Ltd 619

Africa: Publishers (UK)
Bowker-Saur Ltd 20
Cass (Frank) 25
Currey (James) Publishers 32
Curzon Press Ltd 32
Evans Brothers Ltd 39
Zed Books Ltd 98

Africa: Agents (UK)
Bolt (David) Associates 160
Eady (Toby) Associates Ltd 165

Africa: Magazines
African Affairs 217

Africa: Bursaries/Fellowship
Sunday Times Fellowship, The 540

Africa: Prizes
Graham (Edgar) Book Prize 553

Africa: Libraries
British Library Oriental and India Office Collections 580

Africa: Picture Libraries
Animal Photography 599
Art Directors Photo Library 600
Camerapix Picture Library 603
Christian Aid Photo Library 603
Colasanti (Stephanie) 604
Dixon (C M) 605
Estall (Robert) Photographs 606
Halliday (Sonia) Photographs 61
Images of Africa Photo Bank 612
Photographers' Library, The 618
Screen Ventures 621

Africa: Small Presses
Peepal Tree Books 143

Agriculture & Farming: Publishers (UK)
Crowood Press Ltd, The 32
Donald (John) Publishers Ltd 35
Farming Press Books 41
Freeman (W. H.) & Co. Ltd 42
Pergamon Press 73
Prism Press Book Publishers Ltd 75

Agriculture & Farming: Magazines
Farmers Weekly 245
Farming News 245
Home Farm 254
Scottish Farmer, The 281
Smallholder (and Small Farmer) 284
What's new in Farming 296

Agriculture & Farming: Film, TV and video producers
Normandy Film Productions 363
Waterfront Productions 374

Agriculture & Farming: Professional Associations
Guild of Agricultural Journalists 496

Agriculture & Farming: Libraries
Farming Information Centre 583
Ministry of Agriculture, Fisheries and Food 587

Agriculture & Farming: Picture Libraries
Aquila Photographics 599
Blake (Anthony) 602
Cash (J. Allan) Ltd 603
Coleman (Bruce) Wildlife & Travel Photo Library 604
Farmers Publishing Group Picture Library 607
Financial Times Picture Collection 607
Frith (Francis) Collection 608
Garland (Leslie) Picture Library 609
Holt Studios International Ltd 611
Hutchison Library, The 611
Impact Photos 612
Natural Science Photos 616
Network Photographers 616
Northern Picture Library, The 616
Ronan (Ann) Picture Library 620

Sefton Photo Library 621
Viewfinder Colour Photo Library 624
Williams (S & I) Power Pix International Picture Library 626

Agriculture & Farming: European Publishers
B L V Verlagsgesellschaft mbH 419
Deutsch (Verlag Harri) 419
Payot Lausanne (Editions) 435
Vogel-Verlag KG 422

Animal Care: Publishers (UK)
Cassell 25
Freeman (W. H.) & Co. Ltd 42
Souvenir Press Ltd 87

Animal Care: Magazines
Animal World 219
FarmWatch 245
Greenscene 251

Animal Care: Agents (US)
ForthWrite Literary Agency 462

Animal Care: Picture Libraries
Cordaiy (Sylvia) Photo Library 604

Animal Care: Small Presses
Fox Press 138

Animal Rights: Publishers (UK)
Centaur Press Ltd 26
HarperCollins Publishers Ltd 49

Animal Rights: Magazines
FarmWatch 245
Greenscene 251

Animation: Film, TV and video producers
Amber Films 337
Bevanfield Films 339
Cartwn Cymru 342
Filmfair Ltd 349
Meditel Productions Ltd 360
Melendez Films 361
Rank Production 366
Siriol Productions 368
Talbot Television Ltd 369

Anthropology: Publishers (UK)
Boyars (Marion) Publishers Ltd 20
Constable & Co. Ltd 30

Currey (James) Publishers 32
Curzon Press Ltd 32
Donald (John) Publishers Ltd 35
Edinburgh University Press 37
Freeman (W. H.) & Co. Ltd 42
Harcourt Brace Jovanovich Ltd 48
Harvard University Press 50
Karnak House 55
Manchester University Press 62
MIT Press Ltd, The 65
Pergamon Press 73
Polity Press 75
Routledge, Chapman & Hall Ltd 81

Anthropology: Publishers (US)
Iowa State University Press 445
Princeton University Press 450
Tennessee (University of) Press 452
Texas (University of) Press 452

Anthropology: Agents (US)
Schwartz (Laurens R.) 475

Anthropology: Picture Libraries
Axel Poignant Archive 601
Coleman (Bruce) Wildlife & Travel Photo Library 604
Natural History Museum Picture Library 616

Anthropology: European Publishers
Beck (Verlag C H) 418
Gruyter (Walter de) & Co 419
Jaca Book (Editoriale) 424
Liguori Editore SRL 424
Presses de la Cité, Les 418

Antiques: Publishers (UK)
Antique Collectors' Club 12
Facts On File 40
Lutterworth Press, The 60
Milestone Publications 64
Random House Publishing Group Ltd 76
Souvenir Press Ltd 87

Antiques: Magazines
Antique and New Art 219
Antique Collector, The 219
Antique Dealer and Collectors' Guide, The 220
Traditional Homes 292

Antiques: Agents (US)
Urstadt (Susan P.), Inc. 478

Antiques: Libraries
Art & Design Library
(Westminster) 577

Antiques: Picture Libraries
Antiquities (Museum of) Picture
Library 599
Financial Times Picture Collection
607

Antiquarian: Publishers (UK)
Batsford (B.T.) Ltd 16
Constable & Co. Ltd 30
Dalesman Publishing Co. Ltd 32
Donald (John) Publishers Ltd 35
Macmillan Publishers Ltd 61
MIT Press Ltd, The 65
Souvenir Press Ltd 87
Thames and Hudson Ltd 90

Antiquarian: Prizes
Taylor (E. Reginald) Essay
Competition 569

Antiquarian: Picture Libraries
Antiquities (Museum of) Picture
Library 599

Antiquarian
Prisma-Verlag421

Archaeology: Publishers (UK)
Athlone Press, The 14
Batsford (B.T.) Ltd 16
British Museum Press 22
Constable & Co. Ltd 30
Council for British Archaeology
31
Curzon Press Ltd 32
Donald (John) Publishers Ltd 35
Edinburgh University Press 37
Exeter (University of) Press 40
Freeman (W. H.) & Co. Ltd 42
Harcourt Brace Jovanovich Ltd 48
Herbert Press, The 51
Leicester University Press 57
Liverpool University Press 59
Macmillan Publishers Ltd 61
Polity Press 75
Random House Publishing Group
Ltd 76
Routledge, Chapman & Hall Ltd
81
Seaby (B. A.) Ltd 84
Souvenir Press Ltd 87
Sutton (Alan) Publishing Ltd 89
Thames and Hudson Ltd 90

Archaeology: Agents (UK)
Bycornute Books 161

Archaeology: Magazines
History Today 253

Archaeology: Publishers (US)
Iowa State University Press 445
Kent State University Press 445
Texas (University of) Press 452

**Archaeology:
Bursaries/Fellowships**
Prometheus Award 539

Archaeology: Prizes
Taylor (E. Reginald) Essay
Competition 569

**Archaeology: Picture
Libraries**
Adkins (Lesley & Roy) Picture
Library 598
Antiquities (Museum of) Picture
Library 599
Colasanti (Stephanie) 604
Coleman (Bruce) Wildlife &
Travel Photo Library 604
Dixon (C M) 605
E. T. Archive 606
Financial Times Picture Collection
607
Halliday (Sonia) Photographs 610
Lessing (Erich) Archive of Fine
Art & Culture, The 614
London (Museum of) Picture
Library 614
National Monuments Record 615
Photo Resources 617
South American Pictures 621

Archaeology: Small Presses
Red Earth Publications 144

**Archaeology: European
Publishers**
Beck (Verlag C H) 418
DuMont Buchverlag GmbH & Co
KG 419
Econ-Verlag GmbH 419
Francisci (Aldo) Editore 423
Jaca Book (Editoriale) 424
Klincksieck (Editions) 417
Laterza (Giuseppe) e Figli SpA
424
Lübbe (Gustav) Verlag GmbH 420
Uniboek BV 427

Architecture: Publishers (UK)
Academy Editions 10
Antique Collectors' Club 12
Athlone Press, The 14
Attic Books 14

Batsford (B.T.) Ltd 16
Boyars (Marion) Publishers Ltd 2◀
Chadwyck-Healey Ltd 26
Constable & Co. Ltd 30
Donald (John) Publishers Ltd 35
Emap Business Publishing Ltd 38
Gollancz (Victor) Ltd 45
Herbert Press, The 51
Little, Brown & Co. (UK) Ltd 59
Lund Humphries Publishers Ltd
60
Lutterworth Press, The 60
Macmillan Publishers Ltd 61
Manchester University Press 62
MIT Press Ltd, The 65
Orion Publishing Group 69
Phaidon Press Ltd 73
Prism Press Book Publishers Ltd
75
Quiller Press 76
Random House Publishing Group
Ltd 76
Scottish Academic Press 84
Tauris (I.B.) & Co. Ltd 90
Thames and Hudson Ltd 90

Architecture: Packagers
Alphabet & Image Ltd 148
Gardenhouse Editions Ltd 151

Architecture: Agents (UK)
Davidson (Caroline) and Robert
Ducas Literary Agency 164

Architecture: Magazines
*Architects' Journal/The
Architectural Review* 220
Architectural Design 220
Blueprint 224
RIBA Journal, The 279
Traditional Homes 292
What's New in Interiors 296

Architecture: Publishers (US)
ABC-Clio, Inc. 436
Iowa State University Press 445
Massachusetts (University of)
Press 447
MIT Press 447
Pelican Publishing Company 449
Princeton University Press 450
Texas (University of) Press 452
Van Nostrand Reinhold 453

Architecture: Agents (US)
Urstadt (Susan P.), Inc. 478
Van der Leun & Associates 478

Architecture: Prizes
Fletcher Award, Sir Banister 551

Architecture: Libraries
Art & Design Library
(Westminster) 577
British Architectural Library 579

**Architecture: Picture
Libraries**
Adkins (Lesley & Roy) Picture
Library 598
Ancient Art and Architecture
Collection 599
Arcaid 599
Architectural Association Slide
Library 600
Cordaiy (Sylvia) Photo Library 604
Edifice 606
Garland (Leslie) Picture Library
609
Geonex UK Ltd 609
Harding (Robert) Picture Library
610
Holford (Michael) 611
Hutchison Library, The 611
Laubier (André) Picture Library
614
National Monuments Record 615
National Trust Photographic
Library, The 616
Pictures Colour Library 618
Strang (Jessica) Library 622
Whiting (Elizabeth) & Associates
625
Woodmansterne Ltd 626

**Architecture: European
Publishers**
Artemis Verlags AG 434
Bauverlag GmbH 418
Calderini (Edizioni) 422
Casterman (Editions) 415
E U N S A (Ediciones Universidad
de Navarra SA) 431
Gili (Gustavo) SA 431
Grafis Edizioni 423
Hachette 416
Jaca Book (Editoriale) 424
Kohlhammer (Verlag W) GmbH
420
Laterza (Giuseppe) e Figli SpA
424
Niederösterreichisches
Pressehaus, Verlag 411
Paris Musées 418
V C H Verlagsgesellschaft mbH
422

Art: Publishers (UK)
Academy Editions 10
Allardyce, Barnett, Publishers 11
Ashgate Publishing Co. Ltd 13

Athlone Press, The 14
Bellew Publishing Co. Ltd 17
British Academy, The 22
California University Press 24
Cassell 25
Chadwyck-Healey Ltd 26
David & Charles Publishers 33
Dragon's World 35
Enitharmon Press 38
Faber & Faber Ltd 40
Gay Men's Press (GMP Publishers
Ltd), The 44
Golden Cockerel Press Ltd 44
Harvard University Press 50
Herbert Press, The 51
King (Laurence) 55
Little, Brown & Co. (UK) Ltd 59
Lund Humphries Publishers Ltd
60
Lutterworth Press, The 60
Manchester University Press 62
Medici Society Ltd, The 63
MIT Press Ltd, The 65
Orion Publishing Group 69
Pavilion Books Ltd 71
Phaidon Press Ltd 73
Plexus Publishing Ltd 75
Random House Publishing Group
Ltd 76
Routledge, Chapman & Hall Ltd
81
Sangam Books Ltd 82
Search Press Ltd/Burns & Oates
Ltd 84
Silent Books 86
Studio Editions Ltd 88
Thames and Hudson Ltd 90
Women's Press, The 96

Art: Packagers
Albion Press Ltd, The 148
Bison Books Ltd 149
Breslich & Foss 150
Calmann & King Ltd 150
Cameron Books (Production) Ltd
150
New England Editions Ltd 154
Quarto Publishing 155

Art: Agents (UK)
Bycornute Books 161
Davidson (Caroline) and Robert
Ducas Literary Agency 164
Futerman (Vernon) Associates
166
Higham (David) Associates Ltd
168
Kelly (Frances) 169
Martinez (M. C.) Literary Agency
171

Art: Magazines
Antique and New Art 219
Antique Dealer and Collectors'
Guide, The 220
Art & Design 221
Artist, The 221
Art Monthly 221
Art Newspaper, The 221
RA 277
Women's Art Magazine 298

**Art: Film, TV and video
producers**
Poseidon Productions Ltd 365
Riverfront Pictures Ltd 367

Art: Publishers (US)
ABC-Clio, Inc. 436
Abrams (Harry N.), Inc. 436
Chronicle Books 440
Iowa State University Press 445
McFarland & Company, Inc.,
Publishers 446
Pelican Publishing Company 449
Princeton University Press 450
Rosen Publishing Group, Inc., The
450
Texas (University of) Press 452
Walker & Co 453

Art: Agents (US)
Chester (Linda) Literary Agency
458
Nathan (Ruth) Agency 470
Van der Leun & Associates 478

Art: Professional Associations
Personal Managers' Association
Ltd, The 500

Art: Prizes
Fletcher Award, Sir Banister 551
Yorkshire Post Art and Music
Awards 573

Art: Libraries
Art & Design Library
(Westminster) 577
Westminster Reference Library
593

Art: Picture Libraries
Ace Photo Agency 598
Ancient Art and Architecture
Collection 599
Artbank International 600
Aspect Picture Library Ltd 600
Bridgeman Art Library 602
Dixon (C M) 605
E. T. Archive 606

Financial Times Picture Collection 607
Fotomas Index, The 608
Harding (Robert) Picture Library 610
Holford (Michael) 611
Laubier (André) Picture Library 614
Lessing (Erich) Archive of Fine Art & Culture, The 614
Miller (Lee) Archives 615
National Trust Photographic Library, The 616
Photo Resources 617
Retrograph Archive Ltd 619
Rex Features Ltd 620
Strang (Jessica) Library 622
Traeger (Tessa) 623
V&A Picture Library 624
Wingfield Sporting Art Library, The 626
Woodmansterne Ltd 626

Art: Small Presses
Businesslike Publishing 135
Crescent Moon Publishing 136
Redstone Press 145
Stride 146

Art: Festivals
Brighton Festival 404

Art: European Publishers
Adelphi Edizioni SpA 422
Age d'Homme – La Cité (Editions L') 433
Alianza Editorial SA 430
Amalthea-Verlag Gesellschaft mbH 410
Ansgar Forlag A/S 427
Artemis Verlags AG 434
Athesia (Verlagsanstalt) 422
Beck (Verlag C H) 418
Belfond (Editions Pierre) 415
Benteli Verlag 434
Bertrand Editora Lda 429
Bölau Verlag Gesellschaft mbH & Co KG 410
Bompiana 422
Bonnier Fakta Bokforlag AB 432
Borgens Forlag A/S 412
Cappelli (Nuova Casa Editrice Licinio) SpA 422
Carinthia, Universitätsverlag 410
Casterman (Editions) 411
Casterman (Editions) 415
Delta (Editions) SA 411
Denoël (Editions) Sàrl 416
Destino SL 430
Différence, La 416

Diogenes Verlag AG 434
Dreyers Forlag A/S 428
D T V Deutscher Taschenbuch Verlag GmbH & Co KG 419
DuMont Buchverlag GmbH & Co KG 419
Econ-Verlag GmbH 419
Elsevier Librico NV 411
Europa-America (Publicaoes) Lda 429
Ex Libris Forlag A/S 428
Fischer (S) Verlag GmbH 419
Flammarion et Cie 416
Forum (Bokförlaget) AB 433
Francisci (Aldo) Editore 423
Gallimard (Editions) 416
Garzanti Editore 423
G.E.C. Gad Publishers 413
Gili (Gustavo) SA 431
Giunti Publishing Group 423
Grafis Edizioni 423
Gremese Editore SRL 423
Grijalbo SA 431
Gründ (Librairie) 416
Guida Editori SpA 423
Gyldendal Norsk Forlag 428
Gyldendalske Boghandel, Nordisk Forlag A/S 413
Hachette 416
Hatier (Editions) SA 417
Herder (Verlag) GmbH & Co KG 420
Hoffmann und Campe Verlag 420
Horay (Pierre) Editeur 417
Incafo (Editorial) SA 431
Istituto Geografico de Agostini SpA 423
Istituto per l'Enciclopedia del Friuli Venezia Giulia 424
Jaca Book (Editoriale) 424
Klett-Cotta Verlag 420
Kofod (Forlaget Per) ApS 413
Kohlhammer (Verlag W) GmbH 420
Kok (Uitgeversmaatschappij J H) BV 426
Laffont (Editions Robert) 417
Lalli (Antonio) Editore 424
Landesverlag Buchverlag 410
Landi (Luciano) Editore SRL 424
Lannoo (Uitgeverij) Drukkerij 412
Laterza (Giuseppe) e Figli SpA 424
Leykam Buchverlagsgesellschaft mbH 410
Longanesi & C 424
Maule (Michel de) 417
Meulenhoff International 426
Mondadori (Arnoldo) Editore SpA 424

Nathan (Fernand) 418
Neff (Paul), Verlag 410
Niederösterreichisches Pressehaus, Verlag 411
Nyt Nordisk Forlag Arnold Busck A/S 414
Orell Füssli Verlag 435
Österreichischer Bundesverlag Gesellschaft mbH 411
Paoline (Edizioni) SRL 425
Paris Musées 418
Payot Lausanne (Editions) 435
Politikens Forlag A/S 414
Presses Universitaires de France (PUF) 418
Rabēn och Sjögren Bokforlag AB 433
RCS Rizzoli Libri SpA 425
Rhodos, International Science and Art Publishers 414
S A I E Editrice SRL 425
Schönbergske (Det) Forlag A/S 414
S E I (Società Editrice Internationale) 425
Seuil (Editions du) 418
Skira (Editions d'Art Albert) SA 435
Teide (Editorial) SA 432
Time-Life Books BV 427
Tusquets Editores 432
Ugo (Gruppo) Mursia Editore SpA 425
Ullstein (Buchverlage) GmbH 421
Uniepers BV 427
Vanderlinden (Librairie) SA 412
V C H Verlagsgesellschaft mbH 422
Zytglogge Verlag 435

Art History: Publishers (UK)
British Academy, The 22
British Museum Press 22
Herbert Press, The 51
King (Laurence) 55
Lutterworth Press, The 60
MIT Press Ltd, The 65
Phaidon Press Ltd 73

Art History: Magazines
Art Monthly 221
Burlington Magazine, The 227

Art History: Publishers (US)
New England (University Press of) 448
Universe Publishing, Inc. 453

Art History: Agents (US)
Schulman (Susan) Literary Agency
475

Art History: Prizes
Taylor (E. Reginald) Essay
Competition 569

Art History: Picture Libraries
Holford (Michael) 611

**Art History: European
Publishers**
Skira (Editions d'Art Albert) SA
435

**Arts & Entertainment:
Publishers (UK)**
Carlton Books Ltd 25
Fourth Estate Ltd 42
Gordon & Breach Science
Publishers 45
Oxford University Press 70
Phaidon Press Ltd 73
Plexus Publishing Ltd 75
Spellmount Ltd 87
Summersdale Publishers 89
Virgin Publishing 93

**Arts & Entertainment:
Packagers**
Bison Books Ltd 149

**Arts & Entertainment: Agents
(UK)**
Radala & Associates 175

**Arts & Entertainment:
Magazines**
Arena 220
Chapman 230
City Limits 232
Day by Day 237
Face, The 244
London Magazine 260
Outlook 272
Time Out 290
What's On in London 296

**Arts & Entertainment:
Television**
Carlton Television 308

**Arts & Entertainment: Film,
TV and video producers**
After Image Ltd 337
Artifax Ltd 338
Brook Productions 341
Cadenza 342
Electric Picture Machine 348

Illuminations 356
Landseer Film and Television
Productions Ltd 358
Lucida Productions 359
Mentorn Films 361
Mirus Productions 361
MJW Productions 362
Normandy Film Productions 363
Oxford Film & Video Makers 363
Riverfront Pictures Ltd 367
Schonfeld Productions
International/SPI 80 Ltd 367
Signals, Essex Media Centre 368
Talbot Television Ltd 369

**Arts & Entertainment:
Publishers (US)**
Kent State University Press 445
McFarland & Company, Inc.,
Publishers 446
Players Press 449
Simon & Schuster 451

**Arts & Entertainment: Agents
(US)**
Chester (Linda) Literary Agency
458
Schwartz (Laurens R.) 475
Urstadt (Susan P.), Inc. 478

**Arts & Entertainment:
Professional Associations**
Association for Business
Sponsorship of the Arts (ABSA)
490
British American Arts Association
493
Critics' Circle, The 495
Federation of Entertainment
Unions 496
Office of Arts and Libraries 499

**Arts & Entertainment:
Bursaries/Fellowships**
McColl Arts Foundation Bursaries
538

Arts & Entertainment: Prizes
BP Arts Journalism Awards 545

**Arts & Entertainment:
Libraries**
Barbican Library 577
BBC Data Enquiry Service 578
French Institute Library 583
Liverpool City Libraries 586
Newcastle upon Tyne Central
Library 588
Sheffield Libraries and
Information Services 591

**Arts & Entertainment: Picture
Libraries**
All-Action Picture Library 599
Art Directors Photo Library 600
Cinema Museum, The 603
Dominic Photography 605
Financial Times Picture Collection
607
Hunt (Robert) Library, The 611
Network Photographers 616
Newsfocus Press Photograph
Agency Ltd 616
Performing Arts Library 617
Universal Pictorial Press & Agency
Ltd 624

**Arts & Entertainment:
Festivals**
Arundel Festival 403
Brighton Festival 404

**Asia/Asian Interest:
Publishers (UK)**
California University Press 24
Columbia University Press 30
Curzon Press Ltd 32
Routledge, Chapman & Hall Ltd
81
Zed Books Ltd 98

**Asia/Asian Interest: Theatre
producers**
Theatre Royal Stratford East 397

**Asia/Asian Interest:
Publishers (US)**
McFarland & Company, Inc.,
Publishers 446

**Asia/Asian Interest: Agents
(US)**
Writers' Productions 480

**Asia/Asian Interest:
Bursaries/Fellowships**
Sunday Times Fellowship, The
540

Asia/Asian Interest: Prizes
Graham (Edgar) Book Prize 553

Asia/Asian Interest: Libraries
British Library Oriental and India
Office Collections 580

**Asia/Asian Interest: Picture
Libraries**
Art Directors Photo Library 600
Cable & Wireless Visual Resource
602

Camerapix Picture Library 603
Cephas Picture Library 603
Christian Aid Photo Library 603
Colasanti (Stephanie) 604
Dickins (Douglas) Photo Library 605
Format Partners Photo Library 608
Greenhill (Sally and Richard) 610
Photographers' Library, The 618
Screen Ventures 621
Strang (Jessica) Library 622
V&A Picture Library 624

Asia/Asian Interest: Small Presses
Peepal Tree Books 143

Astrology: Publishers (UK)
Foulsham (W.) & Co. 42
HarperCollins Publishers Ltd 49
Penguin Books Ltd 71

Astrology: Magazines
Prediction 276

Astrology: Libraries
Price (Harry) Library of Magical Literature 590

Astrology: Picture Libraries
Walker (Charles) Collection, The 624

Astronomy: Publishers (UK)
Harvard University Press 50
Macmillan Publishers Ltd 61
Reed International Books 78

Astronomy: Picture Libraries
Financial Times Picture Collection 607
Galaxy Picture Library 609
Science Photo Library 620

Astronomy: European Publishers
Kluwer Academic Publishers BV 426
Liguori Editore SRL 424

Atlases: Publishers (UK)
AA Publishing 9
Allan (Ian) Ltd 11
HarperCollins Publishers Ltd 49
Macmillan Publishers Ltd 61
Nelson (Thomas) & Sons Ltd 66
RAC Publishing 76
Reed International Books 78

Atlases: Packagers
Andromeda Oxford Ltd 148
Ilex Publishers Ltd 152
Marshall Editions Ltd 153

Atlases: Publishers (US)
Rand McNally & Co. 450

Atlases: Prizes
Library Association McColvin Medal, The 557

Atlases: European Publishers
Cappelens (J W) Forlag A/S 428
Droemersche Verlagsanstalt Th Knaur Nachf 419
Fayard (Librarie Arthème) 416
Mairs Geographischer Verlag 420
Michelin et Cie (Services de Tourisme) 417
Politikens Forlag A/S 414

Australia: Picture Libraries
Axel Poignant Archive 601
Colasanti (Stephanie) 604
E. T. Archive 606
NHPA (Natural History Photographic Agency) 616
Thurston (Patrick) PhotoLibrary 623
Williams (S & I) Power Pix International Picture Library 626

Autobiography: Publishers (UK)
Acair Ltd 10
Allan (Ian) Ltd 11
Boyars (Marion) Publishers Ltd 20
Calder Publications Ltd 23
Chapmans Publishers 27
Commonword Ltd 30
Constable & Co. Ltd 30
Ellis (Aidan) Publishing 37
Free Association Books 42
Gay Men's Press (GMP Publishers Ltd), The 44
Halban (Peter) Publishers 48
Little, Brown & Co. (UK) Ltd 59
Macmillan Publishers Ltd 61
Mainstream Publishing Co. (Edinburgh) Ltd 62
MIT Press Ltd, The 65
Orion Publishing Group 69
Penguin Books Ltd 71
Pen & Sword Books Ltd 71
Smith Gryphon Ltd 86
Solo Books Ltd 87
Souvenir Press Ltd 87

Thames Publishing/Autolycus Press 90
Virago Press Ltd 93
Virgin Publishing 93
Yorkshire Arts Circus Ltd 97

Autobiography: Agents (UK)
Anderson (Darley) Books 159
Cochrane (Elspeth) Agency 162
Davis-Poynter (Reg) 164
Doyle (Colleen) 165
Judd (Jane) Literary Agency 169
Penman Literary Agency 173
Simmons (Jeffrey) 177
Solo Syndication & Literary Agency Ltd 177
Tauber (Peter) Press Agency 178
Wiener (Dinah) Ltd 179

Autobiography: Publishers (US)
Carol Publishing 440
Iowa State University Press 445

Autobiography: Agents (US)
Andrews (Bart) & Associates 455
Author Aid Associates 456
Boates (Reid) Literary Agency 45?
Lampack (Peter) Agency, Inc. 46?
Living Faith Literary Agency 468
Protter (Susan Ann) Literary Agent 472
Rees (Helen) Literary Agency 473

Autobiography: Prizes
Ackerley (J.R.) Prize 542
GPA Book Award 553
Hughes (John Edeyrn) Prize 554
Irish Times-Aer Lingus International Fiction Prize 555
Stanford (Winifred Mary) Prize, The 568

Autobiography: Small Presses
Korvet Publishing and Distribution 140

Aviation: Publishers (UK)
Airlife Publishing Ltd 11
Allan (Ian) Ltd 11
Argus Books 13
Aston Publications 14
Brooks Books 22
Cassell 25
Dalton (Terence) Ltd 32
Fountain Press Ltd 42
Greenhill Books/Lionel Leventhal Ltd 46
Grub Street 47
Haynes Publishing Group 50

Jane's Information Group 54
Midland Publishing Ltd 64
Reed International Books 78
Salamander Books Ltd 82

Aviation: Magazines
Airforces Monthly 218
Air International 218
Flight International 246
FlyPast 247
Pilot 273
Popular Flying 275

Aviation: Publishers (US)
Iowa State University Press 445
TAB Books 452

Aviation: Agents (US)
Author Aid Associates 456
Wieser & Wieser, Inc. 479

Aviation: Picture Libraries
Allan (Chris) Aviation Library 599
Aviation Photographs
   International 600
Aviation Picture Library 600
Moving Image Research & Library
   Services 615
Williams (S & I) Power Pix
   International Picture Library
   626

**Bibles/Biblical Studies:
   Publishers (UK)**
Bible Society Publishing 17
Cambridge University Press 24
Darton, Longman & Todd Ltd 33
Epworth Press 38
HarperCollins Publishers Ltd 49
Kingsway Publications 56
Oxford University Press 70
SPCK 86

**Bibles/Biblical Studies:
   Publishers (US)**
NavPress Publishing Group 447

**Bibles/Biblical Studies:
   Agents (US)**
Living Faith Literary Agency 468

Bibles/Biblical Studies: Prizes
Stanford (Winifred Mary) Prize,
   The 568

**Bibles/Biblical Studies:
   Picture Libraries**
Halliday (Sonia) Photographs 610
Lessing (Erich) Archive of Fine
   Art & Culture, The 614

Bibliography: Publishers (UK)
Ashgate Publishing Co. Ltd 13
Bowker-Saur Ltd 20
British Library, The 22
Library Association Publishing 58
MIT Press Ltd, The 65
Pergamon Press 73
St Paul's Bibliographies 82

**Bibliography: Professional
   Associations**
Bibliographical Society, The 491
Edinburgh Bibliographical Society
   495

Bibliography: Prizes
Library Association Besterman
   Medal, The 556
Oldman (C.B.) Prize 562

Bibliography: Small Presses
Alembic Press, The 133
Dragonby Press, The 136
Galactic Central Publications 138

**Bilingual Reference:
   Publishers (UK)**
HarperCollins Publishers Ltd 49

**Bilingual Reference:
   Packagers**
Holtkamp and Whitlam Ltd 152
Lexus Ltd 153

**Bilingual Reference:
   European Publishers**
D T V Deutscher Taschenbuch
   Verlag GmbH & Co KG 419
Langenscheidt KG 420

**Biochemistry: Publishers
   (UK)**
Freeman (W. H.) & Co. Ltd 42

Biochemistry: Libraries
Royal Society of Medicine Library
   591

Biography: Publishers (UK)
Acair Ltd 10
Allan (Ian) Ltd 11
Aurum Press Ltd 15
Berg Publishers Ltd 17
Berkswell Publishing Co. Ltd 17
Bowker-Saur Ltd 20
Boyars (Marion) Publishers Ltd 20
Breese (Martin) Publishing 21
Calder Publications Ltd 23
Carcanet Press Ltd 25
Cathie (Kyle) Ltd 26

Chapmans Publishers 27
Collins & Brown 29
Constable & Co. Ltd 30
Davies (Christopher) Publishers
   Ltd 33
Deutsch (André) Ltd 34
Ellis (Aidan) Publishing 37
Free Association Books 42
Gay Men's Press (GMP Publishers
   Ltd), The 44
Gollancz (Victor) Ltd 45
Graham-Cameron Publishing 46
Grosvenor Books 47
Halban (Peter) Publishers 48
Hale (Robert) Ltd 48
Headline Book Publishing 50
Herbert Press, The 51
Kensal Press, The 55
Little, Brown & Co. (UK) Ltd 59
Lochar Publishing Ltd 59
Macmillan Publishers Ltd 61
Mainstream Publishing Co.
   (Edinburgh) Ltd 62
Melrose Press Ltd 63
MIT Press Ltd, The 65
Orion Publishing Group 69
Owen (Peter) Ltd 69
Pavilion Books Ltd 71
Penguin Books Ltd 71
Pen & Sword Books Ltd 71
Plexus Publishing Ltd 75
Quartet Books 76
Quiller Press 76
Ramsay Head Press, The 76
Random House Publishing Group
   Ltd 76
Reinhardt Books Ltd 80
Robson Books Ltd 81
Serpent's Tail 84
Smith Gryphon Ltd 86
Solo Books Ltd 87
Souvenir Press Ltd 87
Spellmount Ltd 87
Stone Flower Ltd 88
Sutton (Alan) Publishing Ltd 89
Thames and Hudson Ltd 90
Thames Publishing/Autolycus
   Press 90
Virago Press Ltd 93
Virgin Publishing 93
Windrush Press, The 96

Biography: Packagers
Berkswell Publishing Co. Ltd 149

Biography: Agents (UK)
Anderson (Darley) Books 159
Bolt (David) Associates 160
Bookworms Literary Agency 160

Bromley (Rosemary) Literary Agency 160
Bryan (Felicity) 160
Clarke (Serafina) 162
Clarson-Leach (Robert) 162
Cochrane (Elspeth) Agency 162
Coles (Dianne) Agency 162
Conway (Vernon) Ltd 163
Davidson (Caroline) and Robert Ducas Literary Agency 164
Davis-Poynter (Reg) 164
Denniston & Lownie 164
Doyle (Colleen) 165
Fox & Howard Literary Agency 166
Higham (David) Associates Ltd 168
Jarvie (Gordon), Literary Agent 169
Judd (Jane) Literary Agency 169
Kelly (Frances) 169
Knight Features 170
Manuscript ReSearch 171
Nye (Alexandra) (Writers & Agents) 173
Pawsey (John) 173
Pearlstine (Maggie) 173
Penman Literary Agency 173
Reynolds (Jim) Associates 175
Robertson (Patricia) 175
Sayle (Tessa) Agency 176
Sheil Land Associates Ltd* 176
Simmons (Jeffrey) 177
Solo Syndication & Literary Agency Ltd 177
Tauber (Peter) Press Agency 178
Wiener (Dinah) Ltd 179

Biography: Publishers (US)
Academy Chicago Publishers 436
Addison-Wesley Publishing Co., Inc. 436
Avon Books 438
Carol Publishing 440
Carroll & Graf Publishers, Inc. 440
Harcourt Brace Jovanovich 443
Houghton Mifflin Co. 444
Iowa State University Press 445
Kent State University Press 445
Little, Brown & Co., Inc. 445
Louisiana State University Press 446
New England (University Press of) 448
New Mexico (University of) Press 448
Paragon House Publishers 449
Princeton University Press 450
Random House, Inc. 450

Rosen Publishing Group, Inc., The 450
St Martin's Press, Inc. 451
Scholastic, Inc. 451
Simon & Schuster 451
Times Books 453
Walker & Co 453
Warner Books 453

Biography: Agents (US)
Acton & Dystel 455
Andrews (Bart) & Associates 455
Appleseeds Management 455
Author Aid Associates 456
Boates (Reid) Literary Agency 457
Borchardt (Georges), Inc. 457
Casselman (Martha), Literary Agent 458
Chester (Linda) Literary Agency 458
Dijkstra (Sandra) Literary Agency 460
Dykeman Associates, Inc. 460
Ellenberg (Ethan), Literary Agency, The 461
Elmo (Ann) Agency, Inc. 461
Fuhrman (Candice) Literary Agency 462
Hawkins (John) & Associates, Inc. 463
Heacock Literary Agency, Inc. 464
Hull House Literary Agency 464
Kohner (Paul), Inc. 465
Lampack (Peter) Agency, Inc. 465
Lazear Agency, Inc., The 466
Leone (Adele) Agency, Inc. 466
Lincoln (Ray) Literary Agency 467
Literary & Creative Artists Agency 467
Living Faith Literary Agency 468
McBride (Margret) Literary Agency 468
Miller (Peter) Agency, Inc., The 469
Multimedia Product Development, Inc. 470
Nathan (Ruth) Agency 470
Nelson (B.K.) Literary Agency 470
New England Publishing Associates, Inc. 470
Noetzli (Regula) Literary Agency 471
Peter (James) Associates, Inc. 472
Protter (Susan Ann) Literary Agent 472
Quicksilver Books, Literary Agents 473
Rees (Helen) Literary Agency 473
Schaffner Agency, Inc. 474

Schwartz (Laurens R.) 475
Siegel (Bobbe), Literary Agency 475
Singer (Evelyn) Literary Agency, Inc., The 476
Singer Media Corporation 476
Spitzer (Philip G.) Literary Agency 477
Stern (Gloria) Agency (New York) 477
Stuhlmann (Gunther) Author's Representative 477
Urstadt (Susan P.), Inc. 478
Van der Leun & Associates 478
Ware (John A.) Literary Agency 479
Wright (Stephen) Authors' Representative 480
Writers House, Inc. 480

Biography: Prizes
Black (James Tait) Memorial Prizes 544
Cooper (Duff) Prize, The 548
GPA Book Award 553
Hughes (John Edeyrn) Prize 554
Irish Times-Aer Lingus International Fiction Prize 555
Marsh Christian Trust Award 559
Royal Heinemann Award 565
Stanford (Winifred Mary) Prize, The 568
Whitbread Book of the Year and Literary Awards 571

Biography: Libraries
BBC Data Enquiry Service 578
Newcastle Literary and Philosophical Society Library 588
Nottingham Subscription Library Ltd 589

Biography: European Publishers
Abadia de Montserrat (Publicaciones de l') 430
Actes Sud (Editions) 415
Adelphi Edizioni SpA 422
Age d'Homme – La Cité (Editions L') 433
Ansgar Forlag A/S 427
Artemis Verlags AG 434
Balland (André) 415
Belfond (Editions Pierre) 415
Bertelsmann AG 418
Brockhaus (F A) 419
Calmann-Lévy (Editions) SA 415
Capitol Editrice Dischi CEB 422

Cappelli (Nuova Casa Editrice Licinio) SpA 422
Det Norske Samlaget 428
D T V Deutscher Taschenbuch Verlag GmbH & Co KG 419
Econ-Verlag GmbH 419
Elsevier Librico NV 411
Europa-America (Publicaoes) Lda 429
Fayard (Librarie Arthème) 416
Fischer (S) Verlag GmbH 419
Flammarion et Cie 416
Forum (Bokförlaget) AB 433
Gallimard (Editions) 416
Garzanti Editore 423
Gedisa (Editorial) SA 431
Grijalbo SA 431
Gyldendalske Boghandel, Nordisk Forlag A/S 413
Hanser (Carl) Verlag 420
Herder (Verlag) GmbH & Co KG 420
Heyne (Wilhelm) Verlag 420
Hoffmann und Campe Verlag 420
Horay (Pierre) Editeur 417
Kok (Uitgeversmaatschappij J H) BV 426
Laffont (Editions Robert) 417
Lalli (Antonio) Editore 424
Landesverlag Buchverlag 410
Lannoo (Uitgeverij) Drukkerij 412
Laterza (Giuseppe) e Figli SpA 424
Lattes (Editions Jean-Claude) 417
Longanesi & C 424
Lübbe (Gustav) Verlag GmbH 420
Manteau (Uitgeversmaatschappij A) NV 412
Mondadori (Arnoldo) Editore SpA 424
Mondadori Espana SA 432
Natur och Kultur (Bokförlaget) 433
Neff (Paul), Verlag 410
Nyt Nordisk Forlag Arnold Busck A/S 414
Oglio (Dall') Editore SRL 425
Orell Füssli Verlag 435
Paoline (Edizioni) SRL 425
Presses de la Cité, Les 418
Presses Universitaires de France (PUF) 418
RCS Rizzoli Libri SpA 425
Samlerens Forlag A/S 414
Sauerlander AG 435
Scherz Verlag AG 435
Schibsteds (Chr.) Forlag A/S 428
Schönbergske (Det) Forlag A/S 414

S E I (Società Editrice Internationale) 425
Seuil (Editions du) 418
Sperling e Kupfer Editori SpA 425
Styria (Verlag) 411
Suhrkamp Verlag 421
Table Ronde (Les Editions de la) 418
Tusquets Editores 432
Ugo (Gruppo) Mursia Editore SpA 425
Ullstein (Buchverlage) GmbH 421
Versal (Ediciones) SA 432
Zsolnay (Paul), Verlag GmbH 411

Biology/Bioscience: Publishers (UK)
Edinburgh University Press 37
Freeman (W. H.) & Co. Ltd 42
Harcourt Brace Jovanovich Ltd 48
Harvard University Press 50
Jai Press Ltd 54
MIT Press Ltd, The 65
Pergamon Press 73
Princeton University Press 75

Biology/Bioscience: Magazines
Naturalist, The 268

Biology/Bioscience: Publishers (US)
Iowa State University Press 445
Krieger Publishing Co., Inc. 445
Princeton University Press 450
Texas (University of) Press 452
Van Nostrand Reinhold 453

Biology/Bioscience: Picture Libraries
GeoScience Features 609
Science Photo Library 620

Biology/Bioscience: European Publishers
B L V Verlagsgesellschaft mbH 419
Deutsch (Verlag Harri) 419
Didactica Editora 429
McGraw-Hill Interamericana de España SA 432
Parey (Verlag Paul) 421
Springer-Verlag GmbH & Co KG 421
Thieme (Georg) Verlag 421
V U Boekhandel/Uitgeverij BV 427

Biotechnology: Film, TV and video producers
Chapel Broadcast Productions Ltd 343

Birds: Publishers (UK)
Black (A. & C.) (Publishers) Ltd 18
Cassell 25
Gollancz (Victor) Ltd 45

Birds: Magazines
Birds 224
British Birds 225
Budgerigar World 227

Birds: Libraries
Natural History Museum Library 588

Birds: Picture Libraries
Aquila Photographics 599
Ardea London Ltd 600
Camera Ways Ltd Picture Library 603
GeoScience Features 609
Grace (Martin and Dorothy) 609
Natural Science Photos 616
Premaphotos Wildlife 618
RSPB Picture Library 620

Black Writing/Issues: Publishers (UK)
Sheba Feminist Press 85

Black Writing/Issues: Packagers
Beanstalk Books Ltd 149

Black Writing/Issues: Magazines
Black Beauty & Hair 224
Voice, The 294

Black Writing/Issues: Theatre producers
Contact Theatre Company 381
Gay Sweatshop 383
Temba Theatre Company Ltd 396
Tricycle Theatre 398
Umoja Theatre Company 398

Black Writing/Issues: Publishers (US)
Massachusetts (University of) Press 447
Temple University Press 452

Black Writing/Issues: Agents (US)
Connor Literary Agency 459

Black Writing/Issues: Professional Associations
New Playwrights Trust 498

Black Writing/Issues: Bursaries/Fellowships
Sunday Times Fellowship, The 540

Black Writing/Issues: Prizes
King (Martin Luther) Memorial Prize, The 556

Black Writing/Issues: Picture Libraries
Format Partners Photo Library 608
Wiedel (Janine) 625

Black Writing/Issues: Small Presses
Peepal Tree Books 143
Tamarind Ltd 146

Blindness: Magazines
New Beacon 268

Book Arts & Booktrade: Publishers (UK)
Ashgate Publishing Co. Ltd 13
British Library, The 22
estamp 39

Book Arts & Booktrade: Magazines
Book and Magazine Collector 224
Bookdealer 225
Books 225
Bookseller, The 225
British Book News 225
Logos 260
London Review of Books 261
Orbis 272
Publishing News 277
Small Press World 284

Book Arts & Booktrade: Professional Associations
Bibliographical Society, The 491
Book House Ireland 492
Book Packagers Association 492
Booksellers Association 492
Book Trust 492
Book Trust Scotland 492
British Amateur Press Association 492

Independent Publishers Guild 497
Private Libraries Association 500
Publishers Association, The 501
Scottish Print Employers' Federation 502
Scottish Publishers Association, The 502
Small Press Group of Britain (SPG) 502
Society of Young Publishers 503
Welsh Books Council $51(Cyngor Llyfrau Cymraeg) 505
Women in Publishing 505

Book Arts & Booktrade: Bursaries/Fellowships
Lewis (Ralph) Award 538

Book Arts & Booktrade: Prizes
British Book Awards 545

Book Arts & Booktrade: Libraries
British Library Reading Room 580
St Bride Printing Library 591

Book Arts & Booktrade: Small Presses
Aard Press 133
Alembic Press, The 133
Bracken Press 135
Previous Parrot Press 143

Book Arts & Booktrade: Festivals
Edinburgh Book Festival 406

Botany: Publishers (UK)
Batsford (B.T.) Ltd 16

Botany: Libraries
Natural History Museum Library 588

Botany: Picture Libraries
Angel (Heather)/Biofotos 599
Ardea London Ltd 600
A–Z Botanical Collection Ltd 601
Camera Ways Ltd Picture Library 603
Foord (Ron & Christine) Colour Picture Library 608
Footprints Colour Picture Library 608
GeoScience Features 609
Grace (Martin and Dorothy) 609
Mathews (S & O) Photography 615
Natural History Museum Picture Library 616

Natural Science Photos 616
Northern Picture Library, The 61
Oxford Scientific Films Photo Library 617
Photo Flora 617
Photos Horticultural 618
Premaphotos Wildlife 618
Reflections PhotoLibrary 619
Retna Pictures Ltd 619
Science Photo Library 620

Botany: European Publishers
Balkema (A A) 426

Boy Scouts/Guides: Publishers (UK)
Brown, Son & Ferguson, Ltd 23

Boy Scouts/Guides: Magazines
Brownie, The 226
Guide Patrol 251
Guiding 251
Scouting Magazine 282

Britain: Publishers (UK)
Phillimore & Co. Ltd 73
Reed International Books 78

Britain: Packagers
Berkswell Publishing Co. Ltd 14

Britain: Professional Associations
British Council, The 493

Britain: Prizes
Whitfield Prize 572

Britain: Libraries
English Folk Dance and Song Society Library 583
Liverpool City Libraries 586

Britain: Picture Libraries
Aird (Malcolm) Associates 598
Andes Press Agency 599
Axel Poignant Archive 601
Belcher (Ivan J.) Colour Picture Library 601
Cephas Picture Library 603
Collections 604
Cordaiy (Sylvia) Photo Library 6
Craven (Philip) Worldwide Phot Library 605
Cunningham (Sue) 605
English Heritage Photographic Library 606
Estall (Robert) Photographs 606
Frith (Francis) Collection 608

Guy (V. K.) Ltd 610
Hanley (Tom) 610
National Monuments Record 615
Noble (David) Photography 616
Sealand Aerial Photography 621
Skyscan Balloon Photography 621
Spectrum Colour Library 621
Swift Picture Library Ltd 623
Thurston (Patrick) PhotoLibrary
 623
Viewfinder Colour Photo Library
 624
Visionbank Library/England
 Scene 624
West Air Photography 625
Williams (Andy) Photo Library
 625
Williams (S & I) Power Pix
 International Picture Library
 626
Woodmansterne Ltd 626
Woolverton Colour Library 626

Broadcasting: Magazines
British Journalism Review 226
Broadcast 226
Television Week 289

**Broadcasting: Professional
 Associations**
Association of Independent Radio
 Companies 490
Campaign for Press and
 Broadcasting Freedom 494
Chartered Institute of Journalists
 494

Broadcasting: Prizes
OWG/COLA Awards for
 Excellence 562

**Broadcasting: Picture
 Libraries**
Financial Times Picture Collection
 607

Building: Publishers (UK)
Attic Books 14
Batsford (B.T.) Ltd 16
Prism Press Book Publishers Ltd
 75

Building: Magazines
Building 227
What's New in Building 296

**Building: Film, TV and video
 producers**
Visual Connection (TVC) Ltd, The
 374

Building: Publishers (US)
Van Nostrand Reinhold 453

Building: Libraries
British Architectural Library 579

Building: Picture Libraries
Financial Times Picture Collection
 607
Garland (Leslie) Picture Library
 609
QA Photos 618

**Business & Commerce:
 Publishers (UK)**
Blackwell Publishers 18
Boyars (Marion) Publishers Ltd 20
Brealey (Nicholas) Publishing Ltd
 21
Business Education Publishers Ltd
 23
Cassell 25
Chapman (Paul) Publishing Ltd 27
Donald (John) Publishers Ltd 35
D. P. Publications 35
Economist Books 36
Elm Publications 37
Emap Business Publishing Ltd 38
Ensign Publications 38
Euromonitor 39
Gower Publishing Ltd 45
Graham & Trotman Ltd 45
Harcourt Brace Jovanovich Ltd 48
IBC Publishing 53
Jai Press Ltd 54
Kogan Page Ltd 56
Longman Group Ltd 60
Macmillan Publishers Ltd 61
McGraw-Hill Book Co. Europe 60
Mercury Business Books 63
Milestone Publications 64
MIT Press Ltd, The 65
Northcote House Publishers Ltd
 67
Penguin Books Ltd 71
Pergamon Press 73
Piatkus Books 73
Pitman Publishing 74
Quiller Press 76
Random House Publishing Group
 Ltd 76
Reed International Books 78
Rosendale Press Ltd 81
Routledge, Chapman & Hall Ltd
 81
Scope International Ltd 83
Smith Gryphon Ltd 86
Solo Books Ltd 87
Souvenir Press Ltd 87
Tolley Publishing Co. Ltd 91

Weavers Press Publishing 95

**Business & Commerce:
 Packagers**
Archival Facsimiles Ltd 148
Hamilton House Mailings Ltd 152

**Business & Commerce:
 Agents (UK)**
Chris (Teresa) Literary Agency
 162
Drexl (Anne) 165
Fox & Howard Literary Agency
 166
Futerman (Vernon) Associates
 166
Martinez (M. C.) Literary Agency
 171
Pawsey (John) 173
Pearlstine (Maggie) 173
Power (Shelley) Literary Agency
 Ltd 174
Watson, Little Ltd* 179

**Business & Commerce:
 Magazines**
Bloomberg Business News 482
Business Week 482
Fortune Magazine 482
Journal of Commerce 482
Business Life 227
Chacom 230
Commerce Magazine 233
Director 239
Executive Strategy 243
InterCity 257
Management Today 262
Mind Your Own Business 264

**Business & Commerce:
 Television**
GMTV 309

**Business & Commerce: Film,
 TV and video producers**
Acacia Productions Ltd 337
Alan Afriat Associates 337
Angel (Greg) (Film and
 Television) 338
ANV Productions 338
Apple Television 338
Artts International 338
Aspect Film and Television
 Productions Ltd 338
Aspen Business Communications
 338
AVC Group 339
Barratt (Michael) Ltd 339
Behr Cinematography 339
BFV Ltd 340

Blackbird Productions 340
Blackrod 340
Black (Stuart) Productions 340
Bould (Penny) Media 340
Broadcast Communications 341
Broadwick Productions 341
Burder (John) (Films) 341
Camerson Television 342
Catlin (Pearl) Associates 342
Chapel Broadcast Productions Ltd 343
Chess Valley Films and Video Ltd 343
CHG Communications 343
Cinecosse Video 344
Clear Picture Company, The 344
Compass Film Productions Ltd 344
Component Television Productions Ltd 345
Convergent Communications Ltd 345
Corporate Communication Consultants Ltd 345
Creative Channel Ltd 345
Creative Film Makers Ltd 345
Creative Television Workshops Ltd 345
Crew Green Associates Ltd 345
Crown Business Communications Ltd 346
Dane Productions 346
Dareks Production House 346
Daring Deeds Ltd 346
Dateline Productions Ltd 346
DBI Communication 347
Directors Video Company 347
Diverse Productions Ltd 347
Dragon Communications Ltd 347
Drake A-V Video Ltd 347
Dunkley (Robert) Associates Ltd 347
Eagle and Eagle Ltd 347
Edric Audio Visual Ltd 348
Electric Picture Machine 348
Espresso TV 348
Fast Forward Productions 349
Filmlt Productions Ltd 349
Filmnova 349
Filmworks 349
First Creative Group Ltd 350
First Freedom Productions Ltd 350
First House Productions Ltd 350
Fitting Images Ltd 350
Five Lamps Group 350
Flying Tiger Film and TV Productions 350
Formula Communications 351
Fourth Wall Productions 351

Fox Television 351
Gall (Ian) Television 351
Gateway Audio Visual and Video 351
Gau (John) Productions 352
GCP 352
Gibb Rose Organisation Ltd 352
Good Film Company, The 352
Grapevine TV 353
Greenpark Productions Ltd 353
Hall (David) Productions 353
Haraco Ltd 354
Harnett Milan Ltd 354
Hawkshead Ltd 354
Head-On Productions Ltd 354
Head to Head Communication Ltd 354
Hines Communications Ltd 355
Hourglass Pictures Ltd 355
Howes (Michael) Productions Ltd 355
HPICM 355
Hubner Films Ltd 355
Illustra Communications Ltd 356
Imagicians Ltd 356
Inca Video & Film Productions 356
In-House Corporate Video 356
Input Video Ltd 356
In Video Productions Ltd 356
Jacaranda Productions Ltd 357
Jenkinson (Brian) Film & Television Productions Ltd 357
Jericho Productions Ltd 357
Kann (Michael) Associates Ltd 357
Lagan Pictures Ltd 358
Lifetime Group 358
Longman Training 359
Main Communications 359
Malachite Ltd 359
Maritz Communications 360
Mayhew Business Communication Ltd 360
Mentorn Films 361
Mills Video Company 361
MNV 362
Mosaic Film & Video Productions 362
Moving Direction 362
Mulberry Ltd 362
New Decade Productions 362
Normandy Film Productions 363
Original Film & Video Productions Ltd 363
Ovation Productions Ltd 363
Pace Productions Ltd 363
Pentagon Communications 364
PGP Films 364
Pretty Clever Pictures Ltd 365

Principal Film Company Ltd, The 365
Priory Film Productions 366
Purchasepoint Video 366
Purkis Neale Productions Ltd 366
Quad Production Co. 366
Quay Productions Ltd 366
Red Lion Communications Ltd 367
Renaissance Vision 367
Roymark Ltd 367
Scope Picture Productions Ltd 367
Skippon Video Associates 368
Skyline Film & TV Productions Ltd 368
SMI Business Television 368
Solo Vision Ltd 369
Spectel Productions Limited 369
Spectrum Communications Ltd 369
Steel (Tom) Productions 369
Strawberry Productions Ltd 369
Swanlind Ltd 369
Tabard Productions 369
Television in Business Ltd 370
Television Visualeyes 370
Tern Television Productions Ltd 370
Topaz Productions Ltd 371
Town House Productions Ltd 371
United Television Artists Ltd 372
VATV 372
Vera Productions 372
Video Arts (Production) Ltd 372
Video At Work 373
Video Enterprises 373
Videoplus Productions Ltd 373
Video Presentations 373
Vidox Video Productions Ltd 373
Viewpoint Group Ltd 373
Visual Connection (TVC) Ltd, The 374
Wadlow Grosvenor 374
Walnut Partnership, The 374
Waterfront Productions 374
Watershed Television Ltd 374
Worldview Pictures 375
WSTV Productions Ltd 375

Business & Commerce: Publishers (US)
Adams (Bob) Publishers, Inc. 436
Addison-Wesley Publishing Co., Inc. 436
AMACOM 437
Avon Books 438
Berkley Publishing Group 439
Iowa State University Press 445
Krieger Publishing Co., Inc. 445

McFarland & Company, Inc.,
  Publishers 446
Prima Publishing and
  Communications 450
Random House, Inc. 450
Sterling Publishing 452
TAB Books 452
Times Books 453
Walker & Co 453
Warner Books 453

**Business & Commerce:
  Agents (US)**
Authors Resource Center & Tarc
  Literary Agency, The 456
Carvainis (Maria) Agency, Inc.
  457
Catalog Literary Agency, The 458
Chester (Linda) Literary Agency
  458
Dijkstra (Sandra) Literary Agency
  460
Flannery, White & Stone 462
ForthWrite Literary Agency 462
Gelles-Cole Literary Enterprises
  463
Heacock Literary Agency, Inc.
  464
Kern (Natasha) Literary Agency,
  Inc. 464
Lazear Agency, Inc., The 466
Literary/Business Associates 467
Marcil (Denise) Literary Agency,
  Inc. 469
Nelson (B.K.) Literary Agency 470
Nolan (Betsy) Literary Agency,
  The 471
Rees (Helen) Literary Agency 473
Rights Unlimited, Inc. 473
Sebastian Agency 475
Shepard Agency, The 475
Singer Media Corporation 476
Snell (Michael) Literary Agency
  476
Spieler Literary Agency 477
Steele (Lyle) & Co. Ltd 477
Waterside Productions, Inc. 479
Wieser & Wieser, Inc. 479

Business & Commerce: Prizes
Wadsworth Prize for Business
  History 571

**Business & Commerce:
  Libraries**
British Library Business
  Information Service 579
City Business Library 582
Hatfield Polytechnic Library 584
Liverpool City Libraries 586

Newcastle upon Tyne Central
  Library 588
Sheffield Libraries and
  Information Services 591
Westminster Reference Library
  593

**Business & Commerce:
  Picture Libraries**
Ace Photo Agency 598
Art Directors Photo Library 600
Evans (Greg) International Photo
  Library 606
Independent Newspaper Picture
  Library, The 612
Monitor Syndication 615
Sefton Photo Library 621
Telegraph Colour Library, The 623

**Business & Commerce:
  European Publishers**
Bohmann Druck und Verlag
  GmbH & Co 410
E U N S A (Ediciones Universidad
  de Navarra SA) 431
Gruyter (Walter de) & Co 419
Hanser (Carl) Verlag 420
Haufe (Rudolf) Verlag GmbH &
  Co KG 420
Liber AB 433
Payot Lausanne (Editions) 435
V N U Business Press Group BV
  427

Calligraphy: Publishers (UK)
Black (A. & C.) (Publishers) Ltd
  18
Search Press Ltd/Burns & Oates
  Ltd 84
Shepheard-Walwyn (Publishers)
  Ltd 85

Calligraphy: Picture Libraries
Sanders (Peter) Photography 620

Canada: Picture Libraries
Estall (Robert) Photographs 606
Hanley (Tom) 610
Williams (S & I) Power Pix
  International Picture Library
  626

**Careers & Employment:
  Publishers (UK)**
Hobsons Publishing 52
Kogan Page Ltd 56
NCVO Publications 66
Northcote House Publishers Ltd
  67
Pergamon Press 73

Trotman & Co. Ltd 92
Weavers Press Publishing 95

**Careers & Employment:
  Packagers**
Hamilton House Mailings Ltd 152

**Careers & Employment:
  Magazines**
Escape: The Career Change
  Magazine 242
Ms London 266
Office Secretary 271
Platform Magazine 274

**Careers & Employment:
  Publishers (US)**
Adams (Bob) Publishers, Inc. 436
AMACOM 437
Rosen Publishing Group, Inc., The
  450

**Careers & Employment:
  Agents (US)**
Sebastian Agency 475

**Careers & Employment: Small
  Presses**
Cheverell Press, The 135

**Cartoons/Comics: Publishers
  (UK)**
Titan Books 91

Cartoons/Comics: Packagers
Creative Comics 151

**Cartoons/Comics: Agents
  (UK)**
Knight Features 170

Cartoons/Comics: Agents (US)
Gusay (Charlotte) Literary
  Agency, The 463

**Cartoons/Comics: Small
  Presses**
Aard Press 133
Businesslike Publishing 135

**Cartoons/Comics: European
  Publishers**
Casterman (Editions) 411
Casterman (Editions) 415
Dom Quixote (Publicacoes) Lda
  429
D T V Deutscher Taschenbuch
  Verlag GmbH & Co KG 419
Glenat (Editions J.) SA 416
Heyne (Wilhelm) Verlag 420

Lalli (Antonio) Editore 424
Nebelspalter Verlag 434
70 (Edições) Lda 430
Standaard Uitgeverij 412

Celtic: Publishers (UK)
Davies (Christopher) Publishers
  Ltd 33
Wales (University of) Press 94

Celtic: Libraries
National Library of Wales 588

Celtic: Small Presses
CNP Publications/Lyfrow
  Trelyspen 136

Ceramics: Publishers (UK)
Antique Collectors' Club 12

Ceramics: Packagers
Alphabet & Image Ltd 148

Ceramics: Libraries
Art & Design Library
  (Westminster) 577

Ceramics: Picture Libraries
Bridgeman Art Library 602
Collections 604
Holford (Michael) 611
V&A Picture Library 624

Chemistry: Publishers (UK)
Freeman (W. H.) & Co. Ltd 42
Gordon & Breach Science
  Publishers 45
Harcourt Brace Jovanovich Ltd 48
Jai Press Ltd 54
MIT Press Ltd, The 65
Pergamon Press 73

Chemistry: Publishers (US)
Krieger Publishing Co., Inc. 445
Van Nostrand Reinhold 453

Chemistry: Picture Libraries
GeoScience Features 609
Science Photo Library 620

**Chemistry: European
  Publishers**
Giunti Publishing Group 423
Hanser (Carl) Verlag 420
Kluwer Academic Publishers BV
  426
Springer-Verlag GmbH & Co KG
  421
Thieme (Georg) Verlag 421

V C H Verlagsgesellschaft mbH
  422

Children's
Österreichischer Bundesverlag
  Gesellschaft mbH 411
Pinguin-Verlag Pawlowski
  GmbH 411

Children's: Publishers (UK)
ABC - All Books For Children 9
Acair Ltd 10
Allardyce, Barnett, Publishers 11
Andersen Press Ltd 12
Atlantic Europe Publishing Co. Ltd
  14
Barny Books 15
Black (A. & C.) (Publishers) Ltd
  18
Book Guild, The 20
Boxtree 20
Brown Watson Ltd 23
Byway Books 23
Canongate Press 24
Chapmans Publishers 27
Cherrytree Press Children's Books
  28
Child's Play (International) Ltd 28
Coleman (Frank) Publishing 29
Cressrelles Publishing Co. Ltd 31
Dorling Kindersley Ltd 35
Dragon's World 35
East-West Publications 36
Exley Publications Ltd 40
Faber & Faber Ltd 40
Gollancz (Victor) Ltd 45
Graham-Cameron Publishing 46
Grosvenor Books 47
Haddock (Peter) Ltd 48
HarperCollins Publishers Ltd 49
Henderson Publishing Ltd 51
Hodder & Stoughton Ltd 52
Hunt & Thorpe 53
Karnak House 55
Kingfisher Books 55
Ladybird Books Ltd 57
Liber Press 58
Lincoln (Frances) Ltd 58
Lutterworth Press, The 60
Macmillan Publishers Ltd 61
Magi Publications 62
Medici Society Ltd, The 63
O'Mara (Michael) Books Limited
  68
Oxford University Press 70
Pavilion Books Ltd 71
Penguin Books Ltd 71
Piccadilly Press 74
Quiller Press 76

Random House Publishing Group
  Ltd 76
Reed International Books 78
Reinhardt Books Ltd 80
Salamander Books Ltd 82
Scholastic Publications Ltd 83
Sheba Feminist Press 85
Simon & Schuster Ltd 86
Souvenir Press Ltd 87
Spindlewood 87
Studio Editions Ltd 88
Three Hills Books 91
Transworld Publishers Ltd 91
Two-Can Publishing Ltd 92
Usborne Publishing Ltd 93
Walker Books Ltd 94
Watts Group, The 95
Wayland (Publishers) Ltd 95
World International Publishing L
  97
Yates (Roy) Books 97
Young Library Ltd 98

Children's: Packagers
Albion Press Ltd, The 148
AS Publishing 148
Autumn Publishing Ltd 149
Beanstalk Books Ltd 149
Belitha Press Ltd 149
Bennett (David) Books Ltd 149
BLA Publishing Ltd 150
Breslich & Foss 150
Brown Wells and Jacobs Ltd 150
Grisewood & Dempsey Ltd 152
Lionheart Books 153
Morris (Neil & Ting) 154
Oyster Books Ltd 154
Price (Mathew) Ltd 155
Sadie Fields Productions Ltd 155
Salariya Book Company Ltd 155
Templar Company 156
Twin Books UK Ltd 156
Victoria House Publishing Ltd 1
Zoe Books Ltd 156

Children's: Agents (UK)
Bookworms Literary Agency 160
Bryant (Peter) (Writers) 161
Comstock-Smith Literary Agency
  163
Curtis Brown Group Ltd 163
Film Link Literary Agency 165
Greene (Elaine) Ltd 167
Hodgson (Pamela) Writers'
  Agency 168
Jarvie (Gordon), Literary Agent
  169
Manuscript ReSearch 171
Martinez (M. C.) Literary Agency
  171

Martin (Judy) 171
Noach (Maggie) Literary Agency,
    The 172
Peters Fraser & Dunlop Group
    Ltd* 174
Pollinger (Laurence) Ltd 174
Rogers, Coleridge & White Ltd*
    175
Ryder (Herta) 175
Sheldon (Caroline) Literary
    Agency 177
Watt (A. P.) Ltd 179

Children's: Magazines
Early Times 240
Look-in 261
Plus 274
Young Telegraph 301

Children's: Television
Carlton Television 308
Children's Channel, The 313
GMTV 309
Meridian Broadcasting 311
Westcountry Television Ltd 312

**Children's: Film, TV and video
    producers**
BFV Ltd 340
Blackbird Productions 340
Black Tulip 340
Broadsword Television 341
Cartwn Cymru 342
Catlin (Pearl) Associates 342
Chapman Clarke Television 343
Childsplay Productions Ltd 343
Chrysalis Television Productions
    Ltd 344
Crystalvision Ltd 346
CTR Productions 346
Eagle and Eagle Ltd 347
Flying Pig Productions Ltd 350
Grasshopper Productions Ltd 353
Henson (Jim) Productions 354
Landseer Film and Television
    Productions Ltd 358
Lifetime Group 358
Main Communications 359
MCEG Virgin Vision 360
Normandy Film Productions 363
Open Mind Productions 363
Picturehead Productions 365
Primetime Television Ltd 365
Ragdoll Productions 366
Talbot Television Ltd 369
Verronmead Ltd 372
World Wide International
    Television 375

Children's: Theatre producers
Borderline Theatre Company 378
Hazemead Ltd 384
Norwich Puppet Theatre 390
Polka Children's Theatre 392
Q20 Theatre Company 392
Redroofs Associates 393
Roundabout Theatre in Education
    393
Snap People's Theatre Trust 395
Theatr Clwyd 396
Thorndike Theatre (Leatherhead)
    Ltd 397
Unicorn Theatre for Children 398
Whirligig Theatre 399

Children's: Publishers (US)
Avon Books 438
Bantam Doubleday Dell
    Publishing Group 438
Barron's Educational Series 439
Boyds Mills Press 439
Carolrhoda Books, Inc. 440
Charlesbridge Publishing 440
Chronicle Books 440
Clarion Books 441
Dial Books for Young Readers 441
Farrar, Straus & Giroux, Inc. 443
Harcourt Brace Jovanovich 443
HarperCollins Publishers, Inc. 443
Harvest House Publishers 444
Holiday House, Inc. 444
Houghton Mifflin Co. 444
Lerner Publications Co. 445
Macmillan Children's Book Group
    446
Morrow (William) and Co., Inc.
    447
Pelican Publishing Company 449
Putnam Publishing Group 450
Random House, Inc. 450
Scholastic, Inc. 451
Simon & Schuster 451
Sterling Publishing 452
Stevens (Gareth) Children's Books
    452
Walker & Co 453

Children's: Agents (US)
Browne (Pema) Ltd 457
Casselman (Martha), Literary
    Agent 458
Catalog Literary Agency, The 458
Cohen (Ruth), Inc. 458
Daves (Joan) Agency 459
Elek (Peter) Associates 461
Ellen Lively Steele & Associates
    461
Elmo (Ann) Agency, Inc. 461
Flannery, White & Stone 462

ForthWrite Literary Agency 462
Gusay (Charlotte) Literary
    Agency, The 463
Hawkins (John) & Associates, Inc.
    463
Kern (Natasha) Literary Agency,
    Inc. 464
Kouts (Barbara S.), Literary Agent
    465
Lazear Agency, Inc., The 466
Lighthouse Literary Agency 467
Lincoln (Ray) Literary Agency 467
Living Faith Literary Agency 468
McIntosh & Otis, Inc. 468
Mews Books Ltd 469
Pegasus International, Inc. 471
Picard (Alison J.) Literary Agent
    472
Rights Unlimited, Inc. 473
Rosenstone/Wender 473
Rosenthal (Jean) Literary Agency
    473
Schlessinger–Van Dyck Agency
    474
Schwartz (Laurens R.) 475
Shepard Agency, The 475
Singer (Evelyn) Literary Agency,
    Inc., The 476
Wright (Stephen) Authors'
    Representative 480
Writers House, Inc. 480

**Children's: Professional
    Associations**
Book Trust 492
Book Trust Scotland 492

Children's: Prizes
Andersen (Hans Christian)
    Awards 542
Children's Book Award 547
Children's Book Circle Eleanor
    Farjeon Award 547
Earthworm Award 550
Fidler (Kathleen) Award, The 551
Guardian Children's Fiction
    Award, The 553
Jones (Mary Vaughan) Award 555
Kelpie Competition 555
Kent Young Writers of the Year
    Award 556
Library Association Carnegie
    Medal, The 556
Library Association Kate
    Greenaway Medal, The 557
Macmillan Prize for a Children's
    Picture Book 558
Maschler (Kurt) Award (Emil) 559
Mother Goose Award, The 560

Nottinghamshire Children's Book Award 562
Signal Poetry for Children Award 567
Smarties Prize for Children's Books 567
Tir Na N-Og Award, The 570
Unicorn Theatre Young Playwrights' Competition 570
Whitbread Book of the Year and Literary Awards 571

Children's: Libraries
Barbican Library 577
Children's Book Foundation Reference Library 581

Children's: Picture Libraries
Adlib Specialist Picture Source 598
Birdsall (John) Photographic Library 601
Bubbles Photolibrary 602
Children's Library, The 603
Cunningham (Sue) 605
Fairclough (Chris) Colour Library 607
Financial Times Picture Collection 607
Format Partners Photo Library 608
Harding (Robert) Picture Library 610
Jessel (Camilla) Photo Library 613
Lupe Cunha Photos 614
PictureBank Photo Library Ltd 618
Pictures Colour Library 618
Reflections PhotoLibrary 619

Children's: Small Presses
Feather Books 137
Indelible Inc 140
Stride 146
Tamarind Ltd 146

Children's: Festivals
Bath Fringe Festival 403
Cardiff Literature Festival 404
Edinburgh Book Festival 406
Kent Literature Festival 407
Lancaster Literature Festival 407

Children's: European Publishers
Alhambra (Editorial) SA 430
Ansgar Forlag A/S 427
Apostrof (Forlaget) ApS 412
Ark Boeken Publishing House 425

Armando Armando (Editore) SRL 422
Artemis Verlags AG 434
Aschehoug (H) & Co (W Nygaard) 427
Aventura Forlag 427
Belin (Editions) 415
Benziger AG 434
Bertelsmann AG 418
Bertrand Editora Lda 429
Bompiana 422
Bonniers Juniorforlag AB 433
Borgens Forlag A/S 412
Born NV Uitgeversmaatschappij 426
Caminho (Editorial) SARL 429
Capitol Editrice Dischi CEB 422
Cappelens (J W) Forlag A/S 428
Cappelli (Nuova Casa Editrice Licinio) SpA 422
Casals (Editorial) SA 430
Casterman (Editions) 411
Casterman (Editions) 415
Ceac (Ediciones) SA 430
Città Nuova Editrice 423
Damm (N W) & Son A/S 428
Davidsfonds VZW 411
De Agostini Ragazzi SpA 423
Debate SA 430
Delagrave Sàrl (Librarie) 416
Destino SL 430
Det Norske Samlaget 428
Diogenes Verlag AG 434
Dom Quixote (Publicacoes) Lda 429
Droemersche Verlagsanstalt Th Knaur Nachf 419
D T V Deutscher Taschenbuch Verlag GmbH & Co KG 419
Elsevier Librico NV 411
Europa-America (Publicaoes) Lda 429
Ex Libris Forlag A/S 428
E – Elle (Edizioni) SRL 423
Fabbri (Gruppo Editoriale) SpA 423
Facet NV 412
Fehmers (Frank) Productions 426
Flammarion et Cie 416
Forum (Forlaget) A/S 412
Fremad (Forlaget) A/S 413
Gallimard (Editions) 416
Garzanti Editore 423
Gauthier-Languereau (Les Editions) SA 416
Giunti Publishing Group 423
Gradiva – Publicacoes Lda 429
Grafisk Forlag A/S 413
Grasset et Farquelle (Société des Editions) 416

Gründ (Librairie) 416
Gyldendal Norsk Forlag 428
Gyldendalske Boghandel, Nord Forlag A/S 413
Haase (P.) & Søns Forlag A/S 4
Hachette 416
Hatier (Editions) SA 417
Herder (Verlag) GmbH & Co K(420
Hernovs Forlag 413
Horay (Pierre) Editeur 417
Horizonte (Livros) Lda 429
Høst & Søns Forlag A/S 413
hptH Verlagsgesellschaft mbH & Co KG 410
Istituto per l'Enciclopedia del Friuli Venezia Giulia 424
Jaca Book (Editoriale) 424
Kofod (Forlaget Per) ApS 413
Kok (Uitgeversmaatschappij J H BV 426
Korch's (Morten A.) Forlag 413
Laertes SA de Ediciones 431
Lalli (Antonio) Editore 424
Lannoo (Uitgeverij) Drukkerij 4
Larousse (Librairie) 417
Lello e Irmão 429
Lohses Forlag 414
Magnard Sàrl (Les Editions) 417
Mallings ApS 414
Medici (Cartiere Binda de) SpA 424
Mondadori (Arnoldo) Editore S 424
Nathan (Fernand) 418
Natur och Kultur (Bokförlaget) 433
Neptun-Verlag 434
Norstedts Forlag AB 433
Orell Füssli Verlag 435
Presses de la Cité, Les 418
Rabên och Sjögren Bokforlag A 433
RCS Rizzoli Libri SpA 425
Richters Fölag AB 433
Rowohlt Tashenbuch 421
S A I E Editrice SRL 425
Santillana SA 432
Sauerlander AG 435
Schibsteds (Chr.) Forlag A/S 42
S E I (Società Editrice Internationale) 425
Seuil (Editions du) 418
70 (Edições) Lda 430
Solum Forlag A/S 428
Standaard Uitgeverij 412
Suhrkamp Verlag 421
Texto Editora 430
Thienemanns (K.) Verlag 421
Tiden (Bokförlags) AB 433

Tiden Norsk Forlag 428
Timun Mas (Editorial) SA 432
Toorts (Uitgeverij De) 427
Tyrolia (Verlagsanstalt)
  Gesellschaft mbH 411
Ugo (Gruppo) Mursia Editore SpA
  425
Uniboek BV 427
Vanderlinden (Librairie) SA 412
Verbo (Editorial) SA 430
Vives (Editorial Luis) (Edelvives)
  432
Vuibert (Librairie) SA 418
Wahlströms Bokfölag AB 433
West-Friesland (Uit-Mij) 427
Zytglogge Verlag 435

China: Agents (UK)
Eady (Toby) Associates Ltd 165

China: Picture Libraries
Aspect Picture Library Ltd 600
Greenhill (Sally and Richard) 610
Hanley (Tom) 610
Harding (Robert) Picture Library
  610
Photo Flora 617
21Abadia de Montserrat
  (Publicaciones de l') 430

Cinema: Publishers (UK)
Batsford (B.T.) Ltd 16
BFI Publishing 17
Black Spring Press Ltd 18
Boyars (Marion) Publishers Ltd 20
Headline Book Publishing 50
Little, Brown & Co. (UK) Ltd 59
Macmillan Publishers Ltd 61
MIT Press Ltd, The 65
Plexus Publishing Ltd 75
Robson Books Ltd 81
Roundhouse Publishing Ltd 81
Smith Gryphon Ltd 86

Cinema: Agents (UK)
Simmons (Jeffrey) 177

Cinema: Magazines
Empire 241
Sight & Sound 283

**Cinema: Film, TV and video
  producers**
Amber Films 337
Bevanfield Films 339
British Lion Screen Entertainment
  Ltd 341
Elstree (Production) Co. Ltd 348
Flamingo Pictures 350

Forstater (Mark) Productions Ltd
  351
Frontroom Films Ltd 351
HandMade Films 353
Illustra Communications Ltd 356
Lucida Productions 359
Mentorn Films 361
Palace Productions 363
Picturehead Productions 365
Rank Production 366
Schonfeld Productions
  International/SPI 80 Ltd 367
Twentieth Century Fox
  Productions Ltd 371
Twin Continental Films Ltd 371
Wickes (David) Productions Ltd
  375

Cinema: Publishers (US)
Players Press 449

**Cinema: Professional
  Associations**
PACT (Producers Alliance for
  Cinema and Television) 499

**Cinema:
  Bursaries/Fellowships**
Funding for Script Development
  537

Cinema: Libraries
Barbican Library 577
British Film Institute Library and
  Information Services 579
Northumberland County Library
  588
Westminster Reference Library
  593

Cinema: Picture Libraries
BFI Stills, Posters and Designs 601
Cinema Museum, The 603
Kobal Collection, The 613

Cinema: Small Presses
Crescent Moon Publishing 136

Cinema: European Publishers
Age d'Homme – La Cité (Editions
  L') 433
Bulzoni Editore SRL (Le Edizioni
  Universitarie d'Italia) 422
Casterman (Editions) 415
Fundamentos (Editorial) 431
Gremese Editore SRL 423
Hatier (Editions) SA 417
Laertes SA de Ediciones 431
Lalli (Antonio) Editore 424

**Classical Studies: Publishers
  (UK)**
Aris & Phillips Ltd 13
Exeter (University of) Press 40

**Classical Studies: Publishers
  (US)**
Longman Publishing Group 446
Oklahoma (University of) Press
  448
Texas (University of) Press 452

Classical Studies: Prizes
Routledge Ancient History Prize
  565

**Classical Studies: European
  Publishers**
Beck (Verlag C H) 418
Gruyter (Walter de) & Co 419
Laertes SA de Ediciones 431
Laterza (Giuseppe) e Figli SpA
  424

Collecting: Publishers (UK)
Antique Collectors' Club 12
Golden Cockerel Press Ltd 44
Lutterworth Press, The 60
Milestone Publications 64
Random House Publishing Group
  Ltd 76
Salamander Books Ltd 82
Seaby (B. A.) Ltd 84
Souvenir Press Ltd 87

Collecting: Packagers
Cameron Books (Production) Ltd
  150

Collecting: Magazines
Antique Collector, The 219
*Antique Dealer and Collectors'
  Guide, The* 220
Book and Magazine Collector 224
Coin News 233
Gibbons Stamp Monthly 248
Map Collector 262
Medal News 263
Record Collector 279
Stamps 286

**Commonwealth: Publishers
  (UK)**
Exeter (University of) Press 40

Commonwealth: Prizes
Commonwealth Writers Prize 548
Reese (Trevor) Memorial Prize
  564

Commonwealth: Libraries
Commonwealth Resource Centre
582
Commonwealth Secretariat
Library 582
Foreign and Commonwealth
Office Library 583

**Commonwealth: Picture
Libraries**
Compix 604

Computing: Publishers (UK)
Addison-Wesley Publishers Ltd
10
Chapman (Paul) Publishing Ltd 27
D. P. Publications Ltd 35
Edinburgh University Press 37
Emap Business Publishing Ltd 38
Freeman (W. H.) & Co. Ltd 42
Fulton (David) (Publishers) Ltd 43
Gordon & Breach Science
Publishers 45
Harcourt Brace Jovanovich Ltd 48
Hobsons Publishing 52
Jai Press Ltd 54
McGraw-Hill Book Co. Europe 60
MIT Press Ltd, The 65
Penny Press 72
Pergamon Press 73

Computing: Magazines
Computer Weekly 233
Computing 233
Network 268
PC User 272
PCW Plus 272
What Personal Computer 295
Which Computer? 297

**Computing: Film, TV and
video producers**
Epic Interactive Media Company
348

Computing: Publishers (US)
Addison-Wesley Publishing Co.,
Inc. 436
Bantam Doubleday Dell
Publishing Group 438
Krieger Publishing Co., Inc. 445
MIT Press 447
Prima Publishing and
Communications 450
Princeton University Press 450
TAB Books 452
Van Nostrand Reinhold 453

Computing: Agents (US)
Catalog Literary Agency, The 458

Snell (Michael) Literary Agency
476

Computing: Picture Libraries
Art Directors Photo Library 600
Financial Times Picture Collection
607
Harding (Robert) Picture Library
610
Science Photo Library 620

Computing: Small Presses
Intellect Books 140

**Computing: European
Publishers**
Bohmann Druck und Verlag
GmbH & Co 410
Borgens Forlag A/S 412
Calderini (Edizioni) 422
Falken-Verlag GmbH 419
Hanser (Carl) Verlag 420
Sikkel (Uitgeverij De) NV 412
Springer-Verlag GmbH & Co KG
421
Strandbergs Forlag ApS 415
Tano AS 428
V C H Verlagsgesellschaft mbH
422
V N U Business Press Group BV
427

Cookery: Publishers (UK)
Appletree Press Ltd 12
Cassell 25
Cathie (Kyle) Ltd 26
Chapmans Publishers 27
Constable & Co. Ltd 30
Davies (Christopher) Publishers
Ltd 33
Dorling Kindersley Ltd 35
Elliot Right Way Books 37
Faber & Faber Ltd 40
Foulsham (W.) & Co. 42
Grub Street 47
Letts (Charles) & Co. Ltd 58
Little, Brown & Co. (UK) Ltd 59
Macmillan Publishers Ltd 61
Merehurst Ltd 64
New Holland (Publishers) Ltd 67
Orion Publishing Group 69
Pavilion Books Ltd 71
Piatkus Books 73
Prism Press Book Publishers Ltd
75
Quiller Press 76
Ramsay Head Press, The 76
Random House Publishing Group
Ltd 76

Reader's Digest Association Ltd
78
Reed International Books 78
Robson Books Ltd 81
Salamander Books Ltd 82
Search Press Ltd/Burns & Oates
Ltd 84
Smith Gryphon Ltd 86
Souvenir Press Ltd 87
Summersdale Publishers 89

Cookery: Packagers
Bison Books Ltd 149
Cameron Books (Production) L
150
Gardenhouse Editions Ltd 151
Quarto Publishing 155
Sheldrake Press Ltd 155
Toucan Books Ltd 156

Cookery: Agents (UK)
Anderson (Darley) Books 159
Bromley (Rosemary) Literary
Agency 160
Chilcote (Judith) Agency 161
Chris (Teresa) Literary Agency
162
Clarke (Serafina) 162
Davidson (Caroline) and Rober
Ducas Literary Agency 164
Judd (Jane) Literary Agency 16
Martinez (M. C.) Literary Agenc
171
Pearlstine (Maggie) 173
Sheil Land Associates Ltd* 176
Wiener (Dinah) Ltd 179

Cookery: Publishers (US)
Adams (Bob) Publishers, Inc. 4
Arkansas (University of) Press 4
Avery Publishing Group, Inc. 43
Bergh Publishing, Inc. 439
Chronicle Books 440
Little, Brown & Co., Inc. 445
Lyons & Burford, Publishers 44
Pelican Publishing Company 44
Prima Publishing and
Communications 450
Random House, Inc. 450
Simon & Schuster 451
Sterling Publishing 452
Texas (University of) Press 452
Times Books 453
Van Nostrand Reinhold 453
Warner Books 453

Cookery: Agents (US)
Casselman (Martha), Literary
Agent 458

Ellen Lively Steele & Associates 461

Kern (Natasha) Literary Agency, Inc. 464

Lee Allan Agency, The 466

Mews Books Ltd 469

Nolan (Betsy) Literary Agency, The 471

Schlessinger-Van Dyck Agency 474

Stern (Gloria) Agency (New York) 477

2M Communications Ltd 478

Urstadt (Susan P.), Inc. 478

Wieser & Wieser, Inc. 479

Cookery: Prizes
Glenfiddich Awards 552

Cookery: Picture Libraries
Ronan (Ann) Picture Library 620

Wright (George) 626

Cookery: Small Presses
Logaston Press 141

Southover Press 145

Cookery: European Publishers
Athesia (Verlagsanstalt) 422

B L V Verlagsgesellschaft mbH 419

Bonnier Fakta Bokforlag AB 432

Calderini (Edizioni) 422

Ceac (Ediciones) SA 430

Falken-Verlag GmbH 419

Glenat (Editions J.) SA 416

Gremese Editore SRL 423

Hallwag Verlag AG 434

Heyne (Wilhelm) Verlag 420

Landesverlag Buchverlag 410

Mosaik Verlag 421

Orac Verlag Gesellschaft mbH 411

Rosinante/Munksgaard 414

Sigloch (Edition Helmut) GmbH & Co 421

Texto Editora 430

Time-Life Books BV 427

Trauner (Rudolf) Verlag 411

Tusquets Editores 432

Uniboek BV 427

Uniepers BV 427

Cosmology: Agents (UK)
Bycornute Books 161

Countryside/Landscape: Publishers (UK)
Ashford, Buchan & Enright 13

Ensign Publications 38

Farming Press Books 41

Headline Book Publishing 50

Moorland Publishing Co. Ltd 65

Sumach Press, The 88

Sunflower Books 89

Sutton (Alan) Publishing Ltd 89

Tabb House 89

Thornhill Press 91

Whittet Books Ltd 96

Countryside/Landscape: Packagers
Cameron Books (Production) Ltd 150

Countryside/Landscape: Magazines
Country Life 234

Country Living 235

Countryman, The 235

Country Quest 235

Cumbria 236

Field, The 245

Great Outdoors, The 250

Natural World 268

This England 290

Countryside/Landscape: Film, TV and video producers
Bird (Martin) Productions 340

Normandy Film Productions 363

Waterfront Productions 374

Countryside/Landscape: Prizes
Hughes (John Edeyrn) Prize 554

Lakeland Book of the Year 556

Countryside/Landscape: Picture Libraries
Adkins (Lesley & Roy) Picture Library 598

Adlib Specialist Picture Source 598

Aird (Malcolm) Associates 598

Alba Pictures 598

Ancient Art and Architecture Collection 599

Angel (Heather)/Biofotos 599

Calendar Concepts & Design 602

Camera Ways Ltd Picture Library 603

Cleare (John)/Mountain Camera 604

Cordaiy (Sylvia) Photo Library 604

Country Life Library 605

Craven (Philip) Worldwide Photo-Library 605

Dixon (C M) 605

Edifice 606

Evans (Greg) International Photo Library 606

Felix (Paul) 607

Garland (Leslie) Picture Library 609

GeoScience Features 609

Grace (Martin and Dorothy) 609

Harding (Robert) Picture Library 610

Heseltine (John) Picture Library 610

Hutchison Library, The 611

Impact Photos 612

Landscape Only 613

Mathews (S & O) Photography 615

National Trust Photographic Library, The 616

Noble (David) Photography 616

Northern Picture Library, The 616

Oxford Scientific Films Photo Library 617

Paterson (David) Library 617

Photographers' Library, The 618

PictureBank Photo Library Ltd 618

Pictures Colour Library 618

Planet Earth Pictures/Seaphot 618

Reflections PhotoLibrary 619

Rex Features Ltd 620

Science Photo Library 620

Skyscan Balloon Photography 621

Spectrum Colour Library 621

Swift Picture Library Ltd 623

Viewfinder Colour Photo Library 624

Williams (S & I) Power Pix International Picture Library 626

Wright (George) 626

Crafts & Decorative Arts: Publishers (UK)
Anaya Publishers Ltd 12

Batsford (B.T.) Ltd 16

Bellew Publishing Co. Ltd 17

Black (A. & C.) (Publishers) Ltd 18

Cassell 25

Chapmans Publishers 27

Collins & Brown 29

Crowood Press Ltd, The 32

Dalesman Publishing Co. Ltd 32

David & Charles Publishers 33

Dorling Kindersley Ltd 35

Dragon's World 35

Fountain Press Ltd 42

Herbert Press, The 51

King (Laurence) 55

Letts (Charles) & Co. Ltd 58
Lincoln (Frances) Ltd 58
Little, Brown & Co. (UK) Ltd 59
Macmillan Publishers Ltd 61
Merehurst Ltd 64
New Holland (Publishers) Ltd 67
Pavilion Books Ltd 71
Penguin Books Ltd 71
Quiller Press 76
Random House Publishing Group
  Ltd 76
Reed International Books 78
Salamander Books Ltd 82
Search Press Ltd/Burns & Oates
  Ltd 84
Souvenir Press Ltd 87
Studio Editions Ltd 88
Thames and Hudson Ltd 90

**Crafts & Decorative Arts:
Packagers**
Breslich & Foss 150
Cameron Books (Production) Ltd
  150
Quarto Publishing 155
Savitri Books Ltd 155

**Crafts & Decorative Arts:
Agents (UK)**
Coles (Dianne) Agency 162
Martinez (M. C.) Literary Agency
  171
Pearlstine (Maggie) 173
Robertson (Patricia) 175

**Crafts & Decorative Arts:
Magazines**
Art & Craft 220
Embroidery 241
Evergreen 243
Machine Knitting Monthly 261
Modern Machine Knitting 264
Popular Crafts 275
Workbox 299

**Crafts & Decorative Arts:
Publishers (US)**
TAB Books 452

**Crafts & Decorative Arts:
Agents (US)**
Authors Resource Center & Tarc
  Literary Agency, The 456
Connor Literary Agency 459
ForthWrite Literary Agency 462
Heacock Literary Agency, Inc.
  464
Urstadt (Susan P.), Inc. 478

**Crafts & Decorative Arts:
Picture Libraries**
Bridgeman Art Library 602
Felix (Paul) 607
Financial Times Picture Collection
  607
Holford (Michael) 611
Hurst (Jacqui) 611
Laubier (André) Picture Library
  614
Retrograph Archive Ltd 619
V&A Picture Library 624

**Crafts & Decorative Arts:
European Publishers**
Borgens Forlag A/S 412
Calderini (Edizioni) 422
Ceac (Ediciones) SA 430
Kok (Uitgeversmaatschappij J H)
  BV 426
Mosaik Verlag 421
Paris Musées 418
Schibsteds (Chr.) Forlag A/S 428

Crime: Publishers (UK)
Breese (Martin) Publishing 21
Ensign Publications 38
Gay Men's Press (GMP Publishers
  Ltd), The 44
Gollancz (Victor) Ltd 45
HarperCollins Publishers Ltd 49
Henry (Ian) Publications Ltd 51
Little, Brown & Co. (UK) Ltd 59
Macmillan Publishers Ltd 61
Penguin Books Ltd 71
Polity Press 75
Random House Publishing Group
  Ltd 76
Robinson Publishing 80
Routledge, Chapman & Hall Ltd
  81
Serpent's Tail 84
Severn House Publishers 85
Smith Gryphon Ltd 86
Souvenir Press Ltd 87
Titan Books 91
Virago Press Ltd 93
Virgin Publishing 93

Crime: Agents (UK)
Anderson (Darley) Books 159
Burston (Diane) Literary Agency
  161
Chris (Teresa) Literary Agency
  162
Dorian Literary Agency 164
Doyle (Colleen) 165
Drexl (Anne) 165
Fox & Howard Literary Agency
  166

Gregory & Radice Authors'
  Agents* 167
Holt (Vanessa) Associates Ltd
Judd (Jane) Literary Agency 16
Little (Christopher) 170
Manuscript ReSearch 171
Motley (Michael) Ltd 172
Pawsey (John) 173
Pearlstine (Maggie) 173
Pollinger (Laurence) Ltd 174
Power (Shelley) Literary Agenc
  Ltd 174
Reynolds (Jim) Associates 175
Robertson (Patricia) 175
Simmons (Jeffrey) 177
Solo Syndication & Literary
  Agency Ltd 177
Tauber (Peter) Press Agency 1

Crime: Publishers (US)
Academy Chicago Publishers 4
Bergh Publishing, Inc. 439
Gardner Press, Inc. 443
Plenum Publishing 449
St Martin's Press, Inc. 451
Warner Books 453

Crime: Agents (US)
Anthony (Joseph) Agency 455
Appleseeds Management 455
Authors Resource Center & Tar
  Literary Agency, The 456
Boates (Reid) Literary Agency
Dijkstra (Sandra) Literary Agen
  460
Ellenberg (Ethan), Literary
  Agency, The 461
Hull House Literary Agency 464
Kern (Natasha) Literary Agency
  Inc. 464
King (Daniel P.) 465
Kohner (Paul), Inc. 465
Lazear Agency, Inc., The 466
Lee Allan Agency, The 466
Lee (L. Harry) Literary Agency
  466
Literary & Creative Artists Agen
  467
McBride (Margret) Literary
  Agency 468
Miller (Peter) Agency, Inc., The
  469
Morrison (Henry) Inc. 470
New England Publishing
  Associates, Inc. 470
Noetzli (Regula) Literary Agenc
  471
Quicksilver Books, Literary Age
  473

Schlessinger–Van Dyck Agency 474

Siegel (Bobbe), Literary Agency 475

Steele (Lyle) & Co. Ltd 477

Wright (Stephen) Authors' Representative 480

Writer's Consulting Group 480

Zelasky (Tom) Literary Agency 481

Crime: Professional Associations

Crime Writers' Association (CWA) 495

Crime: Bursaries/Fellowships

Fulbright-Chandler Arts Fellowship Award 537

Crime: Prizes

Creasey (John) Memorial Award 549

Gold Dagger Award for Non-Fiction 552

Gold, Silver & Diamond Dagger Awards for Fiction 552

Last Laugh Award 556

Crime: Libraries

Sherlock Holmes Collection (Westminster) 585

Crime: Picture Libraries

Financial Times Picture Collection 607

Hunt (Robert) Library, The 611

Popperfoto 618

Crime: Small Presses

Sherlock Publications 145

Crime: European Publishers

Garzanti Editore 423

Scherz Verlag AG 435

Spectrum (Uitgeverij Het) BV 427

Current Affairs: Publishers (UK)

Cathie (Kyle) Ltd 26

Chapmans Publishers 27

Claridge Press 29

Deutsch (André) Ltd 34

Fourth Estate Ltd 42

Gollancz (Victor) Ltd 45

Grosvenor Books 47

Lawrence & Wishart Ltd 57

Macmillan Publishers Ltd 61

Mainstream Publishing Co. (Edinburgh) Ltd 62

Penguin Books Ltd 71

Random House Publishing Group Ltd 76

Tauris (I.B.) & Co. Ltd 90

Current Affairs: Agents (UK)

Bryan (Felicity) 160

Futerman (Vernon) Associates 166

Higham (David) Associates Ltd 168

Jarvie (Gordon), Literary Agent 169

Pawsey (John) 173

Pearlstine (Maggie) 173

Reynolds (Jim) Associates 175

Sayle (Tessa) Agency 176

Current Affairs: Magazines

Illustrated London News, The 256

Outlook 272

Time 290

Tribune 292

Current Affairs: Television

Carlton Television 308

GMTV 309

Meridian Broadcasting 311

Westcountry Television Ltd 312

Current Affairs: Film, TV and video producers

Barony Film and Television Productions Limited 339

Broadcast Communications 341

Brook Productions 341

Clark Production 344

Diverse Productions Ltd 347

Fourth Wall Productions 351

Landseer Film and Television Productions Ltd 358

Lucida Productions 359

Peake Productions 364

Schonfeld Productions International/SPI 80 Ltd 367

Sevenday Productions 367

Worldwide Television News 375

Current Affairs: Publishers (US)

Carroll & Graf Publishers, Inc. 440

Eerdmans (William B.) Publishing Co. 442

Harcourt Brace Jovanovich 443

Harvest House Publishers 444

Houghton Mifflin Co. 444

Times Books 453

Current Affairs: Agents (US)

Acton & Dystel 455

Boates (Reid) Literary Agency 457

Casselman (Martha), Literary Agent 458

Kern (Natasha) Literary Agency, Inc. 464

Multimedia Product Development, Inc. 470

New England Publishing Associates, Inc. 470

Sebastian Agency 475

Spitzer (Philip G.) Literary Agency 477

Urstadt (Susan P.), Inc. 478

Ware (John A.) Literary Agency 479

Current Affairs: Prizes

Irish Times-Aer Lingus International Fiction Prize 555

Current Affairs: Picture Libraries

Empics Ltd 606

Express Newspapers Picture Library 607

Hulton Picture Company, The 611

Impact Photos 612

Independent Newspaper Picture Library, The 612

Magnum Photos Ltd 614

Network Photographers 616

Outram (George) Picture Library 617

Popperfoto 618

Rex Features Ltd 620

Select Photos 621

Spooner (Frank) Pictures 622

Sygma 623

Topham Picture Source 623

Universal Pictorial Press & Agency Ltd 624

Current Affairs: European Publishers

Artemis Verlags AG 434

Bertelsmann AG 418

Droemersche Verlagsanstalt Th Knaur Nachf 419

Europa Verlag GmbH 410

Lalli (Antonio) Editore 424

Lannoo (Uitgeverij) Drukkerij 412

Styria (Verlag) 411

Dance: Publishers (UK)

Gordon & Breach Science Publishers 45

Northcote House Publishers Ltd 67

Dance: Agents (UK)
Radala & Associates 175

Dance: Magazines
Dance & Dancers 236
Dance Theatre Journal 236
Dancing Times, The 236

Dance: Film, TV and video producers
MJW Productions 362

Dance: Professional Associations
Arvon Foundation 489

Dance: Libraries
Barbican Library 577
English Folk Dance and Song Society Library 583
Theatre Museum Library & Archive 592
Westminster Reference Library 593

Dance: Picture Libraries
Dominic Photography 605
Performing Arts Library 617
Williams (Vaughan) Memorial Library 626
Woodmansterne Ltd 626

Dance: Festivals
Brighton Festival 404
Bury St Edmunds Arts Festival 404
Cambridge Festival 404
Exeter Festival 406
Glasgow Mayfest 406
Lancaster Literature Festival 407
Windsor Festival 409
York Festival 409

Defence: Publishers (UK)
Allan (Ian) Ltd 11
Grosvenor Books 47
Jane's Information Group 54
Leicester University Press 57

Defence: Magazines
Jane's Defence Weekly 258

Defence: Film, TV and video producers
Chapel Broadcast Productions Ltd 343

Defence: Picture Libraries
Financial Times Picture Collection 607

Demography: Libraries
Population Censuses & Surveys Library, Office of 589
Public Record Office 590

Dentistry: Publishers (UK)
Dunitz (Martin) Ltd 36
Mosby Year Book Europe Ltd 65

Design: Publishers (UK)
Batsford (B.T.) Ltd 16
Bellew Publishing Co. Ltd 17
Boyars (Marion) Publishers Ltd 20
Cassell 25
Constable & Co. Ltd 30
Cornerhouse Publications 31
Donald (John) Publishers Ltd 35
Dragon's World 35
Emap Business Publishing Ltd 38
Fountain Press Ltd 42
Fourth Estate Ltd 42
Headline Book Publishing 50
Herbert Press, The 51
King (Laurence) 55
Little, Brown & Co. (UK) Ltd 59
Lund Humphries Publishers Ltd 60
Lutterworth Press, The 60
Macmillan Publishers Ltd 61
MIT Press Ltd, The 65
Phaidon Press Ltd 73
Tauris (I.B.) & Co. Ltd 90
Thames and Hudson Ltd 90
Trentham Books Ltd 92

Design: Packagers
Calmann & King Ltd 150
Cameron Books (Production) Ltd 150
Quarto Publishing 155

Design: Agents (UK)
Davidson (Caroline) and Robert Ducas Literary Agency 164

Design: Magazines
Art & Design 221
Big Paper, The 224
Blueprint 224
Creative Review 235
Design 238
Designers' Journal 238
DESIGNING 238

Design: Publishers (US)
Abrams (Harry N.), Inc. 436
Chronicle Books 440
Iowa State University Press 445
TAB Books 452
Van Nostrand Reinhold 453

Design: Agents (US)
Kroll (Lucy) Agency 465

Design: Libraries
Art & Design Library (Westminster) 577
Westminster Reference Library 593

Design: Picture Libraries
Design Council Picture Library 605
Strang (Jessica) Library 622

Design: European Publisher
Gili (Gustavo) SA 431
Uniboek BV 427

Dictionaries: Publishers (UK
Acair Ltd 10
Allan (Ian) Ltd 11
Chambers (W & R) 27
HarperCollins Publishers Ltd 49
Macmillan Publishers Ltd 61
Nelson (Thomas) & Sons Ltd 66
Oxford University Press 70
Penguin Books Ltd 71
Routledge, Chapman & Hall Ltd 81

Dictionaries: Packagers
Holtkamp and Whitlam Ltd 152
Lexus Ltd 153
Market House Books Ltd 153

Dictionaries: Publishers (US
Hippocrene Books, Inc. 444

Dictionaries: Agents (US)
Leone (Adele) Agency, Inc. 466

Dictionaries: Prizes
Library Association McColvin Medal, The 557

Dictionaries: European Publishers
Bauverlag GmbH 418
Bertrand Editora Lda 429
Bompiana 422
Bonnier Fakta Bokforlag AB 43:
Bordas (Editions) 415
Brockhaus (F A) 419
Deutsch (Verlag Harri) 419
Droemersche Verlagsanstalt Th Knaur Nachf 419
Garzanti Editore 423
Giunti Publishing Group 423
Kunnskapsforlaget I/S 428
Langenscheidt KG 420

Larousse (Librairie) 417
Larousse (Suisse) SA 434
Lello e Irmão 429
Liber AB 433
Nathan (Fernand) 418
Norstedts Forlag AB 433
Paoline (Edizioni) SRL 425
Porto Editora Lda 429
S A I E Editrice SRL 425
Standaard Uitgeverij 412
Teide (Editorial) SA 432
VEB Verlag Enzyklopädie Leipzig
    422

Directories: Publishers (UK)
Associated Publicity Holdings Ltd
    14
CBD Research Ltd 26
Elvendon Press 38
Euromonitor 39
Graham & Trotman Ltd 45
Headline Book Publishing 50
Hobsons Publishing 52
IBC Publishing 53
Jane's Information Group 54
Macmillan Publishers Ltd 61
NCVO Publications 66
Weavers Press Publishing 95

Directories: Packagers
Ink Inc. Ltd 152
MM Productions Ltd 154

**Directories: Professional
    Associations**
Directory Publishers Association
    495

Directories: Prizes
Library Association McColvin
    Medal, The 557

Disability: Publishers (UK)
Souvenir Press Ltd 87

Disability: Magazines
Disability Now 239
Disabled Driver 239

**Disability: Film, TV and video
    producers**
Ideas Factory, The 356

Disability: Theatre producers
Gay Sweatshop 383
Graeae Theatre Company 383

Disability: Picture Libraries
Birdsall (John) Photographic
    Library 601

Financial Times Picture Collection
    607
Format Partners Photo Library
    608
Photofusion 617

D.I.Y.: Publishers (UK)
Cassell 25
Consumers' Association 30
Dragon's World 35
Elliot Right Way Books 37
Foulsham (W.) & Co. 42
Fountain Press Ltd 42
Little, Brown & Co. (UK) Ltd 59
Penguin Books Ltd 71
Quiller Press 76
Random House Publishing Group
    Ltd 76
Reader's Digest Association Ltd
    78

D.I.Y.: Agents (UK)
Drexl (Anne) 165
Martinez (M. C.) Literary Agency
    171

D.I.Y.: Magazines
Practical Householder 276

D.I.Y.: Picture Libraries
Houses & Interiors Photographic
    Features Agency 611

Documentary: Agents (UK)
Creative Tone Ltd 163
Peters Fraser & Dunlop Group
    Ltd* 174
Sales (Ian) Associates 176

Documentary: Television
Carlton Television 308

**Documentary: Film, TV and
    video producers**
Acacia Productions Ltd 337
Aisling Films Ltd 337
Alan Afriat Associates 337
Amber Films 337
Angel (Greg) (Film and
    Television) 338
Antelope Films Ltd 338
ANV Productions 338
Artifax Ltd 338
Aspect Film and Television
    Productions Ltd 338
Barony Film and Television
    Productions Limited 339
Batty (Peter) Productions 339
Behr Cinematography 339
Berriff (Paul) Productions Ltd 339

BFV Ltd 340
Blackbird Productions 340
Black (Stuart) Productions 340
Blossom Productions Ltd 340
Boney (Matt) Associates 340
Box Clever 341
Brilliant Ideas Productions 341
Broadsword Television 341
Broadwick Productions 341
Brook Productions 341
Cadenza 342
Caravel Film Techniques Limited
    342
Catlin (Pearl) Associates 342
Chameleon Television Ltd 342
Chapman Clarke Television 343
Cinecosse Video 344
Cinexsa Film Productions Limited
    344
Cirrus Films 344
Clark Production 344
Clear Picture Company, The 344
Cleveland Productions 344
Commercial Facilities Ltd (Colstar
    International) 344
Compass Film Productions Ltd
    344
Component Television
    Productions Ltd 345
Creative Film Makers Ltd 345
Creative Television Workshops
    Ltd 345
Cromdale Films Ltd 346
Crown Business Communications
    Ltd 346
Crystalvision Ltd 346
CTR Productions 346
Dateline Productions Ltd 346
DBA Television 346
Deptford Beach Productions Ltd
    347
Dibgate Productions Ltd 347
Dunkley (Robert) Associates Ltd
    347
Eagle and Eagle Ltd 347
Edinburgh Film & Video
    Productions 348
Electric Picture Machine 348
Espresso TV 348
Ettinger Brothers Productions 349
Eyewitness Ltd 349
Farnham Film Company Ltd 349
Fast Forward Productions 349
FilmIt Productions Ltd 349
Filmworks 349
First Freedom Productions Ltd
    350
Flashback Television Ltd 350
Flying Pig Productions Ltd 350

Flying Tiger Film and TV Productions 350
Fourth Wall Productions 351
Fox Television 351
Gall (Ian) Television 351
Gau (John) Productions 352
Gibb Rose Organisation Ltd 352
Greenpark Productions Ltd 353
Griffin Productions 353
Hall (David) Productions 353
Hawkshead Ltd 354
Hemson (John) 354
Highgate Films 355
Holmes Associates 355
Holmes & Moriarty 355
Horntvedt Television 355
Hourglass Pictures Ltd 355
Howes (Michael) Productions Ltd 355
Hubner Films Ltd 355
Illuminations 356
Imagicians Ltd 356
Insight Productions Ltd 356
Interesting Television Ltd 357
Isaac (Peter) Ltd 357
Isolde Films Ltd 357
Jenkinson (Brian) Film & Television Productions Ltd 357
Lagan Pictures Ltd 358
Landseer Film and Television Productions Ltd 358
Lifetime Group 358
Lodestar Productions Ltd 358
Lombard Productions Ltd 358
London Scientific Films 359
LTV Productions 359
Lucida Productions 359
Main Communications 359
Malachite Ltd 359
Malone Gill Productions Ltd 360
Marking Inc Productions 360
Meditel Productions Ltd 360
Mentorn Films 361
MIlls (John) Film and Television 361
Mirus Productions 361
MJW Productions 362
Morrison Company, The 362
Mosaic Film & Video Productions 362
Mother Films 362
Moving Direction 362
New Decade Productions 362
Normandy Film Productions 363
Open Mind Productions 363
Pace Productions Ltd 363
Panoptic Productions 364
Paper Moon Productions 364
Parallax Pictures Ltd 364

PCP - Production Centre Productions 364
Peake Productions 364
Pelicula Films 364
Pentagon Communications 364
Picturehead Productions 365
Picture Palace Productions 365
Pilley (Phil) Productions 365
Poseidon Productions Ltd 365
Primetime Television Ltd 365
Principal Film Company Ltd, The 365
Priory Film Productions 366
Purchasepoint Video 366
Quanta Ltd 366
Riverfront Pictures Ltd 367
Roymark Ltd 367
Schonfeld Productions International/SPI 80 Ltd 367
Scope Picture Productions Ltd 367
Sevenday Productions 367
Seventh House Films 367
Signals, Essex Media Centre 368
Smith & Watson Productions 368
Solo Vision Ltd 369
Spectel Productions Limited 369
Strawberry Productions Ltd 369
Talbot Television Ltd 369
Team Two Ltd 370
Television in Business Ltd 370
Teliesyn 370
Third Eye Productions Ltd 370
Tiger Television Ltd 370
Touch Productions 371
Twin Continental Films Ltd 371
United Television Artists Ltd 372
Vera Productions 372
Verronmead Ltd 372
Videoplus Productions Ltd 373
Viewpoint Group Ltd 373
Wadlow Grosvenor 374
Wall to Wall Television 374
Warner Sisters 374
Waterfront Productions 374
White City Films 374
Worldview Pictures 375
Worldwide Television News 375
Younger (Greg) Associates 375
Yo-Yo Films 375
Zoom Production Co. Ltd, The 376

Documentary: European Publishers
Balland (André) 415
Elsevier Librico NV 411
Laffont (Editions Robert) 417
Politikens Forlag A/S 414

Dogs: Publishers (UK)
Crowood Press Ltd, The 32
Random House Publishing Grou Ltd 76

Dogs: Magazines
Dog World 239
Kennel Gazette 259

Dogs: Picture Libraries
Animal Photography 599
Kennel Club Library, The 613
Natural Science Photos 616

Drama/Theatre: Publishers (UK)
Absolute Press 9
Amber Lane Press Ltd 11
Black (A. & C.) (Publishers) Ltd 18
Black Spring Press Ltd 18
Bloodaxe Books Ltd 19
Boyars (Marion) Publishers Ltd
Brown, Son & Ferguson, Ltd 23
Calder Publications Ltd 23
Faber & Faber Ltd 40
French (Samuel) Ltd 43
Garnet Miller (J.) Ltd 43
Macmillan Publishers Ltd 61
Northcote House Publishers Ltd 67
Oberon Books 68
Penguin Books Ltd 71
Random House Publishing Grou Ltd 76
Robson Books Ltd 81
Roundhouse Publishing Ltd 81
Souvenir Press Ltd 87
Warner Chappell Plays Ltd 95

Drama/Theatre: Agents (UK)
Anderson (Darley) Books 159
Baker (Yvonne) Associates 160
Bryant (Peter) (Writers) 161
Casarotto Ramsay Ltd 161
Cochrane (Elspeth) Agency 162
Colin (Rosica) Ltd 162
Comstock-Smith Literary Agenc 163
Conway-Gordon (Jane) 163
Conway (Vernon) Ltd 163
Creative Tone Ltd 163
Curtis Brown Group Ltd 163
Daish (Judy) Associates Ltd 164
Davis-Poynter (Reg) 164
Fitch (Laurence) Ltd 165
Foster (Jill) Ltd 165
Gardner (Kerry) Management 1
Glass (Eric) Ltd 166
Hancock (Roger) Ltd 167

Hoskins (Valerie) 168
ICM 168
Imison (Michael) Playwrights Ltd 168
International Copyright Bureau Ltd 169
International Scripts 169
Jarvie (Gordon), Literary Agent 169
Lemon, Unna and Durbridge Ltd 170
L'Epine Smith & Carney Associates 170
Mann (Andrew) Ltd 171
Martinez (M. C.) Literary Agency 171
Marvin (Blanche) 171
MBA Literary Agents Ltd* 172
McLean (Bill) Personal Management 170
Milne (Richard) Ltd 172
Morris (William) Agency UK Ltd 172
Peters Fraser & Dunlop Group Ltd* 174
Radala & Associates 175
Sales (Ian) Associates 176
Sayle (Tessa) Agency 176
Sharland Organisation Ltd, The 176
Shaw (Vincent) Associates 176
Sheil Land Associates Ltd* 176
Simmons (Jeffrey) 177
Steel (Elaine) 177
Steinberg (Micheline) Playwrights' Agent 178
Thurley (J. M.) 178
Ware (Cecily) Literary Agents 179
Warner Chappell Plays Ltd 179
Watt (A. P.) Ltd 179

Drama/Theatre: Magazines
Amateur Stage 218
Plays and Players 274
Stage and Television Today 286
Sunk Island Review 287

Drama/Theatre: Television
Carlton Television 308

Drama/Theatre: Film, TV and video producers
Aisling Films Ltd 337
Alan Afriat Associates 337
Amber Films 337
Angel (Greg) (Film and Television) 338
Antelope Films Ltd 338
Aspect Film and Television Productions Ltd 338

Barclay (Humphrey) Productions/First Choice 339
Barony Film and Television Productions Limited 339
Blackbird Productions 340
Blossom Productions Ltd 340
Brook Productions 341
Cadenza 342
Carnival Films & Theatre Ltd 342
Catlin (Pearl) Associates 342
Chameleon Television Ltd 342
Chapman Clarke Television 343
Chatsworth Television Ltd 343
CHG Communications 343
Childsplay Productions Ltd 343
Chrysalis Television Productions Ltd 344
Cirrus Films 344
Commercial Facilities Ltd (Colstar International) 344
Component Television Productions Ltd 345
Cromdale Films Ltd 346
Crown Business Communications Ltd 346
Crystalvision Ltd 346
Dunkley (Robert) Associates Ltd 347
Eagle and Eagle Ltd 347
Edinburgh Film & Video Productions 348
Electric Picture Machine 348
Elstree (Production) Co. Ltd 348
Enigma Productions Ltd 348
Eyewitness Ltd 349
Farnham Film Company Ltd 349
FilmIt Productions Ltd 349
Flying Pig Productions Ltd 350
Gau (John) Productions 352
GCP 352
Gilpin (Adrian) Television 352
Grasshopper Productions Ltd 353
Griffin Productions 353
Grundy (Reg) Productions (GB) Ltd 353
Hall (David) Productions 353
Hat Trick Productions Ltd 354
Highgate Films 355
Hines Communications Ltd 355
Holmes Associates 355
Holmes & Moriarty 355
Hourglass Pictures Ltd 355
ICE International Video Films Ltd 356
Insight Productions Ltd 356
Interesting Television Ltd 357
Isolde Films Ltd 357
Jericho Productions Ltd 357
Knaves Acre Productions 358
Lagan Pictures Ltd 358

Landseer Film and Television Productions Ltd 358
Lawson Productions Ltd 358
Lifetime Group 358
Lodestar Productions Ltd 358
Lombard Productions Ltd 358
London Film Productions Ltd 359
LTV Productions 359
Lucida Productions 359
Mac Films 359
Main Communications 359
Malone Gill Productions Ltd 360
Marking Inc Productions 360
Meditel Productions Ltd 360
Mentorn Films 361
Mersey Television Company Ltd 361
Morrison Company, The 362
Mother Films 362
Oxford Film & Video Makers 363
Pace Productions Ltd 363
Parallax Pictures Ltd 364
Paramount Revcom 364
PCP - Production Centre Productions 364
Peake Productions 364
Pentagon Communications 364
Picture Base International 364
Picturehead Productions 365
Picture Palace Productions 365
Polygram Filmed Entertainment 365
Primetime Television Ltd 365
Principal Film Company Ltd, The 365
Quanta Ltd 366
Riverfront Pictures Ltd 367
Roymark Ltd 367
Schonfeld Productions International/SPI 80 Ltd 367
Smith & Watson Productions 368
Strawberry Productions Ltd 369
Talbot Television Ltd 369
Talisman Films Ltd 369
Television in Business Ltd 370
Television Visualeyes 370
Teliesyn 370
Touch Productions 371
Tyburn Productions Ltd 371
Vera Productions 372
Verronmead Ltd 372
Wall to Wall Television 374
Warner Sisters 374
White (Michael) Productions Ltd 374
Working Title Films Ltd/WTTV Ltd 375
Worldview Pictures 375
World Wide International Television 375

Younger (Greg) Associates 375
Yo-Yo Films 375
ZED Ltd 376
Zenith Productions Ltd 376
Zoom Production Co. Ltd, The 376

Drama/Theatre: Publishers (US)
French (Samuel), Inc. 443
Players Press 449

Drama/Theatre: Agents (US)
Artists Group, The 456
Author Aid Associates 456
Berman (Lois) 457
Creative Concepts Literary Agency 459
Curtis Brown Ltd 459
Ellen Lively Steele & Associates 461
Fields (Marje)/Rita Scott 462
Fishbein (Frieda) Ltd 462
Freedman (Robert A.) Dramatic Agency, Inc. 462
Kroll (Lucy) Agency 465
Lee (L. Harry) Literary Agency 466
Lord (Sterling) Literistic, Inc. 468
Nelson (B.K.) Literary Agency 470
Rosenstone/Wender 473
Schwartz (Laurens R.) 475
Swanson (H. N.), Inc. 478
Tantleff Office, The 478
Writer's Consulting Group 480

Drama/Theatre: Professional Associations
Arvon Foundation 489
Independent Theatre Council 497
New Playwrights Trust 498
Personal Managers' Association Ltd, The 500
Player-Playwrights 500
Playwrights Co-operative 500
Playwrights' Workshop 500
Theatre Writers' Union 504

Drama/Theatre: Bursaries/Fellowships
Arts Council Theatre Writing Bursaries 535
Mobil Bursary 538
Thames Television Theatre Writers' Scheme 540

Drama/Theatre: Prizes
Anderson (Eileen) Central Television Drama Award 542
Bargate (Verity) Award 543

Beckett (Samuel) Award 544
Devine (George) Award 550
King (Martin Luther) Memorial Prize, The 556
LWT Plays on Stage 557
Markham (Arthur) Memorial Prize 559
Questors Theatre Student Playwright Competition 564
Radio Times Drama & Comedy Awards 564
Unicorn Theatre Young Playwrights' Competition 570
Wandsworth Writers London Competition 571
Whiting (John) Award 572
Young Playwright of the Year Award 573

Drama/Theatre: Libraries
Theatre Museum Library & Archive 592
Westminster Reference Library 593

Drama/Theatre: Picture Libraries
Dominic Photography 605
Performing Arts Library 617
V&A Picture Library 624

Drama/Theatre: Small Presses
Businesslike Publishing 135
Cheverell Press, The 135
Paranoia Press (Teesside) 142
Peepal Tree Books 143

Drama/Theatre: Festivals
BBC Radio Drama Young Playwright's Festival 403
Brighton Festival 404
Cambridge Festival 404
Contact Young Playwrights' Festival 405
Coventry Festival 405
Doncaster Literature Festival 405
Exeter Festival 406
Glasgow Mayfest 406
Greenwich Festival 406
Hay-on-Wye Festival of Literature 406
King's Lynn, The Drama Festival 407
Lancaster Literature Festival 407
London New Play Festival 407
Ludlow Festival 407
Royal Court Young Writers' Festival 408
South London Playwrighting Festival 408

Worcester Festival of Literature 409
Write Around $92 A Celebration of Cleveland Writing 409
York Festival 409

Drama/Theatre: European Publishers
Actes Sud (Editions) 415
Bompiana 422
Bulzoni Editore SRL (Le Edizioni Universitarie d'Italia) 422
Cappelli (Nuova Casa Editrice Licinio) SpA 422
Don Quijote (Editorial) 430
Fundamentos (Editorial) 431
Gremese Editore SRL 423
Lalli (Antonio) Editore 424
Mulino (Societe Editrice Il) 425
Seix Barral SA 432

Eastern Europe: Publishers (UK)
Forest Books 41
Quartet Books 76

Eastern Europe: Agents (UK)
Radala & Associates 175

Eastern Europe: Picture Libraries
Panos Pictures 617

Ecology: Publishers (UK)
Crabtree Publishing 31
Gaia Books Ltd 43
Gateway Books 43
Little, Brown & Co. (UK) Ltd 59
Merlin Press Ltd 64

Ecology: Agents (UK)
O'Leary (David) Literary Agents 173
Solo Syndication & Literary Agency Ltd 177

Ecology: Magazines
Ecologist, The 240

Ecology: Television
Discovery Channel, The 313

Ecology: Agents (US)
Quicksilver Books, Literary Agents 473
Spieler Literary Agency 477

Ecology: Picture Libraries
Coleman (Bruce) Wildlife & Travel Photo Library 604

Ecoscene 606
Garland (Leslie) Picture Library
  609
GeoScience Features 609
Grace (Martin and Dorothy) 609
Hoffman (David) Photo Library
  611
Hutchison Library, The 611

Ecology: Small Presses
Dark Diamonds Publications 136

Ecology: European Publishers
Hovedland (Forlaget) 413
Incafo (Editorial) SA 431
Klett-Cotta Verlag 420
Kluwer Academic Publishers BV
  426
Miraguano SA Ediciones 432

Economics: Publishers (UK)
Athlone Press, The 14
Berg Publishers Ltd 17
Blackwell Publishers 18
Bookmarks Publications 20
Boyars (Marion) Publishers Ltd 20
Business Education Publishers Ltd
  23
Chapman (Paul) Publishing Ltd 27
Currey (James) Publishers 32
Donald (John) Publishers Ltd 35
Economist Books 36
Elgar (Edward) Publishing Ltd 37
Freeman (W. H.) & Co. Ltd 42
Gordon & Breach Science
  Publishers 45
Harcourt Brace Jovanovich Ltd 48
Harvard University Press 50
Jai Press Ltd 54
Lawrence & Wishart Ltd 57
Macmillan Publishers Ltd 61
Manchester University Press 62
McGraw-Hill Book Co. Europe 60
Merlin Press Ltd 64
Milestone Publications 64
MIT Press Ltd, The 65
Pergamon Press 73
Polity Press 75
Random House Publishing Group
  Ltd 76
Routledge, Chapman & Hall Ltd
  81
Shepheard-Walwyn (Publishers)
  Ltd 85
Verso Ltd 93

Economics: Magazines
Economist, The 240
Euromoney 243
Forbes Magazine 482

Wall Street Journal 485

Economics: Publishers (US)
Addison-Wesley Publishing Co.,
  Inc. 436
Avon Books 438
Iowa State University Press 445
Krieger Publishing Co., Inc. 445
Longman Publishing Group 446
MIT Press 447
Random House, Inc. 450
Times Books 453

**Economics:
  Bursaries/Fellowships**
Blundell (K.) Trust, The 535

Economics: Prizes
Royal Economic Society Prize 565

Economics: Libraries
Bank of England Reference
  Library 577

**Economics: European
  Publishers**
Beck (Verlag C H) 418
Calmann-Lévy (Editions) SA 415
Casterman (Editions) 415
Denoël (Editions) Sàrl 416
Deutsch (Verlag Harri) 419
E U N S A (Ediciones Universidad
  de Navarra SA) 431
Flammarion et Cie 416
Francisci (Aldo) Editore 423
FSRs Forlag 413
Hachette 416
Kohlhammer (Verlag W) GmbH
  420
Lannoo (Uitgeverij) Drukkerij 412
Liber AB 433
Liguori Editore SRL 424
Masson Editeur 417
Mulino (Societe Editrice Il) 425
Orac Verlag Gesellschaft mbH
  411
Orell Füssli Verlag 435
Paludans (Jörgen) Forlag ApS 414
Rabén och Sjögren Bokforlag AB
  433
RCS Rizzoli Libri SpA 425
Rosinante/Munksgaard 414
S A I E Editrice SRL 425
Sperling e Kupfer Editori SpA 425
Springer-Verlag GmbH & Co KG
  421
V U Boekhandel/Uitgeverij BV
  427
Vuibert (Librairie) SA 418

Education: Publishers (UK)
Acair Ltd 10
Accent Educational Publishers Ltd
  10
Atlantic Europe Publishing Co. Ltd
  14
Batsford (B.T.) Ltd 16
Black (A. & C.) (Publishers) Ltd
  18
Brooks Books 22
Business Education Publishers Ltd
  23
Cambridge University Press 24
Cassell 25
Cass (Frank) 25
Chapman (Paul) Publishing Ltd 27
Child's Play (International) Ltd 28
Clare (John) Books 28
Consumers' Association 30
Crabtree Publishing 31
Donald (John) Publishers Ltd 35
Drake Educational Associates 35
Elm Publications 37
Evans Brothers Ltd 39
Falmer Press 41
Freeman (W. H.) & Co. Ltd 42
Fulton (David) (Publishers) Ltd 43
Gibson (Robert) & Sons 44
Glasgow (Mary) Publications Ltd
  44
Graham-Cameron Publishing 46
Grosvenor Books 47
Harcourt Brace Jovanovich Ltd 48
HarperCollins Publishers Ltd 49
Hodder & Stoughton Ltd 52
Karnak House 55
Kingsley (Jessica) Publishers Ltd
  56
Kogan Page Ltd 56
Lawrence & Wishart Ltd 57
Liverpool University Press 59
Longman Group Ltd 60
Lutterworth Press, The 60
Macmillan Publishers Ltd 61
Manchester University Press 62
MIT Press Ltd, The 65
Murray (John) (Publishers) Ltd 66
Nelson (Thomas) & Sons Ltd 66
NFER-NELSON Publishing Co. Ltd
  67
Open University Press 69
Pergamon Press 73
Pitman Publishing 74
Reed International Books 78
Routledge, Chapman & Hall Ltd
  81
Sangam Books Ltd 82
Scholastic Publications Ltd 83
Scottish Academic Press 84

Search Press Ltd/Burns & Oates
  Ltd 84
Souvenir Press Ltd 87
Thornes (Stanley) (Publishers) Ltd
  90
Trentham Books Ltd 92
Trotman & Co. Ltd 92
Vision Press Ltd 94
Ward Lock Educational 94
Weavers Press Publishing 95

Education: Packagers
Chancerel Publishers Ltd 151

Education: Agents (UK)
Clarson-Leach (Robert) 162
Fox & Howard Literary Agency
  166
Futerman (Vernon) Associates
  166
Jarvie (Gordon), Literary Agent
  169

Education: Magazines
Child Education 231
Education 240
Education & Training 241
Mensa Magazine 263
Report 279
*Times Educational Supplement
  Scotland, The* 290
*Times Educational Supplement,
  The* 290
*Times Higher Education
  Supplement, The* 291

**Education: Film, TV and video
  producers**
Apple Television 338
Barratt (Michael) Ltd 339
Behr Cinematography 339
Broadwick Productions 341
Childsplay Productions Ltd 343
Compass Film Productions Ltd
  344
Creative Television Workshops
  Ltd 345
Crown Business Communications
  Ltd 346
Diverse Productions Ltd 347
Dunkley (Robert) Associates Ltd
  347
Edric Audio Visual Ltd 348
Electric Picture Machine 348
First House Productions Ltd 350
Flying Pig Productions Ltd 350
Gall (Ian) Television 351
Hawkshead Ltd 354
In Video Productions Ltd 356
Jacaranda Productions Ltd 357

Main Communications 359
MCEG Virgin Vision 360
Meditel Productions Ltd 360
Open Mind Productions 363
Oxford Film & Video Makers 363
Purchasepoint Video 366
Rank Production 366
Sevenday Productions 367
Skyline Film & TV Productions Ltd
  368
Sonoptics Communications Group
  369
Talbot Television Ltd 369
United Television Artists Ltd 372
VATV 372
Video Arts (Production) Ltd 372
Videotel Productions/Living Tape
  Productions 373
Wadlow Grosvenor 374
Zoom Production Co. Ltd, The
  376

Education: Theatre producers
Humberside Theatre in Education
  385
Roundabout Theatre in Education
  393

Education: Publishers (US)
ABC–Clio, Inc. 436
Barron's Educational Series 439
Charlesbridge Publishing 440
Iowa State University Press 445
Krieger Publishing Co., Inc. 445
Longman Publishing Group 446
New England (University Press of)
  448
Open Court Publishing Co. 448
Schocken Books, Inc. 451
Times Books 453

Education: Agents (US)
Brandenburgh & Associates
  Literary Agency 457
Educational Design Services, Inc.
  460
Singer (Evelyn) Literary Agency,
  Inc., The 476
Stern (Gloria) Agency (New York)
  477
Writer's Consulting Group 480

Education: Prizes
International Reading Association
  Literacy Award 555
SCSE Book Prizes 567
Times Educational Supplement
  Information Book Awards 570

Education: Libraries
Hatfield Polytechnic Library 584

Education: Picture Libraries
Fairclough (Chris) Colour Library
  607
Financial Times Picture Collectio
  607
Format Partners Photo Library
  608
Greater London Photograph
  Library 609
Greenhill (Sally and Richard) 610
Photofusion 617
Reflections PhotoLibrary 619
Walmsley (John) Picture Library
  625
Wiedel (Janine) 625

Education: Small Presses
Education Now Publishing
  Cooperative Ltd 137
Oriflamme Publishing 142
QED Books 144
Robinswood Press, The 145
Tamarind Ltd 146
Tufnell Press, The 146
Whyld Publishing Co-op 147
Yoffroy Publications 147

**Education: European
  Publishers**
Anaya (Ediciones) SA 430
Armando Armando (Editore) SR
  422
Belin (Editions) 415
B L V Verlagsgesellschaft mbH
  419
Bordas (Editions) 415
Borgens Forlag A/S 412
Capitol Editrice Dischi CEB 422
Ceac (Ediciones) SA 430
Città Nuova Editrice 423
Davidsfonds VZW 411
Delagrave Sàrl (Librarie) 416
Diesterweg (Verlag Moritz) 419
Dom Quixote (Publicacoes) Lda
  429
Elsevier 426
Eumo Editorial 431
E U N S A (Ediciones Universida
  de Navarra SA) 431
Flammarion et Cie 416
G.E.C. Gad Publishers 413
Gedisa (Editorial) SA 431
Gjellerup & Gad Publishers Ltd
  413
Gradiva – Publicacoes Lda 429
Gyldendalske Boghandel, Nordis
  Forlag A/S 413

Haase (P.) & Søns Forlag A/S 413
Hachette 416
Herder (Verlag) GmbH & Co KG
420
Jover (Ediciones) SA 431
Keesing Uitgeversmaatschappij
BV 426
Klett-Cotta Verlag 420
Kluwer Group 426
Kok (Uitgeversmaatschappij J H)
BV 426
Lalli (Antonio) Editore 424
Magnard Sàrl (Les Editions) 417
Mallings ApS 414
Mondadori (Arnoldo) Editore SpA
424
Nathan (Fernand) 418
Natur och Kultur (Bokförlaget)
433
Nelissen (Uitgeverij H) BV 426
NKS-Forlaget (Ernst G.
Mortensens stiftelse) 428
Orell Füssli Verlag 435
Österreichischer Bundesverlag
Gesellschaft mbH 411
Paludans (Jörgen) Forlag ApS 414
Porto Editora Lda 429
S A I E Editrice SRL 425
Sauerlander AG 435
S E I (Società Editrice
Internationale) 425
Servire BV Uitgevers 426
Sikkel (Uitgeverij De) NV 412
Skira (Editions d'Art Albert) SA
435
Styria (Verlag) 411
Suhrkamp Verlag 421
Swets en Zeitlinger BV 427
Tano AS 428
Teide (Editorial) SA 432
Texto Editora 430
Timun Mas (Editorial) SA 432
Ugo (Gruppo) Mursia Editore SpA
425
Ullstein (Buchverlage) GmbH 421
Verbo (Editorial) SA 430
Vives (Editorial Luis) (Edelvives)
432

Electronics: Publishers (UK)
Addison–Wesley Publishers Ltd
10
Argus Books 13
Artech House 13
Helicon Publishing 51
Oxford University Press 70
Woodhead Publishing Ltd 97

Electronics: Magazines
Hi-Fi News & Record Review 253

Practical Electronics 275
What Hi-Fi 295

Electronics: Publishers (US)
TAB Books 452

Electronics: Agents (US)
Catalog Literary Agency, The 458

**Electronics: European
Publishers**
Kohlhammer (Verlag W) GmbH
420
Vogel-Verlag KG 422
Hachette 416

**Encyclopedias: Publishers
(UK)**
Cambridge University Press 24
Longman Group Ltd 60
Macmillan Publishers Ltd 61
Oxford University Press 70
Reed International Books 78

Encyclopedias: Packagers
Andromeda Oxford Ltd 148
BLA Publishing Ltd 150
Market House Books Ltd 153

Encyclopedias: Agents (US)
Rosenthal (Jean) Literary Agency
473

Encyclopedias: Prizes
Library Association McColvin
Medal, The 557

**Encyclopedias: European
Publishers**
Bompiana 422
Bonnier Fakta Bokforlag AB 432
Bordas (Editions) 415
Bra Bocker (Bokforlaget) AB 433
Brockhaus (F A) 419
Cappelens (J W) Forlag A/S 428
Damm (N W) & Son A/S 428
Debate SA 430
E U N S A (Ediciones Universidad
de Navarra SA) 431
Fabbri (Gruppo Editoriale) SpA
423
Garzanti Editore 423
Istituto per l'Enciclopedia del
Friuli Venezia Giulia 424
Kluwer Group 426
Kunnskapsforlaget I/S 428
Lademann (Det Ny) A/S 414
Landi (Luciano) Editore SRL 424
Larousse (Librairie) 417
Paoline (Edizioni) SRL 425

S A I E Editrice SRL 425
Spectrum (Uitgeverij Het) BV 427
Standaard Uitgeverij 412
Verbo (Editorial) SA 430

Engineering: Publishers (UK)
Attic Books 14
Freeman (W. H.) & Co. Ltd 42
Gordon & Breach Science
Publishers 45
McGraw-Hill Book Co. Europe 60
MIT Press Ltd, The 65
Pergamon Press 73
Woodhead Publishing Ltd 97

Engineering: Magazines
Engineering 242
Engineer, The 241

**Engineering: Film, TV and
video producers**
Chapel Broadcast Productions Ltd
343

Engineering: Publishers (US)
Iowa State University Press 445
Krieger Publishing Co., Inc. 445
Van Nostrand Reinhold 453

Engineering: Picture Libraries
Evans (Mary) Picture Library 606
Outram (George) Picture Library
617
QA Photos 618

**Engineering: European
Publishers**
Bauverlag GmbH 418
Born NV Uitgeversmaatschappij
426
Bulzoni Editore SRL (Le Edizioni
Universitarie d'Italia) 422
Calderini (Edizioni) 422
CEDAM (Casa Editrice Dr A
Milani) 423
Elsevier 426
E U N S A (Ediciones Universidad
de Navarra SA) 431
Europa-America (Publicaoes) Lda
429
Kohlhammer (Verlag W) GmbH
420
NKI Forlaget 428
Presses Universitaires de France
(PUF) 418
Springer-Verlag 411
Springer-Verlag GmbH & Co KG
421
Swets en Zeitlinger BV 427
Vogel-Verlag KG 422

English Language Teaching (ELT): Publishers (UK)
Cambridge University Press 24
Glasgow (Mary) Publications Ltd 44
Harcourt Brace Jovanovich Ltd 48
Longman Group Ltd 60
Macmillan Publishers Ltd 61
Nelson (Thomas) & Sons Ltd 66
Oxford University Press 70
Penguin Books Ltd 71
Reed International Books 78
Simon & Schuster Ltd 86
Thornes (Stanley) (Publishers) Ltd 90
Ward Lock Educational 94

English Language Teaching (ELT): Agents (UK)
Jarvie (Gordon), Literary Agent 169

English Language Teaching (ELT): Publishers (US)
Longman Publishing Group 446

Entomological Studies: Publishers (UK)
Harley Books 48

Entomological Studies: Libraries
Natural History Museum Library 588

Entomological Studies: Picture Libraries
Camera Ways Ltd Picture Library 603
Foord (Ron & Christine) Colour Picture Library 608
Natural Science Photos 616
Premaphotos Wildlife 618
RSPB Picture Library 620

Entomological Studies: Small Presses
Fitzgerald Publishing 137

Environment/Conservation: Publishers (UK)
Athlone Press, The 14
Green Books 46
Kogan Page Ltd 56
Lutterworth Press, The 60
Penguin Books Ltd 71
Pinter Publishers Ltd 74
Prism Press Book Publishers Ltd 75

Routledge, Chapman & Hall Ltd 81
Zed Books Ltd 98

Environment/Conservation: Packagers
Belitha Press Ltd 149
Cameron Books (Production) Ltd 150
Greenpeace Books 152
New England Editions Ltd 154

Environment/Conservation: Agents (UK)
Dorian Literary Agency 164

Environment/Conservation: Magazines
BBC WILDLIFE Magazine 223
Birds 224
Country-Side 235
English Heritage Magazine 242
FarmWatch 245
Green Magazine 250
Greenscene 251
Hertfordshire Countryside 253
Home and Country 254
Naturalist, The 268

Environment/Conservation: Film, TV and video producers
Acacia Productions Ltd 337
International Broadcasting Trust 357
Mosaic Film & Video Productions 362
Waterfront Productions 374

Environment/Conservation: Publishers (US)
Kansas (University of) Press 445
Massachusetts (University of) Press 447
NorthWord Press, Inc. 448
Random House, Inc. 450
Texas (University of) Press 452
Van Nostrand Reinhold 453

Environment/Conservation: Agents (US)
Fishbein (Frieda) Ltd 462
Quicksilver Books, Literary Agents 473
Singer (Evelyn) Literary Agency, Inc., The 476
Urstadt (Susan P.), Inc. 478

Environment/Conservation: Bursaries/Fellowships
Thomas (David) Prize 540

Environment/Conservation: Prizes
Earthworm Award 550
Kent (Sir Peter) Conservation Book Prize, The 555
Michelin Award 559

Environment/Conservation: Libraries
Barbican Library 577

Environment/Conservation: Picture Libraries
Aquila Photographics 599
Ardea London Ltd 600
Camera Ways Ltd Picture Library 603
Circa Photo Library 604
Cordaiy (Sylvia) Photo Library 6[?]
Ecoscene 606
Financial Times Picture Collectio[n] 607
Garland (Leslie) Picture Library 609
GeoScience Features 609
Greenpeace Communications Lt[d] 610
Hutchison Library, The 611
Impact Photos 612
Oxford Scientific Films Photo Library 617
Panos Pictures 617
Photofusion 617
Planet Earth Pictures/Seaphot 6[?]
Reflections PhotoLibrary 619
Retna Pictures Ltd 619
Select Photos 621
Still Pictures Environmental Agency 622
Swift Picture Library Ltd 623
Tropix Photographic Library 623
Wilderness Photographic Library 625

Environment/Conservation: European Publishers
Bauverlag GmbH 418
Orac Verlag Gesellschaft mbH 411
Parey (Verlag Paul) 421

Epidemiology: Libraries
Population Censuses & Surveys Library, Office of 589

Equal Opportunities: Libraries
Equal Opportunities Commission Library 583

Equal Opportunities: Small Presses
Whyld Publishing Co-op 147

Essays: Publishers (UK)
Random House Publishing Group Ltd 76

Essays: Magazines
London Review of Books 261

Essays: Publishers (US)
New England (University Press of) 448

Essays: Prizes
Alexander Prize 542
Berry (David) Prize 544
GPA Book Award 553
Holliday (Dan) Prize 554
Markham (Arthur) Memorial Prize 559
Rogers Prize 564
Taylor (E. Reginald) Essay Competition 569

Essays: Small Presses
CNP Publications/Lyfrow Trelyspen 136
Dark Diamonds Publications 136

Etiquette: Publishers (UK)
Debrett's Peerage Ltd 34
Headline Book Publishing 50

Europe/EC: Publishers (UK)
Brealey (Nicholas) Publishing Ltd 21
Dedalus Ltd 34
Sunflower Books 89

Europe/EC: Film, TV and video producers
Chapman Clarke Television 343
Hawthornden Films 354

Europe/EC: Bursaries/Fellowships
European Cultural Foundation 536

Europe/EC: Prizes
Bentinck (Adolphe) Prize 544
European Literary and Translation Prizes 550

Europe/EC: Libraries
Westminster Reference Library 593
Wiener Library, The 594

Europe/EC: Picture Libraries
Art Directors Photo Library 600
Cephas Picture Library 603
Colasanti (Stephanie) 604
Dixon (C M) 605
Garland (Leslie) Picture Library 609
Hanley (Tom) 610
Photographers' Library, The 618
Spectrum Colour Library 621
Wiedel (Janine) 625
Williams (S & I) Power Pix International Picture Library 626
Woodmansterne Ltd 626
Woolverton Colour Library 626
Wright (George) 626

Family Reference: Publishers (UK)
Elite Words & Image 37
Elliot Right Way Books 37
Guinness Publishing Ltd 47
Rosendale Press Ltd 81

Family Reference: Packagers
Zoe Books Ltd 156

Family Reference: Magazines
First Choice 246
Home & Family 254
Lifestyle Magazine 260
Living 260
Weekly News 294

Family Reference: Theatre producers
Thorndike Theatre (Leatherhead) Ltd 397

Family Reference: Publishers (US)
Gardner Press, Inc. 443

Family Reference: Agents (US)
Living Faith Literary Agency 468

Family Reference: Picture Libraries
Collections 604
Evans (Greg) International Photo Library 606
Financial Times Picture Collection 607

Hutchison Library, The 611
Photofusion 617
Photographers' Library, The 618
PictureBank Photo Library Ltd 618
Reflections PhotoLibrary 619
Stockphotos 622

Fashion & Costume: Publishers (UK)
Batsford (B.T.) Ltd 16
Herbert Press, The 51
Thames and Hudson Ltd 90

Fashion & Costume: Packagers
Gardenhouse Editions Ltd 151

Fashion & Costume: Agents (UK)
Anderson (Darley) Books 159
Solo Syndication & Literary Agency Ltd 177

Fashion & Costume: Magazines
Arena 220
Black Beauty & Hair 224
Harpers & Queen 252
ID Magazine 256
Looking Good 261
Vogue 294

Fashion & Costume: Publishers (US)
Players Press 449

Fashion & Costume: Libraries
Art & Design Library (Westminster) 577

Fashion & Costume: Picture Libraries
Art Directors Photo Library 600
Express Newspapers Picture Library 607
Frith (Francis) Collection 608
Harding (Robert) Picture Library 610
Miller (Lee) Archives 615
Retrograph Archive Ltd 619
Spooner (Frank) Pictures 622
V&A Picture Library 624
Victory Archive, The 624

Fashion & Costume: European Publishers
Gremese Editore SRL 423
Paris Musées 418

**Feminism & Women's Studies:
Publishers (UK)**
Athlone Press, The 14
Bloodaxe Books Ltd 19
Boyars (Marion) Publishers Ltd 20
Harvard University Press 50
Open Letters 68
Open University Press 69
Penguin Books Ltd 71
Piatkus Books 73
Pluto Press Ltd 75
Polity Press 75
Prism Press Book Publishers Ltd
75
Routledge, Chapman & Hall Ltd
81
Scarlett Press 83
Sheba Feminist Press 85
Souvenir Press Ltd 87
Verso Ltd 93
Virago Press Ltd 93
Volcano Press 94
Women's Press, The 96
Zed Books Ltd 98

**Feminism & Women's Studies:
Theatre producers**
Gay Sweatshop 383

**Feminism & Women's Studies:
Publishers (US)**
ABC-Clio, Inc. 436
Kansas (University of) Press 445
Massachusetts (University of)
Press 447
McFarland & Company, Inc.,
Publishers 446
New England (University Press of)
448
Oklahoma (University of) Press
448
Schocken Books, Inc. 451
Temple University Press 452
Tennessee (University of) Press
452
Times Books 453
Universe Publishing, Inc. 453

**Feminism & Women's Studies:
Agents (US)**
Carvainis (Maria) Agency, Inc.
457
Catalog Literary Agency, The 458
Gusay (Charlotte) Literary
Agency, The 463
Heacock Literary Agency, Inc.
464
Kern (Natasha) Literary Agency,
Inc. 464

New England Publishing
Associates, Inc. 470
Sebastian Agency 475
Stern (Gloria) Agency (New York)
477
Waterside Productions, Inc. 479

**Feminism & Women's Studies:
Prizes**
Fawcett Society Book Prize 551

**Feminism & Women's Studies:
Libraries**
Fawcett Library 583

**Feminism & Women's Studies:
Picture Libraries**
Evans (Mary) Picture Library 606
Format Partners Photo Library
608
London (Museum of) Picture
Library 614

**Feminism & Women's Studies:
Small Presses**
AK Press/AKA Books 133
Pythia Press 143

**Feminism & Women's Studies:
European Publishers**
LaSal (Edicions de les Dones) 431
Tiderne Skifter 415

Feminism & Women's Studies
Prisma-Verlag 421

Fiction: Publishers (UK)
Bellew Publishing Co. Ltd 17
Black Spring Press Ltd 18
Blackstaff Press Ltd 18
Blake Publishing 19
Book Guild, The 20
Boyars (Marion) Publishers Ltd 20
Breese (Martin) Publishing 21
Carcanet Press Ltd 25
Chapmans Publishers 27
Clio Press Ltd 29
Commonword Ltd 30
Constable & Co. Ltd 30
Dedalus Ltd 34
Deutsch (André) Ltd 34
Duckworth (Gerald) & Co. Ltd 36
Edinburgh University Press 37
Ellis (Aidan) Publishing 37
Faber & Faber Ltd 40
Fourth Estate Ltd 42
Gay Men's Press (GMP Publishers
Ltd), The 44
Gollancz (Victor) Ltd 45
Hale (Robert) Ltd 48

HarperCollins Publishers Ltd 49
Headline Book Publishing 50
Hodder & Stoughton Ltd 52
Karnak House 55
Little, Brown & Co. (UK) Ltd 59
Macmillan Publishers Ltd 61
Mainstream Publishing Co.
(Edinburgh) Ltd 62
MCM Publishing 61
O'Mara (Michael) Books Limited
68
Orion Publishing Group 69
Penguin Books Ltd 71
Piatkus Books 73
Quartet Books 76
Ramsay Head Press, The 76
Random House Publishing Group
Ltd 76
Reed International Books 78
Reinhardt Books Ltd 80
Robinson Publishing 80
Sangam Books Ltd 82
Serpent's Tail 84
Settle Press 85
Severn House Publishers 85
Simon & Schuster Ltd 86
Smith Gryphon Ltd 86
Souvenir Press Ltd 87
Stone Flower Ltd 88
Sumach Press, The 88
Swift Children's Books 89
Tabb House 89
Transworld Publishers Ltd 91
Virago Press Ltd 93
Women's Press, The 96
Yorkshire Arts Circus Ltd 97

Fiction: Packagers
MM Productions Ltd 154

Fiction: Agents (UK)
Abacus Literary Agency 159
Aitken & Stone Ltd* 159
Alexander (Jacintha) Associates
159
Anderson (Darley) Books 159
Blake Friedmann Literary Agency
Ltd* 160
Bolt (David) Associates 160
Bookworms Literary Agency 160
Bromley (Rosemary) Literary
Agency 160
Bryan (Felicity) 160
Burston (Diane) Literary Agency
161
Campbell Thomson & McLaughlin
Ltd* 161
Carnell Literary Agency* 161
Casarotto Ramsay Ltd 161
Chilcote (Judith) Agency 161

Chris (Teresa) Literary Agency 162
Clarke (Serafina) 162
Clarson-Leach (Robert) 162
Clowes (Jonathan) Ltd 162
Cochrane (Elspeth) Agency 162
Conway-Gordon (Jane) 163
Conway (Vernon) Ltd 163
Crew (Rupert) Ltd 163
Cruickshank Cazenove Ltd 163
Curtis Brown Group Ltd 163
Davidson (Caroline) and Robert Ducas Literary Agency 164
Davidson (Merric) Literary Agency 164
Dorian Literary Agency 164
Doyle (Colleen) 165
Eady (Toby) Associates Ltd 165
Evans (Faith) Associates 165
Film Link Literary Agency 165
Fox & Howard Literary Agency 166
French's 166
Futerman (Vernon) Associates 166
Gabriel (Jüri) 166
Glass (Eric) Ltd 166
Green (Christine) (Authors' Agent) Ltd 167
Greene (Elaine) Ltd 167
Gregory & Radice Authors' Agents* 167
Grossman (David) Literary Agency Ltd 167
Heath (A. M.) & Co Ltd 167
Higham (David) Associates Ltd 168
Holt (Vanessa) Associates Ltd 168
Howard Seddon Associates 168
Howarth (Tanja) 168
Jarvie (Gordon), Literary Agent 169
Judd (Jane) Literary Agency 169
Levy (Barbara) Literary Agency 170
Little (Christopher) 170
London Independent Books Ltd 170
Mann (Andrew) Ltd 171
Manuscript ReSearch 171
Marjacq Scripts Ltd 171
Martinez (M. C.) Literary Agency 171
Martin (Judy) 171
MBA Literary Agents Ltd* 172
Millstone Lit 172
Morris (William) Agency UK Ltd 172
Motley (Michael) Ltd 172

O'Leary (David) Literary Agents 173
Owen (Deborah) Ltd 173
Pawsey (John) 173
Pearlstine (Maggie) 173
Penman Literary Agency 173
Peters Fraser & Dunlop Group Ltd* 174
Pollinger (Laurence) Ltd 174
Pollinger (Murray) 174
Power (Shelley) Literary Agency Ltd 174
PVA Management Ltd 174
Radala & Associates 175
Robertson (Patricia) 175
Rogers, Coleridge & White Ltd* 175
Ryder (Herta) 175
Sharkey (James) Associates Ltd 176
Sharland Organisation Ltd, The 176
Sheil Land Associates Ltd* 176
Sheldon (Caroline) Literary Agency 177
Simmons (Jeffrey) 177
Smith (Carol) Literary Agency 177
Stein (Abner) 178
Sugg (Belinda) Literary Agency 178
Tauber (Peter) Press Agency 178
Thurley (J. M.) 178
Victor (Ed) Ltd 178
Walker (S.) Literary Agency 179
Watson, Little Ltd* 179
Wiener (Dinah) Ltd 179

Fiction: Magazines
Active Life 217
Annabel 219
Bella 223
Challenge 230
Cosmopolitan 234
Essentials 242
Family Circle 244
Good Housekeeping 249
Harpers & Queen 252
HIM 253
Just Seventeen 258
LOOKS 261
Million: The Magazine About Popular Fiction 264
Mosaic 265
My Weekly 267
North, The 270
People's Friend, The 273
Sunk Island Review 287
Take a Break 288

Fiction: Publishers (US)
Academy Chicago Publishers 436
Aegina Press, Inc. 436
Arkansas (University of) Press 438
Atlantic Monthly Press 438
Avon Books 438
Bantam Doubleday Dell Publishing Group 438
Berkley Publishing Group 439
British American Publishing 440
California (University of) Press 440
Carol Publishing 440
Carroll & Graf Publishers, Inc. 440
Chronicle Books 440
Evans (M.) & Co., Inc. 442
Harcourt Brace Jovanovich 443
HarperCollins Publishers, Inc. 443
Harvest House Publishers 444
Illinois (University of) Press 444
Iowa (University of) Press 445
Little, Brown & Co., Inc. 445
Louisiana State University Press 446
Morrow (William) and Co., Inc. 447
Norton (W. W.) & Company 448
Putnam Publishing Group 450
Random House, Inc. 450
Rutgers University Press 451
St Martin's Press, Inc. 451
Simon & Schuster 451
Walker & Co 453

Fiction: Agents (US)
The majority of US agents listed in *The Writer's Handbook* handle fiction. See listing pp 455–481.

Fiction: Bursaries/Fellowships
Fulbright-Chandler Arts Fellowship Award 537
Trask (Betty) Awards, The 541

Fiction: Prizes
Angel Literary Award 543
Authors' Club First Novel Award 543
Black (James Tait) Memorial Prizes 544
Boardman Tasker Memorial Award 544
Booker Prize for Fiction 545
Constable Trophy, The 548
Cookson (Catherine) Fiction Prize 548
Encore Award, The 550
Faber (Geoffrey) Memorial Prize 551

Fawcett Society Book Prize 551
GPA Book Award 553
Guardian Fiction Prize, The 553
Heinemann Fiction Award 553
Higham (David) Prize for Fiction 554
Holtby (Winifred) Memorial Prize 554
Irish Times-Aer Lingus International Fiction Prize 555
Irish Times Aer Lingus Irish Literature Prizes 555
Lichfield Prize 557
Mail on Sunday/John Llewellyn Rhys Prize, The 559
Mail on Sunday Novel Competition, The 559
Markham (Arthur) Memorial Prize 559
McKitterick Prize 558
McVitie's Prize for Scottish Writer of the Year 559
People's Prize, The 563
Portico Prize, The 563
Stanford (Winifred Mary) Prize, The 568
Sunday Express Book of the Year Award 568
Sunday Times Special Award for Excellence in Writing 569
Sunday Times Young British Writer of the Year Award 569
Toonder (Marten) Award 570
Wingate (H. H.) Prize 572
Yorkshire Post Book of the Year Award 573
Young Writers' Competition 573

Fiction: Small Presses
Crescent Moon Publishing 136
Littlewood Arc 141
Maypole Editions 141
Peepal Tree Books 143
Quay Books Exeter 144
Stride 146

Fiction: Festivals
Birmingham Readers and Writers Festival 404
Canterbury Festival 404
King's Lynn, The Fiction Festival 407
Write Around – A Celebration of Cleveland Writing 409

Fiction: European Publishers
Many of the European publishers listed in *The Writer's Handbook* publish fiction. See section pp 410–435.

Film: Publishers (UK)
Aurum Press Ltd 15
BFI Publishing 17
Boxtree 20
Boyars (Marion) Publishers Ltd 20
Faber & Faber Ltd 40
Golden Cockerel Press Ltd 44
Harvard University Press 50
Headline Book Publishing 50
Reed International Books 78
Robinson Publishing 80
Titan Books 91
Virgin Publishing 93

Film: Packagers
Cameron Books (Production) Ltd 150

Film: Agents (UK)
Baker (Yvonne) Associates 160
Blake Friedmann Literary Agency Ltd* 160
Bryant (Peter) (Writers) 161
Casarotto Ramsay Ltd 161
Clowes (Jonathan) Ltd 162
Cochrane (Elspeth) Agency 162
Colin (Rosica) Ltd 162
Cruickshank Cazenove Ltd 163
Curtis Brown Group Ltd 163
Daish (Judy) Associates Ltd 164
Doyle (Colleen) 165
Fitch (Laurence) Ltd 165
Futerman (Vernon) Associates 166
Gardner (Kerry) Management 166
Glass (Eric) Ltd 166
Hoskins (Valerie) 168
ICM 168
Imison (Michael) Playwrights Ltd 168
International Copyright Bureau Ltd 169
International Scripts 169
Lemon, Unna and Durbridge Ltd 170
Little (Christopher) 170
Mann (Andrew) Ltd 171
Martin (Judy) 171
Marvin (Blanche) 171
MBA Literary Agents Ltd* 172
McLean (Bill) Personal Management 170
Milne (Richard) Ltd 172
Morris (William) Agency UK Ltd 172
Noach (Maggie) Literary Agency, The 172
Peters Fraser & Dunlop Group Ltd* 174

Power (Shelley) Literary Agency Ltd 174
PVA Management Ltd 174
Sales (Ian) Associates 176
Sayle (Tessa) Agency 176
Seifert Dench Associates 176
Shaw (Vincent) Associates 176
Sheil Land Associates Ltd* 176
Steel (Elaine) 177
Steinberg (Micheline) Playwrights Agent 178
Thurley (J. M.) 178
Ware (Cecily) Literary Agents 179
Watt (A. P.) Ltd 179

Film: Magazines
Amateur Film and Video Maker 218
Creative Review 235
Empire 241
Film Monthly 246
Film Review 246
Screen 282
Screen International 282
Sight & Sound 283
Video World Magazine 294
Watch It! 294

Film: Television
Bravo 313
Sky Television (BSkyB) 314

Film: Film, TV and video producers
Amber Films 337
Barclay (Humphrey) Productions/First Choice 339
Black Tulip 340
British Film Institute Production 341
British Lion Screen Entertainment Ltd 341
Burrill Productions 341
Carnival Films & Theatre Ltd 342
Chapman Clarke Television 343
Chrysalis Television Productions Ltd 344
Cromdale Films Ltd 346
Edinburgh Film & Video Productions 348
Elstree (Production) Co. Ltd 348
Enigma Productions Ltd 348
Euston Films 349
Forstater (Mark) Productions Ltd 351
Freeway Films 351
Frontroom Films Ltd 351
Gibb Rose Organisation Ltd 352
Goldcrest Films and Television Ltd 352

Greenpark Productions Ltd 353
Greenpoint Films 353
Gregg (Colin) Films Ltd 353
Hall (David) Productions 353
Hammer Film Productions 353
HandMade Films 353
Henson (Jim) Productions 354
Highgate Films 355
Hubner Films Ltd 355
ICE International Video Films Ltd 356
Illustra Communications Ltd 356
Isolde Films Ltd 357
Lombard Productions Ltd 358
London Film Productions Ltd 359
Mac Films 359
MCEG Virgin Vision 360
Midnight Films Ltd 361
Palace Productions 363
Paramount Pictures (UK) Ltd 364
Picture Base International 364
Polygram Filmed Entertainment 365
Portman Entertainment 365
Rakoff (Alvin) Productions Ltd 366
Rose Partnership (David & Kathy) 367
Schonfeld Productions International/SPI 80 Ltd 367
Twentieth Century Fox Productions Ltd 371
UBA Ltd 372
Uden Associates Ltd 372
Visionventures International Ltd 373
Warner Sisters 374
White City Films 374
White (Michael) Productions Ltd 374
Working Title Films Ltd/WTTV Ltd 375
Zenith Productions Ltd 376

Film: Publishers (US)
Iowa State University Press 445
Players Press 449
Texas (University of) Press 452

Film: Agents (US)
Amsterdam (Marcia) Agency 455
Andrews (Bart) & Associates 455
Appleseeds Management 455
Artists Group, The 456
Author Aid Associates 456
Browne (Pema) Ltd 457
Connor Literary Agency 459
Creative Concepts Literary Agency 459
Curtis Brown Ltd 459

Dupree/Miller & Associates, Inc., Literary Agency 460
Dykeman Associates, Inc. 460
Ellen Lively Steele & Associates 461
Feiler (Florence) Literary Agency 462
Fishbein (Frieda) Ltd 462
Flannery, White & Stone 462
Freedman (Robert A.) Dramatic Agency, Inc. 462
Gladden Unlimited 463
Kroll (Lucy) Agency 465
Lampack (Peter) Agency, Inc. 465
Lazear Agency, Inc., The 466
Lee Allan Agency, The 466
Lee (L. Harry) Literary Agency 466
Lighthouse Literary Agency 467
Literary & Creative Artists Agency 467
Lord (Sterling) Literistic, Inc. 468
Mann (Carol) Agency 468
Marshall Cameron Agency 469
Marshall (Evan) Agency 469
Nelson (B.K.) Literary Agency 470
Pegasus International, Inc. 471
Radley-Regan (D.) & Associates 473
Rosenstone/Wender 473
SBC Enterprises, Inc. 474
Scagnetti (Jack) Literary Agency 474
Schwartz (Laurens R.) 475
Shapiro-Lichtman Talent Agency 475
Shore (Lee) Agency 475
Stern (Gloria) Agency (Hollywood) 477
Tantleff Office, The 478
Wright (Ann) Representatives, Inc. 480
Wright (Stephen) Authors' Representative 480
Writer's Consulting Group 480

Film: Professional Associations
BAFTA (British Academy of Film and Television Arts) 491
British Film Commission, The 493
British Film Institute 493
British Screen Finance 494
London Screenwriters' Workshop 498

Film: Prizes
Frankel (Anne) Prize 552
King (Martin Luther) Memorial Prize, The 556

McVitie's Prize for Scottish Writer of the Year 559
Powell (Michael) Book Award 563

Film: Libraries
British Film Institute Library and Information Services 579

Film: Picture Libraries
Spooner (Frank) Pictures 622

Film: Festivals
Brighton Festival 404
Bury St Edmunds Arts Festival 404
Cambridge Festival 404
Coventry Festival 405

Film: European Publishers
Cappelli (Nuova Casa Editrice Licinio) SpA 422
Heyne (Wilhelm) Verlag 420

Finance: Publishers (UK)
Blackwell Publishers 18
Chapman (Paul) Publishing Ltd 27
Consumers' Association 30
Economist Books 36
Kogan Page Ltd 56
Longman Group Ltd 60
Macmillan Publishers Ltd 61
Random House Publishing Group Ltd 76
Scope International Ltd 83
Smith Gryphon Ltd 86
Woodhead Publishing Ltd 97

Finance: Agents (UK)
Clarson-Leach (Robert) 162

Finance: Magazines
Banker, The 222
Brokers' Monthly & Insurance Adviser 226
Dimensions 238
Euromoney 243
Giroscope 248
Investors Chronicle 257
Moneycare 265
Money Week 264
Moneywise 265
Wall Street Journal 483
What Investment 295
What Mortgage 295

Finance: Film, TV and video producers
Broadcast Communications 341
Broadwick Productions 341

Chapel Broadcast Productions Ltd 343

Finance: Publishers (US)
Adams (Bob) Publishers, Inc. 436

Finance: Agents (US)
Carvainis (Maria) Agency, Inc. 457
Catalog Literary Agency, The 458
Marcil (Denise) Literary Agency, Inc. 469
Snell (Michael) Literary Agency 476
Wieser & Wieser, Inc. 479

Finance: Libraries
Bank of England Reference Library 577
Barbican Library 577

Finance: Picture Libraries
Financial Times Picture Collection 607

Finance: European Publishers
Elsevier 426
Haufe (Rudolf) Verlag GmbH & Co KG 420

Firearms: Publishers (UK)
Crowood Press Ltd, The 32

Firearms: Magazines
Handgunner 252

Firearms: Libraries
Imperial War Museum 585

Fish/Fishing: Publishers (UK)
Black (A. & C.) (Publishers) Ltd 18
Cassell 25
Crowood Press Ltd, The 32
Elliot Right Way Books 37
Gollancz (Victor) Ltd 45
Reed International Books 78

Fish/Fishing: Agents (UK)
Eady (Toby) Associates Ltd 165

Fish/Fishing: Magazines
Angling Times 219
David Hall's Coarse Fishing Magazine 237
David Hall's Match Fishing Magazine 237
Practical Fishkeeping 275
Shooting Times & Country 283
Trout Fisherman 292

World Fishing 299

Fish/Fishing: Publishers (US)
Lyons & Burford, Publishers 446

Fish/Fishing: Libraries
Ministry of Agriculture, Fisheries and Food 587

Fish/Fishing: Picture Libraries
Ardea London Ltd 600
Blake (Anthony) 602
Camera Ways Ltd Picture Library 603
Footprints Colour Picture Library 608
Natural Science Photos 616
Scottish Highland Photo Library, The 621
Waterways Photo Library 625

Folklore: Publishers (UK)
Blackstaff Press Ltd 18
Dragon's World 35
Ensign Publications 38
Swift Children's Books 89

Folklore: Agents (UK)
Howard Seddon Associates 168

Folklore: Magazines
Evergreen 243
Scots Magazine, The 281
This England 290

Folklore: Publishers (US)
Tennessee (University of) Press 452

Folklore: Agents (US)
Ware (John A.) Literary Agency 479

Folklore: Prizes
Briggs (Katharine) Folklore Award 545

Folklore: Libraries
English Folk Dance and Song Society Library 583

Folklore: Picture Libraries
Fortean Picture Library 608
International Photobank 613
Laubier (André) Picture Library 614
Williams (Vaughan) Memorial Library 626

Folklore: Small Presses
Broadside 135
Hisarlik Press 139

Food & Drink: Publishers (UK)
Absolute Press 9
Associated Publicity Holdings Ltd 14
Consumers' Association 30
Headline Book Publishing 50
Lochar Publishing Ltd 59
Rosendale Press Ltd 81
Smith Gryphon Ltd 86

Food & Drink: Agents (UK)
Kelly (Frances) 169

Food & Drink: Magazines
BBC Good Food 222
Decanter 237
Expression 244
Good Food Retailing 249
Good Housekeeping 249
Homebrew Supplier 254
Homebrew Today 255
House & Garden 256
Infusion 257
Taste 288
Wine 297

Food & Drink: Publishers (US)
Chronicle Books 440
Random House, Inc. 450
Van Nostrand Reinhold 453

Food & Drink: Agents (US)
Casselman (Martha), Literary Agent 458
Shepard Agency, The 475

Food & Drink: Prizes
Glenfiddich Awards 552
Simon André Memorial Fund Book Awards 567

Food & Drink: Libraries
Ministry of Agriculture, Fisheries and Food 587

Food & Drink: Picture Libraries
Blake (Anthony) 602
Boys Syndication 602
Financial Times Picture Collection 607
Heseltine (John) Picture Library 610
Hurst (Jacqui) 611
Pictures Colour Library 618

Retrograph Archive Ltd 619
Stockphotos 622
Traeger (Tessa) 623

Food & Drink: Small Presses
Southover Press 145

Football: Publishers (UK)
Headline Book Publishing 50

Football: Magazines
First Down 246
Football Monthly 247
Gridiron 251
Match 262
Scottish Football Today 282
Shoot Magazine 283
World Soccer 299

Football: Film, TV and video producers
Cheerleader Productions 343
Scope Picture Productions Ltd 367

Football: Picture Libraries
Action Plus 598
Allsport (UK) Ltd 599
Associated Sports Photography 600
Colorsport 604
Empics Ltd 606
Professional Sport 618

France: Prizes
McLeod (Enid) Prize 558
Moncrieff (Scott) Prize 560

France: Libraries
French Institute Library 583

France: Picture Libraries
Baxter (Colin) Photography Ltd 601
Estall (Robert) Photographs 606
Noble (David) Photography 616
Strang (Jessica) Library 622
Woolverton Colour Library 626

Freelancing: Publishers (UK)
St John Thomas (David) Publisher 82

Freelancing: Magazines
Freelance Market News 247
Freelance, The 247
Freelance Writing & Photography 247
Quartos Magazine 277
Writers' Monthly 299

Writers News 300
Writers' Rostrum, The 300
Writing Magazine 300

Freelancing: Professional Associations
British Amateur Press Association 492
IVCA Writers Group 497
Montpelier Society, The 498
Penman Literary Club, The 500
Society of Civil Service Authors 502
The Society of Authors 502
Union of Welsh Writers, The 504
Women Writers Network (WWN) 505
Writers' Guild of Great Britain, The 505

Gaelic: Publishers (UK)
Acair Ltd 10
Gairm Publications 43
Gomer Press 45

Gaelic: Professional Associations
Gaelic Books Council (An Comann Leabhraichean) 496

Gaelic: Prizes
An Duais don bhFiliocht i nGaelige (Prize for Poetry in Irish) 542
Irish Times-Aer Lingus International Fiction Prize 555
Irish Times Aer Lingus Irish Literature Prizes 555
McVitie's Prize for Scottish Writer of the Year 559

Gaelic: Libraries
Scottish Poetry Library 591
Western Isles Libraries 593

Games: Publishers (UK)
Acair Ltd 10
Batsford (B.T.) Ltd 16
Crowood Press Ltd, The 32
Donald (John) Publishers Ltd 35
Gollancz (Victor) Ltd 45
Haynes Publishing Group 50
Macmillan Publishers Ltd 61
Random House Publishing Group Ltd 76
Robson Books Ltd 81

Games: Packagers
MM Productions Ltd 154

Games: Agents (UK)
Drexl (Anne) 165

Games: Magazines
Bridge Magazine 225
British Chess Magazine 226
Chess 231
Darts World 237
Snooker Scene 285

Games: Film, TV and video producers
Action Time 337
Celador Productions Ltd 342
CTR Productions 346
Solo Vision Ltd 369
Talbot Television Ltd 369

Games: Theatre producers
Hindin (Philip) 384

Games: Publishers (US)
Adams (Bob) Publishers, Inc. 436
Prima Publishing and Communications 450
Sterling Publishing 452

Games: Small Presses
Yoffroy Publications 147

Gardening & Horticulture: Publishers (UK)
Antique Collectors' Club 12
Batsford (B.T.) Ltd 16
Cassell 25
Collins & Brown 29
Consumers' Association 30
Crowood Press Ltd, The 32
David & Charles Publishers 33
Dorling Kindersley Ltd 35
Foulsham (W.) & Co. 42
HarperCollins Publishers Ltd 49
Haynes Publishing Group 50
Letts (Charles) & Co. Ltd 58
Lincoln (Frances) Ltd 58
Little, Brown & Co. (UK) Ltd 59
Lutterworth Press, The 60
Macmillan Publishers Ltd 61
New Holland (Publishers) Ltd 67
Orion Publishing Group 69
Pavilion Books Ltd 71
PBI Publications 71
Quiller Press 76
Random House Publishing Group Ltd 76
Reader's Digest Association Ltd 78
Reed International Books 78
Robson Books Ltd 81

Search Press Ltd/Burns & Oates Ltd 84
Silent Books 86
Souvenir Press Ltd 87

Gardening & Horticulture: Packagers
Alphabet & Image Ltd 148
Breslich & Foss 150
Cameron Books (Production) Ltd 150
Gardenhouse Editions Ltd 151
Quarto Publishing 155

Gardening & Horticulture: Agents (UK)
Anderson (Darley) Books 159
Clarke (Serafina) 162
Davidson (Caroline) and Robert Ducas Literary Agency 164
Pawsey (John) 173
Pearlstine (Maggie) 173

Gardening & Horticulture: Magazines
Amateur Gardening 218
BBC Gardeners' World Magazine 222
Flora 246
Garden Answers 248
Garden News 248
Homes and Gardens 255
Horticulture Week 255
House & Garden 256
Practical Gardening 276

Gardening & Horticulture: Publishers (US)
Atlantic Monthly Press 438
Chronicle Books 440
Lyons & Burford, Publishers 446

Gardening & Horticulture: Agents (US)
Nolan (Betsy) Literary Agency, The 471
Urstadt (Susan P.), Inc. 478

Gardening & Horticulture: Professional Associations
Guild of Agricultural Journalists 496

Gardening & Horticulture: Libraries
Ministry of Agriculture, Fisheries and Food 587

Gardening & Horticulture: Picture Libraries
Boys Syndication 602
Coleman (Bruce) Wildlife & Travel Photo Library 604
Collections 604
Craven (Philip) Worldwide Photo-Library 605
Foord (Ron & Christine) Colour Picture Library 608
Garden Picture Library, The 609
Harpur Garden Library 610
Holt Studios International Ltd 611
Houses & Interiors Photographic Features Agency 611
Impact Photos 612
Mathews (S & O) Photography 615
National Trust Photographic Library, The 616
Natural Science Photos 616
Palmer (Hugh) 617
Photos Horticultural 618
Strang (Jessica) Library 622
Swift Picture Library Ltd 623
Traeger (Tessa) 623
Whiting (Elizabeth) & Associates 625
Wright (George) 626

Gardening & Horticulture: Small Presses
New Arcadian Press 142

Gardening & Horticulture: European Publishers
B L V Verlagsgesellschaft mbH 419
Falken-Verlag GmbH 419
Mosaik Verlag 421
Parey (Verlag Paul) 421
Time-Life Books BV 427

Gay/Lesbian: Publishers (UK)
Gay Men's Press (GMP Publishers Ltd), The 44
Open Letters 68
Scarlett Press 83
Sheba Feminist Press 85

Gay/Lesbian: Magazines
Capital Gay 228
Gay Times 248
HIM 253
Pink Paper, The 274

Gay/Lesbian: Theatre producers
Gay Sweatshop 383

Gay/Lesbian: Publishers (U
Alyson Publications, Inc. 437

Gay/Lesbian: Professional Associations
Gay Authors Workshop 496

Gay/Lesbian: Small Presse
Third House (Publishers) 146

Genealogy: Publishers (UK
Barracuda Books Ltd/Quotes L 15
Countryside Books 31
Manchester University Press 6:

Genealogy: Magazines
Family Tree Magazine 244

Genealogy: Libraries
Guildhall Library 584
Newcastle upon Tyne Central Library 588
Northumberland County Libra 588

Genealogy: Picture Librari
Science Photo Library 620

Geography: Publishers (UK
Chapman (Paul) Publishing Ltc
Dalesman Publishing Co. Ltd 3
Darf Publishers Ltd 33
Freeman (W. H.) & Co. Ltd 42
Fulton (David) (Publishers) Ltc
Harcourt Brace Jovanovich Ltc
Liverpool University Press 59
MIT Press Ltd, The 65
Pergamon Press 73
Routledge, Chapman & Hall Lt 81
Ward Lock Educational 94

Geography: Publishers (US
Iowa State University Press 445
Rosen Publishing Group, Inc., 450

Geography: Libraries
Royal Geographical Society Library 590

Geography: Picture Librari
Dixon (C M) 605
Garland (Leslie) Picture Library 609
GeoScience Features 609
Natural Science Photos 616
RIDA Photo Library 620

Royal Geographical Society
Picture Library 620

**Geography: European
Publishers**
Abadia de Montserrat
(Publicaciones de l') 430
Bra Bocker (Bokforlaget) AB 433
Istituto Geografico de Agostini
SpA 423
Knorr und Hirth Verlag GmbH
420
Kummerly und Frey
(Geographischer Verlag) 434
Orell Füssli Verlag 435
Presses Universitaires de France
(PUF) 418
Teide (Editorial) SA 432

Geology: Publishers (UK)
Dalesman Publishing Co. Ltd 32
Freeman (W. H.) & Co. Ltd 42
Harcourt Brace Jovanovich Ltd 48
MIT Press Ltd, The 65
Pergamon Press 73
Scottish Academic Press 84

Geology: Publishers (US)
Iowa State University Press 445

Geology: Picture Libraries
Alba Pictures 598
Dixon (C M) 605
Garland (Leslie) Picture Library
609
GeoScience Features 609
RIDA Photo Library 620
Wilderness Photographic Library
625

Geology: Small Presses
Geological Society Publishing
House 138
Red Earth Publications 144

Germany: Agents (UK)
Ryder (Herta) 175

Germany: Picture Libraries
Weimar Archive 625
Woolverton Colour Library 626

Glaciers: Picture Libraries
Alba Pictures 598
Wilderness Photographic Library
625

**Global Warming: Picture
Libraries**
Angel (Heather)/Biofotos 599

Greenpeace Communications Ltd
610
Still Pictures Environmental
Agency 622

Government: Publishers (UK)
Elvendon Press 38
HMSO Books 52
Hobsons Publishing 52

**Government: Film, TV and
video producers**
Roymark Ltd 367

Government: Publishers (US)
ABC-Clio, Inc. 436
New England (University Press of)
448

Government: Libraries
Bank of England Reference
Library 577
Belfast Public Libraries: Central
Library 578
Greater London History Library
584
Guildhall Library 584
Public Record Office 590
Westminster Reference Library
593

Greece: Picture Libraries
Hanley (Tom) 610
Wood (Roger) Library 626
Woolverton Colour Library 626

Guidebooks: Publishers (UK)
AA Publishing 9
Allan (Ian) Ltd 11
Cicerone Press 28
Constable & Co. Ltd 30
Dalesman Publishing Co. Ltd 32
Donald (John) Publishers Ltd 35
Economist Books 36
HarperCollins Publishers Ltd 49
Haynes Publishing Group 50
Little, Brown & Co. (UK) Ltd 59
Macmillan Publishers Ltd 61
Moorland Publishing Co. Ltd 65
Penguin Books Ltd 71
Quiller Press 76
Reed International Books 78
Robson Books Ltd 81
Settle Press 85
Thornhill Press 91
Weavers Press Publishing 95

Guidebooks: Small Presses
Cheverell Press, The 135
Crescent Moon Publishing 136

Kittiwake Press 140
Meridian Books 141

**Guidebooks: European
Publishers**
Athesia (Verlagsanstalt) 422
Calderini (Edizioni) 422
DuMont Buchverlag GmbH & Co
KG 419
Elsevier Librico NV 411
Francisci (Aldo) Editore 423
Giunti Publishing Group 423
Høst & Søns Forlag A/S 413
Istituto per l'Enciclopedia del
Friuli Venezia Giulia 424
Lannoo (Uitgeverij) Drukkerij 412
Michelin et Cie (Services de
Tourisme) 417
Nathan (Fernand) 418

**Health & Beauty: Publishers
(UK)**
Macmillan Publishers Ltd 61
Random House Publishing Group
Ltd 76
Robson Books Ltd 81
Souvenir Press Ltd 87

Health & Beauty: Agents (UK)
Anderson (Darley) Books 159
Solo Syndication & Literary
Agency Ltd 177

Health & Beauty: Magazines
Looking Good 261
New Woman 270

Health & Beauty: Agents (US)
Heacock Literary Agency, Inc.
464
New Age World Services & Books
470
Siegel (Bobbe), Literary Agency
475

**Health & Beauty: Picture
Libraries**
Financial Times Picture Collection
607

**Health & Nutrition:
Publishers (UK)**
Argus Books 13
Cathie (Kyle) Ltd 26
Consumers' Association 30
Dorling Kindersley Ltd 35
Elite Words & Image 37
Elliot Right Way Books 37
Foulsham (W.) & Co. 42
Gaia Books Ltd 43

Gay Men's Press (GMP Publishers Ltd), The 44
Harcourt Brace Jovanovich Ltd 48
HarperCollins Publishers Ltd 49
Lincoln (Frances) Ltd 58
Little, Brown & Co. (UK) Ltd 59
Mainstream Publishing Co. (Edinburgh) Ltd 62
Mason (Kenneth) Publications Ltd 63
Open University Press 69
Penguin Books Ltd 71
Piatkus Books 73
Prism Press Book Publishers Ltd 75
Robinson Publishing 80
Rosendale Press Ltd 81
Routledge, Chapman & Hall Ltd 81
Women's Press, The 96

Health & Nutrition: Packagers
Aspect 149
Breslich & Foss 150

Health & Nutrition: Agents (UK)
Anderson (Darley) Books 159
Aspect 160
Chilcote (Judith) Agency 161
Chris (Teresa) Literary Agency 162
Fox & Howard Literary Agency 166
Judd (Jane) Literary Agency 169
Pearlstine (Maggie) 173

Health & Nutrition: Magazines
ADviser 217
Health & Fitness 252
Health Now 252
Here's Health 253
Home Economics & Technology 254
Infusion 257
Lifestyle Magazine 260
Slimming 284
Weight Watchers Magazine 295
What Diet & Lifestyle 295

Health & Nutrition: Film, TV and video producers
Medical & Scientific Productions 360
Paper Moon Productions 364
Skippon Video Associates 368

Health & Nutrition: Publishers (US)
Addison-Wesley Publishing Co., Inc. 436
Avery Publishing Group, Inc. 438
Avon Books 438
Berkley Publishing Group 439
Chronicle Books 440
Houghton Mifflin Co. 444
Llewellyn Publications 446
Plenum Publishing 449
Prima Publishing and Communications 450
Random House, Inc. 450
Rosen Publishing Group, Inc., The 450
Sterling Publishing 452
Temple University Press 452

Health & Nutrition: Agents (US)
Catalog Literary Agency, The 458
Chester (Linda) Literary Agency 458
Dijkstra (Sandra) Literary Agency 460
Ellenberg (Ethan), Literary Agency, The 461
ForthWrite Literary Agency 462
Heacock Literary Agency, Inc. 464
Kern (Natasha) Literary Agency, Inc. 464
Leone (Adele) Agency, Inc. 466
Literary/Business Associates 467
Literary & Creative Artists Agency 467
Marcil (Denise) Literary Agency, Inc. 469
Mews Books Ltd 469
Nolan (Betsy) Literary Agency, The 471
Peter (James) Associates, Inc. 472
Protter (Susan Ann) Literary Agent 472
Quicksilver Books, Literary Agents 473
Rees (Helen) Literary Agency 473
Schulman (Susan) Literary Agency 475
Singer (Evelyn) Literary Agency, Inc., The 476
Snell (Michael) Literary Agency 476
Steele (Lyle) & Co. Ltd 477
2M Communications Ltd 478
Ware (John A.) Literary Agency 479
Wreschner (Ruth), Authors' Representative 479

Writer's Consulting Group 480

Health & Nutrition: Libraries
Health Information Library (Westminster) 585

Health & Nutrition: Picture Libraries
Birdsall (John) Photographic Library 601
Format Partners Photo Library 608
Photofusion 617
Reflections PhotoLibrary 619

Health & Nutrition: Small Presses
Daniels Publishing 136
Tufnell Press, The 146

Health & Nutrition: European Publishers
Borgens Forlag A/S 412
Ennsthaler (Wilhelm), Verlag 41
Francisci (Aldo) Editore 423
Haase (P.) & Søns Forlag A/S 4
McGraw-Hill Interamericana de España SA 432
Mosaik Verlag 421
Orac Verlag Gesellschaft mbH 411
Sperling e Kupfer Editori SpA 42
Texto Editora 430
Toorts (Uitgeverij De) 427

Heritage: Publishers (UK)
Berkswell Publishing Co. Ltd 17
Routledge, Chapman & Hall Ltd 81
Thornhill Press 91

Heritage: Packagers
Berkswell Publishing Co. Ltd 14

Heritage: Magazines
English Heritage Magazine 242

Heritage: Picture Libraries
Adkins (Lesley & Roy) Picture Library 598
Belcher (Ivan J.) Colour Picture Library 601
English Heritage Photographic Library 606
Garland (Leslie) Picture Library 609
Guy (V. K.) Ltd 610
Skyscan Balloon Photography 6

Heritage: Editorial Services
Adkins (Lesley & Roy) 531

History: Publishers (UK)
Aberdeen University Press 9
Academy Books 10
Acair Ltd 10
Ashgate Publishing Co. Ltd 13
Athlone Press, The 14
Batsford (B.T.) Ltd 16
Berg Publishers Ltd 17
Blackstaff Press Ltd 18
British Academy, The 22
British Museum Press 22
Cassell 25
Cass (Frank) 25
Chapmans Publishers 27
Collins & Brown 29
Constable & Co. Ltd 30
Currey (James) Publishers 32
Curzon Press Ltd 32
Dalesman Publishing Co. Ltd 32
Darf Publishers Ltd 33
Davies (Christopher) Publishers
   Ltd 33
Deutsch (André) Ltd 34
Donald (John) Publishers Ltd 35
Edinburgh University Press 37
Elm Publications 37
Exeter (University of) Press 40
Golden Cockerel Press Ltd 44
Gollancz (Victor) Ltd 45
Grey Seal Books 47
Halban (Peter) Publishers 48
Hambledon Press, The 48
Harvard University Press 50
Hurst (C.) & Co. 53
Karnak House 55
Lawrence & Wishart Ltd 57
Leicester University Press 57
Little, Brown & Co. (UK) Ltd 59
Liverpool University Press 59
Macmillan Publishers Ltd 61
Mainstream Publishing Co.
   (Edinburgh) Ltd 62
Manchester University Press 62
Merlin Press Ltd 64
MIT Press Ltd, The 65
Orion Publishing Group 69
Penguin Books Ltd 71
Polity Press 75
Princeton University Press 75
Random House Publishing Group
   Ltd 76
Routledge, Chapman & Hall Ltd
   81
Scottish Academic Press 84
Seaby (B. A.) Ltd 84
Search Press Ltd/Burns & Oates
   Ltd 84

Shepheard-Walwyn (Publishers)
   Ltd 85
Smythe (Colin) Ltd 86
Souvenir Press Ltd 87
Sutton (Alan) Publishing Ltd 89
Swift Children's Books 89
Tauris (I.B.) & Co. Ltd 90
Thames and Hudson Ltd 90
Verso Ltd 93
Virago Press Ltd 93
Windrush Press, The 96

History: Packagers
Alphabet & Image Ltd 148
Bison Books Ltd 149
Lionheart Books 153
Quarto Publishing 155

History: Agents (UK)
Bolt (David) Associates 160
Bryan (Felicity) 160
Clarke (Serafina) 162
Davidson (Caroline) and Robert
   Ducas Literary Agency 164
Davis-Poynter (Reg) 164
Denniston & Lownie 164
Futerman (Vernon) Associates
   166
Higham (David) Associates Ltd
   168
Jarvie (Gordon), Literary Agent
   169
Kelly (Frances) 169
Martin (Judy) 171
O'Leary (David) Literary Agents
   173
Pearlstine (Maggie) 173
Robertson (Patricia) 175
Sayle (Tessa) Agency 176
Simmons (Jeffrey) 177

History: Magazines
Contemporary Review 233
History Today 253

History: Publishers (US)
ABC–Clio, Inc. 436
Academy Chicago Publishers 436
Addison-Wesley Publishing Co.,
   Inc. 436
Arkansas (University of) Press 438
Avon Books 438
Carol Publishing 440
Carroll & Graf Publishers, Inc. 440
Harcourt Brace Jovanovich 443
Houghton Mifflin Co. 444
Iowa State University Press 445
Kent State University Press 445
Krieger Publishing Co., Inc. 445
Little, Brown & Co., Inc. 445

Longman Publishing Group 446
Louisiana State University Press
   446
McFarland & Company, Inc.,
   Publishers 446
Missouri (University of) Press 447
New England (University Press of)
   448
Oklahoma (University of) Press
   448
Paragon House Publishers 449
Princeton University Press 450
Random House, Inc. 450
St Martin's Press, Inc. 451
Schocken Books, Inc. 451
Simon & Schuster 451
Temple University Press 452
Tennessee (University of) Press
   452
Times Books 453
Walker & Co 453

History: Agents (US)
Acton & Dystel 455
Author Aid Associates 456
Chester (Linda) Literary Agency
   458
Ellenberg (Ethan), Literary
   Agency, The 461
ForthWrite Literary Agency 462
Garon-Brooke (Jay) Associates,
   Inc. 463
Kohner (Paul), Inc. 465
Lincoln (Ray) Literary Agency 467
Literary & Creative Artists Agency
   467
Mann (Carol) Agency 468
Multimedia Product Development,
   Inc. 470
New England Publishing
   Associates, Inc. 470
Noetzli (Regula) Literary Agency
   471
Peter (James) Associates, Inc. 472
Protter (Susan Ann) Literary
   Agent 472
Rees (Helen) Literary Agency 473
Schwartz (Laurens R.) 475
Sebastian Agency 475
Spieler Literary Agency 477
Steele (Lyle) & Co. Ltd 477
Stern (Gloria) Agency (New York)
   477
Ware (John A.) Literary Agency
   479
Writers House, Inc. 480

**History:
   Bursaries/Fellowships**
Prometheus Award 539

History: Prizes
Alexander Prize 542
Berry (David) Prize 544
Cooper (Duff) Prize, The 548
GPA Book Award 553
Irish Times-Aer Lingus
  International Fiction Prize 555
Mackenzie (Agnes Mure) Award
  558
Reese (Trevor) Memorial Prize
  564
Routledge Ancient History Prize
  565
Whitfield Prize 572
Wolfson History Awards 572

History: Libraries
Guildhall Library 584
Newcastle Literary and
  Philosophical Society Library
  588
Penzance Library 589
Williams's (Dr) Library 594

History: Picture Libraries
Barnaby's Picture Library 601
Evans (Mary) Picture Library 606
Fotomas Index, The 608
Hulton Picture Company, The 611
London (Museum of) Picture
  Library 614
Popperfoto 618
Royal Photographic Society, The
  620

History: Small Presses
AK Press/AKA Books 133
Bozo 134
Korvet Publishing and Distribution
  140
Partizan Press 143
QueenSpark Books 144
Wakefield Historical Publications
  147

History: European Publishers
Abadia de Montserrat
  (Publicaciones de l') 430
Alhambra (Editorial) SA 430
Alianza Editorial SA 430
Ambo (Uitgeverij) BV 425
Armado (Armenio), Editore de
  Simoes, Belrao & Cia Lda 429
Artemis Verlags AG 434
Arthaud (Editions) SA 415
Athesia (Verlagsanstalt) 422
Aubier-Montaigne (Editions) SA
  415
Balkema (A A) 426
Beck (Verlag C H) 418

Belfond (Editions Pierre) 415
Benteli Verlag 434
Bölau Verlag Gesellschaft mbH &
  Co KG 410
Bra Bocker (Bokforlaget) AB 433
Brockhaus (F A) 419
Calmann-Lévy (Editions) SA 415
Cappelli (Nuova Casa Editrice
  Licinio) SpA 422
Casterman (Editions) 411
Découverte, La 416
Denoël (Editions) Sàrl 416
Destino SL 430
Det Norske Samlaget 428
Dom Quixote (Publicacoes) Lda
  429
Don Quijote (Editorial) 430
Droz (Librairie) SA 434
D T V Deutscher Taschenbuch
  Verlag GmbH & Co KG 419
Econ-Verlag GmbH 419
Elsevier 426
Elsevier Librico NV 411
Ennsthaler (Wilhelm), Verlag 410
Eumo Editorial 431
Europa-America (Publicaoes) Lda
  429
Fabbri (Gruppo Editoriale SpA)
  423
Fayard (Librarie Arthème) 416
Fischer (S) Verlag GmbH 419
Flammarion et Cie 416
Forum (Forlaget) A/S 412
Francisci (Aldo) Editore 423
Gallimard (Editions) 416
Garzanti Editore 423
Giunti Publishing Group 423
Gradiva – Publicacoes Lda 429
Grijalbo SA 431
Gruyter (Walter de) & Co 419
Guida Editori SpA 423
Gyldendalske Boghandel, Nordisk
  Forlag A/S 413
Hachette 416
Hallwag Verlag AG 434
Hatier (Editions) SA 417
Herder (Verlag) GmbH & Co KG
  420
Heyne (Wilhelm) Verlag 420
Hiperión (Ediciones) SL 431
Hoffmann und Campe Verlag 420
Horay (Pierre) Editeur 417
Incafo (Editorial) SA 431
Istituto Geografico de Agostini
  SpA 423
Istituto per l'Enciclopedia del
  Friuli Venezia Giulia 424
Jaca Book (Editoriale) 424
Klett-Cotta Verlag 420
Klincksieck (Editions) 417

Kohlhammer (Verlag W) GmbH
  420
Kok (Uitgeversmaatschappij J H
  BV 426
Laffont (Editions Robert) 417
Landesverlag Buchverlag 410
Landi (Luciano) Editore SRL 42
Lannoo (Uitgeverij) Drukkerij 4
Laterza (Giuseppe) e Figli SpA
  424
Lavoro Editoriale, Il 424
Lello e Irmão 429
Liguori Editore SRL 424
Longanesi & C 424
Lübbe (Gustav) Verlag GmbH 4
Manesse Verlag GmbH 434
Mercure de France SA 417
Mondadori (Arnoldo) Editore S
  424
Mondadori Espana SA 432
Mulino (Societe Editrice Il) 425
Nathan (Fernand) 418
Natur och Kultur (Bokförlaget)
  433
Neptun-Verlag 434
Niederösterreichisches
  Pressehaus, Verlag 411
Nyt Nordisk Forlag Arnold Busc
  A/S 414
Oglio (Dall') Editore SRL 425
Oldenbourg (R) Verlag GmbH
  421
Orell Füssli Verlag 435
Österreichischer Bundesverlag
  Gesellschaft mbH 411
Paludans (Jörgen) Forlag ApS 4
Paoline (Edizioni) SRL 425
Payot Lausanne (Editions) 435
Politikens Forlag A/S 414
Presses de la Cité, Les 418
Presses Universitaires de France
  (PUF) 418
Rabēn och Sjögren Bokforlag A
  433
RCS Rizzoli Libri SpA 425
S A I E Editrice SRL 425
Samlerens Forlag A/S 414
Sauerlander AG 435
Scherz Verlag AG 435
Schönbergske (Det) Forlag A/S
  414
S E I (Società Editrice
  Internationale) 425
Seuil (Editions du) 418
Spectrum (Uitgeverij Het) BV 4
Styria (Verlag) 411
Table Ronde (Les Editions de la
  418
Teide (Editorial) SA 432
Tiden (Bokförlags) AB 433

Time-Life Books BV 427
Tusquets Editores 432
Ugo (Gruppo) Mursia Editore SpA 425
Ullstein (Buchverlage) GmbH 421
Uniepers BV 427
V C H Verlagsgesellschaft mbH 422
Verbo (Editorial) SA 430
V U Boekhandel/Uitgeverij BV 427
Zsolnay (Paul), Verlag GmbH 411

Home Interests: Publishers (UK)
Cassell 25
Merehurst Ltd 64

Home Interests: Packagers
Book Packaging and Marketing 150

Home Interests: Agents (UK)
Pearlstine (Maggie) 173

Home Interests: Magazines
Brides and Setting Up Home 225
Country Homes and Interiors 234
Family Circle 244
Good Housekeeping 249
Halifax Building Society Magazine 252
Home Economics & Technology 254
Homes and Gardens 255
House Beautiful 255
House Buyer 256
House & Garden 256
Ideal Home 256
Practical Householder 276
Traditional Homes 292
Woman and Home 297

Home Interests: Publishers (US)
Iowa State University Press 445
TAB Books 452

Home Interests: Agents (US)
ForthWrite Literary Agency 462

Home Interests: Picture Libraries
Houses & Interiors Photographic Features Agency 611
Whiting (Elizabeth) & Associates 625

Horses: Publishers (UK)
Allen (J.A.) & Co. Ltd 11

Batsford (B.T.) Ltd 16
Crowood Press Ltd, The 32
Elliot Right Way Books 37
Kenilworth Press Ltd 55

Horses: Magazines
Horse and Hound 255
Horse and Rider 255
Horse & Pony Magazine 255
Pony 275
Riding 279
Sporting Life, The 286
Sporting Life Weekender 286
Your Horse 301

Horses: Film, TV and video producers
Bird (Martin) Productions 340
Normandy Film Productions 363

Horses: Picture Libraries
Animal Photography 599
Eyeline Photography 607
Jones (Trevor) Thoroughbred Photography 613
Only Horses Picture Agency 616

Housing: Picture Libraries
Adkins (Lesley & Roy) Picture Library 598
Financial Times Picture Collection 607
Greater London Photograph Library 609
Hoffman (David) Photo Library 611
Photofusion 617

How To: Publishers (UK)
Consumers' Association 30
Elliot Right Way Books 37
How To Books Ltd 53

How To: Agents (UK)
Drexl (Anne) 165

How To: Publishers (US)
ABC-Clio, Inc. 436
Addison-Wesley Publishing Co., Inc. 436
Avon Books 438
Berkley Publishing Group 439
Carol Publishing 440
Little, Brown & Co., Inc. 445
Llewellyn Publications 446
Sterling Publishing 452
Walker & Co 453
Warner Books 453

How To: Agents (US)
Browne (Pema) Ltd 457
Catalog Literary Agency, The 458
Connor Literary Agency 459
Feiler (Florence) Literary Agency 462
Fishbein (Frieda) Ltd 462
Fuhrman (Candice) Literary Agency 462
Kern (Natasha) Literary Agency, Inc. 464
Literary/Business Associates 467
Marcil (Denise) Literary Agency, Inc. 469
Multimedia Product Development, Inc. 470
New Age World Services & Books 470
Schwartz (Laurens R.) 475
Shore (Lee) Agency 475
Siegel (Bobbe), Literary Agency 475
Singer (Evelyn) Literary Agency, Inc., The 476
Snell (Michael) Literary Agency 476
Wreschner (Ruth), Authors' Representative 479

How To: Small Presses
Cheverell Press, The 135
Dragonfly Press 136

How To: European Publishers
Born NV Uitgeversmaatschappij 426
Calmann-Lévy (Editions) SA 415
Droemersche Verlagsanstalt Th Knaur Nachf 419
Falken-Verlag GmbH 419
Flammarion et Cie 416
Forum (Bokförlaget) AB 433
Gauthier-Languereau (Les Editions) SA 416
Gründ (Librairie) 416
Gyldendalske Boghandel, Nordisk Forlag A/S 413
Hachette 416
Hallwag Verlag AG 434
Heyne (Wilhelm) Verlag 420
Horay (Pierre) Editeur 417
Kok (Uitgeversmaatschappij J H) BV 426
Lattes (Editions Jean-Claude) 417
Longanesi & C 424
Lübbe (Gustav) Verlag GmbH 420
Mondadori (Arnoldo) Editore SpA 424
Nyt Nordisk Forlag Arnold Busck A/S 414

Orell Füssli Verlag 435
Paoline (Edizioni) SRL 425
Politikens Forlag A/S 414
Presses de la Cité, Les 418
Rabén och Sjögren Bokforlag AB 433
Seuil (Editions du) 418
Sperling e Kupfer Editori SpA 425
Standaard Uitgeverij 412
Time-Life Books BV 427

Humanities: Publishers (UK)
Ashgate Publishing Co. Ltd 13
Berg Publishers Ltd 17
Blackwell Publishers 18
British Academy, The 22
Cambridge University Press 24
Clio Press Ltd 29
Fourth Estate Ltd 42
Hodder & Stoughton Ltd 52
Liverpool University Press 59
Manchester University Press 62
Oxford University Press 70
Oxford University Press 70
Pergamon Press 73
Routledge, Chapman & Hall Ltd 81
Wales (University of) Press 94
Yale University Press (London) 97

Humanities: Magazines
New Humanist 269

Humanities: Publishers (US)
Illinois (University of) Press 444
Missouri (University of) Press 447
Stanford University Press 452

Humanities: Bursaries/Fellowships
British Academy Small Personal Research Grants 536

Humanities: Libraries
Birmingham and Midland Institute 578
British Library Reading Room 580
Commonwealth Secretariat Library 582
Fawcett Library 583
Hatfield Polytechnic Library 584
London Library, The 587
National Library of Wales 588
Newcastle upon Tyne Central Library 588

Humanities: European Publishers
Bölau Verlag Gesellschaft mbH & Co KG 410

Brill (A J) 426
Gedisa (Editorial) SA 431
Gradiva – Publicacoes Lda 429
Hatier (Editions) SA 417
Kluwer Academic Publishers BV 426
Kohlhammer (Verlag W) GmbH 420
Lavoro Editoriale, Il 424
70 (Edições) Lda 430
Toorts (Uitgeverij De) 427

Human Rights: Publishers (UK)
Volcano Press 94

Humour: Publishers (UK)
Bridge Studios 22
Dalesman Publishing Co. Ltd 32
Exley Publications Ltd 40
Farming Press Books 41
Fourth Estate Ltd 42
Grub Street 47
Little, Brown & Co. (UK) Ltd 59
Macmillan Publishers Ltd 61
Piccadilly Press 74
Quiller Press 76
Random House Publishing Group Ltd 76
R & B Publishing 77
Reed International Books 78
Robson Books Ltd 81
Souvenir Press Ltd 87
Stone Flower Ltd 88
Summersdale Publishers 89
Thames Publishing/Autolycus Press 90
Virgin Publishing 93

Humour: Packagers
Lennard Books 153

Humour: Agents (UK)
Anderson (Darley) Books 159
Clarson-Leach (Robert) 162
Clowes (Jonathan) Ltd 162
Doyle (Colleen) 165
Foster (Jill) Ltd 165
Fox & Howard Literary Agency 166
Judd (Jane) Literary Agency 169
Martin (Judy) 171
Milne (Richard) Ltd 172
Sales (Ian) Associates 176
Sheil Land Associates Ltd* 176
Ware (Cecily) Literary Agents 179

Humour: Magazines
Club International 232

Humour: Film, TV and video producers
Barclay (Humphrey) Productions/First Choice 339
Black Tulip 340
Cadenza 342
Channel X 343
Dibgate Productions Ltd 347
Elstree (Production) Co. Ltd 348
GCP 352
Gilpin (Adrian) Television 352
Knaves Acre Productions 358
Lawson Productions Ltd 358
MCEG Virgin Vision 360
Mother Films 362
Peake Productions 364
Quad Production Co. 366
Riverfront Pictures Ltd 367
Talkback Productions 370
Tiger Television Ltd 370
Ty Gwyn Films Ltd 371

Humour: Theatre producers
Bristol Old Vic Company 379
Hazemead Ltd 384
Hiss & Boo Company, The 384
Jones (Pola) Associates Ltd 385
Marcellus Productions Ltd 388
Murray (Norman) & Anne Chudleigh Ltd 389
Quill Theatre Productions 392
Theatre of Comedy Company 395
Theatre Royal Windsor 397

Humour: Publishers (US)
Adams (Bob) Publishers, Inc. 437
Carol Publishing 440
Random House, Inc. 450
Simon & Schuster 451
Warner Books 453

Humour: Agents (US)
Amsterdam (Marcia) Agency 455
Browne (Pema) Ltd 457
Gusay (Charlotte) Literary Agency, The 463
Lee Allan Agency, The 466
Lee (L. Harry) Literary Agency 466
Literary/Business Associates 467

Humour: Professional Associations
Association of Comics Enthusiasts 490
Comedy Writers' Association of Great Britain 494

Humour: Prizes
Radio Times Drama & Comedy
Awards 564

Humour: Picture Libraries
Rex Features Ltd 620

Humour: Small Presses
Bozo 134
QueenSpark Books 144

Humour: Festivals
Bath Fringe Festival 403
Brighton Festival 404
Glasgow Mayfest 406
Greenwich Festival 406

Humour: European Publishers
Apostrof (Forlaget) ApS 412
Balland (André) 415
Calmann-Lévy (Editions) SA 415
Dom Quixote (Publicacoes) Lda
429
Haase (P.) & Søns Forlag A/S 413
Lalli (Antonio) Editore 424
Navers (Rasmus) Forlag A/S 414
Nebelspalter Verlag 434
Strandbergs Forlag ApS 415

**Illustrated & Fine Editions:
Publishers (UK)**
Blackstaff Press Ltd 18
Mainstream Publishing Co.
(Edinburgh) Ltd 62
Random House Publishing Group
Ltd 76
Souvenir Press Ltd 87
Thames and Hudson Ltd 90

**Illustrated & Fine Editions:
Small Presses**
Alembic Press, The 133
Bracken Press 135
New Arcadian Press 142
Previous Parrot Press 143
Redlake Press, The 144

**Illustrated & Fine Editions:
European Publishers**
Andersens (Carit) Forlag A/S 412
Denoël (Editions) Sàrl 416

**Indexing: Professional
Associations**
Society of Indexers 503

Indexing: Prizes
Carey Award 546
Library Association Wheatley
Medal, The 557

Indexing: Editorial Services
Jarvie (Gordon) Editorial 532

India: Publishers (UK)
Sangam Books Ltd 82

India: Agents (UK)
Eady (Toby) Associates Ltd 165

India: Libraries
British Library Oriental and India
Office Collections 580

India: Picture Libraries
Dickins (Douglas) Photo Library
605
Hanley (Tom) 610
Hurst (Jacqui) 611
Photo Flora 617
Royal Photographic Society, The
620
Sanders (Peter) Photography 620
V&A Picture Library 624
Williams (S & I) Power Pix
International Picture Library
626
Wright (George) 626

**Industrial Relations:
Publishers (UK)**
Bookmarks Publications 20
Kogan Page Ltd 56

**Industrial Relations:
Publishers (US)**
Van Nostrand Reinhold 453

Industrial Relations: Libraries
Trades Union Congress Library
593

Industry: Publishers (UK)
Boyars (Marion) Publishers Ltd 20
Donald (John) Publishers Ltd 35
Harcourt Brace Jovanovich Ltd 48
Longman Group Ltd 60
Macmillan Publishers Ltd 61
MIT Press Ltd, The 65
Pergamon Press 73
Quiller Press 76

Industry: Magazines
Chacom 230

**Industry: Film, TV and video
producers**
BFV Ltd 340
Chapel Broadcast Productions Ltd
343
Five Lamps Group 350

FM Television Ltd 351
Gamble (Ken) Productions 351
Harnett Milan Ltd 354
Kay Communications Ltd 358

**Industry: Professional
Associations**
British Association of Industrial
Editors 493

**Industry:
Bursaries/Fellowships**
Thomas (David) Prize 540

Industry: Prizes
Wadsworth Prize for Business
History 571

Industry: Libraries
BBC Data Enquiry Service 578

Industry: Picture Libraries
Ace Photo Agency 598
Aird (Malcolm) Associates 598
Art Directors Photo Library 600
Art Resource Illustration Library
600
Aspect Picture Library Ltd 600
Barnaby's Picture Library 601
Cash (J. Allan) Ltd 603
Comstock Photofile Ltd 604
Evans (Greg) International Photo
Library 606
Financial Times Picture Collection
607
Forsythe (Robert) Picture Library
608
Garland (Leslie) Picture Library
609
Hutchison Library, The 611
Illustrated London News Picture
Library 612
Impact Photos 612
Laubier (André) Picture Library
614
Network Photographers 616
Northern Picture Library, The 616
Photographers' Library, The 618
Photo Library International Ltd
617
PictureBank Photo Library Ltd
618
Pictures Colour Library 618
Science Photo Library 620
Sefton Photo Library 621
Spectrum Colour Library 621
Stockphotos 622
Stone (Tony) Worldwide 622
Telegraph Colour Library, The 623

Viewfinder Colour Photo Library 624

Walmsley (John) Picture Library 625

Wiedel (Janine) 625

Interior Design: Publishers (UK)
Cassell 25
Lincoln (Frances) Ltd 58

Interior Design: Packagers
Gardenhouse Editions Ltd 151

Interior Design: Agents (UK)
Martinez (M. C.) Literary Agency 171

Interior Design: Magazines
Country Homes and Interiors 234
Design 238
RIBA Journal, The 279
Traditional Homes 292
What's New in Interiors 296
World of Interiors, The 299

Interior Design: Publishers (US)
Van Nostrand Reinhold 453

Interior Design: Libraries
Art & Design Library (Westminster) 577
British Architectural Library 579

Interior Design: Picture Libraries
Arcaid 599
Boys Syndication 602
Country Life Library 605
Houses & Interiors Photographic Features Agency 611
National Trust Photographic Library, The 616
Pictures Colour Library 618
Strang (Jessica) Library 622
Whiting (Elizabeth) & Associates 625
Woodmansterne Ltd 626

Ireland/Irish Interest: Publishers (UK)
Appletree Press Ltd 12
Blackstaff Press Ltd 18
Smythe (Colin) Ltd 86
Swift Children's Books 89

Ireland/Irish Interest: Agents (UK)
Comstock-Smith Literary Agency 163
Jarvie (Gordon), Literary Agent 169
O'Leary (David) Literary Agents 173

Ireland/Irish Interest: Magazines
Irish Post 257

Ireland/Irish Interest: Theatre producers
Field Day Theatre Company 382
Tricycle Theatre 398
Tron Theatre Company 398

Ireland/Irish Interest: Professional Associations
Book House Ireland 492

Ireland/Irish Interest: Bursaries/Fellowships
Aosdàna Scheme 535
Bursaries in Literature 536
Macaulay Fellowship 538

Ireland/Irish Interest: Prizes
An Duais don bhFiliocht i nGaelige (Prize for Poetry in Irish) 542
Devlin (Denis) Award 550
GPA Book Award 553
Irish Times-Aer Lingus International Fiction Prize 555
Rooney Prize for Irish Literature 565
Toonder (Marten) Award 570

Ireland/Irish Interest: Libraries
Belfast Public Libraries: Central Library 578
Linen Hall Library 586

Ireland/Irish Interest: Picture Libraries
Brown (Hamish) Scottish Photographic 602

Islam: Publishers (UK)
Edinburgh University Press 37
Grey Seal Books 47
Volcano Press 94

Islam: Picture Libraries
Camerapix Picture Library 603
Sanders (Peter) Photography 620

V&A Picture Library 624

Islam: Small Presses
Quilliam Press Ltd 144

Italy: Prizes
Florio (John) Prize 551

Italy: Libraries
Italian Institute Library 585

Italy: Picture Libraries
Venice Picture Library, The 624

Japan: Publishers (UK)
Athlone Press, The 14
Routledge, Chapman & Hall Ltd 81

Japan: Agents (US)
Stuhlmann (Gunther) Author's Representative 477
Writers' Productions 480

Japan: Picture Libraries
Dickins (Douglas) Photo Library 605
Hanley (Tom) 610
Strang (Jessica) Library 622
Williams (S & I) Power Pix International Picture Library 626

Jewish Interest: Publishers (UK)
Cass (Frank) 25
Golden Cockerel Press Ltd 44

Jewish Interest: Magazines
Jewish Chronicle 258
Jewish Quarterly 258

Jewish Interest: Publishers (US)
Schocken Books, Inc. 451

Jewish Interest: Agents (US)
Authors Resource Center & Tarc Literary Agency, The 456

Jewish Interest: Prizes
Sunlight (Edith & Joseph) Award 569
Wingate (H. H.) Prize 572

Jewish Interest: Libraries
Wiener Library, The 594

Jewish Interest: European Publishers
Suhrkamp Verlag 421

Journalism: Agents (UK)
Coles (Dianne) Agency 162
Crew (Rupert) Ltd 163
Davidson (Caroline) and Robert Ducas Literary Agency 164
Greene (Elaine) Ltd 167
Judd (Jane) Literary Agency 169
Martin (Judy) 171
Reynolds (Jim) Associates 175
Write Stuff, The 180

Journalism: Magazines
British Journalism Review 226
Journalist, The 258

Journalism: Publishers (US)
Iowa State University Press 445

Journalism: Agents (US)
Boates (Reid) Literary Agency 457
Marks (Betty) 469
Sebastian Agency 475
Ware (John A.) Literary Agency 479

Journalism: Professional Associations
Association of British Editors 489
Campaign for Press and Broadcasting Freedom 494
Chartered Institute of Journalists 494
Foreign Press Association in London 496
National Union of Journalists 498
Newspaper Society, The 499
Scottish Newspaper Publishers' Association 502
Society of Women Writers and Journalists 503

Journalism: Bursaries/Fellowships
Economist/Richard Casement Internship, The 536
Guardian Research Fellowship, The 537
Independent Student Journalist Bursary, The 537
Newspaper Press Fund 539
Rhondda (Margaret) Award, The 539
Stern (Lawrence) Fellowship 540

Journalism: Prizes
BP Arts Journalism Awards 545
Cameron (James) Award 546
Lyons (Sir William) Award 557
OWG/COLA Awards for Excellence 562
Pakenham (Catherine) Award 563
Pulitzer Prizes 563
Regional Press Awards 564
RTZ David Watt Memorial Prize, The 565
Vogue Talent Contest 571

Journalism: Libraries
British Library Newspaper Library 580
Press Association Library 590

Journalism: Festivals
Write Around – A Celebration of Cleveland Writing 409

Journals: Publishers (UK)
Blackwell Publishers 18
Blackwell Scientific Publications Ltd 19
Cambridge University Press 24
Churchill Livingstone 28
Clark (T. & T.) 29
Elsevier Science Publishers Ltd 38
Emap Business Publishing Ltd 38
Glasgow (Mary) Publications Ltd 44
Gordon & Breach Science Publishers 45
Graham & Trotman Ltd 45
Jai Press Ltd 54
Kluwer Academic Publishers 56
Kogan Page Ltd 56
Macmillan Publishers Ltd 61
Manchester University Press 62
Oxford University Press 70
Paternoster Press Ltd 70
Pergamon Press 73
Reed International Books 78
Routledge, Chapman & Hall Ltd 81
Scholastic Publications Ltd 83
Scottish Academic Press 84
Sweet & Maxwell Ltd 89
Wiley (John) & Sons Ltd 96

Journals: Publishers (US)
New England (University Press of) 448

Journals: Professional Associations
Periodical Publishers Association (PPA) 500

Journals: European Publishers
Almqvist och Wiksell International 432
Athesia (Verlagsanstalt) 422
Bauverlag GmbH 418
Belin (Editions) 415
Bohmann Druck und Verlag GmbH & Co 410
Bonniers (Albert) Forlag AB 433
Braun (Verlag G) GmbH 419
Det Norske Samlaget 428
Elsevier 426
E U N S A (Ediciones Universidad de Navarra SA) 431
Francisci (Aldo) Editore 423
Fremad (Forlaget) A/S 413
Kluwer Group 426
Lavoro Editoriale, Il 424
Liguori Editore SRL 424
Manteau (Uitgeversmaatschappij A) NV 412
Mulino (Societe Editrice Il) 425
Munksgaard International Publishers Ltd 414
Nebelspalter Verlag 434
Oldenbourg (R) Verlag GmbH 421
Parey (Verlag Paul) 421
Sikkel (Uitgeverij De) NV 412
Springer-Verlag GmbH & Co KG 421
Thieme (Georg) Verlag 421
Universitetsforlaget 428
V C H Verlagsgesellschaft mbH 422
Vogel-Verlag KG 422
Westermann (Georg) Verlag GmbH 422

Languages: Publishers (UK)
Aberdeen University Press 9
Abson Books 9
Accent Educational Publishers Ltd 10
Brealey (Nicholas) Publishing Ltd 21
Chambers (W & R) 27
Curzon Press Ltd 32
Darf Publishers Ltd 33
Donald (John) Publishers Ltd 35
Exeter (University of) Press 40
Glasgow (Mary) Publications Ltd 44
Grevatt & Grevatt 46
Harcourt Brace Jovanovich Ltd 48
Karnak House 55
Lund Humphries Publishers Ltd 60
Macmillan Publishers Ltd 61

Manchester University Press 62
MIT Press Ltd, The 65
Pergamon Press 73
Wales (University of) Press 94

Languages: Packagers
Chancerel Publishers Ltd 151
Holtkamp and Whitlam Ltd 152
Lexus Ltd 153

Languages: Magazines
Verbatim, The Language Quarterly
293

Languages: Publishers (US)
Hippocrene Books, Inc. 444
Iowa State University Press 445
Longman Publishing Group 446
Princeton University Press 450
Times Books 453

**Languages: Professional
Associations**
English Association, The 495
Yorkshire Dialect Society 506

Languages: Libraries
Leeds Library 586
Liverpool City Libraries 586

Languages: Small Presses
Glosa 138

**Languages: European
Publishers**
Alhambra (Editorial) SA 430
Armado (Armenio), Editore de
   Simoes, Belrao & Cia Lda 429
Aubier-Montaigne (Editions) SA
   415
CEDAM (Casa Editrice Dr A
   Milani) 423
Didactica Editora 429
Elsevier 426
Hachette 416
Høst & Søns Forlag A/S 413
Keesing Uitgeversmaatschappij
   BV 426
Langenscheidt KG 420
Larousse (Suisse) SA 434
Porto Editora Lda 429
Teide (Editorial) SA 432
VEB Verlag Enzyklopädie Leipzig
   422
Vogel-Verlag KG 422
V U Boekhandel/Uitgeverij BV
   427

Large Print: Publishers (UK)
Clio Press Ltd 29

Law: Publishers (UK)
Boyars (Marion) Publishers Ltd 20
Brealey (Nicholas) Publishing Ltd
   21
Business Education Publishers Ltd
   23
Clark (T. & T.) 29
Consumers' Association 30
Dartmouth Publishing Co. Ltd 33
Edinburgh University Press 37
Graham & Trotman Ltd 45
Grotius Publications 47
Leicester University Press 57
Longman Group Ltd 60
Manchester University Press 62
MIT Press Ltd, The 65
NCVO Publications 66
Prism Press Book Publishers Ltd
   75
Reed International Books 78
Stone Flower Ltd 88
Sweet & Maxwell Ltd 89
Tolley Publishing Co. Ltd 91

Law: Agents (UK)
Simmons (Jeffrey) 177

Law: Magazines
Solicitors Journal 285

Law: Publishers (US)
Iowa State University Press 445
Temple University Press 452

Law: Bursaries/Fellowships
Neave (Airey) Trust, The 538

Law: Prizes
New Law Journal Rumpole Award
   561

Law: Libraries
Holborn Library 585

Law: Picture Libraries
Hoffman (David) Photo Library
   611
Monitor Syndication 615

Law: European Publishers
Armado (Armenio), Editore de
   Simoes, Belrao & Cia Lda 429
Athesia (Verlagsanstalt) 422
Beck (Verlag C H) 418
Bosch Casa Editorial SA 430
Bulzoni Editore SRL (Le Edizioni
   Universitarie d'Italia) 422
CEDAM (Casa Editrice Dr A
   Milani) 423
Davidsfonds VZW 411

Elsevier 426
E U N S A (Ediciones Universidad
   de Navarra SA) 431
FSRs Forlag 413
G.E.C. Gad Publishers 413
Gruyter (Walter de) & Co 419
Haufe (Rudolf) Verlag GmbH &
   Co KG 420
Kluwer Group 426
Kohlhammer (Verlag W) GmbH
   420
Liber AB 433
Masson Editeur 417
Mulino (Societe Editrice Il) 425
Orac Verlag Gesellschaft mbH
   411
Payot Lausanne (Editions) 435
Porto Editora Lda 429
Springer-Verlag 411
Springer-Verlag GmbH & Co KG
   421
V C H Verlagsgesellschaft mbH
   422
V U Boekhandel/Uitgeverij BV
   427
Vuibert (Librairie) SA 418

**Leisure & Hobbies: Publishers
(UK)**
AA Publishing 9
Allan (Ian) Ltd 11
Argus Books 13
Batsford (B.T.) Ltd 16
Carlton Books Ltd 25
Cassell 25
Consumers' Association 30
Crowood Press Ltd, The 32
Dalesman Publishing Co. Ltd 32
David & Charles Publishers 33
Foulsham (W.) & Co. 42
Fountain Press Ltd 42
Gay Men's Press (GMP Publishers
   Ltd), The 44
Haynes Publishing Group 50
Herbert Press, The 51
Jarrold Publishing 54
Letts (Charles) & Co. Ltd 58
Little, Brown & Co. (UK) Ltd 59
Lochar Publishing Ltd 59
Macmillan Publishers Ltd 61
Merehurst Ltd 64
Northcote House Publishers Ltd
   67
Quiller Press 76
Random House Publishing Group
   Ltd 76
Reed International Books 78
Souvenir Press Ltd 87
Springfield Books Ltd 88
Transworld Publishers Ltd 91

Weavers Press Publishing 95

Leisure & Hobbies: Packagers
Clark (Philip) Ltd 151
Eddison Sadd Editions 151
Ink Inc. Ltd 152
Marshall Cavendish Books Ltd 153
Marshall Editions Ltd 153
MM Productions Ltd 154
Morgan Samuel Editions 154
Parke Sutton Publishing Ltd 154
Quarto Publishing 155
Savitri Books Ltd 155
Toucan Books Ltd 156

Leisure & Hobbies: Agents (UK)
Bromley (Rosemary) Literary Agency 160
Coles (Dianne) Agency 162
Drexl (Anne) 165
Pearlstine (Maggie) 173

Leisure & Hobbies: Magazines
Aquarist & Pondkeeper 220
Bicycle 223
In Britain 257
Sailplane and Gliding 280

Leisure & Hobbies: Television
GMTV 309

Leisure & Hobbies: Publishers (US)
Chronicle Books 440
Iowa State University Press 445
Random House, Inc. 450
Sterling Publishing 452
Walker & Co 453

Leisure & Hobbies: Agents (US)
Authors Resource Center & Tarc Literary Agency, The 456
Literary & Creative Artists Agency 467

Leisure & Hobbies: Picture Libraries
Action Plus 598
Financial Times Picture Collection 607
Garland (Leslie) Picture Library 609
Hutchison Library, The 611
Network Photographers 616
Retna Pictures Ltd 619
Stockphotos 622
Viewfinder Colour Photo Library 624

Leisure & Hobbies: European Publishers
Borgens Forlag A/S 412
Fabbri (Gruppo Editoriale SpA) 423
Gremese Editore SRL 423
Høst & Søns Forlag A/S 413
Politikens Forlag A/S 414
RCS Rizzoli Libri SpA 425

Library Science: Publishers (UK)
Ashgate Publishing Co. Ltd 13
Bowker-Saur Ltd 20
Library Association Publishing 58
Pergamon Press 73
Routledge, Chapman & Hall Ltd 81

Library Science: Publishers (US)
McFarland & Company, Inc., Publishers 446

Library Science: Professional Associations
Association of Independent Libraries 490
Library Association, The 498
Office of Arts and Libraries 499
Scottish Library Association 501

Library Science: Prizes
Oldman (C.B.) Prize 562

Library Science: Libraries
British Library Information Sciences Service 579

Library Science: European Publishers
Francisci (Aldo) Editore 423
Jackson (Gruppo Editoriale) SpA 424
Saur (KG) Verlag GmbH & Co KG 421
V N U Business Press Group BV 427

Light Entertainment: Publishers (UK)
R & B Publishing 77

Light Entertainment: Agents (UK)
Hancock (Roger) Ltd 167
Power (Shelley) Literary Agency Ltd 174

Light Entertainment: Television
Sky Television (BSkyB) 314
Super Channel 314

Light Entertainment: Film, TV and video producers
Action Time 337
Artifax Ltd 338
Broadsword Television 341
Celador Productions Ltd 342
Chameleon Television Ltd 342
Chapel Broadcast Productions Ltd 343
Chatsworth Television Ltd 343
Cwmni'r Castell Cyf 346
Electric Picture Machine 348
First Freedom Productions Ltd 350
Fourth Wall Productions 351
Grundy (Reg) Productions (GB) Ltd 353
Henson (Jim) Productions 354
Insight Productions Ltd 356
PCP - Production Centre Productions 364
Talbot Television Ltd 369
Wall to Wall Television 374
World Wide International Television 375
Worldwide Television News 375

Linguistics: Publishers (UK)
Aberdeen University Press 9
Batsford (B.T.) Ltd 16
Curzon Press Ltd 32
Donald (John) Publishers Ltd 35
Edinburgh University Press 37
Exeter (University of) Press 40
Grevatt & Grevatt 46
Harcourt Brace Jovanovich Ltd 48
Karnak House 55
Macmillan Publishers Ltd 61
MIT Press Ltd, The 65
Pergamon Press 73
Routledge, Chapman & Hall Ltd 81

Linguistics: Magazines
Verbatim, The Language Quarterly 293

Linguistics: Publishers (US)
MIT Press 447

Linguistics: Prizes
Baal Book Prize 543

Linguistics: European Publishers
Armando Armando (Editore) SRL 422
Beck (Verlag C H) 418
Bulzoni Editore SRL (Le Edizioni Universitarie d'Italia) 422
Elsevier 426
Giunti Publishing Group 423
Istituto per l'Enciclopedia del Friuli Venezia Giulia 424
Klincksieck (Editions) 417
Kluwer Academic Publishers BV 426
Langenscheidt AG 434
Larousse (Librairie) 417
Liguori Editore SRL 424
Mulino (Societe Editrice Il) 425

Literature: Publishers (UK)
Aberdeen University Press 9
Allardyce, Barnett, Publishers 11
Bloodaxe Books Ltd 19
Bloomsbury Publishing Ltd 19
Boyars (Marion) Publishers Ltd 20
Calder Publications Ltd 23
Campbell (David) Publishers Ltd 24
Canongate Press 24
Cass (Frank) 25
Collins & Brown 29
Darf Publishers Ltd 33
Davies (Christopher) Publishers Ltd 33
Dedalus Ltd 34
Deutsch (André) Ltd 34
Exeter (University of) Press 40
Fourth Estate Ltd 42
Gay Men's Press (GMP Publishers Ltd), The 44
Granta Publications 46
Halban (Peter) Publishers 48
Leicester University Press 57
Little, Brown & Co. (UK) Ltd 59
Liverpool University Press 59
Macmillan Publishers Ltd 61
Mainstream Publishing Co. (Edinburgh) Ltd 62
Manchester University Press 62
Orion Publishing Group 69
Owen (Peter) Ltd 69
Penguin Books Ltd 71
Polity Press 75
Princeton University Press 75
Quartet Books 76
Reed International Books 78
Scottish Academic Press 84
Skoob Books Publishing Ltd 86
Smythe (Colin) Ltd 86
Tabb House 89

Virgin Publishing 93

Literature: Packagers
Albion Press Ltd, The 148

Literature: Agents (UK)
Alexander (Jacintha) Associates 159
Blake Friedmann Literary Agency Ltd* 160
Chris (Teresa) Literary Agency 162
Clarke (Serafina) 162
De Wolfe (Felix) 164
Fox & Howard Literary Agency 166
Green (Christine) (Authors' Agent) Ltd 167
Howard Seddon Associates 168
Judd (Jane) Literary Agency 169
Noach (Maggie) Literary Agency, The 172
Nye (Alexandra) (Writers & Agents) 173
O'Leary (David) Literary Agents 173
Pollinger (Laurence) Ltd 174
Pollinger (Murray) 174
Sayle (Tessa) Agency 176
Sheldon (Caroline) Literary Agency 177
Simmons (Jeffrey) 177

Literature: Magazines
Acumen 217
Ambit 219
Chapman 230
Contemporary Review 233
Edinburgh Review 240
Granta 250
Literary Review 260
London Magazine 260
Spectator, The 285
Times Literary Supplement, The 291

Literature: Publishers (US)
Carroll & Graf Publishers, Inc. 440
Eerdmans (William B.) Publishing Co. 442
Houghton Mifflin Co. 444
Little, Brown & Co., Inc. 445
New England (University Press of) 448
Princeton University Press 450
Tennessee (University of) Press 452

Literature: Agents (US)
Acton & Dystel 455

Author Aid Associates 456
Chester (Linda) Literary Agency 458
Creative Concepts Literary Agency 459
Deering Literary Agency, The 460
Ellenberg (Ethan), Literary Agency, The 461
Flannery, White & Stone 462
Herner (Susan) Rights Agency, Inc. 464
Lampack (Peter) Agency, Inc. 465
Lazear Agency, Inc., The 466
Lee (L. Harry) Literary Agency 466
Lord (Sterling) Literistic, Inc. 468
McDonough (Richard P.), Literary Agent 468
Noetzli (Regula) Literary Agency 471
Picard (Alison J.) Literary Agent 472
Quicksilver Books, Literary Agent 473
Sandum & Associates 474
Schaffner Agency, Inc. 474
Schulman (Susan) Literary Agency 475
Sebastian Agency 475
Siegel (Bobbe), Literary Agency 475
Snell (Michael) Literary Agency 476
Spieler Literary Agency 477
Stern (Gloria) Agency (New York) 477
Stuhlmann (Gunther) Author's Representative 477
Ware (John A.) Literary Agency 479
Wecksler-Incomco 479
Wieser & Wieser, Inc. 479
Writers' Productions 480
Zeckendorf (Susan) Associates 481

Literature: Professional Associations
Alliance of Literary Societies 489
Arvon Foundation 489
Authors' Club, The 491
Royal Society of Literature 501
South Bank Board: Literature Office 503
Welsh Academy 504

Literature: Bursaries/Fellowships
Arts Council Writers' Bursaries 535

Head (Francis) Bequest 537
Northern Arts Literary Fellowship
  539
Royal Literary Fund, The 540
Southern Arts Literature Bursaries
  540
Tom-Gallon Trust 541
Welton (Arthur) Scholarship 541

Literature: Prizes
Calvin & Rose G. $Hoffman Prize
  554
Cheltenham Prize 546
Cohen (David) British Literature
  Prize 547
Crawshay (Rose Mary) Prize 549
European Literary and Translation
  Prizes 550
Hawthornden Prize, The 553
King (Martin Luther) Memorial
  Prize, The 556
McLeod (Enid) Prize 558
Nobel Prize 561
Pulitzer Prizes 563
Rooney Prize for Irish Literature
  565
Royal Heinemann Award 565
Smith (W. H.) Literary Award 567
Southern Arts Literature Prize 568
Welsh Arts Council Book of the
  Year Awards 571
Whitbread Book of the Year and
  Literary Awards 571

Literature: Small Presses
AK Press/AKA Books 133
BB Books 134
Crescent Moon Publishing 136
Dragonfly Press 136
Frontier Publishing 138
Redstone Press 145
Tyrannosaurus Rex Press 147

Literature: Festivals
Arundel Festival 403
Bath Fringe Festival 403
Belfast Festival at Queen's 403
Birmingham Readers and Writers
  Festival 404
Brighton Festival 404
Bury St Edmunds Arts Festival 404
Cambridge Festival 404
Canterbury Festival 404
Cardiff Literature Festival 404
Chester Literature Festival 404
Colchester–Essex Festival 405
Daily Telegraph Cheltenham
  Festival of Literature, The 405
Dartington Literary Festival (Ways
  with Words) 405

Doncaster Literature Festival 405
Durham Literary Festival 406
Glasgow Mayfest 406
Hay-on-Wye Festival of Literature
  406
Hull Festival 406
Ilkley Literature Festival 406
Kent Literature Festival 407
Lancaster Literature Festival 407
Liverpool Festival 407
Ludlow Festival 407
Rye Festival 408
Salisbury Festival 408
Windsor Festival 409
Word For Word, Berkshire
  Literature Festival 409

**Literature: European
Publishers**
Abadia de Montserrat
  (Publicaciones de l') 430
Actes Sud (Editions) 415
Alhambra (Editorial) SA 430
Ambo (Uitgeverij) BV 425
Apostrof (Forlaget) ApS 412
Arche Verlag AG 434
Arthaud (Editions) SA 415
Bertrand Editora Lda 429
Bosch Casa Editorial SA 430
Bulzoni Editore SRL (Le Edizioni
  Universitarie d'Italia) 422
CEDAM (Casa Editrice Dr A
  Milani) 423
Davidsfonds VZW 411
Delta (Editions) SA 411
Différence, La 416
Droz (Librairie) SA 434
D T V Deutscher Taschenbuch
  Verlag GmbH & Co KG 419
E C I G (Edizioni Culturali
  Internazionali Genova) 423
E D H A S A 430
Elsevier 426
Elsevier Librico NV 411
Eumo Editorial 431
Europa Verlag GmbH 410
Francisci (Aldo) Editore 423
Fundamentos (Editorial) 431
Garzanti Editore 423
Hatier (Editions) SA 417
Istituto Geografico de Agostini
  SpA 423
Jaca Book (Editoriale) 424
Klincksieck (Editions) 417
Laia (Editorial) SA 431
Landesverlag Buchverlag 410
Landi (Luciano) Editore SRL 424
Lavoro Editoriale, Il 424
Manesse Verlag GmbH 434
Maule (Michel de) 417

Métaillié (A.M.) 417
Meulenhoff International 426
Minuit (Les Editions de) SA 418
Miraguano SA Ediciones 432
Niederösterreichisches
  Pressehaus, Verlag 411
Presses de la Cité, Les 418
Seuil (Editions du) 418
Toorts (Uitgeverij De) 427
Uniboek BV 427
Versal (Ediciones) SA 432
Zytglogge Verlag 435

**Literary Criticism: Publishers
(UK)**
Batsford (B.T.) Ltd 16
Black Spring Press Ltd 18
Bloodaxe Books Ltd 19
Boyars (Marion) Publishers Ltd 20
Calder Publications Ltd 23
Currey (James) Publishers 32
Edinburgh University Press 37
Enitharmon Press 38
Golden Cockerel Press Ltd 44
Halban (Peter) Publishers 48
Harvard University Press 50
Karnak House 55
Macmillan Publishers Ltd 61
Mainstream Publishing Co.
  (Edinburgh) Ltd 62
Northcote House Publishers Ltd
  67
Penguin Books Ltd 71
Routledge, Chapman & Hall Ltd
  81
Smythe (Colin) Ltd 86
Women's Press, The 96

Literary Criticism: Magazines
Literary Review 260

**Literary Criticism: Publishers
(US)**
Arkansas (University of) Press 438
Kent State University Press 445
Louisiana State University Press
  446
Massachusetts (University of)
  Press 447
Missouri (University of) Press 447
New England (University Press of)
  448
Oklahoma (University of) Press
  448
Tennessee (University of) Press
  452
Texas (University of) Press 452

Literary Criticism: Prizes
Crawshay (Rose Mary) Prize 549

GPA Book Award 553
Hardy (Thomas) Society Prize 553
Irish Times-Aer Lingus
International Fiction Prize 555
Royal Heinemann Award 565

Literary Criticism: Small Presses
Brentham Press 135
Crescent Moon Publishing 136
Indelible Inc 140
Paranoia Press (Teesside) 142
Paupers' Press 143
Zzero Books 147

Literary Criticism: European Publishers
Age d'Homme - La Cité (Editions L') 433
Fundamentos (Editorial) 431
Gremese Editore SRL 423
Gruyter (Walter de) & Co 419
Hiperión (Ediciones) SL 431
Kohlhammer (Verlag W) GmbH 420
Liguori Editore SRL 424
Mulino (Societe Editrice Il) 425
S A I E Editrice SRL 425
Tiderne Skifter 415

Local Interest/History: Publishers (UK)
Abson Books 9
Airlife Publishing Ltd 11
Barracuda Books Ltd/Quotes Ltd 15
Batsford (B.T.) Ltd 16
Berkswell Publishing Co. Ltd 17
Bridge Studios 22
Countryside Books 31
Dalton (Terence) Ltd 32
Ensign Publications 38
Exeter (University of) Press 40
Henry (Ian) Publications Ltd 51
Manchester University Press 62
Phillimore & Co. Ltd 73
S. B. Publications 82
Sumach Press, The 88
Sutton (Alan) Publishing Ltd 89
Tabb House 89
Wharncliffe Publishing Ltd 95
Windrush Press, The 96
Yorkshire Arts Circus Ltd 97

Local Interest/History: Packagers
Berkswell Publishing Co. Ltd 149

Local Interest/History: Magazines
Bedfordshire Magazine 223
Cambridgeshire Life 227
Cheshire Life 231
Cornish Life 234
Cotswold Life 234
Cumbria 236
Dalesman, The 236
Derbyshire Life and Countryside 238
Devon Life 238
Dorset Life 239
Essex Countryside 243
Evergreen 243
Exeter Life 243
Hampshire, The County Magazine 252
Hertfordshire Countryside 253
Lancashire Magazine 259
Lincolnshire Life 260
Mayfair Times 263
Norfolk Life 270
Northamptonshire Image 271
North East Times 270
Red Rose Magazine 279
Shropshire Magazine 283
Somerset & Avon Life 285
Somerset Magazine 285
Staffordshire Life 286
Suffolk Life 287
Surrey County Magazine 288
Tees Valley Writer 289
Wiltshire Life 297
Yorkshire Ridings Magazine 301

Local Interest/History: Television
Westcountry Television Ltd 312

Local Interest/History: Radio
Wear FM, 103.4 329

Local Interest/History: Publishers (US)
Iowa (University of) Press 445
Nevada (University of) Press 447
New England (University Press of) 448

Local Interest/History: Agents (US)
Southern Writers 476

Local Interest/History: Professional Associations
Coventry Writers' Association 495
Humberside Writers' Association (HWA) 497

Lancashire Authors' Association 498
South Eastern Writers' Association 503
West Country Writers' Association 505
Yorkshire Dialect Society 506

Local Interest/History: Prizes
Angel Literary Award 543
Holtby (Winifred) Memorial Prize 554
Lakeland Book of the Year 556
Lichfield Prize 557
Northern Poetry Award 561
Northern Stories Award 562
Portico Prize, The 563

Local Interest/History: Libraries
Armitt Trust & Library 577
Athenaeum, Liverpool 577
Barnsley Public Library 578
Derby Central Library 582
Devon & Exeter Institution Library 582
Highgate Literary and Scientific Institution Library 585
Liverpool City Libraries 586
Newcastle Literary and Philosophical Society Library 588
Newcastle upon Tyne Central Library 588
Nottingham Subscription Library Ltd 589
Penzance Library 589
Sheffield Libraries and Information Services 591
Wolverhampton Central Library 594
York Central Library 594

Local Interest/History: Picture Libraries
Baxter (Colin) Photography Ltd 601
Besley (Andrew) PhotoLibrary 601
County Visuals 605
Innes Photographic Library 612
Insight Picture Library, The 613
Oxford Picture Library 617

Local Interest/History: Small Presses
Amra Imprint 133
Aussteiger Publications 134
Baldwin (M. & M.) 134
Book Castle, The 134

Broadside 135
Castleden Publications 135
CNP Publications/Lyfrow
Trelyspen 136
Dragonfly Press 136
Ellenbank Press 137
Feather Books 137
Fortress Books 138
Fox Press 138
Heart of Albion Press 139
Hisarlik Press 139
Logaston Press 141
Marine Day Publishers 141
Meridian Books 141
Partizan Press 143
Power Publications 143
Quay Books Exeter 144
QueenSpark Books 144
Red Earth Publications 144
Stepney Books Publications 145
Wakefield Historical Publications
147

London: Publishers (UK)
HarperCollins Publishers Ltd 49
Spellmount Ltd 87

London: Magazines
City Limits 232
Illustrated London News, The 256
London Magazine 260
Ms London 266
Time Out 290
What's On in London 296

London: Libraries
Barbican Library 577
British Library Map Library 579
Greater London History Library
584
Guildhall Library 584
Highgate Literary and Scientific
Institution Library 585
Westminster Archives & Local
History Collection 593

London: Picture Libraries
Evans (Mary) Picture Library 606
Fotomas Index, The 608
Greater London Photograph
Library 609
Greenhill (Sally and Richard) 610
Hanley (Tom) 610
Illustrated London News Picture
Library 612
London (Museum of) Picture
Library 614
Miller (Lee) Archives 615
Newsfocus Press Photograph
Agency Ltd 616

Skyscan Balloon Photography 621
Strang (Jessica) Library 622
Williams (Andy) Photo Library
625

Magic: Publishers (UK)
Breese (Martin) Publishing 21
Souvenir Press Ltd 87

Magic: Publishers (US)
Llewellyn Publications 446

Magic: Agents (US)
Pegasus International, Inc. 471

Magic: Libraries
Price (Harry) Library of Magical
Literature 590

Magic: Small Presses
Mandrake 141

Maps: Publishers (UK)
AA Publishing 9
Allan (Ian) Ltd 11
Constable & Co. Ltd 30
Dalesman Publishing Co. Ltd 32
Ensign Publications 38
HarperCollins Publishers Ltd 49
Herbert Press, The 51
Macmillan Publishers Ltd 61
Macmillan Publishers Ltd 61
MIT Press Ltd, The 65
RAC Publishing 76
Reed International Books 78
Robson Books Ltd 81
Studio Editions Ltd 88
Sutton (Alan) Publishing Ltd 89
Thames and Hudson Ltd 90

Maps: Agents (UK)
Abacus Literary Agency 159

Maps: Magazines
Map Collector 262

Maps: Publishers (US)
Hippocrene Books, Inc. 444
Rand McNally & Co. 450

Maps: Libraries
British Library Map Library 579
Royal Geographical Society
Library 590
Westminster Reference Library
593

Maps: Picture Libraries
Aviation Picture Library 600

Brown (Hamish) Scottish
Photographic 602
Fotomas Index, The 608
Frith (Francis) Collection 608
Geonex UK Ltd 609
Northern Picture Library, The 616
Popperfoto 618
Topham Picture Source 623

Maps: European Publishers
Athesia (Verlagsanstalt) 422
Cappelens (J W) Forlag A/S 428
D T V Deutscher Taschenbuch
Verlag GmbH & Co KG 419
Hallwag Verlag AG 434
Istituto Geografico de Agostini
SpA 423
Kummerly und Frey
(Geographischer Verlag) 434
Liber AB 433
Mairs Geographischer Verlag 420
Michelin et Cie (Services de
Tourisme) 417
Politikens Forlag A/S 414
Porto Editora Lda 429

**Maritime/Nautical: Publishers
(UK)**
Airlife Publishing Ltd 11
Allan (Ian) Ltd 11
Ashford, Buchan & Enright 13
Black (A. & C.) (Publishers) Ltd
18
Brooks Books 22
Brown, Son & Ferguson, Ltd 23
Cassell 25
Dalton (Terence) Ltd 32
Ensign Publications 38
Exeter (University of) Press 40
Fernhurst Books 41
Haynes Publishing Group 50
Little, Brown & Co. (UK) Ltd 59
Mason (Kenneth) Publications Ltd
63
S. B. Publications 82

**Maritime/Nautical: Agents
(UK)**
London Independent Books Ltd
170

Maritime/Nautical: Magazines
Boat International 224
Canal and Riverboat 228
Motor Boat and Yachting 265
Practical Boat Owner 275
Sea Breezes 282
Waterways World 294
Yachting Monthly 300
Yachts and Yachting 301

Maritime/Nautical: Publishers (US)
Morrow (William) and Co., Inc. 447
TAB Books 452

Maritime/Nautical: Libraries
British Library Map Library 579

Maritime/Nautical: Picture Libraries
Adlib Specialist Picture Source 598
Beken of Cowes Ltd 601
Calendar Concepts & Design 602
Christel Clear Marine Photography 603
Cordaiy (Sylvia) Photo Library 604
Eyeline Photography 607
Footprints Colour Picture Library 608
FotoFlite 608
Garland (Leslie) Picture Library 609
Kos Image Library 613
National Maritime Museum Picture Library 615
Photographers' Library, The 618
PictureBank Photo Library Ltd 618
Planet Earth Pictures/Seaphot 618
Premaphotos Wildlife 618
Railfotos 619
Wilderness Photographic Library 625
Williams (S & I) Power Pix International Picture Library 626

Maritime/Nautical: European Publishers
Balkema (A A) 426
Hoffmann und Campe Verlag 420
Teide (Editorial) SA 432
Ugo (Gruppo) Mursia Editore SpA 425

Marketing/PR: Publishers (UK)
Kogan Page Ltd 56
Random House Publishing Group Ltd 76

Marketing/PR: Magazines
Export Sales and Marketing 244
Marketing Week 262
PR Week 275
Sales and Marketing Director 280
Sales and Marketing Management 281

Sales Direction 281

Marketing/PR: Film, TV and video producers
Adam Video Productions 337
Apple Television 338
Artts International 338
Aspen Business Communications 338
Aurora Sound and Vision 338
AVC Group 339
Broadwick Productions 341
Chess Valley Films and Video Ltd 343
Cinecosse Video 344
Compass Film Productions Ltd 344
Component Television Productions Ltd 345
Creative Channel Ltd 345
Creative Television Workshops Ltd 345
Crew Green Associates Ltd 345
Cricket Ltd 345
DBI Communication 347
Directors Video Company 347
Drake A-V Video Ltd 347
Dunkley (Robert) Associates Ltd 347
Edric Audio Visual Ltd 348
Electric Picture Machine 348
Enlightenment AV & Video 348
Fitting Images Ltd 350
Flying Pig Productions Ltd 350
Gateway Audio Visual and Video 351
Harnett Milan Ltd 354
Hawkshead Ltd 354
Head to Head Communication Ltd 354
Hourglass Pictures 355
Inca Video & Film Productions 356
In-House Corporate Video 356
In Video Productions Ltd 356
LTV Productions 359
Maiden Films Ltd 359
Main Communications 359
Mayhew Business Communication Ltd 360
New Decade Productions 362
Peake Productions 364
Pretty Clever Pictures Ltd 365
Priory Film Productions 366
Renaissance Vision 367
Signals, Essex Media Centre 368
Sonoptics Communications Group 369
Television Visualeyes 370
Triangle Two Ltd 371

United Television Artists Ltd 37?
Vera Productions 372
Video Enterprises 373
Videoplus Productions Ltd 373
Video Production Associates 37?
Zoom Production Co. Ltd, The 376

Marketing/PR: Publishers (US)
AMACOM 437

Marketing/PR: European Publishers
Moderne Industrie (Verlag) AG Co 420
V N U Business Press Group BV 427

Martial Arts: Publishers (UK)
Kime Publishing 55

Martial Arts: Packagers
Berkswell Publishing Co. Ltd 14?

Marxist Studies: Publishers (UK)
Pluto Press Ltd 75

Marxist Studies: Magazines
New Left Review 269

Marxist Studies: Prizes
Deutscher (Isaac & Tamara) Memorial Prize 549

Mathematics & Statistics: Publishers (UK)
D. P. Publications Ltd 35
Freeman (W. H.) & Co. Ltd 42
Gordon & Breach Science Publishers 45
Harcourt Brace Jovanovich Ltd
MIT Press Ltd, The 65
Pergamon Press 73
Ward Lock Educational 94

Mathematics & Statistics: Publishers (US)
Iowa State University Press 445
Krieger Publishing Co., Inc. 445
Open Court Publishing Co. 448
Van Nostrand Reinhold 453

Mathematics & Statistics: Agents (US)
Schwartz (Laurens R.) 475

Mathematics & Statistics:
Small Presses
QED Books 144

Mathematics & Statistics:
European Publishers
Alianza Editorial SA 430
Deutsch (Verlag Harri) 419
Didactica Editora 429
Giunti Publishing Group 423
Kluwer Academic Publishers BV
426
Liguori Editore SRL 424
Springer-Verlag GmbH & Co KG
421
Vuibert (Librairie) SA 418

Media & Cultural Studies:
Publishers (UK)
Cornerhouse Publications 31
Emap Business Publishing Ltd 38
Libbey (John) & Co. Ltd 58
Manchester University Press 62
Pluto Press Ltd 75
Polity Press 75
Roundhouse Publishing Ltd 81
Routledge, Chapman & Hall Ltd
81
Serpent's Tail 84
Thames and Hudson Ltd 90
Verso Ltd 93
Virgin Publishing 93

Media & Cultural Studies:
Agents (UK)
Dorian Literary Agency 164

Media & Cultural Studies:
Magazines
Media Week 263

Media & Cultural Studies:
Publishers (US)
Iowa State University Press 445
Walker & Co 453

Media & Cultural Studies:
Agents (US)
Boates (Reid) Literary Agency 457

Media & Cultural Studies:
Professional Associations
Campaign for Press and
Broadcasting Freedom 494
Chartered Institute of Journalists
494

Media & Cultural Studies:
Picture Libraries
Newsfocus Press Photograph
Agency Ltd 616

Medical: Publishers (UK)
Athlone Press, The 14
Blackwell Scientific Publications
Ltd 19
Boyars (Marion) Publishers Ltd 20
Cambridge University Press 24
Churchill Livingstone 28
Dunitz (Martin) Ltd 36
Faber & Faber Ltd 40
Freeman (W. H.) & Co. Ltd 42
Harcourt Brace Jovanovich Ltd 48
Hodder & Stoughton Ltd 52
Kluwer Academic Publishers 56
Libbey (John) & Co. Ltd 58
Longman Group Ltd 60
Macmillan Publishers Ltd 61
Meadow Books 63
MIT Press Ltd, The 65
Mosby Year Book Europe Ltd 65
Oxford University Press 70
Pergamon Press 73
Plenum Publishing Ltd 74
Reed International Books 78
Souvenir Press Ltd 87
Starke Publishers (Harold) Ltd 88
Tarragon Press 90
Wiley (John) & Sons Ltd 96

Medical: Packagers
MM Productions Ltd 154

Medical: Agents (UK)
Futerman (Vernon) Associates
166

Medical: Magazines
Balance 222
British Medical Journal 226
European Medical Journal 243

Medical: Film, TV and video
producers
BFV Ltd 340
Dragon Communications Ltd 347
Isaac (Peter) Ltd 357
London Scientific Films 359
Medical & Scientific Productions
360
Meditel Productions Ltd 360
Paper Moon Productions 364
Visual Connection (TVC) Ltd, The
374
Zoom Production Co. Ltd, The
376

Medical: Publishers (US)
Chronicle Books 440
Iowa State University Press 445
Krieger Publishing Co., Inc. 445
Times Books 453

Medical: Agents (US)
Mews Books Ltd 469

Medical: Professional
Associations
General Practitioner Writers
Association 496
Medical Journalists' Association
498
Medical Writers Group 498

Medical: Prizes
Glaxo Prize for Medical Writing &
Illustration 552
MIND Book of the Year – The
Allen Lane Award 560
Rogers Prize 564

Medical: Libraries
Health Information Library
(Westminster) 585
Royal Society of Medicine Library
591

Medical: Picture Libraries
Audio Visual Services 600
Barts Medical Picture Library 601
Financial Times Picture Collection
607
National Medical Slide Bank 615
Science Photo Library 620
Stockphotos 622
Telegraph Colour Library, The 623
Walmsley (John) Picture Library
625

Medical: European Publishers
Alhambra (Editorial) SA 430
Born NV Uitgeversmaatschappij
426
Braun (Verlag G) GmbH 419
Capitol Editrice Dischi CEB 422
CEDAM (Casa Editrice Dr A
Milani) 423
D T V Deutscher Taschenbuch
Verlag GmbH & Co KG 419
Econ-Verlag GmbH 419
Elsevier 426
E U N S A (Ediciones Universidad
de Navarra SA) 431
Europa-America (Publicaoes) Lda
429
Fabbri (Gruppo Editoriale) SpA
423

Flammarion et Cie 416
Gruyter (Walter de) & Co 419
Karger (S) GmbH 420
Kohlhammer (Verlag W) GmbH 420
Kok (Uitgeversmaatschappij J H) BV 426
Laffont (Editions Robert) 417
Lavoro Editoriale, Il 424
Liguori Editore SRL 424
Longanesi & C 424
Miraguano SA Ediciones 432
Mondadori (Arnoldo) Editore SpA 424
Mosaik Verlag 421
Munksgaard International Publishers Ltd 414
Nyt Nordisk Forlag Arnold Busck A/S 414
Paoline (Edizioni) SRL 425
Parey (Verlag Paul) 421
Presses Universitaires de France (PUF) 418
RCS Rizzoli Libri SpA 425
S A I E Editrice SRL 425
Sauerlander AG 435
Springer-Verlag 411
Springer-Verlag GmbH & Co KG 421
Swets en Zeitlinger BV 427
Thieme (Georg) Verlag 421
Toorts (Uitgeverij De) 427
Trauner (Rudolf) Verlag 411
Universitetsforlaget 428
Urban und Schwarzenberg GmbH 421
V C H Verlagsgesellschaft mbH 422
V U Boekhandel/Uitgeverij BV 427

Medicine: Publishers (UK)
Athlone Press, The 14
Polity Press 75
Prism Press Book Publishers Ltd 75
Routledge, Chapman & Hall Ltd 81
Sangam Books Ltd 82

Medicine: Packagers
Aspect 149

Medicine: Agents (UK)
Aspect 160
Kelly (Frances) 169

Medicine: Publishers (US)
Evans (M.) & Co., Inc. 442

Medicine: Agents (US)
Carvainis (Maria) Agency, Inc. 457
Fishbein (Frieda) Ltd 462
Lincoln (Ray) Literary Agency 467
Menza (Claudia) Literary Agency 469
Singer (Evelyn) Literary Agency, Inc., The 476
Wieser & Wieser, Inc. 479
Wreschner (Ruth), Authors' Representative 479

Medicine: Picture Libraries
Audio Visual Services 600
National Medical Slide Bank 615
Rex Features Ltd 620
Ronan (Ann) Picture Library 620
Science Photo Library 620

Medicine: Small Presses
Daniels Publishing 136

Medicine: European Publishers
Gyldendalske Boghandel, Nordisk Forlag A/S 413
Masson Editeur 417
B L V Verlagsgesellschaft mbH 419

Memoirs: Publishers (UK)
Aurum Press Ltd 15
Carcanet Press Ltd 25
Free Association Books 42
Gollancz (Victor) Ltd 45
Halban (Peter) Publishers 48
Penguin Books Ltd 71
Random House Publishing Group Ltd 76
Tabb House 89
Windrush Press, The 96

Memoirs: Agents (UK)
Robertson (Patricia) 175

Memoirs: Publishers (US)
Bergh Publishing, Inc. 439

Memoirs: Agents (US)
Dijkstra (Sandra) Literary Agency 460
Lazear Agency, Inc., The 466
McBride (Margret) Literary Agency 468

Memoirs: European Publishers
Calmann-Lévy (Editions) SA 415
Forum (Bokförlaget) AB 433

Lalli (Antonio) Editore 424
Tiden (Bokförlags) AB 433

Men's Interests: Magazines
Arena 220
Esquire 242
GQ 250
Mayfair 263
Penthouse 273
Titbits 291

Metaphysics: Publishers (UK
Daniel (C. W.) Co. Ltd, The 32
Gateway Books 43

Metaphysics: Agents (UK)
Bycornute Books 161

Metaphysics: Film, TV and video producers
Mosaic Film & Video Production 362

Metaphysics: Publishers (US
Llewellyn Publications 446
Missouri (University of) Press 44

Metaphysics: Agents (US)
Ellen Lively Steele & Associates 461
New Age World Services & Boo 470

Metaphysics: Small Presses
Barton House Publishing 134

Mexico: Publishers (US)
Texas (University of) Press 452

Mexico: Picture Libraries
South American Pictures 621

Middle East: Publishers (UK
Cass (Frank) 25
Darf Publishers Ltd 33
Routledge, Chapman & Hall Ltd 81
Scorpion Publishing Ltd 84
Tauris (I.B.) & Co. Ltd 90
Volcano Press 94
Zed Books Ltd 98

Middle East: Agents (UK)
Eady (Toby) Associates Ltd 165
Reynolds (Jim) Associates 175

Middle East: Magazines
Jewish Quarterly 258

Middle East: Publishers (US)
Texas (University of) Press 452

Middle East: Libraries
British Library Oriental and India
Office Collections 580

Middle East: Picture Libraries
Aspect Picture Library Ltd 600
Camerapix Picture Library 603
Casement Collection, The 603
Dixon (C M) 605
Halliday (Sonia) Photographs 610
Miller (Lee) Archives 615
Screen Ventures 621
Spooner (Frank) Pictures 622
Wood (Roger) Library 626

Military: Publishers (UK)
Allan (Ian) Ltd 11
Barracuda Books Ltd/Quotes Ltd
15
Cassell 25
Cass (Frank) 25
Donald (John) Publishers Ltd 35
Fountain Press Ltd 42
Greenhill Books/Lionel Leventhal
Ltd 46
Haynes Publishing Group 50
Macmillan Publishers Ltd 61
Mainstream Publishing Co.
(Edinburgh) Ltd 62
Midland Publishing Ltd 64
Milestone Publications 64
Owl Press 70
Pen & Sword Books Ltd 71
Reed International Books 78
Salamander Books Ltd 82
Souvenir Press Ltd 87
Spellmount Ltd 87
Studio Editions Ltd 88

Military: Packagers
Bison Books Ltd 149
MM Productions Ltd 154
Wordwright Books 156

Military: Agents (UK)
Bolt (David) Associates 160
Fox & Howard Literary Agency
166
Reynolds (Jim) Associates 175
Ryder (Herta) 175
Watson, Little Ltd* 179

Military: Magazines
Jane's Defence Weekly 258

**Military: Film, TV and video
producers**
Tomahawk Films Ltd 371

Military: Publishers (US)
ABC–Clio, Inc. 436
Avery Publishing Group, Inc. 438
Kansas (University of) Press 445
Sterling Publishing 452

Military: Agents (US)
Authors Resource Center & Tarc
Literary Agency, The 456
Hull House Literary Agency 464
Lee (L. Harry) Literary Agency
466
Leone (Adele) Agency, Inc. 466
Schulman (Susan) Literary Agency
475

Military: Picture Libraries
Allan (Chris) Aviation Library 599
Aviation Photographs
International 600
E. T. Archive 606
Financial Times Picture Collection
607
FotoFlite 608
Greenpeace Communications Ltd
610
Imperial War Museum
Department of Photographs
612
Victory Archive, The 624
Young (John Robert) Collection
627

Military: Small Presses
Partizan Press 143

Military: European Publishers
Österreichischer Bundesverlag
Gesellschaft mbH 411
Ullstein (Buchverlage) GmbH 421

**Mineralogy/Mining:
Publishers (UK)**
Exeter (University of) Press 40
Woodhead Publishing Ltd 97

Mineralogy/Mining: Libraries
Natural History Museum Library
588

**Mineralogy/Mining: Picture
Libraries**
GeoScience Features 609
Natural History Museum Picture
Library 616
RIDA Photo Library 620

**Mineralogy/Mining: Small
Presses**
Red Earth Publications 144

**Mineralogy/Mining: European
Publishers**
Balkema (A A) 426

**Motoring & Cars: Publishers
(UK)**
AA Publishing 9
Aston Publications 14
Bay View Books Ltd 16
Brooks Books 22
Crowood Press Ltd, The 32
Elliot Right Way Books 37
Fernhurst Books 41
Haynes Publishing Group 50
Hazleton Publishing 50
Motor Racing Publications 66
Reed International Books 78

Motoring & Cars: Agents (UK)
Knight Features 170

Motoring & Cars: Magazines
Autocar & Motor 221
Car 228
Car Mechanics 229
*Cars and Car Conversions
Magazine* 229
Fast Car 245
Fast Lane 245
Practical Motorist 276
Veteran Car 293
What Car? 295

**Motoring & Cars: Publishers
(US)**
TAB Books 452

**Motoring & Cars: Professional
Associations**
Guild of Motoring Writers 497

Motoring & Cars: Prizes
Dreyfus (Pierre) Award 550
Lyons (Sir William) Award 557
Michelin Award 559
Montagu Trophy 560
Rover Group Award 565
Vauxhall Trophy 570

**Motoring & Cars: Picture
Libraries**
Adlib Specialist Picture Source
598
Art Directors Photo Library 600
Calendar Concepts & Design 602
Quadrant Picture Library 619

Motoring & Cars: European Publishers
B L V Verlagsgesellschaft mbH 419
Vogel-Verlag KG 422

Motor Cycling: Publishers (UK)
Aston Publications 14
Bay View Books Ltd 16
Fernhurst Books 41
Haynes Publishing Group 50
Hazleton Publishing 50
Motor Racing Publications 66

Motor Cycling: Agents (UK)
Knight Features 170

Motor Cycling: Magazines
Dirt Bike Rider (DBR) 239
Motor Cycle News 266
Mountain Biking UK 266

Motor Cycling: Prizes
Montagu Trophy 560

Motor Cycling: Picture Libraries
Quadrant Picture Library 619

Motor Cycling: European Publishers
B L V Verlagsgesellschaft mbH 419
Falken-Verlag GmbH 419

Music: Publishers (UK)
Acair Ltd 10
Allardyce, Barnett, Publishers 11
Ashgate Publishing Co. Ltd 13
Athlone Press, The 14
Black Spring Press Ltd 18
Boxtree 20
Boyars (Marion) Publishers Ltd 20
Breese (Martin) Publishing 21
Calder Publications Ltd 23
Cassell 25
Donald (John) Publishers Ltd 35
Faber & Faber Ltd 40
Golden Cockerel Press Ltd 44
Gollancz (Victor) Ltd 45
Gordon & Breach Science Publishers 45
Harvard University Press 50
Kahn & Averill 54
Karnak House 55
Macmillan Publishers Ltd 61
MIT Press Ltd, The 65
Omnibus Press 68
Oxford University Press 70

Plexus Publishing Ltd 75
Quartet Books 76
Reed International Books 78
Smith Gryphon Ltd 86
Souvenir Press Ltd 87
Spellmount Ltd 87
Stainer & Bell Ltd 88
Thames and Hudson Ltd 90
Thames Publishing/Autolycus Press 90
Virgin Publishing 93

Music: Agents (UK)
Davidson (Merric) Literary Agency 164
Higham (David) Associates Ltd 168
Judd (Jane) Literary Agency 169
Pawsey (John) 173
Ryder (Herta) 175

Music: Magazines
British Bandsman, The 225
Church Music Quarterly 232
Classical Guitar 232
Classical Music 232
Crescendo & Jazz Music 235
Early Music 240
Folk Roots 247
Gramophone 250
Hi-Fi News & Record Review 253
Jazz Journal International 258
Keyboard Review 259
Making Music 262
Melody Maker 263
Musical Opinion 267
Musical Times 267
Music Review, The 267
Music Week 267
New Musical Express 269
Q 277
Record Collector 279
Smash Hits 285
Strad, The 287

Music: Television
MTV Europe 314

Music: Radio
Classic FM 317
Independent Music Radio 317

Music: Film, TV and video producers
Artifax Ltd 338
Broadwick Productions 341
Cadenza 342
Crystalvision Ltd 346
CTR Productions 346
Electric Picture Machine 348

Eyewitness Ltd 349
Gibb Rose Organisation Ltd 352
Good Film Company, The 352
Holmes Associates 355
Knaves Acre Productions 358
Landseer Film and Television Productions Ltd 358
Lucida Productions 359
Mansfield (Mike) Television Ltd 360
MCEG Virgin Vision 360
Medialab Ltd 360
Mentorn Films 361
Midnight Films Ltd 361
MIlls (John) Film and Television 361
Mirus Productions 361
MJW Productions 362
Normandy Film Productions 363
Pelicula Films 364
Polygram Filmed Entertainment 365
Primetime Television Ltd 365
Riverfront Pictures Ltd 367
Talbot Television Ltd 369
Teliesyn 370

Music: Theatre producers
Century Theatre Touring 379
Jones (Pola) Associates Ltd 385
Newpalm Productions 389
Theatr Clwyd 396
Wallbank (John) Associates Ltd 398

Music: Publishers (US)
Iowa State University Press 445
Louisiana State University Press 446
McFarland & Company, Inc., Publishers 446
Princeton University Press 450
Rosen Publishing Group, Inc., Th 450
Walker & Co 453

Music: Agents (US)
Nolan (Betsy) Literary Agency, The 471
Writers House, Inc. 480

Music: Professional Associations
Arvon Foundation 489
Performing Right Society 500

Music: Prizes
Oldman (C.B.) Prize 562
Yorkshire Post Art and Music Awards 573

Music: Libraries
Barbican Library 577
British Library Music Library 580
British Library National Sound
Archive 580
Central Music Library
(Westminster) 581
Liverpool City Libraries 586
Newcastle Literary and
Philosophical Society Library
588
Sheffield Libraries and
Information Services 591

Music: Picture Libraries
All-Action Picture Library 599
E. T. Archive 606
Hanley (Tom) 610
London Features International Ltd
614
Performing Arts Library 617
Redferns 619
Relay Photos Ltd 619
Repfoto London 619
Retna Pictures Ltd 619
Sefton Photo Library 621
Syndication International 623
V&A Picture Library 624
Vintage Magazine Company Ltd,
The 624
Williams (Vaughan) Memorial
Library 626

Music: Small Presses
Alan (Richard) Publications 133
Stride 146
Works Publishing 147

Music: Festivals
Arundel Festival 403
Bath Fringe Festival 403
Brighton Festival 404
Buxton International Festival 404
Cambridge Festival 404
Doncaster Literature Festival 405
Glasgow Mayfest 406
Greenwich Festival 406
Hay-on-Wye Festival of Literature
406
Lancaster Literature Festival 407
London (City of) Festival 407
Ludlow Festival 407
Worcester Festival of Literature
409
York Festival 409

Music: European Publishers
Adelphi Edizioni SpA 422
Age d'Homme – La Cité (Editions
L') 433

Alianza Editorial SA 430
Amalthea-Verlag Gesellschaft
mbH 410
Beck (Verlag C H) 418
Belfond (Editions Pierre) 415
Brockhaus (F A) 419
Cappelli (Nuova Casa Editrice
Licinio) SpA 422
Casterman (Editions) 415
Dreyers Forlag A/S 428
D T V Deutscher Taschenbuch
Verlag GmbH & Co KG 419
Econ-Verlag GmbH 419
Europa-America (Publicaoes) Lda
429
Fabbri (Gruppo Editoriale) SpA
423
Fayard (Librarie Arthème) 416
Fischer (S) Verlag GmbH 419
Gallimard (Editions) 416
Gremese Editore SRL 423
Gyldendal Norsk Forlag 428
Gyldendalske Boghandel, Nordisk
Forlag A/S 413
Hachette 416
Hoffmann und Campe Verlag 420
Horay (Pierre) Editeur 417
Klincksieck (Editions) 417
Laffont (Editions Robert) 417
Lattes (Editions Jean-Claude) 417
Longanesi & C 424
Maule (Michel de) 417
Mondadori (Arnoldo) Editore SpA
424
Mulino (Societe Editrice Il) 425
Neff (Paul), Verlag 410
Nyt Nordisk Forlag Arnold Busck
A/S 414
Österreichischer Bundesverlag
Gesellschaft mbH 411
Paoline (Edizioni) SRL 425
Payot Lausanne (Editions) 435
Politikens Forlag A/S 414
Presses Universitaires de France
(PUF) 418
Rabën och Sjögren Bokforlag AB
433
RCS Rizzoli Libri SpA 425
Seuil (Editions du) 418
70 (Edições) Lda 430
Sikkel (Uitgeverij De) NV 412
Swets en Zeitlinger BV 427
Ullstein (Buchverlage) GmbH 421
Uniepers BV 427

Mythology: Publishers (UK)
HarperCollins Publishers Ltd 49
Thames and Hudson Ltd 90

Mythology: Picture Libraries
Dixon (C M) 605
Halliday (Sonia) Photographs 610
Photo Resources 617
Walker (Charles) Collection, The
624

**Nature/Natural History:
Publishers (UK)**
Airlife Publishing Ltd 11
Barracuda Books Ltd/Quotes Ltd
15
Blackstaff Press Ltd 18
Cassell 25
Cathie (Kyle) Ltd 26
Constable & Co. Ltd 30
David & Charles Publishers 33
Dorling Kindersley Ltd 35
Dragon's World 35
Freeman (W. H.) & Co. Ltd 42
Gollancz (Victor) Ltd 45
Harley Books 48
HarperCollins Publishers Ltd 49
Herbert Press, The 51
Letts (Charles) & Co. Ltd 58
Little, Brown & Co. (UK) Ltd 59
Lutterworth Press, The 60
Macmillan Publishers Ltd 61
Medici Society Ltd, The 63
MIT Press Ltd, The 65
New Holland (Publishers) Ltd 67
Orion Publishing Group 69
Random House Publishing Group
Ltd 76
Reader's Digest Association Ltd
78
Reed International Books 78
Souvenir Press Ltd 87
Studio Editions Ltd 88
Swift Children's Books 89
Whittet Books Ltd 96

**Nature/Natural History:
Packagers**
Belitha Press Ltd 149
Brown Wells and Jacobs Ltd 150
Calmann & King Ltd 150
Cameron Books (Production) Ltd
150
Lionheart Books 153
New England Editions Ltd 154
Savitri Books Ltd 155

**Nature/Natural History:
Agents (UK)**
Bromley (Rosemary) Literary
Agency 160
Davidson (Caroline) and Robert
Ducas Literary Agency 164

Solo Syndication & Literary
Agency Ltd 177

**Nature/Natural History:
Magazines**
Bee World 223
Country-Side 235
Naturalist, The 268
Nature 268

**Nature/Natural History: Film,
TV and video producers**
Waterfront Productions 374

**Nature/Natural History:
Publishers (US)**
Abrams (Harry N.), Inc. 436
Chronicle Books 440
Houghton Mifflin Co. 444
Little, Brown & Co., Inc. 445
Lyons & Burford, Publishers 446
Nevada (University of) Press 447
NorthWord Press, Inc. 448
Random House, Inc. 450
Sterling Publishing 452
Texas (University of) Press 452
Walker & Co 453

**Nature/Natural History:
Agents (US)**
Lincoln (Ray) Literary Agency 467
Urstadt (Susan P.), Inc. 478
Wecksler-Incomco 479

**Nature/Natural History:
Prizes**
BBC WILDLIFE Magazine Awards
for Nature Writing 544
Natural World Book of the Year
Award 561

**Nature/Natural History:
Libraries**
Natural History Museum Library
588

**Nature/Natural History:
Picture Libraries**
Ace Photo Agency 598
Adlib Specialist Picture Source
598
Angel (Heather)/Biofotos 599
Aquila Photographics 599
Ardea London Ltd 600
Barnaby's Picture Library 601
Camera Ways Ltd Picture Library
603
Cash (J. Allan) Ltd 603
Coleman (Bruce) Wildlife &
Travel Photo Library 604

Comstock Photofile Ltd 604
Ecoscene 606
Evans (Greg) International Photo
Library 606
Garland (Leslie) Picture Library
609
Grace (Martin and Dorothy) 609
Lane (Frank) Picture Agency Ltd
614
Laubier (André) Picture Library
614
Michael & Patricia Fogden 608
Natural History Museum Picture
Library 616
Natural Science Photos 616
NHPA (Natural History
Photographic Agency) 616
Oxford Scientific Films Photo
Library 617
Paterson (David) Library 617
Planet Earth Pictures/Seaphot 618
Premaphotos Wildlife 618
Press-tige Pictures 618
RSPB Picture Library 620
Spooner (Frank) Pictures 622
Survival Anglia Photo Library 622
Telegraph Colour Library, The 623
Topham Picture Source 623
Williams (S & I) Power Pix
International Picture Library
626
Woodmansterne Ltd 626

**Nature/Natural History: Small
Presses**
Ellenbank Press 137
Logaston Press 141

**Nature/Natural History:
European Publishers**
B L V Verlagsgesellschaft mbH
419
Brockhaus (F A) 419
Elsevier Librico NV 411
Fabbri (Gruppo Editoriale) SpA
423
Falken-Verlag GmbH 419
Forum (Bokförlaget) AB 433
Gründ (Librairie) 416
Hatier (Editions) SA 417
Høst & Søns Forlag A/S 413
Incafo (Editorial) SA 431
Kok (Uitgeversmaatschappij J H)
BV 426
Nathan (Fernand) 418
Politikens Forlag A/S 414
Rabén och Sjögren Bokforlag AB
433
Spectrum (Uitgeverij Het) BV 427

Naturalism: Magazines
Health and Efficiency 252

New Age: Publishers (UK)
Breese (Martin) Publishing 21
Cassell 25
Daniel (C. W.) Co. Ltd, The 32
Foulsham (W.) & Co. 42
Gateway Books 43
HarperCollins Publishers Ltd 49
Penguin Books Ltd 71

New Age: Publishers (US)
Avery Publishing Group, Inc. 438
Sterling Publishing 452

New Age: Agents (US)
Elek (Peter) Associates 461
Leone (Adele) Agency, Inc. 466
Literary/Business Associates 467
New Age World Services & Books
470
Pegasus International, Inc. 471
Quicksilver Books, Literary Agent
473
Schwartz (Laurens R.) 475
Shore (Lee) Agency 475
Steele (Lyle) & Co. Ltd 477

New Age: Small Presses
Barton House Publishing 134

**New Age: European
Publishers**
Fayard (Librarie Arthème) 416
Servire BV Uitgevers 426
Spectrum (Uitgeverij Het) BV 427

**New Zealand: Picture
Libraries**
Colasanti (Stephanie) 604

Nursing: Publishers (UK)
Churchill Livingstone 28
Faber & Faber Ltd 40
Mosby Year Book Europe Ltd 65

Nursing: Magazines
Nursing Times 271

Nursing: Agents (US)
Fishbein (Frieda) Ltd 462

Nursing: European Publishers
Alhambra (Editorial) SA 430
Armando Armando (Editore) SRl
422
E U N S A (Ediciones Universidad
de Navarra SA) 431
Liber AB 433

Munksgaard International
Publishers Ltd 414

**Occult/Mysticism: Publishers
(UK)**
HarperCollins Publishers Ltd 49
Karnak House 55
Penguin Books Ltd 71
Prism Press Book Publishers Ltd
75
Skoob Books Publishing Ltd 86
Souvenir Press Ltd 87

**Occult/Mysticism: Agents
(UK)**
Howard Seddon Associates 168

Occult/Mysticism: Magazines
*Fortean Times: The Journal of
Strange Phenomena* 247
Prediction 276
Psychic News 277

**Occult/Mysticism: Film, TV
and video producers**
Mosaic Film & Video Productions
362

**Occult/Mysticism: Publishers
(US)**
Llewellyn Publications 446

**Occult/Mysticism: Agents
(US)**
Appleseeds Management 455
Author Aid Associates 456
Dijkstra (Sandra) Literary Agency
460
Ellen Lively Steele & Associates
461
Garon-Brooke (Jay) Associates,
Inc. 463
Jarvis (Sharon) and Co., Inc. 464
Lee Allan Agency, The 466
Lee (L. Harry) Literary Agency
466
Literary/Business Associates 467
New Age World Services & Books
470
Pegasus International, Inc. 471
Steele (Lyle) & Co. Ltd 477

Occult/Mysticism: Libraries
Leeds Library 586

**Occult/Mysticism: Picture
Libraries**
Fortean Picture Library 608
Walker (Charles) Collection, The
624

**Occult/Mysticism: Small
Presses**
Gothic Press 139
Haunted Library 139
Mandrake 141
Spacelink Books 145
Temple Press Ltd 146

**Occult/Mysticism: Literary
Societies**
Gothic Society, The 510

**Occult/Mysticism: European
Publishers**
Bogans Forlag 412
Haase (P.) & Søns Forlag A/S 413
Heyne (Wilhelm) Verlag 420
B L V Verlagsgesellschaft mbH
419

Opera: Publishers (UK)
Calder Publications Ltd 23

Opera: Magazines
Opera 271
Opera Now 271

**Opera: Film, TV and video
producers**
MJW Productions 362

Opera: Picture Libraries
Dominic Photography 605
Performing Arts Library 617
Woodmansterne Ltd 626

Opera: Festivals
Brighton Festival 404
Buxton International Festival 404
Ludlow Festival 407
York Festival 409

**Ophthalmology/Optometry:
Film, TV and video
producers**
Adam Video Productions 337

**Oriental Studies: Publishers
(UK)**
Aris & Phillips Ltd 13
Athlone Press, The 14
Curzon Press Ltd 32
Darf Publishers Ltd 33
East-West Publications 36
Octagon Press Ltd 68
Scorpion Publishing Ltd 84

**Oriental Studies: Publishers
(US)**
Open Court Publishing Co. 448

Oriental Studies: Libraries
British Library Oriental and India
Office Collections 580

**Outdoor & Country Pursuits:
Publishers (UK)**
Airlife Publishing Ltd 11
Ashford, Buchan & Enright 13
Barracuda Books Ltd/Quotes Ltd
15
Batsford (B.T.) Ltd 16
Berkswell Publishing Co. Ltd 17
Cassell 25
Cicerone Press 28
Crowood Press Ltd, The 32
Fernhurst Books 41
Lochar Publishing Ltd 59
Thornhill Press 91
Wharncliffe Publishing Ltd 95

**Outdoor & Country Pursuits:
Packagers**
Berkswell Publishing Co. Ltd 149
Leading Edge Press & Publishing
Ltd 153

**Outdoor & Country Pursuits:
Agents (UK)**
Clarke (Serafina) 162

**Outdoor & Country Pursuits:
Magazines**
Camping and Caravanning 228
Camping Magazine 228
Caravan Magazine 229
Caves & Caving 230
Climber and Hill Walker 232
Country Life 234
Country Sports 235
Descent 238
Great Outdoors, The 250
*Motorcaravan & Motorhome
Monthly (MMM)* 266
Motor Caravan World 266
Motor Home 266
On The Edge 271
Rambling Today 278
Shooting and Conservation 283
Shooting News & Country Weekly
283
Shooting Times & Country 283
Survival and Outdoor Techniques
288

**Outdoor & Country Pursuits:
Publishers (US)**
Abrams (Harry N.), Inc. 436
Lyons & Burford, Publishers 446
NorthWord Press, Inc. 448

Outdoor & Country Pursuits: Professional Associations
Outdoor Writers Guild 499
Yachting Journalists' Association 506

Outdoor & Country Pursuits: Prizes
Boardman Tasker Memorial Award 544
OWG/COLA Awards for Excellence 562

Outdoor & Country Pursuits: Picture Libraries
Alba Pictures 598
Bonington (Chris) Library 602
Cleare (John)/Mountain Camera 604
Whitehead (Eric) Picture Library and Agency 625
Wilderness Photographic Library 625

Outdoor & Country Pursuits: Small Presses
Aussteiger Publications 134
Footmark Publications 138
Logaston Press 141
Meridian Books 141
Power Publications 143

Outdoor & Country Pursuits: European Publishers
Arthaud (Editions) SA 415
Athesia (Verlagsanstalt) 422
Parey (Verlag Paul) 421
Rabén och Sjögren Bokforlag AB 433

Palaeontology: Publishers (UK)
Freeman (W. H.) & Co. Ltd 42

Palaeontology: Libraries
Natural History Museum Library 588

Parenting: Publishers (UK)
Elite Words & Image 37
HarperCollins Publishers Ltd 49
Piatkus Books 73
Reed International Books 78
Usborne Publishing Ltd 93

Parenting: Magazines
Baby Magazine 222
Home Economics & Technology 254
Home & Family 254

Maternity and Mothercraft 262
Mother and Baby 265
Parents 272

Parenting: Publishers (US)
Adams (Bob) Publishers, Inc. 436
Avery Publishing Group, Inc. 438
NavPress Publishing Group 447
Prima Publishing and Communications 450
Walker & Co 453

Parenting: Agents (US)
Heacock Literary Agency, Inc. 464
Marcil (Denise) Literary Agency, Inc. 469
Schulman (Susan) Literary Agency 475

Parenting: Picture Libraries
Bubbles Photolibrary 602
Greenhill (Sally and Richard) 610
Hutchison Library, The 611
Jessel (Camilla) Photo Library 613
Lupe Cunha Photos 614
Photofusion 617
Reflections PhotoLibrary 619
Wiedel (Janine) 625

Pets: Publishers (UK)
Elliot Right Way Books 37
HarperCollins Publishers Ltd 49
Salamander Books Ltd 82

Pets: Magazines
Animal World 219
Cat World 229

Pets: Publishers (US)
Sterling Publishing 452

Pets: Picture Libraries
Animal Photography 599
Aquila Photographics 599
Financial Times Picture Collection 607
Spectrum Colour Library 621

Philosophy: Publishers (UK)
Athlone Press, The 14
Boyars (Marion) Publishers Ltd 20
Cathie (Kyle) Ltd 26
Claridge Press 29
Clark (T. & T.) 29
Curzon Press Ltd 32
Edinburgh University Press 37
Golden Cockerel Press Ltd 44
Halban (Peter) Publishers 48
HarperCollins Publishers Ltd 49

Harvard University Press 50
Macmillan Publishers Ltd 61
Merlin Press Ltd 64
MIT Press Ltd, The 65
Octagon Press Ltd 68
Open Gate Press 68
Pergamon Press 73
Polity Press 75
Prism Press Book Publishers Ltd 75
Random House Publishing Group Ltd 76
Routledge, Chapman & Hall Ltd 81
SCM Press Ltd 83
Search Press Ltd/Burns & Oates Ltd 84
Shepheard-Walwyn (Publishers) Ltd 85
Souvenir Press Ltd 87
Verso Ltd 93
Virago Press Ltd 93

Philosophy: Agents (UK)
Denniston & Lownie 164
Howard Seddon Associates 168

Philosophy: Magazines
Edinburgh Review 240
New Humanist 269

Philosophy: Publishers (US)
Iowa State University Press 445
Kansas (University of) Press 445
Massachusetts (University of) Press 447
Missouri (University of) Press 447
MIT Press 447
New England (University Press of) 448
Open Court Publishing Co. 448
Paragon House Publishers 449
Princeton University Press 450
Simon & Schuster 451
Temple University Press 452

Philosophy: Agents (US)
Literary/Business Associates 467
Stern (Gloria) Agency (New York) 477

Philosophy: Libraries
Liverpool City Libraries 586
Williams's (Dr) Library 594

Philosophy: Small Presses
Paupers' Press 143
Tyrannosaurus Rex Press 147
Zzero Books 147

Philosophy: European Publishers
Adelphi Edizioni SpA 422
Age d'Homme – La Cité (Editions L') 433
Alhambra (Editorial) SA 430
Alianza Editorial SA 430
Ambo (Uitgeverij) BV 425
Armado (Armenio), Editore de Simoes, Belrao & Cia Lda 429
Armando Armando (Editore) SRL 422
Artemis Verlags AG 434
Aubier-Montaigne (Editions) SA 415
Beck (Verlag C H) 418
Born NV Uitgeversmaatschappij 426
Bulzoni Editore SRL (Le Edizioni Universitarie d'Italia) 422
Calmann-Lévy (Editions) SA 415
Cappelli (Nuova Casa Editrice Licinio) SpA 422
CEDAM (Casa Editrice Dr A Milani) 423
Città Nuova Editrice 423
Davidsfonds VZW 411
Découverte, La 416
Denoël (Editions) Sàrl 416
Det Norske Samlaget 428
Dom Quixote (Publicacoes) Lda 429
D T V Deutscher Taschenbuch Verlag GmbH & Co KG 419
E C I G (Edizioni Culturali Internazionali Genova) 423
E U N S A (Ediciones Universidad de Navarra SA) 431
Europa-America (Publicaoes) Lda 429
Europa Verlag GmbH 410
Fischer (S) Verlag GmbH 419
Flammarion et Cie 416
Francisci (Aldo) Editore 423
Gallimard (Editions) 416
Gedisa (Editorial) SA 431
Gradiva – Publicacoes Lda 429
Grasset et Farquelle (Société des Editions) 416
Grijalbo SA 431
Gruyter (Walter de) & Co 419
Guida Editori SpA 423
Gyldendalske Boghandel, Nordisk Forlag A/S 413
Hachette 416
Hanser (Carl) Verlag 420
Herder (Verlag) GmbH & Co KG 420
Hiperión (Ediciones) SL 431
Hoffmann und Campe Verlag 420

Jaca Book (Editoriale) 424
Kluwer Academic Publishers BV 426
Kok (Uitgeversmaatschappij J H) BV 426
Laffont (Editions Robert) 417
Lalli (Antonio) Editore 424
Liguori Editore SRL 424
Longanesi & C 424
Maule (Michel de) 417
Mercure de France SA 417
Minuit (Les Editions de) SA 418
Mondadori (Arnoldo) Editore SpA 424
Mulino (Societe Editrice Il) 425
Nathan (Fernand) 418
Nelissen (Uitgeverij H) BV 426
Nyt Nordisk Forlag Arnold Busck A/S 414
Paoline (Edizioni) SRL 425
Presses Universitaires de France (PUF) 418
Reitzels (Hans) Forlag A/S 414
S A I E Editrice SRL 425
Scherz Verlag AG 435
Schönbergske (Det) Forlag A/S 414
S E I (Società Editrice Internationale) 425
Seuil (Editions du) 418
Springer-Verlag GmbH & Co KG 421
Styria (Verlag) 411
Suhrkamp Verlag 421
Teide (Editorial) SA 432
Tusquets Editores 432
Ugo (Gruppo) Mursia Editore SpA 425
V U Boekhandel/Uitgeverij BV 427

Photography: Publishers (UK)
Bloodaxe Books Ltd 19
Cassell 25
Collins & Brown 29
Cornerhouse Publications 31
Countryside Books 31
Deutsch (André) Ltd 34
Dragon's World 35
Enitharmon Press 38
Fountain Press Ltd 42
Gay Men's Press (GMP Publishers Ltd), The 44
Haynes Publishing Group 50
Herbert Press, The 51
King (Laurence) 55
Little, Brown & Co. (UK) Ltd 59
Macmillan Publishers Ltd 61
Mainstream Publishing Co. (Edinburgh) Ltd 62

MIT Press Ltd, The 65
Phaidon Press Ltd 73
Quartet Books 76
Random House Publishing Group Ltd 76
Thames and Hudson Ltd 90

Photography: Packagers
Berkswell Publishing Co. Ltd 149

Photography: Agents (UK)
Davidson (Caroline) and Robert Ducas Literary Agency 164

Photography: Magazines
Amateur Photographer 218
Creative Camera 235
Freelance Writing & Photography 247
Practical Photography 276

Photography: Publishers (US)
Chronicle Books 440
Temple University Press 452

Photography: Agents (US)
Wieser & Wieser, Inc. 479

Photography: Picture Libraries
Royal Photographic Society, The 620

Photography: Small Presses
Frontier Publishing 138

Photography: European Publishers
Casterman (Editions) 415
Falken-Verlag GmbH 419
Flammarion et Cie 416
Grafis Edizioni 423
Gremese Editore SRL 423
Herder (Verlag) GmbH & Co KG 420
Jaca Book (Editoriale) 424
Lannoo (Uitgeverij) Drukkerij 412
Paris Musées 418
Tiderne Skifter 415
Time-Life Books BV 427

Phrenology: Libraries
National Library of Scotland 587

Physics: Publishers (UK)
Edinburgh University Press 37
Freeman (W. H.) & Co. Ltd 42
Gordon & Breach Science Publishers 45
Harcourt Brace Jovanovich Ltd 48

Jai Press Ltd 54
MIT Press Ltd, The 65
Pergamon Press 73
Pinter Publishers Ltd 74
Wiley (John) & Sons Ltd 96

Physics: Publishers (US)
Iowa State University Press 445
Krieger Publishing Co., Inc.
445
Princeton University Press 450

Physics: Picture Libraries
Science Photo Library 620

Physics: European Publishers
Springer-Verlag GmbH & Co KG
421
V C H Verlagsgesellschaft mbH
422
Vuibert (Librairie) SA 418

Poetry: Publishers (UK)
Acair Ltd 10
Anvil Press Poetry Ltd 12
Blackstaff Press Ltd 18
Bloodaxe Books Ltd 19
Boyars (Marion) Publishers Ltd 20
Calder Publications Ltd 23
Canongate Press 24
Carcanet Press Ltd 25
Cassell 25
Chapman 27
Commonword Ltd 30
Deutsch (André) Ltd 34
Edinburgh University Press 37
Enitharmon Press 38
Faber & Faber Ltd 40
Gay Men's Press (GMP Publishers
Ltd), The 44
Grevatt & Grevatt 46
Hale (Robert) Ltd 48
HarperCollins Publishers Ltd 49
Jarrold Publishing 54
Oxford University Press 70
Penguin Books Ltd 71
Random House Publishing Group
Ltd 76
Scottish Academic Press 84
Skoob Books Publishing Ltd 86
Smythe (Colin) Ltd 86
Souvenir Press Ltd 87
Swift Children's Books 89
Thames Publishing/Autolycus
Press 90
Virago Press Ltd 93
Virgin Publishing 93

Poetry: Poetry Presses
See section pp 119–128.

Poetry: Packagers
Beanstalk Books Ltd 149

Poetry: Agents (UK)
Eady (Toby) Associates Ltd 165
Motley (Michael) Ltd 172

Poetry: Magazines
Acumen 217
London Review of Books 261
Mosaic 265
North, The 270
Poetry Review 274
Stand Magazine 286
Staple Magazine 287
Sunk Island Review 287
Tees Valley Writer 289
Working Titles 299

Poetry: Publishers (US)
Aegina Press, Inc. 436
Arkansas (University of) Press 438
California (University of) Press
440
Harcourt Brace Jovanovich 443
Iowa (University of) Press 445
Louisiana State University Press
446
Massachusetts (University of)
Press 447
Missouri (University of) Press 447
Morrow (William) and Co., Inc.
447
New England (University Press of)
448
Paragon House Publishers 449

Poetry: Agents (US)
Author Aid Associates 456
Living Faith Literary Agency 468
New Age World Services & Books
470

**Poetry: Professional
Associations**
Arvon Foundation 489
Association of Little Presses 490
Ver Poets 504

Poetry: Bursaries/Fellowships
Cholmondeley Awards 536
Gregory (Eric) Trust Fund 537
Masefield (John) Memorial Trust,
The 538
National Poetry Foundation
Grants 538

Poetry: Prizes
Aldeburgh Poetry Festival Prize
542

An Duais don bhFiliocht i
nGaelige (Prize for Poetry in
Irish) 542
Arthur (Rosemary) Award 543
Arvon Foundation International
Poetry Competition 543
Boardman Tasker Memorial
Award 544
Bridport Arts Centre Creative
Writing Competition 545
Cardiff (The City of) International
Poetry Competition 546
Cooper (Duff) Prize, The 548
Crabbe Memorial Poetry
Competition 549
Devlin (Denis) Award 550
Envoi Poetry Competition 550
European Prize for the Translation
of Poetry 551
Faber (Geoffrey) Memorial Prize
551
Farmer (Prudence) Award 551
GPA Book Award 553
Hemans (Felicia) Prize for Lyrical
Poetry 554
Hughes (John Edeyrn) Prize 554
Irish Times-Aer Lingus
International Fiction Prize 555
Irish Times Aer Lingus Irish
Literature Prizes 555
Kent & Sussex Poetry Society
Open Competition 555
King (Martin Luther) Memorial
Prize, The 556
Leek Arts Festival International
Poetry Competition 556
Literary Review Grand Poetry
Competition 557
Markham (Arthur) Memorial Prize
559
National Poetry Competition 561
Northern Poetry Award 561
Outposts Poetry Competition 562
Peterloo Poets Open Poetry
Competition 563
Poetry Business Competition 563
Rhyme International Prize 564
Royal Heinemann Award 565
Signal Poetry for Children Award
567
Smith (W. H.) Young Writers'
Competition 568
Southern Arts Literature Prize 568
Southport Writers' Circle Poetry
Competition 568
Staple Open Poetry Competition
568
Sunday Times Young British
Writer of the Year Award 569

Tibble (Ann) Poetry Competition 569
Tripp (John) Award 570
Tutin (Dorothy) Award 570
Ver Poets Poetry Competitions 571
Wandsworth Writers London Competition 571
Whitbread Book of the Year and Literary Awards 571
Wilkins (Alfred & Mary) Memorial Poetry Competition, The 572
Wingate (H. H.) Prize 572
Yorkshire Open Poetry Competition 573
Young Writers' Competition 573

Poetry: Libraries
Northumberland County Library 588
Poetry Library 589
Scottish Poetry Library 591

Poetry: Small Presses
Aard Press 133
AK Press/AKA Books 133
Alembic Press, The 133
Amra Imprint 133
BB Books 134
Brentham Press 135
Businesslike Publishing 135
CNP Publications/Lyfrow Trelyspen 136
Crescent Moon Publishing 136
Dark Diamonds Publications 136
Diamond Press 136
Dragonfly Press 136
Feather Books 137
Fox Press 138
Hilltop Press 139
Indelible Inc 140
Littlewood Arc 141
Maypole Editions 141
Paranoia Press (Teesside) 142
Peepal Tree Books 143
Poetry Business, The 143
Previous Parrot Press 143
QueenSpark Books 144
Redlake Press, The 144
Stride 146

Poetry: Festivals
Aldeburgh Poetry Festival 403
Arundel Festival 403
Avon Poetry Festival 403
Bath Fringe Festival 403
Bury St Edmunds Arts Festival 404
Cley Little Festival of Poetry 405
Daily Telegraph Cheltenham Festival of Literature, The 405

Greenwich Festival 406
Hay-on-Wye Festival of Literature 406
King's Lynn, The Poetry Festival 407
Salisbury Festival 408
Stratford-upon-Avon Poetry Festival 409
Windsor Festival 409
Worcester Festival of Literature 409
Word For Word, Berkshire Literature Festival 409
Write Around – A Celebration of Cleveland Writing 409
York Festival 409

Poetry: European Publishers
Actes Sud (Editions) 415
Age d'Homme – La Cité (Editions L') 433
Alianza Editorial SA 430
Athesia (Verlagsanstalt) 422
Aubier-Montaigne (Editions) SA 415
Belfond (Editions Pierre) 415
Benteli Verlag 434
Cappelli (Nuova Casa Editrice Licinio) SpA 422
Casterman (Editions) 415
Découverte, La 416
Différence, La 416
Dom Quixote (Publicacoes) Lda 429
Don Quijote (Editorial) 430
Droz (Librairie) SA 434
D T V Deutscher Taschenbuch Verlag GmbH & Co KG 419
Empeño (Editoria) 431
Ennsthaler (Wilhelm), Verlag 410
Europa-America (Publicaoes) Lda 429
Fischer (S) Verlag GmbH 419
Flammarion et Cie 416
Francisci (Aldo) Editore 423
Gallimard (Editions) 416
Garzanti Editore 423
Gyldendalske Boghandel, Nordisk Forlag A/S 413
Hanser (Carl) Verlag 420
Heyne (Wilhelm) Verlag 420
Hiperión (Ediciones) SL 431
Hoffmann und Campe Verlag 420
Kok (Uitgeversmaatschappij J H) BV 426
Lalli (Antonio) Editore 424
Lannoo (Uitgeverij) Drukkerij 412
Manteau (Uitgeversmaatschappij A) NV 412
Mercure de France SA 417

Mondadori (Arnoldo) Editore SpA 424
Oglio (Dall') Editore SRL 425
Payot Lausanne (Editions) 435
Sauerlander AG 435
Schönbergske (Det) Forlag A/S 414
Seix Barral SA 432
Seuil (Editions du) 418
Suhrkamp Verlag 421
Todariana Editrice 425
Ugo (Gruppo) Mursia Editore SpA 425
Ullstein (Buchverlage) GmbH 421
Vindrose (Forlaget) A/S 415
Zsolnay (Paul), Verlag GmbH 411

Poetry: Writers Circles
Many Writer's Circles listed in *The Writer's Handbook* cover poetry. See section pp 522–550.

Poland: Libraries
Polish Library 590

Polar Studies: Publishers (UK)
Erskine Press/Bluntisham Books 39

Polar Studies: Publishers (US)
Alaska (University of) Press 437

Polar Studies: Libraries
National Library of Scotland 587

Polar Studies: Picture Libraries
Alexander (Bryan & Cherry) Photography 598
Angel (Heather)/Biofotos 599
Wiedel (Janine) 625
Wilderness Photographic Library 625

Politics: Publishers (UK)
Athlone Press, The 14
Bellew Publishing Co. Ltd 17
Blackstaff Press Ltd 18
Bloodaxe Books Ltd 19
Bookmarks Publications 20
Bowker–Saur Ltd 20
Boyars (Marion) Publishers Ltd 20
Calder Publications Ltd 23
Cassell 25
Cass (Frank) 25
Chapmans Publishers 27
Claridge Press 29
Currey (James) Publishers 32
Darf Publishers Ltd 33

Dartmouth Publishing Co. Ltd 33
Deutsch (André) Ltd 34
Dunrod Press 36
Economist Books 36
Freeman (W. H.) & Co. Ltd 42
Grey Seal Books 47
Halban (Peter) Publishers 48
Harvard University Press 50
Hurst (C.) & Co. 53
Lawrence & Wishart Ltd 57
Leicester University Press 57
Macmillan Publishers Ltd 61
Mainstream Publishing Co.
  (Edinburgh) Ltd 62
Manchester University Press 62
Merlin Press Ltd 64
MIT Press Ltd, The 65
Open Gate Press 68
Open University Press 69
Penguin Books Ltd 71
Pergamon Press 73
Pluto Press Ltd 75
Polity Press 75
Prism Press Book Publishers Ltd
  75
Routledge, Chapman & Hall Ltd
  81
Swift Children's Books 89
Verso Ltd 93
Virago Press Ltd 93
Volcano Press 94

Politics: Agents (UK)
Davis-Poynter (Reg) 164
Futerman (Vernon) Associates
  166
Gregory & Radice Authors'
  Agents* 167
Pawsey (John) 173
Reynolds (Jim) Associates 175
Simmons (Jeffrey) 177

Politics: Magazines
Contemporary Review 233
Granta 250
Labour Party News 259
Liberal Democrat News 259
New Internationalist 269
New Left Review 269
New Statesman and Society 270
Salisbury Review 281
Spectator, The 285
Tribune 292

**Politics: Film, TV and video
  producers**
Smith & Watson Productions 368

Politics: Publishers (US)
ABC–Clio, Inc. 436

Addison-Wesley Publishing Co.,
  Inc. 436
Arkansas (University of) Press 438
Avon Books 438
Eerdmans (William B.) Publishing
  Co. 442
Iowa State University Press 445
Kansas (University of) Press 445
Longman Publishing Group 446
Louisiana State University Press
  446
Massachusetts (University of)
  Press 447
Paragon House Publishers 449
Princeton University Press 450
Random House, Inc. 450
St Martin's Press, Inc. 451

Politics: Agents (US)
Acton & Dystel 455
Browne (Pema) Ltd 457
Carvainis (Maria) Agency, Inc.
  457
Garon-Brooke (Jay) Associates,
  Inc. 463
Hawkins (John) & Associates, Inc.
  463
Literary & Creative Artists Agency
  467
Menza (Claudia) Literary Agency
  469
Peter (James) Associates, Inc. 472
Schwartz (Laurens R.) 475
Sebastian Agency 475
Singer (Evelyn) Literary Agency,
  Inc., The 476
Spitzer (Philip G.) Literary Agency
  477
Steele (Lyle) & Co. Ltd 477

Politics: Prizes
Bentinck (Adolphe) Prize 544
Cooper (Duff) Prize, The 548
Irish Times-Aer Lingus
  International Fiction Prize 555
Mackenzie (W. J. M.) Book Prize
  558
RTZ David Watt Memorial Prize,
  The 565
Utley (T. E.) Award 570

Politics: Libraries
BBC Data Enquiry Service 578

Politics: Picture Libraries
All-Action Picture Library 599
Financial Times Picture Collection
  607
Fotomas Index, The 608
Impact Photos 612

London Features International L
  614
Monitor Syndication 615
Network Photographers 616
Newsfocus Press Photograph
  Agency Ltd 616
Popperfoto 618
Rex Features Ltd 620
Select Photos 621
Spooner (Frank) Pictures 622
Universal Pictorial Press & Agence
  Ltd 624
Visnews Still Service 624

Politics: Small Presses
AK Press/AKA Books 133
Bozo 134
CNP Publications/Lyfrow
  Trelyspen 136
Dark Diamonds Publications 136
Fortress Books 138
Paranoia Press (Teesside) 142
QueenSpark Books 144
Tufnell Press, The 146

Politics: European Publishers
Alianza Editorial SA 430
Armado (Armenio), Editore de
  Simoes, Belrao & Cia Lda 429
Armando Armando (Editore) SR
  422
Brombergs Bokförlag AB 433
Caminho (Editorial) SARL 429
Casterman (Editions) 415
CEDAM (Casa Editrice Dr A
  Milani) 423
Davidsfonds VZW 411
Découverte, La 416
Denoël (Editions) Sàrl 416
Econ-Verlag GmbH 419
Europa Verlag GmbH 410
Francisci (Aldo) Editore 423
Grijalbo SA 431
Hachette 416
Lalli (Antonio) Editore 424
Lannoo (Uitgeverij) Drukkerij 411
Mulino (Societe Editrice Il) 425
Nelissen (Uitgeverij H) BV 426
Orac Verlag Gesellschaft mbH
  411
Paludans (Jörgen) Forlag ApS 41
Presses Universitaires de France
  (PUF) 418
Rosinante/Munksgaard 414
Samlerens Forlag A/S 414
Seuil (Editions du) 418
Standaard Uitgeverij 412
Tiden (Bokförlags) AB 433
Tiderne Skifter 415
Time-Life Books BV 427

Ullstein (Buchverlage) GmbH 421
Uniboek BV 427
V U Boekhandel/Uitgeverij BV 427
Zytglogge Verlag 435

Pollution: Picture Libraries
Angel (Heather)/Biofotos 599
Ecoscene 606
Financial Times Picture Collection 607
Greenpeace Communications Ltd 610
Hoffman (David) Photo Library 611
Oxford Scientific Films Photo Library 617
Planet Earth Pictures/Seaphot 618
Reflections PhotoLibrary 619
Still Pictures Environmental Agency 622

Professional: Publishers (UK)
Ashgate Publishing Co. Ltd 13
Blackwell Publishers 18
Blackwell Scientific Publications Ltd 19
Longman Group Ltd 60
Macmillan Publishers Ltd 61
McGraw-Hill Book Co. Europe 60
Open University Press 69
Pergamon Press 73
Pitman Publishing 74
Plenum Publishing Ltd 74
Reed International Books 78
Routledge, Chapman & Hall Ltd 81
Sage Publications Ltd 82
Sweet & Maxwell Ltd 89
Tolley Publishing Co. Ltd 91
Wiley (John) & Sons Ltd 96

Professional: Magazines
Electrical Times 241
Office Secretary 271
Personnel Management 273
PM Plus 274

Professional: Publishers (US)
Longman Publishing Group 446
Pennsylvania (University of) Press 449
Van Nostrand Reinhold 453

Professional: Agents (US)
Catalog Literary Agency, The 458
Snell (Michael) Literary Agency 476

Professional: European Publishers
Elsevier 426

Psychology: Publishers (UK)
Boyars (Marion) Publishers Ltd 20
BPS Books 21
Constable & Co. Ltd 30
Free Association Books 42
Freeman (W. H.) & Co. Ltd 42
Gateway Books 43
Gordon & Breach Science Publishers 45
Harcourt Brace Jovanovich Ltd 48
HarperCollins Publishers Ltd 49
Harvard University Press 50
James (Arthur) Ltd 54
Kingsley (Jessica) Publishers Ltd 56
Little, Brown & Co. (UK) Ltd 59
Macmillan Publishers Ltd 61
MIT Press Ltd, The 65
Octagon Press Ltd 68
Open Gate Press 68
Open University Press 69
Pergamon Press 73
Piatkus Books 73
Polity Press 75
Random House Publishing Group Ltd 76
Routledge, Chapman & Hall Ltd 81
Souvenir Press Ltd 87
Virago Press Ltd 93
Women's Press, The 96

Psychology: Agents (UK)
Abacus Literary Agency 159
Anderson (Darley) Books 159
Paterson (Mark) & Associates 173
Radala & Associates 175
Watson, Little Ltd* 179

Psychology: Publishers (US)
Addison-Wesley Publishing Co., Inc. 436
Avon Books 438
Carroll & Graf Publishers, Inc. 440
Evans (M.) & Co., Inc. 442
Gardner Press, Inc. 443
Houghton Mifflin Co. 444
Iowa State University Press 445
Krieger Publishing Co., Inc. 445
New England (University Press of) 448
Open Court Publishing Co. 448
Plenum Publishing 449
Prima Publishing and Communications 450
Random House, Inc. 450

Schocken Books, Inc. 451
Walker & Co 453

Psychology: Agents (US)
Authors Resource Center & Tarc Literary Agency, The 456
Brandenburgh & Associates Literary Agency 457
Carvainis (Maria) Agency, Inc. 457
Chester (Linda) Literary Agency 458
Dijkstra (Sandra) Literary Agency 460
Hawkins (John) & Associates, Inc. 463
Heacock Literary Agency, Inc. 464
Kern (Natasha) Literary Agency, Inc. 464
Lincoln (Ray) Literary Agency 467
Literary/Business Associates 467
Mann (Carol) Agency 468
Multimedia Product Development, Inc. 470
New Age World Services & Books 470
New England Publishing Associates, Inc. 470
Noetzli (Regula) Literary Agency 471
Quicksilver Books, Literary Agents 473
Schulman (Susan) Literary Agency 475
Sebastian Agency 475
Siegel (Bobbe), Literary Agency 475
Snell (Michael) Literary Agency 476
2M Communications Ltd 478
Ware (John A.) Literary Agency 479
Waterside Productions, Inc. 479

Psychology: Prizes
MIND Book of the Year – The Allen Lane Award 560

Psychology: Libraries
British Psychological Society Library 581
Population Censuses & Surveys Library, Office of 589

Psychology: Small Presses
Zzero Books 147

Psychology: European Publishers
Adelphi Edizioni SpA 422
Alhambra (Editorial) SA 430
Ambo (Uitgeverij) BV 425
Apostrof (Forlaget) ApS 412
Armado (Armenio), Editore de Simoes, Belrao & Cia Lda 429
Armando Armando (Editore) SRL 422
Aubier-Montaigne (Editions) SA 415
Calmann-Lévy (Editions) SA 415
Ceac (Ediciones) SA 430
Città Nuova Editrice 423
Denoël (Editions) Sàrl 416
Diesterweg (Verlag Moritz) 419
D T V Deutscher Taschenbuch Verlag GmbH & Co KG 419
E C I G (Edizioni Culturali Internazionali Genova) 423
Econ-Verlag GmbH 419
Europa-America (Publicaoes) Lda 429
Fischer (S) Verlag GmbH 419
Francisci (Aldo) Editore 423
Fundamentos (Editorial) 431
G.E.C. Gad Publishers 413
Gedisa (Editorial) SA 431
Giunti Publishing Group 423
Grijalbo SA 431
Gyldendalske Boghandel, Nordisk Forlag A/S 413
Herder (Verlag) GmbH & Co KG 420
Heyne (Wilhelm) Verlag 420
Hoffmann und Campe Verlag 420
Horizonte (Livros) Lda 429
Karger (S) GmbH 420
Klett-Cotta Verlag 420
Kok (Uitgeversmaatschappij J H) BV 426
Laffont (Editions Robert) 417
Laia (Editorial) SA 431
Longanesi & C 424
Mercure de France SA 417
Mondadori (Arnoldo) Editore SpA 424
Mulino (Societe Editrice Il) 425
Munksgaard International Publishers Ltd 414
Nathan (Fernand) 418
Natur och Kultur (Bokförlaget) 433
Nyt Nordisk Forlag Arnold Busck A/S 414
Oldenbourg (R) Verlag GmbH 421
Paludans (Jörgen) Forlag ApS 414
Paoline (Edizioni) SRL 425

Payot Lausanne (Editions) 435
Presses Universitaires de France (PUF) 418
Rabēn och Sjögren Bokforlag AB 433
Reitzels (Hans) Forlag A/S 414
Scherz Verlag AG 435
S E I (Società Editrice Internationale) 425
Servire BV Uitgevers 426
Seuil (Editions du) 418
Springer-Verlag GmbH & Co KG 421
Suhrkamp Verlag 421
Swets en Zeitlinger BV 427
Table Ronde (Les Editions de la) 418
Tiden (Bokförlags) AB 433
Todariana Editrice 425
Toorts (Uitgeverij De) 427
V U Boekhandel/Uitgeverij BV 427

Puzzles, Quizzes & Crosswords: Publishers (UK)
Abson Books 9
Elliot Right Way Books 37

Puzzles, Quizzes & Crosswords: Agents (UK)
Drexl (Anne) 165

Puzzles, Quizzes & Crosswords: Magazines
Good Stories 250

Puzzles, Quizzes & Crosswords: Television
GMTV 309

Puzzles, Quizzes & Crosswords: Film, TV and video producers
Winnick (Maurice) Associates Ltd 375

Puzzles, Quizzes & Crosswords: Publishers (US)
Sterling Publishing 452

Radio: Radio Companies
See section pp 315–330.

Radio: Agents (UK)
Anderson (Darley) Books 159
Baker (Yvonne) Associates 160
Blake Friedmann Literary Agency Ltd* 160

Bromley (Rosemary) Literary Agency 160
Bryant (Peter) (Writers) 161
Casarotto Ramsay Ltd 161
Cochrane (Elspeth) Agency 162
Colin (Rosica) Ltd 162
Conway-Gordon (Jane) 163
Cruickshank Cazenove Ltd 163
Curtis Brown Group Ltd 163
Daish (Judy) Associates Ltd 164
Dorian Literary Agency 164
Film Link Literary Agency 165
Fitch (Laurence) Ltd 165
Futerman (Vernon) Associates 166
Gabriel (Jüri) 166
Gardner (Kerry) Management 1[
Gillis (Pamela) Management 16[
Glass (Eric) Ltd 166
Hoskins (Valerie) 168
Imison (Michael) Playwrights Lt[168
International Copyright Bureau Ltd 169
International Scripts 169
Juvenilia 169
Lemon, Unna and Durbridge Ltd 170
Levy (Barbara) Literary Agency 170
Mann (Andrew) Ltd 171
Manuscript ReSearch 171
Marjacq Scripts Ltd 171
Martinez (M. C.) Literary Agency 171
Martin (Judy) 171
Marvin (Blanche) 171
MBA Literary Agents Ltd* 172
McLean (Bill) Personal Management 170
Milne (Richard) Ltd 172
Morris (William) Agency UK Ltd 172
Peters Fraser & Dunlop Group Ltd* 174
Sharland Organisation Ltd, The 176
Shaw (Vincent) Associates 176
Sheil Land Associates Ltd* 176
Steinberg (Micheline) Playwrigh[Agent 178
Thurley (J. M.) 178
Ware (Cecily) Literary Agents 1[

Radio: Magazines
Practical Wireless 276
Radio Communication 278
Radio Times 278

Radio: Film, TV and video producers
CTR Productions 346

Radio: Agents (US)
Artists Group, The 456
Creative Concepts Literary Agency 459
Curtis Brown Ltd 459
Ellen Lively Steele & Associates 461
Kroll (Lucy) Agency 465
Lord (Sterling) Literistic, Inc. 468
Schwartz (Laurens R.) 475
Swanson (H. N.), Inc. 478
Tantleff Office, The 478
Writer's Consulting Group 480

Radio: Professional Associations
Association of Independent Radio Companies 490

Radio: Prizes
Cooper (Giles) Awards, The 548
Radio Times Drama & Comedy Awards 564

Radio: Libraries
Westminster Reference Library 593

Radio: Festivals
New London Radio Playwrights Festival 408

Railways: Publishers (UK)
Haynes Publishing Group 50
Midland Publishing Ltd 64
S. B. Publications 82
St John Thomas (David) Publisher 82
Unicorn Books 92

Railways: Packagers
Sheldrake Press Ltd 155

Railways: Magazines
RAIL 278
Railway Magazine, The 278

Railways: Publishers (US)
TAB Books 452

Railways: Picture Libraries
Collections 604
Frith (Francis) Collection 608
National Railway Museum Picture Library 615
Railfotos 619

Railways: Small Presses
Terminus Publications 146

Reference
Pinguin-Verlag Pawlowski GmbH 411

Reference: Publishers (UK)
Acair Ltd 10
Allan (Ian) Ltd 11
Black (A. & C.) (Publishers) Ltd 18
Cambridge University Press 24
Cassell 25
Chambers (W & R) 27
Chapmans Publishers 27
Columbia University Press 30
Consumers' Association 30
Economist Books 36
Euromonitor 39
Europa Publications Ltd 39
Facts On File 40
Fourth Estate Ltd 42
Gaia Books Ltd 43
Graham-Cameron Publishing 46
HarperCollins Publishers Ltd 49
Harvard University Press 50
Helicon Publishing 51
Library Association Publishing 58
Little, Brown & Co. (UK) Ltd 59
Macmillan Publishers Ltd 61
Melrose Press Ltd 63
Milestone Publications 64
MIT Press Ltd, The 65
O'Mara (Michael) Books Limited 68
Oxford University Press 70
Penguin Books Ltd 71
Pergamon Press 73
Plenum Publishing Ltd 74
Quiller Press 76
Reed International Books 78
Routledge, Chapman & Hall Ltd 81
Search Press Ltd/Burns & Oates Ltd 84
Starke Publishers (Harold) Ltd 88
Virago Press Ltd 93
Virgin Publishing 93
Watts Group, The 95
Wiley (John) & Sons Ltd 96

Reference: Packagers
Book Packaging and Marketing 150
Cameron Books (Production) Ltd 150
Diagram Visual Information Ltd 151
Market House Books Ltd 153

Morgan Samuel Editions 154
Zoe Books Ltd 156

Reference: Agents (UK)
Davidson (Caroline) and Robert Ducas Literary Agency 164
Fox & Howard Literary Agency 166

Reference: Publishers (US)
ABC-Clio, Inc. 436
Adams (Bob) Publishers, Inc. 436
Bowling Green State University Popular Press 439
Facts on File, Inc. 442
Hippocrene Books, Inc. 444
Krieger Publishing Co., Inc. 445
McFarland & Company, Inc., Publishers 446
Paragon House Publishers 449
Pennsylvania (University of) Press 449
Random House, Inc. 450
Rosen Publishing Group, Inc., The 450
St Martin's Press, Inc. 451
Scarecrow Press, Inc. 451
Simon & Schuster 451
Sterling Publishing 452
Walker & Co 453
Warner Books 453

Reference: Agents (US)
Boates (Reid) Literary Agency 457
Browne (Pema) Ltd 457
Herman (Jeff) Agency, Inc., The 464
New England Publishing Associates, Inc. 470
Protter (Susan Ann) Literary Agent 472
Snell (Michael) Literary Agency 476
Urstadt (Susan P.), Inc. 478

Reference: Prizes
Library Association McColvin Medal, The 557
Oldman (C.B.) Prize 562
Times Educational Supplement Information Book Awards 570

Reference: Libraries
Bishopsgate Library 578
British Library Manuscripts Department 579
Manchester Central Library 587

Reference: European Publishers
Amanda 412
Aschehoug (H) & Co (W Nygaard) 427
Aubier-Montaigne (Editions) SA 415
Benteli Verlag 434
Bonniers (Albert) Forlag AB 433
Bordas (Editions) 415
Born NV Uitgeversmaatschappij 426
Capitol Editrice Dischi CEB 422
Cappelli (Nuova Casa Editrice Licinio) SpA 422
Damm (N W) & Son A/S 428
Denoël (Editions) Sàrl 416
Det Norske Samlaget 428
Deutsch (Verlag Harri) 419
Dom Quixote (Publicacoes) Lda 429
Droemersche Verlagsanstalt Th Knaur Nachf 419
Droz (Librairie) SA 434
Econ-Verlag GmbH 419
Elsevier Librico NV 411
Fabbri (Gruppo Editoriale) SpA 423
Fayard (Librarie Arthème) 416
Fischer (S) Verlag GmbH 419
Flammarion et Cie 416
Forum (Bokförlaget) AB 433
Garzanti Editore 423
G.E.C. Gad Publishers 413
Gjellerup & Gad Publishers Ltd 413
Grijalbo SA 431
Gyldendalske Boghandel, Nordisk Forlag A/S 413
Hachette 416
Herder (Verlag) GmbH & Co KG 420
Holkenfeldts Forlag A/S 413
Høst & Søns Forlag A/S 413
Istituto Geografico de Agostini SpA 423
Komma & Clausen 413
Larousse (Librairie) 417
Larousse (Suisse) SA 434
Laterza (Giuseppe) e Figli SpA 424
Mondadori (Arnoldo) Editore SpA 424
Mosaik Verlag 421
Nathan (Fernand) 418
Oldenbourg (R) Verlag GmbH 421
Österreichischer Bundesverlag Gesellschaft mbH 411
Paludans (Jörgen) Forlag ApS 414

Paoline (Edizioni) SRL 425
Presses Universitaires de France (PUF) 418
RCS Rizzoli Libri SpA 425
S A I E Editrice SRL 425
Saur (KG) Verlag GmbH & Co KG 421
Schibsteds (Chr.) Forlag A/S 428
Schönbergske (Det) Forlag A/S 414
Springer-Verlag GmbH & Co KG 421
Styria (Verlag) 411
Ugo (Gruppo) Mursia Editore SpA 425
Uniboek BV 427

Religion & Theology: Publishers (UK)
Acair Ltd 10
Athlone Press, The 14
Barracuda Books Ltd/Quotes Ltd 15
Bellew Publishing Co. Ltd 17
Boyars (Marion) Publishers Ltd 20
Cambridge University Press 24
Cassell 25
Christian Focus Publications 28
Clark (T. & T.) 29
Curzon Press Ltd 32
Darf Publishers Ltd 33
Darton, Longman & Todd Ltd 33
Donald (John) Publishers Ltd 35
Epworth Press 38
Gresham Books 46
Grevatt & Grevatt 46
Grey Seal Books 47
Grosvenor Books 47
Halban (Peter) Publishers 48
Harcourt Brace Jovanovich Ltd 48
HarperCollins Publishers Ltd 49
Hodder & Stoughton Ltd 52
Hunt & Thorpe 53
Inter Publishing Ltd 53
James (Arthur) Ltd 54
Kingsway Publications 56
Lion Publishing 58
Lutterworth Press, The 60
Octagon Press Ltd 68
Paternoster Press Ltd 70
Polity Press 75
Routledge, Chapman & Hall Ltd 81
St Paul Publications 82
SCM Press Ltd 83
Scottish Academic Press 84
Search Press Ltd/Burns & Oates Ltd 84
Shepheard-Walwyn (Publishers) Ltd 85

Society for Promoting Christian Knowledge (SPCK) 86
Souvenir Press Ltd 87
Stainer & Bell Ltd 88

Religion & Theology: Agents (UK)
Abacus Literary Agency 159
Anderson (Darley) Books 159
Bolt (David) Associates 160
Howard Seddon Associates 168

Religion & Theology: Magazines
Catholic Herald 229
Challenge 230
Christian Herald 231
Church of England Newspaper 231
Church Times 232
Contemporary Review 233
Logos, The Welsh Theological Review 260
Sign, The 284
Tablet, The 288
Theologia Cambrensis 289
Universe, The 292

Religion & Theology: Television
Carlton Television 308
Meridian Broadcasting 311
Westcountry Television Ltd 312

Religion & Theology: Film, T and video producers
Mosaic Film & Video Production 362
Tern Television Productions Ltd 370

Religion & Theology: Publishers (US)
Abingdon Press 436
CSS Publishing Co. 441
Dimensions for Living 442
Eerdmans (William B.) Publishing Co. 442
Harvest House Publishers 444
NavPress Publishing Group 447
Open Court Publishing Co. 448
Paragon House Publishers 449
Princeton University Press 450
Random House, Inc. 450
Tennessee (University of) Press 452
Trinity Press International 453

Religion & Theology: Agents (US)
Brandenburgh & Associates Literary Agency 457
Browne (Pema) Ltd 457
Living Faith Literary Agency 468
New Age World Services & Books 470

Religion & Theology: Prizes
Collins Biennial Religious Book Award 547
Deo Gloria Award 549
Stanford (Winifred Mary) Prize, The 568

Religion & Theology: Libraries
Catholic Central Library 581
Library of the Religious Society of Friends 590
Liverpool City Libraries 586
National Library of Scotland 587
Penzance Library 589
Williams's (Dr) Library 594

Religion & Theology: Picture Libraries
Ancient Art and Architecture Collection 599
Andes Press Agency 599
Circa Photo Library 604
Dixon (C M) 605
Fairclough (Chris) Colour Library 607
Financial Times Picture Collection 607
Halliday (Sonia) Photographs 610
Hutchison Library, The 611
Impact Photos 612
Monitor Syndication 615
Photo Resources 617
Young (John Robert) Collection 627

Religion & Theology: Small Presses
Chapter Two 135
Romer Publications 145
Stride 146
Tyrannosaurus Rex Press 147

Religion & Theology: European Publishers
Abadia de Montserrat (Publicaciones de l') 430
Adelphi Edizioni SpA 422
Ambo (Uitgeverij) BV 425
Ansgar Forlag A/S 427
Ark Boeken Publishing House 425

Armado (Armenio), Editore de Simoes, Belrao & Cia Lda 429
Aubier-Montaigne (Editions) SA 415
Beck (Verlag C H) 418
Benziger AG 434
Borgens Forlag A/S 412
Cappelli (Nuova Casa Editrice Licinio) SpA 422
Carinthia, Universitätsverlag 410
Città Nuova Editrice 423
Davidsfonds VZW 411
Det Norske Samlaget 428
Droz (Librairie) SA 434
D T V Deutscher Taschenbuch Verlag GmbH & Co KG 419
Econ-Verlag GmbH 419
E U N S A (Ediciones Universidad de Navarra SA) 431
Fayard (Librarie Arthème) 416
G.E.C. Gad Publishers 413
Gruyter (Walter de) & Co 419
Herder (Verlag) GmbH & Co KG 420
Istituto Geografico de Agostini SpA 423
Jaca Book (Editoriale) 424
Kohlhammer (Verlag W) GmbH 420
Kok (Uitgeversmaatschappij J H) BV 426
Laffont (Editions Robert) 417
Lalli (Antonio) Editore 424
Lannoo (Uitgeverij) Drukkerij 412
Laterza (Giuseppe) e Figli SpA 424
Lohses Forlag 414
Longanesi & C 424
Mondadori (Arnoldo) Editore SpA 424
Nelissen (Uitgeverij H) BV 426
Nyt Nordisk Forlag Arnold Busck A/S 414
Presses Universitaires de France (PUF) 418
RCS Rizzoli Libri SpA 425
S A I E Editrice SRL 425
S E I (Società Editrice Internazionale) 425
Seuil (Editions du) 418
Styria (Verlag) 411
Table Ronde (Les Editions de la) 418
Tyrolia (Verlagsanstalt) Gesellschaft mbH 411
Ugo (Gruppo) Mursia Editore SpA 425
V U Boekhandel/Uitgeverij BV 427

Romantic Fiction: Publishers (UK)
Gay Men's Press (GMP Publishers Ltd), The 44
Mills & Boon Ltd 64
Severn House Publishers 85

Romantic Fiction: Agents (UK)
Abacus Literary Agency 159
Clarke (Serafina) 162
Drexl (Anne) 165
Pollinger (Laurence) Ltd 174

Romantic Fiction: Magazines
Loving 261

Romantic Fiction: Publishers (US)
Avalon Books 438
Avon Books 438
Bantam Doubleday Dell Publishing Group 438
Dorchester Publishing Co., Inc. 442
Evans (M.) & Co., Inc. 442
Simon & Schuster 451

Romantic Fiction: Agents (US)
Acton & Dystel 455
Anthony (Joseph) Agency 455
Browne (Pema) Ltd 457
Creative Concepts Literary Agency 459
Deering Literary Agency, The 460
Ellenberg (Ethan), Literary Agency, The 461
Elmo (Ann) Agency, Inc. 461
Herner (Susan) Rights Agency, Inc. 464
Jane $Rotrosen Agency 474
Jarvis (Sharon) and Co., Inc. 464
Kern (Natasha) Literary Agency, Inc. 464
Kidde, Hoyt & Picard Literary Agency 465
Lee (L. Harry) Literary Agency 466
Leone (Adele) Agency, Inc. 466
Literary/Business Associates 467
MacCampbell (Donald), Inc. 468
Panettieri Agency, The 471
Pegasus International, Inc. 471
Picard (Alison J.) Literary Agent 472
Schulman (Susan) Literary Agency 475
Shore (Lee) Agency 475
Sierra Literary Agency 476
Singer Media Corporation 476
Southern Writers 476

Weiner (Cherry) Literary Agency 479

Zelasky (Tom) Literary Agency 481

Romantic Fiction: Professional Associations
Romantic Novelists' Association, The 501

Romantic Fiction: Prizes
Romantic Novelists' Association Major Award 564
Romantic Novelists' Association/Netta Muskett Award 565

Royal Family: Publishers (UK)
Berkswell Publishing Co. Ltd 17
O'Mara (Michael) Books Limited 68
Reed International Books 78

Royal Family: Packagers
Berkswell Publishing Co. Ltd 149

Royal Family: Magazines
Hello! 252
Royal Dempster's 280
Weekly News 294

Royal Family: Picture Libraries
All-Action Picture Library 599
Camera Press 602
Express Newspapers Picture Library 607
Frith (Francis) Collection 608
Hulton Picture Company, The 611
Hunt (Robert) Library, The 611
London Features International Ltd 614
Monitor Syndication 615
Newsfocus Press Photograph Agency Ltd 616
Popperfoto 618
Rex Features Ltd 620
Syndication International 623
Topham Picture Source 623
Universal Pictorial Press & Agency Ltd 624
Weimar Archive 625
Woodmansterne Ltd 626

Russia & Soviet Studies: Publishers (UK)
Routledge, Chapman & Hall Ltd 81
Tauris (I.B.) & Co. Ltd 90

Russia & Soviet Studies: Agents (UK)
O'Leary (David) Literary Agents 173

Russia & Soviet Studies: Film, TV and video producers
Poseidon Productions Ltd 365

Russia & Soviet Studies: Publishers (US)
Texas (University of) Press 452

Russia & Soviet Studies: Picture Libraries
Dixon (C M) 605
Evans (Mary) Picture Library 606
USSR Photo Library 624
Weimar Archive 625

Safety: Film, TV and video producers
Adam Video Productions 337
AVC Group 339
Broadcast Communications 341
Chapel Broadcast Productions Ltd 343
DBI Communication 347
Fitting Images Ltd 350
Skippon Video Associates 368

Safety: Publishers (US)
Van Nostrand Reinhold 453

Safety: Picture Libraries
RoSPA (Royal Society for the Prevention of Accidents) 620

Scandinavia: Picture Libraries
Axel Poignant Archive 601
Thurston (Patrick) PhotoLibrary 623

Scandinavia: Small Presses
Hisarlik Press 139
Norvik Press Ltd 142

Science: Publishers (UK)
Athlone Press, The 14
Blackwell Scientific Publications Ltd 19
Cambridge University Press 24
Cassell 25
Elsevier Science Publishers Ltd 38
Gordon & Breach Science Publishers 45
Harvard University Press 50
Oxford University Press 70
Penny Press 72

Routledge, Chapman & Hall Ltd 81
Sangam Books Ltd 82
Tarragon Press 90
Ward Lock Educational 94
Wiley (John) & Sons Ltd 96

Science: Packagers
Brown Wells and Jacobs Ltd 150
Lionheart Books 153
New England Editions Ltd 154

Science: Agents (UK)
Bryan (Felicity) 160
Davidson (Caroline) and Robert Ducas Literary Agency 164
O'Leary (David) Literary Agents 173
Watson, Little Ltd* 179
Wiener (Dinah) Ltd 179

Science: Magazines
Mensa Magazine 263
Nature 268
New Scientist 269

Science: Film, TV and video producers
BFV Ltd 340
Dragon Communications Ltd 347
Illuminations 356
London Scientific Films 359
Meditel Productions Ltd 360

Science: Publishers (US)
Addison-Wesley Publishing Co., Inc. 436
Carol Publishing 440
Harcourt Brace Jovanovich 443
Houghton Mifflin Co. 444
Iowa State University Press 445
Krieger Publishing Co., Inc. 445
Little, Brown & Co., Inc. 445
Open Court Publishing Co. 448
Plenum Publishing 449
Simon & Schuster 451
Times Books 453
Walker & Co 453

Science: Agents (US)
Authors Resource Center & Tarc Literary Agency, The 456
Boates (Reid) Literary Agency 45
Carvainis (Maria) Agency, Inc. 457
Catalog Literary Agency, The 458
Chester (Linda) Literary Agency 458
Dijkstra (Sandra) Literary Agency 460

Ellenberg (Ethan), Literary
Agency, The 461
Kern (Natasha) Literary Agency,
Inc. 464
Leone (Adele) Agency, Inc. 466
Lincoln (Ray) Literary Agency 467
Multimedia Product Development,
Inc. 470
New England Publishing
Associates, Inc. 470
Noetzli (Regula) Literary Agency
471
Protter (Susan Ann) Literary
Agent 472
Schulman (Susan) Literary Agency
475
Sebastian Agency 475
Spieler Literary Agency 477
Van der Leun & Associates 478
Ware (John A.) Literary Agency
479
Waterside Productions, Inc. 479
Writers House, Inc. 480

**Science: Professional
Associations**
Association of British Science
Writers (ABSW) 489

**Science:
Bursaries/Fellowships**
Economist/Richard Casement
Internship, The 536
Glaxo Science Writers'
Fellowships 537

Science: Prizes
Mackenzie (Agnes Mure) Award
558
Science Book Prizes 566

Science: Libraries
Liverpool City Libraries 586
Newcastle upon Tyne Central
Library 588
Royal Society Library 591
Science Museum Library 591
Sheffield Libraries and
Information Services 591

Science: Picture Libraries
Coleman (Bruce) Wildlife &
Travel Photo Library 604
Comstock Photofile Ltd 604
Financial Times Picture Collection
607
Network Photographers 616
Rex Features Ltd 620
Ronan (Ann) Picture Library 620
Science Photo Library 620

Science: European Publishers
Adelphi Edizioni SpA 422
Age d'Homme - La Cité (Editions
L') 433
Alhambra (Editorial) SA 430
Alianza Editorial SA 430
Almqvist och Wiksell International
432
Belin (Editions) 415
Bogans Forlag 412
Bompiana 422
Bosch Casa Editorial SA 430
Braun (Verlag G) GmbH 419
Brill (A J) 426
Brockhaus (F A) 419
Brombergs Bokförlag AB 433
Bulzoni Editore SRL (Le Edizioni
Universitarie d'Italia) 422
Calderini (Edizioni) 422
CEDAM (Casa Editrice Dr A
Milani) 423
Delagrave Sàrl (Librarie) 416
Deutsch (Verlag Harri) 419
Didactica Editora 429
Dom Quixote (Publicacoes) Lda
429
Droemersche Verlagsanstalt Th
Knaur Nachf 419
D T V Deutscher Taschenbuch
Verlag GmbH & Co KG 419
Econ-Verlag GmbH 419
Elsevier 426
Empeño (Editoria) 431
Europa-America (Publicaoes) Lda
429
Fabbri (Gruppo Editoriale) SpA
423
Fayard (Librarie Arthème) 416
Flammarion et Cie 416
G.E.C. Gad Publishers 413
Giunti Publishing Group 423
Gradiva - Publicacoes Lda 429
Gruyter (Walter de) & Co 419
Gyldendalske Boghandel, Nordisk
Forlag A/S 413
Hachette 416
Hallwag Verlag AG 434
Hanser (Carl) Verlag 420
Hoffmann und Campe Verlag 420
Jover (Ediciones) SA 431
Karger (S) GmbH 420
Klincksieck (Editions) 417
Kluwer Academic Publishers BV
426
Kohlhammer (Verlag W) GmbH
420
Kok (Uitgeversmaatschappij J H)
BV 426
Laffont (Editions Robert) 417
Larousse (Librairie) 417

Laterza (Giuseppe) e Figli SpA
424
Levrotto e Bella Libreria Editrice
Universitaria SAS 424
Liguori Editore SRL 424
Longanesi & C 424
Mondadori (Arnoldo) Editore SpA
424
Mondadori Espana SA 432
Nathan (Fernand) 418
Natur och Kultur (Bokförlaget)
433
Oldenbourg (R) Verlag GmbH
421
Österreichischer Bundesverlag
Gesellschaft mbH 411
Payot Lausanne (Editions) 435
Presses Universitaires de France
(PUF) 418
Rhodos, International Science
and Art Publishers 414
S A I E Editrice SRL 425
Sauerlander AG 435
S E I (Società Editrice
Internationale) 425
Seuil (Editions du) 418
70 (Edições) Lda 430
Solum Forlag A/S 428
Spectrum (Uitgeverij Het) BV 427
Springer-Verlag 411
Standaard Uitgeverij 412
Suhrkamp Verlag 421
Swets en Zeitlinger BV 427
Thieme (Georg) Verlag 421
Time-Life Books BV 427
Trauner (Rudolf) Verlag 411
Tusquets Editores 432
Ugo (Gruppo) Mursia Editore SpA
425
Ullstein (Buchverlage) GmbH 421
Universitetsforlaget 428
Vanderlinden (Librairie) SA 412
Verbo (Editorial) SA 430
Vindrose (Forlaget) A/S 415
V U Boekhandel/Uitgeverij BV
427
Vuibert (Librairie) SA 418
West-Friesland (Uit-Mij) 427

**Science Fiction/Fantasy:
Publishers (UK)**
Dragon's World 35
Gay Men's Press (GMP Publishers
Ltd), The 44
Gollancz (Victor) Ltd 45
Little, Brown & Co. (UK) Ltd 59
Orion Publishing Group 69
Penguin Books Ltd 71
Random House Publishing Group
Ltd 76

Robinson Publishing 80
Severn House Publishers 85
Titan Books 91
Women's Press, The 96

**Science Fiction/Fantasy:
Agents (UK)**
Carnell Literary Agency* 161
Dorian Literary Agency 164
Doyle (Colleen) 165
Martin (Judy) 171

**Science Fiction/Fantasy:
Magazines**
Back Brain Recluse (BBR) 222
Foundation: The Review of
Science Fiction 247
Interzone: Science Fiction &
Fantasy 257
Matrix 263
New Moon Science Fiction 269
Paperback Inferno 272
Vector 293
Xenos 300

**Science Fiction/Fantasy:
Publishers (US)**
Avon Books 438
Baen Books 438
Bantam Doubleday Dell
Publishing Group 438
Berkley Publishing Group 439
Carroll & Graf Publishers, Inc. 440
DAW Books, Inc. 441
Random House, Inc. 450
Simon & Schuster 451

**Science Fiction/Fantasy:
Agents (US)**
Appleseeds Management 455
Creative Concepts Literary
Agency 459
Deering Literary Agency, The 460
Dijkstra (Sandra) Literary Agency
460
Ellenberg (Ethan), Literary
Agency, The 461
Evans & Associates 461
Gladden Unlimited 463
Hawkins (John) & Associates, Inc.
463
Herner (Susan) Rights Agency,
Inc. 464
King (Daniel P.) 465
Lee Allan Agency, The 466
Lee (L. Harry) Literary Agency
466
Leone (Adele) Agency, Inc. 466
McBride (Margret) Literary
Agency 468

Morrison (Henry) Inc. 470
Pegasus International, Inc. 471
Protter (Susan Ann) Literary
Agent 472
Shore (Lee) Agency 475
Siegel (Bobbe), Literary Agency
475
Weiner (Cherry) Literary Agency
479

**Science Fiction/Fantasy:
Professional Associations**
British Science Fiction
Association 494
Science Fiction Foundation 501

**Science Fiction/Fantasy:
Prizes**
British Fantasy Awards 546
British Science Fiction Award 546
Clarke (Arthur C.) Award for
Science Fiction 547

**Science Fiction/Fantasy:
Libraries**
Science Fiction Foundation
Research Library 591

**Science Fiction/Fantasy:
Picture Libraries**
Art Resource Illustration Library
600

**Science Fiction/Fantasy:
Small Presses**
Galactic Central Publications 138
Hilltop Press 139
Works Publishing 147

**Science Fiction/Fantasy:
Festivals**
Cardiff Literature Festival 404

**Science Fiction/Fantasy:
Literary Societies**
British Fantasy Society 507

**Science Fiction/Fantasy:
European Publishers**
Calmann-Lévy (Editions) SA 415
Denoël (Editions) Sàrl 416
Heyne (Wilhelm) Verlag 420
Lübbe (Gustav) Verlag GmbH 420
Meulenhoff International 426
Miraguano SA Ediciones 432
Presses de la Cité, Les 418
70 (Edições) Lda 430
Spectrum (Uitgeverij Het) BV 427
Todariana Editrice 425

**Scientific & Technical:
Publishers (UK)**
Addison–Wesley Publishers Ltd
10
Elsevier Science Publishers Ltd
Hodder & Stoughton Ltd 52
Kluwer Academic Publishers 56
Macmillan Publishers Ltd 61
MIT Press Ltd, The 65
Plenum Publishing Ltd 74
Reed International Books 78
Wiley (John) & Sons Ltd 96

**Scientific & Technical:
Packagers**
MM Productions Ltd 154

**Scientific & Technical:
Publishers (US)**
Van Nostrand Reinhold 453

**Scientific & Technical: Agen
(US)**
Mews Books Ltd 469

**Scientific & Technical:
Libraries**
Newcastle Literary and
Philosophical Society Library
588

**Scientific & Technical:
European Publishers**
Ceac (Ediciones) SA 430
Delagrave Sàrl (Librarie) 416
Deutsch (Verlag Harri) 419
Europa-America (Publicaoes) L
429
Larousse (Librairie) 417
Masson Editeur 417
Parey (Verlag Paul) 421
Springer-Verlag GmbH & Co KC
421

**Scotland/Scottish Interest:
Publishers (UK)**
Aberdeen University Press 9
Acair Ltd 10
Brown, Son & Ferguson, Ltd 23
Chambers (W & R) 27
Chapman 27
Edinburgh University Press 37
Lochar Publishing Ltd 59
Mercat Press 63
Ramsay Head Press, The 76
Shepheard-Walwyn (Publishers
Ltd 85
St John Thomas (David) Publish
82

Scotland/Scottish Interest:
Agents (UK)
Denniston & Lownie 164
Jarvie (Gordon), Literary Agent
169

Scotland/Scottish Interest:
Magazines
Chapman 230
Edinburgh Review 240
Scotland's Runner 281
Scots Magazine, The 281
Scottish Farmer, The 281
Scottish Field 281
Scottish Football Today 282
Scottish Golf Magazine 282
Scottish Home & Country 282
*Times Educational Supplement
Scotland, The* 290

Scotland/Scottish Interest:
Theatre producers
Communicado Theatre Company
380
Theatre Workshop Edinburgh 397
Tron Theatre Company 398
Winged Horse Touring
Productions 399

Scotland/Scottish Interest:
Agents (US)
ForthWrite Literary Agency 462

Scotland/Scottish Interest:
Professional Associations
Book Trust Scotland 492
Scottish Newspaper Publishers'
Association 502
Scottish Print Employers'
Federation 502
Scottish Publishers Association,
The 502

Scotland/Scottish Interest:
Prizes
Berry (David) Prize 544
Mackenzie (Agnes Mure) Award
558
McVitie's Prize for Scottish Writer
of the Year 559
People's Prize, The 563
Scottish Arts Council Book
Awards 566
Scottish Book of the Year 566

Scotland/Scottish Interest:
Libraries
National Library of Scotland 587
Scottish Poetry Library 591

Scotland/Scottish Interest:
Picture Libraries
Alba Pictures 598
Aviemore Photographic Scotland
600
Baxter (Colin) Photography Ltd
601
Brown (Hamish) Scottish
Photographic 602
Edinburgh Photographic Library
606
Garland (Leslie) Picture Library
609
Henderson (Jim) Photographer
610
Moving Picture Library, The 622
Outram (George) Picture Library
617
Scottish Highland Photo Library,
The 621
Williams (David) Picture Library
626

Scotland/Scottish Interest:
Small Presses
Forth Naturalist & Historian 138
Luath Press Ltd 141

Scotland/Scottish Interest:
Editorial Services
Jarvie (Gordon) Editorial 532

Self-Help: Publishers (UK)
Gateway Books 43
How To Books Ltd 53
Letts (Charles) & Co. Ltd 58
Routledge, Chapman & Hall Ltd
81
Society for Promoting Christian
Knowledge (SPCK) 86

Self-Help: Packagers
Marshall Editions Ltd 153

Self-Help: Agents (UK)
Fox & Howard Literary Agency
166
Kelly (Frances) 169
Power (Shelley) Literary Agency
Ltd 174
Watson, Little Ltd* 179

Self-Help: Publishers (US)
Adams (Bob) Publishers, Inc. 436
Avery Publishing Group, Inc. 438
Avon Books 438
Carol Publishing 440
Dimensions for Living 442
Gardner Press, Inc. 443
Llewellyn Publications 446

Random House, Inc. 450
Rosen Publishing Group, Inc., The
450
St Martin's Press, Inc. 451
TAB Books 452
Walker & Co 453
Warner Books 453

Self-Help: Agents (US)
Appleseeds Management 455
Authors Resource Center & Tarc
Literary Agency, The 456
Boates (Reid) Literary Agency 457
Catalog Literary Agency, The 458
Chester (Linda) Literary Agency
458
Creative Concepts Literary
Agency 459
Dijkstra (Sandra) Literary Agency
460
Elmo (Ann) Agency, Inc. 461
ForthWrite Literary Agency 462
Fuhrman (Candice) Literary
Agency 462
Garon-Brooke (Jay) Associates,
Inc. 463
Kern (Natasha) Literary Agency,
Inc. 464
Lazear Agency, Inc., The 466
Lee Allan Agency, The 466
Literary & Creative Artists Agency
467
Living Faith Literary Agency 468
Marcil (Denise) Literary Agency,
Inc. 469
Multimedia Product Development,
Inc. 470
Nelson (B.K.) Literary Agency 470
New Age World Services & Books
470
Quicksilver Books, Literary Agents
473
Sebastian Agency 475
Shepard Agency, The 475
Shore (Lee) Agency 475
Sierra Literary Agency 476
Singer Media Corporation 476
Snell (Michael) Literary Agency
476
Steele (Lyle) & Co. Ltd 477
Writer's Consulting Group 480

Self-Help: Small Presses
Whyld Publishing Co-op 147

**Self-Help: European
Publishers**
Casterman (Editions) 415
Droemersche Verlagsanstalt Th
Knaur Nachf 419

Sex: Publishers (UK)
Reed International Books 78
Sheba Feminist Press 85

Sex: Magazines
New Woman 270
Penthouse 273

Sex: Agents (US)
Snell (Michael) Literary Agency
476

Sex: Small Presses
Mandrake 141

Short Stories: Publishers (UK)
Chapman 27
Commonword Ltd 30
Yorkshire Arts Circus Ltd 97

Short Stories: Magazines
Acumen 217
Best 223
Good Stories 250
Literary Review 260
London Review of Books 261
Mosaic 265
People's Friend, The 273
Quartos Magazine 277
Scottish Field 281
Stand Magazine 286
Sunk Island Review 287
Tees Valley Writer 289
Woman's Own 298
Woman's Realm 298
Woman's Weekly 298
Working Titles 299
Writers' Monthly 299

Short Stories: Publishers (US)
Chronicle Books 440
Illinois (University of) Press 444
Iowa (University of) Press 445
Louisiana State University Press
446
Missouri (University of) Press 447
New England (University Press of)
448

Short Stories: Prizes
Bates (H. E.) Short Story
Competition 543
Bridport Arts Centre Creative
Writing Competition 545
Carmarthen Writers' Circle Short
Story Competition 546
Commonwealth Writers Prize 548
Davies (Rhys) Award 549
Gemmell (David) Cup 552

Higham (David) Prize for Fiction
554
Irish Times-Aer Lingus
International Fiction Prize 555
Irish Times Aer Lingus Irish
Literature Prizes 555
Macmillan Silver Pen Award 558
Mail on Sunday/John Llewellyn
Rhys Prize, The 559
Markham (Arthur) Memorial Prize
559
Northern Stories Award 562
St James (Ian) Awards 566
Smith Corona Prize 567
Stand Magazine Short Story
Competition 568
Wandsworth Writers London
Competition 571
Young Writers' Competition 573

Short Stories: Small Presses
Businesslike Publishing 135
Dark Diamonds Publications 136
Feather Books 137

Short Stories: Festivals
Write Around – A Celebration of
Cleveland Writing 409

**Show Business: Publishers
(UK)**
Solo Books Ltd 87
Virgin Publishing 93

Show Business: Agents (UK)
Aquarius Literary Agency &
Picture Library 159
Chilcote (Judith) Agency 161
Futerman (Vernon) Associates
166
Pawsey (John) 173
Peters Fraser & Dunlop Group
Ltd* 174

Show Business: Magazines
Hello! 252
Titbits 291
Weekly News 294

Show Business: Television
GMTV 309

Show Business: Agents (US)
Acton & Dystel 455
Andrews (Bart) & Associates 455
Dykeman Associates, Inc. 460
Kern (Natasha) Literary Agency,
Inc. 464
Miller (Peter) Agency, Inc., The
469

Nathan (Ruth) Agency 470
Singer (Evelyn) Literary Agency,
Inc., The 476

**Show Business: Picture
Libraries**
Ace Photo Agency 598
All-Action Picture Library 599
Camera Press 602
Dominic Photography 605
Express Newspapers Picture
Library 607
Hunt (Robert) Library, The 611
Kobal Collection, The 613
London Features International L
614
Monitor Syndication 615
Retna Pictures Ltd 619
Rex Features Ltd 620
Spooner (Frank) Pictures 622
Sygma 623
Syndication International 623
Vintage Magazine Company Ltd
The 624

Social Work: Publishers (UK
Ashgate Publishing Co. Ltd 13
Batsford (B.T.) Ltd 16
James (Arthur) Ltd 54
NCVO Publications 66

Social Work: Publishers (US
Gardner Press, Inc. 443

Socialism: Publishers (UK)
Bookmarks Publications 20
Merlin Press Ltd 64
Pluto Press Ltd 75

**Sociology/Social Issues:
Publishers (UK)**
Ashgate Publishing Co. Ltd 13
Athlone Press, The 14
Berg Publishers Ltd 17
Blackwell Publishers 18
Boyars (Marion) Publishers Ltd ?
Calder Publications Ltd 23
Cambridge University Press 24
Clare (John) Books 28
Claridge Press 29
Clio Press Ltd 29
Columbia University Press 30
Constable & Co. Ltd 30
Currey (James) Publishers 32
Curzon Press Ltd 32
Donald (John) Publishers Ltd 35
Edinburgh University Press 37
Elgar (Edward) Publishing Ltd 3
Freeman (W. H.) & Co. Ltd 42
Golden Cockerel Press Ltd 44

Gordon & Breach Science
Publishers 45
Graham-Cameron Publishing 46
Harcourt Brace Jovanovich Ltd 48
Harvard University Press 50
Hurst (C.) & Co. 53
Jai Press Ltd 54
Kingsley (Jessica) Publishers Ltd
56
Liverpool University Press 59
Macmillan Publishers Ltd 61
Manchester University Press 62
MIT Press Ltd, The 65
Open Gate Press 68
Open University Press 69
Owen (Peter) Ltd 69
Oxford University Press 70
Pergamon Press 73
Pinter Publishers Ltd 74
Pluto Press Ltd 75
Polity Press 75
Random House Publishing Group
Ltd 76
Routledge, Chapman & Hall Ltd
81
Sangam Books Ltd 82
Scottish Academic Press 84
Souvenir Press Ltd 87
Trentham Books Ltd 92
Verso Ltd 93
Wales (University of) Press 94

**Sociology/Social Issues:
Packagers**
Albion Press Ltd, The 148
Cameron Books (Production) Ltd
150
Wordwright Books 156

**Sociology/Social Issues:
Agents (UK)**
Davis-Poynter (Reg) 164
Holt (Vanessa) Associates Ltd 168
Howard Seddon Associates 168
Reynolds (Jim) Associates 175
Robertson (Patricia) 175
Sayle (Tessa) Agency 176

**Sociology/Social Issues: Film,
TV and video producers**
Meditel Productions Ltd 360
Mosaic Film & Video Productions
362

**Sociology/Social Issues:
Publishers (US)**
Academy Chicago Publishers 436
Arkansas (University of) Press 438
Eerdmans (William B.) Publishing
Co. 442

Iowa State University Press 445
Kansas (University of) Press 445
Longman Publishing Group 446
Massachusetts (University of)
Press 447
New England (University Press of)
448
Plenum Publishing 449
Random House, Inc. 450
Schocken Books, Inc. 451
Stanford University Press 452
Temple University Press 452
Texas (University of) Press 452

**Sociology/Social Issues:
Agents (US)**
Casselman (Martha), Literary
Agent 458
Mann (Carol) Agency 468
Multimedia Product Development,
Inc. 470
Popkin/Cooke 472
Schulman (Susan) Literary Agency
475
Schwartz (Laurens R.) 475
Spieler Literary Agency 477
Steele (Lyle) & Co. Ltd 477
Stern (Gloria) Agency (New York)
477

**Sociology/Social Issues:
Bursaries/Fellowships**
Blundell (K.) Trust, The 535
British Academy Small Personal
Research Grants 536

**Sociology/Social Issues:
Prizes**
Irish Times-Aer Lingus
International Fiction Prize 555
Odd Fellows (Manchester Unity)
Social Concern Book Award
562
Williams (Raymond) Community
Publishing Prize 572

**Sociology/Social Issues:
Libraries**
Barbican Library 577
British Library Reading Room 580
Fawcett Library 583
Hatfield Polytechnic Library 584
Sheffield Libraries and
Information Services 591

**Sociology/Social Issues:
Picture Libraries**
Andes Press Agency 599
Birdsall (John) Photographic
Library 601

Coleman (Bruce) Wildlife &
Travel Photo Library 604
Eye Ubiquitous 607
Financial Times Picture Collection
607
Fotomas Index, The 608
Hoffman (David) Photo Library
611
Hulton Picture Company, The 611
Illustrated London News Picture
Library 612
MacQuitty International
Photographic Collection 614
Network Photographers 616
Photofusion 617
Popperfoto 618
Wiedel (Janine) 625

**Sociology/Social Issues: Small
Presses**
Daniels Publishing 136
Dark Diamonds Publications 136
Fortress Books 138
Logaston Press 141
Tufnell Press, The 146
Zzero Books 147

**Sociology/Social Issues:
European Publishers**
Age d'Homme – La Cité (Editions
L') 433
Alianza Editorial SA 430
Ambo (Uitgeverij) BV 425
Armado (Armenio), Editore de
Simoes, Belrao & Cia Lda 429
Armando Armando (Editore) SRL
422
Aubier-Montaigne (Editions) SA
415
Beck (Verlag C H) 418
Bertrand Editora Lda 429
Born NV Uitgeversmaatschappij
426
Bulzoni Editore SRL (Le Edizioni
Universitarie d'Italia) 422
Calmann-Lévy (Editions) SA 415
Caminho (Editorial) SARL 429
CEDAM (Casa Editrice Dr A
Milani) 423
Città Nuova Editrice 423
Davidsfonds VZW 411
Découverte, La 416
Diesterweg (Verlag Moritz) 419
Dom Quixote (Publicacoes) Lda
429
Droz (Librairie) SA 434
D T V Deutscher Taschenbuch
Verlag GmbH & Co KG 419
Econ-Verlag GmbH 419
Empeño (Editoria) 431

Europa-America (Publicaoes) Lda 429
Europa Verlag GmbH 410
Fayard (Librairie Arthème) 416
Fischer (S) Verlag GmbH 419
Flammarion et Cie 416
Francisci (Aldo) Editore 423
Fundamentos (Editorial) 431
Gedisa (Editorial) SA 431
Grijalbo SA 431
Gyldendalske Boghandel, Nordisk Forlag A/S 413
Hachette 416
Haufe (Rudolf) Verlag GmbH & Co KG 420
Hoffmann und Campe Verlag 420
Horizonte (Livros) Lda 429
Hovedland (Forlaget) 413
Jaca Book (Editoriale) 424
Klett-Cotta Verlag 420
Klincksieck (Editions) 417
Kok (Uitgeversmaatschappij J H) BV 426
Laffont (Editions Robert) 417
Laia (Editorial) SA 431
Lalli (Antonio) Editore 424
Larousse (Librairie) 417
Laterza (Giuseppe) e Figli SpA 424
Liber AB 433
Liguori Editore SRL 424
Longanesi & C 424
Masson Editeur 417
Métaillié (A.M.) 417
Minuit (Les Editions de) SA 418
Mulino (Societe Editrice Il) 425
Nathan (Fernand) 418
Nelissen (Uitgeverij H) BV 426
Nyt Nordisk Forlag Arnold Busck A/S 414
Oldenbourg (R) Verlag GmbH 421
Presses Universitaires de France (PUF) 418
Rabén och Sjögren Bokforlag AB 433
RCS Rizzoli Libri SpA 425
Rhodos, International Science and Art Publishers 414
Sauerlander AG 435
S E I (Società Editrice Internationale) 425
Seuil (Editions du) 418
70 (Edições) Lda 430
Table Ronde (Les Editions de la) 418
Tiden (Bokförlags) AB 433
Time-Life Books BV 427
Todariana Editrice 425
Tusquets Editores 432

Ugo (Gruppo) Mursia Editore SpA 425
Ullstein (Buchverlage) GmbH 421
Vindrose (Forlaget) A/S 415
V U Boekhandel/Uitgeverij BV 427

Sound: Libraries
British Library National Sound Archive 580
Imperial War Museum 585

South America: Picture Libraries
Colasanti (Stephanie) 604
Cunningham (Sue) 605
Hanley (Tom) 610
Lupe Cunha Photos 614
South American Pictures 621

Space: Picture Libraries
Art Directors Photo Library 600
Aspect Picture Library Ltd 600
Cash (J. Allan) Ltd 603
Dixon (C M) 605
Galaxy Picture Library 609
Genesis Space Photo Library 609
Harding (Robert) Picture Library 610
Science Photo Library 620
Sefton Photo Library 621
Telegraph Colour Library, The 623
Woodmansterne Ltd 626

Spain/Hispanic Interest: Publishers (UK)
Aris & Phillips Ltd 13
Dolphin Book Co. Ltd 35
Liverpool University Press 59

Spain/Hispanic Interest: Publishers (US)
Nevada (University of) Press 447

Spain/Hispanic Interest: Libraries
Spanish Institute Library 592

Spain/Hispanic Interest: Picture Libraries
Cunningham (Sue) 605
Strang (Jessica) Library 622
Travel Library, The 623
Wright (George) 626

Sport & Fitness: Publishers (UK)
Acair Ltd 10
Associated Publicity Holdings Ltd 14

Barracuda Books Ltd/Quotes Ltd 15
Batsford (B.T.) Ltd 16
Black (A. & C.) (Publishers) Ltd 18
Book Guild, The 20
Boxtree 20
Cassell 25
Crowood Press Ltd, The 32
Darf Publishers Ltd 33
Donald (John) Publishers Ltd 35
Foulsham (W.) & Co. 42
Gollancz (Victor) Ltd 45
Guinness Publishing Ltd 47
Haynes Publishing Group 50
Headline Book Publishing 50
Kime Publishing 55
Lochar Publishing Ltd 59
Macmillan Publishers Ltd 61
Mainstream Publishing Co. (Edinburgh) Ltd 62
Pavilion Books Ltd 71
Penguin Books Ltd 71
Quiller Press 76
Random House Publishing Group Ltd 76
Reed International Books 78
Robson Books Ltd 81
Salamander Books Ltd 82
Souvenir Press Ltd 87
Springfield Books Ltd 88
Thornhill Press 91
Transworld Publishers Ltd 91

Sport & Fitness: Packagers
Autumn Publishing Ltd 149
Bison Books Ltd 149
Breslich & Foss 150
Lennard Books 153
MM Productions Ltd 154
Wordwright Books 156

Sport & Fitness: Agents (UK)
Chris (Teresa) Literary Agency 162
Fox & Howard Literary Agency 166
Pawsey (John) 173
Reynolds (Jim) Associates 175
Simmons (Jeffrey) 177
Solo Syndication & Literary Agency Ltd 177

Sport & Fitness: Magazines
Amateur Golf 218
Athletics Weekly 221
Country Sports 235
Cricketer International, The 236
Cycling Weekly 236
Golf Monthly 249

Golf Weekly 249
Golf World 249
Good Ski Guide 249
*Ice Hockey World and Skating
Review* 256
Netball 268
New Cyclist 268
Racing Pigeon, The 278
Rugby Leaguer 280
Rugby World & Post 280
Running Magazine 280
Scotland's Runner 281
Scottish Golf Magazine 282
Ski Survey 284
Sport and Leisure Magazine 285
Sporting Life, The 286
Sporting Life Weekender 286
Squash Player Magazine 286
Swimming Times 288
Tennis Times, The 289
Tennis World 289
Today's Golfer 291
Today's Runner 291
Wisden Cricket Monthly 297

Sport & Fitness: Television
GMTV 309
Sky Television (BSkyB) 314

**Sport & Fitness: Film, TV and
video producers**
Boney (Matt) Associates 340
Chapel Broadcast Productions Ltd
343
Cheerleader Productions 343
Creative Film Makers Ltd 345
Crystalvision Ltd 346
Ettinger Brothers Productions 349
FM Television Ltd 351
Ideas Factory, The 356
Pilley (Phil) Productions 365
Scope Picture Productions Ltd
367
Tomahawk Films Ltd 371
Worldwide Television News 375

**Sport & Fitness: Publishers
(US)**
Adams (Bob) Publishers, Inc. 436
Avon Books 438
Little, Brown & Co., Inc. 445
McFarland & Company, Inc.,
Publishers 446
NorthWord Press, Inc. 448
Random House, Inc. 450
Sterling Publishing 452
Walker & Co 453

Sport & Fitness: Agents (US)
Acton & Dystel 455

Nelson (B.K.) Literary Agency 470
Siegel (Bobbe), Literary Agency
475
Spitzer (Philip G.) Literary Agency
477
Urstadt (Susan P.), Inc. 478
Ware (John A.) Literary Agency
479
Wieser & Wieser, Inc. 479

**Sport & Fitness: Professional
Associations**
Sports Writers' Association of
Great Britain 504

Sport & Fitness: Prizes
Hill (William) Sports Book of the
Year 554

**Sport & Fitness: Picture
Libraries**
Ace Photo Agency 598
Action Images Ltd 598
Action Plus 598
All-Action Picture Library 599
Allsport (UK) Ltd 599
Art Resource Illustration Library
600
Associated Sports Photography
600
Cash (J. Allan) Ltd 603
Colorsport 604
Dazeley (Peter) Photography 605
Eager (Patrick) Photography 606
Empics Ltd 606
Evans (Greg) International Photo
Library 606
Express Newspapers Picture
Library 607
Eyeline Photography 607
Financial Times Picture Collection
607
Footprints Colour Picture Library
608
Harding (Robert) Picture Library
610
Hobbs Golf Collection 611
Hulton Picture Company, The 611
Hunt (Robert) Library, The 611
Impact Photos 612
Independent Newspaper Picture
Library, The 612
Laubier (André) Picture Library
614
London Features International Ltd
614
Moving Picture Library, The 622
Muscroft (David) Photography
and Picture Library 615
Network Photographers 616

Northern Picture Library, The 616
Outram (George) Picture Library
617
Photographers' Library, The 618
Popperfoto 618
Professional Sport 618
Retna Pictures Ltd 619
Sefton Photo Library 621
Sheldon (Phil) Golf Picture
Library 621
Skishoot Offshoot 621
Spectrum Colour Library 621
Split Second 622
Spooner (Frank) Pictures 622
Sporting Pictures (UK) Ltd 622
Stockfile 622
Stockphotos 622
Stock Shot 622
Stone (Tony) Worldwide 622
Telegraph Colour Library, The 623
Totterdell (B.M.) Photography
623
Universal Pictorial Press & Agency
Ltd 624
Viewfinder Colour Photo Library
624
Whitehead (Eric) Picture Library
and Agency 625
Williams (S & I) Power Pix
International Picture Library
626
Wingfield Sporting Art Library,
The 626

Sport & Fitness: Small Presses
Grant Books 139

**Sport & Fitness: European
Publishers**
Arthaud (Editions) SA 415
B L V Verlagsgesellschaft mbH
419
Calderini (Edizioni) 422
Calmann-Lévy (Editions) SA 415
Denoël (Editions) Sàrl 416
Didactica Editora 429
Gedisa (Editorial) SA 431
Glenat (Editions J.) SA 416
Gremese Editore SRL 423
Hachette 416
Landi (Luciano) Editore SRL 424
Mosaik Verlag 421
Orac Verlag Gesellschaft mbH
411
Payot Lausanne (Editions) 435
Politikens Forlag A/S 414
Sikkel (Uitgeverij De) NV 412
Sperling e Kupfer Editori SpA 425

Technology: Publishers (UK)
Academy Books 10
Gordon & Breach Science
  Publishers 45
Penny Press 72
Routledge, Chapman & Hall Ltd
  81
Sangam Books Ltd 82
Trentham Books Ltd 92

Technology: Packagers
Sheldrake Press Ltd 155

Technology: Publishers (US)
Iowa State University Press 445
Krieger Publishing Co., Inc. 445
Simon & Schuster 451

Technology: Agents (US)
Catalog Literary Agency, The 458
Schwartz (Laurens R.) 475

**Technology:
  Bursaries/Fellowships**
Economist/Richard Casement
  Internship, The 536

Technology: Prizes
Science Book Prizes 566

Technology: Libraries
Liverpool City Libraries 586
Science Museum Library 591
Sheffield Libraries and
  Information Services 591

Technology: Picture Libraries
Art Directors Photo Library 600
Financial Times Picture Collection
  607
Harding (Robert) Picture Library
  610
Hutchison Library, The 611
PictureBank Photo Library Ltd
  618
Ronan (Ann) Picture Library 620
Science Photo Library 620

**Technology: European
  Publishers**
Almqvist och Wiksell International
  432
Bosch Casa Editorial SA 430
Empeño (Editoria) 431
Fayard (Librarie Arthème) 416
Gili (Gustavo) SA 431
Grijalbo SA 431
Gruyter (Walter de) & Co 419
Levrotto e Bella Libreria Editrice
  Universitaria SAS 424

Liber AB 433
Liguori Editore SRL 424
Oldenbourg (R) Verlag GmbH
  421

Teenagers: Publishers (UK)
Piccadilly Press 74
Reed International Books 78
Transworld Publishers Ltd 91
Usborne Publishing Ltd 93
Women's Press, The 96

Teenagers: Agents (UK)
Blake Friedmann Literary Agency
  Ltd* 160
Drexl (Anne) 165
Juvenilia 169

Teenagers: Magazines
Catch 229
Jackie 257
Just Seventeen 258
LOOKS 261
Mizz 264
My Guy 267
Smash Hits 285
19 270

Teenagers: Publishers (US)
Avon Books 438
Farrar, Straus & Giroux, Inc. 443
Lerner Publications Co. 445
Macmillan Children's Book Group
  446
Morrow (William) and Co., Inc.
  447
Random House, Inc. 450
Rosen Publishing Group, Inc., The
  450
Scholastic, Inc. 451
Simon & Schuster 451

Teenagers: Agents (US)
Author Aid Associates 456
Browne (Pema) Ltd 457
Lazear Agency, Inc., The 466
Lee Allan Agency, The 466
New Age World Services & Books
  470
Picard (Alison J.) Literary Agent
  472
Rosenstone/Wender 473
Shepard Agency, The 475
Singer (Evelyn) Literary Agency,
  Inc., The 476
Southern Writers 476
Writers House, Inc. 480

Teenagers: Prizes
Nottinghamshire Children's Book
  Award 562

Teenagers: Picture Libraries
Children's Library, The 603
Financial Times Picture Collection
  607
Reflections PhotoLibrary 619

**Television: Television
  Companies**
See section pp 305–314.

Television: Publishers (UK)
BFI Publishing 17
Boxtree 20
Headline Book Publishing 50
Titan Books 91
Virgin Publishing 93

Television: Packagers
Lennard Books 153

Television: Agents (UK)
Anderson (Darley) Books 159
Baker (Yvonne) Associates 160
Blake Friedmann Literary Agency
  Ltd* 160
Bromley (Rosemary) Literary
  Agency 160
Bryant (Peter) (Writers) 161
Casarotto Ramsay Ltd 161
Clowes (Jonathan) Ltd 162
Cochrane (Elspeth) Agency 162
Colin (Rosica) Ltd 162
Conway-Gordon (Jane) 163
Creative Tone Ltd 163
Cruickshank Cazenove Ltd 163
Curtis Brown Group Ltd 163
Daish (Judy) Associates Ltd 164
Dorian Literary Agency 164
Doyle (Colleen) 165
Film Link Literary Agency 165
Fitch (Laurence) Ltd 165
Foster (Jill) Ltd 165
Futerman (Vernon) Associates
  166
Gabriel (Jüri) 166
Gardner (Kerry) Management 166
Gillis (Pamela) Management 166
Glass (Eric) Ltd 166
Hoskins (Valerie) 168
ICM 168
Imison (Michael) Playwrights Ltd
  168
International Copyright Bureau
  Ltd 169
International Scripts 169
Juvenilia 169

Lemon, Unna and Durbridge Ltd 170
L'Epine Smith & Carney Associates 170
Levy (Barbara) Literary Agency 170
Little (Christopher) 170
Mann (Andrew) Ltd 171
Manuscript ReSearch 171
Marjacq Scripts Ltd 171
Martinez (M. C.) Literary Agency 171
Martin (Judy) 171
Marvin (Blanche) 171
MBA Literary Agents Ltd* 172
McLean (Bill) Personal Management 170
Milne (Richard) Ltd 172
Morris (William) Agency UK Ltd 172
Noach (Maggie) Literary Agency, The 172
Peters Fraser & Dunlop Group Ltd* 174
PVA Management Ltd 174
Sales (Ian) Associates 176
Sayle (Tessa) Agency 176
Seifert Dench Associates 176
Sharland Organisation Ltd, The 176
Shaw (Vincent) Associates 176
Sheil Land Associates Ltd* 176
Steinberg (Micheline) Playwrights' Agent 178
Thurley (J. M.) 178
Ware (Cecily) Literary Agents 179
Watt (A. P.) Ltd 179

Television: Magazines
Empire 241
Film Monthly 246
Radio Times 278
Screen 282
Screen International 282
Stage and Television Today 286
Television Week 289
TV Times 292
What Satellite 296

Television: Film, TV and video producers
Action Time 337
After Image Ltd 337
Amber Films 337
Barratt (Michael) Ltd 339
Bevanfield Films 339
BFV Ltd 340
Black Tulip 340
Broadcast Communications 341
Broadsword Television 341

Burder (John) (Films) 341
Cadenza 342
Camerson Television 342
Caravel Film Techniques Limited 342
Carnival Films & Theatre Ltd 342
Celador Productions Ltd 342
Chameleon Television Ltd 342
Chapel Broadcast Productions Ltd 343
Chatsworth Television Ltd 343
CHG Communications 343
Childsplay Productions Ltd 343
Chrysalis Television Productions Ltd 344
Cinexsa Film Productions Limited 344
Cirrus Films 344
Clark Production 344
Compass Film Productions Ltd 344
Creative Film Makers Ltd 345
Crown Business Communications Ltd 346
CTR Productions 346
Dareks Production House 346
Deptford Beach Productions Ltd 347
Edinburgh Film & Video Productions 348
Electric Picture Machine 348
Elstree (Production) Co. Ltd 348
Ettinger Brothers Productions 349
Euston Films 349
Filmnova 349
Filmworks 349
First House Productions Ltd 350
Flamingo Pictures 350
Forstater (Mark) Productions Ltd 351
Fourth Wall Productions 351
Fox Television 351
Frontroom Films Ltd 351
Gall (Ian) Television 351
Gamble (Ken) Productions 351
Gau (John) Productions 352
Gay (Noel) Television 352
Gibb Rose Organisation Ltd 352
Gregg (Colin) Films Ltd 353
Griffin Productions 353
Grundy (Reg) Productions (GB) Ltd 353
Hall (David) Productions 353
Hat Trick Productions Ltd 354
Hawkshead Ltd 354
Henson (Jim) Productions 354
Highgate Films 355
Holmes Associates 355
Holmes & Moriarty 355
Horntvedt Television 355

Illuminations 356
Illustra Communications Ltd 356
Imagicians Ltd 356
Input Video Ltd 356
Insight Productions Ltd 356
Interesting Television Ltd 357
In Video Productions Ltd 356
Jericho Productions Ltd 357
Kingfisher Television Productions Ltd 358
Knaves Acre Productions 358
Lodestar Productions Ltd 358
Lombard Productions Ltd 358
London Film Productions Ltd 359
Lucida Productions 359
Mansfield (Mike) Television Ltd 360
Medialab Ltd 360
Mentorn Films 361
Mosaic Pictures Ltd 362
Moving Direction 362
Normandy Film Productions 363
Open Mind Productions 363
Original Film & Video Productions Ltd 363
Oxford Film & Video Makers 363
Palace TV 363
Pelicula Films 364
Pentagon Communications 364
Picturehead Productions 365
Picture Palace Productions 365
Polygram Filmed Entertainment 365
Portman Entertainment 365
Pretty Clever Pictures Ltd 365
Priory Film Productions 366
Quanta Ltd 366
Rakoff (Alvin) Productions Ltd 366
Rank Production 366
Riverfront Pictures Ltd 367
Rose Partnership (David & Kathy) 367
Roymark Ltd 367
Siren Film & Video Co-op 368
Skyline Film & TV Productions Ltd 368
Steel (Tom) Productions 369
Topaz Productions Ltd 371
Twin Continental Films Ltd 371
UBA Ltd 372
Uden Associates Ltd 372
United Television Artists Ltd 372
VATV 372
Verronmead Ltd 372
Viewpoint Group Ltd 373
Visionventures International Ltd 373
Wadlow Grosvenor 374
Wall to Wall Television 374

Warner Sisters 374
Watershed Television Ltd 374
Wickes (David) Productions Ltd
375
Younger (Greg) Associates 375
Yo-Yo Films 375
Zenith Productions Ltd 376

Television: Publishers (US)
Players Press 449

Television: Agents (US)
Amsterdam (Marcia) Agency 455
Andrews (Bart) & Associates 455
Anthony (Joseph) Agency 455
Appleseeds Management 455
Artists Group, The 456
Author Aid Associates 456
Connor Literary Agency 459
Creative Concepts Literary
Agency 459
Curtis Brown Ltd 459
Dupree/Miller & Associates, Inc.,
Literary Agency 460
Ellen Lively Steele & Associates
461
Feiler (Florence) Literary Agency
462
Freedman (Robert A.) Dramatic
Agency, Inc. 462
Gladden Unlimited 463
Kroll (Lucy) Agency 465
Lampack (Peter) Agency, Inc. 465
Lazear Agency, Inc., The 466
Lee (L. Harry) Literary Agency
466
Literary & Creative Artists Agency
467
Lord (Sterling) Literistic, Inc. 468
Mann (Carol) Agency 468
Marshall Cameron Agency 469
Marshall (Evan) Agency 469
Nelson (B.K.) Literary Agency 470
Pegasus International, Inc. 471
Radley-Regan (D.) & Associates
473
Rosenstone/Wender 473
Scagnetti (Jack) Literary Agency
474
Schwartz (Laurens R.) 475
Shapiro-Lichtman Talent Agency
475
Swanson (H. N.), Inc. 478
Tantleff Office, The 478
Wright (Ann) Representatives,
Inc. 480
Wright (Stephen) Authors'
Representative 480
Writer's Consulting Group 480

**Television: Professional
Associations**
BAFTA (British Academy of Film
and Television Arts 491
British Film Institute 493
Educational Television
Association 495
London Screenwriters' Workshop
498
PACT (Producers Alliance for
Cinema and Television 499
Player-Playwrights 500
Royal Television Society 501
Television History Centre 504

**Television:
Bursaries/Fellowships**
Funding for Script Development
537

Television: Prizes
King (Martin Luther) Memorial
Prize, The 556
McVitie's Prize for Scottish Writer
of the Year 559
Powell (Michael) Book Award
563
Radio Times Drama & Comedy
Awards 564

Television: Libraries
BBC Written Archives Centre 578
Westminster Reference Library
593

Television: Picture Libraries
BFI Stills, Posters and Designs 601

Textiles: Publishers (UK)
Antique Collectors' Club 12

Textiles: Magazines
Corporate Clothing & Textile Care
234
Home Economics & Technology
254
Text 289

Textiles: Libraries
Art & Design Library
(Westminster) 577

Textiles: Picture Libraries
Financial Times Picture Collection
607
V&A Picture Library 624

Textbooks: Publishers (UK)
Acair Ltd 10

Addison-Wesley Publishers Ltd
10
Cambridge University Press 24
Cassell 25
Chambers (W & R) 27
Donald (John) Publishers Ltd 35
D. P. Publications Ltd 35
Elm Publications 37
Glasgow (Mary) Publications Ltd
44
Harcourt Brace Jovanovich Ltd 4
HarperCollins Publishers Ltd 49
Hobsons Publishing 52
Library Association Publishing 58
Lutterworth Press, The 60
Macmillan Publishers Ltd 61
MIT Press Ltd, The 65
Murray (John) (Publishers) Ltd 6
Nelson (Thomas) & Sons Ltd 66
Oxford University Press 70
Pergamon Press 73
Reed International Books 78
Simon & Schuster Ltd 86
Thornes (Stanley) (Publishers) L
90
Ward Lock Educational 94
Wiley (John) & Sons Ltd 96

Textbooks: Packagers
Diagram Visual Information Ltd
151

Textbooks: Publishers (US)
Avery Publishing Group, Inc. 438
Bowling Green State University
Popular Press 439
HarperCollins Publishers, Inc. 44
Longman Publishing Group 446
Paragon House Publishers 449
Pennsylvania (University of) Pres
449
Rosen Publishing Group, Inc., Th
450
University Press of America 453

Textbooks: Agents (US)
Catalog Literary Agency, The 458
Educational Design Services, Inc
460
Feiler (Florence) Literary Agency
462
Herman (Jeff) Agency, Inc., The
464
Nelson (B.K.) Literary Agency 47
Shore (Lee) Agency 475

Textbooks: Prizes
Times Educational Supplement
Information Book Awards 570

Textbooks: Small Presses
Oriflamme Publishing 142

**Textbooks: European
Publishers**
Alhambra (Editorial) SA 430
Amanda 412
Anaya (Ediciones) SA 430
Armando Armando (Editore) SRL
422
Artemis Verlags AG 434
Aschehoug Dansk Forlag A/S 412
Aschehoug (H) & Co (W
Nygaard) 427
Athesia (Verlagsanstalt) 422
Aubier-Montaigne (Editions) SA
415
Belin (Editions) 415
Benteli Verlag 434
Bonnier Fakta Bokforlag AB 432
Borgens Forlag A/S 412
Born NV Uitgeversmaatschappij
426
Braun (Verlag G) GmbH 419
Bulzoni Editore SRL (Le Edizioni
Universitarie d'Italia) 422
Calderini (Edizioni) 422
Capitol Editrice Dischi CEB 422
Cappelens (J W) Forlag A/S 428
Cappelli (Nuova Casa Editrice
Licinio) SpA 422
CEDAM (Casa Editrice Dr A
Milani) 423
Città Nuova Editrice 423
Debate SA 430
Delagrave Sàrl (Librarie) 416
Deutsch (Verlag Harri) 419
Diesterweg (Verlag Moritz) 419
Don Quijote (Editorial) 430
E C I G (Edizioni Culturali
Internazionali Genova) 423
Europa-America (Publicaoes) Lda
429
Fabbri (Gruppo Editoriale) SpA
423
Flammarion et Cie 416
Fremad (Forlaget) A/S 413
FSRs Forlag 413
Garzanti Editore 423
G.E.C. Gad Publishers 413
Giunti Publishing Group 423
Gjellerup & Gad Publishers Ltd
413
Grafisk Forlag A/S 413
Gyldendal Norsk Forlag 428
Gyldendalske Boghandel, Nordisk
Forlag A/S 413
Hachette 416
Haufe (Rudolf) Verlag GmbH &
Co KG 420

Horizonte (Livros) Lda 429
Kok (Uitgeversmaatschappij J H)
BV 426
Laffont (Editions Robert) 417
Larousse (Librairie) 417
Larousse (Suisse) SA 434
Laterza (Giuseppe) e Figli SpA
424
Levrotto e Bella Libreria Editrice
Universitaria SAS 424
Leykam Buchverlagsgesellschaft
mbH 410
Liber AB 433
Liviana Editrice SpA 424
Magnard Sàrl (Les Editions) 417
Manteau (Uitgeversmaatschappij
A) NV 412
Mondadori (Arnoldo) Editore SpA
424
Mulino (Societe Editrice Il) 425
Munksgaard International
Publishers Ltd 414
Nathan (Fernand) 418
Natur och Kultur (Bokförlaget)
433
Nelissen (Uitgeverij H) BV 426
Neue Zurcher Zeitung AG
Buchverlag 434
NKI Forlaget 428
NKS-Forlaget (Ernst G.
Mortensens stiftelse) 428
Nyt Nordisk Forlag Arnold Busck
A/S 414
Oldenbourg (R) Verlag GmbH
421
Österreichischer Bundesverlag
Gesellschaft mbH 411
Presses Universitaires de France
(PUF) 418
RCS Rizzoli Libri SpA 425
Schönbergske (Det) Forlag A/S
414
S E I (Società Editrice
Internationale) 425
Seuil (Editions du) 418
Solum Forlag A/S 428
Springer-Verlag 411
Standaard Uitgeverij 412
Tano AS 428
Teide (Editorial) SA 432
Trauner (Rudolf) Verlag 411
Ugo (Gruppo) Mursia Editore SpA
425
Unicopli (Edizione Scolastiche)
SpA 425
Universitetsforlaget 428
Urban und Schwarzenberg GmbH
421
Vanderlinden (Librairie) SA 412

V C H Verlagsgesellschaft mbH
422
Vives (Editorial Luis) (Edelvives)
432
Vuibert (Librairie) SA 418
Yrkesopplaering I/S 429

Third Age: Magazines
Active Life 217
Choice 231
Fifty Plus 245
Oldie, The 271
Saga Magazine 280
Yours Magazine 301

Third Age: Prizes
Sagittarius Prize 566

Third Age: Picture Libraries
Format Partners Photo Library
608

Third World: Publishers (UK)
Currey (James) Publishers 32
Evans Brothers Ltd 39
Hurst (C.) & Co. 53
Kogan Page Ltd 56
Tauris (I.B.) & Co. Ltd 90
Zed Books Ltd 98

Third World: Packagers
Beanstalk Books Ltd 149

Third World: Magazines
Catholic Herald 229
New Internationalist 269

**Third World: Film, TV and
video producers**
International Broadcasting Trust
357

**Third World:
Bursaries/Fellowships**
Thomas (David) Prize 540

Third World: Prizes
Graham (Edgar) Book Prize 553

Third World: Picture Libraries
Christian Aid Photo Library 603
Panos Pictures 617
Still Pictures Environmental
Agency 622

Third World: Small Presses
Peepal Tree Books 143

**Thrillers & Suspense:
Publishers (UK)**
Gollancz (Victor) Ltd 45
O'Mara (Michael) Books Limited
68
Penguin Books Ltd 71
Random House Publishing Group
Ltd 76
Severn House Publishers 85

**Thrillers & Suspense: Agents
(UK)**
Anderson (Darley) Books 159
Blake Friedmann Literary Agency
Ltd* 160
Clarke (Serafina) 162
Davidson (Merric) Literary
Agency 164
Dorian Literary Agency 164
Doyle (Colleen) 165
Fox & Howard Literary Agency
166
Gregory & Radice Authors'
Agents* 167
Judd (Jane) Literary Agency 169
Little (Christopher) 170
Manuscript ReSearch 171
Nye (Alexandra) (Writers &
Agents) 173
Pawsey (John) 173
Pearlstine (Maggie) 173
Tauber (Peter) Press Agency 178

**Thrillers & Suspense: Film,
TV and video producers**
Ty Gwyn Films Ltd 371

**Thrillers & Suspense: Theatre
producers**
Hiss & Boo Company, The 384
Marcellus Productions Ltd 388
Theatre Royal Windsor 397

**Thrillers & Suspense:
Publishers (US)**
Academy Chicago Publishers 436
Avon Books 438
Bantam Doubleday Dell
Publishing Group 438
Bergh Publishing, Inc. 439
Carroll & Graf Publishers, Inc. 440
Dorchester Publishing Co., Inc.
442
Random House, Inc. 450
Simon & Schuster 451
Walker & Co 453

**Thrillers & Suspense: Agents
(US)**
Acton & Dystel 455

Amsterdam (Marcia) Agency 455
Appleseeds Management 455
Connor Literary Agency 459
Creative Concepts Literary
Agency 459
Deering Literary Agency, The 460
Dijkstra (Sandra) Literary Agency
460
Ellenberg (Ethan), Literary
Agency, The 461
Ellen Lively Steele & Associates
461
Elmo (Ann) Agency, Inc. 461
Evans & Associates 461
Fishbein (Frieda) Ltd 462
Garon-Brooke (Jay) Associates,
Inc. 463
Gladden Unlimited 463
Herner (Susan) Rights Agency,
Inc. 464
Hull House Literary Agency 464
Jane Rotrosen Agency 474
Jarvis (Sharon) and Co., Inc. 464
Lampack (Peter) Agency, Inc. 465
Lazear Agency, Inc., The 466
Lee Allan Agency, The 466
Lee (L. Harry) Literary Agency
466
Leone (Adele) Agency, Inc. 466
Literary/Business Associates 467
Marcil (Denise) Literary Agency,
Inc. 469
McBride (Margret) Literary
Agency 468
McDonough (Richard P.), Literary
Agent 468
Noetzli (Regula) Literary Agency
471
Panettieri Agency, The 471
Peekner (Ray) Literary Agency,
Inc., The 471
Pegasus International, Inc. 471
Picard (Alison J.) Literary Agent
472
Protter (Susan Ann) Literary
Agent 472
Quicksilver Books, Literary Agents
473
Radley-Regan (D.) & Associates
473
Schlessinger–Van Dyck Agency
474
Schulman (Susan) Literary Agency
475
Sebastian Agency 475
Siegel (Bobbe), Literary Agency
475
Snell (Michael) Literary Agency
476
Southern Writers 476

Spitzer (Philip G.) Literary Agent
477
Steele (Lyle) & Co. Ltd 477
Stern (Gloria) Agency (New York)
477
Swanson (H. N.), Inc. 478
Ware (John A.) Literary Agency
479
Weiner (Cherry) Literary Agency
479
Wright (Stephen) Authors'
Representative 480
Writers House, Inc. 480
Zeckendorf (Susan) Associates
481
Zelasky (Tom) Literary Agency
481

**Thrillers & Suspense:
Bursaries/Fellowships**
Fulbright-Chandler Arts
Fellowship Award 537

**Thrillers & Suspense: Small
Presses**
Aard Press 133

**Thrillers & Suspense:
European Publishers**
Denoël (Editions) Sàrl 416
Ex Libris Forlag A/S 428
Forum (Forlaget) A/S 412
Heyne (Wilhelm) Verlag 420
Lalli (Antonio) Editore 424
Lübbe (Gustav) Verlag GmbH 42
Mondadori (Arnoldo) Editore Sp
424
Scherz Verlag AG 435
70 (Edições) Lda 430
Sonzogno 425
Spectrum (Uitgeverij Het) BV 42
Uniboek BV 427

**Trade Unions: Publishers
(UK)**
Bookmarks Publications 20

**Trade Unions: Film, TV and
video producers**
Oxford Film & Video Makers 36.

Trade Unions: Libraries
Trades Union Congress Library
593

**Trade Unions: Picture
Libraries**
Financial Times Picture Collectic
607
Monitor Syndication 615

Training: Publishers (UK)
Gower Publishing Ltd 45
Kogan Page Ltd 56
NFER-NELSON Publishing Co. Ltd
    67
Northcote House Publishers Ltd
    67

Training: Magazines
Education & Training 241
Personnel Management 273
Platform Magazine 274

**Training: Film, TV and video
    producers**
Acacia Productions Ltd 337
Adam Video Productions 337
Angel (Greg) (Film and
    Television) 338
ANV Productions 338
Apple Television 338
Aspen Business Communications
    338
Aurora Sound and Vision 338
AVC Group 339
Barratt (Michael) Ltd 339
Bould (Penny) Media 340
Box Clever 341
Broadcast Communications 341
Broadwick Productions 341
Burder (John) (Films) 341
Chess Valley Films and Video Ltd
    343
CHG Communications 343
Convergent Communications Ltd
    345
Creative Channel Ltd 345
Crew Green Associates Ltd 345
DBI Communication 347
Drake A-V Video Ltd 347
Dunkley (Robert) Associates Ltd
    347
Edric Audio Visual Ltd 348
Enlightenment AV & Video 348
Fitting Images Ltd 350
Flying Pig Productions Ltd 350
Formula Communications 351
Gateway Audio Visual and Video
    351
Gower Training 352
Harnett Milan Ltd 354
Hawkshead Ltd 354
Hemson (John) 354
In-House Corporate Video 356
Jacaranda Productions Ltd 357
Kay Communications Ltd 358
Longman Training 359
LTV Productions 359
Mayhew Business Communication
    Ltd 360

Melrose Film Productions 361
Mills Video Company 361
MNV 362
New Decade Productions 362
Peake Productions 364
Pretty Clever Pictures Ltd 365
Priory Film Productions 366
Red Lion Communications Ltd
    367
Renaissance Vision 367
Skippon Video Associates 368
Sonoptics Communications Group
    369
Tern Television Productions Ltd
    370
Vera Productions 372
Video Arts (Production) Ltd 372
Video At Work 373
Video Enterprises 373
Videoplus Productions Ltd 373
Videotel Productions/Living Tape
    Productions 373
Vidox Video Productions Ltd 373
Viewpoint Group Ltd 373
Visual Connection (TVC) Ltd, The
    374
Watershed Television Ltd 374
Zoom Production Co. Ltd, The
    376

Training: Picture Libraries
Walmsley (John) Picture Library
    625

**Training: European
    Publishers**
NKI Forlaget 428
Yrkesopplaering I/S 429

Translations: Publishers (UK)
Absolute Press 9
Carcanet Press Ltd 25
Dedalus Ltd 34
Forest Books 41
Owen (Peter) Ltd 69
Quartet Books 76
Random House Publishing Group
    Ltd 76
Serpent's Tail 84
Skoob Books Publishing Ltd 86

Translations: Agents (UK)
Howarth (Tanja) 168
Imison (Michael) Playwrights Ltd
    168
Marsh & Sheil Ltd 171

Translations: Magazines
*Storm: New Writing from East and
    West* 287

Sunk Island Review 287

**Translations: Theatre
    producers**
Gate Theatre Company Ltd 383

Translations: Publishers (US)
Princeton University Press 450
Texas (University of) Press 452

Translations: Agents (US)
Feiler (Florence) Literary Agency
    462
Pegasus International, Inc. 471

**Translations: Professional
    Associations**
Institute of Translation and
    Interpreting 497
Translators' Association, The 504

Translations: Prizes
European Literary and Translation
    Prizes 550
European Prize for the Translation
    of Poetry 551
Florio (John) Prize 551
Independent Award for Foreign
    Fiction, The 554
Moncrieff (Scott) Prize 560
Schlegel-Tieck Prize 566

Translations: Small Presses
Atlas Press 133

**Translations: European
    Publishers**
Bertelsmann AG 418
Bertrand Editora Lda 429
D I F E L – Difusao Editorial Lda
    429
Laertes SA de Ediciones 431
Laffont (Editions Robert) 417
Manesse Verlag GmbH 434
Maule (Michel de) 417
Métaillié (A.M.) 417
Meulenhoff International 426
Plaza Y Janés SA 432
Rosinante/Munksgaard 414
Rowohlt Tashenbuch 421
Santillana SA 432
Seix Barral SA 432

Transport: Publishers (UK)
Academy Books 10
Allan (Ian) Ltd 11
Ashgate Publishing Co. Ltd 13
Barracuda Books Ltd/Quotes Ltd
    15
Bay View Books Ltd 16

Cassell 25
Countryside Books 31
Dalesman Publishing Co. Ltd 32
Donald (John) Publishers Ltd 35
Ensign Publications 38
Haynes Publishing Group 50
Henry (Ian) Publications Ltd 51
Jane's Information Group 54
Kogan Page Ltd 56
Random House Publishing Group
Ltd 76
Salamander Books Ltd 82
Sutton (Alan) Publishing Ltd 89
Unicorn Books 92
Whittet Books Ltd 96

Transport: Packagers
Bison Books Ltd 149
Leading Edge Press & Publishing
Ltd 153

Transport: Prizes
Michelin Award 559
Rover Group Award 565
Vauxhall Trophy 570

Transport: Picture Libraries
Barnaby's Picture Library 601
Financial Times Picture Collection
607
Forsythe (Robert) Picture Library
608
Garland (Leslie) Picture Library
609
Greater London Photograph
Library 609
Harding (Robert) Picture Library
610
Hutchison Library, The 611
Laubier (André) Picture Library
614
Photographers' Library, The 618
Popperfoto 618
Quadrant Picture Library 619
Retrograph Archive Ltd 619
Ronan (Ann) Picture Library 620
Victory Archive, The 624
Viewfinder Colour Photo Library
624
Woodmansterne Ltd 626

Transport: Small Presses
Ferry Publications 137
Terminus Publications 146

**Transport: European
Publishers**
Orell Füssli Verlag 435

Travel: Publishers (UK)
Airlife Publishing Ltd 11
Allan (Ian) Ltd 11
Aston Publications 14
Aurum Press Ltd 15
Black (A. & C.) (Publishers) Ltd
18
Boyars (Marion) Publishers Ltd 20
Cadogan Books Ltd 23
Chapmans Publishers 27
Constable & Co. Ltd 30
Consumers' Association 30
Dalesman Publishing Co. Ltd 32
Darf Publishers Ltd 33
Fourth Estate Ltd 42
Gollancz (Victor) Ltd 45
Granta Publications 46
HarperCollins Publishers Ltd 49
Haynes Publishing Group 50
Herbert Press, The 51
Jarrold Publishing 54
Letts (Charles) & Co. Ltd 58
Little, Brown & Co. (UK) Ltd 59
Macmillan Publishers Ltd 61
Moorland Publishing Co. Ltd 65
New Holland (Publishers) Ltd 67
Northcote House Publishers Ltd
67
Octagon Press Ltd 68
Orion Publishing Group 69
Pavilion Books Ltd 71
Penguin Books Ltd 71
Quiller Press 76
RAC Publishing 76
Random House Publishing Group
Ltd 76
Reader's Digest Association Ltd
78
Reed International Books 78
Robson Books Ltd 81
Rosendale Press Ltd 81
S. B. Publications 82
Settle Press 85
Studio Editions Ltd 88
Summersdale Publishers 89
Sutton (Alan) Publishing Ltd 89
Tauris (I.B.) & Co. Ltd 90
Thames and Hudson Ltd 90
Windrush Press, The 96

Travel: Packagers
Bison Books Ltd 149
Book Packaging and Marketing
150
Clark (Philip) Ltd 151
MM Productions Ltd 154
Sheldrake Press Ltd 155

Travel: Agents (UK)
Bookworms Literary Agency 160

Chris (Teresa) Literary Agency
162
Clarke (Serafina) 162
Coles (Dianne) Agency 162
Davidson (Caroline) and Robert
Ducas Literary Agency 164
Fox & Howard Literary Agency
166
Futerman (Vernon) Associates
166
Judd (Jane) Literary Agency 169
London Independent Books Ltd
170
Martinez (M. C.) Literary Agency
171
Martin (Judy) 171
Pawsey (John) 173
Sheil Land Associates Ltd* 176
Simmons (Jeffrey) 177

Travel: Magazines
Business Traveller 227
Executive Travel 243
Expression 244
Good Holiday Magazine 249
High Life 253
Holiday Which? 254
In Britain 257
Lady, The 259
Signature 284
Traveller 292

Travel: Television
GMTV 309

**Travel: Film, TV and video
producers**
Boney (Matt) Associates 340
Dibgate Productions Ltd 347
Ideas Factory, The 356
Inca Video & Film Productions
356
Priory Film Productions 366

Travel: Publishers (US)
Academy Chicago Publishers 438
Arkansas (University of) Press 43
Chronicle Books 440
Harcourt Brace Jovanovich 443
Hippocrene Books, Inc. 444
Morrow (William) and Co., Inc.
447
Pelican Publishing Company 449
Van Nostrand Reinhold 453

Travel: Agents (US)
Lazear Agency, Inc., The 466
Rosenthal (Jean) Literary Agency
473
Schaffner Agency, Inc. 474

Shepard Agency, The 475
Wieser & Wieser, Inc. 479

**Travel: Professional
Associations**
British Guild of Travel Writers 493

Travel: Bursaries/Fellowships
Trask (Betty) Awards, The 541

Travel: Prizes
Cook (Thomas) Travel Book
Awards 548
Hughes (John Edeyrn) Prize 554
Irish Times-Aer Lingus
International Fiction Prize 555
Naipaul (Shiva) Memorial Prize
560

Travel: Libraries
Newcastle Literary and
Philosophical Society Library
588
Nottingham Subscription Library
Ltd 589
Royal Geographical Society
Library 590

Travel: Picture Libraries
Adlib Specialist Picture Source
598
Alba Pictures 598
Art Directors Photo Library 600
Aspect Picture Library Ltd 600
Aviation Picture Library 600
BMV Picturebank International
602
Boys Syndication 602
Brown (Hamish) Scottish
Photographic 602
Calendar Concepts & Design 602
Casement Collection, The 603
Cash (J. Allan) Ltd 603
Comstock Photofile Ltd 604
Cordaiy (Sylvia) Photo Library 604
Craven (Philip) Worldwide Photo-
Library 605
Davis (James) Travel Photography
605
Evans (Greg) International Photo
Library 606
Fairclough (Chris) Colour Library
607
Footprints Colour Picture Library
608
Garland (Leslie) Picture Library
609
Harding (Robert) Picture Library
610

Heseltine (John) Picture Library
610
Hutchison Library, The 611
Illustrated London News Picture
Library 612
Images Colour Library 612
International Photobank 613
Joel Photographic Library 613
Laubier (André) Picture Library
614
MacQuitty International
Photographic Collection 614
Paterson (David) Library 617
PictureBank Photo Library Ltd
618
Pictures Colour Library 618
Raleigh International Picture &
Features Library 619
Remote Source 619
Retna Pictures Ltd 619
Royal Geographical Society
Picture Library 620
Skishoot Offshoot 621
Spectrum Colour Library 621
Spooner (Frank) Pictures 622
Stockfile 622
Stockphotos 622
Stock Shot 622
Stone (Tony) Worldwide 622
Swift Picture Library Ltd 623
Syndication International 623
Telegraph Colour Library, The 623
Traeger (Tessa) 623
Travel Library, The 623
Viewfinder Colour Photo Library
624
World Pictures/Feature-Pix Colour
Library 626
Wright (George) 626
Young (John Robert) Collection
627

Travel: Small Presses
Crescent Moon Publishing 136
Ellenbank Press 137
Frontier Publishing 138
QED Books 144

Travel: European Publishers
Abadia de Montserrat
(Publicaciones de l') 430
Andersen (Carit) Forlag A/S 412
Artemis Verlags AG 434
Arthaud (Editions) SA 415
Athesia (Verlagsanstalt) 422
Bohmann Druck und Verlag
GmbH & Co 410
Brockhaus (F A) 419
Calderini (Edizioni) 422
Différence, La 416

D T V Deutscher Taschenbuch
Verlag GmbH & Co KG 419
DuMont Buchverlag GmbH & Co
KG 419
Econ-Verlag GmbH 419
Elsevie. Librico NV 411
Falken-Verlag GmbH 419
Forum (Bokförlaget) AB 433
Glenat (Editions J.) SA 416
Gremese Editore SRL 423
Gründ (Librairie) 416
Hachette 416
Hallwag Verlag AG 434
Hatier (Editions) SA 417
Høst & Søns Forlag A/S 413
Knorr und Hirth Verlag GmbH
420
Kohlhammer (Verlag W) GmbH
420
Laertes SA de Ediciones 431
Mairs Geographischer Verlag 420
Michelin et Cie (Services de
Tourisme) 417
Neptun-Verlag 434
NKS-Forlaget (Ernst G.
Mortensens stiftelse) 428
Politikens Forlag A/S 414
Presses de la Cité, Les 418
Rot-Weiss (Verlag) AG 435
Schibsteds (Chr.) Forlag A/S 428
Schönbergske (Det) Forlag A/S
414
Spectrum (Uitgeverij Het) BV 427
Sperling e Kupfer Editori SpA 425
Strandbergs Forlag ApS 415
Tyrolia (Verlagsanstalt)
Gesellschaft mbH 411
Ullstein (Buchverlage) GmbH 421

Tropics: Picture Libraries
Angel (Heather)/Biofotos 599
Art Directors Photo Library 600
Footprints Colour Picture Library
608
Michael & Patricia Fogden 608
Wilderness Photographic Library
625

USA: Publishers (UK)
Exeter (University of) Press 40

USA: Magazines
American, The 219
USA Today 219

USA: Television
Cable News Network - CNN 313

USA: Publishers (US)
Illinois (University of) Press 444
Kansas (University of) Press 445
Louisiana State University Press
446
Paragon House Publishers 449
Random House, Inc. 450
Temple University Press 452
Texas (University of) Press 452
Walker & Co 453
Washington State University Press
454

USA: Agents (US)
Ware (John A.) Literary Agency
479

**USA: Professional
Associations**
Association of American
Correspondents in London 489

USA: Prizes
Pulitzer Prizes 563

USA: Picture Libraries
Art Directors Photo Library 600
Cable & Wireless Visual Resource
602
Casement Collection, The 603
Cephas Picture Library 603
Colasanti (Stephanie) 604
Greenhill (Sally and Richard) 610
Hanley (Tom) 610
Noble (David) Photography 616
Photographers' Library, The 618
Sanders (Peter) Photography 620
Strang (Jessica) Library 622
Wiedel (Janine) 625
Williams (S & I) Power Pix
International Picture Library
626

Vegetarian: Publishers (UK)
HarperCollins Publishers Ltd 49

Vegetarian: Magazines
FarmWatch 245
Greenscene 251
Vegan, The 293
Vegetarian Living 293

Veterinary: Publishers (UK)
Freeman (W. H.) & Co. Ltd 42
Harcourt Brace Jovanovich Ltd 48
Liverpool University Press 59
Mosby Year Book Europe Ltd 65

Veterinary: Publishers (US)
Iowa State University Press 445

Veterinary: Picture Libraries
Cordaiy (Sylvia) Photo Library 604

**Veterinary: European
Publishers**
Parey (Verlag Paul) 421
Thieme (Georg) Verlag 421

Video: Video Companies
See section pp 337–376.

Video: Publishers (UK)
Macmillan Publishers Ltd 61
Picture Publishing Co. Ltd 74

Video: Magazines
Amateur Film and Video Maker
218
Camcorder User 227
Empire 241
Film Monthly 246
Screen International 282
Sight & Sound 283
Video and Satellite Today 293
Video Trade Weekly 293
Video World Magazine 294
Watch It! 294
What Video 296

Video: Television
Home Video Channel 314

**Video: Film, TV and video
producers**
Angel (Greg) (Film and
Television) 338

**Video: Professional
Associations**
British Film Institute 493
London Screenwriters' Workshop
498

Volcanoes: Picture Libraries
Alba Pictures 598
GeoScience Features 609
Wilderness Photographic Library
625
Woodmansterne Ltd 626

**Voluntary Sector: Publishers
(UK)**
NCVO Publications 66

**Voluntary Sector: Film, TV
and video producers**
Black (Stuart) Productions 340
Signals, Essex Media Centre 368

**Wales/Welsh Interest:
Publishers (UK)**
Davies (Christopher) Publishers
Ltd 33
Wales (University of) Press 94

**Wales/Welsh Interest:
Magazines**
Country Quest 235

**Wales/Welsh Interest: Film,
TV and video producers**
Cwmni'r Castell Cyf 346
Teliesyn 370
Ty Gwyn Films Ltd 371

**Wales/Welsh Interest:
Theatre producers**
Cwmni Theatr Gwynedd 381
Made in Wales Stage Company,
The 388
Swansea Little Theatre Ltd 396
Theatr Powys 396

**Wales/Welsh Interest:
Professional Associations**
Union of Welsh Writers, The 504
Welsh Academy 504
Welsh Books Council (Cyngor
Llyfrau Cymraeg) 505
Yr Academi Gymreig 506

Wales/Welsh Interest: Prizes
Davies (Rhys) Award 549
Hughes (John Edeyrn) Prize 554
Jones (Mary Vaughan) Award 55
Tir Na N-Og Award, The 570
Tripp (John) Award 570
Welsh Arts Council Book of the
Year Awards 571
Williams (Griffith John) Memoria
Prize 572

**Wales/Welsh Interest:
Libraries**
National Library of Wales 588

**Wales/Welsh Interest: Pictur
Libraries**
Celtic Picture Library 603
Fortean Picture Library 608
Hylton Warner Photography/Bar
Webb Associates 612
Waterways Photo Library 625
West Air Photography 625

**Wales/Welsh Interest: Small
Presses**
Iolo 140

War: Publishers (UK)
Cassell 25
Macmillan Publishers Ltd 61
Mainstream Publishing Co.
 (Edinburgh) Ltd 62
Milestone Publications 64

War: Publishers (US)
ABC-Clio, Inc. 436
Avon Books 438
Bantam Doubleday Dell
 Publishing Group 438

War: Agents (US)
Author Aid Associates 456
Lee Allan Agency, The 466
Lee (L. Harry) Literary Agency
 466
Pegasus International, Inc. 471

War: Libraries
Imperial War Museum 585

War: Picture Libraries
Greater London Photograph
 Library 609
Hanley (Tom) 610
Hulton Picture Company, The 611
Hunt (Robert) Library, The 611
Illustrated London News Picture
 Library 612
Imperial War Museum
 Department of Photographs
 612
Laubier (André) Picture Library
 614
Miller (Lee) Archives 615
Outram (George) Picture Library
 617
Popperfoto 618
Topham Picture Source 623
Victory Archive, The 624

War: Small Presses
Korvet Publishing and Distribution
 140

Westerns: Agents (UK)
Abacus Literary Agency 159
Burston (Diane) Literary Agency
 161

Westerns: Publishers (US)
Avalon Books 438
Avon Books 438
Bantam Doubleday Dell
 Publishing Group 438
Dorchester Publishing Co., Inc.
 442
Evans (M.) & Co., Inc. 442

Simon & Schuster 451
Walker & Co 453

Westerns: Agents (US)
Authors Resource Center & Tarc
 Literary Agency, The 456
Browne (Pema) Ltd 457
Evans & Associates 461
Kern (Natasha) Literary Agency,
 Inc. 464
Lee Allan Agency, The 466
Lee (L. Harry) Literary Agency
 466
Leone (Adele) Agency, Inc. 466
Peekner (Ray) Literary Agency,
 Inc., The 471
Shore (Lee) Agency 475
Weiner (Cherry) Literary Agency
 479
Zelasky (Tom) Literary Agency
 481

Wildlife: Publishers (UK)
Aston Publications 14

Wildlife: Packagers
Bison Books Ltd 149

Wildlife: Agents (UK)
Solo Syndication & Literary
 Agency Ltd 177

Wildlife: Magazines
BBC WILDLIFE Magazine 223
Birds 224
Country Life 234
Natural World 268

Wildlife: Publishers (US)
NorthWord Press, Inc. 448

Wildlife: Prizes
BBC WILDLIFE Magazine Awards
 for Nature Writing 544

Wildlife: Picture Libraries
Angel (Heather)/Biofotos 599
Aquila Photographics 599
Ardea London Ltd 600
Calendar Concepts & Design 602
Camerapix Picture Library 603
Camera Ways Ltd Picture Library
 603
Cordaiy (Sylvia) Photo Library 604
Craven (Philip) Worldwide Photo-
 Library 605
GeoScience Features 609
Hutchison Library, The 611
Martin Library, The 614

NHPA (Natural History
 Photographic Agency) 616
Planet Earth Pictures/Seaphot 618
Reflections PhotoLibrary 619
Stone (Tony) Worldwide 622
Swift Picture Library Ltd 623
Wilderness Photographic Library
 625

**Wine & Spirits: Publishers
 (UK)**
Absolute Press 9
Argus Books 13
Constable & Co. Ltd 30
Gollancz (Victor) Ltd 45
Headline Book Publishing 50
Macmillan Publishers Ltd 61
Orion Publishing Group 69
Quiller Press 76
Reed International Books 78
Salamander Books Ltd 82
Smith Gryphon Ltd 86

Wine & Spirits: Packagers
Berkswell Publishing Co. Ltd 149
Clark (Philip) Ltd 151

Wine & Spirits: Agents (UK)
Kelly (Frances) 169

Wine & Spirits: Magazines
Decanter 237
Expression 244
House & Garden 256
Taste 288
Wine 297

**Wine & Spirits: Publishers
 (US)**
Sterling Publishing 452

**Wine & Spirits: Professional
 Associations**
Circle of Wine Writers 494

Wine & Spirits: Prizes
Glenfiddich Awards 552
Simon André Memorial Fund
 Book Awards 567

**Wine & Spirits: Picture
 Libraries**
Blake (Anthony) 602
Boys Syndication 602
Cephas Picture Library 603
Eager (Patrick) Photography 606

**Wine & Spirits: European
 Publishers**
Hallwag Verlag AG 434

Uniepers BV 427

Women's Interests:
Publishers (UK)
Elite Words & Image 37
HarperCollins Publishers Ltd 49
Reed International Books 78
Sheba Feminist Press 85
Virago Press Ltd 93
Women's Press, The 96

Women's Interests: Packagers
Wordwright Books 156

Women's Interests: Agents
(UK)
Burston (Diane) Literary Agency
161
Dorian Literary Agency 164
Doyle (Colleen) 165
Judd (Jane) Literary Agency 169
Sheldon (Caroline) Literary
Agency 177
Tauber (Peter) Press Agency 178

Women's Interests: Magazines
Annabel 219
Bella 223
Best 223
Black Beauty & Hair 224
Brides and Setting Up Home 225
Chat 230
Company 233
Cosmopolitan 234
Elle 241
Essentials 242
Everywoman 243
Family Circle 244
First Choice 246
Girl About Town 248
Hair 251
Hairflair 251
Harpers & Queen 252
Home and Country 254
Living 260
marie claire 262
Me 263
More! 265
My Weekly 267
New Woman 270
Options 272
Prima 277
She Magazine 283
Tatler, The 289
Townswoman 291
Vogue 294
Wedding and Home 294
Woman 297
Woman and Home 297
Woman's Journal 297

Woman's Own 298
Woman's Realm 298
Woman's Weekly 298
Women's Art Magazine 298

Women's Interests: Film, TV
and video producers
Vera Productions 372
Verronmead Ltd 372

Women's Interests: Theatre
producers
Contact Theatre Company 381
Monstrous Regiment Ltd 388
Sphinx, The 395
Tricycle Theatre 398

Women's Interests:
Publishers (US)
ABC-Clio, Inc. 436
Princeton University Press 450
Texas (University of) Press 452

Women's Interests: Agents
(US)
Siegel (Bobbe), Literary Agency
475

Women's Interests:
Professional Associations
Society of Women Writers and
Journalists 503
Women in Publishing 505
Women Writers Network (WWN)
505

Women's Interests:
Bursaries/Fellowships
Rhondda (Margaret) Award, The
539

Women's Interests: Picture
Libraries
Harding (Robert) Picture Library
610
Wiedel (Janine) 625

Woodwork: Publishers (UK)
Argus Books 13

Woodwork: Magazines
Woodworker 298

Woodwork: Publishers (US)
Sterling Publishing 452
TAB Books 452

World Affairs/International:
Publishers (UK)
Bookmarks Publications 20

Bowker-Saur Ltd 20
Boyars (Marion) Publishers Ltd 2(
Cassell 25
Cass (Frank) 25
Dartmouth Publishing Co. Ltd 33
Dunrod Press 36
Economist Books 36
Freeman (W. H.) & Co. Ltd 42
Halban (Peter) Publishers 48
Leicester University Press 57
Macmillan Publishers Ltd 61
Mainstream Publishing Co.
(Edinburgh) Ltd 62
MIT Press Ltd, The 65
Pergamon Press 73
Pluto Press Ltd 75
Tauris (I.B.) & Co. Ltd 90
Zed Books Ltd 98

World Affairs/International:
Agents (UK)
Simmons (Jeffrey) 177

World Affairs/International:
Magazines
Day by Day 237
New Internationalist 269
New Statesman and Society 270
Time 290

World Affairs/International:
Publishers (US)
ABC-Clio, Inc. 436

World Affairs/International:
US Press and Journals
US News and World Report 483

World Affairs/International:
Prizes
RTZ David Watt Memorial Prize,
The 565

World Affairs/International:
Libraries
BBC Data Enquiry Service 578
United Nations London
Information Centre 593

World Affairs/International:
Picture Libraries
Magnum Photos Ltd 614
Network Photographers 616

World Affairs/International:
Small Presses
Minority Rights Group 142

Zoology: Publishers (UK)
Athlone Press, The 14
Edinburgh University Press 37
Facts On File 40
Freeman (W. H.) & Co. Ltd 42
Harcourt Brace Jovanovich Ltd 48
MIT Press Ltd, The 65
Pergamon Press 73

**Zoology: Film, TV and video
producers**
Isaac (Peter) Ltd 357

Zoology: Libraries
Natural History Museum Library
588

Zoology: Picture Libraries
E. T. Archive 606
GeoScience Features 609
Science Photo Library 620